The People's Republic of China

1979-1984

A Documentary Survey

Volume

1

The People's Republic of China 1979-1984

A Documentary Survey

Harold C. Hinton

Editor

SR *Scholarly Resources Inc.*

WILMINGTON, DELAWARE

∞™

The paper used in this publication meets the minimum requirements of the American National Standard for permanence of paper for printed library materials, Z39.48, 1984.

Scholarly Resources Inc.
104 Greenhill Avenue
Wilmington, Delaware 19805-1897

Library of Congress Cataloging-in-Publication Data
Main entry under title:

The People's Republic of China, 1979–1984.

1. China—History—1976– —Sources. I. Hinton, Harold C.   DS779.17.P46   1986   951.05'8
85-30391   ISBN 0-8420-2253-8

Publisher's Note

Scholarly Resources has reproduced the following collection of translated speeches, government reports, and news releases exactly as they were printed, and in their entirety, from the originals published in or by the People's Republic of China. Variant spellings, as well as inconsistencies in editorial style, punctuation, and capitalization, therefore have been retained. The Chinese names used throughout these documents reflect the official Pinyin spelling system, adopted by the PRC in 1979.

FOR CAROLYN

Contents

Ideology and Party History

Rectifying the Party

Evolution of the State System

The Party and the Military

Intellectuals, Dissent, and Human Rights

Introduction

This two-volume work, covering the history of the People's Republic of China from October 1979 to October 1984, begins with strong man Deng Xiaoping's political comeback following his purge in April 1976 in the aftermath of the death of his patron, Premier Zhou Enlai. Along the way to regaining his power, Deng had promised in 1977 not to seek any post higher than those he had held prior to 1976, a pledge he observed, or was compelled to observe. He therefore has never been elected to any office above that of vice-chairman of the Communist Party Central and until 1980 vice-premier of the State Council. Another pledge that he made at the same time was to respect the leadership of Party Chairman and Premier Hua Guofeng which he was evidently determined to, and in fact did, violate.

In 1978, perceiving a threat from Deng, Hua began to pose increasingly as the leader and spokesman of the remaining Maoist, or radical, elements in the Communist Party, which included some of the leading army commanders. He also proposed in that year a dramatic acceleration of China's projected rate of economic growth, probably as a means to enhance his own role as a constructive statesman. These various ploys failed, however. From the Third Plenary Session of the Eleventh Communist Party Central Committee in December 1978, Deng was clearly the ascendant and Hua in decline.

After the remaining radicals, apart from Hua, were eliminated from the Politburo in February 1980 (Doc. 5), Hua's turn was not long in coming. He was eased out as premier in September 1980 and as Party chairman in June 1981. At the Twelfth Party Congress in September 1982 (Docs. 30–34), he also lost his seat on the Central Committee. He was replaced as premier by Zhao Ziyang, a Deng man and a competent administrator who has concerned himself mainly with the economy, and as the former senior Party official by General Secretary (the chairmanship was abolished) Hu Yaobang, another Deng man. Despite numerous problems, this new leadership seems to have things under reasonable control. A congenial group has been brought up to second-level positions in the Party and government, and elderly or otherwise unacceptable figures are being retired in large numbers. Younger radicals are gradually being weeded out of the Party.

Deng's pragmatism and general pushiness have inevitably aroused concern and some outright opposition among Party leaders who object to him on general, power, personal, or ideological grounds. Until about 1980 they had clustered around the elderly Marshal Ye Jianying, now retired (Doc. 9). More recently, they have found something of a spokesman in Chen Yun, a very senior Party official, although not quite so powerful as Deng. Chen Yun appears to have particular reservations about Deng's freewheeling approach to the economy and to favor more centralized, bureaucratic, and Soviet-style procedures.

One of Chen Yun's protégés, a radical named Deng Liqun, who headed the Party Secretariat's Propaganda Department, evidently decided in 1983 to discredit and, if possible, replace General Secretary Hu Yaobang by alleging that the open-door policy toward the outside world was bringing spiritual pollution into the country. During the last few months of 1983 and the beginning of 1984 (Docs. 78–81), Deng Liqun received enough support to generate a propaganda campaign against this alleged evil, but it was then called off, to the definite detriment of his career. The campaign had raised fears at home and abroad of a revival of radical Maoism, something to which Deng, most of his colleagues, and apparently a majority of the population are strongly opposed.

Mao Zedong's posthumous reputation has had its ups and downs under Deng Xiaoping. At first, Mao was somewhat downgraded as a way of getting at Hua Guofeng, but, as Hua fell in 1980–81, Mao was authoritatively appraised as a great statesman before 1949 but as one who had generated a "cult of personality" after that and had committed a colossal blunder in the Cultural Revolution and another somewhat lesser one in the Great Leap Forward (Doc. 17). Similarly, Mao's widow Jiang Qing and the other members of the so-called Gang of Four, plus six more, were given a Stalin-style show trial in 1980–81, partly as a means of attacking Hua Guofeng by attributing the excesses of the late Mao period indirectly to him as well as more directly to those on trial (Docs. 75–76).

Like any other Marxist-Leninist leader, Deng Xiaoping runs a taut ship, built around the dominance of the Communist Party's apparatus, or internal bureaucracy headed by the Secretariat. This has inevitably aroused some popular opposition and intellectual dissent, but these have been dealt with rather sternly. The brief Beijing Spring (1978–79), during which critics were permitted to write posters and put them up on the so-called Democracy Wall in Beijing, was terminated after it had served Deng's apparent purpose of helping to undermine Hua Guofeng (Docs. 58–63).

From about 1979 the Chinese economy went into a phase of readjustment; that is, a program of tinkering with the nonessentials of the overly centralized, highly bureaucratized system, in the hope of obtaining better results without the mental effort and probable erosion of political control inherent in something more thoroughgoing. Deng and his colleagues apparently hoped that a saving injection of capital and technology from abroad would flow from the large-scale operations, which began around 1980, of foreign oil companies in the South China Sea. Inevitably, readjustment had only limited success, but it had two bright aspects. One was the virtual decollectivization of agriculture, which has gone beyond readjustment and into true reform, with beneficial effects on agricultural production (Docs. 92–95). The second was the open-door policy toward the outside world, which included not only the offshore oil program just mentioned but also a general receptivity to foreign, including U.S., capital and technology.

By 1984 it had become reasonably clear that the offshore oil program was likely to prove much less of a bonanza than had been hoped originally by all concerned. Probably not by coincidence it was also in 1984 that first the State Council (Doc. 110), and then the Party Central Committee (Doc. 111), announced a potentially revolutionary policy of reforming the industrial sector of the economy. Prices were to be fixed rationally, rather than arbitrarily; consumer subsidies were to be cut back; and authority over industrial enterprises was to be decentralized, although to lower level administrative organs more than to the enterprises themselves. At present, China's economic system is in a confused transition to the state of affairs desired by the Deng leadership, or to its nearest attainable approximation.

Barring some improbable catastrophe, such as massive food shortages, serious civil disorder, a major Soviet attack, or a cutoff of foreign credits and technology (a possible outcome if Beijing should decide to blockade or attack Taiwan), the Chinese economy is likely in time to muddle through. If so, the result in the next century almost certainly will be a China that, even if not fully modern or a superpower, is at least significantly stronger, both absolutely and relatively, than the China of today. Such a country presumably will tend to carry increased weight in the international community.

Since the end of the 1970s, Beijing has continued to try to manipulate the superpower balance to the benefit of its own security and development. The Soviet Union has remained a mortal threat, as Beijing was reminded by the December 1979 invasion of Afghanistan. China's fairly impressive military modernization program (Docs. 119–120) is designed mainly to deter or, if necessary, defend against a Soviet attack, as well as to cope with Moscow's informal ally, Vietnam. On the one hand, since about October 1982, when regular Sino-Soviet talks began at the vice-foreign minister level, Beijing has been trying to ease tension with Moscow, increase the level of Sino-Soviet trade, and moderate its potential dependence on the United States, all of which have been achieved to a significant, although not spectacular, degree without giving up its demand for a reduction of Soviet military presence near China's borders and without accepting any kind of political subordination to Moscow.

On the other hand, and despite continuing tensions over U.S. arms sales to Taiwan and related issues, Beijing has continued to cultivate, without quite admitting it, a preferential relationship with the United States, which it sees as a necessary counterweight to the Soviet Union and a valuable source of high technology (Docs. 123–130). Japan is similarly cultivated, also despite certain issues and tensions, but with the emphasis on economic, rather than strategic, factors (Doc. 140). Other non-Communist industrial countries, such as those of Western Europe and South Korea, also play significant roles in Beijing's open-door policy and its drive for modernization. Vietnam is treated as an adversary because it has "tilted" toward Moscow and has invaded Cambodia (Kampuchea) in order to displace a Chinese client regime under Pol Pot (Doc. 141). North Korea, however, is wooed, but mainly in the hope of discouraging it from attacking South Korea again or tilting toward Moscow more than it is doing already since the unfortunate shooting down by Soviet forces of the South Korean airliner on 1 September 1983 (Doc. 135).

Harold C. Hinton

Deng Xiaoping: More Equal Than His Colleagues

On the Current Situation and Tasks, 16 January 1980

By the beginning of 1980, Deng was about ready to begin his final moves to get rid of Party Chairman and Premier Hua Guofeng, and therefore Deng's words began to carry even more weight than before. The main points of interest in this speech, which was delivered at a conference of some ten thousand cadres (Party workers and officials), are his definition of China's main "tasks" for the 1980s (the maintenance of internal stability, unification with Taiwan, and modernization, with emphasis on the latter); the four problems or premises of modernization (political control, stability and unity, "arduous struggle," and reliable cadres); and the need for strong leadership by the Party.

Comrades: I spoke for about 15 minutes to the CPPCC [Chinese People's Political Consultative Conference] on New Year's Day; Hu Yaobang and other comrades want me to speak to more of the comrades in order to put forward our hopes for the work of this year. At present there are indeed certain questions in the party and among the people which need answers. I cannot talk about every problem today, and there are also certain problems which I cannot speak about very well. As everyone hopes that I will speak, I will now speak.

I intend my speech to be in three parts. In the first part I will talk about the three major tasks for the 1980's and the situation as we enter the decade. In the second part, I will talk about four problems which must be solved in order to accomplish the four modernizations, which could also be called the four necessary premises. In part three, I will talk about upholding and improving party leadership.

PART I

In Part One, I will talk about the three major tasks for the 1980's and the domestic situation as we enter the decade.

I will begin with the major things which we must do in the 1980's. The main thing is to accomplish three major tasks in this decade:

The first is to oppose hegemonism and safeguard world peace in international affairs. The whole world estimates that the 1980's will be a dangerous decade. The task of opposing hegemonism will be on our agenda every day. The decade has started off badly with the Afghan incident; there is also the Iranian incident, and there is still less need to mention the Vietnam and Middle East incidents, which occurred a little before the decade began. There will

[Hong Kong *Cheng Ming*, 1 March 1980. *Cheng Ming* is one of the most important of the left-wing, although unofficial, newspapers and journals, generally with good sources on developments in Beijing, that have sprung up in Hong Kong in recent years.]

be many more such problems in the future. In short, the struggle against hegemonism is constantly a major task, which must be on the agenda of our state and the people of the whole country.

The second task is to bring about the return of Taiwan to the motherland and accomplish the unification of the motherland. We must strive to attain this target in the 1980's, and even though there may be twists and turns of various kinds, it will remain an important task on our agenda.

The third task is to step up economic construction, that is, to step up the building of the four modernizations. In a nutshell, the four modernizations mean economic construction. National defense construction cannot be carried out without a certain economic foundation. The main aim of science and technology is to serve economic construction.

Modernization is the core of the three major tasks. This is our main condition for solving international and internal problems. Everything depends on whether we make a success of running our affairs, and the size of the role we play in international affairs depends on the speed and range of our economic development. If our country develops and becomes more prosperous, we will play a great role in international affairs. Our current role in international affairs is by no means small, but if our material foundation and strength grow powerful, the role we play will be still greater. To bring about the return of Taiwan to the motherland and accomplish the unification of the motherland also mean in the final analysis that we must run our affairs well. Our politics and our economic system are superior to Taiwan's, and we must also achieve a certain degree of superiority over Taiwan in economic development; we cannot succeed without this. If our four modernizations are carried out well and our economy develops, our strength for accomplishing unification will be different from what it is now. Therefore, in the final analysis, to oppose hegemonism in international affairs, bring about the return of Taiwan to the motherland and accomplish the unification of the motherland all depend on our doing a good job in economic construction. Of course, many other things must also be done well, but the most important thing is to do a good job in economic construction.

Today is 16 January 1980, and we are already 16 days into the 1980's. This will be an extremely important decade both in international and in internal affairs. It is very hard to predict what international problems will crop up, but one can say that this will be a decade of extremely great turmoil and filled with danger. Of course we have confidence in being able to put off the outbreak of war and in striving for a somewhat longer period of peace, if we make a success of our struggle against hegemonism. This is possible, and this is precisely what we are currently striving for. We ourselves as well as the people of the world really do need a peaceful environment. Therefore, our strategy in foreign affairs, as far as our country is concerned, is to seek a peaceful environment for carrying out the four modernizations. This is not a lie, it is the truth. This is a great affair that conforms to the interests of both the Chinese and world peoples.

We have only 20 years—the 1980's and 1990's—in which to accomplish the four modernizations before the end of the century. Unless decisive success is scored in building the four modernizations in the 1980's, that will be the equivalent of a setback. The 1980's is therefore a very important and decisive decade as far as our economic construction is concerned. If we can successfully lay the foundation in this decade, when we enter the next decade, our achieving the Chinese-style four modernizations in the next 20 years will be feasible and will truly have good prospects. Twenty years seem a long time, but they are very soon past. Therefore, from New Year's Day of the first year of the 1980's, we must not delay things for even 1 day and must concentrate all our efforts and energy on building the four modernizations. We have firmly laid down the general task of building the four modernizations, and we will certainly not permit any more dissipation of effort.

What is our internal situation as we enter the 1980's? Our targets and tasks have been set, and we should have a look at and estimate our situation. Some of the masses and party members, and even some cadres, are not too clear about our accomplishments since the "gang of four" were smashed.

They are dissatisfied, feeling that progress is too slow; since they are dissatisfied, they feel that there is not much chance of carrying out the political line we have laid down and accomplishing the four modernizations. Of course, there are still people around who take a hostile attitude toward our ideological, political and organizational lines; I will not talk about the problems of those people. I want to put forward some opinions to those comrades who feel that our prospects are not bright enough and who are confused.

We should say that our situation is very favorable. The situation in the whole country has developed rapidly, exceeding people's expectations, in the 3 years and 2 months since the "gang of four" were overthrown and especially in the 1 year since the third plenary session. In the first 2 of the 3 years following the smashing of the "gang of four," we did a lot of work, and without the preparations made during those 2 years, the third plenary session would not have been able to lay down in a clear-cut way the party's ideological and political lines. Therefore, the previous 2 years we made active preparations for the third plenary session. Apart from solving problems of the 10 years of the Great Cultural Revolution, the third plenary session also solved to a very great extent the problems of more than 20 years. Everyone should ask: As a result of the work of the past 3 years, have there not been fundamental changes in the condition of the party, in the leadership groups, and in the ideological line? This does not mean that all problems have been solved, nevertheless a fundamental change has taken place which is the most important fact. Of course there are still many problems and they must all be solved; we are now gradually solving them, and will continue to solve them in the future. In short, we should certainly not doubt this fundamental change. We have done a lot of work in turning chaos into order in the past 3 years, and our successes are tremendous. It is wrong to underestimate them.

Let us now recall the main work we have carried out in politics, economics and foreign affairs.

What basis do we have for saying that there has been a fundamental change in the political situation? First, we have investigated the "gang of four" and carried out a nationwide purge of the "gang of four's" factional network and ultraleftist line. We have fundamentally rectified the leadership groups of organizations at all levels throughout the country. This has been the political guarantee for the achievements we scored in the past 3 years. Secondly, democratic life in the country and the party has started to get onto the right track. The democratic system has been put on a sounder basis each year, and democratic life has been expanded each year. Although there are still many important problems which require deepgoing study and demand that we must continue to make efforts to promote what is beneficial and eliminate what is harmful, we must look at the main current and the essence. In the 29 years after the founding of the country, we did not even have a criminal code; we have worked on this over and over again and written more than 30 drafts, but in fact, they were never adopted for use. The criminal law and the law of criminal procedure have now been approved and promulgated and have been put into effect. The people of the whole country have seen their hopes of strictly enforcing the socialist legal system realized. This is certainly not a small matter! Thirdly, in these 3 years, and especially in the past 1 year, the central authorities and the localities throughout the country have reversed the verdicts on a large number of miscarriages of justice. According to incomplete statistics, 2.9 million people have now been rehabilitated, and many more have been rehabilitated whose cases were not put on file or tried. We have reversed the verdict on the Tiananmen incident and on miscarriages of justice concerning a large number of comrades including Peng Dehuai, Zhang Wentian, Tao Zhu, Bo Yibo, Xi Zhongxun, Wang Renzhong, Huang Kecheng, Yang Shangkun, Lu Dingyi and Zhou Yang. In addition, we are about to restore the good name of Comrade Liu Shaoqi. We have also corrected a large number of cases of wrongly labelling people rightists in 1957. I want to mention in passing that antirightist movement in 1957 was necessary and was not erroneous. Comrades should ask themselves: What was the problem in 1957? From 1949 to 1957, we spent 8 years in basically completing the socialist transformation of agriculture, handicrafts and capitalist industry and commerce, and entered socialism. A trend of thought arose during this period, centered on opposition to socialism and party leadership.

Certain people went about with murderous looks on their faces! It was imperative to counterattack this trend of thought at that time. Where did the problem arise then? The problem was that as the movement developed it became inflated, too many people were hit, and they were hit with too much force. Large numbers of people were indeed treated improperly and too harshly, they nursed their grievances for many years and were unable to bring into play their wisdom and talent for the benefit of the people. This was a loss for the whole country, not just of those individuals. Therefore, removing all the labels from the rightists, correcting the handling of the great majority of them and assigning them suitable work was a very necessary and important political measure, but one should not conclude from this that there was no antisocialist trend of thought in 1957 or that we should not have launched a counterattack against such a trend. In short, the 1957 antirightist movement was not erroneous in itself, the problem is that it became inflated. Fourth, we have removed the "stinking ninth category" label from intellectuals and removed the labels from the great majority of landlords, rich peasants and capitalists throughout the country. Is this not a great event in the political life of the people of the whole country? Fifth, we have basically summed up the experiences and lessons of the Great Cultural Revolution and the past 30 years and restored the good name and traditions of the eighth party congress. The National Day speech delivered by Comrade Ye Jianying on behalf of the Central Committee was not only significant in summing up the Great Cultural Revolution; it actually summed up, or basically at any rate, the experiences and lessons of the 30 years since the founding of the state. Our party history will probably be written in this tone. If it is written too meticulously, I am afraid it will not be appropriate. Are we not saying that we should be a bit rough and not too meticulous in solving the problems of the past? We should also hold firm to this sense of propriety in the future. In evaluating figures and history, we must advocate an all-round and scientific viewpoint and guard against onesidedness and emotionalism; in this way, we will conform to Marxism and the interests and desires of the people of the whole country. We may issue formal resolutions this year on a number of historical problems. Sixth, within these 3 years, we have given a correct explanation of Mao Zedong Thought and restored Mao Zedong Thought to its original state. This is something that everyone knows. Through the discussion on practice as the criterion for testing truth, we have laid down our party's ideological line, or one could say that we have revived the ideological line of Marxism-Leninism-Mao Zedong Thought. Because of this, the principle of correctly distinguishing and handling the two different kinds of contradictions, the double hundred principle, and the principle of not sticking labels on people, beating them with sticks or grabbing them by their pigtails—all of which Chairman Mao advocated for many years—have been seriously and correctly carried out. Seventh, our education, science and cultural work has started to get on the right track. Eighth, our public security, procuracy and judicial work, nationalities work, united front work, work concerning workers, youths and women, and much other work have started to get on the right track. I have not mentioned everything, just these few things. It was certainly not easy to solve so many problems in so short a time, and it would have been almost unimaginable 3 years

ago. With these problems solved, our party and state have been transformed and the political situation has become one of stability and unity and liveliness and vigor. Thus, we are able to shift the focus of work and concentrate our energy on promoting socialist modernization with peace of mind; otherwise, such a thing would have been impossible. The facts have proved that we have indeed done a great deal of intense work in the past 3 years and scored tremendous achievements.

We have also scored much success in the economic field in the past 3 years. We often say that our economic work suffered 10 years of interference and sabotage by Lin Biao and the "gang of four," and that there was also a great deal of confusion before those 10 years. As a result of 3 years of efforts, things have recovered to what they are today. This is a major achievement. For more than 20 years, the work focus was never seriously shifted to economic construction, and many problems accumulated in economic work. Some people now heap blame on our previous economic work. We lacked experience in many things in the past, and the good experiences we have gained have not been properly arranged or systematized. There are very many problems which have never been solved well; in particular, during the Great Cultural Revolution, Lin Biao and the "gang of four" threw everything into chaos during their 10 years' tyranny. Hence, frankly speaking, our previous economic work was not done well. First of all, we must not blame the economic departments; apart from the sabotage done by Lin Biao and the "gang of four," the central authorities are to blame. Of course, there are also shortcomings in the work of the economic departments, and it is necessary to sum up these experiences and lessons. Now everyone must concentrate on looking ahead and must put forward positive suggestions. People should not grumble and reproach others. We must realize that in the past 3 years, on the one hand the comrades undertaking leadership work at all levels have done a great deal of work. On the other hand, the situation in which many comrades had to stand aside for many years has been stopped; it has not been long since they returned to their work posts. The comrades who have been at their posts all the time are also facing new problems, and they cannot become familiar with these things all at once. They do not have a very good understanding of conditions at home and abroad, and it is inevitable that there should be shortcomings of various kinds in their work. As long as everyone humbly studies the new situation and problems, work will constantly improve.

After 2 years of work, we put forward the eight-character principle of readjusting, restructuring, rectifying and improving the national economy. This principle was not put forward by accident; it was put forward after summing up experiences of the past and analyzing the current situation, with the goal of promoting still better and faster development of work in the future. Today we can see ever more clearly that it was completely necessary and correct to put forward this principle.

The third plenary session adopted two resolutions on rural work, stipulated a whole series of policy measures, and decided to raise the procurement prices of grain and other agricultural products. The wages of workers have been increased as well. We have opened up all kinds of employment opportunities on a considerable scale; last year we arranged jobs for over 7 million people, and we must continue with this work this year. We have strengthened the light and textile industries, reduced the capital construction front, and set up trial points in enterprise self-management rights. The financial system is being gradually reformed, and we have also decided on trial measures for the gradual reform of other systems. We still have many problems to solve, and we must continue carrying out readjustment and restructuring in the future. However, we should say that we have scored tremendous achievements in the economy in the past 3 years, and especially in the past 1 year. Take a look at the rural areas. The characteristic of China is, as before, that 80 percent of the population lives in the rural areas. The great majority of the rural areas throughout the country have now been transformed, and the minds of the peasants are considerably at ease. Is this not the result of the role played by the party and state policies? Conditions in the towns are relatively complicated; in particular, there is some confusion in commodity prices. However, there has been a great improvement in production order in the great majority of factories and enterprises, and some improvement is starting to be made in the people's living standards, thanks to the wage readjustment and the increases in employment and housing. All this is the result of the great amount of work we have done.

In our economic development, we are currently seeking a road suited to the actual conditions in China by which we can promote the economy a bit faster and a bit more economically. This road includes expanding enterprise self-management rights and democratic management, developing specialization and coordination, combining planning regulation with market regulation, combining advanced and medium technology, making rational use of foreign investment and technology and so on. We have paid the price for our lessons and suffered some losses, but the important thing is that we are now accumulating skills which have already started to yield results. We must now sum up experiences, run things a bit faster and better, formulate principles for restructuring the economic system, and draw up long-term plans. These are all major affairs. We must be neither impetuous nor tardy. The central authorities hope that the comrades engaged in actual and theoretical work on the economic front will, working in concert and in coordination, learn others' good points to compensate for their own weak points, carry out investigations and studies, hold repeated discussions, and utter less empty talk in order to submit several practical plans and a long-term plan to the central authorities before the end of this year.

As far as foreign affairs are concerned, during these 3 years we have established diplomatic relations with the United States, signed the Sino-Japanese treaty of peace and friendship and paid state visits to Japan and the United States. Comrade Hua Guofeng has visited Korea, Romania, Yugoslavia, and four Western European countries. Comrade Li Xiannian and I have visited a number of countries in Asia and Africa. There have also been a large number of foreign visits of various categories, involving several score countries on the five continents. Almost all our vice premiers have been abroad as have many of the NPC Standing Committee vice chairmen. In the past 3 years, and especially in the past 1 year, we have paid an unprecedented number of visits to foreign countries, while there seems to have been a constant stream of foreign leaders visiting China. These activities have set a new pattern in our country's diplomacy, giving us comparatively good international conditions for accomplishing the four modernizations while expanding the lineup in the struggle against hegemonism. Our cooperation with Third World countries continues to increase. We won a military and political victory in the self-defense counterattack against Vietnam. This has already played a major role in the international antihegemonist struggle and in stabilizing the Southeast Asia situation and will continue to do so in the future.

I have given a political, economic and diplomatic outline of the work we have done in the past 3 years and especially in the 1 year since the third plenary session. We should perceive our successes. We should see that we have spent 3 years in laying a very good foundation as we enter the 1980's in all fields, in internal politics and economics and in international affairs.

In short, the situation as we enter the 1980's is very good. We have prepared our positions in all respects for victorious advance. We are filled with confidence as we enter the 1980's. It is completely wrong and baseless to harbor doubts about the international situation and about the future of the four modernizations. Of course, due to the 10 years' tyranny of Lin Biao and the "gang of four," some of the masses were poisoned and there are many things they do not understand because we have not carried out sufficient education. Some people even feel disappointed in certain ways with regard to the party and socialism. This is understandable. We must work with patience and confidence to gradually change their mental attitude. However, our cadres, especially the high-ranking cadres, must possess full awareness and must not waver in the slightest on fundamental issues. Only in this way can we unite and educate the whole party and the people of the whole country to enable everyone to be filled with confidence as we enter the 1980's.

PART II

In Part Two, I will talk about four problems which must be solved in order to accomplish the four modernizations, which could also be called the four necessary premises.

This is the way I spoke at the CPPCC, and everyone feels that this way of putting things is good enough. The four problems are: 1) There must be an unswerving political line which is implemented all the time; 2) there must be a political situation of stability and unity; 3) there must be a pioneering spirit of arduous struggle amid difficulties; and 4) there must be a force of cadres which persistently follows the socialist road and possesses specialized knowledge and ability. Of course, these four points cannot cover everything, but they outline what we have to do and point out the current orientation for our efforts.

First, we must have an unswerving political line which is implemented all the time. We have already stipulated this line. Comrade Ye Jianying's National Day speech summarized our general task or general line in these terms: Unite the people of all nationalities throughout the country, mobilize all positive factors, work in concert, go all out, aim high, and achieve greater, faster, better and more economical results in building a powerful modern socialist state. This is the first time that our current general line was summarized in a relatively complete way. This is the current greatest politics. [as published] Is the general line not the greatest politics? This is a long-term task. If a large-scale war breaks out, we will have to fight and halt the implementation of this general line. Otherwise, we must follow this line and concentrate all our efforts on its constant implementation. In the past 30 years, as a result of several upheavals we have never shifted our work focus to socialist construction. The result is that the superiority of socialism has been brought into too little play, the social productive forces have not developed rapidly, steadily or in concert, and the people's living standards have not had much improvement. We suffered still more during the 10 years of the Great Cultural Revolution, which caused a very great disaster. Now we must be resolved to devote all our efforts to constantly implementing this general line, unless a large-scale war breaks out. Everything must revolve around this, and it must suffer no interference. Even if a major war does break out, we must continue to implement this line after the war, or start to implement it again. The whole party and the people of the whole country must firmly establish this heroic ambition, never turn from it, and be a bit "stubborn" about it without the slightest wavering. Except for the "leftist" interference of the past, the upheaval of 1958, and especially the Great Cultural Revolution, our industrial and agricultural production and science and education would have developed greatly and there would have been a relatively great improvement in people's living standards—even without the advanced experiences of the world we are now absorbing, and even without heroic ambitions—provided that we had honestly kept to the conventional ways of doing things. Take steel for instance, if development had been steady we could have produced at least 50 to 60 million tons, and it would moreover have been usable. We now possess very good international conditions, and the whole party and the people of the whole country are truly working in concert and resolutely following the political line stipulated by the central authorities. We can say with great confidence that our prospects are very good.

There are many tasks involved and many things to be done to build a powerful modern socialist state. There is also interdependence between various tasks. For instance, there is such interdependence between economics and education and science, and between economics and politics and law and so on. We must not attend to only one thing and lose sight of others. A very great shortcoming in our planning work for a long time in the past was that we failed to do a good job of balancing things. There are imbalances between agriculture and industry; between agriculture, forestry, animal husbandry, sideline production and fishery; between light and heavy industries; between coal, power, fuel and transport and other industries; and between the "bones" and the "flesh" (that is, between industry on the one hand and housing construction, communications, urban construction, and commercial services construction on the other), and between accumulation and consumption. Planning work for this year has been done a bit better, but we will have to go on making very great efforts to fundamentally transform this state of affairs. Apart from these imbalances, another very important one is the imbalance between economic development on the one hand and the development of education, science, culture and public

health on the other. Expenditures for education, science, culture and public health are too small and are out of balance. There are even some Third World countries which have attached more importance to this aspect than we have. India spends more on education than we do. A country such as Egypt has a population of only 40 million, but they spend several times more per capita on education than we do. In short, it is absolutely imperative that we increase our spending on education, science, culture, and public health. Due to financial difficulties, we can only take care of the key points this year, but beginning next year, or the year after that at the latest, no matter what the circumstances, we must increase our emphasis on this aspect. Otherwise, modernization cannot be accomplished. There are many aspects of modernization and it is essential to achieve a comprehensive balance of all of them. We must not overemphasize one aspect. However, in the final analysis, it remains necessary to treat economic construction as the central task. If we depart from this, we will be in danger of losing our material foundation. All other tasks must serve and revolve around this central task and must certainly not interfere with it or squeeze it aside. Our lessons in this respect in the past 20 years and more have been really too painful.

At present some people, especially some young people, doubt the socialist system and babble that socialism is inferior to capitalism. We must vigorously correct this idea. The socialist system is not equivalent to the concrete methods of building socialism. Since the October 1917 Revolution, the Soviet Union has been pursuing socialism for 63 years. However, it has nothing to boast about in the way it pursues socialism. We really lack experience, but perhaps we can now seriously explore a relatively good road. However, no matter what we do, the superiority of socialism has already been proven. We must prove this to a greater, better and more forceful extent. We must and can produce many things in the future which prove that the socialist system is superior to the capitalist system. This should be expressed in many aspects, but first in the speed and efficiency of economic development. Without that, all our boasting will be useless. To achieve success like this, we must constantly, unswervingly and unwaveringly implement our political line.

Second, we must have a political situation of stability and unity.

Without a political situation of stability and unity, we cannot carry out construction with peace of mind. The experiences of the past 20 years and more have proved this point. The experiences of last year have also proved this point. We now have, or basically have, a political situation of stability and unity. This political situation of stability and unity was not easily gained, and it is still very far from being consolidated. There are still factors of instability from various aspects. Comrades at every work post must shoulder their responsibilities together and safeguard, insure and develop this political situation of stability and unity.

We want stability and unity, and we also want liveliness and vigor. Liveliness and vigor are not easily gained either, but develop in the wake of stability and unity. Under our socialist system, stability and unity and liveliness and vigor form an entity. Fundamentally speaking, there is no contradiction between them, nor should there be. What should we do if contradictions occur at certain times and in certain circumstances between stability and unity on the one hand, and liveliness and vigor on the other? We should attain liveliness and vigor under the premise that stability and unity are not hindered. At present, some comrades are somewhat confused on this question, having apparently forgotten what we suffered. In the past, after successfully completing socialist transformation, we had organizing movements of various kinds, each movement delaying so many things and harming so many people. In the final analysis, bringing in the superiority of socialism means greatly developing the social productive forces and gradually improving and raising the people's material and spiritual living standards. This cannot be achieved, not even liveliness and vigor can be attained, unless there is a political situation of stability and unity.

There are currently certain trends of thought in society, especially among certain young people, to which we must pay serious attention. For instance, could many things at the "Xidan Wall" last year be described as liveliness and vigor? What would happen if we allowed such things to spread unchecked? There are examples of this in the world, and also in China. Do not imagine that acting in this way will not lead to chaos and do not regard the matter as of little importance. A few people can sabotage our great cause. Therefore, if contradictions occur between stability and unity on the one hand, and liveliness and vigor on the other, liveliness and vigor can only be attained under the premise that stability and unity are not hindered. Only in this way can everyone advance in order. The experiences of the Great Cultural Revolution proved that turmoil can lead only to retrogression, not to progress, and that progress can only be achieved if there is order. Under the present conditions in our country, we can say that without stability and unity we would have nothing, including democracy, the double hundred principle and so on. In the past we suffered for more than 10 years, and the people cannot take and will not tolerate any more turmoil. On the contrary, on the basis of socialist stability and unity, we will be able to attain in a planned and measured way everything that is attainable and satisfy the people's demands to the maximum extent.

We have already said that there are still factors of instability. The organizational and ideological remnants of the "gang of four" still exist. We must not underestimate the strength of these remnants, otherwise we will be making a mistake. Factionalist elements still exist. There are also some new beaters, smashers and looters. There are various kinds of gangs of thugs and criminal elements. There are also counterrevolutionaries who have contacts with foreign forces and Taiwan spy organs and who carry out underground activities. There are also so-called "democrats" and "dissidents" who openly oppose the socialist system and the CCP leadership, such as Wei Jingsheng and his ilk. We cannot underestimate them either. That banner of theirs is quite distinctive. Although they sometimes say that they too support Chairman Mao and the CCP, they actually want to oppose CCP leadership and socialism. The real ideology of this bunch is to regard socialism as inferior to capitalism and the mainland as inferior to Taiwan. Of course, they know nothing about what capitalism is or what the true state of affairs is on Taiwan. Many of them have gone astray and need educating and saving. However, we must clearly understand and not be innocent about

the general tendencies and the true aims of the so-called "democrats" and "dissidents". There are also anarchists, extreme individualists and so on who sabotage social order. All these are factors of instability. Although these people do not all have the same nature, but [sic] under certain conditions they are completely capable of banding together to form a sabotage force which could cause a great deal of turmoil and damage. This situation occurred last year, and may also occur again in the future. Some people ask, since the exploiting of class as a class has been wiped out, how can there still be class struggle? Now we can see that these two aspects are both objective facts. Although our current struggle against all kinds of counterrevolutionaries, elements engaged in serious sabotage and crime, and cliques engaged in serious crime is not all class struggle, it does include ingredients of class struggle. Of course, we must resolutely draw clear distinctions between the two different kinds of contradictions and must educate all those who can be educated among the great majority of people who sabotage social order. However, if we cannot educate them or cannot educate them effectively, we must adopt resolute and merciless legal action against the various kinds of criminals. A few places and a few comrades are still acting in a soft-handed way toward these people. Some places adopt very ineffective measures or fail to take action. The people will not be satisfied with us if we indulge these people, these remnants of the "gang of four," and these counterrevolutionaries and other criminals. We have recently taken some steps to strike at them, but only initial results have been produced; we must continue to deal resolute blows at all kinds of criminal elements and strive to insure and consolidate a sound and stable social order. We must learn how to use the weapon of law and use it well. To act in a soft-handed way towards those who violate the law can only endanger the interests of the great majority of the people and jeopardize the overall situation of the four modernizations.

Party members and party cadres, especially high-ranking cadres, must take a firm and clear-cut stand in this struggle against all kinds of criminal elements. It is absolutely impermissible to publicize any freedom of speech, publication or assembly or to form associations which include counterrevolutionaries. It is absolutely impermissible for any person to have liaison with these people behind the party's back. What I mean here is the kind of liaison which involves sympathy for them. Certain comrades who have to contact them for reasons of work are of course excluded. There are indeed liaisons which involve a feeling of sympathy for those people.

For instance, certain secret publications are printed so beautifully. Where did they get the paper? These people do not have any printing plants. Are there any party members in the printing plants which print those things? Some of those who support those activities are party members, and quite a few of them are even cadres. We must clearly tell these party members that their standpoint is extremely erroneous and dangerous, and if they do not correct it immediately and thoroughly, they will be subjected to party disciplinary punishment. In short, on the issue of waging struggle against counterrevolutionaries, sabotage elements and all kinds of criminal elements, the attitude of the party organizations at all levels, right down to the party branches, must be very firm. There must be no sign of wavering or hesitation.

Some people might ask if this is another "retraction". We have never actually "relaxed" on this question so there is no need to talk about "retraction". When did we ever say we would tolerate the activities of counterrevolutionaries and all kinds of sabotage elements? When did we ever say we should abolish the dictatorship of the proletariat? Frankly speaking, we should currently act with severity, not lightly, on these issues because too much awful commotion has been caused. The state cannot just ignore these things. We must be severe in applying legal action against these elements; in this way, we can educate and save a number of young people. We must proclaim the legal system and truly insure that people can understand the law so more and more people will not only refrain from crime but will also actively uphold the law. In dealing severely with these people now, we are carrying out a kind of education not only for the great majority of criminal elements but also for the whole party and the people of the whole country. We must resolutely enforce these principles throughout the whole country: Laws must be obeyed, violators must be prosecuted, law enforcement must be strict, and everyone is equal before the law.

To truly consolidate stability and unity, the main thing is naturally to rely on positive and fundamental measures and also to rely on developing the economy and education. At the same time, we must rely on a complete legal system. If the economy and education are promoted well, if the legal system is placed on a sound basis, and if judicial work is perfected, we can insure the orderly advance of society to a very great extent. However, the legal system must be gradually perfected in the course of its implementation; we cannot wait until it is perfected. What is the point of talking about a legal system unless all these large numbers of criminal elements are severely dealt with? We must deal severely with people who sabotage stability and unity according to the circumstances.

To achieve stability and unity, the comrades of the propaganda, education, theory, literature and art departments must make great efforts together in all aspects. Without doubt, if work in these fields is done well, it can play an extremely great role in insuring, safeguarding and developing the political situation of stability and unity. However, if great deviations occur in this work, they can also assist the growth of factors of instability. We hope newspapers and publications will carry more ideological and theoretical explanations of the necessity for stability and unity. This means they should vigorously publicize the superiority of socialism, the correctness of Marxism-Leninism-Mao Zedong Thought, the powerful strength of the unity of party leadership and of the unity of party and masses, and the tremendous achievements and limitless future of socialist China. They must publicize that to strive for the future of socialist China is the supreme mission and honor of the current younger generation. In short, we must make our party's newspapers and publications the ideological center of the stability and unity of the whole country. Newspapers and publications, radio and television must regard promoting stability and unity and enhancing the socialist awareness of young people as their regular and basic task. Newspapers and publications, radio and television have scored great success over the past 3 years, and their work is generally good; however, there are also shortcomings. The comrades working in these departments must regularly listen to differing views from all quarters and analyze and improve their work. Literature and art circles have just held a congress. We say there should be no forceful interference in the questions of what to write and how to write it; therefore, this increases the responsibility of literature and art workers and the demands on their own work. We will persistently follow the double hundred principle and the principle of not sticking labels on people, beating them with sticks or grabbing them by their pigtails. Also, we will not go on putting forward the slogan that literature and art belongs to politics because this slogan is liable to become a theoretical pretext for forceful interference. Experience has proved that it does little benefit but great harm to the development of literature and art. However, this naturally does not mean that literature and art can be divorced from politics. Literature and art cannot be divorced from politics. No progressive revolutionary literature and art worker can fail to consider the social influence of his works or to consider the interests of the people, state and the party. Cultivating new socialist men is politics. New socialist men must naturally strive to fulfill the people's interests, defend the honor of the socialist motherland, and boldly sacrifice themselves for the future of the socialist motherland. Literature and art work has a very great effect on the ideological trends of people, especially of young people, and also on stability and unity. We sincerely hope all comrades in literature and art circles, and the comrades engaged in education, journalism, theoretical work and other work in the ideological field will regularly and spontaneously regard the overall situation as the most important thing and ceaselessly strive to enhance the socialist awareness of the people and of young people.

Will the demand for stability and unity hamper letting a hundred flowers blossom? No, it will not. We must forever uphold the principle of letting a hundred flowers blossom and a hundred schools of thought contend. However, this does not mean this principle may be allowed to be used to the disadvantage of the overall situation of stability and unity. To say this principle disregards stability and unity is a misunderstanding and a misuse of it. What we are implementing is socialist democracy, not capitalist democracy. Therefore, we say upholding stability, unity and the four basic principles are completely in line with upholding the principle of letting a hundred flowers blossom and a hundred schools of thought contend. Some people say the third plenary session of the party Central Committee means letting go and the four basic principles mean pulling in the reins. This kind of talk is an outright distortion. We communists can never tolerate this distortion and must resolutely oppose it. Upholding socialism is the first of the four basic principles. Is it conceivable that we can afford not to uphold socialism? If we do not uphold socialism, will there be stability and unity and will there be the socialist four modernizations? The third plenary session of the party Central Committee called for stability and unity and called for promoting socialist modernization on the basis of stability and unity. This concerns the greatest interests of people throughout the country. The principle of letting a hundred flowers blossom and a hundred schools of thought contend must, of course, serve and not oppose the greatest interests.

It is our party's unswerving principle to persevere in developing democracy and the legal system. However, in realizing democracy, the legal system and the four modernizations, we must not apply the "Great Leap Forward" methods and the "free airing of views" methods. In other words, they must be carried out step by step and in a guided way. Otherwise, they can only encourage turmoil and hamper the four modernizations, democracy and the legal system. The "four greats," namely, speaking out freely, airing views fully, holding great debates and writing big-character posters, are stated in the Constitution. After summing up historical experiences, we are compelled to admit that the "four greats" as a whole have never played a positive role. (applause) The masses should be given full right and every opportunity to make responsible criticisms of leaders and to offer positive proposals. But methods of the free airing of views are obviously inappropriate to attaining this goal. Therefore, according to practices carried out over a long period of time and in accordance with the view of the great majority of cadres and people, the party Central Committee is prepared to submit to the NPC Standing Committee and the NPC a motion to abolish the Constitution's articles concerning the "four greats." (applause)

Third, we must have the pioneering spirit of plain living and hard work.

In realizing China's four modernizations, we must make unrelenting and strenuous efforts to do pioneering work with sincerity and candor. Our country is poor. It has a poor foundation to start with. Its education, science and culture are backward. All these mean we have to go through a process of plain living and hard work. Because of their self-interest, some developed countries in the past offered capital-support and technology-support to some relatively small countries and regions where wages are low. As a result, their cheap products availed themselves of gaps in the international market with a relative ease at a certain period. Capitalists distributed a bit of their huge profits to workers in those countries and regions, thus greatly improving the workers' livelihood. China is such a big socialist country, but it is impossible for China to take this kind of "shortcut." We must also make use of foreign capital and technology and energetically develop foreign trade. However, we must emphasize self-reliance. Lin Biao and the "gang of four" promoted the so-called "socialism with poverty," "transition to poverty" and "making revolution with poverty." We oppose these absurd and reactionary viewpoints. However, we also oppose the impracticable viewpoint that China must now become a so-called welfare state. We can only gradually improve our livelihood on the basis of developing production. Developing production without improving people's livelihood is not right. Without the development of production, calling for improving livelihood is not right. It is also impossible.

We advocate distribution according to labor and offering moral encouragement and material reward to those individuals and units which make special contributions. We also advocate offering more pay for more work done by some people and areas and enabling them to become prosperous first. These are what we persistently advocate. However, we must not lose sight of the following tendency: Some people and units only pay attention to getting more pay. They not only do not give consideration to neighbors but even disregard the whole country's interests and discipline. For example, due to our negligence, a trend of indiscriminately giving bonuses was begun last year. Over 5 billion yuan of bonuses were handed out. Most of them were properly handed out but many were improperly handed out. Some units which failed to fulfill their

production and profit plans were also given bonuses. To strive for more bonuses, some enterprises arbitrarily increased the prices of some commodities. Due to indiscriminately giving bonuses, the actual wages of workers in several areas increased by 100 percent. On the other hand, several professions, particularly education units, scientific research organs, government organs and the army were not given bonuses. This created an unreasonable inequality between the bitter have-nots and the happy recipients. Thus, it created new social problems. If we had paid out 2 billion yuan less in bonuses last year, people's lives would be much better this year and there would have been no need to stop work on many capital construction projects. This trend of indiscriminate payment of bonuses "improved" the life of a few, but it imposed many more difficulties on the people of the whole country. I want to mention in passing that our measure in raising the procurement prices of agricultural products was extremely correct, and it has played a tremendous role in stimulating agricultural production. However, if we further sum up experiences, perhaps we should have done it in two steps to insure a somewhat lesser effect on finances and prices. Similar problems may crop up in our work in the future. Hence, we must again conduct education for the cadres and masses. We are a poor and large country and we must struggle hard to improve our situation. Gradual improvement of the people's living standards and increases in their incomes must be made on the basis of developing production while insuring more pay for more work. It is also necessary to take care of the whole country and to take care of those around us. We must work at a steady pace in solving this problem. We must do very well in providing guidance for the masses, and we must absolutely not make promises and arouse the masses in an irresponsible way. For instance, a recent short report said a television plant in Beijing produced 20,000 black and white 9-inch TV sets last year, an average of over 50 a day, and then organized a production line for manufacturing Japanese 12-inch black and white TV sets with a designed capacity of producing 600 a day. They are now already producing more than 400 a day. Thus, people there are talking about paying out more bonuses. It would be impossible to issue bonuses there if the payment was made on the basis of the rate of increase in labor productivity. The laboring people, who are the masters, have to create more profit for the state and increase the state's financial income for use in other fields, in expanded production and in capital construction to further speed up the development of our economy. One should be paid more for working more, but it is necessary to consider the whole society. Citing this one plant as an example, even in organizing one production line it is also necessary to consider other workshops. More and more practical problems like this are confronting us, and everyone must consider this point.

We must have a clear understanding of struggling hard to build our affairs. With the foundation it has, its huge population and its small area of arable land, China cannot achieve a large and rapid increase in labor productivity, financial income, and imports and exports. Also the people's income cannot grow rapidly. Therefore, when I am talking to foreigners I say our four modernizations are Chinese-style. A foreign visitor talking to me not long ago asked, "What do your four modernizations actually mean?" I told him that a society which could achieve a total national output value averaging 1,000 U.S. dollars per capita before the end of the century would be considered a comfortably well-off society. Of course, this reply was not accurate, but it was not just my wishful thinking. Now we have only something over 200 U.S. dollars. An increase to 1,000 dollars would mean a three-fold increase. The Singapore figure is almost 3,000 dollars, and it is over 2,000 in Hong Kong. It would not be easy for us to attain that level because our land is vast and our population great. Our conditions differ greatly from theirs. However, we should say that if our total national output value can truly reach 1,000 U.S. dollars per person, our life will be much better than theirs, better than their 2,000 dollars. This is because there is no exploiting class system here. The national income is completely used for the whole society, and a large part of it is directly distributed to the people. Those places have great contrasts between rich and poor, and the majority of the wealth is in the hands of the capitalists.

We must often remember that our country is vast, its population huge and its foundation weak; we can only catch up with the developed countries by long-term efforts. Take coal production for instance. In 1978, the United States produced over 599 million tons of commodity coal, the Soviet Union produced over 724 million tons, and we produced 620 million tons of crude coal last year. This looks quite good. However, calculating output according to population, our production was much less than theirs. Again, take steel. Japan produces almost 1 ton per person. The United States and Soviet Union produce 1 ton for every 2 persons. Many European countries also produce 1 ton for every 2 persons; that is more or less the case in Britain, France and West Germany. To reach that level, assuming our population at the end of the century would be only 1.2 or 1.3 billion, we would have to produce 600 million tons of steel, which is neither possible nor necessary. If we were able to produce 100 or 200 million tons of steel, we would have 1 ton to every 12 or 16 persons [as published]. In short, we possess various favorable conditions and we will certainly be able to catch up with the advanced countries of the world. However, we must also realize that we must be resolved to wage a long-term struggle in order to reduce or eliminate the gap of two or three centuries, or at least more than one century. We absolutely must advocate and practice struggling hard to build our affairs for a rather long time to come.

Struggling hard to build our affairs first requires that our party members and cadres, especially high-ranking cadres, take the lead. Are we not opposed to the pursuit of privilege? This is a severe struggle. Pursuit of privilege does not just exist among high-ranking cadres; it exists at all levels and in all departments. In fact, some of our cadres have turned into Mandarins. Our party members and cadres, especially high-ranking cadres, must strive to revive the glorious traditions of Yanan, strive to learn from the example of Zhou Enlai and other comrades, and play a model role in struggling hard to improve our situation. The central authorities have already laid down a number of regulations and will issue more—more stringent ones—in the future. Party members and cadres who violate the central regulations must undergo serious education. In cases where education is ineffective, organizational measures and even disciplinary action must be taken.

Opposing the pursuit of privilege is only one issue in struggling hard to improve our situation. The biggest issue is to block all kinds of waste, raise labor productivity, reduce the number of waste products which do not meet requirements, cut production costs, and improve the rate of use of investment. We must enable everyone to understand that our investment is not easily raised, that our products are not easily produced and that all waste is criminal. When production develops, we must also consider future development, carry out capital construction, achieve a comprehensive balance of the national economy and repay the debts of many years. For instance, our towns need construction, water pipes, housing, transport and schools. There are many difficulties which urgently need solving in the daily life of our teachers and scientific workers. There are many fine intellectuals whose income is only a few score yuan, who would be able to solve more problems and create a large amount of wealth for the state and people if their living and working conditions could be made just a little better, and so on. Therefore, there must not be the slightest waste and extravagance either before production and construction are undertaken, in the course of production and construction, or after products are manufactured. Great successes were scored in increasing production and practicing economy last year. That is very good, but there is still a lot of waste. It is the cadres who are mainly responsible for this and that includes those bonuses I spoke of a while ago. Not long ago the departments concerned of the State Council drew up a new charter on the question of bonuses. It must be resolutely acted on after being conveyed to the lower levels. It will not do for everyone to act as they please, as is happening now; if this occurs there can be no hope of accomplishing the four modernizations.

Fourth, we must have a force of cadres which persistently follows the socialist road and possesses specialized knowledge and ability.

It goes without saying that, to accomplish the four modernizations under China's socialist system, our force of cadres must persistently follow the socialist road, possess the basic Marxist viewpoints and abide by party and state discipline. We should say that there have been some nonsocialist ideas in the state and the party. Due to the 10 years of tyranny of Lin Biao and the "gang of four" and many other causes, plus the existence of diplomatic and trading relations with capitalist countries—relations which are still in the course of development—the penetration of the influence of bourgeois ideology is inevitable. Hence, we must constantly emphasize the need for our cadre force to persistently follow the socialist road. It is of particular significance to reiterate this point today. It is impermissible to turn our learning of certain technical and management experiences of capitalist society into the worship of capitalist foreign countries, to be corrupted and seduced by capitalism and to lose the national pride and self-confidence of socialist China. A Chinese scholar living abroad recently said that he hoped that, no matter what happened, China would not follow the road of Taiwan and would not carry out modernization in the manner of Taiwan, where the economy is actually under the control of the United States. When we select and promote a cadre, we must be sure to find out whether he persistently follows the socialist road. It is necessary to step up education for cadres who do not meet this condition, and transfer them to other work if necessary. We must with planning and leadership vigorously promote socialist virtues and habits throughout the whole party and the whole country, warmly love the socialist motherland and enhance national self-respect. In the towns we must also conduct education in the revolutionary qualities of following the socialist road and opposing corruption by capitalism. At present some young people tend to neglect politics; the whole party must realize the gravity of this problem. It is necessary to analyze the causes and find ways of seriously solving the problem.

However, the four modernizations cannot be accomplished if we merely rely on persistently following the socialist road and lack talent and learning. No matter what position one holds, it is essential to possess a certain degree of specialized knowledge and ability; if one does not have this one must learn it, and if one does have it one must continue to learn it. Readjustments must be made in the case of those who really cannot or will not learn. We must organize leadership groups in accordance with the demands of specialization, bring the role of specialized personnel into full play and also lead the masses to study and work in accordance with the demands of specialization.

I want to talk here about the relationship between Red and expert. Being expert certainly does not mean being Red; however, to be Red, it is also necessary to be expert. No matter what your trade, if you are not expert, if you do not understand things and if you give blind orders which damage the people's interests and delay the development of production and construction, it is out of the question to say that you are Red. We cannot accomplish the four modernizations unless we solve this problem. Both internationally and internally there is a universal feeling that we are overstaffed and bureaucratic, take a long time to deal with things and rely on holding meetings and describing circles; many problems which could have been solved by one phone call cannot be solved in 6 months. How can we carry out the four modernizations like this! Therefore, many foreigners say that China has no hope of accomplishing the four modernizations in this way. People at home also say this. This is indeed true; it is not false. How can we improve things? We must change the cadres' attitude of lack of specialized knowledge and ability. Do we have many cadres now? As an absolute figure, 18 million cadres in a country as large as ours is not a large number. The problem is that the cadre structure is irrational, there are too many cadres who lack specialized knowledge and ability and too few who possess these things. For example, we are at least 1 million short—I think it is 2 million—in the number of cadres capable of doing judicial work, including judges, lawyers, judicial officers, procurators and special policemen. There are very few cadres who can act as judges and lawyers, who have studied law and understand it and who also can enforce the law in a fair and impartial way. Again, take our teachers; an increase of 2 or 3 million in the number of qualified university, secondary and primary school teachers could not be called great. We have many secondary and primary students but not many university students; there are less than 1 million of those now in college. The United States has 10 million university students. In a population of 220 million, this means that 1 in every 22 persons is a university student. We would be able to cultivate more people with specialized talents if we had 2 to 3 million students studying at university. This requires an increase in the number of talented people running schools and of teachers. We are also short of secondary and primary school teachers. The burdens of many of them are too heavy, which affects the standard of teaching. We also need large numbers of qualified school administrators; these too are specialized personnel. For instance, should the leading comrade of a school party committee be a specialized person? He ought to be. He need not be a teacher, but he should at least be a specialist who understands education and is able to administer the school, to administer a certain category of school. In short, the current problem is certainly not that there are too many cadres, but that the structure is irrational, with too few of them being specialists in their work. The way to deal with this is to learn. One way is to run schools and organize training courses to teach people; another way is self-study. In short, great efforts are needed. No matter what your work or your age, you must strive to learn all about your work. You will just have to be readjusted if you cannot or will not learn. There is no other way, because you are delaying things. In future cadre selection, we must attach particular importance to specialized knowledge. For a long time we have not attached importance to this, and if we fail to attach special importance to it now we will be unable to carry out modernization. If you have no specialized knowledge and also fail to study seriously, even though you may be fired with great enthusiasm for building socialism, you will be unable to make your proper contribution or play your proper role. You may even play a contrary role. Things today are different from the past. In the past we spent a rather long time mechanically copying the experiences of the army during the war years. Actually if we carry out serious research into those experiences, we will find that they are a unity of Redness and expertise. Which of those many comrades here today who took part in the revolution during the years of war is not specialized in military affairs? Of course, there are many methods of waging war, including logistics. Carrying out logistics work is also for the purpose of fighting. At that time Redness and expertise were united which was relatively easy to do. Things are different now. We are carrying out construction and there is an extremely large number of different trades, every one of which needs specialized knowledge. It is also necessary to ceaselessly acquire new knowledge. Even the army today is different. In the past the army was a matter of millet plus rifles and you could go to battle if you knew how to fire your gun, use the bayonet and throw a grenade. Now the navy needs specialized marine knowledge, and the air force needs specialized aviation knowledge. General staff duties are also different from those days, and the area of knowledge required is much broader. Today's army cannot manage by using its past experiences, which is precisely the problem we must strive to solve. As for carrying out economic construction and education, science, political and legal work and so on, we should say that we are indeed far too short of specialized people of talent. We must therefore build a cadre force which persistently follows the socialist road and possesses specialized knowledge and ability. It must be a vast force.

We need more and more specialists, but does this mean that we have no people of talent now? No. The problem is that the party committees at all levels, especially certain old comrades, have not paid sufficient attention to this point and have failed to consciously discover, select, promote, cultivate and assist a number of talented people. A particle physics seminar was convened in Guangzhou a few days ago, and one item of news from it gives us great joy. The standard of our particle physics is very close to advanced world standards, that is to say, we have already attained a fairly advanced standard. We also have a number of young people who have scored achievements from self-study, but their numbers are much smaller than in some advanced countries. This shows that it is certainly not the case that we don't have anyone. Many people of talent have not yet been discovered; their work conditions are too poor, their pay is too low and their role cannot be brought into full play. Certain old comrades must show awareness on this point and not despise young people or always think that the young ones are not as good as we are. Actually, how old were we when we worked in the past? We were already doing great work in our 20's. Are people today less intelligent than we? We must open our minds a bit more, take stock of the overall situation and look at things from the viewpoint of the future of our cause. We must actively discover people of talent and seriously help them when we have discovered them. We should gradually attain a situation in which people with specialized knowledge are undertaking leadership work in professional organs at all levels, including the party committees at all levels. At present we should pay particular attention to selecting and promoting people around the age of 40. What is the significance of "around the age of 40"? Broadly speaking, these are people who went to university in the 1950's. It has been 30 years since the founding of the state, and those who graduated between 1961 and 1966 at the age of about 25 are now 40–45. Of course we should also select and promote cadres in their 50's. These people are our major treasure. I am afraid there are not many of that age here today. That is very regrettable. It will be a sign of the prospering of our cause if one day the majority of comrades sitting and listening to a report like this are in their 40's. We cannot comfort ourselves with the idea that we can still get by in a mediocre sort of way. We must view the future of our cause. We never did have many people of talent, and we absolutely cannot waste any more of them. We will be unable to bear such waste. The chief and most important task of the old comrades is to promote cadres who are relatively young. If other things are not done so well while this is done well, we will be able to render a good account of ourselves to Marx; otherwise, we will be unable to do so.

PART III

In Part Three, I will talk about upholding and improving party leadership.

The three major tasks and the four premises I have been speaking about pose a very great burden of work. However, I hold that so long as we uphold and improve party leadership and proceed from that to lead forward all other work, our tasks can be fulfilled.

The core of upholding the four basic principles—socialism, the dictatorship of the proletariat, Marxism-Leninism-Mao Zedong Thought, and party leadership—is to uphold party leadership. This party is a party of Marxism-Leninism-Mao Zedong Thought, the force at the core leading the socialist cause and exercising the dictatorship of the proletariat. It is a proletarian vanguard force with socialist and communist awareness and revolutionary discipline. Our party's ties with the masses and its leadership over China's socialist cause have formed during the history of 60 years of struggle. The party cannot be separated from the people, and the people cannot be separated from the party; this is something which no force can change. Actually, there is now a great deal of ideological confusion on this question. Some young people have blind faith in the so-called democracy of capitalist society. In 1957 there was talk of "taking turns to be banker," and now there are those so-called "dissidents" and those "Xidan Wall" people who are also making a fuss about this. Therefore, we must clearly explain this point. Fundamentally speaking, without party leadership, there would not be a correct political line or a political situation of stability and unity, the spirit of struggling hard to build our affairs could not be brought into play and it would be impossible to build a truly Red and expert force of cadres, especially one with specialized knowledge and ability. Thus, there would be no force able to lead the building of the four modernizations, the unification of the motherland and the struggle against hegemonism. This is an objective fact that nobody can deny. Those innocent young people who temporarily harbor some doubts about this will agree after they have gained a bit more experience.

Let us recall the road we have traversed. Could the Chinese revolution have succeeded but for the CCP? No. Don't disdain our party. I recently saw some material which said that the 4th party congress represented some 900 party members, including Comrades Mao Zedong and Zhou Enlai who were delegates; and that that party of some 900 members achieved cooperation between the CCP and the KMT and impelled the war of the northern expedition. Afterward, the revolution was defeated. Only our party could have withstood 10 years of bloody terror, "encirclement" by an army of 1 million and the Long March of 25,000 li. Thanks to the party's leadership, after struggling against all kinds of difficulties and adversities, the Chinese people finally established the PRC. Our party has also made serious mistakes, but these were always corrected by the party itself, not by any other force. Even the smashing of the "gang of four" was carried out by the party on behalf of the interests and demands of the people. China has always been called a tray of loose sand, but our party became the ruling party and the core force uniting the whole country, bringing to an end the countless splits and little kingdoms. So long as the leadership of our party is correct, it can gather together the strength of the whole people as well as the whole party to achieve tremendous accomplishments. What is the advantage of the multiparty system in the capitalist countries? That kind of multiparty system is determined by the situation of internal strife and contest within the bourgeoisie. None of them can represent the interests of the laboring people. In capitalist countries, people do not and cannot have communist ideals, and many people have no ideals at all. This situation is a weakness, not a strong point, in the struggle between them and Soviet hegemonism. It means that the strength of each country cannot be fully concentrated, and a very great part of their strength is mutually pinned down and cancelled out. Ours too is a multiparty country, but the other parties in China serve the socialist cause under the premise of acknowledging the leadership of the CCP. The people of the whole country have common interests and lofty ideals, which are to build and develop socialism and finally realize communism; we can therefore unite under the leadership of the CCP. Our party has coexisted with other parties for a long time and they exercise mutual supervision. We must persistently follow this principle. However, China is led by the CCP and China's cause of socialist modernization is carried out under the leadership of the CCP. This principle cannot be shaken. If it is, China will retrogress into divisions and confusion and will then be unable to accomplish modernization.

On the other hand we must realize that it is essential to work hard to improve party leadership in order to uphold it. Lin Biao and the "gang of four" did tremendous damage to our party. It is apparent that our party's prestige among the people is not as high as it used to be. In the past, to overcome difficulties the party just issued one call and the Central Committee uttered one sentence, and the whole country acted accordingly. In this way the purpose was served extremely well. Under the unified leadership of the CCP, we very quickly overcame the grave difficulties of 1959, 1960 and 1961. It is very worthwhile to recall that. When over 20 million workers were sent down to the rural areas, we followed the mass line and explained things clearly, and nobody complained. Things are not so easy today. Why? Lin Biao and the "gang of four" exercised tyrannical rule for 10 years, kicked aside the party committees to create "revolution," and threw the party into chaos. The "gang of four" exercised gang leadership and rule. The urgent task facing us now is to revive the party's fighting strength. The party should be a fighting force, the vanguard force of the proletariat, and it should be a united force with a high degree of awareness and discipline. The party can only have fighting strength if it is restored to this state.

There are several problems here. First, some of our party members are not up to standard. Some of the new members who joined the party under the ultraleftist line never received party education and thus cannot become models for the masses; they are not up to standard. Some old party members were up to standard for a long time, but now they too cannot become models for the masses; they too are not really up to standard. We advocate party spirit and oppose factionalism, but some people cling to factions like grim death. There are people, including certain old party members, who regard factionalism as higher than party spirit. How can one consider them to be up to standard? When fighting the war we always said that if a company consists of 30 percent party members it must be a good company with powerful fighting strength. Why? Because the party members led the charge and were the last to retreat; they were the first to suffer in daily life and the last to enjoy material things. Thus, they became models for the masses and the core of the masses. It is as simple as that. It was not easy to become a party member at that time. A party cadre, the commander of a company, or a platoon leader had to carry two or three rifles on his back when on the march. Some party members are not like that now. They joined the party to be the first to enjoy material benefits and the last to suffer. In opposing the pursuit of privileges, we are actually opposing the pursuit of privileges by some party members and cadres. So we now propose that our party must revive its fine traditions and work style. There is a problem with bringing party members up to standard. Whether one meets the standards and criteria for a party member is not just a problem facing new party members, it is also a problem for some of the old ones.

Therefore, there is indeed a problem with rectifying the party. We now have 38 million party members. If all of these 38 million were up to standard, what a tremendous force that would be! The problem is that some party members are not up to standard, and it is necessary to carry out rectification on the basis of education. The central committee is now considering revising the party constitution. The constitutions adopted by the 9th and 10th party congresses were not actually constitutions; they failed to lay down good regulations on the rights and duties of party members, guidelines for judging good party members and procedures to be followed if a party member does not meet the criteria. Revision is needed. We must certainly set strict demands on party members. Through discussion of the draft party constitution we should carry out education throughout the party, and then officially adopt it at the 12th party congress.

In improving party leadership, apart from improving the organizational state of the party we must also improve the state of its leadership work and leadership system. This is a complex problem. Everyone knows that just after we entered the cities, Chairman Mao said that we would soon have to put aside the things we were familiar with, as the things facing us were becoming unfamiliar. Because it has not been seriously solved over a long period of time, this problem is now all the more urgent and grave. The work of leading an area, a department, a factory, a school or a PLA unit is now much more complex and difficult than in the past. For instance, in economic work we have of course done a lot of good things, but have we really systematically studied and built socialist economy in a planned way? To build a socialist economy in a planned way throughout the whole country is very different from economic work in the liberated areas. Problems in economic work now are also much more complex than in the 1950's. The conditions are different and the tasks we face are also different. Science and technology has developed, international exchange has developed, our economy must be internationally competitive and we must measure it by international standards. In the face of the new problems that are constantly cropping up, our party members and our people must always study. Nobody can be content with being backward; if we are backward, we cannot exist. But how many party members possess specialized knowledge? In particular, how many of our leading cadres possess specialized knowledge? Can we get by without changing the current state of affairs? Of course, even if party members possess specialized knowledge, the party cannot replace and monopolize everything. This is particularly true now. The party must hold the leading position, but it is necessary to seriously study and solve these problems I have spoken of. I think that the party congresses at all levels should emphasize studies on this problem and that preparations should be made now; everyone should join in the discussion. We must solve this problem in a systematic and proper way.

There are currently many problems to solve in improving the party leadership. For instance, we have always said that a factory should implement the system of division of responsibilities for managers under the leadership of the party committee; the army should implement the system of division of responsibilities for commanders under the leadership of the party committee, and schools should implement the system of division of responsibilities for headmaster under the leadership of the party committee. If we continue to carry out this system in the future, do factory workshops need to be led by their party general branches? Do the work shifts and groups need to be led by their party branches or groups? Similarly, do school faculties need to be led by their party general branches? Is this beneficial for the work of the factory or school? Can it express the role of party leadership? If this problem is not solved well, party leadership may be damaged and weakened instead of being strengthened. What methods should the CCP adopt to exercise leadership? Should it use this organizational form or other methods? For instance, the model role played by party members, including making great efforts to learn specialized knowledge, becoming adept in all kinds of specialities and being the first to suffer and the last to enjoy material comforts, means that their work burden is heavier than that of other people. The party committee of a factory must insure that plans are fulfilled with respect to quantity and quality of output and production costs, that technology and management are advanced, that management is advanced and that management is democratic, that all management personnel have duties and powers and can work in an effective and disciplined way, that all the workers enjoy democratic rights and reasonable labor, living and study conditions, and that they can cultivate, select and promote talented people without allowing any sectarianism and make full use of able people, whether or not they are party members. If the party committee can insure all this, it is exercising effective and efficient leadership. This way of doing things is much better than trying to do everything at the same time and interfering in everything. The party's prestige will naturally be enhanced.

In short, we are facing the major question of how to improve party leadership. Unless we study and solve this question well we will be unable to uphold party leadership or enhance the party's prestige.

To uphold and improve party leadership, it is necessary to strengthen party discipline. Party discipline fell to pieces during the Great Cultural Revolution and has still not been completely restored; this too is an important factor why the party cannot play its proper role. Because discipline is rather poor, many party members can do as they please and need not carry out or need not completely carry out the party's line, principles, policies, decisions and stipulated tasks. If a party allows its members to say and do whatever strikes their fancy, that party naturally cannot have unified will or fighting strength, and the party's tasks cannot be smoothly carried out. Therefore, to uphold and improve party leadership, it is necessary to strictly promote party discipline and strengthen the sense of discipline to a very great extent. The individual must obey the organization, the minority the majority, the lower levels the upper levels, and the whole party the Central Committee. It is essential to strictly enforce this. Otherwise, the party cannot become a combat collective and will not be qualified to act as the vanguard force.

I want to say here that the most important thing is that the whole party must obey the Central Committee. The Central Committee has made mistakes, but it corrected these long ago. Nobody is allowed to resist the leadership of the Central Committee by using the Central Committee's mistakes as a pretext. Only if the whole party strictly obeys the Central Committee can the party lead all the party members and all the people of the country to struggle to accomplish the great task of modernization. If anyone seriously sabotages this regulation, the party committees and the discipline inspection committees at all levels must mete out disciplinary punishment, because this embodies the highest interests of the party and also of the people of the whole country. We must resolutely bring party democracy into play and insure party democracy. If party members have differing views of party decisions, they can reserve their opinions and also make their opinions known via their organization right up to the Central Committee. Party organizations at all levels, from the Central Committee downward, must seriously consider these opinions. However, it is necessary to obey the decisions of the Central Committee and the party organization until those decisions are changed. It is necessary to present one's opinions in accordance with the party's decisions. It is forbidden to arbitrarily spread opinions which show lack of trust in, dissatisfaction with and opposition to the Central Committee's line, principles and policies. The party's newspapers and publications must unconditionally publicize the party's proposals. Party members naturally have the right to criticize shortcomings and mistakes in party work, but this must be constructive criticism. They must propose positive ideas for improving things. I am not saying that problems of various kinds cannot be discussed. They can be discussed, but the scope and forms of discussion must conform to party principles and observe party discipline. Otherwise, if everyone does as he pleases and fails to carry out in his action the Central Committee's principles, policies and decisions, the party will become slack and cannot possess unity and fighting strength. Hence, it is necessary to eliminate the anarchist trend of thought brought into the party by the "gang of four" and the various bourgeois liberalist trends of thought which have recently appeared in the party. Only by resolutely insuring the unity and fighting strength of the party can we accomplish all the tasks proposed today.

In the final analysis, all the major tasks and principles which I have been talking about mean that we must have a good party to lead things. We have always said that the CCP is a great, glorious and correct party. Various shortcomings have appeared due to historical twists and turns. However, as a result of 3 years of effort, these shortcomings have either been basically eliminated or we are currently making efforts to eliminate them. We must strive to act more correctly in our future work, or at any rate to make fewer mistakes, avoid great twists and turns and great mistakes and correct mistakes as rapidly as possible. I fully believe that our party and our Central Committee will certainly be able to succeed in this. We are full of confidence. Building China's modernization needs our party; China's international struggle against hegemonism and its important position in the effort to promote the advance of mankind requires our party. We must uphold and strengthen party leadership and strengthen the party's discipline and fighting strength to enable us to victoriously fulfill our tremendous task of leading the whole country and the people of all nationalities. (warm applause)

An Introduction to Deng Xiaoping's Selected Works, 30 June 1983

Once Deng had become both the strong man and the elder statesman of the regime, as he had by 1981, it was more or less inevitable that his Selected Works should be published as Mao Zedong's had been after 1949. This official introduction to, or summary of, these works is both authoritative and convenient. The introduction, followed by the table of contents, is also easy to use. Deng emerges for what he is: a vigorous, pragmatic leader trying to combine enhanced control by the Party and its apparatus, with increased all-round efficiency. Not being a quasi-megalomaniac like Mao, Deng has caused, or permitted, the selected works of some other prominent Chinese Communist leaders, living and dead, also to be published.

1975, YEAR OF STRUGGLE AGAINST THE GANG OF FOUR

Supported by Comrade Mao Zedong, Comrade Deng Xiaoping took care of the day-to-day work of the party Central Committee in 1975, while Comrade Zhou Enlai was seriously ill. Upholding the party's correct leadership and waging a sharp struggle against the gang of four, Deng Xiaoping called a number of important meetings to solve problems in industry, agriculture and the Army and made great efforts to straighten things out in various fields.

He worked hard to eliminate the chaos created by the "Cultural Revolution" and promote stability, unity and growth of the national economy, bringing about a significant improvement in the situation. Eight of his speeches that year are included in the "Selected Works." Among them:

"The Army Needs Consolidation" was delivered at a meeting of cadres of the headquarters of the General Staff of the Chinese People's Liberation Army in January 1975 after Deng Xiaoping was appointed vice-chairman of the Central Committee's Military Commission and chief of the General Staff. In view of the serious sabotage of Army building by Lin Biao and the gang of four, Deng Xiaoping pointed out that the Army should be consolidated, party spirit enhanced, factionalism eliminated and discipline strengthened. This was one of his earliest proposals to set things in order, which was followed by efforts to this end.

"The Whole Party Should Take the Overall Interest Into Account and Push Forward the National Economy" was presented in March 1975 at a meeting of secretaries in charge of industry from the provincial, municipal and autonomous region Communist Party committees. Deng Xiaoping urged the whole party and nation to strive for the ambitious goal of making China a powerful socialist state with modern agriculture, industry, national defense, and science and technology by the end of the century, which

[New China News Agency, 30 June 1983.]

represented the nation's overall interest. Deng Xiaoping sharply criticized the erroneous view that "it is safe to make revolution but dangerous to engage in production." Pinpointing railroad transportation as a weak link in the national economy, he proposed such effective measures to straighten up the railroad service as strengthening centralized and unified leadership, establishing necessary rules and regulations and opposing factionalism. At the same time, the party Central Committee made a decision to improve the railroad service. The speech exerted a great impact throughout the country. The breakthrough scored in solving the problems in the railroad system sparked efforts to straighten things out in all industry, including iron and steel, coal mining and national defense industry, with good results.

"Things Must Be Straightened Out in All Fields" was delivered at a rural work meeting in September and October 1975. In this speech, Deng Xiaoping touched on agriculture, industry, science, education, art and literature, all of which, he said, had serious problems that needed to be straightened out. Consolidation of the party and leading bodies at various levels should be the center of the effort. He also criticized Lin Biao's practice of vulgarizing and fragmenting Mao Zedong Thought, pointing out that this problem was yet to be solved. This criticism was actually aimed at the gang of four. The effort initiated by Deng Xiaoping to straighten things out in all fields was aimed at systematically correcting the errors of the "Cultural Revolution," and Mao Zedong found this unbearable. An erroneous movement to criticize Deng Xiaoping thereafter again plunged the country into chaos.

THE FIRST TWO YEARS AFTER THE SMASHING OF THE GANG OF FOUR

During the two years following the smashing of the gang of four, the party's work advanced hesitatingly. Hua Guofeng, then chairman of the party Central Committee, persisted in the errors of Mao Zedong in his late years by pursuing the line of "two-whatever's" (i.e., whatever policy decisions Chairman Mao made should be firmly upheld and whatever instructions Chairman Mao gave should be unswervingly adhered to). In these circumstances, Deng Xiaoping energetically opposed the personality cult, advocated emancipation of the mind and seeking truth from facts, and waged an arduous struggle to reestablish the Marxist ideological line in the party. He volunteered to take charge of science and education, making a breakthrough in setting distorted things to rights in this area. Deng Xiaoping and other proletarian revolutionary veterans jointly made full preparations for the success of the third plenary session of the 11th party Central Committee toward the end of 1978. Thirteen of his speeches and talks during those two years are included in the "Selected Works." Among them:

"The Two Whatever's Does Not Accord With Marxism," is part of a talk he had with two comrades on the party Central Committee in May 1977. Deng Xiaoping had not yet resumed his work at that time, because of procrastination and obstruction by Hua Guofeng. Deng Xiaoping said pointedly in his talk that the "two whatever's" would not do. He reiterated the important view he had expressed in a letter to the party Central Committee in April 1977 that Mao Zedong Thought must be applied accurately and in its entirety as the guiding principle for the whole party, Army and nation. The talk, which reflected his scientific attitude and dauntlessness in safeguarding Mao Zedong Thought, heralded the emancipation of thinking in the party.

"Grasp Mao Zedong Thought as a Whole and Accurately" is part of Deng Xiaoping's first formal speech after he resumed his leading positions at the third plenary session of the 10th Central Committee in July 1977. He again expounded the necessity of having an all-round and accurate understanding of Mao Zedong Thought and of being good at studying and mastering Mao Zedong Thought as a system and applying it to guiding work in various fields.

"Respect Knowledge and Able People" and "Some Views on Work in Science and Education" were two talks given in May and August of 1977. Deng Xiaoping pointed out in these talks that the political line represented by Comrade Mao Zedong had predominated scientific and educational work during the 17 years after the founding of the People's Republic of China and that the overwhelming majority of intellectuals had served socialism with great successes under the correct leadership of the party. He thus refuted the erroneous assessments at the time of scientific and educational work during the 17 years and of the intellectuals. He emphasized that respect for knowledge and able people should be fostered as a trend within the party, that mental workers should be regarded as part of the working people and that the erroneous notion of looking down on intellectuals should be opposed.

"Speech at the Plenary Session of the Military Commission of the Party Central Committee" was made in December 1977. Deng Xiaoping again voiced important views on consolidating the Army and stressed that the people and events involved in the conspiracy of the gang of four to usurp the supreme party leadership and state power must be thoroughly investigated and that leading bodies should never accept in their ranks those who had taken part in these activities and those with bad political character and anti-Marxist ideology.

"Speech at the Opening Ceremony of the National Science Conference" was made in March 1978. Deng Xiaoping pointed out that mastery of modern science and technology is the key to achieving the four modernizations. He called for tremendous efforts to develop scientific research and education and to bring into full play the revolutionary enthusiasm of scientific and educational workers. He dwelt at length on the Marxist view that science and technology are part of the productive forces. He declared that in socialist society, those who labor, whether by hand or by brain, are all working people. He affirmed that the overwhelming majority of brain workers have become intellectuals of the working class and the laboring people, and therefore can be regarded as part of the working class.

"Speech at the All-Army Political Work Conference" was made in June 1978, at a time when the debate on the criterion for judging what is truth had just started. Deng Xiaoping stated that some people regarded seeking truth from facts, proceeding from reality and integrating theory with practice as wrong, but this was a question involving how to look at Marxism-Leninism and Mao Zedong Thought. He said that seeking truth from facts, proceeding in all cases from reality and integrating theory with practice are basic viewpoints and methods of Marxism-Leninism and Mao Zedong Thought. Running counter to this will only lead to idealism and metaphysics, as well as losses in work and failure of the revolution. He said it was a serious task to get rid of the pernicious influence of Lin Biao and the gang of four, set to rights what had been distorted, throw off mental shackles and bring about a great emancipation of thinking. The speech provided important ideological and theoretical preparations for reestablishing the ideological line of seeking truth from facts and in bringing about a great strategic shift at the third plenary session of the 11th Central Committee of the party.

FROM THE THIRD PLENARY SESSION OF THE 11TH CENTRAL COMMITTEE TO THE 12TH PARTY CONGRESS

The third plenary session of the 11th Central Committee of the party put an end to the difficult situation of the party's work advancing hesitatingly from October 1976 and began a conscientious and comprehensive correction of the "left" errors of the "Cultural Revolution" and earlier. From that plenary session to the 12th party congress, Deng Xiaoping played an even more outstanding policy-making role in the work of the party and the state in various fields. The many theories and policies he set forth or elaborated on for building socialism with Chinese characteristics in accordance with the basic principles of Marxism-Leninism and Mao Zedong Thought and China's conditions are very important for guiding the triumphant progress in China's socialist modernization. The 26 works of this period contained in the selection include:

"Emancipate the Mind, Seek Truth From Facts, Unite as One and Look Forward," a speech in December 1978 at the closing session of a work conference of the party Central Committee in preparation for the third plenary session. Deng Xiaoping summed up the previous two years' criticism of the "two-whatevers" and discussions on the criterion for judging what is truth and set the task of continuing to emancipate the mind in the future. The article said emancipation of thinking is an important political question at present. Only when one's thinking is emancipated can one correctly use Marxism-Leninism and Mao Zedong Thought as the guide in solving the problems left over from the past and new ones, correctly reform those aspects of the relations of production and the superstructure that are not in harmony with the rapid growth of the productive forces, and determine the concrete road, principles, methods, and measures to achieve the four modernizations in the light of China's conditions. Unless the rigid way of thinking was broken and the minds of the cadres and the people were fully emancipated, there could be no hope of achieving the four modernizations. The speech also stressed that democracy is an important condition for emancipating thinking and that the handling of leftover problems is aimed at going forward and smoothly shifting the focus of the party's work to socialist construction. The speech served as the keynote for the third plenary session.

"Adhere to the Four Cardinal Principles," a speech at a conference on the party's theoretical work in March 1979. The article clearly sets modernization as a major task for the present and a considerably long period in the future and calls for blazing a path for modernization with Chinese characteristics. This requires ideological and political adherence to the four cardinal principles of upholding the socialist road, the dictatorship of the proletariat, leadership by the Communist Party, and Marxism-Leninism and Mao Zedong Thought. As the fundamental prerequisites for ensuring stability and unity and carrying out the four modernizations, these principles conform to the spirit of the third plenary session. The four cardinal principles were later written into the Constitutions of the party and the state, becoming the common political foundation for the unity of the whole party and the people of all nationalities in China.

"The Tasks of the United Front and the People's Political Consultative Conference in the New Period," which was the opening address to the Second Session of the Fifth National Committee of the Chinese People's Political Consultative Conference in June 1979. Deng Xiaoping made a scientific analysis of the changes in the social classes in China over the 30 years since the People's Republic was founded. He pointed out that China's united front had become a broad alliance of socialist workers and patriots who support socialism. ("Patriots who uphold reunification of the motherland" was added in his speech to the Third Session of the Fifth CPPCC National Committee.) He also described that alliance as led by the working class and based on the worker-peasant alliance.

"The Organizational Line Is the Guarantee for Implementing the Ideological and Political Lines," a talk to people attending an enlarged meeting of the Standing Committee of the Navy's party committee in July 1979. Deng Xiaoping said that, once the ideological and political lines are established, the most urgent question to be solved is the organizational line, of which the most important and pressing issue is selection of worthy successors. The problem should be solved while the veteran cadres are still active and in good health. The two major criteria for choosing cadres are: 1) they support the political and ideological lines of the third plenary session, and 2) they uphold party spirit instead of factionalism.

"Greetings to the Fourth National Congress of Chinese Writers and Artists," delivered in October 1979. The article refutes the slanders spread by Lin Biao and the gang of four that China's literature and art in the 17 years up to the "Cultural Revolution" was "a field in which the sinister line exercised dictatorship." While urging party committees at all levels to provide good leadership on literature and art, Deng Xiaoping pointed out that party leadership does not mean issuing orders nor requiring literature and art to be subordinated to temporary, concrete and specific political tasks. It means providing writers and artists with the conditions to enrich socialist literature and art according to their characteristics and inherent laws of development.

"Senior Cadres Should Take the Lead in Carrying Forward the Party's Fine Traditions," a report made in November 1979 at a meeting of cadres working in the central party, government and army organizations at the vice-ministerial level and above. Drawing attention to the tendency of certain cadres, especially senior cadres, to seek privilege, Deng Xiaoping urged them to set strict demands on themselves and to restore and carry forward the party's fine traditions of hard work, plain living and close contacts with the masses. He asked them to set an example in rectifying the party's style of work and improving social conduct.

"The Present Situation and Our Tasks," a speech at a cadres' meeting called by the party's Central Committee in January 1980. Deng Xiaoping listed three major tasks for China in the 1980s: combating hegemonism and defending world peace in international affairs; getting Taiwan back to the motherland and reunifying the country; and intensifying the four modernizations program. The core of the tasks is modernization, which is the most essential condition for China's efforts to solve both internal and international problems. It is imperative to uphold and improve party leadership, tighten party discipline and raise the party's combat worthiness if these tasks are to be accomplished.

"Opinions on Drafting the 'Resolution on Certain Questions in the History of Our Party Since the Founding of the People's Republic of China'," a collection of excerpts from nine talks Deng Xiaoping made between March 1980 and June 1981. In these talks he repeatedly stressed that the three focal points in the draft should be: defining the place of Comrade Mao Zedong in history and upholding and developing Mao Zedong Thought; analyzing the major historical events in the 30 years since the founding of the People's Republic of China by seeking truth from facts and giving them fair appraisals; and making a basic summation of the past so as to encourage people to look forward in unity. He said that the first point is the most important and fundamental: the very core of the issue. Explaining Mao Zedong Thought is not just a theoretical issue but, above all, a major political issue internally and internationally. These views were instrumental to unifying the understanding of the entire party membership and to summing up historical experiences correctly.

"An Important Principle for Handling Relations Between Fraternal Parties," which was part of a talk in May 1980 with senior personnel working in the party Central Committee. The situation in various countries differs in a thousand ways. And revolution in different countries cannot proceed according to a set model, Deng Xiaoping said. There must be respect for the party and people of each country to find their own way, and they must not be subject to commands by a self-appointed paternal party. The major points of the talk laid the foundation for formulating the party's correct principles of "independence, complete equality, mutual respect and non-interference in each other's internal affairs" in handling relations between fraternal parties.

"Reforms in Party and State Leadership Systems," a speech in August 1980 at an enlarged meeting of the Political Bureau of the party Central Committee. The speech raised the point that the system of leadership of the party and the state must be reformed in order to give full play to the superiority of the socialist system and speed up the progress of modernization. Efforts must be made in the following aspects: economically, expanding the productive forces rapidly and improving the material and cultural well-being of the people step by step; politically, fully developing people's democracy and building up a socialist legal system; organizationally, training large numbers of qualified people needed by China's socialist modernization who adhere to the four cardinal principles, whose average age is relatively young and who have professional knowledge.

"Implement the Principle of Readjustment and Ensure Stability and Unity," a speech in December 1980 at the Central Committee work conference. It analyzes the need to carry out the principle of readjustment, which is to provide a solid basis for steady advance so that China will reach its goal of the four modernizations with a greater certainty of success. The speech stresses the importance of consolidating and increasing political stability and unity as the key to the success of this readjustment. The policy advanced by Deng Xiaoping for "furthering the economic readjustment and enhancing political stability" has since guided China's economy onto the path of healthy development.

"On Opposing Erroneous Ideology Tendencies" and "On Questions on the Ideological Front," containing the main points of talks by Deng Xiaoping in March and July of 1981, on separate occasions with leaders of the People's Liberation Army General Political Department and central propaganda units. Pointing to the tendency at the time toward bourgeois liberalization that deviates from the socialist path and leadership by the Communist Party, Deng Xiaoping said: The call for emancipation of thinking was raised at the third plenary session of the 11th Central Committee, with emphasis on correcting "left" errors. Right tendencies occurred later, and they, too, must be corrected. The emancipation of thinking requires combating both "left" and right deviations. Efforts to correct erroneous ideological tendencies must proceed from reality and adhere to correct principles. Slackness and weakness shown by party organizations in exercising leadership over the ideological front and their timidity in criticizing erroneous tendencies at present call for particular attention. This problem must be dealt with seriously.

"Build a Powerful, Modern and Regular Revolutionary Army," a speech delivered by Deng Xiaoping in September 1981 when he reviewed the troops participating in military exercises in north China as chairman of the Central Committee's Military Commission. Taking into consideration the situation at home and abroad and the Army's glorious mission of defending the socialist motherland and the modernization program, he raised the higher demand of building the Army into a powerful, modern and regular revolutionary Army.

"Streamlining Government Institutions Is a Revolution," a speech to a meeting of the party Central Committee's Political Bureau in January 1982. Deng Xiaoping said that streamlining institutions is a major event, a revolution in its own right. It does not, of course, mean revolution against persons, but a revolution against the set-up. Streamlining government institutions requires determination and meticulous work. Attention should be paid not only to the issue involving those who are leaving, but even more to the issue involving those coming in. It is essential to choose the right persons. The key point is to select younger cadres who have both ability and political integrity and get them into leading bodies. Choosing good persons and giving responsibility to competent people is also a revolution.

"Resolutely Strike at Criminal Activities in the Economic Sphere," a speech to a meeting of the Political Bureau of the party Central Committee in April 1982. Analyzing criminal activities in the economic sphere after adoption of the policy of opening to the outside world and taking flexible measures to invigorate the economy domestically, Deng Xiaoping pointed out that, unless the party took firm steps to check such activities, the problem might arise as to whether or not there would be a "change of political color." He said the party must pay attention to two aspects: persisting in the policy of opening to the outside world and invigorating the economy domestically, and resolutely striking at criminal activities in the economic sphere. He also raised four assurances for keeping to the socialist road, namely, restructuring government institutions, building socialist culture and ethics, striking at criminal offenses in the economic sphere, and rectifying the party's style of work and consolidating the party organization.

"Opening Speech to the 12th National Congress of the Communist Party of China," delivered in September 1982. Deng Xiaoping listed the tasks of the congress which he described as the most important meeting since the party's seventh national congress in 1945. While the seventh congress laid the foundation for the nationwide victory of the new-democratic revolution, he said, the 12th congress would create a new situation in all fields of socialist modernization and guide it toward victory. The basic conclusion China has reached in summing up its long historical experience is, he said, to integrate the universal truth of Marxism with the concrete realities of China, to blaze China's own path and build socialism with Chinese characteristics.

CONTENTS OF "SELECTED WORKS"

Following are the contents of "Selected Works of Deng Xiaoping" (1975–1982), with editor's notes explaining the occasions on which the speeches were made:

The Army Needs Consolidation (January 25, 1975)—Speech at a meeting of cadres of the headquarters of the General Staff of the Chinese People's Liberation Army

The Whole Party Should Take the Overall Interest Into Account and Push Forward the National Economy (March 5, 1975)—Speech at a meeting of secretaries in charge of industry from the provincial, municipal and autonomous region party committees

Some Problems To Be Solved in the Iron and Steel Industry (May 29, 1975)—Speech at a meeting on the iron and steel industry

Strengthen Party Leadership and Rectify the Party's Style of Work (July 4, 1975)—Speech to the students of the fourth study class arranged by the party Central Committee

Tasks for Consolidating the Army (July 14, 1975)—Speech at an enlarged meeting of the Military Commission of the party Central Committee

On Consolidation of Enterprise in the National Defense Industry (August 3, 1975)—Speech at a meeting of the major enterprises in the national defense industry

Some Views on the Development of Industry (August 18, 1975)—Talk at the State Council's discussion on the document, "Some Problems in Accelerating the Development of Industry," drafted by the State Planning Commission

Things Must Be Straightened Out in All Fields (September 27 and October 4, 1975)—Talks at a rural work meeting

The "Two-Whatever's" Does Not Accord With Marxism (May 24, 1977)—Part of a talk with two comrades on the party Central Committee

Respect Knowledge and Able People (May 24, 1977)—ditto

Grasp Mao Zedong Thought as a Whole and Accurately (July 21, 1977)—Part of a speech at the third plenary session of the 10th party Central Committee

Some Views on Work in Science and Education (August 8, 1977)—Speech at a meeting on the work in the fields of science and education

The Army Should Attach Strategic Importance to Education and Training (August 23, 1977)—Part of a speech at a meeting of the Military Commission of the party Central Committee

Put To Rights What Have Been Distorted in the Field of Education (September 19, 1977)—Talk to the principal leading members of the Ministry of Education

Speech at the Plenary Session of the Military Commission of the Party Central Committee (December 28, 1977)

Speech at the Opening Ceremony of the National Science Conference (March 18, 1978)

Adhere to the Principle of Distribution According to Work (March 28, 1978)—Part of a talk to leading members of the Politics Research Office of the State Council

Speech at the National Educational Work Conference (April 22, 1978)

Speech at the All-Army Political Work Conference (June 2, 1978)

Hold Aloft the Banner of Mao Zedong Thought and Adhere to the Principle of Seeking Truth From Facts (September 16, 1978)—Part of the talk while hearing reports on work by members of the Standing Committee of the Jilin provincial party committee

The Working Class Should Make Outstanding Contributions to the Four Modernizations (October 11, 1978)—Speech at the ninth national congress of Chinese trade unions

Emancipate the Mind, Seek Truth From Facts, Unite as One and Look Forward (December 13, 1978)—Speech at the closing session of the work conference of the party Central Committee

Adhere to the Four Cardinal Principles (March 30, 1979)—Speech at a conference on the party's theoretical work

The Tasks of the United Front and the People's Political Consultative Conference in the New Period (June 15, 1979)—Opening address to the Second Session of the Fifth National Committee of the Chinese People's Political Consultative Conference

The Organizational Line Is the Guarantee for Implementing the Ideological and Political Lines (July 29, 1979)—Talk to people attending an enlarged meeting of the Standing Committee of the Navy's party committee

Greetings to the Fourth National Congress of Chinese Writers and Artists (October 30, 1979)

Senior Cadres Should Take the Lead in Carrying Forward the Party's Fine Traditions (November 2, 1979)—Report to a meeting of cadres working in the central party, government and Army organizations at the vice-ministerial level and above

The Present Situation and Our Tasks (January 16, 1980)—Speech at a cadres' meeting called by the party Central Committee

Persist in the Party Line and Improve Working Methods (February 29, 1980)—Speech at the third meeting of the fifth plenary session of the 11th party Central Committee

Streamline the Army To Raise its Combat Effectiveness (March 12, 1980)—Speech at an enlarged meeting of the Standing Committee of the Military Commission of the party Central Committee

Opinions on Drafting the "Resolution on Certain Questions in the History of Our Party Since the Founding of the People's Republic of China" (March 1980–June 1981)—Excerpts from nine talks during this period on the drafting and revision of the resolution

On Questions Concerning the Rural Policies (May 31, 1980)—Part of a talk with senior personnel working in the party Central Committee

An Important Principle for Handling Relations Between Fraternal Parties (May 31, 1980)—ditto

Reforms in Party and State Leadership Systems (August 18, 1980)—Speech at an enlarged meeting of the Political Bureau of the party Central Committee

Interviews with the Italian Journalist Oriana Fallaci (August 21 and 23, 1980)

Implement the Principle of Readjustment and Ensure Stability and Unity (December 25, 1980)—Speech at a work conference of the party Central Committee

On Opposing Erroneous Ideological Tendencies (March 27, 1981)—Main points of a talk with leaders of the P.L.A. General Political Department

Speech at the Closing Ceremony of the Sixth Plenary Session of the 11th Party Central Committee (June 29, 1981)

The Primary Task for Veteran Cadres Is To Select Young and Middle-Aged Cadres (July 2, 1981)—Speech at a meeting of secretaries of the provincial, municipal and autonomous region party committees

On Questions on the Ideological Front (July 17, 1981)—Main points of a talk with leaders of central propaganda units

Build a Powerful, Modern and Regular Revolutionary Army (September 19, 1981)—Speech at a review of the troops participating in military exercises in north China

Streamlining Government Institutions Is a Revolution (January 13, 1982)—Speech at a meeting of the party Central Committee Political Bureau on streamlining the central leading organs

Resolutely Strike at Criminal Activities in the Economic Sphere (April 10, 1982)—Speech at a meeting of the party Central Committee Political Bureau to discuss the "Decision of the C.P.C. Central Committee and State Council on Struggle Against Criminal Activities in the Economic Sphere"

China's Historical Experience in Economic Construction (May 6, 1982)—Talk with Samuel Kanyon Doe, head of state of Liberia

Speech at a Meeting of the Military Commission of the Party Central Committee (July 4, 1982)

Establishing of Advisory Commissions Is an Interim Measure Toward Abolition of Life-Long Tenure for Leading Cadres (July 30, 1982)—Part of a speech at an enlarged meeting of the Political Bureau of the party Central Committee

Opening Speech to the 12th National Congress of the Communist Party of China (September 1, 1982)

An Official Plug for Deng Xiaoping's Selected Works, 12 July 1983

3

If there could be any doubt as to the authoritative character of Deng's Selected Works, this circular dispels it.

"Selected Works of Deng Xiaoping (1975–1982)" has been published; the whole party must study it earnestly. Party committees at all levels must strengthen their leadership over the study.

The study of "Selected Works of Deng Xiaoping" is an important ideological preparation for an overall party consolidation to be started this fall and winter. Party consolidation should primarily be ideological consolidation. It aims at reaching a common understanding of the whole party along the Marxist lines established at the 3d Plenary Session of the 11th CPC Central Committee and the 12th CPC Congress.

Studying "Selected Works of Deng Xiaoping" is an extremely significant aspect of the strengthening of the party's ideological unity. "Selected Works of Deng Xiaoping" systematically reflects the party's correct leadership represented by Comrade Deng Xiaoping; the struggle in 1975 to put things in various quarters in good order following the ravages by the "gang of four;" the struggle during the period between the crushing of the "gang of four" and the 3d Plenary Session of the 11th CPC Central Committee to correct the errors of the "two whatevers" and reestablish the Marxist ideological, political and organizational lines; and the struggles carried out after the 3d Plenary Session of the 11th CPC Central Committee to set things right in

all fields, to earnestly sum up historical experiences, particularly the lessons learned from the "Cultural Revolution" and from the "leftist" mistakes committed before it, and to ascertain that socialist modernization and building socialism with Chinese characteristics will be the focus of party work.

This magnificent book, while manifesting the creative initiative Comrade Deng Xiaoping displayed in handling a whole series of vital issues, also demonstrates his style of drawing on the collective wisdom and absorbing all useful ideas, upholding democratic centralism and the mass line, and opposing personality cults and arbitrary decisions. In this sense, this work is also a collection of the party Central Committee's correct opinions.

Earnest study of "Selected Works of Deng Xiaoping" will help us to better understand the history of the party during this great transitional period, the origin and development of the lines set by the 3d Plenary Session of the 11th CPC Central Committee, the principal substance and assurances of the correct course set by the 12th CPC Congress toward the building of a socialism with Chinese characteristics, and our party's new accomplishments in upholding and developing Mao Zedong Thought under new historical conditions.

While studying "Selected Works of Deng Xiaoping," we must adhere to the principle of integrating theory with practice. Comrades engaged in the study—particularly leading cadres at and above county and regimental-level units—must, on the basis of studying the "Selected Works"

[Central Committee Circular on the Study of the *Selected Works of Deng Xiaoping*, New China News Agency, 12 July 1983.]

assiduously and understanding their concept thoroughly, review their experiences in recent years (certain veteran comrades may also reexamine their experiences gained over the past 30 years or so since the founding of the republic) in connection with their actual thinking and work, sum up their experiences and lessons, and combat all types of erroneous ideas so as to raise their consciousness of implementing the lines set by the 3d Plenary Session of the 11th CPC Central Committee and the 12th CPC Congress and raise their consciousness of being politically at one with the party Central Committee.

It is particularly necessary to link the present situation and the tasks before us, stressing the basic idea of building a socialism with Chinese characteristics and paying special attention to resolving the following issues of understanding during the last half of this year:

1. The need to concentrate financial and material resources to ensure the construction of key projects.

2. The need for reform as well as the principles and policies for this purpose (including the reform of various administrative organs and the economic system).

3. The need to build simultaneously a material civilization and a spiritual civilization.

4. The need for party building and consolidation.

In the course of study, all party members must strive to increase their understanding, give impetus to work in all fields, and make sure that the forthcoming full-scale party consolidation can be carried out smoothly.

With regard to the specific requirements and plans for the study of "Selected Works of Deng Xiaoping," the Propaganda Department of the CPC Central Committee had already issued a circular prior to the publication of the book, and further plans will be made in the near future. All localities and departments may follow the plans formulated by the Propaganda Department of the CPC Central Committee.

A Boost from an Old Colleague, 12 July 1983

4

This article, originally published on 12 July in the Liberation Army Daily *(which does not circulate legally outside the PRC), is by an important veteran Party official who, like Deng, had been purged during the Cultural Revolution. It gives a somewhat more personal perspective than does the preceding article.*

The "Selected Works of Deng Xiaoping," published according to a decision made by the CPC central authorities, is a collection of magnificent writings which embodies Marxism-Leninism-Mao Zedong Thought and which emerges at the great historical turning point in our country, and is a summary of the experiences of the whole Army and the people throughout the country in their pioneer practice in socialist construction. These writings faithfully reflect Comrade Deng Xiaoping's decisive role and his outstanding contributions in guiding the whole party to set to rights things which had been thrown into disorder, realizing the great historical change, and building socialism with Chinese characteristics. The "Selected Works" shows a high theoretical standard and a close adherence to policy. Based strictly on actual reality, it fully reflects the needs of our times and the will of the broad masses of people, and is of great value as guidance to the building of our

party, state, and Army. I would like to conscientiously study this book together with all comrades of our Army.

The "Selected Works of Deng Xiaoping" has a rich content involving all fronts. In putting forth and providing a solution to the essential problems concerning the theory, guidelines, and policies to be adopted in the building of the party and the state during the period witnessing the great historical turning point, the "Selected Works" plays an extremely important role in helping all comrades of the Army to raise their levels of knowledge in political and ideological theory, to conscientiously implement the political line, principles, and policies laid down by the 12th CPC Congress, and to more closely keep in line politically with the CPC central authorities. The "Selected Works" includes 10 speeches delivered by Comrade Deng Xiaoping to the Army. Presenting the correct analysis of and the solution to a series of important problems in the revolutionization, modernization, and regularization of our Army, these speeches are programmatic documents for the building of the Army in the new period. We have not yet completely carried out those ideas so far on the rectification and building of the Army and on war readiness, as well as those tasks mentioned by Comrade Deng Xiaoping. Now,

---

[Yang Shangkun, "A Typical Example of Unity Between Revolutionary Boldness and the Spirit of Seeking Truth from Facts—Notes on Studying the *Selected Works of Deng Xiaoping*," *People's Daily*, 13 July 1983.]

in restudying Comrade Deng Xiaoping's important thinking in these many fields, we will more thoroughly understand Comrade Deng Xiaoping's foresight and correctness in making a series of important decisions.

I have been working directly under Comrade Deng Xiaoping for many years. While reading this "Selected Works", in light of my personal experience, I had a particularly strong feeling that his words touched my heart. And, what impressed me most deeply was the revolutionary boldness and the spirit of seeking truth from facts of Comrade Deng Xiaoping.

1

All of us still remember the situation in that unforgettable year, 1975: As the "gang of four" was running amok and Comrade Zhou Enlai was critically ill, proletarian revolutionaries of the older generation and the vast number of cadres were suffering persecution. When our motherland was faced with crisis, Comrade Deng Xiaoping was entrusted with the task of taking care of the routine work of the party and state. At that time, by vigorously publicizing the absurd theory of "retaining socialist grasses rather than capitalist seedlings," Jiang Qing, Zhang Chunqiao, and their like unbridledly undermined the national economy to the verge of collapse. They banned all criticism of their practice, but forced people against their conscience to sing the praise of the excellent and ever-improving situation. They promoted the ruthless "white terror," thus giving rise to an apathetic atmosphere and forcing people to keep their resentment to themselves. Despite the slander on him of "restoring capitalism," Comrade Deng Xiaoping waged a tit-for-tat struggle against the "gang of four" at the risk of being overthrown again. Counter to the theory advocated by the "gang of four" of "kicking away the party committee and carrying out revolution alone," which was aimed at undermining and abolishing the party's leadership, Comrade Deng Xiaoping put forth that it was necessary to build a strong leading body and to appoint some people who were not afraid of being overthrown to undertake posts in the leading body. Counter to the practice of the "gang of four" of promoting factionalism and upsetting the state, Comrade Deng Xiaoping put forth that it was necessary to resolutely mobilize the masses to struggle against factionalism.

Considering that the "gang of four" had fabricated a large number of unjust, false, and wrong cases, Comrade Deng Xiaoping put forth that it was necessary to conscientiously implement the policy: Not only the problems concerning those who had been wrongly labelled but also the problems concerning those who had been involved in the former's cases had to be solved. To cope with the so-called method of "imprisonment, restriction, and suppression" practiced by the "gang of four," Comrade Deng Xiaoping advocated that necessary rules and regulations had to be set up and improved, and organizational discipline had to be strengthened. Comrade Deng Xiaoping said: "Now we are faced with quite a lot of problems. Without determination and real actions, we will not be able to solve them. We must be courageous and must make up our mind." "We must deal with all wrong things, and we must touch all rumps, whether that of a 60-year-old tiger, or that of a 40-year-old tiger, or that of a 30- or 20-year-old tiger." He

first took actions to rectify the army, and then dealt with railway transport, industry, agriculture, and other fronts. He made every effort to eliminate disorder, to consolidate stability and unity, and to push ahead the national economy. Comrade Deng Xiaoping resolutely and courageously safeguarded truth against the "trend." His dauntless spirit, which is the feature of a proletarian revolutionary, his courage to turn the tide, and his correct viewpoints to redeem the party and the state raised the consciousness and courage of the vast number of cadres and the masses of people and provided the important basis for the following struggle to smash the "gang of four."

2

In the first 2 years after the smashing of the "gang of four," our country suffered setbacks in its movement ahead. The party's work in many fields deviated from the Marxist ideological line on the one hand, because of the profound and evil influence of the Lin Biao and Jiang Qing counter-revolutionary cliques, who went all out to publicize personality cult, and wantonly distorted, tampered with, garbled, and forged Mao Zedong Thought, and, on the other hand, of the mistake of Comrade Hua Guofeng, who upheld the erroneous principle of the "two whatevers" and hesitated giving it up. At that time, as the people were shackled by old conventions, Comrade Deng Xiaoping and many elderly cadres were prevented from taking up their posts, unjust, false, and wrong verdicts left over by history could not be reversed, and the discussion of great significance concerning the criterion for truth was suppressed.

Under these circumstances, Comrade Deng Xiaoping far-sightedly put forth that it is necessary to wholly and accurately understand and apply Mao Zedong Thought and to correctly understand the relations between the leader and the masses. He castigated the "two whatevers" for its incompatibility with Marxism. In his speech to the all-army political work conference held in June 1978, he incisively elucidated our party's ideological line of seeking truth from facts, pointing out that this line is the starting and basic point of Mao Zedong Thought. He took a clear-cut stand by supporting the discussion of the question about the criterion of truth. In December of the same year he again delivered a speech, entitled "Emancipate the Mind, Seek Truth From Facts, Unite as One, and Look Ahead," to the party's central work conference. He pointed out that emancipating the mind and seeking truth from facts concern the future and destiny of the party and state and that "a party, a state, or a nation which proceeds from book worship in doing everything and is ossified ideologically and superstitious, cannot advance but will become lifeless, and the party and the state will be subjugated." He called on the whole party to emancipate their mind, smash the fetters, and go back to the ideological line of seeking truth from facts. All these were all-round ideological and theoretical preparations for the 3d Plenary Session of the 11th CPC Central Committee and played an immeasurable role in helping the whole party reestablish the Marxist ideological, political, and organizational lines, completely rectifying the "leftist" mistakes during and before the "Great Cultural Revolution," systematically solving many old problems left from the past and new problems met in daily life, and realizing the far-reaching, historic change in the history of our party since the founding of the PRC.

3

Due to Comrade Mao Zedong's mistakes in his later years, the evaluation of Comrade Mao Zedong and Mao Zedong Thought attracted the attention of people inside and outside the party, at home and abroad. Quite a few comrades had confused ideas on this problem. Some of them, due to Comrade Mao Zedong's mistakes in his later years, attempted to negate the scientific value of Mao Zedong Thought and its guiding role in China's revolution and construction. But others held that what Comrade Mao Zedong said was the irrefutable truth and went so far as to strictly adhere to Comrade Mao Zedong's mistakes in his later years. There were also various opinions abroad and some even alleged that we would carry out de-Maoization. How to correctly evaluate and expound Comrade Mao Zedong and Mao Zedong Thought was not only a problem concerning the individual person, Comrade Mao Zedong, but also a matter of overall importance concerning the history and future development of our party and country. This was not only a theoretical problem, but also a political problem, a very important political problem in both domestic and international fields. On this extremely important problem in our party's history, Comrade Deng Xiaoping, with Marxist vision and sagacity, made an appropriate analysis, rendered scientific exposition, and made a reasonable evaluation, thus properly resolving this complicated and sensitive problem of great importance. When we read the "Selected Works," we will find that there are as many as tens of important arguments made by Comrade Deng Xiaoping on Comrade Mao Zedong's historical position and Mao Zedong Thought. Especially in his nine talks during the process of drafting "The Resolution on Certain Questions in the History of the Party Since the Founding of the PRC," he time and again stressed that the most essential thing of the "Resolution" was to establish Comrade Mao Zedong's historical position and to uphold and develop Mao Zedong Thought. If we failed to write this part well, we might as well give up writing the whole resolution. Comrade Deng Xiaoping pointed out: Comrade Mao Zedong was the principal founder of our party and state; he had saved our party and state from crisis on several occasions, and his great achievements were to integrate the universal truth of Marxism with the practice of the Chinese revolution and to point out a road for the Chinese revolution to achieve victory.

Although he made mistakes in his later years, they were, after all, mistakes made by a great Marxist. His merits were primary and his mistakes secondary. Mao Zedong Thought was the application and development of Marxism-Leninism in China, as well as the crystallization of the experience drawn by the party and people in revolutionary struggles. We absolutely cannot abandon the banner of Mao Zedong Thought. If we fail to uphold Mao Zedong Thought, we will make serious historical mistakes. Under the guidance of Comrade Deng Xiaoping's comprehensive, dialectical, and practical ideas of Marxism, the 6th Plenary Session of the 11th CPC Central Committee adopted the "Resolution on Certain Questions in the History of the Party Since the Founding of the PRC" and unified the thinking of the whole party and the people throughout the country, thus guaranteeing that our cause would continue to march forward along the scientific path of Marxism-Leninism-Mao Zedong Thought.

Comrade Deng Xiaoping's great contributions to establishing Comrade Mao Zedong's historical position and to upholding and developing Mao Zedong Thought are indelible forever.

4

What road China should take in building socialist modernization is an important problem concerning the success and failure of the four modernizations, and the prosperity and perishing of the state. Comrade Deng Xiaoping threw great energy into this problem. Together with many leading comrades of the party, he seriously researched China's conditions, summed up both historical and practical experiences, creatively sought for and explored the road of building Chinese-style modernization, and took it in concrete practice. In his opening speech to the 12th CPC National Congress, he explicitly and completely described the road, saying: "Integrate the universal truth of Marxism with the concrete practice of our country, take our own road, and build socialism with Chinese characteristics." He emphatically pointed out: In building modernization, we must proceed from China's reality, and mechanically copying foreign experiences and patterns has never been successful. We must carry out China's affairs according to China's conditions and relying on the strength of the Chinese people. Whether in the past, present, or future, it is our starting point to maintain independence and keep the initiative in our hands, and to rely on our own efforts. Our fighting goal is to build China into a modernized socialist country with a high degree of civilization and democracy. Comrade Deng Xiaoping pointed out that while building a high degree of material civilization, we must build a high degree of socialist spiritual civilization with communist ideology at its core. Ideologically and politically, we must uphold the four basic principles and have four important guarantees. In order to build socialism with Chinese characteristics, we must break the old and create the new, and carry out reforms in all fields. Comrade Deng Xiaoping time and again said: Without reforms, it is impossible to achieve the four modernizations. Reforms must be carried out in the whole process of building the four modernizations. We are carrying out and will carry out various reforms to improve old systems not adapted to the development of socialist productive forces and harmful to the people's interests, to eliminate defects and overcome shortcomings in the system, to establish gradually a new system suited to China's conditions, and to build socialism with Chinese characteristics. Comrade Deng Xiaoping's idea of taking our own road to build socialism with Chinese characteristics is the concentrated expression and high development of his Marxist ideological line of seeking truth from facts.

5

Comrade Deng Xiaoping not only takes up heavy tasks as a leader of our party and country, but is also the chairman of the Central Military Commission, who commands our country's Armed Forces. He has all along paid great attention to the modernization of national defense and the nation's security, and showed loving care for our Army.

Shortly after taking charge of the routine work of the Military Commission, he analyzed the new historical conditions and many new changes within the Army, pointed out that it was necessary to study and analyze the new situation and to resolve new problems in the new historical conditions with a spirit of seeking truth from facts, called on cadres, high-ranking cadres in particular, to be examples of seeking truth from facts and of integrating Marxism-Leninism-Mao Zedong Thought with revolutionary practice.

Just as Comrade Deng Xiaoping has pointed out, the work focus of our Army has been shifted to modernization. The present situation of our Army is different not only from that in the years of war and the early period after the liberation, but also from that in the 1960's and 1970's. Rapidly changing modern science and technology have been extensively and expeditiously applied to military affairs. This has brought about a series of changes to the theories and forms of modern warfare, strategy, tactics, and command, as well as to the establishment of our troops. All these changes have demanded that we enhance the capability of the coordinated fighting and fast reaction of our troops. Various kinds of modern scientific knowledge are before us and we must study them. Cultural, scientific, and technical knowledge is playing a more and more important role in the building of our Army. Comrade Deng Xiaoping said: "The present warfare is a joint operation which occurs in the sky, on the ground, and in the water. It is no longer a war of millet and rifles." Our cadres at various levels are not competent enough to command modern warfare. Even a company commander is required to acquire more knowledge than he did before. Comrade Deng Xiaoping pointed out: Our troops should assign education and training a strategical position. They should work hard to study knowledge of modern warfare and other necessary knowledge on politics, culture, and science and technology. We should run military institutes and schools well and train more cadres in schools. We should have scientific and rational establishments for Army units. We should speed up the work of improving the facilities of our troops in light of our present national power. We should also have powerful rear services and a good reserve service system. All this has clearly shown the orientation of our Army modernization.

Our Army's political work is also facing a number of new situations and problems. Comrade Deng Xiaoping stressed: "The Basic tasks and contents of our political work have not changed. All these are our fine traditions. However, the time, conditions, and targets have changed. Therefore, we should adopt different methods to solve problems." Our Army has many valuable historical traditions. With the development of the situation, all these traditions will also change and be enriched. Only thus can they have vitality. While strengthening political work, we should improve it to satisfy the demands of Army building in the new period. Comrade Deng Xiaoping has always attached importance to the establishment of the Army's leading bodies at various levels and the work of making cadre corps revolutionized, professional, younger, and more educated. Although we have achieved some results in our work, it is still far from what the Central Military Commission and Comrade Deng Xiaoping have demanded. We should continue to strengthen the building of new leading bodies and trust middle-aged and young cadres who are assigned to work in the new leading bodies. We should help and train them so that they raise their working ability. We should also make proper arrangements for veteran comrades who have retired from the leading bodies. We should show concern for them politically and in their daily life so that they continue to play their role in the revolutionary cause. Comrade Deng Xiaoping pointed out: In order to promote Army building and to enable our Army to support the state's economic construction, we should turn our Army into a big school so that our comrades and soldiers will be able to study knowledge of modern warfare and knowledge of modern science and production. In such a way they will become qualified personnel suitable for both the Army and localities. Practice has proved that the work of training qualified personnel suitable for the Army and localities and the integrating of civilian and military affairs, the Army and the people, as well as the demands of peacetime and war, is a matter of primary importance which is beneficial to the state, Army, and people. It is continuation and development of the fine traditions of our Army under the new historical conditions. Joint efforts of the Army and people to build socialist spiritual civilization are also new development and creation of the fine tradition of maintaining close ties between the Army and people in the new period. This has added new contents to the activities of supporting the government and cherishing the people.

Comrade Deng Xiaoping has also paid close attention to the Army's ideological and political building in the new period. While talking with leading comrades of the PLA General Political Department on opposing erroneous ideological trends, he stressed: "We should also follow the practice of seeking truth from facts in solving ideological problems of the Army. Ideological work should be carried out in light of circumstances of different units and individuals." We should strengthen the propaganda and education of upholding the four basic principles. While criticizing "leftist" erroneous ideology, we should also repudiate right erroneous ideology. Comrade Deng Xiaoping pointed out that the "leftist" influence in the Army should not be ignored. His appraisal is in accord with the practical conditions in our Army. Although we have done some work to eliminate the "leftist" influence and the situation has somewhat improved, it cannot be completely eliminated overnight because it was deeply rooted in the Army. Very often the "leftist" influence consciously or unconsciously manifests itself in some units and some comrades. In the process of studying the "Selected Works," we should continue to eliminate the "leftist" influence in the military field. In the meantime, we should not ignore the right erroneous tendencies, and the erroneous views and attitudes toward the four basic principles and the party's line, guiding principles, and policies. At the present stage, class struggle still exists within a certain scope in our country and there is a danger of being infiltrated by capitalism. We should heighten our vigilance against the activities of some hostile elements who intend to sabotage our motherland.

Under the leadership of the Central Military Commission and Comrade Deng Xiaoping, our Army has made great progress in its various work. We have enhanced the level of our revolutionization, modernization, and regularization. Through initial structural reform and streamlining the institutions, our troops have become more capable and well-organized. We have also achieved marked results in making our cadre corps younger. The work of promoting the new formation of our troops and our command ability for joint operations has been further carried out. In the meantime we have strengthened our military training, ideological and political work, military schools and institutes, rear services, and military academic research work. Our research work for national defense and sophisticated weapons has entered a new stage. New changes have taken place in the entire Army.

The important reason why our Army has made relatively great achievements within a comparatively short period of time and has made new developments and progress under new historical conditions is that it has implemented Comrade Deng Xiaoping's guiding ideology concerning Army building and a series of principles and measures in striving to build itself into a modern and regular revolutionary Army with Chinese characteristics. In guiding the party and the country in construction in various aspects, Comrade Deng Xiaoping has upheld dialectical materialism and historical materialism, sought truth from facts, and always proceeded from reality. In leading the building of the Army, he has also upheld dialectical materialism and historical materialism, sought truth from facts, and always proceeded from reality. This is clearly shown in the "Selected Works of Deng Xiaoping."

What is mentioned above is only a brief review on several major questions as a result of studying the "Selected Works of Deng Xiaoping." From this alone, we can clearly see that Deng Xiaoping is good at integrating the universal truth of Marxism with the concrete practice of socialist modernization in our country. In handling each important issue of the party, the country, and the Army, he has always paid great attention to analyzing concrete historical conditions, proceeding from the conditions of our country, proceeding from existing reality, and putting the interests of the party, the people, and the overall situation above all other things. Therefore, he may have a penetrating and thorough insight of problems, handle affairs in a decisive manner, present correct solutions, always have a comprehensive and dialectical understanding of matters, grasp the key links, and push forward step-by-step the great cause of socialist modernization. He has a very high level of Marxism and has greatly emancipated his mind. He dares to abandon conventions and old styles which do not meet the needs of the new historical mission and revolutionary practice, is good at quickly absorbing new ideas, new creations, and new experiences which are in line with the people's interests and the demands of the time, and dares to realistically negate what should be negated and affirm what should be affirmed. Therefore, he is always able to replace outdated conclusions with new viewpoints and to replenish and enrich existing basic principles with new experience in practice. Comrade Deng Xiaoping is a thorough dialectical materialist, an example of a high degree of integration of revolutionary boldness with a realistic spirit, and an example of upholding the ideological line of seeking truth from facts. This is what is most worthy of our understanding and study and most necessary for us to understand and study the "Selected Works of Deng Xiaoping."

Marx said: "Once theory is grasped by the masses, it turns into a material force." Since the whole party, the whole Army, and all the people of the country are seriously studying the "Selected Works of Deng Xiaoping," there will certainly be an outburst of tremendous force for opening a new situation in socialist modernization.

Overhauling the Leadership

The Purge of the "Little Gang of Four," February 1980

Deng Xiaoping had been constrained by the presence on the Politburo of the so-called "Little Gang of Four," the radicals Wang Dongxing, Ji Dengkui, Wu De, and Chen Xilian, who were all deprived of their posts at this February 1980 meeting, although not expelled from the Party. Other important decisions formalized at the meeting were the "election" of Deng's lieutenant Hu Yaobang as general secretary and of other Deng men to the Party Secretariat; the posthumous rehabilitation of Liu Shaoqi, the most prominent leader purged by Mao Zedong during the Cultural Revolution; and the convening in September 1982 of the Twelfth Party Congress.

The 11th Central Committee of the Communist Party of China held its 5th plenary session in Beijing from 23 to 29 February 1980. Present were 201 members and 118 alternate members of the Central Committee. In addition, 37 leading comrades of various localities and departments attended the session as observers. Chairman Hua Guofeng and Vice Chairmen Ye Jianying, Deng Xiaoping, Li Xiannian and Chen Yun of the CCP Central Committee attended the session and delivered important speeches. Comrade Hua Guofeng presided over the session. To a great extent the agenda of the 5th plenary session concerned strengthening and improving party leadership so as to adapt it to the development of socialist modernization. The agenda covered: 1) discussing and approving the draft resolution on holding the 12th National CCP Congress; 2) electing additional Standing Committee members of the CCP Central Committee's Political Bureau, and discussing and approving the draft resolution on the establishment of the Secretariat of the CCP Central Committee; 3) discussing and approving "certain criteria for political life inside the party"; 4) discussing the revised draft of the "Constitution of the Communist Party of China."

The plenary session held: Since the 11th National CCP Congress, particularly since the 3d plenary session of the 11th CCP Central Committee, there have been important changes and developments in the domestic and international situations. Since the shift in the focus of the work of the whole party, the socialist modernization program has started on a course of sound development. The party's political, ideological and organizational lines laid down by the 3d and the 4th plenary sessions have taken root in the hearts of the people. The counterrevolutionary crimes of Lin Biao, the "gang of four" and their ilk, the ultra-leftist line they peddled and their remnant influence in organization and ideology have been further exposed and criticized. A large number of cases left over from the past in

[Communiqué of the Fifth Plenary Session of the Eleventh Central Committee, 29 February 1980, New China News Agency, 29 February 1980.]

which people were wronged, misjudged or framed have been redressed. The party's various policies have been extensively implemented throughout the country.

It is on this basis that the whole party, the entire army and the people throughout the country have closely rallied around the party Central Committee, worked hard for the realization of the great cause of the four modernizations and for the implementation of the policy of readjustment, restructuring, consolidation and improvement of the national economy. This has caused good news to pour in from all fields of endeavor, including agriculture, industry, finance and trade, education, science, culture, politics and judicial affairs, national defense and others. A situation of stability and unity and of liveliness and vigor is developing. All these facts have proved that the line, principles and policies implemented by the party Central Committee are correct and that the serious chaotic situation which was created in our country by Lin Biao and the "gang of four," who held sway for 10 years, has basically changed into a situation in which there is proper leadership, good order, a direction and target on the road of advance, conditions for winning victories and confidence. This is a tremendous victory that was won by our party in overcoming formidable difficulties.

The plenary session pointed out: The great practice of the people of all nationalities in the whole country in their advance toward the four modernizations has raised a series of important issues for the party that demand prompt and speedy resolution. These include working out a long-term program for development of the national economy, an economic system, educational plans and an educational system suited to the needs of this development.

In view of the rapid changes in the domestic situation, a number of important issues in the political life of the state and in party life and a number of important ideological and theoretical problems also need to be solved in a manner which is conducive to stability and unity, to the development and consolidation of a vigorous political situation of stability and to the smooth advance of the modernization program.

In order to solve all these pressing issues, it is necessary for the Central Committee to convene the party's 12th National Congress before the due date. The plenary session of the CCP Central Committee unanimously adopted a resolution to convene the 12th National CCP Congress before the due date. The specific date for the congress will be decided by the Political Bureau of the CCP Central Committee.

The fifth plenary session held: In order to strengthen the party's leadership over socialist modernization, the party's leading organizations at various levels must strive to absorb those comrades into the leadership who are capable of firmly implementing the party line, possess ability to work independently and are in the prime of life. This is not only to meet the needs of the heavy workloads of modernization, but also to guarantee the long-term continuity of the party line, principles and policies and to insure the long-term stability of the party's collective leadership. After serious and earnest discussions, the plenary session decided to increase the membership of the Standing Committee of the Political Bureau of the Central Committee and to elect Comrades Hu Yaobang and Zhao Ziyang to the Standing Committee.

After serious and earnest discussions, the plenary session decided to restore the system established at the Eighth CCP National Congress, which had been necessary and effective during the 10-year period. Thus the central Secretariat was established as a permanent office under the leadership of the Political Bureau of the Central Committee and its Standing Committee. Comrade Hu Yaobang was elected general secretary of the Central Committee and (listed in the order of strokes in their surnames) Wan Li, Wang Renzhong, Fang Yi, Gu Mu, Song Renqiong, Yu Qiuli, Yang Dezhi, Hu Qiaomu, Hu Yaobang, Yao Yilin, and Peng Chong were the 11 comrades elected as secretaries to the central Secretariat.

The plenary session held that the election of additional members to the Standing Committee of the Political Bureau of the Central Committee and the establishment of the central Secretariat are major policy decisions of the party which demonstrate both the vitality of the great socialist and communist undertakings initiated by Comrade Mao Zedong and other proletariat revolutionaries of the older generation and the great number of talented people in these undertakings. The strengthening of the party's central leading organization will positively promote the development and consolidation of the lively political situation of stability and unity throughout the country and the smooth progress of socialist modernization.

The plenary session discussed the draft of the "Revised Constitution of the Chinese Communist Party." After its revision based on the views put forth at the plenary session, this document will be widely discussed by the whole party, further revised based on the views raised during the discussions and examined and adopted by the party's 12th National Congress. The revised draft Constitution sets rigid demands on the conditions of party members and at the same time sets fairly complete regulations regarding the party's democratic centralism. The revised draft Constitution sums up historical experience and, in meeting the needs during the period of socialist modernization building, sets a series of new provisions about the party's cadre system, including the abolition of the existing system of lifetime jobs for cadres.

The plenary session discussed and unanimously adopted "Some Criteria About the Political Life Within the Party." It has 12 items. Its draft was adopted in principle by the Central Committee's Political Bureau in February 1979 and was widely discussed within the party since March. After repeated revisions it was once again adopted by the Central Committee's Political Bureau and then sent for discussion at the fifth plenary session. The plenary session held that the 12 criteria sum up the experiences and lessons our party has learned in the past decades in handling the relations within the party, in particular those experiences and lessons learned in the struggle against Lin Biao and the gang of four during the 10-year period of the Great Cultural Revolution. They are necessary supplements to the party constitution and are of great significance in bringing the positive factors into play and eliminating the passive factors within the party and for bringing the party members leading an exemplary role into play. The plenary session decided to publish the "criteria" after its conclusion and to implement them throughout the party.

The plenary session, in the course of implementing "Some Criteria About the Political Life Within the Party," asked for political and ideological education of the party. This education should persist in the party's political and ideological line, strengthen the party's unification and consolidate its democratic centralism and the sense of its organization and discipline. The education should be conducted together with discussions of the revised draft party constitution.

Party organizations at all levels and each and every party member should check their own performance and work style against the provisions of the criteria, continue their achievements and overcome shortcomings. Anything running counter to the provisions of the criteria must be corrected in good time and effectively. Such phenomena as continuing to practice factionalism and acting without a sense of organization and discipline by individual party organizations and certain party members must be thoroughly changed. The plenary session reiterated that by upholding the principle that individual party members should submit to party organizations, the minority to the majority, the lower levels to the higher levels and the whole party to the party Central Committee, the whole party will, under the leadership of the party Central Committee, be able to unify thinking and action and insure the smooth progress of the socialist modernization program.

To redress Comrade Liu Shaoqi was another major item on the agenda of the fifth plenary session of the CCP Central Committee. The session held that Comrade Liu Shaoqi, former vice chairman of the CCP Central Committee, chairman of the People's Republic of China and a great Marxist and proletarian revolutionist, was loyal to the party and the people at all times over the past decades. He devoted all his energy to the revolutionary cause of the proletariat and made indelible contributions to China's new democratic revolution and socialist revolution and construction. Because the appraisal on the eve of the Great Cultural Revolution of the situation in the party and the country was contrary to fact, an entirely wrong and groundless inference was made asserting that there was a counterrevolutionary revisionist line within the party. It also was asserted that there was a so-called bourgeois headquarters headed by Comrade Liu Shaoqi. Seizing upon this to serve their counterrevolutionary purpose of usurping supreme party and state leadership and subverting the dictatorship of the proletariat, Lin Biao, the "gang of four" and company concocted false evidence and deliberately subjected Comrade Liu Shaoqi to a political frame-up and physical persecution. Furthermore, they overthrew a large number of leading party, government and army cadres on the false charge of being Liu Shaoqi's agents. This brought extremely grave consequences. This is the biggest frame-up our party has ever known and must be completely overturned.

For almost a year the Central Commission for Inspecting Discipline under the CCP Central Committee has conducted a thorough investigation and study concerning the facts of various "crimes" of Comrade Liu Shaoqi set forth by the 12th plenary session of the 8th CCP Central Committee. After repeatedly checking the related materials, it submitted a detailed and accurate examination report to the Central Committee. The Political Bureau of the CCP Central Committee unanimously approved the report and, based on it, adopted a draft resolution on the rehabilitation of Comrade Liu Shaoqi. Following serious and earnest discussion, the plenary session unanimously adopted the resolution and decided to remove the labels "renegade, traitor and scab" which the 12th plenary session of the 8th CCP Central Committee imposed on Comrade Liu Shaoqi; to cancel the erroneous resolution expelling him "from the party once and for all and dismissing him from all posts both inside and outside the party"; to cancel the original report on the examination and clear the name of Comrade Liu Shaoqi as a great Marxist and proletarian revolutionary and one of the principal leaders of the party and the state; to hold a memorial meeting at an appropriate time for Comrade Liu Shaoqi; to redress the cases of people implicated with Comrade Liu Shaoqi on unjust, false and wrong charges or sentences by the departments concerned; and, on the basis of the spirit of uniting and looking ahead, to convey the resolution of the plenary session to the whole party and people of the country and to eradicate the influence caused by the erroneous handling of the case of Comrade Liu Shaoqi in the past. The session also decided to inspire all comrades in the party and the people all over the country to act with one mind and one heart and to devote themselves to the grand cause of the four modernizations with complete confidence.

The 5th plenary session of the 11th CCP Central Committee hereby solemnly declares to the whole party and the people of the whole country: The rehabilitation of Comrade Liu Shaoqi shows the Chinese Communist Party is a Marxist revolutionary party which seeks truth from facts, corrects mistakes whenever found and is serious, earnest and aboveboard. It shows that the party is determined to restore Mao Zedong Thought to what it is and that this is not an empty slogan but a principled stand unswervingly adhered to by the party throughout all its activities. The party committed a distressingly serious mistake during the Great Cultural Revolution, a mistake that was used by counterrevolutionary careerists Lin Biao and the "gang of four." It resulted in a serious consequence unprecedented in the history of the party. Since smashing the "gang of four," the party Central Committee has exposed and criticized the counterrevolutionary crimes of Lin Biao and the "gang of four" and the serious mistakes of the Great Cultural Revolution and, at the same time, it has redressed the series of cases of people unjustly, falsely and wrongly charged or sentenced. The rehabilitation of Comrade Liu

Shaoqi by the 5th plenary session of the 11th CCP Central Committee is not only for his own sake. It is for the purpose of engraving this bitter lesson permanently in the minds of the party and the people so every effort will be made henceforth to safeguard, consolidate and perfect socialist democracy and the socialist legal system, so frame-ups such as the one which befell Comrade Liu Shaoqi and many other comrades inside and outside the party shall never happen again and so our party and state shall never change their color.

In accordance with the opinion of the broad masses inside and outside the party, the fifth plenary session decided to approve the resignations of Comrades Wang Dongxing, Ji Dengkui, Wu De and Chen Xilian and decided to remove and proposed to remove them from their leading party and state posts.

The rehabilitation of Comrade Liu Shaoqi and the actions taken to seriously and appropriately deal with comrades who made grave mistakes reflect the aspirations of the comrades of the whole party and the people throughout the country.

The plenary session calls on party organizations at all levels to actively and responsibly continue to resolve, in line with this spirit, similar problems which have remained unresolved or partly resolved and to educate the party members and the masses to unite closely under the leadership of the party Central Committee. The plenary session also called on the party organizations to strengthen organizational discipline and wholeheartedly strive for the great future of socialist modernization.

The plenary session held that it is our party's unswerving policy to promote socialist democracy, perfect the socialist legal system and to guarantee that the masses have the full right and opportunity to express their views on state affairs and raise suggestions to and criticize party and government leaders. However, experience shows that the practices of speaking out freely, airing views fully, holding great debates and writing big-character posters are not good ways to achieve this. These practices as a whole never played a positive role in safeguarding the people's democratic rights. On the contrary, they hampered the people in the normal exercise of their democratic rights. To help eliminate these destabilizing factors, the plenary session decided to propose to the National People's Congress that the stipulation in Article 45 of the Constitution of the People's Republic of China, that citizens "have the right to 'speak out freely, air their views fully, hold great debates and write big-character posters'" be deleted.

The 5th plenary session of the 11th CCP Central Committee is another important meeting following the convocation of the 3d and 4th plenary sessions. The main theme of the session is to uphold and improve party leadership and enhance the party's combat strength. These are the most important guarantees for the smooth progress of the socialist modernization program. The session did not specifically discuss economic work. This was because the national planning conference, held under the leadership of the party Central Committee and the State Council from November to December 1979, had already formulated the national economic plan for 1980. Also, after Comrade Deng Xiaoping had given the report on the current situation and tasks on 16 January 1980, Comrade Li Xiannian again on 10 February gave a report on current economic problems. Now the central tasks on the country's economic front are to strive to fulfill and overfulfill this year's national economic plan in accordance with the various policies laid down by the party Central Committee. Obviously, the tasks facing the whole party on all fronts in 1980 are very difficult. Fulfilling these tasks will play an enormous role in determining the success of the 12th National Party Congress. The 5th plenary session of the 11th CCP Central Committee called on comrades of the whole party to unite with the people throughout the country, closely rally around the party Central Committee, work energetically with one heart and one mind and make outstanding achievements on all fronts to greet the convocation of the 12th National Party Congress.

DENG XIAOPING

On Reforming the Party and State Leadership, 18 August 1980

6

By the summer of 1980, Deng was strong enough to begin the ouster of Hua Guofeng as premier. As this speech, delivered to the Politburo, shows, he had some other more sweeping ideas in mind as well, such as reduction in the level of multiple officeholding that had characterized the PRC since 1949, the separation to a degree of the Party and state leaderships, and the incorporation of younger men.

Comrades: The main topic to be discussed in this enlarged meeting is the reform of the party and state leadership system and some problems relating to this reform.

The reshuffle of the leading members of the State Council will be one of the chief items on the agenda of the coming Third Session of the Fifth NPC. This reshuffle will result in Comrade Hua Guofeng being dismissed from his concurrent post of premier, which will be taken up by Comrade Zhao Ziyang; Comrades Li Xiannian, Chen Yun, Xu Xiangqian, Wang Zhen, and myself being dismissed from our concurrent posts of vice premiers, which will be taken over by comrades with more energy; and Comrade Wang Renzhong also being dismissed from his concurrent post as vice premier because he has been appointed to an important post in the party. The Central Committee has decided to approve Comrade Chen Yonggui's application for resignation from his post as a vice premier. We will also propose, after consulting with relevant people, some reshuffles related to the posts of NPC vice chairmen and CPPCC National Committee vice chairmen. The Standing Committee of the CPC Central Committee Political Bureau has discussed this matter time and again. Now the committee will put forward a formal proposal in the name of the CPC Central Committee for the NPC and CPPCC sessions to discuss this matter and make their decisions.

Why does the Central Committee decide the reshuffle of responsible persons of the State Council?

The first reason for this decision is that our power should not be overcentralized. Overcentralization of power impedes the implementation of our socialist democracy and the party's democratic centralism. It also hinders the development of our socialist construction and blocks the way for collective wisdom to play its role. This will lead to the malpractice of people acting arbitrarily as individuals and make it impossible for collective leadership to work. Thus it constitutes one of the major causes that give rise to bureaucracy in the new conditions.

Our second reason is that a person should not undertake too many posts concurrently. A man has but limited knowledge, experience, and energy; therefore, if he holds too many jobs concurrently, it will be very hard for him to carry out his work in depth. Furthermore, this blocks the way for appointing a greater number of more appropriate people to be responsible for the leadership work.

A third reason is that we are tackling the problems of confusing the party with the government and substituting the party for the government. When some of the major leading comrades of the Central Committee are freed from their concurrent posts in the government, they will be able to concentrate their energy on dealing with matters related to the party, the line, the principles, and policies. This will facilitate the strengthening and improvement of the unified leadership of the Central Committee and the establishment of a powerful work system of our government which can exercise its management from above level by level, in order to satisfactorily discharge the responsibility within the scope of the government.

[Deng Xiaoping, "The Reform of the Party and State Leadership System," 18 August 1980, *People's Daily*, 2 July 1983.]

The fourth reason is that we want to solve the problem related to handing over the leadership power to our successors in view of our long-term interests. Our old comrades are a valuable treasure for our party and state and they are shouldered with heavy responsibilities. However, the task of first priority for them is to help our party organizations correctly select successors. This is a solemn task. Letting young comrades take up posts at the first line and appointing old comrades to satisfactorily act as their advisers and support their work is a major strategic measure to maintain the continuity and stability of the correct leadership of our party and government.

These decisions of the Central Committee are aimed at carrying out necessary reform in the leadership system of our party and state. The Central Committee has taken a first step toward this by deciding to set up a Secretariat in its fifth plenary session. This Secretariat has done its work effectively since its establishment. The reshuffle of the leading members of the State Council will be a first step toward improving the leadership system of our government. In order to meet the demand of the socialist modernization, in order to meet the needs resulting from the democratization of the political life of the party and state, and in order to develop favorable factors and remove unfavorable factors, it is still necessary for us to carry out reform in many aspects of the leadership and other systems of our party and state. We should continuously sum up our historical experience, carry out deep-going investigation and study, solicit and collect correct opinions, and vigorously and systematically continue to carry out reform in both our central and local organizations.

2

The reform in the leadership and other systems of our party and state is aimed at giving full play to the superiority of the socialist system and speeding up the development of our socialist modernization.

In order to give full play to the superiority of our socialist system, at present and in a time to come, we should strive to satisfy the following three requirements: 1) in the economic field, we should quickly develop the productive force of the society and gradually improve our people's material and cultural standard of living; 2) in the political field, we should fully develop our people's democracy and ensure that all our people really enjoy the power to manage our country through various effective means, particularly, to manage the basic-level local government and the various enterprises and institutions and that they enjoy all their rights as citizens. At the same time, we should perfect our revolutionary legal system, correctly handle the contradictions among the people, deal blows at all antagonistic forces and criminal activities, give play to the initiative of the masses of people, and consolidate and develop the lively political situation of stability and unity; 3) in order to achieve the above-mentioned two requirements, in the area related to our organizations, there is an urgent need to train, discover, promote, and employ for our socialist modernization a large number of people of ability who adhere to the four basic principles and are relatively young and professionally competent.

In carrying out our socialist modernization program,

our aim is to economically catch up with developed capitalist countries, to politically create a democracy that is superior to and more realistic than that of the capitalist countries, and to train a large number of more brilliant people of ability than that of those countries. Some aspects of the above-mentioned three requirements can be satisfied in a short time, but others take a longer time to meet. However, since ours is a great socialist country, we can and must meet all these requirements. Therefore, we must judge whether or not the various systems of our party and state are satisfactory and perfect by the criterion of whether or not these systems facilitate meeting these three requirements.

Here, I should like to emphatically expound on the problem of giving play to the superiority of the socialist system in the aspect of organization, consciously renewing the leading organs of the party and government at all levels, and gradually achieving the aim of making our leaders younger and professionally competent.

For many years we failed to boldly promote and employ, under the prerequisite of adhering to the four basic principles, people of abilities who are younger, professionally competent, and practically experienced. During the "Great Cultural Revolution," a large number of our cadres were persecuted by Lin Biao and the "gang of four" and our work related to cadres was seriously undermined. This has given rise to the current situation whereby our leading cadres in all levels are universally aged. Our personnel problem is mainly a problem concerned with our organizational line. It is necessary to train a large number of new personnel. However, the chief task at present is to be good at discovering, promoting, and bravely breaking a rule to promote fine middle-aged and young cadres. This is an urgent objectively existing demand of the state modernization program. It is not a question put forward by some elderly comrades in a whimsical mood.

Some comrades worry that in promoting middle-aged and young cadres, we will perhaps promote some factionalists and even some elements who have engaged in beating, smashing, and looting. This is a reasonable worry. For even by now we have not yet satisfactorily reorganized the leading groups in some areas and departments. Therefore, it is possible that some factionalists will use the excuse of promoting middle-aged and young cadres to promote members of their factions. In a speech that I gave on 16 January this year, I said that we must not underestimate the remnant force of the "gang of four" in our organizations and ideology. In this area, we must be sober-minded. We must never promote anyone who began his career by following the Lin Biao and Jiang Qing cliques to rebel, who has a serious factionalist idea, or who is an element engaging in beating, smashing, and looting. We should resolutely dismiss all such people who have already been in leading posts. If we fail to be on our guard and allow these people to occupy our leading posts, play again their double-dealing tricks, strike their roots, build up their connections, and stay hidden in our ranks, they may cause inestimably great evils to us even though their number is small.

Some comrades say that it is better to promote cadres step by step. In 1975, I made such remarks aimed at the erroneous method practiced during the "Great Cultural Revolution." We must no longer promote our cadres like launching a rocket or helicopter. Our cadres should be promoted step by step. In a general sense, it would mean that our cadres should undergo a course of immersing themselves among the masses, have an intimate knowledge of their profession, accumulate experience, and withstand all trials and tribulations. However, we cannot stick to the old idea of promoting cadres by steps. The promotion of cadres must not be restricted to the steps of district, county, prefecture, and province, in which our party and government cadres are promoted at present. All trades and professions should have different kinds of grades, posts, and titles. Along with the development of our construction, we must also stipulate new requirements and methods for promoting cadres and utilizing people in different trades. Most of the posts and titles in the future should be provided and conferred on those who can pass the qualifying examinations. Only when we have smashed the out-dated idea of promoting by grades and formulated new ideas that suit the new situation and task can we boldly break the rule in making promotions. Furthermore, we cannot go on further than just talking about either the new or old steps. It is imperative to earnestly promote to leading posts those outstanding middle-aged and young cadres as soon as possible. We cannot be hasty in promoting cadres. However, if we are too slow, we may delay the major work of the building of modernization. We have already delayed too much! We must provide a light and convenient ladder to those outstanding comrades so that they can be promoted by skipping the regular grades. We have proposed to transform the phenomenon of holding too many concurrent posts and overcentralization in power.

Our aim was to release more posts for the middle-aged and young comrades. How can they be promoted if the posts are all fully occupied? How can they be promoted if the vacant posts are not transferred to them?

Some comrades fear that the young people lack experience and are not competent. I think such worries are unnecessary. Experience, sufficient or not, is a relative matter. To be frank, did not our veteran cadres lack experience in the new problems of building modernization and also committed some mistakes? Generally speaking, young people lack experience; this is true. However, I hope that you comrades will think it over. Were many of us, who are now senior cadres and handling major work, not 20–30 years old when we started? We should admit that the middle-aged and young comrades at present possess more knowledge than we did in those years. Although they lack experience in leadership work and undergoing the test of struggle, it is a result of objective conditions. It is because they did not have practical experience in specific work. If they are placed in a specific post, their work can be gradually improved. After liberation, there were 7–8 million students graduating from the institutions of higher learning and special secondary schools. Most of them were from workers' and peasants' families and were tempered for over 10 years. Those middle-aged and young cadres who did not receive education in institutions of higher learning and special secondary schools had practical experience although their educational level was a bit low. Provided we train them in a planned way, many of them can certainly become both Red and expert cadres. Moreover, there are large numbers of outstanding middle-aged and young talented people who have assiduously studied on their own. There are also many people of ability among the educated urban youth working in the countryside and mountain areas who went deep into the masses and studied hard. As a matter of fact, there are large numbers of middle-aged and young cadres who have become backbones working at various fronts. Compared with those cadres who stand high above the masses and who are unwilling to go to the grassroots levels, they are more acquainted with the masses and reality. We rely mainly on them in most of our work. It is because they were not promoted and did not have the right in making decisions that many of the problems had to be reported time and again to the higher levels for instructions. This became one of the main sources of our bureaucratic practices. In a word, we must never underestimate this contingent of middle-aged and young cadres. Since the political quality of many of the middle-aged and young cadres is good, they are not factionalists, they have the correct way of thinking, and possess certain professional knowledge, why should we not select, promote and use them? Many of the enterprises and units have achieved quick results in letting the masses elect their cadres and letting cadres recommend themselves and voluntarily take on the responsibility of the work. This was much better than appointing cadres. Should we not wake up to the truth of these facts? There are fine middle-aged and young cadres everywhere. There are middle-aged and young cadres in all trades, professions, localities, and units, who were discontented, and positively or negatively resisted the practices of Lin Biao, Jiang Qing, and their followers, who politically behaved well and had professional knowledge, and were willing to work hard. The problem is we did not make any attempts to discover and promote them. We must also not desert those people who have genuine talent, and who were once deceived by Lin Biao, Jiang Qing, and their followers, and committed mistakes, but later became aware of their mistakes and corrected them. There are some comrades who only look upon and deal with the people around them, but are not willing to go deep into the masses to select talented people. This is also one of the bureaucratic practices.

We must draw lessons from the "Great Cultural Revolution," and at the same time we must be soberly aware that our country confronts the enormous task and situation of building modernization, and that large numbers of cadres cannot meet the actual demands of building modernization. Therefore, we must resolutely rectify the outlook of not judging problems from the long-term point of view.

We have the correct ideological, political, and organizational line. Provided we work with great courage and meticulous care, carry out thorough investigation and studies, and heed the wide range of opinions from the masses, we will certainly be able to promote large numbers of middle-aged and young cadres, ensure that our cause lacks no successors, and let the latecomers surpass the old-timers.

Comrade Chen Yun said that we must pay attention to both political integrity and ability in selecting cadres. With regard to political integrity, the most important thing is to adhere to the socialist road and party leadership. On this premise, the cadres' ranks should be more revolutionary, younger in average age, better educated, and more professionally competent. We must also institutionalize such a system in promoting and utilizing cadres. These opinions are very good. There are some comrades who did not pay attention to the younger cadre ranks, and did not attach importance to better education and the professional competence of cadre ranks. This is the evil result of the "leftist" ideology which existed in the intellectual problem for a long time in the past.

At present, the problem is that the organizational system in force and the method of thinking of a number of cadres are not advantageous to the promotion and utilization of talented people, which is urgently needed for the building of the four modernizations. I hope that the party committees and organizational departments at all levels will shift their ground on this matter, resolutely emancipate their minds, remove all sorts of obstacles, break with old conventions, have courage to reform the inappropriate organizational and personnel system, energetically train, discover, and utilize outstanding talented people, and resolutely fight against all practices that suppress and ruin talented people. After more than a decade's trial, the leading comrades and masses are quite clear of the political feature of the middle-aged and young comrades. Our elderly comrades are still alive, so by adopting the method of judging cadres from the top and lower levels, we will certainly be able to select the proper people. To be sure, this work should be carried out step-by-step, but we must not be too slow. If we miss the opportunity and start dealing with the problem when the elderly comrades pass away, it will be too late and the work will become more difficult than at present. It will then be a grave mistake committed by our elderly comrades.

3

There still exist many defects and shortcomings in the concrete regulations of our party and state which seriously hinder the superiority of socialism. If they are not reformed in earnest, it will be impossible to meet the urgent needs of building modernization and we will be seriously divorced from the masses.

The main defects in the leadership and cadre system of the party and state are the practices of bureaucratism, overcentralization of power, paternalism, leading comrades holding lifelong posts, and privileges of every description.

The practice of bureaucratism is a major problem that exists in a wide range in the political life of the party and state. Its principal manifestation and harm are as follows: standing high above the masses, abusing power, divorcing from the actual conditions and the masses, being fond of keeping up appearances and empty talk, rigid thinking, sticking to conventions, organizations being overstaffed, having more hands than needed, being dilatory in doing things, paying no attention to efficiency, not keeping promises, passing documents from one department to the other, shifting responsibility onto each other which leads to having bureaucratic airs, blaming people at every turn, retaliating, oppressing democracy, deceiving the superiors and deluding the subordinates, being imperious and despotic, practicing favoritism and resorting to bribery, corrupting and perverting the law, and so on. All these practices, whether in our internal affairs or international contacts, have reached an intolerable state.

Bureaucracy is a long-standing and complicated historical phenomenon. While bearing features common to bureaucracy in history, the bureaucratic phenomena existing in our country today also have their own characteristics, which differ from the bureaucracy of old China, as well as from the bureaucracy of capitalist countries. They are closely related to our long-standing adherence to the concept that the socialist system and planned administrative system must impose highly centralized control on the economic, political, cultural, and social fields. Our leading organizations at all levels must be engaged in too many matters, which they in fact should not have their hands in, or cannot handle properly, or simply cannot manage. All these things can in fact be handled smoothly by the lower levels, by enterprises, nonproductive institutions, and social service units themselves, strictly according to the procedure of democratic centralism and under the guidance laid down by certain rules and regulations. However, when all these things are covered by party and governmental leading organs, and the department directly under the central authorities, all of them become knotty problems. Nobody is so versatile as to handle all alone all these arduous and unfamiliar tasks. And all the current phenomena derived from our peculiar bureaucracy can be attributed to this general origin. Another origin of our bureaucracy lies in the fact that for a long time we have lacked some strict administrative regulations and personal responsibility system which stipulates the work procedure from the higher levels to the grassroots, and strict rules to clearly define the duties and the authorities of every organ and every individual. As a result, when faced with problems, minor or major, most people have no rules and regulations to follow. Usually they cannot independently handle what they are expected to handle and exhaust themselves in writing reports, asking for instructions, reading over, and conveying documents. Some people who are seriously influenced by selfish departmentalism even shift responsibilities onto others, scramble for power and interests, and always argue over trifles. Furthermore, there is no system stipulating the regular recruitment, reward and punishment, retirement, resignation, and discharge of cadres. All cadres, whether they are or are not doing a good job, can keep their iron rice bowls, and will never be dismissed or downgraded once they are employed. Such circumstances will naturally lead to the overstaffing of organizations, create redundant levels, and bring about many positions of deputies, and lots of unoccupied staffers. An overstaffed organization will inevitably aggravate the bureaucracy. Therefore, it is necessary to thoroughly change these systems. Of course, bureaucracy also shows itself in the aspect of ideological styles. However, as long as the problem concerning systems remains unsolved, the problem concerning ideological style cannot be solved. That is why our efforts in opposing bureaucracy repeatedly failed to score results in the past. Solving the above-mentioned problem concerning systems needs a great deal of work, including strengthening education and waging ideological struggle, which are indispensable. Without completing these tasks, it is impossible to effectively push ahead our economic undertaking and other works.

Overcentralization of power is manifested in the following practice: Under the pretext of strengthening the unified leadership of the party, all authorities are inappropriately and indiscriminately centralized under party committees, and the power of party committees is in turn held in the hands of several secretaries, in particular in the hands of first secretaries. The first secretaries make decisions for everything. Consequently, the unified leadership of the party always becomes leadership by individuals. All levels throughout the country are faced with this problem to a different extent. As the authorities are overcentralized to individuals or a small number of people, the majority of people who are actually in charge of the affairs do not have the decisionmaking power, and a small number of people with power are overloaded with duties. This will inevitably lead to bureaucracy, bring about various mistakes, jeopardize the normal practice of democracy of party organizations and governments at all levels, the collective leadership system, democratic centralism, the responsibility system of division of labor for the individual, and so forth.

These phenomena are related to the influence of feudal autocracy in the history of our country, as well as the tradition of a high degree of centralization of power to individual leaders in the party work of various countries which prevailed during the period of the Communist International. In the history of our party, undue emphasis was repeatedly placed on the centralized leadership of the party, and on the opposition to decentralism and to the assertion of one's independence. Meanwhile, we seldom emphasized the necessary decentralization of authority and decisionmaking power of the individual. In the past, several times we tried to divide power between the central authorities and the locality. However, we never touched the division of responsibilities between the party and the government, economic organizations, mass organizations, and so on. I do not oppose the emphasis on the centralized leadership of the party, nor negate centralized leadership for all cases and the necessity of opposition to decentralism and assertion of the individual's independence. After the party became the ruling party of our country, and particularly after the socialist transformation of the private ownership of the means of production was basically completed, the party had to undertake a central task different from that in the past. As the task of building socialism is extremely arduous and complicated, overcentralization of power is more and more unadaptable to the development of the socialist cause. Our overlooking of this problem for a long period of time was one of the important causes of the "Great Cultural Revolution," which brought us enormous losses. Now we can no longer ignore this problem.

While giving rise to a high degree of centralization of power to the individual, paternalism within the revolutionary ranks helped the individual to dominate the organization, and turned the organization into the tool of the individual. Paternalism is an outmoded social phenomenon with a very long history whose influence caused tremendous damages in our party's history. Chen Duxiu (Chen Duxiu (1879–1942) was a native of Huaining in Anhui Province. He became the chief editor of *Youth* journal, later renamed *New Youth*, in September 1915. In 1918, he and Li Dazhao founded the journal *Meizhou Pinglun*, [*Weekly Commentary*] by which he publicized a new culture and became one of the principal leaders of the May 4th new cultural movement. After the May 4th movement, Chen Duxiu accepted and began to publicize Marxism and became one of the principal founders of the CPC. He remained the principal leader of the party during the first 6 years after the founding of the party. In the later period of the first revolutionary civil war, he committed serious

rightist capitulationist mistakes. After that, being pessimistic and disappointed in the prospect of the revolution, he embraced the Trotskyite viewpoint, organized small groups within the party, and engaged in antiparty activities. In November 1929, he was expelled from the party, and publicly participated later in the activities of Trotskyite organizations. Chen was arrested by the Kuomintang in October 1932 and released in August 1937. He died of illness in Jiangjin, Sichuan Province, in 1942), Wang Ming (Wang Ming, alias Chen Shaoyu (1904–1974), was a native of Jinzhai in Anhui Province. Joining the CPC in 1924, he was appointed member of the CPC Central Committee, member of the Political Bureau of the CPC Central Committee, and secretary of the Changjiang River bureau of the CPC. He was the major representative of the erroneous line of "leftist" adventurism within the CPC during the period from January 1931 to January 1935 before the Zunyi meeting. In the initial period of the anti-Japanese war, Wang Ming again committed the rightist capitulationist mistake. Denying criticism and help by the party for a long time, Wang Ming degenerated into a traitor to the Chinese revolution in the 1960's), Zhang Guotao (Zhang Guotao (1897–1979) was a native of Pingxiang in Jiangxi Province. In 1921, he participated in the first CPC National Congress. He was then elected a member of the CPC Central Committee, the Political Bureau of the CPC Central Committee, and the Standing Committee of the Political Bureau.

(In 1931, he was appointed secretary of the central subbureau of the CPC in Hubei, Henan, and Anhui Provinces, vice chairman of the provisional central government of the soviet republic of China, and to other posts. He was appointed general political commissar of the Red Army after the 1st and the 4th Front Armies of the Red Army joined forces with each other in the Maogong area of Sichuan Province in June 1935. Taking objection to the central authorities' decision concerning the northward operation of the Red Army, Zhang Guotao engaged in activities to split the party as well as the Red Army and plotted to set up a new Central Committee of the party. He was forced to abolish the second Central Committee of the party in June 1936. And then he moved northward together with the 2d and 4th Front Armies of the Red Army and arrived in northern Shaanxi in December. He held the posts of vice chairman and acting chairman of the government of the Shaanxi-Gansu-Ningxia border region since September 1937. In April 1938, taking advantage of the occasion of the memorial ceremony for Huangdi at his tomb, Zhang Guotao fled the Shaanxi-Gansu-Ningxia border region, and went to Wuhan via Xian. He joined the secret service of the Kuomintang and thus became traitor to the Chinese revolution, and was expelled from the CPC immediately. He died in Canada in 1979.) and some others had promoted paternalism. From the Zunyi meeting to the socialist transformation period, the CPC central authorities and Comrade Mao Zedong did a relatively good job in upholding collective leadership and democratic centralism, and thus managed to maintain a relatively normal practice of democracy with the party. However, these fine traditions were not carried forward later and were never shaped into a strict and complete system. For example, when discussing important issues within the party, we often failed to thoroughly adhere to democratic procedure and have a full exchange of views, and decisions were usually made hastily by an individual or a small number of people. We seldom put issues to the vote according to the principle of the minority being subordinate to the majority. This showed that the democratic centralist practice had not yet been shaped into a strict system. Beginning with the criticism of opposition to adventurous advance in 1958 (based on the opinion of the Political Bureau of the CPC Central Committee, *Renmin Ribao* published an editorial entitled "It is Necessary To Oppose Conservatism and Also Impetuosity" on 20 June 1956, pointing out that certain phenomena of impetuous and rash advance, going beyond the bounds of practical possibility, had appeared in the process of the vigorous development of the cause of socialist construction. In accordance with this spirit, stress was laid on correcting problems in this respect. At the enlarged third plenary session of the eighth central committee in the autumn of 1957, Mao Zedong in his speech started to criticize the 1956 drive against adventurous advance. At the Nanning conference in January 1958 and the Chengdu conference in March 1958, Mao Zedong went further in severely criticizing the 1956 opposition to adventurous advance. The 1958 criticism of opposition to adventurous advance brought about a rapid development of "leftist" ideology in the party), and the "antirightist" drive of 1959 (this refers to the struggle launched in 1959 against the so-called rightist opportunist line of Peng Dehuai. See item 17 of "Resolution of the CPC Central Committee on a Number of Problems in the History of the Party Since the Founding of the PRC"), democratic life in the party and state gradually became abnormal, and there was a continuous growth in phenomena of the patriarchal system such as one person alone having the say and deciding on major issues, personality cult, and the individual overriding the organization. Lin Biao preached the theory of "the peak," saying that Chairman Mao's words were supreme instructions; such an expression became extremely common in the whole party, the whole Army, and the whole country. After the "gang of four" were smashed, the personality cult was still practiced for a time. Commemorations of the other leaders were also sometimes tinged with personality cult.

The Central Committee recently issued instructions on some issues in practicing "less publicity for the individual," pointing out that these inappropriate ways of commemorating people not only caused extravagance and waste and were divorced from the masses, but were also tinged with the idea that history is created by the individual; they do not help to carry out education in Marxism inside and outside the party or to sweep away the influence of feudal and bourgeois ideology. This instruction has also made some stipulations on correcting shortcomings of this type. This is a very important document. It should also be mentioned that after 1958 houses were built everywhere for Comrade Mao Zedong and other central comrades, and after the downfall of the "gang of four," surface construction work was undertaken at Zhongnanhai, which had a very bad effect and caused very great waste. Apart from that, certain high-ranking cadres, everywhere they go, either attend welcome or farewell banquets, or block traffic, or are given great publicity. These things are very improper. These serious instances of being divorced from the masses cannot be permitted to occur again, from the Central Committee right down to all levels.

In many places and units there are patriarchal-type figures; there is no limit to their power, and others have to show them absolute obedience and even form personal attachments with them. One of our organizational principles is that the lower levels must obey the upper, which means that the lower levels must carry out the decisions and instructions of the upper, but we cannot negate the relations of equality between party comrades on that account. Party members engaged in leadership work and ordinary party members must all treat each other as equals, and enjoy all their proper rights and carry out all their duties as equals. The upper levels cannot be insufferably arrogant toward the lower levels, and in particular cannot allow the lower levels to do things that violate the party Constitution and state laws; while the lower levels should not toady to and flatter the upper levels, obey them in an unprincipled way, and show "utmost loyalty." Relations between upper and lower levels should not turn into the cat-and-mouse relations criticized by Comrade Mao Zedong on many occasions, or into the relations between monarch and minister and father and son as in the old society, or into factional relations. The serious mistakes made by certain comrades are linked to this patriarchal-type work style surviving in the party. In short, unless we totally eliminate this patriarchal-type work style, there can be no question whatever of democracy in the party or socialist democracy.

The formation of the lifelong tenure system for leading cadres is related to a certain degree to feudalist influences and also to the fact that our party has never had a proper method for retirement and relieving people of their duty. During the years of revolutionary war everyone was relatively young, and in the 1950's everyone was in the prime of life, and there was no retirement problem; however it was a mistake that the issue has never been solved in good time. It should be acknowledged that under the specific historical conditions at the time, this problem could not be solved, or not completely solved. The draft of the party Constitution discussed by the fifth plenary session proposes abolishing the lifelong tenure system for cadres; as I see it now, this should be further revised and supplemented. The key lies in putting on a sound basis the systems of electing, examining, appointing and dismissing, impeaching, and rotating the cadres. Appropriate and specific regulations should be laid down according to the circumstances governing the length of office of leading cadres of all categories and at all levels (including those elected, those assigned, and those recruited), together with their retirement. No leading cadres should have an indefinite term of office.

During the "Great Cultural Revolution," Lin Biao and the "gang of four" went in for special powers in a big way, bringing great calamity on the masses. At present there are also some cadres who, instead of regarding themselves as servants of the people, see themselves as their masters and pursue special powers and privileges; this causes strong discontent among the masses and ruins the party's prestige.

Unless these practices are resolutely corrected, they are bound to cause corruption of our cadre force. The special powers we oppose today mean political and economic powers not covered by the law and the system. Pursuing special powers is a sign that the remnant influences of feudalism have not yet been eliminated. From old China, we inherited many traditions of feudal autocracy and few traditions of democracy and the legal system. Since liberation, we have not conscientiously and systematically set up systems guaranteeing the people's democratic rights; the legal system is far from complete and is given little attention, and phenomena of special powers are sometimes restricted, criticized, and hit, and sometimes grow anew. To overcome the phenomena of special powers, it is necessary to solve the ideological questions of equal rights and duties stipulated by the law, and nobody is allowed to gain an advantage or break the law. No matter who breaks the law, he must be investigated by the public security organs according to the law, and handled by the judicial organs according to the law; nobody is allowed to interfere in the execution of the law, and nobody who has broken the law may remain at large. Nobody is allowed to violate the party Constitution and discipline, and anyone who does must be subjected to disciplinary punishment; nobody is allowed to interfere in the execution of party discipline, and nobody who had violated party discipline may remain at large without being subject to legal sanctions. Only by genuinely and resolutely succeeding in these respects can we completely solve the problems of pursuing special powers and violating law and discipline. There must be a system of mass supervision, and the masses and party members must be allowed to supervise the cadres, especially the leading cadres. In the case of those who pursue special powers and privileges and do not mend their ways after being criticized and educated, the people have the right to expose, accuse, impeach, replace, and dismiss them, demand that they make economic restitution, and also subject them to punishment by the law and discipline. It is necessary to lay down regulations governing the scope of powers of cadres of all levels and their political and daily life treatment. The most important thing is that there should be special organs exercising utterly impartial supervision and inspection.

The mistakes of all kinds that we made in the past were of course connected with the thinking and work style of certain leaders, but the problems in organizational and work systems were even more serious. If these systems are good, we can ensure that bad people are unable to act as tyrants at will; and if the systems are bad, it is impossible for good people to do nothing but good things, and they may even take the wrong direction. Even such a great figure as Comrade Mao Zedong was seriously affected by certain bad systems, and the result was great calamity for the party, the state, and himself. If we today go on failing to put the socialist system on a sound basis, people will say, why is the socialist system unable to solve certain problems that the capitalist system has been able to solve? Although such a comparison is incomplete, we cannot fail to pay attention to it on that account. Stalin seriously damaged the socialist system; Comrade Mao Zedong said that such a thing could not have happened in Western countries such as Britain, France, and America. Although he understood this point, yet the 10-year catastrophe of the "Great Cultural Revolution" followed because the problems in the leadership system were not actually solved, and also on account of certain other reasons. This is an extremely profound lesson. I am not saying that the individual had no responsibility for what happened, but that the problems in leadership and organizational system are even more fundamental, allround, unchanging, and protracted. These problems in the system are related to whether the party and state will change color; the whole party must attach a high degree of importance to them.

If we fail to resolutely reform the defects in our current systems, certain serious problems that occurred in the past may appear anew in the future. Only by carrying out resolute and total reform of these defects in a planned and measured way will the people have faith in our leadership and in the party and socialism, and will our cause enjoy boundless prospects.

When talking of the defects in our party and state leadership system, we cannot but touch on the mistakes made by Comrade Mao Zedong in his last years. The resolution on a number of problems in the history of the party since the founding of the state, which is now being drafted, will make a systematic exposition on Mao Zedong Thought and also a relatively all-round appraisal of Comrade Mao Zedong's merits and faults, including a criticism of his mistakes during the "Great Cultural Revolution." We communists are thoroughgoing materialists; we can only affirm in a truth-seeking way those things that should be affirmed and negate those things that should be negated. During his life Comrade Mao Zedong gained undying merit for our party, state, and people. His achievements are primary and his mistakes secondary. It is not a materialist approach to conceal his faults on account of his merits. Nor is it a materialist approach to negate his merits on account of his errors. The reason why the "Great Cultural Revolution" was erroneous and was defeated was precisely because it ran counter to the scientific principles of Mao Zedong Thought. The scientific principles of Mao Zedong Thought, which have been proven correct in the course of long testing in practice, not only guided us in winning victory in the past, but will also remain our guiding ideology for a long period of struggle in the future. It is incorrect to show any doubt or wavering over this important party principle; to do so runs counter to the fundamental interests of the Chinese people.

4

Now I would like to talk about the problem of eliminating feudal and bourgeois ideological influence.

Various kinds of malpractices which I mentioned above have a more or less feudal coloration. Of course, the scope of the residual influence of feudalism is much wider, which includes the residual patriarchal mentality in social relations and hierarchy; certain unequal relations between the higher and lower levels on the one hand, and between the cadres and masses on the other; weak concepts on citizens' rights and duties; system and work style of certain "bureaucratic industry," "bureaucratic commerce," and "bureaucratic agriculture" in the economic field; undue stress on the administrative division and jurisdiction of areas and departments in economic work, which leads to restricting the activities of some areas and departments to a designated sphere and shifting troubles onto others. Sometimes, two socialist enterprises or two socialist regions might encounter difficulties when they make representations, and these difficulties can be avoided at the start. Some people practice autocracy in the cultural field. Some people do not admit the great importance of science and education concerning socialism and refuse to recognize the truth that without science and education, there will be no socialism. While dealing with foreign countries, some people follow a closed-door policy and adopt an attitude of parochial arrogance. With regard to patriarchal mentality, during the "Great Cultural Revolution," when a man became a mighty official, all his friends and relations got to the top. When a person had bad luck, all the members of his nine clans were adversely affected. The situation was very serious. Even now, the abominable practice of appointing people by favoritism and factionalism is still prevalent in some areas, departments, and units. Such a bad practice has not yet been corrected. Some cadres abuse their power in order to allow their relatives and friends to live and work in towns or cities or to promote them to higher positions. It is obvious that we should not neglect the pernicious influence of the patriarchal mentality. We should make great efforts to completely solve the above-mentioned problems.

We completed the new democratic revolution in 28 years. We did a successful and complete job in overthrowing the reactionary rule of feudalism and in eliminating the feudal land ownership system. However, due to the fact that we underestimated the importance of the task of eliminating the residual feudal influence in the ideological and political field, we did not complete this task. Thereafter, we entered the socialist revolution.

Now we should explicitly put forth the task of continuing to eliminate the residual feudal influence in the ideological and political field. In the meantime, we should carry out a series of reforms of the system. Otherwise, our country and people will suffer from losses.

To accomplish this task, we should adopt a scientific attitude of seeking truth from facts. We should make use of Marxism-Leninism-Mao Zedong Thought to specifically, accurately, and practically analyze the manifestations of the pernicious influence of feudalism. First of all, we should draw a clear line of demarcation between socialism and feudalism. Nobody is allowed to oppose socialism on the pretext of opposing feudalism; neither is he allowed to pursue feudalism by using the stuff of the fake socialism advocated by the "gang of four." Furthermore, we should draw a clear line of demarcation between the democratic essence of our cultural heritage and the feudal dross. We should also draw a clear line of demarcation between the pernicious influence of feudalism and some of our unscientific methods which we adopted due to a lack of experience. We should avoid doing things like a gust of wind and regarding all things as feudal without making any analyses.

To the broad masses of cadres and people, eliminating the residual feudal influence should be regarded as a drive of self-education and self-reform. Our purpose in doing so is to free ourselves from the pernicious influence of feudalism, to emancipate our minds, and to enhance our consciousness so that we will be able to satisfy the demands of the modernization and make contributions to the people, the society, and mankind. To eliminate the residual influence of feudalism, we should place our stress on truly reforming and improving the system of our party and state so as to ensure the democratization of the political life of the party and state, economic management, and the entire social life. To do so, we can promote the smooth progress of our modernization. To accomplish our task, we should conscientiously carry out study and investigation, compare the experiences of other countries with ours, and draw on collective wisdom and absorb all useful ideas

so that we can formulate effective plans and adopt useful measures. We should not think that destruction comes first and that construction will come in the course of destruction. It should be clearly pointed out that we should not launch any political movement or propagate the movement of so-called opposing feudalism. We should not carry out a political campaign to criticize certain people as we did in the past. We are not allowed to direct the spearhead of attack on cadres and masses. Historical experiences have proved that we never succeed in solving ideological problems of the masses if we adopt the method of mass campaign rather than the methods of reasoning and discussion. We will never succeed in reforming the existing system and establishing the new one if we fail to adopt a down-to-earth manner and take the method of steady progress. In socialist society, the matter of solving ideological problems of the masses and reforming specific organizational and work systems is completely and entirely different from attacking counterrevolutionary elements and sabotaging the reactionary system during the revolutionary period.

While eliminating the residual feudal influence, we should not slacken our efforts or neglect criticism of the bourgeois and petty bourgeois ideology and repudiation of extreme individualism and anarchism. Whether the residual feudal influence is more serious than the bourgeois influence is determined by practical conditions in different areas and departments, different issues, and people with different ages, experiences, and education. We should not treat different matters as the same. In addition, our country was a semifeudal and semicolonial society for more than a hundred years. Sometimes, feudal ideology, capitalist ideology, and the colonial slave ideology lump together, with one intermingling with another. In recent years, due to the expansion of international contacts, some people have been influenced by the decadent bourgeois ideology and way of life of foreign countries. The practice of worshipping and having blind faith in things foreign has already occurred, and things will become more serious in the future. This is an important problem which we should solve conscientiously.

China is economically and culturally backward, but it is not backward in everything. Some foreign countries are advanced in science, technology, and management, but they are not advanced in everything. Our party and people fought a bloody battle to establish the socialist system. In spite of the fact that this system is not perfect and that it was sabotaged, it is much better than the capitalist system, in which the weak are the prey of the strong and some people benefit themselves at the expense of others. Our system is getting better and better because it can absorb the advanced factors of various countries in the world. It will become the best system in the world. This is the thing that capitalism can never do. We committed mistakes in the history of our socialist revolution and construction. If we lose faith in socialism and think that socialism is inferior to capitalism because of this, this is completely wrong. It is equally wrong if we think that we should propagate capitalist ideas in order to eliminate the residual influence of feudalism. We should thoroughly repudiate these erroneous ideas and never let them spread unchecked. We should advocate the principle of distribution according to work and admit material interests and strive for the material interests of the entire people. Everybody must have his own material interests. However, this does not mean that we encourage people to strive for their own material interests at the expense of the interests of the state, collective, and other people. We never encourage people to regard "money" as everything. Otherwise, what is the difference between socialism and capitalism? We always maintain that in the socialist society, the interests of the state, the collective, and individuals are basically identical. If there is a conflict, one's personal interests must be subordinated to the interests of the state and collective. When necessary, all revolutionary conscious and advanced elements should sacrifice their own interests in order to promote the interests of the state, collectives, and the people. We should do our best to propagate such lofty ethics among the whole people and youths.

In an attempt to go abroad or to make money, some youths, some children of cadres, and even some cadres themselves do not hesitate to sacrifice their personalities, the integrity of the state, and the national sense of self-respect by violating the law and discipline, engaging in smuggling activities, taking bribes, or engaging in speculation and profiteering. This is quite shameful. In the past 1 to 2 years, some obscene, dirty, salacious, and ugly photos, films, books, and magazines have been imported into the country through various channels. They corrupt our social values and some of our youths and cadres. If we allow this pestilence to spread unchecked, many people who do not have a strong will will be corrupted morally or degenerated spiritually. The party organizations at various levels should pay serious attention to this problem and adopt resolute and effective measures to ban and destroy them. Under no circumstances should we allow them to flow into the country continuously. In domestic economic work, the individuals, small cliques, and even enterprises and units distorting current economic policies and engaging in various illegal activities by taking advantage of the loopholes in economic management have also increased to some extent. It is also necessary to be highly vigilant and to struggle resolutely against the criminals who engage in antisocialist illegal activities.

In short, it is necessary to integrate the work of eliminating the remnant influence of feudalism and the criticism of bourgeois ideas characterized by benefiting oneself at the expense of others and putting profit-making first and other corrupt ideas.

Naturally, it is also necessary to adopt a scientific attitude toward capitalist and bourgeois ideology. Some time in the past, in an effort to conduct education in revolutionary ideas, some localities again put forward the slogan of "fostering proletarian ideology and liquidating bourgeois ideology." I have read the relevant documents but did not notice any problems at that time. It now seems that this old slogan is neither sufficiently comprehensive nor accurate.

Due to their failure to conduct ample investigation and study, some comrades have criticized some reforms beneficial to the development of production and the socialist cause as if they were capitalist ones. This is incorrect. In order to avoid committing previous mistakes, it is quite necessary to continue to study the elements in bourgeois ideology which should be resolutely criticized and prevented from spreading, and the capitalist tendencies in our economic life which should be resolutely overcome,

resisted, and correctly criticized, and then make appropriate stipulations about them.

5

The CPC Central Committee has deliberated on many occasions the reform of the leadership system of the party and state. Some of the reforms have been implemented since the fifth plenary session, some will be put forward at the Third Session of the Fifth NPC, and specific measures for some others will be taken one after another when conditions are ripe. In addition to those mentioned above, we are now considering the question of gradually conducting the following major reforms:

1. The CPC Central Committee will propose to the Third Session of the Fifth NPC a revision of the Constitution. Our Constitution should be made more complete, well conceived, and accurate to ensure that the people truly enjoy the right to manage state organizations at various levels, enterprises, and institutions and to ensure the ample rights of citizens. Efforts should be made to ensure that the various nationalities truly practice regional national autonomy, to improve the system of people's congresses at various levels, and so on. The principle of not permitting overconcentration of power will also be reflected in the Constitution.

2. The CPC Central Committee has set up a Discipline Inspection Commission and is considering the setting up of an advisory commission (the name can be further considered), which, together with the Central Committee, are elected by the party's national congress with clear-cut stipulations regarding their respective tasks, functions, and power. Thus, we can fully utilize the experiences of a large number of old comrades who formerly worked in the Central Committee and the State Council, and give scope to their guiding, supervisory, and advisory role. At the same time, we can also make the everyday working bodies of the Central Committee and the State Council more rational and efficient, and gradually make the ranks of the cadres younger in average age.

3. Truly set up a powerful working system from the State Council down to local governments at various levels. In the future, all work which comes within the scope of the functions and power of the government should be discussed and decided upon by the State Council and local governments at various levels, which will issue the relevant documents; the CPC Central Committee and local CPC committees at various levels will no longer issue instructions or make decisions on them. Government work, naturally, should be conducted under the political leadership of the party. When government work is strengthened, party leadership will also be strengthened.

4. All enterprises and institutions should set up extensively the system of workers' congresses or workers' representative conferences. This issue was decided long ago, and the issue now is to popularize and perfect this system. The workers' congress or workers' representative conference has the right to discuss and make decisions on major issues concerning its own unit, to propose to the higher authorities the dismissal of unqualified administrative leading personnel in its own unit, and gradually to elect leaders within the appropriate scope.

5. Party committees at various levels should truly institute the system of integrating collective leadership with the division of labor with individual responsibility. It is necessary to make clear which issues should be collectively discussed and which should come under individual responsibility.

Major issues must be discussed and decided upon by the collective. When making a decision, it is necessary to abide strictly by the principle that the minority is subordinate to the majority, with each person having one vote. Each secretary only has the right to cast one vote; the first secretary should not decide everything. The work decided upon by the collective should be carried out separately, with each person having his own responsibility; under no circumstances should we shift responsibility among one another. It is necessary to investigate and affix the responsibility of those who neglect their duties. There should be a head even in collective leadership. The first secretaries of party committees at various levels should be responsible primarily for the daily work. It is necessary to emphasize individual responsibility among the other members of the party committees. We should promote the practice of leading cadres being brave in shouldering responsibilities. This is entirely different from changing the system of making arbitrary decisions, and these two questions should not be mixed up.

I ask you to discuss and study the above-mentioned five points, conscientiously and amply airing your views, including differing views. With respect to some questions, after the CPC Central Committee has made a decision on them in principle, it is still necessary to conduct experiments in order to gain experience and to pool collective wisdom. We will solve the questions one by one when the conditions are ripe. Respectively, the CPC Central Committee makes official decisions on them, formulates well-conceived and feasible systems and regulations which will work for a considerably long period of time, and puts them into effect step by step. Before the CPC Central Committee formulates and officially issues new systems and regulations, the work on various aspects should still be carried out according to the existing systems.

In reforming the leadership system of the party and state, we do not aim at weakening party leadership and slackening party discipline, but at abiding by and strengthening party leadership and party discipline. In a great country like China, it would be impossible to unify the ideas and strength of several hundred million people for building socialism without a party which can truly represent and unite the masses of people and which is formed by party members with a high degree of consciousness, discipline, and the spirit of self-sacrifice and without the unified leadership of such a party. It will only result in disunity and nothing will be accomplished. This is a truth which the people of all nationalities throughout the country have profoundly understood through protracted struggle and practice. The unity of our people, the stability of our society, the development of democracy, the reunification of our country rely on the leadership of the party. The kernel of the four basic principles is to abide by the leadership of the party. The issue is that our party should be good at leadership; only by constantly improving leadership is it possible to strengthen leadership.

The extremely arduous and complicated task of socialist modernization lies before us. A lot of old problems constantly need to be solved and, what is more, new problems are emerging one after another. Only by closely relying on the masses, maintaining close contacts with them, listening to their voice at all times, understanding their sentiments, and representing their interests will it be possible for our party to form a powerful force and successfully accomplish all our tasks. There are now numerous ideological problems among the masses which should be solved, and this applies to the ideological problems within the party. It is absolutely necessary for us to place ideological and political work at a very important position and conscientiously do a good job of them, never slackening our efforts. It is necessary for party committees and leading cadres at various levels and for all party members to do this work. They should do the work in accordance with the special characteristics of these problems and in a meticulous and deep-going way so that the masses are happy to receive the education.

What is most important is that if it is necessary to mobilize the masses to do something, all party members, particularly those assuming leading posts, should take the lead in doing so. Therefore, in order to do a good job of ideological and political work, it is also necessary to improve party leadership and the leadership system of the party.

Comrades! Reforming and perfecting various systems of the party and state is an arduous and protracted task; the key to achieving this task lies in reforming and perfecting the leadership system of the party and state. We should have an ample understanding of this point. Comrade Mao Zedong and other revolutionaries of the older generation who passed away have not been able to accomplish this task. This load has now been placed on our shoulders. All party members, particularly elderly party members, should put all their energy into this. Since the 3d Plenary Session of the 11th CPC Central Committee, we have done a lot of work, solved a lot of problems, and attained numerous achievements. We now have a very good forward position. We now set forward the task for reforming and perfecting the leadership system of the party and state in order to meet the needs of modernization. The conditions for this are ripe. It is perhaps impossible for our generation to accomplish this task completely, but we have at least the duty to lay a solid foundation for its accomplishment and establish a correct orientation for it. I believe we can assuredly achieve this.

Hua Guofeng's Last Speech as Premier, 7 September 1980

The proceedings of the third session of the Fifth National People's Congress in September 1980 reflected Deng Xiaoping's victory over Hua, although it was rendered a trifle less brusque by the resignation of seven vice-premiers, including Deng, as well as that of Hua himself in favor of Deng's man Zhao Ziyang. The speech focuses on the policies of Deng rather than on those of Hua.

Deputies, the present NPC session has been going on for 9 days. Entrusted by the State Council, Comrades Yao Yilin and Wang Bingqian have delivered reports on the national economic plans, and on the state budget and the final state accounts, respectively. Comrades Peng Zhen, Jiang Hua, Huang Huoqing, Wu Xinyu and Gu Ming have respectively given reports or explanations of the work of the NPC Standing Committee, the Supreme People's Court and the Supreme People's Procuratorate and on several draft laws. I am now going to express some opinions primarily on the work of the government.

On planning and finance, people hold that the economic growth and various economic quotas set for 1980 and 1981 in the report on planning are comparatively appropriate and will be conducive to achieving better economic results. The financial report explains the causes for the financial deficit in 1979 and for the financial deficit in 1980 and 1981 and comes up with measures for further reducing and eventually eliminating financial deficits. People hold that it is possible to gradually restore a balance between revenues and expenditures through effort.

Efforts have been made so that both the national economic plans and the financial revenue plans for this year and the next are geared to actual circumstances. However, it is still necessary for all workers, peasants, PLA commanders and fighters, intellectuals, cadres and patriotic personages of all nationalities throughout the country to make concerted and vigorous efforts to realize them.

Since last year, serious natural disasters have occurred or are occurring in some areas of our country. Here I extend my cordial regards to the elders, brothers and sisters in these disaster areas and to the cadres, masses, and PLA commanders and fighters who have heroically done relief work and rushed to deal with the emergencies. Like you deputies, I believe that people throughout the country can certainly overcome these difficulties and other temporary difficulties caused by the natural disasters and score new brilliant achievements on the road ahead.

During the past few days of discussions deputies have also affirmed the achievements and pointed out existing problems in the work of the government and in work in other fields over the past year and more, and have made many important criticisms and suggestions. On behalf of the State Council, I thank you deputies from the bottom of my heart for your trust in the government. The State Council and the departments concerned should seriously study the criticism and suggestions made by deputies and make vigorous efforts to do what should be done and to correct what should be corrected.

The last session of the Fifth NPC was held 1 year or so ago. Since then the stress of work of the whole nation has been gradually shifted to socialist modernization. The handling of many political and social problems left by history is continuing. The stable, united and lively political situation continues to consolidate and develop. Although there are still many problems that need to be noted and resolved, the political and social environment required for modernization is basically fine.

Thanks to the joint efforts of the public security, judicial, educational, and ideological and cultural work departments, the Youth League and the society as a whole, the order in our society has become more stable and a gratifying progress in our moral practices has also begun to appear. On this basis, government departments at various levels have begun to concentrate their main energy on economic construction, researching the new situation, resolving new problems and making solid strides on the road of probing specific measures for realizing our country's socialist modernization.

New conditions have emerged in our national economy after more than one year of readjustment, restructuring, consolidation and improvement: The relations among major sectors of the economy are gradually becoming harmonious; agricultural production which remained backward for a long time began to take a turn for the better in the past 2 years; the growth rate of light industry is now faster than that of heavy industry; heavy industry has shown progress in readjusting the commodity structure and in serving agriculture, light industry and the people's livelihood; state financed capital construction is now under control; the accumulation rate which used to be too high is beginning to slow down; and the living standard of the majority of the people in urban and rural areas is somewhat improved.

Preliminary reforms have been carried out in the economic system: the decisionmaking right of rural communes, production brigades and production teams is guaranteed; industrial and commercial enterprises' authority over their own management has been expanded; the principle of regulation through planning combined with

[New China News Agency, 14 September 1980.]

regulation by the market has been implemented in some areas; competition and joint operation among enterprises within the limits allowed by socialism is being encouraged; development of the collective economy in towns and cities is being given assistance; legitimate individual economy in urban and rural areas is allowed to exist and, to a limited extent, develop; and the two-tier financial system—at the central and local levels—has been put into effect. These things have changed the overcentralized situation in production, circulation and distribution and, as a result, the entire national economy has been stimulated.

Progress has been achieved in enterprise consolidation: The leading bodies of many enterprises have been adequately staffed and strengthened; democratic management prevails in enterprises; all technical and economic targets are being better fulfilled; the number of enterprises running at a loss due to mismanagement is decreasing; and fairly good achievements have been made in creating greater social wealth with a smaller labor force and less material consumption. Many areas, departments and enterprises have strengthened their control over cadres and the training of technical personnel and production workers. They have carried out education in economic management and scientific and technical education. In some places, technical renovation and innovation centered around energy conservation have started. The enterprises' organizational management and technical level have improved. All these are preliminary steps; we must unswervingly continue these efforts.

The proposition and implementation of the principle of readjustment, restructuring, consolidation and improvement signals the beginning of a fundamental change in the governing concept of our economic construction work. For a long time in the past, a left-deviationist tendency prevailed in many aspects of our economic work. We departed from the basic principle of Mao Zedong Thought, divorced ourselves from reality, flouted objective laws and blindly went after and rashly set high targets. As a result, investment in all sectors of heavy industry, with the exception of energy and transportation, was too high and capital construction was overextended, resulting in low speed and efficiency. Thus, development of energy, transport, agriculture, light industry, commerce, science and technology, culture and education, and the improvement of the people's living standard were seriously impaired and even the environment and ecological equilibrium were damaged.

We imposed excessive and too rigid controls. This inhibited the initiative of grassroots administrative offices and the masses of workers and obstructed the smooth flow between the various links in production and circulation.

There are also many serious defects in investment methods in sharing the earnings of industry, in labor management and in the principles of distribution. In some cases, we were encouraging waste not thrift, slipshod and not quality products, backwardness and not advancement, and laziness and not industriousness. All these hampered our efforts to bring into full play the superiority of socialism and even distorted the basic principles of socialism. Fundamentally speaking, implementation of the principle of readjustment, restructuring, consolidation and improvement means eliminating the influence of left-deviationist thinking in our economic work and carrying out the principle of starting from reality, seeking truth from facts and suiting the task to our capability in economic construction,

which is a principle of Mao Zedong Thought. Thus all economic activities will conform more fully to objective economic laws. Facts show that the principle of readjustment, restructuring, consolidation and improvement is correct and that it injects new vitality into our economy and propels our economy onto a sound course of development.

For the past year and more, conditions for scientific research work have improved, bringing about a number of important achievements in scientific research. The work of popularizing science has also been strengthened. In education, the quality of teaching in primary schools, middle schools and universities has been raised in general compared with past years. A number of reforms have been made in the structure of secondary school education, and secondary vocational schools are being continuously restored. The number of TV universities, correspondence universities and night universities are on the increase. New major achievements have been attained in the fields of science, health and physical education. All these achievements are inseparable from the diligent work of the comrades in the fields of science, education, culture, health, and physical education. For the past year and more, there have been new developments in promoting socialist democracy and a legal system. Based on the four fundamental principles of upholding the socialist road, the dictatorship of the proletariat, the leadership of the Communist Party and Marxism-Leninism-Mao Zedong Thought, the broad masses of cadres and people have emancipated their minds, sought truth from facts, developed the style of daring to speak and conduct criticism, and daring to do things that they had dared not do before, although these were things that needed doing and they were things they had always wanted to do. Many government organs have further strengthened their ties with the masses, paid attention and listened to the masses' criticisms and proposals, and accepted their supervision. The enforcement of the seven laws adopted by the Second Session of the Fifth National People's Congress is playing an important role in bringing into full play the enthusiasm of the people of the whole country for socialism, in striking at criminal offenders, in safeguarding the people's interests and in ensuring the smooth development of the modernization program. To meet the needs for economic development, legislative and judicial work in the economic field is being developed step by step. The State Council and the departments concerned have proclaimed more than 40 economic laws and regulations, and are working out, examining and revising some 20 more. A great deal of work needs to be done in this regard. It is only a beginning at present.

Here, I would like to dwell upon the issues of safeguarding the democratic and economic rights of the people of national minorities and of strengthening unity among all nationalities in particular. Owing to shortcomings and errors in our work—particularly the serious sabotage of the policies on nationalities and religions as well as other related policies of the party and the government by the two counterrevolutionary cliques headed by Lin Biao and Jiang Qing respectively during the 10 years of turmoil— the rights of many minority nationalities for regional national autonomy and their other democratic rights have been trampled on, their economy and culture have been ruined, and the masses have encountered difficulties in their livelihood.

To fundamentally change this situation, the party and the government are adopting a series of practical and effective measures to help the people in these areas have a breathing space, to progress healthily and to earnestly protect their political, economic and cultural rights, particularly their rights for regional national autonomy. All of us firmly believe that by relying on the joint efforts of all our nationalities, we will definitely be able to heal, within a fairly short period, the grievous wounds left from the past and unprecedentedly consolidate and develop the close friendship and unity among our people of all nationalities.

For the past year and more, we have actively carried out our work in dealing with foreign countries, strengthened friendship and cooperation and exchanges in the fields of economy, science and technology and culture with many countries, and enhanced friendly relations between the Chinese peoples and the peoples in various countries. We hoist aloft the banner of opposing hegemonism and safeguarding world peace, support the just struggle of the peoples in various countries, and internationally create favorable conditions for China's socialist modernization program.

Judging from the situation in the political, economic, scientific, technological and other fields and in foreign affairs, we can declare with good reason that thanks to the common efforts of the people of all nationalities, governments at all levels and personalities of all circles throughout the country, the various resolutions adopted and the various policies set forth at the Second Session of the Fifth NPC have been or are being implemented.

The major task for 1980 and 1981, in broad terms, is to continue developing the current favorable situation; to continue implementing the policy of readjusting, reforming, consolidating and improving the national economy; and in accordance with the plans presented by the State Council to this session, to press ahead with the modernizations on the basis of achievements to date. This is a very complex and arduous task. It requires us to do a lot of work and to solve a great many problems.

Now, I would like to express a few opinions on the following five issues for the deliberation of the deputies:

I. THE DRAFTING OF A LONG TERM PROGRAM

To draft a long term plan is a necessary prerequisite for developing a socialist planned economy. Since the founding of the nation, the First 5-Year Plan for development of the national economy worked out after the 3 years of economic recovery was fine from drafting to implementation. The contents of the Second 5-Year Plan were also fairly good. However, it is regrettable that owing to the trend of "being boastful," "stirring up a communist wind" and "giving arbitrary directions" in 1958 and the effect of the "anti-right deviationist" struggle after September 1959, this Second 5-Year Plan failed to play its proper role. In the several years after 1961, the work of readjusting the national economy was carried out smoothly, and we attained remarkable achievements and accumulated rich experiences. However, no 5-year plans for the development of the economy were mapped out. The economy during that period was basically one of recovery. After 1966, the whole national economy, together with work of the State Planning Commission itself were seriously battered by the "Great Cultural Revolution." The necessary reference materials and organs for formulating plans were destroyed. It was almost impossible to carry out planning work. Therefore, only outlines were put forward for the Third, Fourth and Fifth 5-Year Plans during the 15 years from 1966 to 1980. It was impossible to work out complete plans.

As a result, our nation was always short of a long term program for the development of the national economy—an ambitious and well-planned program with clear targets and careful and precise steps that took into consideration both past experiences and situations that could possibly arise in the future and that struck an overall balance. Exerting strenuous efforts, the workers, peasants, PLA intellectuals and the broad masses of cadres in the whole country have overcome various difficulties, done a great deal of arduous work and attained many outstanding achievements during the past 10 years and more. However, in the development of economic construction, there was no way we could implement the correct plans or avoid doing things blindly. Thus, we inevitably suffered some undeserved major losses. Under this situation, it was difficult to demonstrate the superiority of the socialist economic system. There is no doubt that socialism is far superior to capitalism. However, history has substantiated that to give full scope to this superiority, we must have a correct line, principles and policies, and draw up correct long term programs and annual plans under the correct line, principles and policies. Now we have a correct line, principles and policies. To achieve modernization, the mapping out of a long term program or its draft outline has become the order of the day. There are still many obstacles in outlining a long term program under the present conditions. However, we must map out such an outline, because it is our guide for realizing the four modernizations.

In the "Report on the Work of the Government" delivered at the Second Session of this National People's Congress, I had already put forward the necessary supplements and revisions for the outline of the 10-year program from 1976 to 1985. After repeated study, the State Council held that after the smashing of the "gang of four," we adopted a series of measures and did a great deal of arduous work in eliminating chaos and restoring order and brought about the rapid recovery and development of the national economy. At that time, everyone wanted to make up the losses which we had suffered during the 10 years of turmoil. It is necessary to reaffirm this kind of revolutionary enthusiasm. However, the 10-year program outline was made under the influence of conditions prevailing at the time. Difficulties arising from the prolonged sabotage by Lin Biao, Jiang Qing and their ilk and their ultraleft ideology was underestimated. Not enough work had been done to sum up the positive and the negative experiences and lessons in economic construction over the last 30 years. Some targets were too high. The scale of capital construction was too large. Comprehensive balance was lacking for many projects. The deputies raised many correct criticisms of the original draft at this session. However, more than 4 years had already elapsed for this draft of the 10-year program. To revise this draft would be meaningless. Therefore, we decided not to revise the original 10-year program outline, but to start drafting a 10-year program outline for the 1981–1990 period and to draw up the Sixth 5-Year Plan for the 1981–1985 period accordingly.

Drawing a lesson from our past experience, we think

that in order to map out a good long term program, we must emphasize the solution of the following several problems:

It is necessary to act according to the objective laws of socialist society. Socialist society will exist for a considerably long historical period. In this period, the existence and development of a commodity economy is an objective reality that is inevitable. Of course, our commodity economy is a socialist and planned one and our enterprises are relatively independent commodity producers. Under the guidance of the unified state plan and within the limits of the principles, policies and decrees of the state, enterprises should have the right to engage independently in such economic activities as production and trade, according to social needs and the law of value. During a specific part of the socialist period, the state-owned economy and the collective economy are the basic forms of the socialist economy, and the individual economy of labor guided by the state is a necessary supplement to the socialist economy. Any change in prolonged coexistence of these economic sectors depends solely on the development of the social forces of production.

One of the salient manifestations of left deviationist thinking in China's economic work in the past was rejection of the need to develop commodity production and commodity exchange and the rejection of the historical role of the prolonged coexistence of the multiple sectors of the economy after the socialist transformation was, in the main, completed. The overly rigid and excessive control of the economic system, the attempt to narrow the scope of socialist commodity economy quickly, instead of expanding it, and the attempt to eliminate the necessary individual economy and to speed up the transition of collective ownership to ownership by the whole people in disregard of the need to expand the social forces of production—these have already done China grievous harm and even now confront the country with many difficulties. While formulating the long term program, we must conscientiously sum up experience and lessons, eliminate the influence of left deviationist thinking, other idealist thinking and metaphysics and act honestly according to the objective law of socialist society.

It is necessary to proceed from reality and work within the limits of our capability. China has a vast territory with an abundance of natural resources, but the natural conditions and economic development in various regions of China are uneven. China has a large population and the Chinese people are diligent, brave and intelligent, but the scientific and cultural level of our people is low. We have developed an independent and comparatively complete economic system of a certain dimension; but our per capita income is very low, our commodity economy is underdeveloped and our technology management is backward. When we draft the outline of the 10-year plan, we must fully consider these salient features of China's natural conditions, economy and culture. We must take full advantage of our favorable conditions, open up more avenues of production and exploit our superior features. At the same time we must strive to overcome our shortcomings and work hard for the prosperity of our country. Whether we are making positive, full and effective efforts or not will, of course, play an important role in deciding how much we can accomplish in the next 10 years and what level we can attain after 10 years. However, we must know that the effects of our efforts have certain limits; that is they are not unlimited, because the conditions that our efforts can rely on, use and create are decided solely by the existing objective reality, not by our subjective wishes. Therefore, after this conference is over, all departments of the State Council and the local governments at all levels will continue to make thorough, systematic investigations and studies of the current national situation of resources—including manpower resources—that can be exploited and explored in the next 10 years, and of the ways to exploit and explore them, so that our 10-year plan can be placed on a scientific and practical basis as far as possible.

It is necessary to pay full attention to the improvement of the people's living standards. The fundamental aim of our modernization program is to gradually raise the people's material and cultural living standards on the basis of the development of production. The State Council should fully consider this when it begins to formulate the draft outline of the 10-year plan.

We closely combine our production development plan with our plan for gradually raising the people's living standards on the basis of the development of production so that the 10-year plan outline will be an overall, balanced and complete plan dealing with both economic and social development in China. To raise the people's material and cultural living standards, we of course need to work in many fields. Some work does not seem to be directly relevant to the improvement of the people's living standards, but it actually is indispensable to that improvement. For example, to step up the building of the People's Liberation Army, strengthen the defense of our great motherland and protect our peaceful construction is precisely one such indispensable task. The same is true of certain basic scientific research. All this is not hard to understand. Anyway, we must make the development of production show its effects on the improvement of the living standards of all the people. In this way, people throughout the country will be able to see what developments China can make in its socialist economy and what improvement they can make in their livelihood in the next 10 years, after they take a look at the plan.

Then, they will understand the relationship between the modernization program and their present and future interests and the relationship between the partial and local interest and the general interest. Then, everyone will take the plan as his own undertaking, continue to carry forward the hard-working and pioneering spirit and make all efforts to realize it.

It is necessary to pay special attention to the exploitation of intellectual resources and to make efforts to develop scientific and educational institutions. The level of development of a country is to a great extent decided by the degree of its exploitation of intellectual resources. The modernization of science and technology is the key to the three other modernizations. Scientific research must anticipate the needs of economic construction and be conducted to solve the scientific and technological problems concerning the modernization program, particularly significant key problems. In connection with the management system, economic interests and our ideas and understanding, we should take necessary measures to widely and rapidly popularize and use the results of scientific research. The development of educational institutions of various types and at various levels has a bearing on the scientific and cultural level of those who undertake the modernization program. This includes the level of knowledge, skill, proficiency, discipline, vitality and morality of physical laborers and mental workers in urban and rural areas of our country. It also has a bearing on the development of China's scientific and technological undertakings. While science is a productive force, education, as a means of improving the laborers' knowledge and skills, is also an indispensable productive force. It is impossible to undertake the modernization program by relying on illiterate or semiliterate persons. The governments at all levels and the entire society should pay attention to science and education, respect the teachers of kindergartens, primary schools, middle schools and colleges and scientists for their lofty and arduous work and raise their social position. On 2 September, Ye Shengtao and seven other deputies wrote *Renmin Ribao* a letter. They exposed the mistakes of some workers at two restaurants in Dalian who treated some primary school teacher without proper respect. They sternly criticized those workers and called on people in all walks of life to respect primary school teachers. I completely agree with and support the letter. I hope that government personnel and people throughout the country make concerted efforts to foster a common practice of respecting all teachers and scientists in our society. The neglect, or even the rejection of science and education was an important aspect of the left-deviation which made us suffer heavy losses. We must resolutely correct such mistakes. Therefore, the tremendous importance of science and education to the cause of modernization must be duly reflected in the 10-year plan draft outline. The State Council plans to devote more funds to science and education step by step in the coming decade and hopes that the governments of various provinces, municipalities and autonomous regions will do likewise. We should take various paths to strive to make a faster and better development of science and education and, in the course of time, train generation after generation of healthy laborers with socialist consciousness and scientific and cultural knowledge and skills, and group after group of experts in the fields of science, technology, social science, organization, management, literature and art, who satisfy the demands of the four modernizations.

Family planning should be included in the long-term program. Population is an issue of general concern to the people nationally at present. In drawing up the long term program, we must plan not only on the growth of material production but also on population growth, making the two compatible to each other. For a considerably long period in the past (chiefly in the 1960's), efforts were slackened with regard to family planning. As a result, the population has grown too rapidly, and the trend is continuing. Now people under 30 account for about 65 percent of the population, totalling about 630 million. Some have already reached childbearing age, and most of the rest will reach childbearing age successively in 10 to 20 odd years from now. If population growth is not controlled, there will be an ultrahigh peak, to which the economy and social life as a whole cannot possibly be adapted.

After careful study, the State Council deems it imperative to adopt firm measures on the population issue for the coming 20 or 30 years. That is, except in sparsely populated areas inhabited by the minority nationalities, it

should be widely encouraged for each couple to have only one child so that the rate of population growth will be brought under control as soon as possible, striving to limit the total population of the country to under 1.2 billion by the end of the century. It is very common in developed countries for a couple to have only one child, but in the rural areas in our country this indeed will be a big change in prevailing habits and customs. To promote this end, we must rely mainly on publicity and implementing the policies of the party and government and on ideological and political work, and not resort to compulsion and arbitrary orders. It should be pointed out that since the beginning of the 1970's, particularly in the last few years, remarkable achievements have been made in family planning both in cities and in the countryside. Cadres at various levels, particularly the comrades in women's organizations at all levels, and public health, family planning and other departments who have directly participated in this work, have done a great deal. We must fully affirm their achievements. However, we must also see that in some places, for more reasons than one, there are instances of compulsion and even violations of law and discipline in this work. This must be resolutely corrected. The State Council declares to the people of the whole country: In the interests of the people of the whole country themselves, family planning work must continue. It is necessary to continue to encourage every couple to have only one child. Party and CYL members and cadres should resolutely take the lead. The policies and measures for carrying out the task must be suitable. Full use must be made of persuasion and education, and safety of birth control techniques must be guaranteed. We hope that, through patient propaganda and education, the people, particularly the young people, will recognize the interests of the whole nation and warmly respond to this important call.

The mass line is the essential method by which to map out the long-term program. It is imperative to unite those at higher levels with those at lower levels and extensively mobilize government departments at all levels, all enterprises and institutions, the masses of workers and peasants and specialists in all fields to take part in this work. The socialist economy as well as each big enterprise and project are all entities composed of various elements. The interrelations between these elements and the advantages or disadvantages and gains or losses that may result from these relations are very complicated and have far-reaching effects, and for the most part cannot be seen at a glance but must be figured out through precise calculations and scientific predictions. Therefore, decisions on major projects and programs, the formulation of yearly plans and particularly the drawing up of long-term plans must be made through discussions by relevant departments according to legal procedures following repeated investigations, surveys, calculations, studies, discussions, debates and comparisons by many specialists. They must not be made in a hurry. Mistakes and losses are unavoidable, but efforts must be made to avoid them as much as possible. To bring into full play the role of specialists in all fields in mapping out the 10-year plan outline, we invite specialists in all fields, including economists, technical economists, technological experts and natural scientists, to attend the long-term planning forum held in March and April this year. We should continue to do this in the future.

II. CONTINUED ECONOMIC MANAGEMENT REFORM

The existing management systems in our national economy, including financial and monetary systems, labor and wage systems, the price system, systems of goods and materials control and many others, were to a large extent copied from foreign countries when we had very little experience. Some were inherited from practices prevailing under special historical conditions in the period of revolutionary wars.

The systems have never undergone the necessary reforms that would take into consideration the specific conditions of our country's developing socialist construction and the scientific and democratic principles of socialism and, therefore, are encountering more and more problems. The shortcomings and defects of our economic management systems show themselves mainly in the over-concentration of power, in excessive and rigid control, in the denial of necessary independence for socialist enterprises in their operations, in improper use of government authority (both central and local) to make direct decisions and in interference by administrative means, and in no separation of the party from the government and of the government from the enterprises in the work of management, which make it impossible for the enterprise to establish a system of independent production command and management. Over a long period of time, we advocated and upheld, instead of reforming, some methods that restricted or even sabotaged the development of productive forces and regarded them as socialist principles. At the same time, we denied the independence and rights which trade union organizations are entitled to have. As a result, the enterprises (including those in industry, communications, commerce, service industry, state-run agriculture and collectively-owned agriculture, which consists of most of the population), have lacked the intrinsic motivation to expand production and improve operations. The enthusiasm, initiative and creativity of the workers have been dampened. The superiority of the socialist system has not been given full play. We neglected the education of cadres, workers and staff members in production technology and management and failed to put talented people with professional knowledge in important positions. Consequently, nonprofessionals have led professionals for a long time. Arbitrary and impractical directions have often been given. And, it has been difficult to raise technical and management levels. In the 10 years of turmoil, Lin Biao and the "gang of four" virtually destroyed all the effective systems and policies we had formulated based on our many years of experience. The left-deviationist line they peddled in economic work and the whole set of policies and methods related to the line threw our country's already problem-stricken economic system into great chaos. Although important improvements have been made in the whole economic situation through consolidation over the past 3-odd years, there are still many problems. In short, the shortcomings and defects of our economic management systems seriously impede the progress of the four modernizations and must be eliminated by thorough-going reform.

Our general orientation for the structural reform of economic management is to transform the overcentralized system of management by the state (both central and local authorities) and to expand the decisionmaking power of enterprises and the power of their workers and staff members to participate in management, to transform unitary regulation by planning into regulation by planning combined with regulation by the market, and to transform management relying mainly on administrative organs and methods into management relying mainly on economic agencies as well as on economic and legal methods. The reform that has been going on for the past year is only a small first step in this direction. From now on, we must protect, improve and perfect the reforms on the basis of initial achievements made in this regard. However, it must be pointed out that structural reform is a complex task which involves work in many fields. Therefore, it is necessary to give careful consideration and make thorough preparations. We must map out an overall plan for reform and implement it prudently and step by step after a trial period.

Fundamentally speaking, reforming the economic system is for the purpose of bringing into full play the superiority of the socialist system. Naturally in the course of the reform, new problems unavoidably will crop up. We should make investigations, studies and serious efforts to solve the problems in good time, but we must not panic, even stop or retreat on the road toward economic reform because of these problems.

Government personnel at all levels, leading personnel in particular, must further emancipate their minds and, working together enthusiastically with the masses of the people and on the basis of investigations and studies and pooling the wisdom of the masses, courageously blaze new trails while acting with caution, continue to push forward the reform of the economic system and bring about a new situation in which the socialist modernization develops vigorously. This kind of reform serves to increase the efficiency of economic work, to speed up modernization, to consolidate and perfect the socialist system and, in the final analysis, to improve the people's living standards. Therefore, we believe that this reform will surely receive the support of the people of the whole country.

III. OVERCOME BUREAUCRACY AND IMPROVE GOVERNMENT WORK

While restructuring the economic system, we must strive to improve the work of the government at all levels. At present, widespread bureaucracy in government organizations at all levels presents a very serious problem. To a very large extent this phenomenon is interrelated with the irrational economic system, each being both the cause and effect of the other. Restructuring the economic management system will eliminate a large part of the bureaucratic phenomenon, but bureaucracy will hinder the restructuring of the economic system and even continue to cause problems in a new economic system. Therefore, elimination of bureaucracy must go hand in hand with restructuring the economic system. Bureaucracy has not only impeded economic reform and the progress of the four modernizations program but has hampered all kinds of work and has long aroused strong popular discontent. Unless we eliminate all kinds of bureaucratic practices in the system, it is impossible for our government at all levels to establish an efficient and respected working system, impossible to bring into full play the enthusiasm of government personnel and the broad masses and impossible to bring into full play the superiority of the socialist system. Therefore, I would like to say a little more about how to effectively overcome bureaucracy.

Bureaucracy is an old social phenomenon with a long history. There are many similarities as well as essential differences between bureaucracy in present-day China and that in the old society. Bureaucracy in the old society served the ruling class by exploiting and oppressing the working people, and it could not possibly be eliminated in the old society. Bureaucracy in real life today makes it difficult to bring into play the superiority of socialism and runs against the interests of the socialist system. It must be and can be overcome by socialism. In addition to, and more important than, the bad habits left over from the old society, the social causes that have created and abetted the new bureaucratic phenomenon in our government organizations today are that our socialist system itself is still far from perfect and that our understanding of the laws governing the development of socialism is still very immature. Although we have in the past made repeated efforts to combat bureaucratic phenomenon, little has been accomplished. Why? It is mainly because in the past we placed the main stress only on ideological education, seeing only the aspect of bureaucracy that was left over from the old society, and failed to look for causes for the generation of bureaucracy and ways to overcome it in our present systems. In fact, under the present far-from-perfect socialist system, our government organizations improperly control by administrative means almost all aspects of social life and shoulder arduous and complicated tasks never attempted before in history. This unreasonable state of affairs is where the crux of the matter lies. Unless this state of affairs is changed, not only is it impossible for us to concentrate our efforts on eliminating the old forms of bureaucracy but it is unavoidable that bureaucracy will be created under the new conditions. Here I do not plan to say more about the old forms of bad bureaucratic habits and about all kinds of bad bureaucratic work styles in dealing with the masses to which we ordinarily refer. I want to say something emphatically about the serious defects and faults that exist in the present administrative system of our country that engender bureaucracy. These defects and faults are mainly as follows:

1. Overconcentration of power. The individual enterprises and production units do not have the reasonable power to independently carry out economic activities. Many important powers are concentrated in the multileveled administrative organizations above these enterprises and production units. This often leads to this phenomenon: The farther these organizations are separated from productive activities, the greater their powers become, and the more organizations there are, the more difficult the work becomes. The situation—in which the powers of enterprises and production units are improperly concentrated in government departments, local powers are improperly concentrated in the central level, and the powers of government departments are improperly concentrated in party committees—is more and more seriously impeding the effective development of socialist construction. The situation in fields of work other than economics is generally the same.

To be sure, in a socialist country such as ours, especially in its developing stages, a certain degree of concentration in management work is essential. Of course, the practice of necessary centralized control in accordance with the national economic development plan and the coordination of the interests of all sectors of society by the unified leadership of the administration and the party are important manifestations of the superiority of the socialist system. However, when power is overconcentrated, the outcome will be the opposite. We have all encountered this situation: Those at the lower levels who understand the actual situation are often not in a position to make the decisions they should make. On the other hand those at the higher levels who do not quite understand the actual situation often have to make decisions before they have the time to understand the necessary conditions. This not only reduces work efficiency and dampens the enthusiasm of those working at lower levels but it lowers the leading standard of those working at higher levels. Thus, mistakes in their work become inevitable. They are excessively entangled in trivial and routine details from which they should free themselves, and they do not have sufficient time to investigate, study and carefully consider major problems in finding proper solutions. Because those at the higher levels are far removed from the complexities of the actual situation, more often than not they tend to oversimplify matters, think in absolute terms and handle diverse problems with a single solution when handling concrete problems at lower levels. Many new bureaucratic practices in real life today are caused by this important factor.

2. Confusion regarding the limits of power and responsibility. From the State Council down to local governments at various levels, no systematic and practical administrative rules and regulations have been formulated. There are no clear definitions or concrete stipulations on the scope of work, the limits of power and the rules of work for different departments, localities, units and individuals. As a result, various departments and units often have no rules to follow and are not clear about their duties and responsibilities. Furthermore, when there are no precedents to follow, they have no alternative but to report to the higher authorities, seek instructions and pass reports from one echelon to another. The result is an odyssey of official papers, a deluge of reports and meetings, disputes over trivial matters and a dilatory work style.

3. The incompatibility of the cadre system with the requirements of the period of socialist construction. At all levels of the government, there is no sound system for selecting, appointing, assessing and training cadres. Also, there is no system for weeding out incompetents, meting out rewards or disciplinary sanctions and so forth. The various departments and units seldom recruit cadres strictly through advertisement or examination. This would ensure they are used in a way commensurate with their abilities. Instead, they are generally appointed by the organization and personnel departments. The formation of this system has its historical reasons, and it has played a positive role.

However, this system is now becoming more and more inadequate in meeting the tasks of modernization. There is no practical plan for training cadres, and the training is often out of keeping with the requirements of the work. There is no regular and strict assessment of cadres' work performance and no rewards or penalties given accordingly. It makes no difference whether one does his work well or poorly, or whether one is qualified for the job or not. Once a person becomes a cadre, he has a lifelong job, an "iron rice bowl." Even if he proves really incompetent or does not apply himself to his work, he remains a cadre unless he is dismissed from public office. Indeed, this system can prevent some people from becoming unemployed and can maintain a stable life for them but the price is too high. If this state of affairs is not thoroughly reformed, how can we realize modernization?

4. Overstaffing, overlapping, proliferation of deputies and nominal posts and low job efficiency. The aforesaid three conditions—overconcentration of power, confusion of work and responsibilities, and the unsuitable cadre system inevitably cause overstaffing. In return overstaffing inevitably causes the further growth of many bureaucratic maladies. Our administrative organizations often overlap, and the number of permanent and temporary organizations and government personnel is now larger than at any time in history. This explains the seriousness of the problem. Now is the time when we must seriously study the problem and find solutions.

I must stress here that most of our administrative organizations have indeed done a great deal of work which is indispensable for the cause of socialist construction, and all our accomplishments cannot be separated from their efforts. Even in the future we must have powerful state organs and an authoritative government, and a government certainly cannot dispense with all sorts of necessary administrative work, which is done basically to serve the people.

I also want to stress that the majority of our personnel are willing to bear the burden of office and work selflessly for the public interest. Also, many people are professionally knowledgeable and have practical experience, and they often make on-the-spot study and are good at maintaining close ties with the masses. Criticizing bureaucracy in our work, our principal task should be to study the cause of bureaucracy and improve our work system.

A bad system often keeps many of our local and devoted personnel from exerting their efforts, or makes them do a lot of work which produces very little effect. This responsibility, of course, does not rest on them. There are indeed some personnel whose ideology and work style are bad but changing these people's malpractices is often ineffective without the system. To combat bureaucracy, the key lies first in earnestly reforming the irrational phenomena in the state administrative system, the work system of organizations, the cadre system and the structure of organs. The specific measures are:

1. The power of enterprises and undertakings should be transferred to the lower levels. Under the centralized leadership of the state, enterprises and undertakings should have the necessary power to make independent decisions on management and operations. This experiment, which has been carried out in some enterprises since last year with good results, will be popularized step by step in the future and enterprises' power to make independent decisions will be expanded. So far, it has only been carried out in a few selected undertakings. Their experiences will be summed up and popularized steadily.

Once the enterprises and undertakings have more power to make their own decisions, the work of many administrative departments can be reduced. Some of these departments may be transformed into enterprises or undertakings; others may be merged. Thus the administrative organs can be greatly simplified and the foundation of bureaucracy will be reduced immensely.

Of course, the power to make independent decisions cannot be given only to those who are in charge of enterprises and undertakings; it should also be given to the proper democratic management and supervision organs which can truly represent the broad masses of workers. The transfer of power must be linked with democratic management. All enterprises and undertakings should establish congresses or conferences of their workers and staff, and these congresses or conferences have the right to discuss and decide important matters concerning their units and to elect their leading administrative personnel or make recommendations for their appointment to and removal from office. In daily work all matters affecting the vital interests of the workers and staff must be handled with the consent and cooperation of the trade unions.

The transfer of power should by no means weaken the necessary centralized management, but as far as enterprises are concerned, such centralized management should be economic management and not the kind using principally administrative means as in the past. While carrying out democratic management within an enterprise, it is doubtless that the necessary centralized management and command are essential for production and technical and economic aspects. In principle, this also applies to various undertakings.

2. The functions and duties of each administrative organ and its subordinate units and individuals should be clearly defined by administrative statutes. This task must be carried out in two respects simultaneously: 1) All departments and units mobilize the masses to formulate various kinds of regulations and rules and work out the details stipulating the work of various posts so that everybody knows his responsibility and what should be taken care of by whom. In case there are surplus personnel, they can leave their jobs temporarily for training or they can be reassigned. Some units are already doing this, and this practice has been proven to be quite effective; 2) the State Council as well as the local governments at all levels should organize special forces to formulate systematic administrative laws and regulations in order to explicitly define the limits of functions and powers of various departments and units and the principles of exercising these functions and powers as well as measures for handling certain special problems. With such laws and regulations, the number of reports requesting instructions will be greatly reduced. Many things can be resolved by various departments and units independently according to the limits of their functions and powers and work principles. After the functions and powers are specified for each unit and person, a rigorous checking system should be established so that there can be both rewards and disciplinary measures. Those who seriously neglect their duties should be dealt with according to law.

3. Efforts should be made to improve the cadre system. We must, on the basis of conscientiously summing up historical experience and conducting penetrating investigation and study, work out a concrete and feasible system for appointment, reassignment, retirement, dismissal and so on, for all cadres at all levels and in all categories. As ours is a socialist country, we must do all

we can to give all the working personnel the necessary protection regarding their livelihood and make proper arrangements for them upon their retirement and dismissal.

4. We must establish and perfect a system of inspection and supervision. Implementation of the above-mentioned three measures will correct the overconcentration of power, the confusion regarding the limits of power and responsibility and the inadequate cadre system as well as the overstaffing. This will greatly curb bureaucracy. However, since bureaucracy is a historical phenomenon, our struggle against it has to be protracted and tenacious.

Rigid checks and supervision should be constantly conducted. At present, the forms, channels and systems of the work and staff of the governments at various levels for checking and supervising the government staff at various levels are far from perfect, and it is very difficult and uncommon for the people to actually exercise their power of supervision. This situation must be changed. In order to check and supervise the work of the governments and their staff at various levels and in order for party organizations and committees to supervise inspection of discipline at all levels, letters and visits from the masses should be seriously handled. Furthermore, exposure and criticism in newspapers and magazines should be adequately supported. Checks by the people's deputies and governments at higher levels and exposure reports from governments at lower levels all have a powerful influence and should be extensively encouraged. Some government organizations have done so. Some have experimented with letting the masses recommend and appraise cadres with good results. These methods may be popularized. In short, governments at all levels must continue to pool the wisdom of the masses and strive to create more methods of supervision which are both more effective and easier to follow. This will facilitate, in accordance with the people's will, timely praise, reward and promotion of cadres who have made outstanding contributions to the cause of socialism. At the same time, it will facilitate the exposure and correction of faults and errors of cadres as well as replacement and recall of bureaucrats who are guilty of serious dereliction of duty.

I must make it clear here that what I have just said about the causes of engendering bureaucracy and the methods to overcome it are not exhaustive. Moreover, some of the above-mentioned methods can be applied relatively sooner, while a rather larger part of them cannot be applied so readily. This makes it necessary to conduct rather complete and thorough reforms of our working and organization systems. Therefore, it is necessary to make certain preparations. However since we are determined to realize modernization, we have to make up our mind to carry out reforms. Otherwise, our modernization program will inevitably be hampered by these irrational systems. Of course, the vestiges of the bureaucratic practice of the old society have something to do with the level of development of the social production forces and the educational and cultural levels of the people and cadres. As a result, thorough elimination of all bureaucratic practices is a protracted and arduous task. However, the major bureaucratic and other maladies can surely be overcome provided that governments at all levels recognize the dangers of bureaucracy and pay the greatest attention to the four key problems— reform of the system of state management, reform of the working system of the administrative organs at all levels, reform of the cadre system and the strengthening of the system of checks and supervision of cadres. These problems must be solved step by step in a planned way and training and education work must be strengthened. Bureaucracy is by no means an incurable disease of socialism. Socialism will certainly become a system full of vitality. At least we must make it so and will certainly be able to do so in China. The basic theory of Marxism inherently requires this. For our part, we have the longstanding revolutionary tradition of the mass line and we can rely on the broadest masses of people. This will surely enable us to achieve the goal of eliminating bureaucracy. With the power effectively and reliably delegated to the grassroots units and to the masses—the power that should be delegated to them—they surely will be able to help and supervise our government in carrying out necessary reforms to enable it to adapt to the needs of modernization until it becomes a modern socialist government. The masses will also enable it to become the most streamlined, responsible and efficient government maintaining the closest links with the masses in history.

IV. STRENGTHENING SOCIALIST DEMOCRACY AND THE SOCIALIST LEGAL SYSTEM

An indispensable political prerequisite for the smooth progress of socialist modernization is to make further efforts to establish and strengthen the democratic system and perfect the socialist legal system so the people can effectively exercise their rights to manage political, economic and other social affairs and so any illegal activities obstructing and damaging the cause of socialism can be quickly and effectively punished.

We should effect structural reform on economic management, improve the situation of overconcentration of power, change the situation of making no distinction between party and government and between government and enterprises, grant more power to the localities and grassroots units, shift power to enterprises and institutions, expand the necessary decisionmaking power of enterprises and institutions in independent management and operation, perfect such democratic management and supervision agencies as staffers' and workers' congresses and trade unions and strengthen democratic management and supervision of enterprises and institutions; we should develop and protect the regional autonomy and other democratic rights of the minority nationalities; we should oppose bureaucracy, improve government leadership, and strengthen mass inspection and supervision over the work of government organs and their personnel; we should abolish the system of permitting leading cadres to hold lifetime jobs, strengthen collective leadership in leading organs at all levels, and oppose arbitrary decisions by individuals. All these are important steps and measures for further developing socialist democracy.

In order to systematize and legalize socialist democracy, we need to make continued and great efforts. Revising the Constitution is the most important of these tasks. The Constitution is our country's fundamental charter, on which all our government functions are based. The First Session of the Fifth NPC had made some amendments to the Constitution, but we did not have enough time to comprehensively sum up the experience and lessons gained since the founding of the PRC, nor did we have enough time to evaluate and eliminate the influence exerted by certain ultraleftist thinking on the Constitution during the 10 chaotic years. As a result, the Constitution contains quite a number of provisions that are not appropriate. Moreover, many provisions of this fundamental charter are not free of flaws, nor are they as well-defined as they should be. For this reason, the CCP Central Committee has proposed that the current session consider and begin an overall revision of the Constitution to more fully reflect the interests and aspirations of the people of all nationalities throughout the country in the new historical period of development and to better meet the demands of socialist modernization and state democratization.

The rule of law in the country is required not only for consolidating and developing the stability and unity of our country but also for ensuring the smooth progress of modernization. This calls for continued strengthening of legislative and judicial work. We should, first of all, formulate laws that are much more complete than what we have now, and in particular, we should devote much of our energy to legislation concerning economic affairs. For this reason, it is proposed that the NPC Standing Committee call on specialists to successively draw up such important laws as a civil code, a law of civil procedures, a law of regional national autonomy, a planning law, a factory law, a labor law, a contract law, and an energy law. The State Council shall also take an active part in drafting relevant laws and continuously formulate and promulgate various statutes and regulations, particularly administrative regulations governing the terms of reference and duties of different organizations and those for reforming their employment system. According to the principles laid down by law, the provincial, municipal and autonomous regional people's congresses and their Standing Committee should also work out and promulgate various local statutes and regulations. Only in this way can our cadres and other citizens have laws and regulations to abide by in every field of work.

Governments at all levels should firmly ensure the enforcement of all the laws, statutes and ordinances already promulgated. Based on the provisions of the election law, direct elections of the county-level people's deputies and the choosing of county leaders by directly elected county-level people's deputies are going on throughout the country. This is a major event of far-reaching significance in the political life of the Chinese people and it marks the further extension of the Chinese people's democratic system. Governments at all levels must do this work well.

Our cadres and senior cadres in particular must set an example in observing discipline and abiding by law and must never think that they can flout laws or discipline because of their authority or past meritorious services. Comrades, by so doing they would make serious mistakes! The greater the authority and meritorious services of our cadres, the greater their political and moral obligation to set an example for the people, their subordinates, their children and posterity and lead the entire people in creating an entire generation imbued with revolutionary spirit. Comrades, we must resolutely eliminate bureaucratic

practices and privileges and foster a revolutionary spirit of serving the people wholeheartedly. This is our sacred mission toward the people and the younger generation. People who only pursue their own interests or those of their children, relatives and friends at the expense of the interests of the state and people will eventually be punished by law and discipline. Our cadres must wage a resolute struggle against the evil practice of tailoring the law to suit one's selfish ends and against bureaucrats shielding one another in wrongdoing. Under all circumstances, we must keep to the principle that "all are equal before the law," and there must never be any "special citizens" who can violate state laws or discipline with impunity. We must see to it that the public security organs, the people's procuratorates and the people's courts exercise their respective authority independently, allowing no illegal interference whatsoever by any administrative institutions, mass organizations, or individuals. Only by so doing can we guard the sanctity of socialist legality and make it a truly powerful weapon in the defense of socialist democracy.

In order to carry out reforms correctly and effectively in our existing economic and political systems and in other areas, we must strengthen ideological and political work. We must also strengthen education on revolutionary traditions, on socialist morality, on the socialist legal system and on attitudes toward communist labor among cadres and masses at all levels. In this way, we will help them combat the influence of the residual feudalist ideology and the influence of the bourgeois, petty bourgeois and all kinds of nonproletarian ideologies. We must also realize that, following the increase of international exchange, the corrosion of some people by the bourgeois ideology of foreign countries has already appeared along with the shameful behavior of worshipping and having blind faith in foreign things and losing one's national dignity. This is what we must guard against and oppose. Eliminating the influence of the ideologies of the exploiting classes and other nonproletarian classes is an essential and important task not only for the time being but for a considerably long time to come in developing our socialist democracy.

V. REALIZING THE GOAL OF HAVING YOUNGER, KNOWLEDGEABLE AND PROFESSIONAL GOVERNMENT LEADERS AT ALL LEVELS

Following the shift of emphasis from work in the country, it has become increasingly evident that the advanced age and lack of professional knowledge of many government leaders at various levels have made them unequal to the task of the four modernizations. Now the party's work is to be separated from the government's, and the responsible personnel of government at all levels and of various enterprises and establishments must directly shoulder the heavy burden of organizing the people to engage in the work of modernization. The smooth progress of the four modernizations will be severely affected if the present composition of the various leading bodies is not changed by promoting a large number of professionally competent cadres who uphold the four basic principles and who are in the prime of life to various leading posts. Therefore, under the prerequisite of upholding the four basic principles, the selection and promotion to leading posts of a large number of young, knowledgeable and professionally competent cadres has a direct bearing on the continuity and stability of the government's correct leadership and on the success or failure of the modernization program.

Since the beginning of last year, the CCP Central Committee has repeatedly emphasized that resolute measures must be taken to select and promote a large number of cadres who firmly adhere to the party's line, who are professionally knowledgeable and capable and who are in the prime of their lives.

In this way, we can replenish and reinforce the leading groups of party committees at various levels. These guidelines also apply to governments at all levels. Over the country as a whole, this task of strategic significance has been going on at a rather slow pace. Now it is time we solve this problem.

The three criteria put forward by the party Central Committee for selecting and promoting middle-aged and young cadres are not complex. As long as we emancipate our minds and take the mass line, it will not be difficult to select and promote the middle-aged and young cadres who meet these three criteria.

Over the past 30 years, we have trained more than 3 million college graduates and 5 million graduates from secondary technical schools. In addition, there are many middle-aged and young cadres, who were formerly workers and peasants, who have raised their scientific and educational levels and acquired professional knowledge through tests in the protracted and complicated practice of revolution and construction. Many qualified people are there to be found. The trouble is that some people rarely try to find them. Many capable people have been placed in posts where, unable to use their specialized knowledge, they have long had a sense of frustration. Yet the leaders of their departments have paid little heed to their situation. What a great loss to the state! This shows how important it is to do away with the longstanding leftist contempt for knowledge and intellectuals. Forty years ago, Comrade Mao Zedong said with regard to selecting cadres for economic work: "Discard this mistaken view and you will see cadres all around you." This remark is really well said and it is still true today.

Our old cadres have an especially important duty to select and train middle-aged and young cadres. Braving untold dangers and working under very difficult conditions in the course of protracted revolutionary struggle and construction, our many old cadres have made tremendous contributions. They are the precious assets of our party and state and rightfully deserve the people's respect and love. By younger leadership, we mean increasing the number of younger people and gradually forming a majority of them in leadership. We do not mean replacing all the old people in their leading posts. Also, the age requirements for leading cadres at different levels should vary. Old cadres who can continue to work are still our backbone leading cadres. However, some of the old cadres are after all physically weak and less than vigorous.

Nobody can escape natural laws. It is correct to ask the old comrades to be our chiefs of staff and advisers; it would be difficult to demand them to shoulder heavy burdens of duty on the first line as they did in the old days. Therefore, we should earnestly make good arrangements for a large number of old and physically weak comrades who have contributed to the state and people to move to the second or third line and maintain intact the political treatment and treatment in living conditions they now enjoy so that they may continue to contribute to the people in their lifetime. Our old cadres have rich experience in discovering, selecting and training people of great promise. A supremely glorious heavy duty assigned to our old cadres by history is to enthusiastically discover and select fine middle-aged and young cadres, voluntarily and willingly vacate their posts for younger comrades in their prime of life and encourage and support these young comrades to boldly carry out their work. This is also the best and most valuable contribution our old comrades can make toward the four modernizations. It is our firm belief that our old cadres will never fail to live up to the expectations of the people of the whole country!

In order that the large numbers of the government staff and the cadres of all trades and services may acquire and improve the general and professional knowledge necessary for the four modernizations, we should prepare for them necessary study facilities, including regular professional schools and other study methods such as fulltime or on-the-job study. In this respect, we have both positive and negative experiences and lessons. Shortly after the founding of the PRC, we adopted many forms to train the worker-peasant-soldier cadres to improve their general and professional knowledge. Very good results were achieved. Unfortunately, this tremendously significant task was later abandoned.

Now we should resume and expand this task so that all the worker-peasant-soldier cadres who still can pursue studies may painstakingly learn all professional knowledge through all possible channels to suit the needs of the four modernizations. Leading persons and the great numbers of cadres of governments at all levels must assiduously study in an indomitable and enterprising spirit. We believe that more and more of these comrades will become specialists both Red and expert in various fields!

Comrade Mao Zedong said in his report at the Second Plenary Session of the Seventh Central Committee: "If we do not know production and do not master it quickly, if we cannot restore and develop production as speedily as possible and achieve solid successes so that the livelihood of the workers, first of all, and that of the people in general is improved, we will be unable to maintain our political power, we will be unable to stand on our feet, we shall fail." After winning nationwide victory, we splendidly accomplished this task. Today, under the new circumstances, and to realize the four modernizations, we again are faced with a similar task. We must accomplish this task. We surely will accomplish it.

Deputies! The people of the whole country are deeply concerned over the problems just mentioned above. They are the new problems under the new conditions. So far our understanding of these problems is very superficial. Now will all deputies please discuss them together so that a common and correct understanding may be reached. I should say that these problems are just being pointed out and that extremely arduous efforts are needed to solve them. After this session, the State Council and local governments of various levels should take effective steps to make investigation and study, and, proceeding from reality, propose feasible and concrete principles, policies and measures. The priority work of governments at all levels is to enforce reforms, eliminate bureaucracy and truly become state administrative organs leading the four modernizations and serving the people.

Entrusted by the CCP Central Committee, I hereby make an explanation of the changes of the members of the State Council.

In order to strengthen and improve the party's leadership to meet the needs of socialist modernization, a number of important measures were proposed at the 5th Plenary Session of the 11th CCP Central Committee held not long ago. One of them is to place in leading posts at all levels those people who unswervingly carry out the party's line, who are capable of using their initiative and are in the prime of life. Another measure is to strengthen the collective leadership and put an end to the practice of providing lifelong posts for leading cadres. The basic spirit underlying these measures is applicable to the strengthening and improvement of government leadership. The CCP Central Committee, learning from history, decided that, as a rule, the first secretary of a party committee should not concurrently be provincial governor, or chairman of an autonomous region or head of an autonomous prefecture, or of a county or city. This was aimed at preventing overconcentration of power and the holding of too many posts concurrently by one person and at effectively and clearly separating party work from government work. Thus, such comrades would be able to concentrate their time and energy on solving the party's major problems while all levels of government under the State Council would have a complete and efficient administrative system from top to bottom. In line with this principle, I proposed to the party Central Committee and the party Central Committee decided that I cease concurrently holding the premiership of the State Council. The party Central Committee simultaneously decided that the five veteran comrades of the party including Comrades Deng Xiaoping, Li Xiannian, Chen Yun, Xu Xiangqian and Wang Zhen should no longer concurrently hold vice premierships of the State Council and that Comrade Wang Renzhong should also cease holding the vice premiership of the State Council because of his taking up an important post in the party. The congress is hereby asked to consider and decide on all these proposals. Furthermore, Comrade Chen Yonggui asked to be relieved of his spot as vice premier, and the party Central Committee agreed to this. The congress is also asked to consider and decide on this matter.

After careful consideration, the CCP Central Committee decided to propose to the NPC that Zhao Ziyang be appointed premier of the State Council. The party Central Committee believes that Zhao Ziyang is a suitable choice and worthy of trust. The congress is requested to consider and decide on this matter.

The changes in leading members of the State Council constitute an excellent beginning to the transformation of the system of leadership of our government. It is our belief that the current changes will surely help to strengthen and improve government leadership, raise the quality and efficiency of its work and hasten the progress of modernization.

Fellow deputies! China needs a lasting peaceful international environment to carry out its modernization program. Opposing hegemony and safeguarding world peace is not only in line with the Chinese people's interests but also in keeping with the interests of the people throughout the world. Soviet hegemonists have sent their troops to occupy Afghanistan and they supported Vietnam

in its continued invasion and occupation of Kampuchea. This not only directly endangers the peace and security of the Persian Gulf, the Middle East and Southeast Asia but also threatens the peace and security of the whole world. The Chinese Government and people resolutely support the just struggle of the Kampuchean and Afghan peoples against aggression and will, as in the past, resolutely join the people throughout the world to tirelessly work for opposing hegemony and safeguarding world peace.

The Chinese PLA is a strong pillar of the dictatorship of the proletariat and a loyal defender of the socialist motherland and its modernization program. It is also an important force for safeguarding the peaceful cause of the world. In the coming years, it will be impossible to sharply increase our defense spending, but our national defense must nevertheless be strengthened. The PLA should continue to strengthen military and political training and cadre training, step up political and ideological work, intensify all kinds of preparations against aggression, carry forward its fine traditions and consolidate and enhance its combat strength. It is necessary to continuously do a good job in militia training and all kinds of work concerning supporting the army and giving preferential treatment to army dependents. Representatives of the people in all walks of life, governments at all levels and people of all nationalities should show concern for and love their own army and actively support and help the PLA to accomplish all its tasks. We must make concerted efforts to build our army into a great iron wall.

We will work energetically for the return of Taiwan to the motherland, fulfilling our lofty aim of reunifying our homeland at an early date. The "Message to Compatriots on Taiwan" issued by the NPC Standing Committee on New Year's day 1979 has had an increasing influence on the people there, from the top to the grassroots, and on the overseas compatriots and people in other countries. Patriots on Taiwan and overseas compatriots the world over have made enthusiastic efforts for the reunification of China over the past year and more. Compatriots on both sides of the straits, in particular, desire to establish regular links between the mainland and Taiwan in postal service, sea and air transport and trade at an early date. We are convinced that the historical trend of reunification of the motherland is irrevocable, and that this sacred goal will surely be attained.

There is but one China in this world, and Taiwan is a province of China and inseparable from it. This is the immutable position consistently held by the Chinese Government and people and is also a basic principle governing the establishment of diplomatic relations between China and all other countries.

Any argument for "two Chinas" or "one China, one Taiwan" is bound to be opposed unanimously by the Chinese Government and all Overseas Chinese compatriots.

Comrades! Friends! The situation after the smashing of the "gang of four" proves that the future of our country and people is bright, and this fact is more obvious today. The most important reason why we can achieve victory is because all patriotic fellow countrymen throughout the country have rallied together under the leadership of the CCP Central Committee's correct line. The unity of our great Chinese PLA, the people of the whole country and the people's governments in all localities has been, and always will be, the most reliable guarantee for the victory of our revolutionary cause. All nationalities of our country will forever rally together as one big family of our great motherland. No forces whatsoever can undermine our lofty fraternal bond which has gone through protracted tests.

Over the past few years, our various democratic parties and nonparty democratic personages have made new important contributions to the prosperity of our motherland, and they will continue to play an important role in the four modernizations in the future. The slogan "long-range coexistence and mutual supervision" put forward by Comrade Mao Zedong will forever be the CCP's standard in handling its relations with all democratic parties. The patriotic religious leaders have made precious efforts in leading the followers of all religions of the country to defend religious freedom on a patriotic footing. As the cause of our motherland advances victoriously, we must exert still greater efforts to consolidate and develop the united front of all our socialist workers, patriots who support socialism and patriots who support the unification of our motherland.

We will rally still more closely around the CCP and the people's government, hold high the revolutionary banner of Marxism-Leninism-Mao Zedong Thought and unswervingly carry out the lines, principles and policies of our party and state. Let us join hands and make concerted efforts to win great victories in our cause of socialist modernization!

Hua Guofeng's Ouster as Party Chairman, 29 June 1981

Once he had lost the premiership, which he had clearly wanted to retain, Hua's days as Party chairman were inevitably numbered, although he became a vice-chairman until September 1982. He was replaced as chairman (pending the subsequent abolition of that title which had been tailor-made for Mao Zedong in 1943) by General Secretary Hu Yaobang, a Deng man.

The Eleventh Central Committee of the Communist Party of China held its Sixth Plenary Session in Beijing from June 27 to 29, 1981. It was attended by 195 members and 114 alternate members of the Central Committee and 53 non-voting members of the Central Committee and 53 non-voting participants. Members of the Standing Committee of the Political Bureau of the Central Committee, Comrades Hu Yaobang, Ye Jianying, Deng Xiaoping, Zhao Ziyang, Li Xiannian, Chen Yun and Hua Guofeng, presided at the session.

Items on the agenda of the plenary session were:

1) Discussion and approval of "The Resolution on Certain Questions in the History of our Party Since the Founding of the People's Republic of China";

2) Reelection of principal leading members of the Central Committee and election of new ones.

The above-mentioned agenda was thoroughly deliberated and conscientiously discussed at a preparatory meeting held before the plenary session. This session is another meeting of great significance in the history of our party following the third plenary session of the eleventh Central Committee, a meeting for summing up experience and closing the ranks to press forward. This session will go down in history for fulfilling the historic mission of setting to right things which have been thrown into disorder in the guiding ideology of the party.

[Communiqué of the Sixth Plenary Session of the Eleventh Central Committee, 29 June 1981, New China News Agency, 29 June 1981.]

Applying Marxist dialectical materialism and historical materialism, "The Resolution on Certain Questions in the History of our Party Since the Founding of the People's Republic of China" unanimously adopted by the plenary session correctly sums up the major historical events of the party in the 32 years since the founding of the People's Republic of China, particularly the "Great Cultural Revolution." The resolution scientifically analyzes the rights and wrongs in the party's guiding ideology during these events, analyzes the subjective factors and social causes that gave rise to mistakes, realistically evaluates the historical role played by Comrade Mao Zedong, the great leader and teacher, in the Chinese Revolution and fully elaborates the great significance of Mao Zedong Thought as the guiding ideology of our party. The resolution affirms the correct path for building a modern and powerful socialist country, a path which has been gradually established since the third plenary session and which conforms to the realities in China, and further points out the orientation for the continued advance of our country's socialist cause and the work of our party. The plenary session believes that the adoption and publication of the resolution will exert great and far-reaching influence on unifying the thinking and understanding of the party, the army and the people of all nationalities throughout the country so that they will strive with one heart and one mind to carry out our new historical task.

The plenary session unanimously approved Comrade Hua Guofeng's request to resign his posts as chairman of the Central Committee and chairman of its Military Commission. The plenary session reelected the principal leading members of the Central Committee and elected new ones by secret ballot. The results of the elections are:

1) Comrade Hu Yaobang—chairman of the Central Committee;

2) Comrade Zhao Ziyang—vice-chairman of the Central Committee;

3) Comrade Hua Guofeng—vice-chairman of the Central Committee;

4) Comrade Deng Xiaoping—chairman of the Military Commission of the Central Committee;

5) A standing committee of the Political Bureau of the Central Committee made up of the chairman and vice-chairmen of the central committee. They are Hu Yaobang, Ye Jianying, Deng Xiaoping, Zhao Ziyang, Li Xiannian, Chen Yun and Hua Guofeng.

6) Comrade Xi Zhongxun—member of the Secretariat of the Central Committee.

The plenary session holds that the election and re-election of the principal leading members of the Central Committee will play an important part in strengthening the Central Committee's collective leadership and unity on the basis of Marxism and ensuring the full implementation of the party's correct line and policies formulated since the third plenary session.

The plenary session gave full play to democracy. All comrades present spoke out freely, adopted the scientific approach of seeking truth from facts and displayed the spirit of criticism and self-criticism in summing up historical experience and discussing and deciding the choice of persons as leading members of the Central Committee. This restored and carried forward the fine tradition formed by our party during the Yanan rectification period. The session vividly demonstrated our party's strong unity and fully reflects the growing and flourishing of our cause.

The plenary session believes that, just as the party's correct summing up of historical experience in the period of the democratic revolution brought great revolutionary victories, the correct summing up of the party's historical experience since the founding of the People's Republic of China will help bring about new great victories in our future socialist construction. The plenary session calls on the party, the army and the people of all nationalities throughout the country to hold high the banner of Marxism-Leninism-Mao Zedong Thought, rally more closely around the party Central Committee, carry forward the spirit of "the foolish old man who removed the mountain," be resolute, surmount all difficulties and work hard to turn China step by step into a modern and powerful socialist country with a high degree of democracy and civilization.

A Senior Leader Requests Retirement, 25 February 1983

9

Ye Jianying, an elderly and ailing former marshal who had acted like a counterbalance to Deng Xiaoping, announces his intended retirement from some of his state posts. (He also retired from his Party offices at about the same time.) This act, which did not reflect a purge, was intended to set a precedent for further "voluntary" retirement by other senior officials regarded by the Deng leadership as obsolete.

Dear Comrades, It is five years since I assumed the post as chairman of the Standing Committee of the Fifth National People's Congress and the term will expire. The Sixth National People's Congress will be convened soon. It is my long-cherished wish to fight to the end for the socialist cause, but I am old, failing in health and unable to do as much as I wish. At a time when the Fifth National People's Congress is being replaced by the new, I request the present meeting of the Standing Committee to take into consideration my practical conditions and to suggest to the

[New China News Agency, 2 March 1983.]

electoral units during the election of deputies to the Sixth National People's Congress that I not be nominated and elected again as a deputy to the National People's Congress. Thus, I will naturally not be nominated by the Sixth National People's Congress as a candidate for the chairmanship of its Standing Committee. I sincerely hope that my request will be accepted.

Things in our socialist motherland are getting better and better. The political situation is stable, economy has grown, culture has further developed, great successes have been scored in foreign affairs, and thousands of middle-aged and young good cadres have been promoted to the leading posts at various levels. When I am saying good-bye to my colleagues in the N.P.C. Standing Committee, I feel most gratified at all this.

A new Constitution that can guarantee and promote China's socialist modernization was adopted at the Fifth Session of the Fifth National People's Congress held last year. In ancient times, laws were cast on bronzes so as to be faithfully observed for long. [sentence as received] We should continue to give wider publicity to the new constitution so as to make it rooted in the hearts of all our people and turn it into a powerful weapon of the people for safeguarding the socialist system and the people's democracy and to ensure that it will be fully implemented. This is my heartfelt wish!

Ye Jianying
February 25, 1983

Retirement Accepted, 5 March 1983

Retirement from office has been much less common in Communist countries than purging or death in office.

Respected and beloved Chairman Ye Jianying:

We have conscientiously read and discussed your letter. All of us have agreed to grant your request and decided to suggest to all the electoral units that you not be nominated and elected again as a deputy to the Sixth National People's Congress during the election of deputies to the congress.

You are highly esteemed and trusted by the people of the whole country for the monumental contributions you have made in the revolutionary struggles, filled with hardship and difficulties, in more than half a century and for the important contribution you added in the severe struggle to smash the gang of four. We, together with the people of the whole country, all wish that you could continue your leadership over the work of the Standing Committee of the National People's Congress. At the same time, considering your advanced age, you should have more rest to enjoy health and longevity for the greater benefit of the nation and the people. Therefore, it is with high respect that we grant your request contained in the letter you have sent us.

In the past five years, the Standing Committee of the Fifth National People's Congress has, under your leadership, successfully done important work of setting things to rights in order to bring the country in order and develop economy, and fulfilling various tasks entrusted by the people of the whole country. Above all, you personally headed the Committee for Revision of the Constitution and guided the revision work and the formulation of the Constitution of the People's Republic of China which was adopted at the Fifth Session of the Fifth National People's Congress. It was also under your leadership that the Criminal Law, the Law of Criminal Procedure and the Law of Civil Procedure and 13 other laws were made and promulgated. With the promulgation of the Constitution and other laws, China has increased the number of statutes and established a better legal system, creating a situation in which "there are laws to be observed and law breakers are to be dealt with", a situation which the people have longed for for many years. The people are most gratified. When being implemented, the new Constitution, as a fundamental law, will guarantee the further consolidation and development of our socialist system, guarantee the advance of the national economy along the road of Chinese-type modernization and ensure that the people of the whole country enjoy full democratic rights without being infringed on. We believe that your foresighted and brilliant idea of giving wider publicity and fully implementing the new Constitution raised in your letter will be resolutely put to practice in the future.

To strive for the great cause of reunifying the motherland including Taiwan, you personally presided over a meeting of the Standing Committee of the National People's Congress in January 1979 to adopt and issue the message to compatriots in Taiwan, which states that "reunification of China fits in with the direction of popular feeling and the general trend of development," and puts forward the policy of developing trade, making up what the other lacks and creating "economic interflow" and that "both sides will bring about at an early date the setting up of transportation and postal services."

On September 30, 1981, you issued the significant statement "Elaborations on Policy Concerning the Return of Taiwan to the Motherland and Peaceful Reunification", laying down the nine-point concrete policy for the reunification of the motherland. The two documents express the ardent aspirations of the people of all nationalities of our country including the people in Taiwan, compatriots in Hong Kong and Macao and overseas Chinese, and have

[Letter to Ye Jianying from the Standing Committee of the National People's Congress, New China News Agency, 5 March 1983.]

played an enormous and positive role in promoting the great cause of reunifying the motherland.

Your wise leadership during the long tenure as the chairman of the Fifth N.P.C. Standing Committee and your hard and effective work have contributed outstandingly to the cause of socialist construction. We hereby express our deep thanks. The people will never forget them. The attitude of practicing democracy and of being modest and prudent you have taken in your work has given us a deep education. The manner of revolutionary statesman you have demonstrated as a state leader will impel us forward constantly. We are sure that the Standing Committee of the next National People's Congress will work still harder and win still greater victories in fulfilling the tasks defined by the new Constitution.

We heartily wish you good health and a long life!

[Signed] The Standing Committee of the
Fifth National People's Congress

March 5, 1983

Ideology and Party History

An Unofficial Blast at the Nine Open Letters of 1963–64, 1 November 1979

In the nine open letters from the Chinese Central Committee to the Soviet Central Committee, Mao and, according to recent statements, the dead and disgraced Kang Sheng cited the "revisionism" allegedly rampant in the Soviet Union and other Communist countries, such as Yugoslavia, as a warning to Chinese leaders like Liu Shaoqi and Deng Xiaoping, who were considered guilty of the same ideological sin. Here the open letters are appraised as a major episode in the development of the ultraleftist line in the history of the Party.

In the "big polemic" with the Soviet Communist Party 16 years ago, the Chinese Communist Party published a series of "antirevisionist" articles. While lashing out at the Soviet Communist Party, these articles actually produced a greater impact on China.

In these articles certain authoritative theoreticians of the Chinese Communist Party theoretically described and criticized "revisionism." These theories were accepted by the vast majority of the people in the country. For this reason, when the Cultural Revolution broke out 3 years later, almost all the slogans used by the Red Guards in their "rebellion" and "destroying the four olds" were derived from the "nine comments." The theoretical basis of the ultraleftist line spreading unchecked in the Cultural Revolution originated from the "nine comments" in the vast majority of cases.

Ye Jianying recently said at a meeting celebrating the 30th anniversary of National Day: "The Cultural Revolution was launched with the aim of preventing and combating revisionism." "But the point is that, at the time the Cultural Revolution was launched, the estimate made of the situation within the party and the country ran counter to reality" and "no accurate definition was given of revisionism. . . ." This shows that a leader of the Chinese Communist Party himself has come to realize that the wrong interpretation of "revisionism" was an important cause of the 10-year calamity.

How did this wrong interpretation come about? The "nine comments" were its most important source.

THE QUESTION OF CLASS STRUGGLE

At the 10th plenary session of the 8th CCP Central Committee in 1962, Mao Zedong put forward the slogan "never forget class struggle." He also put forward the general line for the transition period, that is: Throughout the historical period of socialism there are classes, class contradiction

and class struggle; struggle between the socialist and capitalist roads; and the danger of capitalist restoration. We should know the protractedness and complexity of this struggle. We should sharpen our vigilance. We should conduct socialist education, correctly understand the deal with the question of class contradiction and class struggle and correctly distinguish and handle the contradictions between the enemy and ourselves and the contradictions among the people. Otherwise, our socialist state will change into its opposite and degenerate, and restoration will appear. From now on, we must remind ourselves of this every year, every month and every day so that we shall have a sober understanding of this question and the Marxist-Leninist line.

The "nine comments" which were published beginning September 1963 expounded this general line in detail and extensively propagated it. The "nine comments" stated: "Throughout the socialist period, class struggle between the proletariat and the bourgeoisie in the political, economic, ideological, cultural and educational spheres cannot possibly cease. This struggle will be protracted, changeable, tortuous and complicated." "Politically, as the force opposed to the proletariat, they will long exist and always attempt to overthrow the dictatorship of the proletariat." "Throughout the socialist period, the struggle of Marxism-Leninism against various forms of opportunism, mainly revisionism, will inevitably exist within communist parties in socialist countries. This revisionism is characterized by attacks on the proletariat in the name of negating classes and class struggle, taking the stand of the bourgeoisie and changing the dictatorship of the proletariat into the dictatorship of the bourgeoisie."

It was precisely with the aid of propaganda and exposition by the "nine comments" that "the theory that class struggle will never die out" was extensively disseminated in society, shaping public opinion in favor of "enlarging class struggle" and pushing the ultraleftist line in days to come.

Although the "nine comments" raised "class struggle" to a very high plane, they did not give a concrete answer

[Hong Kong *Cheng Ming*, 1 November 1979.]

to the question of "how to differentiate classes after completion of the transformation of ownership." However, the "nine comments" did make a "class differentiation" in tracing the cause of "class struggle." "1) The overthrown exploiters will always attempt to regain their lost 'paradise' by every conceivable means. 2) The spontaneous force of the petty-bourgeoisie will regularly produce new capitalist elements. 3) Under the influence of the bourgeoisie and the encirclement and corrosive effect of the spontaneous force of petty-bourgeoisie, the contingent of workers and office workers of state organs will also produce some degenerate elements and new bourgeois elements...." ("On Khrushchev's Phoney Communism and Its Lesson for World History"—ninth comment on the open letter from the Soviet Communist Party Central Committee.) This "class differentiation" subconsciously exerted a tremendous influence when the Chinese Communist Party waged "class struggle" afterward. To begin with, landlords, rich peasants and capitalists and "the overthrown exploiting classes" became targets of permanent class struggle as did their children. Beginning in 1963, the Chinese Communist Party increasingly placed emphasis on implementing the "class line," "the theory that class status is everything" and the "theory of blood lineage." When the Cultural Revolution broke out, Red Guards of "five red category" origin, swinging leather belts, fell on the "five black categories" and killed landlords, rich peasants, reactionaries, bad elements and rightists without anyone stopping them. Did these overthrown classes really always attempt to regain their lost paradise? To be sure, these people whose "property was expropriated" nursed a grievance. But cowed by the powerful "dictatorship of the proletariat," none dared attempt to regain their lost paradise. How many cases in the 30 years since the Chinese Communist Party founded the republic have been attributed to these overthrown exploiting classes? Probably their number is next to nothing. Did practice not make the best test and give the best answer? Furthermore, the term "spontaneous force of petty bourgeoisie" was used indiscriminately by the Chinese Communist Party. Middle peasants, "office workers" in cities and large numbers of intellectuals were placed in the category of "petty-bourgeoisie." (Although office workers and intellectuals are not defined in explicit terms, in usual practice they are placed in this category.) Private plots and the remunerations of authors were regarded as hotbeds spontaneously engendering capitalism. Even those who hunted wild ducks during their spare time and sold them to stores were denounced as traversing the capitalist road. (See the modern drama "Never Forget" which was popular in the early 1960's.) During the Cultural Revolution, the tails of capitalism were cut off here and there with the result that the economy was on the verge of collapse and people lost almost all their enthusiasm and confidence. Finally, "degenerate elements and new bourgeois elements emerge from among the working class contingent and office workers of state organs"—this way of putting things evolved during the Cultural Revolution into the theory that "capitalist roaders" and "the bourgeoisie are inside the Communist Party."

This shows that from its presentation to its practice, the theory "never forget class struggle" produced bad results. This also shows that the "nine comments" played an evil role in forming a connecting link between what went before and what followed and in adding fuel to the flames.

THE QUESTION OF PRIVATE ECONOMY

At the same time it was preaching "class struggle," the "nine comments" repeatedly underlined the danger of "capitalist restoration."

What is "capitalist restoration?" The "nine comments" gave a concrete description through criticism of the Soviet Union and Yugoslavia.

1. The existence of private economy. The first evidence cited by the "nine comments" to demonstrate that Yugoslavia is not a socialist state is that private economy exists on a massive scale in Yugoslavia and that the government encourages and aids it. (Concerning the specific socioeconomic state of Yugoslavia, the writer does not propose to narrate it further here. The focal point of this article is to probe into the impact of the "nine comments" produced on the history of China.) This attack of the "nine comments" on private economy "dragged the reputation of private economy in the dust." Small merchants, peddlers, practicing doctors as well as casual workers were made targets of suppression. At the outbreak of the Cultural Revolution, these people were almost at the point of becoming targets of "rebellion" and went instantly into complete hiding. "Private plots," "free market" and "household sideline production" were also regarded as hotbeds of private economy and "capitalist restoration" and were "cut off" during the Cultural Revolution. This way of eliminating private economy was not in conformity with the objective laws of economic development. This point has been completely borne out by the reality of China's economic development. To save China's economy which was on the verge of collapse following the Cultural Revolution, the Chinese Communist Party not only permitted restoration of "free market," "private plots" and "household sideline production" but also permitted educated youths, while solving their employment problems, to run photo studios, wine stores and carpenter shops. The Chinese Communist Party clearly expressed its intention to learn the experience of Yugoslavia. According to the logic of the "nine comments," this meant "capitalist restoration."

THE QUESTION OF WORKERS' SELF-GOVERNMENT

2. "Workers' self-government" makes "the socialist economy owned by the whole people degenerate into capitalist economy." Dwelling on capitalist restoration in Yugoslavia, the "nine comments" said: "The restoration of capitalism in Yugoslavia does not find its expression only in the unchecked spread of private capitalism in cities and rural capitalism. What is more important, the 'public-operated' economy occupying a decisive position in Yugoslavia's economy has generated. The Tito clique's so-called economy under the system of 'workers' self-government' is a special type of state capitalism. It is not state capitalism under the dictatorship of the proletariat but state capitalism under the dictatorship of the bureaucrat-compradore bourgeoisie into which the Tito clique has degenerated the dictatorship of the proletariat. The means of production of these enterprises under the system of 'workers' self-government' are not owned by a certain capitalist or several private ones but actually by the new bureaucrat-compradore bourgeoisie represented by the Tito clique and including bureaucrats and managers. This bureaucrat-compradore

bourgeoisie, usurping the name of the state, attaching itself to U.S. imperialism and putting on the cloak of 'socialism,' seizes the property originally belonging to the working people. The so-called system of 'workers' self-government' is actually a system of brutal exploitation under the rule of bureaucrat-compradore capital." "The so-called system of 'workers' self-government' pushed by the Tito clique has completely cut the enterprises originally owned by the whole people out of the orbit of socialist economy. This is mainly expressed in: 1) cancellation of the unified economic plans of the state; 2) use of profits as the fundamental means to stimulate enthusiasm for enterprise operation . . . ; 3) carrying out a policy of encouraging capitalist free competition; 4) use of credit loans and banks as an important lever to support capitalist free competition; and 5) considering the relations between various enterprises not as socialist relations of mutual aid and cooperation under unified state plans but capitalist ones who harass each other on the free market." ("Is Yugoslavia a Socialist State?"—third comment on the open letter from the Soviet Communist Party Central Committee.) This series of criticisms leveled by the "nine comments" at the enterprises under the system of "workers' self-government" placed "profits," "bonuses" and "enterprise rights to act on their own" entirely into the category of "capitalist restoration." Since then, nobody within the Chinese Communist Party has dared mention "bonuses," "profits" and so forth.

After the conclusion of the Cultural Revolution, many people still did not dare mention profits and bonuses lest they be accused of "restoring capitalism." This shows the deep influence exerted by the "nine comments." However, in recent years the Chinese Communist Party has strongly promoted "manage the economy by economic means." The tactics proposed are similar to those criticized by the "nine comments."

THE QUESTION OF AMERICAN AID AND FOREIGN LOANS

3. "Accept American aid," "accept American loans," "learn American ways of operation." The "nine comments" said: "The process of restoring capitalism in Yugoslavia is intermingled with the process in which the Tito clique throws in their lot with U.S. imperialism and with the process in which Yugoslavia is reduced to the status of an appendage of U.S. imperialism. . . . From the end of World War II to January 1963, the aid from the United States and other imperialist nations to the Tito clique totaled $5.46 billion according to incomplete statistics. American aid accounted for more than 60 percent, or approximately $3.5 billion." "To obtain American aid, the Tito clique, in addition to signing a series of unequal treaties with the United States and bartering away their national sovereignty, has taken a series of steps in their internal and external policies to meet the demand of Western monopoly capital to invade Yugoslavia." "What have been the economic consequences since the Tito clique accepted huge amounts of American aid and opened their door to imperialism?" First, Yugoslavia has become a dumping market for imperialism. Second, Yugoslavia has become an outlet for imperialist investments. . . . Third, Yugoslavia has become an imperialist base of raw materials. Fourth, Yugoslavia's industrial enterprises have become assembly shops of Western

monopoly capital. . . . Under such circumstances, Yugoslavia has become a component of the world Western monopoly capital market. Financially and economically, Yugoslavia has forged unbreakable links with the capitalist world market and has been reduced to the status of an appendage to imperialism, particularly to U.S. imperialism. That a socialist state barters away its independence and sovereignty and depends on imperialism will inevitably lead to the restoration of the capitalist system." (Extracted from "Is Yugoslavia a Socialist State?"—third comment on the open letter from the Soviet Communist Party Central Committee.) The "nine comments" held that Khrushchev also wanted to depend on the United States to build "goulash communism." "Taking the United States as the chief course, he elevated the issue of learning U.S. capitalist ways of business and the bourgeois way of life to the position of national policy. Furthermore, he looked forward to using U.S. imperialist loans to build communism." "When he visited the United States and Hungary Khrushchev repeatedly expressed his desire to 'obtain loans from devils.' This shows that Khrushchev's 'communism' was 'goulash communism,' 'communism of following the American way of life' and the 'communism of seeking loans from devils.'" ("Concerning Khrushchev's Pseudocommunism and Its Lesson in World History"—ninth comment on the open letter from the Soviet Communist Party Central Committee.) According to the logic of the "nine comments," to "accept American aid," "accept American loans" and "learn the American ways of operation" would mean restoring capitalism. This logic tightly bound the hands of China's economy in its development. The China of the 1960's began to carry out a policy of "isolation" under the slogan of "self-reliance." This policy was fundamentally contrary to the objective laws governing the development of modern production. For this reason, it was bound to lead to slowness, stagnation and even the retrogression of economic development. China has now awakened since learning these bitter lessons and economically put into effect a series of reforms. These reforms are exactly the things condemned by the "nine comments" as capitalist restoration.

THE QUESTION OF A PRIVILEGED STRATUM

"The emergence of a privileged stratum." The "nine comments" said: "What Khrushchev puts into effect is an out-and-out revisionist line. Under this line, not only the old bourgeois elements run wild but also a large number of new ones have emerged from among the leading Soviet party and government cadres, responsible persons of state enterprises and collective farms and higher intellectuals of the departments of culture, art, science and technology." "In the Soviet Union, the new bourgeois elements have not only increased in number as never before but have also undergone fundamental changes in social position. Before Khrushchev came to power, they did not occupy dominant positions in the Soviet society and their activities were subject to various restrictions and attacks. After Khrushchev came to power, in the wake of Khrushchev's gradual usurpation of party and state leadership, they occupied a dominant position in the party, government and economic and cultural departments, forming a privileged stratum in Soviet society." ("On Khrushchev's Phoney Communism and Its Lesson for World History"—ninth comment on the open letter from the Soviet Communist Party Central Committee.) The existence of a privileged stratum in a socialist state is a ruthless reality which is confirmed by the history of all socialist states. It is precisely because it is an attribute common to all socialist states that it is not a symbol of "capitalist restoration." Some people are probing into and studying the question of how to restrict the prerogatives of the "privileged stratum," but, unfortunately they have not come to a perfect conclusion. During the Cultural Revolution, leading exponents of the ultraleftist line of the Chinese Communist Party exploited the inherent contradiction between the privileged stratum and the masses and disguised themselves as those leading the people to the left. The aftermath of this mistake was that some changes were made in the personnel of the CCP Central Committee and that the ultraleftist deviation was temporarily restrained.

Mao Zedong put forward the slogan "never forget class struggle" in 1962. This slogan gave the ultraleftist line its most important theoretical core. Centering on this core, a series of ultraleftist theories came into being. The "nine comments" which were published beginning in 1963 (the "first comment" was published on 6 September 1963 and the "ninth comment" on 14 July 1964) enabled the leading opponents to the privileged stratum to incite the masses to rebel and seize power and to strike down their political enemies who held different views. The result was that cadres in the privileged stratum became "capitalist roaders" and the intellectuals in the "privileged stratum" became the "stinking ninth category." The old privileged stratum was struck down but a new, bigger privileged stratum took shape. If prerogatives were distributed in the whole stratum in the past, they were now monopolized by a handful. The "nine comments" raised the question of the "privileged stratum" but did not settle it. On the contrary, certain theories advanced in the "nine comments" became the tools of the "monopoly privileged stratum."

THE POSITION OF THE "NINE COMMENTS" IN THE HISTORY OF THE ULTRALEFTIST LINE

The ultraleftist line of the Chinese Communist Party emerged at the end of the 1950's. The "antirightist" struggle in 1957, the "Big Leap Forward" in 1958 and the "antirightist" movement in 1959 were major demonstrations of ultraleftist deviation. However, beginning in 1960, the ruthless reality of the 3 years of difficulties confirmed the systematic, comprehensive, theoretical exposition previously made of the ultraleftist line. At that time, the Chinese Communist Party organized the whole nation to study the "nine comments." Factories and organs studied the "nine comments," and schools suspended political study and devoted themselves to studying the "nine comments." In the course of nationwide theoretical study, the "four clean-ups" movement and the criticism of "combine two into one" and "ghost plays," "honest officials" and "the fig, the foreign and the old" were unfolded. The "four clean-ups" movement was a rehearsal of the Cultural Revolution. It was a movement for "preventing capitalist restoration" and "seizing the capitalist roaders" launched according to the "theory that class struggle will never die out." In criticizing "combine two into one," "ghost play" and "honest officials," the theories advanced in the "nine comments" were fully applied. This nationwide study of the "antirevisionist" theory produced a tremendous impact on the dissemination of the ultraleftist theory.

By the first half of 1966 the ultraleftist theory was accepted by the vast majority of people. It dominated the entire public opinion. Thereupon, the ultraleftist line moved from theoretical propagation to social practice. When the ultraleftist theory was at the theoretical stage, the majority of people were misled by its beautiful and radical words and were not yet able to identify its harm. At that time, criticism was leveled at "Yugoslav revisionism" and "Soviet revisionism." You reproached others, without feeling hurt yourself. People could not possibly know what the ultraleftist line would look like when it was put into practice. The Cultural Revolution put the ultraleftist theory into practice, and only then did the people see the ultraleftist line from their personal experiences as it was. Suddenly they saw light after a practice filled with tears and blood. The history of the Cultural Revolution is the history of the practice of the ultraleftist theory as well as the history of its bankruptcy.

At the later stage of the Cultural Revolution, the ultraleftist theory was generalized into the "theory of continuing the revolution under the dictatorship of the proletariat." This theory and the "nine comments" came down in one continuous line. The vast part of the viewpoints of this theory could be seen in the "nine comments." It is precisely these viewpoints that laid the foundation of the ultraleftist theory. The "nine comments" expounded on ultraleftist theory in the greatest detail (no article as all-embracing as the "nine comments" has appeared since the Cultural Revolution) from internal affairs to external affairs, from politics and economics to culture and education. Therefore, the "nine comments" may be regarded as the most complete literature of the ultraleftist theory. In the history of the ultraleftist line of the Chinese Communist Party, the role of the "nine comments" must not be underestimated.

Deng Xiaoping's Posthumous Rehabilitation of Liu Shaoqi, 17 May 1980

Liu, who had been purged by Mao Zedong in 1966–67 and who had died in disgrace in 1969, was a close senior colleague of Deng. By rehabilitating him, Deng struck a blow at the jailed Gang of Four, whom he held responsible for Liu's fall, and only indirectly at Mao, whom Deng still needs as the only possible adequate source of legitimacy, apart from Marxism-Leninism, for the regime and himself.

We are gathered here today to mourn with profound grief Comrade Liu Shaoqi, a great Marxist and proletarian revolutionary, who dedicated the whole of his militant life to the cause of communism. He was a long-tested and outstanding party and state leader loved and respected by the whole party and the people of all our nationalities.

Actuated by their reactionary motives of scheming to usurp supreme leadership of the party and the state during the Cultural Revolution, Lin Biao, Jiang Qing and company, taking advantage of our party's shortcomings and mistakes, deliberately framed Comrade Liu Shaoqi and persecuted him cruelly. He died of illness in Kaifeng, Henan Province, on November 12, 1969. His death was a great loss to our party and our people. On the basis of a wealth of conclusive evidence accumulated in the course of meticulous investigation and review, the 11th party Central Committee, at its fifth plenary session, thoroughly repudiated the accusations made against Comrade Liu Shaoqi, and solemnly redressed the wrongs done him and rehabilitated his reputation. This principled stand of our party, that is, seeking truth from facts and correcting mistakes whenever discovered, won hearty support from the whole party, the whole army and the people of all our nationalities.

Comrade Liu Shaoqi was one of the earliest members of the Communist Party of China. Born in 1898 in Ningxiang County, Hunan Province, he took part in the 1919 May 4th movement in his youth, joined the Socialist Youth League in 1920 and became a member of the Chinese Communist Party in 1921, shortly after its founding. From 1922 to 1932, he was involved mainly with the workers movement and underground party work. He participated in leading, one after another, the general strike of coal miners and railway workers in Anyuan, the May 30th general strike in Shanghai, the general strike of Guangzhou and Hong Kong workers and the heroic struggle of Wuhan workers to seize back the British Concession there. He was elected a member of the Central Committee at the Fifth National Congress of the C.P.C. held in April 1927. After the failure of the great revolution (the first revolutionary civil war), he did underground party work in Shanghai, Tianjin, northeast China and north China under ferocious white terror, being one of the leaders of the Hebei provincial party committee at

one time and secretary of the Manchuria provincial party committee at another. In January 1931, he was elected a member of the Political Bureau of the Central Committee at the fourth plenary session of the Sixth Central Committee of the party. In the autumn of that year, he became director of the Workers' Department of the party Central Committee and secretary of the party group in the All-China Federation of Trade Unions.

In the winter of 1932, Comrade Liu Shaoqi arrived in the central revolutionary base area in Jiangxi and served as chairman of the All-China Federation of Trade Unions and later as secretary of the Fujian provincial party committee. He took part in the Long March of 25,000 li, serving as the representative of the party Central Committee in the eighth and then the Fifth Army Corps of the Red Army and director of the Political Department of the Third Army Corps. At the Zunyi meeting held in January 1935, which was vital to the Chinese revolution, Comrade Liu Shaoqi gave firm support to the correct line represented by Comrade Mao Zedong.

In the spring of 1936, Comrade Liu Shaoqi, as secretary of the Northern Bureau of the party Central Committee, correctly implemented in north China the party's policy of national united front against Japanese aggression, consolidating and extending the victories of the 1935 December 9th movement led by the party. During the early period of the war against Japanese aggression, he went far behind enemy lines, boldly arousing the masses to carry out the national salvation movement against Japanese aggression in accordance with the strategic policy put forward by the party Central Committee and Comrade Mao Zedong for independent guerrilla warfare in the enemy's rear areas, and effectively leading the work of founding the new anti-Japanese armed forces in Shaanxi and establishing anti-Japanese base areas in north China. In the winter of 1938, Comrade Liu Shaoqi went south, serving as secretary of the Central Plains Bureau of the party Central Committee and helping to organize and establish anti-Japanese base areas in central China. Receiving an assignment at a critical moment following the south Anhui incident in 1941, he became political commissar of the New Fourth Army and, in May of the same year, secretary of the Central China Bureau of the party Central Committee. He worked alongside Chen Yi and other comrades and quickly

[New China News Agency, 17 May 1980.]

ended the difficult situation of the New Fourth Army and revived and expanded the revolutionary forces in central China.

Comrade Liu Shaoqi was one of the principal leaders of our party for a long time. He returned to Yanan in 1943 and then became a member of the Secretariat of the party Central Committee and vice-chairman of the Revolutionary Military Commission. At the seventh national party congress in 1945, he was elected a member of the Political Bureau of the Central Committee and a member of the Secretariat of the Central Committee. When the enemy attacked Yanan in the spring of 1947, Comrade Mao Zedong and Comrades Zhou Enlai, Ren Bishi and Peng Dehuai remained in north Shaanxi to direct the nationwide liberation war and campaign to defend the Shaanxi-Gansu-Ningxia border region. In these circumstances, Comrade Liu Shaoqi, on order of the party Central Committee and Comrade Mao Zedong, moved to north China as secretary of the working committee of the C.P.C. Central Committee and joined Comrade Zhu De in taking charge of the party Central Committee's day-to-day work.

Comrade Liu Shaoqi was elected vice-chairman of the central people's government at the Chinese People's Consultative Conference in September 1949. He was elected chairman of the Standing Committee of the National People's Congress at the first session of the first National People's Congress in 1954. At the eighth national party congress in 1956, he was elected a member of the Central Committee, a member and Standing Committee member of the Political Bureau of the Central Committee and vice-chairman of the party Central Committee. At the first session of the Second National People's Congress in April 1959, Comrade Liu Shaoqi was elected chairman of the People's Republic of China. He held the post until his death.

For decades, Comrade Liu Shaoqi waged unremitting struggle and made immortal contributions to the consolidation and development of the party, to the victory of the new democratic revolution, to the victory of the socialist revolution and socialist construction, to the struggle against imperialism and colonialism and to the expansion of the international communist movement, winning love and respect from the whole party, the whole army and the people of all our nationalities.

Comrade Liu Shaoqi was a Marxist theorist of our party. He consistently stressed the importance of uniting theory and practice, was diligent in investigation, study and the summing up of experience, and was good at raising practical experience to the height of theory. He made important contributions in both practice and theory to our party building, to the workers movement in our country and to party work in the white areas. The theoretical viewpoints and ideological principles he advanced in these respects crystallized the experience accumulated by the party and the people in their heroic struggle over the past decades; and were a component of the scientific system of Mao Zedong Thought.

Comrade Liu Shaoqi dedicated his life's energy to making our party a Marxist-Leninist party, to defending the party's ideological and organizational purity, to consolidating and expanding its ranks, to safeguarding its solidarity and unity, to establishing fundamental guiding principles for inner-party life and to strengthening the party's ties with the masses. Being the first to advance the concept of Mao Zedong Thought, he publicized it energetically at the seventh national congress of the party. "How To Be a Good Communist" and his other works on party building, which have educated vast numbers of our party members, have become our party's invaluable spiritual wealth.

One of the principal leaders and organizers of China's workers movement over a long period, Comrade Liu Shaoqi was good at combining the party's political tasks with the workers' vital interests and organizing them in fruitful struggles. The ideas he advocated tirelessly in the early stage of China's labour movement, of emphasizing the trade union's organizational role, of raising the workers' political consciousness and of paying attention to their vital interests, continue to be of guiding significance.

China was hurled into the white terror after the failure of the great revolution in 1927. Confronted with Kuomintang counter-revolutionary suppression, some cadres in the party developed a tendency towards rash resistance. Comrade Liu Shaoqi advocated the need in the work among the masses to make use of public and legal means as far as possible, exploit the contradictions in the enemy's ranks, win over allies and be careful to wage appropriate struggles in light of the political awareness of the masses so as to preserve and expand the party's revolutionary forces in the white areas. Although his correct position was repressed and vilified at the time, the experience he summed up about work in the white areas on the eve of the war of resistance against Japan won attention in the party and played an important role in the white areas during that war and in the subsequent war of liberation.

Comrade Liu Shaoqi upheld a correct stand in the major struggles over the political line of the party during the new democratic revolution. He waged firm struggles against the "left" adventurism of Li Lisan, the "left" opportunism of Wang Ming, the criminal activities of Zhang Guotao to split the party during the Long March and the right opportunism of Wang Ming in the early stage of the resistance against Japan. History shows that Comrade Liu Shaoqi deserved to be called a staunch and mature proletarian revolutionary.

After the founding of the People's Republic, Comrade Liu Shaoqi, as one of the principal leaders of the party and state, took an active part in formulating and implementing the political lines, principles and policies for the socialist revolution and socialist construction. He upheld the socialist road, the dictatorship of the proletariat, the leadership of the Communist Party and Marxism-Leninism-Mao Zedong Thought. In the report he made on behalf of the Central Committee to the party's eighth national congress, which was convened after the socialist transformation of the ownership of the means of production in China had been completed in the main, he proposed shifting the focus of the party's work to economic construction and making every effort to raise the social forces of production. During the period of economic difficulties in the early sixties, he made a deep-going study of the actual situation, heeded the views of the masses, showed deep concern for the safety of the country and the weal and woe of the people, and justly supported the correct policy of readjustment, consolidation, filling out and raising of standards, and achieved outstanding success in his efforts.

Like any other proletarian revolutionary who could not be without flaws and errors of this sort or that, Comrade Liu Shaoqi, too, had some shortcomings and mistakes in his work. However, he always faithfully implemented the party Central Committee's political line and domestic and foreign policies and unswervingly adhered to the party's mass line and democratic centralism.

Comrade Liu Shaoqi was a communist with a lofty moral character. He always paid great attention to studying Marxist-Leninist theory and was good at integrating theory with practice, thoroughly investigating and concretely analyzing problems, in line with theoretical principles. He was a person with political foresight and sagacity. We should learn from his scientific attitude of combining theory and practice.

Comrade Liu Shaoqi shared weal and woe with the people. He stressed that the chairman of the state was a servant of the people, that in revolutionary work no job should be regarded as superior to another, and that one should serve the people wholeheartedly at every post. Proceeding from the interests of the people, he always had the courage to correct shortcomings and mistakes in work and to accept responsibility for them. He maintained his revolutionary faith as a communist even in the bitterly hard time when he was cruelly persecuted by Lin Biao, Jiang Qing and company. We should learn from his revolutionary attitude of boundless faith in the party and the people.

His words were matched by his deeds. He set an example in fulfilling what he required in "How To Be a Good Communist" of all party members in cultivating party spirit. He was fearless in upholding truth and resisting erroneous ideas, never concealing his own views. He respected collective leadership and obeyed party decisions, always placing himself in the midst of the organization. We should learn from his revolutionary style of firmly adhering to principles and strictly observing discipline.

Comrade Liu Shaoqi was calm, resourceful and staunch in struggle against the enemy. He remained faithful and unyielding during his two arrests by reactionary authorities. He never evaded hardship or danger at the critical moment of the revolution, but instead, always chose to go to the most difficult place and shoulder the heaviest task. We should learn from his valiant and indomitable revolutionary spirit.

Respected and beloved Comrade Liu Shaoqi left us more than ten years ago. Lin Biao, Jiang Qing and company fabricated evidence, concealed the truth and made false charges against him, trying to erase his name from the history of the Chinese revolution. But, as Comrade Liu Shaoqi said in his hardest time: "However, history is written by the people." Now history has declared the complete bankruptcy of the plot of Lin Biao, the gang of four and company. History is just towards every founding member and leader of New China, and the merit of no one shall be forgotten. Comrade Liu Shaoqi, like Comrades Mao Zedong, Zhou Enlai and Zhu De, will always live in the hearts of the people of all our nationalities.

In this new period of historical development, the whole party, the whole army and the people of all our nationalities face the arduous task of the four modernizations. The fundamental guarantee for accomplishing this historical task is upholding and improving leadership by the party and strengthening its fighting power. Commemorating Comrade Liu Shaoqi means first and foremost carrying out his behests and building our party into a fine party, restoring and developing our party's good traditions and style of work in every respect, and making our party truly the force at the core of China's socialist cause, so that it will lead the people of all our nationalities, with one heart and one mind, in working for the great goal of socialist modernization.

Eternal glory to Comrade Liu Shaoqi.

DENG XIAOPING
Interview with Yugoslav Correspondent, 17 December 1980

13

This interview is interesting as a source on Deng's views, both on the past and the present. In particular, he foreshadows the official evaluation of Mao Zedong which was to be promulgated the following year.

Mitevic: Many people all over the world support China's "four modernizations" policy. What do you think is the main difficulty in carrying out this policy?

Deng: As you all know, we will complete the Chinese-style four modernizations plan by the end of this century.

[Hong Kong *Wen Wei Po*, 18 December 1980.]

What do I mean by Chinese-style four modernizations? First, our modernizations are not being carried out according to the standard ways used in the Western world, with which everyone is familiar. Our national income remains one of the lowest in the world. Hence, although we will develop very rapidly in the future, our income per capita will still be low at the end of the century. It is precisely because of this that we want to double the national income in the next decade, and we should continue to proceed in that fashion in the decade after that. Only in this way can we develop to the level of Yugoslavia by the end of the century, that is, to the level of a prosperous and happy society. With a prosperous society, our life will be much better. China has socialist ownership over the means of production; in these circumstances, the aim of increasing production is to improve the people's living standards, not to practice exploitation. As a fruit of the four modernizations, the national income level should be directly reflected in the people's living standards. This is the fundamental difference between us and the West.

Mitevic: Do you have enough experts for accomplishing the four modernizations?

Deng: Just now you asked me what difficulties there were. There are many difficulties. It is not at all easy to accomplish our target. We have both favorable and unfavorable conditions.

The favorable conditions are that China has a large population, so we possess a mighty labor force, and the Chinese people are also hard-working and brave. Another favorable condition is that China is very rich in natural resources. In addition we have been building socialism for more than 30 years and have laid the foundation for further development. However, there are also many unfavorable conditions, our standards of science and technology are low, our management efficiency cannot keep up with demand, while in addition for a rather long time in the past, especially during the Cultural Revolution, the many stupid "leftist" policies produced a whole series of bad effects. There is duplication of leadership organs, work efficiency that is falling all the time, and massive development of bureaucracy. That is why we cannot accomplish the four modernizations without carrying out political reforms in society.

There are also many other difficulties. However, I hold that we will gradually enhance the productive force and improve our work in the course of accomplishing the four modernizations.

Mitevic: There is now a lot of talk in China about the question of promoting democracy. This process is evident; it penetrates into every field. Can you tell us what is the most important reason for separating party and government? Is it aimed, as you said, at improving work management efficiency? Is it also necessary to eliminate factional struggles at the same time?

Deng: Yes. We are now eliminating bureaucratism and encouraging and bringing into play the masses' enthusiasm. This is because, to accomplish the four modernizations, we must put socialist democracy into effect and establish our legal system. I want to stress this point, we must strengthen the legal system while strengthening democracy. This is certainly not an easy thing to do. China has historically lacked traditions of democracy and a legal system.

Hence, we cannot just talk about the necessity of bringing democracy into play without talking of the question of the legal system. That is impossible. At the same time, it is necessary to realize that the Cultural Revolution lasted more than 10 years and caused enormous damage. One of its consequences is that problems such as anarchism and extreme individualism have appeared among young people. This is a special feature of China. This is

another reason why we must strengthen the legal system while bringing democracy into greater play.

Mitevic: Will you also separate party and government in the enterprises?

Deng: We are currently thinking of switching the enterprises, including production units and rural production teams, to the system of manager or production team leader responsibility under party committee leadership. We don't want to allow the party to interfere in the management system, that is to say, the party committees should not take charge of this system. This is because, to carry out the four modernizations, it is necessary to mobilize the enthusiasm of staff and workers and also to institute democratic management. Hence, we should expand enterprise decisionmaking powers to a considerable extent. We are advocating enterprise decisionmaking powers and powers that the enterprise staff and workers should possess. At the same time, enterprise leaders too should have the right to handle their affairs independently. The managerial personnel should have the power and responsibility to do their work as well as possible. Naturally the party committee is there too, but the party committee should certainly not take charge of everything.

Mitevic: The party committee should not take charge?
Deng: Correct.

Mitevic: I mentioned just now, you were acting premier in 1975. At that time I had the opportunity to see the late Chairman Mao. Chairman Mao made tremendous contributions to China; you worked with him for many years. I want to know, what do you think Mao's chief mistakes were as a revolutionary, a theoretician and a practical person?

Deng: As you know, the seventh party congress in 1945 established Mao Zedong Thought as the guiding ideology for the whole party. You also know that Mao Zedong himself was the most typical representative of Mao Zedong Thought. Mao Zedong Thought is the crystallization of the ideology of the whole party. His greatest contribution was to successfully integrate Marxism-Leninism with China's realities. This led to our victory in the Chinese revolution. This is a precious treasure of the Chinese party and revolution. This is why we will always uphold Mao Zedong Thought. However, he made a number of mistakes in his declining years, and some of them were even great mistakes.

Mitevic: Are you mainly referring to the Cultural Revolution period?

Deng: Yes. Especially during the Cultural Revolution period. The Cultural Revolution was from every angle a great mistake which has caused many severe difficulties for us. However, when we evaluate Comrade Mao Zedong, we always hold that his achievements were primary and his mistakes secondary. We cannot underestimate his achievements. At the same time, we cannot neglect his mistakes. We have successfully educated our party and people in this attitude. We have summed up our experiences in this attitude, in order to advance more rapidly.

Mitevic: Comrade Deng, we have heard that the gang of four will soon be put on trial. The Chinese people are familiar with their errors. So I want to ask, what are the gang of four actually going to be tried for?

Deng: We shall try them for their crimes. One cannot exaggerate in talking about the gang of four's crimes. You can say that they were evil incarnate. The question of Comrade Mao Zedong will inevitably be involved when the gang of four are tried, and so when trying them we will mainly try them for their own crimes without getting involved in the question of the responsibility of Comrade Mao Zedong. We will judge them according to the proven crimes that they have committed. This is because their deeds were criminal, while the mistakes committed by Comrade Mao Zedong were political.

Mitevic: They broke the law. Will the new criminal code you just mentioned apply to them?

Deng: They were involved in thousands and thousands of criminal deeds.

Mitevic: Comrade Deng, China is gradually opening up to the world. This is also your achievement. However, some people in the world say that this opening up has come about because of the Soviet challenge. I want to ask, under what circumstances will China seek a way of easing or overcoming this confrontation?

Deng: One thing is that we are opening up to the world in order to speed up China's own development. A country cannot develop if it isolates and insulates itself; its development then will be rather slow. After the establishment of the PRC, we were blockaded for a long time by the Western world, so all we could do was to shut the door and carry out construction ourselves.

Mitevic: Do you mean in the years after 1949?

Deng: Yes. The Soviet Union helped us for a time after the establishment of our state, but after Khrushchev came to power, 700 agreements and contracts were torn up overnight; beginning from that time, we operated on our own for many years. As you know, in autumn 1974 the situation started to change, and this gave us the conditions for instituting a policy of opening up to the world and strengthening our international exchanges. We have the conditions for absorbing foreign experiences and strengthening cooperation with the developed countries, and even for making use of their technology, science and capital to help us speed up our development. We have engaged in this business for 2 or 3 years now. Summing it up, we find that this orientation is correct. However, we lack sufficient experience. But never mind, we will continue to implement this policy.

On the question of Sino-Soviet relations, the Soviet Union has deployed 1 million troops on our border, beginning in the Khrushchev era and developing to the time of Brezhnev. The way to understand China's foreign policy can be explained in two phrases: "opposition to hegemonism, and preservation of world peace." The question of Sino-Soviet relations is a question of preserving world peace and opposing hegemonism. Therefore, it is something entirely different from China's economic policy of opening up to the world.

Mitevic: You have said that Taiwan will return to China by the end of the century. Can it return a bit earlier than that, considering that Reagan is now taking office?

Deng: We have not mentioned any particular time for accomplishing that, but we have designated the 1980's as the era when it should happen. However, we should as far as possible devise ways to accomplish the peaceful return of Taiwan to the motherland in a relatively short period of time. However, as far as the PRC is concerned, every day we have not accomplished the unification of the motherland means that we have not yet completed our task and are unable to justify ourselves to our posterity.

Mitevic: I have two further questions. China is now restoring the good name of many people, and Liu Shaoqi has been rehabilitated. The Chinese people support this point. What in fact is the scale of this rehabilitation?

Deng: Lin Biao and the gang of four overthrew 70 to 80 percent of the members and alternate members of the eighth Central Committee. They also toppled many scientists, men of letters, artists, and people in every field. We were able to rehabilitate them after the gang of four were smashed. This task is now basically completed, but there is still some left to do.

Mitevic: If you were 20 years old now, and in France, what things would you like to change in life? What would you like to do?

Deng: At that time, when we started going to France, ours was a kind of bourgeois reformist ideology. At the time we called it saving the country by industry and commerce, but after arriving in France we came into contact with the international workers' movement and were influenced by the October Revolution. We also accepted Marxism and strengthened our proletarianization.

Mitevic: You were a political commissar on the Long March and a well-known commander during the war. What was your most difficult period?

Deng: I returned to China at the end of 1920. I held a responsible post in a Kuomintang military officers' school. After that I went to work in the party Central Committee. I became party secretary-general in 1927, when I was 22. In 1929 the Central Committee sent me to lead an uprising in Guangxi. I was instructor of the 7th Red Army until the liberation.

Mitevic: Comrade Deng Xiaoping, you have never been to Yugoslavia. I believe you will visit that country one day. Through this interview, you are actually speaking to the Yugoslav people; it is as though you have come to Yugoslavia.

Deng (laughs): Yes, our country and people enjoy high international prestige. I am very happy to meet the Yugoslav people through the medium of television. We grieve at the death of Comrade Tito, but we are particularly happy to see that in the past half year the Yugoslav people have persistently followed the cause of Tito and have scored excellent achievements in this endeavor. I congratulate the Yugoslav party and people!

Mitevic: I thank you for this interview and your words of friendship on behalf of the Yugoslav television station. We have talked for quite a long time, but it is all right for our friendly talk to be a bit long.

Deng: Thank you very much.

On the Publication of the First Volume of Zhou Enlai's Selected Works, 27 December 1980

14

As the patron of the Four Modernizations of Deng Xiaoping and of much that has gone into the making of post-Mao Zedong China, Zhou occupies a place in the history of the Chinese Communist movement and the PRC second only to that of Mao himself. By publishing Zhou's writings up until 1949, Deng not only celebrates Zhou's memory but also helps to enhance his own legitimacy.

The Chinese language edition of volume 1 of the two-volume "Selected Works of Zhou Enlai," edited by the editorial committee on party literature of the Central Committee of the Communist Party of China, has been published by the People's Publishing House. Copies will be available in major Chinese cities starting from January 1, 1981.

The first volume contains 60 works that Zhou Enlai wrote during the new democratic revolution, from the period of the first revolutionary civil war (1924–1927) to the eve of the founding of the People's Republic of China in 1949. They are chronologically arranged. Forty of them have not been published before.

The works are a record of Zhou Enlai's heroic struggle for the Chinese people's revolutionary cause, reflect his thought and fine qualities, and illustrate his outstanding contribution to the work of integrating Marxism-Leninism with the practice of the Chinese revolution.

Chinese theoretical circles describe the issuance of the "Selected Works of Zhou Enlai" as a great event in theoretical work and the dissemination of Marxism-Leninism in China. The selected works will be of immediate importance and historical significance. It will become a powerful ideological weapon for studying and doing research on Marxism-Leninism-Mao Zedong Thought and the history of the Chinese revolution, and for advancing the socialist modernization of China.

Editions in five foreign languages, English, French, Russian, Spanish and Japanese, are being prepared.

CONTENTS LIST

The Chinese Communist Party in the Present Political Struggle (11 December 1926)

On Taking Prompt Punitive Action Against Chiang Kai-shek (April 1927)

On Firmly Eliminating Non-Proletarian Ideology From the Party (11 November 1928)

Some Questions Concerning the Development of the Soviet Areas in Western Hunan and Hubei (17 March 1929)

[New China News Agency, 27 December 1980.]

On How To Strengthen the Party's Organizational Work Under the White Terror (25 March 1929)

On How Comrades Peng Pai, Yang Yin, Yan Changyi and Xing Shizhen Were Arrested and Killed by the Enemy (14 September 1929)

The Chinese Communist Party's Letter of Instruction to the Party Front Committee of the 4th Army of the Red Army (28 September 1929)

The Reasons of the Emergence and the Future of the Trotskiyite Opposition Faction in China (October 1929)

On the Work in Wuhan (4 September 1930)

On the Rationale of the Lisan Line (1 December 1930)

Telegrams Relating to the Smashing of the Fourth "Encirclement and Suppression" Campaign (January–March 1933)

Three Telegrams Relating to the Xian Incident (December 1936)

The Chinese Communist Party Central Committee's Declaration on Kuomintang-Communist Cooperation (15 July 1937)

On Opposing the Pursuit of Peace Through Compromise and Persistently Waging a War of Resistance in North China (13 November 1937)

The Present Crises in the War of Resistance and the Tasks in Persistently Waging a War of Resistance in North China (16 November 1937)

On the Nature and Tasks of the Youth Movement at the Present Stage (31 December 1937)

On the Political Work of the Army in the War of Resistance (10 January 1938)

On the Present Situation and the Tasks of the New 4th Army (March 1939)

On Building a Strong and Militant Party Organization in the Southwest (January 1942)

On the Party's Relations With the Kuomintang 1924–26 (Spring 1943)

The Main Points of Self-Cultivation for Myself (18 March 1943)

Letter of Condolence to the Family of Dr. Kotivis (22 March 1943)

How To Be a Good Leader (22 April 1943)

Speech at a Meeting of Welcome in Yanan (2 August 1943)

On China's Fascism–Neo-Despotism (16 August 1943)

A Study on the Party's "Sixth National Congress" (3, 4 March 1944)

Opinions on the Party Rectification Campaign in the Cultural Circles in the Rear Area (18 January 1945)

On the United Front (30 April 1945)

An Urgent Call at Present (August 1945)

On Vigorously Carrying Out Propaganda Against Civil War and Dictatorship and Exposing Chiang Kai-shek's Deceptive Conspiracy (16 August 1945)

Letter of Condolence to Shen Cuizhen, Wife of Zou Taofen (12 September 1945)

Talk on the Second Plenary Session of the Kuomintang Central Committee (18 March 1946)

Eternal Glory to the "8 April" Martyrs (19 April 1946)

A Solemn Statement on Opposing the Spreading of Civil War and Political Assassinations (17 July 1946)

Take Better Care of the Progressive Friends (25 July 1946)

A Poem for Mourning Li Gongpu and Wen Yiduo (4 October 1946)

Speech at a Shanghai Meeting in Commemoration of Lu Xun's 10th Death Anniversary (19 October 1946)

A Solemn Statement on the Convocation of the "National Assembly" by the Kuomintang (16 November 1946)

Congratulatory Speech in Celebration of Commander in Chief Zhu's 60th Birthday (30 November 1946)

Speech at a Yanan Meeting of All Circles in Commemoration of the "12 December" Day (12 December 1946)

On the Negotiations in the Past Year and their Future (18 December 1946)

A Comment on Marshall's Statement Before his Departure From China (10 January 1947)

Two Documents on the Principles of the Work and the Tactics of Struggle in Areas Dominated by Chiang Kai-shek (28 February, 5 May 1947)

On Launching Nationwide Counterattack and Overthrowing Chiang Kai-shek (28 September 1947)

Opinions on the Present Work of the Democratic Parties and Groups (January 1948)

An Important Question in Leadership Style (5 February 1948)

On Land Reform and Party Consolidation in the Old and Semi-Old Liberated Areas (22 February 1948)

Telegram to the Fuping Central Bureau on the Questions of Land Reform and Party Consolidation (23 February 1948)

The Party's Policies Should Be Made Known to the Masses in Good Time (7 March 1948)

On Organizing Soldiers' Committees in Army Units on a Trial Basis (8 March 1948)

On the Economic Construction of the New Democratic Period (21 June 1948)

On Foiling the Enemy's Plot in the Sham Peace Movement (27 July 1948)

Sober-Mindedness and Flexible Tactics Are Needed for the Struggles in Areas Dominated by Chiang Kai-shek (22 August 1948)

A Letter to Zheng Dongguo (18 October 1948)

Report on the Question of Peace Negotiations (17 April 1949)

On Uniting the Broad Masses of People and Advancing Together With Them (22 April 1949)

Learn from Mao Zedong (7 May 1949)

Political Report at the Congress of All-China Literary and Art Workers (6 July 1949)

On Restoring Production and Constructing China (23 July 1949)

Special Features of the Draft Common Outline of the People's Political Consultative Conference (22 September 1949)

SHORT DESCRIPTION OF "WORKS"

The first volume of the "Selected Works of Zhou Enlai" edited by the editorial committee on party literature of the CCP Central Committee has been published by the People's Publishing House.

Comrade Zhou Enlai was a great Marxist, a proletarian revolutionary and an outstanding leader of the CCP. Comrade Zhou Enlai's works recorded his revolutionary achievements and reflected his brilliant thought, lofty qualities and fine work style. On a series of important issues, it profoundly summed up the experience of the Chinese revolution and it showed a valuable achievement in making use of Marxist theory to solve the problems of the Chinese revolution.

The first volume of the "Selected Works of Zhou Enlai" contains 60 articles written during the period of new democratic revolution up to the founding of the PRC. Forty of the articles have never been published before.

Two of Comrade Zhou Enlai's articles written during the first revolutionary civil war were selected. "The CCP in the Present Political Struggle" was written in the winter of 1926, a critical juncture when successive victories were being won in the northern expedition and the right wing of the Kuomintang was stepping up its counterrevolutionary activities. It elucidated the stratagem and line of the CCP on the united front during the first revolutionary civil war. This article points out: The CCP is working hard for the interests of the most oppressed and suffering worker-peasant class. It is necessary to lead the revolutionary force of the worker-peasant class to promote the national revolution and overcome the tendency among other classes towards compromise. Communists join the Kuomintang, but the Communist Party must not lose its own independence.

The article was a blow to the attack of the Kuomintang right wing and at the same time resisted the capitulationist trend within the CCP, Chen Duxiu being the chief exponent.

"On Taking Punitive Action Against Chiang Kai-shek" analyzes the political and military situation after Chiang Kai-shek staged the 12 April 1927 counterrevolutionary coup d'etat in Shanghai. It points out: The entire revolution would end in total failure, if the revolutionary force continued to vacillate and compromise. It advocated the adoption of resolute measures to save the resolution.

The second revolutionary civil war period was an important historical period in which the party developed and matured in the course of extremely arduous and tortuous struggles. During this period, the Chinese people had preserved and developed the revolutionary force, established new positions and found the road to the victory of the revolution. Under very complicated conditions, Comrade Zhou Enlai waged arduous struggles on many sides. He had left with us his enriched works dealing with party building, work in the white areas and building the Red Army and revolutionary base areas.

A total of 11 articles written during this period were included in the selected works. Follows a listing of the main articles.

"On Firmly Eliminating Nonproletarian Ideology From the Party" was written in November 1928 when Comrade Zhou Enlai was director of the Organization Department of the CCP Central Committee and secretary of the Military Commission of the CCP Central Committee. This article is an important document in the history of the CCP on party building. The article summed up the experience in party building accumulated by the Communist Party since its inception. It analyzed the various manifestations of the petit-bourgeois ideas in the party and pointed out that these petit-bourgeois ideas had always undermined the party's organs and impeded the party's work and that the comrades in the whole party must resolutely rise to eliminate all nonproletarian ideology. Many of the important ideas contained in the article are still of great current significance in building the party at present.

"Several Questions on the Development of the Soviet Areas in Western Hunan and Hubei" was a directive Comrade Zhou Enlai drafted for the party Central Committee in March 1929 to Comrade He Long and the front committee in western Hunan and Hubei. The article summed up the experience in waging guerrilla war, building party organizations and doing mass work in the Soviet areas; and affirmed and recommended the practice of the 4th Army of the Red Army in establishing party branches at the company level. The article was aimed at the remnant influence of putschism, pointing out: The main task at that time was to mobilize the masses and carry out, in the rural areas, the agrarian revolution in depth and expand guerrilla areas, instead of going beyond the strength of the Red Army subjectively by trying to take key industrial and commercial cities right away.

"How To Improve the Party's Organizational Work Under the White Terror" was a directive drafted by Comrade Zhou Enlai for the CCP Central Committee in March 1929 to the Shunzhi Provincial CCP Committee and Comrade Wang Ming. The article pointed out: workers in the white area must enter factories, rural areas and the society to look for jobs and go deep among the masses. They must carry out mass work in a down-to-earth manner and correct the state of affairs of party organs being mere skeletons under the white terror and completely isolated with the life of the masses.

"The Directive of the CCP Central Committee to the Front Committee of the 4th Army of the Red Army" was the famous "September Letter from the Central Authorities" drafted by Comrade Chen Yi in 1929 for the CCP Central Committee on the basis of several talks made by Comrade Zhou Enlai and the guidelines laid down by a meeting of the central authorities after Comrade Chen Yi went to Shanghai to report to the CCP Central Committee on the work of the Red 4th Army. The directive was approved by Comrade Zhou Enlai.

This article analyzed the political situation at that time. It pointed out that Red Army forces should be built in the countryside first and political power seized in the cities later—this was the characteristic of the Chinese revolution and a product of its economic base. It summed up the experience of the Red Army and explained the fundamental task of the Red Army and many issues in the course of development. This letter played an important

role in doing a good job in convening the Gutian congress. In the resolution of the ninth party congress of the 4th Army of the Red Army drafted by Comrade Mao Zedong, he pointed out: "Based on the guidelines laid down by the September letter of the central authorities, the congress pointed out the manifestations, sources and corrective methods of the nonproletarian ideology of all kinds within the party organs of the 4th Army and called on the comrades to rise to thoroughly eliminate such ideology."

"On Problems of Work in Wuhan" was a directive drafted by Comrade Zhou Enlai in September 1930 for the CCP Central Committee to its Changjiang bureau. The article stressed correcting the erroneous thinking flowing from Comrade Li Lisan's "left" line, which consisted of empty talk about major actions and armed insurrection. It pointed out that without the necessary fighting strength and organizational foundation for major actions, especially without strong party leadership, it was absolutely impossible to carry out any major actions. The article criticized the erroneous idea that maintained that "left" was better than right and that feared right deviation but not "left" deviation. It pointed out that "left" deviations could obstruct and destroy the revolution just as surely as right errors could.

"Telegrams Relating to the Smashing of the Fourth 'Encirclement and Suppression' Campaign" consisted of eight telegrams sent by Comrade Zhou Enlai, then directing operations at the front after his arrival in the central Soviet area, to the CCP Central Committee and its Soviet bureau, and an order jointly issued by Comrades Zhou Enlai and Zhu De. At the time when the fourth counter-campaign against "encirclement and suppression" began, Comrade Mao Zedong had been forced out of the Red Army by the leadership of the "left" opportunist line. From practice Comrades Zhou Enlai, Zhu De and others realized that the orders of the party Central Committee and its Soviet bureau—which called on the Red Army to gain the initiative by striking first, and to attack and take the cities of Nanfeng and Nancheng, which were defended by massive enemy forces—were wrong. The telegrams proposed the principle of concentrating a superior force to destroy enemy forces one by one in mobile warfare. The fourth counter-campaign against "encirclement and suppression" was victorious under the command of Comrades Zhou Enlai and Zhu De.

The war of resistance against Japanese aggression was an extremely important period in the history of the Chinese revolution. During this period, the Chinese nation waged a life-and-death struggle against Japanese imperialism. After 8 years of bloody fighting, the Chinese people defeated the aggressors. In the meantime, the people's armed forces grew stronger, powerful revolutionary base areas were established and the united front was developed. Through the rectification campaign and the "seventh party congress," the Chinese Communist Party summed up historical experience and united the whole party, and the party's leadership became more mature, ensuring victory in the war of resistance against Japanese aggression and laying the foundation for defeating the U.S.-Chiang reactionaries and later winning nationwide victory. Included in the "selected works" are 15 articles written during this period, mainly the following:

"Oppose Seeking Peace Through Compromise, Persist in the War of Resistance in North China" was a telegram sent to the party Central Committee from Linfen, Shanxi

Province, soon after the outbreak of the war of resistance against Japanese aggression. The article pointed out that after the Japanese aggressors occupied Taiyuan, there was a growing atmosphere of defeatism and peace-seeking in Chiang Kai-shek's Kuomintang, and that it was imperative to oppose seeking peace through compromise and to persist in the war of resistance in north China. The article stressed that, in that stage of the war, guerrilla warfare must be the main form of operations, and that it was necessary to expand the Red Army, win over and influence friendly forces, realize democratization in local politics, and so forth. After the telegram was sent, Comrade Zhou Enlai made his well-known speech, "Current Crisis in the War of Resistance and the Task of Persisting in the War of Resistance in North China," at a mass rally in Linfen, in which he further expounded his thinking in the telegram. The telegram produced a great impact on mobilizing the people in north China to persist in fighting the war of resistance behind enemy lines.

"The Current Situation and the Tasks of the New 4th Army" was the gist of a speech at a cadre meeting at the headquarters of the new 4th Army in southern Anhui in March 1939. The article set forth the new 4th Army's strategic principles and, in view of the situation that the new 4th Army was located in the special surroundings south of the Changjiang River where both the Japanese aggressors and the Kuomintang had strong forces, clearly pointed out that the new 4th Army must fear no difficulties, ignore the Kuomintang's restrictions, go deep among the masses, develop itself behind enemy lines, stress guerrilla warfare, create base areas and boldly build a powerful force.

"On Building a Strong and Militant Party Organization in the Southwest" was written in 1942. In accordance with the CCP Central Committee's guidelines for work in white areas—long-term underground work, building up strength and biding one's time—and experience gained in work in white areas, the article set forth the necessary conditions for building a strong and militant party organization in the southwest. It had a universal significance to building party organizations in various places in white areas.

"On the Party's Relationship With the Kuomintang Between 1924 and 1926" was written in 1943. The article reviewed the historical course of the cooperation between the Kuomintang and the Communist Party from 1924 to 1926, analyzed the three major concessions made by the right opportunists within the Chinese Communist Party to Chiang Kai-shek politically, militarily and in party affairs, and pointed out that Chen Duxiu's right opportunist mistakes were an important cause for the failure of the great revolution. This was an important article for studying the experience and lessons of the first revolutionary civil war period.

"How To Be a Good Leader" put forward all-round demands on leading cadres of the party at all levels. It pointed out that a correct leader must relate the party's general tasks of the characteristics of a given time and place on the basis of thorough investigation and study of concrete conditions to determine the tasks and policies for a given period, formulate suitable slogans and tactics, and prove through practice that the party's line and tactics were correct. The experience gained by the leaders and the masses must be pooled, for only in this way can there be correct leadership. The article also pointed out that

leaders should raise their prestige by correcting their mistakes, and not by covering them up; and by immersing themselves in hard work, not by bragging and boasting.

"Speech at a Meeting of Welcome in Yanan" was written in 1943. The article described the changes in the international and domestic situation in the 3 years following his departure from Yanan and the great achievements made by the whole party under the leadership of the party Central Committee and Comrade Mao Zedong. It stressed that Comrade Mao Zedong's leadership ensured that our party did not lose its bearings or take the wrong course at many critical junctures and on many key questions.

"On China's Fascism—New Despotism" was written in 1943, when Chiang Kai-shek published his book "China's Destiny" to peddle fascism and start the third anticommunist upsurge. The article incisively analyzed the essence of the rule of Chiang Kai-shek's Kuomintang and pointed out that China's fascism was a compradore, feudalistic fascism. The article discussed the ideological system, historical origin, political program and tactics and organizational activities of China's fascism. It pointed out that world fascism was heading for its doom, and that China's fascism could not possibly survive alone.

"A Study on the Party's 'Sixth Congress'" was a report made at the central party school in Yanan in 1944. Comrade Zhou Enlai took part in the work of the "sixth congress" and was one of the principal responsible persons at that time. The article scientifically discussed the "sixth congress" and a number of important issues in the history of the party prior to the "sixth congress"; studied the understanding of the "sixth congress" of the nature, tasks, motive force and other things of the Chinese revolution; looked into the experience and lessons of the great revolution; and analyzed the tactics, principles and some policies laid down by the "sixth congress." The article affirmed that the "sixth congress" was basically correct and had played a progressive role in the history of the Chinese Communist Party and the Chinese revolution. It pointed out at the same time that the "sixth congress" also made mistakes. This is a valuable historical document for the study of the party's history.

"On the United Front" was a speech Comrade Zhou Enlai gave at the seventh CCP national congress in 1945, systematically analyzing the formation and development of the anti-Japanese national united front and the Communist Party's experience on the question of the united front during the period of democratic revolution. The article pointed out that the enemies of the new democratic revolution were the imperialist and feudal forces, which would not change for the entire period of the new democratic revolution. However, there was more than one imperialist country, and the big landlord class and the big bourgeoisie were also divided into different factions and cliques. These enemies were often in disunity. Therefore, the enemy camp was changing, and particularly the representatives of various classes were far from fixed and unchanging. Because of this, we must be good at recognizing and analyzing the enemies. The new democratic revolutionary ranks included the proletariat, the peasantry, the petty bourgeoisie, the liberal bourgeoisie, and sometimes even part of the big landlord class and the big bourgeoisie. The commander of the new democratic revolution was the proletariat, which should lead the other classes that had joined the revolution. The question of leadership was the most focal question in the united front. Leadership must be seized by force. In the war of resistance against Japan, the Kuomintang ruling clique representing the big landlord class and the big bourgeoisie was the most important contender for leadership with the Communist Party. With correct understanding of these three questions—the enemies, the revolutionary ranks and the commander—and adoption of correct policies, the united front would succeed. Otherwise, "left" or right mistakes would occur.

The period of the third revolutionary civil war, from the end of the war of resistance against Japan to the founding of the People's Republic of China, was the period of final, decisive battles between the people of the whole country led by the proletariat and the big landlord class and the big bourgeoisie represented by Chiang Kai-shek. Under the correct leadership of the Chinese Communist Party headed by Comrade Mao Zedong, the Chinese people, after 4 years of hard and valiant struggle, finally won a great victory, overthrowing nationwide the rule of imperialism and its lackeys and establishing new China. Thirty-two works written by Comrade Zhou Enlai during this period are included in the "selected works," mainly the following:

"Urgent Demands at Present" was written in August 1945 just after Japan announced its surrender. At that time, the people throughout the country longed for peace and democracy. Chiang Kai-shek, however, deliberately stirred up a civil war and strengthened his dictatorial rule. The article put forth 14 demands, including the withdrawal of the Kuomintang forces encircling and attacking the liberated areas to avoid civil war, the convocation of a political conference attended by representatives of all parties and people without party affiliation, the establishment of a coalition government and so forth. These demands were reflected in the "Declaration of the CCP Central Committee on the Current Situation" issued on 25 August 1945, and played a tremendous role in calling on and encouraging the people of the whole country to uphold peace, democracy and unity and fight for building an independent, free, prosperous and powerful new China.

"Speech on the Second Plenary Session of the Kuomintang Central Committee," "Stern Statement on the 'National Assembly' Convened by the Kuomintang" and "The Talks Over the Past Year and Their Future" are the historical records of Comrade Zhou Enlai's struggle against the Kuomintang reactionaries while holding talks with them after the victory of the war of resistance against Japan. At that time, in order to deceive the people and prepare for civil war, Chiang Kai-shek had no choice but to agree to hold the talks and sign the double 10 agreement [the agreement signed in Chongqing on 10 October 1945], the cease-fire agreement and the resolution on political consultation. Shortly afterward, however, the agreements and resolution were breached by Chiang Kai-shek. The above-mentioned articles analyze the characteristics of the talks at different stages, expose Chiang Kai-shek's reactionary acts of totally breaching the agreements and undermining the peace talks, and expound the firm stand of the Chinese Communist Party.

"The Documents Concerning the Principles of Work in Chiang-Ruled Areas and the Strategy of the Struggle" was written in the spring of 1947. In view of Chiang Kai-shek's policy of fiercely suppressing the patriotic democratic movement in the wake of the breaking of the peace

talks between the Kuomintang and the Communist Party, the article points out that the party work in the Chiang-ruled areas should aim at making more widespread propaganda and averting hard confrontation. It points out the necessity to win over intermediate elements and legally build a broad front against national betrayal, civil war, autocracy, espionage and terrorism on the basis of trying to struggle for the masses' immediate interests. In the struggle, the article says, it is necessary to be firm and brave, vigilant and cautious, and to protect our party and democratic progressive forces so as to make continued, increased efforts in developing the people's movement.

"Let the Whole Country Launch a Large-Scale Counterattack To Overthrow Chiang Kai-shek" is a report on the situation on which Comrade Zhou wrote at Shenquanbao, Jia County, in 1947 when he was fighting in northern Shaanxi. The article sums up the great victories in the self-defensive war during the past year or so and analyzes the favorable situation in which the People's Liberation Army was going to launch a nationwide counterattack after smashing Chiang Kai-shek's all-round attack and attacks on key points of the liberated areas. It expounds the strategic principle of annihilating Chiang Kai-shek's troops in the Chiang-ruled areas.

"The Work of Land Reform and Party Consolidation in the Old and Semi-Old Liberated Areas" and "The Telegram to the Central Bureau in Fuping on the Questions of Land Reform and Party Consolidation" set forth the principles and policies for the work of land reform and party consolidation in the old and semi-old liberated areas. The articles point out the need to take into consideration the specific conditions at different localities in determining whether [sic] the method of dividing land or making adjustments of land requirements of poor peasants and farm laborers, but also to take into account the interests of the middle peasants. Moreover, the articles say, land reform should be combined with the work of party consolidation, and in both cases it is necessary to pay attention to certain key aspects of the work and to expand its scale step by step and wave upon wave.

"New Democratic Economic Construction" is an outline written in June 1948. It points out that the essential criterion for distinguishing between the new democratic economy and the capitalist economy is to see whether the economy is led by the proletariat or by the bourgeoisie, whether it is for the interests of the majority or for the interests of a few people, and whether it is essentially a planned economy or an entirely liberalist economy. It says that the new democratic economic construction is also opposed to the principles of agrarian socialism and extreme egalitarianism. This is still of vital significance to our socialist construction today.

"Smash the Enemy's Plot of a Sham Peace Movement" exposes the reactionary nature of the United States and certain factions and individuals in the Kuomintang reactionary ruling clique in planning a sham peace movement to oppose Chiang and open up peace negotiations. It points out the necessity of distinguishing the anti-Chiang peace plot of those within the reactionary ruling clique from the demand for peace made by the people and the democratic persons; to translate the enemy's sham peace movement into the people's real peace movement; and to change the enemy's deceptive slogans into slogans for action of the masses; so as to push the people's revolutionary movement forward in coordination with the people's revolutionary war to win a nationwide victory.

"Report on the Question of Peace Negotiations" was a statement to some patriotic personages and some professors of the universities in Beijing. In view of the total collapse of the Kuomintang's rule, Chiang Kai-shek was forced to "retire from office." Acting President Li Zongren sent a delegation to Beijing for peace negotiations, and as a result of the negotiations, an agreement for domestic peace was drawn up. The article points out that even though victory was at hand, we still held the peace negotiations with the Kuomintang government so that our country would suffer less damage and preserve more manpower and materials for peaceful construction in the future. If the Kuomintang government in Nanjing refused to accept this domestic peace agreement, the article adds, we would fight and cross the Changjiang River.

"Learn From Mao Zedong" is an excerpt from a report made at the first All-China Youth Congress in May 1949. The article pointed out that Comrade Mao Zedong was a leader who had emerged from the masses in the course of a protracted revolutionary movement, and he should never be regarded as a chance leader, a born leader, a demigod or a leader impossible to emulate, and he should not be turned into a deity apart. Mao Zedong Thought took shape as a result of a process of historical development. Comrade Mao Zedong, by integrating the universal truth of Marxism-Leninism with the practice of the Chinese revolution, indicated the correct orientation for the Chinese people's revolutionary struggle. The article called on youth in the whole country to unite and advance under Mao Zedong's banner.

The "Political Report at the National Congress of Chinese Writers and Artists" pointed out that creative literature and art should depict the great People's Liberation Army of the great era; describe the outstanding achievements of the hundreds of millions of peasants overcoming extreme hardships and difficulties and fighting heroically; and take the working class, which is gradually becoming the major force in our country's construction, as the subject of literary and art creations. Literary and art workers are mental laborers and a part of the working class. The article also elaborated on questions of the unity of the ranks of literary and art workers, how literature and art should serve the people, popularizing and raising standards of literature and art, how to reform old literature and art, and so forth.

"The Characteristics of the Draft Common Program of the People's Political Consultative Conference" is an excerpt from the report at the first plenary session of the Chinese People's Political Consultative Conference on the eve of the birth of the People's Republic of China. The article expounded the nature of the political power of the People's Republic of China and its basic internal and external policies. It pointed out that the goal of the Chinese people's revolution against imperialism, feudalism and bureaucrat-capitalism is to build an independent, democratic, peaceful, unified, prosperous and powerful new China. Under the leadership of the working class, all classes and all nationalities must form the broadest united front and practice the people's democratic dictatorship. New China's system of political power is one of democratic centralism, the system of the People's Congress. In the structure of the five economic sectors of new democracy, the state-owned economy is the leading sector. The future of new China must develop toward socialism and communism.

The publication of the "Selected Works of Zhou Enlai" is of great significance for the whole party and the people of the whole country to study and do research on Marxism-Leninism-Mao Zedong Thought and the history of the Chinese revolution. If we cherish the memory of the esteemed and beloved Comrade Zhou Enlai, we must strive to learn from him and draw on the wisdom and strength of his works.

The "Selected Works of Zhou Enlai" assuredly will become a powerful ideological weapon for us to push forward our socialist modernization program.

Here some major figures connected with recent Chinese Communist history are clearly sorted out into the good leaders—Mao Zedong, Zhou Enlai, Liu Shaoqi, Zhu De, and Deng Xiaoping in particular, all referred to as comrade— and the bad, including the late security tsar Kang Sheng, who has been posthumously expelled from the Party, Nikita Khrushchev, Lin Biao, and the Gang of Four, all of whom were denied the appellation of comrade. This is clearly both Deng's personal view and the official interpretation.

Marxism must be combined with the specific features of various countries and it can be realized only through a certain national form. The Chinese people found the universal truth of Marxism after arduous struggles and after they had paid a high price. They combined it with the practice of the Chinese revolution and used it as their weapon in the struggle they launched. Mao Zedong Thought is the result of the practical struggles of the Chinese people and it has become the invaluable treasure of our party and our country. The ways in which Mao Zedong Thought is presented and its recognition by the whole party is the result of a protracted and tortuous process. We have compiled this material for study and for further reference for our comrades.

I. THE FORMULATION OF MAO ZEDONG THOUGHT AND THE WAYS IN WHICH IT WAS PRESENTED BEFORE AND AFTER THE "SEVENTH PARTY CONGRESS"

In his "Preface to 'Communists'" in October 1939, Comrade Mao Zedong put forth for the first time the formula of "combining the theory of Marxism and Leninism with the practice of the Chinese revolution."

During the party rectification movement in Yanan in 1942, Comrades Zhou Enlai, Liu Shaoqi and Zhu De pointed out in their articles and reports that Comrade Mao Zedong was a great revolutionary who combined the universal truth of Marxism with the practice of the Chinese revolution. Comrade Liu Shaoqi even put forth the concept of the "Thought of Comrade Mao Zedong."

In his article "Settle Accounts With Menshevist Ideology Within the Party" that was written to mark the 22d anniversary of the founding of the party, Comrade Liu Shaoqi said: "All cadres and party members must study hard the historical experiences of the Chinese Communist Party over

the past 22 years, must study hard the theory of Comrade Mao Zedong about the Chinese revolution and other aspects and must arm themselves with the thought of Comrade Mao Zedong and use the system of his thought in settling the account with the ideology of Menshevism within the party."

"The resolution on some historical questions" that was adopted by the seventh enlarged plenary session of the sixth party Central Committee in April 1945 pointed out: "The Chinese Communist Party has, since its founding in 1921, combined the universal truth of Marxism and Leninism with the practice of the Chinese revolution using it as the guide in all of its work. Comrade Mao Zedong's theory about and practice in the Chinese revolution represent this combination."

In his speech to the seventh national party congress in May 1945, Comrade Liu Shaoqi was the first to put forth the concept of "Mao Zedong Thought." He said: "Mao Zedong Thought is the continuous development of Marxism in the present era of the national democratic revolution in a colonial, semicolonial and semifeudal country. It is an excellent example of the nationalization of Marxism." The constitution of the party definitively states that "the Chinese Communist Party has Mao Zedong Thought—the thought of the unification of Marxist and Leninist theory with the practice of the Chinese revolution as the guide in all its work and in opposing any tendency of dogmatism and adventurism."

In January and February of 1947 Comrade Liu Shaoqi had talks in Yenan with American reporter Anna Louise Strong and she said: "Mao Zedong is great because he has turned European-style Marxism into Asian-style Marxism." "Not only has he interpreted various questions under new conditions with Marxism . . . he has also caused Marxism to make a new development. He has created a Chinese-style or Asian-style Marxism."

When the first national youth congress was convened on 7 May 1949, Comrade Zhou Enlai made a report entitled "Young People Throughout the Country Unite and Advance Under the Banner of Mao Zedong" and he said: "Chairman Mao has practiced in China the truth of the

["Some Ways in Which Mao Zedong Thought was Presented During the Past Forty Years," *Red Flag*, no. 2, 16 January 1981.]

world revolution—the universal truth of Marxism and combined it with the practice of the Chinese revolution to form Mao Zedong Thought." "The features of Mao Zedong Thought are to concretize universal truth and practice it on Chinese soil. Our young people must study this."

Comrade Mao Zedong himself did not regard Mao Zedong Thought as his personal ideology but as the collective wisdom of the party and the people. And when some comrades suggested changing Mao Zedong Thought into Mao Zedongism, he would say such suggestions were improper.

During the rectification movement in Yenan in 1942, the cadets of the party school under the party Central Committee discussed what was the thought of Comrade Mao Zedong who himself also expressed his own views on this question. He said, It is not my personal ideology; it has been written with the blood of hundreds of millions of martyrs and it is the collective wisdom of the party and the people. He said, my ideology is developing and I will also make mistakes. For example, when I write some articles, I rewrite them again and again. Why? Because there are mistakes in them.

In 1943 when Comrade Mao Zedong was 50, some comrades in the party suggested marking his birthday and disseminating Mao Zedong Thought. Comrade He Kaifeng, minister of propaganda of the party Central Committee conveyed their suggestion to Comrade Mao Zedong. On 22 April, Comrade Mao Zedong replied in a letter: "The consciousness of our ideology (Marxism) is not ripe yet and we must continue to study and not to brag about it. If we are to brag, we can do so about some aspects (for example, those that are included in rectification documents); we cannot brag about it as a system because my system is not ripe."

In August 1948, Comrade Wu Yuzhang was planning to use Mao Zedongism instead of Mao Zedong Thought in his speech on the inauguration of Huabei University and to call for "mainly studying Mao Zedongism." He sent a telegram to Comrade Mao Zedong for instruction and Comrade Mao Zedong replied in a telegram: "Such a presentation is very improper. There is neither Mao Zedongism nor 'mainly to study Mao Zedongism.' We must call on students to study the theories of Marx, Engels, Lenin and Stalin and the experiences of the Chinese revolution. Here [*sic*] the experiences of the Chinese communists (including Mao Zedong) based on the theories of Marx, Engels, Lenin and Stalin and the documents about the line and policies that have been defined by the party Central Committee."

II. THE WAYS OF PRESENTATION IN THE EARLY DAYS OF LIBERATION AND BEFORE AND AFTER THE EIGHTH PARTY CONGRESS

Since the early days after the founding of new China, our party has insisted on the ways in which Mao Zedong Thought was represented in the seventh party congress and stressed the importance of disseminating Mao Zedong Thought properly and modestly.

In his article "The World Significance of the Chinese Revolution" that was written in 1951 to mark the 30th anniversary of the party, Comrade Lu Dingyi, propaganda minister of the party Central Committee, said: "Mao Zedong

Thought is the combination of the universal truth of Marxism and Leninism with the practice of the Chinese revolution."

In 1954, Comrade Mao Zedong suggested: Do not use the concept of "Mao Zedong Thought" any longer so as to prevent misunderstanding. Therefore the Ministry of Propaganda of the party Central Committee issued a circular: "The party constitution has already explicitly pointed out that 'Mao Zedong Thought' is the 'unified ideology of the combination of Marxist and Leninist theory with the practice of the Chinese revolution' and its content is the same as Marxism and Leninism." "We suggest that in the future when comrades in the party are writing articles or making reports that they follow the instruction of Comrade Mao Zedong. But in explaining the party constitution and the past important documents and resolutions of the party they may do so according to the originals and it is not necessary to change them. But we must pay attention to explaining that 'Mao Zedong Thought' is Marxist and Leninist ideology so as to avoid misunderstanding in the content of the two. When it is necessary to mention Comrade Mao Zedong in writing articles or making reports, we suggest using 'Mao Zedong's works.' "

During the national conference on intellectuals in 1955, some comrade suggested changing Mao Zedong Thought to Mao Zedongism. But Comrade Mao Zedong disagreed and said: "Marxism is the trunk and we are the branches and leaves."

When preparations were under way for the eighth party congress in 1956, Comrade Mao Zedong once again suggested not using "Mao Zedong Thought" in official party documents. Consequently, the party constitution adopted by the eighth party congress did not use the concept of "Mao Zedong Thought." Instead, the concept was changed to "the Chinese Communist Party has taken Marxism and Leninism as the guide in its actions." "In carrying out activities, the party persists in the principle of combining the universal truth of Marxism and Leninism with the practice of the Chinese revolutionary struggles and opposes any tendency of dogmatism and adventurism."

III. THE WAYS OF PRESENTING BEFORE AND AFTER THE ENLARGED MEETING OF THE MILITARY COMMISSION OF THE PARTY CENTRAL COMMITTEE IN 1960

In the late 1950's, Khrushchev went all out to attack Mao Zedong Thought and there appeared an international anti-China adverse current. Internally, we were then launching a momentous struggle against the so-called "opportunism" and party and state political life became abnormal. Following the Lushan meeting, some leading members in the party Central Committee once again used the concept of "Mao Zedong Thought" in their articles and speeches. This situation was taken advantage of by Lin Biao and Kang Sheng to create confusion and they tried in every way to distort Mao Zedong Thought.

From September to October 1959, Lin Biao said with ulterior motives in the all-army meeting of senior cadres: "What is Marxism and Leninism today? It is the thought of our Chairman Mao. This thought now stands at the top of the world and at the peak of ideology of the present era." "How should we study Marxism and Leninism? I suggest that you comrades mainly study the works of Comrade Mao Zedong. It is a short cut way to studying Marxism and Leninism," "it reaps large profits from a small capital investment." In January 1961, Lin Biao ridiculously said in the "Instruction on Stepping Up Political and Ideological Work in the Army": "In studying Mao Zedong Thought we must achieve instant results." In September, he said: "In the study of Mao Zedong's works, we should not just read each of his articles, we must study them intensely." With ulterior motives, Lin Biao went further in early 1966 to make Mao Zedong Thought absolute when he said: "Mao Zedong Thought is the top of Marxism and Leninism of the present era, it is the highest and the liveliest Marxism and Leninism." "Chairman Mao's words are of highest standards with highest prestige and strongest power. Each of his sentences represent truth and one of his words is the equivalent of ten thousand words."

Kang Sheng also played a sinister role when Lin Biao was distorting Mao Zedong Thought. In summer of 1958, Kang Shang said in his report to the conference of political teachers in Beijing that "Mao Zedong Thought is the top of Marxism." On 2 December 1959 he once again said in a meeting of cadres that "Mao Zedong Thought is Marxism and Leninism of the era in which the world has been divided into the two big camps of imperialism and socialism, and socialist revolution and socialist construction have developed into a new historical era." Later he again said in a meeting that "Mao Zedong Thought is the highest and last standard of Marxism."

During this period, some party leading comrades and some comrades from the Ministry of Propaganda of the party Central Committee countered the fallacies of Lin Biao and Kang Sheng and expressed their views as how to disseminate Mao Zedong Thought in a correct way and they said "not to put Mao Zedong Thought side by side with Marxism and Leninism," "not to regard Mao Zedong's works and speeches as dogma," "not to oversimplify and vulgarize."

In 1961, Comrade Mao Zedong aired his views. He opposed putting Mao Zedong Thought side by side with Marxism and Leninism and he defined the formulation for newspaper propaganda: It is all right to say to study Mao Zedong Thought independently. But if it is mentioned together with Marxism and Leninism, we must say to study Marxism and Leninism and the works of Comrade Mao Zedong and not to say to study Marxism and Leninism and Mao Zedong Thought.

On 15 November 1963, Comrade Zhou Enlai explicitly said when he referred to the experiences and problems of socialist construction in his speech "International and Internal Situations and our Tasks" to the supreme state conference: "Experience can be gained only through our own practice." "Mao Zedong Thought has emerged and has been established in the process of persisting in what is correct and correcting what is wrong, and this should be followed in our construction."

On 30 September 1964 Comrade Liu Shaoqi said when he replied to a letter from Comrade Jiang Weiqing: "Our principle is to learn from all the people who hold truth. We should just not learn from those in high positions." "We cannot regard the theory of Marxism and Leninism as dogma. Also we cannot regard Mao Zedong's works and speeches as dogma. You must use the spiritual essence of Mao Zedong Thought to analyze the actual conditions in your place, correctly sum up your practical experiences and correctly define the principle, planning and measures for future work." Having read Comrade Liu Shaoqi's letter, Comrade Mao Zedong attached this comment to it: I have read your letter and I think it is excellent.

In 1960, a leading member of the Ministry of Propaganda of the party Central Committee pointed out in a meeting: We must not say that Mao Zedong Thought is the "top" of Marxism and Leninism. In drafting its own restricted document, the ministry itself regarded the above-mentioned concept as wrong. The document "investigation report on some problems in disseminating Mao Zedong Thought and revolutionary deeds of leaders" that was worked out by the ministry and issued by the party Central Committee on 15 March 1961 explicitly pointed out: "In disseminating Mao Zedong Thought there has been oversimplification and vulgarization. In some articles, certain scientific and technical innovations, inventions and discoveries have been simply, forcibly and directly linked with Mao Zedong Thought or they have been said to be the results of Mao Zedong Thought." In October 1961, a leading member of the ministry once again said: There is another new label now, it is called "Mao Zedong Thought" and is used everywhere. It seems that anything that has been attached with this label is Mao Zedong Thought. He also said: Do not oversimplify the thinking of the generation of young people and make it absolute. Do not make them believe in anything that is labeled with "Mao Zedong Thought." He said, what is the good of bringing up young people in a way which makes them lie, to have a rigid way of thinking and to talk big without carrying out investigations and studies. In June 1964, a leading member of the Ministry again said: Those who have studied well have spent several years; there is no "instant result" in the study.

IV. THE WAYS OF PRESENTATION DURING THE 10 TURBULENT YEARS

In order to seize party and political power during the "Great Cultural Revolution," Lin Biao, the "gang of four" and Kang Sheng went all out to indulge in the personality cult and wracked their brains to distort Mao Zedong Thought in an attempt to turn Mao Zedong Thought into a religious doctrine.

On 18 May 1966, Lin Biao said in the enlarged meeting of the Political Bureau of the party Central Committee: "Chairman Mao has inherited, defended and developed Marxism and Leninism in a talented and creative way and developed it into a new stage. Mao Zedong Thought is Marxism and Leninism of the era in which imperialism is heading for total collapse and socialism is advancing for worldwide victory." This concept was later inserted by Chang Chunqiao into the preface of the second edition of the "Quotations From Chairman Mao Zedong" which was compiled by Lin Biao.

In August 1966, Lin Biao said during the work conference of the party Central Committee: "Chairman Mao is the axis and we are the grinder; we will do everything according to the thought of Chairman Mao." "We must resolutely carry out the instructions of Chairman Mao whether we understand these instructions or not." On 18 September 1966, he said: "A genius like Chairman Mao occurs only once in several hundred years in the world and several thousand years in China. Chairman Mao is the greatest genius in the world." "The books written by Marx and Engels are too many for us to read and they were too far from us. In reading the classic works of Marxism and Leninism, we must study 99 percent of the works of Chairman Mao because his works are revolutionary teaching books."

On 10 August 1966, Kang Sheng said in a group meeting during the 11th plenary session of the 8th party Central Committee: "I said in the enlarged meeting of the Political Bureau in May this year that accurately speaking Mao Zedong Thought should be Mao Zedongism." On 19 January 1967, he said in talks with foreign guests: "Mao Zedong Thought has become the banner of the international communist movement of the present era." Later he said: "It has become the line of demarcation and 'watershed' between Marxism and revisionism whether to agree or oppose the Chinese Great Cultural Revolution and whether to agree or oppose Mao Zedong Thought."

On 18 May 1967, an article "A Great Historical Document" that was jointly compiled by the editorial boards of *Hongqi* and *Renmin Ribao* pointed out: "Marx and Engels established the theory of the scientific socialism and Lenin and Stalin developed Marxism and solved a series of problems of the proletarian revolution in the era of imperialism as well as the theory and practice of how the dictatorship of the proletariat is realized in a country; Comrade Mao Zedong has developed Marxism and Leninism and solved a series of problems of the proletarian revolution of the present era as well as solved the theory and practice of how to carry out the revolution under the dictatorship of the proletariat and to prevent the restoration of capitalism. These are the three great milestones in the historical development of Marxism."

During this period, Comrade Mao Zedong had criticized Lin Biao, the "gang of four" and Kang Sheng and denied some of their conceptions. On 25 July 1966, Comrade Mao Zedong wrote on a document: "In the future, please do not use the words like 'the highest and the most living . . . ,' 'top,' and the 'highest instructions.'" With regard to Lin Biao's words of the "absolute authority of Mao Zedong Thought," Comrade Mao Zedong once said in a written instruction: "The wording of absolute authority is not correct." "The wording of establishing in an extraordinary big way is also not correct. Authority and prestige can naturally only be established in the practice of struggles and not artificially. The prestige that is established artificially will naturally collapse." With regard to the concept that was put forth by Lin Biao in his speech on 18 May 1966 and was later widely spread in the preface of the second edition of the "Quotations From Chairman Mao Zedong," Comrade Mao Zedong said: "We are still in the era of imperialism and proletarian revolution." He asked that it be changed and he himself deleted the phrase "in a talented way." With regard to foreign propaganda, Comrade Mao Zedong stressed that whether a party in another country is good or bad must not be judged from whether or not this party accepts Mao Zedong Thought, this should not be the standard. He also said that in our contact with other parties from various countries, we can only and must persist in this concept: the combination of the universal truth of Marxism and Leninism with the revolutionary practice of those countries.

V. THE PRESENTATION AFTER THE DOWNFALL OF THE "GANG OF FOUR"

Following the downfall of the "gang of four," our party has gradually corrected Mao Zedong Thought that had been distorted by Lin Biao, the "gang of four" and Kang Sheng and criticized their poisonous influence. But the struggle has always existed around the question of how to correctly deal with Mao Zedong Thought.

On 7 February 1977, the editorial "Study Well Documents and Grasp the Key" that was jointly compiled by *Renmin Ribao*, *Hongqi* and *Jiefangjun Bao* put forth the two "whatevers": "we resolutely support whatever policies made by Chairman Mao; we resolutely follow whatever directives made by Chairman Mao."

On 10 April 1977, Comrade Deng Xiaoping wrote a letter to the party Central Committee and he said with regard to the two "whatevers": "We must, for generations to come, guide our whole party, whole army and whole people with accurate and complete Mao Zedong Thought so as to victoriously push ahead the cause of the party and socialism as well as the cause of the international communist movement."

On 2 June 1978, Comrade Deng Xiaoping said at the all-army political work conference: "Many comrades in our party have persisted in studying Marxism and Leninism and Mao Zedong Thought and have persisted in the principle of combining the universal truth of Marxism and Leninism with the practice of the revolution. This is a good attitude that we must continue to develop. But there are other comrades who are talking about Mao Zedong Thought every day but they often forget or have even discarded the basic Marxist and Leninist viewpoint and method of Chairman Mao: Proceed from reality and combine theory with practice. Furthermore, some people have gone even further as to regard those who persist in proceeding from reality and in combining theory with practice as having committed a heinous crime."

On 22 December 1978, the 3d plenary session of the 11th party Central Committee pointed out: "The lofty task of the party Central Committee in theoretical line is to guide and educate the whole party and the whole people to understand historically and scientifically the great contributions of Comrade Mao Zedong and completely and accurately grasp the scientific system of Mao Zedong Thought so as to combine the universal truth of Marxism and Leninism and Mao Zedong Thought with the practice of the socialist modernization construction and develop them under the new historical conditions."

In September 1979, the 4th plenary session of the 11th party Central Committee adopted the following words of Comrade Ye Jianying in his "Speech at the Rally To Mark the 30th Anniversary of the Founding of the People's Republic of China": "The victory of the Chinese revolution is the victory of Marxism and Leninism and Mao Zedong Thought. Marxism and Leninism is constantly developing in the revolutionary struggles of the people of various countries and no one is able in any form to monopolize and transfix it. Mao Zedong Thought is the practice and development of Marxism in the Chinese revolution. It is the fruit of combining the universal truth of Marxism and Leninism with the practice of the Chinese revolution." "The Chinese communists and Chinese people have termed the development of Marxism in the Chinese revolution as Mao Zedong Thought and that without Mao Zedong Thought there would have been no new China. This understanding completely accords with history. Of course, Mao Zedong Thought is not only the fruit of the wisdom of Comrade Mao Zedong himself, it is also the fruit of the wisdom of his comrades in arms, the party and the people. He himself said that it has emerged 'during the collective struggles by the party and the people.' Mao Zedong Thought is the crystallization of the experiences of the Chinese revolution and the experiences of the new social construction over the past half a century. It is the crystallization of the collective wisdom of the Chinese Communist Party. Comrade Mao Zedong was the most outstanding representative of the great Chinese Communist Party and the great Chinese people."

On 29 February 1980, Comrade Deng Xiaoping pointed out in the 5th plenary session of the 11th party Central Committee: The discussions on the question of the criterion of truth are directed against the two "whatevers," with connotation that Marxism and Leninism and Mao Zedong Thought must not be treated as dogma. The formulation of the third plenary session is to study new situations and solve new problems. We said last year that the discussion of this question in various places must be combined with their actual conditions so as to solve problems. That is to say in upholding the ideological line of the party, we must also look forward.

From 21 to 23 August 1980, Comrade Deng Xiaoping answered the questions put to him by Italian reporter Oriana Fallaci and said: "The greatest contribution of Chairman Mao is that he combined the principle of Marxism and Leninism with the actual conditions of the Chinese revolution and pointed out the road to victory for the Chinese revolution. It is right to say that before the 1960's or before the end of the 1950's, much of his ideology brought great achievements to us and some of the basic principles formulated by him are no doubt correct. He creatively used Marxism and Leninism in various aspects of the Chinese revolution that included philosophy, politics, military, culture and arts and other sectors with creative viewpoints. But unfortunately, in the latter period of his life and particularly during the 'Great Cultural Revolution,' he made mistakes and, these were not minor mistakes, that have brought many misfortunes to our party, state and people. You know that when we were in Yanan, our party summarized the ideology of Chairman Mao in various aspects into Mao Zedong Thought and we used it as the guiding ideology of our party. It is because we followed this road that we finally won the great victory of the revolution. Of course, Mao Zedong Thought is not the creation of only Comrade Mao Zedong; the older generation of the revolutionaries had their share in establishing and developing Mao Zedong Thought. But in the main, it is the thought of Comrade Mao Zedong. But because of these achievements, he became less prudent and in his later years there gradually appeared some unhealthy factors and unhealthy thinking, mainly 'leftist' thinking. Quite a considerable part of this thinking ran counter to his original thinking and to his correct advocations that were originally very good, including his own style of work." "We will continue to persist in Mao Zedong Thought. Mao Zedong Thought represents the correct part in the life of Chairman Mao. Mao Zedong Thought led us to win victory in our revolution in the past. It remains the invaluable treasure of the Chinese party and state now and in the future."

In his speech to the work conference of the party Central Committee on 25 December 1980, Comrade Deng Xiaoping said: "Mao Zedong Thought that has been proven correct in the tests of practice is still our guiding ideology which we must persist in and develop by combining it with reality. With self-confidence, we must disseminate it and there will be no slowing down in doing this."

An Appraisal of Mao Zedong by a General He Purged, 10 April 1981

16

Huang Kecheng had been chief of staff of the People's Liberation Army under Defense Minister Peng Dehuai until they were both purged by Mao in the summer of 1959. This article, originally a speech, clearly foreshadows the more authoritative verdict on Mao to be promulgated by the Party Central Committee in 1981: Mao was a great revolutionary statesman until 1949. After that, although still a constructive figure of major importance, he espoused his own brand of authoritarian radicalism and committed some serious mistakes, the most significant of which was the Cultural Revolution, which is referred to here only in passing.

How to understand and appraise Chairman Mao, or how to treat Mao Zedong Thought is a fundamental question of our party and our state. Comrade Deng Xiaoping has expressed principled views in regard to the question on behalf of the party Central Committee. Comrade Deng Xiaoping has said on numerous occasions that in the context of the history of our party and the state, Chairman Mao's merits are primary and his mistakes are secondary. Comrade Deng Xiaoping also said: Chairman Mao "saved the party and the state from crises. Without Chairman Mao, the Chinese people would have had to grope in the dark for an even longer period of time." With regard to the mistakes Chairman Mao made in his old age, Comrade Deng Xiaoping said: We cannot attribute all past mistakes to Chairman Mao alone, as we of the older generation are equally responsible. We must continue to uphold Mao Zedong Thought from now on. I fully agree with all these principled remarks made by Comrade Deng Xiaoping on behalf of the party Central Committee. I am of the opinion that all communists should appraise Chairman Mao and take an attitude toward Mao Zedong Thought in this spirit.

Some comrades recently have taken a radical attitude toward this question. Some individuals have even wantonly vilified Mao Zedong Thought and defamed Comrade Mao Zedong. I have been extremely concerned over such attitudes. As a veteran Communist Party member, I am obliged to express my views. To help you understand Comrade Deng Xiaoping's principled views, I wish to first discuss history.

Chairman Mao Performed Immortal Deeds for the Party and the People in the Period of Red Army Building

During the period of Chen Duxiu's right-leaning opportunism the peasants in Hunan rose to revolution. At that time the majority of the party Central Committee leaders and public opinion above middle social stratum opposed the peasant movement in Hunan. For instance, Tan Ping-shan and others, who had gone to Hunan to solve the peasants' problem, unduly criticized the peasant movement, as did Chen Duxiu. Only a handful of people stood fast on the revolutionary stand in supporting the peasant movement. Moreover only Chairman Mao conducted an on-the-spot investigation and then wrote the "Report on an Investigation of the Peasant Movement in Hunan," which warmly praised the peasant movement in Hunan, regarded the attitude toward the movement as a principled issue and repudiated various criticisms of the movement. In this way Chairman Mao enabled many revolutionary Communist Party members to arm their minds on this major question. The report indeed played an important role at that time.

After the failure of the major revolution the party Central Committee at the "7 August" conference put forward the general policy on waging armed resistance against the Kuomintang reactionaries and carrying out land revolution and decided to incite armed rebellions in Hunan, Hubei, Guangdong and Jiangxi. Chairman Mao was sent to Hunan to start rebellion in the Liuyang and Pingjiang areas during the autumn harvest and originally planned to attack Changsha. During the rebellion a former guard regiment of the nationalist government in Wuhan joined us.

Regiment Commander Lu Deming was a very good comrade of our party. After passing through various places he led the regiment to the Xiushui area and made contact with Chairman Mao. Luo Ronghuan and other comrades also organized small contingents and led the peasant riots in Chongyang and Tongcheng. In addition there were the peasant volunteer army in Pingjiang and Liuyang, a workers' self-defense force in Pingjiang and Anyuan and an insurrectionary army in Liling. Chairman Mao assembled all these troops and organized the uprising in Pingjiang, Liuyang and Liling during the autumn harvest. But the plan to attack Changsha did not materialize. Realizing that the Pingjiang and Liuyang areas were too close to Changsha and that it would be difficult for a large number of troops

[New China News Agency, 10 April 1981.]

to be stationed there for a long period of time, Chairman Mao decided to give up the plan to seize the city center and to start the march toward Jinggangshan. This was a great strategic policy decision.

During the well-known reorganization of troops in Sanwan, Chairman Mao set up party organizations at all levels of the army. After arriving in Jinggangshan Chairman Mao put forward the program to found the revolutionary regime in the central section of the Luoxiao Mountain Range and to raise the red flag in Jinggangshan. During the autumn harvest uprising, rebellions also took place in Hubei's Huangma, Jiangxi, western Hunan and Jiangxi and many other places. But due to a lack of experience most rebellions were suppressed by the enemy. In some places weapons were buried. The armed force that openly upheld the red flag without defeat consisted mainly of troops led by Chairman Mao and a small section led by Comrade Fang Zhimin in northwestern Jiangxi.

The raising of the red flag in Jianggangshan had an important meaning. It represented the direction and hope of the Chinese revolution. The fact that this armed force was able to hold its ground greatly encouraged many communists and enhanced their revolutionary confidence, frustrated under the perilous situation arising from the failure of the great revolution.

The 1 August Nanchang uprising led by Zhou Enlai, He Long, Ye Ting, Zhu De, Liu Bocheng and other comrades was the beginning of the revolutionary war independently led by our party and had very important meaning. Some 30,000 people who took part in the Nanchang rebellion were later defeated and almost annihilated at Tangkeng and Sanheba. Comrades Zhu De and Chen Yi assembled the remaining 800–900 soldiers and officers to set up a new regiment and later carried out the rebellion in southern Hunan, thereby expanding the armed forces and gaining more troops than Chairman Mao. However, without the red flag raised by Chairman Mao in Jinggangshan and his correct political and military line, it would have been very difficult for the troops led by Comrades Zhu De and Chen Yi to persevere.

Peng Dehuai, Teng Daiyuan, Huang Gonglue and other comrades heroically led the rebellion in Pingjiang. After the rebellion Huang Gonglue and a few other comrades were ordered to stay in Pingjiang to lead a small armed force to continue the struggle in Pingjiang and Liuyang while comrades Peng Dehuai and Teng Daiyuan led the main force to Jinggangshan. After they learned in Jinggangshan the whole set of things by Chairman Mao, namely, founding the revolutionary regime, the revolutionary base, the party and the army, they returned to the Pingjiang and Liuyang areas to develop the Hunan-Hubei-Jiangxi revolutionary base.

After the failure of the rebellion in Guangzhou, which was led by Zhang Tailei, Su Shaozheng, Ye Ting, Ye Jianying and other comrades, Comrades Yuan Guoping, Ye Xiao and Lu Gengfu took the remaining troops to Hailufeng. Retaining party organizations, this group was a high-quality force, which consisted of many Communist Party members and mostly students with high educational level, political consciousness and military and technical proficiency, and was better than the two forces led by Chairman Mao and Comrade Zhu De. Comrade Peng Pai, who led the struggle in Hailufeng, was an outstanding comrade. The soviet system set up in Hailufeng had a good revolutionary base and mass foundations.

But because of the lack of correct military and political line, plus the influence of pessimism within the party caused by the dismissal of personnel from other parts of the country from the soviet base, this good regime, with the support of such high-quality troops, failed. How could the force led by Chairman Mao, which was smaller in strength than those taking part in the Nanchang and the Guangzhou rebellions, which traversed twists and turns and suffered losses too, survive in Jinggangshan by itself ahead of other forces? It was because at the crucial moment after the failure of the great revolution, Chairman Mao alone could correctly solve in theory and practice the key questions concerning whether and how the Red Army and the Red regime could survive and develop. Major progress achieved by the Red Army in the Hubei-Henan-Anhui and Hunan-western Hubei areas later was also inseparable from the influence of the red flag in Jinggangshan.

The whole set of political and military line, principles and policies created by Chairman Mao at that time looks simple today. But without experience at that time it was very difficult to formulate a whole set of correct elements. This had never been achieved by the party Central Committee at that time, including before and after the sixth national party congress. Chairman Mao was indeed several times wiser than we were.

Let me give another example. After I arrived in Jinggangshan, Chairman Mao suggested that the army issue no pay and practice the supply system [of providing working personnel and their dependents with the primary necessities of life] instead. I wondered if the system could work. It would be no problem for conscientious Communist Party members. But how about the fighters? Issuing pay to officers and soldiers was a regular practice of the army of old times. For example, a major of the national revolutionary army during the northern expedition received a monthly pay of over $100 silver. Would the army accept the system? I doubted it. But the system worked. The system could work so long as the cadres took the lead and officers and soldiers acted in unison. At the beginning in Jinggangshan, we had a smaller army and more chances to raid local despots and thus were able to issue a monthly pay of $3 per person. A month or two later, we had fewer financial sources, as local despots were almost gone, and thus issued a monthly pay of $1, later 50 cents, to each person. Later on we could not even issue the 50 cent monthly pay. Each person was given only 5 cents in allowance for food, including edible oil, salt, soy sauce and vinegar. Under such difficult conditions, the army did not dissolve, but only became stronger and stronger in the course of fighting and finally developed into a new-type people's army. The supply system was difficult to implement and no one else would have suggested it.

In short, Chairman Mao performed immortal deeds for the party and the people of our country during the perilous historical turning point after the failure of the great revolution. Obviously without his arduous and far-sighted struggle and the red flag of Jinggangshan raised under his leadership, the Chinese revolution would have been unimaginable. Who else made a greater contribution or performed more meritorious deeds than Chairman Mao during this historical period? If anyone insists that some other people were wiser or contributed more, it would be a mockery to history.

Thanks Primarily to Chairman Mao's Correct Decision, the Red Army Was Able To Smash the Enemy's First, Second and Third Encirclement and Suppression

In February 1929 the party Central Committee in Shanghai instructed Zhu De and Chairman Mao to leave the army for Shanghai and organize the troops into company and platoon units so as to scatter the army and reduce the target of enemy attack. The revolution was at its low ebb at that time. Chairman Mao replied to the party Central Committee: We cannot afford to leave the army because the army will dissolve in our absence. If you insist that we go, please send Comrades Yun Daiying and Liu Bocheng to act on our behalf. Later on the situation changed as a result of the outbreak of the war among warlords.

"There is a sudden change in the situation; the warlords have renewed the war. . . ." was a poem written by Chairman Mao at that time. Had Chairman Mao not adhered to his correct stand at this crucial moment, it would be hard to predict the fate of the army.

An argument concerning some major issues of principle took place within the party in 1929 when the main force of the Red Army was in western Fujian. Although I did not take part in the argument, I discussed it in detail with Comrades Luo Ronghuan and Chen Yi. The result of heated debates during the argument showed that the majority of people disagreed with Chairman Mao. He was relieved of the post of secretary of the frontline party committee and had to rest at home. Later Chairman Mao was invited to rejoin the army because the fighting had not been successful. The ninth party congress of the 4th Army of the Red Army was convened. The resolution of the Gutian conference, which was drafted by Chairman Mao, was adopted at the congress. The main portion of the resolution was the article "On Correcting Mistaken Ideas in the Party" in the "Selected Works of Mao Zedong." The resolution solved many key issues concerning the ideology and line in the party. Correct policy decisions made by Chairman Mao on many issues concerning life or death of our party and the army played a great role in the building of the party and the army. The allegation that the Gutian conference was not led by Chairman Mao is not historical fact. It is not right to say that Chairman Mao never did anything correct or to attribute all mistakes to him whenever a mistake made by him is mentioned.

In 1930 Li Lisan's line emerged. He wanted to concentrate the Red Army's main force to seize Wuhan. At that time the Red Army was in very good shape. It controlled more than 10 counties in Jiangxi and all of western Jiangxi. Many comrades suggested that Nanchang should be taken first and then Wuhan. At the time an important decision was needed. Chairman Mao keenly sensed indications of a change in the situation. He determined that the war among the warlords was going to end soon and that Chiang Kai-shek would concentrate his forces to attack the Red Army. At that time only Chairman Mao realized that. Through Comrade Zhou Yili he persuaded the 3d Army of the Red Army not to risk an attack on Nanchang, to swiftly return to its old base by crossing the Ganjiang River in the east and to attack the enemy only after the enemy attacked

first. After more than a month's argument and persuasion, leading comrades of the 3d Army of the Red Army withdrew the troops to the old base. At that time our intelligence work was poorly done and Chairman Mao made his analysis on the Kuomintang offensive by reading newspapers. That was yet another major policy decision. Thanks to that correct decision, the Red Army was able to smash the enemy's first, second and third "encirclement and suppression." If we had not returned to the soviet area and instead fought the enemy in the area under its control, the result would be hard to tell and we would probably have suffered grave losses.

In 1931 the Red Army in Jiangxi used Chairman Mao's tactic of luring the enemy deep into our territory and then smashed Chiang Kai-shek's first "encirclement and suppression." The party Central Committee then dispatched Xiang Ying and other comrades to the soviet area to set up the Central Bureau with the Military Commission under it. Comrade Xiang Ying assumed the post of secretary of the Central Bureau and concurrently served as chairman of the Military Commission. He dissolved the frontline party committee of the 1st Army, of which Chairman Mao was the secretary. Immediately afterward the enemy's second "encirclement and suppression" occurred. Chiang Kai-shek consolidated his position by advancing gradually and entrenching his troops at every step. Having no combat experience, Xiang Ying and other comrades wanted to flee and order the army to leave the soviet area with them. At first only Chairman Mao opposed fleeing and leaving the soviet area. He favored fighting the enemy on the spot. After debates for more than a month, no conclusion was reached although he gained more supporters. But the enemy had already arrived at the mountains between Futian and Donggu in Jiangxi and they were building fortresses there.

The situation was pressing. Chairman Mao decisively ordered an attack on the enemy, annihilating several enemy divisions at one stroke. In his poem to the tune of "Yu Jia Ao" he said: "In 15 days we have marched 700 li crossing misty Gan waters and green Fujian hills, rolling back the enemy as we would a mat." This was the situation at that time. If the method advocated by Xiang Ying and other comrades had been followed, it would have been a disaster—the revolutionary base would have been lost and the Red Army would have been in a predicament. It is an obvious historical fact that Chairman Mao's decision was wiser than others'. He never mentioned this part of the history, nor did other comrades. Therefore many comrades do not know about this. When the third "encirclement and suppression" occurred, there was no argument. Everyone listened to Chairman Mao, whose prestige had been greatly enhanced because of the previous two "encirclement and suppression" campaigns.

Rejecting Chairman Mao's Leadership, the Revolution Suffered Great Losses

The "18 September incident" of 1931 took place following the smashing of the third "encirclement and suppression." The majority of the comrades on the party Central Committee went to the central soviet area from Shanghai and set up the Central Bureau to lead the struggle in the central soviet area. The situation at that time was very good. On the one hand, after smashing the third "encirclement and suppression," Chairman Mao used the main force of the Red Army for the struggle to consolidate the base area, and attacked many fortified villages in the next 2 to 3 months and wiped out most strongholds of white terror in the base area. This brought about an excellent situation in the central soviet area.

On the other hand, after the outbreak of the "28 January" war in Shanghai in 1932, Chiang Kai-shek was beset with difficulties both at home and abroad because he had to cope with the Japanese and to deal with various groups of forces in his camp. It was a pity that a debate then occurred within our party: The strategic principles set forth by Chairman Mao called for keeping a part of the Red Army in the soviet area and using its main force to get through and establish contact with the forces of the Red Army in northeast Jiangxi in order to develop forces in the Fujian-Zhejiang-Jiangxi region, and the slogan Chairman Mao raised was to support the 19th Route Army of the Kuomintang in the war of resistance against Japanese aggression. However, comrades of the provisional party Central Committee and the Central Bureau in Shanghai did not agree to this correct view. Because Wang Ming's left-deviationist line held the dominant position in the party Central Committee, Chairman Mao was pushed out again. But Chairman Mao's military thinking and strategic principles had already produced a profound influence on the Red Army. Under the command of Comrades Zhou Enlai and Zhu De, the Red Army was victorious in the fourth "encirclement and suppression." The provisional party Central Committee with Bo Gu as its secretary also moved to the central soviet area in 1933. Later the Communist International sent Li De to the central soviet area to take command of the army. By that time Wang Ming's left-deviationist opportunist line was in complete control of the Red Army. They changed Chairman Mao's correct principles of leadership and military direction. As a result the whole soviet area was lost.

Then the Central Red Army was forced to undertake the Long March. Before setting out, it was 80,000 strong. It had only 20,000 members left when it crossed the marshlands and only several thousand were left when it reached northern Shaanxi. Tens of thousands of troops remained in the central soviet area, but they were finally reduced to only a very small number of troops under the command of Chen Yi, Xiang Ying and other comrades. Comrades can see from this that we built a large soviet area under Chairman Mao's leadership, but the revolution suffered great losses once his leadership was absent. For several years after being pushed out in 1932, Chairman Mao could only make some investigation and study, read some books, practice calligraphy and write poems. He served as chairman of the soviet in name only. In his own words, he "had no say at all." His poems, such as "Dabodi" and "Huichang" were written during that period.

Chairman Mao Saved the Revolution From Crises and Led the Chinese Revolution From Victory to Victory

The Long March had begun. After the Red Army suffered serious losses in battles in Guangxi, approximately around the Liping meeting held in Guizhou, Chairman Mao began to ask a number of comrades of the central authorities to study issues with regard to our party leadership and military guidelines. At the Zunyi meeting, his policy decision

was once again very wise. I personally heard from Chairman Mao at the 3d Army Group about the situation in the Zunyi meeting. At that time, I was not very satisfied with the meeting on the basis of what I heard, because Comrade Zhang Wentian (Luofu) assumed the post of secretary general, although this meeting reorganized the leadership of the central authorities and reaffirmed Chairman Mao's leading position at the central level. The meeting only criticized the mistakes of the military line without criticizing the mistakes of the political line. At that time I thought that what the meeting did was not enough. Only half a year passed before I gave up my original views and realized that by only criticizing mistakes in military command without mentioning the political line at that time, not too many comrades were subject to criticism. This was conducive to unity. At that time only Bo Gu was relieved from his post as secretary general, and Li De relieved from the military command, while other comrades of the Political Bureau of the CCP Central Committee retained their leading posts. Comrade Bo Gu was also retained in the Political Bureau. Particularly during the time of the struggle against Zhang Guotao I was even more conscious that this policy decision made by Chairman Mao was absolutely correct. If the issue of the political line was brought up at the Zunyi meeting, more leading comrades would be subject to criticism. That would be harmful to the revolutionary cause. At that time the military struggle constituted the key issue of life and death to the revolution. The Red Army was also in a desperate predicament. This policy decision made by Chairman Mao was conducive not only to concentrating efforts in tackling military issues, but also to safeguarding the party's unity. Thus the Political Bureau was basically united at the time of our struggle against Zhang Guotao's warlordism, flightism and splittism.

The struggle against Zhang Guotao was another major issue of life and death for the Chinese revolution. When the 1st and 4th Front Armies joined forces at Maogong in northwest Sichuan, the 4th Front Army had more than 80,000 men. Considering himself as powerful with many men and guns, Zhang Guotao sought to force the central authorities to implement his line and even intended to murder Chairman Mao and Comrades Zhang Wentian and Zhou Enlai. Had Chairman Mao followed Zhang Guotao's line and gone to Xikang instead of firmly opposing Zhang Guotao's flightism and resolutely leading the 1st and 3d Army Groups and other units to go north and arrive in northern Shaanxi, the Red Army would have been faced with the risk of being completely wiped out.

After fighting bitterly in the Xikang area for more than a year, the 80,000 men of the 4th Front Army plus a portion of the 1st Front Army were reduced to 30,000. Owing to the joint struggle waged by Zhu De, Ren Bishi, He Long, Xu Xiangqian and other comrades as well as many comrades of the 4th Front Army, Zhang Guotao was forced to agree to go north. In the course of pressing north, he again went on a westward expedition. As a result another 20,000 men were lost. Ultimately, only some 10,000 men of the 4th Front Army arrived in northern Shaanxi.

The Xian incident at the end of 1936 successfully realized the guideline of achieving a peaceful solution and laid the foundation for the establishment of the anti-Japanese National United Front, with the Kuomintang and the communists cooperating with each other for the second time. This was a wise policy decision of historical significance made by the party Central Committee with Chairman Mao at its head.

In developing the United Front together with the Kuomintang during the war of resistance against Japanese aggression, the Communist International had a difference of views with our party's Central Committee. It wanted us to "do everything through the United Front and subordinate ourselves to the United Front in everything." Chairman Mao objected to doing things in such a manner, but he did not criticize the Communist International. He only criticized Wang Ming. Thus he adhered to our united front policy of maintaining independence and keeping the initiative in our own hands, while fostering unity with the Communist International. During that period he made a series of policy decisions on how to independently carry out guerrilla warfare and to go behind enemy lines to open up anti-Japanese base areas and do other things. Our party and army developed greatly under the leadership of Chairman Mao's correct line. Xiang Ying and other comrades refused to carry out Chairman Mao's directive ordering them to boldly drive into the areas behind enemy lines. In 1941, when they led troops north under the strict supervision of the central authorities, they once again changed without authorization the line formulated by the central authorities, to cross the river and drive northward, thus suffering the disastrous south Anhui incident. On the contrary, Comrade Chen Yi implemented Chairman Mao's directive and crossed the river to go north after leading a part of the new 4th Army to drive eastward into the areas behind enemy lines south of the Yangtze River between April and May 1938. His army grew rapidly.

After the conclusion of the war against Japanese aggression, Stalin asked our party to surrender its armed forces, reorganize them into the national defense army, and form a coalition government with the Kuomintang in exchange for our party's "legal" status. Despite the fact he went to Chongqing, Chairman Mao remained adamant in adhering to the policy of "giving tit for tat" and "not surrendering a single gun." Chairman Mao not only guided the war of liberation with correct strategic and tactical principles, but also personally took command of all major decisive battles. In less than 4 years, he had wiped out the Kuomintang reactionaries' army of 8 million, liberated the vast motherland, and established the People's Republic of China.

All the policy decisions made by our party during the early stage after the nationwide liberation under the leadership of Chairman Mao, such as land reform, aiding Korea against U.S. aggression, the realization of three major transformations, the development of socialist revolution and socialist construction and so on, are wise and correct. I will not talk about these policy decisions in detail since many comrades are familiar with this.

Chairman Mao's contributions to the Chinese Revolution have far exceeded what I mentioned here. I mention these historical facts, as I intend to specifically illustrate that what Comrade Deng Xiaoping said, namely, "Without Chairman Mao, the Chinese people would have had to grope in the dark for an even longer period of time," is definitely not an eulogistic remark, but a just and scientific conclusion to the historical fact. Making such remarks, he had no intention of praising Chairman Mao as our savior. Nor did he try to negate the merits of other revolutionaries. As the principal founder of our party and state, Chairman Mao saved the revolution from crises. In this respect, no one else in the party can match him.

We Must Proceed From the Fundamental Interests of 1 Billion People and Appraise Chairman Mao With a Correct Attitude

In his later years, Chairman Mao had some shortcomings and made some mistakes, and even some serious mistakes. Our party is now correcting those mistakes and summing up the experiences and lessons since we established political power in the whole country. This is, of course, a necessary thing.

However, we must proceed from a correct attitude. We can remember that following the 20th Congress of the CPSU in 1956, a secret report from Khrushchev reached the party Central Committee.

When the article "On the Historical Experience of the Dictatorship of the Proletariat" was being discussed at the party Central Committee, Chairman Mao read a poem by Du Fu to us. The poem said: "Wang, Yang, Lu and Luo wrote articles of that time; they were ridiculed by frivolous articles. Your bodies and names would be forgotten one day; the indestructible river would flow forever." The meaning of the poem is: The articles by Wang Bo and three others were forms of literature of that era, but now some people ridicule their articles contemptuously. When you all die and are forgotten by the people, the articles by Wang, Yang and Lu and Luo will go on for many generations like indestructible rivers. I think that this poem can still teach us a lesson. It will caution us not to evaluate Chairman Mao with a frivolous attitude.

In my opinion, Chairman Mao made two main mistakes in his later years. After socialist political power was established and the socialist transformation of agriculture, handicrafts and capitalist industry and commerce was completed, the focus of work was not shifted explicitly and promptly to socialist construction, and he committed the mistake of becoming impatient for more and quicker results in giving concrete guidance to the socialist revolution and socialist construction. The second mistake is that he mixed up two kinds of contradictions that differ in nature. He treated a number of contradictions among the people like contradictions between the people and the enemy, viewed class struggle in absolute terms and exaggerated its scope. He handled many contradictions within the party like contradictions with the enemy, so that bad elements were able to take him in. This resulted in 10 years of great disorder during the "Great Cultural Revolution." Its consequences are known to everyone and I do not have to talk any more. Of course, if we count everything in detail, he might have made other mistakes. But all these mistakes basically derived from these two main errors.

If we impute all the mistakes committed by our party since the founding of the People's Republic to Chairman Mao and attribute the responsibility to him alone, this does not conform to the historical facts. Comrade Deng Xiaoping has rightly said that, including himself, all of us old comrades are responsible for many mistakes.

One of our comrades asked me: "If we do not attribute the responsibility for committing mistakes to Chairman Mao alone, do you assume the responsibility?" I replied: "I must also share some responsibility. However, I cannot assume responsibility for carrying out the 'Great Cultural

Revolution' because I was not working at the party Central Committee and had no right to speak at that time." In my opinion, if I did not express my view to oppose erroneous decisions when I had the right to speak, then I could not shirk my responsibility later. For example, the antirightist struggle was necessary, but its scope was exaggerated and we erroneously struggled against many people. We must not attribute the responsibility to Chairman Mao alone. I was a member of the Secretariat at that time, considered some people as rightists and hastily joined others in passing the resolution during the discussion without careful thinking. How can I attribute my own mistake to Chairman Mao? During the Great Leap Forward, many comrades were prone to boasting and exaggerating and distorted facts to a frightening extent. They were also responsible for the serious mistakes developed during the movement. The party Central Committee should be responsible for everything decided and approved at its plenary sessions and be held responsible when they are wrong. Of course, Chairman Mao was chairman of the party Central Committee and he should be responsible as its principal leader.

In the past we veteran Communist Party members fulfilled our responsibility in liberating the whole country and building the new China, and we shared all the merit. Now we attribute the responsibility of all mistakes to one man alone, as if the mistakes have nothing to do with us. This is not fair. All of us should share the responsibility, and we should share it to be truthful to historical facts and materialism.

Chairman Mao has passed away and the revolutionary cause must be continued by us, the living. By summing up our own experience and lessons, it will only help us work for the people in a better way.

I think there are many reasons for Chairman Mao's mistakes in his later years, including profound historical and social reasons. It is an extremely arduous task to build socialism in China, a poor, backward and big country with a huge population. Besides, we had no experience. Even today there are still many things we have not understood, we are still groping our way, and we may still commit certain mistakes. I will not talk too much about this problem. I would only like to speak briefly about personal reasons for Chairman Mao's mistakes and the attitude we should adopt. In his later years Chairman Mao ceased to be prudent. He had little direct contact with day-to-day life or the masses, and the democratic style became poor, and so forth. This is why he made mistakes, and the whole party ought to draw lessons from this.

Our comrades should know that Chairman Mao worked intensely and wracked his brains for the cause of the people throughout his life. After the failure of the great revolution in China, he started to wrack his brains to think about problems day and night. When I had the chance of being with him in 1958, I felt that he had overtaxed his brain. When a person overtaxes his brain he is apt to make mistakes. I also have this experience now. Whenever I got excited, I did not know what to say and what not to say. Chairman Mao had noble aspirations even in his later years. He hoped to accomplish things in a few years or dozens of years during his life that could take several hundred years to accomplish. This resulted in some disorder. Despite the disorder and unfortunate harm to the party and the people, his intention was to do things well for the people and push the revolutionary cause forward. He devoted his whole life to this ideal. Chairman Mao's mistakes are those of a great revolutionary. Therefore when we correct the mistakes committed by him and sum up past experience, we should make allowances for him with feelings of love and respect.

Some people criticize Chairman Mao to the extreme, and some even talk of him as if he had no single redeeming feature. I think this is not right. Not only does it run contrary to essential facts, it is a disservice to the party and the people. Some comrades, especially those who were attacked and persecuted, have some indignant feelings. This is quite understandable. You all know that during Chairman Mao's later years I myself had some bitter experiences. However, I feel that we must not be emotional and be swayed by personal feelings toward such an important issue. We should consider the issue in light of the fundamental interests of the whole party, the whole country and the 1 billion people. We should also proceed from the interests of our future generations and the cause of socialist revolution.

For many years Chairman Mao was recognized by the whole world as the leader of our party and state and the symbol of revolution. This conforms to the actual situation. Defaming and distorting Chairman Mao can only defame and distort the party and our socialist motherland. This will endanger the fundamental interests of the party, the state, and the 1 billion people. At present the hostile forces at home and abroad all hope that we will totally negate Chairman Mao in order to confuse our thinking and lead our country to capitalism. There are also some people within our own country who have been influenced by Western individualism and liberalism and sing the same tune as the hostile forces. We must heighten our vigilance against this.

The History of Contemporary China Shows That Only Marxism-Leninism-Mao Zedong Thought Can Save China

Chairman Mao has passed away. He left us valuable wealth and also some negative factors. However, these negative factors only played a temporary role, and we can overcome them after some work. At present we are effectively overcoming these negative factors. His most valuable legacy, namely, Mao Zedong Thought, will guide our actions for a long time.

Now some people want to discard the banner of Mao Zedong Thought and even criticize Chairman Mao's correct thinking and words. I think this will lead China on a dangerous road. It will make us suffer and end in disaster.

For instance, some people are now criticizing Chairman Mao's "Talks at the Yanan Forum on Literature and Art." The fundamental thinking of the talks was the proposal that literature and art should serve the workers, peasants and soldiers, and play the role of uniting and educating the people. This in essence is the same as our present proposal that literature and art should serve the people and socialism. How can we set one proposal against the other? How can we talk about the people if we disregard the workers, peasants and soldiers? And how can literature and art serve socialism if they do not play the role of uniting and educating the people?

In recent years many good works of literature and art have emerged, and they have played a very good role in promoting the revolutionary cause. However, there are also a small number of people who, under the pretext of liberating our thinking, negate the principle for literature and art formulated by Chairman Mao. Those people do not want to serve the peasants, who account for 80 percent of our population; the broad masses of workers; the intellectuals who have been working hard; and the four modernizations. On the contrary, they are very much interested in those not so good things and even low class stuff from Hong Kong, Japan and the United States.

Our country is now in a difficult period of opening new roads and building the four modernizations. When we open our door to foreign countries, we should introduce the good points of people of foreign countries to our own people so that we can learn advanced things from others. We should introduce to our own people the spirit of hard struggle of the people of those countries in building up their countries. And we should introduce to our own people the needs and spirit of those scientists in the world who dedicated their entire lives to their cause and to benefiting mankind. We should note that there are tendencies that some of our young people only seek for the Western way of life and material enjoyment and that some are even infatuated with things that are considered as rotten and senseless stuff by the people in capitalist countries. What kind of spiritual food should our literary and art creations and foreign literature and art provide for the Chinese people? What should be used to cultivate our young people and juniors? We must seriously consider these questions.

Just imagine: What would take the place of Mao Zedong Thought if it were abandoned? Mao Zedong Thought was not a fortuitous thing. It was the product of several decades of revolutionary struggle by hundreds of millions of people.

In Chinese history Confucius' thought dominated for as long as 2,000 years. Now, more than 60 years after the democratic revolution in our country, this thought can no longer play any significant role. Another thought is that of Dr. Sun Yat-sen. A great democratic revolutionary pioneer, Dr. Sun Yat-sen advanced the three people's principles, which played a positive role in the Chinese democratic revolution. Many people of the older generation, including myself, were believers in the three people's principles when they were young, but these principles can in no way be compared with Marxism-Leninism-Mao Zedong Thought. The history of contemporary China has borne out that only Marxism-Leninism-Mao Zedong Thought can save China. From the very day our party was founded we Chinese Communists have used the banner of Marxism-Leninism to arouse, unite and organize the Chinese people to rise up to struggle. Basing himself on the fundamental tenets of Marxism-Leninism, Chairman Mao led the Chinese revolution and summed up its experience in a series of works. Mao Zedong Thought came into being in the course of Chinese revolutionary struggles and has become the ideological weapon of the Chinese Communists and the people of our country. It is an invaluable treasure resulting from the blood and sweat of the tens of millions of Communist Party members and hundreds of millions of revolutionary masses. We all feel that it is closer to us and more effective for our purposes than any other thought. We must have an ideological weapon to guide our big party and our big country with a population of 1 billion. Some people want to discard our own invaluable treasure. Do they mean to call back Confucius or the three people's principles?

Both have been proved by history to be out of date and impractical. If neither Confucius nor the three people's principles are what they want, do they mean to introduce into our country capitalist things from the West? In my opinion this is absolutely impractical. I am by no means an isolationist advocate. We should learn advanced things from abroad, such as science and technology and the scientific management of enterprises. As regards social science, we should in no way copy capitalist things. The bourgeois ideology serves the capitalist private-ownership system, and it is impossible for this ideology to serve our socialist system based on public ownership. Now some people worship capitalist things. Of course, people's living standards in Western countries are higher than ours, but it should be noted that they have practiced capitalism for hundreds of years, while it has been only 30 years since we began our socialist system. Also, if we had made fewer mistakes, our situation would be much better. Moreover, we should not describe everything in the West as being so beautiful. There are many things on the dark side in the West. According to American press reports on the U.S. mafia's "production" figures, the revenue for 1979 was $150 billion, with a net profit of $50 billion. This was second only to the oil industry in production value. What is that organization? It is an organization engaging in narcotics, gambling, prostitution and other criminal activities. What would be the outcome if our country were like that? Is that so-called civilization and happiness? If Mao Zedong Thought were discarded there would be ideological chaos in the party and in the people's minds, our socialist state would probably change its nature, and generations to come would suffer. We must see the danger of this matter.

Some comrades said that Marxism-Leninism would be enough. The comrades holding this opinion actually ignored the fact that Mao Zedong Thought is a product combining the basic principles of Marxism-Leninism with the concrete practice of the Chinese revolution, that it has developed Marxism-Leninism in the practice of the Chinese revolution, and that it has Chinese peculiarities and its own unique contents. Under the banner of Marxism-Leninism-Mao Zedong Thought, we Chinese Communists have made great contributions to the people and have tempered our own party style. Today we must still depend on Mao Zedong Thought to unite the people, overcome difficulties and concentrate to work with one mind and one heart toward the four modernizations. For example, to get rid of bad practices within the party, we have to promote the party's traditional fine style of work that Chairman Mao always advocated, namely, integrating theory with practice, maintaining close ties with the masses, criticism and self-criticism and hard struggle. In no way should we discard this valuable tradition, seek personal comfort, indulge in lavish feasting and entertainment and watch vulgar movies because we are now taking charge and have become "officials." These are not trivialities in life. Failing to check such unhealthy trends and bad practices, we would divorce ourselves from the masses and become corrupt.

The fundamental principles of Mao Zedong Thought are the guiding ideology for our party and country. This has been written into our party constitution and the "Guiding Principles for Inner-Party Political Life" and is an important principle that the central authorities have reiterated again and again. Acts to deny and defame Mao Zedong

Thought violate the party constitution and party discipline. We veteran communists, as well as all party members truly fighting for the cause of the people, must struggle against tendencies to defame Mao Zedong Thought and smear Chairman Mao's image in order to safeguard the fundamental interests of the party and the people.

At present a "crisis of belief" exists in many countries of the world. A great number of young people feel that there is no proper thought to depend upon, and that they lack spiritual sustenance. We Chinese Communists have fostered our own noble ideals and beliefs in the course of long struggle and have used such ideals and beliefs to unite and educate the broad masses of people. We should not destroy our own beliefs. Of course, I am not saying that every word of Chairman Mao was correct. Some of his statements were incorrect or out of date.

However, the essence and basic principles of Mao Zedong Thought will forever remain a spiritual weapon for the Chinese Communists and the Chinese revolutionary people and will continue to guide us in pushing the revolution forward. As a scientific system, Mao Zedong Thought has to be continuously enriched and developed. We must not place excessive demands on our predecessor. What we must do is use our practice of struggle to make up for what our predecessor did not accomplish. We must continue to enrich and develop Mao Zedong Thought so as to add a new chapter to this brilliant banner.

The Official Dengist Interpretation of Party History and Mao Zedong, 27 June 1981

17

This authoritative statement from Deng Xiaoping's perspective argues that Mao was a heroic figure until 1949 and for a while after that. The year 1956, when Mao had not yet turned into an extreme radical, the Party apparatus was essentially ruling the country, and Deng was elected general secretary, is looked back upon as halcyon. Soon afterwards, however, Mao began to commit "leftist" errors, one of which was the Great Leap Forward and the most serious of which was the Cultural Revolution. Another disaster threatened when the Gang of Four allegedly tried to seize power after Mao's death in 1976 but were averted. Hua Guofeng then proceeded to commit his own "leftist" mistakes. The Third Plenary Session of the Eleventh Central Committee in December 1978 marked the point of no return in Deng's ascent to power in the post-Mao period. Since then things have gone well. Mao's Thought and career are creative outgrowths of Marxism-Leninism and are still the sources of legitimacy for the Party, the PRC, and, by implication, for Deng's leadership and policies.

REVIEW OF THE HISTORY OF THE TWENTY-EIGHT YEARS BEFORE THE FOUNDING OF THE PEOPLE'S REPUBLIC

1. The Communist Party of China has traversed sixty years of glorious struggle since its founding in 1921. In order to sum up its experience in the thirty-two years since the founding of the People's Republic, we must briefly review the previous twenty-eight years in which the party led the people in waging the revolutionary struggle for new democracy.

2. The Communist Party of China was the product of the integration of Marxism-Leninism with the Chinese workers' movement and was founded under the influence of the October Revolution in Russia and the May 4th movement in China and with the help of the Communist International led by Lenin. The revolution of 1911 led by Dr. Sun Yat-sen, the great revolutionary forerunner, overthrew the Qing Dynasty, thus bringing to an end over 2,000 years

[Resolution on Certain Questions in the History of Our Party Since the Founding of the People's Republic of China, adopted at the Sixth Plenary Session of the Eleventh Central Committee, 27 June 1981, New China News Agency, 30 June 1981.]

of feudal monarchical rule. However, the semi-colonial and semi-feudal nature of Chinese society remained unchanged. Neither the Kuomintang nor any of the bourgeois or petty-bourgeois political groupings and factions found any way out for the country and the nation, nor was it possible for them to do so. The Communist Party of China and the Communist Party of China alone was able to show the people that China's salvation lay in overthrowing once and for all the reactionary rule of imperialism and feudalism and then switching over to socialism. When the Communist Party of China was founded, it had less than sixty members. But it initiated the vigorous workers' movement and the people's anti-imperialist and anti-feudal struggle and grew rapidly and soon became a leading force such as the Chinese people had never before known.

3. In the course of leading the struggle of the Chinese people with its various nationalities for new democracy, the Communist Party of China went through four stages: the northern expedition (1924–27) conducted with the co-operation of the Kuomintang, the agrarian revolutionary war (1927–37), the war of resistance against Japan (1937–45) and the nationwide war of liberation (1946–49). Twice, first in 1927 and then in 1934, it endured major setbacks. It was not until 1949 that it finally triumphed in the revolution, thanks to the long years of armed struggle in conjunction with other forms of struggle in other fields closely co-ordinated with it.

In 1927, regardless of the resolute opposition of the left wing of the Kuomintang with Soong Ching Ling as its outstanding representative, the Kuomintang controlled by Chiang Kai-shek and Wang Jingwei betrayed the policies of Kuomintang-Communist co-operation and of anti-imperialism and anti-feudalism decided on by Dr. Sun Yat-sen and, in collusion with the imperialists, massacred communists and other revolutionaries. The party was still quite inexperienced and, moreover, was dominated by Chen Duxiu's right capitulationism, so that the revolution suffered a disastrous defeat under the surprise attack of a powerful enemy. The total membership of the party, which had grown to more than 60,000, fell to a little over 10,000.

However, our party continued to fight tenaciously. Launched under the leadership of Zhou Enlai and several other comrades, the Nanchang uprising of 1927 fired the opening shot for armed resistance against the Kuomintang reactionaries. The meeting of the Central Committee of the party held on August 7, 1927 decided on the policy of carrying out agrarian revolution and organizing armed uprisings. Shortly afterwards, the autumn harvest and Guangzhou uprisings and uprisings in many other areas were organized. Led by Comrade Mao Zedong, the autumn-harvest uprising in the Hunan-Jiangxi border area gave birth to the first division of the Chinese workers' and peasants' revolutionary army and to the first rural revolutionary base area in the Jinggang mountains. Before long, the insurgents led by Comrade Zhu De arrived at the Jinggang mountains and joined forces with it. With the progress of the struggle, the party set up the Jiangxi central revolutionary base area and the western Hunan-Hubei, the Haifeng-Lufeng, the Hubei-Henan-Anhui, the Qiongya, the Fujian-Zhejiang-Jiangxi, the Hunan-Hubei-Jiangxi, the Hunan-Jiangxi, the Zuojiang-Youjiang, the Sichuan-Shaanxi, the Shaanxi-Gansu and the Hunan-Hubei-Sichuan-Guizhou and other base areas. The First, Second and Fourth Front

Armies of the workers' and peasants' Red Army were also born, as were many other Red Army units. In addition, party organizations and other revolutionary organizations were established and revolutionary mass struggles unfolded under difficult conditions in the Kuomintang areas. In the agrarian revolutionary war, the First Front Army of the Red Army and the central revolutionary base area under the direct leadership of Comrades Mao Zedong and Zhu De played the most important role. The front armies of the Red Army defeated in turn a number of "encirclement and suppression" campaigns launched by the Kuomintang troops. But because of Wang Ming's "left" adventurist leadership, the struggle against the Kuomintang's fifth "encirclement and suppression" campaign ended in failure. The First Front Army was forced to embark on the 25,000-li Long March and made its way to northern Shaanxi to join forces with units of the Red Army which had been persevering in struggles there and with its Twenty-Fifth Army which had arrived earlier. The Second and Fourth Front Armies also went on their Long March, first one and then the other arriving in northern Shaanxi. Guerrilla warfare was carried on under difficult conditions in the base areas in south China from which the main forces of the Red Army had withdrawn. As a result of the defeat caused by Wang Ming's "left" errors, the revolutionary base areas and the revolutionary forces in the Kuomintang areas sustained enormous losses. The Red Army of 300,000 men was reduced to about 30,000 and the Communist Party of 300,000 members to about 40,000.

In January 1935, the Political Bureau of the Central Committee of the party convened a meeting in Zunyi during the Long March, which established the leading position of Comrade Mao Zedong in the Red Army and the Central Committee of the party. This saved the Red Army and the Central Committee of the party which were then in critical danger and subsequently made it possible to defeat Zhang Guotao's splittism, bring the Long March to a triumphant conclusion and open up new vistas for the Chinese revolution. It was a vital turning point in the history of the party.

At a time of national crisis of unparalleled gravity when the Japanese imperialists were intensifying their aggression against China, the Central Committee of the party headed by Comrade Mao Zedong decided on and carried out the correct policy of forming an anti-Japanese national united front.

Our party led the students' movement of December 9, 1935 and organized the powerful mass struggle to demand an end to the civil war and resistance against Japan so as to save the nation. The Xian incident organized by Generals Zhang Xueliang and Yang Hucheng on December 12, 1936 and its peaceful settlement which our party promoted played a crucial historical role in bringing about renewed co-operation between the Kuomintang and the Communist Party and in achieving national unity for resistance against Japanese aggression. During the war of resistance, the ruling clique of the Kuomintang continued to oppose the Communist Party and the people and was passive in resisting Japan. As a result, the Kuomintang suffered defeat after defeat in front operations against the Japanese invaders. Our party persevered in the policy of maintaining its independence and initiative within the united front, closely relied on the masses of the people, conducted guerrilla warfare behind enemy lines and set up many anti-Japanese base areas. The Eighth Route Army and the New Fourth Army—the reorganized Red Army—grew rapidly and became the mainstay in the war of resistance. The northeast anti-Japanese united army sustained its operations amid formidable difficulties. Diverse forms of anti-Japanese struggle were unfolded on a broad scale in areas occupied by Japan or controlled by the Kuomintang. Consequently, the Chinese people were able to hold out in the war for eight long years and win final victory, in co-operation with the people of the Soviet Union and other countries in the anti-fascist war.

During the anti-Japanese war, the party conducted a rectification movement, a movement of Marxist education. Launched in 1942, it was a tremendous success. It was on this basis that the seventh plenary session of the sixth Central Committee of the party in 1945 adopted the resolution on certain questions in the history of our party and soon afterwards the party's seventh national congress was convened. These meetings summed up our historical experience and laid down our correct line, principles and policies for building a new-democratic new China, enabling the party to attain an unprecedented ideological, political and organizational unity and solidarity. After the conclusion of the war of resistance against Japan, the Chiang Kai-shek government, with the aid of U.S. imperialism, flagrantly launched an all-out civil war, disregarding the just demand of our party and the people of the whole country for peace and democracy. With the wholehearted support of the people in all the liberated areas, with the powerful backing of the students' and workers' movements and the struggles of the people of various strata in the Kuomintang areas and with the active co-operation of the democratic parties and non-party democrats, our party led the People's Liberation Army in fighting the three-year war of liberation and in wiping out 8,000,000 Chiang Kai-shek troops in the Liaoxi-Shenyang, Beiping-Tianjin and Huai-Hai campaigns and in the successful crossing of the Chang Jiang (Yangtze) River. The end result was the overthrow of the reactionary Kuomintang government and the establishment of the great People's Republic of China. The Chinese people had stood up.

4. The victories gained in the twenty-eight years of struggle fully show that:

1) Victory in the Chinese revolution was won under the guidance of Marxism-Leninism. Our party had creatively applied the basic tenets of Marxism-Leninism and integrated them with the concrete practice of the Chinese revolution. In this way, the great system of Mao Zedong Thought came into being and the correct path to victory for the Chinese revolution was charted. This is a major contribution to the development of Marxism-Leninism.

2) As the vanguard of the Chinese proletariat, the Communist Party of China is a party serving the people whole-heartedly, with no selfish aim of its own. It is a party with both the courage and the ability to lead the people in their indomitable struggle against any enemy. Convinced of all this through their own experience, the Chinese people of whatever nationality came to rally around the party and form a broad united front, thus forging a strong political unity unparalleled in Chinese history.

3) The Chinese revolution was victorious mainly because we relied on a people's army led by the party, an army of a completely new type and enjoying flesh-and-blood ties with the people, to defeat a formidable enemy through protracted people's war. Without such an army, it would have been impossible to achieve the liberation of our people and the independence of our country.

4) The Chinese revolution had the support of the revolutionary forces in other countries at every stage, a fact which the Chinese people will never forget. Yet it must be said that, fundamentally, victory in the Chinese revolution was won because the Chinese Communist Party adhered to the principle of independence and self-reliance and depended on the efforts of the whole Chinese people, whatever their nationality, after they underwent untold hardships and surmounted innumerable difficulties and obstacles together.

5) The victorious Chinese revolution put an end to the rule of a handful of exploiters over the masses of the working people and to the enslavement of the Chinese people of all nationalities by the imperialists and colonialists. The working people have become the masters of the new state and the new society. While changing the balance of forces in world politics, the people's victory in so large a country having nearly one-quarter of the world's population has inspired the people in countries similarly subjected to imperialist and colonialist exploitation and oppression with heightened confidence in their forward march. The triumph of the Chinese revolution is the most important political event since World War II and has exerted a profound and far-reaching impact on the international situation and the development of the people's struggle throughout the world.

5. Victory in the new-democratic revolution was won through long years of struggle and sacrifice by countless martyrs, party members and people of all nationalities. We should by no means give all the credit to the leaders of the revolution, but at the same time we should not underrate the significant role these leaders have played. Among the many outstanding leaders of the party, Comrade Mao Zedong was the most prominent. Prior to the failure of the revolution in 1927, he had clearly pointed out the paramount importance of the leadership of the proletariat over the peasants' struggle and the danger of a right deviation in this regard. After its failure, he was the chief representative of those who succeeded in shifting the emphasis in the party's work from the city to the countryside and in preserving, restoring and promoting the revolutionary forces in the countryside. In the twenty-two years from 1927 to 1949, Comrade Mao Zedong and other party leaders managed to overcome innumerable difficulties and gradually worked out an over-all strategy and specific policies and directed their implementation, so that the revolution was able to switch from staggering defeats to great victory. Our party and people would have had to grope in the dark much longer had it not been for Comrade Mao Zedong, who more than once rescued the Chinese revolution from grave danger, and for the Central Committee of the party which was headed by him and which charted the firm, correct political course for the whole party, the whole people and the people's army.

Just as the Communist Party of China is recognized as the central force leading the entire people forward, so Comrade Mao Zedong is recognized as the great leader of the Chinese Communist Party and the whole Chinese people, and Mao Zedong Thought, which came into being through the collective struggle of the party and the people, is recognized as the guiding ideology of the party. This is the inevitable outcome of the twenty-eight years of historical development preceding the founding of the People's Republic of China.

BASIC APPRAISAL OF THE HISTORY OF THE THIRTY-TWO YEARS SINCE THE FOUNDING OF THE PEOPLE'S REPUBLIC

6. Generally speaking, the years since the founding of the People's Republic of China are years in which the Chinese Communist Party, guided by Marxism-Leninism and Mao Zedong Thought, has very successfully led the whole people in carrying out socialist revolution and socialist construction. The establishment of the socialist system represents the greatest and most profound social change in Chinese history and is the foundation for the country's future progress and development.

7. Our major achievements in the thirty-two years since the founding of the People's Republic are the following:

1) We have established and consolidated the people's democratic dictatorship led by the working class and based on the worker-peasant alliance, namely, the dictatorship of the proletariat. It is a new type of state power, unknown in Chinese history, in which the people are the masters of their own house. It constitutes the fundamental guarantee for the building of a modern socialist country, prosperous and powerful, democratic and culturally advanced.

2) We have achieved and consolidated nationwide unification of the country, with the exception of Taiwan and some other islands, and have thus put an end to the state of disunity characteristic of old China. We have achieved and consolidated the great unity of the people of all nationalities and have forged and expanded a socialist relationship of equality and mutual help among the more than fifty nationalities. And we have achieved and consolidated the great unity of the workers, peasants, intellectuals and people of other strata and have strengthened and expanded the broad united front which is led by the Chinese Communist Party in full co-operation with the patriotic democratic parties and people's organizations, and comprises all socialist working people and all patriots who support socialism and patriots who stand for the unification of the motherland, including our compatriots in Taiwan, Hong Kong and Macao and Chinese citizens overseas.

3) We have defeated aggression, sabotage and armed provocations by the imperialists and hegemonists, safeguarded our country's security and independence and fought successfully in defence of our border regions.

4) We have built and developed a socialist economy and have in the main completed the socialist transformation of the private ownership of the means of production into public ownership and put into practice the principle of "to each according to his work." The system of exploitation of man by man has been eliminated, and exploiters no longer exist as classes since the overwhelming majority have been remoulded and now live by their own labour.

5) We have scored signal successes in industrial construction and have gradually set up an independent and fairly comprehensive industrial base and economic system. Compared with 1952 when economic rehabilitation was completed, fixed industrial assets, calculated on the basis of their original price, were more than 27 times greater in 1980, exceeding 410,000 million yuan; the output of cotton yarn was 4.5 times as great, reaching 2,930,000 tonnes; that of coal 9.4 times, reaching 620 million tonnes; that of electricity 41 times, exceeding 300,000 million kwh; and the output of crude oil exceeding 105,000,000 tonnes and that of steel 37 million tonnes; the output value of the engineering industry was 54 times as great, exceeding 127,000 million yuan. A number of new industrial bases have been built in our vast hinterland and the regions inhabited by our minority nationalities. National defence industry started from scratch and is being gradually built up. Much has been done in the prospecting of natural resources. There has been a tremendous growth in railway, highway, water and air transport and post and telecommunications.

6) The conditions prevailing in agricultural production have experienced a remarkable change, giving rise to big increases in production. The amount of land under irrigation has grown from 300 million mu in 1952 to over 670 million mu. Flooding by big rivers such as the Chang Jiang, Huang He (Yellow River), Huai He, Hai He, Zhu Jiang (Pearl River), Liao He and Songhua Jiang has been brought under initial control. In our rural areas, where farm machinery, chemical fertilizers and electricity were practically non-existent before liberation, there is now a big increase in the number of agriculture-related tractors and irrigation and drainage equipment and in the quantity of chemical fertilizers applied, and the amount of electricity consumed is 7.5 times that generated in the whole country in the early years of liberation. In 1980, the total output of grain was nearly double that in 1952 and that of cotton more than double. Despite the excessive rate of growth in our population, which is now nearly a billion, we have succeeded in basically meeting the needs of our people in food and clothing by our own efforts.

7) There has been a substantial growth in urban and rural commerce and in foreign trade. The total value of commodities purchased by enterprises owned by the whole people rose from 17.5 billion yuan in 1952 to 226.3 billion yuan in 1980, registering an increase nearly 13-fold; retail sales rose from 27.7 billion yuan to 214 billion yuan, an increase of 7.7 times. The total value of the state's foreign trade in 1980 was 8.7 times that of 1952. With the growth in industry, agriculture and commerce, the people's livelihood has improved very markedly, as compared with pre-liberation days. In 1980, average consumption per capita in both town and country was nearly twice as much as in 1952, allowing for price changes.

8) Considerable progress has been made in education, science, culture, public health and physical culture. In 1980, enrollment in the various kinds of full-time schools totalled 204 million, 3.7 times the number in 1952. In the past 32 years, the institutions of higher education and vocational schools have turned out nearly 9 million graduates with specialized knowledge or skills. Our achievements in nuclear technology, man-made satellites, rocketry, etc. represent substantial advances in the field of science and technology. In literature and art, large numbers of fine works

have appeared to cater to the needs of the people and socialism. With the participation of the masses, sports have developed vigorously, and records have been chalked up in quite a few events. Epidemic diseases with their high mortality rates have been eliminated or largely eliminated, the health of the rural and urban populations has greatly improved, and average life expectancy is now much higher.

9) Under the new historical conditions, the People's Liberation Army has grown in strength and in quality. No longer composed only of ground forces, it has become a composite army, including the naval and air forces and various technical branches. Our armed forces, which are a combination of the field armies, the regional forces and the militia, have been strengthened. Their quality is now much higher and their technical equipment much better. The PLA is serving as the solid pillar of the people's democratic dictatorship in defending and participating in the socialist revolution and socialist construction.

10) Internationally, we have steadfastly pursued an independent socialist foreign policy, advocated and upheld the five principles of peaceful coexistence, entered into diplomatic relations with 124 countries and promoted trade and economic and cultural exchanges with still more countries and regions. Our country's place in the United Nations and the Security Council has been restored to us. Adhering to proletarian internationalism, we are playing an increasingly influential and active role in international affairs by enhancing our friendship with the people of other countries, by supporting and assisting the oppressed nations in their cause of liberation, the newly-independent countries in their national construction and the people of various countries in their just struggles and by staunchly opposing imperialism, hegemonism, colonialism and racism in defence of world peace. All of which have served to create favourable international conditions for our socialist construction and contributed to the development of a world situation favourable to the people everywhere.

8. New China has not been in existence for very long, and our successes are still preliminary. Our party has made mistakes owing to its meagre experience in leading the cause of socialism and subjective errors in the party leadership's analysis of the situation and its understanding of Chinese conditions. Before the "Cultural Revolution" there were mistakes of enlarging the scope of class struggle and of impetuosity and rashness in economic construction. Later, there was the comprehensive, long-drawn-out and grave blunder of the "Cultural Revolution." All these errors prevented us from scoring the greater achievements of which we should have been capable. It is impermissible to overlook or whitewash mistakes, which in itself would be a mistake and would give rise to more and worse mistakes. But after all our achievements in the past thirty-two years are the main thing. It would be a no less serious error to overlook or deny our achievements or our successful experiences in scoring these achievements. These achievements and successful experiences of ours are the product of the creative application of Marxism-Leninism by our party and people, the manifestation of the superiority of the socialist system and the base from which the entire party and people will continue to advance. Uphold truth and rectify error—this is the basic stand of dialectical-materialism our party must take. It was by taking this stand that we saved our cause from danger and defeat and won

victory in the past. By taking the same stand, we will certainly win still greater victories in the future.

THE SEVEN YEARS OF BASIC COMPLETION OF THE SOCIALIST TRANSFORMATION

9. From the inception of the People's Republic of China in October 1949 to 1956, our party led the whole people in gradually realizing the transition from new democracy to socialism, rapidly rehabilitating the country's economy, undertaking planned economic construction and in the main accomplishing the socialist transformation of the private ownership of the means of production in most of the country. The guidelines and basic policies defined by the party in this historical period were correct and led to brilliant successes.

10. In the first three years of the People's Republic, we cleared the mainland of bandits and the remnant armed forces of the Kuomintang reactionaries, peacefully liberated Tibet, established people's governments at all levels throughout the country, confiscated bureaucrat-capitalist enterprises and transformed them into state-owned socialist enterprises, unified the country's financial and economic work, stabilized commodity prices, carried out agrarian reform in the new liberated areas, suppressed counter-revolutionaries, and unfolded the movements against the "three evils" of corruption, waste and bureaucracy and against the "five evils" of bribery, tax evasion, theft of state property, cheating on government contracts and stealing of economic information, the latter being a movement to beat back the attack mounted by the bourgeoisie. We effectively transformed the educational, scientific and cultural institutions of old China. While successfully carrying out the complex and difficult task of social reform and simultaneously undertaking the great war to resist U.S. aggression and aid Korea, protect our homes and defend the country, we rapidly rehabilitated the country's economy which had been devastated in old China. By the end of 1952, the country's industrial and agricultural production had attained record levels.

11. On the proposal of Comrade Mao Zedong in 1952, the Central Committee of the party advanced the general line for the transition period, which was to realize the country's socialist industrialization and socialist transformation of agriculture, handicrafts and capitalist industry and commerce step by step over a fairly long period of time. This general line was a reflection of historical necessity.

1) Socialist industrialization is an indispensable prerequisite to the country's independence and prosperity.

2) With nationwide victory in the new-democratic revolution and completion of the agrarian reform, the contradiction between the working class and the bourgeoisie and between the socialist road and the capitalist road became the principal internal contradiction. The country needed a certain expansion of capitalist industry and commerce which were beneficial to its economy and to the people's livelihood. But in the course of their expansion, things detrimental to the national economy and the people's livelihood were bound to emerge. Consequently, a struggle between restriction and opposition to restriction was inevitable. The conflict of interests became increasingly apparent between capitalist enterprises on the one hand and the economic policies of the state, the socialist

state-owned economy, the workers and staff in these capitalist enterprises and the people as a whole on the other. An integrated series of necessary measures and steps, such as the fight against speculation and profiteering, the readjustment and restructuring of industry and commerce, the movement against the "five evils", workers' supervision of production and state monopoly of the purchase and marketing of grain and cotton, were bound to gradually bring backward, anarchic, lop-sided and profit-oriented capitalist industry and commerce into the orbit of socialist transformation.

3) Among the individual peasants, and particularly the poor and lower-middle peasants who had just acquired land in the agrarian reform but lacked other means of production, there was a genuine desire for mutual aid and co-operation in order to avoid borrowing at usurious rates and even mortgaging or selling their land again with consequent polarization, and in order to expand production, undertake water conservancy projects, ward off natural calamities and make use of farm machinery and new techniques.

The progress of industrialization, while demanding agricultural products in ever increasing quantities, would provide stronger and stronger support for the technical transformation of agriculture, and this also constituted a motive force behind the transformation of individual into co-operative farming.

As is borne out by history, the general line for the transition period set forth by our party was entirely correct.

12. During the period of transition, our party creatively charted a course for socialist transformation that suited China's specific conditions. In dealing with capitalist industry and commerce, we devised a whole series of transitional forms of state capitalism from lower to higher levels, such as the placing of state orders with private enterprises for the processing of materials or the manufacture of goods, state monopoly of the purchase and marketing of the products of private enterprise, the marketing of products of state-owned enterprises by private shops, and joint state-private ownership of individual enterprises or enterprises of a whole trade, and we eventually realized the peaceful redemption of the bourgeoisie, a possibility envisaged by Marx and Lenin. In dealing with individual farming, we devised transitional forms of co-operation, proceeding from temporary or all-the-year-round mutual-aid teams, to elementary agricultural producers' co-operatives of a semi-socialist nature and then to advanced agricultural producers' co-operatives of a fully socialist nature, always adhering to the principles of voluntariness and mutual benefit, demonstration through advanced examples, and extension of state help. Similar methods were used in transforming individual handicraft industries. In the course of such transformation, the state-capitalist and co-operative economies displayed their unmistakable superiority. By 1956, the socialist transformation of the private ownership of the means of production had been largely completed in most regions. But there had been shortcomings and errors. From the summer of 1955 onwards, we were over-hasty in pressing on with agricultural cooperation and the transformation of private handicraft and commercial establishments; we were far from meticulous, the changes were too fast, and we did our work in a somewhat summary, stereotyped manner, leaving open a number of questions for a long time. Following the basic completion of the trans-

formation of capitalist industry and commerce in 1956, we failed to do a proper job in employing and handling some of the former industrialists and businessmen. But on the whole, it was definitely a historic victory for us to have effected, and to have effected fairly smoothly, so difficult, complex and profound a social change in so vast a country with its several hundred million people, a change, moreover, which promoted the growth of industry, agriculture and the economy as a whole.

13. In economic construction under the first five-year plan (1953–57), we likewise scored major successes through our own efforts and with the assistance of the Soviet Union and other friendly countries. A number of basic industries, essential for the country's industrialization and yet very weak in the past, were built up. Between 1953 and 1956, the average annual increases in the total value of industrial and agricultural output were 19.6 and 4.8 percent respectively. Economic growth was quite fast, with satisfactory economic results, and the key economic sectors were well-balanced. The market prospered, prices were stable. The people's livelihood improved perceptively. In April 1956, Comrade Mao Zedong made his speech "On the Ten Major Relationships," in which he initially summed up our experiences in socialist construction and set forth the task of exploring a way of building socialism suited to the specific conditions of our country.

14. The first National People's Congress was convened in September 1954, and it enacted the Constitution of the People's Republic of China. In March 1955, a national conference of the party reviewed the major struggle against the plots of the careerists Gao Gang and Rao Shushi to split the party and usurp supreme power in the party and the state; in this way it strengthened party unity. In January 1956, the Central Committee of the party called a conference on the question of the intellectuals. Subsequently, the policy of "letting a hundred flowers blossom and a hundred schools of thought contend" was advanced. These measures spelled out the correct policy regarding intellectuals and the work in education, science and culture and thus brought about a significant advance in these fields. Owing to the fact that the party enjoyed high prestige among the people for its correct policies and fine style of work, the vast numbers of cadres, masses, youth and intellectuals earnestly studied Marxism-Leninism and Mao Zedong Thought and participated enthusiastically in revolutionary and construction activities under the leadership of the party, so that a healthy and virile revolutionary morality prevailed throughout the country.

15. The eighth national congress of the party held in September 1956 was very successful. The congress declard that the socialist system had been basically established in China, that while we must strive to liberate Taiwan, thoroughly complete socialist transformation, ultimately eliminate the system of exploitation and continue to wipe out the remnant forces of counter-revolution, the principal contradiction within the country was no longer the contradiction between the working class and the bourgeoisie but between the demand of the people for rapid economic and cultural development and the existing state of our economy and culture which fell short of the needs of the people; that the chief task confronting the whole nation was to concentrate all efforts on developing the productive forces, industrializing the country and gradually meeting the people's incessantly growing material and cultural

needs; and that although class struggle still existed and the people's democratic dictatorship had to be further strengthened, the basic task of the dictatorship was now to protect and develop the productive forces in the context of the new relations of production. The congress adhered to the principle put forward by the Central Committee of the party in May 1956, the principle of opposing both conservatism and rash advance in economic construction, that is, of making steady progress by striking an over-all balance. It emphasized the problem of the building of the party in office and the need to uphold democratic centralism and collective leadership, oppose the personality cult, promote democracy within the party and among the people and strengthen the party's ties with the masses. The line laid down by the eighth national congress of the party was correct and it charted the path for the development of the cause of socialism and for party building in the new period.

THE TEN YEARS OF INITIALLY BUILDING SOCIALISM IN ALL SPHERES

16. After the basic completion of socialist transformation, our party led the entire people in shifting our work to all-round, large-scale socialist construction. In the ten years preceding the "Cultural Revolution" we achieved very big successes despite serious setbacks. By 1966, the value of fixed industrial assets, calculated on the basis of their original price, was 4 times that in 1956. The output of such major industrial products as cotton yarn, coal, electricity, crude oil, steel and mechanical equipment all recorded impressive increases.

Beginning in 1965, China became self-sufficient in petroleum. New industries such as the electronic and petrochemical industries were established one after another. The distribution of industry over the country became better balanced. Capital construction in agriculture and its technical transformation began on a massive scale and yielded better and better results. Both the number of tractors for farming and the quantity of chemical fertilizers applied increased over 7 times and rural consumption of electricity 71 times. The number of graduates from institutions of higher education was 4.9 times that of the previous seven years. Educational work was improved markedly through consolidation. Scientific research and technological work, too, produced notable results.

In the ten years from 1956 to 1966, the party accumulated precious experience in leading socialist construction. In the spring of 1957, Comrade Mao Zedong stressed the necessity of correctly handling and distinguishing between the two types of social contradictions differing in nature in a socialist society, and made the correct handling of contradictions among the people the main content of the country's political life. Later, he called for the creation of "a political situation in which we have both centralism and democracy, both discipline and freedom, both unity of will and personal ease of mind and liveliness." In 1958, he proposed that the focus of party and government work be shifted to technical revolution and socialist construction. All this was the continuation and development of the line adopted by the eighth national congress of the party and was to go on serving as a valuable guide. While leading

the work of correcting the errors in the "Great Leap Forward" and the movement to organize people's communes, Comrade Mao Zedong pointed out that there must be no expropriation of the peasants; that a given stage of social development should not be skipped; that egalitarianism must be opposed; that we must stress commodity production, observe the law of value and strike an overall balance in economic planning; and that economic plans must be arranged with the priority proceeding from agriculture to light industry and then to heavy industry. Comrade Liu Shaoqi said that a variety of means of production could be put into circulation as commodities and that there should be a double-track system for labour as well as for education in socialist society. The double-track system for labour refers to a combination of the system of the eight-hour day in factories, rural areas and government offices with a system of part-time work and part-time study in factories and rural areas. The double-track system for education means a system of full-time schooling combined with a system of part-time work and part-time study. Comrade Zhou Enlai said, among other things, that the overwhelming majority of Chinese intellectuals had become intellectuals belonging to the working people and that science and technology would play a key role in China's modernization. Comrade Chen Yun held that plan targets should be realistic, that the scale of construction should correspond to national capability, considerations should be given to both the people's livelihood and the needs of state construction, and that the material, financial and credit balances should be maintained in drawing up plans. Comrade Deng Xiaoping held that industrial enterprises should be consolidated and their management approved and strengthened, and that the system of workers' conferences should be introduced. Comrade Zhu De stressed the need to pay attention to the development of handicrafts and of diverse undertakings in agriculture. Deng Zihui and other comrades pointed out that a system of production responsibility should be introduced in agriculture. All these views were not only of vital significance then, but have remained so ever since.

In the course of economic readjustment, the Central Committee drew up draft rules governing the work of the rural people's communes and work in industry, commerce, education, science and literature and art. These rules which were a more or less systematic summation of our experience in socialist construction and embodied specific policies suited to the prevailing conditions remain important as a source of reference for us to this very day.

In short, the material and technical basis for modernizing our country was largely established during that period. It was also largely in the same period that the core personnel for our work in the economic, cultural and other spheres were trained and that they gained their experience. This was the principal aspect of the party's work in that period.

17. In the course of this decade, there were serious faults and errors in the guidelines of the party's work, which developed through twists and turns.

Nineteen fifty-seven was one of the years that saw best results in economic work after the founding of the People's Republic owing to the conscientious implementation of the correct line formulated at the eighth national congress of the party. To start a rectification campaign throughout the party in that year and urge the masses to offer criticisms and suggestions were normal steps in developing socialist democracy. In the rectification campaign a handful of bourgeois rightists seized the opportunity to advocate what they called "speaking out and airing views in a big way" and to mount a wild attack against the party and the nascent socialist system in an attempt to replace the leadership of the Communist Party. It was therefore entirely correct and necessary to launch a resolute counter-attack. But the scope of this struggle was made far too broad and a number of intellectuals, patriotic people and party cadres were unjustifiably labelled "rightists," with unfortunate consequences.

In 1958, the second plenum of the eighth national congress of the party adopted the general line for socialist construction. The line and its fundamental aspects were correct in that it reflected the masses' pressing demand for a change in the economic and cultural backwardness of our country. Its shortcoming was that it overlooked the objective economic laws. Both before and after the plenum, all comrades in the party and people of all nationalities displayed high enthusiasm and initiative for socialism and achieved certain results in production and construction. However, "left" errors, characterized by excessively high targets, the issuing of arbitrary directions, boastfulness and the stirring up of a "communist wind," spread unchecked throughout the country. This was due to our lack of experience in socialist construction and inadequate understanding of the laws of economic development and of the basic economic conditions in China. More important, it was due to the fact that Comrade Mao Zedong and many leading comrades, both at the centre and in the localities, had become smug about their successes, were impatient for quick results and overestimated the role of man's subjective will and efforts. After the general line was formulated, the "Great Leap Forward" and the movement for rural people's communes were initiated without careful investigation and study and without prior experimentation. From the end of 1958 to the early stage of the Lushan meeting of the Political Bureau of the party's Central Committee in July 1959, Comrade Mao Zedong and the Central Committee led the whole party in energetically rectifying the errors which had already been recognized. However, in the latter part of the meeting, he erred in initiating criticism of Comrade Peng Dehuai and then in launching a party-wide struggle against "right opportunism."

The resolution passed by the eighth plenary session of the eighth Central Committee of the party concerning the so-called anti-party group of Peng Dehuai, Huang Kecheng, Zhang Wentian and Zhou Xiaozhou was entirely wrong. Politically, this struggle gravely undermined inner-party democracy from the central level down to the grass roots; economically, it cut short the process of rectification of the "left" errors, thus prolonging their influence. It was mainly due to the errors of the Great Leap Forward and of the struggle against "right opportunism" together with a succession of natural calamities and the perfidious scrapping of contracts by the Soviet Government that our economy encountered serious difficulties between 1959 and 1961, which caused serious losses to our country and people.

In the winter of 1960, the Central Committee of the party and Comrade Mao Zedong set about rectifying the "left" errors in rural work and decided on the principle of "readjustment, consolidation, filling out and raising standards" for the economy as a whole. A number of correct policies and resolute measures were worked out and put into effect with Comrades Liu Shaoqi, Zhou Enlai, Chen Yun and Deng Xiaoping in charge. All this constituted a crucial turning point in that historical phase. In January 1962, the enlarged central work conference attended by 7,000 people made a preliminary summing-up of the positive and negative experience of the "Great Leap Forward" and unfolded criticism and self-criticism. A majority of the comrades who had been unjustifiably criticized during the campaign against "right opportunism" were rehabilitated before or after the conference. In addition, most of the "rightists" had their label removed. Thanks to these economic and political measures, the national economy recovered and developed fairly smoothly between 1962 and 1966.

Nevertheless, "left" errors in the principles guiding economic work were not only not eradicated, but actually grew in the spheres of politics, ideology and culture. At the tenth plenary session of the party's eighth Central Committee in September 1962, Comrade Mao Zedong widened and absolutized the class struggle existing only within certain limits in a socialist society and carried forward the viewpoint he had advanced after the anti-rightist struggle in 1957 that the contradiction between the proletariat and the bourgeoisie remained the principal contradiction in our society. He went a step further and asserted that, throughout the historical period of socialism, the bourgeoisie would continue to exist and would attempt a comeback and become the source of revisionism inside the party. The socialist education movement unfolded between 1963 and 1965 in some rural areas and at the grass-roots level in a small number of cities did help to some extent to improve the cadres' style of work and economic management. But, in the course of the movement, problems differing in nature were all treated as forms of class struggle or its reflections inside the party. As a result, quite a number of the cadres at the grass-roots level were unjustly dealt with in the latter half of 1964, and early in 1965 the erroneous thesis was advanced that the main target of the movement should be "those party persons in power taking the capitalist road." In the ideological sphere, a number of literary and art works and schools of thought and a number of representative personages in artistic, literary and academic circles were subjected to unwarranted, inordinate political criticism. And there was an increasingly serious "left" deviation on the question of intellectuals and on the question of education, science and culture. These errors eventually culminated in the "Cultural Revolution," but they had not yet become dominant.

Thanks to the fact that the whole party and people had concentrated on carrying out the correct principle of economic readjustment since the winter of 1960, socialist construction gradually flourished again. The party and the people were united in sharing weal and woe. They overcame difficulties at home, stood up to the pressure of the Soviet leading clique and repaid all the debts owed to the Soviet Union, which were chiefly incurred through purchasing Soviet arms during the movement to resist U.S. aggression and aid Korea. In addition, they did what they could to support the revolutionary struggles of the people of many countries and assist them in their economic construction. The third National People's Congress, which met between the end of 1964 and the first days of 1965, announced that the task of national economic readjustment had in the main been accomplished and that the economy as a whole would soon enter a new stage of development. It called for energetic efforts to build China step by step into a socialist power with modern agriculture, national defence and science and technology. This call was not fulfilled owing to the "Cultural Revolution."

18. All the successes in these ten years were achieved under the collective leadership of the Central Committee of the party headed by Comrade Mao Zedong. Likewise, responsibility for the errors committed in the work of this period rested with the same collective leadership. Although Comrade Mao Zedong must be held chiefly responsible, we cannot lay the blame on him alone for all those errors. During this period, his theoretical and practical mistakes concerning class struggle in a socialist society became increasingly serious, his personal arbitrariness gradually undermined democratic centralism in party life, and the personality cult grew graver and graver. The Central Committee of the party failed to rectify these mistakes in good time. Careerists like Lin Biao, Jiang Qing and Kang Sheng, harbouring ulterior motives, made use of these errors and inflated them. This led to the inauguration of the "Cultural Revolution."

THE DECADE OF THE "CULTURAL REVOLUTION"

19. The "Cultural Revolution", which lasted from May 1966 to October 1976, was responsible for the most severe setback and the heaviest losses suffered by the party, the state and the people since the founding of the People's Republic. It was initiated and led by Comrade Mao Zedong. His principal theses were that many representatives of the bourgeoisie and counter-revolutionary revisionists had sneaked into the party, the government, the army and cultural circles, and leadership in a fairly large majority of organizations and departments was no longer in the hands of Marxists and the people; that party persons in power taking the capitalist road had formed a bourgeoisie headquarters inside the Central Committee which pursued a revisionist political and organizational line and had agents in all provinces, municipalities and autonomous regions, as well as in all central departments; that since the forms of struggle adopted in the past had not been able to solve this problem, the power usurped by the capitalist-roaders could be recaptured only by carrying out a Great Cultural Revolution, by openly and fully mobilizing the broad masses from the bottom up to expose these sinister phenomena; and that the Cultural Revolution was in fact a great political revolution in which one class would overthrow another, a revolution that would have to be waged time and again. These theses appeared mainly in the "May 16 circular," which served as the programmatic document of the "Cultural Revolution," and in the political report to the ninth national congress of the party in April 1969.

They were incorporated into a general theory—the "theory of continued revolution under the dictatorship of the proletariat"—which then took on a specific meaning. These erroneous "left" theses, upon which Comrade Mao Zedong based himself in initiating the "Cultural Revolution," were obviously inconsistent with the system of Mao Zedong Thought, which is the integration of the universal principles of Marxism-Leninism with the concrete practice of the Chinese revolution. These theses must be thoroughly distinguished from Mao Zedong Thought. As for Lin Biao, Jiang Qing and others, who were placed in important positions by Comrade Mao Zedong, the matter is of an entirely different nature. They rigged up two counter-revolutionary cliques in an attempt to seize supreme power and, taking advantage of Comrade Mao Zedong's errors, committed many crimes behind his back, bringing disaster to the country and the people. As their counter-revolutionary crimes have been fully exposed, this resolution will not go into them at any length.

20. The history of the "Cultural Revolution" has proved that Comrade Mao Zedong's principal theses for initiating it conformed neither to Marxism-Leninism nor to Chinese reality. They represent an entirely erroneous appraisal of the prevailing class relations and political situation in the party and state.

1) The "Cultural Revolution" was defined as a struggle against the revisionist line or the capitalist road. There were no grounds at all for this definition. It led to the confusing of right and wrong on a series of important theories and policies. Many things denounced as revisionist or capitalist during the "Cultural Revolution" were actually Marxist and socialist principles, many of which had been set forth or supported by Comrade Mao Zedong himself. The "Cultural Revolution" negated many of the correct principles, policies and achievements of the seventeen years after the founding of the People's Republic. In fact, it negated much of the work of the Central Committee of the party and the people's government, including Comrade Mao Zedong's own contribution. It negated the arduous struggles the entire people had conducted in socialist construction.

2) The confusing of right and wrong inevitably led to confusing the people with the enemy. The "capitalist-roaders" overthrown in the "Cultural Revolution" were leading cadres of party and government organizations at all levels, who formed the core force of the socialist cause. The so-called bourgeois headquarters inside the party headed by Liu Shaoqi and Deng Xiaoping simply did not exist. Irrefutable facts have proved that labelling Comrade Liu Shaoqi a "renegade, hidden traitor and scab" was nothing but a frame-up by Lin Biao, Jiang Qing and their followers. The political conclusion concerning Comrade Liu Shaoqi drawn by the twelfth plenary session of the eighth Central Committee of the party and the disciplinary measure it meted out to him were both utterly wrong. The criticism of the so-called reactionary academic authorities in the "Cultural Revolution" during which many capable and accomplished intellectuals were attacked and persecuted also badly muddled up the distinction between the people and the enemy.

3) Nominally, the "Cultural Revolution" was conducted by directly relying on the masses. In fact, it was divorced both from the party organizations and from the masses. After the movement started, party organizations at different levels were attacked and became partially or wholly paralysed, the party's leading cadres at various levels were subjected to criticism and struggle, inner-party life came to a standstill, and many activists and large

numbers of the basic masses whom the party has long relied on were rejected.

At the beginning of the "Cultural Revolution," the vast majority of participants in the movement acted out of their faith in Comrade Mao Zedong and the party. Except for a handful of extremists, however, they did not approve of launching ruthless struggles against leading party cadres at all levels. With the lapse of time, following their own circuitous paths, they eventually attained a heightened political consciousness and began to adopt a sceptical or wait-and-see attitude towards the "Cultural Revolution," or even resisted and opposed it. Many people were assailed either more or less severely for this very reason. Such a state of affairs could not but provide openings to be exploited by opportunists, careerists and conspirators, not a few of whom were escalated to high or even key positions.

4) Practice has shown that the "Cultural Revolution" did not in fact constitute a revolution or social progress in any sense, nor could it possibly have done so. It was we and not the enemy at all who were thrown into disorder by the "Cultural Revolution." Therefore, from beginning to end, it did not turn "great disorder under heaven" into "great order under heaven," nor could it conceivably have done so. After the state power in the form of the people's democratic dictatorship was established in China, and especially after socialist transformation was basically completed and the exploiters were eliminated as classes, the socialist revolution represented a fundamental break with the past in both content and method, even its tasks remained to be completed. Of course, it was essential to take proper account of certain undesirable phenomena that undoubtedly existed in party and state organisms and to remove them by correct measures in conformity with the constitution, the laws and the party constitution. But on no account should the theories and methods of the "Cultural Revolution" have been applied. Under socialist conditions, there is no economic or political basis for carrying out a great political revolution in which "one class overthrows another." It decidedly could not come up with any constructive programme, but could only bring grave disorder, damage and retrogression in its train. History has shown that the "Cultural Revolution," initiated by a leader labouring under a misapprehension and capitalized on by counter-revolutionary cliques, led to domestic turmoil and brought catastrophe to the party, the state and the whole people.

21. The "Cultural Revolution" can be divided into three stages.

1) From the initiation of the "Cultural Revolution" to the ninth national congress of the party in April 1969. The convening of the enlarged Political Bureau meeting of the Central Committee of the party in May 1966 and the eleventh plenary session of the eighth Central Committee in August of that year marked the launching of the "Cultural Revolution" on a full scale. These two meetings adopted the "May 16 circular" and the "Decision of the Central Committee of the Communist Party of China Concerning the Great Proletarian Cultural Revolution" respectively. They launched an erroneous struggle against the so-called antiparty clique of Peng Zhen, Luo Ruiqing, Lu Dingyi and Yang Shangkun and the so-called headquarters of Liu Shaoqi and Deng Xiaoping. They wrongly reorganized the central leading organs, set up the "Cultural Revolution group under the Central Committee of the Chinese Communist Party"

and gave it a major part of the power of the Central Committee. In fact, Comrade Mao Zedong's personal leadership characterized by "left" errors took the place of the collective leadership of the Central Committee, and the cult of Comrade Mao Zedong was frenziedly pushed to an extreme.

Lin Biao, Jiang Qing, Kang Sheng, Zhang Chunqiao and others, acting chiefly in the name of the "Cultural Revolution group," exploited the situation to incite people to "overthrow everything and wage full-scale civil war." Around February 1967, at various meetings, Tan Zhenlin, Chen Yi, Ye Jianying, Li Fuchun, Li Xiannian, Xu Xiangqian, Nie Rongzhen and other Political Bureau members and leading comrades of the Military Commission of the Central Committee sharply criticized the mistakes of the "Cultural Revolution." This was labelled the "February adverse current," and they were attacked and repressed. Comrades Zhu De and Chen Yun were also wrongly criticized. Almost all leading party and government departments in the different spheres and localities were stripped of their power or reorganized. The chaos was such that it was necessary to send in the People's Liberation Army to support the left, the workers and the peasants and to institute military control and military training. It played a positive role in stabilizing the situation, but it also produced some negative consequences. The ninth congress of the party legitimatized the erroneous theories and practices of the "Cultural Revolution," and so reinforced the positions of Lin Biao, Jiang Qing, Kang Sheng and others in the Central Committee of the party. The guidelines of the ninth congress were wrong, ideologically, politically and organizationally.

2) From the ninth national congress of the party to its tenth national congress in August 1973. In 1970–71 the counter-revolutionary Lin Biao clique plotted to capture supreme power and attempted an armed counter-revolutionary coup d'etat. This was the outcome of the "Cultural Revolution" which overturned a series of fundamental party principles. Objectively, it announced the failure of the theories and practices of the "Cultural Revolution." Comrades Mao Zedong and Zhou Enlai ingeniously thwarted the plotted coup. Supported by Comrade Mao Zedong, Comrade Zhou Enlai took charge of the day-to-day work of the Central Committee and things began to improve in all fields. During the criticism and repudiation of Lin Biao in 1972, he correctly proposed criticism of the ultra-left trend of thought. In fact, this was an extension of the correct proposals put forward around February 1967 by many leading comrades of the Central Committee who had called for the correction of the errors of the "Cultural Revolution." Comrade Mao Zedong, however, erroneously held that the task was still to oppose the "ultra-right." The tenth congress of the party perpetuated the "left" errors of the ninth congress and made Wang Hongwen a vicechairman of the party. Jiang Qing, Zhang Chunqiao, Yao Wenyuan and Wang Hongwen formed a gang of four inside the Political Bureau of the Central Committee, thus strengthening the influence of the counter-revolutionary Jiang Qing clique.

3) From the tenth congress of the party of October 1976. Early in 1974 Jiang Qing, Wang Hongwen and others launched a campaign to "criticize Lin Biao and Confucius." Jiang Qing and the others directed the spearhead at Comrade Zhou Enlai, which was different in nature from the campaign conducted in some localities and organizations where individuals involved in and incidents connected with

the conspiracies of the counter-revolutionary Lin Biao clique were investigated. Comrade Mao Zedong approved the launching of the movement to "criticize Lin Biao and Confucius." When he found that Jiang Qing and the others were turning it to their advantage in order to seize power, he severely criticized them. He declared that they had formed a "gang of four" and pointed out that Jiang Qing harboured the wild ambition of making herself chairman of the Central Committee and "forming a cabinet" by political manipulation.

In 1975, when Comrade Zhou Enlai was seriously ill, Comrade Deng Xiaoping, with the support of Comrade Mao Zedong, took charge of the day-to-day work of the Central Committee. He convened an enlarged meeting of the Military Commission of the Central Committee and several other important meetings with a view to solving problems in industry, agriculture, transport and science and technology, and began to straighten out work in many fields so that the situation took an obvious turn for the better. However, Comrade Mao Zedong could not bear to accept systematic correction of the errors of the "Cultural Revolution" by Comrade Deng Xiaoping and triggered the movement to "criticize Deng and counter the right deviationist trend to reverse correct verdicts," once again plunging the nation into turmoil. In January of that year, Comrade Zhou Enlai passed away. Comrade Zhou Enlai was utterly devoted to the party and the people and stuck to his post till his dying day. He found himself in an extremely difficult situation throughout the "Cultural Revolution," he always kept the general interest in mind, bore the heavy burden of office without complaint, wracking his brains and untiringly endeavouring to keep the normal work of the party and the state going, to minimize the damage caused by the "Cultural Revolution" and to protect many party and non-party cadres. He waged all forms of struggle to counter sabotage by the counter-revolutionary Lin Biao and Jiang Qing cliques. His death left the whole party and people in the most profound grief. In April of the same year, a powerful movement of protest signalled by the Tienanmen incident swept the whole country, a movement to mourn for the late Premier Zhou Enlai and oppose the gang of four. In essence, the movement was a demonstration of support for the party's correct leadership as represented by Comrade Deng Xiaoping. It laid the ground for massive popular support for the subsequent overthrow of the counter-revolutionary Jiang Qing clique. The Political Bureau of the Central Committee and Comrade Mao Zedong wrongly assessed the nature of the Tienanmen incident and dismissed Comrade Deng Xiaoping from all his posts inside and outside the party. As soon as Comrade Mao Zedong passed away in September 1976, the counter-revolutionary Jiang Qing clique stepped up its plot to seize supreme party and state leadership. Early in October of the same year, the Political Bureau of the Central Committee, executing the will of the party and the people, resolutely smashed the clique and brought the catastrophic "Cultural Revolution" to an end. This was a great victory won by the entire party, army and people after prolonged struggle. Hua Guofeng, Ye Jianying, Li Xiannian and other comrades played a vital part in the struggle to crush the clique.

22. Chief responsibility for the grave "left" error of the "Cultural Revolution," an error comprehensive in magnitude and protracted in duration, does indeed lie with Comrade Mao Zedong. But after all it was the error of a great proletarian revolutionary. Comrade Mao Zedong paid constant attention to overcoming shortcomings in the life of the party and state. In his later years, however, far from making a correct analysis of many problems, he confused right and wrong and the people with the enemy during the "Cultural Revolution." While making serious mistakes, he repeatedly urged the whole party to study the works of Marx, Engels and Lenin conscientiously and imagined that his theory and practice were Marxist and that they were essential for the consolidation of the dictatorship of the proletariat. Herein lies his tragedy. While persisting in the comprehensive error of the "Cultural Revolution," he checked and rectified some of its specific mistakes, protected some leading party cadres and non-party public figures and enabled some leading cadres to return to important leading posts. He led the struggle to smash the counter-revolutionary Lin Biao clique.

He made major criticisms and exposures of Jiang Qing, Zhang Chunqiao and others, frustrating their sinister ambition to seize supreme leadership. All this was crucial to the subsequent and relatively painless overthrow of the gang of four by our party. In his later years, he still remained alert to safeguarding the security of our country, stood up to the pressure of the social-imperialists, pursued a correct foreign policy, firmly supported the just struggles of all peoples, outlined the correct strategy of the three worlds and advanced the important principle that China would never seek hegemony. During the "Cultural Revolution" our party was not destroyed, but maintained its unity. The State Council and the People's Liberation Army were still able to do much of their essential work. The fourth National People's Congress which was attended by deputies from all nationalities and all walks of life was convened and it determined the composition of the State Council with Comrades Zhou Enlai and Deng Xiaoping at the core of its leadership. The foundation of China's socialist system remained intact and it was possible to continue socialist economic construction. Our country remained united and exerted a significant influence on international affairs. All these important facts are inseparable from the great role played by Comrade Mao Zedong. For these reasons, and particularly for his vital contributions to the cause of the revolution over the years, the Chinese people have always regarded Comrade Mao Zedong as their respected and beloved great leader and teacher.

23. The struggle waged by the party and the people against "left" errors and against the counterrevolutionary Lin Biao and Jiang Qing cliques during the "Cultural Revolution" was arduous and full of twists and turns, and it never ceased. Rigorous tests throughout the "Cultural Revolution" have proved that standing on the correct side in the struggle were the overwhelming majority of members of the eighth Central Committee of the party and the members it elected to its Political Bureau, Standing Committee and Secretariat. Most of our party cadres, whether they were wrongly dismissed or remained at their posts, whether they were rehabilitated early or late, are loyal to the party and people and steadfast in their belief in the cause of socialism and communism. Most of the intellectuals, model workers, patriotic democrats, patriotic Overseas Chinese and cadres and masses of all strata and all nationalities who had been wronged and persecuted, did not waver in

their love for the motherland and in their support for the party and socialism. Party and state leaders such as Comrades Liu Shaoqi, Peng Dehuai, He Long and Tao Zhu and all other party and non-party comrades who were persecuted to death in the "Cultural Revolution" will live forever in the memories of the Chinese people. It was through the joint struggles waged by the entire party and the masses of workers, peasants, PLA officers and men, intellectuals, educated youth and cadres that the havoc wrought by the "Cultural Revolution" was somewhat mitigated. Some progress was made in our economy despite tremendous losses. Grain output increased relatively steadily. Significant achievements were scored in industry, communications and capital construction and in science and technology. New railways were built and the Changjiang River bridge at Nanjing was completed; a number of large enterprises using advanced technology went into operation; hydrogen bomb tests were successfully undertaken and man-made satellites successfully launched and retrieved; and new hybrid strains of long-grained rice were developed and popularized. Despite the domestic turmoil, the People's Liberation Army bravely defended the security of the motherland. And new prospects were opened up in the sphere of foreign affairs. Needless to say, none of these successes can be attributed in any way to the "Cultural Revolution," without which we would have scored far greater achievements for our cause.

Although we suffered from sabotage by the counter-revolutionary Lin Biao and Jiang Qing cliques during the "Cultural Revolution," we won out over them in the end. The party, the people's political power, the people's army and Chinese society on the whole remained unchanged in nature. Once again history has proved that our people are a great people and that our party and socialist system have enormous vitality.

24. In addition to the above-mentioned immediate cause of Comrade Mao Zedong's mistake in leadership, there are complex social and historical causes underlying the "Cultural Revolution" which dragged on for as long as a decade. The main causes are as follows:

1) The history of the socialist movement is not long and that of the socialist countries even shorter. Some of the laws governing the development of socialist society are relatively clear, but many more remain to be explored. Our party had long existed in circumstances of war and fierce class struggle. It was not fully prepared, either ideologically or in terms of scientific study, for the swift advent of the new-born socialist society and for socialist construction on a national scale. The scientific works of Marx, Engels, Lenin and Stalin are our guide to action, but can in no way provide ready-made answers to the problems we may encounter in our socialist use. Even after the basic completion of socialist transformation, given the guiding ideology, we were liable, owing to the historical circumstances in which our party grew, to continue to regard issues unrelated to class struggle as its manifestations when observing and handling new contradictions and problems which cropped up in the political, economic, cultural and other spheres in the course of the development of socialist society. And when confronted with actual class struggle under new conditions, we habitually fell back on the familiar methods and experiences of the large-scale, turbulent mass struggle of the past, which should no longer have been mechanically followed. As a result, we substantially broadened the scope of class struggle. Moreover, this subjective thinking and practice divorced from reality seemed to have a "theoretical basis" in the writings of Marx, Engels, Lenin and Stalin because certain ideas and arguments set forth in them were misunderstood or dogmatically interpreted. For instance, it was thought that equal right, which reflects the exchange of equal amounts of labour and is applicable in the distribution of the means of consumption in socialist society, or "bourgeois right" as it was designated by Marx, should be restricted and criticized, and so the principle of "to each according to his work" and that of material interest should be restricted and criticized: that small production would continue to engender capitalism and the bourgeoisie daily and hourly on a large scale even after the basic completion of socialist transformation, and so a series of "left" economic policies and policies on class struggle in urban and rural areas were formulated; and that all ideological differences inside the party were reflections of class struggle in society, and so frequent and acute inner-party struggles were conducted. All this led us to regard the error in magnifying class struggle as an act in defense of the purity of Marxism. Furthermore, Soviet leaders started a polemic between China and the Soviet Union, and turned the arguments between the two parties on matters of principle into a conflict between the two nations, bringing enormous pressure to bear upon China politically, economically and militarily. So we were forced to wage a just struggle against the big-nation chauvinism of the Soviet Union. In these circumstances, a campaign to prevent and combat revisionism inside the country was launched, which spread the error of broadening the scope of class struggle in the party, so that normal differences among comrades inside the party came to be regarded as manifestations of the revisionist line or of the struggle between the two lines. This resulted in growing tension in inner-party relations. Thus it became difficult for the party to resist certain "left" views put forward by Comrade Mao Zedong and others, and the development of these views led to the outbreak of the protracted "Cultural Revolution."

2) Comrade Mao Zedong's prestige reached a peak and he began to get arrogant at the very time when the party was confronted with the new task of shifting the focus of its work to socialist construction, a task for which the utmost caution was required. He gradually divorced himself from practice and from the masses, acted more and more arbitrarily and subjectively, and increasingly put himself above the Central Committee of the party. The result was a steady weakening and even undermining of the principle of collective leadership and democratic centralism in the political life of the party and the country. This state of affairs took shape only gradually and the Central Committee of the party should be held partly responsible. From the Marxist viewpoint, this complex phenomenon was the product of given historical conditions. Blaming this on only one person or on only a handful of people will not provide a deep lesson for the whole party or enable it to find practical ways to change the situation. In the communist movement, leaders play quite an important role. This has been borne out by history time and again and leaves no room for doubt. However, certain grievous deviations, which occurred in the history of the international communist movement owing to the failure to handle the relationship

between the party and its leader correctly, had an adverse effect on our party, too. Feudalism in China has had a very long history. Our party fought in the firmest and most thoroughgoing way against it and particularly against the feudal system of land ownership and the landlords and local tyrants, and fostered a fine tradition of democracy in the anti-feudal struggle. But it remains difficult to eliminate the evil ideological and political influence of centuries of feudal autocracy. And for various historical reasons, we failed to institutionalize and legalize inner-party democracy and democracy in the political and social life of the country, or we drew up the relevant laws but they lacked due authority. This meant that conditions were present for the over-concentration of party power in individuals and for the development of arbitrary individual rule and the personality cult in the party. Thus, it was hard for the party and state to prevent the initiation of the "Cultural Revolution" or check its development.

A GREAT TURNING POINT IN HISTORY

25. The victory won in overthrowing the counter-revolutionary Jiang Qing clique in October 1976 saved the party and the revolution from disaster and enabled our country to enter a new historical period of development. In the two years from October 1976 to December 1978 when the third plenary session of the eleventh Central Committee of the party was convened, large numbers of cadres and other people most enthusiastically devoted themselves to all kinds of revolutionary work and the task of construction. Notable results were achieved in exposing and repudiating the crimes of the counter-revolutionary Jiang Qing clique and uncovering their factional setup. The consolidation of party and state organizations and the redress of wrong suffered by those who were unjustly, falsely and wrongly charged began in some places. Industrial and agricultural production was fairly swiftly restored. Work in education, science and culture began to return to normal. Comrades inside and outside the party demanded more and more strongly that the errors of the "Cultural Revolution" be corrected, but such demands met with serious resistance.

This, of course, was partly due to the fact that the political and ideological confusion created in the decade-long "Cultural Revolution" could not be eliminated overnight, but it was also due to the "left" error in the guiding ideology that Comrade Hua Guofeng continued to commit in his capacity as chairman of the Central Committee of the Chinese Communist Party. On the proposal of Comrade Mao Zedong Comrade Hua Guofeng had become first vice-chairman of the Central Committee of the party and concurrently premier of the State Council during the "movement to criticize Deng Xiaoping" in 1976. He contributed to the struggle to overthrow the counter-revolutionary Jiang Qing clique and did useful work after that. But he promoted the erroneous "two-whatever's" policy, that is, "we firmly uphold whatever policy decisions Chairman Mao made, and we unswervingly adhere to whatever instructions Chairman Mao gave," and he took a long time to rectify the error. He tried to suppress the discussions on the criterion of truth unfolded in the country in 1978, which were very significant in setting things

right. He procrastinated and obstructed the work of reinstating veteran cadres in their posts and redressing the injustices left over from the past (including the case of the "Tienanmen incident" of 1976). He accepted and fostered the personality cult around himself while continuing the personality cult of the past. The eleventh national congress of the Chinese Communist Party convened in August 1977 played a positive role in exposing and repudiating the gang of four and mobilizing the whole party for building China into a powerful modern socialist state. However, owing to the limitations imposed by the historical conditions then and the influence of Comrade Hua Guofeng's mistakes, it reaffirmed the erroneous theories, policies and slogans of the "Cultural Revolution" instead of correcting them. He also had his share of responsibility for impetuously seeking quick results in economic work and for continuing certain other "left" policies. Obviously, under his leadership it is impossible to correct "left" errors within the party, and all the more impossible to restore the party's fine traditions.

26. The third plenary session of the eleventh Central Committee in December 1978 marked a crucial turning point of far-reaching significance in the history of our party since the birth of the People's Republic. It put an end to the situation in which the party had been advancing haltingly in its work since October 1976 and began to correct conscientiously and comprehensively the "left" errors of the "Cultural Revolution" and earlier. The plenary session resolutely criticized the erroneous "two-whatever's" policy and fully affirmed the need to grasp Mao Zedong Thought comprehensively and accurately as a scientific system. It highly evaluated the forum on the criterion of truth and decided on the guiding principle of emancipating the mind, using our brains, seeking truth from facts and uniting as one in looking forward to the future. It firmly discarded the slogan "take class struggle as the key link" which had become unsuitable in a socialist society, and made the strategic decision to shift the focus of work to socialist modernization. It declared that attention should be paid to solving the problem of serious imbalances between the major branches of the economy and drafted decisions on the acceleration of agricultural development. It stressed the task of strengthening socialist democracy and the socialist legal system. It examined and redressed a number of major unjust, false and wrong cases in the history of the party and settled the controversy on the merits and demerits, the rights and wrongs, of some prominent leaders. The plenary session also elected additional members to the party's central leading organs. These momentous changes in the work of leadership signify that the party has re-established the correct line of Marxism ideologically, politically and organizationally. Since then, it has gained the initiative in setting things right and is able to solve step by step many problems left over since the founding of the People's Republic and the new problems cropping up in the course of practice and carry out the heavy tasks of construction and reform, so that things are going very well in both the economic and political spheres.

1) In response to the call of the third plenary session of the eleventh Central Committee of the party for emancipating the mind and seeking truth from facts, large numbers of cadres and other people have freed themselves from the spiritual shackles of the personality cult and the dogmatism that prevailed in the past. This has stimulated thinking inside and outside the party, giving rise to a lively

situation where people try their best to study new things and seek solutions to new problems. To carry out the principle of emancipating the mind properly, the party reiterated in good time the four fundamental principles of upholding the socialist road, the people's democratic dictatorship (i.e., the dictatorship of the proletariat), the leadership of the Communist Party, and Marxism-Leninism and Mao Zedong Thought. It reaffirmed the principle that neither democracy nor centralism can be practised at each other's expense and pointed out the basic fact that, although the exploiters had been eliminated as classes, class struggle continued to exist within certain limits. In his speech at the meeting in celebration of the 30th anniversary of the founding of the People's Republic of China, which was approved by the fourth plenary session of the eleventh Central Committee of the party, Comrade Ye Jianying fully affirmed the gigantic achievements of the party and people since the inauguration of the People's Republic while making self-criticism on behalf of the party for errors in its work and outlined our country's bright prospects. This helped to unify the thinking of the whole party and people. At its meeting in August 1980, the Political Bureau of the Central Committee set the historic task of combating corrosion by bourgeois ideology and eradicating the evil influence of feudalism in the political and ideological fields which is still present. A work conference convened by the Central Committee in December of the same year resolved to strengthen the party's ideological and political work; make greater efforts to build a socialist civilization, criticize the erroneous ideological trends running counter to the four fundamental principles and strike at the counter-revolutionary activities disrupting the cause of socialism. This exerted a most salutary countrywide influence in fostering a political situation characterized by stability, unity and liveliness.

2) At a work conference called by the Central Committee in April 1979, the party formulated the principle of "readjusting, restructuring, consolidating and improving" the economy as a whole in a decisive effort to correct the shortcomings and mistakes of the previous two years in our economic work and eliminate the influence of "left" errors that had persisted in this field. The party indicated that economic construction must be carried out in the light of China's conditions and in conformity with economic and natural laws; that it must be carried out within the limits of our own resources, step by step, after due deliberation and with emphasis on practical results, so that the development of production will be closely connected with the improvement of the people's livelihood; and that active efforts must be made to promote economic and technical co-operation with other countries on the basis of independence and self-reliance. Guided by these principles, light industry has quickened its rate of growth and the structure of industry is becoming more rational and better co-ordinated. Reforms in the system of economic management, including extension of the decision-making powers of enterprises, restoration of the workers' congresses, strengthening of democratic management of enterprises and transference of financial management responsibilities to the various levels, have gradually been carried out in conjunction with economic readjustment. The party has worked conscientiously to remedy the errors in rural work since the later stage of the movement for agricultural co-operation, with the result that the purchase prices of farm

and sideline products have been raised, various forms of production responsibility introduced whereby remuneration is determined by farm output, family plots have been restored and appropriately extended, village fairs have been revived, and sideline occupations and diverse undertakings have been developed.

All these have greatly enhanced the peasants' enthusiasm. Grain output in the last two years reached an all-time high, and at the same time industrial crops and other farm and sideline products registered a big increase. Thanks to the development of agriculture and the economy as a whole, the living standards of the people have improved.

3) After detailed and careful investigation and study, measures were taken to clear the name of Comrade Liu Shaoqi, former vice-chairman of the Central Committee of the Communist Party of China and chairman of the People's Republic of China, those of other party and state leaders, national minority leaders and leading figures in different circles who had been wronged, and to affirm their historical contributions to the party and the people in protracted revolutionary struggle.

4) Large numbers of unjust, false and wrong cases were re-examined and their verdicts reversed. Cases in which people had been wrongly labelled bourgeois rightists were also corrected. Announcements were made to the effect that former businessmen and industrialists, having undergone remoulding, are now working people; that small tradespeople, pedlars and handicraftsmen, who were originally labourers, have been differentiated from businessmen and industrialists who were members of the bourgeoisie; and that the status of the vast majority of former landlords and rich peasants, who have become working people through remoulding, has been re-defined. These measures have appropriately resolved many contradictions inside the party and among the people.

5) People's congresses at all levels are doing their work better and those at the provincial and county levels have set up permanent organs of their own. The system according to which deputies to the people's congresses at and below the county level are directly elected by the voters is now universally practised. Collective leadership and democratic centralism are being perfected in the party and state organizations. The powers of local and primary organizations are steadily being extended. The so-called right to "speak out, air views and hold debates in a big way and write big-character posters," which actually obstructs the promotion of socialist democracy, was deleted from the constitution. A number of important laws, decrees and regulations have been reinstated, enacted or enforced, including the criminal law and the law of criminal procedure which had never been drawn up since the founding of the People's Republic. The work of the judicial, procuratorial and public security departments has improved and telling blows have been dealt at all types of criminals guilty of serious offences. The ten principal members of the counter-revolutionary Lin Biao and Jiang Qing cliques were publicly tried according to law.

6) The party has striven to readjust and strengthen the leading bodies at all levels. The fifth plenary session of the eleventh Central Committee of the party, held in February 1980, elected additional members to the Standing Committee of its Political Bureau and re-established the Secretariat of the Central Committee, greatly strengthening the central leadership. Party militancy has been enhanced

as a result of the establishment of the central commission for inspecting discipline and of discipline inspection commissions at the lower levels, the formulation of the "guiding principles for inner-party political life" and other related inner-party regulations, and the effort made by leading party organizations and discipline inspection bodies at the different levels to rectify unhealthy practices. The party's mass media have also contributed immensely in this respect. The party has decided to put an end to the virtually lifelong tenure of leading cadres, change the over-concentration of power and, on the basis of revolutionization, gradually reduce the average age of the leading cadres at all levels and raise their level of education and professional competence, and has initiated this process. With the reshuffling of the leading personnel of the State Council and the division of labour between party and government organizations, the work of the central and local governments has improved.

In addition, there have been significant successes in the party's effort to implement our policies in education, science, culture, public health, physical culture, nationality affairs, united front work, Overseas Chinese affairs and military and foreign affairs.

In short, the scientific principles of Mao Zedong Thought and the correct policies of the party have been revived and developed under new conditions and all aspects of party and government work have been flourishing again since the third plenary session of the eleventh Central Committee. Our work still suffers from shortcomings and mistakes, and we are still confronted with numerous difficulties. Nevertheless, the road of victorious advance is open, and the party's prestige among the people is rising day by day.

COMRADE MAO ZEDONG'S HISTORICAL ROLE AND MAO ZEDONG THOUGHT

27. Comrade Mao Zedong was a great Marxist and a great proletarian revolutionary, strategist and theorist. It is true that he made gross mistakes during the "Cultural Revolution," but, if we judge his activities as a whole, his contributions to the Chinese revolution far outweigh his mistakes. His merits are primary and his errors secondary. He rendered indelible meritorious service in founding and building up our party and the Chinese People's Liberation Army, in winning victory for the cause of liberation of the Chinese people, in founding the People's Republic of China and in advancing our socialist cause. He made major contributions to the liberation of the oppressed nations of the world and to the progress of mankind.

28. The Chinese communists, with Comrade Mao Zedong as their chief representative, made a theoretical synthesis of China's unique experience in its protracted revolution in accordance with the basic principles of Marxism-Leninism. This synthesis constituted a scientific system of guidelines befitting China's conditions, and it is this synthesis which is Mao Zedong Thought, the product of the integration of the universal principles of Marxism-Leninism with the concrete practice of the Chinese revolution. Making revolution in a large eastern semi-colonial, semi-feudal country is bound to meet with many special, complicated problems, which cannot be solved by reciting the general principles of Marxism-Leninism, or by copying foreign experience in every detail. An erroneous tendency of making Marxism a dogma and deifying Comintern resolutions and the experience of the Soviet Union prevailed in the international communist movement and in our party mainly in the late 1920s and early 1930s, and this tendency pushed the Chinese revolution to the brink of total failure. It was in the course of combating this wrong tendency and making a profound summary of our historical experience in this respect that Mao Zedong Thought took shape and developed. It was systematized and extended in a variety of fields and reached maturity in the latter part of the agrarian revolutionary war and the war of resistance against Japan, and it was further developed during the war of liberation and after the founding of the People's Republic of China. Mao Zedong Thought is Marxism-Leninism applied and developed in China; it constitutes a correct theory, a body of correct principles and a summary of the experiences that have been confirmed in the practice of the Chinese revolution, a crystallization of the collective wisdom of the Chinese Communist Party. Many outstanding leaders of our party made important contributions to the formation and development of Mao Zedong Thought, which are synthesized in the scientific works of Comrade Mao Zedong.

29. Mao Zedong Thought is wide-ranging in content. It is an original theory which has enriched and developed Marxism-Leninism in the following respects:

1) On the new-democratic revolution. Proceeding from China's historical and social conditions, Comrade Mao Zedong made a profound study of the characteristics and laws of the Chinese revolution, applied and developed the Marxist-Leninist thesis of the leadership of the proletariat in the democratic revolution, and established the theory of new-democratic revolution—a revolution against imperialism, feudalism and bureaucrat-capitalism waged by the masses of the people on the basis of the worker-peasant alliance under the leadership of the proletariat. His main works on this subject include: "Analysis of the Classes in Chinese Society," "Report on an Investigation of the Peasant Movement in Hunan," "A Single Spark Can Start a Prairie Fire," "Introducing 'The Communist'," "On New Democracy," "On Coalition Government" and "The Present Situation and Our Tasks." The basic points of this theory are:

I) China's bourgeoisie consisted of two sections, the big bourgeoisie (that is, the comprador bourgeoisie, or the bureaucrat-bourgeoisie) which was dependent on imperialism, and the national bourgeoisie which had revolutionary leanings but wavered. The proletariat should endeavour to get the national bourgeoisie to join in the united front under its leadership and, in special circumstances, to include even part of the big bourgeoisie in the united front, so as to isolate the main enemy to the greatest possible extent. When forming a united front with the bourgeoisie, the proletariat must preserve its own independence and pursue the policy of "unity, struggle, unity through struggle"; when forced to split with the bourgeoisie, chiefly the big bourgeoisie, it should have the courage and ability to wage a resolute armed struggle against the big bourgeoisie, while continuing to win the sympathy of the national bourgeoisie or keep it neutral.

II) Since there was no bourgeois democracy in China and the reactionary ruling classes enforced their terroristic dictatorship over the people by armed force, the revolution could not but essentially take the form of protracted armed struggle. China's armed struggle was a revolutionary war led by the proletariat with the peasants as the principal force. The peasantry was the most reliable ally of the proletariat. Through its vanguard, it was possible and necessary for the proletariat, with its progressive ideology and its sense of organization and discipline, to raise the political consciousness of the peasant masses, establish rural base areas, wage a protracted revolutionary war and build up and expand the revolutionary forces.

Comrade Mao Zedong pointed out that "the united front and armed struggle are the two basic weapons for defeating the enemy." Together with party building, they constituted the "three magic weapons" of the revolution. They were the essential basis which enables the Chinese Communist Party to become the core of leadership of the whole nation and to chart the course of encircling the cities from the countryside and finally winning countrywide victory.

2) On the socialist revolution and socialist construction. On the basis of the economic and political conditions for the transition to socialism ensuing on victory in the new-democratic revolution, Comrade Mao Zedong and the Chinese Communist Party followed the path of effecting socialist industrialization simultaneously with socialist transformation and adopted concrete policies for the gradual transformation of the private ownership of the means of production, thereby providing a theoretical as well as practical solution of the difficult task of building socialism in a large country such as China, a country which was economically and culturally backward, with a population accounting for nearly one-fourth of the world's total. By putting forward the thesis that the combination of democracy for the people and dictatorship over the reactionaries constitutes the people's democratic dictatorship, Comrade Mao Zedong enriched the Marxist-Leninist theory of the dictatorship of the proletariat.

After the establishment of the socialist system, Comrade Mao Zedong pointed out that, under socialism, the people had the same fundamental interests, but that all kinds of contradictions still existed among them, and that contradictions between the enemy and the people and contradictions among the people should be strictly distinguished from each other and correctly handled. He proposed that among the people we should follow a set of correct policies. We should follow the policy of "unity—criticism—unity" in political matters, the policy of "long-term coexistence and mutual supervision" in the party's relations with the democratic parties, the policy of "let a hundred flowers blossom, let a hundred schools of thought contend" in science and culture, and, in the economic sphere the policy of overall arrangement with regard to the different strata in town and country and of consideration for the interests of the state, the collective and the individual, all three. He repeatedly stressed that we should not mechanically transplant the experience of foreign countries, but should find our own way to industrialization, a way suited to China's conditions, by proceeding from the fact that China is a large agricultural country, taking agriculture as the foundation of the economy, correctly handling the relationship between heavy industry on the one hand and agriculture and light industry on the other and attaching due importance to the development of the latter. He stressed that in socialist construction we

should properly handle the relationships between economic construction and building national defence, between large-scale enterprises and small and medium-scale enterprises, between the Han nationality and the minority nationalities, between the coastal regions and the interior, between the central and the local authorities, and between self-reliance and learning from foreign countries, and that we should properly handle the relationship between accumulation and consumption and pay attention to overall balance. Moreover, he stressed that the workers were the masters of their enterprises and that cadres must take part in physical labour and workers in management, that irrational rules and regulations must be reformed and that the three-in-one combination of technical personnel, workers and cadres must be effected. And he formulated the strategic idea of bringing all positive factors into play and turning negative factors into positive ones so as to unite the whole Chinese people and build a powerful socialist country. The important ideas of Comrade Mao Zedong concerning the socialist revolution and socialist construction are mainly contained in such major works as "Report to the Second Plenary Session of the Seventh Central Committee of the Communist Party of China," "On the People's Democratic Dictatorship," "On the Ten Major Relationships," "On the Correct Handling of Contradictions Among the People" and "Talk at an Enlarged Work Conference Convened by the Central Committee of the Communist Party of China."

3) On the building of the revolutionary army and military strategy. Comrade Mao Zedong methodically solved the problem of how to turn a revolutionary army chiefly made up of peasants into a new type of people's army which is proletarian in character, observes strict discipline and forms close ties with the masses. He laid it down that the sole purpose of the people's army is to serve the people whole-heartedly. He put forward the principle that the party commands the gun and not the other way round. He advanced the three main rules of discipline and the eight points for attention and stressed the practice of political, economic and military democracy and the principles of the unity of officers and soldiers, the unity of army and people and the disintegration of the enemy forces. Thus he formulated by way of summation a set of policies and methods concerning work in the army. In his military writings such as "On Correcting Mistaken Ideas in the Party," "Problems of Strategy in China's Revolutionary War," "Problems of Strategy in Guerrilla War Against Japan," "On Protracted War" and "Problems of War and Strategy," Comrade Mao Zedong summed up the experience of China's protracted revolutionary war and advanced the comprehensive concept of building a people's army and of building rural base areas and waging people's war by employing the people's army as the main force and relying on the masses.

Raising guerrilla war to the strategic plane, he maintained that guerrilla warfare and mobile warfare of a guerrilla character would for a long time be the main forms of operation in China's revolutionary war. He explained that it would be necessary to effect an appropriate change in military strategy simultaneously with the changing balance of forces between the enemy and ourselves and with the progress of the war. He worked out a set of strategies and tactics for the revolutionary army to wage people's war in conditions when the enemy was strong and we were weak.

These strategies and tactics include fighting a protracted war strategically and campaigns and battles of quick decision, turning strategic inferiority into superiority in campaigns and battles and concentrating a superior force to destroy the enemy forces one by one. During the war of liberation, he formulated the celebrated ten major principles of operation. All these ideas constitute Comrade Mao Zedong's outstanding contribution to the military theory of Marxism-Leninism. After the founding of the People's Republic, he put forward the important guideline that we must strengthen our national defence and build modern revolutionary armed forces (including the navy, the air force and technical branches) and develop modern defence technology (including the making of nuclear weapons for self-defense).

4) On policy and tactics. Comrade Mao Zedong penetratingly elucidated the vital importance of policy and tactics in revolutionary struggles. He pointed out that policy and tactics were the life of the party, that they were both the starting-point and the end-result of all the practical activities of a revolutionary party and that the party must formulate its policies in the light of the existing political situation, class relations, actual circumstances and the changes in them, combining principle and flexibility. He made many valuable suggestions concerning policy and tactics in the struggle against the enemy, in the united front and other questions. He pointed out among other things:

That, under changing subjective and objective conditions, a weak revolutionary force could ultimately defeat a strong reactionary force;

That, we should despise the enemy strategically and take the enemy seriously tactically;

That, we should keep our eyes on the main target of the struggle and not hit out in all directions;

That, we should differentiate between and disintegrate our enemies, and adopt the tactic of making use of contradictions, winning over the many, opposing the few and crushing our enemies one by one;

That, in areas under reactionary rule, we should combine legal and illegal struggle and, organizationally, adopt the policy of assigning picked cadres to work underground;

That, as for members of the defeated reactionary classes and reactionary elements, we should give them a chance to earn a living and to become working people living by their own labour, so long as they did not rebel or create trouble; and

That the proletariat and its party must fulfill two conditions in order to exercise leadership over their allies: (A) lead their followers in waging resolute struggles against the common enemy and achieving victories; (B) bring material benefits to their followers or at least avoid damaging their interests and at the same time give them political education.

These ideas of Comrade Mao Zedong's concerning policy and tactics are embodied in many of his writings, particularly in such works as "Current Problems of Tactics in the Anti-Japanese United Front," "On Policy," "Conclusions on the Repulse of the Second Anti-Communist Onslaught," "On Some Important Problems of the Party's Present Policy," "Don't Hit Out in All Directions" and "On the Question of Whether Imperialism and All Reactionaries Are Real Tigers."

5) On ideological and political work and cultural work. In his "On New Democracy," Comrade Mao Zedong stated:

Any given culture (as an ideological form) is a reflection of the politics and economics of a given society, and the former in turn has a tremendous influence and effect upon the latter; economics is the base and politics the concentrated expression of economics.

In accordance with this basic view, he put forward many significant ideas of far-reaching and long-term significance. For instance, the theses that ideological and political work is the life-blood of economic and all other work and that it is necessary to unite politics and economics and to unite politics and professional skills, and to be both Red and expert; the policy of developing a national, scientific and mass culture and of letting a hundred flowers blossom, weeding through the old to bring forth the new, and making the past serve the present and foreign things serve China; and the thesis that intellectuals have an important role to play in revolution and construction, that intellectuals should identify themselves with the workers and peasants and that they should acquire the proletarian world out-look by studying Marxism-Leninism, by studying society and through practical work. He pointed out that "this question of 'for whom?' is fundamental; it is a question of principle" and stressed that we should serve the people whole-heartedly, be highly responsible in revolutionary work, wage arduous struggle and fear no sacrifice. Many notable works written by Comrade Mao Zedong on ideology, politics and culture, such as "The Orientation of the Youth Movement," "Recruit Large Numbers of Intellectuals," "Talks at the Yanan Forum of Literature and Art," "In Memory of Norman Bethune," "Serve the People" and "The Foolish Old Man Who Removed the Mountains," are of tremendous significance even today.

6) On party building. It was a most difficult task to build a Marxist, proletarian party of a mass character in a country where the peasantry and other sections of the petty bourgeoisie constituted the majority of the population, while the proletariat was small in number yet strong in combat effectiveness. Comrade Mao Zedong's theory on party building provided a successful solution to this question. His main works in this area include "Combat Liberalism," "The Role of the Chinese Communist Party in the National War," "Reform Our Study," "Rectify the Party's Style of Work," "Oppose Stereotyped Party Writing," "Our Study and the Current Situation," "On Strengthening the Party Committee System" and "Methods of Work of Party Committees." He laid particular stress on building the party ideologically, saying that a party member should join the party not only organizationally but also ideologically and should constantly try to reform his non-proletarian ideas and replace them with proletarian ideas. He indicated that the style of work which entailed integrating theory with practice, forging close links with the masses and practising self-criticism was the hallmark distinguishing the Chinese Communist Party from all other political parties in China. To counter the erroneous "left" policy of "ruthless struggle and merciless blows" once followed in inner-party struggle, he proposed the correct policy of "learning from past mistakes to avoid future ones and curing the sickness to save the patient," emphasizing the need to achieve the objective of clarity in ideology and unity among comrades in inner-party struggle. He initiated the rectification campaign as a

form of ideological education in Marxism-Leninism throughout the party, which applied the method of criticism and self-criticism.

In view of the fact that our party was about to become and then became a party in power leading the whole country, Comrade Mao Zedong urged time and again, first on the eve of the founding of the People's Republic and then later that we should remain modest and prudent, guard against arrogance and rashness and keep to plain living and hard struggle in our style of work and that we should be on the lookout against the corrosive influence of bourgeois ideology and should oppose bureaucratism which would alienate us from the masses.

30. The living soul of Mao Zedong Thought is the stand, method and viewpoint embodied in its component parts mentioned above. This stand, viewpoint and method boil down to three basic points: to seek truth from facts, the mass line, and independence. Comrade Mao Zedong applied dialectical and historical materialism to the entire work of the proletarian party, giving shape to this stand, viewpoint and method so characteristic of Chinese communists in the course of the Chinese revolution and its arduous, protracted struggles and thus enriching Marxism-Leninism. They find expression not only in such important works as "Oppose Book Worship," "On Practice," "On Contradictions," "Preface and Postscript to 'Rural Surveys'," "Some Questions Concerning Methods of Leadership" and "Where Do Correct Ideas Come From?", but also in all his scientific writings and in the revolutionary activities of the Chinese communists.

1) Seeking truth from facts. This means proceeding from reality and combining theory with practice, that is, integrating the universal principles of Marxism-Leninism with the concrete practice of the Chinese revolution. Comrade Mao Zedong was always against studying Marxism in isolation from the realities of Chinese society and the Chinese revolution. As early as 1930, he opposed blind book worship by emphasizing that investigation and study is the first step in all work and that one has no right to speak without investigation. On the eve of the rectification movement in Yanan, he affirmed that subjectivism is a formidable enemy of the Communist Party, a manifestation of impurity in party spirit. These brilliant theses helped people break through the shackles of dogmatism and greatly emancipate their own minds. While summarizing the experience and lessons of the Chinese revolution in his philosophical works and many other works rich in philosophical content, Comrade Mao Zedong showed great profundity in expounding and enriching the Marxist theory of knowledge and dialectics. He stressed that the dialectical materialist theory of knowledge is the dynamic, revolutionary theory of reflection and that full scope should be given to man's conscious dynamic role which is based on and is in conformity with objective reality. Basing himself on social practice, he comprehensively and systematically elaborated the dialectical materialist theory on the sources, the process and the purpose of knowledge and the criterion of truth. He said that as a rule, correct knowledge can be arrived at and developed only after many repetitions of the process leading from matter to consciousness and then back to matter, that is, leading from practice to knowledge and then back to practice. He pointed out that truth exists by contrast with falsehood and grows in struggle with it, that truth is inexhaustible and that the truth of any piece

of knowledge, namely, whether it corresponds to objective reality, can ultimately be decided only through social practice. He further elaborated the law of the unity of opposites, the nucleus of Marxist dialectics. He indicated that we should not only study the universality of contradiction in objective existence, but, what is more important, we should study the particularity of contradiction, and that we should resolve contradictions which are different in nature by different methods. Therefore, dialectics should not be viewed as a formula to be learned by rote and applied mechanically, but should be closely linked with practice and with investigation and study and should be applied flexibly.

He forged philosophy into a sharp weapon in the hands of the proletariat and the people for knowing and changing the world. His distinguished works on China's revolutionary war, in particular, provide outstandingly shining examples of applying and developing the Marxist theory of knowledge and dialectics in practice. Our party must always adhere to the above ideological line formulated by Comrade Mao Zedong.

2) The mass line means everything for the masses, reliance on the masses in everything and "from the masses, to the masses." The party's mass line in all its work has come into being through the systematic application in all its activities of the Marxist-Leninist principle that the people are the makers of history. It is a summation of our party's invaluable historical experience in conducting revolutionary activities over the years under difficult circumstances in which the enemy's strength far outstripped ours. Comrade Mao Zedong stressed time and again that as long as we rely on the people, believe firmly in the inexhaustible creative power of the masses and hence trust and identify ourselves with them, no enemy can crush us while we can eventually crush every enemy and overcome every difficulty. He also pointed out that in leading the masses in all practical work, the leadership can form its correct ideas only by adopting the method "from the masses, to the masses" and by combining the leadership with the masses and combining the general call with particular guidance. This means concentrating the ideas of the masses and turning them into systematic ideas, then going to the masses so that the ideas are persevered in and carried through, and testing the correctness of these ideas in the practice of the masses. And this process goes on, over and over again, so that the understanding of the leadership becomes more correct, more vital and richer each time. This is how Comrade Mao Zedong united the Marxist theory of knowledge with the party's mass line. As the vanguard of the proletariat, the party exists and fights for the interests of the people. But it always constitutes only a small part of the people, so that isolation from the people will render all the party's struggles and ideals devoid of content as well as impossible of success. To persevere in the revolution and advance the socialist cause, our party must uphold the mass line.

3) Independence and self-reliance are the inevitable corollary of carrying out the Chinese revolution and construction by proceeding from Chinese reality and relying on the masses. The proletarian revolution is an internationalist cause which calls for the mutual support of the proletariats of different countries. But for the cause to triumph, each proletariat should primarily base itself on its own country's realities, rely on the efforts of its own masses and revolutionary forces, integrate the universal

principles of Marxism-Leninism with the concrete practice of its own revolution and achieve victory. Comrade Mao Zedong always stressed that our policy should rest on our own strength and that we should find our own road of advance in accordance with our own conditions. In a vast country like China, we must all the more rely mainly on our own efforts to promote the revolution and construction. We must be determined to carry the struggle through to the end and must have faith in the hundreds of millions of Chinese people and rely on their wisdom and strength. Otherwise, it will be impossible for our revolution and construction to succeed or to be consolidated even if success is won. Of course, China's revolution and national construction are not and cannot be carried on in isolation from the rest of the world. It is always necessary for us to try to win foreign aid and, in particular, to learn all that is advanced and beneficial from other countries.

The closed-door policy, blind opposition to everything foreign and any theory or practice of great-nation chauvinism are all entirely wrong. At the same time, although China is still comparatively backward economically and culturally, we must maintain our own national dignity and confidence and there must be no slavishness or submissiveness in any form in dealing with big, powerful or rich countries. Under the leadership of the party and Comrade Mao Zedong, we never wavered, whether before or after the founding of new China, in our determination to remain independent and self-reliant and, no matter what difficulty we encountered, we never submitted to any pressure from outside; we showed the dauntless and heroic spirit of the Chinese Communist Party and the Chinese people. We stand for the peaceful co-existence of the people of all countries and their mutual assistance on an equal footing. While upholding our own independence, we respect other people's right to independence. The road of revolution and construction suited to the characteristics of a country has to be explored, decided on and blazed by its own people. No one has the right to impose his views on others. Only under these conditions can there be genuine internationalism. Otherwise, there can only be hegemonism. We will always adhere to this principled stand in our international relations.

31. Mao Zedong Thought is the valuable spiritual asset of our party. It will be our guide to action for a long time to come. The party leaders and the large group of cadres nurtured by Marxism-Leninism and Mao Zedong Thought were the backbone forces in winning great victories for our cause; they are and will remain our treasured mainstay in the cause of socialist modernization. While many of Comrade Mao Zedong's important works were written during the periods of new-democratic revolution and of socialist transformation, we must still constantly study them. This is not only because one cannot cut the past off from the present and failure to understand the past will hamper our understanding of present-day problems, but also because many of the basic theories, principles and methodology set forth in these works are of universal significance and provide us with valuable guidance now and will continue to do so in the future. Therefore, we must continue to uphold Mao Zedong Thought, study it in earnest and apply its stand, viewpoint and method in studying the new situation and solving the new problems arising in the course of practice. Mao Zedong Thought has added much that is new to the treasure-house of Marxist-Leninist theory. We must combine our study of the scientific works of Comrade Mao Zedong with that of the scientific writings of Marx, Engels, Lenin and Stalin. It is entirely wrong to try to negate the scientific value of Mao Zedong Thought and to deny its guiding role in our revolution and construction, just because Comrade Mao Zedong made mistakes in his later years. And it is likewise entirely wrong to adopt a dogmatic attitude towards the sayings of Comrade Mao Zedong, to regard whatever he said as the unalterable truth which must be mechanically applied everywhere, and to be unwilling to admit honestly that he made mistakes in his later years, and even try to stick to them in our new activities. Both these attitudes fail to make a distinction between Mao Zedong Thought—a scientific theory formed and tested over a long period of time—and the mistakes Comrade Mao Zedong made in his later years. And it is absolutely necessary that this distinction should be made. We must treasure all the positive experience obtained in the course of integrating the universal principles of Marxism-Leninism with the concrete practice of China's revolution and construction over fifty years or so, apply and carry forward this experience in our new work, enrich and develop party theory with new principles and new conclusions corresponding to reality, so as to ensure the continued progress of our cause along the scientific course of Marxism-Leninism and Mao Zedong Thought.

UNITE AND STRIVE TO BUILD A POWERFUL, MODERN SOCIALIST CHINA

32. The objective of our party's struggle in the new historical period is to turn China step by step into a powerful socialist country with modern agriculture, industry, national defence and science and technology and with a high level of democracy and culture. We must also accomplish the great cause of reunification of the country by getting Taiwan to return to the embrace of the motherland. The fundamental aim of summing up the historical experience of the thirty-two years since the founding of the People's Republic is to accomplish the great objective of building a powerful and modern socialist country by further rallying the will and strength of the whole party, the whole army and the whole people on the basis of upholding the four fundamental principles, namely, upholding the socialist road, the people's democratic dictatorship (i.e., the dictatorship of the proletariat), the leadership of the Communist Party and Marxism-Leninism and Mao Zedong Thought. These four principles constitute the common political basis of the unity of the whole party and the unity of the whole people as well as the basic guarantee for the realization of socialist modernization. Any word or deed which deviates from these four principles is wrong. Any word or deed which denies or undermines these four principles cannot be tolerated.

33. Socialism and socialism alone can save China. This is the unalterable conclusion drawn by all our people from their own experience over the past century or so; it likewise constitutes our fundamental historical experience in the thirty-two years since the founding of our People's Republic. Although our socialist system is still in its early phase of development, China has undoubtedly established a socialist system and entered the stage of socialist society.

Any view denying this basic fact is wrong. Under socialism, we have achieved successes which were absolutely impossible in old China. This is a preliminary and at the same time convincing manifestation of the superiority of the socialist system. The fact that we have been and are able to overcome all kinds of difficulties through our own efforts testifies to its great vitality. Of course, our system will have to undergo a long process of development before it can be perfected. Given the premise that we uphold the basic system of socialism, therefore, we must strive to reform those specific features which are not in keeping with the expansion of the productive forces and the interests of the people, and to staunchly combat all activities detrimental to socialism. With the development of our cause, the immense superiority of socialism will become more and more apparent.

34. Without the Chinese Communist Party, there would have been no new China. Likewise, without the Chinese Communist Party, there would be no modern socialist China. The Chinese Communist Party is a proletarian party armed with Marxism-Leninism and Mao Zedong Thought and imbued with a strict sense of discipline and the spirit of self-criticism, and its ultimate historical mission is to realize communism. Without the leadership of such a party, without the flesh-and-blood ties it has formed with the masses through protracted struggles and without its painstaking and effective work among the people and the high prestige it consequently enjoys, our country—for a variety of reasons, both internal and external—would inexorably fall apart and the future of our nation and people would inexorably be forfeited. The party leadership cannot be free from mistakes, but there is no doubt that, by relying on the close unity between the party and the people, it can correct its mistakes, and in no case should one use the party's mistakes as a pretext for weakening, breaking away from or even sabotaging its leadership. That would only lead to even greater mistakes and court grievous disasters. We must improve party leadership in order to uphold it.

We must resolutely overcome the many shortcomings that still exist in our party's style of thinking and work, in its system of organization and leadership and in its contacts with the masses. So long as we earnestly uphold and constantly improve party leadership, our party will definitely be better able to undertake the tremendous tasks entrusted to it by history.

35. Since the third plenary session of its eleventh Central Committee, our party has gradually mapped out the correct path for socialist modernization suited to China's conditions. In the course of practice, the path will be broadened and become more clearly defined, but, in essence, the key pointers can already be determined on the basis of the summing up of the negative as well as positive experiences since the founding of the People's Republic, and particularly of the lessons of the "Cultural Revolution."

1) After socialist transformation was fundamentally completed, the principal contradiction our country has had to resolve is that between the growing material and cultural needs of the people and the backwardness of social production. It was imperative that the focus of party and government work be shifted to socialist modernization centering on economic construction and that the people's material and cultural life be gradually improved by means

of an immense expansion of productive forces. In the final analysis, the mistake we made in the past was that we failed to persevere in making this strategic shift. What is more, the preposterous view opposing the so-called "theory of the unique importance of productive forces," a view diametrically opposed to historical materialism, was put forward during the "Cultural Revolution." We must never deviate from this focus, except in the event of large-scale invasion by a foreign enemy (and even then it will still be necessary to carry on such economic construction as wartime conditions require and permit). All our party work must be subordinated to and serve this central task—economic construction. All our party cadres, and particularly those in economic departments, must diligently study economic theory and economic practice as well as science and technology.

2) In our socialist economic construction, we must strive to reach the goal of modernization systematically and in stages, according to the conditions and resources of our country. The prolonged "left" mistakes we made in our economic work in the past consisted chiefly in departing from Chinese realities, trying to exceed our actual capabilities and ignoring the economic returns of construction and management as well as the scientific confirmation of our economic plans, policies and measures, with their concomitants of colossal waste and losses. We must adopt a scientific attitude, gain a thorough knowledge of the realities and make a deep analysis of the situation, earnestly listen to the opinions of the cadres, masses and specialists in the various fields and try our best to act in accordance with objective economic and natural laws and bring about a proportionate and harmonious development of the various branches of economy. We must keep in mind the fundamental fact that China's economy and culture are still relatively backward. At the same time, we must keep in mind such favourable domestic and international conditions as the achievements we have already scored and the experience we have gained in our economic construction and the expansion of economic and technological exchanges with foreign countries, and we must make full use of these favourable conditions. We must oppose both impetuosity and passivity.

3) The reform and improvement of the socialist relations of production must be in conformity with the level of the productive forces and conducive to the expansion of production. The state economy and the collective economy are the basic forms of the Chinese economy.

The working people's individual economy within certain prescribed limits is a necessary complement to public economy. It is necessary to establish specific systems of management and distribution suited to the various sectors of the economy. It is necessary to have planned economy and at the same time give play to the supplementary, regulatory role of the market on the basis of public ownership. We must strive to promote commodity production and exchange on a socialist basis. There is no rigid pattern for the development of the socialist relations of production. At every stage our task is to create those specific forms of the relations of production that correspond to the needs of the growing productive forces and facilitate their continued advance.

4) Class struggle no longer constitutes the principal contradiction after the exploiters have been eliminated as classes. However, owing to certain domestic factors and

influences from abroad, class struggle will continue to exist within certain limits for a long time to come and may even grow acute under certain conditions. It is necessary to oppose both the view that the scope of class struggle must be enlarged and the view that it has died out. It is imperative to maintain a high level of vigilance and conduct effective struggle against all those who are hostile to socialism and try to sabotage it in the political, economic, ideological and cultural fields and in community life. We must correctly understand that there are diverse social contradictions in Chinese society which do not fall within the scope of class struggle and that methods other than class struggle must be used for their appropriate revolution. Otherwise, social stability and unity will be jeopardized. We must unswervingly unite all forces that can be united with and consolidate and expand the patriotic united front.

5) A fundamental task of the socialist revolution is gradually to establish a highly democratic socialist political system. Inadequate attention was paid to this matter after the founding of the People's Republic, and this was one of the major factors contributing to the initiation of the "Cultural Revolution." Here is a grievous lesson for us to learn. It is necessary to strengthen the building of state organs at all levels in accordance with the principle of democratic centralism, make the people's congresses at all levels and their permanent organs authoritative organs of the people's political power, gradually realize direct popular participation in the democratic process at the grass roots of political power and community life and, in particular, stress democratic management by the working masses in urban and rural enterprises over the affairs of their establishments. It is essential to consolidate the people's democratic dictatorship, improve our constitution and laws and ensure their strict observance and inviolability. We must turn the socialist legal system into a powerful instrument for protecting the rights of the people, ensuring order in production, work and other spheres, punishing criminals and cracking down on the disruptive activities of class enemies. The kind of chaotic situation that obtained in the "Cultural Revolution" must never be allowed to happen again in any sphere.

6) Life under socialism must attain a high ethical and cultural level. We must firmly eradicate such utterly fallacious views as denigrate education, science and culture and discriminate against intellectuals, views which had long existed and found extreme expression during the "Cultural Revolution"; we must strive to raise the status and expand the role of education, science and culture in our drive for modernization. We unequivocally affirm that, together with the workers and peasants, the intellectuals are a force to rely on in the cause of socialism and that it is impossible to carry out socialist construction without culture and the intellectuals.

It is imperative for the whole party to engage in a more diligent study of Marxist theories, of the past and present in China and abroad, and of the different branches of the natural and social sciences. We must strengthen and improve ideological and political work and educate the people and youth in the Marxist world outlook and communist morality; we must persistently carry out the educational policy which calls for an all-round development morally, intellectually and physically, for being both Red and expert, for integration of the intellectuals with the workers and peasants and the combination of mental and physical labour; and we must counter the influence of decadent bourgeois ideology and the decadent remnants of feudal ideology, overcome the influence of petty-bourgeois ideology and foster the patriotism which puts the interests of the motherland above everything else and the pioneer spirit of selfless devotion to modernization.

7) It is of profound significance to our multi-national country to improve and promote socialist relations among our various nationalities and strengthen national unity. In the past, particularly during the "Cultural Revolution," we committed, on the question of nationalities, the grave mistake of widening the scope of class struggle and wronged a large number of cadres and masses of the minority nationalities. In our work among them, we did not show due respect for their right to autonomy. We must never forget this lesson. We must have a clear understanding that relations among our nationalities today are, in the main, relations among the working people of the various nationalities. It is necessary to persist in their regional autonomy and enact laws and regulations to ensure this autonomy and their decision-making power in applying party and government policies according to the actual conditions in their regions. We must take effective measures to assist economic and cultural development in regions inhabited by minority nationalities, actively train and promote cadres from among them and resolutely oppose all works and deeds undermining national unity and equality. It is imperative to continue to implement the policy of freedom of religious belief. To uphold the four fundamental principles does not mean that religious believers should renounce their faith but that they must not engage in propaganda against Marxism-Leninism and Mao Zedong Thought and that they must not interfere with politics and education in their religious activities.

8) In the present international situation in which the danger of war still exists, it is necessary to strengthen the modernization of our national defence. The building up of national defence must be in keeping with the building up of the economy. The People's Liberation Army should strengthen its military training, political work, logistic service and study of military science and further raise its combat effectiveness so as gradually to become a still more powerful modern revolutionary army. It is necessary to restore and carry forward the fine tradition of unity inside the army, between the army and the government and between the army and the people. The building of the people's militia must also be further strengthened.

9) In our external relations, we must continue to oppose imperialism, hegemonism, colonialism and racism, and safeguard world peace. We must actively promote relations and economic and cultural exchanges with other countries on the basis of the five principles of peaceful coexistence. We must uphold proletarian internationalism and support the cause of the liberation of oppressed nations, the national construction of newly independent countries and the just struggles of the peoples everywhere.

10) In the light of the lessons of the "Cultural Revolution" and the present situation in the party, it is imperative to build up a sound system of democratic centralism inside the party. We must carry out the Marxist principle of the exercise of collective party leadership by leaders who have emerged from mass struggles and who combine political integrity with professional competence, and we must prohibit the personality cult in any form. It is imperative

to uphold the prestige of party leaders and at the same time ensure that their activities come under the supervision of the party and the people. We must have a high degree of centralism based on a high degree of democracy and insist that the minority is subordinate to the majority, the individual to the organization, the lower to the higher level and the entire membership to the Central Committee. The style of work of a political party in power is a matter that determines its very existence. Party organizations at all levels and all party cadres must go deep among the masses, plunge themselves into practical struggle, remain modest and prudent, share weal and woe with the masses and firmly overcome bureaucratism. We must properly wield the weapon of criticism and self-criticism, overcome erroneous ideas that deviate from the party's correct principles, uproot factionalism, oppose anarchism and ultra-individualism and eradicate such unhealthy tendencies as the practice of seeking perks and privileges. We must consolidate the party organization, purify the party ranks and weed out degenerate elements who oppress and bully the people. In exercising leadership over state affairs and work in the economic and cultural fields as well as in community life, the party must correctly handle its relations with other organizations, ensure by every means the effective functioning of the organs of state power and administrative, judicial and economic and cultural organizations and see to it that trade unions, the youth league, the women's federation, the science and technology association, the federation of literary and art circles and other mass organizations carry out their work responsibly and on their own initiative. The party must strengthen its co-operation with public figures outside the party, give full play to the role of the Chinese People's Political Consultative Conference, hold conscientious consultations with democratic parties and personages without party affiliation on major issues of state affairs and respect their opinions and the opinions of specialists in various fields. As required of other social organizations, the party's organizations at all levels must conduct their activities within the limits permitted by the constitution and the law.

36. In firmly correcting the mistake of the so-called "continued revolution under the dictatorship of the proletariat," a slogan which was advanced during the "Cultural Revolution" and which called for the overthrow of one class by another, we absolutely do not mean that the tasks of the revolution have been accomplished and that there is no need to carry on revolutionary struggles with determination. Socialism aims not just at eliminating all systems of exploitation and all exploiting classes but also at greatly expanding the productive forces, improving and developing the socialist relations of production and the superstructure and, on this basis, gradually eliminating all class differences and all major social distinctions and inequalities which are chiefly due to the inadequate development of the productive forces until communism is finally realized. This is a great revolution, unprecedented in human history. Our present endeavour to build a modern socialist China constitutes but one stage of this great revolution. Differing from the revolutions before the overthrow of the system of exploitation, this revolution is carried out not through fierce class confrontation and conflict, but through the strength of the socialist system itself, under leadership, step by step and in an orderly way. This revolution which has entered the period of peaceful development is more profound and arduous than any previous revolution and will not only take a very long historical period to accomplish but also demand the unswerving and disciplined hard work and heroic sacrifices of many generations.

In this historical period of peaceful development, revolution can never be plain sailing. There are still overt and covert enemies and other saboteurs who watch for opportunities to create trouble. We must maintain high revolutionary vigilance and be ready at all times to come out boldly to safeguard the interests of the revolution. In this new historical period, the whole membership of the Chinese Communist Party and the whole people must never cease to cherish lofty revolutionary ideals, maintain a dynamic revolutionary fighting spirit and carry China's great socialist revolution and socialist construction through to the end.

37. Repeated assessment of our successes and failures of our correct and incorrect practices of the thirty-two years after the founding of our People's Republic, and particularly deliberation over and review of the events of the past few years, have helped to raise immensely the political consciousness of all party comrades and of all patriots. Obviously, our party now has a higher level of understanding of socialist revolution and construction than at any other period after liberation. Our party has both the courage to acknowledge and correct its mistakes and the determination and ability to prevent repetition of the serious mistakes of the past. After all, from a long-term historical point of view the mistakes and setbacks of our party were only temporary whereas the consequent steeling of our party and people, the greater maturity of the core force formed among our party cadres through protracted struggle, the growing superiority of our socialist system and the increasingly keen and common aspiration of our party, army and people for the prosperity of the motherland will be decisive factors in the long run. A great future is in store for our socialist cause and for the Chinese people in their hundreds of millions.

38. Inner-party unity and unity between the party and the people are the basic guarantee for new victories in our socialist modernization. Whatever the difficulties, as long as the party is closely united and remains closely united with the people, our party and the cause of socialism it leads will certainly prosper day by day.

The resolution on certain questions in the history of our party unanimously adopted in 1945 by the enlarged seventh plenary session of the sixth Central Committee of the party unified the thinking of the whole party, consolidated its unity, promoted the rapid advance of the people's revolutionary cause and accelerated its eventual triumph. The sixth plenary session of the eleventh Central Committee of the party believes that the present resolution it has unanimously adopted will play a similar historical role. This session calls upon the whole party, the whole army and the people of all our nationalities to act under the great banner of Marxism-Leninism and Mao Zedong Thought, closely rally around the Central Committee of the party, preserve the spirit of the legendary foolish old man who removed mountains and work together as one in defiance of all difficulties so as to turn China step by step into a powerful modern socialist country which is highly democratic and highly cultured. Our goal must be attained! Our goal can unquestionably be attained!

HU YAOBANG
Speech on the Party's Sixtieth Anniversary, 1 July 1981

This speech by Deng Xiaoping's choice as Party general secretary is briefer, more ideological, and more impressionistic than the Central Committee resolution. Hu's position as the former senior Party officer, and therefore his right to make the principal speech on this ceremonious important occasion, had only just been validated by the ouster of Hua Guofeng as Party chairman.

Comrades and friends:

We are gathered here today to celebrate the 60th anniversary of the founding of the Communist Party of China. At this moment, we are all deeply aware that our party and state are in an important historical period, a period in which we are bringing order out of chaos, carrying on our cause and forging ahead.

To bring order out of chaos, carry on our cause and forge ahead, we must undo all the negative consequences of the "Cultural Revolution," advance the great cause pioneered by the party under the leadership of Comrade Mao Zedong and other proletarian revolutionaries of the older generation, and pave the way further to socialism and communism for the Chinese people.

The sixth plenary session of the eleventh Central Committee of the Communist Party of China, which has just ended, adopted the "Resolution on Certain Questions in the History of Our Party Since the Founding of the People's Republic of China." The resolution reviews the party's sixty years of struggle, sums up the basic experience it has gained in the thirty-two years since the founding of the People's Republic, makes a concrete and realistic evaluation of a whole train of crucial historical events, analyses what was right and what was wrong in the ideology behind these events and the subjective factors and social roots giving rise to them, evaluates Comrade Mao Zedong's role in history and expounds Mao Zedong Thought scientifically, and indicates our way forward more clearly. The plenary session also took decisions on other important matters. History will prove that it too was a meeting of paramount importance for our party—a new milestone for our party and state in the course of bringing order out of chaos, carrying on our cause and forging ahead.

Looking back over the path our party has traversed, we are keenly conscious of the fact that the Chinese revolution has not been smooth sailing. We can say that the sixty years since the founding of the Communist Party of China have been years of unflinching, heroic struggle for the liberation of the Chinese nation and the happiness of the Chinese people, years of ever closer integration, through repeated application, of the universal truth of Marxism-Leninism with the concrete practice of the Chinese revolution, and years when right prevailed over wrong and positive aspects prevailed over negative aspects in the party. They have been years during which we marched on to a number of victories despite untold hardships and setbacks.

Why do we say that the history of the Chinese Communist Party is one of unflinching, heroic struggle for the liberation of the Chinese nation and the happiness of the Chinese people?

In modern Chinese history, between the opium war of 1840–42 and the outbreak of the May 4th movement of 1919, the Chinese people waged protracted, heroic struggles against imperialism and feudalism. The 1911 revolution led by the great revolutionary Dr. Sun Yat-sen overthrew the Qing Dynasty monarchy, thus bringing to an end more than 2,000 years of feudal autocracy. However, the way to China's salvation was not discovered through any of these struggles. It was not until the Communist Party of China was born after the October Socialist Revolution in Russia and the May 4th movement in China that new vistas were opened up for the Chinese revolution, as a result of the integration of Marxism-Leninism with the rising workers' movement in China, and with the help of the international proletariat.

The enemy of the Chinese revolution was formidable and ferocious. But none of the hardships overwhelmed the Chinese people and the Communist Party of China. In a dauntless revolutionary spirit, our party led the people in rising up to fight the enemy. We communists and the people depended on each other for survival; we relied closely on the people, and the people had deep faith in us. Our party steeled itself in the grim struggle and became the most advanced and most powerful leading force in the history of the Chinese revolution and built a new and well-trained people's army.

After twenty-eight years of arduous struggle in four great people's revolutionary wars (the northern expedition, 1924–27, the agrarian revolutionary war, 1927–37, the war of resistance against Japan, 1937–45, and the war of liberation, 1946–49), our party led the people of all our nationalities in finally overthrowing in 1949 the reactionary rule of imperialism, feudalism and bureaucrat-capitalism and winning the great victory of the new-democratic revolution,

[New China News Agency, 1 July 1981.]

a victory which led to the founding of the People's Republic of China, a state of the people's democratic dictatorship.

After the founding of the People's Republic, our party led the entire people in sustained advance. We thwarted the threats, attempts at subversion, sabotage and armed provocations of the imperialists and hegemonists, and safeguarded the independence and security of our great motherland. Except for Taiwan province and a few other islands, we have achieved and consolidated the unification of our country. We have achieved and strengthened the great unity of the Chinese people of whatever nationality and of the workers, peasants and intellectuals throughout the country. We have formed and consolidated the broadest possible united front of all socialist workers, patriots who support socialism and other patriots who uphold the reunification of the motherland—a united front led by the Chinese Communist Party in full cooperation with all the democratic parties. And we smoothly effected the decisive transition of our society from new democracy to socialism. Thanks to the arduous struggle of the whole party and people, we in the main completed the socialist transformation of the private ownership of the means of production and embarked on large-scale, planned socialist economic construction. Thus, our economy and culture registered an advance unparalleled in Chinese history. However numerous the shortcomings and mistakes in our work and however imperfect some aspects of our social system, we have eliminated the system of exploitation and the exploiting classes and have established the socialist system. Hence, with nearly a quarter of the world's population, China has entered upon a socialist state of society, a state of society new in the history of mankind. Beyond a shadow of a doubt, this is the most radical social change in Chinese history. It is a leap of the most far-reaching significance in the progress of mankind and a tremendous victory for and a further development of Marxism.

The change is indeed striking. In the eighty years between the opium war and the birth of the Chinese Communist Party, the ceaseless struggles of the people had all failed despite their heroism, and their hopes and lofty aspirations were sadly frustrated. The picture has been altogether different in the sixty years since the birth of the Chinese Communist Party. A new epoch in Chinese history was ushered in. The Chinese people have taken their destiny into their own hands; they have stood up in the East. Never again will the Chinese nation be bullied and oppressed.

In celebrating the 60th anniversary of the founding of the Chinese Communist Party, it is with deep emotion that we feel that the splendid fruits of the Chinese people's revolution have been truly hard-won. They have been won by the Chinese people in sixty long years of hard struggle under the leadership of the Chinese Communist Party. They have been nurtured with the blood of millions of communists and non-party revolutionaries who died before the firing squad, on the battlefield or at their posts.

Let us rise and pay our sincere tribute to the memory of all the revolutionary martyrs: All the revolutionary leaders and cadres, communists and Communist Youth League members, veteran revolutionaries and young fighters, non-party comrades-in-arms and foreign friends who laid down their lives for the Chinese people at different stages of the Chinese revolution over the past six decades.

Why do we say that the history of the Chinese Communist Party is one of ever closer integration, through repeated application, of the universal truth of Marxism-Leninism with the concrete practice of the Chinese revolution?

From the moment of its inception, our party adopted Marxism-Leninism as its guiding ideology. However, the general principles of Marxism provide no ready-made recipe for revolution in a particular country, especially a big, oriental, semi-feudal and semi-colonial country like China. During its formative years, the 1920's and the 1930's, our party suffered again and again from the "infantile malady" of turning Marxism into a dogma and deifying foreign experience—a malady which could not but leave the Chinese revolution groping in the dark and even lead it into a blind alley. Comrade Mao Zedong's great contribution lies in the fact that, in the course of combating this erroneous tendency and in the struggles waged collectively by the party and the people, he succeeded in integrating the universal truth of Marxism with the concrete practice of the Chinese revolution and in summing up freshly gained experiences. In this way Mao Zedong Thought took shape as the guiding scientific ideology conforming to Chinese conditions. It is this scientific ideology that has guided the sweeping advance of the Chinese revolution from one triumph to another.

Mao Zedong Thought, coming into being and developing in the course of the Chinese revolution, is the crystallization of the collective wisdom of our party and a summing-up of the victories in the gigantic struggles of the Chinese people. Its theories on the new-democratic revolution, on the socialist revolution and socialist construction, on the strategy and tactics of revolutionary struggle, on the building of a revolutionary army, on military strategy, on ideological and political work, on cultural work, and on the building of the party, as well as its theories concerning scientific modes of thought, work and leadership which will be even more important in guiding all our work in the future, have all added new and original ideas to the treasure-house of Marxism. As a theory and as the summing-up of experiences verified in practice, as the application and development of Marxism in China, Mao Zedong Thought has been and will remain the guiding ideology of our party.

However, Comrade Mao Zedong had his shortcomings and mistakes just like many other outstanding figures in the forefront of the march of history. Chiefly in his later years, having been admired and loved for so long by the whole party and people, he became over-confident and more and more divorced from reality and the masses and, in particular, from the party's collective leadership, and often rejected and even suppressed correct opinions that differed from his. Thus, he inevitably made mistakes, including the comprehensive, long-drawn-out and gross blunder of initiating the "Cultural Revolution"; this was a tremendous misfortune for the party and the people. Of course, it must be admitted that both before the "Cultural Revolution" and at the time of its inception, the party failed to prevent Comrade Mao Zedong's erroneous tendency from growing more serious but, instead, accepted and approved some of his wrong theses. We veterans who had been working together with him for a long time as his comrades-in-arms, or who had long been following him in revolutionary struggle as his disciples, are keenly aware of our own responsibility in this matter, and we are determined never to forget this lesson.

Although Comrade Mao Zedong made grave mistakes in his later years, it is clear that if we consider his life work as a whole, his contributions to the Chinese revolution far outweigh his errors. He had dedicated himself to the Chinese revolution since his youth and had fought for it all his life. He was one of the founders of our party and the chief architect of the glorious Chinese People's Liberation Army.

At the most trying times in the Chinese revolution, he was the first to discover the correct road for the revolution, work out a correct over-all strategy and gradually formulate a whole set of correct theories and tactics, thus guiding the revolution from defeat to victory. After the founding of the People's Republic, under the leadership of the party Central Committee and Comrade Mao Zedong, new China quickly consolidated its position and embarked on the great cause of socialism. Even in the last few years of his life, when his errors had become very serious, Comrade Mao Zedong still remained alert to the nation's independence and security and had a correct grasp of the new developments in the world situation. He led the party and people in standing up to all pressures from hegemonism and instituted a new pattern for our foreign relations. In the long years of struggle, all comrades in our party drew wisdom and strength from Comrade Mao Zedong and Mao Zedong Thought which nurtured successive generations of our party's leaders and large numbers of its cadres and educated the whole Chinese people. Comrade Mao Zedong was a great Marxist, a great proletarian revolutionary, theorist and strategist, and the great national hero in Chinese history. He made major contributions to the cause of the liberation of the world's oppressed nations and to the cause of human progress. His immense contributions are immortal.

While celebrating the 60th anniversary of the founding of the Communist Party of China, we deeply cherish the memory of Comrade Mao Zedong. We deeply cherish the memory of the great Marxists, Comrades Zhou Enlai, Liu Shaoqi and Zhu De, and the memory of Comrades Ren Bishi, Dong Biwu, Peng Dehuai, He Long, Chen Yi, Luo Ronghuan, Lin Boqu, Li Fuchun, Wang Jiaxiang, Zhang Wentian, Tao Zhu and others, all of whom were outstanding leaders of our party and, together with Comrade Mao Zedong, made important contributions to the victorious Chinese revolution and to the formation and development of Mao Zedong Thought. We deeply cherish the memory of Comrades Li Dazhao, Qu Qiubai, Cai Hesen, Xiang Jingyu, Deng Zhongxia, Su Zhaozheng, Peng Pai, Chen Yannian, Yun Daiying, Zhao Shiyan, Zhang Tailei, Li Lisan and other prominent leaders of our party in its formative years. We deeply cherish the memory of Comrades Fang Zhimin, Liu Zhidan, Huang Gonglue, Xu Jishen, Wei Baqun, Zhao Bosheng, Dong Zhentang, Duan Dechang, Yang Jingyu, Zuo Quan, Ye Ting and other outstanding commanders of the people's army who early laid down their lives for the party and the country. We deeply cherish the memory of Comrade Soong Ching Ling, a great contemporary woman fighter who fought together with us over a long period of time and became a member of the glorious Chinese Communist Party before her death, of Cai Yuanpei, the prominent

Chinese intellectual forerunner, and of Lu Xun, the great standard-bearer of our proletarian revolutionary culture. We deeply cherish the memory of Comrades Liao Zhongkai, He Xiangning, Deng Yanda, Yang Xingfo, Shen Junru and other close non-party comrades-in-arms of ours who consistently supported our party. We deeply cherish the memory of Comrades Zou Taofen, Wen Yiduo, Guo Moruo, Mao Dun, Li Siguang and other distinguished fighters in the fields of science and culture. We deeply cherish the memory of Yang Hucheng, Tan Kah Kee, Zhang Zhizhong, Fu Zuoyi and other renowned patriots who made important contributions to the victorious Chinese people's revolution. We deeply cherish the memory of Norman Bethune, Agnes Smedley, Anna Louise Strong, Dwarkanath S. Kotnis, Edgar Snow, Inejiro Asanuma, Kenzo Nakajima and other close friends of the Chinese people and eminent internationalist fighters.

Why do we say that the history of the Chinese Communist Party is also the history of the triumph of right over wrong and of the triumph of the party's positive aspects over its negative ones?

The revolutionary cause our party has embarked upon is a sacred cause involving the radical transformation of Chinese society, a completely new cause never undertaken by our forefathers. The enemy of the revolution was formidable and the social conditions under which the revolution took place were extremely complex. Therefore, it was only natural that we should make mistakes of one kind or another, and even grievous ones, in the course of our revolutionary struggles. The important thing is to be good at learning through practice once a mistake has been made, to wake up in good time and endeavour to correct it, to strive to avoid a blunder which is long-drawn-out and comprehensive in character, and to avoid repetition of the same grievous blunder.

Our party was born and grew to maturity in the old society. At the high tide of the revolution, large numbers of revolutionaries joined our ranks. This boosted our strength, but a few careerists and opportunists, too, wormed their way into the party. This could hardly be avoided. The point is that while transforming society, our party must pay attention to remoulding itself, and be good at educating and remoulding those who have diverse non-proletarian ideas when they join our party and good at recognizing careerists and conspirators for what they are, so as to be able to foil their schemes and conspiracies.

The greatness of the party does not lie in any readiness to guarantee complete freedom from any negative phenomena but in its ability to overcome shortcomings and rectify errors and to defeat sabotage by all alien forces. Let us look back: Isn't this precisely how our party has fought in the past? Its history contains the grave errors of Chen Duxiu's right capitulationism and Wang Ming's "left" dogmatism. There were also conspiracies to split the party hatched by Zhang Guotao and by Gao Gang and Rao Shushi. There were even the Lin Biao and Jiang Qing counter-revolutionary cliques. However, none succeeded in destroying our party. The extremely treacherous careerists and conspirators Lin Biao and Jiang Qing exploited the "Cultural Revolution" to seize supreme power; they committed every conceivable sin against our nation and people, with the gravest consequences. Yet they were finally unmasked and swept into the garbage bin of history by the party and the people. Isn't this an incontrovertible historical fact? Instead of being destroyed by sabotage or crippled by reverses of one kind or another, our party has emerged each time refreshed and reinvigorated from the struggle to overcome mistakes and prevail over what is negative. It is our party that is invincible.

The past sixty years prove that our party is indeed a proletarian party armed with Marxism-Leninism and Mao Zedong Thought and a party wholeheartedly serving the people, entirely dedicated to their interests and with no particular interest of its own. It is truly a long-tested party which has acquired rich experience, learned many lessons and is capable of leading the people in braving difficulties to win victory after victory in the revolution. The role of this great party as the force at the core of the Chinese people's revolutionary cause and its leadership in this cause are the dictates of history and of the will and interests of the people of all our nationalities, dictates which no force on earth can change or shake.

Comrades and Friends:

With widespread popular support, our party smashed at one stroke the Jiang Qing counterrevolutionary clique in October 1976. This saved the revolution and our socialist state and ushered in a new period of historical development. The third plenary session of the eleventh Central Committee held in December 1978 marked a decisive turning point in the post-1949 history of our party.

The tremendous significance of this plenary session lies in the fact that it really started to correct matters in an all-round, determined and well-considered way by relying on the masses. Since then, right through the fourth, fifth and sixth plenary sessions, our party has been working hard with concentrated energy and attention and under difficult and complex conditions, and has adopted and implemented step by step a series of major policy decisions in ideological, political and organizational matters and all aspects of socialist construction, thus correcting the erroneous "left" orientation. Moreover, in the light of the new historical conditions, our party has gradually charted a correct course for socialist modernization that is suited to China's conditions.

The most striking change of all is the shift of the focus of work of the whole party and nation after the liquidation and repudiation of the Lin Biao and Jiang Qing counterrevolutionary cliques. The leading organs from the central down to local levels are now concentrating their energy and attention on socialist modernization. Now that liquidation of the long prevalent "left" deviationist guiding ideology is under way, our socialist economic and cultural construction has been shifted to a course of development that takes into account the basic conditions of the country and the limits of our ability, proceeds step by step, and seeks practical results and steady advance. With the implementation of the party's policies, the introduction of the system of production responsibilities and the development of a diversified economy, an excellent situation has developed in the vast rural areas in particular, a dynamic and progressive situation seldom seen since the founding of the People's Republic.

In sociopolitical relations, our party has resolutely and appropriately solved many important issues which had been wrongly handled over a long period of time, eliminated a number of major factors detrimental to stability and unity and put an end to the social unrest and upheaval fomented in the "Cultural Revolution." We are now striving to foster socialist democracy, improve the socialist legal system and reform and perfect the socialist political system. This gives a powerful impetus to the consolidation and development of a political situation of stability, unity and liveliness.

Through organizational consolidation and rectification of the style of work, tangible progress has been made in the normalization of party life, the development of inner-party democracy and the strengthening of the party's ties with the masses. The party's prestige, grievously damaged during the "Cultural Revolution," is gradually being restored.

To ensure the proper implementation of the principle of emancipating the mind, our party has reiterated that it is necessary to uphold the four fundamental principles of the socialist road, the people's democratic dictatorship (i.e., the dictatorship of the proletariat), the Communist Party's leadership, and Marxism-Leninism and Mao Zedong Thought. These principles constitute the common political basis for the unity of the whole party and the unity of the entire people and provide the fundamental guarantee for the success of socialist modernization.

The great change which began with the third plenary session of the party's eleventh Central Committee and our correct line and policies fulfill the common aspirations of the people and the party. Speaking of the general orientation and major policy decisions taken since the session, many comrades have said, "they suit us fine." These words reflect the thoughts and feelings of the masses and of the majority of cadres. They explain why the change is so dynamic and irresistible.

Needless to say, many difficulties confront us. We have yet to finish the process of correction, and in various fields many problems remain to be resolved. Our material resources, expertise and experience are far from adequate for the achievement of the four modernizations. The people's living standards are still very low and many pressing problems demand solution. We have yet to introduce further improvements in the party's leadership and style of work. It is wrong to take these difficulties lightly. Only by taking them into full account will we be invincible. The road before us is still long and tortuous. It is like climbing the Taishan Mountain; when we have reached the halfway gate to heaven, we find that the three eighteen bends lie ahead of us, demanding Herculean efforts. Until we have negotiated these bends, however, we won't be able to reach the south gate to heaven. Still climbing, we will find it relatively easy to mount the peak of the jade emperor, our destination, and only then can we claim to have accomplished the splendid cause of socialist modernization. Once at the south gate to heaven, we shall be in a position to appreciate the great Tang Dynasty poet Du Fu's well-known lines, "Viewed from the topmost summit, all mountains around are dwarfed." The hardships that once towered like "mountains" will then look small and we will be able to negotiate the obstacles on the way to the "topmost summit" more or less easily. In the course of our long journey, we will certainly be able to conquer the eighteen bends, reach the south gate to heaven and then ascend the peak of the jade emperor. Once there, we shall push towards new summits.

Comrades and friends:

The historical experience of the past sixty years can be summed up in one sentence: There must be a Marxist, revolutionary line and a proletarian party capable of formulating and upholding this line. Faced with the gigantic task of socialist modernization centering around economic construction in the new historical period, we are deeply aware that the key to the fulfillment of this task lies in our party.

Now, the entire people has placed its hopes on our party, and other peoples of the world are closely watching it. Whether or not we can steer the ship of the Chinese revolution onward through storm and stress in the new historical period, whether or not we can modernize our agriculture, industry, national defence and science and technology fairly smoothly, avoid suffering such serious setbacks and paying such a huge price as in the past, and achieve results that will satisfy the people and win the praise of posterity, all depends on the efforts of all comrades in the party in the next decade or two. We must not let our people down.

With higher political awareness, we must make our party a solid core which is more mature politically, more unified ideologically and more consolidated organizationally, and more able to unite with all our nationalities and lead them in socialist modernization.

1. All Members of the Party Must Work With Selfless Devotion for China's Socialist Modernization and in the Service of the People.

We Chinese communists must always proceed from our basic standpoint with the objective of wholeheartedly serving the people. Serving the people in essence means that our party must rally the masses round it and, by virtue of its correct guidelines and policies, its close ties with the masses, its members' exemplary role and its propaganda and organizational work, help them to see where their fundamental interests lie and to get united to strive for them.

The people are the makers of history. Both the people's revolution and the construction of socialism led by our party are the people's very own cause. At all times party members comprise only a small minority of the population; so we must rely on the people in all our work, have faith in them, draw wisdom from them, set store by their creativeness and subject ourselves to their supervision. Otherwise, we will accomplish nothing, we will fail. Since victory was won in the revolution, the people have become the masters of the country and society. To organize and support them in fulfilling this role and building a new life under socialism is the very essence of the party's leadership over affairs of state.

For us communists, serving the people means primarily dedication to the cause of communism and readiness to sacrifice ourselves for the interests of the people. In the years of war, many of our party members were the first to charge at the enemy and the last to pull back; they remained staunch and unyielding in captivity, dying as martyrs; and they were invariably the first to bear hardships and the last to enjoy comforts. What an inspiration and encouragement they were to millions upon millions of our people! Today, in peacetime construction, and particularly after the decade of havoc of the "Cultural Revolution," we need this revolutionary spirit even more. Although our party's fine style of work was corroded by the counter-revolutionary cliques of Lin Biao and Jiang Qing, there are still large numbers of fine party members who have maintained and carried forward this revolutionary spirit, a spirit characterized by readiness to sacrifice one's individual interests and even one's own life, for the interests of the people. They have won high praise from the people, and they have earned it. It is utterly wrong to think and act as though the revolutionary spirit may be discarded in peacetime construction and party members no longer need to share weal and woe with the masses whose interests they may subordinate to their own. That would be to debase our party spirit.

The style of work of a party in power vitally affects its very existence. As Comrade Mao Zedong pointed out in 1942, "Once our party's style of work is put completely right, the people all over the country will learn from our example. Those outside the party who have the same kind of bad style will, if they are good and honest people, learn from our example and correct their mistakes, and thus the whole nation will be influenced. So long as our communist ranks are in good order and march in step, so long as our troops are picked troops and our weapons are good weapons, any enemy, however powerful, can be overthrown." Let us firmly resolve to strive to our utmost to restore and carry forward the fine style of work which our party and Comrade Mao Zedong cultivated, and to lead the whole Chinese nation in building a high level of socialist civilization.

2. We Must Be Good at Carrying Forward Marxism-Leninism and Mao Zedong Thought in the Light of the New Historical Conditions.

We have obtained great successes in revolution and construction in the past under the guidance of Marxism-Leninism and Mao Zedong Thought. We will obtain new and greater successes in our long march into the future by relying on Marxism-Leninism and Mao Zedong Thought for guidance. If we communists have any family heirlooms to speak of, by far the most important one is Marxism-Leninism and Mao Zedong Thought. It has always been our basic and unshakable principle to uphold Marxism-Leninism and Mao Zedong Thought and persist in taking the tenets of Marxism as our guideline.

Marxism is the crystallization of scientific thinking on proletarian revolution; it is our most powerful weapon for understanding and transforming the objective world. Its tenets are truths that have been repeatedly verified in practice. However, it does not embrace all the truths in the unending course of human history, nor can it possibly do so. For us revolutionaries, the theory of Marxism is the guide to action and by no means a rigid dogma to be followed unthinkingly. All revolutionaries true to Marxism have the responsibility to ensure that it does not become divorced from social life and does not stagnate, wither or ossify; they must enrich it with fresh revolutionary experiences so that it will remain full of vitality. Therefore, our fundamental approach to Marxism is that we should apply and advance Marxism-Leninism and Mao Zedong Thought; such is our unshirkable historical duty as Chinese communists. This is not easy of course. It requires us to make an arduous, lifelong effort to achieve a better integration of the tenets of Marxism with the concrete practice of China's socialist modernization.

We must continue to apply ourselves to the study and investigation of the history of the Chinese revolution. For the China of today has grown out of the China of yesterday, a China about which we know, not too much, but too little. We should especially study present-day China because our efforts to create a radiant future must first of all be based on a comparatively correct understanding of the present. And the trouble is that we don't know much; in fact we still know very little about Chinese realities today and the objective laws governing the building of socialism.

Our cause is an integral whole and has a single goal. Yet, ours is a vast country with extremely diverse conditions. Therefore, our study and understanding of the overall situation and of the situation in different regions must be closely co-ordinated. If we overlook the whole and disregard uniformity, we shall make the mistake of acting blindly and thoughtlessly and with no consideration for the whole in directing the work in specific regions. If we ignore the regions' specific conditions in directing the work of the whole country, we shall make the mistake of being guided by our own conjectures and fancies which may have no relation to reality. We Chinese communists should be revolutionaries who are at once far-sighted and realistic in our approach.

We lay stress on self-reliance and strive to solve our problems by our own efforts and treasure our own experience. But we must never be conceited and underrate the experience of others. We should through analysis absorb whatever is useful in others' experience and lessons. We must therefore earnestly study and analyse the experience of other countries, other regions and other people while studying and summing up our own.

The integration of the universal truth of Marxism with Chinese reality is a long process of repeated cycles of practice, knowledge, again practice and again knowledge. In the new historical period, we should emancipate our minds and constantly identify and grapple with the new conditions and problems in our practice and thus equip ourselves with rich, varied and living perceptual knowledge. At the same time, we must set our minds to work and learn more social and natural sciences and their methods in order to raise perceptual knowledge to the plane of rational knowledge, logical knowledge that is more or less systematic, and verify it again and again in practice. We must therefore study diligently, learn from specialists and heed differing views and opinions and, at the same time, delve deep into reality and carry out thorough, systematic investigation and study so as to successfully synthesize our direct and indirect experience.

So long as we proceed in study and work in accordance with this stand, viewpoint and method, we shall be able to put all our party work on a scientific foundation, make discoveries and function creatively for socialist modernization, thus ensuring the triumphant advance of our great cause.

3. We Must Put Democratic Life in the Party on a Sounder Basis and Strengthen Party Organization and Discipline.

One of the fundamental reasons why the grievous errors of the "Cultural Revolution" remained unrectified for so long is that the regular political life of our party, inner-party democratic centralism and the collective leadership of the Central Committee in particular, had been disrupted. As a result, the personality cult, anarchism and ultra-individualism all prevailed. This afforded the Lin Biao and Jiang Qing counter-revolutionary cliques and other scoundrels an opportunity they exploited to the full. No comrade in the party must ever forget this bitter lesson and we must all take warning from it.

We are historical materialists. We do not deny the significant role that outstanding individuals play in history or the significant role of outstanding leaders in a proletarian party. But at the same time we maintain that our party must be placed under collective leadership to be exercised by those who combine ability with political integrity and who have emerged in the course of mass struggles, and that we must ban all forms of the personality cult. Party organizations should commend all comrades, irrespective of their rank or position, who have made special contributions and achieved outstanding results in their work, so as to encourage other party members and people to learn from their example. But such public commendation must be truthful and unvarnished.

Appropriate relationships should be established between the leaders and the led in our party organizations at all levels. Comrades at a lower level must respect and obey the leadership of comrades at a higher level. They must not feign compliance while actually violating or resisting instructions from the higher level. On the other hand, comrades at a higher level must heed the opinions of their subordinates, respect their functions and powers and accept their supervision. Leaders should take part in inner-party activities just like ordinary party members, abide by party rules and discipline and the law of the state, and maintain their ties with the rank-and-file and the masses in general; they must not put themselves in a special category just because they are in leading positions.

Decisions concerning important matters must be made after collective discussions by the appropriate party committee, and no one individual is allowed to have the final say. All members of a party committee must abide by its decisions. Party committees at all levels must practice a division of labour and responsibilities to be discharged under the collective leadership of the party committee, with each member doing his share conscientiously and responsibly and in the best and most efficient way possible.

All party members are entitled to criticize, at party meetings, any individuals within the party, including leading members of the Central Committee; retaliation is impermissible. Party organizations at all levels and all party members should give full play to their initiative and dare to work independently and conscientiously in a spirit characterized by boldness in thinking and action. But no party member is allowed to impair the party's interests and the common goal by turning the department or unit entrusted to him by the party into his own independent kingdom.

Our party's fighting strength lies in its vitality and strict discipline. Now that we are committed to the socialist modernization of the country and our task is most challenging and difficult, we have still greater need to promote this fine party tradition.

4. We Must Be Good at Keeping Ourselves Politically Pure and Healthy and Under All Circumstances Maintain Our Revolutionary Vigour as Members of a Party in Power.

Ours is a large party with a membership of 39 million and it is a party in power. This can easily make some of our comrades feel conceited and succumb to bureaucratic practices. Confronted as we are with so many new things and new problems, we can hardly avoid making mistakes. Besides, class struggle continues to exist to a certain extent in our society, and the ideological influences of the exploiting and other non-proletarian classes still survive. These facts, combined as they are with the complexities of contemporary international relations, put us in daily contact with the undesirable phenomena of capitalism, feudalism and small production. The contradictions between proletarian and non-proletarian ideology and between correct and erroneous thinking within our party demand that we make more effective use of the best weapon communists have for remoulding themselves, namely, the practice of criticism and self-criticism.

Communists should take a clear-cut stand on questions of principle and should uphold truth. Every party member should uphold the party spirit and be unequivocal in his position on questions of right and wrong which involve the interests of the party and the people and should show clearly what he is for and what he is against. The rotten and vulgar practice of trying to be on good terms with everybody at the expense of principle is incompatible with the proletarian character of our party.

Our party's fine tradition of criticism and self-criticism, gravely undermined in previous years, is now being revived and carried forward, and some new and useful experience has been gained in this respect. In making either criticism or self-criticism, one should base oneself on facts and rectify existing mistakes without trying to hide or magnify them. Criticisms should be offered in a well-reasoned way and should be instructive so that they can help the comrades concerned raise their level of political consciousness; they must not be based on speculation or aimed at intimidating others. We should induce the comrades concerned voluntarily to examine themselves and correct their mistakes. In our criticisms we must not make far-fetched interpretations and unduly involve other comrades at a higher or lower level. So long as the comrades concerned have recognized their mistakes and are willing to correct them, we should encourage them to go on working boldly. Our main mistake in the past was to engage in excessive struggle that yielded results contrary to our expectations; people became reluctant to make self-criticism and were afraid to criticize others. We must change this unhealthy tendency.

We communists need to practice criticism and self-criticism so that our party will become more, not less, united and militant. Provided we fully revive and carry forward this fine tradition, our party will undoubtedly continue to show inexhaustible vitality and will never show signs of decay.

5. We Must Select More Cadres Who Combine Ability and Political Integrity and Who Are in the Prime of Life and Appoint Them to Leading Posts at All Levels.

Insofar as experience in struggle is concerned, it may be said that our party's cadres belong to three or four generations, which shows that ours is a long-standing and well-established cause. It is indeed fortunate that our leading cadres at all fronts are largely veterans who have been tempered in prolonged revolutionary struggle. If cadres can be called valuable party assets, then these numerous senior comrades are most valuable.

But the laws of nature cannot be changed and, after all, most of our senior comrades are physically not as strong and active as before. In order to make sure that there is an adequate number of successors to carry on our cause and guarantee continuity in our party's guidelines and policies, we must devote much of our energy from now on to the selection and training of thousands upon thousands of cadres who combine ability and political integrity and are in their prime and give these comrades the opportunity to take part in leadership in various fields so that they may be better and more effectively tempered through practice. It is now a pressing strategic task facing the whole party to build up a large contingent of revolutionary, well-educated, professionally competent and younger cadres.

The older comrades have an especially significant role to play in fulfilling this strategic task. Comrades Ye Jianying, Deng Xiaoping, Chen Yun and Li Xiannian have said more than once that although the old comrades may be pardoned for other mistakes, they would be committing an unforgivable historical error if they did not redouble their efforts to train younger successors. The old comrades should work personally with the organizational departments of the party and the masses in the selection and training of younger cadres and eagerly and enthusiastically guide them to front-line posts of leadership. At the same time, they should free themselves from the onerous pressure of day-to-day work and advance their views and judgments on key and long-range problems. The Central Committee of the party earnestly hopes that all veteran party comrades will have the depth of insight and foresight to discharge this crucial historic responsibility to the best of their ability. Meanwhile, it hopes that party organizations at all levels and all comrades in their prime who have been selected for higher posts will respect and take good care of our veterans and learn as much as possible from them.

At present, we are facing the major task of learning anew. It is the hope of the Central Committee of the party that all party comrades and the younger comrades in particular will brace up, strengthen their party spirit, enhance their political consciousness, set stricter demands on themselves, diligently study Marxist-Leninist works and works by Mao Zedong and the history of the party, our nation and the world, acquire more theoretical and practical knowledge, and learn more about management and technology as required by their own occupations and specific jobs. The results of our study will determine the quality of our leadership and work and will have a direct bearing on the progress of the socialist modernization of our country. Since we have successfully learned to destroy the old world, we can surely learn even more successfully how to build a new one.

6. *We Must Forever Uphold Internationalism and Cast in Our Lot With the Proletariat and the People of the Whole World.*

We Chinese communists have always integrated patriotism with internationalism.

We are patriots. We have invariably fought might and main for our national liberation, for the well-being of our people and the unification and prosperity of our motherland. We have never knuckled under to any pressure from any foreign power. We have never flinched in our determination to be independent and to rely on ourselves, no matter how formidable the difficulties we have faced. Our country is still relatively backward economically and culturally; but we have always maintained our national self-respect in the face of hegemonist threats of force or in our relations with all stronger and richer countries, and will not tolerate any servility in thought or deed.

As it is, Taiwan still stands apart from its reunified motherland and we are resolved to strive together with the people of the whole country, not least including those in Taiwan, for its return and for the sacred cause of the complete reunification of our motherland.

At the same time we are proletarian internationalists. We have always cast in our own lot with the other peoples of the world in their just struggles and with the cause of human progress. Our struggles have throughout enjoyed the support of the other peoples of the world, and we on our part have always supported the struggles of the world's oppressed nations and people for emancipation, the cause of world peace and the cause of human progress, and we have consistently opposed imperialism, hegemonism, colonialism and racism. Our cause of socialist modernization is at once patriotic and internationalist. Its success will be a tremendous contribution to the cause of world peace and human progress. We hereby wish solemnly to proclaim once again that the Communist Party of China will always live in friendship and cooperation and on an equal footing with all the political parties and organizations in the world which are dedicated to human progress and to national liberation and will learn from their useful experience, and that we will never interfere in the internal affairs of any foreign political party. Even when it becomes stronger and more prosperous, socialist China will belong to the Third World and forever stand by the other peoples of the world, strive for world peace and friendly intercourse among peoples, abide faithfully by the five principles of peaceful co-existence, and continue to promote more economic, cultural, scientific and technological exchange and cooperation with other nations; it will never seek advantage at the expense of others or bully weaker nations and will never under any circumstances seek hegemony.

Comrades and friends:

The decisions of the sixth plenary session of the eleventh Central Committee of the party were adopted after ample and extensive exchanges of views and discussions both prior to and during the session. Its outcome fully testifies to our party's ability to safeguard and strengthen its unity on the basis of Marxist principles and to the fact that the political life of our party has now become much healthier.

Some well-intentioned friends at home and abroad have been worried about our party's ability to achieve complete unity, while a handful of people harbouring evil designs placed their hopes on successfully sowing dissension so as to undermine the unity of our party. Now, reality has given them a clear answer: No force on earth can break the Chinese Communist Party's strong unity based on Marxist principles.

Comrades and friends:

We, the proletariat, are the class which commands the future, and our party has lofty ideals and aspirations. The best way for us to celebrate this grand festival, our party's birthday, is to learn from historical experience and thus unite and look forward, focusing our attention on unresolved problems.

Socialist modernization is a great revolution. We are undertaking this great revolution in a huge oriental nation left economically and culturally backward by ruthless imperialist oppression and plunder. The fact that China entered upon socialism before developed capitalist countries is due to its specific historical conditions, to the correct leadership exercised by our party and the arduous struggles of the entire people. It represents a development of scientific socialism and is a credit to our party and the Chinese people. On the other hand, our socialist cause is bound to meet many difficulties arising from our economic and cultural backwardness. This in turn calls for more strenuous and protracted struggle.

We are still living under the threat of aggression and sabotage from outside. Therefore, our whole party, our whole army and our whole people must more actively apply their revolutionary spirit, heighten their revolutionary vigilance and steel their revolutionary will so as to win victory in this great revolution.

We have suffered severe setbacks in our advance to socialism and paid heavily for our errors. However, these errors and setbacks have made us firmer, more experienced, more mindful of our actual conditions, more sober and more powerful. We have learned much from our reverses and mistakes and shall go on learning more. In this sense, our grievous errors and reverses are but fleeting phenomena. We must not overlook that we have a vast contingent of cadres steeled in struggle, that we have built up a substantial material base, that the whole party, army and people fervently desire a prosperous motherland, and that we enjoy the superiority of our socialist system. All this and the fact that we now have correct ideological, political and organizational lines, constitute the decisive factor that will apply for a long time to come. There is no doubt whatsoever that our socialist cause and the hundreds of millions of Chinese people have a bright future.

The internal unity of the party and the party's unity with the people are the essential condition for the triumph of our cause. While celebrating the 60th anniversary of the founding of the Communist Party of China, we wish to pay our sincere respects to the workers, peasants and intellectuals who are fighting valiantly on the different fronts, to the glorious People's Liberation Army, the great wall of steel that defends our motherland, to the vast numbers of hard-working cadres, to our party's close aides, the Communist Youth League members who are full of vigour and vitality, and to our fellow-countrymen in Taiwan, Hong Kong and Macao and to Chinese citizens overseas! We wish to extend our heartfelt thanks to all the democratic parties and non-party personages and friends of all circles who have cooperated with our party and rendered invaluable support to the people's revolution and to construction.

The unity of the Chinese people with the other peoples of the world is another essential condition for the triumph of our cause. In celebrating the 60th anniversary of the founding of the Communist Party of China, we wish to express our deep gratitude to all friendly countries which have entered into relations of equality and mutual assistance with us, and to all our foreign friends and comrades who have rendered our party and people invaluable help.

Let all comrades in the party and the people of all nationalities in our country unite as one under the great banner of Marxism-Leninism and Mao Zedong Thought and work hard to make China a modern and powerful socialist country which is prosperous, highly democratic and culturally advanced! Let us all strive for the supreme ideal of communism!

HU YAOBANG   19
On Ideological Questions, 24 April 1982

The publication of this speech, almost one year after its delivery, may have reflected a sense of growing challenge from Hu's radical rival Deng Liqun, who, according to an editorial note prefixed to this article but not reprinted here, had been present when the speech was originally given. Hu's main theme is the necessary organic interconnection between Marxist-Leninist-Maoist ideology and "political work," and by clear implication the domination of both by the Party, with Hu himself as its general secretary.

Our party's achievements in leading and uniting the masses to wage great struggles and constantly win victory are inseparable from the fact that the party has consistently attached importance to ideological and political work. After its founding, the party used various types of newspapers and publications, books and other forms to extensively publicize Marxism-Leninism and the victory of the October Revolution in Russia. This played an effective role in enlightening China's worker-peasant masses and intellectuals. We first set up a political work system in the Red Army during the Jinggangshan period. The cardinal link in political work was to educate the cadres and fighters in revolutionary ideology and arouse their revolutionary consciousness. During the entire period of the 10-year land revolution, despite very poor material and other conditions, we defeated frequent encirclements by the enemy, expanded the Red Army and the bases, completed the unprecedented 25,000-li Long March, and in the end carried on. After that we experienced the 8-year war of resistance to Japan and the liberation war, which lasted more than 3 years, and gained victory throughout the land. What did we depend on? Fundamentally speaking, our victory was gained because our party's line, principles and policies were correct, and our party closely integrated the universal truth of Marxism-Leninism with the concrete reality of the Chinese revolution; and because our party represented the interests of the people of the whole country, and our party members and fighters fought hard and made bloody sacrifices to liberate the people of the whole country, and were thus able to mobilize and lead the masses to wage victorious struggles. An important method adopted by the whole party throughout this period was to enhance the masses' revolutionary consciousness by means of ideological and political work. The entire historical experience of our party shows that the development and victory of our cause were built on the foundation of correct leadership and conscious masses; and after the condition of correct leadership had been gained, the masses' consciousness was the decisive factor. We therefore say that skill in ideological and political work is an important characteristic distinguishing our party from other political parties and is an extremely important condition for winning victory in revolution and construction.

At present, our party's ideological and political work is in many respects and links not done as well as in the past. It could be said that many of the party's fine traditions have been discarded. Failure to attach importance to ideological and political work and an inability to do this work are universal phenomena. Of course there are many reasons for this, and one of them is that we have not summed up well, systematically and profoundly, the experiences in

[Hu Yaobang, "On Questions of Ideological and Political Work," *People's Daily*, 2 January 1983.]

ideological and political work in light of the practice of revolution and construction since the founding of the state.

A major task that ought to be carried out by the party organizations of every place, department and unit is to investigate seriously and study, sum up the positive and negative historical experiences in ideological and political work, and form a complete set of correct viewpoints and methods. This task should in particular be grasped well by the party's propaganda departments.

In a talk in July 1981, Comrade Deng Xiaoping clearly pointed out that there was laxity and weakness in party leadership over ideological and political work. This criticism hit the nail right on the head and raised a key question on our ideological front. The central authorities therefore convened the forum on problems on the ideological front and afterwards issued documents; these were conveyed and discussed in all departments and localities. At that time, apart from tackling problems of bourgeois liberalization in a few aspects, including literature and art creation, the other fields were basically untouched. It is evident that it is by no means easy to solve the problems in connection with reality in all aspects in accordance with the Central Committee's demand. That is to say, people did not think that the central authorities' guiding principles applied in their case. Is this not called taking one's seat according to the ticket number? Certain comrades can often never find room for the central instructions in their units or implement them in their actions. Right at the start of 1982, the Central Committee emphasized promoting the building of socialist spiritual civilization, hitting at serious economic crimes, and carrying out structural reforms. As soon as these three issues were tackled, the laxity and weakness in ideological and political work was further changed. Ideological and political work cannot be tackled in a general way; instead we should relentlessly grasp one or two main issues at a time. In this respect, our party's ideological and political work has still not been properly implemented in many ways, and the problems of laxity and weakness still exist among the leaders of many departments and places.

The work of many departments and places has improved in recent years, but ideological and political work has still not been well grasped. This is a basic matter. This does not mean that the comrades doing ideological and political work are no good; the great majority of them are good comrades. Nor does it mean that our comrades have no standards; many of them do. It seems that a main problem on the ideological front is that there is not enough systematic summation of experiences and not enough study of the current ideological state and characteristics of the cadres and masses, while the methods used are not very apt. Hence the whole party must systematically and deeply ponder this question. On this occasion I am just raising questions and giving a few personal views; I hope everyone will study them.

WHAT IS OUR PARTY'S IDEOLOGICAL AND POLITICAL WORK?

In order to sum up experiences, we must first have a clear idea of what ideological and political work is. There would seem to be no problem here. The targets of ideological and political work are people and their thinking, viewpoint and

standpoint. Our party's ideological and political work is aimed at solving problems in people's thinking, viewpoint and political standpoint, and mobilizing the cadres and masses to attain the current and the long-term goals of the revolution. Is there anything unclear about this? But actually there is. In fact, the thinking of many comrades is still muddled and even stupid. It is therefore extremely important to truly clarify this issue.

We are faced with the problem of method in our study of things. The method told us by Marx is to start with the most universal and basic things in order to reveal their essence. In studying capitalist society, Marx precisely started with the most simple, universal and basic relationship, that is, the exchange of commodities. He wrote "Das Kapital," which became a classic in political economy.

The historical materialism of Marxist philosophy began with people's food, clothing and housing needs, which meant that people have to engage in production, and reached the conclusion that productive force determines production relations and the economic base determines the superstructure. It will be recalled that when Comrade Mao Zedong criticized dogmatism and subjectivism at the central revolutionary base, he said that people have to eat, roads are for people to walk on, after walking people need to sleep, and bullets can kill people. Why did Comrade Mao Zedong say these things? Because the dogmatists at that time issued an order requiring the army to march 120 li in 1 night and then wipe out the enemy. Was this possible? And so Comrade Mao Zedong used the most universal and basic reasoning to refute them; this was using materialism to oppose subjectivism. The theory of scientific socialism also begins with class analysis and clarifies the issues of how there were no classes at the start of human history, how classes formed, developed and changed, and how to eliminate classes and attain the communist society of the proletariat, and so on.

Therefore, when studying how to strengthen ideological and political work, we must grasp the fundamental and essential parts of this work by utilizing Marxist methods and analyzing phenomena and at the same time, we should point out and clarify many confused ideas.

For example, is it right to say that ideological and political work is to organize people to study the central leadership's documents? This answer of course includes some truth, but it does not touch the essence of ideological and political work.

For another example, some people say that ideological and political work is to commend good people and good things, advanced figures and deeds and to sum up and publicize advanced experiences. This is also somewhat true, but it does not touch the essence of ideological and political work either.

For another example, it is said that ideological and political work is to carry out criticism and self-criticism. Of course, criticism and self-criticism constitute an important method in ideological and political work, but this definition again does not reveal the essence of this work.

The above propositions do point out some important facts and forms of ideological and political work from different angles, but they fail to explain the most essential aspect of ideological and political work. Therefore, it is necessary for us to discuss and study ideological and political work so as to enable people to truly realize the essence of ideological and political work, that is, the purpose and task of this work and the relationship of this work with other work, and first of all, with economic work. Through study and discussion, we can correct various confused ideas about this question.

WHAT IS THE PURPOSE AND TASK OF IDEOLOGICAL AND POLITICAL WORK?

In a word, the purpose and task of ideological and political work is to enhance people's capacity for understanding and remolding the world. To say this in more detail, it is to educate party members and cadres, educate the broad masses, the working class as a whole and the people as a whole in revolutionary ideology and spirit, that is, in communist ideology, in Marxist basic theory and Mao Zedong Thought, which combines the universal truth of Marxism and the concrete practice of the revolution and construction in China so as to enlighten and enhance people's revolutionary consciousness, to enable people to establish correct standpoints and viewpoints and master correct thinking methods and work methods and to improve people's capacity for understanding and reforming the world through repeated practice.

In the essay "On Practice," Comrade Mao Zedong points out: "The struggle of the proletariat and the revolutionary people to change the world comprises the fulfillment of the following tasks: to change the objective world and at the same time, their own subjective world—to change their cognitive ability and change the relations between the subjective and the objective world." ("Selected Works of Mao Zedong," vol. 1, pp. 272–273) We communists, as the vanguards of the proletariat, should not only play an exemplary role in fulfilling the tasks of changing both the objective and their own subjective world, but should also, through ideological and political work, influence and attract more and more people to fulfill these tasks. We should make more and more people understand: "Discover the truth through practice, and again through practice verify and develop the truth. Start from perceptual knowledge and actively develop it into rational knowledge; then start from rational knowledge and actively guide revolutionary practice to change both the subjective and the objective world." (ibid., p. 273) We must get a good grasp of this epistemology of dialectical materialism so as to ensure our party's ideological and political work is closely related around the fundamental purpose and task of understanding and remolding the world.

It is of course not easy to enhance the capacity for understanding the objective world, including the capacity for observation, analysis and distinguishing. This is because the objective world is so complex that nobody can acquire a clear knowledge of it in a short while. Moreover, since social practice is developing continuously, as individuals, no person can have complete knowledge. On this issue, we have committed many errors for a fairly long time. For example, some people and some things were said to be constantly and absolutely correct. Of course, this was at variance with the facts. "The movement of change in the world of objective reality is never ending and so is man's cognition of truth through practice." (ibid., p. 272) All truths are relative in the long course of human cognition with absolute truth being included in relative truth. Absolute truth is a sum total of innumerable relative truths. Man's

cognition can merely approach absolute truth through relative truths while the limits and degrees of the approach have to be conditioned by historical circumstances. Therefore, it is impossible that some people are omniscient and omnipotent and it is not possible that some people are always correct.

Our ideological and political work is to publicize the party's line, principles and policies for revolution and construction and struggle objectives, strategies and methods among the vast number of party members, cadres and the masses, and to educate them in these things so as to enlighten and enhance their revolutionary consciousness and enable them to consciously and willingly follow the party's political leadership. In this way, it can effect ideological and political mobilization which arouses great strength so as to ensure the fulfillment of the tasks of revolution and construction. Comrade Mao Zedong underlined the great importance of ideological and political work in his essay "On Protracted War." Apart from a special section on "Political Mobilization for the War of Resistance," he also pointed out in the section entitled "The Army and the People Are the Foundation of Victory": "The reform of our military system requires its modernization and improved technical equipment, without which we cannot drive the enemy back across the Yalu Jiang. In our employment of troops we need progressive, flexible strategies and tactics, without which we likewise cannot win victory. Nevertheless, soldiers are the foundation of an army; unless they are imbued with a progressive political spirit, and unless such a spirit is fostered through progressive political work, it will be impossible to achieve genuine unity between officers and men, impossible to arouse to the full their enthusiasm for the war of resistance, and impossible to provide a sound basis for the most effective use of all our technical equipment and tactics." ("Selected Works of Mao Zedong," vol. 2, p. 278) Though here Mao Zedong referred to a war, the principle expounded by him still holds true in the building of socialist material and spiritual civilization.

In order to build socialism, we should not only build a high level of material civilization, continuously develop and improve the material and technical foundation for the socialist system, but should also build a high level of spiritual civilization with communist ideology as its core, which is also an essential requirement of the socialist system. Our construction will not be able to go on smoothly without improving the revolutionary consciousness of the vast number of workers, peasants, intellectuals and other masses, without enlightening their firm belief in communism, without encouraging them to show initiative, creativity and enthusiasm in building socialism, without arousing their senses of honor, pride and responsibility toward their work, and particularly without requiring the vast number of our party members, league members and cadres to play an exemplary role in these areas. It will even be very difficult for us to achieve our goals if we fail to do a good job in the above areas, because there are various ideas in people's minds; both communist and noncommunist ideology exist simultaneously. There are capitalist ideology, feudal ideology as well as the backward ideology of the petty bourgeoisie. All kinds of nonproletarian ideology will impede our correct implementing of the party's line, principles and policies and hinder us from carrying out unswerving struggle which is necessary for the realization of the tasks set forth by our party. It will also prevent us from remolding both the objective world and our own subjective world. Without eliminating nonproletarian ideology, our revolution will not succeed and our construction will not be successful. The purpose of ideological and political work is to sweep away these things. This is also a sanitation and hygiene movement and a movement of general cleaning. All of us should set to work and do cleaning every day and only by sweeping in a proper way can we achieve results.

Thus, our party's ideological and political work should first function in strengthening, encouraging and arousing people's belief, enthusiasm, willpower and morale. That is what we often say—firm and scientific faith, revolutionary enthusiasm, staunch willpower and high morale. If ideological and political work remain only at the stage of understanding the world and fail to encourage people to change the world in practice, then it will only be empty talk. Enhancing people's revolutionary consciousness means that we should strengthen and enhance the revolutionary faith, enthusiasm, fighting will and resolution of a vast number of party members, cadres and masses. It should be noticed that in the course of revolution and construction, various erroneous ideas and actions will continually arise among the people, such as actions of excess, cowardliness and retrogression. Our comrades who are engaged in ideological and political work should be good at promptly perceiving new situations and studying new problems so as to correctly and effectively educate and help people to promptly correct their erroneous understanding, standpoint and method in the course of understanding and changing the world. They should even do this work in advance and take preventive measures so as to solve problems in their embryonic stage or enable people to have sufficient mental preparation before problems appear. Thus, through repeated practice, deepening our cognition and enhancing our capacity for changing the world are the fundamental purposes and tasks of ideological and political work of our party which take the changing of the world as its own mission. All of our comrades engaging in ideological and political work must clearly realize this point and should never lump together some specific parts and methods of ideological and political work with our fundamental purposes and tasks. The specific parts and concrete methods and means of ideological and political work may be diverse and changeable with different historical conditions, circumstances and specific objects. If we only pay attention to means and methods or only remember some individual and concrete items but forget the fundamental purpose and task, our ideological and political work will not reap good results and the comrades who are engaging in this work cannot improve themselves either.

WHAT ARE THE FEATURES OF IDEOLOGICAL AND POLITICAL WORK?

Any work or any department has its own features. To understand things, we must begin with their features. Anyone who has a clear understanding of the features of his own department and its relationship to other things can do his work with good results. The features of ideological and political work are derived from the object of its given tasks. As mentioned above, the object of ideological and political work is men. We must straighten out the thinking, viewpoint and standpoint of men. This is different from economic work. It is also not completely like the work of the organizational department.

The scope of ideological and political work is very broad. There are people in every department or unit. People think. Therefore, every department or unit must do ideological and political work. All work is done by people. In the process of physical or mental work, people would think this way or that. Therefore, in doing anything, we must do ideological and political work. Comrade Mao Zedong said that ideological and political work is a guarantee for economic work. In a broad sense, ideological and political work should be the guarantee for all work. Given a good performance in ideological problems, half the battle is won. No department or unit can ever forget ideological and political work in doing any work.

Ideological and political work calls for, first of all, the solution of the problem of ideological awareness and the problem of a political stand. Lenin said many times that Marxism cannot automatically spring up in workers' minds but must be instilled into them. Later, Comrade Mao Zedong also said on many occasions that we must enlighten and educate people. We must advocate such virtues as love for the motherland, love for the people, love for labor, love for science and love for socialism and carry out education in patriotism, internationalism, collectivism, communism and education in dialectical materialism and the world outlook represented by historical materialism. We must resist capitalist, feudalist and other decadent ideas. We must imbue people with revolutionary ideals, moral principles and a sense of discipline. We must raise people's consciousness as the masters. These are undoubtedly the most constant and most general contents of ideological and political work.

In "On Protracted War," Comrade Mao Zedong pointed out that the three major principles of political work in the army—unity between officers and men, unity between the army and the people and the disintegration of the enemy troops. What is meant here is actually the correct handling of the relationship between men. In building socialist material civilization and spiritual civilization, we must also pay good attention to the proper handling of relationships of this kind, such as the relationship between workers and peasants, the relationship between the worker-peasant masses and intellectuals, the relationship between cadres and the masses, the relationship among people of all nationalities of the country, the relationship between the Chinese people and the people of various countries, the relationship between the Chinese proletariat and the bourgeoisie in foreign countries, and so forth. We must also correctly handle the relationship between various kinds of people in the political, economic, ideological and cultural fields and in social life. Of course, also involved here are some fundamental policies of our party and state. It is not just the business of the ideological and political work department. But our ideological and political work must be conducive to unity among people of all nationalities of the country and people in all circles and to unity between the Chinese people and the people of various countries in the world. Given firm unity at home and international unity, we can, in the process of socialist construction, overcome various difficulties, effectively resist domestic and external enemies and achieve our goals in a relatively short period of time and at a relatively small cost.

Unlike economic, technical and other material things, changes in people's thinking are governed by different laws.

Therefore, unlike the economic department, we, in doing ideological and political work, cannot formulate annual plans or 5-year plans and set clear-cut goals. A few years ago, I told the comrades of the propaganda department that the work of the propaganda department could not be just a matter of calling one conference a year. The planning department can call just one conference a year and take care of such matters as what are the goals for the year, how much money is to be spent, how large are the supplies of things required and how to bring about a balance. The organization department generally can also meet once a year. If the propaganda department meets just once a year, setting forth several tasks in a sweeping manner, many problems cannot be properly solved. The propaganda department must call many meetings a year—large, medium-sized and small meetings. Mainly small meetings must be called. A meeting should be held with a particular problem in mind. The comrades concerned must be brought together for a joint discussion. Concerning how to understand and approach things, how to carry out publicity and education and how to adhere to principle and foster a sense of propriety, we must seek actual results; and in a word, where there are existing problems and especially where an ideological trend of a general nature is discovered, we must immediately call a meeting, make an analysis and work out a few rules for implementation. The results of certain kinds of work must be summed up promptly. For example, the "civilization and courtesy month," "five stresses and four beauties" and other campaigns launched throughout the country must be summed up in time. We must study what effects have been produced, determine if there is any typical example, if there is any problem and what are the future plans. In my opinion, the propaganda departments at all levels must, in light of the progress of work and changes in people's thinking, tackle a number of problems in a given year and make studies to find 5 solutions.

The fundamental principle of ideological and political work means conducting education and persuasion of people and does not mean adopting coercive and forceful methods or issuing administrative orders. Concerning the problems of ideology and understanding among the people, we must adopt the principle of clearing the way and providing guidance and opposing the principle of blocking it. The principle of clearing the way and providing guidance is the correct principle for ideological and political work. We must guide while clearing the way and clear the way while guiding, and both clear the way and guide. Clearing the way means providing wide opportunities for airing views and pooling the wisdom of the masses. Guiding means teaching with skill and patience and conducting education by persuasion. We must seek truth from facts, convince people with reason, and stress practical results. We must go deep among the people and patiently conduct arduous and meticulous work in light of the ideological state of the masses. If we rely on coercion and force regarding people's ideological problems, and if we rely on big and empty talk, boasting and lies over matters for which it is necessary to mobilize the masses, we are acting in a way totally opposite to all of our party's principles, including the correct principle of ideological education.

Since ideological and political work means educating and persuading people and raising their revolutionary consciousness and their ability to understand things, apart from relying on the broad masses of party members and people to do it, we must rely on cadres to tackle the large amount of work. Therefore, the propaganda and political work departments' organizing and guiding such work must first properly do the work concerning cadres, educating and persuading them and raising their revolutionary consciousness and their ability to understand things. The first four volumes of "Selected Works of Mao Zedong" mentioned the theory of the Chinese revolution and pointed out the line, strategies and general and specific policies for work at all stages. As far as the object of education is concerned, we must first carry out ideological and political work among cadres, educating and convincing them, so that they understand the principle of revolution. Then through the cadres, we must educate, unite and guide the masses, thus achieving victory in revolution.

Of the articles in which Comrade Mao Zedong systematically defined ideological and political work, the earliest was the Gutian congress resolution written in 1929. At that time, subjectivism prevailed and nonproletarian ideas were rife. This resolution enabled the worker-peasant Red Army to be built on the basis of Marxism-Leninism and to basically eliminate the influences of the old-type army. This was also first aimed at cadres. When it came to the problem of mistreating and beating and taunting soldiers, who was mentioned? It was the cadres who were mentioned. Such articles as "The Situation and Tasks of the Anti-Japanese War After the Fall of Shanghai and Taiyuan" and "On Protracted War" also first mentioned the need to convince cadres. Given the correct thinking of cadres and a raised level on their part, the job of carrying out ideological education among workers, peasants and fighters is rendered relatively easy.

The time our party did ideological and political work well was the period of the Red Army, the period of Yanan or the period shortly after the founding of the PRC. Later, for a period of time, under the influence of "leftist" mistakes, ideological and political work was gradually turned into a means used by leaders in coping with ordinary workers, peasants, fighters and intellectuals. The reputation of ideological and political work became stained, with very bad consequences. To certain cadres, it seemed that only the common people had incorrect ideas and that they themselves were all right. To them, it seemed that raising revolutionary consciousness and the ability to understand things involved only the common people and that this had nothing to do with themselves. Certain leadership cadres also think that they themselves were many times wiser than ordinary ones and that there was basically no need for them to undergo transformation. Comrade Mao Zedong criticized this erroneous trend many times. Facts proved to be the opposite of what they had thought. Many kinds of work were not done well and even chaos and losses resulted. This was first blamed on the problem of ideological awareness and political stand involving cadres and party members, or on the problem of style. With the thinking of cadres raised and wrong things overcome, the job was made easy.

Therefore, in doing ideological and political work, we must first solve the ideological problems among cadres. To change the state of a lack of organization and discipline in the production of coal and charcoal, the leaders of the Ministry of Coal Industry first worked on cadres at all levels. The first rule was for cadres to work side by side with the rank and file. The second was to transfer those cadres originally working on the surface of the ground to work below the surface. The third rule was to criticize the lethargic state of cadres. Did not Comrade Mao Zedong often mention the need to "move the god"? The god means the common people. To "move the god" means doing ideological and political work, including the need for cadres to set personal examples by taking part in collective production and labor and mingling with the masses as one.

After the founding of the PRC, we paid relatively serious attention in the first few years to the training of cadres on a rotating basis, their education and the elevation of their cultural, scientific and theoretical levels. The pity was that we did not stick it out. We missed many favorable opportunities. This was a great mistake. Now, the party Central Committee is determined to carry out education and training for cadres, give them training on a rotating basis and improve their caliber. It has called on all our cadres to think more of the affairs of the state and of the people and not to place their personal affairs first. Those people who become obsessed with subjectivism all day can get nowhere. We must encourage cadres to devote the great part of their time after work to reading. They must pick up some books on theory, on science and on particular trades and raise their cultural and ideological levels.

Only by understanding and grasping the features of ideological and political work can we work out correct methods. Without understanding China's features, our party could not have guided the Chinese revolution to victory and cannot guide socialist modernization to victory.

Without understanding the features of ideological and political work, we cannot possibly improve and strengthen ideological and political work and bring about the vigorous development of this kind of work to achieve marked new progress.

EDUCATORS MUST FIRST BE EDUCATED

Since ideological and political work consists chiefly of education this is in fact a question of how to strengthen the ranks of ideological and political workers. It is necessary for educators to have not only a correct ideological viewpoint and political stand but also correct ways and methods.

There are two forms of education: one is education by argument and reasoning and another is education in terms of images (chiefly through literature and art). It is necessary for educators to be familiar with these two forms of education and to be good at applying them in their work.

How is our education by argument and reasoning at present? The problem in this respect lies chiefly in the lack of conviction. What is referred to as lack of conviction is that we do not sufficiently explain the truth, that it does not produce vigorous agitation and that it fails to move the people. There are only two forms of education by argument and reasoning; one is orally, such as speeches, reports, transmission of documents, talks, arguments, criticism and self-criticism; another is by writing, such as resolutions, instructions, theoretical works, popular literature, commentaries and news reports. There are two major common failings in many of our articles and speeches: The first is that we only apply the deductive method and that we do not or seldom apply the method of analysis. We often infer from one concept what and how we should do without

so much as presenting the facts and reasoning things out or making concrete analyses according to facts or reasoning things out while recounting. Lenin and Comrade Mao Zedong were different. When we read their major works, we become aware of an outstanding feature, that is, they make concrete analyses of concrete problems and are very convincing. Take Comrade Mao Zedong's article, "On Protracted War," for example. First it analyzes and compares the actual conditions of both China and Japan and their strong and weak points and says that the theory of national subjugation is wrong and that the theory of quick victory is likewise wrong. Then it amply presents the facts and reasons things out through detailed analysis, argument and reasoning. The second common failing is that we load our articles or speeches with too many concepts, with one concept linked with another and big concepts linked with small ones. Why is it that many people are unwilling to listen to a report or a speech or a thesis or an editorial? We should find the cause not only from the audience or readers but also from ourselves, which is chiefly because we do not penetratingly analyze and dissect problems and clearly reason things out.

Our education in terms of images is chiefly reflected in the problems that exist in literature and art. In addition to bad political tendencies, unhealthy ideology and feelings and a bad social effect in some works, there are also some works which lack appeal and have little social effect. The CPC Central Committee pointed out before the "Cultural Revolution" that there was a defect of formalism and generalization in our literary and art creation. This hit home as far as the literary and art features are concerned. Our education in terms of images lacks appeal so that people do not want to read them. It fails to strike a sympathetic chord in their ideas and feelings and in the depth of their souls after they read it and it fails to produce repercussions and exert a perceptible influence.

Why is it that our education by argument and reasoning carry little conviction and that our education in terms of images lacks appeal? This is because our educators fail to master the laws governing these two kinds of education.

Therefore, it is necessary for all trades and services, first of all the propaganda, cultural and educational departments that have a direct relationship with ideological and political work, to receive some training in basic methods. All trades and services, whether in party work or in ideological and political work, should have their own basic knowledge and professional skills. We should not consider that only those who engage in economic and technical work face a problem of specialization.

It will be impossible for our cadres in various trades and services, and the leading cadres in particular, to do their work well if they do not have some basic training in professional knowledge, do not have professional skills and do not become experts.

Educators must first be educated. As far as ideological viewpoint and political stand are concerned, there are three main requirements:

1. Our revolutionary consciousness, knowledge in various aspects and our abilities in recognizing some aspects of objective things should always be higher, greater and stronger than other people's and we should be a little ahead of them. If you want to persuade other people to have confidence in socialism, you should first have

conviction. If you vacillate and have no conviction, how can you enhance other people's conviction?

2. It is necessary to understand the specific law governing ideological and political work, be familiar with the specific features of our work and, proceeding from practice, correctly apply the objective law in our work. This is not merely a professional question for it is first of all a question of ideological and political standards.

3. We should set an example not only by giving verbal directions but also by teaching others by our own examples and by integrating both of them. If you do not match your deeds with your words, no matter how well you talk, people will not listen to you; if you talk about wholehearted service to the people but you do not serve the people even half-heartedly, this will exert a very bad influence. Why is it that, at present, some people do not have strength and good effect in doing ideological and political work? An important reason is that they do not set an example. If a person can set an example, his speech can carry weight. This is a most important condition in doing a good job of ideological and political work. In mobilizing the masses to do something, all party members, particularly party cadres holding leading positions, should first be able to do it.

SOME PROBLEMS WE SHOULD PAY ATTENTION TO ON THE CURRENT IDEOLOGICAL FRONT

The CPC Central Committee has repeatedly pointed out that it is still necessary to continuously eliminate "leftist" things on the political, economic and ideological fronts. At the same time it is necessary to pay serious attention to and deal seriously with bourgeois liberalization and pay attention to overcoming feudal things. We should never lower our guard. The idea that "leftist" things have been completely eliminated as a result of bringing order out of chaos is not correct. Actually, we should still exert great efforts to fight against them in the future. Some people who were extremely "leftist" during the "Cultural Revolution" are now extremely rightist. They jump from one extreme to another. Of course, this kind of person is very few in number. We should make a practical analysis that conforms with principles in order to determine which are "leftist" and which are rightist things on the political, economic and ideological fronts and in various different tasks and specific problems. We should oppose either "leftist" or "rightist" things, as appropriate. We should not treat different things as the same.

The open-door policy has brought us many beneficial things. But it has also brought us many germs. Therefore, we should adopt dual tactics. On the one hand, we should resolutely implement the open-door policy, because this policy is correct. On the other hand, we should resolutely resist decadent capitalist things, including the bourgeois ideology and way of life. There are at least two kinds of "sugar-coated bullets," including money, beautiful women, foreign goods and so forth, which corrupt us materially. The other kind is spiritual "sugar-coated bullets," including decadent capitalist ideological viewpoints, culture, art, way of life and so forth, which corrode us ideologically, erode our fighting will and convictions, and confuse our minds. Every nation has its advanced and backward things. With respect to all foreign things, we should acquire the concept of one divides into two. In

other words, we should absorb good things from others, but resolutely resist those decadent and backward things. Socialism and capitalism are two different worlds. We are building a socialist spiritual civilization which is, by and large, much loftier than capitalism. With respect to the open-door policy we are now implementing, there are also various comments from the outside world. We should also adopt the attitude of analysis by adhering to our Marxist stand, viewpoints, methods and principles without being swayed by comments from the outside world.

With respect to press reporting, first, we should not report news worshipping things foreign; second, we should pay attention to policy; third, we should clearly check on things before publishing reports and avoid boastful and exaggerated reports. With respect to reports from the capitalist world, our newspapers and periodicals should be very serious and careful and should adopt an attitude of analysis and criticism. We should never eulogize them or engage in so-called pure objective reporting. Being an ideological matter, the press cannot be without a class nature. When class is eliminated in the future throughout the world, there will still be rights and wrongs, let alone not only when class struggle is still very acute and complicated, as at present on the world scale. With regard to the achievements of scientific research, advanced technology and rational methods of management in the capitalist world, we may report them and advocate learning from them but we should absorb, digest or develop them in light of the actual conditions in our country and according to our specific conditions. As to its social system, its decadent ideological viewpoints and all things diametrically opposed to socialism, we should never eulogize them.

With regard to literature and art, particularly films, operas and novels, we should avoid indiscriminate and excessive learning from the skill and art of the West. We should not completely and uncritically accept artistic viewpoints of the West. To deal with those who wantonly and brazenly spread bourgeois poison, the first step we should take is to criticize them. If they turn a deaf ear to our criticism, we should transfer them to other posts. If they refuse to mend their ways despite repeated admonitions or persist in their mistakes, the third step we should take is to take disciplinary measures against them. Those who deliberately spread ideological poison, slander our socialist system, instigate the worship of foreign things and fawning on foreign powers and carry out feudal and superstitious activities should be condemned by the public opinion of society. Those who truly cause serious consequences should be legally accountable. What do we rely on to maintain popular morale if we do not rely on Marxism in practicing socialism and in building our country into a powerful modern socialist country with a high degree of civilization and democracy? Once our spiritual pillar of fighting for communism collapses and once the four pillars of abiding by the four fundamental principles collapse, will it still be possible for the great building of our Chinese nation not to topple? Once a nation has collapsed spiritually, its politics, economy and culture will also break down completely. There are many lessons drawn from such incidents. Under the conditions of implementing the open-door policy toward foreign countries, Communist Party members and party cadres, our middle-ranking and senior cadres in particular, should keep a clear head.

They should firmly believe in Marxism, pay attention

to communist purity and apply the proletarian world out-look to observe and handle problems. We should stick to the patriotic stand and the stand of the masses and proletariat. We should never fall captive to bourgeois ideology.

Finally, I would like to stress that since ideological and political work is so important, its task is so arduous and it is so indispensable to the victory of revolution and construction, it is necessary for our party organizations at various levels to put this work in an important position, place it on the important agenda of the party committees, strengthen their leadership over ideological and political work, and attach importance to strengthening the ranks of ideological and political workers. Comrade Mao Zedong said: "All departments and organizations should shoulder their responsibilities in ideological and political work. This applies to the Communist Party, the youth league, government departments in charge of this work, and especially to heads of educational institutions and teachers." ("On the Correct Handling of Contradictions Among the People") "The first secretaries of the party committees in all provinces, municipalities and autonomous regions should personally tackle this question." ("Speech at the CPC's National Conference on Propaganda Work") Only by paying attention to and studying this question will it be possible to energetically overcome the lax and weak situation that exists in the leadership over ideological and political work; to correctly solve the various problems that exist in the ranks of ideological and political workers; and to bring into full play the role of ideological and political work in mobilizing and ensuring the realization of the party's tasks in the new period.

HU YAOBANG   20
On the Karl Marx Centennial, 13 March 1983

To commemorate the centennial of Marx's death, General Secretary Hu delivered this speech at a meeting in Beijing. It appears to possess no theoretical originality or interest. Hu apparently intended to show that, at least in China, the reports of the death of Marxist ideology were greatly exaggerated.

Comrades and friends:

We are gathered here today at this grand meeting to commemorate the centenary of the death of Karl Marx, founder of scientific communism, great teacher of the proletariat and of the exploited and oppressed masses throughout the world, and the most outstanding revolutionary and scientist in human history.

Marx was a German of the 19th century, but his influence far exceeds the limitations of time and place. He belongs to the whole of progressive mankind as well as to the proletariat of the world and all oppressed peoples and nations. As Frederick Engels said following Marx's death, Marx had fertilized with his powerful thought the proletarian movement of both the Western and Eastern hemispheres. (1) [see notes at end of speech] It was under the guidance of Marx's theory that the communists, the proletariat and the people of all nationalities in China embarked on the correct path of revolution and liberation in this enormous yet backward country of the East. The Chinese people have now accomplished the new-democratic and the socialist revolution and become masters of this great socialist country. We are creating a new situation in all fields of socialist modernization, striving to build a socialist material and spiritual civilization and to fulfill the splendid programme set forth at the Twelfth National Congress of the Communist Party of China. All of us feel more deeply now that, without Marx's theory, China could not possibly have become what she is today. We have learned from Marx, conscientiously studied and drawn wisdom and strength from his works, and shall continue to do so. Therefore, as we honour the memory of Karl Marx, who rests in eternal peace in London, let us today, at this commemorative meeting held in the East, express our deepest gratitude to him.

Comrades and friends:

Marx's greatest contribution to mankind is his theory of scientific communism, which, formulated by Marx together with his closest comrade-in-arms Frederick Engels, equipped the proletariat and progressive people of the

[Hu Yaobang, "The Radiance of the Great Truth of Marxism Lights Our Way Forward," New China News Agency, 13 March 1983.]

world with the most powerful ideological weapon for criticizing the old world, creating a new world and struggling for their own emancipation.

Marx was the first to combine materialism with dialectics and to apply dialectical materialism to the observation and examination of the history of human society, bringing to light the truths that, in the final analysis, material production constitutes the basis of man's social, political and ideological life taken as a whole and that the contradiction between the productive forces and the relations of production constitutes the real motive force of historical development. He scientifically explained the role of class struggle in human history and the conditions under which classes come into being, develop and die out.

Marx was the first to discover the secret of the exploitation of labour by capital, namely, the law of surplus value, and to bring to light the circumstances of the birth and development of capitalism and its final historically inevitable replacement by communism.

He was thus the first to transform utopian socialism into scientific socialism, proving that the modern proletariat represents the new social force for the overthrow of the old system and the establishment of the new, and that it is the most promising and thoroughly revolutionary class.

Thereby, he brought about the most radical change in history, economics and philosophy and established a truly scientific world outlook and the most thorough theory of social revolution.

From its very birth, Marxism has demonstrated its mighty power with which no other ideological system can compare. Marx joined the revolution in his youth, and after he became a communist, he directly led the workers' movement, identified himself with it and dedicated his whole life to the emancipation of the proletariat. His revolutionary activity was carried on in the 19th century, when European society was in the throes of violent upheavals and revolutionary storms. Under the test of these storms, particularly the severe test of the great struggle for the Paris Commune in 1871, a motley variety of previously vociferous schools of socialism gradually died out. Marx's theory alone rapidly spread far and wide, because it truly represented the interests of the proletariat and the people at large and brilliantly summarized the experience of both the old and the new revolutionary movements. The proletarian party personally created by Marx developed from a small group of exiled revolutionaries into a "powerful party that made the whole official world tremble". (2)

Marx and Engels have passed away, but Marxism has developed with increasing vigour. The past century has demonstrated, again and again, that the history of Marxism is one of triumph over successive onslaughts by various antagonistic ideological trends and over "encirclement and suppression" by reactionary forces. However serious the setbacks and violent the storms, its revolutionary drive has remained invincible. The past century has also repeatedly shown that the history of Marxism is one in which it has overcome various erroneous tendencies within the Marxist movement, thus continuing its forward march. Revisionism is erroneous because it discards the universal truth of Marxism; dogmatism, too, is erroneous because it regards Marxism as a set of rigid tenets. Both revisionism and dogmatism run counter to Marxism in that they separate the subjective from the objective world and divorce theory from

practice. Marxism is a developing science; it is the guide to revolution. Its vitality lies in its constant analysis and study of new situations and problems that arise in the course of practice and in its integration with concrete revolutionary practice at different times and in different countries. This is the well-spring of the unceasing enrichment and development of Marxism and the basic guarantee for its ever-growing revolutionary vigour.

The victory of the October Revolution led by V. I. Lenin and the Bolshevik Party of Russia represented the first momentous development of Marxism after the death of Marx and Engels. Lenin and his party formulated their own line and policies by integrating the universal truth of Marxism with the then latest developments of the world situation in the era of imperialism and with the concrete realities of Russia. From this arose the new development of Marxism, the birth of Leninism, the victory of the October Revolution and the realization of socialist revolution first in one country. If Lenin and the Russian Bolshevik Party had failed to act in the light of the actual conditions in Russia but had held rigidly to Marx's specific conclusion that the proletarian revolution must win victory simultaneously in the major capitalist countries, what would have been the result? There would have been no victory of the October Revolution.

The triumph of the Chinese revolution is the most significant event in the history of Marxism's development after the October Revolution. Under the conditions then prevailing in the world's East, Comrade Mao Zedong and our party integrated the universal truth of Marxism-Leninism with the concrete realities in China, relied closely on the peasants—the powerful ally of the working class in the rural areas and the main revolutionary force against feudalism—and found the correct path of encircling the cities from the countryside.

From this flowed the birth of Mao Zedong Thought and the triumph of the Chinese revolution. If we had not taken this path, but had held rigidly to the traditional mode of revolution in modern Europe, that is, the seizure of state power through urban armed uprisings, what would have been the result? There would have been no triumph of the Chinese revolution.

It follows that a basic lesson to draw from the history of the development of Marxism is that the Marxist party of each country cannot succeed in revolution and construction unless it formulates its own line and policies in accordance with its own concrete conditions and with the international and domestic circumstances in which it finds itself.

For more than three decades since the Second World War, the world Communist movement has followed a tortuous course of development. It has scored magnificent successes and victories, but has also experienced severe setbacks and failures, undergoing a bewildering process of turbulence and division. This complex historical phenomenon has given rise to a wide variety of reactions throughout the world. Some people have gloated over the setbacks, whereas others have lost their confidence, describing Marxism as being in a state of "crisis". However, amidst such shouts of "crisis", the Marxist parties and organizations of many countries, braving all kinds of attacks, have heroically and calmly carried on the fight. In the tortuous course of development all true Marxists and far-sighted people are discerning a most essential positive factor, i.e., politically and ideologically more and more Marxist parties and organizations have dared to break with blind faith, to emancipate their minds and to think for themselves, thus becoming able independently to integrate the universal truth of Marxism with the concrete practice of the revolution in their own countries. Facts have proved that on the questions of how to handle correctly the relations between the parties of various countries and of what specific road of revolution to take, the Marxist parties in different countries have a much deeper understanding and are richer in experience and their level is clearly higher than before. Fundamentally, this has created the most important condition for the greater development of Marxism.

In our own Communist Party of China, a change of historic significance has taken place since the Third Plenary Session of its Eleventh Central Committee in late 1978. Our party fell into dire straits in the ten years (1966–76) of the "Cultural Revolution". However, in spite of all the difficulties the Chinese people did not lose faith in Marxism; on the contrary, they were able to acquire a better understanding of its truth. In the short span of four years or so from the Third Plenary Session to the Twelfth National Congress of the C.P.C. in September 1982, we fulfilled the arduous task of setting things to rights in our guiding ideology. In essence, this means that we have re-embarked on the road of integrating the universal truth of Marxism with the actual realities in China under the new historical conditions. This is the only correct road opened up for us by Comrade Mao Zedong. Our personal experience has made us appreciate keenly the brilliance of his thinking and practice and the tremendous wisdom and strength he brought to the party and people when he adhered to this correct road through decades of activity. It has also made us realize that, deviating or departing from this correct road in the evening of his life, even such a great Marxist as Comrade Mao Zedong could not avoid going astray and making distressing mistakes. Therefore, by setting things to rights we mean restoring Mao Zedong Thought to its true essence and upholding and developing it. Some people are prattling right up to now that we have abandoned Mao Zedong Thought. This only shows that they have no idea of what Mao Zedong Thought means, that is, no idea of what Marxism means.

In setting things to rights in ideology, we have resolutely shaken off the "left" tendency and the personality cult that long fettered us, re-established the principle of seeking truth from facts, scientifically appraised the historical role of Mao Zedong Thought and Comrade Mao Zedong, and restored and developed the Marxist principles guiding our party life.

In setting things to rights politically, we have courageously discarded the erroneous theory of "continued revolution under the dictatorship of the proletariat" that did us so much harm, correctly re-analysed the contradictions in China's socialist society, achieved political stability and unity and shifted the focus of work of the whole party.

In setting things to rights in the agricultural system, we have resolutely corrected certain grave and prolonged misunderstandings regarding such questions as the socialist public economy and mass production, overcome the serious egalitarian error of "everyone eating from the same big pot" and created the system of responsibility for agricultural production characterized by contracting for specialized work and by payment being linked to output. In such ways the Marxist principle of "to each according to his work" and the principle of integrating the interests of the state, the collective and the individual are being genuinely implemented in the vast rural areas in the light of China's concrete conditions. The bold reform in agriculture has pioneered a correct road and given our 800 million peasants a free hand to fully tap their tremendous labour potential, develop a diversified economy and expand production in breadth and depth. It has led to a steady rise in purchasing power for means of production as well as for consumer goods and thus to the building up of an extensive socialist market. This has lent tremendous impetus to our socialist modernization drive as a whole, and will continue to do so. Far from losing its foothold or slipping back as some half-baked critics have claimed, socialism has become greatly consolidated and is taking big strides forward in our rural areas. This is because we have given up old forms that were divorced from realities—forms that were either uncritically copied from other countries or arbitrarily devised by ourselves—and have found new forms that are truly Chinese and suited to China's current rural conditions.

We have now entered the stage of creation of a new situation in all fields of socialist modernization. But in our economic, social and other activities, there still exist many erroneous ideas and models that do not suit China's actual conditions and that have long fettered people's minds and seriously hampered the development of the productive forces. Only by proceeding from realities, breaking away from such ideas and models and instituting properly guided reforms step by step and in an all-round, systematic, resolute and orderly way can we create a new situation in all fields, better integrate the fundamental principles of Marxism with the concrete reality of our modernization drive and develop scientific socialism even further. In order to achieve the four modernizations (modernization of China's industry, agriculture, national defence and science and technology), and to vigorously develop the productive forces, it is imperative to carry out reforms in both the relations of production and the superstructure.

We are convinced that, by readjusting those links in the relations of production that are not in correspondence with the growth of the productive forces and those links in the superstructure that are not in correspondence with the requirements of the economic base, always provided that we adhere to the four cardinal principles (those principles refer to adherence to the socialist road, the people's democratic dictatorship [i.e., the dictatorship of the proletariat], the leadership of the Communist Party, and Marxism-Leninism and Mao Zedong Thought), and the basic system of socialism, we will surely succeed in building socialism with distinctive Chinese characteristics and bring out to the full the immense creativeness latent in our hundreds of millions of people, so that the superiority of the socialist system will display itself still better. This, of course, cannot be accomplished in a short time, for it involves a process of constant improvement and progress. But it can be predicted that through one or two decades of hard struggle China, as an economically and culturally backward developing country with a population of one billion, will make historic progress in its modernization programme under the socialist system and that this will bring a new major victory for Marxism in the East at the turn of the century.

Comrades and friends:

Marx was not only a great revolutionary, but also a great scientist. One extremely important factor which enabled him to found scientific communism was that he mastered all that was best in the culture and knowledge of mankind and integrated it firmly with the workers' movement. As Lenin said, the ideological sources of Marxism lay in its critical assimilation of three main trends of thought prevailing in the three most advanced countries of the time, that is, German classical philosophy, English classical political economy and French utopian socialism. (3) And Marx's theory was able to "win the hearts and minds of millions and tens of millions of the most revolutionary class" because he based himself "on the firm foundation of the human knowledge acquired under capitalism," knowledge which enriched his conclusions. (4) Marx's knowledge was extensive and expert. Rarely in the history of the world has any person achieved such breadth of scope and accomplished so much. Marx won the admiration of many honest scientists, thinkers and historians. The apologists of the old world tried to write him off or branded his theory as being thoroughly "outdated," but facts proved that this was mere wishful thinking. Generation after generation of scholars, young people, activists in the workers' movement, national revolutionaries and other people seeking change have continued to draw inexhaustible strength and confidence from Marxism. This would be inconceivable in regard to any flash-in-the-pan "new trend of thought." Marx's diligence and tenacity were amazing, and particularly in his rigorous approach to scholarly research, he set a worthy example for all scientific workers. Often persecuted by reactionary governments, he had to live abroad in exile, drifting from place to place. But his fighting will became even firmer and he never ceased to strive on along the road of revolution and science. All his life he was plagued by poverty, somewhat alleviated only with help from Engels. Four of his children died either in infancy or childhood and he could not even afford a small coffin for one daughter. (5) He dedicated all his energies and wisdom and the choicest fruits of his scientific research to the working class and to all mankind. This spirit of utter devotion can move one to song and tears. Marx was indeed a working-class intellectual par excellence, and the most outstanding intellectual representing the wisdom and conscience of mankind.

In speaking here of the importance of the mastery of humanity's cultural heritage to the success of Marx's great cause and of Marx as the most outstanding intellectual, I would like to take the opportunity to discuss at some length the correct attitude our party, the Chinese working class and other working people should take towards knowledge and intellectuals.

Since our party's founding more than 60 years ago, its main efforts have gone into leading the people of all our nationalities in the performance of two major tasks.

One is the overthrow of the old world, the three big mountains (imperialism, feudalism and bureaucrat-capitalism), and the other is the building of a new world, or the building of a powerful, modern socialist China. Knowledge and intellectuals were necessary for overthrowing the old world, and they are even more necessary for building the new. Furthermore, in a country like China with its low economic and cultural level, whether or not we are able to master modern science and culture is a pivotal factor determining success or failure in our construction. But it is precisely with regard to this key question that our understanding has been inadequate for so long and that we have for years been obsessed with erroneous ideas that depart from Marxism. Today, the correct attitude towards knowledge and intellectuals has therefore become a vital and urgent question, in the integration of the universal truth of Marxism with the concrete practice of China's socialist modernization.

It must be affirmed that our party has had marked successes in handling the question of intellectuals. The founding and development of our party cannot be separated from the efforts of revolutionary intellectuals. In 1939, when the war of resistance against Japan (1937–45) entered a more arduous stage, a decision was taken, drafted by Comrade Mao Zedong, on "recruiting large numbers of intellectuals," and in this well-known document he made an incisive Marxist analysis of the characteristics of the intellectuals in semi-colonial and semi-feudal China and laid down the policy of recruiting them boldly. History has already proved the importance of this strategic decision to the winning of victories in the anti-Japanese war, in the war of liberation (1946–49) and in our cause after the founding of the People's Republic. In the early years after the birth of New China, our party was, for some time, rather prudent and basically correct in its attitude towards intellectuals. In 1956, that is, after the basic completion of the socialist transformation of the private ownership of the means of production, Comrade Zhou Enlai, in his report at a meeting on the question of intellectuals convened on the proposal of Comrade Mao Zedong, systematically expounded the relationship between this question and the acceleration of socialist construction. For the first time, he pointed out in explicit terms that the overwhelming majority of China's intellectuals had already become a part of the working class, and issued the great call to "scale the heights of science." Under the party's leadership, progress without parallel in Chinese history has been made in science, education and culture. There have been major achievements in science and technology, including such sophisticated items as the atomic bomb, the hydrogen bomb, rocket carriers and man-made satellites. Not only have we recruited large numbers of intellectuals who were educated before liberation, but we have trained an even larger number of new intellectuals, among whom more than four million have received higher education. They constitute the backbone of our intellectuals' force today, and this contingent is growing steadily. They, along with the workers and peasants with whom they have identified themselves, are people we should rely on, for in their joint efforts lies our hope of attaining, by the end of this century, the advanced world levels of the 1970's and 1980's in science and technology.

But it should be noted that, from the late 1950s onwards, we gradually swerved away from the correct orientation and committed serious "left" errors in our attitude towards knowledge and intellectuals. The principal manifestations were contempt for knowledge and specialized studies, the stigmatizing as "bourgeois" of large numbers of intellectuals who loved their socialist motherland and had made important contributions to socialist construction, and discrimination and attacks against them. The result was that many intellectuals felt depressed and not a few were wronged. At the same time, efforts to carry out the strategic task of making our cadres at large better educated and professionally more competent were slackened or abandoned altogether. During the "Cultural Revolution" these tendencies reached heights of absurdity and whoever attached importance to knowledge and intellectuals was described as going "revisionist" and creating the danger of "subjugating the party and nation". Thus, the effects of the "left" mistakes concerning knowledge and intellectuals became an important component of the catastrophic upheaval of that distressing decade.

Since the smashing of the Jiang Qing counterrevolutionary clique in 1976, and especially since the Third Plenary Session of the Eleventh Central Committee of the Party, there has been a marked turn for the better. In 1978, Comrade Deng Xiaoping further expounded the thesis that the overwhelming majority of the intellectuals have become a part of the working class, thus bringing the party's policy towards intellectuals back onto the right track of Marxism, as is now generally known. At the same time, however, it must be noted that the grave consequences of the prolonged "left" mistakes are far from being liquidated either in our ideology and public opinion or in various political, economic and organizational measures adopted. The working class and other working people throughout the country, all party comrades and primarily the leading cadres at different levels must gain a profound understanding of the Marxist concept on this major issue, so as to meet the urgent needs of vigorous expansion in our cause of socialist modernization. Time is as precious as gold to us. It is high time we solved this question thoroughly and without any hesitation.

Comrades and friends:

What lessons should we draw from the past twists and turns on the question of knowledge and intellectuals? And what truly revolutionary and scientific Marxist concepts should we establish in the light of them?

First, it is imperative that we fight against the incorrect tendency of isolating Marxism from the cultural achievements of mankind and setting it against the latter, that we establish the correct concept of valuing scientific and general knowledge and that we mobilize the whole party and the whole people to strive to acquire knowledge of modern science and culture.

Where does Marxism come from? Fundamentally, it is no doubt the product of contradictions and of the workers' movements in capitalist society; at the same time it is the result of absorbing human knowledge accumulated over several thousand years. If the cultural achievements of mankind had not been applied to the scientific discovery of the laws governing historical development and to the definition of the fundamental and long-term interests of the working class, the movement of the workers could only

have given rise to various kinds of theories such as syndicalism, economism, reformism and anarchism, but not to Marxism. Moreover, our comrades have all learned through personal experience that to study Marxism one has to have a certain amount of knowledge. Simple class feeling can make one receptive to some isolated Marxist concepts, but is inadequate for a systematic understanding and good command of Marxism.

In order to build a new world under the guidance of Marxism, apply and develop it in the great cause of China's modernization and use it to educate all the builders of socialism, it is all the more necessary that we make sustained efforts to critically assimilate new knowledge and the new achievements of modern science and culture. "Knowledge is power." (6) It should be part of the fine qualities of us communists and all builders of the future to value knowledge, embrace it, thirst after it and turn it into immense power for building a new world.

A fallacy that prevailed during the "Cultural Revolution" was that "the more learned one becomes, the more reactionary he will be". It must be pointed out explicitly that human knowledge, that is, the knowledge of natural sciences, of production and technology, of history and geography, of different branches of modern social sciences studied under the guidance of Marxism and of operation and management as a reflection of the laws governing mass social production, as well as various other kinds of knowledge embodying the progress of mankind and the demands of progressive classes in history—all such knowledge contains truths accumulated by mankind in the long process of understanding and changing the world, is the product of its hard labour and can be a weapon in its fight for freedom. The more knowledge people acquire, the better able they will be to know the world and to change it. This is a sign of social progress. Even certain things which played an important role in history, but are imbued with prejudices of the reactionary classes, should be critically analysed by Marxists and whatever is useful in them can be assimilated. What really matters is the standpoint, views and methods people apply in regard to knowledge. In general, it is always better to have more knowledge than less, and it definitely must not be said that "the more learned one becomes, the more reactionary he will be."

When we state that Marxism is based on the fine cultural achievements of mankind, we naturally include natural sciences in that basis. It is particularly important to make this point clear today when we are concentrating on socialist modernization. Here I would like to stress the importance Marx and Engels attached to natural sciences, by delving deeply into the theories of mathematics and natural sciences and into a wealth of technical material, and by applying the results of natural sciences, especially of the three great discoveries. (7) In the 19th century, they substantiated the theory that things in nature develop through interconnection and mutual transformation, thereby laying a solid foundation in natural sciences for the Marxist world outlook. Two works by Engels, "Dialectics of Nature" and "Anti-Duhring," give concentrated expression to the results of their studies in this area. Particularly noteworthy is Marx's famous thesis that science constitutes a productive force and has always played the role of a revolutionary motive force of history. Taking his stand with the proletariat which represents the advanced productive forces, Marx highly valued the role of science and technology in propelling social development and vividly referred to certain epoch-making achievements in these fields as "revolutionists of a rather more dangerous character" (8) than some famous revolutionary persons of his time. When the techniques for generating electricity were still in an embryonic stage, he perceived discerningly that mankind would soon see the dawn of the epoch of electricity. When the world's first experimental electric transmission line was set up, Marx and Engels gave it the closest attention, foreseeing that in the future electricity would reach remote corners of the world and "become the most powerful lever in eliminating antithesis between town and country". (9) So Marx, while fighting for the overthrow of the old world, already paid great heed to developments in science and technology.

Should not we, who today shoulder the great historical responsibility of building a New China, give science and technology still greater attention and all the more conscientiously study and master modern science and culture? There can be no doubt that once our hundreds of millions of working people, who have become masters of their country, are armed with Marxism and modern science and culture, they will become more powerful and dynamic productive forces and be able to perform world-shaking deeds.

Second, it is imperative that we oppose the erroneous tendency of separating intellectuals from the working class, counterposing them to the workers and regarding them as an "alien force", that we confirm the correct concept of intellectuals as a part of the working class and that we strengthen a hundredfold the unity between workers and peasants on the one hand and intellectuals on the other.

We must respect and rely on the intellectuals as much as we respect and rely on the workers and peasants in the great cause of socialist construction. In the Marxist view, intellectuals do not constitute an independent class. Before the founding of New China, ours was a semi-colonial and semi-feudal society. Although intellectuals were for the most part linked to the bourgeoisie or the petty bourgeoisie in their social status, the overwhelming majority of them were at the same time oppressed by imperialism and the Kuomintang reactionaries. Therefore a number joined the revolution directly, others sympathized with it and a great many cherished anti-imperialist and patriotic aspirations. Those reactionary intellectuals who did obdurately range themselves against the revolutionary people and served the ruling classes were of course a force alien to the proletariat. But they were very few in number. When our socialist society was built, the conditions of China's intellectuals underwent a fundamental change. The overwhelming majority of them coming over from the old society have been working energetically for socialism and have been educated in Marxism and tempered and tested over a long period since the founding of New China. Moreover, over 90 per cent of our intellectuals today have been trained in the new society and, in their overwhelming majority, come from worker, peasant or intellectual families. Although major differences in their form of labour still exist between intellectuals on the one hand and workers and peasants on the other, this does not keep us from stating that in terms of their means of living and whom they serve, on the whole the intellectuals in our country have definitely become a part of the working class. This change is a great achievement in the history of the Chinese revolution and in our socialist development.

In the new period of socialist modernization, intellectuals have a particularly important role to play. In the Marxist view and judging from the latest trend in the development of science and industry, essential differences between manual and mental labour will gradually diminish and eventually disappear, and there will be successive generations of new people in whom manual labour is integrated with mental labour on an ever higher level. But this is a long-range perspective and will not happen right away. In other words, for a fairly long time to come scientific and cultural knowledge and mental work will continue to be relatively concentrated among one section of the population—the intellectuals. Therefore, the intellectuals, who constitute the trained mental power indispensable to socialist modernization, are a valuable asset to our country. In our society we must create an atmosphere in which knowledge and intellectuals are valued, and we must take effective steps to improve their working and living conditions.

This should be taken as "capital construction," and of the most essential kind at that. We should make it clear to our people at large that, generally speaking, in socialist society it is an essential condition for mental labour that people who engage in it, or who have attained a relatively high scientific and educational level, should receive more material remuneration than those who do manual labour or whose scientific and educational level is relatively low and, more importantly, that this will greatly contribute to the expansion of production and to the improvement of the material and cultural life of the people as a whole. At the same time, this will serve to encourage the working class and all other working people to become more educated and the children of workers and peasants to seek education and study science, thus swelling the ranks of the intellectuals. It is obvious that this policy conforms to the law of the development of socialism and to the immediate and long-term interests of the working class and the whole people and that it is a Marxist policy. Conversely, the previous erroneous "left" policy ran counter to the principles of Marxism and socialism.

When we speak of respect for knowledge and intellectuals, in no sense do we mean that manual labour and manual workers may be disdained or belittled. This is absolutely impermissible in our socialist society. Any type of labour, manual or mental, is great and glorious in itself so long as it benefits society. In China, more than 90 per cent of our working people are engaged in different kinds of manual labour. In the final analysis, all our wealth is jointly produced by both manual and mental labour. Naturally, with progress in modernization, the fruits of mental labour will take on ever increasing prominence and the proportion of mental workers in the working population will gradually grow. However, this process will itself involve a steady improvement in the educational and scientific level of manual workers, a steady increase of the elements of mental labour in manual labour and a switch from manual to mental work by group after group of people according to society's needs. At the same time, the productive activities pursued with creativeness by the masses of workers and peasants, particularly skilled veteran workers as well as dexterous artisans in the rural areas, constitute an inexhaustible source of scientific and technological progress.

Any idea or practice that isolates mental from manual labour and pits one against the other is utterly wrong. In socialist society, intellectuals who hold workers and peasants in contempt and are divorced from them will find it hard to play their due role and will be corrected by society. It should furthermore be borne in mind that however high the technological level in production that may be reached in the future, the elements of manual labour can never be completely eliminated from man's labour, much less can technical and artistic handwork or heavy manual labour under special circumstances and in emergencies ever disappear. In this sense there will still be manual labour even ten thousand years from now. All in all, the distinction between manual and mental labour in socialist society is nothing more than a division of work and a difference in degree of complexity. In no way is one superior and noble and the other inferior and ignoble. I am making this point because now, as we lay emphasis on valuing knowledge and intellectuals, we must guard against the wrong tendency of disdaining and belittling manual labour and also because in China, with its thousands of years of feudal history, the outworn concept of social hierarchy expressed in the saying "those who do mental labour rule and those who do manual labour are ruled" is deeply entrenched. Engels referred to the pernicious habit of disdaining labour as a poisoned sting left behind by the slave system. (10) We must at all times keep a watchful eye on this poisoned sting and see to its removal.

In saying that knowledge and intellectuals should be valued, we certainly do not imply that intellectuals are perfect in every way, or that they have no weaknesses to overcome. Our workers, peasants and intellectuals have each come, under specific historical circumstances, to possess certain strengths and weaknesses. Whether ideologically, professionally or in work performance, our intelligentsia taken as a whole cannot as yet fully meet the new and higher demands set by our socialist modernization drive. In the new period, we hope that while taking Marx and Engels, the most outstanding intellectuals, as shining models, inheriting and carrying forward the glorious traditions of revolutionary Chinese intellectuals since the May Fourth Movement of 1919 and the December Ninth Movement of 1935, and learning from the spirit of dedication of comrades like Peng Jiamu, Luan Fu, Jiang Zhuying, Luo Jianfu, Lei Yushun and Sun Yefang, our intellectuals will study Marxism more diligently, apply themselves more assiduously to the pursuit of new knowledge, go among the masses and dig into practical work, consciously strengthen their sense of organization and discipline and strive to transform their own subjective world and become both Red and expert in the course of the great struggle to transform the objective world. The experience of all advanced intellectuals has testified to the fact that none of them, not even highly prestigious specialists and scholars, can rest on their laurels in the face of rapid scientific and social progress, but have constantly to raise their ideological and professional levels. It has also proved that only when intellectuals identify themselves more closely with the workers and peasants and wholeheartedly serve the people can they put their talents to the best use, bring their initiative into full play and truly turn their knowledge into a mighty force for enhancing the people's well-being.

Ninety years ago, Engels wrote a letter to the International Congress of Socialist Students, expressing the ardent hope that from among them "the intellectual proletariat" would emerge. Taking their place in the same ranks as the manual workers, he added, such intellectuals could play a great role in revolution alongside their brothers, the manual workers. (11) Today, under the new historical conditions in China, Engels' hope is being realized on a countrywide scale. However, some people now say that "while number one has been shunted aside, number nine is soaring to the skies." (Translator's note: Here "number one" refers to the workers whereas "number nine" refers to the intellectuals because, during the "Cultural Revolution", they were placed ninth, after the landlords, the rich peasants, the counter-revolutionaries, the bad elements, the rightists, the renegades, the special agents, and the inveterate capitalist-roaders.) It is not right to describe workers as "number one" and intellectuals as "number nine". As for the assertion that "number nine" is soaring to the skies, this is not true. We maintain that under the leadership of the party, workers, peasants and intellectuals join hands and work shoulder to shoulder so that they can all soar to the skies, the new skies of socialist modernization.

Third, it is imperative that we oppose the erroneous tendency of divorcing party leadership from expert leadership or setting the former against the latter, that we implant the correct concept that all leading personnel must strive to be experts and that we ensure that our cadres become better educated and more professionally competent on the basis of becoming more revolutionary-minded.

That our socialist modernization needs knowledge and needs intellectuals is a guiding idea which must be embodied, first and foremost, in the reform of the leading organs at all levels and of all departments, so that our cadres will be younger, better educated and more professionally competent on the basis of becoming more revolutionary-minded. People may ask: Didn't we win our revolutionary wars even though the educational level of our cadres wasn't very high? True, due to the protracted rural guerrilla fighting, our party cadres lacked knowledge of modern science and culture during the war years. Even in those circumstances, however, our party laid great stress on the planned training of large numbers of cadres and troops. We ran many kinds of cadre schools in Yanan and other base areas and in the liberated areas. We studied diligently and conscientiously and acquired much knowledge about military, social, economic and cultural affairs urgently needed in the revolutionary wars, the building of revolutionary base areas and work in the Kuomintang areas. Thousands upon thousands of fine leaders were brought up at different levels from among the cadres of both worker-peasant and intellectual origins, and many of them became specialists in military affairs, agrarian reform, united front work, financial and economic affairs, propaganda, cultural and educational work, and so on. And the comrades forming the leading core of the Central Committee of the party that directed our entire struggle and the large numbers of outstanding party leaders all attained a high educational and theoretical level. They studied questions concerning the Chinese revolution comprehensively and profoundly and summed up the laws of development of Chinese society, thus evolving the set of systematic and scientific theories on the Chinese revolution known as Mao Zedong Thought. History shows that, far from being uneducated and ignorant, the cadres of our party were intelligent and capable people who had a good command of the knowledge urgently needed in the revolutionary struggles of the time and were, therefore, able to vanquish the enemy. The situation today is radically different from that in the past. Socialist modernization, being an entirely new task, is much broader in scale and far more complex in nature, involving many more branches of learning than the tasks we faced before. Military work, too, has become more specialized. Under these circumstances, to rely merely on past knowledge and experience is far from adequate. It is a pressing necessity of the current struggle to master modern science, technology and culture. Is it not, then, entirely correct, necessary and in conformity with the requirements of historical development for us now to set the higher demands of training better educated and more professionally competent cadres?

Party leadership involves political, ideological and organizational leadership, leadership in matters of principle and policy, and inspection and supervision of work in various fields. It cannot—and should not—monopolize specific professional, technical and administrative work. This being so, what need is there for the party's leading cadres at all levels to become more professionally competent and turn into experts? In our socialist modernization drive today, correct political leadership means adhering to the four cardinal principles in all fields, integrating the party's principles and policies with the concrete practice and professional work of the given locality or department and mobilizing and organizing the positive factors in various quarters so as to effectively fulfill the tasks advanced by the party. To achieve this, it is imperative not only that the leading party cadres at all levels master the basics of general and scientific knowledge, but also that they acquire the professional knowledge needed by the particular work they lead, understand the actual conditions in the relevant professions and grasp their specific laws.

Otherwise, their leadership will be nothing more than armchair politics, pointless and fruitless effort, or arbitrary direction. Our modernization programme would get nowhere if we were to rely on such leadership. To lead, therefore, one must strive to be expert.

From the viewpoint of the theory of knowledge, we must correctly understand and handle the relationship between the general and the particular if we are properly to integrate the universal truth of Marxism with the concrete practice of our socialist modernization and properly integrate the party's principles and policies with concrete professional work in various fields. Marxism holds that the general and the particular are interrelated and that the former resides in the latter. Only with a deep understanding of the particular will it be possible to have a better grasp of the general; and an understanding of the general should be followed up with a continuous deepening of knowledge of the particular. Comrade Mao Zedong regarded this dialectical relationship between the general and the particular as part of the quintessence of the dialectical materialist theory of knowledge and as an important principle of method of thinking and of leadership which we must always bear in mind. It will be very dangerous if our leading comrades rest content with generalized "political leadership" without trying to gain a deep understanding of the particular and to acquire the professional knowledge necessary for effective leadership, or if they simply refuse to do so, thinking that it is perfectly normal for laymen to lead experts. For to act thus will be to negate outright the necessity for greater professional competence and to obstruct both the steady deepening of knowledge and the continuous improvement of leadership.

In fact, the question of making our party and government functionaries better educated and more professionally competent was raised as early as in the 1950s. At the first session of the party's Eighth National Congress held in September 1956, Comrade Mao Zedong stressed that, reflecting the course of development of the Chinese revolution, the composition of the Central Committee would change later to include many engineers and scientists. However, this question, along with that of lowering the average age of leading cadres at various levels, was not solved in good time. With the present organizational reform as a good start, the Central Committee of the party is determined to solve all these questions gradually in conjunction with one another and through the succession of new cadres to the old. They will be solved by the following methods: Large numbers of old cadres are mobilized to leave their posts and help and guide young and middle-aged cadres and pass on experience to them; many intellectuals who possess both political integrity and professional competence and are in the prime of life are recruited into the leading bodies at all levels; and middle-aged cadres fairly experienced in leadership and having a fairly high level of political understanding but little schooling are warmly encouraged and helped to improve their level of education. These are strategic measures of far-reaching import for ensuring the incessant vigorous development of our party's cause.

Comrades and friends:

As we commemorate the centenary of the death of Karl Marx, we are happy to see that, in China today, the central task of the communist movement initiated by Marx and Engels has become the struggle to bring about a new situation in all fields of socialist modernization and to turn the country into a modern, powerful socialist state with a high level of democracy and civilization. This grand and arduous task is one of the greatest creative undertakings in the history not only of the east but also of all mankind. Some of the major problems involved in accomplishing this task have never before been encountered by the world's Marxists and hence there is no precedent for solving them. This demands that we Chinese communists and cadres in all fields learn anew in the unfolding great struggle.

On the eve of the founding of our People's Republic, our party put forward the slogan of learning anew. In his article, "On the People's Democratic Dictatorship", Comrade Mao Zedong said emphatically: "The serious task of economic construction lies before us. We shall soon put aside some of the things we know well and be compelled to do things we don't know well. This means difficulties." He added: "We must overcome difficulties, we must learn what we do not know. We must learn to do economic work from all who know how, no matter who they are." Facts have proved that our learning anew in that period ensured the success of our party's shift from fighting a revolutionary war to seizing state power and ensured the establishment and consolidation of our People's Republic. It is regrettable that we did not persevere in such study and, particularly, that we did not put before our leading cadres at all levels the specific task of systematically learning modern science and culture, and especially of acquiring varied professional knowledge—even less did we adopt any long-term and effective measures for that purpose. Faced with the task of socialist modernization in this new historical period, our party has now once again put forward the slogan of learning anew. This effort to learn anew—the second following the founding of our People's Republic—has two equally important aspects: one is to acquire a better grasp of Marxism-Leninism and Mao Zedong Thought on which the theory guiding our thinking and all our actions is based, and the other is to acquire a better grasp of various branches of social and natural sciences, modern technology and scientific operation and management. This effort, which will run through the whole process of China's four modernizations, must be organized in a planned and systematic way and persisted in for a long time. Together with the planned vigorous expansion of all our educational and cultural undertakings, it will mean a great, nationwide march towards the heights of science, involving hundreds of millions of workers, peasants and intellectuals in all fields of endeavour.

At this commemorative meeting, as we put forward the task of learning anew we think naturally of the brilliant example Marx and Engels set for us in this respect. For more effective research in political economy, Marx, in his forties, reviewed his knowledge of algebra and learned calculus, an advanced branch of mathematics in his time; in addition, he made a point of attending lectures on technology. In the course of establishing the dialectical materialist outlook on nature, Engels determinedly embarked on a systematic study of mathematics and natural sciences when already past fifty. Recalling this experience, Engels said, "I went through as complete as possible a 'moulting,' as Liebig calls it, in mathematics and natural sciences." (12) What was meant by this "moulting"? The famous 19th-century German chemist Justus Liebig had said: "Chemistry is moving forward at an incredible speed, and chemists, wishing to keep up with it, are in a state of constant moulting. The first feathers, unsuitable for flight, fall out of the wings, but new ones grow in their stead and flight becomes more powerful and easier." (13) This refers to the precious enterprising spirit of scientists who strive constantly to update their knowledge, never cease in their research effort and dare to destroy the old and establish the new. Why can't the effort being made by us Chinese Communists and people to learn anew be compared to moulting? China, with its one billion people, is like a giant roc whose "wings obscure the sky like clouds". (14) Once the old feathers unsuitable for flight fall out of the wings and new ones grow in their stead in the process of learning anew, our country is bound to soar to the skies more powerfully and with greater ease, flying over one peak after another towards its goal.

Comrades and friends:

A full century has elapsed since the death of Marx. For more than a hundred years, Marx's theory, at first a "spectre" haunting Europe, has grown into a mighty force that has profoundly changed world history and will continue to do so. Since its birth, Marxism has been a compass guiding the world proletarians in their united struggle and guiding the oppressed nations of the world in their struggle for political and economic independence. At present, although there are many obstacles on their road of advance, both these forces are a thousand times more powerful than in Marx's time. Marxism also enables us scientifically to pinpoint the source of war and find the only way to eliminate it. Although today mankind is still faced with the menace of a massive war of aggression, we are convinced that through the common struggle of the working class, the oppressed nations and the whole progressive mankind, light will eventually triumph over darkness.

The great ideal of communism advanced by Marx and Engels inspires the world proletariat and all oppressed peoples and nations in their struggle for emancipation and inspires all progressive mankind in its struggle for a bright future. These struggles are converging into a worldwide, irresistible historical tide propelling social progress.

Marxism is immortal. Let the radiance of the great truth of Marxism forever light our way forward!

NOTES

(1) See Frederick Engels' letter to Wilhelm Liebknecht of March 14, 1883, in Wilhelm Liebknecht, "Karl Marx—Biographical Memoirs," Eng. ed., Charles H. Kerr and Company Co-operative, Chicago, 1901, p. 46.

(2) See Frederick Engels, "Closing Speech Delivered at the International Congress of Socialist Workers", in "Karl Marx and Frederick Engels, Collected Works," German ed., Dietz Verlag, Berlin, 1963, Vol. 22, p. 408.

(3) V. I. Lenin, "The Three Sources and Three Component Parts of Marxism", "Collected Works," Eng. Ed., Foreign Languages Publishing House, Moscow, 1963, Vol. 19, pp. 23–24.

(4) V. I. Lenin, "The Tasks of the Youth Leagues", "Collected Works," Eng. ed., Progress Publishers, Moscow, 1966, Vol. 31, p. 286.

(5) See Jenny Marx, "Short Sketch of An Eventful Life", "Reminiscences of Marx and Engels," Eng. ed., FLPH, Moscow.

(6) See Francis Bacon, "Advancement of Learning and Novum Organum," The Colonial Press, 1900, p. 315.

(7) These refer to the discovery of the law of the conservation and conversion of energy, the discovery of the cell and the discovery of the evolution of living beings.

(8) See Marx, "Speech at the Anniversary of the People's Paper", in "Karl Marx and Frederick Engels, Collected Works," Eng. ed., Progress Publishers, Moscow, 1980, Vol. 14, p. 655.

(9) See "Engels to E. Bernstein, February 27–March 1, 1883", in "Karl Marx and Frederick Engels, Collected Works," German ed., Dietz Verlag, Berlin, 1967, Vol. 35, p. 445.

(10) See Frederick Engels, "The Origin of the Family, Private Property and the State," Eng. ed., Foreign Languages Press, Beijing, 1978, p. 181.

(11) See Engels, "To the International Congress of Socialist Students", "Karl Marx and Frederick Engels, Collected Works," German ed., Dietz Verlag, Berlin, 1963, Vol. 22, p. 415.

(12) Frederick Engels, "Prefaces to the Three Editions",

"Anti-Duhring," Eng. ed., Progress Publishers, Moscow, 1969, pp. 15–16.

(13) Ibid., note 12, p. 449.

(14) See Chapter I, "Transcendental Bliss", "Chuang Tzu," edited by H. A. Giles, Eng. ed., Kelly and Walsh Ltd., Shanghai, 1926, p. 1.

HU YAOBANG **21**
On Mao Zedong's Ninetieth Birthday, 26 December 1983

Here Hu does his best to enhance his own aspirations to be the successor to both Mao and Deng Xiaoping.

December 26 is an unforgettable day for the Chinese people of all nationalities. Ninety years ago today, our Comrade Mao Zedong was born.

For China, the century and more before and after Comrade Mao Zedong's birth has been a tumultuous and eventful one, during which the Chinese people have repeatedly tested their courage in their difficult struggle against powerful enemies—imperialism from abroad and feudalism at home. A great militant epoch inevitably brings forth its outstanding people, who, in turn, help drive history forward. Comrade Mao Zedong was clearly the greatest and most outstanding figure China has had in the past century and more.

The great struggle of the Chinese people has long commanded the interest of progressives the world over. In 1857, on learning of the rising of the revolution of the Taiping Heavenly Kingdom and the Chinese people's tenacious struggle against foreign invaders, Marx and Engels excitedly predicted that even greater struggles would take place in China in a few years, which would show people the dawn of a new era for all of Asia. In 1913, when Lenin witnessed the new storm of the Chinese revolution led by Dr. Sun Yat-sen, he said with equal enthusiasm that a new source of great world storms has opened up in Asia. As he saw it, the revolution in Asia would eventually influence Europe.

The pioneers of the democratic revolution failed to change the destiny of China, but the predictions of the international Marxist teachers did not come to nothing. In 1921, the Chinese Communist Party was born. Led by Comrade Mao Zedong and many other Marxist revolutionaries, the Chinese Communist Party fulfilled, with brand-new ideas, the wishes of the high-minded patriots of modern Chinese history, after 28 years of heroic, unremitting struggle fought on a scale unmatched by any waged by our forefathers. The triumph of the Chinese revolution represented yet another leap forward in mankind's revolutionary history, following the Russian October Revolution [1917]. As it took place in a nation which accounts for one-quarter of the world's population, the victory of the Chinese revolution was bound to have a great impact on the course of world history. It not only put an end to feudal rule, which had lasted two millennia, and the century-and-more-long imperialist oppression of China, but also opened up a new road which will lead the Chinese people to the magnificent communist society. The great victory of the Chinese revolution boosted the morale of people of all nationalities in China, and struck a deep chord in the hearts of the oppressed people and progressives the world over.

Comrade Mao Zedong's position and role in the Chinese Communist Party and the Chinese revolution were unparalleled. He was one of the founders of our Party, and the chief founder of the Chinese People's Liberation Army. He was the first to discover the correct road for the Chinese revolution during its most difficult years. By constantly pooling the wisdom of everyone in the Party, he combined the universal truth of Marxism-Leninism with the concrete practice of the Chinese revolution, formulated a correct general strategy and set forth, step by step, a whole series of correct theories and policies which form what we now call Mao Zedong Thought. Mao Zedong Thought was the ideological weapon with which the Chinese revolution emerged victorious from many setbacks, and advanced from victory to victory. Its stand, views and methods for understanding and remoulding the world serve as a guide for us to continue to win victories in socialist revolution and construction. Comrade Mao Zedong's contributions are immortal, and Mao Zedong Thought will shine for ever.

That Comrade Mao Zedong could score such great achievements was not accidental. When he was a teenager he had already made up his mind to do what he could to save the nation from peril. After he became a Marxist in his youth, he devoted himself heart and soul to the emancipation of the Chinese people. Fighting one battle after another in the long years of revolution, he never slackened his efforts to investigate, read and think. Whenever and wherever he could, he sought knowledge from the people,

[Hu Yaobang, "The Best Way to Remember Mao Zedong," *Beijing Review*, no. 1, 2 January 1984.]

society and his forefathers. While learning, he also taught others; he was indeed both a student and a teacher. He never forgot to foster a fine style of work and study in the Party. His erudition impressed and inspired respect in whoever met him. His energy, surpassing that of many others, was attributed to his lofty revolutionary aspirations. With his revolutionary spirit, he is for ever the fine example for us to follow.

Comrade Mao Zedong's scientific ideas and revolutionary spirit have nurtured generations of Chinese Marxists. It can be said that every one of us who form the core of the Party leadership today has been influenced, nurtured and tempered by his scientific ideas and revolutionary spirit. I, for one, grew up under his direct teaching.

I first met him in 1933 and first listened to his earnest teachings in 1936. In 1937, when I was studying at the Chinese People's Anti-Japanese Military and Political College in Yanan, he lectured about his two articles "On Practice" and "On Contradiction" in my class as part of our philosophy course. In autumn that year, it was he who suggested that I become secretary of the college's general Party branch. He told me that to do the work of the Party general branch well, the first thing was to run a good college journal. On reading the first issue of this journal, he criticized us for not having written anything by ourselves, and volunteered to contribute his celebrated militant article "Combat Liberalism." This was only one of my many contacts with him before I reached the age of 21. In fact, he instructed me many times in those years. My experience is only one of the examples which show how he loved and helped young Party cadres. Ours is a party which controls its own future. To ensure continuity of the Party's cause, our veteran comrades should act as Comrade Mao Zedong did, considering it their important historical mission to love the young cadres and care for their progress.

Like many other great figures in history, Comrade Mao Zedong also made mistakes. The serious mistakes he made in his later years put our Party in a very difficult situation for a time. We wondered how to appraise the mistakes made by such a prestigious and great leader just after he passed away. Some people in the Party, particularly those holding certain leading positions at that time, did not restore and carry forward the extremely precious heritage left over by Comrade Mao Zedong. Instead, they attempted to follow the wrong policies he adopted in his later years. Some comrades with good intentions argued that they had followed Chairman Mao for several decades, and they could not overcome their emotional barriers enough to criticize him. Some worried that open exposure of his mistakes would throw the Party into confusion and cause a crisis of confidence.

There were also some who went to the other extreme, wanting to throw out all the great contributions made by Comrade Mao Zedong along with his errors in his later years. This would have led the Party astray.

Our Party did not succumb to such interference. We understood clearly that emotion could never replace revolutionary reason, and metaphysical methods were not the strict dialectical and historical materialism we upheld. Inspired and repeatedly persuaded by the revolutionaries of the older generation, our Party has made a comprehensive appraisal of Comrade Mao Zedong, after penetratingly analysing the reasons for his successes and failures and the lessons to be drawn. Through our efforts in recent years to set things to rights, we have restored the original features of Mao Zedong Thought and developed it in certain ways under new conditions. The whole Party, the army and all the Chinese people, as well as all upright people the world over, have come to see that our state can stand any test, and that there is no crisis in our Party, which is, instead, full of vigour.

It is true that we still face many problems. The ferocious destruction caused by the Lin Biao and Jiang Qing counter-revolutionary cliques in making use of Comrade Mao Zedong's mistakes inflicted serious wounds on the body of our Party, and contaminated it with filth and dust. As soon as the task of setting things to rights had been basically accomplished, we timely proposed to start a Party consolidation, with the sole purpose of carrying forward the fine traditions of our Party, improving the Party's political life, healing the wounds which we have not yet had time to heal, and eliminating the filth and dust there has not yet been time to clean away. All comrades engaged in theoretical, literary and artistic work should treasure their glorious responsibility as "engineers of the soul," work hard to develop socialist culture and ethics and eliminate and prevent ideological contamination.

Ours is a big party with 40 million members and occupies the leading position in the political life of the state. People throughout the country are extremely concerned about a fundamental turn for the better of the style of the Party. Now, the detailed plans we have made for the Party consolidation have won support from the broad masses both in and outside the Party. We are convinced that our Party will be able, after three years of Party consolidation, to grow stronger and more vital, and lead the 1,000 million people of China towards the splendid goal set by the Party's 12th National Congress.

The most arduous task now facing us is to build China into a strong and modernized socialist country, in line with China's conditions. This is what Comrade Deng Xiaoping has called socialism with Chinese characteristics. Some comrades ask: Can you give a ready definition for "socialism with Chinese characteristics"? We say that there is no pre-prepared, ready definition. It is impossible to have one. We can only enrich our knowledge constantly through practice, under the guidance of correct theory. Just as Lenin pointed out, theory must achieve vitality from practice, and be revised and tested by it.

Some other people say that since there are no ready answers, a certain existing model should be followed. We say this will not do either. The conditions in different countries vary, and the socialist construction in each country must inevitably have its own features. A big country like ours, where the economic and cultural development is backward, is bound to meet specific problems in its socialist construction, and it must adopt specific measures to deal with them.

Those comrades who hold that it is enough to follow the beaten path to socialism forget the famous remark by Lenin, "The more variety there will be, the better and richer will be our general experience, the more certain and rapid will be the success of socialism, and the easier it will be for practice to devise—for only practice can devise—the best methods and means of struggle." Practice is a great school. Let us carry forward the revolutionary style of bold exploration in our work, to scale new heights of Marxism-Leninism and Mao Zedong Thought.

Comrade Mao Zedong's monumental contributions in cutting a path through difficulties over the past several decades will always be a source of admiration and encouragement for us, and inspire us to advance courageously in accomplishing the tasks he left unfinished. We must exert ourselves.

On the Need to Thoroughly Negate the Cultural Revolution, 28 July 1984

22

Factionalism, a cardinal sin in the Communist demonology, is here equated explicitly with the Cultural Revolution and implicitly with opposition to Deng Xiaoping's current policies.

1. Question: As the "Cultural Revolution" has been concluded for 8 years, why is it still necessary to raise the question of thoroughly negating the "Cultural Revolution" at present?

Answer: The "Cultural Revolution" constituted a civil commotion that produced serious, harmful influences in all fields. It is true that 8 years have passed since the conclusion of the "Cultural Revolution," and 3 years have elapsed since the "resolution on certain historical questions" was adopted at the 6th Plenary Session of the 11th CPC Central Committee. However, the poisonous influence of the "leftist" mistakes caused by the "Cultural Revolution" has not yet been thoroughly eliminated. First, some comrades still hold some erroneous or confused ideas about the "Cultural Revolution." For example, some people argue that the "Cultural Revolution" should not be regarded as devoid of any merit; some people contend that the "Cultural Revolution" did play a positive role in "opposing and preventing revisionism"; and still others maintain that the achievements of the "Cultural Revolution" must be affirmed even though its mistakes should be repudiated. Second, some people are still unable to realize their own mistakes committed during the "Cultural Revolution" and are even adhering to factionalism and continuing their factional activities. Their factionalism will become particularly obvious in matters of redressing mishandled cases, reorganizing leading bodies, promoting cadres, and clearing away "people of the three categories." Some people even pose as representatives of the "correct line" so as to demand higher positions and official ranks in leading bodies. Third, the residual influence of "leftism" left over by the "Cultural Revolution" still time and again obstructs the implementation of the party's line, principles, and policies formulated since the 3d Plenary Session of the 11th CPC Central Committee and, in particular, disturbs the ongoing reforms in all fields. All this shows that it is absolutely necessary to thoroughly negate the "Cultural Revolution" and to make this an important ingredient of party rectification. Only by thoroughly negating the "Cultural Revolution" can it be possible to eliminate the poisonous influence of "leftism," ensure implementation of the party's line, principles, and policies since the third plenary session, fulfill the general tasks and general objective established by the 12th CPC National Congress.

And only through complete repudiation of the "Cultural Revolution" can it be possible to eradicate factionalism, strengthen party spirit, overcome the ideological, behavioral, and organizational impurities of party organizations, expel "people of the three categories" from the party, and build up the "third echelon." Therefore, we must thoroughly negate the "Cultural Revolution" and take this as a matter of importance in party rectification.

2. *Question*: Some people argue that in spite of serious mistakes, the "Cultural Revolution" still played a positive role in "opposing and preventing revisionism." Why is this an erroneous viewpoint?

Answer: The actual fact is that the "Cultural Revolution" did not and would never have been able to play a role in "opposing and preventing revisionism."

When one opposes and criticizes a thing, he must first frame a categorical definition of this thing and give a correct explanation of its connotations. The "Cultural Revolution" was launched and carried out in the name of "opposing and preventing revisionism," but the explanation of "revisionism" was greatly confusing and misleading. As Comrade Ye Jianying said in his speech at the rally to mark the 30th anniversary of the PRC, "When the 'Cultural Revolution' was launched, the assessment of the inner-party and domestic situations was unrealistic, and no accurate and categorical explanation was made with regard to the term revisionism." Since the "Cultural Revolution pursued a "leftist" line, truth and falsehood in many questions were confused. In those days many correct things were denounced as "revisionist," things such as negating the so-called continued revolution under the dictatorship of the proletariat, negating the proposition that intense class struggle still exists in socialist society, agreeing to allowing

---

["Questions and Answers About Thoroughly Negating the Cultural Revolution, Eliminating Factionalism, and Strengthening Party Spirit," Beijing *Guangming Daily*, 28 July 1984. Reprinted from *Liberation Army Daily*.]

the individual economy to exist under the socialist system, acknowledging that the principle of distribution according to work must be carried out under the socialist system, showing respect for knowledge and people of learning, and advocating that communists should pay attention to ideological self-cultivation. It was precisely the criticism of such "revisionist" things that exacerbated the "leftist" mistakes of our party and brought about serious consequences because it provided a theoretical foundation for the "Cultural Revolution." The "Resolution on Historical Questions" points out: "A campaign to prevent and combat revisionism inside the country was launched, which spread the error of broadening the scope of class struggle in the party, so that normal differences among comrades inside the party came to be regarded as manifestations of the revisionist line or of the struggle between the two lines. This resulted in growing tension in inner-party relations. Thus it became difficult for the party to resist certain 'leftist' views put forward by Comrade Mao Zedong and others, and the development of these views led to the outbreak of the protracted 'Cultural Revolution.'" Many things denounced as revisionist or capitalist during the "Cultural Revolution" were actually Marxist and socialist principles, many of which had been proposed or supported by Comrade Mao Zedong himself. During the "Cultural Revolution," selecting "successors" was taken as an important measure for "opposing and preventing revisionism." However, instead of resolving the issue of selecting "successors," the "Cultural Revolution" only provided openings to be exploited by a number of careerists, conspirators, and villains, who usurped part of the state power from the central to local leaderships. Therefore, it is quite wrong to think that the "Cultural Revolution" was contributive to "preventing and combating revisionism."

3. *Question*: "One dividing into two" long has been accepted as a universal truth. Is the thorough repudiation of the "Cultural Revolution" opposed to the viewpoint of "one dividing into two"?

Answer: To clarify this question, we should first have a correct understanding of the connotations of the term "one dividing into two." By "the division of one into two," it is meant that everything in the world consists of two opposite sides existing in unity or that inner contradictions exist in all things, which thus can be analyzed.

However, things in the world are extremely complicated and intricate. The way to apply the viewpoint of "one dividing into two" to analyze a thing must be determined by the specific character of this thing. For example, an electron consists of positrons and negatrons; a war consists of offense and defense or of advance and retreat; and our work has achievements and mistakes or has merits and demerits. All this manifests the "division of one into two." However, it is not right to consider the unity of merits and demerits or of achievements and mistakes as a sole manifestation and the entire connotation of the viewpoint of "one dividing into two." So it is not correct to think that everything must have merits and demerits. Precisely because of their misunderstanding of the philosophic term "one dividing into two," some people have thought that thorough repudiation of the "Cultural Revolution" does not conform with this viewpoint.

Does a thorough negation of the "Great Cultural Revolution" run against the viewpoint of one dividing into two? No, it does not. We can analyze, in the manner of one

dividing into two, the "Great Cultural Revolution" from the point of view of bad things being able to be transformed into good ones. The "Great Cultural Revolution" was a civil disorder and a great calamity causing disastrous destruction to our country. Precisely in that serious disaster and destruction, our party and people began to understand that it was entirely wrong to launch the "Great Cultural Revolution" and that the set of "leftist" theory that guided the "Great Cultural Revolution" had to be entirely negated. As a result, we have become able to draw on lessons from it and prevent a repetition of this historical tragedy. Thus a bad thing has been turned into a good one. Just as Comrade Hu Yaobang said: There was nothing correct, nothing of a positive role but only things of a negative role in the "Great Cultural Revolution." "If we say that there was any positive factor, that was the fact that we learned something from our mistakes. In this sense, it has been turned into a good thing now."

4. *Question*: During the 10 years of the "Great Cultural Revolution," we built the Chang Jiang bridge, launched satellites and developed our industrial and agricultural production. Can we say that the "Great Cultural Revolution" was devoid of anything good?

Answer: True, we made some progress in our economic construction and scientific research in the 10 years of the "Great Cultural Revolution," but this can never be regarded as achievements of the "Great Cultural Revolution." The "Great Cultural Revolution" was not equivalent to the 1-year period in which it took place. The "Great Cultural Revolution" had its specific meaning, that is, it was a so-called major political revolution in which "one class overthrew another class." In the process of this "revolution," the practice of carrying out economic construction and scientific research was criticized and regarded as a practice of the "theory of productive forces," and of "taking the road of becoming bourgeois specialists." "Distribution according to labor" was criticized and regarded as "bourgeois rights" and the practices of "eating out of the same big pot" and of providing people with "iron rice bowls" were in vogue. In our production we negated science and technology and paid no attention to administration and management. The "Great Cultural Revolution" gave rise to a great turmoil all over our country, "suspended our production to let people be engaged in revolution," and undermined the normal production order and regulations in various areas. A large number of old workers and model workers and a large number of talented intellectuals were persecuted. A series of "leftist" urban and rural economic policies seriously dampened the people's labor enthusiasm, caused great destruction to the productive forces, and pushed our national economy onto the verge of collapse. To the present, the people in our country still cannot lead a prosperous life and there is a shortage of transport and residential housing facilities. All those are directly related to the destruction caused by the "Great Cultural Revolution."

The reason why we could still make some progress in our economic construction and scientific research during the 10 years of the "Great Cultural Revolution" was because the whole party and the vast number of the masses of people carried out an arduous struggle against the "leftist" mistakes of the Lin Biao and Jiang Qing counterrevolutionary cliques. Because of this kind of struggle, we were able to preserve the foundation of our socialist system and to carry out some major domestic and foreign policies and our socialist economic construction. In particular, our vast number of cadres and masses of people continued to persist in carrying out socialist construction in all fields under extremely difficult conditions during the tremendously great turmoil. This enabled us to restrict the destruction of the "Great Cultural Revolution" within certain limits. Just as the "Resolution on Certain Questions in the History of the Party Since the Founding of the PRC" states, "If there had not been a 'Great Cultural Revolution,' we would have scored much greater achievements in our undertakings." We can say that all the achievements scored during the period of the "Great Cultural Revolution," including the construction of the Chang Jiang bridge and the launching of the satellites, were precisely the consequence of our resistance against the "Great Cultural Revolution."

5. *Question*: Does a thorough negation of the "Great Cultural Revolution" comply with the principle that we should pay attention to major matters and not to minor ones in handling historical issues? Is it a practice of nitpicking at past mistakes?

Answer: In handling historical issues, the idea that we should pay attention to major matters and not to minor ones was a principle that Comrade Deng Xiaoping presented in drafting the "Resolution on Certain Questions in the History of the Party Since the Founding of the PRC." This principle means that in handling historical issues, we should pay attention only to major issues and should not look into the details; and that we should focus on summing up historical experiences and lessons, but should not focus on discovering who was to blame. Through scientific analysis, in the manner of seeking truth from facts, of the theory, principles, policies, and actual results of the "Great Cultural Revolution," we have concluded that the "Great Cultural Revolution" was a civil disorder that brought serious disasters to the party, the state, and the people of all nationalities that had to be thoroughly negated. By so doing, we have summed up our experiences and lessons, sorted out and corrected our mistakes, heightened our awareness, unified our thinking, and united our people to carry out the four modernizations. This is precisely an actual implementation of the principle that we should pay attention to major matters and not to minor ones in handling historical issues. Therefore, negation of the "Great Cultural Revolution" complies with this principle.

The principle that we should pay attention to major matters and not to minor ones does not mean that we should not make a distinction between right and wrong. In handling historical issues and summing up historical experiences, we should not nitpick over details, but we should make a profound and careful analysis and study of major issues in order to draw scientific conclusions. When we succeed in making a distinction between right and wrong concerning major issues, the other problems related to details will be readily resolved. If we do not thoroughly negate the "Great Cultural Revolution," and if we do not confirm that during the "Great Cultural Revolution" the organizations of both factions were formed and carried out their activities under the guidance of the erroneous theory of the so-called "continuous revolution," and that therefore both factions were fundamentally wrong, it will be impossible for us to end the unprincipled disputes between the two factions on some concrete problems. If we act in this manner, we will precisely run against the principle that we should pay attention to

major matters and not to minor ones in handling historical issues.

Thoroughly negating the "Great Cultural Revolution," continuing to clearly understand what was wrong in the theory and practice of the "Great Cultural Revolution," and consciously drawing on historical lessons differ diametrically from the practice of nitpicking over details in historical incidents in order to gain an upper hand for the private interests of some people as individuals or for the interests of some small factions. Now some people are paying lip service to supporting the evaluation of the "Great Cultural Revolution" contained in the "Resolution." However, as soon as some concrete problems are raised, they begin to engage in endless disputes and nitpicking. One of the important reasons for the emergence of this phenomenon is that we have not thoroughly negated the "Great Cultural Revolution" and thus unified people's thinking and made them conform to the spirit of the "Resolution." Therefore, to avoid nitpicking over historical details, we must thoroughly negate the "Great Cultural Revolution."

6. *Question*: In what aspects is factionalism displayed now? What is its harm?

Answer: Today we say that factionalism took place and developed in the process of the "Great Cultural Revolution." Since the smashing of the "gang of four," and particularly since the 3d Plenary Session of the 11th CPC Central Committee, we have greatly weakened factionalism through bringing order out of chaos in various fields and through carrying out arduous ideological and educational work. However, just as the decision on party rectification says: "Even now we have not yet overcome the factionalism with which some of our party members and party member cadres have been infected during the 10 years of civil disorder." Now, factionalism is committed in a relatively covert form. It is mainly displayed in the following aspects:

1. In thoughts and feelings, people who were previously of the same faction keep no secrets from one another. They will even go so far as to violate organizational principles and disclose to one another the decisions of the organizations and the secrets of the party. People who were previously of different factions are out of tune with one another and on their guard against one another, are seemingly in harmony but actually at odds, or even carry out both open strife and veiled struggle.

2. Concerning their work and work style, they utilize their factionalism to develop the study of relations. Those who were previously of the same faction will help each other in their work and they even develop under-the-counter relations among themselves and use one another's position to seek their private ends. Those who were previously not of the same faction will shift responsibility to one another, refuse to cooperate with one another, or overtly consent with but covertly oppose one another. In a small number of areas where factionalism exists, the cadres who have been newly sent there have encountered the intervention and obstacles of factionalism and are not able to carry out their work smoothly.

3. In building our organizations and carrying out policies related to cadres, factionalists give different treatment to different people of different factions. They appoint people by favoritism and discriminate against those who hold different views. In implementing the policies related to our cadres, they vigorously run about to help those of their own factions to have the policies implemented, but

create a variety of obstacles for those who are members of other factions. In forming leading groups, they do not carry out the party's policy on the "four transformations" of cadres, but select people into the leading groups from a factionalist point of view. They are in favor of selecting anyone of their faction into leading groups, but oppose selecting anyone of the antagonistic faction into leading groups, no matter how virtuous and competent he may be.

4. They also proceed from factionalism in readjusting wages, granting technological titles, and distributing residential housing. They divide people into enemies and friends, and strive to get more for their friends. If anything is not done in a manner that pleases them, they loudly complain and groundlessly accuse the leading groups of "retaliation."

Factionalism has withered away, but its residual influence is still quite dangerous and must not be neglected.

First, it weakens our party spirit. If one adheres to 38ctionalism and proceeds from the interests of his faction, he will never be able to acquire the real party spirit. If factionalism exists in a party organization, this organization will certainly become disunited, party discipline will become slack, and the combat capacity of this organization will be weakened.

Second, factionalism obstructs the implementation of the party's line, principles, and policies. Being influenced by factionalism, some people disregard the overall interests of the party and the state. For the sake of their factions' interests, they may refuse to implement the party's policies or just accept the part that favors their selfish interests. Factionalism is corruptive of the united and stable situation and leads to discord in inner-party relations, thus hindering the fulfillment of various tasks of the party.

Third, factionalism impedes the work of clearing away "people of the three categories" and building up the "third echelon." Without thoroughly clearing away "people of the three categories," it is impossible to select the right candidates for the "third echelon," and it is even likely to nominate "people of the three categories" to the "third echelon."

7. *Question*: Why is it possible to thoroughly smash factionalism only by thoroughly negating the "Cultural Revolution"?

Answer: Because factionalism is a product of the "Cultural Revolution." This can be seen clearly from its appearance and development. At the beginning of the "Cultural Revolution," various kinds of "fighting teams" and "rebel corps" emerged one after another and started rebelling against the so-called "capitalist-roaders." In particular, since the so-called "January storm" in 1967, all rebel organizations attempted to seize power in their own units, resulting in two extremely antagonistic factions and the development from verbal and written fighting to struggles by force. Later there was a so-called "support the left" movement. But "supporting leftists" actually meant supporting factions. So the struggle between the two factions centered on seizing power and further intensified and factionalism further developed. At the end of 1967, Comrade Mao Zedong called on the two factions to unite, so the struggle between the two factions became less fierce. But the two factions, in order to seize power and interests, still maintained and continued to develop factionalism under the garb of union. Such a situation continued until the end of the "Cultural Revolution," but its bad influence remains to date. That is why we say factionalism is a product of the "Cultural Revolution" and that it is necessary to thoroughly negate the "Cultural Revolution" in order to thoroughly eliminate factionalism.

The reason for the existence of factionalism at present is that some comrades still think there were a "correct line" and "correct aspects" in the "Cultural Revolution," and that their faction represented the "correct line" or at least that they themselves were correct. Hence they compete with the other faction whenever there is a chance. By holding such an idea, these comrades still believe that the "Cultural Revolution" was more or less correct. Therefore, in order to thoroughly eliminate factionalism, it is necessary to thoroughly negate the "Cultural Revolution," just like "removing firewood from under a cauldron."

8. *Question*: Why will the failure to thoroughly negate the "Cultural Revolution" and eliminate factionalism directly hamper the work of sorting out "people of the three categories" and selecting the "third echelon"?

Answer: "People of the three categories" are a product of the "Cultural Revolution." During the Cultural Revolution they carried out various sabotages by taking advantage of "leftist" mistakes and under the cover of factionalism. Today, some of them still treat "leftist" ideas and factionalist remnants as their hide-outs. For example, in the current party rectification campaign, some people have done their utmost to protect and shield those who belonged to their faction in the past, and they are unwilling to provide information to relevant authorities. When the "Cultural Revolution" is mentioned, some people are very fond of distinguishing between "rights" and "wrongs," so that those who should be sorted out can be shielded. Some leading cadres judge rights and wrongs based on whether or not the people concerned protected them during the "Cultural Revolution." They protect those who once protected them. Therefore, some of those who should be sorted out, by taking advantage of their protection, absolve themselves from blame on such pretexts as "rebelling as instructed." In some areas and units some of the "people of the three categories" are notorious for their past misdeeds, but they have not yet been dealt with for quite a long time. The reason is none other than factionalism. It is thus clear that without thoroughly negating the "Cultural Revolution" and eliminating factionalism, it will be impossible to see through and expose "people of the three categories" and to purify party organizations.

Likewise, the failure to thoroughly negate the "Cultural Revolution" and eliminate factionalism will also directly hamper the work of selecting the "third echelon." The selection of the "third echelon" is closely linked with sorting out "people of the three categories." If "people of the three categories" are not sorted out thoroughly, they will conceal their identity and disguise themselves to win the trust of the people. If we proceed from factionalism, appoint people by favoritism, cultivate "people of the three categories" as the "third echelon" or even entrust them with important tasks, then there will be no end of trouble in the future. Sorting out "people of the three categories" and building the "third echelon" all aim to put the leading power in the hands of reliable persons. They are two aspects of one problem. Only by thoroughly negating the "Cultural Revolution" and eliminating factionalism will it be possible to fulfill the two tasks in a good manner.

9. *Question*: There were two factions in the "Cultural Revolution." Some organizations rebelled against leading

cadres, and they were obviously wrong. But other organizations protected leading cadres. Were they also wrong?

Answer: Concrete analysis should be made on this problem. First, the "Cultural Revolution," under the guidance of the theory of continuing the revolution under the dictatorship of the proletariat, treated the so-called struggle against "the bourgeoisie within the party" and the rebellion against "capitalist-roaders" as its main content. Therefore, in the "Cultural Revolution" there were no such organizations which merely protected leading cadres and did not rebel against "capitalist-roaders." If there were one or two such organizations at the beginning of the "Cultural Revolution," they were immediately suppressed by Lin Biao and the "gang of four." Therefore, the two factions in the "Cultural Revolution" rebelled against some leading cadres while "protecting" others. There were no such organizations which merely protected leading cadres and did not rebel against "capitalist-roaders." If they had protected some leading cadres, they proceeded from the theory of the "Cultural Revolution." Therefore, in today's view both the "rebelling" and "protecting" factions were wrong. At that time both factions were factionalist organizations and "protected" or "rebelled against" others according to their factionalist ideas. All in all, on the whole it must be admitted that the two factions were products of the "Cultural Revolution." They emerged and carried out activities under the guidance of the so-called theory of "continuing the revolution under the dictatorship of the proletariat" and carried out the "leftist" ideas and line, much to the detriment of the revolutionary cause.

10. *Question* By raising the question of thoroughly negating the "Cultural Revolution" and eliminating factionalism, will factionalism be stirred up again?

Answer: No. On the contrary, only by thoroughly negating the "Cultural Revolution" will it be possible to effectively eliminate factionalism once and for all. A few years ago, the work of opposing factionalism was also carried out in quite a few localities and units. But factionalism has never been uprooted and "the nonexistence of apparent mountain strongholds but the existence of submerged reefs" still exists in many units. A fundamental cause of the weak situation in opposing factionalism lies in the fact that we did not thoroughly negate the "Cultural Revolution" and all its factions. Some units affirmed first and foremost that all the factions were "revolutionary mass organizations" that "made their own contributions but had all sorts of shortcomings or errors" during the "Cultural Revolution." Thus, in opposing factionalism on the major premise of still affirming the "Cultural Revolution," a small number of people with serious factional ideas were very keen on vying with each other to see who was better. As a result, not only was it impossible to oppose factionalism but it became "too tangled to be unraveled."

Now that we take the "Resolution on Certain Questions in the History of Our Party Since the Founding of the PRC" as our criterion in thoroughly negating the "Cultural Revolution" and all its factional organizations, we have grasped the fundamentals for eliminating factionalism. Since the "Cultural Revolution" was completely erroneous and all its factions were also wrong, no factions can claim they were correct. There were only historic errors and bitter lessons. Realizing this, it is possible for certain people still clinging to factionalism to suddenly wake up to the truth

and extricate themselves quickly from the mire of factionalism. Facts prove that the units which have succeeded in doing so have not stirred up fresh factional disputes but have created a new atmosphere of unity and progress. In the past, some leading cadres had profound feelings of estrangement toward one another; now they have heart-to-heart talks on their own initiative and make peace with one another. Some cadres and party members have burned the books originally intended for avenging themselves on other parties because they do not want revenge. The previous practice of throwing mud at others and lodging complaints against each other has disappeared.

Naturally, there are also a very small number of people who have excessively deep-rooted habits. Entertaining serious factional ideas, they only censure others for their factionalism and refuse to examine their own factionalism. With regard to these people, it is necessary to educate them through criticism so they can correct their errors conscientiously.

11. *Question*: Some comrades said they were impartial during the "three supports and two militaries" and supported the opposing factions. Can we say they made no mistakes?

Answer: We cannot say they made no mistakes.

First, taken as a whole, the "three supports and two militaries" was also an outcome of the "Cultural Revolution." It was carried out under the theory of supposedly "continuing the revolution under the dictatorship of the proletariat." The "three supports and two militaries" itself was an outcome and a clear proof that the "Cultural Revolution" was out of control. At that time, dispatching the PLA to engage in "three supports and two militaries" was aimed at stabilizing the situation, but the main purpose was to support the rebel groups. Situated as it was during the "three supports and two militaries," the Army was not keenly aware of the harm of "leftist" ideas. Under the conditions at that time, it was also difficult to resist "leftist" ideas. Therefore, generally speaking, the Army carried out a set of "leftist" policies in the "three supports and two militaries" and vigorously supported the "Cultural Revolution."

The "Resolution on Certain Problems in the History of Our Party Since the Founding of the PRC" pointed out that the "three supports and two militaries" was "necessary under the chaotic situation at that time and played a positive role in stabilizing the situation." This was in keeping with the facts. With the exception of this, however, there is nothing more to be affirmed.

The slogan of "holding level a bowl of water" was raised in the winter of 1967 to promote the so-called "great alliance." But because it contradicted the requirement of supporting the rebel groups, this aim was practically impossible to achieve. Even if the Army had succeeded in supporting the opposing factions, what objective would it have achieved? It was none other than destroying the "bourgeois headquarters," smashing the "counter-revolutionary revisionist line," and overthrowing the "capitalist-roaders." After the autumn of 1968, the work of the PLA propaganda teams and the worker propaganda teams—such as carrying out "struggle-criticism-transformation," establishing the "revolutionary committees," launching criticism and repudiation, purifying the class ranks, and conducting party rectification, which was unexceptionally carried out under the guidance of "leftist" ideas—had similarly the problem of confusing right and wrong and confusing friend with foe. It can thus be seen that the argument that the PLA made no mistakes in "holding level a bowl of water" during the "three supports and two militaries" is not in keeping with historical facts.

12. *Question*: Some comrades say they did not participate in either the movement of "speaking out freely, airing views fully, holding great debates, and writing big-character posters" or in the "three supports and two militaries," that they had nothing to do with the "leftist" influence or factionalism. Why do we say that this argument is wrong?

Answer: The "leftist" errors did not emerge only after the "Cultural Revolution." Neither were the victims confined to people participating in the movement of "speaking out freely, airing views fully, holding great debates, and writing big-character posters" and the "three supports and two militaries." The "leftist" errors emerged prior to the "Cultural Revolution" and the "leftist" slogans and "leftist" viewpoints existed in all fields of social life. It was difficult to prevent people from being imperceptibly influenced by what they constantly saw and heard. As far as the Army is concerned, it had practiced "giving prominence to politics" ever since Lin Biao presided over the routine work of the Central Military Commission, and had been subjected to "leftist" influence even more seriously. During the "Cultural Revolution," "leftist" ideas were further systematized and raised to a theoretical plane. The so-called "theory of continuing the revolution under the dictatorship of the proletariat" was incorporated into the party constitution and the state Constitution and became a guiding principle for the party and state. It also dragged the people throughout the country into the whirlpool of the "Cultural Revolution" through the form of "speaking out freely, airing views fully, holding great debates, and writing big-character posters" in unprecedented scope and depth. The "leftist" influence penetrated all aspects of social life and was characterized by long duration, deep penetration, and extensive scope. Under these circumstances, it was impossible for the Army to be free of "leftist" influence even if it did not participate in "speaking out freely, airing views fully, holding great debates, and writing big-character posters" and in the "three supports and two militaries." Naturally, due to the different specific experiences of different people, there were certain differences in the extent and depth of "leftist" influence among different people.

Neither can factionalism be considered something characteristic of the movement of "speaking out freely, airing views fully, holding great debates, and writing big-character posters" and the "three supports and two militaries." During the "Cultural Revolution," factionalism permeated society, saturated the organism of our party and all organizations in society, and even penetrated families. Comparatively speaking, the comrades who did not participate in the movement of "speaking out freely, airing views fully, holding great debates, and writing big-character posters" and the "three supports and two militaries" did not join a specific "faction" or express their support for a certain faction could detach themselves from reality to a certain extent.

However, they did not live in a vacuum. With respect to the opposing factions in their localities or units, they had their own views and inclinations and sympathized with or supported certain factions ideologically and even in action, in varying degrees either overtly or covertly. There were also people who completely detached themselves from reality, but there were very few of them. We should not regard ourselves as having had nothing to do with factionalism simply because we did not participate in the movement of "speaking out freely, airing views fully, holding great debates, and writing big-character posters" and in the "three supports and two militaries." It can be said that the "Cultural Revolution" was a "dyeing vat" of "leftism" and a "hotbed" of factionalism. It was possible for those taking part in the "Cultural Revolution" to be influenced by "leftist" ideas and factionalism. We should have an ample understanding of this point so we can consciously eliminate it.

To be sure, when we judge the extent and depth of the influence of "leftism" or factionalism on a person, we should look at his actual performance, such as his specific activities and deeds, during the whole process of the "Cultural Revolution." We should not judge him simply by the criterion of whether or not he participated in the movement of "speaking out freely, airing views fully, holding great debates, and writing big-character posters" and the "three supports and two militaries."

13. *Question*: Why cannot the influence of "leftist" thinking be cleared away once and for all unless we thoroughly negate the "Great Cultural Revolution"?

Answer: "Leftist" thinking, though having already influenced our party before the "Cultural Revolution," did not dominate the entire party at that time. However, during the "Cultural Revolution," erroneous "leftist" thinking not only predominated over the CPC central authorities but also formed a complete theoretical system and a whole set of "leftist" principles and methods that influenced every corner and every front throughout the country for fully 10 years. Its widespread influence, formidable harm, as well as long duration, are unprecedented in the history of our party. Our party has launched an all-round drive to set things right after the 3d Plenary Session of the 11th CPC Central Committee. However, erroneous thinking, as soon as it takes shape, will have lasting influence that cannot be eliminated in a short time. And this is exactly the real situation. Although 8 years have passed since the "Cultural Revolution," the influence of "leftist" thinking is still alive to a different extent in the minds of many people. For example, although some comrades admit verbally the full correctness of the line, principles, and policies adopted since the 3d Plenary Session of the 11th CPC Central Committee, they have different worries and doubts about many specific problems. They think the responsibility system does not conform to the principle of "being large in size and collective in nature"; they doubt if the policy of promoting commodity production is a "socialist" policy or a "capitalist" one; they believe the policy to allow some people to get rich before others means encouraging the division of society into two opposing extremes; they are afraid that the long-distance transportation of goods for sale will give rise to speculation and profiteering; and they doubt whether the selection and promotion of cadres of intellectual origin conforms with the party's class line. Moreover, leading people of some units always carry out their work perfunctorily and pay lip service. They never try to implement the line, principles, and policies laid down by the CPC central authorities in light of the actual situation of their own units and departments but copy things mechanically in disregard of specific conditions. Such a practice can also be traced back to the "leftist" thinking prevailing in the "Great Cultural Revolution." Without thoroughly negating the "Great Cultural Revolution," we will fail to completely repudiate and will thereby partially affirm and retain the theory, principles, and struggle methods that guided the whole course of the "Great Cultural Revolution" as well as the work method and work style relating to the "leftist" ideology which drastically developed in the "Great Cultural Revolution."

As a result, we will never be able to completely eliminate the long-standing erroneous "leftist" influences. The "Cultural Revolution" had enabled "leftist" thinking to develop to a very high level. And, at the same time, it was the drastic prevalence of "leftist" thinking that prepared the conditions for the emergence of the "Cultural Revolution" and supported its development. Therefore, in order to eliminate the long-standing pernicious "leftist" influences, it is necessary to thoroughly negate the "Great Cultural Revolution."

14. *Question*: It was once said that "both factions were organizations of the revolutionary masses." But now we say that both sides were wrong and should be negated equally. Does this mean negating the masses?

Answer: During the "Cultural Revolution," the two factions posed as a "revolutionary faction" and denounced each other as a "conservative faction," engaging in endless bloody fighting. It was under such circumstances that both sides were recognized as "organizations of the revolutionary masses" in order to press for the so-called "great unification." Reviewing the issue in retrospect today, we must say that it was completely wrong to recognize as "organizations of the revolutionary masses" these factionalist organizations whose purpose was to overthrow the "capitalist-roaders."

The reason we say that both factions were wrong is because all factionalist organizations emerging in the "Cultural Revolution" were evil, no matter what slogan they were upholding and what banner they were flaunting, and all of these factions should have been negated—the questions of which was right and which was wrong and that of which was superior and which was inferior are completely meaningless. As for the masses who joined these organizations, we have to make specific analyses of them. During the "Cultural Revolution," apart from a small number of "people of the three categories," many people, though having joined organizations of a certain faction, did not take part in the ruthless struggle against leading cadres. Some of them joined a certain "faction," but never participated in factionalist fighting or engaged in the activities of smashing and grabbing. Others had been activists at the initial stage of the "Cultural Revolution" but awoke later. Becoming disgusted with endless struggle, they withdrew from factionalist organizations and boycotted factionalist activities to a different extent and by different means. Most people stuck to their posts on the production front and continued to work even during the period when factionalist trends and bloody fighting were on the upswing. Thanks to their efforts, socialist construction was not interrupted in those days. Therefore, while realizing that both factions emerging in the "Cultural Revolution" were evil,

we must be aware that the majority of the masses are good or relatively good. When saying that both factions were wrong and should be negated, we absolutely do not mean to negate the masses nor to state that everyone who joined any factionalist organization was equally wrong in committing mistakes of the same nature. Of course, all comrades who joined factionalist organizations should draw a lesson from their own experience. By so doing, they can see their mistakes clearly and thus become staunch revolutionaries.

15. *Question*: Eight years have passed since the end of the "Cultural Revolution." Why do factionalist influences still remain in some units today?

Answer: There are two reasons. First of all, the factionalist influence left over from the "Cultural Revolution" has shown all the common die-hard characteristics of all cliques and factions in history. Various types of "fighting teams" and factionalist organizations emerged in some units during the "Cultural Revolution." Although all these organizations were abolished in the latter period of the "Cultural Revolution," most members of these organizations remain in their original units. Some of these people are stubborn factionalists who always regard those who belonged to the same organizations as theirs as "comrades in arms" and place factionalist relationship before party spirit, proceeding from their factionalist "feelings." This shows that eliminating the die-hard influence of factionalism is by no means an easy task but one which calls for persistent and tremendous efforts.

Second, the fact that factionalist influence remains in some units nearly 8 years after the end of the "Great Cultural Revolution" is related to the weak and slack leadership of these units. The leading people of these units have never been determined in eliminating factionalist influence. They dare not face and fight against factionalist influence. Fearing that fighting factionalism may provoke a factionalist confrontation once again, some of them are hesitant to take action but try to evade the problem, while others attempt to gloss over things by compromising on disputes and the balance of power. Some of these leading people themselves are the followers of factionalism. Afraid that thoroughly negating the "Cultural Revolution" and fighting factionalism will mean negating themselves, they openly or secretly encourage a number of people to practice factionalism. As a result, factionalist influence has not yet been completely eliminated.

Yielding to the factionalists will only stimulate the development of factionalism and encourage some people to give fuller play to factionalism. Therefore, it is necessary to educate our party members and cadres to thoroughly negate the "Cultural Revolution," eliminate factionalist influences, and strengthen the party spirit; it is also necessary to severely punish those who continue to practice factionalism and refuse to correct their mistakes despite criticism, as well as those who continue to interfere with the current party rectification and our day-to-day work by practicing factionalism. Everyone must enhance his party spirit and resolutely do away with factionalist influences, and every leading person must be brave in fighting factionalism. Only in this way can we effectively eliminate factionalist influences.

16. *Question*: Some people agree verbally that the "Cultural Revolution" should be thoroughly negated and the two factions in the "Cultural Revolution" were wrong,

but whenever they are involved in concrete problems, they would like to say that the faction they sided with is correct. Why is this so?

Answer: This shows that thorough negation of the "Cultural Revolution" and recognition that both factions in the "Cultural Revolution" were wrong is not only a problem of understanding, but first an ideological problem also. Only when we proceed from the party spirit, keep our distance from personal gains and losses and virtually resolve our ideological problems will we be able to keep our views identical with the spirit of the CPC Central Committee and its Military Commission. In doing this, we will not agree verbally that the "Cultural Revolution" should be thoroughly negated and both of the two factions in the "Cultural Revolution" are wrong and we will not argue that the faction we sided with is correct whenever we are involved in concrete problems.

Why do some comrades argue for the correctness of the faction they sided with whenever they are involved in concrete problems? Behind the "argument," there are some hidden personal objectives and motives. Some of these comrades fear that negating the "Cultural Revolution" may negate themselves, some who did something wrong in the "Cultural Revolution" are afraid of bringing up old scores again, and some argue for the correctness of the faction they sided with in an attempt to fight for promotions in their posts and ask for power from the party with the "capital" that they "are consistently correct." It is thus clear that to argue for correctness is, in fact, to fight for personal gain. To thoroughly negate the "Cultural Revolution," we must jump out of our small circle of people. If comrades who participated in certain factional organizations can really take the interests of the party and people into consideration, and if they will realize that they did more or less make certain mistakes in the "Cultural Revolution," an internal disorder and catastrophe which brought heavy losses to the party and state, they will voluntarily draw lessons, and they will in no way argue for the correctness of the faction they sided with.

17. *Question*: Some comrades said that they did not feel that they had committed mistakes in the hard work of the "three supports and two militaries" and now they feel wronged. Why is the feeling incorrect?

Answer: Some comrades in the Army indeed worked hard and did many useful things in the "three supports and two militaries." Some of them made joint efforts with the masses to maintain the normal order of production and routine work; some of them protected cadres against persecution; and some of them contributed to stopping armed conflicts between mass organizations. Their positive role in stabilizing the situation should be affirmed.

However, it should also be noticed that since the guiding principle and policies of the "Cultural Revolution" were completely wrong, the Army could not but put these erroneous theories, principles, and policies into practice in the course of the "three supports and two militaries." For example, when taking part in the "three supports and two militaries," many comrades brought such "leftist" things as Lin Biao's proposition of "giving prominence to politics" to civilian organizations, and they unavoidably committed some mistakes in the course of doing so. These mistakes definitely impaired our Army's prestige and reputation and adversely affected relations between the Army, the civilian administrative organizations, and people. We hold that there

should be the unity of motives and effects. Although many comrades who participated in the "three supports and two militaries" did not have evil motives and wanted to do a good job in this work, it was still hard for them to avoid mistakes since they were subject to the guidance of erroneous principles and policies. We should now proceed from the interests of the party and the people and clearly realize the negative effects of the "three supports and two militaries." We should look at things from the people's position and acknowledge that our mistakes indeed caused losses to the civilian organizations where we once supported the "leftists." We should not try to defend ourselves because we worked hard in those days. Then we can overcome the feeling of being wronged.

We should also be aware that in the drive of "three supports and two militaries," supporting the "leftists" meant supporting factionalism and was thus a mistake. In saying this, we are not intending to find out who was to blame for the mistake but to distinguish between right and wrong and draw a lesson from our historical experience. Everyone can make mistakes. The most important thing is that every wrongdoer must realize his mistakes, admit his responsibility, and draw a lesson from the mistakes. If someone does not realize his mistakes but feels wronged, he may possibly have the intention of boycotting the act of thoroughly negating the "Cultural Revolution." So, he may make mistakes again in the future. Therefore, those comrades who feel wronged should enhance their ideological understanding in order to get rid of such feelings as soon as possible.

18. *Question*: Some comrades say that they themselves were only innocent children when the "Cultural Revolution" broke out; therefore they have nothing to do with thoroughly negating the "Cultural Revolution" and eliminating "leftist" influences. Is this a wrong viewpoint?

Answer: The "Cultural Revolution" was a serious and lasting "leftist" mistake which had extensive influence on the whole situation, every sector and every family in Chinese society. "Leftist" propaganda which flooded all the newspapers, journals, magazines, and textbooks poisoned the whole country, while bloody fighting in the form of "smashing and grabbing" became a common practice at that time. Those who were innocent children during the "Cultural Revolution" are now young people. Because they experienced the "Cultural Revolution," they could not help but be imperceptibly influenced by "leftist" thinking. Many negative things prevailing in the "Cultural Revolution" have left traces in these youngsters' hearts. In addition, the pernicious influence of "leftist" thinking and the "Cultural Revolution" still remains in the realities of life today. Everyone can be contaminated by these negative things and "leftist" thinking if he fails to guard against them.

It must also be emphasized that we are not aiming at any individual or any group of people in calling for thoroughly negating the "Cultural Revolution" and eliminating the influence of "leftist" thinking. The purpose of the above actions is to ensure a more effective implementation of the line, principles, and policies laid down by the 3d Plenary Session of the 11th CPC Central Committee and the 12th CPC National Congress and to pave the way for the emergence of a new situation in socialist construction. This is the common task for all people throughout the country, a task which is closely linked with every Communist Party member and every comrade, whether old or young. Therefore, those comrades are wrong in saying that they have nothing to do with thoroughly negating the "Cultural Revolution" and eliminating "leftist" influences since they themselves were only innocent children when the "Cultural Revolution" broke out.

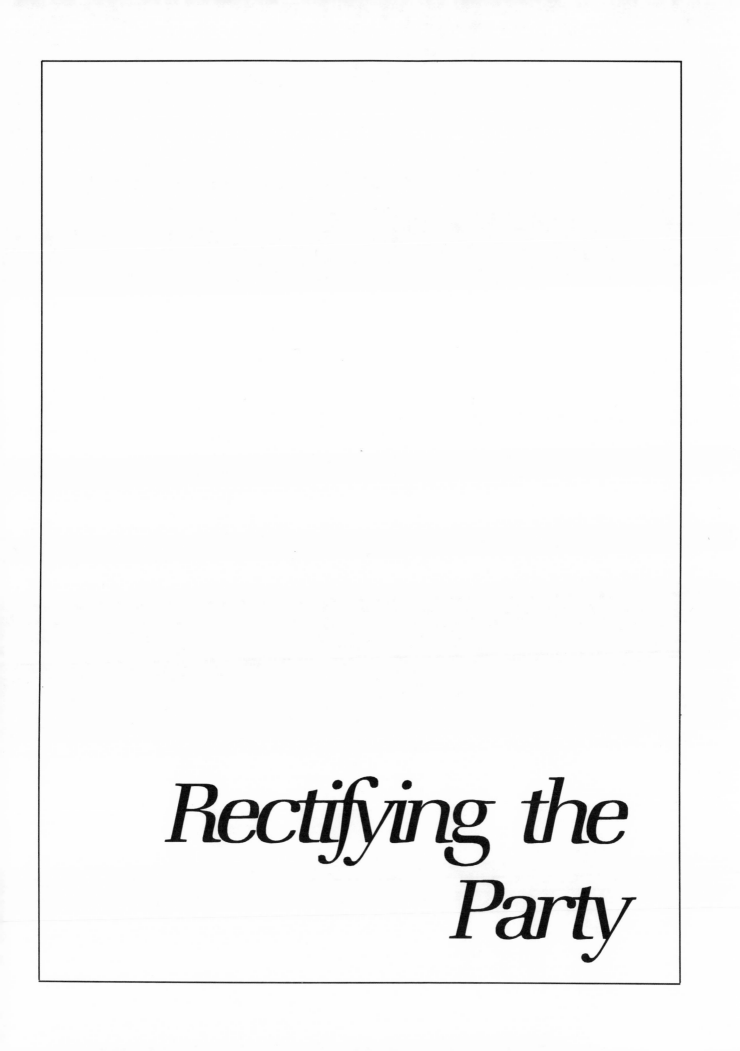

Rectifying the Party

23

A Disciplined Party as the Engine of Modernization, 28 January 1980

This is one of many indications that Deng Xiaoping essentially visualizes the rectified Party to be manager and guarantees successful modernization.

The Central Discipline Inspection Commission held its second plenary session from 7–25 January this year. The session fully discussed the major changes in the political life of the party and the state and the major achievements in all fields of endeavor since the 3d plenary session of the 11th CCP Central Committee. The comrades attending the session were serious and earnest and imbued with confidence.

The session summed up the work of the Central Discipline Inspection Commission in the past year and mapped out the 1980 task for inspecting discipline. It was determined to shift the focus of its work further to insuring the implementation of the party's line, principles and policies formulated since the convocation of the party's third plenary session and to insuring the realization of the four modernizations.

The session also revised and replenished the document: "Certain guiding principles concerning inner-party political life" (draft), which will soon be forwarded to the party Central Committee. Furthermore, the session examined and discussed the several major cases left over from the past and current cases which were handed down by the party Central Committee for solution. This was an important session. The major cases left over from the past and solved by the session and the task and principles formulated by the session will certainly play an active and important role in further improving the party style, strengthening the party's political and organizational discipline and insuring the development of the four modernizations.

The Central Discipline Inspection Commission and the various organs for inspecting discipline in party organizations at all levels were established after the convocation of the party's third plenary session. This is an important measure reflecting the determination of the party Central Committee to improve the party style, safeguard party rules and regulations and restore and advance the party's fine traditions and work style.

During the past year, the Central Discipline Inspection Commission conducted its work and established its organization at the same time. On the one hand, it paid attention to studying and solving the major cases left over from the past; on the other hand, it did a great deal of work in formulating and reaffirming a number of party rules and regulations which were neglected for many years. At the same time, in order to correct unhealthy trends and educate the broad masses of party members and cadres, it also issued many timely circulars and directives and handled a number of current issues.

After a decade of catastrophe created by Lin Biao and the "gang of four," it is absolutely necessary and correct to concentrate our main efforts on solving major problems left over from history and on restoring party rules and regulations—when we start to restore the work of inspecting party discipline.

Actually, this is aimed at clearing the base and laying the foundation for improving party style and strengthening party discipline. The problems left over from the past have now been cleared up, some major issues during the Great Cultural Revolution solved and party rules and regulations restored by actually summing up the important positive and negative experiences of the party's political life during the 30 years since the founding of the nation. This is of tremendous significance. The second plenary session completely reaffirmed the achievements of the Central Discipline Inspection Commission in its work during the past year.

What is more important about the party's discipline inspection work is that, in addition to insuring the party's organizational discipline, it also insures the party's political discipline. In other words, it insures the implementation of the party's line, principles and policies. At present, it insures the implementation of the political line and the series of principles, policies and decisions which have been established since the 3d plenary session of the 11th CCP Central Committee. The political line established by the 3d plenary session of the 11th CCP Central Committee is: Unite the people of all nationalities throughout the country, mobilize all positive factors, work with one mind and one heart, go all out, aim high and build China into a modern socialist power with greater, faster, better and more economic results.

To put it simply, we should work for the four modernizations. This is the historical task of socialist revolution after the question of the system of ownership is settled. It is the correct line which our party, having experienced many twists and turns in the past 30 years, has finally formulated after smashing the "gang of four." During the new historical period, the whole party and the people of the whole country must always and unswervingly work for

["Strengthen Party Discipline and Improve Party Style to Ensure the Development of the Four Modernizations," *People's Daily*, 28 January 1980.]

this with complete attention and single-hearted devotion. Particularly in the 1980's, a decade crucial to the realization of the four modernizations, we must redouble our efforts to win decisive victories. For this reason, our work in all fields must serve this central task.

In accordance with the political line decided by the 3d plenary session of the 11th CCP Central Committee, the Central Discipline Inspection Commission has arranged its work ever since it was formed. Centering on the task of the four modernizations, this year's discipline inspection work will be to make further efforts to perfect the party style, enforce party discipline and fight all erroneous ideas that obstruct, resist and sabotage the four modernizations as well as all violations of law and discipline.

Of course, this does not mean efforts to handle problems left over from history will be relaxed. These problems will still be handled with continued attention. The party's various policies will continue to be implemented in earnest. We must make sure that the steps to redress the cases of unjust, false and wrong charges and sentences will be taken from start to finish. Negligence of or resistance to policy implementation and the redressing of injustices will absolutely not be tolerated. Party organizations must make careful arrangements for this work.

To realize the four modernizations it is necessary to uphold the party's leadership and strengthen the party's fighting power. Party discipline is the guarantee of the party's fighting power. The call for "kicking aside the party committee to make revolution" made by Lin Biao and the "gang of four" during the 10 years when they were running wild was in fact a call for doing away with the party's leadership and for replacing the party with their faction. The problem that now confronts us is how to uphold the party's leadership and revive the party's fighting power. For this purpose, we need to reaffirm and strengthen party discipline.

The fundamental principle of our party's discipline is: "The individual is subordinate to the organization, the minority is subordinate to the majority, the lower level is subordinate to the higher level and the entire membership is subordinate to the Central Committee." Of these four rules, the most important is "the entire membership is subordinate to the Central Committee." In conducting the party's discipline inspection work, we must make sure these principles, particularly the principle, "the entire membership is subordinate to the Central Committee," are implemented throughout the party.

Our party permits a member to express different opinions to the party organizations all the way up to the party Central Committee. However, in the implementation of the party's line, principles and policies, it is absolutely impermissible for anyone to do whatever he thinks is right. No one is permitted to act in this way, whatever the party organization and whoever the party member, regardless of the length of his career or high position. Therefore, while it is certainly necessary for party discipline inspection work to include the inspection of such problems of work and lifestyle as bureaucracy and the practice of asserting privileges, it is even more necessary for it to include the inspection of the practice of stubbornly going in for factionalism and anarchy and the double-dealing behavior of feigning compliance to the party's line, principles and policies in public but opposing them in private.

The organizational and ideological remnants of Lin Biao and the "gang of four" still exist. This is a serious factor that is interfering with and endangering political stability and unity and obstructing and sabotaging the efforts for the four modernizations, and it must not be underestimated. We must not lower our vigilance against those people who continue to engage in factionalism and anarchy and who use double-dealing tactics against the party. We must resolutely take stern measures against these people in accordance with party discipline, and we must never be softhearted. Measures should be taken where they are called for. We must pay special attention to safeguarding the implementation of the important policy decisions and various principles and policies enacted by the party since the 3d plenary session of the 11th CCP Central Committee. We should regard the guarantee of the political-ideological and organizational unification and the unity of action of the entire party as the primary important task in perfecting party style and enforcing party discipline.

The work principle established by the Central Commission for Inspecting Discipline is to emphasize prevention by enacting laws and conducting education first. Then, it is to insure that these laws are observed and that lawbreakers are dealt with. This principle conforms with our party's traditional policy and realities.

There is a phrase in China that praises a good doctor: "Effect a miraculous cure and bring the dying back to life." When Lin Biao and the "gang of four" held sway, our party's rules and regulations were left in a terrible state and organization and discipline ceased to be binding. Many new party members who joined the party during that period do not understand, or they know little of, the party rules and regulations. They also do not understand the party's traditions. After a decade of turmoil, the party concept and sense of organization and discipline of a number of veteran party members are extremely blunted. Unhealthy trends within the party are flourishing. This is a serious disease within our party. To deal with it, we also need a "miraculous cure." This "miraculous cure" is to suit the medicine to the illness. In other words, we must enact laws and conduct education first, and then carry out preventive inoculation among the broad masses of party members. Therefore, we must conduct education within the whole party over a protracted period and in an overall and penetrating manner to help party members strengthen their concept in observing laws and discipline.

It is also necessary to foster the concept of serving the four modernizations. We should do all this to revitalize and strengthen the fighting strength of our party. Even in dealing with those comrades who had committed serious errors when Lin Biao and the "gang of four" held sway, we must pay attention to their actual deeds and follow the principle of "learning from past mistakes to avoid future ones and curing the sickness to save the patient." However, to carry out preventive inoculation first and emphasize education does not mean we can relax our efforts to enforce the party's discipline. We must also insure that "laws are observed and that lawbreakers are dealt with." We must also make sure that "we now deal with lawbreakers strictly, although we treated them with leniency in the past."

As for those who defy the principles and policies of the party Central Committee and who stubbornly refuse to implement them, those who persistently cling to factionalism and undermine unity, those who obstinately commit all kinds of outrages and violate laws and discipline, and those who run counter to financial and economic discipline and obstruct the development of the four modernizations, we must grasp their typical examples, conduct investigations in a penetrating manner and seriously deal with them.

In short, we must be steady and resolute in safeguarding party rules and regulations and enforcing party discipline. This is conducive to healing the wounds of the party, consolidating political stability and unity, bringing into full play the enthusiasm of the party members and improving the party style earnestly.

In the final analysis, the question of party style is one of party spirit. The fundamental approach to perfecting party style lies in raising the consciousness of the broad masses of party members and in strengthening the party spirit. Our party has always attached importance to strengthening the party spirit of its members. Thanks to the initiative, personal example and verbal instructions of Comrade Mao Zedong and other proletarian revolutionaries of the older generation, the party has formed its fine traditions and style of work. However, due to the rabid vilification and disruption by Lin Biao and the "gang of four," there has been no ideological education or strengthening of party spirit among party members for more than 10 years. The spread of lies has harmed the party and (?state) [words indistinct] in no small measure.

Therefore, we have the problem of strengthening the ideological structure and improving the consolidation of the party. "Certain guiding principles concerning inner-party political life" (draft) and other important party regulations and rules formulated or reiterated by the party Central Committee and the Central Discipline Inspection Commission represent a powerful ideological weapon for us to use in strengthening the ideological structure of the party and in perfecting its style. Through ideological education among party members, we should revive and advance the party's fine traditions and work style and promote the strengthening of party spirit among its members. Our party members must uphold the four fundamental principles, act as vanguards and models and display the pioneer spirit of hard struggle in the course of promoting the four modernizations. In this respect, veteran party members and the party's senior cadres should consciously play a leading role.

Since the downfall of the "gang of four," particularly since the 3d plenary session of the 11th CCP Central Committee, our party has already undergone a fundamental change. It is leading the people of all nationalities throughout the country to march toward the four modernizations. To use a literary phrase, spring has returned to our party and country. We are fully confident of the future. We should also see, however, that the lingering cold has yet to pass despite the heavy scent of spring. We still have to exert the greatest efforts. As far as the party's work is concerned, this means we must pay constant attention to the party style, party discipline and its ideological structure to guarantee progress toward the four modernizations. When all these are done well, there will be great prospects for realizing the four modernizations.

Two Resolutions on Strengthening the Party, February 1980

24

The two Central Committee resolutions below, adopted by the Fifth Plenary Session of the Eleventh Central Committee, call for the convening of the first Party Congress (the Twelfth) since Deng Xiaoping became the Party strong man. They also call for the establishment (actually the reestablishment after the Cultural Revolution) of the Secretariat of the Central Committee as a collective entity in charge of Party administration and, consequently, with considerable influence on Party policy.

1. Since the 3d plenary session of the 11th CCP Central Committee decided to shift the party's work emphasis to socialist modernization, the party has made tremendous advances in political, economic, national defense, foreign affairs, ideological, organizational and other fields, and a situation in which the whole party, the whole army and the people of all nationalities throughout the country are working with one heart and one mind, striving to achieve the four modernizations with greater, faster, better and more economical results, is quickly taking shape and forging ahead. To accomplish the great historical task of the

[New China News Agency, 1 March 1980.]

four modernizations, the party is confronted in practice by a series of major new problems that need to be solved quickly without losing any time. Because of this, the 5th plenary session decided to convene the 12th National Congress of the Chinese Communist Party ahead of time. The national congress will convene at a time to be determined by the Political Bureau of the Central Committee.

2. The major items on the agenda of the party's 12th National Congress will be: 1) work report by the party Central Committee; 2) report by the Central Discipline Inspection Commission; 3) revision of the constitution of the party; 4) program for a long-term plan regarding the development of the national economy; and 5) election of the party Central Committee.

3. The number of deputies to the party's 12th national congress is 1,600. The distribution of deputies to be elected by various units should be determined according to the number of party members as well as the state of economic, cultural, scientific and technical development and the situation of the minority nationalities. All comrades of the Central Committee's Political Bureau, those Central Committee members and alternate members who are in Beijing and veteran comrades enjoying great prestige in the party will be assigned to the concerned units to cast their votes. Their candidacy should be included among the number of deputies to be elected by such units.

Alternate deputies should be elected by all units according to the ratio of one-tenth of the total authorized number of deputies to be elected, to fill the vacancies that may be left by the deputies.

4. The deputies to the party's 12th national congress should be elected at the party congresses or representatives' meetings to be convened respectively by all the provinces, municipalities, autonomous regions, organs directly under the central authorities, central state organs as well as all PLA general departments, services and arms and military regions, after sufficient deliberations and following the differential election method and by secret ballot. Among the deputies to be elected there should be economic, sci-

entific and technical, cultural and educational, and public health experts who have made contributions to the four modernizations as well as model workers and combat heroes of nationwide influence. An appropriate ratio should be arranged for national minority and women party members. Deputies to the party's 12th national congress should be elected not later than the end of November 1980.

5. The Central Committee calls on the comrades of the whole party to unite as one, work hard and bring about great progress in socialist construction on all fronts so as to greet the victorious convocation of the party's 12th national congress.

RESOLUTION ON CENTRAL COMMITTEE SECRETARIAT

[Resolution of the 5th plenary session of the 11th CCP Central Committee on establishment of the Secretariat of the Central Committee—adopted on 28 February 1980]

Seeing that the tasks of socialist modernization are extremely arduous and complicated since the shifting of the whole party's work emphasis, in order that the Political Bureau of the Central Committee and its Standing Committee members can concentrate their energies on considering and making decisions on major questions in domestic and foreign affairs, and at the same time in view of the need of the Central Committee to set up an organ to carry out its day-to-day work in a systematic way so that the party's large amount of day-to-day work in all fields can be handled promptly and efficiently, the plenary session decided to establish a Secretariat of the Central Committee. It will apply the system of collective leadership and division of labor with individual responsibility. The Secretariat consists of a general secretary and a number of members and alternate members, all of whom are to be elected directly by the Central Committee.

25

Deng Xiaoping's Concept of a Rectified Party, February 1980

Although his name is not mentioned, this document, adopted by the Fifth Plenary Session of the Eleventh Central Committee, sets forth Deng's idea of a Party similar to Lenin's "democratic centralism"—the reality of centralism under an appearance of democracy.

The 3d plenary session of the 11th CCP Central Committee decided to shift the emphasis of the whole party's work to socialist modernization. In the new historical period, it is imperative to conscientiously uphold party rules and regulations, practically develop good party style, strengthen and improve party leadership and create a political situation of stability and unity throughout the party and the country in which there is centralism and democracy, discipline and freedom, and unity of will and personal ease of mind and liveliness. Only thus can the revolutionary enthusiasm and initiative of the party members be fully displayed and the whole party and all our nationalities united to accomplish the great task of the socialist four modernizations.

Through protracted revolutionary struggles, particularly after the Yanan rectification campaign and the Seventh CCP National Congress, our party has made an all-round analysis of both positive and negative experiences in handling inner-party relations and it gradually formulated the guiding principles for inner-party political life. The main points of this were: Seeking truth from facts, combining theory with practice, forging close ties between party members and leaders and the masses, unfolding criticism and self-criticism and persisting in democratic centralism. By adhering to these principles, all comrades in the party were united and worked in concert with each other as never before, thereby winning victories in the war of resistance against Japan and the war of liberation.

After nationwide liberation, the masses of party members in the main upheld the party's fine traditions and work style in the course of socialist revolution and construction. However, because of the fact that some comrades became arrogant and complacent as a result of the victory of the revolutionary struggle and the position gained by the party as the ruling party for the entire country, because of the imperfect system of democratic centralism in the party and state and because of the influence of the ideology of the feudal and capitalist classes, such unhealthy tendencies as being divorced from reality and the masses, subjectivism, bureaucracy, making arbitrary decisions, taking peremptory actions and seeking privileges had developed. At the same time, there were some shortcomings and mistakes in guiding the inner-party struggle and normal inner-party political life was impaired to a certain extent.

During the Great Cultural Revolution in particular, driven by their attempt to usurp party and state leadership, Lin Biao and the "gang of four" took advantage of the serious mistake committed by the party at the time and vigorously went in for feudal fascism, anarchism and factional splittist activities. They wantonly trampled upon party rules and regulations, did away with party leadership and seriously damaged party organization, the party spirit of the members and the party's fine traditions and work style. Since the downfall of the "gang of four," the party's fine traditions and work style have been revived to some extent as a result of the party Central Committee's vigorous efforts to consolidate party style and discipline. However, extensive and penetrating education and arduous and complicated struggle are still needed to heal the wounds inflicted on the party by Lin Biao and the "gang of four." In order to achieve the all-round revival and further development of the party's fine traditions and work style, strengthen the party's democratic life, safeguard the party as a centralized and unified one, strengthen party unity, consolidate party organization and discipline and enhance the party's fighting capacity, the Central Committee, in view of the present condition of the party, hereby reiterates the following guidelines for inner-party political life to the whole party:

1. ADHERE TO THE PARTY'S POLITICAL AND IDEOLOGICAL LINE

Adherence to the party's political and ideological line is the most fundamental guiding principle for inner-party political life. The basic content of the political line formulated by the party Central Committee is aimed at uniting the people of all nationalities and bringing into play all positive factors so that we can work with one heart and one mind and go all out, aim high and achieve greater, faster, better and more economic results in building a modern, powerful, socialist country. It is a Marxist-Leninist line which reflects the highest interest of the people throughout the country. All party comrades must resolutely implement it.

The ideological line is the basis for the party's formulation and implementation of its political line. The party's ideological line demands upholding the socialist road, the dictatorship of the proletariat, the leadership of the Communist Party and Marxism-Leninism-Mao Zedong Thought. Our party has always advocated the dialectical materialist way of thinking and work method. The basic

["Guiding Principles for Intra-Party Political Life," New China News Agency, 14 March 1980.]

RECTIFYING THE PARTY **151**

point of this is to proceed from reality in everything we do, combine theory with practice and seek truth from facts. For a long time, Lin Biao and the "gang of four" distorted and usurped Marxism-Leninism-Mao Zedong Thought, ran counter to its essential spirit and regarded, in departure from the criterion of practice, Comrade Mao Zedong's every word as truth, law and dogma. This seriously fettered people's minds. Therefore, it is necessary to stress the need for breaking down blind faith, emancipating the minds and—using practice as the sole criterion for testing truth—earnestly study new phenomena and resolve new problems. Only thus can we develop Marxism-Leninism-Mao Zedong Thought and truly defend and hold high the great banner of Marxism-Leninism-Mao Zedong Thought.

In order to adhere to the correct political and ideological lines, it is necessary to oppose two erroneous ideological tendencies.

First, it is necessary to oppose ossification of the mind and proceeding by the book in everything we do. The mentality that whatever is written in the book is unchangeable and whatever is not written in the book is not allowed to be said or done is anti-Marxist and a big obstacle to implementing the party's political line. In analyzing a situation, considering a question and handling affairs, we must proceed from the objective reality. We must link the fundamental principle of Marxism-Leninism with the development of the current situation at home and abroad and with the concrete practice of socialist modernization. We must link the party's line, principles and policies with the specific situation in our own locality and unit and make objective studies in order to resolve the various theoretical and practical problems in our present revolutionary struggle and modernization process.

Second, it is essential to oppose and repudiate the erroneous view and revisionist ideological trend of negating the socialist road, the dictatorship of the proletariat, party leadership and Marxism-Leninism-Mao Zedong Thought. Socialism is the only correct road leading to a rich, strong and prosperous China; the dictatorship of the proletariat is the guarantee for the victory of the socialist revolution and construction; the party is the force at the core leading the people throughout the country to implement the four modernizations; and Marxism-Leninism-Mao Zedong Thought is the theoretical basis for guiding our revolution and construction. It is imperative to always uphold the four fundamental principles in the struggle for the realization of the four modernizations.

Party organizations and departments at all levels and each and every party member must consciously and unswervingly implement the party's political and ideological lines. Opposition or passive resistance to the party's lines and leadership or taking a double-dealing attitude of feigning compliance is not permitted by party discipline.

2. UPHOLD COLLECTIVE LEADERSHIP AND OPPOSE ARBITRARY DECISIONMAKING BY A SINGLE PERSON

Collective leadership is one of the highest principles guiding party leadership. Party committees from the center down to the grassroots must follow the system of combining collective leadership with a division of labor and individual responsibility in accordance with this principle. All major issues concerning the party's line, principles and policies, the assignment of important tasks, major appointments, removals, transfers and other decisions in handling the cases of individual cadres, important issues involving the people's interests, and matters which leading organs at higher levels assign to lower party committees for collective decision—on the merits of each case, all these issues should be submitted to the party committees concerned, their standing committees or secretariats, or to the leading party groups for discussion and decision collectively, and no individual is allowed to act arbitrarily.

Under no circumstances must any other type of organization be allowed to substitute for the leadership of a party committee and its standing committee. Any organization set up by a party committee to study and handle special issues must do its work under the leadership of the party committee and it must not substitute for the party committee, and still less place itself above the latter. In deciding on matters within a party committee, it is essential to act in strict accordance with the principle that the minority is subordinate to the majority. The relationship between the secretary and other members of a party committee is not one between a superior and a subordinate, and the secretary is a member of the party committee on an equal footing with its other members. The secretary or the first secretary should be good at summing up others' views and is not allowed to practice "what I say goes" or a patriarchal system.

All leading members should support and cooperate with one another and seek mutual understanding. They all should consciously uphold the prestige of their party committees' collective leadership. In performing criticism and self-criticism, it is necessary to uphold principle and to help others as well. In discussing major issues, a party committee should let people speak out freely and air their views fully. When differences of opinion occur during the discussion, it is essential to give serious consideration to the opinions of the minority and it is impermissible to discuss something without reaching a decision, so as not to delay work. Upholding collective leadership does not mean downgrading or negating the role of individuals. Collective leadership must be combined with a division of labor and individual responsibility. It is essential to explicitly define the specific responsibility of each leading member so that everything is taken care of by someone and everyone has his specific responsibility. Not all matters, big and small, should be submitted to the party committee for discussion.

As far as a division of labor and individual responsibility are concerned, the secretary or the first secretary bears the main responsibility of organizing the party committee's activities and handling its day-to-day work. The important role of the secretary or the first secretary in the party committee must not be downgraded or even written off under the pretext of collective leadership.

It is essential to correctly understand and handle the interrelationships of the leaders, party, class and masses. Publicity for leading members should be factual and no unprincipled glorification of them is allowed. It is impermissible to praise leading members of the proletariat in the flattering terms of the exploiting classes. It is impermissible to distort history or fabricate facts in publicizing the contributions of leading members. There is to be no celebration of the birthdays of leading members, nor are they to be sent gifts or congratulatory messages. No museum should be built for any living person, and few museums should be built for deceased leaders. No street, location, enterprise or school is to be named for a leading member of the party. Except where diplomatic protocol requires, it is forbidden to greet or send off any leader with drums and gongs, put up slogans and lay on a feast for such an occasion.

3. SAFEGUARD THE PARTY'S UNITY AND CENTRALIZED LEADERSHIP AND STRICTLY ABIDE BY PARTY DISCIPLINE

Democratic centralism is the party's fundamental principle of organization. The ultraleftist line and anarchism pursued by Lin Biao and the "gang of four" undermined both democracy and centralism and both freedom and discipline. The pernicious influence of this anarchism has yet to be completely eliminated. It is therefore necessary to solemnly reiterate the principle that "the individual is subordinate to the organization, the minority is subordinate to the majority, the lower level is subordinate to the higher level and the entire party is subordinate to the Central Committee." Each and every party member must consider safeguarding the party's unity and centralized leadership and strictly abiding by party discipline to be the guiding principle for his words and deeds. Each and every Communist Party member, especially the members of party committees at all levels, must resolutely implement the decisions of the party committees. If there are differing views, they may be reserved or reported to the party committee at the next higher level. However, before the party committee or that at the next higher level changes the original decision, it must be unconditionally implemented except in an extremely urgent situation in which implementation of the decision will immediately cause grave consequences.

It is essential to oppose and prevent decentralism. That the entire party is subordinate to the Central Committee is the first prerequisite for safeguarding the party's unity and centralized leadership and the basic guarantee for implementing the party's line, principles and policies. Any department, lower party organization or party member which takes an each-goes-his-way attitude toward the party's decisions, implements only those to its or his liking, refuses to carry out those not to its or his liking, openly or covertly resists them or even presumptuously overturns them is in grave violation of party discipline.

With regard to differing views on theoretical and policy matters of great political importance concerning the vital interests of the party and state and concerning the situation as a whole, they may be discussed within the party on proper occasions. As for when and in what manner they should be discussed in the press, this should be decided by the party Central Committee. The party's newspapers and journals must unconditionally publicize the party's line, principles, policies and political views. If party members have views on theoretical and policy matters of great political importance on which the party Central Committee has made a decision, they may present their views according to the specified organizational procedure. But under no circumstances must anyone be allowed to express in the press or on the radio any views contrary to the party

Central Committee's decision, nor must anyone be allowed to spread among the masses any views contrary to the party's line, principles, policies and decisions. This is what party discipline requires.

Each and every Communist Party member and party cadre must handle their personal affairs in accordance with the principle that the party's interests are above all else. They must consciously obey the party organizations' decisions in their work assignments, transfers and other arrangements. If they consider their work assignment improper, they may express their views. But when party organizations have considered their views and reach a final decision, they must obey it.

Each and every party member must strictly guard party and state secrets and wage a resolute struggle against any divulgence of such secrets. In reading documents, hearing or relaying reports and attending party meetings, all party members must strictly abide by discipline concerning the guarding of secrets. It is strictly forbidden to reveal party secrets to one's family members, relatives and friends and to those who are not supposed to know such secrets. One must pay attention to making a distinction between those inside the party and those outside it, and whatever is not allowed to be publicized outside the party must not be spread outside the party.

Communist Party members, in particular leading cadres at various levels, should be models in obeying the law, observing labor or work discipline and adhering to communist morality. At all times and in handling any matter, Communist Party members must take the interests of the party, the state and the people as a whole into consideration and educate the masses in this spirit. This is an important expression of a Communist Party member's revolutionary consciousness as well as an important guarantee for consolidating the stability and unity of the entire country. When a few people cause trouble, party members should perform propaganda work with them, give explanations and carefully handle them in accordance with the party's policies in order to calm them down. If they present some reasonable demands, it is necessary to convince them by helping them satisfy their demands through normal channels. Under no circumstances must Communist Party members instigate or assist people in creating disturbances or troublemaking.

4. UPHOLD PARTY SPIRIT AND ROOT OUT FACTIONALISM

The party is a united militant collective composed of the advanced elements of the proletariat. It is imperative to uphold the unity of the party on the basis of the principles of Marxism-Leninism-Mao Zedong Thought and to oppose any factionalism and factional activities which undermine party unity. Organizing secret groups within the party is a crime of splitting and subverting the party. No Communist Party member is allowed to join any secret organization or participate in any secret activities to oppose the party. Party organizations at all levels and every Communist Party member must draw lessons from Lin Biao and the "gang of four's" acts of inciting factionalism, organizing secret groups and plotting to usurp party and state leadership, heighten their vigilance and prevent recurrence of similar incidents.

Factionalism is basically incompatible with proletarian party spirit. Organizing a factional group or forming a clique to pursue selfish interests is a manifestation of the exploiting classes' ultraindividualism and anarchism and a reflection in the party of ideas of the guilds of the feudal classes and small producers. If some party members carry out organized activities which deviate from the party's line and decisions behind the party's back, these are factional activities. Engaging in factional activities will inevitably impede implementation of the party's line, principles and policies and will undermine the political situation of stability and unity. If such activities are not resolutely checked and are allowed to run their course, they will lead to the splitting of the party.

Although there are now no overt factions within the party, some cadres and party members who were more deeply influenced by Lin Biao and the "gang of four" still harbor factionalism and are even still carrying out factional activities. In some areas, departments and units "there are no visible mountain strongholds, but there are hidden shoals." The "specter" of factionalism is still there, and factionalists often resist implementation of the party's principles and policies and of higher level decisions. Party organizations at all levels and each and every Communist Party member must uphold party spirit and wage an unremitting struggle to root out factionalism. Severe disciplinary actions must be taken against those who cling to factionalism and refuse to mend their ways after repeated education. Such people must not be allowed to join leading bodies and those in leading positions must be replaced.

In handling the inner-party relations, the party's cadres—the leading cadres in particular—must adhere to the principle that it is "our practice to avoid exclusiveness." That is to say that we must unite with all the comrades who are loyal to the interests of the party and unite with the majority. A communist should have the communist trait of great broadmindedness, being strict with himself and broadminded with others. In handling interrelations among comrades, we should judge a person only as to whether or not he resolutely implements the party's line and observes party discipline.

We must not always feel sick at heart because of personal grudges and try to push him aside and strike at others. We should not treat a person differently on the basis of different personal relations. We must absolutely ban factionalist activities and the practice of forming small coteries. We must not allow ourselves to draw some people in while pushing others out and build up some people while suppressing others. We must not squabble endlessly over past grudges.

On the relations between the party and the masses, we must guard against and oppose the sectarianist trend in the same manner. Communists are a minority among the masses. It is necessary to rally hundreds of millions of the masses around the party and work with one heart and one mind for the realization of the four modernizations. A communist must play an exemplary role among the masses, be the first to bear hardships and the last to enjoy comforts, and enthusiastically unite with those comrades who are not affiliated with the party to carry out work together.

In doing work with regard to cadres, we must be honest and upright in our ways and persevere in appointing people on their merits and oppose the practice of appointing people by favoritism. It is strictly forbidden to practice factionalism and draw a demarcation line between one group and another and to make use of one's position and authority to establish personal influence within the party. A communist should be loyal to the party organizations and to the party's principles and should not pledge loyalty to a certain individual. Nobody should regard cadres of the party as his personal property. Nor should he turn the relationships between cadres of the higher level and those of the lower level into relationships of personal dependence.

5. SPEAK THE TRUTH AND MATCH WORDS WITH DEEDS

To be loyal to the cause of the party and the people; to be honest in thought, word and deed; to be open and aboveboard; and to think and act in one and the same way are qualities that a communist must possess. The comrades throughout the party must strive to eradicate the unhealthy trend of telling lies created during the period when Lin Biao and the "gang of four" held sway, and restore and bring into full play the fine work style of telling the truth, refusing to tell lies and matching words with deeds—a style of work always recommended by the party. A communist must be faithful and candid and never hide his own mistakes and his own thinking and views from the party organizations. He should speak frankly and sincerely in dealing with people and things. He must put on the table whatever opinion or criticism he has. He should not keep quiet during a meeting while making irresponsible remarks after the meeting. He must not act in one way to one's face, while acting in another way behind one's back. He must not say yes and mean no, and he must not comply in public but oppose in private.

It is essential to resolutely oppose the work style of a bureaucratic politician and the philistine practice of resorting to boasting, flattery and touting; of talking about and doing things on the basis of hints given by the leadership; of bartering away principles; of securing personal gain by fraud; and of asking the party for honor and position. A communist must respect facts and truthfully reflect the situation according to the true features of things at any time and in any place and in dealing with himself and others. He should not provide whatever the leadership needs and report only the good news, but not the bad. Still less should he resort to deception to win confidence, honor and rewards by fraud. A communist is not allowed to abet, suggest, induce, order or force his subordinates to tell lies for any reason or under any pretext.

Disciplinary actions of the party must be taken against those who practice fraud and create serious losses to the party and the people, those who have won honor and position by telling lies, those who tell lies to cover up their grave mistakes or achieve other individual goals and those who abet or induce their subordinates to tell lies. Those who are not afraid of retaliation and dare to speak the truth for the sake of safeguarding the interests of the party and the people should be commended. The party's leading organs and leading cadres at all levels must play their exemplary role well in seeking truth from facts. In carrying out our work, we must listen to different views and understand both achievements and shortcomings. We must encourage the comrades at the lower level to say what they have on their minds and reflect the true situation. We must strive to create and maintain the atmosphere of letting people air their views face to face, including sharp views, and unhurriedly discuss those views.

6. PROMOTE INNER-PARTY DEMOCRACY AND TAKE A CORRECT ATTITUDE TOWARD DISSENTING VIEWS

To promote inner-party democracy, we must, first of all, allow party members to express different views, fully discuss the issues and make a reality of the maxim: Say all you know and say it without reserve. Those who made wrong remarks or wrote erroneous articles owing to their wrong understanding should not be regarded as violating party discipline, and disciplinary actions should not be taken against them as long as they do not oppose the party's basic political stand; intrigue and conspire; carry out factionalist and splittist activities among the masses; spread among the masses the fallacies that run counter to the party's line, principles and policies; and betray the secrets of the party and the state. It is necessary to strictly uphold the principle of "three nots"—not seizing on others' faults, not putting labels on people and not using the big stick. The so-called principle of not seizing on others' faults, not putting labels on people and not using the big stick is aimed at forbidding any practice of exaggerating a person's errors at will, using such errors as criminal evidence to cook up charges, and striking at and even persecuting an individual politically and organizationally.

The patriarchal behaviour of a number of leading cadres must be corrected. Such cadres lack the democratic spirit, turn a deaf ear to criticism or even suppress it. Criticism and suggestions put forward by any party member should be accepted as long as they are correct ones. If such criticism and suggestions are indeed mistaken, they should be pointed out by seeking truth from facts. It is impermissible to trace and investigate the so-called motive and background. Attention must be paid to distinguishing among the following: To oppose the opinion of a certain comrade is not equivalent to opposing this comrade and to oppose a certain comrade of a certain leading organ is not the same as opposing this organ. It is not equivalent to opposing the leadership. Still less should it be interpreted as opposing the party.

Leading cadres who make use of their position and power for retaliation or who bring false charges against comrades because of personal grudges, adopt measures such as "making things tough for them" and "filling them with data," and punish these comrades for "opposing the party," "opposing the leadership," "launching vicious attacks" and "committing errors in political line" are acting in violation of the inner-party democratic system and revolutionary ethics and qualities. Those who make false charges of committing counterrevolutionary crimes against comrades who dare to uphold truth, those who wantonly adopt the measures of dictatorship and those who carry out ruthless persecution are committing serious crimes against the law. They must be severely punished in accordance with party discipline and state laws.

It is not abnormal for there to be different ideological and theoretical views and disputes within the party. The only way to settle an ideological or theoretical dispute is to present facts and reason things out, hold democratic discussions and not take coercive measures. Disputes over some ideological theories cannot be solved within a short period of time. Hasty conclusions should not be made in such debates, unless on realistic and urgent problems of significant political nature. Further studies should be made later and solutions should be worked out through practice. To arbitrarily put such political labels as "pulling down the banner," "poisonous weeds," "bourgeoisie," and "revisionism" on problems concerning ideology and understanding and to arbitrarily title problems which arise between ourselves and enemies as political will not only undermine the correct inner-party political life but cause ossification of thinking. Those ambitious people who oppose the party may easily take advantage of these labels to undermine the democratic order of a socialist country. Such a practice should be checked.

7. PROTECT THE RIGHTS OF PARTY MEMBERS AGAINST ANY ENCROACHMENT

Party organizations at all levels must protect various rights of party members in an effective way. Any encroachment on the rights of party members constitutes a serious violation of party discipline. Party members have the right to participate in discussion on formulating or implementing party policies either at party meetings or in the papers published by the party. They have the right to criticize any party organization or any individual at the party meetings. Those party members who have different opinions regarding party principles, policies or resolutions may make reports, either orally or in written form, to party organizations at all levels up to the Central Committee. Party organizations should welcome criticism and suggestions from the masses of party members and encourage them to express their creative opinions and propositions on promoting the cause of socialism.

Party members have the right to propose that those cadres who refuse to correct their serious mistakes or who are incompetent be recalled or transferred. Party members have the right to present their statements, appeals, accusations and defense on the party organizations' manner of handling them or other persons at party meetings or to higher organizations up to the party Central Committee. Regarding the party members' statements, appeals, accusations and defense, party organizations must process them or pass them on in due time and must not withhold them, and those responsible must not shift their responsibility onto others. The letters of appeals and accusations should not be turned over to the accused and be handled by them. Retaliation against the appealing party and the accusers is not allowed. The accusers and the accused are not allowed to frame up charges against others, and those who do will be seriously handled according to party discipline and state law.

Party members must be informed of a party organization's appraisal, conclusion and decision on disciplinary action for them. Except for certain cases, the party member concerned must be notified to be present at the meeting while the decision on disciplinary action against him is being adopted. The party organization must earnestly listen to and consider his opinion. If he holds a different opinion, it should file the organization's decision along with his opinion to the higher authorities for determination.

8. ELECTIONS SHOULD FULLY EMBODY THE ELECTORS' WISHES

Only when there are genuine democratic elections within the party can prestigious and strong leading groups be established among the party members and the masses. Party organizations at all levels must convene general membership meetings and party congresses at regular intervals in accordance with the regulations of the party constitution.

Party committees at various levels must be reelected according to schedule. At each session a certain number of delegates and members should be reelected. Elections should give full play to democracy and genuinely reflect the electors' wishes. Namelists of the candidates should be presented after full consultations and discussions among the party members or delegates. In elections, the number of candidates shall be greater than the number of delegates to be elected. This election method may also be used to produce candidates in preelections, which precede formal elections. This method of election and preelections can be skipped in units which have a small number of party members. The electors should be clearly informed of the basic status of the candidates. All elections shall be held by secret ballot.

The electors must pay attention to electing to leading groups those cadres who resolutely support and implement the party's political and ideological lines, who are perfectly impartial, who strictly observe law and discipline, who uphold the party spirit, who have a strong sense of the revolutionary cause and political responsibility and who are professionally knowledgeable and capable. The electors should pay particular attention to electing middle-aged and young cadres who meet the above requirements.

There should be no regulations stipulating who should or should not be elected. Even individuals whose cases are special and who need the recommendation of party organizations to be elected must also be truly approved by the majority of electors. Infringement of the party members' right of election and acts which make the elections a mere formality and which keep the electors from expressing their wishes must be resolutely opposed and guarded against. When the various party congresses are not in session, the higher party committees may appoint, dismiss and transfer the responsible persons of the lower party committees when necessary. With the approval of the higher party organizations, elections can be tentatively postponed in those units which must be consolidated and which do not yet have the conditions for a democratic election, and their leaders will be appointed by the higher authorities.

9. STRUGGLE AGAINST ERRONEOUS TENDENCIES, BAD PEOPLE AND BAD ACTIONS

It is imperative to struggle against erroneous tendencies, bad people and bad actions to straighten out the party's work style, consolidate the dictatorship of the proletariat, promote a fine social custom and unite all the people to dedicate heart and soul to the four modernizations. Party organizations at all levels must give full play to the role of being the fighting fortresses and lead the party members and the masses to resolutely expose and strike at the counterrevolutionaries, embezzlers, thieves, criminals and serious violators of law and discipline. Factionalism, anarchism, ultraindividualism, bureaucracy, seeking privileges and other erroneous tendencies must be solemnly criticized and denounced. The unhealthy trends and evil practices and the erroneous and reactionary ideas in society must be criticized and denounced.

If Communist Party members assume a liberal attitude of being worldly wise and playing safe toward the erroneous tendencies, bad people and bad actions, and avoid them instead of stopping, contesting and denouncing them, then they have shirked their fighting responsibility and have demonstrated a lack of party spirit. In struggling against the erroneous tendencies, bad people and bad actions, the Communist Party members, particularly the leading cadres at all levels, must have a dauntless revolutionary spirit, dare to step out, have no fear of offending people and expressing their true feelings, and have no fear of retaliation and persecution. Only thus can they combat and rectify the erroneous tendencies, rescue those who have committed mistakes and punish the bad people according to what they deserve.

10. TREAT COMRADES WHO HAVE MADE MISTAKES CORRECTLY

In carrying out inner-party struggle, our party's fine tradition is to follow the principle of "learning from past mistakes to avoid future ones and curing the sickness to save the patient" and the principle of "unity-criticism-unity," because this helps us to achieve the dual purpose of uniting our comrades and clarifying their thinking. For those comrades who have erred, we must historically and comprehensively evaluate their contributions, mistakes, rights and wrongs, and must not totally repudiate their contributions just because of a mistake; nor should we continue quibbling over old problems and mistakes that have already been investigated and corrected. We must, on the basis of having clarified the facts, specifically analyze the nature and seriousness of their mistakes and in a comradely manner, warmly help them understand why they made the mistakes, point out how to correct these mistakes and enlighten them to make necessary self-criticism. We must believe that most of the comrades who have erred are willing to correct their mistakes, so we must give them the assistance they need to correct their mistakes and continue to work for the party.

In analyzing a comrade's mistakes, we must first strictly distinguish the two types of contradictions. This means that we should not interpret the common errors in work or mistakes in thinking and understanding as political mistakes; neither should we interpret the general political mistakes as mistakes concerning the political line, nor mix up the mistakes concerning the political line, which still belong to the question of inner-party struggle, with the counterrevolutionary issue of attempting to subvert the party and the socialist state.

The contradictions between the conspirators, careerists and counterrevolutionary double-dealers, who attempt to subvert the party and the socialist state, and the party and the people are contradictions between the enemy and ourselves. The number of such people is extremely small. We must distinguish between those who have followed the higher authorities and principal leaders and have committed mistakes concerning the political line and those who have participated in the conspiracy of usurping party and state power.

In carrying out inner-party struggle, ruthless struggle and merciless blows are impermissible. Although criticism of those comrades who have erred is entirely necessary, methods which arouse the masses to besiege them, forbid them to explain and forbid other comrades to hold "public accusation meetings" to express different opinions should not be adopted, because such methods in fact suppress people by force and do not convince people through reasoning. Within the party, acts of handling party members with anything more than party discipline and acts of violating state law are not allowed. The feudalistic and fascist method employed by Lin Biao and the "gang of four" to settle inner-party issues must by all means be prohibited. The so-called "drag out and struggle against" is strictly forbidden, as is physical humiliation and persecution and inducing and coercing a person to make a confession.

The handling of people must be very scrupulous. If contradictions between the enemy and ourselves and contradictions among the people cannot be immediately distinguished, such contradictions should first be handled as contradictions among the people. Particular caution must be exercised in handling the contradictions between the enemy and ourselves and in handling matters which concern expulsion from the party, which must be handled by judicial organs. Under no circumstances should innocent family members, relatives and friends be implicated. All frame-ups and false and erroneous cases that occurred after the founding of the country—no matter which organization or which leader made a decision on and approved them—must be corrected in the spirit of seeking truth from facts, for all false accusations must be overturned.

Those comrades who have committed mistakes should sincerely accept criticism, education and disciplinary action given by party organizations and fellow comrades. They should draw lessons from their mistakes, correct them earnestly and work for the party in a still better way. For those who have committed mistakes, but refuse to admit them and keep on causing trouble, the punishment should be even harsher.

11. ACCEPT SUPERVISION BY THE PARTY AND THE MASSES; NO ONE IS ALLOWED TO SEEK PRIVILEGES

Leading cadres at all levels are public servants. They have the obligation of serving the people diligently and sincerely, but not the right to seek privileges in livelihood. Although it is necessary to provide leaders with certain rational conveniences and insure their security according to the necessity of work, violating the system to seek special privileges is by no means permissible. In our country, there are only differences in the division of work and there is no such thing as one who is higher and more noble than anyone else. No one is an inferior slave or of superior nobility. The idea that one who has power will not be restricted in any

way is the idea of craving for the corrupted and feudalistic privileges, and such an idea must be denounced and corrected. Communist Party members and cadres must regard seeking privileges and private interests as the most shameful thing to do.

It is essential to uphold the principle that everyone stands equal before truth and everyone stands equal before party discipline and state laws. Party members who do not keep themselves within the bounds of party discipline and state laws and place themselves above party organizations are absolutely not allowed to exist within the party. Communist Party members are absolutely not allowed to seek private interests by utilizing their authority.

Leading cadres are not allowed to exceed the limits of authority bestowed on them by party organizations to violate the limits of authority of the collective and other individuals. All the party members are comrades and comrades-in-arms on an equal footing. The party's leading cadres should treat others as equals, and should not take for granted that others will follow their words whether they are correct or not, nor should they put on bureaucratic airs and frequently give people a dressing down and swear at them. If the shortcomings and mistakes of the upper-level leading personnel create problems in lower-level work, the upper-level personnel must take the initiative in shouldering the responsibility for lower-level personnel by first undergoing self-criticism themselves.

Leading cadres at all levels should maintain and develop our party's glorious tradition of hard struggle and share weal and woe with the masses. The bad tendency of some leading cadres to seek special treatment for themselves and their family must be overcome. Leading personnel are prohibited from wantonly approving the use of funds and materials in violation of financial and economic discipline. They are prohibited from using their position and power to seek preference for their family or relatives in such matters as enrollment in schools, transferring from one school to another, promotions, employment and going abroad. It is prohibited to use public funds for giving banquets, sending gifts in violation of rules and regulations, and building private houses for leading personnel in violation of rules and regulations. It is also prohibited to mix public and private interests, use public service for private gain, and appropriate and squander state and collective property under any pretext or by any means.

The party's leading personnel at various levels must consciously and strictly abide by the stipulations on livelihood and wages and conduct intensified education among their children at the same time. Disciplinary action by the party must be taken against those who violate related stipulations but still do not correct themselves after receiving criticism and education.

No leading cadre is permitted to violate the party's norms for the selection of cadres and organizational principles by promoting his family members or relatives to leading positions. He must not allow them to overstep their authority and meddle in party and state affairs, nor should he place them in key posts that are associated with him.

To maintain the intimate relations between the party and the broad masses of the people and to prevent the party's leading cadres and party members from converting themselves from public servants of the people into bureaucrats riding roughshod over the people, it is essential to adopt the method of achieving integration from lower to higher levels and from higher to lower levels as well as between those inside and outside the party, and to strengthen the supervision of party organizations and masses over the party's leading cadres and party members. They must be supervised in such matters as whether they are conscientiously studying and implementing the line, principles and policies laid down by the party; whether they are abiding by party discipline and state laws; whether they are upholding the party's fine tradition and work style; whether they are seeking special privileges; whether they have played an exemplary role in relation to production, work, study and struggle against the enemy; and whether they have maintained close relationships with the masses and serve the interests of the people. It is essential to commend those comrades who, with higher conscientiousness and stronger party spirit, have performed their duties well and criticize and educate the comrades who have achieved less results in performing their duties.

It is essential to establish and perfect, on the basis of fully following the mass line, a complete system for the examination, review, award and punishment, rotation, retirement and dismissal of cadres and, by enforcing this system, to clearly register a person's contributions and faults, to fairly mete out rewards and punishments and to encourage the advanced and urge on those who are backward.

Leading cadres at all levels should periodically solicit views and comments from party members and people in their unity. Party organizations at all levels should value the people's criticism and views of the leading cadres and party members which are expressed in their visits or letters. Party organizations should report, after verification, the comments, criticisms and views of party members and people to the party committee of the higher level to be used as an important basis for the review of cadres. Every party member, regardless of position, shall be put in a party organization to take part in organizational life. Party committees or their standing committees at all levels should periodically hold a democratic life meeting to exchange ideas and to conduct criticism and self-criticism.

12. STUDY HARD AND STRIVE TO BE RED AND EXPERT

The arduous task of the four modernizations demands the training and bringing up of a magnificent contingent of cadres who uphold the socialist road and possess professional knowledge. It demands, at the same time, the bold promotion to leading posts of middle-aged and young cadres (including party members and nonmembers) who meet this requirement in order to give full play to their strong points and to amend their weak points in the course of work. This is an urgent and important political task confronting the whole party. A communist must be a vanguard fighter for the realization of the four modernizations and must strive to become both Red and expert. "Red" means the possession of a firm, correct political orientation and the upholding of the four fundamental principles. "Expert" means to learn and master a professional understanding of modernization and to become a professional and good at one's work. To become expert does not nec-

essarily mean one has become Red, but to become Red one must be expert. If a communist does not seriously learn his professional affairs but rests content with being a layman in his field indefinitely, then his so-called "political consciousness" and "advanced feature" become nothing but empty talk.

To improve and strengthen the party's leadership over modernization, it is essential to greatly raise the cultural, scientific and technological and vocational levels of the whole party. All communists—especially leading cadres at various levels—must tenaciously and arduously learn and master professional affairs with a high revolutionary, enterprising spirit and become experts in their fields. They must be proficient at whatever they do. To be content with exercising vague leadership in general terms, to be satisfied with being laymen indefinitely, to be ignorant and incompetent, to act in contradiction with objective laws or to give arbitrary and impracticable directions will undoubtedly seriously harm modernization. Persons who act like this should be removed from leading posts, if they cannot correct themselves through criticism and education.

A communist must be strict with himself, use the standard of a proletarian vanguard fighter, strive to study and grasp Marxism-Leninism-Mao Zedong Thought and continuously raise his awareness and the skills for modernization in order to make greater contributions to the four modernizations.

Certain party members and leading cadres, with the waning of their revolutionary will, are not studying hard or working enthusiastically and are unable to play a vanguard and exemplary role in production, work, study and the struggle against the enemy. Their behavior is not worthy of the honorable name of a communist and is harmful to the party's prestige among the people. Such comrades must be given a rigorous education and criticism. They should be persuaded to withdraw from the party, if they fail to correct themselves after a long period of education and, therefore, are disqualified as communists.

The "guiding principles for inner-party political life" is an important party regulation. All party members must seriously study and consciously observe these principles. They should earnestly examine their work and conduct in the light of the guiding principles. Leading organizations or bodies at all levels must take the lead in adhering to the guiding principles. Any party member who violates these guiding principles should be criticized and educated and, in serious cases, punished according to party discipline, up to expulsion from the party.

Party committees and discipline inspection commissions at all levels should periodically check up on the observance of these guiding principles. The discipline inspection commissions shall report the progress to the party congress or party committees at their respective levels. All party comrades must enhance their revolutionary vigor, eliminate the pernicious influence of Lin Biao and the "gang of four" and remove all kinds of interference and obstacles to insure the adherence of party regulations and rules and the improvement of party style—a task that has a vital bearing on the success of the four modernizations and the future of the party and country—so that our party can become a vanguard organization of the proletariat with greater unity and vitality and a higher fighting capacity.

26

Draft of the Revised Party Constitution, April 1980

It was virtually inevitable that the first Party Congress under Deng Xiaoping should be asked to approve a new Party constitution. (For comments on the differences between this draft and the final version, see Doc. 32.) By stressing discipline, the constitution makes it somewhat easier to deny admission or to expel individuals suspected of being opposed to Deng's leadership and/or policies.

General Program

The Chinese Communist Party is the advance force of the Chinese working classes; it is the core of leadership for all China's socialist undertakings, and it is the true representative of the interests of the people of all nationalities in China.

The CCP takes Marxism-Leninism and Mao Zedong Thought as the guiding principles for its actions.

Using the methods of dialectical materialism and historical materialism, established by themselves, Marx and Engels analyzed the rules governing the development of the capitalist economy, and pointed out that, having undergone the revolutionary struggle of the proletariat, having passed through the dictatorship of the proletariat, the capitalist society must, of necessity, be transformed into a socialist society where the means of production are publicly owned, where exploitation has been eliminated, and where there is a system of distribution according to labor. They further pointed out that, having undergone a vast development in the forces of production and a vast advance in politics and culture, this socialist society must necessarily and finally develop into a communist society where all distinctions of class have been abolished, and a state where each contributes according to his ability, and each takes what he needs, has become a reality. At the beginning of the 20th century, Lenin pointed out that, since capitalism had already developed to the imperialist stage, the liberation struggle of the proletariat should be united with the liberation struggle of the oppressed peoples of the world, and that socialism might first win victories by attacking the weak links in the rule of imperialism. After the First and Second World Wars, the socialist system was established and developed in several countries, proving the truth of the scientific Marxist-Leninist theory of socialism.

Although the history of the socialist system is not very long, it is inevitable that some complicated twists and turns have occurred in the process of its development. Basically speaking, only when a socialist system exists is it possible to grasp the insurmountable contradictions inherent in the capitalist system; only then is it possible to bring about the unanimity of the fundamental interests of the whole body of the people; only then can the enthusiasm and creativity of the working people be given full play, and the socialist forces of production developed rapidly and in a planned way, in order to satisfy the daily increasing requirements of the material and cultural life of the members of society. Socialism is advancing at this very moment and must gradually attain final victory throughout the whole world, by the peoples of each country of their own free will following the path chosen, the path which is most suitable for the special features of each particular country.

Mao Zedong Thought represents the application and development of Marxism-Leninism within the context of the Chinese revolution; it constitutes the product of the integration of the universal truth of Marxism-Leninism with the concrete practice of the revolution in China, and it is the crystallization of the collective wisdom of the CCP. The CCP and Comrade Mao Zedong led the people of all nationalities throughout the country to victory in the new democratic revolution, through protracted revolutionary struggles against imperialism, feudalism and bureaucratic capitalism, establishing the People's Republic of China, a state of the dictatorship of the proletariat. After the establishment of the PRC, moreover, they successfully carried out socialist reconstruction, using methods suited to conditions in China. They introduced the systems of socialist public ownership and distribution according to labor, developed the socialist economy, and set up the basis for industrialization.

China has now entered a new stage in its historical development. Excluding Taiwan and other such areas, landlords, rich peasants and capitalists no longer exist as classes. Because of elements left over by history, and the influence of the international environment, class struggle still exists within a limited scope, but the large-scale tempestuous class struggle of the masses is now a part of history. The development of China's productive forces is still at a very low level, material goods are still not plentiful, and education, science and culture are by no means advanced, and will not be able to satisfy the needs of the people for many years to come. Our party must lead the people of all nationalities of the whole country, bringing into play the pioneering spirit of bitter struggle, to resolutely bring about modernization in the fields of

---

[Hong Kong *Chan Wang*, October 1980.]

agriculture, industry, national defense and science and technology. At the same time as establishing a high level of material civilization, our party must set up a high-level civilization in the spirit of socialism, and, while improving and perfecting the socialist economic system, improve and perfect the socialist political system.

In order to ensure the successful establishment of socialist modernization, the CCP upholds the dictatorship of the proletariat within the political life of the country. It is essential to fully realize socialist democracy, to perfect the socialist legal system, to rigorously distinguish and correctly deal with contradictions among the people and between ourselves and the enemy, to attack, and also to reform, counter-revolutionary elements and other criminal elements who carry out disruptive activities, and to consolidate and develop unified security and a lively and vigorous political situation. It is essential to unite with the working people, peasants and intellectuals of every nationality throughout the country, to unite with all democratic political parties and with the patriotic forces of all nationalities, and to steadily develop and strengthen the most extensive united front of the entire body of socialist workers, patriots supporting socialism, and patriots backing the unity of the motherland. It is essential to accomplish the great task of returning Taiwan to the motherland and completing the unification of the motherland. It is essential to strengthen national defense, so as to be ready at all times to resist attack and wipe out any invaders.

At present, the overall duties of the CCP are: to unite the peoples of all nationalities throughout the country, with hearts and minds dedicated to the same cause, in a planned and properly proportioned manner; to develop the socialist economy in such a way as to achieve greater, faster, better and more economical results; and to build up a powerful, modernized, socialist country with a high level of democracy and a high level of culture. The party's ultimate goal is the establishment of communism.

The CCP's basic standpoint on international affairs is as follows: it upholds proletarian internationalism; it upholds the solidarity of the whole world's proletariat with oppressed nationalities and oppressed peoples, and is united in opposition against imperialism, colonialism and racialism, striving for the advancement of humanity; in common with all countries which oppose hegemonism and military intimidation, it supports the cause of world peace and national sovereignty. On the basis of the five-point principle of mutual respect for each other's rights and territorial integrity, mutual abstention from violation of each other's sovereignty, noninterference in each other's internal affairs, equality and mutual benefit, and peaceful coexistence, the CCP advocates that China maintain and develop friendly relations with all countries, to promote economic, technological, scientific and cultural exchanges.

The CCP's leadership of the dictatorship of the proletariat and of socialist undertakings in China has taken shape over a period of 60 years of struggle. The party is inseparable from the people, and the people are inseparable from the party. Only under the party's leadership is it possible to mold the forces of the people in their hundreds of millions into a united and organized fighting force struggling in the great cause of socialism. Strengthening the party ideologically and organizationally and raising the party's fighting capacity is a basic guarantee of achieving victory in the country's task of socialist modernization, as well as a basic guarantee of realizing the unification of the motherland and the defense of China's independence and security.

Important points where the CCP differs from other political parties and organizations are:

First, the entire party insists on a high level of ideological unanimity; it adheres to the socialist road, upholds the dictatorship of the proletariat, the party leadership, and Marxism-Leninism and Mao Zedong Thought. The party must completely and correctly understand, and apply, the scientific theories of Marxism-Leninism and Mao Zedong Thought; setting out from a completely practical basis, integrating theory with practice, seeking truth from facts, through the truth of practical experience and the truth of development, by continually summing up historical experience, and by carefully investigating and studying the present situation, the party must scientifically resolve all new problems arising from domestic and international affairs. The party is opposed to revisionism, dogmatism, idealism and metaphysics.

Second, apart from seeking the widest interests of the broad masses of the people, the party has no special interests of its own. The party forever shares all the comforts and hardships of the masses of the people and maintains the closest links with them; it upholds the democratic rights of the people, and does not permit any party member to stand above the masses. In its own activities, the party works purely for the masses, and relies completely on the masses. The party must consolidate the wisdom of the masses and organize the masses so as to strive to realize and maintain its own interests. All correct suggestions pertaining to the masses must be guided toward vigorous fulfillment, whereas incorrect opinions concerning the masses must be rectified through education; moreover, the party is opposed to commandism, as well as tailism. These, then, are the basic points of the party's mass line.

Third, the party has a strict organization and discipline; it practices a high degree of centralism, on the basis of fully encouraging democracy, thus ensuring unanimity of action, and guaranteeing that the party's decisions will be carried out to the letter, both quickly and effectively. Within its own political life, the party must regularly carry out conscientious, and not perfunctory, criticism and self-criticism, and must constantly overcome weaknesses and correct its mistakes. The party must not only regularly carry on ideological education directed at the people, and lead the people of the entire country in opposing all hostile forces harmful to the interests of the people; it must also expel all those elements within the party who persist in opposing, corrupting or harming the party, so that the party's own purity and its fighting capacity may be maintained.

On the basis of these three important features the party's three great styles of working are formed: seeking truth from facts, the mass line, and criticism and self-criticism. If the party is to accomplish the gigantic aim of realizing socialist modernization, it must steadfastly uphold these important features, vigorously encourage the three great work styles which embody these special features and encourage all the fine traditions which have been formed through protracted struggle.

In order to accomplish the party's fighting tasks, the

leadership organization of the party must, in accordance with objective laws and actual conditions, formulate and put into operation the correct line, correct guiding principles, policies and all kinds of significant measures, thus bringing to fruition the party's work of organization and propaganda education. It must require the entire membership of the party, each mobilizing his own consciousness, discipline and spirit of self-sacrifice, to give free rein to their role as a mainstay and as an exemplary vanguard in every aspect of political and social life. The party must ensure the ability of the legislative, judiciary and administrative organs, of economic and cultural organizations, and of people's organizations to work on their own positive initiative with independent responsibility and complete coordination.

The party must educate its members, so they always remember that they constitute only a very small proportion of the population of the entire country, that, irrespective of time or place, they must closely cooperate with the broad masses of the people, and with persons from all walks of life outside the party, thus enabling all patriots to bring their ingenuity and wisdom into full play, to carry out work of a positive, creative nature, and to join together in making our great motherland daily more prosperous and powerful, thereby ultimately bringing communism into being.

CHAPTER I: PARTY MEMBERSHIP

Article 1. Any Chinese worker, peasant, soldier, intellectual or other revolutionary element, who has reached the age of 18, may become a member of the CCP provided he supports the party's general program and accepts the party constitution, and is willing to join a party organization and work actively in it, carry out the party's decisions and pay membership fees punctually.

Article 2. The members of the CCP are the pioneer fighters of the Chinese working class, who possess revolutionary consciousness and awareness, and who conform to revolutionary discipline.

Communist Party members must not hesitate to give their all, fighting to the end of their lives to bring communism into being.

Members of the CCP in positions of power remain ordinary working people. All Communist Party members must serve the people wholeheartedly; they must all strive to set an example to the people, and to receive the trust of the people, they must on no account seek any private gain outside the stipulations of the system; nor must they on any account seek any privileges outside the limits of their official powers.

Article 3. Besides adhering to the conditions stipulated in articles 1 and 2 of this constitution, party members must discharge the following obligations:

1.   Conscientiously study Marxism-Leninism-Mao Zedong Thought, study the party's line, guiding principles, policies and resolutions, study science and culture, technical skills and professional knowledge.

2.   Support the interests of the party and the people

above all else, subordinating individual interests to those of the party and the people; be the first to bear hardships and the last to enjoy comforts; distinguish clearly between public and private interests; work selflessly for the public good; never, on any account, use public office for private gain, seek private gain at public expense, or run a business for private profit.

3.   Be undaunted by repeated setbacks in carrying out the party line, its guiding principles, policies and decisions; strictly observe party discipline and the laws of the state; strictly guard party and state secrets, and uphold and protect the interests of the party and the state.

4.   Uphold the solidarity and unity of the party, be resolute in eliminating factionalism; oppose the activities of all factional organizations and cliques, and oppose all double-dealing behavior of those who feign compliance with party rules, as well as all scheming and intrigues.

5.   Be truthful and honest to the party; be as good as your word; do not conceal your own views; do not distort the facts and the truth; conscientiously practice criticism and self-criticism; have the courage to expose and correct weaknesses and errors at work, and have the courage to support good people and good deeds, and to oppose evil people and evil deeds.

6.   Maintain close links with the masses; consult with the masses when matters arise; uphold the rights and interests of the masses; respect the specialized knowledge and rational proposals of the masses; listen to the suggestions and requirements of the masses with an open mind, and promptly report them to the party.

7.   Play an exemplary vanguard role in production work and in all social activities; work selflessly; have the courage to make innovations; uphold the revolutionary order; comply with communist moral principles, and take the lead in setting up new socialist customs.

8.   In the struggle to defend the motherland and to safeguard the people's interests, and in all times of difficulty and danger, they must possess the spirit of, first, not fearing hardships and, second, not fearing death; they must be the first to attack and the last to yield, and they must step forward bravely, steadfast to the end.

If a party member fails to carry out these duties, he should be criticized and educated, and, in serious cases, disciplinary action should be taken against him.

Article 4. Party members enjoy the following rights:

1.   The right to attend relevant meetings of the party, to read relevant party documents, and to receive the party's training and instruction.

2.   The right to participate in discussions, at party meetings and in party newspapers and periodicals, concerning the formulation and implementation of party policies.

3. The right to put forward proposals and recommendations as to the work of the party, and to give free rein to initiative in their work.

4. The right, at party meetings, to criticize any party organization, member or leading cadres; the right to expose, in a responsible manner, any party member to the party organization, to provide information about his offenses to the organization, and to demand his punishment, and the right to demand the punishment, recall or replacement of leading cadres who violate the law and discipline, or who are incompetent.

5. The right, within the party, to elect, to be elected, and to vote.

6. When a party organization is discussing the punishment according to party discipline or the judgment of a party member, that member has the right to participate in the discussion and to defend himself, and other comrades are permitted to testify in his favor and to speak in his defense.

7. The right to continue to hold a contrary opinion concerning resolutions and policies of the party, even when those resolutions and policies have been put into execution, and the right of being permitted to communicate one's personal opinion to party organizations at all levels, right up to the Central Committee.

8. The right to submit questions, requests, declarations, appeals and complaints to party organizations at any level, up to the party Central Committee, and the right to demand that the relevant organization provide a responsible reply without delay.

No party organization at whatever level, right up to organizations of the party Central Committee, has the power to deprive party members of the above rights.

If the above-mentioned rights of party members are not respected by responsible persons of party organizations, or by any other party members, then these persons should be subjected to disciplinary action.

Article 5. In expanding the membership of the party, the principle of individual admission must be adhered to. It is not permitted to bring into the party, by any means, persons who do not conform to the conditions of membership of the party; nor is it permitted, on any pretext, to refuse admission to those who genuinely do conform to the conditions of membership of the party.

Applications for party membership must fill in an application form for party membership, and must be recommended by two full party members.

Those persons who recommend an applicant must be fully aware of his or her ideological background, character and experience; they must explain to him or her the party's general program and the party constitution, meticulously explain the rights and duties of party members, and help him or her to gain the determination to struggle to the end of their days for the communist cause. When those recommending a person believe that he or she conforms to the conditions of admission to the party, then they should make a responsible report to the party organization.

A party branch committee must extensively seek the opinions of the masses, inside and outside the party, about an applicant for party membership, and only when the applicant's standard has been reviewed, when his or her case has been submitted for discussion by a general membership meeting of the party branch committee, and reported to the next higher party organization for approval, may the applicant be admitted as a probationary member of the party.

Before approving the admission of an applicant for party membership, the higher party organization must appoint someone to talk with the applicant, in order to gain further knowledge of the applicant and also to increase his or her understanding of the party.

In special cases, the party committees at or above the level of provinces, municipalities and autonomous regions have the power to grant membership directly.

Article 6. On the occasion of his or her first attendance at a party meeting, a probationary member must take the oath of admission to the party. This oath is as follows: In applying to join the Chinese Communist Party, I will uphold the general program of the party, fulfill the duties of a party member, carry out the party's resolutions, submit to party discipline, deep party secrets, be loyal to and honest with the party, accept the job assigned to me by the organization, work enthusiastically and responsibly, fight for communism to the end of my days, be prepared to sacrifice everything for the party and the people, and I will never betray the party.

Article 7. The probationary period for a probationary member is 1 year. The party organization should make further efforts to educate and observe him or her.

The duties of a probationary member are the same as those of a full member of the party. The rights of a probationary member, with the exception of the rights of election, being elected, and voting, are also the same as those of a full member of the party.

When the probationary period has expired, the party branch must promptly discuss whether the probationary member is qualified for full membership. If he or she has conscientiously fulfilled the duties of a party member, and is qualified for party membership, he or she should be given full membership as scheduled. If it is necessary to continue to observe and educate him or her, the probationary period may be extended, but by no more than 1 year. If he or she has not fulfilled the duties of a party member, or if he or she is found to be really unfit for party membership, his or her status as a probationary member should be annulled. Any decision to transfer a probationary member to full party membership, to prolong the probationary period, or to annul his or her status as a probationary member must be adopted by the general membership meeting of the party branch, and approved by the next higher organization.

The probationary period of a probationary member begins from the day when the general membership meeting approves his or her admission to the party. The party standing of a party member begins from the day when he or she is transferred to full membership.

Article 8. Whether his or her duties are at a high or a low level, every party member must belong to a party branch or group, must participate in the organized life of the party, and put himself or herself under the surveillance of the masses both inside and outside the party. The existence of privileged party members who do not participate in the organized life of the party, and who do not put themselves under the surveillance of the masses both inside and outside the party, is not permitted.

Article 9. Party members have the freedom to resign from the party. On the resignation of a party member, the removal of his name from the records should be discussed and approved by the general membership meeting of the party branch and reported to the next higher party organization for the record.

A party member whose revolutionary will has degenerated, who refuses to carry out his duties as a party member, and who no longer conforms to the conditions for party membership, remaining unchanged despite repeated education, should be persuaded to withdraw from the party. If a party member is to be persuaded to withdraw, the case must be decided by the general membership meeting of the party branch, and submitted to the next higher party organization for approval. If the person concerned persists in not withdrawing from the party, the case may then be submitted for discussion by the general membership meeting of the party branch, and a decision made to strike his or her name from the records. Any such decision must be submitted to the next higher party organization for approval.

A party member who, without legitimate excuse, fails to participate in the organized life of the party, or to pay membership fees over a period of six consecutive months, or who fails to do the work assigned by the party over a similar period, is to be regarded as having relinquished membership of his or her own accord. The party branch should, with the approval of its general membership meeting, remove the names of any such party members from the records, and report the case to the next higher party organization for the record.

CHAPTER II: THE ORGANIZATIONAL SYSTEM OF THE PARTY

Article 10. The party is organized according to the system of democratic centralism, and the fundamental principles of the party's system of democratic centralism are as follows:

1. The party is an integrated whole: it has a unified general program, constitution and high-level leading bodies, and it requires unanimity of thought and unanimity of action throughout the entire party. Every organization and member of the party is a part of this integrated whole. In order to guarantee the unity and centralism of the party, individual party members must subordinate themselves to party organizations; the minority must be subordinated to the majority; lower-level organizations must be subordinated to higher-level organizations; every organization in the entire party must unite in subordinating themselves to the national party congress and to the Central Committee.

2. The party's general program and constitution are adopted by the national congress of the party. The leading bodies of the party, at all levels, are elected. The highest leading body of the party is the national party congress and the Central Committee which is chosen by the former body. The leading bodies of party organizations at all levels in the localities are the party congresses at the various levels and the committee elected by them, and the party committees at all levels are responsible for reporting on their work to the party congresses at the same level.

3. The leading bodies at all levels of the party must constantly take note of the suggestions of lower-level organizations and of the broad masses of party members, resolve matters brought up by them, and circulate reports to the lower levels of important details and plans concerning their own work.

4. Lower-level party organizations must constantly report on their work to the higher organizations, and they must promptly ask for instructions from the higher levels on all questions which should be decided by a higher-level organization. They must act on their own responsibility in deciding those questions which they themselves should decide.

5. Party committees at all levels operate on the principle of combining collective leadership with individual responsibility under a division of labor. All important issues are to be decided collectively by the party committees, and at the same time each individual committee member is enabled to play his or her role.

Article 11. The representatives to party congresses at all levels and members of committees should be elected with due respect for the democratic rights of party members and representatives and the voters should be allowed to express their true wills. The number of candidates should be larger than the number of persons to be elected. Lists of candidates should be drawn up on the basis of full consideration and discussion by the party organization and the voters, and should be formally finalized after being agreed upon by the majority. The method of election by a simple majority may also be used to make a preliminary selection of candidates, after which their election should be put to a formal vote. A conscientious and responsible introduction of the basic circumstances of the candidates should be made to the voters. Every effort should be made to safeguard the rights of the voters to have a clear understanding of the candidates' circumstances, to alter the list of candidates, not to vote, and to change each candidate, and to ensure that no organization or individual is in any way able to compel a voter to vote, or not to vote, for a particular person.

The secret ballot method is to be used for voting.

The voting body of the party has the right to make changes, at any time, in respect of those elected to be full party committee members at the same level, and in respect of those elected to be representatives on the party congress at the next higher level.

Article 12. If a party organization at any level has important matters which require urgent discussion and settlement, and is unable to convene a congress, it may call a meeting of representatives. The number of deputies to be elected to the meeting of representatives and the method of electing them are to be determined by the party committee calling the meeting.

Article 13. At times when congresses at all levels in the

localities are not in session, party organizations at the next higher level may, where they deem it to be necessary, transfer or appoint responsible persons of the lower-level organizations.

Article 14. When they are making decisions on important matters relevant to lower-level organizations, leading bodies at all levels of the party should, where this is necessary and possible, solicit the opinions of the lower-level organizations. The lower-level organizations should be assured of being able to exercise their functions and powers in a normal way, of being able to sum up their own particular circumstances, deal with problems correctly, and give full play to their initiative and creativity. Higher-level leading bodies should generally not presume to interfere in any matters which should properly be dealt with by lower-level organizations, unless there are special circumstances.

Decisions of lower-level organizations must not conflict with the decisions of higher-level organizations. If it is necessary to make alterations in the light of special circumstances, prior approval should be obtained from a higher level; a decision should be made as a matter of urgency. After the matter has been dealt with, a report should be submitted to the higher level, and approval sought.

Article 15. Only the leading bodies of the Central Committee have the power to issue propositions and make decisions on matters concerning national policy. The representatives of all departments, and of all local organizations, may engage in discussion at party meetings, and submit proposals to the leading bodies of the Central Committee, but, except where approval has been obtained from the Central Committee, lower-level organizations are not permitted to make contrary decisions on their own account, or to publish contrary propositions for outside distribution.

Before a decision has been made on matters of policy under consideration by leading bodies at the higher levels of the party, lower-level party organizations may engage in discussion of these matters within the party, and may also submit proposals to higher-level organizations, but, once a decision has been issued by the higher-level organization, it must be strictly adhered to. If a lower-level organization considers that a decision of a higher-level organization is not appropriate to the actual situation in its own particular area or department, then it should request that the higher-level organization alter its decision; if the superior organization adheres to its original decision, the lower-level organization has the right to continue to hold its own opinion, but it must resolutely implement the decision, and must on no account openly publish its disagreement.

The newspapers and periodicals of organizations at all levels must disseminate the party line, and publicize the work plans, policies and resolutions of the party Central Committee, of higher-level organizations and of organizations at their own level.

Article 16. All party organizations, in discussions on the resolution of problems, must always strictly adhere to the principle of the subordination of the minority to the majority. Disagreements on the part of a minority should be conscientiously considered. If controversy arises on an important point, and voting is very close, then, except in urgent cases where the majority opinion must be put into effect, the decision should be postponed and discussion continued. Controversial cases where opinion is evenly divided should be referred to a higher-level organization for arbitration.

Every party member, including those carrying out responsible leadership duties, must carry out his work under the leadership of the party. If an important announcement is made in the name of a party organization, whose scope exceeds that already decided on by the party, it must be referred to the relevant party organization for discussion and a decision, or a report submitted to a superior party organization. No party member, whether his duties are at a high or low level, can make an individual decision on an important matter. Where an individual decision has to be made in an urgent case, the facts should afterwards be speedily reported to the party organization. No leading person is permitted to make arbitrary decisions in an individual capacity, nor is an individual permitted to place himself above the organization.

Article 17. The setting up of any new party organization, or the disbanding of any existing one, must be decided upon by the next highest organization.

Whenever they consider it necessary to do so, all party committees at county level and above may form their own representative bodies.

In forming their own administrative bodies, party committees at all levels should take care to closely relate things to the masses, to work efficiently, to streamline organization, and not to let the party take the place of the government.

CHAPTER III: CENTRAL ORGANIZATIONS OF THE PARTY

Article 18. The national congress of the party is elected for a term of 5 years; it is convened by the Central Committee, and it must hold at least two meetings in each tenure of office.

If one-third or more of the delegates, or one-third or more of the organizations at the provincial level, call for the convening of the national congress, then the Central Committee is obliged to convene it. The date and agenda for a meeting of the national congress should generally be announced 3 months prior to the meeting.

Drafts of important documents discussing work reports and schedules for the first meeting of each session of the national congress should be issued for discussion by the delegates or by the whole party at least 1 month prior to the meeting.

Article 19. The duties of the national party congress are:

1. To listen to and review the reports of the Central Committee;

2. To listen to and review the reports of the Central Committee's Discipline Inspection Commission;

3. To discuss and make decisions on important matters concerning the party;

4. To revise the party constitution; and

5. To elect the Central Committee.

Article 20. The party Central Committee is elected for a term of 5 years. The list of members and alternate members of the Central Committee is decided by the national congress. If vacancies occur in the membership of the Central Committee, these vacancies should be filled by alternate members of the Central Committee, in order of precedence according to the number of votes cast in their favor.

When the national congress is not in session, the Central Committee guides all the work of the party, carries out the resolutions of the national congress, and has to set up all kinds of party Central Committee organizations and guide their activities, and has to forge links with other political parties and organizations on the party's behalf.

Article 21. Plenary sessions of the party Central Committee are convened by the Politburo of the Central Committee, and there should be at least one plenary session every year.

Plenary sessions of the Central Committee elect the Politburo of the Central Committee, the Standing Committee of the Politburo of the Central Committee, the Central Committee Secretariat and the Central Discipline Inspection Commission. They also elect one person to be chairman of the Central Committee, a certain number of vice-chairmen, and one general secretary. The chairman, vice-chairmen and general secretary of the Central Committee are automatically members of the Standing Committee of the Politburo of the Central Committee.

When the Central Committee is not in plenary session, the Politburo of the Central Committee and its Standing Committee exercise the functions and powers of the Central Committee.

The Central Committee Discipline Inspection Commission, under the guidance of the Politburo of the Central Committee and its Standing Committee, regulates the everyday work of the Central Committee.

The chairman and vice chairmen of the Central Committee are concurrently the chairman and vice chairmen of the Politburo of the Central Committee.

The Central Committee decides on elections to the Central Committee's Military Affairs Commission.

Article 22. The party organization of the Chinese People's Liberation Army carries out its work in accordance with the instructions of the Central Committee. The General Political Department of the Chinese People's Liberation Army, under the leadership of the Central Committee and of the Central Committee's Military Affairs Commission, organizes party work and political work among the troops.

CHAPTER IV: PARTY ORGANIZATIONS IN THE LOCALITIES

Article 23. The party congresses of provinces, autonomous regions and municipalities directly under the central government are elected for a period of 5 years, and must be convened at least twice during this period.

The party congresses of autonomous prefectures, counties (banners), autonomous counties and municipalities are elected for a period of 3 years, and are convened twice during this period.

Article 24. The powers and functions of party congresses of provinces, autonomous regions, municipalities directly under the central government, autonomous prefectures, and of counties (banners) and autonomous counties are as follows:

1. Listening to and reviewing the reports of committees on the same level;

2. Listening to and reviewing the reports of the Central Committee's Discipline Inspection Commission;

3. The discussion of, and the issuing of resolutions on, important matters within the scope of their own particular region; and

4. The election of party committees on their level, and of delegates to attend the party congresses of higher levels.

Article 25. The party committees of provinces, autonomous regions and municipalities directly under the central government are elected for a period of 5 years, and the party committees of autonomous prefectures, counties (banners), autonomous counties and municipalities are elected for a period of 3 years. The lists of members and alternate members of committees at all levels are decided by the respective committee at the next higher level. If vacancies arise in the membership of committees at any level, they are to be filled by the alternate members in order of precedence according to the number of votes cast in their favor.

When the congresses are not in session, the committees at all levels, within the scope of their own particular regions, carry out the instructions of party organizations at the next higher level and the resolutions of the party congress on their own levels, give guidance in all kinds of work of a regional nature, and report on their work at regular intervals to the party committee at the next higher level.

Article 26. Plenary sessions of the party committees of provinces, autonomous regions, municipalities directly under the central government, and of autonomous prefectures, are convened twice a year. Plenary sessions of the party committees of counties (banners), autonomous counties and municipalities are convened twice a year. The plenary sessions of party committees at all levels in the localities elect standing committee members, secretaries and deputy secretaries, elect commissions for the inspection of discipline at their own levels, and submit these respectively to the Central Committee and to the higher-level committees for examination and approval. When the committees are not in plenary session, the standing committees at all levels in the localities exercise the functions and powers of the committees. The secretaries and deputy secretaries of the committees of provinces, autonomous regions and municipalities directly under the central government form their secretariats, and deal with day-to-day work, under the guidance of their standing committees.

CHAPTER V: PRIMARY ORGANIZATIONS OF THE PARTY

Article 27. All people's communes, factories, mines, and communications, commercial, educational and scientific research organizations, as well as other primary units and companies of the armed forces, which have more than three full party members, should all set up primary organizations of the party.

According to their working needs and the number of party members, and subject to the approval of the next higher party organizations, primary organizations of the party should set up party branch committees, general branch committees, or primary committees. Primary committees are elected by a general meeting of party members or by a congress. General branch committees and branch committees are elected by a general meeting of party members.

The formation and competence of party organizations within enterprises and institutions playing an important part in national construction are determined by party organizations at the next higher level.

Article 28. General meetings of party members or congresses which set up primary committees of the party and primary organizations are convened once a year. General meetings of party members in general branches are convened twice a year. General meetings of party members in branches are convened once every three months.

Congresses or general meetings of party members in primary organizations of the party discuss matters relating to the execution of the directives of the Central Committee and of higher-level organizations, discuss matters relating to the work and organization of their own units, make decisions and put forward proposals. Primary committees of the party are elected for a period of 2 years, and general branch committees and branch committees for a period of 1 year. The secretaries and deputy secretaries elected by the party's primary committees, general branch committees and branch committees are all subject to approval by the party organizations of the next higher levels.

Article 29. The primary organizations of the party should play the role of a fighting bastion. Their main tasks are:

1. To educate and organize party members, to strictly regulate the organized life of the party, to supervise party members in the conscientious performance of their duties, and to guard against violation of the rights of party members.

2. To publicize and implement the party's line, guiding principles and policies, to publicize and implement the resolutions of the party Central Committee, of higher-level organizations and of their own organizations, to give full play to the exemplary vanguard role of party members, to unite and organize cadres and the masses both inside and outside the party and to strive to fulfill the tasks entrusted to their own units.

3. To organize party members in earnestly studying Marxism-Leninism-Mao Zedong Thought, gaining a basic understanding of the party, and learning about the party's line, guiding principles and policies, as well as in studying science and culture, work skills and professional knowledge.

4. To fully mobilize the enthusiasm and creativity of party members and of the masses, to encourage and support innovation and creativity in professional work and in technology, and to strive to keep up with and to surpass advanced levels both at home and abroad.

5. To maintain close links with the masses, to carry out ideological and political work among the masses, to uphold the political and economic rights and interests of the masses, and to improve their material and cultural life.

6. To enroll party members, collect party dues, inspect and judge party members, praise the exemplary actions of activities among the party membership, and take disciplinary action within the party against party members who act contrary to the duties of party members, or who violate party discipline or the laws of the state.

7. To carry out criticism and self-criticism, to expose and eliminate weaknesses and mistakes at work, to correctly deal with contradictions within the party and with internal contradictions among the people, and to oppose harmful trends which threaten the interests of the party and the people.

8. To teach party members and the masses to raise revolutionary vigilance, and to continue the struggle against the disruptive activities of class enemies and other criminal elements.

Article 30. In setting up the enterprises and institutions of party committees, the system of responsibility by leading administrative cadres should be put into operation under the guidance of the party committee. Party committees discuss, and issue decisions on, important matters of principle at party meetings. They are not to intervene in day-to-day work which is the responsibility of the administration, and they are to ensure that persons responsible for administration are fully able to exercise their functions and powers. The principles of the system of responsibility by leading administrative cadres are not suitable for application in those general branch committees and branch committees under the leadership of party committees. These party organizations should play a protective and supervisory role in the proper fulfillment of the work assignments of their own units.

Within offices, the system of responsibility by leading administrative cadres under the leadership of the party committee is not put into operation, but the organizations of the party within these offices should supervise such aspects as the ideology, workstyle and moral qualities of every party member, including responsible persons in administration, as well as their operation of the system, their respect for the law and discipline, and their relations with the masses; they should help the administrative leadership to improve their work, to increase efficiency, overcome bureaucracy, and also to promptly inform the responsible persons in the administration of weaknesses and problems in their work, or report them to the next higher party organization.

CHAPTER VI: THE PARTY'S CADRES

Article 31. The party's leading cadres, including all grades of leading cadres above the administrative level, or full-time party branch secretaries, whether democratically elected, appointed by leading bodies, or accepted for employment through examination, do not have lifelong tenure of office. All of them may be transferred, demoted or removed from their posts. If a leading cadre has lost his capacity for work, or if he ought to retire, then he should not continue to hold a leading post.

The party's leading cadres, however many offices they hold, and at whatever level they hold them, are not permitted to exercise any privileges beyond those stipulated in the party constitution or in the rules and regulations; nor are they allowed to treat other people as unequal to them. If the offices entrusted to them are too high, then the responsibility will be too heavy for them to shoulder, and the demands made on them by the party too great.

The qualifications which should be possessed by all grades of leading cadres of the party are as follows:

1. They must possess a certain level of understanding of the theoretical principles of Marxism-Leninism-Mao Zedong Thought, and have the ability to continue their struggle while adhering to the socialist road;

2. In their own leadership work, they should be able to base themselves on the actual situation, and firmly and specifically put into practice the party's political, ideological and organizational lines, as well as all of its guiding principles and policies;

3. They should have an intense dedication to their revolutionary duty, and should have such specialized capacities and organizational abilities, as well as a sufficient level of knowledge as will render them competent for the work of leadership;

4. They should be selfless, should not use their positions in order to gain personal privilege, and they should uphold the party spirit, and not use their position to encourage factionalism or cliques;

5. They should maintain close links with the masses, be good at uniting their comrades, including those whose opinions differ from their own, and they should be able to accept criticism and carry out self-criticism; and

6. They should be physically healthy and able to cope with a fairly heavy workload.

Article 32. In order to be completely fit for our vital task of constructing modernization, the average age of members of the party Central Committee should be between 55 and 65 years old; the average age of full members of the standing committees of provincial committees should be between 50 and 60 years old; the average age of full members of the standing committees of the party committees of municipalities directly under the provincial governments (zhou) should not exceed 50 years, and that of full members of the standing committees of county committees should not exceed 45 years.

The party's leading cadres of all grades should abide by the principle of not holding concurrent posts. If a few comrades have to hold concurrent posts under special circumstances, the number of jobs actually entrusted to them should not exceed three, and they must, moreover, be fully responsible for the work of the posts which they hold concurrently.

Article 33. Members and alternate members of the party Central Committee and of the committees at all levels in the localities may be reappointed or reelected consecutively, but they must not be reappointed or reelected to more than three sessions in a row.

Party members who have lost their capacity for work may not be entered on the list of candidates for election to party committees at any level.

Article 34. Party organizations at all levels should set up and perfect a system of assessment for cadres. They should bring into operation the methods of integration of assessment by the leadership and election by the masses, and of the integration of routine inspection with assessment at regular intervals, and they should emphasize the assessment of cadres in such aspects as ideology and moral character, professional ability and tangible achievements in work and study. As to the results of these assessments, those showing outstanding results may be promoted or rewarded, while those whose results are not up to standard in two consecutive assessments should be demoted or removed from office.

Article 35. Cadres who are party members should be adept at cooperating and working together with cadres who are not party members; they should treat them with respect, safeguard their functions and powers, modestly learn from their special knowledge, and allow them to play their role to the full.

Party organizations at all levels should have the ability to search out and recommend reliable and learned nonparty cadres and to entrust them with leadership work.

Article 36. Advisory committees are to be established in organizations at the Central Committee and provincial committee levels of the party. Party organizations at the level of autonomous prefecture committees, municipal committees and county committees should set up advisers, and those with more than three advisers should set up advisory groups. Those comrades appointed as advisers should be cadres with extensive work experience and political enthusiasm, who have prestige and are healthy, and who, although they can no longer cope with a heavy workload, are nevertheless still capable of doing some work.

Advisers at all levels must in general be cadres from the same level. Responsible people on advisory committees and advisory groups at all levels may attend meetings of the party committee on the same level as nonvoting delegates.

Advisory committees, advisory groups and advisers should carry out their work under the aegis of the party committees on their respective levels; advisory committees and groups and advisers should actively and responsibly inform the party organization of the situation and raise proposals.

Party organizations at all levels should allow advisory groups to play their parts fully and, in studying and making decisions on matters of importance, should ask for suggestions from them. They should ensure good working, studying and living conditions for the advisers.

Article 37. Those cadres, (including advisers), who for reasons of age or health are not fit to continue in office, should, in accordance with the state ruling, either take convalescent leave or retire from their posts. The relevant party organizations should conscientiously ensure that they continue to receive the political and other benefits to which they are entitled.

When cadres who have made important contributions to the history of the revolution retire from office, the party organizations concerned should make an appropriate appraisal of their past achievements and merits and treat them with the honor they deserve.

CHAPTER VII: PARTY DISCIPLINE

Article 38. Discipline is a powerful weapon for safeguarding the operation of the party line, the party's guiding principles, policies and resolutions, for upholding the party's solidarity and unity, for strengthening the party's close links with the masses and for maintaining the party's fighting ability. To be able to accept the limitations imposed by party discipline and strictly abide by party discipline are qualities which must be possessed by every Communist Party member. To uphold the strict enforcement of party discipline is a responsibility of party organizations at all levels which must not be shirked. If a party organization is remiss in the field of upholding discipline, then it must be put under surveillance.

Party members must set an example in upholding state laws and statutes, and the legal sanction of the state must be imposed without exception on any party members who break the law.

Article 39 Party members must be subjected to disciplinary action by the party if they are guilty of serious violation of party discipline by dint of having committed any of the following actions: Disrupting the solidarity and unity of the party, refusing to carry out the party's line, guiding principles, policies and resolutions; publishing views abroad not endorsed by the party which oppose the party's line, guiding principles, policies, resolutions or basic political standpoint, whether openly or in secret; secretly forming cliques within the party, carrying on factional activities or conspiracies or joining illegal organizations outside the party; serious violation of the party constitution or of the laws and statutes of the state; revealing party and state secrets; intentionally damaging the interests of the party or the people; concealing from the party their own or other people's serious errors or other important matters, or practicing deception, the framing of cases against people, or intimidation; suppressing criticism or exposure by party members or by the masses, carrying out retaliation against them, or depriving party members or the masses of their rights or impinging on them, or taking advantage of their powers and functions to seek private gain.

Article 40. In dealing with violations of party discipline by party members, party organizations at all levels should, according to the seriousness of the case, issue a warning, a serious warning, strip the offenders of their party powers and functions and propose to extraparty organizations that they withdraw the offenders' powers and functions outside the party, place them under party surveillance, or expel them from the party.

Party members must not remain under party surveillance for more than 2 years. During the period of surveillance, the rights of party members and their powers and functions are the same as those of probationary party members. Party members under surveillance by the party should resume their rights as full party members if they

prove to have actually rectified their errors, and should be expelled from the party if they are recalcitrant and persist in their errors.

Expulsion from the party is the harshest punishment which may be inflicted within the party. When they are deciding on and approving the expulsion of a member from the party, party organizations at all levels should thoroughly examine the evidence and testimony on both sides of the case and should adopt an entirely conscientious attitude.

In dealing with party members within the party, it is not permissible to use methods which go against the constitution of the party or the laws of the state; organizations or individuals acting in this manner must be investigated in accordance with party discipline and the laws of the state.

Article 41. Disciplinary action against party members must be discussed and decided by a general membership meeting of a party branch and approved by the next higher party organization; if the matters involved are relatively important or complex, then they should be reported to a discipline inspection commission above the county level for investigation and approval. In special cases, party committees and discipline inspection commissions at all levels are empowered to take disciplinary action against party members.

The revocation of the functions and powers of members and alternate members of the Central Committee and of party committees at all levels in the localities, their subjection to party surveillance, or their expulsion from the party must be decided on by the congress which elected them, but if there is a pressing need, such action may be decided on by a majority of more than two-thirds in a plenary meeting of their respective committees; however, the infliction of the above punishments on members and alternate members of the Central Committee must be subsequently endorsed by the next meeting of the National Congress; the above-mentioned punishment of members and alternate members of regional committees at all levels must be ratified by the party committee at the next higher level.

Article 42. In making the decision to punish a party member, a party organization should seek truth from facts in checking up on the actual circumstances, listen to the member's own explanation of the case and allow him to defend himself; after the decision has been taken, if the member does not submit to the sentence, he may lodge an appeal, in which case the organization concerned must take responsibility for dealing with the matter or pass it on without delay; it may not be withheld.

CHAPTER VIII: THE PARTY'S MECHANISM FOR INSPECTING DISCIPLINE

Article 43. The party Central Committee's Discipline Inspection Commission carries out its work under the guidance of the party Central Committee. The commissions for the inspection of discipline at all levels in the localities carry out their work under the guidance of the party delegates at their respective levels and of the discipline inspection commission at the next higher level.

Article 44. The duties of the discipline inspection commission of the Central Committee and in the localities are: To uphold the rules and regulations of the party; to assist the party committees in consolidating the party's workstyle; to ensure the thoroughgoing execution of the party line, guiding principles, policies and resolutions; to regularly educate party members in respecting discipline, and to make necessary decisions, to investigate and deal with organizations and members of the party that violate the party constitution; to take disciplinary action against or absolve those party members involved in relatively serious or complex cases of breaches of party discipline or infringements of the laws and statutes of the state, and to accept and hear the complaints and appeals of party members.

The party's central and local commissions for the inspection of discipline should report to the party committees on their respective levels the problems encountered in and the results of their handling of especially significant or involved cases. Local commissions for the inspection of discipline should, whenever necessary, make reports to the discipline inspection commissions at the next higher levels.

Article 45. Higher-level commissions for the inspection of discipline have the power to examine the work of like committees at lower levels; they also have the power to ratify and alter the decisions on cases made by like commissions at lower levels. If a higher-level discipline inspection commission wishes to alter a decision of a like commission at a lower level which has already been approved by the latter commission's party committee, the said alteration must then receive the approval of the higher-level commission's party committee.

Lower-level commissions for the inspection of discipline should make reports on their work to the like commissions at the next higher levels and should also accurately report cases of breach of discipline by party members and by the party's cadres, (including responsible cadres at their own and higher levels).

If commissions for the inspection of discipline at any level in the localities discover cases of breach of party discipline by party committees or their members at their respective levels, when such cases are not resolved or not correctly resolved by the committees on their own levels, these commissions have the power to report the said cases to the like commissions at the next higher levels and to request them to deal with them.

CHAPTER IX: LEADING PARTY GROUPS

Article 46. The leading bodies in state institutions, people's organizations, economic and cultural organizations or other nonparty organizations are to set up leading party groups. These leading party groups should take responsibility for keeping things in strict accordance with the general and specific policies of the party, for guiding the work of the party committees in their organizations, uniting nonparty cadres and the masses outside the party and for

fulfilling the duties entrusted to them by the party and the state.

If their work so requires, departments which should establish leading party groups may, with the approval of the Central Committee or of the committees on their respective levels, set up party committees instead.

Article 47. Members of leading party groups within the leading bodies of central and regional state institutions and people's organizations are appointed by the party committees of their respective levels from among the responsible cadres of the organizations in question who are party members. Leading party groups are to appoint secretaries and deputy secretaries.

Leading party groups must place themselves under the guidance of the party committees on their respective levels.

CHAPTER X: THE PARTY'S RELATIONSHIP WITH THE COMMUNIST YOUTH LEAGUE

Article 48. The Communist Youth League of China is the advanced youth organization of the leadership of the Chinese Communist Party. The Central Committee of the Communist Youth League receives the guidance of the party Central Committee. The Communist Youth League's regional organizations at all levels simultaneously receive guidance from the party committees on their own levels and from the league's organizations at the next higher levels.

Article 49. The Communist Youth League is the support of the party and it is a school where advanced youth study communism in action. The Communist Youth League should educate and organize its members, actively publicize and conscientiously execute the party's line and its general and specific policies, and should play a leading role in production, work, study and in struggling against the enemy; it should assist the party and government in inculcating young people with a revolutionary moral character and should take the lead in disseminating new socialist customs and habits; it should center itself on the crucial tasks of the party, unite young people of all nationalities throughout the country, be in keeping with the special qualities of young people, encourage independent activities and assist the party in carrying out all aspects of its work; it should raise, train and supply young cadres for the party and the state.

Article 50. Party committees at all levels should increase the guidance they give to the Communist Youth League, pay attention to the selection and training of the league's cadres and perfect the organizational leadership of the league. It is desirable to strongly support the Communist Youth League in accordance with the needs of the broad masses of young people, and it should carry out its work in a flexible and lively manner and in such a way as to encourage creativity in order to bring the league's role fully into play as a shock brigade and as a bridge linking the broad masses of young people together.

27

Against Life Tenure for Party and State Leaders, 28 October 1980

This article, written by an authoritative "contributing commentator," elaborates on the serious problems of aged leading cadres remaining in office until their death or purgation.

The call for an end to the de facto practice of life tenure of leading cadres was raised at the 5th Plenary Session of the 11th Central Committee of the party. This is an important reform in the leadership system and the cadres system of the party and the state. All Communist Party members, cadres in particular, should pay attention to the interests of the party and the people, take a correct approach to this question and be conscious promoters of this reform.

I

There is no sanction for the life tenure of leading cadres either in the party constitution or in the Constitution of the state. However, for a long time, the terms of office for leaders of government organizations and party committees at all levels, the highest level in particular, have not been specified. While cadres have been "reelected" at regular intervals, there has been no mention of terms of office. On the other hand, we do not have a retirement system for the leading cadres. The leading cadres can remain in their posts indefinitely although they are old and weak and may even have lost their working abilities. Thus, any leading cadre, a party or state leader in particular, may enjoy life tenure provided he or she commits no grave mistakes and is not regarded as having a serious problem. As time goes by, the negative aspects of this de facto practice of life tenure are seen more and more clearly.

First, the leading cadres are old. During the early days of liberation, most of the leading comrades at the central and provincial levels were 30 to 35 years old. The leading bodies at all levels at that time were full of vigor and vitality. All comrades came to the forefront to solve problems. One of the important factors behind the rapid development of the national reconstruction on the bed of ashes left behind by the Kuomintang was the presence of a youthful and vigorous leading body. Over the past 30 years, the terms of office of leading cadres were not specified and young cadres were seldom drawn into the leading bodies, with the result that the average age of the leading cadres has risen considerably. Many leading cadres at the higher levels have difficulty even in walking. Quite a number of the leading cadres at the basic level are hoary with age. Most of them are still willing to make a contribution, but their advanced age frustrates their intentions. They can

no longer work vigorously as they did years ago. This situation is in sharp contradiction with the requirements of the four modernizations. Without specifying the terms of office of leading cadres and establishing a system concerning replacement, leave of absence and retirement for the leading cadres, we cannot prevent the recurrence of old age of the leading bodies a few years later on even though we have now taken measures to admit young cadres into the leading bodies. The question of age of the leading bodies will emerge from time to time.

Second, the practice of life tenure of leading cadres obstructs the training and maturing of talented people. On the one hand, if the leading cadres remain in their posts indefinitely, the young people who have real ability and education cannot be admitted into the leading bodies to receive training. On the other hand, the practice of life tenure hinders the leading cadres themselves from making progress and maturing. Life tenure, equivalent to guaranteed posts, cannot stimulate people to strive hard. On the contrary, it encourages some people to muddle along so that they make no progress in their thinking, professional knowledge and work after serving many years in their posts.

Third, the most serious shortcoming of the practice of life tenure is the harm it does to the implementation of democratic centralism. After serving many years in a place, a leading cadre becomes the "old party secretary" or the "old department chief" and the subordinate cadres are promoted primarily through him. It is easy for him in such circumstances to stand above both the leading body and the masses. This gives rise to a situation in which one man at the top makes arbitrary decisions while those under him just do as they are told. This situation exists in reality. Having served for a long time in a unit, one can hardly avoid substituting the principle of "appointing the favorites" for the principle of "appointing the capable," and will gradually form a circle of associates. This gives rise to sectarianism and impairs the unity and solidarity of party organizations.

Experience also tells us that the practice of life tenure of the highest leaders of the party and the state will do even greater harm. It often happens that when a state leader remains in his post for a long time, he will receive more titles and be given more publicity. Thus, the concentration of power in one man is inevitable. As time goes by, the power of the party and the state will be concentrated in him alone and inner-party democracy and people's democracy will become empty talk. When coupled with the cult of the individual, the concentration of power

["An Important Reform in the Leadership System of Party and State," *People's Daily*, 28 October 1980.]

in one man places the future of the party and the state in the hands of a single person. This is a very dangerous situation. When this person makes a mistake (which is almost inevitable in these circumstances), the whole situation will be jeopardized and it will be difficult to correct this mistake. If anything happens to this person who manipulates the country, it can bring about unrest and confusion in the national political situation. This has occurred time and again in the history of the communist movement. Especially in a vast and populous country like ours where the conditions are complicated, if an old man whose health is declining has to handle the numerous affairs of state every day, he will be overburdened and can hardly avoid making a grave mistake. The practice of life tenure of the highest leaders invariably gives rise to the various unhealthy, abnormal phenomena in the political life of the party and the state. In this situation, it is easy for careerists and conspirators to bluff and deceive the people and to fish in troubled waters. The atrocious crimes committed by Lin Biao and the "gang of four" have been an impressive lesson for us. Thus, it is necessary to put an end to the life tenure of leading cadres and, first and foremost, the life tenure of the highest leading cadres of both the party and the state.

II

The abolition of life tenure for cadres in their leadership posts is of immediate and realistic significance in perfecting party and government leadership, improving the quality and efficiency of leadership work, overcoming bureaucratism and achieving the four modernizations. Moreover, this is also an important problem concerning the improvement of our country's basic political system.

Historically speaking, life tenure is for supreme state rulers and is linked with the despotic political system. In slave societies and feudal societies, with a few exceptions including the Roman Republic, the supreme ruler enjoyed life tenure. As far as the conditions of the Chinese feudal society were concerned, with "divine power vested in the ruler," the emperor was the son of the emperor of heaven (son of heaven). He was authorized by heaven to rule, and no other person had the right to the throne. Therefore, as head of a feudal state, the emperor had supreme power and remained in office for life, with no tenure limit. (There are only a few exceptions, as far as historical facts are concerned.) Even toward the end of the Qing Dynasty, despite the so-called "outline of the constitution" and the "19 credos," the basic principle of the "holy emperor" still prevailed. In feudal states, various officials were only the emperor's pawns in maintaining rule. Generally speaking, the appointment of officials was based on "merit and talents," without any stipulation about life tenure. To guard against dishonest practices on the part of officials, some dynasties clearly stipulated that an official could not stay long in his post and had to be duly transferred or promoted after a period of time. But as a feudal bureaucrat, one could stay on as an official for life so long as he served the supreme ruler. Therefore, in feudal society, it was still common for one to be an official for life. There was no lack of high-ranking officials who remained in office throughout their lives.

With the rise of the bourgeoisie, advocates of the enlightenment severely criticized feudal despotism. Based on the principle of inherent rights, they held that if the government could not protect the people's interests and even encroached upon them, the people should oppose and replace it. This not only negated the despotic rule of feudal rulers but also basically negated life tenure for the highest state office. Bourgeois thinkers also seriously studied the problem of tenure for state leaders and officials. In a study of ancient Roman history, Montesquieu noted, "every king in his life is for a time full of ambition. But this is followed by a period of dissipation and even indifference. Yet the leaders of a republic change every year. They always strive to achieve something during their tenure, so that they can be reelected. Therefore, they never for a moment give up their own ambitions." ("On the Causes of the Rise and Fall of Rome," p. 4.) He believed that given long tenure, all government posts would be dangerous. After overthrowing the rule of feudal rulers, the bourgeoisie established a republic and wrote a constitution, stipulating that state leaders must be elected with a tenure limit. Lenin said: "The bourgeois republic, parliament, and general election— all these represent a big step forward, as far as the social development of the whole world is concerned." ("Selected Works of Lenin," Vol. 4, p. 55.) One salient feature of such a bourgeois system in relation to feudal life tenure is the exercise of control over the state by the whole class. The most capable and talented elements in the class are selected for state leadership posts to serve its own interests in a most effective way. This is unlike feudal life tenure allowing an individual to exercise dictatorship all the time, no matter how stupid and incapable he was.

However, equality as advocated by the bourgeoisie is only a political reflection of the principle of exchange of equal values. A general election, as far as the bourgeoisie is concerned, is also just a political manifestation of free competition. On the basis of free competition, there have gradually formed various groups of politicians representing different sectors of capitalist interests. Bourgeois state power is exercised in turn by these groups of politicians. The parliamentary system, general elections, and all such systems and rules cannot overcome these limitations of a bourgeois republic.

A proletarian socialist republic is a new-type democratic state. Given the principle of democracy, the tenure of any leadership post cannot be indefinite and, still less, life long. As part of a republican system of government, the highest leadership office must have a clear-cut tenure limit. This is an important mark of distinction between the democratic political system and the despotic political system. Moreover, according to Marxist theory on the state, a proletarian socialist republic must not only eliminate all remnants and traces of the feudal despotic system but also overcome the limitations of a bourgeois [one] and basically do away with the phenomenon of distinguishing people as those in control and those under control. This should be our basic principle and object in reforming the leadership system for the party and the state and perfecting the political system of our people's republic.

At present, we must seriously sum up experiences and lessons and draw on the valuable experiences and methods of other countries in practicing democracy. We must establish and perfect such systems as election, recruitment, appointment and dismissal, assessment, censorship, rotation, and so forth for all leading cadres at all levels. We must lay down clear-cut stipulations about the tenure of office, leave of absence and retirement. We must also take measures to ensure that the masses of people and their representatives can exercise such rights as supervision, criticism, accusation and dismissal, as far as leading cadres at all levels are concerned. We must not only firmly abolish life tenure for leadership posts but also strive to create a democratic system more sublime and realistic than that of a Western bourgeois republic.

III

Many questions in our daily life have not been created by the people deliberately, but have been formed unconsciously due to various factors. Therefore, it is necessary for people to go through a certain process before they understand these questions. The de facto life tenure is a question of this nature.

The existence in practice of the life tenure of leaders has various causes. Objectively, there is no mature experience to learn from on how to build up a socialist people's republic. Even when new China was founded, the establishment of a perfect political system in a socialist republic was still a new question. Moreover, we have failed to make a deepgoing study of this problem in connection with our country's development.

In the actual situation of the revolutionary war years, abolishing life tenure was not a question. In the early years after the founding of the PRC, most party and state leaders of China, including Mao Zedong, Zhou Enlai, Liu Shaoqi and Zhu De were in their prime of life. At that time, numerous tasks remained to be undertaken and our leaders, who had always regarded revolution as their career, persistently devoted themselves to our cause. The question of retirement did not then exist, and it was almost impossible for these leaders to consider the problem of limiting their period of office. This is completely understandable. However, as the time passes and the situation changes, things have become complicated. In the early 1960's, we began to touch upon this question and put forth the task of training tens of millions of successors to the revolutionary cause of the proletariat. However, we have not handled this problem in the correct direction by solving it institutionally.

As a system, the de facto life tenure bears the taint of feudalism and is a manifestation of the survival of feudalism. Historical traditions constitute an inertia force. China has been under the feudal autocratic rule for several thousand years. Although the people have thoroughly done away with the feudal system through revolution, they have not completely eliminated the influence of feudal autocratic rule and the habits, mentality and lifestyle adapted to such rule. There is still a great influence by small production—the foundation of feudal autocratic rule. It is inevitable that these things exert their influence on the political life of the party and state. Since the founding of the PRC, we have failed to make a thorough study of democratic systems and have failed to establish a complete and proper cadre system. This was not accidental negligence. In the absence of a tradition and the habits of democratic life, it is almost inevitable that leaders who have performed great feats hold their post throughout their lives. During the "Great Cultural Revolution," Lin Biao, Jiang Qing, Kang Sheng and company even said that life tenure of highest

leaders was sacred and inviolable and was an unalterable principle. While deifying a man, they simultaneously made the people's leader an alienated feudal emperor.

Through several years of experience, particularly the bitter lessons of the "Great Cultural Revolution," we have realized the severe harm caused by life tenure. Now, our party Central Committee has not only clearly put forward the task of eliminating the pernicious influence of feudalism, but also correctly decided to abolish life tenure. This is a great improvement we have made on our way forward.

IV

The abolition of life tenure is an important link in reforming the leadership system of the party and the state and in perfecting the socialist democratic system. To solve this problem, we must start from the actual conditions in our country and seriously conduct studies. We must institutionalize a new system while also raising the people's consciousness to actively and prudently seek a solution.

As a first step, clear stipulations must be made on the tenure of the highest leaders of the party and the state. To perfect the political system of our People's Republic, our Constitution must contain clear stipulations on the tenure of the highest leaders of the state. As the ruling party, the constitution of our party must also have clear provisions on the subject in order to meet the requirement of the democratization of political life.

The most experienced and prestigious persons should be chosen to assume the highest leading posts of both our party and our state, but this does not mean that these leaders should remain in their posts all their lives. In a socialist country, outstanding leaders will continuously come forth if the democratic life is normal, and the democratic system of a socialist country will enable the people to choose from among themselves the most outstanding and suitable persons in terms of capability, wisdom, character, health and energy to assume the highest posts of the party and the state. On the other hand, in a country like ours, a leader or an outstanding statesman will be able to, and ought to, make contributions to the party and the people in various ways.

As a second step, concrete analysis should be made with regard to the tenure of cadres at various levels and proper stipulations must be made accordingly. Considering that units vary greatly in their nature and characteristics, mechanical stipulations concerning tenure are improper. But the tenure of the leadership in any department or unit should certainly not be indefinite. Thus, there must be a system governing the retirement of cadres so as to ensure that all retiring cadres are able to leave their posts happily and still continue to contribute what they can to the people. At present, this is an important issue in implementing the party's organizational line. Of course, we must not be overly rigid in dealing with this problem. Old cadres who are still able to work will remain the backbone of the leadership.

Another thing is to take care to cultivate the fine practice of respect and concern for the old comrades in the party and in society. At present, the bad tendency of flattering the powerholders and treating those not in power coldly exists not only in society but also in some party organizations. Great efforts are needed on our part to change this tendency. Today, the de facto system of life tenure has virtually become a tradition and custom. Some people are reluctant and feel that it will be difficult to abolish this system.

There are many reasons for this phenomenon. Objectively speaking, because this question has not been raised for years, many people are not psychologically prepared for solving this problem now. Furthermore, we lack an adequate system and method to handle the great number of outgoing or resigning old cadres. It would be natural for some comrades to worry about what will happen to them in the future. On the other hand, there are also ideological reasons for this phenomenon. Here, I will only point out two.

One is the superstition concerning the state. Marx said: There used to be "a delusion as if administration and political governing were mysteries, transcendent functions only to be trusted to the hands of a trained caste." ("The Civil War in France," p. 141.) For a long time, people have looked at the administration of the state as a mystery. Actually, such ignorance was created by those who monopolized political administrative power. In the feudal society in our country, people's superstition about the feudal state was absolutely absurd. Not only was the emperor, the head of the feudal state, regarded as the true son of heaven, other high civil or military officials were often said to be celestial beings who had descended to earth. Only these extraordinary deities were believed to be capable of administering the totally mysterious state affairs. With the victory of the revolution in our country, a great number of ordinary people who had been tempered through revolutionary practice participated in the administration of the state. This fact in itself was a forceful attack on decadent prejudice and superstition. However, superstition regarding the state is deeprooted and difficult to eliminate completely at one stroke. Under certain conditions, if superstition regarding the state coupled with personality cult becomes rampant, the situation where a position is believed to be "belonging to none other than so-and-so" will surely emerge. People will piously think that certain important posts can be assumed only by particular persons. Thus, the system of life tenure is thought to be a matter of course. During the 10 years of chaos, this situation was prevalent for a time. Memories of that time are still fresh in people's minds. Was this also not fashionable for a time after the smashing of the "gang of four"? Today, such ideas have not totally disappeared and they still affect some localities. Therefore, eliminating superstition about the state ideologically is an important condition for abolishing the system of life tenure for leading positions and reforming the leadership system of the state.

Of course, when we say we must eliminate superstition regarding the state, we certainly do not mean that important leading positions of the state can easily be assumed by just anyone, nor that we can take a reckless attitude toward making decisions regarding important personnel changes. We mean that we must not surround the administration of state affairs with mystery.

Another question is the pernicious influence of feudalism. An overwhelming majority of our comrades in leading positions faithfully serve the people. However, due to the imperfections of our system and the fact that some people do not set strict demands on themselves, some influence of old ideas has sneaked in. Thus, the traditional feudal concept that "once a person becomes an official, he can enjoy a handsome salary for a lifetime" has found acceptance. In the minds of some people, the distinction between being an official and a revolutionary becomes blurred. Then, unhealthy tendencies begin to grow in our ranks and a very small minority even degenerate to the point of regarding themselves as feudal officials and overlords, becoming obsessed with power and crazy for privilege. Therefore, when the party Central Committee put forth the abolition of the system of life tenure in leading positions, they could not accept it. They are not correctly analyzing this question from the standpoint of the interests of the party and the people. Instead, they put their personal position, income and the interests and future of their family and children first. Some even take the erroneous attitude of fishing for benefits before anything else. This shows that some of our comrades have been seriously affected by the pernicious influence of feudalism.

A good start has been made in abolishing de facto life tenure and in improving the systems relating to the leadership and cadres. With the guidance of the party Central Committee and the joint efforts of all party members, success in this field will surely be achieved.

The use here of quotations to drive home Deng's point, which is that the Party must be disciplined and responsive to his leadership, is somewhat reminiscent of the approach adopted in Mao Zedong's famous Little Red Book.

1. IT IS NECESSARY TO COMPLETELY AND ACCURATELY MASTER AND APPLY MAO ZEDONG THOUGHT

The editorial of the "two newspapers and one magazine" of 7 February 1977, entitled "Study the Documents Well and Grasp the Key Link," mentioned the erroneous guiding principle of the "two whatevers." On 10 April, Comrade Deng Xiaoping wrote a letter to the Central Committee in which he clearly pointed out, "We must forever apply accurate and complete Mao Zedong Thought to guide the whole party, the whole army and the people of the whole country, to triumphantly press forward the cause of the party and socialism and the cause of the international communist movement."

On 21 July 1977, Comrade Deng Xiaoping, addressing the 3d plenary session of the 10th Central Committee, dwelt specifically on the question of applying accurate and complete Mao Zedong Thought to guide the party's cause. He said, "We must have a complete and accurate understanding of the system of Mao Zedong Thought, and we must be good at studying, mastering and applying the system of Mao Zedong Thought in order to guide all our work. Only thus can we avoid separating and distorting Mao Zedong Thought and damaging it." "We cannot understand Mao Zedong Thought just from individual sentences; we must gain a correct understanding from the entire system of Mao Zedong Thought. The 'gang of four', especially the so-called theorist Zhang Chunqiao, distorted and tampered with Mao Zedong Thought. They quoted various fragments of Chairman Mao in order to deceive people and frighten them. We must truly appreciate Mao Zedong Thought. As far as problems in a field or an aspect are concerned, we must also accurately and completely understand Mao Zedong Thought." "Therefore I suggest that apart from doing a good job in compiling and publishing selected works of Mao Zedong, the comrades engaged in theoretical work should devote plenty of effort to expounding on the system of Mao Zedong Thought in every field. We must apply the system of Mao Zedong Thought to educate our party and guide us to forge ahead."

On 27 November 1978, Comrade Deng Xiaoping pointed out when receiving some foreign friends: Marxism-Leninism-Mao Zedong Thought is the guiding ideology for our country to accomplish the four modernizations. He also said, in the course of accomplishing the four modernizations, we must be good at completely and accurately mastering and applying Mao Zedong Thought.

In his speech at the closing session of the central work conference on 13 December 1978, Comrade Deng Xiaoping said, "The ideological system of Comrade Mao Zedong has nurtured our entire generation. It can be said that all the comrades present today were instructed by Mao Zedong Thought. It is not the slightest exaggeration to say that we would not have our Chinese Communist Party as it is today but for Mao Zedong Thought. Mao Zedong Thought will forever be the most precious spiritual treasure of the whole party, the whole army and the people of the whole country. We must completely and accurately understand and master the scientific system of Mao Zedong Thought, and also develop it in the new historical conditions. Of course, Comrade Mao Zedong was not without shortcomings and errors; it is not Marxist to demand that a revolutionary leader be without shortcomings or errors. We must lead and educate the whole body of party members, the whole body of PLA commanders and fighters and the people of all nationalities throughout the country to understand Comrade Mao Zedong's tremendous achievements in a scientific and historical way."

In his 30 March 1979 speech at the party's meeting to discuss ideological guidelines for theoretical work, Comrade Deng Xiaoping proposed that it is necessary to uphold the four basic principles.

Speaking on the necessity of upholding Marxism-Leninism-Mao Zedong Thought, he pointed out: "One of the key points of our struggle with Lin Biao and the 'gang of four' is that we opposed them in forging, tampering with and separating Marxism-Leninism-Mao Zedong Thought. By smashing the 'gang of four,' we have been able to restore afresh the scientific features of Marxism-Leninism-Mao Zedong Thought, and made it the guide for our actions. This is a great victory for the whole party and the people of the whole country. However there is a very small number of people who do not think in this way. They either openly oppose the basic principles of Marxism, or else support it in words but actually oppose Mao Zedong Thought, which is the product of integrating the universal truth of Marxism with the practice of the Chinese revolution. We must oppose all these erroneous trends of thought. Some comrades say, we only support 'correct Mao Zedong Thought,' and we do not support 'erroneous Mao Zedong Thought.' This is also an erroneous way of putting things. What we uphold and must regard as the guide for our action is the basic principles of Marxism-Leninism-Mao Zedong Thought, or

["Comrade Deng Xiaoping Talks on Questions of Rectifying Party Work Style," *Red Flag*, no. 21, 1 November 1981.]

the scientific system formed by these principles. As for individual theses, there are bound to be flaws, whether they come from Marx, Lenin or Mao Zedong. However such things do not come under the category of the scientific system formed by their basic principles." Comrade Deng Xiaoping also pointed out in this speech: "Scientific socialism forges ahead in the course of actual struggle, and so does Marxism-Leninism-Mao Zedong Thought. We obviously will not go back from scientific socialism to utopian socialism, nor will we allow Marxism to stay at the level of individual theses of several decades or a century ago. Therefore we repeatedly say, emancipating the mind means applying the basic principles of Marxism-Leninism-Mao Zedong Thought to study the new situations and solve the new problems." "What is the greatest new situation and the biggest new problem for the whole party today? Obviously, it is to accomplish the four modernizations, or as I said above, to accomplish Chinese-style modernization. We have already spoken of studying in depth the new situations and new problems encountered in accomplishing the four modernizations in China, and have also given an answer of major guiding significance; this will be a major contribution of our ideological and theoretical workers to Marxism, and will mean truly holding aloft Mao Zedong Thought."

2. WE MUST PERSISTENTLY SEEK TRUTH FROM FACTS

In his speech at the 3d plenary session of the 10th Central Committee of 21 July 1977, Comrade Deng Xiaoping pointed out when speaking on studying well Comrade Mao Zedong's theories on party building: "I hold that the mass line and seeking truth from facts are the two most fundamental things in the work style advocated by Chairman Mao. Of course the relationship between democracy and centralism and between freedom and discipline is very important. As far as the present situation in our party is concerned, I personally feel that the mass line and seeking truth from facts are particularly important."

Comrade Deng Xiaoping pointed out in his speech at the all-PLA political work conference on 2 June 1978: "We must never violate the basic principles of Marxism-Leninism-Mao Zedong Thought. There is no doubt at all about that. However we must integrate with reality, we must analyze and study the actual situation and solve the actual problems. To decide on guiding principles for work in accordance with the actual conditions is the most basic ideological and work method which all Communist Party members must remember at all times. Seeking truth from facts is the starting point and the fundamental point of Mao Zedong Thought. This is materialism. Otherwise, when we hold meetings, we could only utter empty talk and would be incapable of solving any problem." Comrade Deng Xiaoping also said, "The living soul of Marxism is to specifically analyze the specific situation. Unless Marxism-Leninism-Mao Zedong Thought is integrated with the actual situation, it has no vitality. The responsibility of our leading cadres is to integrate the instructions of the central authorities and the upper levels with the specific situation in their own units, and solve problems. They cannot act as 'message centers' and simply transmit the instructions in a mechanical way."

He also said, "Please think about it, comrades. Are seeking truth from facts, proceeding from reality in everything, and integrating theory with reality the fundamental viewpoint of Mao Zedong Thought or not? Is this fundamental viewpoint outdated, and can it be outdated? How can we call it Marxism-Leninism-Mao Zedong Thought if we oppose seeking truth from facts, proceeding from reality in everything, and integrating theory with reality in everything, and integrating theory with reality? Where would such actions lead us? Obviously, they could only lead us to idealism and metaphysics, to losses in work and defeat in revolution."

In his talks when inspecting Shenyang, Changchun and other places in September 1978, Comrade Deng Xiaoping pointed out: The basic point of Mao Zedong Thought is to integrate Marxism with the concrete practice of the Chinese revolution. Chairman Mao's inscription for the Yanan party school consisted of four big characters, "seek truth from facts," and these four characters represent the basic point of Mao Zedong Thought. This is the quintessence of Marxism-Leninism. Chairman Mao's greatness and his ability to lead the Chinese revolution to victory rest on this point. We have many conditions for accomplishing the four modernizations; these conditions did not exist during Chairman Mao's lifetime, but we have them now. There are many things we will be unable to undertake if we fail to consider problems in the light of present conditions and to summon up determination. As a result of several years of efforts, there are favorable international conditions for us to absorb advanced technology and capital from abroad. We did not have this condition during Chairman Mao's lifetime. We could not summon up such resolution today if it is said that we should not do anything that Chairman Mao did not mention. We now have conditions that Chairman Mao never encountered, and we should grasp these conditions and make use of them to accomplish the goal of the four modernizations which Chairman Mao proposed and Premier Zhou proclaimed. This is called holding aloft the great banner of Chairman Mao. If we could only do things that Chairman Mao spoke of, what could we do now? Marxism itself must develop! Mao Zedong Thought must develop too! Otherwise it will become ossified!

Comrade Deng Xiaoping pointed out in his speech at the closing session of the central work conference on 13 December 1978: "If a party, a state or a nation proceeds from books in everything, its ideology will become ossified and superstition will run rampant. It will not therefore be able to advance, its life will come to an end, and the party and state will perish. Comrade Mao Zedong repeatedly stressed this point during the rectification movement. Only by emancipating the mind, seeking truth from facts, proceeding from reality in everything and integrating theory with reality can our socialist modernization drive progress smoothly and can our party's Marxist-Leninist-Mao Zedong Thought theory develop." He also said, "Seeking truth from facts is the foundation of the proletarian world outlook and the ideological foundation of Marxism. In the past we relied on seeking truth from facts in all the victories we won in the revolution, we must similarly rely on seeking truth from facts today in accomplishing the four modernizations."

In his 29 February 1980 speech at the 5th plenary session of the 11th Central Committee, Comrade Deng Xiaoping dwelt specifically on problems of the party's ideological line. He said, "The third plenary session established, or, more accurately, reiterated the party's Marxist ideological line. Marx and Engels founded the dialectical and historical materialist ideological line, Chairman Mao summarized it in the Chinese language and wrote 'seek truth from facts,' four big characters, on the party school door. Seeking truth from facts, proceeding from reality in everything, integrating theory with reality, taking practice as the sole criterion for testing truth—this is our ideological line."

Comrade Deng Xiaoping pointed out in a talk on 27 March 1981: "Comrade Chen Yun has said, when he returned to Yanan from Moscow, Chairman Mao said to him on three occasions that he should study philosophy, and laid particular stress on seeking truth from facts. Comrade Chen Yun felt that he benefited greatly from that. Now, certain people utter opinions most of which only look at the phenomena, because their theories are not rooted in practice. Only by laying down such a root can one truly correct errors, including 'leftist' and rightist errors. The Yanan rectification drive opposed subjectivism, sectarianism and stereotyped party writings; it solved the problems fundamentally, not superficially."

3. IT IS NECESSARY TO REVIVE AND CARRY FORWARD OUR PARTY'S FINE TRADITIONS AND WORK STYLE

On 18 August 1977, Comrade Deng Xiaoping pointed out in his "closing address at the 11th national congress of the CCP": "We must revive and carry forward the mass line, the fine tradition and style which Chairman Mao fostered in our party. We must truly have faith in the masses and rely on them, listen to the voice of the people, have their well-being at heart and never for a moment divorce ourselves from them." "We must revive and carry forward the practice of seeking truth from facts, the fine tradition and style which Chairman Mao fostered in our party. The minimum requirement for a communist is to be an honest person, honest in word and honest in deed. Deed and word must correspond and theory and practice must be closely integrated. We must reject flashiness without substance and every sort of boasting. There must be less empty talk and more hard work. We must be steadfast and dedicated." "We must revive and carry forward the practice of criticism and self-criticism, the fine tradition and style which Chairman Mao fostered in our party. Within the party and within the ranks of the people, we should conscientiously apply the principle, 'say all you know and say it without reserve' and 'blame not the speaker but be warned by his words,' as well as the principle of unity-criticism-unity." "We must revive and carry forward the fine tradition and style of modesty and prudence, freedom from arrogance and impetuosity, and plain living and hard struggle, which Chairman Mao fostered in our party. We must wholeheartedly serve the Chinese people and the people of the world." "We must revive and carry forward the practice of democratic centralism, the fine tradition and style which Chairman Mao fostered in our party. We must strive for a political situation in the whole party, the whole army and the whole country, in which there is both centralism and

democracy, both discipline and freedom, both unity of will and personal ease of mind and liveliness."

On 30 March 1979, Comrade Deng Xiaoping pointed out at the meeting to discuss the party's theoretical work: "In order to improve the general mood of society, it is necessary first of all to improve the party's work style. In particular, it is necessary to urge the party's leading comrades at all levels to set an example. The party is the model for the whole society, and the party's leading comrades at all levels are models for the whole party. If the party organization shelves the opinions and interests of the masses and remains indifferent, how can it expect the masses to have faith in and cherish its leadership? If the party's leading cadres do not set strict demands for themselves and do not observe party discipline and state law, if they violate the party's principles, practice factionalism, seek special privileges, secure advantages through pull or influence, indulge in extravagance and waste, feather their nests at public expense, do not share weal and woe with the masses, do not strive to be the first to bear hardships and the last to enjoy comforts, do not follow the decisions of the organization, do not accept supervision from the masses and even resort to retaliation against those who criticize them, how can we expect them to remold the general mood of society? At the present turning point in history, when problems pile up like mountains and a thousand things remain to be done, it is of decisive importance to strengthen party leadership and correctly orientate the party's work style.

"Comrade Mao Zedong said: 'As long as our party is completely honest and upright in work style, the people of the whole country will learn from us. As long as those people outside the party who have these unhealthy ways are good and honest, they will learn from us and rectify their mistakes. In this way, they will influence the whole nation.' Only by improving the party's work style can we change the prevalent social customs and uphold the four basic principles."

With reference to the question of upholding and improving party leadership in his 16 January 1980 report "On the Current Situation and Tasks," Comrade Deng Xiaoping pointed out: "At present, the pressing issue before us is to restore the party's combat capabilities. The party should be a combat force, the vanguard of the proletariat. It should be a unified and well-disciplined contingent with a high sense of discipline. Only by restoring this state of affairs can the party have combat capabilities." "At present, some of our party members are not qualified. Some of the new party members who joined our ranks when the ultra-leftist line held sway have never received any party education. They cannot set an example for the masses and are therefore not qualified. Some of our old party members have measured up to the requirements for a long time. However, they cannot set an example for the masses now and are therefore not so qualified. We advocate the party spirit and oppose factionalism. Some people desperately cling to their faction. There are many people whose factional spirit is higher than their party spirit, and among them are some of our old party members. How can these people qualify? Why was our party so powerful in the past? During the war years we used to say that if 30 percent of the soldiers of a company are party members, this company must be a good one with strong combat capabilities. Why? It is because party members are the first to charge forward and the last to retreat in fighting; because they are the first to bear hardships and the last to enjoy comforts in everyday life. In this way, they can set an example for the masses and become their core." "Some communists are different now. They have joined the party because they wanted to be the first to enjoy comforts and the last to bear hardships. In opposing privileges, we are actually opposing the seeking of personal privileges by some of our party members and party cadres. That is why we say that our efforts to revive and carry forward the party's fine traditions and work style involve a question of party members' qualifications. Whether or not they measure up to the qualifications and requirements is a question that is now put not only before the new party members but also before some old party members. Therefore, there does exist a question of rectification in our party."

In his speech at the enlarged meeting of the Political Bureau of the CCP Central Committee on 18 August 1980, Comrade Deng Xiaoping, when speaking of the malpractices in the leadership system of the party and state, pointed out: "The chief malpractices are the phenomena of bureaucracy, over-concentration of power, patriarchal system, lifelong tenure of office for leading cadres, and special privileges of every description." He said, "Bureaucratic phenomena comprise a big problem that exists extensively in the political life of the party and state. Its chief manifestations and harmful effects are: standing high above the masses, abusing one's power, divorcing oneself from reality and the masses, being keen on keeping up appearances, indulging in idle talk, thinking in a rigid way, sticking to conventions, overstaffing of organizations, having more hands than needed, being dilatory in doing things, not paying attention to efficiency, being irresponsible, not keeping one's promise, sending official documents everywhere, shifting responsibility onto one another, putting on sheer bureaucratic airs, giving people a lecture at the slightest provocation, retaliating, suppressing democracy, deceiving one's superiors and deluding one's subordinates, being imperious and despotic, resorting to bribery for the benefit of relatives or friends, perverting justice for a bribe, and so on. Either in our internal affairs or in our international contacts, this has developed to an intolerable extent." Comrade Deng Xiaoping also pointed out, "During the 'Great Cultural Revolution,' Lin Biao and the 'gang of four' went in for special privileges, bringing about great calamities to the masses. At present, there are also a few cadres who do not regard themselves as the servants but as the masters of the people. They go in for special privileges, bringing about the strong discontent of the masses and damaging the party's prestige. If these are not resolutely corrected, they will certainly corrupt our ranks of cadres."

In his speech at the central work conference on 25 December 1980, Comrade Deng Xiaoping pointed out: "To uphold the leadership of the party, it is imperative to improve the leadership and style of the party. At present, the party's work among the masses is slightly weaker than it was before the 'Great Cultural Revolution,' and the working method is crude in part. These have hindered the party's link with the masses. Only by strengthening vigorously the party's link with the masses and going deep into the masses to conduct ideological and political work will it be easy to overcome the many difficulties in the economic readjustment. The unhealthy tendency among the extremely small number of party members and cadres is very unfavorable to the restoration of the party's prestige among the masses. I agree with what Comrade Chen Yun has said, that the question of the party's work style is one of life and death for a party in power. It is necessary to strictly carry out the 'guiding principles for inner-party political life,' and unswervingly rectify various unhealthy tendencies. It is especially necessary to resolutely oppose the erroneous attitude of feigning compliance and double-dealing toward the line, principles and policies of the CCP Central Committee."

In this speech, Comrade Deng Xiaoping proposed: "It is necessary to educate the comrades in the whole party in promoting the spirit of selflessness, subordinating oneself to the overall situation, carrying out arduous struggle and being honest in performing one's official duties, and to uphold communist ideas and morality. The socialist country that we are building should have not only a high degree of material civilization, but also a high degree of spiritual civilization. Spiritual civilization refers not only to education, science and culture (these are absolutely indispensable), but also communist ideas, ideals, faith, morality and discipline, revolutionary stand and principle, the comradely relationship between one person and another, and so on. These do not require very good material conditions or very high educational standards. Have we not joined the revolution up to now by relying on the scientific theory of Marxism and the revolutionary spirit stated above? From Yanan to new China, in addition to the correct political orientation, have we not relied on this valuable revolutionary spirit to attract the people of the whole country and the friendly personages abroad? Without this spiritual civilization, and without communist ideas and morality, how can we build socialism? The more the party and government carry out various economic reforms and an open foreign policy, the more the party members, especially the senior leading cadres of the party, should pay high attention to and earnestly practice communist ideas and morality. Otherwise, being disarmed spiritually, how can we educate the youths and lead the state and the people in building socialism? During the new democratic revolutionary period, we persisted in guiding the entire work with the communist ideological system and restraining the words and deeds of party members and advanced elements with communist morality. We advocated and commended whole-hearted service to the people, 'the individual subordinating himself to the organization,' 'selflessness,' 'utter devotion to jothers without any thought of self,' and 'fearing neither hardship nor death.' Now that we have entered the socialist period, some people have gone so far as to 'repudiate' these solemn revolutionary slogans, and this preposterous 'repudiation' not only fails to meet effective resistance, but wins the sympathy and support of some people in our ranks. Can a party member who has party and revolutionary spirit tolerate the continued existence of this situation?"

Comrade Deng Xiaoping also said, "Comrade Mao Zedong said that a man should have a little spirit. In protracted revolutionary wars, under the guidance of correct political orientation, we proceeded from analyzing the practical situation and won great victories by carrying forward the revolutionary and death-defying spirit, the spirit of strictly observing discipline and of self-sacrifice, the spirit of selflessness and making things easy for others and taking the difficulties on oneself, the spirit of conquering all enemies and difficulties, and the spirit of upholding revolutionary optimism and surmounting every difficulty to win victory.

"To engage in socialist construction and achieve the four modernizations, it is likewise necessary to vigorously carry forward this spirit under the correct leadership of the CCP Central Committee. A party member who does not have this spirit cannot be regarded as a qualified one. Besides this, we should also spread this spirit among the entire people and youths by giving it great publicity and setting an example, so that it will become the main pillar of spiritual civilization of the PRC, cherished by all people in the world who demand revolution and progress and admired by many people in the world who lack spiritual ballast and suffer spiritual depression."

4. WE SHOULD DEVELOP CRITICISM AND SELF-CRITICISM AND MAINTAIN STRICT DISCIPLINE

On 2 June 1978, Comrade Deng Xiaoping pointed out in his speech at the all-PLA political work conference, "One important point in rectifying and reorganizing the leading groups well is to rectify the work style. During the past years, Lin Biao and the 'gang of four' have seriously destroyed the army's work style, and their pernicious influence has taken deep root. In some units there are serious unhealthy trends and practices, and repeated orders cannot put an end to them. As a result, there is confusion between good and bad, the fragrant and the stinking and right and wrong. This state of affairs has roused the indignation of the masses, gravely impeded the mobilization of all positive factors and destroyed unity. We must criticize and put an end to these unhealthy trends and practices."

On 13 December 1978, Comrade Deng Xiaoping pointed out in his speech at the closing session of the central work conference, "A country must have its laws and a party, its regulations and discipline. The constitution of a party comprises its most fundamental regulations and discipline. Without the regulations and discipline of the party, the laws of the state can hardly be effective. The tasks of the discipline inspection commissions and organizational departments at all levels are not only to handle cases, but also, and more important, to maintain the regulations and discipline of the party so as to earnestly effect a rectification of the party's work style. Anyone who violates the party's discipline should be punished accordingly so as to make a clear distinction between merits and demerits and between reward and punishment, thus fostering the healthy tendencies and dealing blows at the unhealthy tendencies."

On 16 January 1980, Comrade Deng Xiaoping pointed out in his report, "On the Current Situation and Tasks," "In order to uphold and improve the party's leadership, we must intensify its discipline. During the 'Great Cultural Revolution' the party's discipline slackened and it has not yet been completely restored. This is an important reason why the party cannot play its proper role. Owing to the considerable laxity in discipline, many party members act as they please and regard the party's line, principles and

policies and resolutions and the tasks the party assigns them as something they have the right to refuse to carry out or to carry out only partially. If a party allows its members to speak and act absolutely freely according to their individual will, naturally, it will be impossible for it to have a unified will or any combat effectiveness and it will also be impossible for it to successfully fulfill its tasks. Therefore, we should uphold and improve the party's leadership, strictly put the party's discipline into effect in order to greatly heighten our sense of discipline. An individual must obey the organization, the minority must obey the majority, the lower levels must obey the higher levels and the whole party must obey the Central Committee. We should strictly carry out the above principles. Otherwise, the party cannot form a combat collective and will be unqualified for the rank of pioneers." "The most important in the above principles is that the whole party must obey the Central Committee. The Central Committee has made mistakes, but these mistakes have long been corrected by the Central Committee itself. Nobody can be allowed to resist the leadership of the Central Committee on the pretext of its mistakes. Only if the whole party obeys the Central Committee strictly, can the party lead all its members and the people throughout the country to fight for the fulfillment of the great task of modernization.

"Should anyone seriously violate this rule, the party organizations and discipline inspection committees at all levels must strictly enforce disciplinary measures against them because the maximum interests of the party and the people of the whole country are at stake. We must resolutely carry forward and safeguard democracy in the party. Should a party member object to the party's decisions, he can state his views through the organization, or reserve his opinions, or even make suggestions to the Central Committee either through the organization or directly. From the Central Committee down, party organizations at all levels must seriously consider these opinions. However, everything that has been decided on by the Central Committee and by the party organizations must be obeyed until further changes are announced by the party. We must state our views in accordance with the party's decisions and must not willfully spread opinions that show distrust or dissatisfaction with and opposition to the line, principles and policies of the Central Committee. Party papers and journals must unconditionally publicize the party's position." "We must resolutely eliminate anarchist trends of thought which the 'gang of four' introduced into the party as well as all brands of bourgeois liberalism which have newly emerged within the party."

In his speech given at the 5th Plenary Session of the 11th CCP Central Committee on 29 February 1980, Comrade Deng Xiaoping said, "Our party actually needs rectification at present. This matter was put forth 7 years ago and it has not yet been settled. Quite a number of the 38 million party members are not up to the mark. After this plenary session, it will be necessary to carry out education throughout the party linking it with the discussion on the draft of the revised party constitution and the implementation of the guiding principles for inner-party political life." "Those who are not up to the mark should carry out criticism and self-criticism. We should demand changes in them."

At his speech given at the enlarged meeting of the

Political Bureau of the CCP Central Committee on 18 August 1980, Comrade Deng Xiaoping said, "In correcting the phenomenon of privileges, we have to solve both ideological problems and problems in systems. All citizens are equal before the law and all party members are equal before the party constitution and before the party's discipline. Each has equal rights and duties as stipulated by law and no one can gain extra advantages or violate the law. Anyone who breaks the law, no matter who he is, will be investigated by public security organs according to law, and judicial organs will handle his case according to law. No one is permitted to interfere and no one who breaks the law will remain at large. Any party member who violates the party constitution or the party's discipline, no matter who he is, will be punished. No one is permitted to interfere, and no party member who violates the party constitution or the party's discipline will remain at large. Only when these are resolutely enforced can we thoroughly solve the problem of privileges and the problem of discipline. We should establish a system for the masses and party members to supervise cadres, in particular, leading cadres. The people have the right to expose, accuse, impeach, replace and dismiss according to law any cadre who seeks privileges and who does not mend his ways after he is criticized and given education and to demand that he make economic restitution and be punished according to law and discipline. We should lay down rules and regulations for limits of cadres' functions and powers and for their remuneration both politically and in their livelihood. The most important thing is to have a special organization to carry out impartial and incorruptible supervision and checking."

In his speech on problems on the ideological front given on 17 July 1981, Comrade Deng Xiaoping said, "The party has made outstanding achievements in its leadership over the ideological front and the literary and artistic front.

This should be affirmed. There is also a certain tendency toward oversimplification and crudeness in our work. We should not deny or ignore this either. However, I think what needs more attention at present is the lax and weak situation. Erroneous trends cannot be criticized and criticism is regarded as using the big stick.

"At present, we find it difficult to carry out criticism and even more difficult to carry out self-criticism. One of the three essential work styles is self-criticism. This is something that marks the chief difference between our party and other political parties. However, quite a lot of people are still quite unable to carry out criticism and self-criticism."

Comrade Deng Xiaoping also said, "At present, some people regard themselves as heroes. When they have not been criticized, their problem does not appear so serious, but once they are criticized, even more people become attached to them. This is a very abnormal phenomenon and we should strive to put an end to it. Of course, there are social and historical reasons for this phenomenon. It is mainly the sequel of the 10 years of disorder and is also the result of bourgeois erosion from abroad. We should make a concrete analysis of each individual case. But the main problem at present is not in the phenomenon itself but in how we look upon this phenomenon. In handling the problems at present, we should draw a lesson from the past and should not stage movements. We should appropriately handle the mistakes of each individual according to their nature, degree and his understanding of his mistakes. We should pay attention to the way of making criticism and should make appropriate criticism. We should not make joint attacks or stage movements. Nevertheless, it certainly will never do to abandon ideological work, criticism and self-criticism. We certainly should not abandon the weapon of criticism."

On the Party and Modernization, 16 December 1981

29

This editorial urges Party members to recognize the importance of Party discipline as a prerequisite for modernization.

At present, there are several important questions which merit the attention of all comrades of the party. If all party comrades have a unanimous understanding of these questions, they will be able to concentrate their energy and work with concerted efforts to push forward the entire cause of socialist modernization.

["Some Questions that Merit Attention," *Red Flag*, 16 December 1981.]

The First Question Is, What Is the Most Fundamental Task of the Whole Party at Present and in the Future?

Reviewing our development in work over the past few years, we should ask, where did we come from and where do we go from here? How far have we come since the smashing of the "gang of four"? In conclusion, first, we brought about a change in the chaotic situation. This was our first achievement. Second, we restored to order things which had been thrown into disorder in the past. This was our second achievement. So, where do we go from here? First, we should promote the national economy; second, we should promote the building of spiritual civilization. We have already scored two achievements, and we are now going to fulfill the other two targets. This is our strategic ideology and is a major affair of our country.

Promoting the national economy and the building of spiritual civilization are two inseparable targets of struggle which supplement the development of each other. We must struggle for the realization of these two targets. We must stress methods in order to struggle. We will not be able to fulfill our targets if we adopt wrong methods. Comrade Mao Zedong once said: In order to cross the river, we must solve the problem of using a boat or a bridge. In the light of this, we see that methods are of great importance. Similarly, the correct methods, the correct means and correct measures are all very important. However, we must not mix up targets and ends with methods and means. The methods and means are not an end but are the bridges or boats for realizing an end. For instance, our economic readjustment is not an end; and we must not treat readjustment as our end. We only carry out readjustment for the purpose of promoting the economy. We are making use of the method of "readjusting, restructuring, reorganization and upgrading," in order to promote our national economy. Our end is to promote the national economy. Another example is criticism and self-criticism, which is only an important method but not our end. Our end is to strengthen party unity and enhance the party's combat effectiveness. In our actual life, many comrades usually regard methods and means as an end. This is a misconception, and we must always pay attention to it.

All our departments and all our work must struggle for realizing the two great goals of promoting the national economy and promoting building of spiritual civilization. Now, it is necessary to remind all our party comrades of our two great goals and remind them to work closely around them. Everything must be subordinated to the two great goals, and everything must serve the two great goals. This is what we call working with concerted efforts and concentrating all energy to struggle for the building of the four modernizations. Otherwise, no matter what you do, it means promoting decentralism, routinism, and selfish departmentalism. Therefore, all work fronts and party committees at each level cannot forget our fundamental target or forget the fundamental interests of the party and the people. However, some of our comrades always forget this question. They only see partial and immediate matters and cannot realize the overall situation or have a more profound understanding of things. What is considered a relatively higher ideological level? The answer to that is always remembering our target of struggle.

The Second Question Is, What Is the Target That We Demand of Promoting the National Economy? And What Are the Major Demands?

It is impossible for us to suddenly promote the national economy. The national economy will not be promoted by leaps and bounds in a short period of time in the future, particularly in the coming 1 or 2 years or during the sixth 5-year plan period. There are a lot of factors, both subjective and objective, accounting for this. However, the objective factors are the principal ones. The CCP Central Committee is very determined to forbid the pursuit of high quotas and forbid forcing any areas or departments by assigning high production quotas.

This point has been made very clear. However, at the same time, the whole party must also understand that the national economy must be developed at a certain speed in the future. In the words of Comrade Deng Xiaoping, we must have a practical speed which can be attained by means of hard efforts. This is a good remark of Comrade Deng Xiaoping which explains the relationship between quantity and quality. On the other hand, there must be a demand for a certain quantity and on the other, there must also be strict demands for quality. Comrade Zhao Ziyang recently also made a good remark on stressing economic benefits. His remark bore the same significance as that of Comrade Deng Xiaoping. This clearly shows that the kind of speed which fails to fulfill demands of quality and does not take economic benefits into account is a sham speed. If the quality of the products is below average and the products cannot be sold, the more production, the worse the situation will be. This is what we call a sham speed. We made many such mistakes in the past and the lessons taught have been bitter. Nevertheless, we should also realize another aspect. There will not be any real economic benefits without a certain speed or without a certain quantity of production. If productivity is kept low and not much produce is on sale in the markets, how can one say that they bring about economic benefits when production is totally divorced from demand? As Marxists, we uphold the theory of integrating quality with quantity, we must not mechanically separate quantity from quality, and benefit from speed or set one against another.

What speed can we attain in developing the national economy in the next few years? As for agriculture, we are confident that so long as we work in accordance with the present principles and proceed along the present path, the speed of development is very likely to exceed the average annual growth rate of 4 percent fixed during the sixth 5-year plan. For instance, there were 1,622 brigades in 1979 where the per capita income from collective distribution exceeded 300 yuan, and there were 5,569 similar brigades last year, showing an increase of 2.4 percent. And the number of similar brigades is expected to increase this year. Many counties have doubled or increased by several times their agricultural output over the past 2 or 3 years. Many counties have doubled their production in a year, some doubled their production in 2 years, while others increased their production by more than 300 percent in 2 or 3 years. In Shazhou County in Jiangsu Province, the total output of commune and brigade enterprises increased by 270 percent in 3 years, and agricultural and sideline products also increased by more than 150 percent. In Fengyang County in Anhui Province, grain production was so abundant that no one would steal the grain even if it was placed at the door outside the house. *Renmin Ribao* once carried a newsletter entitled "Laughter of People in the Home Village" in which touching scenes of increasing production and income in Feixi County in Anhui Province were vividly portrayed. The family of three mentioned in the newsletter had a total income of 1,500 yuan and the per capita income was 500 yuan. The head of the household humorously said: "I have anticipated the demand put forth by Chairman Hu." In Maduo County in Qinghai Province, the per capita income from collective distribution was above 460 yuan last year.

In Haicheng County in Liaoning Province, the agricultural output was increased to 270 million yuan from 170 million yuan and the total output of commune and brigade enterprises to 220 million yuan from 120 million yuan; the average per capita income of the commune members was 300 yuan. So long as we do not make mistakes and implement the right policies, it is possible for the income of the peasants to be increased by 100, 200 or 300 percent in the coming few years. All of us must pay attention to this question: Agriculture is taking the lead at present and is in the ascendant. Agriculture must speed up development of both industry and commerce. We must not underestimate this question, otherwise we will be thrown into a passive situation.

Then, to what extent can industry grow? So long as we work hard, industry can grow at or above the rate of 5 percent, which is a practical and genuine 5 percent. Under the premise of guaranteeing quality and stressing the economic benefits, a faster speed is advantageous while a lower speed is disadvantageous.

If we maintain a very low speed and do not strive to attain a higher speed which can be attained by means of arduous efforts, we will cause five disadvantages. First, we cannot meet the people's demand, and in particular, the demands of the peasants. At present, the purchasing power of the people and particularly those in the rural areas has been largely increased. By the end of September, the savings of rural inhabitants amounted to more than 48 billion yuan, showing an increase of 12.5 billion yuan over the same period last year. Second, we cannot solve the financial problems. We can increase financial revenue only when production is increased. When the country's production is increased by 1 percent each year, financial revenue will be increased by 1 billion yuan and more. Third, it will be harmful to enhancing morale. Fourth, it will be harmful to improving the broad cadres' level of management and administration. Fifth, it will be harmful to the return of Taiwan to the motherland. Of course, we are taking an approach toward speed and of seeking truth from facts. If a higher speed cannot be attained, we should not force ourselves to do so, for even if we force ourselves to do so, we might not be able to succeed. This is what we call "more haste, less speed." We must on the one hand seek truth from facts and on the other, go all out. Going all out means trying every possible means to tap potential. Each place should compare its present production with its best record, that of its neighbors, and that of foreign countries which possess similar conditions. The potential lies in the comparison of these three things. In Changzhou municipality in Jiangsu Province, the total population is 380,000 and the industrial output scored was 3.8 billion yuan. People there summed up their experience as four thousands: Trying thousands of ways, crossing thousands of crags and torrents, saying thousands of words and undergoing thousands of trials and tribulations. This is a good remark which illustrates the spirit of going all out and tapping potential.

The Third Question Is, What Is the High Degree of Socialist Spiritual Civilization That We Are Going To Build?

The building of socialist spiritual civilization, whether at the present stage or in a certain period of time in the future, demands that we work hard in the following four aspects:

First of all, our party must possess the best work style among all proletarian ruling parties throughout the world. Up until the 1950's our party could be said to be the one which possessed the best work style and had a good reputation because of its good work style. Our party is one which takes wholeheartedly serving the people as its sole aim, and upholds unity and observes strict discipline. It is vigorous and bold in struggling for the interests of the nation and its people and possesses the three great work styles of integrating theory with practice, working in close connection with the masses and unfolding criticism and self-criticism. Over the past few decades, our party has established great prestige and image among the people. However, it is pitiable now that our present party work style has become corrupt due to sabotage during the 10 years of upheaval. So long as we restore our proper party work style, people throughout the country will learn from us. Thus, the entire social mood and appearance will change.

Second, people of all nationalities, at all levels and people belonging to different social groups throughout the country must have a high degree of unity and unanimity in ideology, politics and morality. We must maintain close national unity, unity between the army and the government, unity between the armymen and the people, unity between the workers and peasants, unity between cadres and masses, unity between the party and the masses and unity between party and nonparty which will not be put to rout or broken up. There are a lot of nationalities in such a big country as ours; and some places fail to maintain a harmonious situation regarding relations between nationalities. This has been brought about by history and is a consequence of insufficient education. Our People's Republic has been formed as a result of revolutionary wars, and the army enjoyed great prestige among the masses. However, the army's prestige was infringed upon during the "Great Cultural Revolution," leading to misunderstandings between the army and the people. Hence, the reputation that the army enjoys now is not as good as in the 1950's.

Besides this, various problems also exist in the relations between the workers and peasants, the urban areas and rural areas, the cadres and the masses, party and nonparty and between various places. All these problems can only be solved by means of arduous efforts for a relatively long period of time. If relations between people of all nationalities, at all levels and those belonging to different social groups throughout the country are promoted, and if all people are closely related and mutually dependent and help each other, our country will surely be invincible and will not be defeated by any force or enemy. If we depart from the close unity between people of all nationalities, at all levels and those who belong to different social groups throughout the country, we will not be able to talk about a high degree of socialist spiritual civilization.

Third, our country must on the one hand possess a high degree of democracy and on the other, strict discipline and good social order. At present, our country's democratic life, our legal system and discipline are far from being perfect. We must incessantly improve them. Only by so doing, can stability and unity and a lively political situation be consolidated and developed to a greater extent.

Fourth, we must also have a rich and colorful cultural life, a beautiful environment and sanitation. We must not neglect making the environment green and beautifying it; neither must we neglect sanitation. Comrade Mao Zedong pointed out in the 1950's: We must change prevailing habits and customs and transform China. We should not hold afforestation as a minor affair; it is greatly related to the health of all people and the mental outlook of the whole Chinese nation. It is wrong to look down on these things or not do a good job of them.

Promoting the building of spiritual civilization, we must always grasp these four aspects and must start from the central organs. We must grasp them with both our hands, grasping material civilization on the one hand, and spiritual civilization on the other. Promoting the national economy means grasping material civilization. Analyzing the relationship between the two, the economy forms the basis for spiritual civilization. An effective economy lays a foundation for the building of spiritual civilization. When building of spiritual civilization forges ahead, the people will have a better mental outlook and will make greater efforts which will in turn push forward the development of material civilization. Therefore, we must not separate material civilization from spiritual civilization. Many of our cadres are one-sided; those who are engaged in political and ideological work usually do not understand production, and those who are engaged in economic work are never concerned about spiritual civilization. In the future, no matter what kind of work we are doing, it is necessary to grasp spiritual civilization well.

The Fourth Question Is, What Is the Enhancement of Revolutionary Vigor That We Forcefully Advocate?

Enhancing revolutionary vigor has been put forth by the CCP Central Committee and was directed against certain comrades among our cadres who were lethargic. Advocating enhancement of revolutionary vigor now, we of course should not repeat the erroneous methods which were used in the past. In the past, it seemed that the mention of enhancing revolutionary vigor would mean telling lies and promoting high production quotas; or giving false information, reporting only the good news and hiding all bad news. The enhancement of revolutionary vigor that we talk about today should be manifested mainly in studying the new situation, solving new problems, devising new methods and making a breakthrough. The situation varies every day and there are new problems every day. If we just work in accordance with the old regulations and conventions, we will not be able to devise new methods or make a breakthrough. To enhance revolutionary vigor, we must do a still better job of our studies.

We must read books, including books on theory, history, science, technology, business management; however, we should not read behind closed doors. Although sometimes we must read some books behind closed doors, we should not indulge in it, because it is not of utmost importance. Primarily we must make arduous efforts, go deep into reality and have a thorough understanding of Marxism, modern science, modern technology and modern business management on the basis of integrating theory with practice. Comrade Mao Zedong was correct in calling on us to learn from actual practice. Although learning from actual practice is not the sole approach, it is certainly the principal one.

It is necessary to have a correct understanding of enhancing revolutionary vigor. We must carry out specific analyses when we judge whether a person is vigorous or not; we must not indiscriminately accuse people of being lethargic. Some comrades have become old and are not physically energetic enough for vigorous activities, although they are still mentally enthusiastic. Regarding these people, we should not say that they are lethargic; they are physically weak, as they are influenced by the law of nature. We must take good care of these comrades who have made contributions to the revolution; we must look after both their political treatment and their livelihood. The current problem is that we have not been treating retired comrades well but have been taking very good care of those at their posts. It seems that we have turned things upside down. We should do things in an opposite way: demanding that those at their posts do a good job of their work and taking good care of those who have retired from their posts. Things will not work out as desired if we reverse this relationship. Once at work, people should do a good job at their work until the day they cannot work. By then, they should retreat to the second front. Retreating to the second front means they will be taken good care of by the party organizations. Thus, we will be able to distinguish between right and wrong. This is a question that should be clearly explained.

Some comrades who made mistakes, including serious mistakes, in the past are lethargic because they shoulder heavy burdens. Regarding this, the idea of the CCP Central Committee is to deal leniently with those comrades who made mistakes or serious mistakes in the past and in particular with those who made relatively great contributions to the revolution after they had examined their mistakes to a certain extent. A great number of comrades made mistakes during the "Great Cultural Revolution." Both subjective factors and historical conditions accounted for the mistakes, but in a certain sense, the historical conditions are the major factors. Therefore, dealing with them leniently seems to comply with objective reality. Certainly, dealing with them leniently does not mean taking no action against these comrades or dealing with them too leniently. However, adopting the principle of leniency toward the comrades is conducive to bracing up those comrades who made numerous mistakes in the past. Adopting this policy means encouraging our entire party to work in accordance with dialectics, looking at questions from a dialectical point of view and educating the cadres with dialectics. We must understand that mistakes, under certain conditions, can be transformed and similarly, so long as the comrades who made mistakes in the past conscientiously work and correct their mistakes, they can be transformed into good comrades. On the other hand, those comrades who are relatively correct may also be led astray or become hopeless under certain circumstances. Therefore, we must draw the attention of the comrades who did not make any mistakes during the "Great Cultural Revolution" to the fact that if they do not maintain vigilance, they may make mistakes. There have been numerous examples of people going from right to wrong because they thought they were always correct and were not heedful enough.

In some cases, some comrades who are energetic and are bold in thought and deed slacken off after a certain period of time. What is the factor accounting for this? In order to get the answer, we must carry out specific analyses of these comrades. Perhaps, some of them slacken off because they have been isolated and made fun of. In some places where unsavory trends are practiced, those comrades who are bold in airing their views and doing new things are usually isolated or attacked. There are really some people who like to nitpick other more active comrades and engage in finding trivial errors. Of course, minor problems should also be pointed out. However, minor problems should be solved simply; we should not make a fuss over them or complicate them. Therefore we should help those comrades who are good on the whole but have a few minor problems, under the premise of supporting them, and encourage them to make greater efforts and do a better job of their work. We must primarily support those who are bold in grasping work and working in accordance with the party's policies. Simultaneously, it is necessary to help them overcome minor faults, and we must not attach primary significance to their minor faults. Otherwise, we are in fact infringing upon their morality and infringing upon the revolutionary vigor of the broad masses of cadres. We must pay attention to this point.

Some other comrades are lethargic because they have no confidence, or rather, do not have full confidence in the future. For instance, what is the root of the unsavory trends which exist among some party members and cadres? The root is that they are very calculating. Then why are they so calculating? It is because they think collective interest is unreliable. They do not believe that the state and the party have any prospects and think that they are unreliable. *Renmin Ribao* has carried an article "Political and Ideological Work Must Strengthen People's Confidence" which merits the attention of our comrades who are engaged in political and ideological work. Our propaganda and ideology must always strengthen people's confidence. How can a revolutionary make revolution if he lacks confidence? If we strengthen people's confidence by conducting more propaganda, fewer people will be so calculating; otherwise, there will be more people engaging in such activity. We do not mean that when we do a good job of propaganda, we will be able to prevent everybody from being calculating, but, at least, there will be fewer people engaging in such activity. We should also draw our attention to another problem. There is really a small number of people engaging in promoting severe individualism. They even hate socialism to the marrow of their bones. Although there is only a small number of such people, we cannot neglect them because they exist now and will continue to do so. It is heard that the "gang of four" is going to wreak vengeance; can they do it? The answer is no. However, there will be troublemakers. We must criticize the troublemakers and must punish according to law those who have committed serious offenses. Our party organizations at all levels, masses' organizations at all levels, trade unions and CYL committees must strengthen ideological education on these questions. They must, in particular, promote education in the prospect of, and confidence in, revolution. We must help the masses and in particular, the youths, enhance their awareness, enhance their pride of being a citizen of the PRC and strengthen their confidence in the bright prospects of the socialist motherland.

The Fifth Question Is, What Is Marxist Mass Standpoint?

The mass standpoint is one of our country's fundamental stands and viewpoints. We have been repeatedly taught about this by Comrade Mao Zedong over the past several decades. After the "Great Cultural Revolution," many of our party comrades in fact only had a vague understanding of the mass standpoint and the mass line. The situation has gradually improved over the past few years. However, there is still a large number of party comrades who do not have a correct understanding of the mass standpoint and should be reeducated.

First of all, our party serves the purpose of seeking the interests of the people. Besides the people's interests, our party has no other interests. Comrade Liu Shaoqi said: Our party takes wholeheartedly serving the people as its fundamental goal and we must wholeheartedly serve the people. Our party members and cadres absolutely cannot seek personal privileges by making use of their powers. Regarding this, many comrades have not maintained sharp vigilance, and the situation or party work style has not yet been improved in many places. We must repeatedly stress our party's fundamental goal. This goal is decided by the nature of our party as a proletarian pioneer force.

Second, we must always be concerned about the hardship of the people, hear the voice of the masses, consult with them and try our best to do good things for them. Although there have been improvements in this respect over the last few years, they are far from being sufficient. Simultaneously, we must pay attention to such a phenomenon: When talking about adopting the mass standpoint and doing good things for the masses, many comrades demand money from the state. It seems that they can only manage things with financial support from the state, otherwise they can do nothing. Some cadres even represent certain backward ideas about the masses and "fleece" the state. Here we mean that in some factories, mines and enterprises and in the communes and brigades in the rural areas, a small number of basic level cadres grasp every opportunity to demand money from the state, flaunting the banner of representing the people's interests. This is an erroneous act which infringes upon the interests of the state and violates the overall viewpoint of taking the interests of the state, the collective and the individual into consideration which is consistently advocated by our party. Regarding this question, we must carry out education and criticism within our party. We must point out that in doing this, these people are not representing the masses; that the broad masses never approve of this and that they are only representing the erroneous demands of a very small number of backward people among the broad masses. Currently, we must pay attention to this phenomenon. We must carry out education for the cadres, and in particular, the basic level cadres in taking the interests of the state, the collective and the individual into consideration. Our principle is to simultaneously take the interests of the three into consideration and not to violate the interests of the state and the collective by one-sidedly emphasizing the interest of the individual.

Third, there is another important viewpoint. Representing the interests of the masses, we are not only concerned about the masses' immediate interests but more importantly, we must also be concerned about the masses' long-term interests. Striving for development in production is where the masses' fundamental interest lies. Therefore, we can only gradually promote the masses' livelihood on the basis of developing production. We must not satisfy the masses' immediate interests by means of methods which infringe upon their long-term interests. In addition, we must arouse the enthusiasm of the masses to personally work for their well-being. We call this working for our well-being by ourselves. In saying this, although it does not mean that we can promote our well-being all by ourselves, we can run better and more welfare projects by mobilizing the masses to grasp them with the guidance and support of the state. Our party, trade unions and CYL committees should pay attention to this question. In short, regarding the question of the mass standpoint, we must have a correct and comprehensive Marxist viewpoint.

The Sixth Question Is, What Is the Principal Task of the Leading Organs?

Comrade Mao Zedong said when he was in Yanan that the leading organs had two great tasks to handle: The first one is to understand the situation and the other is to master the policies. He also said: We will have no right to speak if we do not carry out investigations; and if we do not understand the policies, we will not be able to make correct decisions on policies.

Honestly speaking, our party has been suffering great losses over the past few decades because we have not had a thorough understanding of the situation. Comrade Mao Zedong made mistakes himself in his later years because he did not understand the actual situation. This was a very important factor and was a matter of understanding. Comrade Mao Zedong was quite right in saying in "Strategy of China's Revolutionary War" that: "A commander's correct dispositions stem from his correct decisions; his correct decisions stem from his correct judgments; and his correct judgments stem from thorough and necessary reconnaissance and from pondering over and piecing together various kinds of data gathered through reconnaissance." He used the word "reconnaissance" here because he was talking about war. Generally speaking, "reconnaissance" means investigations. Correct understanding stems from investigations and from pondering over and piecing together the data gathered through investigations. This is the most fundamental prerequisite for each level and each leading department to lead work.

Investigations have been relatively more popular over the past few years. However, speaking of the party as a whole, insufficient investigation is still a common problem. On the other hand, most of our investigations are unreliable because the data is usually passed from a lower level to a higher level. For instance, many statistical figures have been invented by the cadres at lower levels and were later reported to the higher levels which believed the figures without doubt. Because the data itself is inaccurate and unreliable, no correct judgments can be made based on it. Therefore, our method of work is to advocate repeated investigations, repeated inspections, independent thought and independent judgment. In other words, it means we must do four things, namely: investigation, study, inspection and supervision. We must treat investigation, study, inspection and supervision as the principal tasks of our leaders at all levels and personnel of all leading organs. We must carry out investigations prior to giving orders.

The shape of China looks like a cock. All is bright when the cock crows. China was liberated and brightened up when the cock in China crowed for the first time. The cock in China crowed for the second time 32 years later, bringing about both merits and flaws. Now, the cock of China is going to crow for the third time for 20 years until the end of this century. The first crow lasted for 28 years, the second crow for 32 years and the third crow will be for another 20 years. In crowing the third time, the cock of China will bring about a strong socialist China, a modern, highly democratic and highly civilized China. Will the third crow resound through the skies? This has to be answered by the whole party, by our 20 million cadres, by our 39 million CCP members and 48 million CYL members, by the 100 million ranks of the working class and the 1 billion people of all nationalities. The Chinese Communist Party which possesses glorious revolutionary traditions, and the Chinese people, our broad masses of party members and CYL members, workers, peasants and intellectuals are bold and hardworking. We will be able to shoulder the great task entrusted to us by history and will victoriously fulfill our goal.

DENG XIAOPING

30

Opening Address to the Twelfth Party Congress, 1 September 1982

Deng again repeats two of his favorite themes—Party rectification and modernization.

Comrades, I now declare the Twelfth National Congress of the Communist Party of China open.

There are three main items on the agenda of our

[New China News Agency, 1 September 1982.]

congress: (1) consideration of the report of the eleventh Central Committee and decision on the party's programme for striving to create a new situation in all fields of socialist modernization; (2) consideration and adoption of the new constitution of the Communist Party of China; and

(3) election of a new Central Committee, a Central Advisory Commission and a new Central Commission for Discipline Inspection in accordance with the provisions of the new party constitution.

With the accomplishment of the tasks of this congress, our party will have a more clear-cut guiding ideology for socialist modernization, the party will be strengthened in a way more suited to the needs of the new historical period, and in the highest leading organs of the party there will be cooperation of old and new cadres and succession of the new to the old, thus making these organs a more vigorous command headquarters.

A review of the party's history will show this congress to be a most important meeting since the seventh national congress.

The seventh congress held in 1945 under the chairmanship of Comrade Mao Zedong was the most important one in the period of democratic revolution since the founding of our party. It summed up the historical experience gained in the tortuous development of China's democratic revolution in the previous twenty years and more, formulated a correct programme and correct tactics and overcame the erroneous ideas within the party so that unity in understanding based on Marxism-Leninism and Mao Zedong Thought was attained. As a result the party became more united than ever before. The seventh congress laid the foundation for the nationwide victory of the new-democratic revolution.

The eighth congress of the party held in 1956 analysed the situation following the basic completion of the socialist transformation of the private ownership of the means of production and put forth the task of all-round socialist construction. The line of the eighth congress was correct. However, because the party was not adequately prepared ideologically for all-round socialist construction at that time, in practice that line and many correct opinions put forward at that congress were not adhered to. After the eighth congress, we suffered serious setbacks, though we also achieved many successes in socialist construction.

The present congress is being held in circumstances vastly different from those at the time of the eighth congress. Just as the twenty-odd years of tortuous development of our democratic revolution before the seventh congress taught the whole party how to grasp the laws governing that revolution in China, so the twenty-odd years of tortuous development of our socialist revolution and construction after the eighth congress taught the whole party profound lessons. Since the third plenary session of the eleventh Central Committee (held in December 1978), our party has restored its correct policies in the economic, political, cultural and other fields of work and adopted a series of new and correct policies after studying the new situation and new experience. By comparison our party has, since the eighth congress, gained a much deeper understanding of the laws governing China's socialist construction, acquired much more experience and become much more conscious and determined in carrying through our correct principles. We have every reason to believe that the correct programme to be formulated at this congress will create a new situation in all fields of socialist modernization and bring prosperity to our party, our socialist cause, our country and all our nationalities.

In our modernization programme, we must proceed from China's realities. Both in our revolution and construction, we should learn from foreign countries and draw on their experience. But mechanical copying and application of foreign experience and models will get us nowhere. We have had many lessons in this respect. To integrate the universal truth of Marxism with the concrete realities of China, blaze a path of our own and build socialism with Chinese characteristics—this is the basic conclusion we have reached in summing up long, historical experience.

China's affairs should be run in our own way and by our own efforts. Independence and self-reliance have always been and will forever be our basic stand. While we Chinese people value our friendship and cooperation with other countries and people, we value even more our hard-won independence and sovereign rights. No foreign country can expect China to be its vassal, nor can it expect China to swallow any bitter fruit detrimental to China's interests. We will unswervingly follow a policy of opening to the outside world and actively increase exchanges with foreign countries on the basis of equality and mutual benefit. At the same time, we will keep a clear head, firmly resist corrosion by decadent ideas from abroad and never permit the bourgeois way of life to spread in our country. We Chinese people have our own national self-respect and pride. We deem it the highest honour to love our country and contribute our all to its socialist construction, and we deem it the deepest disgrace to impair the interests, dignity and honour of our socialist motherland.

The 1980's will be an important decade in the historical development of our party and state. To intensify socialist modernization, to strive for reunification and particularly for the return of Taiwan to the motherland, and to combat hegemonism and safeguard world peace—these are the three major tasks of our people in the 1980's. Economic construction is at the core of these tasks as it is the basis for the solution of China's external and domestic problems. In a long period to come, at least in the eighteen years or more up to the end of this century, we must diligently do the following four things: to restructure the administration and the economic set-up and make the ranks of cadres more revolutionary, younger in average age, better educated and more professionally competent; to build a socialist spiritual civilization; to strike at criminal activities in the economic and other fields that undermine socialism; and to rectify party style and consolidate the party organization on the basis of a conscientious study of the new party constitution. These will be the most important guarantees for our adherence to the socialist road and the concentration of our efforts on modernization.

Ours is now a big party, with a membership of 39 million, that exercises leadership over the whole state power. However, the members of the Communist Party will always be a minority in the whole population. None of the major tasks set forth by our party can be accomplished without the hard work of the masses of the people. Here, on behalf of our party, I wish to pay high tribute to all Chinese workers, peasants and intellectuals who have worked diligently for our socialist modernization, and to the Chinese People's Liberation Army—the Great Wall of steel safeguarding the security and socialist construction of our motherland.

China's democratic parties fought together with our party in the period of the democratic revolution and have advanced and undergone tests together with us in the period of socialism. In the construction work ahead, our party will continue its long-term cooperation with all patriotic democratic parties and all patriotic democrats. Here, on behalf of our party, I wish to express our sincere gratitude to all democratic parties and all our friends without party affiliations.

The cause of our party has enjoyed the support and assistance of the progressive personages and friendly countries throughout the world. Here, on behalf of our party, I wish to express our sincere gratitude to them.

We must do our work well and carefully, strengthen our unity with the people of all nationalities in the country and with the people of the whole world and struggle hard to make China a modern socialist country that is culturally advanced and highly democratic, and to oppose hegemonism, safeguard world peace and promote human progress.

Speeches to the Twelfth Party Congress by Two Other Party Elders, 6 September 1982

31

The still active, although elderly and ailing, Chen Yun and the retiring Ye Jianying stress the need to promote large numbers of worthy members in the Party hierarchy.

CHEN YUN'S SPEECH

I fully agree with the report delivered to this congress by Comrade Hu Yaobang on behalf of the Central Committee, with the draft of the revised party constitution, the opening speech made by Comrade Deng Xiaoping and with the speech made by Comrade Ye Jianying.

After the smashing of the "gang of four", our party set right its course at the third plenary session of its eleventh Central Committee and then, step by step through the fourth, fifth and sixth plenary sessions, it brought the nation's political life and socialist construction onto the correct path of sound development.

However, we must be soberly aware that for various reasons, the ranks of our party's cadres have long faced the problem of aging to varying degrees, and a gap between the old and the young. Unless this problem is solved now, and satisfactorily, the cause of communism may suffer a setback in China. All comrades, particularly the old comrades, should realize the gravity and urgency of this problem.

Therefore, the satisfactory solution of the problem of the smooth succession from old cadres to younger ones is an important task facing the whole party.

The first step in solving this problem is for the old cadres to retire successively from the leading bodies.

In the recent organizational reform of the party central organs and the State Council, some old comrades vacated their "front line" leading posts. And at the recent seventh plenary session of the 11th Central Committee a large number of other old comrades expressed the wish to leave the Central Committee and other leading posts.

This shows that our old cadres have a strong sense of revolutionary responsibility.

When the old cadres withdraw from the "front line", does it mean that they have to come to the end of their revolutionary career? No, it does not. Whether they withdraw to the second line to do such work as they have the strength for or completely retire, they should support the young and middle-aged cadres in their work and take upon themselves the task of helping and guiding the latter and passing on experience to them. Only when the old cadres have fulfilled this task can it be said that they have done their bit to the last for the party and the revolutionary cause.

Besides, since the ranks of our cadres now show a gap between the old and the young, the old comrades cannot leave the leading bodies all at once. As dictated by the actual situation, some old comrades will have to remain at "front line" posts for the time being. Even so, they should devote most of their energy not to the heavy day-to-day work as before, but to helping and guiding younger people, passing on experience to them, giving advice and checking to see that major issues are handled correctly.

To effect the smooth succession from old cadres to younger ones, young and middle-aged cadres must be promoted to the leading bodies at all levels.

In connection with this question, I would like to make two points:

One is that not just a few dozen or a few hundred, but thousands and tens of thousands must be promoted. Why? Because only thus will there be enough people to take over the work of the large numbers of old comrades who retire from the leading bodies; only thus will we have a greater choice and find truly reliable successors; and only thus will it be possible to prevent the trouble-makers who

[New China News Agency, 6 September 1982.]

were promoted to leading posts during the "Cultural Revolution" from stirring up any serious disturbances in the future.

In order to promote thousands and tens of thousands of young and middle-aged cadres, we must take a developmental view in judging them and not just see that they are yet inexperienced. To be sure, the young and middle-aged cadres do not have the rich working experience of the old cadres. But we should ask ourselves the question: Where does experience come from? The answer is, only from tempering in practical work. Placed in posts of responsibility and given a heavy load, the young and middle-aged cadres can certainly gain experience and gradually mature through tempering in three or five years, or at most eight or ten years. In addition, we can create more "assistant" posts. This would help to reduce possible resistance to the promotion of young and middle-aged cadres to full leadership. At the same time, it would enable the party organization to judge their actual leading and organizational ability before they are formally appointed as leaders.

The other point I want to make on the question of promoting young and middle-aged cadres is that none of the following three types of people should be promoted: people who rose to prominence during the "Cultural Revolution" by following Lin Biao, Jiang Qing and their like in "rebellion"; people who are seriously factionalist in their ideas; and people who indulged in beating, smashing and looting. Any of them who have already been promoted must be resolutely removed from the leading bodies.

Why should none of these people be promoted? Because if they are recruited into leading bodies, they will surface to make trouble and again harm the nation and the people when after a number of years, the political climate is right for them, when the party faces any storms.

Of course, we should realize that only a minority of the young and middle-aged people who committed mistakes during the "Cultural Revolution" belong to these three types, while the majority of them merely drifted along. As regards the latter, so long as they have really acknowledged their mistakes, made a clean break with those three types and given a good account of themselves ever since the smashing of the gang of four, the party should trust and use them, and continue to observe and help them in the course of work.

We must also note that there are plenty of young and middle-aged people who behaved well or basically well during the "Cultural Revolution". It is mainly from among them that we should select cadres for promotion.

Apart from the three types mentioned above, there are two other types of people whom we should also not promote to leading posts. I mean people who are opposed to the line followed by the Central Committee of the party since its third plenary session, and people who have seriously violated the law and discipline in the economic and other spheres.

In short, we should on the one hand be bold and quick in promoting young and middle-aged cadres and, on the other, we should strictly insist on the political criteria. As between political integrity and professional competence, we should pay more attention to the former. In other words, we should be sure to promote people who have a strong party spirit, are honest and upright, and dare to stick to principle.

I am convinced that so long as we solve well the problem of succession from old cadres to younger ones, there will be no lack of successors to carry on the cause of our party.

YE JIANYING'S SPEECH

Following is the full text of the speech made by Ye Jianying, vice-chairman of the Central Committee of the Communist Party of China, at the plenary session of the 12th national party congress here this afternoon:

Our present party congress is well prepared, and it is proceeding smoothly. I fully agree with the opening speech made by Comrade Deng Xiaoping. Comrade Hu Yaobang has made a very important report on behalf of the Central Committee, and the revision of the party Constitution has been well done. I fully agree with both.

Our party is full of vigour and vitality. After this congress, a good number of comrades who are in their prime will take up leading positions in the Central Committee and elsewhere. This is a major sign that our party's cause is flourishing, which pleases us old comrades greatly.

The Tang Dynasty poet Li Shangyin wrote the line "The phoenix chick sings sweeter than the older birds" in praise of the poetic talent of a young man. It means that late-comers surpass old-timers, and the young will excel the old. This can be said to be a basic law in the development of history and the progress of society. I hope that the newly promoted young comrades will work in close cooperation with the old comrades, shouldering heavy responsibilities and forging courageously ahead. Man's ability to acquire knowledge is unlimited, but the knowledge of any individual is limited. Hence, one must be good at learning. We believe that, so long as our comrades strive to arm themselves with communist ideology, the party's historical experience and modern science, and so long as they unite with the masses, work hard, know their subordinates well and make good use of them and readily follow good advice, they will certainly be able to do a remarkable job in their leading positions and accomplish glorious feats befitting this great epoch on the march towards China's modernization.

Following this congress, many old comrades will retire from their leading posts, as required by the development of our party's cause. Having worked diligently for scores of years, these old comrades are meritorious contributors to the revolution. The party and the people will never forget their services. The retiring comrades should not retire ideologically. They should, by their deeds, write the last chapter of their lives well, that is to say, they should always keep the interests of the party and the people at heart and continue to do some work that is within their strength.

I am now eighty-five, failing in health and unable to do as much as I would like. For the sake of our party's cause, I have time and again asked to retire from my leading position. However, until the Central Committee decides to grant this, I will do the best I can and devote my all to the party.

After the twelfth national party congress, we shall strive to create a new situation in all fields of socialist modernization. It will be an arduous task. The new Central Committee must do still better in practising democratic centralism and upholding the principle of collective leadership. When the wisdom and strength of the masses are pooled, all affairs become easier to deal with, difficulties are overcome, dangers averted and errors minimized—this has been repeatedly borne out by the past experience of the party. The Political Bureau and the Secretariat of the Central Committee have done fairly well in this respect, and achieved notable results in recent years. All party committees from the central down to the local levels should henceforth do likewise in order to ensure the normal functioning and correct leadership of the party and prolong the political stability in our country. I hope that this fundamental principle in running the affairs of the party and the state will be maintained and passed on from generation to generation. That is all I want to say today. I wish this congress complete success.

The New Party Constitution, 6 September 1982

32

The new constitution adopted by the Twelfth Party Congress does not differ greatly in substance from the draft version (see Doc. 26). Among the new provisions are the enforcement of mandatory meetings of the Party Congress (to be held at least twice during its five-year term), the creation of a Central Advisory Commission composed of Party elders, and the deletion of the article banning lifetime tenure for cadres. There is, however, a balancing provision for the retirement of elderly or ailing cadres.

General Programme

The Communist Party of China is the vanguard of the Chinese working class, the faithful representative of the interests of the people of all nationalities in China, and the force at the core leading China's cause of socialism. The party's ultimate goal is the creation of a communist social system.

The Communist Party of China takes Marxism-Leninism and Mao Zedong Thought as its guide to action.

Applying dialectical materialism and historical materialism, Marx and Engels analysed the laws of development of capitalist society and founded the theory of scientific socialism. According to this theory, with the victory of the proletariat in its revolutionary struggle, the dictatorship of the bourgeoisie is inevitably replaced by the dictatorship of the proletariat, and capitalist society is inevitably transformed into socialist society in which the means of production are publicly owned, exploitation is abolished and the principle "from each according to his ability and to each according to his work" is applied; with tremendous growth of the productive forces and tremendous progress in the ideological, political and cultural fields, socialist society ultimately and inevitably advances into communist society in which the principle "from each according to his ability and to each according to his needs" is applied. Early in the 20th century, Lenin pointed out that capitalism had developed to the stage of imperialism, that the liberation struggle of the proletariat was bound to unite with that of the oppressed nations of the world, and that it was possible for socialist revolution to win victory first in countries that were the weak links of imperialist rule. The course of world history during the past half century and more, especially the establishment and development of the socialist system in a number of countries, has borne out the correctness of the theory of scientific socialism.

The development and improvement of the socialist system is a long historical process. Fundamentally speaking, the socialist system is incomparably superior to the capitalist system, having eliminated the contradictions inherent in the capitalist system, which the latter itself is incapable of overcoming. Socialism enables the people truly to become masters of the country, gradually to shed the old ideas and ways formed under the system of exploitation and private ownership of the means of production, and steadily to raise their communist consciousness and foster common ideals, common ethics and a common discipline in their own ranks. Socialism can give full scope to the initiative and creativeness of the people, develop the productive forces rapidly, proportionately and in a planned way, and meet the growing material and cultural needs of the members of society. The cause of socialism is advancing and is bound gradually to triumph throughout the world along paths that are suited to the specific conditions of each country and are chosen by its people of their own free will.

The Chinese Communists, with Comrade Mao Zedong as their chief representative, created Mao Zedong Thought by integrating the universal principles of Marxism-Leninism with the concrete practice of the Chinese revolution. Mao

[New China News Agency, 8 September 1982.]

Zedong Thought is Marxism-Leninism applied and developed in China; it consists of a body of theoretical principles concerning the revolution and construction in China and a summary of experience therein, both of which have been proved correct by practice; it represents the crystallized, collective wisdom of the Communist Party of China.

The Communist Party of China led the people of all nationalities in waging their prolonged revolutionary struggle against imperialism, feudalism and bureaucrat-capitalism, winning victory in the new-democratic revolution and establishing the People's Republic of China—a people's democratic dictatorship. After the founding of the People's Republic, it led them in smoothly carrying out socialist transformation, completing the transition from new democracy to socialism, establishing the socialist system, and developing socialism in its economic, political and cultural aspects.

After the elimination of the exploiting classes as such, most of the contradictions in Chinese society do not have the nature of class struggle, and class struggle is no longer the principal contradiction. However, owing to domestic circumstances and foreign influences, class struggle will continue to exist within certain limits for a long time, and may even sharpen under certain conditions. The principal contradiction in Chinese society is that between the people's growing material and cultural needs and the backward level of our social production. The other contradictions should be resolved in the course of resolving this principal one. It is essential to strictly distinguish and correctly handle the two different types of contradictions—those contradictions between the enemy and ourselves and those among the people.

The general task of the Communist Party of China at the present stage is to unite the people of all nationalities in working hard and self-reliantly to achieve, step by step, the modernization of our industry, agriculture, national defence and science and technology and make China a culturally advanced and highly democratic socialist country.

The focus of the work of the Communist Party of China is to lead the people of all nationalities in accomplishing the socialist modernization of our economy. It is necessary vigorously to expand the productive forces and gradually perfect socialist relations of production, in keeping with the actual level of the productive forces and as required for their expansion. It is necessary to strive for the gradual improvement of the standards of material and cultural life of the urban and rural population, based on the growth of production and social wealth.

The Communist Party of China leads the people, as they work for a high level of material civilization, in building a high level of socialist spiritual civilization. Major efforts should be made to promote education, science and culture, imbue the party members and the masses of the people with communist ideology, combat and overcome decadent bourgeois ideas, remnant feudal ideas and other non-proletarian ideas, and encourage the Chinese people to have lofty ideals, moral integrity, education and a sense of discipline.

The Communist Party of China leads the people in promoting socialist democracy, perfecting the socialist legal system, and consolidating the people's democratic dictatorship. Effective measures should be taken to protect the people's right to run the affairs of the state and of society, and to manage economic and cultural undertakings; and

to strike firmly at hostile elements who deliberately sabotage the socialist system, and those who seriously breach or jeopardize public security. Great efforts should be made to strengthen the People's Liberation Army and national defence so that the country is prepared at all times to resist and wipe out any invaders.

The Communist Party of China upholds and promotes relations of equality, unity and mutual assistance among all nationalities in the country, persists in the policy of regional autonomy of minority nationalities, aids the areas inhabited by minority nationalities in their economic and cultural development, and actively trains and promotes cadres from among the minority nationalities.

The Communist Party of China unites with all workers, peasants and intellectuals, and with all the democratic parties, non-party democrats and the patriotic forces of all the nationalities in China in further expanding and fortifying the broadest possible patriotic united front embracing all socialist working people and all patriots who support socialism or who support the reunification of the motherland. We should work together with the people throughout the country, including our compatriots in Taiwan, Xianggang (Hong Kong) and Aomen (Macao) and Chinese nationals residing abroad, to accomplish the great task of reunifying the motherland.

In international affairs, the Communist Party takes the following basic stand: It adheres to proletarian internationalism and firmly unites with the workers of all lands, with the oppressed nations and oppressed peoples and with all peace-loving and justice-upholding organizations and personages in the common struggle against imperialism, hegemonism and colonialism and for the defence of world peace and promotion of human progress. It stands for the development of state relations between China and other countries on the basis of the five principles of mutual respect for sovereignty and territorial integrity, mutual non-aggression, non-interference in each other's internal affairs, equality and mutual benefit, and peaceful coexistence. It develops relations with communist parties and working-class parties in other countries on the basis of Marxism and the principles of independence, complete equality, mutual respect and non-interference in each other's internal affairs.

In order to lead China's people of all nationalities in attaining the great goal of socialist modernization, the Communist Party of China must strengthen itself, carry forward its fine traditions, enhance its fighting capacity and resolutely achieve the following three essential requirements:

First, a high degree of ideological and political unity. The Communist Party of China makes the realization of communism its maximum programme, to which all its members must devote their entire lives. At the present stage, the political basis for the solidarity and unity of the whole party consists in adherence to the socialist road, to the people's democratic dictatorship, to the leadership of the party, and to Marxism-Leninism and Mao Zedong Thought and in the concentration of our efforts on socialist modernization. The party's ideological line is to proceed from reality in all things, to integrate theory with practice, to seek truth from facts, and to verify and develop the truth through practice. In accordance with this ideological line, the whole party must scientifically sum up historical experience, investigate and study actual conditions, solve new problems in domestic and international affairs, and oppose all erroneous deviations, whether "left" or right.

Second, whole-hearted service to the people. The party has no special interest of its own apart from the interests of the working class and the broadest masses of the people. The programme and policies of the party are precisely the scientific expressions of the fundamental interests of the working class and the broadest masses of the people. Throughout the process of leading the masses in struggle to realize the ideal of communism, the party always shares weal and woe with the people, keeps in closest contact with them, and does not allow any member to become divorced from the masses or place himself above them. The party persists in educating the masses in communist ideas and follows the mass line in its work, doing everything for the masses, relying on them in every task, and turning its correct views into conscious action by the masses.

Third, adherence to democratic centralism. Within the party, democracy is given full play, a high degree of centralism is practised on the basis of democracy and a sense of organization and discipline is strengthened, so as to ensure unity of action throughout its ranks and the prompt and effective implementation of its decisions. In its internal political life, the party conducts criticism and self-criticism in the correct way, waging ideological struggles over matters of principle, upholding truth and rectifying mistakes. Applying the principle that all members are equally subject to party discipline, the party duly criticizes or punishes those members who violate it and expels those who persist in opposing and harming the party.

Party leadership consists mainly in political, ideological and organizational leadership. The party must formulate and implement correct lines, principles and policies, do its organizational, propaganda and educational work well and make sure that all party members play their exemplary vanguard role in every sphere of work and every aspect of social life. The party must conduct its activities within the limits permitted by the constitution and the laws of the state. It must see to it that the legislative, judicial and administrative organs of the state and the economic, cultural and people's organizations work actively and with initiative, independently, responsibly and in harmony. The party must strengthen its leadership over the trade unions, the Communist Youth League, the women's federation and other mass organizations, and give full scope to their roles. The party members are a minority in the whole population, and they must work in close co-operation with the masses of non-party people in the common effort to make our socialist motherland ever stronger and more prosperous, until the ultimate realization of communism.

CHAPTER I

Membership

Article 1. Any Chinese worker, peasant, member of the armed forces, intellectual or any other revolutionary who has reached the age of eighteen and who accepts the party's programme and constitution and is willing to join and work actively in one of the party organizations, carry out the party's decisions and pay membership dues regularly may apply for membership in the Communist Party of China.

Article 2. Members of the Communist Party of China are vanguard fighters of the Chinese working class imbued with communist consciousness.

Members of the Communist Party of China must serve the people whole-heartedly, dedicate their whole lives to the realization of communism, and be ready to make any personal sacrifices.

Members of the Communist Party of China are at all times ordinary members of the working people. Communist Party members must not seek personal gain or privileges, although they are allowed personal benefits and job functions and powers as provided for by the relevant regulations and policies.

Article 3. Party members must fulfill the following duties:

(1) To conscientiously study Marxism-Leninism and Mao Zedong Thought, essential knowledge concerning the party, and the party's line, principles, policies and decisions; and acquire general, scientific and professional knowledge.

(2) To adhere to the principle that the interests of the party and the people stand above everything, subordinate their personal interests to the interests of the party and the people, be the first to bear hardships and the last to enjoy comforts, work selflessly for the public interest, and absolutely never use public office for personal gain or benefit themselves at the expense of the public.

(3) To execute the party's decisions perseveringly, accept any job and fulfill actively any task assigned them by the party, conscientiously observe party discipline and the laws of the state, rigorously guard party and state secrets and staunchly defend the interests of the party and the state.

(4) To uphold the party's solidarity and unity, to firmly oppose factionalism and all factional organizations and small-group activities, and to oppose double-dealing and scheming of any kind.

(5) To be loyal to and honest with the party, to match words with deeds and not to conceal their political views or distort facts; to earnestly practise criticism and self-criticism, to be bold in exposing and correcting shortcomings and mistakes in work, backing good people and good deeds and fighting against bad people and bad deeds.

(6) To maintain close ties with the masses, propagate the party's views among them, consult with them when problems arise, listen to their views and demands with an open mind and keep the party informed of these in good time, help them raise their political consciousness, and defend their legitimate rights and interests.

(7) To play an exemplary vanguard role in production and other work, study and social activities, take the lead in maintaining public order, promote new socialist ways and customs and advocate communist ethics.

(8) As required by the defence of the motherland and the interests of the people, to step forward and fight

bravely in times of difficulty and danger, fearing neither hardship nor death.

Article 4. Party members enjoy the following rights:

(1) To attend pertinent party meetings and read pertinent party documents, and to benefit from the party's education and training.

(2) To participate in the discussion, at party meetings and in party newspapers and journals, of questions concerning the party's policies.

(3) To make suggestions and proposals regarding the work of the party.

(4) To make well-grounded criticism of any party organization or member at party meetings; to lay information or charges against any party organization or member concerning violations of discipline and of the law to the party in a responsible way, and to demand disciplinary measures against such a member, or to demand the dismissal or replacement of any cadre who is incompetent.

(5) To vote, elect and stand for election.

(6) To attend, with the right of self-defence, discussions held by party organizations to decide on disciplinary measures to be taken against themselves or to appraise their work and behaviour, while other party members may also bear witness or argue in their behalf.

(7) In case of disagreement with a party decision or policy, to make reservations and present their views to party organizations at higher levels up to and including the Central Committee, provided that they resolutely carry out the decision or policy while it is in force.

(8) To put forward any request, appeal or complaint to higher party organizations up to and including the Central Committee and ask the organizations concerned for a responsible reply.

No party organization, up to and including the Central Committee, has the right to deprive any party member of the above-mentioned rights.

Article 5. New party members must be admitted through a party branch, and the principle of individual admission must be adhered to. It is impermissible to drag into the party by any means those who are not qualified for membership, or to exclude those who are qualified.

An applicant for party membership must fill in an application form and must be recommended by two full party members. The application must be accepted by a general membership meeting of the party branch concerned and approved by the next higher party organization, and the applicant should undergo observation for a probationary period before being transferred to full membership.

Party members who recommend an applicant must make genuine efforts to acquaint themselves with the latter's ideology, character and personal history, to explain to each applicant the party's programme and constitution, qualifications for membership and the duties and rights of members, and must make a responsible report to the party organization on the matter.

The party branch committee must canvass the opinions of persons concerned, inside and outside the party, about an applicant for party membership and, after establishing the latter's qualifications following a rigorous examination, submit the application to a general membership meeting for discussion.

Before approving the admission of applicants for party membership, the next higher party organization concerned must appoint people to talk with them, so as to get to know them better and help deepen their understanding of the party.

In special circumstances, the Central Committee of the party or the party committee of a province, an autonomous region or a municipality directly under the central government has the power to admit new party members directly.

Article 6. A probationary party member must take an admission oath in front of the party flag. The oath reads: "It is my will to join the Communist Party of China, uphold the party's programme, observe the provisions of the party constitution, fulfill a party member's duties, carry out the party's decisions, strictly observe party discipline, guard party secrets, be loyal to the party, work hard, fight for communism throughout my life, be ready at all times to sacrifice my all for the party and the people, and never betray the party."

Article 7. The probationary period of a probationary member is one year. The party organization should make serious efforts to educate and observe the probationary members.

Probationary members have the same duties as full members. They enjoy the rights of full members except those of voting, electing or standing for election.

When the probationary period of a probationary member has expired, the party branch concerned should promptly discuss whether he is qualified to be transferred to full membership. A probationary member who conscientiously performs his duties and is qualified for membership should be transferred to full membership as scheduled; if continued observation and education are needed, the probationary period may be prolonged, but by no more than one year; if a probationary member fails to perform his duties and is found to be really unqualified for membership, his probationary membership shall be annulled. Any decision to transfer a probationary member to full membership, prolong a probationary period, or annul a probationary membership must be made through discussion by the general membership meeting of the party branch concerned and approved by the next higher party organization.

The probationary period of a probationary member begins from the day the general membership meeting of the party branch admits him as a probationary member. The party standing of a member begins from the day he is transferred to full membership on the expiration of the probationary period.

Article 8. Every party member, irrespective of position, must be organized into a branch, cell or other specific unit of the party to participate in the regular activities of the party organization and accept supervision by the masses inside and outside the party. There shall be no privileged party members who do not participate in the regular activities of the party organization and do not accept supervision by the masses inside and outside the party.

Article 9. Party members are free to withdraw from the party. When a party member asks to withdraw, the party branch concerned shall, after discussion by its general membership meeting, remove his name from the party rolls, make the removal publicly known and report it to the next higher party organization for the record.

A party member who lacks revolutionary will, fails to fulfill the duties of a party member, is not qualified for membership and remains incorrigible after repeated education should be persuaded to withdraw from the party. The case shall be discussed and decided by the general membership meeting of the party branch concerned and submitted to the next higher party organization for approval. If the party member being persuaded to withdraw refuses to do so, the case shall be submitted to the general membership meeting of the party branch concerned for discussion and decision on a time limit by which the member must correct his mistakes or on the removal of his name from the party rolls, and the decision shall be submitted to the next higher party organization for approval.

A party member who fails to take part in regular party activities, pay membership dues or do work assigned by the party for six successive months without proper reason is regarded as having given up membership. The general membership meeting of the party branch concerned shall decide on the removal of such a person's name from the party rolls and report the removal to the next higher party organization for approval.

CHAPTER II

Organizational System of the Party

Article 10. The party is an integral body organized under its programme and constitution, on the principle of democratic centralism. It practises a high degree of centralism on the basis of a high degree of democracy. The basic principles of democratic centralism as practised by the party are as follows:

(1) Individual party members are subordinate to the party organization, the minority is subordinate to the majority, the lower party organizations are subordinate to the higher party organizations, and all the constituent organizations and members of the party are subordinate to the national congress and the Central Committee of the party.

(2) The party's leading bodies of all levels are elected except for the representative organs dispatched by them and the leading party members groups in non-party organizations.

(3) The highest leading body of the party is the national congress and the Central Committee elected by it. The leading bodies of local party organizations are the party congresses at their respective levels and the party committees elected by them. Party committees are responsible, and report their work, to the party congresses at their respective levels.

(4) Higher party organizations shall pay constant attention to the views of the lower organizations and the rank-and-file party members, and solve in good time the problems they raise. Lower party organizations shall report on their work to, and request instructions from, higher party organizations; at the same time, they shall handle, independently and in a responsible manner, matters within their jurisdiction. Higher and lower party organizations should exchange information and support and supervise each other.

(5) Party committees at all levels function on the principle of combining collective leadership with individual responsibility based on division of labour. All major issues shall be decided upon by the party committees after democratic discussion.

(6) The party forbids all forms of personality cult. It is necessary to ensure that the activities of the party leaders be subject to supervision by the party and the people, while at the same time to uphold the prestige of all leaders who represent the interests of the party and the people.

Article 11. The election of delegates to party congresses and of members of party committees at all levels should reflect the will of the voters. Elections shall be held by secret ballot. The lists of candidates shall be submitted to the party organizations and voters for full deliberation and discussion. There may be a preliminary election in order to draw up a list of candidates for the formal election. Or there may be no preliminary election, in which case the number of candidates shall be greater than that of the persons to be elected. The voters have the right to inquire into the candidates, demand a change or reject one in favour of another. No organization or individual shall in any way compel voters to elect or not to elect any candidate.

If any violation of the party constitution occurs in the election of delegates to a local party congress, the party committee at the next higher level shall, after investigation and verification, decide to invalidate the election and take appropriate measures. The decision shall be reported to the party committee at the next higher level for checking and approval before it is formally announced and implemented.

Article 12. When necessary, party committees of and above the county level may convene conferences of delegates to discuss and decide on major problems that require timely solution. The number of delegates to such conferences and the procedure governing their election shall be determined by the party committees convening them.

Article 13. The formation of a new party organization or the dissolution of an existing one shall be decided upon by the higher party organizations.

Party committees of and above the county level may send out their representative organs.

When the congress of a local party organization at any level is not in session, the next higher party organization may, when it deems it necessary, transfer or appoint responsible members of that organization.

Article 14. When making decisions on important questions affecting the lower organizations, the leading bodies of the party at all levels should, in ordinary circumstances, solicit the opinions of the lower organizations. Measures should be taken to ensure that the lower organizations can exercise their functions and powers normally. Except in special circumstances, higher leading bodies should not interfere with matters that ought to be handled by lower organizations.

Article 15. Only the Central Committee of the party has the power to make decisions on major policies of a nationwide character. Party organizations of various departments and localities may make suggestions with regard to such policies to the Central Committee, but shall not make any decisions or publicize their views outside the party without authorization.

Lower party organizations must firmly implement the decisions of higher party organizations. If lower organizations consider that any decisions of higher organizations do not suit actual conditions in their localities or departments, they may request modification. If the higher organizations insist on their original decisions, the lower organizations must carry out such decisions and refrain from publicly voicing their differences, but have the right to report to the next higher party organization.

Newspapers and journals and other means of publicity run by party organizations at all levels must propagate the line, principles, policies and decisions of the party.

Article 16. Party organizations must keep to the principle of subordination of the minority to the majority in discussing and making decisions on any matter. Serious consideration should be given to the differing views of a minority. In case of controversy over major issues in which supporters of the two opposing views are nearly equal in number, except in emergencies where action must be taken in accordance with the majority view, the decision should be put off to allow for further investigation, study and exchange of opinions followed by another discussion. If still no decision can be made, the controversy should be reported to the next higher party organization for ruling.

When, on behalf of the party organization, an individual party member is to express views on major issues beyond the scope of existing party decisions, the content must be referred to the party organization for prior discussion and decision, or referred to the next higher party organization for instructions. No party member, whatever his position, is allowed to make decisions on major issues on his own. In an emergency, when a decision by an individual is unavoidable, the matter must be reported to the party organization immediately afterwards. No leader is allowed to decide matters arbitrarily on his own or to place himself above the party organization.

Article 17. The central, local and primary organizations of the party must all pay great attention to party building. They shall regularly discuss and check up on the party's work in propaganda, education, organization and discipline inspection, its mass work and united front work. They must carefully study ideological and political developments inside and outside the party.

CHAPTER III

Central Organizations of the Party

Article 18. The national congress of the party is held once every five years and convened by the Central Committee. It may be convened before the due date if the Central Committee deems it necessary or if more than one-third of the organizations at the provincial level so request. Except under extraordinary circumstances, the congress may not be postponed.

The number of delegates to the national congress of the party and the procedure governing their election shall be determined by the Central Committee.

Article 19. The functions and powers of the national congress of the party are as follows:

(1) To hear and examine the reports of the Central Committee;

(2) To hear and examine the reports of the Central Advisory Commission and the Central Commission for Discipline Inspection;

(3) To discuss and decide on major questions concerning the party;

(4) To revise the constitution of the party;

(5) To elect the Central Committee; and

(6) To elect the Central Advisory Commission and the Central Commission for Discipline Inspection.

Article 20. The Central Committee of the party is elected for a term of five years. However, when the next national congress is convened before or after its due date, the term shall be correspondingly shortened or extended. Members and alternate members of the Central Committee must have a party standing of five years or more. The number of members and alternate members of the Central Committee shall be determined by the national congress. Vacancies on the Central Committee shall be filled by its alternate members in the order of the number of votes by which they were elected.

The Central Committee of the party meets in plenary session at least once a year, and such sessions are convened by its Political Bureau.

When the national congress is not in session, the Central Committee carries out its decisions, directs the entire work of the party and represents the Communist Party of China in its external relations.

Article 21. The Political Bureau, the Standing Committee of the Political Bureau, the Secretariat and the general secretary of the Central Committee of the party are elected by the Central Committee in plenary session. The general secretary of the Central Committee must be a member of the Standing Committee of the Political Bureau.

When the Central Committee is not in session, the Political Bureau and its Standing Committee exercise the functions and powers of the Central Committee.

The Secretariat attends to the day-to-day work of the Central Committee under the direction of the Political Bureau and its Standing Committee.

The general secretary of the Central Committee is responsible for convening the meetings of the Political

Bureau and its Standing Committee and presides over the work of the Secretariat.

The members of the Military Commission of the Central Committee are decided on by the Central Committee. The chairman of the Military Commission must be a member of the Standing Committee of the Political Bureau.

The central leading bodies and leaders elected by each Central Committee shall, when the next national congress is in session, continue to preside over the party's day-to-day work until the new central leading bodies and leaders are elected by the next Central Committee.

Article 22. The party's Central Advisory Commission acts as political assistant and consultant to the Central Committee. Members of the Central Advisory Commission must have a party standing of forty years or more, have rendered considerable service to the party, have fairly rich experience in leadership and enjoy fairly high prestige inside and outside the party.

The Central Advisory Commission is elected for a term of the same duration as that of the Central Committee. It elects, at its plenary meeting, its Standing Committee and its chairman and vice-chairmen, and reports the results to the Central Committee for approval. The chairman of the Central Advisory Commission must be a member of the Standing Committee of the Political Bureau. Members of the Central Advisory Commission may attend plenary sessions of the Central Committee as non-voting participants. The vice-chairmen of the Central Advisory Commission may attend plenary meetings of the Political Bureau as non-voting participants and, when the Political Bureau deems it necessary, other members of the Standing Committee of the Central Advisory Commission may do the same.

Working under the leadership of the Central Committee of the party, the Central Advisory Commission puts forward recommendations, on the formulation and implementation of the party's principles and policies and gives advice upon request, assists the Central Committee in investigating and handling certain important questions, propagates the party's major principles and policies inside and outside the party, and undertakes such other tasks as may be entrusted to it by the Central Committee.

Article 23. Party organizations in the Chinese People's Liberation Army carry on their work in accordance with the instructions of the Central Committee. The General Political Department of the Chinese People's Liberation Army is the political work organ of the Military Commission; it directs party and political work in the army. The organizational system and organs of the party in the armed forces will be prescribed by the Military Commission.

CHAPTER IV

Local Organizations of the Party

Article 24. A party congress of a province, autonomous region, municipality directly under the autonomous region, municipality directly under the central government, city divided into districts, or autonomous prefecture is held once every five years.

A party congress of a county (banner), autonomous county, city not divided into districts, or municipal district is held once every three years.

Local party congresses are convened by the party committees at the corresponding levels. Under extraordinary circumstances, they may be held before or after their due dates upon approval by the next higher party committees.

The number of delegates to the local party congresses at any level and the procedure governing their election are determined by the party committees at the corresponding levels and should be reported to the next higher party committees for approval.

Article 25. The functions and powers of the local party congresses at all levels are as follows:

(1) To hear and examine the reports of the party committees at the corresponding levels;

(2) To hear and examine the reports of the commissions for discipline inspection at the corresponding levels;

(3) To discuss and decide on major issues in the given areas; and

(4) To elect the party committees and commissions for discipline inspection at the corresponding levels and delegates to the party congresses at their respective next higher levels.

The party congress of a province, autonomous region, or municipality directly under the central government elects the party advisory committee at the corresponding level and hears and examines its reports.

Article 26. The party committee of a province, autonomous region, or municipality directly under the central government, city divided into districts, or autonomous prefecture is elected for a term of five years. The members and alternate members of such a committee must have a party standing of five years or more.

The party committee of a county (banner), autonomous county, city not divided into districts, or municipal district is elected for a term of three years. The members and alternate members of such a committee must have a party standing of three years or more.

When local party congresses at various levels are convened before or after their due dates, the terms of the committees elected by the previous congresses shall be correspondingly shortened or extended.

The number of members and alternate members of the local party committees at various levels shall be determined by the next higher committees. Vacancies on the local party committees at various levels shall be filled by their alternate members in the order of the number of votes by which they were elected.

The local party committees at various levels meet in plenary session at least once a year.

Local party committees at various levels shall, when the party congresses of the given areas are not in session, carry out the directives of the next higher party organizations and the decisions of the party congresses at the corresponding levels, direct work in their own areas and report on it to the next higher party committees at regular intervals.

Article 27. Local party committees at various levels elect, at their plenary sessions, their standing committees, secretaries and deputy secretaries and report the results to the higher party committees for approval. The standing committees at various levels exercise the powers and functions of local party committees when the latter are not in session. They continue to handle the day-to-day work when the next party congresses at their levels are in session, until the new standing committees are elected.

Article 28. The party advisory committee of a province, autonomous region or municipality directly under the central government acts as political assistant and consultant to the party committee at the corresponding level. It works under the leadership of the party at the corresponding level and in the light of the relevant provisions of Article 22 of the present constitution. The qualifications of its members shall be specified by the party committee at the corresponding level in the light of the relevant provisions of Article 22 of the present constitution and the actual conditions in the locality concerned; it serves a term of the same duration as the party committee at the corresponding level.

The advisory committee of a province, autonomous region or municipality directly under the central government elects, at its plenary meeting, its standing committee and its chairman and vice-chairmen, and the results are subject to endorsement by the party committee at the corresponding level and should be reported to the Central Committee for approval. Its members may attend plenary sessions of the party committee at the corresponding level as non-voting participants, and its chairman and vice-chairmen may attend meetings of the standing committee of the party committee at the corresponding level as non-voting participants.

Article 29. A prefectural party committee, or an organization analogous to it, is the representative organ dispatched by a provincial or an autonomous regional party committee to a prefecture embracing several counties, autonomous counties or cities. It exercises leadership over the work in the given region as authorized by the provincial or autonomous regional party committee.

CHAPTER V

Primary Organizations of the Party

Article 30. Primary party organizations are formed in factories, shops, schools, offices, city neighbourhoods, people's communes, co-operatives, farms, townships, towns, companies of the People's Liberation Army and other basic units, where there are three or more full party members.

In primary party organizations, the primary party committees, and committees of general party branches or party branches, are set up respectively as the work requires and according to the number of party members, subject to approval by the higher party organizations. A primary party committee is elected by a general membership meeting or a delegate meeting. The committee of a general party branch or a party branch is elected by a general membership meeting.

Article 31. In ordinary circumstances, a primary party organization which has set up its own committee convenes a general membership meeting or delegate meeting once a year; a general party branch holds a general membership meeting twice a year; a party branch holds a general membership meeting once in every three months.

A primary party committee is elected for a term of three years, while a general party branch committee or a party branch committee is elected for a term of two years. Results of the election of a secretary and deputy secretaries by a primary party committee, general branch committee or branch committee shall be reported to the higher party organizations for approval.

Article 32. The primary party organizations are militant bastions of the party in the basic units of society. Their main tasks are:

(1) To propagate and carry out the party's line, principles and policies, the decisions of the Central Committee of the party and other higher party organizations, and their own decisions; to give full play to the exemplary vanguard role of party members, and to unite and organize the cadres and the rank and file inside and outside the party in fulfilling the tasks of their own units.

(2) To organize party members to conscientiously study Marxism-Leninism and Mao Zedong Thought, study essential knowledge concerning the party, and the party's line, principles and policies, and acquire general, scientific and professional knowledge.

(3) To educate and supervise party members, ensure their regular participation in the activities of the party organization, see that party members truly fulfill their duties and observe discipline, and protect their rights for encroachment.

(4) To maintain close ties with the masses, constantly seek their criticisms and opinions regarding party members and the party's work, value the knowledge and rationalization proposals of the masses and experts, safeguard the legitimate rights and interests of the masses, show concern for their material and cultural life and help them improve it, do effective ideological and political work among them, and enhance their political consciousness. They must correct, by proper methods, the erroneous ideas and unhealthy ways and customs that may exist among the masses, and properly handle the contradictions in their midst.

(5) To give full scope to the initiative and creativeness of party members and the masses, discover advanced elements and talented people needed for the socialist cause, encourage them to improve their work and come up with innovations and inventions, and support them in these efforts.

(6) To admit new party members, collect membership dues, examine and appraise the work and behaviour of party members, commend exemplary deeds performed by them, and maintain and enforce party discipline.

(7) To promote criticism and self-criticism, and expose and overcome shortcomings and mistakes in work. To educate party and non-party cadres; see to it that

they strictly observe the law and administrative discipline and the financial and economic discipline and personnel regulations of the state; see to it that none of them infringes the interests of the state, the collective and the masses; and see to it that the financial workers including accountants and other professionals who are charged with enforcing laws and regulations in their own units do not themselves violate the laws and regulations, while at the same time ensuring and protecting their right to exercise their functions and powers independently in accordance with the law and guarding them against any reprisals for so doing.

(8) To educate party members and the masses to raise their revolutionary vigilance and wage resolute struggles against the criminal activities of counterrevolutionaries and other saboteurs.

Article 33. In an enterprise or institution, the primary party committee or the general branch committee or branch committee, where there is no primary party committee, gives leadership in the work of its own unit. Such a primary party organization discusses and decides on major questions of principle and at the same time ensures that the administrative leaders fully exercise their functions and powers, but refrains from substituting itself for, or trying to take over from, the administrative leaders. Except in special circumstances, the general branch committees and branch committees under the leadership of a primary party committee only play a guarantory and supervisory role to see that the production targets or operational tasks assigned to their own units are properly fulfilled.

In party or government offices at all levels, the primary party organizations shall not lead the work of these offices. Their task here is to exercise supervision over all party members, including the heads of these offices who are party members, with regard to their implementation of the party's line, principles and policies, their observance of discipline and the law, their contact with the masses, and their ideology, work style and moral character; and to assist the office heads to improve work, raise efficiency and overcome bureaucratic ways, keep them informed of the shortcomings and problems discovered in the work of these offices, or report such shortcomings and problems to the higher party organizations.

CHAPTER VI

Party Cadres

Article 34. Party cadres are the backbone of the party's cause and public servants of the people. The party selects its cadres according to the principle that they should possess both political integrity and professional competence, persists in the practice of appointing people on their merits and opposes favouritism; it calls for genuine efforts to make the ranks of the cadres more revolutionary, younger in average age, better educated and more professionally competent.

Party cadres are obliged to accept training by the party as well as examination and assessment of their work by the party.

The party should attach importance to the training and promotion of women cadres and cadres from among the minority nationalities.

Article 35. Leading party cadres at all levels must perform in an exemplary way their duties as party members prescribed in Article 3 of this constitution and must meet the following basic requirements:

(1) Have a fair grasp of the theories of Marxism-Leninism and Mao Zedong Thought and the policies based on them, and be able to adhere to the socialist road, fight against the hostile forces disrupting socialism and combat all erroneous tendencies inside and outside the party.

(2) In their work as leaders, conduct earnest investigations and study, persistently proceed from reality and properly carry out the line, principles and policies of the party.

(3) Be fervently dedicated to the revolutionary cause and imbued with a strong sense of political responsibility, and be qualified for their leading posts in organizational ability, general education and vocational knowledge.

(4) Have a democratic work style, maintain close ties with the masses, correctly implement the party's mass line, conscientiously accept criticism and supervision by the party and the masses, and combat bureaucratism.

(5) Exercise their functions and powers in the proper way, observe and uphold the rules and regulations of the party and the state, and combat all acts of abusing power and seeking personal gain.

(6) Be good at uniting and working with a large number of comrades, including those who hold differing opinions, while upholding the party's principles.

Article 36. Party cadres should be able to co-operate with non-party cadres, respect them and learn open-mindedly from their strong points.

Party organizations at all levels must be good at discovering and recommending talented and knowledgeable non-party cadres for leading posts, and ensure that the latter enjoy authority commensurate with their posts and can play their roles to the full.

Article 37. Leading party cadres at all levels, whether elected through democratic procedure or appointed by a leading body, are not entitled to lifelong tenure, and they can be transferred from or relieved of their posts.

Cadres no longer fit to continue working due to old age or poor health should retire according to the regulations of the state.

CHAPTER VII

Party Discipline

Article 38. A Communist Party member must consciously act within the bounds of party discipline. Party organizations shall criticize, educate or take disciplinary measures against members who violate party discipline, depending on the nature and seriousness of their mistakes and in the spirit of "learning from past mistakes to avoid future ones, and curing the sickness to save the patient".

Party members who violate the law and administrative discipline shall be subject to administrative disciplinary action or legal action instituted by administrative or judicial organs. Those who have seriously violated criminal law shall be expelled from the party.

Article 39. There are five measures of party discipline: warning, serious warning, removal from party posts and proposals for their removal from non-party posts to the organizations concerned, placing on probation within the party, and expulsion from the party.

The period for which a party member is placed on probation shall not exceed two years. During this period, the party member concerned has no right to vote, elect or stand for election. A party member who during this time proves to have corrected his mistake shall have his rights as a party member restored. Party members who refuse to mend their ways shall be expelled from the party.

Expulsion is the ultimate party disciplinary measure. In deciding on or approving an expulsion, party organizations at all levels should study all the relevant facts and opinions and exercise extreme caution.

It is strictly forbidden, within the party, to take any measures against a member that contravene the party constitution or the laws of the state, or to retaliate against or frame up comrades. Any offending organization or individual must be dealt with according to party discipline or the laws of the state.

Article 40. Any disciplinary measures against a party member must be discussed and decided on at a general membership meeting of the party branch concerned, and reported to the primary party committee concerned for approval. If the case is relatively important or complicated, or involves the expulsion of a member, it shall be reported, on the merit of that case, to a party commission for discipline inspection at or above the county level for examination and approval. Under special circumstances, a party committee or a commission for discipline inspection at or above the county level has the authority to decide directly on disciplinary measures against a party member.

Any decision to remove a member or alternate member of the Central Committee or a local committee at any level from posts within the party, to place such a person on probation within the party or to expel him from the party must be taken by a two-thirds majority vote at a plenary meeting of the party committee to which he belongs. Such a disciplinary measure against a member or alternate member of a local party committee is subject to approval by the higher party committees.

Members and alternate members of the Central Committee who have seriously violated criminal law shall be expelled from the party on decision by the Political Bureau of the Central Committee; members and alternate members of local party committees who have seriously violated criminal law shall be expelled from the party on decision by the standing committees of the party committees at the corresponding levels.

Article 41. When a party organization decides on a disciplinary measure against a party member, it should investigate and verify the facts in an objective way. The party member in question must be informed of the decision to be made and of the facts on which it is based. He must be given a chance to account for himself and speak in his own defence. If the member does not accept the decision, he can appeal, and the party organization concerned must promptly deal with or forward his appeal, and must not withhold or suppress it. Those who cling to erroneous views and unjustifiable demands shall be educated by criticism.

Article 42. It is an important duty of every party organization to firmly uphold party discipline. Failure of a party organization to uphold party discipline must be investigated.

In case a party organization seriously violates party discipline and is unable to rectify the mistakes on its own, the next higher party committee should, after verifying the facts and considering the seriousness of the case, decide on the reorganization or dissolution of the organization, report the decision to the party committee further above for examination and approval, and then formally announce and carry out the decision.

CHAPTER VIII

Party Organs for Discipline Inspection

Article 43. The party's Central Commission for Discipline Inspection functions under the leadership of the Central Committee of the party. Local commissions for discipline inspection at all levels function under the dual leadership of the party committees at the corresponding levels and the next higher commissions for discipline inspection.

The party's central and local commissions for discipline inspection serve a term of the same duration as the party committees at the corresponding levels.

The Central Commission for Discipline Inspection elects, in plenary session, its Standing Committee and secretary and deputy secretaries and reports the results to the Central Committee for approval. Local commissions for discipline inspection at all levels elect, at their plenary sessions, their respective standing committees and secretaries and deputy secretaries. The results of the elections are subject to endorsement by the party committees at the corresponding levels and should be reported to the higher party committees for approval. The first secretary of the Central Commission for Discipline Inspection must be a member of the Standing Committee of the Political Bureau. The question of whether a primary party committee should set up a commission for discipline inspection or simply appoint a discipline inspection commissioner shall be determined by the next higher party organization in the light of the specific circumstances. The committees of general party branches and party branches shall have discipline inspection commissioners.

The party's Central Commission for Discipline

Inspection shall, when its work so requires, accredit discipline inspection groups or commissioners to party or state organs at the central level. Leaders of the discipline inspection groups or discipline inspection commissioners may attend relevant meetings of the leading party organizations in the said organs as non-voting participants. The leading party organizations in the organs concerned must give support to their work.

Article 44. The main tasks of the central and local commissions for discipline inspection are as follows: to uphold the constitution and the other important rules and regulations of the party, to assist the respective party committees in rectifying party style, and to check up on the implementation of the line, principles, policies and decisions of the party.

The central and local commissions for discipline inspection shall carry out constant education among party members on their duty to observe party discipline; they shall adopt decisions for the upholding of party discipline, examine and deal with relatively important or complicated cases of violation of the constitution and discipline of the party or the laws and decrees of the state by party organizations or party members; decide on or cancel disciplinary measures against party members involved in such cases; and deal with complaints and appeals made by party members.

The central and local commissions for discipline inspection should report to the party committees at the corresponding levels on the results of their handling of cases of special importance or complexity, as well as on the problems encountered. Local commissions for discipline inspection should also present such reports to the higher commissions.

If the Central Commission for Discipline Inspection discovers any violation of party discipline by any member of the Central Committee, it may report such an offence to the Central Committee, and the Central Committee must deal with the case promptly.

Article 45. Higher commissions for discipline inspection have the power to check up on the work of the lower commissions and to approve or modify their decisions on any case. If decisions so modified have already been ratified by the party committee at the corresponding level, the modification must be approved by the next higher party committee.

If a local commission for discipline inspection does not agree with a decision made by the party committee at the corresponding level in dealing with a case, it may request the commission at the next higher level to re-examine the case; if a local commission discovers cases of violation of party discipline or the laws and decrees of the state by the party committee at the corresponding level or by its members, and if that party committee fails to deal with them properly or at all, it has the right to appeal to the higher commissions for assistance in dealing with such cases.

CHAPTER IX

Leading Party Members Groups

Article 46. A leading party members group shall be formed in the leading body of a central or local state organ, people's organization, economic or cultural institution or other non-party unit. The main tasks of such a group are: to see to it that the party's principles and policies are implemented, to unite with the non-party cadres and masses in fulfilling the tasks assigned by the party and the state, and to guide the work of the party organization of the unit.

Article 47. The members of a leading party members group are appointed by the party committee that approves its establishment. The group shall have a secretary and deputy secretaries.

A leading party members group must accept the leadership of the party committee that approves its establishment.

Article 48. The Central Committee of the party shall determine specifically the functions, powers and tasks of the leading party members groups in those government departments which need to exercise highly centralized and unified leadership over subordinate units; it shall also determine whether such groups should be replaced by party committees.

CHAPTER X

Relationship Between the Party and the Communist Youth League

Article 49. The Communist Youth League of China is a mass organization of advanced young people under the leadership of the Communist Party of China; it is a school where large numbers of young people will learn about communism through practice; it is the party's assistant and reserve force. The Central Committee of the Communist Youth League functions under the leadership of the Central Committee of the party. The local organizations of the Communist Youth League are under the leadership of the party committees at the corresponding levels and of the higher organizations of the league itself.

Article 50. Party committees at all levels must strengthen their leadership over the Communist Youth League organizations and pay attention to the selection and training of league cadres. The party must firmly support the Communist Youth League in the lively and creative performance of its work to suit the characteristics and needs of young people, and give full play to the league's role as a shock force and as a bridge linking the party with the broad masses of young people.

Those secretaries of league committees, at or below the county level or in enterprises and institutions, who are party members may attend meetings of party committees at the corresponding levels and of their standing committees as non-voting participants.

Report to the Twelfth Party Congress, 7 September 1982

The major document of any Communist Party Congress is the report on behalf of the outgoing Central Committee by the operational head of the Party, usually the general or first secretary. It is considered, at least by its author(s), to have propaganda and even historic, as well as programmatic, significance. In his report, General Secretary Hu develops such Dengist themes as the primacy of modernization, the need for Party rectification, and the independence of China's foreign policy.

Comrades: On behalf of the Eleventh Central Committee of the Communist Party of China, I will now make a report to the twelfth national congress of the party.

I. A HISTORIC CHANGE AND OUR GREAT NEW TASK

Since the smashing of the Jiang Qing counterrevolutionary clique in October 1976 and, in particular, since the third plenary session of the eleventh Central Committee held in December 1978, we have accomplished, through the arduous efforts of the whole party, the whole army and the people of our nationalities, the difficult task of setting the party's guiding ideology to rights and have won major successes in setting right our practical work on all fronts, thereby effecting a great and historic change.

The mission of the present party congress is, through the summing-up of the historic achievements of the past six years, to chart a correct course and define correct strategic steps, principles and policies so that we can more thoroughly eliminate the negative consequences of the decade of domestic turmoil, make further progress and create a new situation in all fields of socialist modernization. The Central Committee of the party is confident that our congress can shoulder this momentous historical task.

What are the main indicators of the historic change that has been brought about?

In the sphere of ideology, we have resolutely broken the fetters of dogmatism and the personality cult which existed for a long time, and have reaffirmed the Marxist ideological line of seeking truth from facts, thus infusing a dynamic and creative spirit into all fields of endeavour. We have restored the original features of Mao Zedong Thought and persisted in and developed it under new historical conditions.

We have put an end to years of social turbulence and brought about a political situation characterized by stability, unity and liveliness. Socialist democracy and the socialist legal system are being gradually perfected, equality and unity among all our nationalities have been strengthened anew, and the patriotic united front has expanded further. Thanks to this political situation, the present period is one of the best since the founding of our People's Republic.

The leading bodies of the party and the state at all levels have been gradually readjusted, improved and strengthened. By and large, the leadership in the party and state organizations at all levels is now in the hands of cadres loyal to the party and the people.

We have resolutely shifted the focus of work of the party and the state to economic construction and, liquidating the "left" mistakes that persisted in our economic work over the years, have conscientiously implemented the correct principle of readjustment, restructuring, consolidation and improvement. Having tided over the most difficult phase, our national economy is now on the sound path of steady growth.

Our endeavours in education, science and culture are on the right track and, with some initial successes, are beginning to thrive. Relations between the party and the intellectuals have improved enormously. Unity among the three main social forces, namely, the workers, peasants and intellectuals is also fairly good now.

We have made tremendous efforts to build a modern regular revolutionary army. The People's Liberation Army has achieved marked successes in improving its military training and its ideological and political work, in bettering its relations with the civil authorities and the people, in defending our frontiers and safeguarding national security and in helping socialist construction. It has further enhanced its military capability and political consciousness in line with new historical conditions.

In the course of leading the people in effecting this historic change, our party has withstood tests and remoulded itself. It has done much to rectify party style, gradually revived its fine traditions and become more mature and firmer in the course of struggle.

Looking back at our path of struggle in these six years, we see that it has been an uneven one. The decade of domestic turmoil inflicted grievous wounds on the party and the state. Our victory has not been easy. It was won

[New China News Agency, 7 September 1982.]

only after the Central Committee led the entire party and people in overcoming enormous difficulties of all kinds.

The "left" mistakes made before and during the "Cultural Revolution" had a deep and extensive influence and caused serious damage. While thoroughly exposing and repudiating the Lin Biao and Jiang Qing counterrevolutionary cliques, we found it necessary to make a clean sweep of all such "left" mistakes. This unavoidably involved the mistakes made by Comrade Mao Zedong in his later years. Comrade Mao Zedong's contributions to the Chinese revolution were great and indelible; that is why over long years he enjoyed enormous prestige in the party and among the people and will continue to do so in the years to come. Whether we had the Marxist courage to conduct self-criticism of our party's mistakes, including those made by Comrade Mao Zedong, and whether we could conduct such self-criticism correctly and in a historical perspective constituted the key issue deciding whether things could be set right. During the two years before the third plenary session of the eleventh Central Committee, the question of rights and wrongs in the party's guiding ideology was not clarified as it should have been and the work of setting things to rights proceeded haltingly; this was because in the early days after the smashing of the Jiang Qing counterrevolutionary clique, our party was not ideologically prepared for an overall liquidation of the "left" mistakes and also because the principal leading comrade in the Central Committee at the time continued to make "left" mistakes on a series of important issues. The eleventh party congress announced the end of the "Cultural Revolution" and reaffirmed the task of building a modern and powerful socialist state, thus playing a positive role in mobilizing the masses. However, the political report to the eleventh party congress still approved of the erroneous theories, policies and slogans of the "Cultural Revolution", thus exerting a negative influence by seriously obstructing our effort to set things right. The historic service of the third plenary session of the eleventh Central Committee was precisely that it thoroughly shattered the heavy chains imposed by the protracted "left" mistakes, set right the guiding ideology of the party and reaffirmed the Marxist ideological, political and organizational lines. Subsequently, our party thoroughly summed up its historical experience in all spheres and scientifically explained numerous questions encountered in practical work, which concerned theory and policy in the building of socialism. The Resolution on Certain Questions in the History of Our Party Since the Founding of the People's Republic of China adopted in June 1981 by the sixth plenary session of the eleventh Central Committee marked the successful conclusion of our work in setting the party's guiding ideology to rights. Drawing on the collective wisdom of the broad sections of cadres and masses, our party subjected the protracted "left" mistakes and Comrade Mao Zedong's mistakes in his later years to scientific analysis and criticism, while firmly upholding the fine traditions developed by the party during long years of struggle, safeguarding the scientific truth of Mao Zedong Thought and affirming Comrade Mao Zedong's historical role. This helped not only to differentiate right from wrong but also to strengthen unity in our ranks, thus providing a basic guarantee for the healthy development of our revolution and construction.

Since the third plenary session, our party has made every effort to conform to objective reality in formulating and implementing a series of principles and policies and to avoid focusing on the criticism of one erroneous tendency to the neglect of another. In times of historic change, people are apt to think one-sidedly because of the profound influence of old ideas and customs and because of lack of experience in dealing with new things, plus the effect of other social and political factors. In recent years, mistaken ideas representing different tendencies have arisen among sections of the party members and cadres with regard to such major questions of principle as the party's policy of mental emancipation, the assessment of Comrade Mao Zedong and Mao Zedong Thought and the appraisal of class struggle at the present stage of socialism. Unable to free themselves completely from the influence of the former "left" mistakes, some comrades wanted to return, wittingly or unwittingly, to the old track of "taking class struggle as the key link". Others, deviating from the Marxist path, went so far as to doubt or even negate the leadership of the party and the socialist road. On such major questions of principle, our party has all along taken a firm stand and waged timely and appropriate ideological struggles on two fronts—against both the "left" and the right deviations. On the one hand, in its effort to prevent the recurrence of mistakes that would lead to the broadening of the scope of class struggle, the Central Committee has systematically liquidated the erroneous theory of "continuing the revolution under the dictatorship of the proletariat" put forth during the "Cultural Revolution", a theory that envisaged a continuing "revolution whereby one class overthrows another", and it has vigorously developed socialist democracy and a socialist legal system and restored and expanded our united front work. On the one hand, the party has reiterated the four cardinal principles centering on upholding the leadership of the party (the four cardinal principles are adherence to the socialist road, to the people's democratic dictatorship, to the leadership of the Communist Party and to Marxism-Leninism and Mao Zedong Thought), criticized and curbed the tendency towards bourgeois liberalism and resolutely cracked down on all types of criminal activity that disrupt socialist construction. In handling various practical problems, we have done our best to act in the scientific and all-sided way as required by Marxism. This has enabled us to deal fairly successfully and relatively speedily with many complex ideological problems and social and political contradictions.

A jumble of problems accumulated during the ten years of domestic turmoil. Many things that needed to be done or needed to be reformed claimed our attention. Moreover, the progress of new work inevitably gives rise to new problems. The party therefore had to draw up a list of priorities, do its work systematically and solve problems step by step.

Take economic work, for example. The third plenary session first grasped the link of agriculture, laying emphasis on overcoming the long-standing "left" mistakes in the guidelines in this sphere. This involved restoring and expanding the power of decision of the rural people's communes and their production brigades and teams; restoring the private plots, family and collective sideline production and village fairs; and gradually introducing, in various forms, the system of responsibility for production in which payment is linked to output. At the same time, the state purchasing prices of grain and some other agricultural products were raised; then the policies providing for a diversified economy were formulated. As a result marked changes have taken place in agriculture, in which vigorous growth has replaced stagnation. For many years, the peasants have not been so happy as they are today. This has done much to start a turn for the better in the whole economic and indeed the whole political situation.

Following the improvement in agriculture, we began to readjust the structure of industry, laying emphasis on remedying the disproportion between light and heavy industries and on readjusting the service orientation of heavy industry. The result has been a rapid expansion of light industry. At the same time, we readjusted the ratio between accumulation and consumption and reduced the scale of capital construction which had been over-extended. This has resulted in improved living standards for the people as well as better proportions between the various branches of the national economy. In other fields, we have, by and large, used the same method—that of tackling the key problem first to facilitate the solution of the rest.

In the final analysis, our party has been successful in the above efforts because it has adhered to the scientific Marxist principles of combining theory with practice and of recognizing the people as the makers of history. The facts are plain enough. The party firmly trusts the people, relies on them and acts in compliance with their wishes and the trend of historical development. With the crushing of the Jiang Qing counterrevolutionary clique, the people placed high hopes on the party. They demanded that wrongs be set right, that stability and unity be achieved, that efforts be concentrated on socialist modernization and that the level of our country's socialist material and spiritual civilization be raised. It is by crystallizing the will of the people and formulating correct lines, principles and policies that the party has been able to bring the cause of socialism in our country back onto the sound path. The people's trust in the party and their support for it are the key to the continuous success of our cause.

Looking back over the course of struggle we have traversed in the past six years, we naturally recall two previous instances of historic change during China's democratic revolution led by the party, namely, the change from the failure of the northern expedition (1924–27) to the outbreak of the agrarian revolutionary war (1927–37) and the change from the failure of the struggle against the Kuomintang's fifth "encirclement and suppression" campaign to the launching of the war of resistance against Japan (1937–45). At both junctures, when the party and the people had suffered heavy losses and the revolution faced grim crises, enemies both at home and abroad concluded that we were doomed to total defeat, and not a few people in our own ranks wavered and grew pessimistic. But the party was not overwhelmed by the enormous difficulties. Under the leadership of a number of outstanding figures of whom Comrade Mao Zedong was representative, the party displayed rare revolutionary courage and fortitude, fought on tenaciously, strove creatively to find a revolutionary path suited to China's specific conditions and finally turned the tide, resuscitating the revolutionary cause and bringing about a new situation of victorious advance.

Compared with the two previous ones, the present change has taken place under vastly different historical conditions. Today, our party is the leading core of nationwide political power and our country has already experienced a long period of socialist revolution and construction. The people are far more powerful than they were in the period of the revolutionary wars. Despite the tremendous damage done to it by the "Cultural Revolution", the cause of socialism retains its great and invincible vitality. Although we have lost Comrades Mao Zedong, Zhou Enlai, Liu Shaoqi and Zhu De and other veteran proletarian revolutionaries, we still have as the mainstay of our cause many other veteran revolutionaries who fought shoulder to shoulder with them. Moreover, we have as our core force many old comrades who went through the test of revolutionary wars and large numbers of young and middle-aged comrades who have been tempered and have matured since the founding of our People's Republic. Under the leadership of the Central Committee, we have at last succeeded in effecting another historic change, thanks to the arduous efforts of the party organizations at all levels and the concerted struggle of all party comrades and millions upon millions of people throughout the country.

Comrades! The great successes we have achieved in the past six years are evident to all. But, instead of resting on our laurels, we must realize that there are still many shortcomings and difficulties and that there is still much to be desired in the work of the party. We must enhance our revolutionary spirit, plunge into work and strive for new and still greater successes.

The general task of the Communist Party of China in this new historical period is to unite the people of all our nationalities in working hard and self-reliantly to achieve, step by step, the modernization of our industry, agriculture, national defence and science and technology and to make China a culturally advanced and highly democratic socialist country. In the five years from the present party congress to the next, we should, as this general task and China's actual conditions require, energetically promote the socialist material and spiritual civilization, continue to strengthen socialist democracy and the socialist legal system, earnestly rectify the party style and consolidate the party organization and strive to bring about a fundamental turn for the better in the country's financial and economic situation, in the standards of social conduct and in the style of the party. At the same time, together with all the patriotic people, our compatriots in Taiwan, Xianggang (Hong Kong) and Aomen (Macao) and including Chinese nationals residing abroad, we shall pursue the great aim of reunifying the motherland. We shall also join the people of the rest of the world in carrying on the struggle against imperialism and hegemonism in defence of world peace. These are the lofty tasks of creating a new situation in all fields that lie before us.

II. BRING ABOUT AN ALL-ROUND UPSURGE OF THE SOCIALIST ECONOMY

Of the various tasks for bringing about an all-round new situation, the most important one is to push forward the socialist modernization of China's economy, For this purpose, the party has formulated the strategic objective, priorities and steps of our economic construction as well as a series of correct principles in a spirit of realism.

The general objective of China's economic construction for the two decades between 1981 and the end of this century is, while steadily working for more and better economic results, to quadruple the gross annual value of industrial and agricultural production—from 710 billion yuan in 1980 to 2,800 billion yuan or so in 2000. This will place China in the front ranks of the countries of the world in terms of gross national income and the output of major industrial and agricultural products; it will represent an important advance in the modernization of her entire national economy; it will increase the income of her urban and rural population several times over; and the Chinese people will be comparatively well-off both materially and culturally. Although China's national income per capita will even then be relatively low, her economic strength and national defence capabilities will have grown considerably, compared with what they are today. Provided that we work hard and in a down-to-earth manner and bring the superiority of the socialist system into fuller play, we can definitely attain our grand strategic objective.

From an overall point of view, what is most important in our effort to realize this objective in economic growth is to properly solve the problems of agriculture, energy and transport and of education and science.

Agriculture is the foundation of the national economy, and provided it grows, we can handle the other problems more easily. At present, both labour productivity and the percentage of marketable products are rather low in our agriculture; our capacity for resisting natural calamities is still quite limited; and, in particular, the contradiction between the huge population and the insufficiency of arable land is becoming ever more acute. From now on, while firmly controlling the population growth, protecting all agricultural resources and maintaining the ecological balance, we must do better in agricultural capital construction, improve the conditions for agricultural production, practise scientific farming, wrest greater yields of grain and cash crops from limited acreage, and secure the all-round development of forestry, animal husbandry, sideline occupations and fishery in order to meet the needs of industrial expansion and of higher living standards for the people.

Energy shortage and the strain on transport are major checks on China's economic development at present. Growth in energy production has slowed down somewhat in the last few years, while waste remains extremely serious. Transport capacity lags far behind the increasing volume of freight, and postal and telecommunications facilities are outmoded. To ensure a fair rate of growth in the national economy, it is imperative to step up the exploitation of energy resources, economize drastically on energy consumption and at the same time strive hard to expand the transport and postal and telecommunications services.

The modernization of science and technology is a key link in our four modernizations. Today, many of our enterprises are backward in production techniques, operation and management; large numbers of workers and staff members lack the necessary scientific knowledge, general education and work skills; and there is an acute shortage of skilled workers, scientists and technicians. In the years to come, we must promote large-scale technical transformation in a planned way, popularize technical measures that have yielded good economic results, and actively introduce new techniques, equipment, technologies and materials. We must step up research in the applied sciences, lay more stress on research in the basic sciences and organize people from all relevant fields to tackle key problems in scientific research. We must improve our study

and application of economics and scientific business management and continuously raise the level of economic planning and administration and of the operation and management of enterprises and institutions. And we must work vigorously to universalize primary education, strengthen secondary vocational education and higher education and develop educational undertakings of all types and at all levels in both urban and rural areas, including training classes for cadres, workers, staff members and peasants and literacy classes in order to train all kinds of specialists and raise the scientific and educational level of the whole nation.

In short, in the next twenty years we must keep a firm hold on agriculture, energy, transport, education and science as the basic links, the strategic priorities in China's economic growth. Effective solution of these problems on the basis of an overall balance in the national economy will lead to a fairly swift rise in the production of consumer goods, stimulate the development of industry as a whole and of production and construction in other fields and ensure a betterment of living standards.

Population has always been an extremely important issue in China's economic and social development. Family planning is a basic policy of our state. We must do our utmost to keep our population within 1.2 billion by the end of this century. The total number of births is now at its peak. Excessive population growth will not only adversely affect the increase of per-capita income but also cause serious difficulties in food supply, housing, education and employment, and it may even disrupt social stability. Consequently, we must never slacken our effort in family planning, especially in the rural areas. We must conduct intensive and meticulous ideological education among the peasants. Provided that we do our work well, we can succeed in bringing our population under control.

In order to realize our objective for the next two decades, we must take the following two steps in our strategic planning: In the first decade, aim mainly at laying a solid foundation, accumulating strength and creating the necessary conditions; and in the second, usher in a new period of vigorous economic development. This is a major policy decision taken by the Central Committee after a comprehensive analysis of the present conditions of China's economy and the trend of its growth.

Our national economy has grown steadily even in the past few years of readjustment, and the achievement is quite impressive. In many fields, however, the economic results have been far from satisfactory, and there has been appalling waste in production, construction and circulation. We have yet to equal our best past records in the materials expended in per unit products, in the profit rate of industrial enterprises, in the construction time for large and medium-sized projects and in the turnover rate of circulating funds in industrial and commercial enterprises. Apart from some objective factors not subject to comparison, the main causes for this are the "left" mistakes of the past, which resulted in blind proliferation of enterprises, an irrational economic structure, defective systems of economic administration and distribution, chaotic operation and management and backward production techniques. Things started to pick up a little in 1982, with the stress laid on better economic results. Nevertheless, it is impossible in a brief space to solve all such problems which have piled up over a long period. We have to bear this basic fact in mind when drawing up the strategic plan for China's economic development.

In the period of the Sixth Five-Year Plan (1981–85), we must continue unswervingly to carry out the principles of readjustment, restructuring, consolidation and improvement, practise strict economy, combat waste and focus all economic work on the attainment of better economic results. We must devote our main efforts to readjusting the economic structure in various fields, streamlining, reorganizing and merging the existing enterprises and carrying out technical transformation in selected enterprises. At the same time, we must consolidate and perfect the initial reform in the system of economic administration and work out at an early date the overall plan for reform and the measures for its implementation. During the Seventh Five-Year Plan (1986–90), we shall carry out the technical transformation of enterprises on an extensive scale and gradually reform the system of economic administration, in addition to completing the rationalization of the organizational structure of enterprises and the economic structure in various fields. We must also undertake a series of necessary capital construction projects in the energy, transport and some other fields, and the concentrated solution of a number of major scientific and technical problems in the 1980's. Therefore, it will not be possible for the national economy to develop very fast in this decade. But if we complete the above tasks, we can solve the problems left over from the past and build a relatively solid basis for economic growth in the decade to follow. The 1990's will witness an all-round upsurge in China's economy which will definitely grow at a much faster rate than in the 1980's. If we publicize and explain this strategic plan adequately to the people, they will see the bright future more clearly and be inspired to work with greater drive to usher in the new period of vigorous economic growth.

In the five years between this party congress and the next, we shall complete the Sixth Five-Year Plan and start on the seventh. To strive for a fundamental turn for the better in China's financial and economic situation in this period means that we must, under the strategic plan outlined above, achieve significantly better economic results, a steady basic balance in finance and credit and basic stability in commodity prices. Clearly, it is of paramount importance to China's long-term economic development that we do our economic work well in these five years.

To bring about an all-round upsurge in China's socialist economy, we must continue to carry out in all our economic work the ten principles for economic construction approved by the Fifth National People's Congress at its fourth session, paying special attention to solving the following major questions of principle.

First, Concentrating Funds on Key Development Projects and Continuing To Improve the People's Living Standards.

To attain our strategic objective for the coming twenty years, the state must concentrate needed funds on key development projects in their order of importance and urgency. For this purpose, while endeavouring to overcome undue decentralization in the use of funds, we must bring into play the initiative of all concerned to expand production and achieve better economic results, so that the national income may rise more rapidly. In recent years, state revenues have somewhat decreased and there has been a shortage of funds for urgently needed key projects. On the other hand, funds at the disposal of local authorities and enterprises have grown greatly and have been used for many projects which may seem badly needed from a local point of view; but this inevitably makes it difficult to adequately meet the national needs and to prevent and overcome the tendency towards blindness in construction. We must realize that if key national projects are not guaranteed and if such parts of the infrastructure as energy and transport are not developed, the national economy as a whole will not prosper and the individual sectors are bound to be greatly restricted in their development. Even if there should be some growth in a given locality at a given time, it would not last because of difficulties in striking a balance between supply, production and marketing. We must firmly implant the idea of co-ordinating all the activities of the nation like moves on a chessboard. While continuing to enforce the present financial system and ensure the decision-making powers of enterprises, we must appropriately readjust, in the light of the actual conditions of the different localities and trades, the distribution of national and local revenues and the proportion of profits retained by enterprises, and we must encourage local authorities, departments and enterprises to make their funds available for the key projects most urgently needed by the state. While thus pooling funds, we must of course continue to take into consideration the needs of the localities and enterprises. If appropriate financial reserves are left at the disposal of local authorities and enterprises, it will help give scope to their initiative and enable them to embark on those projects which they are best fitted to undertake, especially as regards the technical transformation of existing enterprises. Our country has abundant resources of labour power, so we must pay close attention to increasing the investment of labour. In the rural areas we must put their rich manpower to good use in agricultural capital construction according to their local conditions. In mining, transport and other fields, we must also stress the role of the investment of labour.

The fundamental aim of socialist production and construction is to meet continuously the growing material and cultural needs of the people. A basic principle guiding our economic work is "first, feed the people and second, build the country". The party and government have done a great deal to bring about a marked improvement in the people's livelihood in recent years. Yet on the whole the living standards remain fairly low. In some low-yield rural areas, or those hit by natural disasters, the peasants are still impoverished, and we must actively help them increase production and income. Urban people, too, still have many problems which call for solution—such as pay, employment, housing and public utilities. The state has decided to take effective measures to improve, steadily and group by group, the living and working conditions of middle-aged intellectuals, who play a backbone role in production, construction and all the other fields. Whether in town or country, living standards can rise only by increasing production, and not by cutting into funds indispensable to national construction, a course that would impair the fundamental and long-term interests of the people. Specifically, we can no longer increase peasant incomes mainly through raising the prices of farm produce or through lowering the fixed quotas of state purchases and enlarging the scope of negotiated prices. The increase of the average incomes of the workers and staff must necessarily be less than that of labour productivity. We must put a stop to the indiscriminate handing out of bonuses and subsidies without regard to the actual state of production and profit. As a matter of fact, a constant improvement in the living standards of the people is possible provided the workers and peasants enhance their understanding and make sustained efforts to raise labour productivity, lower consumption and eliminate waste. As for those problems concerning the people's daily life which can be solved by spending very little or even no money, leaders at all levels must take even more energetic measures to solve them. Concern for the well-being of the people is a fine tradition of our party, which we should never neglect.

Second, Upholding the Leading Position of the State Economy and Developing Diverse Economic Forms.

The socialist state sector occupies the leading position in the entire national economy. The consolidation and growth of the state sector are the decisive factors in ensuring that the collective economy of the working people will advance along the socialist road and that the individual economy will serve socialism. As the level of development of the productive forces in our country is on the whole still fairly low and uneven, it is necessary to maintain different economic forms for a long time to come. In rural areas, the principal economic form is the cooperative economy collectively owned by the working people. At present, the state sector alone cannot and should not run all handicrafts, industries, building industry, transport, commerce and the service trades in the cities and towns; a considerable part should be run by the collective. Co-operatives financed and run by young people and other residents have spread to many urban areas in the past few years and played a useful role. The party and government should support and guide them and forbid discrimination or attacks against them from any quarter. We must also encourage the appropriate development of the individual economy of urban and rural working people as a necessary and useful complement to the public economy, within limits prescribed by the state and under supervision by industrial and commercial administrations. Only through the rational distribution and development of diverse economic forms is it possible to invigorate the urban and rural economy and make life more convenient for the people.

To bring the initiative of enterprises and of the working people into play, we must earnestly implement a responsibility system in the operation and management of both state and collective enterprises. The responsibility system for production set up in various forms in the countryside in recent years has further emancipated the productive forces and it must be adhered to for a long time to come. The thing for us to do is to gradually perfect it on the basis of summing up the practical experience of the masses. In no case must we make rash changes against the will of the masses, still less must we backtrack. With the growth of agricultural production and the rising management ability of the peasants, demands for new types of combined management are found to arise. We should promote various forms of inter-unit economic combinations

strictly in accordance with the principle of stimulating production and of voluntary participation and mutual benefit. It can be predicted that in the not too distant future, there will emerge in our rural areas an improved cooperative economy, with a diversity of forms, which will be able to make full use of the advantages in the light of local conditions and facilitate the large scale adoption of advanced production measures. Recently, the economic responsibility system has also been initiated in industrial and commercial enterprises with some good results. Although industry and commerce are vastly different from agriculture, the application of the economic responsibility system (including the system of responsibility for profit or loss in some of the state enterprises) similarly helps to implement the Marxist principle of material benefit, to heighten the workers' sense of responsibility as masters of the country and to promote production. We should adopt a positive attitude to this system, earnestly sum up experience and discover and devise a set of specific rules and methods which are suited to the characteristics of industrial and commercial enterprises and which can both ensure unified leadership by the state and bring into full play the initiative of enterprises and their workers and staff members.

It is impermissible to undermine the public ownership of the means of production, which is our basic economic system. Of late, there have been cases in certain rural areas of damage to farm irrigation works, destructive lumbering and doing away with the accumulation and retention of common funds by the collective, while in some state-owned industrial and commercial enterprises, there have been such acts as violation of unified state plans, arbitrary holding back of materials earmarked for unified distribution, withholding of profits that should be turned over to the state, evasion of taxes, willful inflation of prices and blocking the flow of commodities. All such things, though done by only a small number of people, seriously impair the public economy and the interests of the state and the people, and they must be resolutely corrected.

Third, Correctly Implementing the Principle of the Leading Role of the Planned Economy and the Supplementary Role of Market Regulation.

China has a planned economy based on public ownership. Planned production and circulation cover the main body of our national economy. At the same time, the production and circulation of some products are allowed to be regulated through the market without being planned, that is, by letting the law of value spontaneously play a regulatory role within the limits circumscribed by the state's unified plan and in the light of the specific conditions at different periods. This serves as a supplement to planned production and circulation, subordinate and secondary to it but essential and useful nonetheless. The state ensures proportionate and co-ordinated growth of the national economy through overall balancing by economic planning and the supplementary role of market regulation. In the past few years, we have initiated a number of reforms in the economic system by extending the powers of enterprises in planning and by giving scope to the role of market regulation. This orientation is correct and its gains are apparent. However, as some reform measures have not been well co-ordinated with each other and the corresponding forms of administrative work have lagged behind, cases of weakening and hampering the state's unified planning have been on the increase. This is not good for the normal growth of the national economy. Hereafter, while continuing to give play to the role of market regulation, we must on no account neglect or relax unified leadership through state planning.

In order to make the development of the economy centralized and unified as well as flexible and diversified, planning should take different forms in different circumstances. Plans of a mandatory nature must be enforced in regard to the production and distribution of capital goods and consumer goods in the state sector which are vital to the national economy and the people's livelihood, and especially in key enterprises vital to the whole economy. This is a major manifestation of China's socialist ownership by the whole people in the organization and management of production. For the sector of the economy which is owned by collectives, mandatory targets should also be assigned where necessary, as in the purchase of grain and other important agricultural and sideline products by the state on fixed quota. In addition to plans of a mandatory nature, guidance plans, whose implementation is mainly ensured by means of economic levers, should be used in regard to many products and enterprises. This is because diverse economic forms still exist in China and it is difficult to make precise estimates of the multifold and complex demands of society and of the productive capacity of a vast number of enterprises. But whether in mandatory planning or in guidance planning, we must strive to make it conform to the objective reality, constantly study changes in market supply and demand, consciously make use of the law of value and such economic levers as pricing, taxation and credits to guide the enterprises in fulfilling state plans, and give them varying degrees of powers to make decisions as they see fit. Only in this way can state plans be supplemented and improved as required and in good time in the course of their implementation. As for a number of small commodities which are low in output value, great in variety and produced and supplied only seasonally and locally, it is neither necessary nor possible for the state to control them all by planning. Enterprises may be allowed to arrange their production flexibly in accordance with the changes in market supply and demand. The state, on its part, should exercise control through policies, decrees and administration by industrial and commercial offices and should help those enterprises with the supply of certain important raw and semi-finished materials.

Correct application of the principle of ensuring the leading role of planned economy supplemented by market regulation is of fundamental importance to the reform of China's economic systems. We must correctly define the respective scope and limits of mandatory plans, guidance plans and market regulation and, on the premise that basic stability of commodity prices is maintained, gradually reform the pricing system, price control measures and the labour and wage systems, and establish an economic administrative system suited to China's conditions so as to ensure the healthy growth of the national economy.

Whether commercial work is done well or badly has a direct bearing on industrial and agricultural production and the people's standard of living, and the importance of this truth has become increasingly manifest in China's economic growth. At present, our commercial networks, estab- lishments and facilities are far from adequate, there are too many intermediate links, market forecasting is weak, and many problems related to ideas about business operation and to management remain to be solved. After acquiring all relevant information and earnestly summing up experience, we must effectively improve our commercial work and unclog, broaden and multiply the channels of circulation so that commodities can flow freely, materials are put to good use and commerce can play its full role in stimulating and guiding production and in ensuring supply and invigorating the economy.

Fourth, Persevering in Self-Reliance While Expanding Economic and Technological Exchanges With Foreign Countries.

It is our firm strategic principle to carry out the policy of opening to the outside world and expand economic and technological exchanges with foreign countries in accordance with the principles of equality and mutual benefit. We must speed the entry of Chinese products into the world market and vigorously expand foreign trade. We must as far as possible make more use of foreign funds available for our national construction. To this end, it is necessary to do all the required preparatory work well and make proper arrangements with regard to the necessary domestic funds and supporting measures. We must actively import advanced technologies suited to our national conditions, particularly those helpful to the technical transformation of our own enterprises, and strive to absorb and develop them in order to promote our production and construction.

In our efforts for socialist modernization, we must take a self-reliant stand, relying mainly on our own hard work. There must be no wavering whatsoever in this respect. Our aim in expanding economic and technological exchanges with foreign countries is to enhance our ability to be self-reliant and to promote, and certainly not to impair, the development of our national economy. We must refrain from indiscriminate import of equipment, and particularly of consumer goods that can be manufactured and supplied at home. In our economic relations with foreign countries, on the premise of unified planning and policy and co-ordinated action, we must stimulate the initiative of various localities, departments and enterprises in their foreign business dealings while at the same time opposing all acts detrimental to the interests of our country and people. In no circumstances must we forget that capitalist countries and enterprises will never change their capitalist nature simply because they have economic and technological exchanges with us. While pursuing the policy of opening to the outside, we must guard against, and firmly resist, the corrosion of capitalist ideas and we must combat any worship of things foreign or fawning on foreigners.

Comrades! Lenin said that living creative socialism is the product of the masses themselves. Note (1) Beyond all doubt, it would be impossible for the cause of socialist construction to forge ahead without the soaring labour enthusiasm of the masses in their hundreds of millions, without the initiative of thousands of production units and without the hard work of various localities and departments. To yield the best results, all our economic work, principles, policies, plans and measures must be based on overall arrangement, on taking into consideration the interests of the state, the collective and the individual and on fully arousing and scientifically organizing the initiative of the central authorities, the localities, departments, enterprises and the working people. This is the most important way to bring about an all-round upsurge in the socialist economy. We are confident that the people of all our nationalities will surely exert themselves with one heart and one mind for the realization of the great goal of our country's economic development.

III. STRIVE TO BUILD A HIGH LEVEL OF SOCIALIST SPIRITUAL CIVILIZATION

From the time that the party shifted the focus of its work to the modernization of China's economy, the Central Committee has proclaimed on many occasions that while working for a high level of material civilization, we must strive to build a high level of socialist spiritual civilization. This is a strategic principle for building socialism. The history of socialism and the present situation in China both tell us that the success or failure of socialism depends on whether or not we adhere to this principle.

Spiritual civilization is closely interrelated with material civilization in socialist construction. As Marx put it, in their productive activity to transform the world, "the producers themselves change, they evolve new qualities, by producing they develop and transform themselves, acquire new powers and new conceptions, new modes of intercourse, new needs, and new speech." Note (2) Comrade Mao Zedong, too, pointed out that the proletariat and other revolutionary people face a twofold task in their struggle for the transformation of the world: "To change the objective world and, at the same time, their own subjective world". Note (3) The objective world comprises nature and society. The transformation of society results in the establishment and development of new relations of production as well as a new socio-political system. The transformation of nature results in material civilization, as manifested in improved conditions for material production and in a better material life for the people. In the process of transforming the objective world, people also transform their subjective world, and the production of spiritual values and the spiritual life of society also develop. The latter achievement is what we call the spiritual civilization, as manifested in a higher educational, scientific and cultural level and in higher ideological, political and moral standards. The transformation of society or the progress of a social system will ultimately find expression in both material and spiritual civilization. As our socialist society is still in its initial stage, it is not yet highly developed materially. However, the establishment of the socialist system makes it possible for us to build a high level of socialist spiritual civilization while striving for a high level of material civilization, just as the development of a modern economy to a certain level and the appearance of the most advanced class of our time, the working class, and its vanguard, the Communist Party, make it possible to succeed in socialist revolution. Material civilization provides an indispensable foundation for socialist spiritual civilization which, in its turn, gives a tremendous impetus to the former and ensures its correct orientation. Each is the condition and objective of the other.

Socialist spiritual civilization constitutes an important characteristic of the socialist system and a major aspect of its superiority. In the past, when referring to the characteristics of socialism, people laid stress on the elimination of the system of exploitation, public ownership of the means of production, distribution according to work, planned and proportionate development of the national economy, and political power of the working class and other working people. They also laid stress on another characteristic of socialism, the high development of the productive forces and a labour productivity higher than that under capitalism as both a necessity and the end result of the development of socialism. All this is undoubtedly true, but it does not cover all the characteristics. Socialism must possess one more characteristic, that is, socialist spiritual civilization with communist ideology at its core. Without this, the building of socialism would be out of the question.

Communism as a social system can be completely realized in our country only through the protracted, arduous struggle of several generations. However, communism is above all a movement. Marx and Engels said: "We call communism the real movement which abolished the present state of things." Note (4) The final objective of this movement is the realization of communism as a social system. In our country, the spread of communist ideas and the movement for the ultimate realization of the ideal of communism began long ago when the Communist Party of China was founded, and continued during the new-democratic revolution which it led. This movement has now brought about a socialist society, which is the first phase of communism. As far back as the democratic revolution, Comrade Mao Zedong pointed out that the programme of the Chinese Communist Party in regard to China's social system comprised two stages, the present and the future. "For the present period, new democracy, and for the future, socialism; these are two parts of an organic whole guided by one and the same communist ideology." He added: "Communism is at once a complete system of proletarian ideology and a new social system. ...Without communism to guide it, China's democratic revolution cannot possibly succeed, let alone move on to the next stage." Note (5) Therefore, communist ideas and actions have long been part of our actual life. The view that communism is but a "dim illusion" and that it "has not been tested in practice" is utterly wrong. There is communism everywhere in our daily life, of which it forms an inseparable part. Inside and outside our party, there are so many heroic and exemplary people, so many who are ready to give their all, including their very lives, for the realization of revolutionary ideals. Do they do all this for material rewards? Does not a lofty communist spirit guide them? Socialism is advancing steadily towards the goal of its higher phase—communism. This advance depends not only on the increase of material wealth but also on the steady growth of people's communist consciousness and revolutionary spirit.

True, at the present stage, we must in our economic and social life persist in the system of "to each according to his work" and other socialist systems, and we cannot of course expect every member of our society to be a communist, but we must demand that the party members, the Communist Youth League members and all other advanced elements acquire communist ideology, and we must, through their instrumentality, educate and influence the broad masses. If the great task of building a socialist spiritual civilization guided by communist ideology is overlooked, people will fall into a one-sided understanding of socialism and direct their attention exclusively to the building of material civilization or even only to the pursuit of material gains. In that case, we will not be able to safeguard the socialist orientation of China's modernization, and our socialist society will lose its ideals and objectives, its spiritual motivation and fighting will, lose the ability to resist the inroad of corrupt influences and even develop distortedly and degenerate. Comrades, this is not just alarmist talk but a conclusion drawn from present realities at home and abroad. It is from this high theoretical and political vantage point that we must recognize the significance and role of socialist spiritual civilization and make up our minds to do our utmost to ensure the building of both a material and a spiritual civilization so that our socialist cause will forever retain its revolutionary youth and vigour.

Roughly speaking, socialist spiritual civilization consists of two aspects, the cultural and the ideological, permeating and promoting each other.

The cultural aspect refers to the development of undertakings such as education, science, art and literature, the press and publication, broadcasting and television, public health and physical culture, and libraries and museums, as well as the raising of the level of general knowledge of the people. It is an important requisite both for the building of a material civilization and for the raising of people's political consciousness and moral standards. Cultural development also includes mass recreational activities which are healthy, pleasant, lively and varied so that, after a spell of hard work, people may refresh themselves with entertainments that are in good taste. All our cultural construction must, of course, be guided by communist ideology. In the past, owing to the influence of "left" ideas and the small-producer mentality, erroneous views such as underestimation of the importance of education, science and culture and discrimination against intellectuals were rife in our party over a fairly long time. They seriously hindered the building of material and spiritual civilization in our country. In recent years, we have made great efforts to eliminate these wrong views. We are determined gradually to step up cultural development so that it will no longer lag behind economic growth. We have worked hard to carry out the party's policy concerning intellectuals and to enable the whole party and all society to realize that, like workers and peasants, intellectuals are a force we must rely on in building socialism. We are determined to do everything possible to create favourable conditions in which the mass of intellectuals can work with ease of mind and in high spirits in the interest of the people. In this regard, there is still a good deal of painstaking ideological and organizational work to do.

Universal education is an important precondition for building material and spiritual civilization. In 1980, the party's Central Committee and the State Council took the decision that universal primary education in various forms must in the main be achieved by 1990 and, in areas where the economy and education are more developed, this should be done earlier. In China's vast rural areas, this is an arduous task, but it can be done through unremitting efforts, and must be done, for the sake of the development of agriculture and of the rural areas. Teachers in schools of all levels, and especially rural primary school teachers, are engaged in extremely arduous but truly noble work. On their efforts depends the moral, intellectual and physical development of the next generation of our citizens. We must make sure that the whole society respects and energetically supports them in their noble endeavours. Development plans and goals for other cultural undertakings covering the next five to ten years should also be worked out.

The socialist character of our spiritual civilization is determined by ideological education. This consists mainly of the following: The working-class world outlook and scientific theory of Marxism; communist ideals, beliefs and moral values; the outlook of being masters of the country and collectivism which correspond with the system of socialist public ownership; a concept of rights and duties and a sense of organization and discipline which correspond with the socialist political system; devoted service to the people and a communist attitude towards work; and socialist patriotism and internationalism. In essence, it consists of, above all, revolutionary ideals, morality and discipline. All party members and other advanced persons in our society must continuously propagate advanced ideas and set an example by their own deeds so as to inspire more and more members of our society to become working people with lofty ideals, moral integrity, education and a sense of discipline.

We must try not only to help every member of our society to acquire a broader mental outlook but also to establish and develop throughout its ranks the new type of social relations which embody socialist spiritual civilization. These relations find expression in solidarity, friendship and mutual assistance in common struggle and common progress among all our nationalities, between the workers, peasants and intellectuals, the cadres and the masses, the army and the people, the army and the government, and among the people in general. Lenin has pointed out that it will take many decades to create new forms of social ties between people and that this is a most noble work. Note (6) We can say with full confidence that, relying on our long revolutionary tradition and proceeding from the foundation already laid for this work, we shall certainly be able to foster and develop such new social ties.

To build a socialist spiritual civilization is a task for the whole party and the common task of our people in all fields of endeavour. Ideological education in the party is the pillar of the building of spiritual civilization in the whole society, and party members should, first of all, play an exemplary role morally and ideologically. Ideological and political workers, workers in culture, in the sciences and in education of all types and levels from kindergartens to graduate schools—all shoulder especially heavy responsibilities in building a socialist spiritual civilization. In particular, the Communist Party members among them must unite in thought and deed so as to organize a mighty contingent of militant ideological workers able to persuade and act as a magnet for others. It is necessary to do more to educate the masses of the people, and first of all the cadres and youth, in Marxism-Leninism and Mao Zedong Thought, in the history of our motherland, and especially its modern history; in the programme, history and revolutionary tradition of our party; and in the constitution of our country, the rights and duties of citizens and civic morality. It is necessary to do more to educate people of all trades and lines of work in professional responsibility, ethics and discipline. Education in all the areas enumerated above should be closely related to reality and conducted in vivid and varied ways. In formulating and implementing policies and in all their work, leading cadres in the economic field at various levels should concern themselves not only with the development of production but also with the building of a socialist spiritual civilization. In production and construction, we should try not only to turn out more and better material products, but also train successive generations of socialist-minded people of a new type. We must not allow our policies or work in any field to impede or, still worse, to undermine the building of a socialist spiritual civilization. In the past year or so, mass activities for building such a civilization have been unfolded in the People's Liberation Army and among the people in general. Relevant rules have been formulated for students in schools and for workers and staff members in enterprises, and written pledges have been drawn up by city residents, rural commune members and people in various trades and professions. All these activities have begun to yield gratifying results. We call on every locality and department to promote and persist in them. We must explore all possible ways and adopt all possible effective measures to promote education in ideals, morality and discipline among the entire population, and first of all among the youth, within the next five years. This is essential to our endeavour to bring about a fundamental turn for the better in standards of social conduct. From now on, when checking up on the work of any locality, department or unit, the Central Committee and the local party committees at all levels must take into consideration not only its material side, but also its spiritual side. Every citizen should perform his duties and abide by social morality and professional ethics. Every working person should contribute his share to the building of socialist spiritual civilization.

To build it is no easy task, particularly at the present moment. In the years of the revolutionary wars and those immediately following the founding of the People's Republic, our material life was much harder than it is today, but all party members and the people as a whole were full of vigour. The decade of domestic turmoil confounded the criteria of right and wrong, good and evil, and beauty and ugliness. It is much more difficult to undo its grave spiritual consequences than its material ones. For this and other reasons, many serious problems concerning standards of social conduct now exist in our country. The Central Committee of the party is determined to effect a fundamental turn for the better in standards of social conduct in the next five years. This includes, in the main, the achievement of markedly better public order, generally improved attitudes towards all types of work and a marked decline in the crime rate. It also means putting an effective check on, and arousing universal contempt for, such unhealthy tendencies and practices as benefiting oneself at other's expense, pursuing private interests at the expense of public interests, loving ease and despising work, putting money first in everything, unscrupulous pursuit of personal enjoyment, and attempting to isolate and attack advanced elements. It also includes resolutely eliminating all the vile social evils which had been stamped out long ago by New China but have now cropped up again. We must do our utmost to adapt ourselves to the new conditions and developments in the period of construction, do a good job of building socialist spiritual civilization and arouse, with revolutionary ideas and revolutionary spirit, the immense enthusiasm of the broad masses for building socialism.

IV. STRIVE TO ATTAIN A HIGH LEVEL OF SOCIALIST DEMOCRACY

The steady development of socialist democracy provides the guarantee and support for the building of socialist material and spiritual civilization. To attain a high level of socialist democracy is therefore one of our fundamental goals and tasks.

Our state system is the people's democratic dictatorship. On the one hand, it ensures that the working people, the overwhelming majority of the population, are the masters of the state; on the other, it exercises dictatorship over a tiny minority of hostile elements who try to undermine socialism. Socialism is the common cause of the whole people. Only with a high level of socialist democracy will it be possible to develop all our undertakings in accordance with the will, interests and needs of the people, to enhance the people's sense of responsibility as masters and give full play to their initiative and enthusiasm, and to exercise effective dictatorship over the handful of hostile elements, in order to ensure the smooth progress of socialist construction.

Socialist democracy is incomparably superior to bourgeois democracy. Much time and work are needed to establish the system of socialist democracy and foster democratic ways. What we did in this respect was far from adequate and, moreover, was seriously undermined during the "Cultural Revolution". In recent years, socialist democracy has been restored and developed to some extent in our country. We must continue to reform and improve our political institutions and system of leadership in accordance with the principle of democratic centralism so that the people are better able to exercise state power and the state organs can lead and organize the work of socialist construction more effectively. Socialist democracy should be extended to all spheres of life: political, economic, cultural and social; and it is necessary to extend democratic management to all enterprises and institutions and encourage self-management of community affairs by the masses at the grass-roots level. Democracy should serve as a means by which the masses educate themselves. It is necessary to establish a relationship of equality between man and man and a correct relationship between the individual and society in accordance with the principles of socialist democracy. The state and society guarantee legitimate freedom and rights to the citizens, who should in turn perform their duties to the state and society. While exercising their freedom and rights, citizens must not impair the interests of the state, society and the collective, or the freedom and rights of others. While we strive to develop socialist democracy, all our measures must help to consolidate the socialist system and promote social production and work in other fields. On no account will hostile, anti-socialist elements be given any freedom to carry out sabotage.

We must closely link the building of socialist democracy with that of the socialist legal system so that socialist democracy is institutionalized and codified into laws. In the past few years, notable progress has been made in building our legal system. Under the party's leadership, the state has enacted a series of important laws, including the criminal law, the law of criminal procedure, the draft law of civil procedure for trial implementation and the new marriage law. It is especially noteworthy that the draft constitution, soon to be submitted to the National People's Congress for adoption, contains many new and very important stipulations formulated in the light of the achievements scored and the principles worked out in developing socialist democracy since the third plenary session of the eleventh Central Committee. The adoption of this constitution will mark a new stage in the development of China's socialist democracy and legal system. The problems facing us today are that not only a sizable number of non-party people but also many party members, including some leading cadres, do not have an adequate understanding of the importance of building the legal system and that laws already enacted are in some cases not fully observed or enforced. This situation must be resolutely corrected. The party will continue to lead the people in making and improving various laws, strengthen its leadership over the work of public security, the procuratorate and the judiciary and ensure in every way that these departments enforce the laws strictly. Moreover, through our publicity work we should repeatedly educate the whole people in the importance of the legal system and include instructions in the laws in all the teaching programmes from primary schools to colleges, so that every citizen may know the laws and abide by them. In particular, party members should be educated and urged to take the lead in observing the constitution and laws. The stipulation in the new party constitution that "the party must conduct its activities within the limits permitted by the constitution and the laws of the state" embodies a most important principle. It is impermissible for any party organization or member, from the Central Committee down to the grass roots, to act in contravention of the constitution and laws. The party is part of the people. It leads them in making the constitution and laws which, once adopted by the supreme organ of state power, must be strictly observed by the whole party.

Further promotion of the socialist relations of equality, unity and mutual assistance among all our nationalities constitutes an important aspect of the building of socialist democracy in our country. The Central Committee has in the past few years made a number of significant decisions on the nationalities question and achieved marked successes in correcting "left" errors committed during and before the "Cultural Revolution" and in restoring good relations among China's nationalities. In the light of conditions in this new historical period and the specific circumstances of various nationalities, the Central Committee has adopted many policies helpful to economic and cultural development in the minority nationality areas, to the realization of their right to regional autonomy, and to strengthening of unity among all our nationalities. These policies will have to be further improved and developed. Unity, equality and common prosperity among the nationalities are of vital importance to the destiny of China as a multinational country. The whole party must acquire a better understanding of the nationalities question, oppose great-nation chauvinism, primarily Han chauvinism, and at the same time oppose local-nationality chauvinism. We must educate all party members to strive to fulfill the task of the party in regard to the nationalities.

In the period of the democratic revolution, the united front was an important "magic weapon" for winning victory in our revolution. In the period of socialist construction it still plays a major role. With regard to all China's democratic parties, non-party democrats, national minority personages and patriots in the religious circles, our party will continue to adhere to the policy of "long-term coexistence and mutual supervision" and the principle of "treating each other with all sincerity and sharing weal or woe", and strengthen our co-operation with them. We must do everything possible to strengthen the broadest patriotic united front, embracing all socialist working people and all patriots who support socialism or who support the reunification of the motherland, including our compatriots in Taiwan, Xianggang (Hong Kong) and Aomen (Macao) and Chinese nationals residing abroad.

Correct understanding and handling of the class struggle that still exists in China today is the key to guaranteeing the democratic rights of the overwhelming majority of the people and exercising effective dictatorship over the handful of hostile elements. Hostile elements of different shades are still attempting to undermine or overthrow our socialist system in the economic, political, ideological, cultural and other social spheres. The class struggle at the present stage chiefly takes the form of struggle by the people against these hostile elements. The Central Committee has repeatedly pointed out that following the elimination of the exploiting classes as such, most contradictions in our society do not have the nature of class struggle, and class struggle no longer constitutes the principal contradiction. It is wrong, in a socialist society where the system of exploitation has been abolished and the exploiting classes have been eliminated, to declare and act on the principle of "taking class struggle as the key link". We must be very careful in distinguishing and handling contradictions between the enemy and the people and those within the ranks of the people, so as to avoid repeating the past mistake of enlarging the scope of class struggle. However, within certain limits, class struggle will continue to exist for a long time and may even sharpen under certain conditions. This is not only because pernicious influences left over by the exploitative systems and classes cannot be eradicated within a short time, but also because we have not yet achieved our goal of reunifying our motherland and still live in a complicated international environment in which the capitalist forces and other forces hostile to our socialist cause will seek to corrupt us and harm our country. Our economy and culture are still quite backward and our young socialist system is imperfect in many ways, so that it is not yet possible to prevent in all cases the degeneration of some members of our society and party or block the emergence of a few exploiting and hostile elements. Therefore, we must prepare ourselves mentally for a long-term struggle, see to it that the state of the people's democratic dictatorship exercises its function of dictatorship over enemies, and uphold the Marxist class viewpoint in handling the current social contradictions and other social phenomena that have the nature of class struggle. This is the basic principle of the Central Committee with regard to the question of the class struggle in China at the present stage.

In the new period of the development of our socialist cause, we must attend, both in ideology and in action, to two aspects. On the one hand, we must persist in the policy of opening to the outside as well as in our policies for invigorating the economy domestically and, on the other, we must resolutely strike at the grave criminal activities in the economic, political and cultural spheres that endanger socialism. It would be wrong to attend only to the latter aspect and be skeptical about the former, and it would be dangerous to stress the former aspect to the neglect of the latter. All party comrades must have a clear understanding of this principle without the slightest ambiguity.

Our socialist construction is taking place in a very unstable world in which our national security is under grave threat. In these circumstances, we must never relax our vigilance, but must strengthen our national defence on the basis of vigorous economic development. We must work hard to turn the People's Liberation Army into a regular, modern and powerful revolutionary armed force and enhance its defence capabilities in modern warfare. We must continue to maintain and carry forward the fine traditions of our peoples' armed forces, and strengthen and improve their ideological and political work, so that every member will have a lofty spirit of self-sacrifice, strong sense of discipline and revolutionary style of work and that our army will serve not only as a Great Wall of steel guarding our socialist motherland but also as an important force in building our socialist material and spiritual civilization. We must continue to strengthen the militia. The Chinese People's Liberation Army is a people's armed force created and led by the Chinese Communist Party. After the new draft constitution is discussed and adopted by the forthcoming National People's Congress, the Central Committee will continue to exercise leadership over our armed forces through the State Central Military Commission which is due to be set up. We must stick to the successful practices which the party has long followed in leading the armed forces. This conforms to the supreme interests of the whole nation. We are convinced that, under the leadership of the Central Committee and through the efforts of all the commanders and fighters and the people of all nationalities, our national defence will become still stronger, thus providing a surer guarantee that the whole nation will be able to devote its full energy to socialist construction.

V. ADHERING TO AN INDEPENDENT FOREIGN POLICY

China's future is closely bound up with that of the world as a whole. The successes China has achieved in its revolution and construction provide a powerful support to the world's movement for progress and a bright future, and conversely, our successes would have been impossible without the struggles of the people of other countries for a bright future. China has received help from other countries and peoples, and in turn has helped others. In the early years of our People's Republic, Comrade Mao Zedong pointed out: "Our general task is to unite the whole people and win the support of all our friends abroad in the struggle to build a great socialist country, defend world peace and

advance the cause of human progress." Note (7) Integration of patriotism with internationalism has always been our basic point of departure in handling our external relations.

Being patriots, we do not tolerate any encroachment on China's national dignity or interests. Being internationalists, we are deeply aware that China's national interests cannot be fully realized in separation from the overall interests of mankind. Our adherence to an independent foreign policy accords with the discharging of our lofty international duty to safeguard world peace and promote human progress. In the thirty-three years since the founding of our People's Republic, we have shown the world by deeds that China never attaches itself to any big power or group of powers, and never yields to pressure from any big power. China's foreign policy is based on the scientific theories of Marxism-Leninism and Mao Zedong Thought, and it proceeds from the fundamental interests of the people of China and the rest of the world. It follows an overall long-term strategy, and is definitely not swayed by expediency or by anybody's instigation or provocation. Because we have firmly applied the basic principles of our foreign policy formulated by the late Comrades Mao Zedong and Zhou Enlai, socialist New China has gained prestige, made friends throughout the world and maintained its dignity in its relations with foreign countries.

The five principles of mutual respect for sovereignty and territorial integrity, mutual non-aggression, non-interference in each others' internal affairs, equality and mutual benefit, and peaceful coexistence have consistently guided China in its effort to develop relations with other countries. Having suffered aggression and oppression for over a century, the Chinese people will never again allow themselves to be humiliated as they were before, nor will they subject other nations to such humiliation. The founding of our People's Republic has removed the social causes both of China's submission to foreign aggression and of any possibility of China committing aggression abroad. Frederick Engels said: "A nation cannot become free and at the same time continue to oppress other nations." Note (8) This is an incontestable truth. We Marxists-Leninists are convinced that communism will ultimately be realized throughout the world. However, revolution cannot be exported but can occur only by the choice of the people of the country concerned. It is on the basis of this understanding that we have always abided by the five principles of peaceful coexistence. We do not station a single soldier abroad, nor have we occupied a single inch of foreign land. We have never infringed upon the sovereignty of another country, or imposed an unequal relationship upon it. In no circumstances will we seek hegemony.

The five principles of peaceful coexistence are applicable to our relations with all countries, including socialist countries. On the basis of these principles we have in the past thirty-three years established diplomatic relations with 125 countries. With the friendly socialist countries of Korea, Romania and Yugoslavia, we maintain close co-operation and are steadily strengthening and developing ties of unity and friendship. China and many other developing countries in Asia, Africa and Latin America sympathize with and support one another, and have enhanced their co-operation in all fields. Many Western countries have social systems different from China's, yet we share a common desire to safeguard world peace and a common interest in developing our economic and cultural co-operation, for which the potentials are great, and we have maintained good relations over the years. The past few years have also seen some development in our relations with East European countries.

Japan is China's neighbour. Since ancient times, there have been frequent exchanges and a profound friendship between the Chinese and Japanese peoples. But, during a hundred years of modern history, the Japanese militarists unleashed one war of aggression after another against China, inflicting colossal calamities on the Chinese people and grievous damage on the Japanese people themselves. Thanks to long years of joint efforts made by the Chinese and Japanese peoples, state relations were eventually normalized ten years ago. The development of relations of peace and friendship, equality and mutual benefit, and prolonged stability between China and Japan is in accord with the long-term interests of the two peoples and conducive to the peace and stability of the Asian-Pacific region. Now some forces in Japan are white-washing the past Japanese aggressions against China and other east Asian countries and are carrying out activities for the revival of Japanese militarism. These dangerous developments cannot but put the people of China, Japan and other countries sharply on the alert. Together with the Japanese people and with far-sighted Japanese public figures in and out of government, we will work to eliminate all hindrances to the relations between our two countries and make the friendship between our two peoples flourish from generation to generation.

Since the establishment of diplomatic ties between China and the United States of America in 1978, relations between the two countries have developed in the interests of the two peoples. We have always hoped that these relations will continue to grow, and consider this beneficial to our two peoples and to world peace. However, a cloud has all along hung over the relations between the two countries. This is because the United States, despite having recognized that the Government of the People's Republic of China is China's sole legal government and that there is only one China and Taiwan is part of China, has passed the Taiwan Relations Act which contravenes the principles embodied in the joint communique on the establishment of diplomatic relations, and it has continued to sell arms to Taiwan, treating Taiwan as an independent political entity. As the Chinese Government has repeatedly stated, these are acts of infringement on China's sovereignty and of interference in China's internal affairs. Not long ago, after nearly a year of talks, the Chinese and U.S. Governments issued a joint communique providing for a step-by-step solution of the question of U.S. arms sales to Taiwan, leading to a final thorough settlement.

We hope that these provisions will be strictly observed. Sino-U.S. relations can continue to develop soundly only if the principles of mutual respect for sovereignty and territorial integrity and non-interference in each other's internal affairs are truly adhered to.

The relations between China and the Soviet Union were friendly over a fairly long period. They have become what they are today because the Soviet Union has pursued a hegemonist policy. For the past twenty years, the Soviet Union has stationed massive armed forces along the Sino-Soviet and Sino-Mongolian borders. It has supported Vietnam in the latter's invasion and occupation of Kampuchea, acts of expansion in Indochina and Southeast Asia and constant provocations along China's border. Moreover, it has invaded and occupied Afghanistan, a neighbour of China, by force of arms. All these acts constitute grave threats to the peace of Asia and to China's security. We note that Soviet leaders have expressed more than once the desire to improve relations with China. But deeds, rather than words, are important. If the Soviet authorities really have a sincere desire to improve relations with China and take practical steps to lift their threat to the security of our country, it will be possible for Sino-Soviet relations to move towards normalization. The friendship between the Chinese and Soviet peoples is of long standing, and we will strive to safeguard and develop this friendship, no matter what Sino-Soviet state relations are like.

The main forces jeopardizing peaceful coexistence among nations today are imperialism, hegemonism and colonialism. True, the old system of colonialism has disintegrated with the successive winning of independence by nearly a hundred former colonial and semi-colonial countries. Yet its remnants are far from being eliminated. The superpowers that practise hegemonism pose a new threat to the people of the world. In their pursuit of global domination, the superpowers have been contending on a worldwide scale with military power far exceeding that of any other countries. This is the main source of instability and turmoil in the world. The most important task for the people of the world today is to oppose hegemonism and safeguard world peace. Due to the rivalry between the superpowers, the danger of a world war is growing ever greater. However, experience shows that the people of the world, by persevering in struggle, can upset the strategic plans of the superpowers. World peace can be safeguarded, provided the people truly unite and fight resolutely against all expressions of hegemonism and expansionism. We have always firmly opposed the arms race between the superpowers, stood for the prohibition of the use of nuclear weapons and for their complete destruction and demanded that the superpowers be the first to cut their nuclear and conventional arsenals drastically. We are against the world war being fomented by the superpowers and also against all the local wars of aggression which they instigate or back. We have always firmly supported all victim countries and peoples in their struggle against aggression. We support the Korean people in their struggle to reunify their fatherland. We support the Kampuchean people led by the Coalition Government of Democratic Kampuchea in their struggle against Vietnamese aggression. We support the people of Afghanistan in their struggle against Soviet aggression. We support the African people in their struggle against South Africa's racism and expansionism. We strongly condemn Israel for its heinous aggression and atrocities against the people of Palestine and Lebanon. With support and protection from the U.S. hegemonists, Israel has outrageously occupied Palestine and carried out repeated armed aggression against Arab countries, posing a grave threat to peace in the Middle East and the world as a whole. We continue our resolute support for the Palestinian people in their struggle to return to their homeland and to found their own state and for other Arab peoples in their struggle against Israeli expansionism.

Socialist China belongs to the Third World. China has experienced the same sufferings as most other Third World countries, and she is faced with similar problems and tasks. China regards it as her sacred international duty to struggle resolutely against imperialism, hegemonism and colonialism together with the other Third World countries.

The emergence of the Third World on the international arena after World War II is a primary event of our time. It has changed the United Nations from a mere voting machine manipulated by certain big powers into a forum where imperialism, hegemonism and expansionism are often justly condemned. The struggle initiated by Latin American countries against the maritime hegemony of the superpowers and the struggles of the petroleum exporting countries and other raw material producing countries for permanent sovereignty over their own natural resources, the struggle of the nonaligned countries against power politics and bloc politics and the struggles of the developing countries for the establishment of a new international economic order—all these struggles have converged into a mighty current of forces upholding justice in our time and greatly changed the situation in which the superpowers could wilfully manipulate the fate of the world.

The common task confronting the Third World countries is, first and foremost, to defend their national independence and state sovereignty and actively develop their national economies so that they can back up the political independence they have already won with economic independence. Here, mutual aid among Third World countries is of particular importance. We Third World countries have vast territories, large populations, immense resources and extensive markets. Some of us have accumulated considerable funds, and many have acquired their own distinctive technologies and gained experience in developing their national economies which the others can learn from. Our mutual economic co-operation, commonly known as "South-South co-operation", is no less effective than our co-operation with developed countries so far as some kinds of our technology and equipment are concerned in meeting mutual needs. Such co-operation is of great strategic significance, as it helps us to break out of the existing unequal international economic relations and establish the new international economic order.

China is still a developing country, but we have always done our best to help other Third World countries, with whom we share a common destiny. The Chinese people have always spurned attitudes and actions of despising the poor and currying favour with the rich, bullying the weak and fearing the strong. Our friendship with other Third World countries is sincere. Whether in providing aid or co-operating for mutual benefit, we have always strictly respected the sovereignty of the other party, attaching no strings and demanding no privileges. As our economy grows, we will steadily expand our friendly co-operation with other countries and peoples of the Third World.

We are deeply disturbed by the discords, going as far as armed conflicts, that have occurred between some Third World countries. They often cause heavy losses to both sides and at times allow the hegemonists to pick up easy gains. We always work for increased unity among the Third World countries in the hope that the parties to such disputes will resolve them through consultations and avoid any results that grieve friends and gladden enemies.

Here I would especially like to discuss the question of relationships between the Communist Party of China and those of other countries. Our party develops its relations with other communist or working-class parties in strict conformity with Marxism and the principles of independence, complete equality, mutual respect and non-interference in each other's internal affairs.

The success of the revolution in any country depends on the ripeness of conditions for it and the people's support for the line and policies of that country's communist party. Communist parties should of course help each other, but it is absolutely impermissible for any of them to issue orders or run things for others from the outside. Any attempt by one party to impose its views on other parties or interfere in their internal affairs can only lead to setbacks or failures in the revolutions of the countries concerned. As for the practice of one party compelling other parties to make their policies serve its own party and state policies, or even resorting to armed intervention in other countries, it can only undermine the very foundation of the international communist movement.

The communist parties of all countries are equal. Whether large or small, long or short in their history, in power or out of power, they cannot be divided into superior and inferior parties. Our party has suffered from the attempt of a self-elevated paternal party to keep us under control. As is commonly known, it is through resisting such control that our independent external policy has won its successes.

We hold that all communist parties should respect each other. Each party has its strong and weak points. Being situated in different circumstances, all parties cannot be expected to hold completely identical views on the assessment of situations and on their own tasks. Their differences of opinion can only be resolved gradually through friendly consultations and patiently giving each other time. We are in favour of all communist parties learning from each other's successes and failures, believing that this will help the international communist movement to grow and flourish.

On the principles mentioned above, our party has maintained friendly relations with many other communist parties. We sincerely appreciate their support and help and are conscientiously learning from their experience whatever can be of help to our revolution and construction. And we wish to establish similar contacts with a greater number of progressive parties and organizations. Setting store by their friendship with the people of other countries, the Chinese people have developed extensive contacts with them. In the final analysis, steadily increasing understanding and co-operation among the people of all countries is the basic guarantee of progress and a bright future for the world.

Being a large country with a population of one billion, China ought to make a great contribution to the world community, and it is only natural that people place hopes on us. Yet what we have accomplished falls far short of what we ought to have done. We will redouble our efforts to step up our construction so as to play our due role in safeguarding world peace and promoting human progress.

VI. MAKE THE PARTY A STRONG LEADING CORE, THE CAUSE OF SOCIALIST MODERNIZATION

History has entrusted our party with heavy responsibilities in the great undertaking of China's socialist modernization. In order to step up party building in the new period, we have made many fundamental changes in the party constitution adopted by the eleventh national congress. The general principle guiding the revision of the party constitution is to set more exacting demands on party members, enhance the fighting capacity of the party organizations and uphold and improve party leadership, all in conformity with the characteristics and needs of the new historical period. As required by the new constitution, we must strive to build the party and make it a strong leading core for the cause of socialist modernization.

The draft of the revised party constitution now submitted to this congress for its consideration has discarded the "left" errors in the constitution adopted by the eleventh congress, and carries forward the merits of the party constitutions passed respectively by the seventh and eighth congresses. The general programme section in the draft constitution includes Marxist definitions concerning the character and guiding ideology of the party, the principal contradiction in our society at the present stage and the general task of the party, and the correct way for the party to play its leading role in the life of the state. The ideological, political and organizational requirements this draft constitution sets for party members and cadres are stricter than those in all our previous constitutions. In stipulating the duties of party members, the draft absolutely forbids them to use public office for personal gain or to benefit themselves at the expense of the public interests, and requires that they firmly oppose factionalism and be bold in backing good people and good deeds and in opposing bad people and bad deeds. It sets forth as basic requirements for leading cadres at all levels that they correctly implement the party's line, principles and policies, oppose erroneous tendencies inside and outside the party, have the professional knowledge and organizational ability needed for competent leadership, and adhere to party principles in struggling against all abuses of power and pursuit of personal gain. Most of these are additions, not found in the previous constitutions. In the light of our historical experience and lessons, the draft constitution emphasizes that all party organizations from the central down to the primary level must strictly observe the principles of democratic centralism and collective leadership, and it explicitly stipulates that the party "forbids all forms of personality cult". It makes many new provisions for improving the systems of the central and local organizations, tightening party discipline, reinforcing the discipline inspection organs and strengthening the primary party organizations. According to the draft constitution, the Central Committee is to have no chairman but only a general secretary, who will convene meetings of the Political Bureau and its Standing Committee and preside over the work of the Secretariat. Advisory committees are to be established at the central and provincial levels to give our many veteran comrades rich in political experience a role as consultants in the service of the party's cause. Commissions for discipline inspection are to be elected by party congresses at the respective levels and, within limits prescribed by the party constitution, they are to supervise party committees and their members at the respective levels below the Central Committee, and they may report to the Central Committee any breach of party discipline by any of its members. Party organizations at all levels must pay great attention to party building and must regularly discuss and check up on the party's work in propaganda, education, organization and discipline inspection, and its mass work and united front work. All these stipulations should help to reinforce the party's collective leadership, enhance its fighting capacity and strengthen its ties with the masses. It should be said that the present draft is an improvement on all the previous constitutions and is fuller in content. Being a precious crystallization of the party's historical experience and collective wisdom, it is an important guarantee for making our party still stronger in the new historical period.

All party members must study and strictly observe the new constitution after its adoption by this congress. Whether or not a party member really meets the requirements set by the constitution and can fully discharge the duties of membership will be the fundamental criterion for judging whether he or she is qualified to be a party member.

Before the present revision of the constitution, our party worked out the Guiding Principles for Inner-Party Political Life, a document which has played a salutary role in that regard.

The Guiding Principles will remain in full effect as an important complement to the Constitution. In light of the present conditions in the party and in the spirit of our new party constitution, we must now concentrate on solving the following problems in party building.

First, Improve the Party's System of Democratic Centralism and Further Normalize Inner-Party Political Life.

The history of our party shows that, in the period from its founding to the early years after the establishment of the People's Republic, except for a few years when the party fell into grave right or "left" errors, it implemented the principles of democratic centralism relatively well, and inner-party political life was fairly vigorous and lively. But from the late 1950's, the personality cult gradually appeared and developed, and political life in the party and state, and particularly the Central Committee, grew more and more abnormal, leading eventually to the decade of domestic turmoil. The grave twists and turns of history have taught us that whether there is normal political life in the party, and above all in the Central Committee and other leading bodies of the party at different levels, is indeed a fundamental issue bearing on the destiny of the party and state.

Now, the Central Committee is happy to report to the congress that, thanks to efforts made since the third plenary session of the eleventh Central Committee, political life in the party, and first of all in the Central Committee, after being seriously abnormal for so many years, has now gradually returned to the correct path, the path of Marxism. Generally speaking, the Central Committee, its Political Bureau, the bureau's Standing Committee and the Secretariat have proved able to follow principles of democratic centralism and collective leadership. The practices of "what one person says goes" and of each going his own way are no longer allowed. When important differences of opinion arise, unity in thinking and action can be achieved through full reasoning and criticism and self-criticism. The present Central Committee is a united and harmonious leading body and a strong core able to cope with complicated situations. There has also been marked improvement in the political life of many local party organizations.

While affirming this major progress, we must also realize that in the party as a whole, undemocratic practices and patriarchal ways have still not been eradicated in many organizations, and cases of decentralism and liberalism exist to a serious extent. All this hinders the implementation of the party's line, principles and policies and weakens its fighting capacity. In order to carry forward the normalization of political life throughout the party, we must resolutely get rid of such unhealthy phenomena. All party members, and especially the leading cadres at various levels, must bear the principle of democratic centralism firmly in mind, see to it that collective leadership is established and strengthened first of all in the party committees at various levels, and strive to develop inner-party democracy while ensuring centralism and unity on the basis of democracy.

Party discipline must be strengthened in order to improve the functioning of democratic centralism. A grave problem at present is that in quite a number of organizations party discipline has slackened, right and wrong are confounded, rewards and punishments are misused and there is failure to criticize or punish when necessary. This is a problem of long standing, which has become exacerbated after the decade of domestic turmoil, and no marked improvement has yet occurred in some places. In the last few years the Central Committee, local party committees and party commissions for discipline inspection at all levels have attained notable results in their major efforts to uphold party discipline and correct the style of the party. But they have met considerable, and in some cases shocking, obstruction in their work. If such things are allowed to spread, what will remain of the party's fighting capacity? Party organizations at all levels and all party members must be mobilized to fight resolutely to uphold party discipline. We are confident that after this congress, through concerted efforts by all party organizations and members, we shall certainly be able to fully restore the inviolability of discipline throughout the party before too long and thus win the full trust of the people throughout the country.

Second, Reform the Leading Bodies and the Cadre System and Ensure That the Ranks of the Cadres Become More Revolutionary, Younger in Average Age, Better Educated and More Professionally Competent.

The main aim of reforming the system of leadership and the leading organs of the party and state is to eliminate such defects as overconcentration of power, proliferation of concurrent and deputy posts, organizational overlapping, lack of clear-cut job responsibility, overstaffing and failure to separate party work from government work, and in these ways overcome bureaucracy and increase work efficiency. The first stage of reform of the party and government organs at the central level has been basically completed, and the reform in the provinces, municipalities and autonomous regions is scheduled to start in the second half of this year or in the coming year. This reform is of far-reaching significance, being an important political guarantee for the success of China's modernization and adherence to the socialist road.

To solve correctly the question of party leadership over government organs and over enterprises and institutions is a highly important task in the organizational reform. It is necessary to achieve a proper division of labour between the party and the government and between party work and administrative and production work in enterprises and institutions. The party is not an organ of power which issues orders to the people, nor is it an administrative or production organization. The party should, of course, exercise leadership over production, construction and work in all other fields, and for this leadership to be fully effective it must be exercised in close connection with professional work by cadres who are professionally competent in such work. But party leadership is mainly political and ideological leadership in matters of principle and policy and in the selection, allocation, assessment and supervision of cadres. It should not be equated with administrative work and the direction of production by government organizations and enterprises. The party organizations should not take everything into their own hands. Only in this way can the party ensure that the government organs and enterprises do their work independently and effectively, and can the party itself concentrate its efforts on the study and formulation of major policies, the inspection of their implementation and the strengthening of ideological and political work among cadres and the rank and file both inside and outside the party. For long-standing historical reasons, some members of our party committees think that there will be nothing for them to do if they don't handle concrete administrative work—this is an erroneous idea that impairs party building and weakens the party's leading role. From now on, party committees at all levels should frequently study and discuss the party's major policies and principles regarding socialist construction, matters involving the ideology and education of cadres, party members and the masses, the ideological tendencies of cadres and their observance of discipline, the improvement of the party organization and the recruitment of new members, and so on. Of course, while the division of labour between party and government is emphasized, major policy decisions concerning government and economic work must still be made by the party, and all party members working in government organizations, enterprises and institutions must resolutely submit themselves to party leadership and carry out the party's policies.

To ensure that the ranks of the cadres become more revolutionary, younger in average age, better educated and more professionally competent is a long-established principle of the Central Committee of the party. During the organizational reform, we will relieve our many veteran cadres who are advanced in age of their heavy responsibilities in "front line" posts and at the same time enable them to continue their service to the party, the state and society by utilizing their rich experience in leadership work. We will promote large numbers of energetic young and middle-aged cadres who possess both political integrity and ability to various leading posts in good time, so that they can be tempered over a longer period practically and effectively by working with older cadres and taking over responsibilities from them and so that the leading bodies at all levels can continuously absorb new life-blood and talent to maintain their vigour. As for persons who rose to prominence by "rebellion", who are seriously factionalist in their ideas, who have indulged in beating, smashing and looting, who oppose the line followed by the party's Central Committee since its third plenary session, or who have seriously violated the law and discipline, we must remove with a firm hand those among them who are still in leading posts. Persons who have violated criminal law must be investigated and dealt with according to law. Such people, of course, must never be put up as candidates for promotion to leading posts. The co-operation between old and new cadres and the succession of the new to the old are matters important to the continuation of our socialist cause. We believe that all our party comrades, especially our old comrades, will certainly be able to accomplish this historic task with a high revolutionary sense of responsibility.

We must work strenuously to strengthen the education and training of cadres in order to prepare large numbers of specialized personnel needed for socialist modernization. In the future, in our use and promotion of cadres, we must attach importance to educational background and academic records as well as to experience and achievements in work. Party schools at all levels, cadre schools run by government organizations and enterprises, and especially designated institutions of higher learning and specialized secondary schools should all, as required by socialist modernization and in their different capacities, revise their teaching plans and shoulder the regular training of cadres. All functionaries on the job should be trained in rotation. After such training, appropriate adjustments can be made in their jobs through assessment of their actual performance. The training of all cadres in rotation is an important strategic measure for enhancing their quality. All party members and all cadres should have a full understanding of the needs of our modernization programme and be active in study.

Third, Strengthen the Party's Work Among the Workers, Peasants and Intellectuals and Establish Close Ties Between the Party and the Masses.

Our party is powerful because it represents the interests of the broadest masses of the people. The party's leading position in the life of the state determines that its activities vitally affect the interests of the masses, and at the same time involves the danger that party members, and party cadres in particular, may become isolated from the masses. This requires that we strive all the more consciously to preserve and carry forward the party's fine tradition of applying the mass line and effectively strengthen the party's close ties with the people of all strata of society.

Our party is a party of the working class, and it must make a point of relying on the masses of workers. The composition of the working class in China has undergone a big change in recent years, with large numbers of new workers replacing old ones. Many old workers who are party members have retired, many young people have joined the ranks of the working class, and group after group of workers who are party members have been transferred to managerial jobs. As a result, there are fewer party members on the production front, and the harder the labour, the smaller the number of party members. This grave situation has weakened the direct link between the party and the industrial workers. From now on, we must greatly strengthen party work on the production front, encourage party members fitted for working there to do so, and at the same time admit into the party outstanding workers who are qualified for membership. The party's work in the

trade unions must be greatly strengthened so that they become a strong transmission belt between the party and the masses of workers. The system of congresses of workers and staff must be implemented in earnest so that these congresses and the trade unions can both play an important role in ideological education, enterprise management and the improvement of the workers' living standards.

Effective party work among China's 800 million peasants is a major prerequisite for its modernization. In a number of rural areas at present, some party members are interested only in their own productive activities and neglect the interests of the party and the masses, and some party branches have relinquished leadership among the masses. Effective measures must be taken to check this unhealthy tendency. Party committees at all levels should face up to such new developments, further strengthen the rural party organizations as well as the economic and administrative units and mass organizations at the grass roots and intensify ideological education among the peasants of different ages and in different localities, so that the political, economic and cultural life in the rural areas may develop soundly in the socialist direction.

In order to create a new situation in all fields of socialist modernization, we must lay special stress on the role of the intellectuals, improve the work of ideological and political education among them to suit their special characteristics, and actively recruit into the party intellectuals who are qualified for membership.

China has now 200 million young people, who form the most active force in every field of work. Although the "Cultural Revolution" did them immense harm during their formative years, the overwhelming majority of them are good politically and they have made marked progress in the past few years; the negative features displayed by a small number of the young people can be changed through education. The problem now is that work among the young people falls short of the needs of real life. Party and youth league organizations at all levels should establish closer ties with the masses of young people, become their close friends, show sincere concern for them and give them help politically, ideologically and in their work, study and personal life. The party should be on the lookout for advanced young people, help them to become qualified for membership and then admit them to its ranks so as to bring new blood into the party organizations. It should further strengthen its leadership over the Communist Youth League, support the league in the efforts to suit its work to the characteristics of the young people and help it play to the full its role as the party's assistant and reserve force, so that the league can truly become a school where large numbers of young people will learn about communism through practice.

Women are not only an important force in national economic construction; they also have a particularly significant role to play in building socialist spiritual civilization. Owing to traditional prejudices, many women often do not receive due attention, protection and education. The party must strengthen its work among women, concern itself with their special interests, pay attention to the training, selection and promotion of women cadres, and guide and support the women's federations at all levels in carrying out their tasks. The women's federation should become a prestigious mass organization, representing the interests of women and protecting and educating women and children.

Fourth, Consolidate the Party Organizations Step by Step in a Planned Way so as To Effect a Fundamental Turn for the Better in the Style of the Party.

Our party is the vanguard of the Chinese working class; it has been nurtured over the years by Marxism-Leninism and Mao Zedong Thought and has matured through repeated tempering by successes and failures. Rallied in its ranks are outstanding elements of the Chinese working class and the Chinese people. The main body of our party remains politically pure and strong despite the serious damage inflicted by the "Cultural Revolution". After recovery and consolidation in the past few years, the situation in our party is now much improved, and its prestige is being restored and is rising. In these years, outstanding communists on all fronts have led the masses in working hard to implement the party's line, principles and policies and in many acts of heroism. Everywhere, in production and other work, in battles in defence of our motherland and against natural and other calamities, and in struggles against unhealthy tendencies and crimes, party members have written soul-stirring paeans to communism through their own exemplary deeds. All the splendid successes of the party and the people have been achieved precisely through the inspiring example given by such fine core members of the party. This is the principal aspect of our party, and whoever fails to see it, or deliberately denies it, is committing a grave error.

However, the pernicious influences of the ten years of domestic turmoil have not yet been eradicated, and there has been some increase in the corrosive inroads of exploiting class ideologies under new conditions. It is true that impurities in ideology, style and organization still exist within the party and that no fundamental turn for the better has as yet been made in our party style. In the leadership work of some party organizations, signs of flabbiness and lack of unity abound. Some primary party organizations lack the necessary fighting capacity, and some are even in a state of paralysis. A small number of party members and cadres have become extremely irresponsible or seriously bureaucratic; or live a privileged life and abuse the powers entrusted to them to seek personal gain; or commit acts of anarchism and ultra-individualism in violation of party discipline; or obdurately indulge in factional activities to the detriment of the party's interests. A few party members and cadres have even sunk to corruption, embezzlement and other malpractices, committing serious economic crimes. In addition, a small remnant of the followers of the Lin Biao and Jiang Qing counterrevolutionary cliques still usurp some leading positions and are waiting for a chance to stir up trouble. All these phenomena have greatly impaired our party's prestige. While we must not allow any exaggeration of this dark aspect of our party, on no account should we be afraid to expose it. For ours is a staunch party; we have ample healthy forces on our side to wage an uncompromising struggle against the dark aspects and are confident of our victory in the struggle.

The style of a political party in power determines its very survival. To achieve a fundamental turn for the better in the style of our party, the Central Committee has decided on an overall rectification of party style and consolidation of party organizations, which will proceed by stages and by groups over a period of three years beginning from the latter half of 1983. This task will undoubtedly be of primary importance to the party, and it requires very careful attention and preparation and should be carried out step by step in a planned way. The key link in accomplishing this work must be thoroughgoing ideological education throughout the party. In conjunction with the study and implementation of the report and the new party constitution to be adopted by this party congress, the whole party should study the Resolution on Certain Questions in the History of Our Party Since the Founding of the People's Republic of China and the Guiding Principles for Inner-Party Political Life and carry on an education in the basic theories of Marxism-Leninism and Mao Zedong Thought, in the ideal of communism and the party's line, principles and policies and in essential knowledge concerning the party and the requirements for party membership. We must lay stress on getting every member to understand clearly the character, position and role of the party and to realize that all party members have only the duty to serve the people diligently and conscientiously, and no right whatsoever to take advantage of their power and positions to "fatten" on the state and on the masses. In matters of organization and leadership, the consolidation will start with the leading organs and cadres and then proceed, from top to bottom, with the leading bodies at different levels which have already been consolidated leading the consolidation of the subordinate and primary organizations. Bad elements must on no account be permitted to take this as an opportunity to frame and attack good people. We must act in, and develop further, the spirit of the Yanan rectification movement of 1942, follow its principle of "learning from past mistakes to avoid future ones and curing the sickness to save the patient" and its twofold objective of "clarity in ideology and unity among comrades" in unfolding earnest criticism and self-criticism, and take appropriate measures to solicit opinions from the masses outside the party. In the final stage, there will be a re-registration of all party members and, in strict accordance with the provisions of the new party constitution, those who still fail to meet the requirements for membership after education shall be expelled from the party or asked to withdraw from it. At the same time, concrete measures should be worked out to strengthen and improve party leadership so as to effect an improvement in the work of party organizations at all levels.

Through the proposed consolidation of the party, we must further normalize inner-party political life, place an effective check on unhealthy tendencies and greatly strengthen the ties between the party and the masses. In this way, we will certainly achieve a fundamental turn for the better in our party style.

Comrades! Our Central Committee has explained to this congress the fighting tasks that confront the whole party. We have proposed that in the coming five years a fundamental turn for the better should be made in the financial and economic situation, in standards of social conduct and in party style. Can these tasks be accomplished? The Central Committee is confident that the unanimous reply by our congress will be: yes, the tasks can and definitely shall be accomplished!

The principles and tasks to be defined by this congress will enrich and develop the correct line followed since the third plenary session of the party's eleventh Central Committee. Richer in content and closer to reality, they will be even more persuasive in unifying the thinking of the entire party and the people of all our nationalities and become an even more accurate guide to our action.

At this point, it should be emphasized that our party faces yet another historic task, that of joining hands with all our patriotic fellow-countrymen in a common endeavour to accomplish the sacred task of reunifying our motherland. Taiwan is part of the sacred territory of our motherland, and the people in Taiwan are our kith and kin. The return of Taiwan to the embrace of our great and indivisible motherland with her history of 5,000 years, population of one billion and territory of 9.6 million square kilometers is the common desire of all our compatriots; it will be an inevitable outcome of historical development, which no political party or individual can resist. It is China's internal affair with which no foreign country has the right to interfere. We hope that our compatriots in Taiwan, Xianggang (Hong Kong) and Aomen (Macao) and Chinese nationals residing abroad will urge the Kuomintang authorities to take a realistic view of the situation and put the future of our country and the interests of the nation above all else, instead of persisting in their obdurate stand, so that talks between the Kuomintang and the Communist Party may be held at an early date and, together, we can bring about the peaceful reunification of our motherland.

Socialist modernization is the common will, and is in the fundamental interests, of the people of all our nationalities. Remember what hardships and miseries the Chinese nation went through in the century or more between the opium war of 1840 and liberation! Long years of historical experience have inevitably turned the hearts and minds of all members of our party, army and people to the fundamental goal of the prosperity of the country under socialism and of reunification, particularly the return of Taiwan to the motherland. Socialist China's political situation is stable, and the prospect is that our modernization and reunification will definitely succeed. This prospect accords with the desires of the people and the tide of history. So long as we firmly trust and rely on the overwhelming majority of the masses, maintain close ties with the people and work conscientiously for their interests, our cause will be invincible.

We are, of course, soberly aware that we will come upon all kinds of obstacles and difficulties on the path of socialist modernization. At present, the major problems calling for urgent solution are the unhealthy phenomena in our party style and lowered standards of social conduct, which are the aftermath of the "Cultural Revolution"; the continuance of serious criminal activities undermining the socialist economy, politics and culture; and the unwieldiness, overstaffing and inefficiency in leading bodies at various levels, and the failure of our economic systems to fully meet the needs of the expansion of the productive forces. Consequently, as already said above, in the period to come we must systematically complete the organizational reform and reforms in the economic systems, go all out in building socialist spiritual civilization, hit hard at the serious criminal activities undermining our socialist economy and socialist system, and rectify the party style and consolidate the party organizations. Fulfillment of these four tasks will provide an important guarantee that we can adhere to the socialist system and succeed in socialist modernization.

The whole party, particularly party committees at all levels, must lay great stress on these tasks and work unswervingly to accomplish them.

Our comrades should take a correct approach towards difficulties. It is entirely wrong to see only the bright and not the difficult side of the situation, to the point of mistaking one's subjective desires for objective reality and rushing blindly ahead. We suffered greatly from such an approach in the past and should always remember the lessons learned. On the other hand, it is likewise entirely wrong to fear and cower before difficulties, lose faith in the strength of the party and the masses, and waver and procrastinate even after the Central Committee has correctly analysed the situation and formulated principles and tasks accordingly. Things today are far different from those in past periods when our party encountered tremendous difficulties. When our Red Army was compelled to go on the Long March, it was vastly outnumbered by the enemy, yet we overcame that difficulty. During the "Cultural Revolution" the Lin Biao and Jiang Qing counter-revolutionary cliques ran rampant and the whole country was thrown into chaos, yet we turned the tide. So can there be any difficulties today which we cannot overcome? The correct attitude for Marxists in the face of difficulties, the revolutionary style for communists striving to create a new situation is to throw themselves enthusiastically into the great work of socialist modernization and, going among the masses and digging into the actual work, forge ahead in the struggle with added vigour, indomitably and indefatigably.

Comrades! The historical experience of the party during the past 60-odd years teaches us that the fundamental reason why the party has been able to lead the Chinese people in winning one great victory after another is its integration of the universal truth of Marxism with the concrete practice of the Chinese revolution. The supreme historical contribution of Comrade Mao Zedong and the other proletarian revolutionaries of the older generation is that they succeeded in making such an integration. To turn China with its backward economic and cultural base into a modern and powerful socialist country in this new historical period is one of the most gigantic creative undertakings in human history. Many problems involved in it were not, and would not have been, raised or solved by Marxists in the past. In such an undertaking, ideological and political deviations of one kind or another or deviations in concrete work may occur within our ranks. This is not strange, nor can it be entirely avoided. What is important is that the whole party, party committees at all levels in particular, must uphold the four cardinal principles, adhere to the correct line followed since the third plenary session of the eleventh Central Committee and oppose both the "left" tendency of trying to revert to the erroneous theories and policies which prevailed during and before the "Cultural Revolution" and the right tendency of bourgeois liberalization as reflected in distrust or rejection of the four cardinal principles. We must resolutely take over and learn to use the stand, viewpoint and method of Marxism-Leninism and Mao Zedong Thought, acquire a deeper understanding of the actual work in all fields, make systematic investigations and studies, and be good at conducting appropriate criticism and education and waging necessary struggles against wrong tendencies. Provided we persist in doing this, we can certainly accumulate new experience, break new ground in theory and carry forward Marxism-Leninism and Mao Zedong Thought under new historical conditions and in great new fields of practice.

Comrades! For several decades beginning with the 1920's, China's forerunners in the communist cause and millions of other glorious revolutionary fighters and martyrs shed their blood and gave their lives in heroic struggles to bring China to its present state of progress. In the new historical period, let us carry out the behest of our martyrs and accomplish, in this vast land of ours, the great undertaking never attempted before.

In terms of experience of struggles, our contingent of party cadres consists of people of four generations: those who joined the revolution in the party's early days, during the agrarian revolutionary war, during the war of resistance against Japan and the war of liberation, and after the founding of the People's Republic. This testifies that our cause is of long standing and is assured of successors. The ranks of our party will advance incessantly like the flowing waters of the Chang Jiang. This congress of ours will go down in the party's history as one which has defined the party's principles and tasks for the new period politically and achieved the co-operation of old and new cadres and the succession of the new to the old organizationally, and one which creates a new situation in all fields of socialist modernization.

Let the whole party rally still more closely under the great banner of Marxism-Leninism and Mao Zedong Thought! Let our party unite still more closely with the people of all nationalities in the country, with the democratic parties and all patriotic fellow-countrymen at home and abroad, and with all the progressive forces and friendly public figures in other countries who support our cause! Let us march forward dauntlessly and with one heart and one mind! No force on earth can deter us. Our triumph is certain!

NOTES

(1) Cf. V. I. Lenin, "Meeting of the All-Russia Central Executive Committee, November 4 (17), 1917", collected works, Eng. ed., Progress Publishers, Moscow, 1964, vol. 26, p. 288.

(2) Karl Marx and Frederick Engels, "Economic Manuscripts of 1857–1859", pre-capitalist socioeconomic formations, Eng. ed., Progress Publishers, Moscow, 1979, p. 109.

(3) Mao Zedong, "On Practice", selected works, Eng. ed., Foreign Languages Press, Beijing, 1967, vol. I, p. 308.

(4) Karl Marx and Frederick Engels, "The German Ideology", collected works, Eng. ed., Progress Publishers, Moscow, 1976, vol. 5, p. 49.

(5) Mao Zedong, "On New Democracy", selected works, Eng. ed., Foreign Languages Press, Beijing, 1967, vol. II, p. 361.

(6) Cf. V. I. Lenin, "From the Destruction of the Old Social System to the Creation of the New", collected works, Eng. ed., Progress Publishers, Moscow, 1965, vol. 30, p. 518.

(7) Mao Zedong, "Strive To Build A Great Socialist Country", selected works, Eng. ed., Foreign Languages Press, Beijing, 1977, vol. V, p. 148.

(8) Karl Marx and Frederick Engels, "On Poland", collected works, Eng. ed., Progress Publishers, Moscow, 1976, vol. 6, p. 389.

The Party Constitution Explained by Its Principal Drafter, 13 September 1982

34

The following is an interview with Politburo member Hu Qiaomu, who had been in charge of drafting the new Party constitution. He stresses, from an official perspective, the differences between the new constitution and its 1977 predecessor.

Question: First of all, would you please discuss the constitutional revision process?

Answer: The constitutional revising process was a long one. It began in the winter of 1979. The entire revision was carried out under the leadership of the Standing Committee of the Political Bureau of the CPC Central Committee. In the beginning, the then party Central Committee designated the Organization Department of the CPC Central Committee, the Central Party School and the Research Office of the General Office of the CPC Central Committee to assemble a number of cadres to prepare the revision. They held many meetings to discuss this matter. Later, a considerable number of comrades were dispatched to numerous places to investigate and solicit opinions. Afterwards, a draft was prepared.

In January of 1980 the CPC Central Committee decided to formally begin the revision of the party constitution. Comrade Deng Xiaoping gave many important guidelines regarding the revision of the party constitution and demanded that a draft of the revision be submitted as quickly as possible. Under the CPC Central Committee's leadership, the party constitutional revision group was

[New China News Agency, 13 September 1982.]

established. On the basis of the original draft, this group carried out serious discussion and made many alterations. The first draft revision was thus produced. The CPC Central Committee held that this draft could be used as the basis for discussion and further revision. In February of 1980 it was presented for discussion at the 5th Plenary Session of the 11th CPC Central Committee. In view of the opinions collected at that session, the revision group made the first revisions. In April, the revised draft was distributed throughout the party for discussion by the newly created CPC Central Committee Secretariat. It was also distributed to some nonparty personages whose opinions were sought.

According to the opinions inside and outside of the party, the revision group made the second revision in May of 1982. This time many changes were made. In June of the same year, the CPC Central Committee Secretariat again distributed the revised draft to the party committees of various provinces, municipalities, autonomous regions and various military regions; party organizations of various central party, government and military departments; and to all delegates to the 12th CPC National Congress requesting their opinions on this draft. In July, the revision group made the third revision according to the opinions that had been collected. After discussion, the CPC Central Committee Political Bureau decided that the draft would be discussed at the 7th Plenary Session of the 11th CPC Central Committee scheduled for August. The session approved this draft and decided that it should be reviewed by the 12th CPC National Congress. From 31 August, during the preparatory meeting and the congress regular session, all delegations to the congress earnestly discussed the draft and presented many opinions regarding its revision. The Secretariat of the congress synthesized these opinions and made the final revision. On 5 September the third meeting of the congress presidium heard an explanation on the revision and decided that it should be presented to the congress for approval. On 6 September, the congress plenary session unanimously approved the final revised draft and adopted a special resolution for the new constitution. Therefore, we can say that the new party constitution was extensively and fully researched and discussed, and it has collectively expressed the whole party's opinions and wisdom.

Question: What are the major differences between the new party constitution and the previous party constitutions? What are the major revisions?

Answer: The guiding thought for revising the party constitution was that the revision should be made to suit the special characteristics and needs of socialist modernization so that it would, in accordance with the party's current situation, set forth stricter requirements for party members and party cadres, enhance the party organs' fighting strength, uphold and improve the party's leadership and build the party into a strong core in leading socialist construction. The new party constitution has summed up the many years of experience in party building and made many changes to the party constitution adopted at the previous party congress. The new party constitution has eliminated the "left" mistakes found in the constitution adopted at the 11th CPC National Congress, inherited and fostered the strong points of the party constitutions adopted at the 7th and the 8th CPC National Congresses, systematically summed up the historical experiences in party building and reflected the party's demands in real life. First

of all, it has a more substantial "general program" which, like the "general programs" of the constitution adopted at the 7th CPC National Congress and the constitutions adopted at other congresses that followed, is in fact the most precise basic program of the party. It has quite fully and concisely introduced the party's nature, its long-term and short-term goals, its basic requirements for party members and party organizations as well as the basic principles for the party's leading role.

In terms of content, the constitution adopted at the 11th CPC National Congress had only 5 chapters and 19 articles. Since they could not satisfy the party's needs in real life, the content of the new party constitution has been expanded to 10 chapters and 50 articles. Collectively, the major revisions fall into three important areas:

1. It has set forth stricter requirements for all party members, party cadres and grass-roots organs than the previous party constitutions. The criteria set for party members are stricter than all those stipulated in other constitutions. The new party constitution has a new chapter on cadres and it sets higher demands on party cadres than on ordinary party members.

2. Certain new regulations regarding the party's organizational system have been included.

3. More substantial and more specific regulations regarding the party's democratic centralism and party discipline have been included.

Furthermore, certain new regulations on upholding and improving the party's leadership have also been introduced into the new party constitution.

Question: What are the special characteristics in the "general program" of the new party constitution?

Answer: A political party of the proletariat must have a program that is built on the scientific foundation of Marxism because, as Lenin said: "A program is of important significance for a political party's unity and consistent activities." As mentioned before, the general program of our party constitution is in fact a precise program of the party. The general program of the new party constitution, in accordance with the theory of scientific socialism, has concisely expounded on the progress of the world's historical development, the historical stage our country has now entered, the superiority of the socialist system and its prospects for gradually winning worldwide victory. This general program has stipulated the party's ultimate goal of the struggle to realize communism, the party's general task at the current stage and its basic domestic and international policies, the party's nature of being the vanguard of the proletariat, the party's guiding thought and the three basic requirements that the whole party must meet. These three basic requirements are: high ideological and political unity, wholehearted service to the people, and adherence to democratic centralism.

In its final section, the general program also stipulates the basic principles for the party's leading role and clearly indicates the role of the party leadership in the state and in the lives of the people. (These explanations are basically the same as the relevant content of the draft of the revised constitution, which says that the party is the leading force of the state and the people but that it does its work within the scope defined by the constitution and law and is not above the state and the people.) These are the major points of the general program of the party constitution.

Question: What stricter requirements are set forth in the new party constitution for party members, party cadres and primary organizations?

Answer: The new party constitution sets forth requirements for party members in three aspects:

First, who can apply for party membership? (Article 1 of the party constitution)

Second, what kind of person should a Communist Party member be? (Article 2 of the party constitution) It is particularly emphasized here that members of the Communist Party must be ready to make personal sacrifices and dedicate their whole lives to the realization of communism. Moreover, in view of the change in the status of the party which has become the ruling party, it is stressed that members of the Communist Party are at all times ordinary members of the working people. Party members should fulfill more duties than nonparty persons. Under no circumstances must party members seek personal gain or privileges although they are allowed personal benefits and job functions and powers as provided for by the relevant regulations and policies.

Third, the new party constitution provides eight duties that party members must fulfill. These eight provisions are relatively strict, and every party member must act according to them.

For example, the new party constitution stipulates that party members must "consider the interests of the party and the people above everything; subordinate personal interests to the interests of the party and the people; be the first to bear hardships and the last to enjoy comforts; work selflessly for the public interest; and absolutely never use public office for personal gain or to benefit themselves at the expense of the public." Why is there such a stipulation? This is because some party members, with the party leading the country, might seize various opportunities or take advantage of various conditions to benefit themselves at the expense of the masses, others or the public (including the state and the collective). The recurrence of such attempts must be strictly prohibited in order to bring about a fundamental turn for the better in the party's work style. The new party constitution also requires party members to accept any job assigned by the party; conscientiously observe party discipline and the laws of the state; rigorously guard party and state secrets; firmly oppose factionalism; earnestly practice criticism and self-criticism; be bold in exposing and correcting shortcomings and mistakes in work; back good people and good deeds; fight against bad people and bad deeds; play an exemplary vanguard role in production and other work, study and social activities; step forward and fight bravely in times of difficulty and danger; and so on and so forth. These requirements set forth in the new party constitution should and can be met. However, it should be recognized that it is not easy to be a qualified party member. As the saying goes, when one always walks along a river, he can hardly avoid getting his shoes wet. There are indeed many opportunities for members of the ruling party to use public office for personal gain if they so choose. However, if party members are allowed to do so, the party's prestige among the masses and its leading role are bound to decrease, its links with the masses will weaken and the masses might even drift away from the party. Therefore, we must require that party members not get their shoes wet although they must always walk along the river.

When we started revising the party constitution, Comrade Deng Xiaoping pointed out that first of all, the question of being a qualified party member must be solved. A dividing line must be drawn—only those qualified can be party members, and those unqualified must not be admitted into the party. The new party constitution provides party members with duties to fulfill, precisely with the view of drawing such a dividing line.

Of course, the new party constitution also fully provides for the democratic rights of party members and emphatically points out: "No party organization, up to and including the Central Committee, has the right to deprive any party member of the above-mentioned rights." The party constitution also stipulates: "It is strictly forbidden, within the party, to take any measures against a member that contravene the party constitution or the laws of the state, or to retaliate against or frame comrades. Any offending organization or individual must be dealt with according to party discipline or the laws of the state." Thus, cases of persecuting party members and making things hard for other upright party members through the abuse of one's authority, such as those that occurred in the 10 years of domestic turmoil, should no longer occur. If such cases do occur in some party organizations, they will be investigated.

The new party constitution stipulates the taking of an admission oath by a probationary party member in front of the party flag and the unified content of the oath.

There is a special chapter on cadres. The requirements for party cadres are naturally higher than those for ordinary party members. Comrades must be able to correctly implement the party's lines, principles and policies, to resolutely fight against hostile forces and oppose erroneous trends, both inside and outside the party, to have a democratic work style and conscientiously accept criticism and supervision by the party and the masses, and to totally fulfill their duties in a proper way, as required by their jobs, and not to abuse their power to seek personal gain. The new party constitution also stipulates what ability and qualifications a cadre should possess in the period of building socialism. This chapter also explicitly stipulates that it is necessary to attach importance to nonparty cadres, to ensure that they can fully play their role, and to abolish the system of leading party cadres' lifelong tenure which actually existed in the past.

The new party constitution includes fairly detailed provisions on the tasks of the primary party organizations. Many of the provisions deal with the education, organization and supervision of party cadres in fulfilling their duties and playing their proper role. It should be specially mentioned here: On the tasks of the primary party organizations, clause 7 particularly stipulates that it is necessary to educate and supervise party and nonparty cadres, to see to it that they strictly observe the law and administrative discipline and the financial and economic discipline and personnel regulations of the state; and to see to it that financial workers, including accountants and other professionals who are charged with enforcing laws and regulations in their own unit, do not themselves violate laws and regulations, while at the same time ensuring and protecting their right to exercise their functions and powers independently in accordance with the law and guarding them against any reprisals for so doing. This special provision is clearly laid down realistically, which is of great significance in combatting criminal economic activities, bringing about a fundamental turn for the better in the party's work style and the general mood of society and ensuring that party and government organizations, enterprises and institutions adhere to socialist orientation throughout the new historical period.

When the provisions of this party constitution are strictly implemented, party members and cadres will be able to play their exemplary vanguard role better among the masses, and party organizations will greatly increase their fighting effectiveness.

Question: What are the provisions of the new party constitution on the organizational system of the party?

Answer: The new provisions are mainly:

The national congress of the party is to elect the Central Committee as well as the Central Advisory Commission and the Central Commission for Discipline Inspection. Both the Central Advisory Commission and the Central Commission for Discipline Inspection perform their work under the leadership of the Central Committee. Provincial party congresses are to elect provincial party committees, as well as provincial advisory commissions and provincial discipline inspection commissions. They perform their work under the leadership of provincial party committees.

Advisory commissions at the central and provincial levels are political assistants and advisers to the Central Committee or the provincial party committees. This important measure is taken to give full play to old comrades' roles as advisers and to effect cooperation between new and old cadres and the succession of the old by the new in order to adopt ourselves to the current situation and to meet the needs of the present period. Advisory commissions are to be set up down to provincial level, below which all party organizations will not establish such commissions.

Local party organizations at various levels are to set up discipline inspection commissions, and so are relatively large primary party organizations. As for relatively small primary party organizations, they will have discipline inspection commission members. Higher discipline inspection commissions have the power to modify lower discipline inspection commissions' decisions. Local discipline inspection commissions and all levels function under the dual leadership of the party committees at the corresponding levels and the next higher discipline inspection commissions. Thus, discipline inspection commissions form a complete network from the higher levels to the grass roots. At the same time, the authority of discipline inspection commissions at all levels is greatly strengthened.

There is a major change in the organizational system of the party at the central level; that is, the party Central Committee has only a general secretary, and no chairman or vice chairmen. The general secretary, a member of the Political Bureau Standing Committee, is responsible for convening the meetings of the Political Bureau and its Standing Committee and presides over the work of the Central Committee's Secretariat. The role of a convener is obviously different from that of a chairman. Thus, it will be difficult for the phenomenon, in which power is over-concentrated and arbitrary decisions are adopted by an individual, to occur. Practice at home and abroad shows

that, where there are both a chairman and a general secretary, one of them would usually be nominal. Therefore, it is not necessary to have both posts in the party, still less to pick someone to assume both posts. According to the new party constitution, the core of leadership in the day-to-day work of the party is the Standing Committee of the Central Committee's Political Bureau (this is what has actually been done since the 5th plenary session of the 11th Central Committee). In addition to the general secretary, the chairman of the Central Advisory Commission, the first secretary of the Central Commission for Discipline Inspection and the chairman of the Military Commission of the party Central Committee are also on the Standing Committee of the Political Bureau. All these provisions will help ensure our party's collective leadership and unity.

Incidently, I would like to answer this question here: What is the relationship between the Military Commission of the party Central Committee and the Central Military Council of the state, as prescribed in the draft revised constitution? Our party envisages that the members of the party Central Committee's Military Commission may at the same time be members of the Central Military Council of the state, with the approval of the NPC after consultation with the democratic parties. From the day of its birth, the PLA has been led by the party. It accords with the fundamental interests of the people of the country for the party to continue to lead the PLA and the Central Military Council of the state. For the Chinese people, this is easy to understand. This by no means contradicts the provision that the Central Military Council of the state is answerable to the NPC and its Standing Committee.

According to this thinking, two central military commissions will not occur. Of course, legally speaking, this can become a reality only by decision of the NPC.

The new party constitution also stipulates that the central leading bodies (the Political Bureau, its Standing Committee and the Secretariat) and leaders elected by each Central Committee shall, when the next national congress is in session, continue to preside over the party's day-to-day work until the new central leading bodies and leaders are elected by the next Central Committee. Appropriate provisions are also laid down for local party committees and their standing committees at various levels. This is to ensure in the party constitution that the party's leadership over day-to-day work will not be discontinued at any time. This is absolutely necessary for a party leading a big county, because party congresses at all levels and their presidiums cannot handle a great deal of day-to-day work, which only the party's leading bodies can do.

In regard to the relations between the party and the CYL, it is stipulated that "those secretaries of league committees, at or below the county level or in enterprises and institutions, who are party members may attend meetings of party committees at the corresponding levels and of their standing committees as nonvoting participants." This will help promote close ties between the party and the CYL and enhance maturity of leaders of the CYL organizations. There is no similar provision for those above the county level. This is because the problems discussed in party committees at the central and provincial levels are more wide-ranging and complex and participation by CYL secretaries at the corresponding levels in these meetings generally is not suitable. It would be another matter, of course, if the league secretaries are themselves standing committee members of the party committee meetings are discussing matters concerning youth work (as published).

Question: What are the new provisions with regard to democratic centralism and discipline of the party?

Answer: The new party constitution contains provisions on the basic principles of the party's democratic centralism and these provisions are more systematic and comprehensive than before. The general program contains clear stipulations that there are three essential requirements which the party must strive to fulfill in the future. The first among these is to maintain "a high degree of ideological and political unity" and the third is "adherence to democratic centralism." At the outset of the chapter on the organizational system of the party, it is clearly stipulated that our party is an integral body organized under its program and constitution on the principle of democratic centralism, and that under its program and constitution on the principle of democratic centralism, and that it practices a high degree of centralism on the basis of a high degree of democracy. In this chapter, the new party constitution reaffirms in still more precise terms the principle that "individual party members are subordinate to the party organization, the minority is subordinate to the majority, the lower party organizations are subordinate to the higher party organizations, and all the constituent organizations and members of the party are subordinate to the national congress and the Central Committee of the party" as well as other similar principles set forth in the past party constitutions. In addition, drawing upon past experiences and lessons, the new party constitution also stipulates that "party committees at all levels function on the principle of combining collective leadership with individual responsibility based on division of labor" and that "the party forbids all forms of personality cult. It is necessary to ensure that the activities of the party leaders be subject to supervision by the party and the people, while at the same time to uphold the prestige of all leaders who represent the interests of the party and the people." The new party constitution specifically states that no party member is allowed to make decisions on major issues on his own and that such decisions must be made by the party committee after democratic discussions. There are also many provisions embodying both democracy and centralism that deal with the duties and responsibilities and the limits of authority as well as the mutual relationship between the central and the local organizations and between the upper and the lower ones and the relationship between individual party members and party organizations.

For example, it is stipulated that when making decisions on important questions affecting the lower organizations, the higher organizations of the party should, in ordinary circumstances, solicit the opinions of lower organizations. Moreover, measures should be taken to ensure that the lower organizations can exercise their functions and powers normally. Another example is the provision which says that if lower organizations consider that any decisions of higher organizations do not suit actual conditions in their localities or departments, they may request modification. If the higher organizations insist on their original decisions, the lower organizations must carry out such decisions, but they have the right to report to the next higher party organization.

In its provisions concerning the party organizations' discussions and their making decisions on any matter, the new party constitution both provides the principle of subordination of the minority to the majority and sets forth the stipulation that serious consideration should be given to the views of a minority. It also contains prudent provisions specifically on the handling of cases of controversy over major issues in which supporters of the two opposing views are nearly equal in number. As for matters concerning the individual democratic rights of party members, the stipulations are even more elaborate. All these stipulations will provide guarantees still stricter than ever before that democratic centralism will be practiced within the party.

There are also more specific and rigid provisions in regard to party discipline. These include, for example: 1) practice the principle that every party member is equal before party discipline, and there should be no privileged party members who do not participate in the regular activities of the party and outside the party; 2) in addition to observing party discipline, every party member is required to strictly abide by administrative discipline and state laws. If a party member is found to have violated not only party discipline but also administrative discipline and state law, he should be sanctioned at the same time in accordance with the administrative discipline and state law. All party members who have seriously offended the criminal law will be stripped of their party membership; 3) in case a party organization seriously violates party discipline and is unable to rectify the mistake on its own, the next higher party organization should then, after obtaining approval from the party organization further above, decide on the reorganization or dissolution of the party organization concerned. Besides, as mentioned earlier, the new party constitution has set forth provisions more forceful than before on the functions and rights of the party's commissions for discipline inspection.

Question: What major provisions does the new party constitution offer in regard to upholding and improving party leadership?

Answer: All stipulations in the new party constitution—whether in its stricter demands on the members, cadres and primary organizations of the party, in its provisions concerning the party's organizational system, or in the provisions regarding democratic centralism and party discipline—are for the purpose of upholding and improving party leadership. The new party constitution declares in the very beginning of its "general program" that the Communist Party of China is the force at the core leading China's cause of socialism, thereby defining the leading position of the party in our country. Many provisions under the "general program" and various articles in the party constitution give expression to the necessity and importance of upholding the leadership of the party. At the same time, the party constitution also lays down a series of important provisions on the principles and methods to be followed in upholding and improving leadership of the party.

Party leadership consists mainly in political, ideological and organizational leadership. This leadership must be exercised by the party through formulating and implementing the correct line, principles and policies, through carrying out meticulous and effective ideological and political work and propaganda and educational work, through carrying out tight and prudent organizational work and through giving full play to the exemplary vanguard role of party members.

The party's organizational work mainly involves the training, selection, use and supervision of the cadres. One most important key link here is to see to it that the most suitable persons are selected and assigned to various kinds of leading posts and rely on party organizations and the masses of the people to seriously exercise supervision over leading cadres who are party members at all levels.

In implementing the principle of division of work between the party and the government, development of the party itself should be strengthened. The party must see to it that the legislative, judicial and administrative organs of the state, the economic, cultural and people's organizations work actively and with initiative, independently, responsibly and in harmony. In an enterprise or institution, the primary party committee should discuss and decide on major questions of principle and ensure that the administrative leaders fully exercise their functions and powers, but refrain from substituting itself for, or trying to take over from, the administrative leaders. Except in special circumstances, the general branch committees and branch committees under the leadership of a primary party committee only play a guarantory and supervisory role to see that the production targets or operational tasks assigned to their own units are properly fulfilled.

The central, local and primary organizations of the party must all pay great attention to party building, regularly discuss and check on the party's work in propaganda, education, organization and discipline inspection, in mass work and united front work and carefully study the ideological and political situation inside and outside the party.

Within the party, criticism and self-criticism must be conducted regularly and conscientiously, and on questions of principle, ideological struggle must be persistently launched to oppose erroneous deviations, whether "left" or right. It is necessary to adhere to organizational reform, make efforts to promote cadre training and ensure, step by step, that the ranks of the cadres become more revolutionary, younger in age, better educated and more professionally competent. It is also necessary to regularly rectify the party style and consolidate the party organization, preserve the communist purity of the party in both ideology and organization and strengthen the close ties between the party and the broad masses of the people. All these efforts aim at enabling the party to lead the people to carry out the great cause of socialist modernization in a better and more effective way.

The party must conduct its activities within the limit permitted by the constitution and the law. That is to say, the activities of all party members and organizations, from basic units to central organs, should not contravene the constitution or the law, nor violate the law.

All the above-mentioned regulations are of great importance toward strengthening and improving the party's leadership. The resolution adopted at the party congress on taking the party constitution as a weapon to rectify the party style and consolidate the party organization will particularly provide a most important guarantee for upholding and improving the party's leadership.

Question: Why is it that the new party constitution does not stipulate the system of permanent tenure for delegates?

Answer: The suggestion for practicing the system of permanent tenure for delegates was considered at many discussions of the new party constitution and in the course of its revision. Such a stipulation was made in the draft revision issued in February 1982. However, after the stipulation was considered from different quarters, it was finally decided that the stipulation be dropped. Our party has never practiced the system of permanent tenure for delegates. It was stipulated in the party constitution adopted at the 8th national party congress that the national party congress would practice the system of permanent tenure for delegates. However, the second session of the 8th national party congress was held in 1958 but the third session was never held. This proves that this stipulation could hardly work in practice.

There is a great difference between the national party congress and the National People's Congress. While the National People's Congress has to discuss and adopt resolutions on many important topics for the year, the principal tasks for the national party congress are to decide on the line, principle and basic policies of the party for a period of time and to elect a leading organ of relative stability. Therefore, it is not only unnecessary but also impossible for the national party congress to hold meetings every year. Thus there is no need to practice the system of permanent tenure for delegates. On the contrary, if the system of permanent tenure for delegates is adopted, it will be difficult to clearly and specifically define the tasks, functions and powers of the delegates and the relations between the delegates and the party committees at various levels. It will even cause, rather unnecessarily, the work of party committees at various levels to become more complicated. Therefore, such a regulation ought not be stipulated. Of course, delegates to the party congresses at various levels are different from common party members and holding greater responsibility to the party, it goes without saying that they deserve greater respect of the party.

Question: Why does not the new party constitution set strict restrictions on the tenure of office of party leaders?

Answer: The new party constitution clearly stipulates that leading cadres of our party at all levels, whether elected or appointed by leading organs, are not entitled to lifelong tenure, and they can be transferred from or relieved of their posts. The party constitution also stipulates that cadres no longer fit for work because of age or health conditions should retire according to the regulations of the party and the state. These provisions will help promote the constant renewal of the ranks of the party cadres with the infusion of new blood to meet the needs of the development of the party's cause. The results of the election at the 12th national party congress as well as the voluntary and earnest requests made by veteran cadres and approved by the party Central Committee and the congress not to be delegates or candidates for members to central leading organs prior to and during the 12th national party congress indicate that this provision has come to be put into practice.

At the same time, we must keep in mind that our party has a membership of about 40 million and ours is a large country with a population of 1 billion. The task of the party in exercising leadership is very heavy and complicated. Therefore, at the core of the party's central leading bodies, there must be a number of veteran cadres who have rich experience, deep insight and a wide range of knowledge, who are proficient in dealing with various kinds of complicated situations and enjoy high prestige in the party and among the people for their outstanding contributions.

Only thus, is it possible to ensure the maturity "to pass on their experiences to the younger ones and help and guide them." Only thus, is it possible to ensure the smooth succession of new cadres to old ones and guarantee the long-term stability of the country. The actual situation is fundamentally different from the situation during the early days after the founding of our party. In a large party and country like ours, it is impossible to have such leaders who are proficient and who enjoy popular confidence without going through the test of struggles over a long period.

Therefore, after repeated deliberations in the course of revising the party constitution, it was finally decided that no strict restrictions be set on the tenure of office for leading cadres, which will be decided separately according to the specific conditions of each person and each case. At the same time, the party organizations at all levels will be composed of old, middle-aged and young cadres so as to realize the succession of the new cadres to the old. This conforms better to the fundamental interests of the party, the country and the whole people.

HU YAOBANG
Speech to the Central Committee, 13 September 1982

35

The main business of the first session of a Party Congress's newly elected Central Committee is to elect the Politburo— and its Standing Committee—and the Secretariat. In this instance, there was also a speech by General Hu in which he stressed Party rectification and modernization.

Comrades!

The sole agenda of this plenary session was to elect the central leading organs and approve the results of the election of the leading members of the Central Advisory Commission and Central Commission for Discipline Inspection. The task of the session has been completed. On behalf of the Secretariat, I would like to take the opportunity to make a few suggestions on future work for discussion by comrades, primarily the work for next year, because there are no plans to hold a Central Committee plenary session or a work meeting in the coming winter and next spring.

First, it is necessary to organize the whole party to diligently study the documents of the 12th CPC National Congress, including the report of the Central Committee, the new party constitution, Comrade Deng Xiaoping's opening speech, the speeches by Comrades Ye Jianying and Chen Yun and Comrade Li Xiannian's closing speech. The report of the Central Committee and the new party constitution were the crystallization of the collective creation and wisdom of the party. In view of the great significance in earnestly organizing the study of the 12th congress documents for future work, the Central Committee has transmitted its Propaganda Department's arrangements for studying and publicizing the documents.

In transmitting party documents in the past, we had a problem in that party organizations at various levels would wait and do what they were told by the next higher level. Some localities even put aside the documents and went their own way by making different outlines and airing their work problems. The Secretariat holds that such practices

must be stopped. Party organizations at various levels must take the initiative to organize the study of the 12th congress documents instead of waiting for instructions from the next higher level. Of course, higher authorities should also offer effective and timely guidance and assistance.

In the course of study it is necessary to first grasp the basic spirit of the documents, unify the thinking in light of studying the relevant fundamental theories of Marx, Lenin and Comrade Mao Zedong, and then try to solve some practical problems that can be solved in each locality, department and unit. By paying special attention to the study of the documents for the more than six months from now until the first half of 1983, we will greatly educate and mobilize the broad masses of party members, particularly the cadres, to raise their understanding of the party's fighting goal, their ideological awareness and their confidence in our cause. At the same time we will also be able to overcome some erroneous ideas and unhealthy practices that are incompatible with the spirit of the 12th congress documents. Therefore, we must regard the study of the documents as the most important thing after the conclusion of the 12th congress and try our best to do it and cultivate a good study atmosphere.

Second, it is necessary to pay keen attention to organizational reform. The election of the central leading organs by the 12th CPC National Congress and the current plenary session is, in a broad sense, an organizational reform. It has been the most important organizational reform. In view of the readjustment of the leading bodies and organizational structure of the ministries, departments and bureaus directly under the central authorities, which has been basically completed, the organizational reform of

[*People's Daily*, 22 October 1982.]

the various departments under the party Central Committee and State Council has proceeded rather smoothly and has been fairly successful. Of course, further efforts are required in order to thoroughly complete the rotational training of cadres, the defining of powers and responsibilities of various departments, the solving of some problems in relations among various departments and other tasks in organizational reform.

In our exchanges of views with comrades of various provinces, municipalities and autonomous regions, it is the consensus that organizational reform in the provinces, municipalities and autonomous regions may, on the whole, copy the experience of the central departments. The Sixth NPC Session will be convened in May or June of next year. All localities must elect their deputies to the Sixth NPC in March, April or May. In view of the pressing time, the work of organizational reform in all provinces, municipalities and autonomous regions, as well as at prefectural and municipal levels, should be started as early as possible and not delayed. A delay will have unfavorable effects because the experience is there and no major problem is expected to appear. If the work is started this winter and completed in the first half of next year, party committees of all provinces, municipalities and autonomous regions and prefectures and municipalities under them can rely on themselves in carrying out organizational reform at county and commune levels in the winter of next year and the spring of the following year. In this way, organizational reform throughout the country, the first step in our structural reform, will be completed in the spring of 1984. When this task is achieved, we will be able to make more initiatives in our work.

As Comrade Deng Xiaoping once said: This matter is also a revolution. If it is successfully carried out, we will be able to readjust and strengthen leading cores at various levels, streamline overstaffed organizations, promote a large number of young and capable cadres, rotationally train active duty cadres, greatly increase work efficiency and further eliminate bureaucracy. Success in this work relies mainly on the personal attention and efforts of leading comrades of all provinces, municipalities and autonomous regions.

We have suggested the sending of help to comrades of many provinces, municipalities and autonomous regions. They think this is very good because of two advantages: one, comrades sent by the central authorities can help local comrades make up their minds and speak on their behalf when a difficulty arises; two, they can help local comrades listen to opinions from broad sources and follow the mass line. The Secretariat plans to dispatch some members of the Central Committee, Central Advisory Commission and the Central Commission for Discipline inspection, as well as some retired cadres who formerly held the posts of vice minister or deputy director, to various localities, thus helping these comrades to broaden their visions and gain new experience.

Third, it is necessary to seriously think over how to take a firm hold of party consolidation. The task of party consolidation put forth by the 12th CPC National Congress had received favorable responses at home and abroad, and is deep in the hearts of the people. It is a matter of utmost importance. Since we have announced it, we must not only do it but also do it well. Of course, paying close attention to the study of the 12th congress documents, especially the study of the new party constitution article by article, the organizational reform and readjustment of cadres, and making continuous efforts to strike at economic crimes and handle in good time some major and serious cases which have already come under investigation, will give a strong impetus to changing party style. However, all of this cannot take the place of party consolidation. In view of both the positive experience and negative lessons on the questions of party consolidation in our party's history, a party with its work in extensive areas and many problems accumulated in the past, the Secretariat deems it necessary to make painstaking and meticulous efforts to prepare for, guide and organize the new party consolidation which is to begin next year.

On the basis of the work conducted by both the central authorities and various provinces, municipalities and autonomous regions at selected points this winter and next spring, we should draft a good document for party consolidation. It is estimated that the document will be completed next May or June after the convening of the NPC session, or by the fall of next year at the latest, and discussed as one of the central agenda items of the 2d Plenary Session of the 12th CPC Central Committee. Party consolidation should be carried out by stages and in groups after the 2d Plenary Session of the 12th CPC Central Committee. Efforts must be made to strive to complete party consolidation throughout the country within 3 years beginning from next fall.

Fourth, economic work cannot be slackened at any time. Since the third plenary session, tremendous improvement has been made in economic work and many reforms have been carried out, thereby promoting economic development. The economic situation this year is fairly good; economic results and the rate of growth may very possibly exceed the original estimate. Of course, comrades of economic departments and provinces, municipalities and autonomous regions feel many problems still exist and that the tasks remain strenuous. For example, take the industrial and transportation front. While the potentials there are indeed tremendous, the state of affairs characterized by endless haggling and the fear of assuming responsibility has not been basically reversed. In the final analysis, the reason for this is that the people did not assiduously study many problems. Especially, they did not proceed to the frontline to obtain a thoroughly clear picture of the situation, nor did they show daring and resolution in solving problems in a practical manner. This state of affairs, it seems, has developed to a point that it has left us no choice but to change it drastically and with determination. The industrial and transportation enterprises should make continuous efforts to consolidate themselves and to conscientiously popularize the economic responsibility system in an effort to further improve economic results. Commercial enterprises should also earnestly popularize the economic responsibility system in all forms in order to further open the channel of exchange between the urban and rural areas and to develop a vast socialist market under unified planning.

In the field of agriculture, tremendous development and improvements have been made in the past several years. Many localities, communes and brigades which once lagged behind have managed to double their output value in 1 or 2 years. Even in localities with fairly poor foundations to begin with, many also doubled or tripled their output value in 3 or 4 years. What is particularly gratifying is that the increase in many counties, communes and brigades in the past 2 years was even faster. This is chiefly because these localities grasped and vigorously implemented the economic responsibility system and, at the same time, developed diversified undertakings in earnest while endeavoring to raise grain output. The problem at present is that many localities have not emancipated themselves enough ideologically and they must further widen their field of vision.

The Secretariat is of the opinion that party organizations at all levels on the agricultural front should boldly mobilize and guide the people, while first ensuring the fulfillment of the grain production task, and open all avenues for production so that they may become well-off much sooner. This should be put forth as a central idea for leading comrades at all levels, especially leading comrades engaged in rural work. With 800 million peasants becoming well-to-do sooner through their own labor, more raw materials will be made available to industry by agriculture, the market for selling industrial products will become larger, and construction funds and state revenue receipts will increase more rapidly. All this will naturally become one of the strongest motive forces in promoting the development of industry. Both industry and agriculture must call on cadres to guide the masses in paying attention to technical reform. In short, as long as we are good and conducting investigation and study and solving problems in economic work in a practical manner, economic development can certainly be achieved even better year by year. In this respect, if we can shape up things more next year and the year after, it will be possible for the central authorities and provinces, municipalities and autonomous regions, starting from the year after, that is 1984, to make concentrated efforts to study and carry out comprehensive reform step-by-step in the systems governing education, labor, wages and commodity prices. In so doing and by coupling with party consolidation in an all-round manner and putting social atmosphere and social security under comprehensive control, by 1986—namely, the 10th anniversary of the downfall of the gang of four—we will be able possibly to come close to realizing the three targets of bringing about the basic improvement in economic and social life put forth by the 12th CPC National Congress. If this is the case, it is comparable to the vicissitudes of life in areas east and west of the river which changed alternately in a span of 10 years. During the 10 years of the Cultural Revolution, things went from bad to worse and are unbearable to recall; whereas in the next 10 years after the Cultural Revolution, the course of events was reversed and the future is bright.

Lastly, I would like to stress one point. From now on and in the next 5 years, the destiny of the party and the state is closely linked with our present new central leading collective, the new fighting command. I think each and every member of this leading collective will, without exception, realize the heavy historic responsibility on his shoulders.

Can we shoulder such a heavy responsibility? We have many favorable conditions: First, we have gained much more experience in leadership, especially the successful experience of the central leading collective since the 3d Plenary Session of the 11th CPC Central Committee, which is intimate and harmonious and has been doing things in line with the principles of democratic centralism. The readjustment of the leading groups on the one hand, and organizational restructuring on the other, have also strengthened the fighting capacity of organs at all levels. Second, several old revolutionaries who are at the helm for us are still living and in good health. Third, it is certain that the newly established Central Advisory Commission will become a very good assistant and staff officer of the Central Committee politically; the newly-reinforced Central Commission for Discipline Inspection will certainly be able to play a bigger role in safeguarding party discipline and in straightening out the party work style. With these three factors, our present central leading collective cannot only shoulder this important historic responsibility but also do a much better job than the last one.

Present here today are many newly-elected comrades to the Central Committee. As a result of the election, the work of some of these comrades has been changed somewhat. Coming in and going out and moving up and moving down are normal things in inner-party life. This is particularly true as our party undertakings develop rapidly. Regardless of personal circumstances, as long as everyone can look forward and always think of the needs of the people and our own deficiencies, we can certainly march forward continuously and make new contributions. We also wholeheartedly hope that those relatively young comrades who moved up treasure the great trust placed in them by the party and the people, and study painstakingly, are modest and prudent, work conscientiously, enhance their spirit and do a good job. We are strongly convinced of this truth: The people will make the best judgment. Therefore, let the people, the party and the army morally judge each and every one of us once more.

36

On Party Building,
4 November 1982

This article, signed authoritatively by "commentator," calls for rectification and consolidation of the Party, implicitly through a purge of members who are too radical, incompetent, or otherwise displeasing to the Dengist leadership.

The 12th CPC National Congress has put forward the grand tasks for creating a new situation in all fields of socialist modernization. We have all the necessary conditions for accomplishing these tasks. A decisive condition is the party leadership. Therefore, we must strengthen party building in the new period, strive for a fundamental turn for the better in party style and make efforts to build the party into a strong leading core for the cause of socialist modernization.

I. THE DISTINGUISHING FEATURES AND SIGNIFICANCE OF PARTY BUILDING IN THE NEW PERIOD

Our party's character of being the vanguard of the proletariat and its advanced nature are the primary reasons for its being able to take the historical responsibility of leading the revolution and construction in China and for its being a force at the core which liberated the Chinese people and enabling them to led a new socialist life.

After the publication of the "Manifesto of the Communist Party," the founder of Marxism repeatedly pointed out: The proletariat is the most advanced class and a leading revolutionary force in the present society. The proletariat must set up its own fighting headquarters and form its own independent party in the course of revolutionary struggles. The party should be composed of outstanding elements of the working class with the highest political consciousness, be able to arm itself with a scientific communist world outlook and understand the objective law of social development and revolutionary movement. Fundamentally speaking, the Communist Party is of an advanced nature because it does not seek special interests for itself, it emphasizes and persistently upholds the overall interests of the working class and all the people at all times, and it always keeps to the communist orientation and represents the interests of an entire revolutionary movement in various stages of development when it leads the movement.

The Communist Party of China is precisely such a party. It was the product of the integration of Marxism with the Chinese workers' movement. The new democratic revolution in China was an integral part of the communist

["Strengthen Party Building; Strive for a Fundamental Turn for the Better in Party Style," *People's Daily*, 4 November 1982.]

movement led by our party and was a necessary preparation for realizing socialism in China. Our party established its leading position in the cause of the people's revolution and led the new democratic revolution to a complete victory, thanks to its correct theories and policies and to the innumerable communists playing an exemplary role and displaying a spirit of sacrifice during the revolution. History proves that our party is the most advanced political organization in Chinese society. Its leading role and its invincible strength are primarily attributed to its advanced nature.

The winning of a nationwide victory in the new democratic revolution was immediately followed by the undertaking of socialist transformation and the establishment of a socialist system. The communist movement thus entered a new period—a period for building a socialist society, which is the first phase of communism. To our party, the situation has brought about two important changes. One is that our party has freed itself from being oppressed and "encircled" and has become a party holding state power and a leading core for the entire socialist cause. In conventional words, it has become the ruling party. The other change is in our party's tasks. For a long period in the past, the central task of our party was leading the people in waging revolutionary class struggles to first overthrow the rule of reactionary classes and then wipe out the exploiting systems and exploiting classes. The party's present central task is leading the people to build a new society, undertake socialist modernization, develop the productive forces and enhance the standards of their cultural and material life.

This change has brought new characteristics to the task of party building and set forth fresh requirements for maintaining and heightening our party's progressive nature. They are manifested in the following two principal fields: First, acting in accordance with the conditions and circumstances brought forth by this change, our party must learn how to integrate the universal truth of Marxism-Leninism with the concrete practice of the country's socialist modernizations, master the law of socialist construction and be versed in professional knowledge in various fields so that it will be able to exercise leadership over construction. We say that the party has been a vanguard whose primary duty was to lead the people in waging revolutionary class struggle. Today it should be a vanguard whose primary duty is to lead the people to achieve socialist material and spiritual civilization and promote democracy. Second, as the ruling party in the country, the CPC should constantly remind every party member that he is an ordinary worker and instruct him constantly to guard against the danger of divorcing himself from the masses and never to forget the party's purpose of wholeheartedly serving the people. In exercising leadership over economic construction, our party should be soberly earnest in following the socialist orientation of this endeavor, never forget the goal of realizing communism and maintaining its communist purity.

History has proved that party building is closely linked to the party's political line. In his work "Introducing the Communist," Comrade Mao Zedong expounded this point fully and produced ample evidence. During the socialist period, party building is closely related to our party's understanding and handling of the question of economic construction and of class struggle and other social contradictions that still exist after the elimination of the system of exploitation.

The eighth party national congress correctly analyzed the principal contradictions in the country following the basic completion of socialist transformation and put forward the task of carrying out all-round socialist construction. These questions, however, were not thoroughly understood at that time and the task put forward was not persistently carried out. On the contrary, "left" mistakes were committed one after another with regard to class struggle and the question of economic construction, thereby paving the way for the decade of domestic turmoil known as the "Great Cultural Revolution." These mistakes seriously damaged the party's ideological line, its democratic life and its relations with the masses as well as the party's organizational discipline and work style.

On the other hand, the occurrences of these mistakes could not be separated from the ruling party's lack of correct and deep understanding of building itself up. The eighth party national congress put forward the question of party building and called for efforts to persist in the mass line, oppose bureaucracy, strengthen democratic centralism and collective leadership and oppose the personality cult. But there was no sufficient and profound understanding of these questions, nor were they solved in our institutions or in practice. Subsequently, quite a few mistakes were made in the party's ideological line and its organizational systems and the personality cult phenomenon grew increasingly evident, thus leading the inner party's political life to increasing abnormality. This development caused serious damage to the party's correct leadership over the cause of socialism and made the party impotent in thoroughly correcting the mistakes in class struggle and economic construction in good time.

The historical course of victory since the 3d plenary session of the 11th party Central Committee shows that our understanding of the law of socialist construction and our formulation of the line and program for achieving socialist modernization in all fields runs parallel to our efforts to strengthen party building and that they promote each other. If we had failed to formulate a correct ideological line of the party, to correctly sum up our historical experiences and to reform and improve the party's leading bodies and organizational systems according to the principles of democratic centralism, we could not have promptly and successfully effected such a great and historic change and directed our socialist modernization in all fields onto a correct path.

The entire history of the Chinese revolution and the history of our socialist construction in the past 20 years or so tells us that the success of revolution and construction led by the party hinges on party building which is closely related to the party's political line.

II. THE NEEDS OF PARTY BUILDING IN THE NEW PERIOD

The 12th party national congress drew up not only the tasks and principles for socialist modernization, but also the program, system and organizational principle for party building. In addition, it set out the requirements, principles and measures for strengthening party building in the new historical period. All this embodies the portions of the new party constitution and the report to the party congress concerning the party. In a word, the main purpose of all this is to adapt the ruling party's position to the tasks and characteristics of the new historical period and to further raise the party's consciousness and progressiveness, thereby improving party leadership.

On the one hand, upholding the leadership of the party means affirming its leading position in the political life of the state and in the cause of socialism and really following its leadership. On the other hand, speaking from the point of view of party building, upholding the leadership of the party means maintaining and upgrading its progressiveness and using it to educate, affect and guide the whole working class and the people throughout the country. To assume political, ideological or organizational leadership, the party must rely on its progressiveness. This is most essential in assuming leadership. In the cause of socialist modernization, the party itself must be correct. It must deal with the cause of construction with an earnest scientific approach. It must not only have a good understanding of general theories concerning, and the laws governing, socialist construction, but also be able to pool the wisdom of the masses in practice, explore the specific laws governing the building of socialist spiritual and material civilization and democratic politics and build socialism with Chinese characteristics. In this way, it can lead the masses to advance along the correct socialist path. The party itself must be highly efficient politically, culturally and scientifically so that it will be able to make the party members and cadres, not only believe strongly in communism and serve the people wholeheartedly, but also constantly elevate their educational and scientific level and master consummate knowledge for socialist construction.

Currently, special efforts must be made to overcome the wrong concept of despising education, science and culture and discriminating against intellectuals. It is necessary to make the ranks of cadres more revolutionary, younger in average age, better educated and more professionally competent. In this way they will be able to encourage and guide the masses around them by setting a good example. While the party itself must be strong, united and vigorous, its leading bodies and ranks of cadres must be able to strengthen the party continually through the succession of the new to the old, and its various organizations must be imbued with a vigorous, revolutionary creative spirit as well as a sense of organization and discipline. In this way the party will be able to unite and organize the people of all nationalities throughout the country to strive for the common objective. It was with the objective in mind that the 12th party national congress put forward the requirements for strengthening the party after considering the different circumstances. It is true that the party has committed mistakes, and there is no guarantee that it will not make mistakes in the future. However, the party dares to make open and sincere criticism of itself in the cause of communism and the interests of the people and is good at making progress by learning from its mistakes. This is one of the hallmarks of its progressiveness.

In short, the party cannot lead if it is not progressive. If the party organization of an area or a unit puts forward wrong views, if the understanding and actions of its party members and cadres lag behind those of the masses, and if the party organization is lax, the party's leadership there exists only in form, for no effective leadership actually exists in practice. There are some party members and cadres engaged in improper practices who have even become corrupted. There are also a small number of paralyzed and degenerated grassroots organizations. In fact, they have become captives to the decadent ideas of the bourgeoisie and other exploiting classes. How can there be genuine party leadership over the masses in those areas under these circumstances?

On strengthening party building and maintaining and elevating the party's progressiveness, the new party constitution and the report to the 12th party national congress stressed three basic requirements: a high degree of identical views in political and ideological matters, serving the people wholeheartedly and upholding democratic centralism. These requirements are not new. From the day the party was founded, we have embarked on party building according to them and, in the long years of struggle, have formed the characteristics and traditions embodying these requirements. In the present condition it has become our more urgent task to strengthen party building and restore the party's fine traditions according to these three requirements after suffering the consequences of the decade of domestic turmoil; moreover, the status of the party in power and the tasks for the new period have added new contents to these three requirements and further boosted the party's fine traditions.

A high degree of ideological and political unity of course denotes unity on the basis of a correct ideological and political line. History proves that, with an incorrect ideological and political line, it is impossible to achieve unity of the whole party. However, without the high degree of unity of the whole party on this basis, it is impossible to implement the correct line, and it is impossible for the party to have fighting power, even if we have the correct ideological and political line. Now we have every reason to say that we have had the correct ideological and political basis for achieving the unity of the whole party, but we are not saying that the demand for party building in this respect has been met, because of the following reasons:

1. We have had a correct ideological and political line in terms of the leadership of the party Central Committee and the party as a whole. However, it remains an arduous task to make all localities, primary party organizations and party members consciously accept, understand and implement it in their work. Our experiences in the new democratic revolution can prove this fact. It took us 10 years from the Zunyi meeting to the seventh party national congress to achieve a high degree of ideological and political unity of the whole party. Moreover, the unity was achieved with the help of a Marxist rectification movement conducted during that period. Today, some of our party organizations and party cadres still have not learned how to proceed from reality and consider the local situation to accomplish the line and tasks put forward by the Central Committee. They have the habit of mechanically conveying messages or going their own way according to partial experience and wrong knowledge. Therefore, they have not properly implemented the very good policies adopted by the party Central Committee. In addition, we should not underestimate such a situation—some persons in our party still doubt the correct line pursued by the party Central Committee. Some persons with "left" mentality are reluctant to abandon, and still cling to, the wrong idea of "taking class struggle as the key link," and others, with a rightist mentality, appreciate and advocate the trend of thought of bourgeois liberalism. They often express doubt and dissatisfaction with the correct line over one question or another. The two tendencies objectively use and complement each other. This is one of the important expressions of the unhealthy tendencies in the party's current style. Therefore, to adhere to the correct line and achieve a high degree of ideological and political unity of the whole party requires an arduous ideological education and active ideological struggle.

2. The correct ideological and political line cannot solve problems once and for all, even if it has been formulated and implemented. The principles of proceeding from reality and of seeking truth from facts are a process in doing all work. To integrate the universal truth of Marxism with the realities of China, blaze a path of our own and build socialism with Chinese characteristics is also a process. Although the basic orientation and main points of this process have been clearly defined, we cannot say that we have already completely understood the law of China's socialist construction because we still need to continue our exploration for many concrete systems and measures. Moreover, with the continuation of practice, we must constantly improve and develop the line and policies concerning the undertaking of socialist modernization in all fields, prevent and overcome "left" and rightist erroneous tendencies and guarantee the continuity and stability of the existing correct line. Therefore, to keep and consolidate the high degree of ideological and political unity is also a constantly developing process.

To serve the people wholeheartedly is our party's consistent purpose. All the policies and practices of our party take the fundamental interests of the vast majority of people as their departure point and destination. Our party seeks the interests of the working class and all the people and seeks no special interests for itself. This is the fundamental reason why our party has strength. This is the fundamental reason why political parties seeking interests for a minority of persons, certain factions or themselves have successively been eliminated, while our party alone has won the people's widespread support and will forever remain vigorous before it finally completes its historical mission. Our problem is that, since our party became the party holding state power, it has been put under still more rigorous tests in this respect. Its status as the ruling party makes it possible for some of its members and cadres to become arrogant bureaucrats, divorced from the masses and use the power in their hands and various opportunities to seek personal interests and special privileges at the expense of the people and the government. Its status as the ruling party also attracts opportunists with bad motives who attempt to sneak into the party. This phenomenon will inevitably undermine the party's advanced nature, cause the danger of our party becoming divorced from the masses and even degenerating certain parts and some members of the party if we fail to prevent it from spreading before it is too late. Because our party organizations were destroyed during the 10 years of domestic turmoil, this phenomenon has already spread to a certain extent and become another important expression of the unhealthy tendencies in the current party style.

Therefore, it is imperative to set stricter demands on party members and cadres who are also party members and to stress that Communist Party members are at all times ordinary members of the working people. In addition to serving the people wholeheartedly, they should diligently study culture, science and professional knowledge so that they will be competent for the task of serving the people. They can have only more obligations than nonparty members and must not seek personal gain or privileges, although they are allowed legitimate personal benefits and job functions and powers. If they act otherwise, they cannot be party members. It is vitally important that this be made the central link and a strict line of demarcation in putting forward the question of party members' qualifications and in solving it in the course of practice. The correct solution of this question not only has a bearing on the relationship between the party and the people as well as on the party's prestige and leading role among the masses but also determines the party's ability to maintain its characteristics of being the vanguard of the proletariat.

As for persisting in the party's democratic centralism, the progressive nature and leading role of our party are not only manifested in the ideological and political fields but are also guaranteed in the organizational field. It is necessary to act in line with democratic centralism and to build the party into an entity that acts in unison. In the past, our party relied on its strict organizational nature and sense of discipline to lead the people in defeating enemies much more powerful than ourselves. It has become all the more necessary to persist in democratic centralism since the CPC became the ruling party leading socialist construction in the country. The complex and arduous task of construction has, on the one hand, called for developing inner-party democracy, bringing into play the enthusiasm and creativeness of all party members and cadres and—on the basis of this—promoting socialist democracy in the political life of the state. On the other hand, it has created the need for a high level of centralism on the basis of democracy and for a strict sense of organizational discipline to ensure the unity of the entire party in action and to guarantee the prompt and effective implementation of the party's decisions.

We should also understand that the status of the ruling party has brought with it still greater powers for our party leaders which can easily give rise to patriarchal behavior and the personality cult. When the inner-party political life is torpedoed, it will invariably create a phenomenon in which each goes his own way in a manner of liberalism without regard for discipline or for the party as an organization. This would damage the party's collective leadership and its unity in action.

We have summed up the lessons learned from our party's mistakes that led to the "Great Cultural Revolution." Such mistakes were committed in the ideological and political fields, but the most bitter lesson learned from it was the damage done to democratic centralism and the party's normal inner political life. Paying full attention to this fact and taking it as a lesson, the new party constitution has made supplementary and concrete stipulations on democratic centralism and party discipline. Now, from the party Central Committee to the many local party organizations, political life has gradually become normal, and the principles of democratic centralism and collective leadership have also been implemented. However, the consequences and influence of the decade of domestic turmoil still remain among quite a number of party members, cadres and party organizations and are hindering the implementation of the correct line. This is also an important manifestation of the unhealthy style of the party these days. Therefore, it is necessary for us to strengthen democratic centralism and the party's organizational nature and sense of discipline in accordance with the requirements and stipulations spelled out in the new party constitution.

In a nutshell, the three basic requirements for strengthening party building as mentioned above were designed to improve the political quality of the whole party vigorously, enhance the party organizations' fighting power and persist in and improve party leadership over socialist construction.

III. THE STRUGGLE TO TURN PARTY STYLE FUNDAMENTALLY FOR THE BETTER

The new historical period has set very high demands on party building. But seriously unhealthy party style exists in general. This is a sharp contradiction. Therefore, we must carry out party consolidation step by step and in a planned way and work hard to effect a fundamental turn for the better in party style; this is a central link of party building in the next few years.

The 12th party national congress called for a fundamental turn for the better in the country's financial and economic situation, in the standards of social conduct and in party style. These are organically integrated with one another. This is especially so in effecting a fundamental turn for the better in party style and in the standards of social conduct which have a direct bearing and influence on each other. On the one hand, we should not say that unhealthy social conduct is the result of unhealthy party style. Many social evils are not caused by unhealthy party style. On the other hand, it is true that unhealthy party style does have a great bearing on the standards of social conduct. Only by overcoming the unhealthy practices in the party and consolidating the party can our party convince, educate and unite the masses of the people to correct the unhealthy practices in society and use revolutionary ideology and spirit to arouse the people's enthusiasm for construction so as to ensure the smooth development of socialist modernization and the fundamental turn for the better in the country's financial and economic situation. In this sense, the key to fulfilling the tasks set forth by the 12th party national congress is to effect a fundamental turn for the better in party style.

Party building, like any other work, must proceed from the realities. A correct analysis and appraisal of the present situation in the party and the unhealthy phenomena in our party style is the starting point for consolidating the party and bringing about a turn for the better in party style.

The report to the 12th party congress made a correct and incisive analysis of the present situation in the party: On the one hand, the main body of our party remains politically pure and strong despite the serious damage inflicted by the "Cultural Revolution," and after recovery and consolidation in the past few years, the situation in our party is now greatly improved. This is the dominant aspect. On the other hand, it is true that impurities in ideology, style and organization still exist within the party and that no fundamental turn for the better has as yet been made in our party style.

The report enumerated the various manifestations of the unhealthy tendencies in the party and sharply pointed out: "All these phenomena have greatly impaired our party's prestige. While we must not allow any exaggeration of this dark aspect of our party, we should not on any account be afraid to expose it." This analysis is scientific and conforms to the realities. We have only to look back objectively at the tremendous change brought about by the party and the state in all fields since the downfall of the Jiang Qing counterrevolutionary clique—especially since the 3d plenary session of the 11th party Central Committee—and we cannot but recognize that the main body of our party is politically pure and strong and that the party style has improved markedly in the past few years. Of course, if we similarly objectively observe the realities around us, we must admit that there is indeed a dark aspect in the party. Investigations by many local and primary party organizations on the conditions of party members (including those who are cadres) also indicate that the great majority of party members are qualified or basically qualified; that a small number are not quite qualified or basically not qualified, but the overwhelming majority of them can become qualified party members after education; and that only a handful are absolutely not qualified or downright degenerates. This can also prove from one aspect the correctness of the analysis of the situation in the party given by the report.

In order to understand the report's scientific appraisal and to have a basis to effect a fundamental turn for the better in party style, we must also analyze in depth the cause of the emergence of unhealthy tendencies in the party and why they can surely be overcome.

First, the emergence of all kinds of unhealthy tendencies in the party has its historical and social causes. The party's healthy body is attacked by old ideas and old habits formed under the exploiting system and private ownership of the means of production—as a person's healthy body is attacked by all kinds of germs in the environment. All our party members were not born advanced elements. Some of them had lived in the old society, and some had lived in the new society when it had just been born out of the old society. Unavoidably, they were still more or less under the influence of the old ideas when they joined the party,

and unavoidably, they are still continuously subjected to the influence of old ideas and old habits. They must constantly and consciously remold themselves and pay attention to waging a struggle against these old influences, for only in this way can they maintain their progressiveness. If the active ideological struggle in the party is stopped and all kinds of unhealthy tendencies spread unchecked, the party will not be able to undertake the task of leading the revolution and will itself degenerate gradually till its doom. Therefore, the style of the party determines its very survival. And strengthening the party's own building, resisting attacks by all kinds of old ideas and overcoming the unhealthy tendencies are an indispensable part of the party's great historical task to transform the Chinese society.

In fact, the influence of the ideas and habits from the old system on the party and the unhealthy tendencies in the party have existed all along. In the past, it was exactly in the course of continuous struggles against them that the party had developed and grown. At present, unhealthy tendencies are spreading to a certain extent in the party because the evil consequences of the 10 years of domestic turmoil have not been completely eliminated. It is also a manifestation that the various ideas of the exploiting classes are again spreading and their corrosive effects are increasing under the new conditions. We should see that under present international and domestic conditions, the influence of ideas and habits form the old system will remain widespread for a long time to come. It is much more difficult to eliminate the negative effects of the decade of domestic turmoil on party style than to undo its material consequences. Therefore, we must fully understand that the struggle against the unhealthy tendencies will be arduous and protracted and must not lower our guard in the slightest degree.

But the situations and truths mentioned above can also show that the unhealthy tendencies in the party are illegal. They are absolutely incompatible with the party's proletarian progressive character, are what the party wants to transform and eliminate, and can entirely be overcome. First of all, our party is able to do this because it has no special interests of its own apart from the interests of the working class and the Chinese people. Although some party members and cadres, whose party spirit is impure, may take advantage of various opportunities in the party. As far as the party's purpose, its line, the leadership of the party Central Committee and the party as a whole are concerned, there is no need or reason whatsoever to conceal or protect the shortcomings, mistakes and unhealthy tendencies among the party's own ranks. On the contrary, in the interests of the class and the people, the party will certainly eliminate the dark aspect among its ranks with the greatest determination. This has been and will continue to be proven by history. Next, it is because our party has the most powerful weapon to wage the struggle against unhealthy tendencies among its own ranks; that is, the Marxist method of self-criticism. The Marxist scientific theory and the advanced stand of the proletarian determine that our party can grasp and apply the weapon of self-criticism. Lenin said: "All the extinct revolutionary political parties of the past became extinct because they were arrogant and conceited, failed to see where their strength lay and were afraid to admit their own weaknesses. But we will not become extinct because we are not afraid of admitting our own weaknesses and because we can learn to overcome our weaknesses." This is exactly how our party, by correctly using the weapon of self-criticism, has repeatedly overcome mistakes, dangers and difficulties and in the process recovered and grown stronger. After the 10 years of domestic turmoil, because the party not only has the Marxist courage to conduct self-criticism but the ability to do it historically and correctly, it has brought about a historic change and effected a marked turn for the better in party style. Similarly, by correctly using the weapons of self-criticism, we can certainly continue to eliminate the filth among our own ranks and bring about a fundamental turn for the better in our party style.

Since the emergence of the unhealthy tendencies in the party has its social and historical causes, we should see that our struggle against them will be arduous and long; because of the party's proletarian and progressive character and the weapon of self-criticism it possesses, we should see the inevitability of the unhealthy tendencies being overcome. This is the basic understanding and attitude we should have.

To achieve a fundamental turn for the better in our party style, the 12th party congress decided on an overall rectification of party style and consolidation of party organizations, which will proceed by stages and by groups over a period of 3 years beginning from the latter half of 1983. This is an important move to strengthen party building put forward on the basis of a correct analysis of the situation in the party. In a sense, the work our party has been doing in the past few years in uncovering the factional setup of Lin Biao and Jiang Qing, rectifying the ideological line, implementing the cadre policy, consolidating and leading bodies at various levels, implementing the guiding principles for inner-party political life and so forth, as well as the work to strike at serious crimes in the economic field which began this year, are all for consolidating the party—or to put it another way, all have party consolidation as part of their contents. However, all these cannot substitute a concentrated and overall rectification of party style and consolidation of party organizations, and without such a concentrated and overall rectification and consolidation, it is impossible to achieve a fundamental turn for the better in party style.

Party consolidation is a creation of our party, a form and method to strengthen party building that has been proven effective by history. Its basic contents include widespread and thoroughgoing Marxist ideological and political education, conscientious and responsible criticism and self-criticism and serious and careful organizational cleansing.

Since the Yanan rectification campaign, our party has accumulated rich, successful experience in this area and formed a fine tradition. Of course, we have also learned profound lessons in periods of "left" mistakes. The proposed party consolidation will be an overall party consolidation after the destruction of the 10 years of domestic turmoil and the achievement of a historical change—an overall party consolidation to be carried out when the party is faced with the great tasks in the new period. Therefore, it will certainly play a vitally important role and will be of far-reaching significance. We should pay attention to applying successful past experiences, draw lessons from past mistakes, inherit and carry forward the fine traditions formed since the Yanan rectification campaign and do this work well. In this way, we will certainly be able to achieve a fundamental turn for the better in party style and make the party a strong, leading core for the cause of socialist modernization.

The Party Passes the 40 Million Mark, 27 June 1983

37

Despite Deng Xiaoping's desire to rectify the Party, its membership appears to have shown the effects of this wish less than those of Parkinson's Law. The Chinese Communist Party has long been the largest political party in the world, and its membership is officially announced here as having surpassed 40 million.

According to information from the CPC Central Committee Organization Department, total CPC membership has increased from some 4 million people in early liberation days to over 40 million people.

In the past few years, in order to meet the needs of socialist modernization and in accordance with provisions

["The Party's Ranks Continue to Develop and Grow," *People's Daily,* 27 June 1983.]

stipulated in the party Constitution adopted at the 12th CPC Congress, party organizations at various levels have upheld the requirements for membership in recruiting new party members. This has ensured the quality of party members and has quite successfully overcome the practice in some units of only stressing the growth of the party's ranks but not paying attention to education and quality. Many party organizations at grassroots levels have conducted training and education among political activists, established strict systems for observation and education, and paid attention to raising their political consciousness and correcting their motives for joining the party. In recruiting new party members, they have seriously paid attention to going through relevant procedures and have been careful in giving approval. Therefore, the quality of the overwhelming majority of new party members is quite good. According to reports from various localities, among new party members recruited last year, 40–50 percent have been chosen as model laborers, advanced workers, and advanced producers on various fronts. In some localities and units, the percentage has reached about 70 percent. A large number of outstanding people who uphold faith in communism and have selflessly dedicated themselves to the modernization drive have emerged in various localities. Comrades Jiang Zhuying and Zhang Haidi are typical representatives of these people.

Party organizations at various levels have paid special attention to recruiting new party members from among intellectuals, middle-aged intellectuals in particular, backbone elements on the first line of various trades and professions, and in departments and localities where the party's strength is weak. According to statistics compiled at the end of last year, there was a marked increase in the percentage of various specialities recruited in 1982 as new party members accounted for 23.6 percent of the total number of new party members recruited in the same year (excluding those in the Army), 2.2 percent over 1981 and 170 percent over 1978, which accounted for 8.3 percent. Of the newly recruited intellectual party members, middle-aged intellectuals accounted for more than 70 percent. The percentage of personnel on the first line of various trades and professions who were recruited as party members also increased. Various localities also paid attention to recruiting new party members from among better-educated youths less than 25 years old.

The Central Committee Gets Serious About Party Consolidation, 11 October 1983

38

Perhaps on the principle that over 40 million Chinese Communists can be wrong, and that consolidation was long overdue, the Central Committee in October 1983 began to show signs of serious intent to eliminate undesirables from the Party. This move has been essentially unacceptable to the remaining radicals at various levels, especially those in the middle ranks who would be the main target of a purge. It may be significant that the same session that adopted this resolution also kicked off the campaign, much desired by the radicals, against "spiritual pollution" (see Docs. 78–81).

The 12th National Congress of the Communist Party of China has decided on an overall rectification of party style and a consolidation of party organizations over a period of three years beginning in the latter half of 1983. The second plenary session of the 12th party Central Committee had discussed the question of how to carry out this important decision and decided that the overall consolidation of the party should begin in winter this year.

[Resolution of the Second Plenary Session of the Twelfth Central Committee, 11 October 1983, New China News Agency, 12 October 1983.]

(1) THE NECESSITY AND URGENCY OF PARTY CONSOLIDATION

Ours is a long-tested, great Marxist party. In spite of the serious damage by our party sustained in the 10-year domestic turmoil, the ranks of our party remain, on the whole, politically pure and highly militant. Since the third plenary session of the 11th party Central Committee, our party has reaffirmed the Marxist line, accomplished a shift of the focus of work of the party and state, launched the socialist modernization drive with economic construction as the central task, handled in an appropriate manner many major issues left over from the past, systematically summed up the historical experience gained since the founding of the People's Republic, restructured the government organizations and readjusted the leading bodies at all levels, strengthened the building of socialist democracy and legal system, waged struggles to combat grave criminal activities in the economic sphere and other serious crimes and to rectify various acts detrimental to the interests of the state and the people, and conducted education in reviving and promoting the fine traditions of the party and in socialist and communist ideology.

As a result of such work and struggles, initial success had been achieved in rectifying party style and consolidating the party organizations, the situation in the party has noticeably improved, and the healthy force has gained the dominant position in the party. This abundantly proves that our party, by relying on its own strength, is fully capable of overcoming its seamy side, of correcting its mistakes, and of forging ahead with greater vigour.

However, while carrying out the intense work and struggles mentioned above in the last few years, our party did not have the time to carry on an overall and systematic rectification of the many problems existing in the spheres of ideology, style of work and organization of the party. Education among the party members has been neither widespread nor adequate. The pernicious influence of the 10-year domestic turmoil has not been eradicated. It is entirely correct that we have adopted the policy of opening to the outside world and enlivening the national economy. But, under the new historical conditions there has been an increase in the corrosive influence of decadent bourgeois ideology and remnant feudal ideas, while the work and struggles we have undertaken to resist and overcome such corrosive influence have not been effective enough. For these reasons, there are still many serious problems in the party. Some party members lack a correct understanding of the great significance of setting things to rights and have not shifted their stand on to the Marxist line; other members have a vague and confused idea about the basic principles and superiority of the socialist system and about the bright communist future. On the ideological front, some members turn a blind eye to anti-Marxist and anti-socialist ideas, and some even openly spread these ideas. Some party members and cadres [Beijing *Xinhua* Domestic Service in Chinese at 1150 GMT on 12 October renders this phrase, "Some party members and cadres who are party members" and uses this formulation throughout] have succumbed to individualism in a serious way. Seeking to advance personal interests and the interests of a small group, they have unscrupulously resorted to all means to harm the interests of the state and the people and embarked on the road of committing crimes. A number of party members and cadres have a very weak sense of organization, are lax in discipline, and are listless and inert, failing to play an exemplary vanguard role. Some party organizations are soft, weak and lax, or are even in a state of paralysis, failing to play their role as fighting bastions. The party has not yet cleared its ranks of three types of persons, namely, persons who rose to prominence by following the counterrevolutionary cliques of Lin Biao and Jiang Qing in "rebellion," those who are seriously factionalist in their ideas, and those who indulged in beating, smashing and looting. Such serious impurities in ideology, style of work and organization, which are of great harm to the party, must be resolutely and effectively dealt with.

Our party is faced with the new historical task of carrying out socialist modernization. This is a great, glorious and yet extremely arduous task. The strong leadership of the Communist Party is indispensable to the socialist cause. The party Central Committee pointed out long ago that it is essential to uphold and also to improve party leadership. Today, in addition to the serious impurities in ideology, style of work and organization as mentioned above, there are many other aspects in our party which do not conform to the needs of the new situation and new tasks facing us.

The general aim and requirements of the present party consolidation are, under the guidance of Marxism-Leninism and Mao Zedong Thought and by relying on the revolutionary consciousness of all comrades in the party, correctly using the sharp weapons of criticism and self-criticism and enforcing party discipline, to expose and deal with manifestations of the serious impurities that exist in the party in ideology, style of work and organization, so as to bring about a fundamental turn for the better in the style of the party, raise the ideological level of the whole party and the level of its work, strengthen the ties between the party and the masses of the people, and strive to build the party and make it a strong core of leadership for the cause of socialist modernization.

The present party consolidation is a major step which our party must take to achieve fresh great victories in the new historical period. It is a fundamental guarantee for achieving, under the precondition of constantly raising the economic results, the magnificent goal of quadrupling the nation's gross annual output value of industrial and agricultural production by the end of this century, a goal set forth at the 12th party congress, and it is also a fundamental guarantee for building China into a modern, culturally advanced and highly democratic socialist country.

(2) THE TASKS OF PARTY CONSOLIDATION

The party Central Committee holds that the tasks for the present party consolidation are the achievement of ideological unity, the rectification of the party's style of work, the strengthening of discipline and the purification of the party organization.

First, the Achievement of Ideological Unity Means Making Further Efforts To Bring About a High Degree of Ideological and Political Unity Throughout the Party and Correcting All Erroneous "Left" and Right Tendencies That Run Counter to the Four Basic Principles and to the Party Line That Has Been Adopted Since the Third Plenary Session of the 11th Party Central Committee.

The entire history of our party shows that maintaining a high degree of ideological and political unity is a basic condition to winning victory in revolution and construction.

The line, principles and basic policies of the party since the third plenary session of the 11th party Central Committee have been worked out by combining the four basic principles with the concrete practice under the present historical conditions, through the process of correct "left" errors and combating right mistakes, and in compliance with the requirements of socialist modernization.

Proven correct in practice, they have won the wholehearted support of the masses of party members and cadres. [*Xinhua* Chinese version renders this phrase "... they have won the wholehearted support of the masses of party members."] All party organizations and members must maintain unity with the Central Committee on the basis of persisting in the four basic principles and in the party line adopted since the third plenary session of the 11th party Central Committee. This is required by the party's political discipline. Whether a party organization or party member can do this constitutes the main criterion for judging the ideological and political soundness and the sense of discipline of that party organization or member.

On this question, there are now two erroneous tendencies in the party. One is that a number of party members and cadres who have not yet freed themselves from the shackles of past "left" ideas distort the four basic principles and assume a resisting attitude towards the party line, principles and basic policies adopted since the third plenary session of the 11th party Central Committee; some even feign compliance while covertly opposing the party line, principles and policies or openly refuse to carry them out. The other tendency is that some party members and cadres, who have failed to stand the test of historical setbacks and succumbed to the corrosive influence of bourgeois ideology, doubt and negate the four basic principles, deviate from the party line, principles and basic policies adopted since the third plenary session of the 11th Party Central Committee, and propagate bourgeois liberalization. Both these erroneous "left" and right tendencies are incompatible with the character and programme and historic mission of the party.

Most of those party members and cadres who have committed such mistakes have done so because of their ideology and understanding, and they should be helped to deepen their understanding and correct their mistakes by studying and summarizing the historical experience and through patient criticism and education. As for the few who persist in their wrong political stand and refuse to correct their mistakes, they should be seriously criticized and ideological struggles should be carried out against them; in addition, due disciplinary action should be taken against them.

To maintain political unity with the party Central Committee does not mean professing unity in words alone, but everyone must uphold unity in deeds. It is essential to resolutely change the state of flabbiness in ideological-political work, to correctly and willingly carry out the line, principles and policies of the party Central Committee, and to resolutely resist and overcome the influence of erroneous "left" and right tendencies.

To maintain political unity with the party Central Committee, one must integrate the line, principles and policies of the party Central Committee with the actual conditions of one's locality, department or unit; one must also bring into full play one's own initiative and creativity and work in an independent and responsible way. It is essential to overcome subjectivism, conduct careful investigation and study, proceed from reality and seek truth from facts in all matters, and combine revolutionary vigour with scientific approach. Only thus can we ensure that the line, principles and policies of the party Central Committee be correctly carried out, and only thus can we continuously enrich and develop them with the new experience gained in practice and carry the cause of the party forward.

Second, Rectifying the Party Style Means Promoting the Revolutionary Spirit of Serving the People Wholeheartedly, Checking Various Acts of Seeking Personal Gains by Taking Advantage of One's Power and Position, and Opposing the Bureaucratic Attitude of Not Holding Oneself Responsible to the Party and People.

Our party has no particular interest of its own other than the interests of the working class and the masses of the people. For more than half a century, our party has continuously achieved successes in the revolution and in construction precisely because it has by its deeds demonstrated its selfless character and the spirit of serving the people wholeheartedly, thereby winning the people's sincere love and trust. During the years of revolutionary wars, the party would not have been able to hold its ground and avert defeat if it had not worked for the interests of the masses, won them over, relied on them and obtained their full support. This is easy for our comrades to understand. However, in the long years since our party took over the political power of the whole country, quite a number of our comrades have become unclear in their thinking about such necessity. They fail to understand that the question of the party's style is a question of life and death for a party in power.

Because the party's position has changed, all its activities concern the interests of the people and the destiny of the county; if it is divorced from the masses and does not take resolute measures to correct it, then the party will inevitably lose the people's trust and support and will meet with failure.

Now, some party members and cadres have totally forgotten the basic principle of serving the people wholeheartedly. They are not correctly using the power and working conditions given them by the party and the people to work for the welfare of the masses, but are seeking personal gains by every possible means for themselves and for those close to them. They ask the party for higher positions and better treatment. They openly violate financial regulations and discipline, sabotage state plans, violate state economic policies and illegally retain taxes and profits; they invent all sorts of pretexts to squander, waste and occupy state and collective funds and property. With regard to the distribution of housing, the increase in wages and many other matters—such as the employment, education, promotion, job assignments and changing from rural residence registration to urban residence registration for their children, relatives and friends as well as foreign affairs work—they take advantage of their power and position, conveniences provided by their work and personal relations to seek special privileges, violate the law and discipline, and encroach upon the interests of the state and the masses. They ignore the law, protect and shield criminals, and they even take a direct part in unlawful activities, such as smuggling, selling smuggled goods, corruption, accepting bribes and profiteering.

Some party cadres in leading positions are seriously affected by bureaucratism; their revolutionary will has been waning, eating three full meals a day yet doing no work. They pay no attention at all to the weal and woe of the people; they are unconcerned about the expansion of production, the reform of government structure and the development of socialist ethics and culture; and they argue back and forth, trying to shift the responsibility onto others and even counteracting each other's efforts in their work. Their serious neglect of duty has caused horrifying waste in the country's production and construction, serious errors in state administration and huge economic and political losses for the party and government.

These unhealthy tendencies and decadent phenomena, which are seriously sabotaging the nation's socialist modernization, have greatly impaired our party's image among the people, weakened the confidence of the party members and the masses in the superiority of the socialist system and the bright future of communism, and dampened their enthusiasm for politics, production, work and study. We must be resolved to solve this problem in the present party consolidation and resolutely eradicate these unhealthy tendencies. Party members and cadres who took advantage of their power, position and other conveniences to seek personal gains after the party Central Committee promulgated the rules of conduct for inner-party political life in March 1980 should be required to make self-criticisms. Those who have committed grave mistakes should be dealt with according to party discipline and administrative discipline, and those who have violated the law should be punished according to law. [*Xinhua* Chinese version reads ". . . those who have violated criminal law . . ."] Those who have profited at the government's expense should, on the basis of thorough investigations and on the merit of each case, be required to return what they had unlawfully taken or pay compensations. Those who committed such mistakes before the promulgation of the rules of conduct should also be handled in all seriousness if their mistakes are particularly serious or if they refuse to mend their ways. [*Xinhua* Chinese renders this ". . . if they refuse to mend their ways despite repeated education."]

Necessary disciplinary action should also be taken against bureaucrats who have neglected their duties with serious consequences, and some should be dismissed from the leading posts or expelled from the party. [*Xinhua* Chinese renders this phrase ". . . some should be dismissed from their posts or expelled . . ."]

Third, the Strengthening of Discipline Is To Adhere to the Party's Organizational Principle of Democratic Centralism, Oppose the Patriarchal System, Factionalism, Anarchism and Liberalism Which Completely Ignore Party Organizations and Discipline, and Correct the Softness, Weakness and Laxness of the Party Organizations.

To maintain the party's strict organizational discipline and uphold democratic centralism is an important guarantee for the realization of the party's programme and tasks and for the strengthening of the party's fighting capacity.

At present, the pernicious influence of the 10-year domestic turmoil has not been eradicated among a number of party organizations and members, and violations of the party's system of democratic centralism are rather serious. Some leading cadres place themselves above the party organizations, where collective leadership exists in name only. In fact, only one or two individuals make the final decisions. Some of them have even turned the units under their charge into territories where their will holds sway

and where they rule as overlords. In other cases, some party members and cadres disregard the party's organizational principle and party discipline, and are seriously affected by anarchism, liberalism, decentralism, departmentalism and sectarianism. It should be pointed out in particular that up to now factionalism which developed during the 10-year domestic turmoil among a number of party members and cadres has not yet been overcome. They still maintain factionalism instead of the party spirit. They use their faction as the line of demarcation and appoint people by favouritism while elbowing out of their way those who hold different views; they form cliques to pursue selfish interests, seriously impairing the unity and solidarity of the party and hindering the party from carrying out its line, principles and policies. Party activities in a number of party organizations are far from regular, with neither criticism nor self-criticism; party discipline is not strictly observed, and violations of party discipline and other unhealthy tendencies are not checked and corrected. Instead of taking the lead in criticism and self-criticism and combating unhealthy tendencies, some leading cadres, abiding by the principle of giving no offense to others, evade contradictions wherever possible, while others suppress criticism and retaliate against those who criticize them. These phenomena must be done away with completely during the present consolidation of the party. After the party consolidation, criticism and self-criticism should become an established practice in the party organizations, especially within the leading bodies, so as to bring about a vigorous and lively situation in which there are both democracy and centralism, unity and strict discipline.

Fourth, To Purify the Party Organizations Means To Sort Out Elements Who Persist in Opposing and Harming the Party, and Expel Them From the Party in Accordance With the Party Constitution.

Purifying the party organizations is a major purpose of the present consolidation of the party. Since the three types of persons oppose and harm the party, they are bound to be a hidden peril if they are not thoroughly sorted out and expelled. To sort out and expel the three types of persons is of crucial importance in our effort to purify the party organizations.

The first type, those who rose to prominence during the "Cultural Revolution," refers to those persons who closely followed Lin Biao, Jiang Qing and their ilk, formed factions and cliques, seized political power in "rebellion," rose to high positions, and committed evil with serious consequences. The second type, those who are seriously factionalist in their ideas, refers to those who in the "Cultural Revolution" period vigorously publicized the reactionary ideology of the Lin Biao and Jiang Qing counterrevolutionary cliques, and formed cliques for doing evil. After the downfall of the "gang of four," they have continued, either openly or covertly, with their factionalist activities. The third type, those who indulged in beating, smashing and looting during the "Cultural Revolution," period, refers to those who framed and persecuted cadres and the masses, extorted confessions by torture, and seriously ruined their victims' health; it also refers to those chief elements and those behind the scenes responsible for the smashing of institutions, the seizure of files by force and the damaging of both public and private property; it also refers to those who plotted, organized and directed violent confrontations which resulted in serious consequences. The basis for distinguishing whether a person belongs to the three types of persons is the damage done to the party and the people and not the title or membership in a particular faction during the "Cultural Revolution." A serious and prudent attitude should be taken in determining whether a person belongs to any of the three types, and his performance during the "Cultural Revolution" should be analysed from a historical point of view. Wherever and whenever controversy arises, it should be submitted to the party committee at the higher level for discussion and decision. In principle, the three types of persons should be expelled from the party, except those who have proved to have really mended their ways after a long period of examination.

With the exception of the three types of persons mentioned above, the principle of dealing with different cases in different ways will be applied to party members and leading party cadres who made mistakes or had other problems during the "Cultural Revolution." Mistakes of a general character will not be brought up again during this party consolidation. As for those who committed serious mistakes but conclusions have not yet been drawn and they have not been dealt with, conclusions will be drawn and due measures taken during this party consolidation; as for those who have already received a judgment and have been dealt with, their cases will not be considered again this time if no new major problems have been discovered.

Those who stubbornly resist the policies of the party Central Committee [Xinhua Chinese renders this "Those who stubbornly resist the line of the party Central Committee . . ."] adopted since the Third Plenary Session of the 11th Party Central Committee, those who have committed grave crimes in economic matters and other criminal offenses, and those who have seriously violated the law and discipline must all be expelled from the party.

For those who are expelled, appropriate arrangements should be made in work for those who are still fit to be cadres; those unfit to be cadres should be provided with opportunities to find jobs and earn a living. Ideological help and political concern should be shown them, and they should be encouraged and helped to remould their ideology and make progress.

(3) DEMANDS ON PARTY MEMBERS AND LEADING PARTY CADRES

The party Central Committee requires that all party members take an active part in the party consolidation without exception. The broad masses of party members should strive to enhance their communist consciousness and strengthen their party spirit so that they will become qualified members and then make still greater efforts to become outstanding members of the party. The criteria of a qualified member are the basic demands set by Article 2 and the eight duties prescribed by Article 3 of the party Constitution.

The leading party cadres at all levels shoulder particularly important responsibilities in the political life of the party and the state and in the implementation of the party's line, principles and policies. In addition to meeting the requirements of party members mentioned above, they

must meet the six basic requirements prescribed by Article 35 of the party Constitution. At present, it is particularly important for them to enhance their understanding of the theories of Marxism-Leninism and Mao Zedong Thought and the policies based on them, raise their sense of dedication to the revolutionary cause and their sense of political responsibility, dare to combat all hostile forces disrupting socialism, fight against decadent bourgeois ideology, against acts of creating spiritual pollution as well as against the abuse of power and position for personal gains so that they will set a good example for the broad masses of party members and guide the masses to make efforts to become people with high ideals and morality, cultural knowledge and sense of discipline.

The broad masses of young party members are distinguished for their lively thinking, their courage to blaze new trails and their vigour and vitality. However, the majority of them know little about the basic theories of Marxism and the fundamental knowledge concerning the party; they lack experience in revolutionary practice and in inner-party political life. Because they were ideologically influenced by anarchism and other passive phenomena during the 10-year domestic turmoil when their world outlook was taking shape, their ability to correctly distinguish between right and wrong with regard to political affairs, is, generally speaking, fairly poor. During this party consolidation, close attention should be paid to enhancing their ideological and political consciousness, strengthening their party spirit and raising their ability to resist the corrosive influence of bourgeois ideology so that they will mature as quickly as possible and become capable of really shouldering their historical task as successors to the party's cause.

As far as the broad masses of party members are concerned, in judging whether they conform to the standard set by the party Constitution, the emphasis is on their concrete actions in all aspects since the Third Plenary Session of the 11th Party Central Committee.

(4) STEPS AND BASIC METHODS OF PARTY CONSOLIDATION

The present party consolidation will be carried out according to the following steps: It will proceed from the central level to the grass-roots organizations, from the top downwards by stages and in groups. Rectification of the party organization of each unit should also proceed from the top downwards in the order of the leading bodies, leading cadres and ordinary party members.

The party now has 40 million members, including more than 9 million cadres, and about 2.5 million party organizations at the grass-roots level and above.

Party consolidation will be completed in three years, beginning in this winter, in two stages. During the first stage, beginning in winter this year, the work will be the consolidation of party organizations of the leading bodies at the central level and at the provincial, municipal and autonomous regional level (including the party organizations of the various ministries, commissions and offices, departments and bureaus of these two levels) and the party organizations in the leading bodies of all the general headquarters, services and arms and great military areas of the People's Liberation Army. [Xinhua Chinese renders this

". . . services and arms and military regions of the People's Liberation Army."] During this period, the provincial, municipal and autonomous regional party committees may designate some party organizations at the prefectural and county levels which have already completed structural reforms to carry out party consolidation as pilot cases. Similar experiments may also be conducted in the army. In the second stage, beginning in winter 1984, all the remaining party organizations will be consolidated, and the various provincial, municipal and autonomous regional party committees and the General Political Department of the People's Liberation Army may make concrete arrangements, in accordance with their actual conditions, on the ways of carrying out the work by groups during this stage.

After this decision is released, all the party organizations should organize their members to seriously study the documents on party consolidation decided upon by the party Central Committee in order to enhance their ideological consciousness and put the regular activities of the party organizations on a sound basis. Party members and party cadres who have committed various kinds of mistakes should take the initiative to correct their mistakes and should not wait until party consolidation begins in their respective units.

The basic methods of the present party consolidation are, on the basis of a careful study of documents and enhancement of ideology and understanding [*Xinhua Chinese* renders this "and enhancement of ideological understanding"] to make criticism and self-criticism, distinguish between right and wrong, correct mistakes and purify the party organization. In the process of party consolidation, ideological education should be strengthened from beginning to end so as to raise the ideological consciousness of the broad masses of party members.

To meet the needs of party consolidation, the party Central Committee has decided to edit and publish a must book for party members, a concise edition of important documents since the Third Plenary Session of the 11th Party Central Committee, Comrade Mao Zedong on the party's style of work and party organization. These three books and the Selected Works of Deng Xiaoping will be the documents for study during this party consolidation. For party members who lack the ability to read, the party committees at and above the county level will be responsible for organizing and training people to read and explain to them the main contents of a must book for party members and the Selected Works of Deng Xiaoping. All party members must, through the study of these party consolidation documents, raise their understanding of the character, programme and task of the party, and raise their understanding of the criteria for party members and of the line, principles and policies of the party since the Third Plenary Session of the 11th Party Committee. The party organizations of the leading bodies at the central and provincial, municipal and autonomous regional levels should, after the completion of party consolidation in their own units, organize party cadres to earnestly study some basic Marxist works.

(A list of books will be decided later.) Other party organizations should also organize their party cadres to study these books after party consolidation in their units is completed.

To study the documents and raise understanding is to create the necessary conditions for solving contradictions within the party, while correctly carrying out criticism and self-criticism is an effective method to solve these contradictions. Without conscientious criticism and self-criticism, none of the aims of party consolidation can be achieved. Not daring to criticize and fight against erroneous ideas and acts within the party is a manifestation of impurity in party spirit; suppressing criticism and retaliating against people who have made criticisms is abominable behaviour which violates party discipline. While making criticism and self-criticism, we must strictly follow the principles consistently stressed by our party and Comrade Mao Zedong: We must proceed from the desire for unity, help those who are criticized, and act in the spirit of "learning from past mistakes to avoid future ones and curing the sickness to save the patient;" we must be practical and base our criticism on facts and we should allow the people concerned to defend their cases; we must keep to the truth and not spare the feelings of those who are criticized; we must combine the seriousness and acuteness of criticism and self-criticism with a scientific attitude and attain the goal of clearing up ideology, correcting mistakes and uniting with our comrades to make common progress.

The mass line must be followed in the present party consolidation. First of all, we should take full heed of the opinions of the masses of party members and party organizations at the lower levels and give full play to the positive role of the party members in consolidating the party. In the meantime, we should also fully heed the opinions of non-party members. We should actively consider and accept all correct opinions, and give explanations if the opinions put forward are wrong. All the problems arising in the course of party consolidation should be solved through discussions by the related party organizations. On no account should the past erroneous practice of "letting the masses consolidate the party" or letting non-party members decide issues in the party be repeated.

In the process of consolidating the party organizations, we should resolutely and promptly solve all problems which can be solved immediately so that people both inside the party and out can see in good time the actual results of the party consolidation.

The production and work of all units should not be disrupted by the work of party consolidation. While doing a good job in the party consolidation, all units should strive to promote production and work.

The Communist Youth League, which is the party's assistant and reserve force, should organize its members to study the documents on party consolidation so as to raise their ideological and political levels.

The party consolidation is aimed at solving the problems within our party. The various democratic parties, therefore, are not required to rectify their style of work and readjust their organizations.

(5) ORGANIZATIONAL MEASURES AND REGISTRATION OF PARTY MEMBERS

Organizational measures towards party members should, generally speaking, be taken in the latter period of the party consolidation.

For party members who have committed minor errors,

the stress is placed on criticism and education, and they are required to correct their mistakes in an earnest way. For party members who have made grave mistakes, due disciplinary action should be taken towards them, in addition to criticism and education. Party members who have violated administrative discipline should be dealt with by the administrative departments according to administrative discipline; those who have violated the state law should be dealt with by the judicial organs according to law. If we fail to resolutely expel members who should be expelled from the party, we will not be able to maintain the solemnity of party discipline and purify the party organizations, and this will inevitably affect our party's fighting power.

When taking organizational measures towards party members, we should uphold the principle of seeking the truth from facts and strictly abide by the procedures prescribed in the party Constitution. No ratios or quotas whatsoever should be fixed beforehand in this regard.

After rectifying ideological and organizational matters and work style, and after handling issues that should be handled, every party organization should finally carry out, in a prudent way, the registration of party members.

(a) Party members who are up to, or basically up to, the requirements for party membership are allowed to register.

(b) Party members who are still basically not up to the requirements after education, but who have expressed the determination and have through their deeds shown that they are willing to mend their ways and to be tested by the party, may have their registration postponed for no longer than two years. Registration of party members who have been placed on probation within the party as a disciplinary measure should also be postponed.

(c) Party members whose revolutionary will has waned, who do not honour their obligations as party members, who cannot live up to the requirements for party membership, or who refuse to repent despite repeated help and education should be persuaded to withdraw from the party and should not be allowed to register.

(d) Party members who request to quit the party, or those who have already given up their memberships and refuse to participate in the party consolidation should have their names removed from the party and should not be allowed to register.

Whether a party member should be allowed to register or not or whether his registration should be postponed should be discussed and decided upon at the meeting of all members of the party branch. The names of party members whose registration is to be postponed or who are to be refused registration should be submitted to the party organization at the higher level for approval. Party members whose registration is postponed do not have the right to vote, elect or be elected. Party members who have met the requirements for membership by the time the period of postponement expires should be allowed to register, and those who fail to meet the requirements should have their names removed from the party.

Conscientious ideological and political work should be done among party members whose registration has been postponed so as to help them pull themselves together and strive to make progress and become qualified party members as quickly as possible.

Solicitude should also be shown, ideologically and politically, to those who have been refused registration; they should be united with and encouraged to be good citizens or good cadres.

(6) GUARD AGAINST PERFUNCTORINESS

Leading party cadres at all levels, especially the high-ranking cadres, should play a truly exemplary role in guarding against perfunctoriness in the work of consolidating the party organizations. Leading cadres of every party organization should actively participate in the party consolidation as ordinary members. They should be strict in analysing themselves and be courageous in making sincere, profound and realistic self-criticisms of their own mistakes and shortcomings; and they should also dare to use the same attitude in criticizing other leading cadres' mistakes and shortcomings. In this way they will be able to lead the masses of party members to make party consolidation a success.

To prevent the party consolidation from proceeding perfunctorily, it is also necessary for the party organization at the higher level to supervise its subordinate organizations and vice versa. The party organization at the higher level should strengthen its leadership over its subordinate organizations and strictly supervise their work of party consolidation, as well as study and help solve in good time their problems arising in the course of the party consolidation. Every party member should play a supervisory role and actively report, with a high sense of responsibility, problems in the party consolidation of his own unit to the party organization of his unit or to the party committee at the higher level. The main leading members of every party organization should be held responsible for the success or failure of consolidating their own organization, and the party committee at the higher level should also assume responsibility. The party organization at the higher level should promptly inform its subordinate organizations of the situation in its own consolidation, so that they can exercise supervision and put forward their criticisms.

To guard against perfunctoriness in the party consolidation, the party committee at the higher level should organize acceptance tests whenever a subordinate organization has finished its consolidation work. Such acceptance tests should have the participation of representatives of the party members and should proceed by fully soliciting the opinions of the masses of party members. The standards for the acceptance tests are as follows:

(a) Can the leading body correctly implement the party's line, principles and policies and maintain political unity with the party Central Committee and has it become a united and strong leading core?

(b) Have stern measures been taken against antiparty elements and those who have brought damage to the party, especially the three types of persons?

(c) Have the problems much criticized inside and outside the party been earnestly solved, especially the problem of taking advantage of one's position, power and other conveniences to seek personal gains?

(d)   Has the party members' political quality been raised? Have they heightened their sense of organization and discipline, and are they capable of conscientiously implementing the party Constitution and actively playing an exemplary vanguard role? Have the primary party organizations given full play to their role as fighting bastions and have they strengthened their ties with the masses?

(e)   Has noticeable progress been achieved in the production and work under the charge of the party organization concerned?

Resolute remedial measures should be taken whenever a party organization is found to have failed to fulfill any of these five requirements. The consolidation of party organizations conducted on a trial basis before the announcement of this decision should be recognized as valid if they pass the acceptance tests and are found to be up to the five requirements mentioned above. But those party organizations which are not up to the requirements should make up for what they lack.

While preventing the party consolidation from proceeding perfunctorily, attention should be paid to guard against the erroneous practice of the past of ruthless struggle and merciless attack. It is absolutely impermissible for anyone to take advantage of the party consolidation to whip up factionalism, to use factionalism to persecute others, to make false charges or to retaliate against others against whom he bears a grudge. Anyone who commits any of these offenses will be duly punished.

(7) THE LEADERSHIP OF PARTY CONSOLIDATION

The party Central Committee has decided to establish a Central Commission for Guiding Party Consolidation and to set up competent administrative bodies. The commission will function under the leadership of the party Central Committee and its main tasks include keeping abreast of the situation, firmly grasping the party's policies, supervising and checking up on work, giving guidance and doing publicity work. In the course of party consolidation, the commission will issue in succession various supplementary stipulations and issue in good time, circulars on important matters, problems and experiences concerning party consolidation so as to ensure the implementation of the decision made by the party Central Committee on party consolidation.

In accordance with the plan of the party Central Committee, the party committees of the various provinces, municipalities and autonomous regions will complete the reform of organizations at the county and commune (township) levels in 1984 so as to facilitate the work of party consolidation at these two levels.

The present party consolidation will be conducted under the leadership of the party organizations of the respective localities, departments and units, and the party organization at the higher level should have a clear knowledge of whether the leading bodies of the party organizations at the lower levels have any serious problems. In the course of party consolidation, the higher party organization will, generally speaking, not send any work groups. For those units where the situation is complicated and problems are serious and where the leading bodies are not in a position to take upon themselves the task of party consolidation and therefore work groups must be sent by the higher party organizations, the work groups should be headed by responsible cadres of the higher party organizations. Their task is to help reshuffle the leading bodies, after which the leading bodies that have thus been set up will lead the work of party consolidation.

The party committees at and above the county level should select a number of comrades who are strong in party spirit and good in their style of work, and who have a deep knowledge of the party's ideological and organizational work, including veteran comrades who have retired from work in the "front line."

These comrades will be sent, after study and training in the work of party consolidation, to the subordinate units as liaison men or inspectors. Their main task is to gain a better understanding of the situation, have a firm grasp of the trends, heed the opinions of the people from various quarters, report in good time to the local party organizations and higher party committees and put forward proposals.

The task of the present party consolidation is a very arduous one. The major responsible comrades of the party committees at all levels should, therefore, go deep into the realities, strengthen their investigations and studies, personally lead the work at one or two selected spots to get first-hand material, sum up and popularize in good time the typical experience gained in the work of party consolidation. They should dare to take up and cope with the problems cropping up during the party consolidation, and they should dare to tackle hard and difficult cases and correct errors in good time.

(8) CONSOLIDATE AND DEVELOP THE ACHIEVEMENTS OF PARTY CONSOLIDATION

In the later stage of party consolidation, efforts should be made by party organizations at all levels to consolidate and develop the achievements of party consolidation through ideological education, the institution of appropriate systems and organizational building so that the work of party building will be pushed forward further.

After this party consolidation, we should strengthen our daily ideological and political work among party members. Ideological and political education among party members should be regular and systematized. We should, in the light of the actual conditions of the party organizations and the practice in China's socialist modernization, carry out systematic education among party members in the basic theories of Marxism, in the essential knowledge and fine traditions of the party and in the party's principles and policies. We should also carry out education among party members in the socialist legal system and in scientific and cultural knowledge which is indispensable to the modernization drive.

After this party consolidation, we should strive to establish the various necessary systems to improve and reform life within the party. Regular activities of party organizations should be further improved so that party members and cadres will in this way receive rigorous training and the effective supervision of the party organizations. The struggle against the decadent ideology of the bourgeoisie and other exploiting classes will be a protracted one and comrades throughout the party should on no account relax their vigilance.

During and after the consolidation of the party, attention should be paid to admitting into the party outstanding people who are willing to dedicate themselves to the socialist and communist cause. In view of the fact that there are only a small number of party members in the forefront of industrial production and in transport and communications, finance and trade and only a small number of party members among the young peasants and students, that a number of intellectuals who are already up to the requirements for party membership have not been admitted into the party, and that there are not many women or members of the minority nationalities in the party, the stress of recruiting new party members at present should be laid on the workers and staff members working in the front line of industry, transport and communications, finance and trade, young peasants, PLA soldiers and officers, intellectuals in all trades and professions and students in the universities and colleges and secondary technical schools. Greater attention should be paid to recruiting women and people of minority nationalities as party members. In recruiting new party members, it is necessary to adhere to the requirements for party membership and ensure the quality of the party members. We must see to it that anyone who has met the requirements should be admitted accordingly. Closed-doorism should be avoided and hasty admission into the party without going through the necessary procedures is forbidden.

(9) PARTY ORGANIZATIONS AT VARIOUS LEVELS MUST RESOLUTELY AND CREATIVELY IMPLEMENT THIS DECISION

This decision has put forward the basic principles, tasks, policies and methods for the present party consolidation. Party organizations in the various places, departments and units should combine these principles, policies and methods with their actual conditions and draw up concrete plans for implementation. While faithfully following the various stipulations in the decision, they should creatively implement them. With regard to the four tasks listed in the decision for the present party consolidation, party organizations in the various places, departments and units may put the emphasis on certain aspects in the light of their actual conditions. Party committees at various levels should see to it that the present party consolidation should not under any circumstance obstruct the continuous implementation of the party's various principles and policies on opening to the outside world and enlivening the domestic economy.

In the long years of revolutionary struggle, our party has fostered the fine tradition of strengthening party building mainly through ideological education. Now our party has had the negative experience of the "left" mistakes committed in the 10-year domestic turmoil and before then; it also has had the positive experience of successfully setting things to rights since the third plenary session of the 11th party Central Committee, and it has a complete series of correct principles and policies for party consolidation. Moreover, it has a large number of long-tested loyal proletarian fighters as the mainstay in the present party consolidation, and the majority of the party organizations and party members are good or fairly good, while the broad masses of people actively support our work in consolidating the party. With these conditions and through the concerted efforts of the party organizations at various levels and the party members, our party will surely carry forward its fine traditions and successfully fulfill the tasks of the present party consolidation.

The party Central Committee believes that this party consolidation is certain to raise the level of Marxism of the whole party, enable the party to brim with still greater vitality and vigour, and bring about a new atmosphere of working with a will to make the country strong and close unity throughout the party. If the Yanan rectification movement in 1942 enabled the party to achieve a high degree of unity in thinking, guaranteed victory in the war of resistance against Japan and the war of liberation, and led to the founding of the People's Republic of China, the present party consolidation will certainly enable our party to provide better leadership for the people of all nationalities throughout the country to win great victories in the socialist modernization drive.

The ninetieth anniversary of Mao Zedong's birth fell on 26 December 1983. This article is devoted to his rectification campaign of the early 1940s, a major step in the establishment of his domination over the Party and one clearly designed to reinforce Deng Xiaoping's current Party rectification.

This year, when we are marking the 90th birthday of Comrade Mao Zedong, our party has just begun the all-round party rectification in accordance with the decision of the 2d Plenary Session of the 12th CPC Central Committee. The current party rectification will be another party rectification of great significance and far-reaching effect since the 1942 Yanan rectification. It is very meaningful for us to review the historical experiences of the Yanan rectification and to study in these particular days the relevant discussions of Comrade Mao Zedong. This is also a very good way to commemorate the late Comrade Mao Zedong.

The Yanan rectification was a most brilliant page in our party history; it was also a great pioneering undertaking in the international communist movement. It has played and continues to play a tremendous role in the course of our party building.

It was by no means accidental that the Yanan rectification should have taken place in the early 1940's. It was the inevitable necessity of the development of the Chinese revolution at that time, with a profound historical background.

Our party had a history of two decades from its founding to the early 1940's. During that period, the Chinese revolution had achieved great victories while suffering serious setbacks; there were experiences of successes and also lessons in failure. In order to lead the Chinese resolution to continue marching forward, it was extremely necessary for our party to sum up the experiences of the Chinese revolution so that the whole party might draw a demarcation line between the correct guiding ideology and the wrong one, further master the scientific thinking of combining Marxist-Leninist theory with the practice of the Chinese revolution, heighten the conscientiousness of implementing the correct line, principle, and policy, and on this basis, realize the unification of the whole party in ideology and politics and unanimity in action.

Between the Zunyi meeting and the Sixth Plenary Session of the Sixth CPC Central Committee, our party criticized and corrected Wang Ming's "Leftist" errors in the latter part of the 10-year civil war and his rightist errors at the initial stage of the war of resistance against Japan. Nonetheless, because there was not enough time to sum up systematically on a partywide scope the historical experiences and lessons of the party and to carry on overall

[Feng Xianzhi, "The Yanan Rectification is Comrade Mao Zedong's Contribution to Party Building," *Red Flag*, 1 December 1983.]

ideological education from the top to the grassroots level with leadership, the pernicious effects of Wang Ming's errors, which were mainly subjectivism and sectarianism expressed in the effects of stereotyped party writing in the whole party, had not been eliminated. It impeded the unification and unanimity of the party, and even continued to bring injuries to the revolutionary cause in some regions and some aspects in a certain period. Some comrades within the party lacked correct understanding of Wang Ming's errors, while others, though they understood such errors, were not very clear about why such errors should have taken place and what could have been the causes of them.

After the war of resistance against Japan broke out, a large number of revolutionaries of petite bourgeois origin joined the party. They had revolutionary enthusiasm but had not received a comparatively systematic education in Marxism and had not gone through strict ideological remolding. They had brought with them into the party some petite bourgeois and non-proletarian ideas, feelings, and styles. It was easier for them to accept and appreciate some empty revolutionary phrases and to display shortcomings and defects that were counter to the requirements for the party spirit of the proletariat. These new party members accounted for an overwhelming majority in the party at that time. This provided certain soil for the growth of subjectivism, sectarianism, and party jargon in the party.

The CPC Central Committee and Comrade Mao Zedong initiated the partywide rectification campaign precisely to change the situation of incomplete unanimity in ideological thinking and the rather complicated ideological conditions inside the party. At that time, our party was at the most difficult stage of the anit-Japanese war, which was then locked in a stalemate. In order to overcome the difficulties, it was also necessary and possible to carry out a party-wide rectification.

The universal rectification at that time had gone through long-term preparations in politics, ideology, theory, and organization. As Comrade Mao Zedong put it, such preparations had been in progress since the Zunyi meeting, and the period of preparations could be roughly divided into two stages.

During the period between the Zunyi meeting and the time prior to the Sixth Plenary Session of the Sixth CPC Central Committee, Comrade Mao Zedong summed up the experiences of the Chinese revolution in its political line and military line separately, criticized Wang Ming's political strategy of "leftist" closed-doorism and his military "leftist" dogmatism, and formulated the correct political tactics and the strategy and tactics of the Chinese revolutionary war. He continued to sum up the experiences of the Chinese revolution on the high plane of Marxist world outlook and methodology, revealing the essence of the errors of dogmatism, and thus provided a powerful philosophical-ideological weapon for the party-wide rectification.

During the period between the Sixth Plenary Session of the Sixth CPC Central Committee and the time prior to the beginning of the 1942 party-wide rectification, our party corrected Wang Ming's error of rightist capitulationism at the initial stage of the anti-Japanese War. The dominating position of the correct line, with Comrade Mao Zedong as its representative, was further consolidated and strengthened in the whole party.

Comrade Mao Zedong continued to do a tremendous amount of work in ideological theory, systematically expounded the basic principle of Marxism on combining theory with practice, and criticized the erroneous ideas of subjectivism. At the proposal of Comrade Mao Zedong, the CPC Central Committee organized senior cadres of the party to study the basic theories of Marxism-Leninism, to study and do research on the party history, to sum up the historical experiences of the party, and to clarify what was right or wrong in the political line. As a result, a fundamentally unanimous understanding was reached on the basis of Marxism-Leninism and a basic condition was created for the party-wide rectification.

By the spring of 1942, the condition for a partywide rectification was ripe and the universal unfolding of the rectification campaign was then an inevitability. In February that year, Comrade Mao Zedong made the well-known speeches "Rectify the Party's Style of Work" and "Oppose Stereotyped Party Writing," and explicitly proposed that the tasks for the party-wide rectification should be opposing subjectivism so as to rectify the style in studying, opposing sectarianism so as to rectify the party's style, and opposing stereotyped party writing so as to rectify the style of writing. Thereupon, a party-wide universal rectification campaign began.

II

The most important task of the Yanan rectification was to oppose subjectivism, to solve the contradiction between Marxism and subjectivism inside the party, and to arm the whole party with the principle of combining Marxist-Leninist theory with the practice of the Chinese revolution.

Over a long period of time, our party had been dominated by subjectivism. The injuries inflicted on the party by subjectivism had been extremely grave; it had almost ruined the cause of the Chinese revolution. Whether it was the rightist opportunism of Chen Duxiu or the "leftist" opportunism of Wang Ming, both their ideologies took root in subjectivism.

Nonetheless, people had not understood this problem for a long time. Therefore, errors had continued to take place in succession. Take the period of the Second Civil War. As soon as Comrade Qu Qiubai's error was corrected, there appeared the error of Comrade Li Lisan. No sooner was Comrade Li Lisan's error corrected than there was the error of Wang Ming.

There were mistakes time and again, while in their

ideology there was one thing in common, namely, the divorce of theory from practice and the incongruity between the subjective will and the objective realities. They did not proceed from the actual conditions in understanding and solving problems, but proceeded from books or their subjective will or copied foreign experiences.

Since the Zunyi meeting, the CPC Central Committee, with Comrade Mao Zedong as its representative, had proceeded from the actual conditions and formulated and implemented a line, principles, and policies in conformity with the objective conditions which enabled the Chinese revolution to adopt a road of victorious development. It can be clearly seen from the positive and negative experiences of the Chinese revolution that to oppose and correct subjectivism in the guiding ideology of the party is a matter of life and death of our party.

Under the circumstances at that time, dogmatism, among various forms of the ideological methodology of subjectivism, was the greatest danger to the revolution. Dogmatists had once bewildered and captured many people, and it was not easy to reveal the errors of dogmatism and to eliminate its pernicious effects. The Marxist explanations which Comrade Mao Zedong made on the definitions of theory and theorists played an important role in exposing the deception of dogmatism.

He said: "There is only one genuine theory in the world, namely, the theory drawn from and again proved by objective practice. Save that, no other things in question are worth the name of theory." ("Selected Works of Mao Zedong," Vol. 3, p. 775) Only when we study and solve practical problems with a Marxist view is it possible for us to give the problem a scientific explanation and a theoretical demonstration and for us to become the theorists and needed by our party. ("Selected Works of Mao Zedong," vol. 3, p. 772)

These incisive discussions by Comrade Mao Zedong clarified some muddled ideas which had long existed within the party and raised people's ideological understanding to a new level, enabling some people who had committed errors of dogmatism or who had been deceived by it to widely wake up from their perplexity and to understand that empty theories divorced from practice were not genuine theories and that such "theories" were not only of no help but very harmful to the revolution. People who can only recite some phrases of Marxism-Leninism but do not apply them, or who do not know how to apply them can not be counted as theorists by any means.

In the struggle against subjectivism, with dogmatism as its chief expression, Comrade Mao Zedong specially emphasized that communists should devote their efforts to the study of the actual conditions of China, including its history and present conditions. It was necessary to have a grasp of the spiritual essence of Marxism-Leninism, to apply it to the concrete environment of China, to link Marxist-Leninist theories with the practice of the Chinese revolution, and to create new things in China.

Dogmatists such as Wang Ming precisely ran counter to this. They only talked about the experiences of foreign countries uncritically. They lived only on books and had fundamentally "forgotten their duty to learn and create new things." ("Selected Works of Mao Zedong," Vol. 3, p. 756) They themselves had no positive initiatives, but destroyed the initiatives in others, suppressing the growth of all new ideas.

During their control of the whole party, revolutionary ideas were uninformed and their thinking became ossified. As a result, there was no vitality to speak of in the party, and the Chinese revolution was led almost into a dead alley. Therefore, the Yanan rectification had to primarily aim against dogmatism inside the party, in particular, Wang Ming's "leftist" dogmatism.

Stereotyped party writing was the expression of subjectivism in the style of writing; without the elimination of stereotyped party writing, lively revolutionary ideas would fail to be inspired, the truth-seeking spirit would fail to be carried forward, and there would still be a hiding place for subjectivism. Therefore, in order to thoroughly oppose subjectivism, it was necessary to oppose stereotyped party writing simultaneously.

We should point out: The struggle against subjectivism and dogmatism did not mean in any sense that their study of Marxist-Leninist theories could be relaxed or neglected in the least; instead, stronger stress on the important task of studying theory was made. In the party history, the reason why the erroneous leadership of dogmatism was able to dominate the whole party was precisely the weakness of a low level of understanding of Marxism-Leninism on the part of the whole party (and of course, the low level of understanding in the Chinese revolution). People failed to recognize the pseudo-Marxist-Leninist things spread by dogmatists, and even if they did, they lacked the theoretical weapon to fight against them.

Comrade Mao Zedong had long felt the seriousness of this problem. He not only proposed to the whole party the task of studying Marxist-Leninist theories, but earnestly practiced what he advocated and devoted tremendous efforts in studying Marxist-Leninist theories with China's revolutionary practice, and had written many famous works on Marxism-Leninism. He also gave direct guidance to the leading comrades in the CPC Central Committee on studying Marxist philosophy.

The Yanan rectification was unfolded on the basis of the requirement that senior cadres should work hard to master Marxist-Leninist theories, while the theoretical level of the whole party was heightened in the course of the rectification. At the expanded conference of the Political Bureau held in September 1941, Comrade Mao Zedong proposed the theorization of the Chinese revolution in line with Marxism, so as to expound the importance of summing up the experience of the Chinese revolution with Marxist theories. This idea is of great theoretical value and significance in practice. Together with the idea of "making Marxism concrete in China," it has demonstrated the ideological principle of linking the universal truth of Marxism-Leninism with the concrete practice of the Chinese revolution in two aspects.

"The truth of Marxism-Leninism will rise only when subjectivism is overthrown." (Selected Works of Mao Zedong," Vol. 3, p. 758) The Yanan rectification criticized subjectivism, dogmatism in particular, on the one hand; on the other, it developed the principle of combining Marxism-Leninism with the practice of the Chinese revolution. Thus, the spirit of the broad party members was enabled to be emancipated from the bondage of subjectivism, in particular, dogmatism. That is why the Yanan rectification was said to be a great ideological emancipation campaign, which has opened up a broad way for the development of Marxism-Leninism in China.

The greatest feat of the Yanan rectification was to make the whole party master the fundamental orientation of combining Marxism-Leninism with China's revolutionary practice and to learn the method of solving practical problems of the revolution with Marxist-Leninist theories. Thus, it established the ideological unification of the party on this basis.

III

Opposing sectarianism was another major task for the Yanan rectification.

In order to realize the unification of the whole party, it was not enough to achieve unification in ideology; there also had to be unification in organization, with which to guarantee the unification of ideology. The struggle against sectarianism was to solve the problem of ensuring the unification of the whole party in the organizational line.

In the party history, subjectivism and sectarianism coexisted and were interdependent. While the guiding ideology was subjectivism, the organizational line was inevitably sectarian. Sectarianism developed with the growth of subjectivism, and conversely supported the domination of the leadership of subjectivism, helping the growth of subjectivism. Therefore, in order to thoroughly oppose subjectivism, it was essential to thoroughly oppose sectarianism at the same time.

After the Zunyi Conference, sectarianism no longer played the dominant role inside the party. However, its remnants still existed, for instance, mountain stronghold mentality, small group mentality, disunity between one department or region with another, and so on.

The various expressions of sectarianism within the party, as listed by Comrade Mao Zedong in "Rectify the Style of the Party," all had to be opposed and corrected.

However, the most dangerous of them, which would bring the greatest injury to the party, was the refusal to obey the leadership. It sabotaged the unification of the party, injured the unity of the party, and was fundamentally antagonistic to the organizational principle of the proletarian political party, and it had to be resolutely opposed and corrected in particular.

Those who refuse to obey the leadership fail to acquire an overall point of view. They are incorrect in handling the relation between the interests of the part and the interests of the whole, "they always put undue stress on that part of the work for which they themselves are responsible and always wish to subordinate the interests of the whole to the interests of their own part." ("Selected Works of Mao Zedong," Vol. 3, p. 779) They even injure and sacrifice the interests of the whole for the interests of the part.

They have no sense of discipline. They forget that the minority is subordinate to the majority, that the lower level is subordinate to the higher level, that the part is subordinate to the whole. In particular, they forget the most fundamental principle inside the party—that the whole is subordinate to the party Central Committee. They disregard the principle that the party Central Committee is to concentrate the will of the whole party, holding themselves wiser than the party Central Committee. They attach no attention to the resolutions and instructions of the Central Committee, while going their own way; or obey part of them, while disobeying the rest, obeying the part that suits them, or vice versa. "They have confused the correct things as bringing forward the ability to work independently and the creativity of Marxism with erroneous things such as disobeyance of the higher level, disobeyance of the majority, disobeyance of the party Central Committee, making the individual antagonistic to the party and above the party (making oneself conspicuous), and individualistic heroism (which differs from national heroism and heroism of the masses). (Outline for propaganda drafted by Mao Zedong for the Propaganda Department under the CPC Central Committee, 26 January 1942.)

They have no sense of unity. They fail to understand that the unity of the party is the lifeline of the party and that the unique center of unity of the party is the party Central Committee. The party organizations and work of any region or any department are an inseparable part, under the unified leadership of the Central Committee.

They have no sense of the masses. They are not willing to make the interests of their own minority subject to the interests of the whole party and the whole people. They only think of the interests of a minority of people and totally forget the interests of the whole party and the whole people. In cadre policy, they appoint people by favoritism but not on their merits. They draw people of their kind over to their side, while elbowing out and attacking those who disagree with their opinion. They gang up to be factions, forming a system of their own.

Zhang Guotao was an extremely grave example of asserting independence from the Central Committee of the party. Comrade Mao Zedong often cited this example to warn the whole party, to prevent the occurrence of such a phenomenon, and to eliminate various phenomena of disunification. Comrade Mao Zedong said: "We should encourage comrades to take the interests of the whole into account. Every party member, every branch of work, every statement, and every action must proceed from the interests of the whole party. It is absolutely impermissible to violate this principle." ("Selected Works of Mao Zedong," Vol. 3, p. 779) This should become a motto for every one of us communists.

Comrade Mao Zedong pointed out: Those who assert this kind of "independence" are usually wedded to the doctrine of "me first" and are generally wrong on the question of the relationship between the individual and the party. Although in words they profess respect for the party, in practice they put themselves first and the party second.

This analysis by Comrade Mao Zedong is applicable not only to those who assert independence, but to all who are engaged in sectarianism. To oppose sectarianism is in essence to solve the problem of the relations between the individual and the party and between the part and the whole.

Sectarianism is an expression of individualism of the bourgeoisie and petite bourgeoisie interwoven with the mentality of the feudal guild system inside the party. It is diametrically opposed to the party spirit of the proletariat and the spirit of communism. Those who have not gone through education in Marxism, those who have not been strictly trained in part spirit are easily stained with the mentality of sectarianism and make it grow in them.

Therefore, it is absolutely essential to conduct ideological education within the party in taking the interests of the whole into account, observing discipline, consolidating unity, and setting up ties with the masses, and to conduct education in the party spirit of subjecting personal interests to the interests of the party while advocating the spirit of communism. The struggle against sectarianism in the Yanan rectification was to conduct systematic education in this field among party cadres and the broad party members.

IV

The Yanan rectification was a struggle of Marxism against subjectivism, of proletarian ideology against non-proletarian ideology. In this struggle, various non-proletarian ideologies could not but give expression to themselves, and liberalism was one of the most conspicuous of them.

Liberalism existed rather universally and seriously inside the party at that time. Some people failed to tell right from wrong politically and ideologically, failing to criticize or wage struggle against erroneous speeches, but coexisted with erroneous ideas in peace and went so far as to show sympathy for them. They resented the practice of criticism of erroneous speeches and were sentimental toward those who had been criticized for their erroneous speeches, holding that the criticism had gone to extremes.

Some people advocated absolute freedom of speech and action; they denied and even felt disgusted with the party's principle and the sense of organization and discipline. They put their personal opinions in first place while caring not for organization and discipline. Grounded on the stress for "democracy," some people advocated the free development of various kinds of ideology and opposed the correction of erroneous ideas in accordance with party principle on the part of the leadership. Some people violated the party's principle, arbitrarily spreading all kinds of rumors that injured the party and the interests of the revolution, and so on and so forth. All these expressions of liberalism in ideology, politics, and organization gravely injured the unified will, unified action, and unified discipline of the party.

Therefore, it was very essential for the Central Committee of the party and Comrade Mao Zedong to regard correcting the trend of liberalism as an important part of the rectification to be carried out universally in the whole party.

When speaking of problems concerning the rectification, Comrade Mao Zedong and comrades in leading posts of the localities at that time, such as Comrade Deng Xiaoping, placed the struggle against liberalism on the same important plane as the struggle against subjectivism, sectarianism, and stereotyped party writing.

Directed at the situation of the flood of liberalism and various erroneous ideas, Comrade Mao Zedong proposed that it was essential to refute erroneous ideas in an organized way.

Speaking of this problem in a report made to an advanced study group on 28 May 1942, he said: In a place where communists are in the majority, it happens that no one stands out and refutes erroneous ideas when they appeal. Some people lack the courage to refute erroneous ideas when they actually know those ideas to be wrong. It is essential to expand the effects of Marxism, and erroneous opinions should not be developed. The growth of petite bourgeois ideology has affected the growth of the correct ideology of the proletariat in breadth. When an erroneous opinion occurs, a communist should uphold principle and immediately refute the opinion.

On the one hand, free expression should be given to whatever opinions; on the other, refutation should be organized against erroneous views. These two aspects are inseparable. This statement by Comrade Mao Zedong has demonstrated the firm Marxist stand which a communist should take.

The Zunyi Meeting held in January 1935 ended the domination of the Central Committee of the party by the "leftist" errors with Wang Ming as the representative, and reestablished the correct line.

However, there also appeared some mistakes and deviations after the Zunyi meeting; they were chiefly the growth of liberalism. Comrade Mao Zedong pointed out: Before the Zunyi meeting, the main trend within the party was "leftism" and struggle which had been carried to extremes. After the Zunyi meeting, the chief bad tendency within the party was liberalism. Though struggle which had been carried to extremes still existed, and in some places the phenomenon was still rather grave, it was no longer the main trend in the whole party. Nonetheless, some comrades who had committed "leftist" errors in the past, again committed mistakes of rightist liberalism after the Zunyi conference.

After the Zunyi meeting, our party implemented the correct policy of leniency inside and outside the party in correcting "leftist" errors. For instance, inside the party, whoever had committed a mistake would be dealt with in accordance with the lenient policy so long as he resolutely corrected himself. This policy had achieved a good result. Nonetheless, in the concrete implementation of this policy, it had been incorrectly explained by some localities and departments, resulting in changing the lenient policy into liberalism.

Short of a serious attitude in the treatment of cadres, some departments focused on unity and education while neglecting the criticism of and even necessary struggle against their errors. Comrade Mao Zedong pointed out: This was a misunderstanding of the policy of leniency, resulting in benumbing oneself and making oneself muddleheaded. The party's correct policy on cadres should be: First, unity; second, criticism should be practiced when mistakes occur. ("Mao Zedong's Speech at the Senior Cadres Conference of the Shaanxi-Gansu-Ningxia Border Area," November 1942.) When opposing carrying struggle to extremes inside the party, it did not mean to substitute it with unprincipled peace within the party, eliminating active ideological struggle. We should correctly unfold criticism, uphold the truth, and revise our errors.

Back in 1937, Comrade Mao Zedong published the article "Combat Liberalism," listing the various expressions of liberalism inside the revolutionary contingent, revealing its essence and danger, and analyzing the root cause of its occurrence. This is a militant Marxist document. It inspired and guided the broad party members to carry on effective struggle against liberalism in the rectification campaign.

Comrade Mao Zedong pointed out: Liberalism conflicts fundamentally with Marxism. It is negative and objectively has the effect of helping the enemy. ("Selected Works of Mao Zedong," Vol. 2, p. 332) Marxism is, in essence, critical; it criticizes the old world, the bourgeoisie, and other bad things which are non-proletarian. On the other hand,

liberalism eliminates ideological struggle and takes a laissez-faire attitude toward erroneous and ugly phenomena.

The elimination of ideological struggle means to give up the ideological fight of Marxism and to tolerate the attack of non-proletarian ideas against Marxism, permitting them to occupy the ideological field. The growth of liberalism will inevitably give rise to the spread of a decadent, Philistine attitude, "bringing about political degeneration in certain units and individuals in the party and the revolutionary organizations." ("Selected Works of Mao Zedong," Vol. 2, p. 330)

This problem is worthy of our watchful attention. Liberalism, in particular in politics, which regards the line, principles, and policies of the Central Committee of the party with an attitude of liberalism, is the gravest of dangers. Therefore, waging incessant struggles against trends of liberalism is an indispensable condition for building a unified and consolidated party.

Analyzing from an ideological-methodological view, the rise of liberalism inside the party is the failure to match one's deeds with one's words, "looking upon the principles of Marxism as abstract dogma," as Comrade Mao Zedong pointed out. Regarding its social cause, it is the ideology of the petite bourgeoisie, and from a historical view, it takes root in bourgeois liberalism. Our party has been surrounded for a long time by a multitude of the bourgeoisie. During the period of the war of resistance against Japan, class cooperation was practiced in breadth within the united front, bourgeois and petite bourgeois ideas attacked the party from all directions, decaying its body. Under such circumstances, the struggle against liberalism inside the party possessed a particularly important significance.

The fundamental method of the Yanan rectification was to practice criticism and self-criticism through checking up one's work and ideology on the basis of studying documents. In this sense, the Yanan rectification was a criticism and self-criticism campaign in breadth and depth inside the party. Whether it was possible to correctly unfold criticism and self-criticism was the key to success of the rectification.

Criticism and self-criticism is the chief method of solving contradictions within the party. There always exist the contradictions between the advanced and the backward, correctness and errors within the party. Some of them are the expressions of the contradictions between new and old things within the party, others are expressions of class contradictions within the party, and still others are contradictions in cognition. The party's progress is based on the incessant development and solving of these contradictions.

The party's vitality lies in the capability of adopting the method of self-criticism, continuously eliminating and overcoming its own shortcomings, mistakes, and backward things, and preserving and bringing forward its merits, advanced, and correct things.

If the weapon of self-criticism is done away with, the party will lose its vitality, deteriorate, and will even come to an end of its life. At a time when criticism fails to be carried on smoothly, when criticism and self-criticism have not yet formed an atmosphere within the party, the focus on the importance of criticism should be placed first and foremost.

Comrade Mao Zedong once demonstrated and emphasized criticism and self-criticism in line with Marxist methodology. He said: One of the basic methods of Marxism is analysis. Criticism is to implement the method of analysis. Work is a whole, criticism means to analyze our work, to point out its merits and shortcomings, to bring forward the good, and to get rid of the bad. To make an analysis of one's work and one's own history is to practice self-criticism, and to make an analysis of others is to practice criticism of others.

If one considers himself always in the right, makes no analysis of his own work, speaks only of his merits but does not touch upon his shortcomings and errors, it will be impossible for him to make progress in his work. Some comrades who have committed errors of subjectivism do not know the method of analysis. It is essential to take a modest attitude toward one's work, to understand that there is always room for improvement, and to constantly think of the fact that we have shortcomings and errors and that there is room for improvement in our work; only then is it possible for us to make progress. ("Mao Zedong's Speech at the Senior Cadres Conference of the Shaanxi-Gansu-Ningxia Border Area")

Wang Ming, the self-proclaimed 100 percent Bolshevik, was a person who knew nothing of the method of analysis. He affirmed everything concerning himself, with not the least spirit of self-criticism, while toward others (those who did not agree with his erroneous opinions) he would negate everything, wage cruel struggles against them, and deal relentless blows at them.

There are two kinds of criticism: One conforms to the actual conditions and is conducted with the correct method; the other, does not. Comrade Mao Zedong summed up the experiences and lessons in the party's history while proposing a whole set of correct principles and methods of practicing criticism appearing in the rectification. "Learn from past mistakes to avoid future ones, and cure the sickness to save the patient" is a general principle.

The principle of "learning from past mistakes to avoid future ones, and curing the sickness to save the patient" has two meanings. First, mistakes must be exposed without sparing anyone's sensibilities. It is necessary to analyze and criticize what was bad in the past with a scientific attitude so that work in the future will be done more carefully and done better. Second, our aim in exposing errors and criticizing shortcomings, like that of a doctor curing a sickness, is solely to save the patient and not to doctor him to death. So long as the comrade who has made mistakes sincerely wishes to correct them, we should welcome him and cure his sickness so that he can become a good comrade. These two aspects are inseparable.

We must proceed from unity in criticism, and this is the premise. Nonetheless, it will be impossible to achieve unity without going through criticism and self-criticism, without clarifying what is right or wrong. This is the dialectic of unity and criticism. The formula of unity-criticism-unity is in opposition to the method of inner-party struggle of "cruel struggle and relentless attack" by "leftist" dogmatists, as summed up and generalized by Comrade Mao Zedong.

Of course, what we mean by proceeding from unity is proceeding from the unity of the whole party and from the interests of the people of the whole country, but not from the interests of a small group or a sector. This is an important principle.

We should adopt a good attitude in criticism and aim at helping those criticized. Toward our own comrades, we must adopt a comradely attitude. We should not go in for condemning our comrades in freezing irony and burning satire; we should never treat our comrades as we do the enemy. Comrade Mao Zedong said: "Criticism should be strict and acute, but at the same time it should be sincere, frank, and aimed at helping those criticized. Only with this attitude will it be favorable to unity. Freezing irony and burning satire are another kind of corrosive agent, which is unfavorable to unity." ("Mao Zedong's Speech at the Yanan Forum on the Correcting of Jiefang Ribao," 31 March 1942)

Criticism should be truth-seeking. Criticism should be based on facts and should be practiced correctly by analyzing the root cause and environment leading to the mistake with a scientific attitude. Particularly in dealing with ideological problems, it is necessary to reason fully. The practice of over-simplification and being rough will not help solve problems, but will intensify the contradictions.

As the Yanan rectification had implemented correct but not distorted, serious but not superficial criticism and self-criticism, it finally "achieved the two-fold objective of clarity in ideology and unity among comrades" ("Selected Works of Mao Zedong," Vol. 2, p. 892) and the unprecedented unity of the whole party.

V

It is four decades since the Yanan rectification took place. In looking at this event 40 years afterward, more and more do we find its significance unfathomable.

Shortly after the rectification was universally unfolded, Comrade Mao Zedong expressed much determination, saying: It is necessary to thoroughly oppose subjectivism; it must be done well, and it is imperative for us to make such a determination. If the work is not done well, we will do it again; if a poor job is done in second time, we will do it a third time. To make it short, we will do the work thoroughly. If some people should oppose it, it is necessary for us to make explanations. If they are not convinced, we will make more explanations; we must make them completely convinced. To make it short, we must carry the work through to the end. We must rectify the three styles and let there be a thorough ideological change. (Speech by Mao Zedong concerning the rectification of the three styles, 21 April 1942)

As a result of years of concerted efforts by the whole party, the Yanan rectification achieved the purpose of changing the ideological condition of the whole party as Comrade Mao Zedong had expected. "Ensuring the unanimity of the party in ideology and politics and the purity of the composing elements of party organization" (Speech by Mao Zedong at the soiree marking the 22nd Anniversary of the founding of the CPC and the 6th anniversary of the war of resistance against Japan, 1 July 1943) Our party stood before the Chinese people with a brand new feature.

The initiation and leadership of the Yanan rectification campaign was one of the great contributions of Comrade Mao Zedong in party building. On the basis of summing up the Yanan rectification, he set up a fine ideological style and work style for the CPC, formed a complete doctrine in party building, enriched and developed

Marxism-Leninism in the theory of party building, and left us a precious spiritual wealth that should be passed down generation after generation. The Yanan rectification has educated several generations of Chinese communists, including the older generation of revolutionaries of our party. It is through them that the fine tradition formed in the Yanan rectification is passed down generation after generation, enabling our party to stand whatever test of hardship and danger.

The reasons for the tremendous success of the Yanan rectification were many, and the most important points are: First, the Central Committee of the party, with Comrade Mao Zedong as its representative was united and unanimous, and they were unified in ideological cognition. Second, the party's line, principles, and policies since the Zunyi meeting had been proved to be correct by practice and understood by the broad party members. Third, the main trend of the party was good. Correct style and healthy strength had a dominant place inside the party, while unhealthy tendencies held a secondary place. Fourth, the Central Committee of the party formulated a whole set of correct principles, policies, measures, and methods in guiding the rectification campaign. Fifth, there had been long-standing preparations in ideology and theory.

Historical experiences have demonstrated that after our party corrected an erroneous guiding ideology that had dominated the whole party, reestablished the correct line, and realized a historic change, it was inevitable to unfold an all-round party rectification with unifying ideology and rectifying style as its main target.

This conforms to the law of historical phenomena. On the one hand, it is necessary to eliminate the remnants and efforts of erroneous ideas of the past; on the other, it is necessary to solve new problems emerging under the new historical condition so that the whole party may unite as one in leading the Chinese revolutionary cause to advance in big strides on the basis of Marxism-Leninism. It was so with the Yanan rectification, and it is the same case with the party rectification we are carrying on today.

However, our conditions today are greatly different from those of the Yanan days. Our party has become the leading party of the political power of the whole country, and the contingent of the party has grown much larger. Having gone through the 10 years of turmoil of the "Cultural Revolution," the party's fine style has been greatly sabotaged. The impurity of organization is more serious than it was in the Yanan days. The party is in a more complicated historical environment than it was before. The corrosion of various non-proletarian ideas has grown more serious, ideas which have corrupted and are corrupting some communists.

At the same time, our party is facing the complicated and arduous task of modernization. Therefore, the concrete tasks of our current party rectification are different from those of the Yanan rectification; it possesses new characteristics and new contents. It will not only universally carry on education in Marxism-Leninism and rectify ideological style as it did in the Yanan rectification, but will focus on the weeding out in organization, which will be regarded as an important target in the current party rectification. Even so, the basic experiences of the Yanan rectification are still of realistic significance today; we have the same essential conditions for success as the Yanan rectification. In addition, our party has accumulated many new experiences. Therefore, we are sure to say that the current party rectification will certainly achieve the same great victory as the Yanan rectification.

Back in 1945, Comrade Mao Zedong explained the significance of the Yanan rectification at the height of summing up the historical experiences of the party. He said: We did not win victory either in the northern expedition war or the agrarian revolutionary war. This was because, objectively, the strength of imperialism and the KMT was powerful and, subjectively, it was because we were not spiritually prepared, we were muddleheaded, and there were mistakes in our policies.

At present, regarding the objective conditions at home and abroad, there is the possibility of our winning victory. The question is that we should be spiritually prepared. The rectification in recent years is to make spiritual preparation for the victory, to prepare the CPC for the nationwide victory. (Mao Zedong's speech at the central party school, 25 February 1845) The Yanan rectification in the forties had spiritually prepared conditions for the nationwide victory of the new democratic revolution. Likewise, we can also say that the current party rectification of the eighties is spiritually preparing the conditions for the victory of the socialist modernizations.

In his speech made in April 1942, Comrade Mao Zedong had this to say on the historical role of the Yanan rectification: To overcome the present difficulties, to welcome a bright future, and to create a new world, we should make the same estimation of the party rectification we are carrying on today.

Central Committee Circular No. 7 on Rectification, 4 March 1984

This document makes it clear that the Party consolidation desired by Deng Xiaoping was still very much in progress in March 1984, although the anti-"spiritual pollution" campaign so highly valued by the radicals was being abandoned.

1. Some units that are undertaking party rectification have now entered or are going to enter the comparison and examination stage when criticism and self-criticism should be made. Party committees and leading party members' groups of various provinces, autonomous regions, and municipalities as well as various ministries and commissions at the central level must act according to the three main criteria for studying party rectification documents without perfunctoriness as stipulated by the Central Commission for Guiding Party Rectification—that is, the three main criteria for judging whether a party rectification unit can go from the stage of studying the documents to the stage of comparison and examination—and take up the responsibility to check the work and ensure that the criteria are met. Any unit meeting these three criteria may enter the comparison and examination stage. Those units not meeting them should assign some time to continue the study of the documents and should not enter the comparison and examination stage in a perfunctory and hasty manner. We must ensure that a unit enters the comparison and examination stage only when it has conditions to do so. In no way should we arbitrarily seek "uniformity" or speed up this process.

2. The comparison and examination state is a key stage in the current party rectification. Guarding against perfunctoriness in making comparison and examination has a decisive effect on ensuring that all party rectification work will be carried out without perfunctoriness and achieve the expected goal. Comparison and examination should be carried out in such a way as to center closely on the general objective of the decision on party rectification which was adopted by the CPC Central Committee. The main purpose of comparison and examination is to carry forward strong points and overcome shortcomings, carry forward positive factors and overcome negative factors, carry forward healthy trends and overcome unhealthy and vile trends, and carry forward the spirit of going onward and being bold in blazing new trails and overcome the idea of following conventions and refusing to make progress. In this way our party organizations will become even more staunch, our party style will be even better, and the vast numbers of our party members and party cadres will raise their consciousness, dispel misgivings, eliminate estrangement, and become more united. In a more vigorous spirit and with one mind, they will work hard to fulfill the general task and objective of the party (quadrupling the annual

gross value of industrial and agricultural production, building the spiritual and material civilization, fulfilling the three major tasks for the 1980's or even the 1990's) and to build socialism with Chinese characteristics. Party committees and leading party members' groups of all provinces, autonomous regions, and municipalities as well as all ministries and commissions at the central level must understand this very clearly and must give careful guidance and pay close attention to comparison and examination work.

3. After the comparison and examination stage begins, further efforts should be exerted to make good, sufficient preparations for the comparison and examination work based on the work of the preceding stage. Three tasks should be done: First, continued efforts should be made to study seriously the documents on party rectification and other relevant documents of the CPC Central Committee in order to further deepen and heighten the understanding of the essential spirit of these documents. This will lay a firmer ideological and political foundation for comparison and examination work. Second, it is necessary to find out accurately, through continued in-depth study, the major problems that exist in the respective departments and units concerning ideology, work style, discipline, and organization and that are incompatible with or even against the party's general task and objective. Efforts should be made to unify the understanding in this regard in the leading bodies and among party cadres and party members and to determine the main direction of comparison and examination work. To do this, it is necessary to persistently go among the masses to seriously solicit the opinions of party members, nonparty friends, and the masses of the respective departments and units and the opinions of the lower-level organs. Third, we should do in-depth and meticulous ideology-stimulating work and promote heart-to-heart talks among party cadres and party members and have them open their hearts to each other in order to eliminate the remnant effect of factionalism and unnecessarily being on guard against each other, and to dispel misunderstanding and enhance their understanding of each other. In the meantime, leading cadres should continue to publicize among the masses of party members the principle and policy of party rectification and should conduct patient education among them so that they will enhance their party spirit, become open and aboveboard, trust the party and masses, and be loyal and honest to the party. Leading cadres should also help some party members get rid of various misgivings, increase their determination and consciousness to remold themselves, overcome the passive feeling that they will be rectified anyway, and do away with

[New China News Agency, 4 March 1984.]

the idea of behaving as a good man who never offends others. This will create a good atmosphere for carrying out comparison and examination and for making criticism and self-criticism.

4. Comparison and examination should be conducted from the top down; that is, first by leading bodies and leading cadres and then by the masses of party members. Leading bodies and leading cadres should set an example in conducting comparison and examination. In this way can they use their actual conduct to influence and motivate other party cadres and party members and have the power to take the initiative to lead the party rectification work in their respective localities, departments, or units.

In carrying out examination work, party committees and leading party members' groups of various provinces, autonomous regions, and municipalities as well as various ministries and commissions at the central level should emphasize the examination of major problems that exist in their respective localities and departments in implementing the party's line, principles, and policies. In general, they should check to see if there is a correct attitude toward the four basic principles, toward the line, principles, and policies formulated since the 3d Plenary Session of the 11th CPC Central Committee, and toward the general task and objective set by the 12th CPC National Congress. They should check whether the guiding ideology for their work agrees with the principle and line of the CPC Central Committee, meets the requirement of creating a new situation, and suits the need to build socialism with Chinese characteristics, and whether they have made the work within the scope of their duty and responsibility serve the purpose of fulfilling the party's general task and objective. In addition, they should conduct serious examinations of the major problems in their respective localities and departments concerning work style, discipline, and organization. On the basis of these examinations, they should formulate relevant practical and concrete measures for correcting the problems.

Examinations of individual members of party committees and leading party members' groups should be conducted according to the spirit of the stipulations and principles regarding demands on party members and leading party cadres as stated in the CPC Central Committee's Decision on Party Rectification. These individual members should examine their own problems concerning not only the ideological and political line and the guiding ideology for their work, but also those regarding their party spirit, work style, and discipline. In making the examinations, however, they must grasp the key problems, sum up principal experiences and lessons, and thus decide explicitly what they should do in the days to come. They should not attend to every problem and treat all things equally.

In the current party rectification there are two general demands: One is to eliminate the seamy side of things within our party; the other is to greatly raise the political and ideological consciousness of the broad masses of party members and heighten the level of their thinking about the work in their own fields to suit the needs of socialist modernization. Because of these demands, every party organization and every party member should strive to meet high standards and rigorous requirements in conducting the examination. While checking to see if the first demand

has been met, they should not ignore the second demand; neither should they refrain from making serious efforts to examine themselves just because they think they have no great problem with regard to the first demand.

5. The process of comparison and examination is one of making criticism and self-criticism. Criticism and self-criticism are the principal weapons our party uses to expose and eliminate the seamy side of things within the party, to correct the various mistakes among party members and party cadres, and to improve their style of work. Making earnest and conscientious criticism and self-criticism is the key to the success of comparison and examination work.

In doing comparison and examination work, party committees and groups and their members in various provinces, autonomous regions, and municipalities under the direct administration of the central government and in the various ministries and commissions at the central level must act on the basis of their actual situation, adopt various forms, and actively listen to criticisms and views from all quarters. Every party committee or group member must strictly analyze himself and be brave in criticizing his own mistakes and errors earnestly, profoundly, and realistically. One must neither act perfunctorily nor utter words against one's conscience and accuse oneself in an "exaggerated manner." In criticizing others, it is necessary to proceed from the desire to achieve unity and to treat others openheartedly. In learning from past mistakes in order to avoid future ones and to cure the sickness in order to save the patient, we must listen to facts and convince people by reasoning. We must pay attention to truth while casting aside all considerations for face. At the same time, we must realize that to uphold truth, correct mistakes, and facilitate changes and progress in one's thinking and understanding is a complicated process. We must not act with undue haste. Those comrades who have committed mistakes must seriously deal with them instead of evading the issue and covering them up. However, so long as they have realized their own mistakes and have expressed willingness to conduct self-examination, we should welcome their doing so. For those who still fail to correct their thinking for the time being, we can wait. When we reach a certain stage in conducting examination, we can let them correct their mistakes in the course of practice and keep them under observation. We must not keep bothering them about it.

In the process of conducting criticism and self-criticism, in the work of making preparations to clear out the "three types of persons," and on the issue of dealing with those who erred during the "Great Cultural Revolution," we must strictly follow the various basic policies of the CPC Central Committee decision on party rectification. We must pay attention to eliminating all types of interferences. Particular effort must be made to guard against factionalists who attack those who display party spirit. Any practice of attacking people or shielding people by means of factionalism or lodging false accusations and taking retaliatory actions against others is considered as an action that undermines party rectification work. Such practices should be seriously dealt with after investigation.

6. In order to guard against perfunctoriness in carrying out comparison and examination, we must strengthen supervision at the higher and lower levels. Party organizations at the higher level must, through the proper forms,

earnestly listen to the views of party organizations at the lower level and inform them about the main situation in carrying our comparison and examination in their own organizations at the higher level so that the party organizations at the lower level may exercise supervision and put forward their criticism. After the party organizations at the lower level begin their comparison and examination, they should also report on the situation and developments to the party organizations at the higher level on time so that the party organizations at the higher level may strengthen their guidance, easily check up on things, and in a timely manner, help solve problems that have cropped up.

7. The aforementioned matters to which we must pay attention in carrying out comparison and examination are applicable to not only the party committees and party groups in various provinces, autonomous regions, and municipalities under the direct administration of the central government and various ministers and commissions at the central level. Their basic guidelines are also applicable to party organizations and party members in other units where party rectification work should be carried out during the first stage. All units that have entered the comparison and examination stage should strive to create new experiences in close connection with their own specific conditions. We have already entered the busy spring farming season. Our tasks in other economic work are also extremely arduous. We must make overall arrangements for comparison and examination work and other party rectification work as well as for other vocational work so that they can promote each other.

8. Units that are still studying the documents or making self-examination as prescribed by those documents must step up the work of rectifying their work style and bad practices. Rectifying the party's work style and bad tendencies in conjunction with important work and personnel problems and related matters, with emphasis on attacking bad tendencies, is a very big part of improving relations between the party and the masses, strengthening the ties between the party and the people, and raising the party's fighting capability—not a small matter. It is completely wrong to regard as a small matter the rectifying of the party's work style and bad tendencies by concentrating on problems that concern the interests of the masses. It is necessary to continue to implement Circular No 6 of the Central Commission for Guiding Party Rectification. Rectifying the party's work style and bad tendencies should be followed by achievements in unification of thinking and self-examination as prescribed by party rectification documents. It is also wrong to set unification of thinking and self-examination as prescribed by party rectification documents against the simultaneous rectification of the party's work style and bad tendencies.

Bad tendencies in the form of bureaucratism, such as seeking personal interests by abusing power and by taking advantage of one's work connections, and irresponsibly to the party and the people exist in varying degrees in various departments and trades. In many departments and trades these tendencies have become a special type of bad tendency. This problem has been raised by some departments. For example, petroleum departments have called for a solution to the problem of seeking personal gain by selling oil; Shanxi Province has called for a solution to the problem of seeking personal gain by selling coal; electric power departments have called for a solution to the problem of a warlord work style. They have done the right thing in trying to solve these problems. Quite a number of other departments and trades also have their particular bad tendencies, and the masses are very critical of them. Although these bad tendencies are caused by a small number of people, their influence and harmful effects must not be underestimated. These bad tendencies are gravely contaminating the party's work style and social practice, gravely harming the interests of the state and the people, gravely corrupting the ranks of cadres, staff members, and workers, and are directly assaulting and undermining the state's economic and social development plan. If a Communist Party member commits the mistake of bureaucratism by seeking personal gain by abusing power and by being irresponsible to the party and the people, he is demonstrating that he lacks party spirit and that his existing party spirit is seriously impure. This is incompatible with the nature of the party, its program, and its historical mission. When these problems are examined, they should be understood in this context.

Party committees and party groups of various provinces, autonomous regions, and municipalities directly under the central government and ministries under the central government must rectify the party's work style and bad tendencies in their locations and departments by concentrating on prominent ones and should continue to select some typical major cases and publicize them to spur various areas into action, thereby further pushing forward the work of simultaneously rectifying the party's work style and its bad tendencies. It is hoped that the units that have made little effort to carry out the principle of simultaneous rectification of the party's work style and bad tendencies and use excuses to slacken the struggle against such grave evil tendencies as seeking personal gain by abusing power, thus making little progress in simultaneously rectifying the party's work style and bad tendencies, take immediate action to adopt effective measures for correcting this situation. It is even more necessary to look into the evil phenomenon of a small number of units who verbally promise to simultaneously rectify the party's work style and bad tendencies but, in fact, continue to make mistakes while rectifying the party's work style. Party members and cadres concerned must be given immediate disciplinary punishment on the basis of investigation.

Correcting evil tendencies such as seeking personal gain by taking advantage of one's position and power and bureaucratism is a common task of all party organizations. The first group of units to start party rectification should persist in simultaneously rectifying the party's work style and bad tendencies, while units that have not yet started party rectification should rectify their bad tendencies before they start party rectification. In the course of simultaneously rectifying the party's work style and bad tendencies, it is necessary to apply the principle of seeking truth from facts; it is not permitted to cover up, contract, or enlarge problems concerning bad tendencies. In solving urgent problems of which the masses are most critical, it is necessary to overcome hesitation and guard against the tendency of absolute egalitarianism and dispute over every detail.

41

Rectification as the Main Task of the Party, 1 July 1984

This editorial, keyed to the sixty-third anniversary of the founding of the Party, makes it reasonably clear that Deng Xiaoping regards its streamlining into a disciplined, effective organization that can carry out his policies, and above all modernize the country, as the Party's most important task.

Today marks the 63d anniversary of the birth of the Communist Party of China, and this year is the first year of party rectification at the central level and the provincial, municipal and autonomous regional level. A man 63 years of age is an old man; for a proletarian party whose ultimate goal is the realization of communism, 63 years are but an episode in a long historic play which requires the efforts of many generations. Our cause is just unfolding and we have a great future. In this sense, our party is still quite young. The 2d Plenary Session of the 12th CPC Central Committee decided to launch overall party rectification righteousness and revolutionary vigor which are needed in our endeavor to quadruple the country's total annual industrial and agricultural output value by the turn of the century—a great goal set forth by the 12th National Party Congress. Comrades throughout the party should clearly understand the heavy historic task on their shoulders and, by acting in accordance with the CPC Central Committee's decision on party rectification, make the current party rectification a success in high standards so that our party will be the strong force at the core leading the cause of socialist modernization.

The current party rectification is now 8 months old, its development is generally and relatively healthy. The Central Committee has lost no time in settling the relationship between party rectification and the campaign to combat spiritual pollution, solved the relations between party rectification and economic work, and emphatically pointed out that party rectification will promote the economy and economic achievements will test party rectification. (Of course, this is said in the sense of economic work being the central task of the whole party; it does not mean that this slogan can be mechanically copied by all non-economic work departments.) Guiding the present party rectification to proceed in the correct orientation, these policy decisions have ensured our continuous political stability and promoted economic growth. It is especially true that the Central Committee's decision to further open the country to the outside world and accelerate the pace of administrative reform has boosted popular morale and the situation is getting better and better. This is the most advantageous condition for making the current party rectification a success in high standards.

To make party rectification a success in high standards, we must strictly act in accordance with the Central

["Uphold High Standards in Party Rectification," *People's Daily*, 1 July 1984.]

Committee's decision on party rectification and fulfill its four tasks: the achievement of ideological unity, the rectification of the party's work style, the strengthening of discipline, and the purification of the party organization. In no way should the four tasks proceed perfunctorily. Of these four tasks, the first one is the achievement of ideological unity which means achieving an ideological unity throughout the party according to the four basic principles; unifying the ideas of party members of the basis of the party's line, principles and fundamental policies formulated since the 3d Plenary Session of the 11th CPC Central Committee, unifying them on the general goal set forth by the 12th National Party Congress to quadruple the country's total annual industrial and agricultural output value and on work to achieve the four modernizations with one heart and one mind. Comrade Deng Xiaoping has pointed out for a long time: "What is our primary task at present and for a fairly long historic period to come? In a nutshell, it is modernization. The destiny of our country and the fate of our nation will be decided upon whether or not we can realize the four modernizations. Under the present conditions in China, to ensure a success in the socialist four modernizations, we must adhere to Marxism and hold high the great banner of Mao Zedong Thought. When you fail to promote the four modernizations and proceed from realities, you are divorced from Marxism and indulging in idle talk about it."

Comrades throughout the party must not be vague, but firm on this matter of principle which is related to the destiny of our country and our nation and concerns our adherence to Marxism or our paying lip service to it.

To achieve ideological unity and maintain political unanimity with the Central Committee, the crux lies in acting in accordance with the Central Committee's line, principles and fundamental policies and gearing the guiding ideas on work of one's own department or area to the party's general task and ultimate goal and to the requirements of reform. The Central Committee's decision on party rectification points out: "To maintain political unity with the Central Committee, one must integrate the limit, principles and policies of the Central Committee with the actual conditions of one's locality, department or unit; one must also bring into full play one's own initiative and creativity and work in an independent and responsible way." If the party organization of a department or locality does not quite understand the actual conditions of that department or locality and does not have a pretty clear idea of how to create a new situation and help fulfill the general goal, that party organization cannot be considered to have achieved ideological unity in high standards. The party group in the Ministry of Coal Industry, in carrying out comparison and examination, and the Guizhou provincial party committee, in launching party rectification, have closely integrated the actual conditions of the minstry and Guizhou Province with work to achieve the party's general goal. They have found the discrepancies between themselves and others, defined the guiding ideas and have thus met the Central Committee's requirements for party rectification that one must "discuss important matters, understand the entire situation, and exercise control over one's own department, locality or trade."

An important task in this regard is to continuously eliminate the influence of "leftist" ideology and carry out education in totally disavowing the "Great Cultural Revolution" among party members. The party's line, principles and policies since the 3d Plenary Session of the 11th CPC Central Committee arises from a struggle against erroneous "left" and right tendencies, "leftist" ideology in particular, and from a disavowal of the "Great Cultural Revolution." If one still cherishes "leftist" ideology and still says that he was correct during the "Cultural Revolution" and that the faction he supported was correct or the faction that protected him was correct, one cannot have a correct guiding idea, nor can he make the work to sort out the "three types of persons" and build the "third echelon" successfully. Thus, it is quite possible that party rectification may proceed perfunctorily. Disavowal of the "Great Cultural Revolution" does not mean settling old accounts, but educating all party members in the "Resolution on Certain Questions in the History of the Party Since the Founding of the PRC" adopted by the 6th Plenary Session of the 11th CPC Central Committee.

While continuing to eliminate the influence of "leftist" ideology, there must be resolute struggles against such rights ideologies as bourgeois liberalism, the idea of harming the public to benefit oneself, blind faith in everything foreign and insensitiveness toward hostile elements' corruptive and sabotage activities. In a nutshell, there must be a struggle against "leftist" and right ideologies when they emerge. Only thus can we guarantee the thorough implementation of the correct line of the Central Committee.

Recently, the CPC Central Committee decided to devote several months to reform during party rectification after units undergoing the party rectification process have finished the task of comparison and examination. This will be the continuation and development of the previous task of simultaneous rectification and correction. It is an important step to persist in party rectification in high standards and prevent the party rectification process from proceeding perfunctorily. The CPC Central Commission for Guiding Party Rectification has, in its Circular No 9, spelled out in explicit terms the key points and principal demands with regard to work of rectification and correction.

The correctness or incorrectness and the clear-cut or ambiguous content of the guiding idea of a department or locality will be tested during the stage of rectification and correction. It is correct that simultaneous rectification and correction has been emphasized in the past. Problems discovered during party rectification, especially those bitterly complained about by the masses, will hurt the people's enthusiasm if these problems are shelved and not corrected. They will weaken the confidence of the comrades both inside and outside the party during the current party rectification. Henceforth, the guidelines for simultaneous rectification and correction will still be thoroughly implemented. All problems that can be immediately solved must be solved with determined efforts and there will be no excuses for procrastinating their settlement. Special efforts are needed to deal with cases of power abuse for personal gains and with serious problems of bureaucracy which are not responsible for the party and the people. We must not belittle or neglect these cases and problems. Cadres who have serious problems in this regard must be removed from their posts without hesitation. Simultaneous rectification and correction of some minor issues and offensives is not enough. A new situation in socialist modernization can be created only by grasping the major problems of one's own department, locality, or unit; arousing the masses to discuss these problems thoroughly; drawing up a feasible plan for rectification and correction and putting it into practice.

To persist in party rectification in high standards is a demand presented to us by history. The CPC has been active for 63 years. Of these, 28 years were devoted to democratic revolution and a period of 35 years has been spent in socialist construction. During the democratic revolutionary period, our struggle witnessed twists and turns for 22 years until the Yanan rectification campaign which swept out the influence of Wang Ming's "left" deviation mistakes and achieved a high degree of ideological and political unity of the entire party. Democratic revolution developed like a hot knife cutting through butter until nationwide victory was won. In carrying out socialist construction, we have both positive and negative experiences and particularly many fresh experiences have been gained since the 3d Plenary Session of the 11th CPC Central Committee. We will proceed with the current overall party rectification in high standards, further eliminate the influence of the "Great Cultural Revolution" and of the erroneous "left" and right tendencies before that chaotic event, earnestly start from the actual conditions in China in doing things but not from book worship, persist in the ideological line of seeking truth from facts, and maintain a high degree of ideological and political unity of the entire party. We will certainly be able to take the road of socialist modernization with Chinese characteristics and our cause of socialist modernization will develop like splitting a bamboo. This is the hope of the people of all nationalities in the country and is the fighting goal of all our Communist Party members during the current party rectification.

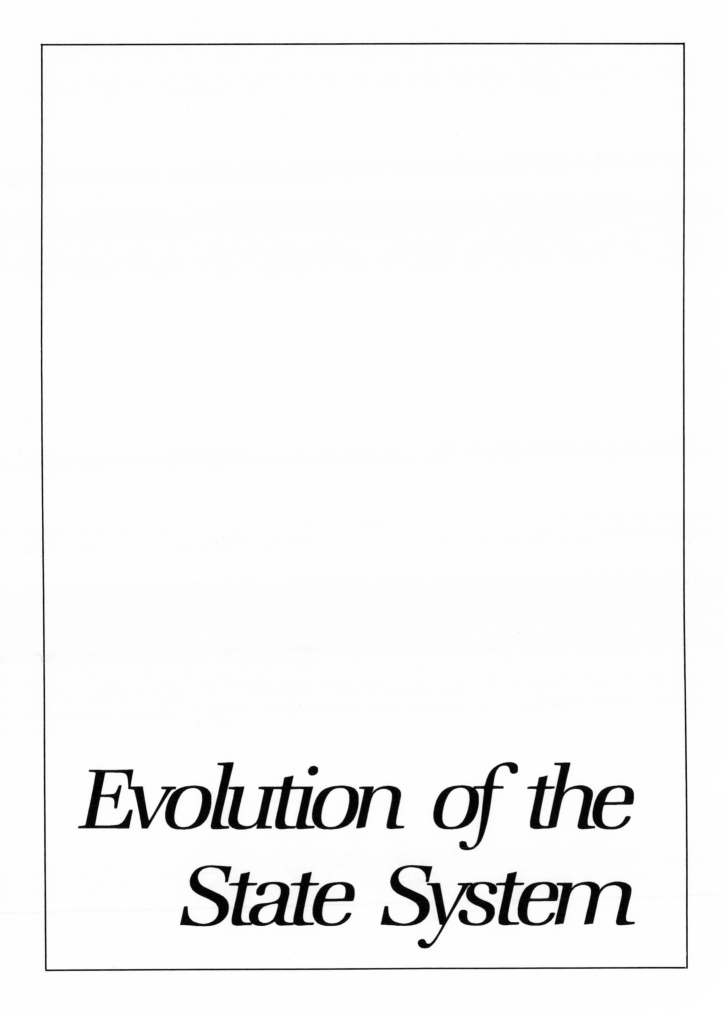

Evolution of the State System

ZHAO ZIYANG
On Streamlining the State Council, 8 March 1982

42

Parallel with the rectification of the Party being undertaken by Deng Xiaoping and Hu Yaobang, Premier Zhao has begun to overhaul the State Council and its subordinate ministries and commissions, or, in other words, the central government and bureaucracy. Massive personnel cuts, especially the retirement of overage officials, are on the agenda.

All Standing Committee members: The work of restructuring government organizations which is being carried out in our country is an important matter that has attracted the attention of the whole nation. In the past 2 months since the closing of the Fourth Session of the Fifth NPC, this work has been making fairly good progress. Its results are better than expected. I now deliver my report on this work for your examination.

1. THE PROGRAM FOR RESTRUCTURING THE STATE COUNCIL'S ORGANIZATIONS AND ITS IMPLEMENTATION:

The policy for our country has now been finally formulated, and the situation of stability and unity has been further consolidated. This calls for the restructuring of government organizations. Moreover, the conditions for this work are ripe. Doing this work well is very important to promoting our country's socialist modernization. As soon as the Fourth Session of the Fifth NPC ended, the State Council, while making an overall arrangement for government work in various spheres, immediately began a systematic restructuring of its various ministries and commissions according to the session's resolution. The CCP Central Committee gave explicit instructions concerning the principle for carrying out this work. Many important suggestions were also given by Comrade Hu Yaobang, Deng Xiaoping and by other Standing Committee comrades of the Political Bureau of the CCP Central Committee. A general program for restructuring the State Council's organizations has been initially formulated after it was discussed many times at State Council meetings, after it was repeatedly studied by responsible comrades of the ministries and commissions under the State Council and after hearing the opinions of and holding consultation meetings with various quarters. The work of restructuring the various ministries and commissions is being carried out actively and in an overall manner. The 12 units which began this work ahead of others have put forward a concrete program for the establishment of various organs, selection of leaders at the department and bureau level and determination of the numbers of staff members.

To restructure the State Council's organizations, it is, first of all, necessary to improve the State Council's system and method of leadership so as to strengthen its unified and centralized leadership and raise work efficiency. Therefore, we suggest that the number of vice premiers be reduced, that state councillors be appointed and that a permanent conference of the State Council be formed consisting of the premier, vice premiers, state councillors and a secretary general. The State Council now has 13 vice premiers. The number should be reduced to two. The position of state councillors will be roughly equal to that of vice premiers. While some state councillors will concurrently head ministries or commissions, others will be responsible for specialized functions. They may be entrusted by the premier or the State Council's permanent conference to carry out assigned work or some other important specialized tasks. In external affairs, they may be entrusted by the premier to play an important role as his representatives. The State Council's permanent conference handles the day-to-day work of the State Council. Chaired by the premier, it will make decisions on various fields of work and give guidance within the functions and powers of the State Council.

To raise work efficiency, it is necessary to pay attention to rational division of work and functions and capability in setting up the various ministries, commissions, agencies with offices under the State Council. In accordance with the principle of abolishing overlapping organizations and merging those that have similar functions, a plan has been drawn up to have the existing 98 ministries, commissions, agencies and offices under the State Council merged and reduced to about 52.

Since the emphasis of the nation's work has been shifted to concentrate on socialist modernization, the State Council has given priority to guiding economic work. The work of the State Planning Commission must be further strengthened in order to boost the socialist planned economy and especially to successfully carry out the long-term plan of strategic importance.

Command of the routine economic activities of the state must be centralized and unified. The present situation of multiple leadership and diversified administration must be changed. It is for this reason that we have decided to reshuffle the State Economic Commission and expand its functions and authority as well as its scope of business. The state Economic Commission is responsible, in an

[New China News Agency, 8 March 1982.]

overall way, for supervising and checking how the national economic plan is implementing in each fiscal year and for organizing and coordinating all economic and technical activities in a particular year for the various departments of agriculture, industry, capital construction, railway transportation, finance and domestic and foreign trade. The State Economic Commission is also responsible for organizing and carrying out changes to the state's economic system each year. The existing State Agricultural Commission, the State Machine Building Industry Commission, the State Energy Commission and the finance and trade group under the State Council will be abolished. Some of their work will be taken over by the reshuffled State Economic Commission, while other work will be carried out by the ministries concerned. The existing State Capital Construction Commission will be abolished. Its work will be shared by the new Ministry of Urban and Rural Construction and Environmental Protection and the reorganized State Economic Commission and the State Planning Commission. The main task of the State Scientific and Technological Commission from now on is to study policy with regard to science and technology, work with the State Economic Commission and the State Planning Commission to put forward major projects for scientific and technical research, and organize and coordinate with scientific and technical forces to tackle key problems. Planning work in the field of science and technology and the work in the field of production technology will be handled respectively by the State Planning Commission and the State Economic Commission so as to link science and technology even more closely with economic construction. The Office of National Defense Industry will merge with the Science and Technology Commission for National Defense to exercise unified control over tests for scientific research and production work in the national defense industry.

On the basis of the plans mapped out by the State Council, various ministries and commissions have taken immediate steps. The 12 units that are among the first restructuring group have already achieved gratifying results. The plan to merge the Ministry of Power Industry with the Ministry of Water Conservancy into a Ministry of Water Conservancy and Power, the plan to merge the Ministry of Commerce with the All-China Federation of Supply and Marketing Cooperatives and the Ministry of Food into a Ministry of Commerce and the plan to merge the Administrative Commission on Import and Export Affairs with the Ministry of Foreign Trade, the Ministry of Economic Relations With Foreign Countries and the Foreign Investment Control Commission into a Ministry of Foreign Trade and Economic Relations have matured one by one. After the merger of the administrative organ of the State Council in charge of the supply and marketing cooperatives with the Ministry of Commerce, the All-China Federation of Supply and Marketing Cooperatives will remain as a mass organization conducting necessary activities at home and abroad. The Ministry of Chemical Industry, the Ministry of Coal Industry and the Ministry of Textile Industry, whose systems will remain unchanged, have separately put forward their plans to simplify their internal structure and to reduce and merge the various departments and offices under each ministry as well as namelists of new ministers.

These plans will be put into effect immediately, and the ministries will begin their work according to the new system as soon as the above-mentioned plans are examined and approved by the current NPC Standing Committee session.

As seen from the reform plans submitted by the aforementioned 12 units, the situation of overstaffing and members of leading groups being too old will be greatly changed. After restructuring these units, the number of units at the ministry level will be reduced from 12 to 6, the number of administrative organs at the department and bureau levels will be reduced from 180 to 112, and their staff will be cut by 33 percent from 8,693 to 5,864. The greatest changes will take place in the leading groups at ministry and bureau levels. They will become smaller but will be highly capable. There will be far fewer deputy posts.

The number of ministers and vice ministers will be reduced from 117 to 27, a 77-percent cut. The number of department and bureau chiefs and deputy chiefs will be reduced from 617 to 304, a 51-percent cut. After restructuring these units, the average age of the leading cadres at the ministry level will be 57 compared with 64 at present. The average age of the cadres at the department and bureau levels will be 53 compared with 59 at present. In the leading group at the ministry level, 48 percent of all cadres will receive college-level education as compared with 31 percent at present. At the department and bureau levels, 45 percent of all cadres will receive college-level education as compared with 32 percent at present. Among the leading cadres, newly promoted are 2 ministers, 5 vice ministers and 57 chiefs and deputy chiefs of various departments and bureaus. The situation has indicated that we have made a gratifying step forward in making our cadres younger, better-educated and professionally more competent.

In the process of restructuring organs, the broad masses of cadres, particularly the old cadres, have displayed a high level of revolutionary awareness. Many veteran comrades have realized that this time we have taken the initiative in restructuring the state organs, done a good job in replacing the old cadres with new ones, abolished the existing system of lifelong tenure for leading cadres and set good examples and rules for our descendants. These are the objective requirements for the development of our socialist cause. They are indeed of immediate importance and of far-reaching historic significance. Many old comrades have happily stepped down from their leading posts and enthusiastically recommended those comrades who are in the prime of their lives to take these posts. They have said it well: In order to advance, individuals must retreat so the cause of our party and state will forge ahead even more rapidly. After taking the initiative in applying for retirement and convalescence leave or retreating to the second line, many old cadres, in an effort to fulfill even better the historic task of restructuring organs, have continued to work hard for the nation. They have gone deep among the masses to conduct investigation and study, pondered various plans, looked for qualified people and conscientiously and responsibly put forward their own views. Many people are deeply touched by the earnest attitude of these old cadres in holding themselves responsible for the revolutionary cause and by their noble qualities in remaining loyal at all times. Many middle-aged and young cadres have expressed their determination to do a good job in learning from the old comrades, to remain prudent and humble, to work hard and to be good revolutionary successors. This contingent of our cadres deserves to be called the contingent cultivated and educated by the Communist Party of China over a protracted period and armed with Mao Zedong Thought. Keeping the entire situation in mind and seeking no personal interests, this contingent is completely trustworthy. The high awareness level of these cadres in setting store by the revolutionary cause constitutes an important guarantee in smoothly carrying out the work of restructuring organs.

Although the task of restructuring organs is arduous and large in scale, it has not disturbed or halted routine work in the past 2 months and more. The actual work of the government in various fields is being done under proper leadership and in good order. Our nation remains stable, and the political and economic situation in the whole country is good. This fully shows that after the implementation of the series of strong measures of setting things straight laid down since the 3d Plenary Session of the 11th CCP Central Committee, the political order has become stable and the political life normal. This also shows that the decision on streamlining government structure has the support of the people.

We are confident we have the ability to accomplish this major reform. The fear of difficulties, pessimism and inertia are completely groundless. Some people abroad who gloat over others' misfortune have commented that China is undergoing a "hopeless" reform. This kind of forecast will only end in complete bankruptcy.

2. BASIC PRINCIPLES AND SEVERAL MAJOR TASKS:

The restructuring of our state government organs has made a good start. The task ahead of us is to sum up experience and push on in the flush of victory.

Early this year, Comrade Deng Xiaoping clearly pointed out at a meeting of the Political Bureau of the CCP Central Committee on the restructuring of organs: In a certain sense, restructuring of organs is a revolution, but this is a revolution in administrative structure, not against anyone. Comrade Deng Xiaoping's judgment is absolutely correct and very important. At present, low efficiency, resulting from overlapping and overstaffed administrations with their multitiered departments and without clearly defined responsibility, has become intolerable. To uphold the socialist road and to realize the four modernizations, it is necessary for us to carry out this revolution. Without it, it would be impossible to fully implement the correct principles and policies of the party and government, nor would the problems of serious bureaucracy and low work efficiency be truly overcome, and our cause would be hopeless. Our basic principle is to carry out this important restructuring in a revolutionary spirit. In carrying it out, we can only advance, we cannot retreat. We must have great determination and our work must be careful and meticulous. First of all, we must have full confidence in victory and at the same time advance steadily and conduct thoroughgoing and painstaking ideological and organizational work well. The State Council's earlier organization restructuring was carried out in this spirit and we should continue to do so.

The State Council held that, in the course of the restructuring of organizations in line with the abovementioned basic principles and earlier practice, we must stress the proper solution of the following four problems through practical work:

First, the tasks and scope of responsibilities of various departments and their subordinate organizations must be clearly defined. We must, through this restructuring of organizations, resolutely change the situation of irrational division of work and poorly defined responsibilities. A person can only be employed for the job, and a job should never be created to accommodate a person. When things can be handled by a single organization, there is no need to set up others; when things can be handled by a single-level organization, there is no need to set up organizations at several levels; when things can be handled by a single person, there is no need to put several persons on the job. There should be rules specifying responsibilities and tasks for each organization and person. The organizational restructuring of the second group of advance units should proceed from serious discussion of the scope of responsibilities of the organizations concerned. From now on, all other units should do the same. After organizations are streamlined, it is necessary to thoroughly study work relations among various departments, from top to bottom and from left to right. For example, relations among ministries and commissions under the State Council; relations between the ministries and commissions of the State Council and the various provincial, municipal and autonomous regional governments and their subordinate departments and bureaus; relations between administrative and economic organizations; and how government organizations can manage and serve enterprises and business units more effectively; all these questions must be thoroughly studied and feasible rules and regulations formulated. The endless haggling and shirking of responsibility among nominal personnel in the past, was no doubt a manifestation of the bureaucratic style of work; nevertheless, this was caused to a large extent by the lack of clearly defined responsibility and division of work. Only by conscientiously solving problems in these areas can we do things for the people more effectively.

Second, able and virtuous persons should be selected to equip and build the leading bodies well. This is an important link. In various ministries and commissions under the State Council, the key is to properly equip the leading bodies in the ministries, commissions and departments and bureaus.

This is a major project of strategic significance. Such a project was emphasized shortly after the founding of the country, but was later interrupted. We suffered a great loss from this seriously unwise move. Now we must put this project on the agenda of important affairs and must be determined to spend money on intellectual investment. Today the state organs are overstaffed by people, many of whom are not professionally proficient for lack of proper training. Certainly, this is not a good phenomenon. Nevertheless, the majority of these people have had considerable work experience and professional capability and can continue to contribute their efforts at their respective posts to socialist modernization. This is also a favorable factor in our rotational training of cadres by groups and by stages after our organs have been streamlined. For this reason, only the number of slots—but not the number of staff workers—for various departments is defined while streamlining our organs. Regardless of regular or nonregular staff workers, so long as they are able to study, we must give them the chance to study and must organize them to study cultural knowledge and various skills needed in modern socialist construction on a rotational basis. After studying for some time, they should return to work; and after working for some time, they should return to study again. Their performance in the course of study and work must be assessed and, during the process, the outstanding cadres will be selected and promoted to more appropriate and more important posts where they are more needed.

Our cause is still developing, and people with various kinds of special new knowledge are urgently needed. When our rotational training of cadres has been carried out and when our cadres have become more capable, our cause will be able to develop in a still better and quicker manner, and the effects arising therefrom will be inestimable.

The State Council holds that government organizations can certainly be restructured in a sound manner by resolutely carrying out the above basic principles and main tasks. When the administrative structure is streamlined, working efficiency will certainly be improved. However, to really meet the requirements of the four modernizations, it is still necessary to further reform the economic management system and the work system and to improve the work style. We should make revolution not only to do away with overstaffing but to eliminate the irrational structure and systems as well as all forms of bureaucracy. As said before, the profound revolution we are making is aimed at restructuring those parts of the state administrative structure that do not meet the requirements of construction in the economic, cultural, political, legal and other fields; it is not a revolution against anyone. To better solve the most difficult problem of reforming the structure, the State Council proposes that a state committee for restructuring the economic system be established, with the premier concurrently serving as its chairman who is to be responsible for the overall design in the restructuring. No matter how big the difficulties and obstructions we will meet in carrying out the various reforms in future, we must overcome them with an indomitable revolutionary spirit and strive to build the State Council into a compact, highly efficient state organ that maintains close ties with the masses and tends very little toward bureaucracy.

3. THE FOLLOWING MEASURES, APPOINTMENTS AND REMOVALS ARE SUBMITTED FOR APPROVAL:

A. The preliminary plan for restructuring the State Council is submitted for approval in principle. Approval is requested for the position of state councillors. Approval is requested for merging the Ministry of Power Industry and the Ministry of Water Conservancy into a Ministry of Water Conservancy and Power; the Ministry of Commerce, the All-China Federation of Supply and Marketing Cooperatives and the Ministry of Food into a Ministry of Commerce; and the State Administrative Commission on Import and Export Affairs, the Ministry of Foreign Trade, the Ministry of Economic Relations With Foreign Countries and the State Foreign Investment Commission into a Ministry of Foreign Trade and Economic Relations.

B. Approval is requested for the establishment of a State Committee for Restructuring the Economic System, with the premier serving concurrently as its chairman.

C. Approval is requested for the appointment of Qian Zhengying as minister of water conservancy and power, Liu Yi as minister of commerce, Chen Muhua as minister of foreign trade and economic relations and Qin Zhongda as minister of chemical industry. Gao Yangwen will continue to serve as minister of coal industry, and Hao Jianxiu as minister of textile industry.

D. Approval is requested for the removal of Li Peng as minister of power industry, Qian Zhengying as minister of water conservancy, Wang Lei as minister of commerce, Niu Yinguan as director of the All-China Federation of Supply and Marketing Cooperatives, Zhao Xinchu as minister of food, Gu Mu as chairman of the State Administrative Commission on Import and Export Affairs and chairman of the State Foreign Investment Commission, Zheng Tuobin as minister of foreign trade, Chen Muhua as minister of economic relations with foreign countries and Sun Jingwen as minister of chemical industry.

Committee members: Streamlining the government structure is a very arduous and complicated task, which we have only just started. As far as restructuring the State Council is concerned, the first group of units has submitted its streamlining plans to the NPC Standing Committee for approval. Upon approval, these plans will be carried out. Then, there will still be a lot of work to do. Other units have not yet submitted their streamlining plans. When they have finalized their plans, the State Council will report them in groups to the NPC Standing Committee. In the course of streamlining the government structure, it is imperative to ensure that both work and restructuring are not delayed. Under no circumstances are phenomena such as slackness in work, dislocation and confusion permitted, nor is it allowed to adversely affect work and production. Restructuring the government organs in the provinces, municipalities and autonomous regions will begin next year, except for in specific areas where conditions are already ripe and experiments may be conducted at some appropriate time with the approval of the State Council. In short, we are determined to overcome all difficulties, to unswervingly do a good job in streamlining the government structure, to continue to perfect the government work system, to get rid of bureaucracy and to raise working efficiency so that our government organizations will take on an entirely new look in their work and work style.

This concludes my report, and I request you committee members to examine and approve it.

On Government Responsiblity for the Economy, 23 April 1982

43

Although wordy and repetitious, this article makes it clear that the government, under the State Council, is expected to play a key role in managing the economy, and that it has not been very successful.

Economic responsibility system is a system of responsibility among the state, the collective and individuals in our socialist economic life. The purpose of forming economic responsibility systems is to define the economic responsibility of various units and individuals in the process of production so that the responsibility system at various levels can be combined with the principle of distribution according to labor at the same time that "power," "responsibility" and "interest" can be unified. As the economic responsibility system is being implemented more widely in our economic life, it has not only reformed labor discipline and mobilized the initiative of the broad masses of producers and management staff, but has also improved the management of producing units and economic effect and vigorously promoted the development of our socialist economy. Although the economic responsibility system needs further development, practice has proved that it is one of the effective systems in our socialist economic life.

As the economic responsibility system has played such a large role in the economic sector, people cannot but consider that it is also necessary to form various forms of responsibility systems in the political sector, particularly in our government work at various levels.

It is a common phenomenon that the efficiency of our government organizations at various levels is low. We understand that the efficiency of government organizations is mainly determined by two factors. One is the factor of the government organizations themselves. The establishment of government organizations, the division of authority among different government organizations, the handling of the relations between lower- and higher-level organizations and the definition of the authority and responsibility among different positions in government departments—all these have a considerable impact on the efficiency of government organizations. The second is the factor of government staff. The way in which government staff members are promoted, the way in which they are used and the fact that there is no complete and effective examination system and punishment system have all affected the efficiency of the government. For quite a long period in the past, we did not pay enough attention to these two aspects. As a result, the formation of government organizations and the actual work of these organizations are characterized by excessive staff, duplication or effort, unclear delineation of responsibility in various positions, and the situation in which people do not care about effi-

ciency is very serious. In order to change these situations, it is imperative in the process of reforming government organizations to set up various forms of responsibility systems in government work.

In appointing people for positions in government work, the "power" must accord with "responsibility" (of course, with regard to "honorary positions" and some "advisory positions," often "power does not accord with the position." The emergence of a few such positions will not create a bad influence on government work; on the contrary and under certain conditions, such positions are necessary). If a government staff member with heavy "responsibility" does not have the corresponding "power," he is not in a position to carry out his job effectively. He can only complete the defined tasks by relying on active and voluntary help from others, and as a result, there is no guarantee that he can carry out his responsibility. On the contrary, if a government staff member is heavily "empowered" and yet without "responsibility," it is possible that he will exercise his power arbitrarily and at will. Because his deeds are not subject to punishment according to law, various incidents may occur that are harmful to the interests of the state and that violate the rights of the people. Of course, it is possible that those who are in power but who have no responsibility do not use their power arbitrarily, but they will be in a state of inertia and they are good at "shifting responsibility onto others." All these situations have not only seriously affected the relations between the government and the people but have also made government inefficient. A government is a tool of a class in exercising its rule and a government of any class has problems of efficacy. A government that is paying attention to regulating its relations with the people and to efficiency consequently puts "power" in the same place with "responsibility." In all of these positions in government organizations, there should be no position that has "responsibility but without power," nor should there be "power without responsibility." It is imperative to make "power" accord with definite "responsibility."

Generally speaking the "responsibility" of government staff refers to "responsibility in work" and this responsibility can be divided into "political responsibility," "administrative responsibility" and "general legal responsibility." In a country with complete administrative rules and regulations for government organizations and other management tasks, the "administrative responsibility" of government staff is also manifested as "legal responsibility." In a country with incomplete administrative rules and regulations for government organizations and other

[Yan Jiaqi, "A Talk on the Responsibility System in Government Work," *People's Daily*, 23 April 1982.]

management tasks, the "administrative responsibility" is not necessarily manifested as "legal responsibility." "General legal responsibility" refers to public "legal responsibility." In many countries now, both government staff and the public will bear legal responsibility if they violate general laws (such as criminal law and civil law).

What is "political responsibility?" Generally speaking, all senior government officials that are elected or appointed have political responsibility. For example, the representatives to the people's congresses at various levels are politically responsible to their electors and the senior officials of the CCP Central Committee and local governments at various levels are politically responsible to the National People's Congress and people's congresses at various levels. The constitution of our country stipulates that "the State Council is responsible to the National People's Congress and it has to make a work report; during the closing period of the NPC, it is responsible to the Standing Committee of the NPC and it is has to make a work report." The local people's governments and people's congresses at various levels and the standing committees of these congresses also have such relationships. Local people's governments at various levels must also be responsible to higher state organizations while local people's governments at various levels are under the unified leadership of the State Council. Such "power-responsibility relations" in fact manifest the "political responsibility system." During an election, electors or representative organizations elect those who have implemented the party's policies, set an example in abiding by law, demonstrated a healthy work style and have close relations with the masses to representative or government organizations.

However, under this "political responsibility system," even if the people's representatives or government staff do not violate laws or neglect their duties, they still may not be reelected to representative or government organizations once the electors or representative organizations no longer trust them. Electors and representative organizations have the right to dismiss from office incompetent representatives or senior government officials. Higher government organizations also have the right to dismiss from office senior government officials in lower levels who are no longer considered competent in their positions. It can be said that losing an election or recalling or removing somebody from office represent important methods in the commitment of "political responsibility" of people's representatives or certain government officials. As the constitution, government organizational law and election law have defined the appointments and dismissals with regard to the emergency of people's representatives and senior government officials, it can be said to a certain extent that "political responsibility" is also "legal responsibility."

Contrary to "political responsibility," the "administrative responsibility" of government staff refers to a kind of responsibility that should be borne by those who have violated the rules and regulations of the related government administrative organizations and their management tasks. The people's representatives who hold no government positions have no "administrative responsibility" for government tasks. The establishment of the system in government work includes the "political responsibility system" and more important, the "administrative responsibility system." In order to establish the "administrative responsibility system," it is necessary to improve and strengthen the party's leadership over cadre tasks, improve government personnel management organizations and define laws and regulations for various administrative organizations and management. The establishment, power and work procedures and the relations of government organizations as well as the power and responsibility of various positions must be defined through administrative legislation so that in their work, all government staff will have rules and regulations to follow and they will be responsible and correctly handle and solve various problems in a timely way. When there is a contradiction of power among government administrative organizations or when they are shifting responsibility onto each other, these problems can be solved through legal procedures.

In establishing the "administrative responsibility system," it is also necessary, through administrative legislation, to define such matters as how to value, check, award, promote and punish government staff. Rules and regulations must also be formulated for regularly evaluating and checking the ideology, deeds, level of implementing policies, level of organizing, professional knowledge and working efficiency of government staff. According to the results of these tasks, measures must be taken to define and readjust the salaries, jobs and grades of government staff. Those who are indolent in their work, disrespectful in their jobs, infringe upon public interest for their own interests and who arbitrarily exercise their power must, according to the rules and regulations of the related government administrative organizations and their management work, bear "administrative responsibility" and they must accordingly be punished and handled. Of course, a complete "administrative responsibility system" must define supervisory methods and punishment procedures for government staff as well as procedures and methods of appeal for the staff who are subject to administrative responsibility and who refuse to accept the punishment.

Premier Zhao Ziyang said in his "report on the question of restructuring the State Council" that through reform, the government organizations must resolutely change the situations that are characterized by irrational division of work and indefinite responsibility. He said: "In the past, the various phenomena such as arguing over trifles, shifting responsibility onto others and no one taking responsibility are a manifestation of bureaucratic work style; but it is also mainly because of indefinite division of responsibility and work." Therefore, in order to enable our governments at various levels to serve the people still better and improve the efficiency of government organizations and their staff, it is necessary to proceed from our specific national conditions and in reforming our government organizations to set up various effective forms of responsibility system in government work.

44

On Constitution Making by the Deng Xiaoping Leadership, 1 May 1982

The PRC has had four state constitutions: 1954, 1975, 1978, and the one of 1982, whose adoption is foreshadowed here. In their particular field, these documents correspond to and reflect the preeminence respectively of Mao Zedong, Zhou Enlai, Hua Guofeng, and Deng Xiaoping.

The "draft of the revised Constitution of the PRC" has been examined and approved by the national constitutional revision committee, and a resolution has been passed by the 23d Meeting of the 5th NPC Standing Committee for its publication and for its discussion by the people of all nationalities throughout the country. This is major event in the state's political life. We must do a good job of the nationwide discussion of the "draft of the revised constitution."

The "draft of the revised constitution" makes substantial revisions to the current constitution. The current constitution of our country was approved at the First Session of the Fifth NPC in March 1978. At that time, the "gang of four" had been smashed only a short time before and the 3d Plenary Session of the 11th CCP Central Committee had not been convened. Owing to the limitations of the historical conditions at that time, there was not enough time to make a comprehensive summing-up of the experiences and lessons of the socialist revolution and construction in the 30 years after the founding of the PRC, and there was not enough time to thoroughly eliminate the influence of some "leftist" ideas emerging during the decade of turmoil on the articles of the constitution. Consequently, in the current constitution there are quite a few elements that reflect outdated and erroneous political theories and viewpoints and quite a few regulations that do not conform to the practical situation. Although the Second and Third Sessions of the Fifth NPC had made some amendments to one or two articles, no great changes had been made. Since the 3d Plenary Session of the 11th CCP Central Committee in December 1978, great changes have taken place and major progress has been made in the political, economic and cultural life of our country. The party and state have shifted the focal point of the work, the party has made a new and scientific analysis of the class situation in the country, the state has scored major achievements in building a socialist democratic system and has set forth further demands, and major reforms of the state leading system and the national economic system are being carried out.

The "Resolution on Certain Questions in the History of Our Party Since the Founding of the PRC" approved by the 6th Plenary Session of the 11th CCP Central Committee in particular has accomplished the task of bringing order out of chaos in the guiding ideology, comprehensively summed up the historical experiences in the socialist revolution and construction and explicitly defined a path and some major points for achieving socialist modernization that are applicable to the situation in our country. All this was not and could not have been reflected in the current constitution. Moreover, as a fundamental law of the state, many of the articles and stipulations in the current constitution are also not complete, well-knit, specific and explicit. In brief, the constitution approved in 1978 does not keep abreast of the political, economic and cultural reality of our country or suit the needs of the modernization drive of our country. In September 1980, at the suggestion of the CCP Central Committee, the Third Session of the Fifth NPC passed a resolution on setting up a constitutional revision committee to take charge of the work of revising the current constitution. In the past year and more, under the solicitude and leadership of the CCP Central Committee, the constitutional revision committee and its secretariat, acting on the principles that "the leadership should integrate itself with the masses" and that "the experiences of our own country should be integrated with international ones" and proceeding from the fundamental interests of the people of the whole country, have carried out extensive investigations and studies to collect opinions from various quarters. After repeated deliberations and discussions, they have set forth the "draft of the revised constitution" for discussion. After examining and revising the draft for discussion chapter by chapter and article by article, the NPC Standing Committee passed a resolution for its publication. After extensive discussions by the people of the whole country and further revisions, it will be submitted to the Fifth Session of the NPC to be held this year for examination and official approval. Revising the constitution is a very serious and earnest job. It is a project of far-reaching significance in building our country politically during the new historical period.

Of the three constitutions we had before, the one approved by the First Session of the First NPC in September 1954 was a fairly good and consummate one. At that time, under the leadership of the CCP Central Committee and Comrade Mao Zedong, the work of drawing up the constitution was carried out in a very serious and solemn manner. It was during the "Great Cultural Revolution" that the constitution was practically annulled. The next two constitutions reflected in different degrees the abnormal situation in the state's life, but they were very imperfect. However, in 1954, when the work of socialist transformation had just started, it was naturally impossible for a

["A Major Event in the State's Political Life," *Red Flag*, no. 9, 1 May 1982.]

constitution that came into being at that time to reflect the situation of the state after the completion of the socialist transformation. The current "draft of the revised constitution" has retained many of the stipulations of the 1954 constitution that are still applicable today. At the same time, in the light of the great changes in the situation of the country since then and under the guidance of the "Resolution on Certain Questions in the History of Our Party Since the Founding of the PRC," it has paid full attention to summing up the great achievements and basic experiences of the socialist revolution and construction in our country in the past three decades and added many new stipulations. The "draft of the revised constitution" has summed up the fundamental experiences in our history in the past 100 years and more, particularly since the beginning of this century, and recorded the achievements of the people of the whole country in their protracted struggle in the course of the new democratic revolution, the socialist revolution and socialist construction. The draft takes as its general guiding ideology the upholding of the four basic principles and, in the form of a fundamental law, defines the fundamental task of the people of the whole country as the building of our country into a modernized state with a high degree of democracy and civilization. It has also showed clearly the domestic guarantee and the international conditions for accomplishing this task—strengthening the unity of all nationalities throughout the country and the unification of the country at home and, in international affairs, upholding the correct foreign policy, strengthening mutual support with the peoples of various countries, safeguarding world peace and promoting the progressive cause of mankind.

Acting on historical experiences and proceeding from reality, the draft has defined fairly completely the fundamental political and economic systems of the state and the principles for developing culture and building spiritual civilization and enriched the contents of the fundamental rights and duties of citizens. In accordance with the principle of democratic centralism and the needs of the new historical period, the draft pays attention to strengthening the building of state organs and makes some important new stipulations on state organization. In brief, the "draft of the revised constitution" has been revised and drawn up under a correct guiding principle after our party had accomplished the task of bringing order out of chaos in the guiding ideology. It has absorbed quite amply historical experiences and lessons and has recorded quite amply the great progress our country has made in various aspects and the orientation of reforms since the third plenary session of the party. It is therefore a fairly consummate and well-considered draft.

As a result of the efforts of the people of the whole country in the past few years, the various aspects of the country have now been restored to normal and have become stable, and the long-term objective of struggle has also been made clear. After being extensively discussed by the people of the whole country, who will sum up their ideas and make further amendments, and after being examined and approved by the NPC, the draft will become the fundamental law of our country during the new historical period. It will be a stable and solemn fundamental law that will function over a very long historical period. It will play a far-reaching and important role in ensuring the long-term stability of our country, in building and improving our socialist political, economic and cultural systems, in ensuring the consolidation of the state and the democratic rights of the people, in achieving the institutionalization of socialist democracy and in building the socialist legal system. Owing to changes in the actual situation, it will perhaps be necessary to make some amendments in the future, but it will only be amendments or supplements to individual articles. The more prudent and careful we are in revising the constitution now, the more likely we are to have a constitution of long-term stability.

It is precisely for this reason that the current discussion of the "draft of the revised constitution" by the whole people is of very great significance. First of all, discussion by the whole people will make the new constitution more complete. A constitution gives expression to the will of the people of the whole country. The revision of the constitution should not be done by a small number of people and it is imperative to sum up correct ideas on the basis of a high degree of democracy. When the people of all nationalities, all localities and all strata throughout the country are engaged in extensive and fully democratic discussions, drawing on collective wisdom and absorbing all useful ideas, the constitution will be in a better position to reflect the conditions of the whole country and the will and aspirations of the entire people. Secondly, the discussion of the "draft of the revised constitution" by the whole people is also a nationwide study or self-education in the fundamental law of the state. Owing to the fact that socialist democracy and the legal system in our country are still incomplete and that, over a considerably long period of time in the past, the constitution has been cast aside or has been incomplete, with the result that no attention has been paid to it, there is quite an extensive lack of knowledge and sense of a constitutional and legal system among the people of our country. It is necessary, by means of discussion by the whole people, to raise the understanding of the cadres at various levels and the broad masses on the status and function of the constitution in the state's life and raise their consciousness in abiding by and defending the honor of the constitution. The discussion of the constitution by the whole people serves as a school for the cadres at various levels and the broad masses to study and grasp the basic spirit and main content of the constitution. It is necessary, by means of discussion by the whole people, to raise the understanding of the cadres at various levels and the broad masses on the four basic principles and the fundamental tasks of the people of the whole country in the future, on our socialist political, economic and cultural systems and the major principles of the state and on the fundamental rights and duties of citizens, and make clear the relationship between an individual citizen and the state as well as his due responsibility and duties to the state and society.

Finally, the discussion by the whole people is in itself a study and training by the entire people in correctly exercising their democratic rights and promoting their democratic life. In building socialist democracy, it is necessary, on the one hand, to institute and improve the various democratic systems. On the other hand, it is necessary to demand that the numerous cadres and the broad masses learn to correctly exercise their democratic rights and respect the democratic rights of other people and that they cultivate the habits of democratic life. The accomplishment of this point is a long-term process of study and training.

It is stipulated in the "draft of the revised constitution" that the people have the right "to manage state affairs, manage economic and cultural undertakings and manage social affairs through various channels and forms." The fact that it will take the people of the whole country several months to discuss the fundamental law of the state fully reflects the socialist democratic nature of our country. It is at the same time an opportunity for the people to learn to manage state affairs. Through their concern for and discussions of the "draft of the revised constitution" the broad masses will be able to raise their sense of responsibility as masters of the country, learn to manage state affairs and cultivate the habits of democratic life.

In brief, doing a good job of discussing the "draft of the revised constitution" is of long-term and great significance to our country. We should attach great importance to this work and, under the leadership of the party, take an active part in the nationwide discussion and revise and draw up the fundamental law of our country together.

On Party Domination of the State Constitution, 24 May 1982

45

Confusion between the Party and state constitutions is possible not only because of the close interrelationship between Party and state in China but also because of the adoption of a constitution for each in 1982. At first this document might appear to deal with the Party constitution, so emphatic is it on the domination of the Party over the political and constitutional life of the state. In fact, however, it is concerned with the state constitution.

At present, the draft of the revised constituion is being enthusiastically discussed among people of all nationalities throughout the country. In the course of this discussion, it is of primary significance to clarify the general principles or guiding thought to which we adhere in revising the constitution. What is the general guiding thought of the draft of the revised constitution? It is the four basic principles of adherence to the socialist road, adherence to the people's democratic dictatorship, adherence of the party's leadership and adherence to Marxism-Leninism-Mao Zedong Thought. These four basic principles put forth by the CCP Central Committee have fundamentally summed up our country's historical experiences and are truths which have been verified by long-term tests in our actual practice. They reflect the laws governing the development of history which is independent of man's will and are the crucial decision of the hundreds of millions of Chinese people made during their long-term struggles. The preamble of the state's fundamental law has recorded and affirmed this fundamental historical experience. It has also explicitly stipulated that, the Chinese people will continue to adhere to the four basic principles and struggle for the completion of the basic tasks of the new period. This is an extremely essential and important task. Hence, this has laid down a general principle for the establishment and perfection of various political and economic systems in the country and has pointed out the correct orientation for our country's development in the future.

["Adhering to the Four Basic Principles is the General Guiding Thought for Revising the Constitution," *People's Daily*, 24 May 1982.]

Only socialism can save China, and only socialism can enable our country to realize the modernization drive and achieve a high degree of democracy and civilization. Adhering to the socialist road means upholding the various socialist economic and political systems, continuing to launch social reforms and economic cultural construction in the socialist orientation, and creating a high degree of socialist material and spiritual civilization. This is a concentrated representation of the will and interests of the working class and the people throughout the country. Adhering to the socialist road cannot do without the system of the people's democratic dictatorship. Our country's system is the system of the people's democratic dictatorship which is under the leadership of the working class and based on the alliance of the workers and peasants. First, our country is under the leadership of the working class because the working class is the most advanced and prosperous class ever to appear in history. Only by working in accordance with the stand and will of the working class can our country unswervingly adhere to the socialist road. Second, the alliance of the working class and the broad masses of peasants is the foundation of our country. This alliance encompasses an extensive area and the foundation of the people's democratic dictatorship is also extensive and sold because 80 percent of our population are peasants and the nonagricultural laborers also belong to the worker-peasant alliance, the majority of the intellectuals have already become intellectuals of the laboring masses, and that the exploiting class has already been eliminated in our country. Third, in a country where the system of people's democratic dictatorship is practiced and where the system of democracy is extensively practiced among the people, the people are the masters of the country and the state organs are the tools to execute the people's will. Fourth, since class struggle will still exist for a long period of time in certain areas, besides safeguarding the motherland and opposing foreign invasion, we must also wage resolute struggles against the remnant elements of our enemies who are hostile to and sabotage the socialist cause. Thus, the function of dictatorship cannot be weakened. Only by practicing the system of dictatorship toward a small number of enemies, can we safeguard the people's country and the people's rights. These are both aspects of a single matter. In short, the system of the people's democratic dictatorship is on the one hand, an important component of our country's socialist system and on the other hand, is a prerequisite for our country's adherence to the socialist road.

The socialist system and the people's democratic dictatorship are our country fundamental systems. Therefore, they are not only affirmed in the preamble of the draft of the revised constitution but also run throughout all its articles and become the basis for all other concrete systems. Article 1 of the general principles of the draft stipulates: "The People's Republic of China is a socialist state of the people's democratic dictatorship led by the working class and based on the alliance of workers and peasants. The socialist system is the basic system of the People's Republic of China. Disruption of the socialist system by any individual and in any form is prohibited." Other articles of the general principles contain concrete stipulations about our country's socialist economic system and political system and how to safeguard, strengthen and perfect these systems.

The socialist system is a completely new social system and is being developed and perfected in practice. We must carry out reforms in the socialist economic structure, political structure and the state leadership structure on the basis of our country's reality and the positive and negative experiences of the past 30 years or so in order that they will be conducive to developing production, raising the level of the people's material and cultural life and to building material and spiritual civilization. Only in this way are we correctly and really adhere to the socialist road. We have been doing so since the 3d Plenary Session of the 11th CCP Central Committee. Various stipulations in the draft of the revised constitution have recorded in principle the positive results of reforms in various fields achieved since the third plenary session and have affirmed the orientation for further reforms. Consequently, after the new constitution is officially adopted, we will further concretize, systemize and legalize the political principles of adhering to the socialist road and upholding the people's democratic dictatorship and will form systems and laws with binding force for the people of all nationalities and all state organs, political parties and mass organizations. These stipulations in the draft of the revised constitution are of great significance in ensuring that our country will develop along the socialist road.

The leadership of the CCP is the basic guarantee for winning victories in the socialist cause. The party's leading position was shaped by history. In China, without the leadership of the CCP, it will be impossible to adhere to the socialist road; whereas whether or not the party's leadership is good and whether or not the party's leadership can win the support of the broad masses depend on whether or not the party can correctly lead the people in adhering to the socialist road. Therefore, the party's leadership is also explicitly affirmed in the preamble of the draft of the revised constitution.

The party is the vanguard of the working class. Apart from the interests of the broad masses of people of the whole country, it has no particular interest of its own. In the past, the party led the people in the struggle to seize political power. At present, it is leading the people in the struggle to consolidate political power and to build a new life. It has all along been wholeheartedly serving the people and struggling for the people's right to become masters of their own affairs. The party's leadership is not at all contradictory to all power belonging to the people. On the contrary, the former ensures the realization of the latter. The party's leadership over the country should not be exercised by means of administrative orders but should be realized mainly by putting forth correct principles and policies which are in conformity with objective reality and the people's interests, relying on the guidance of Marxism-Leninism-Mao Zedong Thought and according to the ideological line of seeking truth from facts. Besides, the party's leadership is realized by means of the positive role and exemplary deeds of its members and cadres in government organs and other organizations, ideological and political education among the broad masses given by party organizations at all levels and their close ties with the masses.

After the party's stand and the principles and policies it puts forth are accepted by state organs of power and become the country's systems and laws, all party members and cadres should struggle to safeguard these systems and laws at their respective posts and take the lead in observing these systems and laws and should establish extensive ties with the masses of people, educate them and lead them in observing these systems and laws. In this sense, observing the country's constitution and laws is upholding the party's leadership. Otherwise, the party's leadership will be damaged. Except stipulating that "all political parties" (of course, the CCP is included) must observe the constitution and laws, that is, must carry out their activities within the limits permitted by the constitution and laws, the articles in the draft of the revised constitution have not made stipulations on the party's leadership. This is because the party's nature and functions are entirely different from those of state organs of power and government administrative organs. The realization of its leadership does not depend on stipulations in articles of the constitution.

We often say that in order to strengthen the party's leadership, we must improve the party's leadership. We must carry out work in various respects to improve the party's leadership. One important aspect in improving the party's leadership is to correctly understand the nature of the party and to correctly understand the relationship between the party and the country and the methods for the party to exercise leadership over the country's life. Some past practices of mixing the party with the government and equating the party's leadership with the functions of state organs of power were not conducive to strengthening the party's leadership but were harmful to the party's correct leadership. The draft of the revised constitution has correctly summed up the historical experiences in this aspect. This will certainly be conducive to strengthening the party's leadership over the country's life.

The reason why the CCP can become the force at the core of the people of the whole country in carrying out socialist construction is that it is the vanguard of the proletariat armed with Marxism-Leninism-Mao Zedong Thought. By using the scientific theory of Marxism-Leninism-Mao Zedong Thought as a tool to observe the country's destiny and to guide the revolution and construction, it is able to lead our country and the people in advancing smoothly along the socialist road and in overcoming any hardships and dangers until final victory. Since the citizens of the PRC support the socialist road and acknowledge the leadership of the CCP, they are bound to acknowledge the guiding role of Marxism-Leninism-Mao Zedong Thought in the country's life. The entire content of the draft of the revised constitution is the product of integrating the basic principles of Marxism-Leninism-Mao Zedong Thought with China's present reality.

In short, upholding the four basic principles is not only affirmed in the preamble of the draft of the revised constitution but is also manifested in all its content and articles. Through the discussion of the draft of the revised constitution by all the people of the country, we should make the whole party and all the people of the country understand better that the four basic principles are four mainstays of our country and are the foundation of our country. As long as we persistently and correctly uphold the four basic principles, we will certainly be able to build our country into a modern and strong socialist country with a high degree of democracy and a high degree of civilization!

An Authoritative Explanation of the New State Constitution, 26 November 1982

46

Peng Zhen was second in seniority only to Deng Xiaoping on the Party Secretariat prior to the Cultural Revolution. He was then purged but was afterward rehabilitated by Zhou Enlai, although he has not regained all the influence he once enjoyed. This report deals with a wide range of Deng's domestic and foreign policies, at least to the considerable extent that they are reflected in the new constitution.

Members of the Presidium and Fellow Deputies,

I am entrusted by Chairman Ye Jianying of the Committee for Revision of the Constitution with the task of reporting on the draft of the revised Constitution on behalf of the Committee.

The Constitution currently in force was adopted by the Fifth National People's Congress at its First Session held in March 1978. Since then, our country has passed through a period of important historical change. After the Third Plenary Session of the 11th Central Committee of the Chinese Communist Party convened in December 1978, the Party and the state led the whole people in rectifying the mistakes of the "cultural revolution" in all fields, summed up in a deep-going way the historical experience gained since the founding of the People's Republic and restored, or in the light of the new situation formulated, a series of correct principles and policies which have enormously changed the country's political, economic and cultural life. The Constitution as it stands in many ways no longer conforms to present realities or meets the needs of the life of the state; thus, all-round revision is necessary. The Reso-

lution on Certain Questions in the History of Our Party Since the Founding of the People's Republic of China adopted last year by the 11th Central Committee of the Chinese Communist Party at its Sixth Plenary Session and the documents adopted by the 12th National Party Congress this year received support from the people of the whole country and provide a sound basis for revising the Constitution.

We have for two years discussed and revised the present Constitution conscientiously, carefully and meticulously. At the suggestion of the Party Central Committee, the Fifth National People's Congress at its Third Plenary Session on September 10, 1980 decided to set up a Committee for Revision of the Constitution to be responsible for the work. After being set up, the committee and its secretariat solicited opinions widely from all localities, departments and quarters and closely studied them and, in February this year, submitted the Draft of the Revised Constitution of the People's Republic of China for discussion. The committee at its second session spent nine days in discussing and revising the draft. Revisions were also proposed by members of the Standing Committee of the National People's Congress, by some members of the Standing Committee of the National Committee of the Chinese People's Political Consultative Conference, by

[Peng Zhen, Report on the Draft of the Revised Constitution of the People's Republic of China, 26 November 1982, *Beijing Review*, no. 50, 13 December 1982.]

leaders of democratic parties and people's organizations, and by leading members of departments under the Chinese Communist Party's Central Committee, of departments under the State Council, of leading bodies of the People's Liberation Army and of provinces, autonomous regions and municipalities directly under the Central Government. The committee at its third session in April carried on a nine-day discussion on the draft and adopted it, which was made public by the Standing Committee of the National People's Congress and submitted to the people of all nationalities in the country for discussion.

The extensive scale of the nationwide discussion, the vast number of participants and the wide impact demonstrate the surging political enthusiasm of the workers, peasants, intellectuals and other sections of the people in managing state affairs. Through the discussion and the exercise of democracy, the wisdom of the people has been pooled more effectively for revising the Constitution. Such discussion was in fact an experience in national mass education in the legal system, and it has raised the consciousness of the cadres and the masses in abiding by the Constitution and upholding its dignity. The consensus is that the draft scientifically sums up the historical experience of development of socialism in China, that it reflects the common will and fundamental interests of the people of all nationalities, conforms to the situation in China and meets the needs of socialist modernization. During the nationwide discussion, many opinions and proposals of all kinds were put forward. The secretariat of the Committee for Revision of the Constitution made further revision of the draft in accordance with them. Many important and rational proposals were adopted. While the substance of the original draft remains unchanged, nearly 100 additions and amendments were made in regard to specific provisions, not including changes in wording. Other proposals, though good, were not incorporated because the conditions for giving them effect do not yet exist or the necessary experience is still lacking, or because it is more appropriate to include them in other laws and documents rather than in the fundamental law of the state. After article-by-article discussion for five days by the committee at its fourth session, the draft was approved after further revisions by the committee at its fifth session on November 23. It is now submitted to the National People's Congress for consideration.

What are the guidelines for the revision of the Constitution?

The drafting was done under the overall guidance of the Four Cardinal Principles, namely, adherence to the socialist road, to the people's democratic dictatorship, to leadership by the Communist Party of China, and to Marxism-Leninism and Mao Zedong Thought. These Cardinal Principles form the common political basis for the advance of the people of all our nationalities in unity and are the fundamental guarantee for the smooth progress of our socialist modernization.

The Preamble of the draft reviews the history of the Chinese revolution in the past century and more. It points out that great and earth-shaking historical changes have taken place in China in the 20th century. Of these, four historical events are of the utmost importance. Apart from the Revolution of 1911 which was led by Dr. Sun Yat-sen, the three others all resulted from the efforts of the entire Chinese people led by the Communist Party of China with

Chairman Mao Zedong as its leader. These three major events are: the overthrow of the rule of imperialism, feudalism and bureaucrat-capitalism and the founding of the People's Republic of China; the elimination of the system of exploitation lasting for several thousand years and the establishment of the socialist system; and the forming, in the main, of an independent and fairly comprehensive system of industry and the development of socialist economy, politics and culture. The Revolution of 1911 was of great historical importance, but it fell short of fulfilling the task of China's national-democratic revolution. The three later events have brought about a fundamental change in the destiny of the Chinese people and in our society and state. These great historical changes led the Chinese people to the fundamental conclusion: But for the Chinese Communist Party there would be no New China, and socialism alone can save China. The Four Cardinal Principles are both a reflection of the law of historical development that is independent of human will and the decisive choice of the hundreds of millions of Chinese people in the course of long years of struggle.

With the establishment of the socialist system, China entered a new period of historical development. The basic characteristic of this new period is that exploiting classes have been eliminated as such and that class struggle is no longer the principal contradiction in Chinese society. This basic characteristic requires a substantial change in the focus or work of the state and in its guiding principles. To adhere to the Four Cardinal Principles under the new historical conditions, it is imperative to integrate the universal truth of Marxism with the concrete practice of China's socialist construction and to blaze a path for socialist construction with distinctive Chinese features. We have scored great successes and also made many mistakes since we began exploring this correct path in the mid-1950s. Initiation and continuation of the "cultural revolution" constituted a grievous mistake. Of course it was not because we adhered to the Four Cardinal Principles that we made mistakes but because we failed to implement them correctly. As for the sabotage by the Lin Biao and Jiang Qing counter-revolutionary cliques during the "cultural revolution," it was carried out under the banner of these principles, but constituted a complete betrayal of them. Overthrow of the two counter-revolutionary cliques and correction of the mistakes of the "cultural revolution" represent a triumph for these principles. Now we have set our guiding ideology to rights and formulated a correct programme for creating a new situation in all fields of socialist modernization. All this has enormous and far-reaching significance for the prosperity of our country. Bringing about this historic change has been a process of restoring the true features of the Four Cardinal Principles and of adhering to them and developing them. These principles have been substantiated to a large degree in the new historical period and have acquired new and richer content.

A major strategic policy in setting things right has been the resolute shifting of the focus of the work of the state to socialist modernization of China's economy. This must be the focal point for all other work which should serve it. The consolidation of the state and the prosperity of our country, the stability and growth of Chinese society and the improvement of the people's material and cultural life will, in the final analysis, be determined by the expansion of production and the success of our modernization programme. We must from now on implement this strategic policy unswervingly unless there should be a massive invasion by the enemy. Even in that event, we must still carry on whatever economic development is required by the war and permitted by the actual situation. The recording of this policy in the Constitution is entirely necessary. While stressing economic development as the focus of our work, we must pay full attention to building a socialist spiritual civilization and to developing socialist democracy. The draft of the revised Constitution clearly stipulates in its Preamble: "The basic task of the nation in the years to come is to concentrate its effort on socialist modernization" and "to modernize industry, agriculture, national defense and science and technology step by step to turn China into a socialist country with a high level of culture and democracy." The people of all our nationalities must work in concert to fulfill this great task.

The first constitution of the People's Republic of China, namely, the Constitution of 1954, was a very good one. But at that time China had just begun socialist transformation and construction. Enormous changes have taken place in our country and society, so it is quite natural that the 1954 Constitution no longer fully suits the current situation. The present draft maintains and develops the fundamental principles of the 1954 Constitution, while incorporating a careful summary of the rich experience of China's socialist development and draws on international experience; it takes into account both the current situation and the prospects for development. Therefore, this Session of the National People's Congress assuredly can enact a new Constitution that is distinctively Chinese and meets the needs of our socialist modernization in the new historical period and that will remain valid for a long period of time.

Now I would like to give some explanations about the basic content of the draft of the revised Constitution in conjunction with opinions and questions raised during the nationwide discussion.

1. OUR STATE SYSTEM: THE PEOPLE'S DEMOCRATIC DICTATORSHIP

The first article of the draft revised Constitution stipulates, "The People's Republic of China is a socialist state under the people's democratic dictatorship led by the working class and based on the alliance of workers and peasants." This defines the nature of our state and sets forth our state system.

Our people's democratic dictatorship is in essence a dictatorship of the proletariat. This is made explicit in the Preamble of the draft. The dictatorship of the proletariat takes different forms in different countries, and the people's democratic dictatorship is a form created by the Chinese people under the leadership of the Chinese Communist Party that suits the conditions and revolutionary traditions of our country. The term the people's democratic dictatorship is used to define our state power in the Common Programme of 1949, in the Constitution of 1954 and in the documents of the Eighth National Congress of the Chinese Communist Party held in 1956, and we continue this usage in the present draft. The working class is the leading class in our country. Although it comprises a minority of the entire population, it has the vast numbers of peasants as its steadfast ally, and an extremely broad united front led by the Communist Party has taken shape in the long years of revolution and construction. Our country is in a position to practice democracy among the greatest number of people while the targets of dictatorship are only a small number of persons. The people's democratic dictatorship is a formulation which accurately states the present condition of the classes in China and the broad basis of our political power, and it clearly shows the democratic nature of our state power.

The term the people's democratic dictatorship in the current draft is not to be taken as mere restoration of the formulation and its content in the 1954 Constitution. The people's democratic dictatorship of the early years of the People's Republic correspond to the circumstances and tasks of that transitional period when the chief task of the state power was to carry the new-democratic revolution to completion, proceed to the socialist transformation of the private ownership of the means of production, and bring about the transition from new democracy to socialism. With the establishment of the socialist system, however, the task of our state power under the people's democratic dictatorship became primarily to safeguard the socialist system and to guide and organize socialist construction. There has already been a significant change in the class composition of this political power. The working class is much bigger, having grown several fold in size, and carries greater weight in the political life of the state. With the socialist transformation, the vast numbers of peasants have changed from peasants engaged in individual farming to those engaged in collective farming. The number of intellectuals has also grown several fold. Taken as a whole, they have become part of the working class. The exploiting classes no longer exist as such; the overwhelming majority of their members have remoulded themselves and become working people earning their own living.

The workers, peasants and intellectuals constitute the three basic social forces in our socialist construction. Summarizing the views put forward in the nationwide discussion of the draft, we have added the following sentence to the Preamble: "In building socialism it is imperative to rely on the workers, peasants and intellectuals and to unite with all the forces that can be united." Here, the intellectuals are placed on a par with the workers and peasants in terms of their mode of work. Then why does the first article of the draft not say "the alliance of workers, peasants and intellectuals?" That is because, under the socialist system, the difference between the intellectuals and the workers and peasants is not one between classes; as regards their relationship to ownership of the means of production, or class character, the intellectuals do not constitute a class distinct from the workers and peasants. The first article defines the nature of our state, that is, our state system, from the viewpoint of class relations. The formulation "based on the alliance of workers and peasants" includes the intellectuals.

The nature of our state as a people's democratic dictatorship determines that in China it is the people and the people alone who are the masters of the state and society. The draft explicitly stipulates, "All power in the People's Republic of China belongs to the people." This is the kernel of our state system and a fundamental principle governing it. The draft specifically stipulates, "The organs through which the people exercise state power are the

National People's Congress and the local people's congresses at different levels. The people administer state affairs and manage the economic, cultural and social affairs through various channels and in various ways in accordance with the law." One billion people wielding the state power provides a reliable guarantee for safeguarding the fundamental interests of the people and ensuring that our state will be able to weather any storm.

The provisions on the fundamental rights and duties of citizens are an extension of the stipulated principles concerning the state system of the people's democratic dictatorship and the socialist social system in the chapter on General Principles. Our state system and social system provide both legal and practical guarantees that our citizens enjoy extensive and genuine freedoms and rights. The draft has reinstated the provision in the 1954 Constitution that all citizens are equal before the law. China's laws are drawn up by the whole nation under the leadership of the working class and are the concentrated expression of the will and interests of the people. All citizens are equal before such laws, which apply to all citizens equally; no citizen is allowed to enjoy the privilege of being above the Constitution and the law. It is imperative to reinstate this provision, for it represents a basic principle that ensures the application of socialist democracy and legality. The right to vote and the right to stand for election are important indicators that the people exercise state power. Since the elimination of the exploiting classes, the number of people enjoying the right to vote and the right to stand for election in proportion to the total population has steadily grown. According to statistics from the 1981 direct elections at the county level throughout the country, 99.97 per cent of the citizens attaining the age of 18 enjoyed these rights. This fully demonstrates the broad scope of our socialist democracy. In the light of historical experience and the lessons of the "cultural revolution," the draft has, in its provisions on the fundamental rights of citizens, not only restored what was relevant in the 1954 Constitution, but made it more specific and explicit and added new content. For example, there is the additional provision on the inviolability of the personal dignity of citizens, and there are more specific provisions than before on citizens' freedom of person and of religious belief, the inviolability of home, the protection of their freedom and privacy of correspondence by law and their right to criticize and make suggestions to any state organ or functionary and to make complaints and charges against, or exposures of, violation of the law or dereliction of duty by any state organ or functionary, and so on. The draft also stipulates relevant basic policies and measures to be adopted by the state to materialize and gradually extend citizens' rights.

Freedoms and rights with absolutely no restrictions have never existed in the world. As ours is a socialist country, the interests of the state and society are in basic accord with the citizens' personal interests. Only when the democratic rights and fundamental interests of the people as a whole are ensured and extended, will it be possible for the freedoms and rights of individual citizens to be effectively ensured and fully realized. Hence the draft stipulates, "The exercise by citizens of the People's Republic of China of their freedoms and rights may not infringe upon the interests of the state, of society and of the collective, or upon the lawful freedoms and rights of other citizens."

The draft stipulates, "Every citizen enjoys the rights and at the same time must perform the duties prescribed by the Constitution and the law." In accordance with this fundamental principle, the draft specifies the duties of citizens to the state and society. Only when all observe and perform their fundamental duties as citizens, can they be sure of enjoying their civic rights as prescribed by the Constitution.

Democracy among the people is one aspect of the people's democratic dictatorship; the other is dictatorship by the entire people over their enemies. After the elimination of the system of exploitation and the exploiting classes, the targets of this dictatorship are no longer complete reactionary classes, and the number of targets has dwindled. However, owing to certain domestic factors and foreign influences, class struggle will continue to exist within certain limits for a long time, and may even sharpen under certain conditions. Our people must still fight against those forces and elements at home and abroad that are hostile to China's socialist system and try to undermine it. Therefore, the function of the state as an instrument of dictatorship cannot be abolished at this time. Suppression of treasonable and other counter-revolutionary activities and striking at dangerous criminals who deliberately attempt to undermine and overthrow the socialist system in the economic and other fields are both functions of the state in exercising dictatorship in accordance with the Constitution and the law. It is imperative to uphold these functions in order to ensure successful implementation of the socialist modernization programme and safeguard and promote socialist democracy.

2. OUR SOCIALIST ECONOMIC SYSTEM

The draft of the revised Constitution truly reflects the fact that a socialist economic system has been established in our country and that it is growing ever stronger. It affirms socialist public ownership of the means of production as the basis of our socialist economic system.

Ownership by the whole people and collective ownership by the working people are the two forms of socialist public ownership in our country. The draft stipulates, "The state economy is the sector of socialist economy under ownership by the whole people; it is the leading force in the national economy." This is the decisive factor ensuring that the collective economy of the working people advances along the socialist road, that individual economy serves socialism and that the growth of the entire national economy conforms to the overall and long-term interests of the working people. The draft stipulates that, among the natural resources, all mineral resources and waters are owned by the state; and that all forests, mountains, grassland, unreclaimed land and beaches are owned by the state, except for those owned by collectives in accordance with the law. With the permission of the state, some natural resources owned by the state may within certain limits be allocated to collective economic organizations or even individuals for their use.

Collective ownership by the working people is the principal economic form in our countryside. It is suited to the present stage of development of our agricultural productive forces. Apart from the people's communes, agricultural producers' co-operatives and other forms of cooperative economy such as producers' supply and marketing, credit, and consumers' co-operatives exist and are growing in our rural areas. Even in the cities and towns, the state economy cannot run everything. The development of co-operative economy under collective ownership is suitable for a fairly big portion of handicrafts, industries, the building trade and transport, as well as commerce and service trades. The draft stipulates, "The state protects the lawful rights and interests of the urban and rural economic collectives and encourages, guides and helps the growth of the collective economy."

On the question of landownership, the draft makes clear-cut stipulations proceeding from the realities in our country. Land in the cities is owned by the state. Land in the rural and suburban areas is owned by collectives except for those portions which belong to the state in accordance with the law. House sites and private plots of cropland and hilly land are for the long-term use of rural households but are not their private property. The state may in the public interest take over for its use in accordance with the law land owned by collectives. "No organization or individual may appropriate, buy, sell or lease land, or unlawfully transfer land in other ways." These provisions of principle are of great significance in ensuring our socialist economic development, and particularly in ensuring the socialist orientation in the growth of our agricultural economy. It should be explained here that in Article 10 of the draft, land in the towns was originally put on a par with land in the rural and suburban areas. During the nationwide discussion, it was pointed out that conditions differ in various parts of the country and some towns of a fairly large scale will continue to grow and actually become small cities. That is why the provision about land in towns has been deleted. The question of landownership in towns can be dealt with in each case in the light of the actual situation.

It will be necessary for the individual economy of the working people to exist for a considerable period in urban and rural areas and to grow to a certain extent. The draft affirms that this individual economy, within the limits prescribed by law, is a complement to the socialist public economy; the state protects the lawful rights and interests of the individual economy, and guides, helps and supervises it by means of administrative control. The draft also stipulates, "Working people who are members of rural economic collectives have the right, within the limits prescribed by law, to farm private plots of cropland and hilly land, engage in household sideline production and raise privately owned livestock."

In short, state economy, collective economy and individual economy all have advantages in different respects and are all indispensable, although they have different status and functions. The presence of individual economy, which occupies only a small part of the national economy, does not prevent socialist public ownership from being the foundation of our economic system or hamper the successful growth of public economy. Given the premise of upholding the leading position of the state economy, we must develop diverse economic forms so as to promote the prosperity of the whole national economy.

The establishment of socialist public ownership makes it objectively possible to eliminate anarchy in social production and to practice economic planning. The planned economy is the basic system of the socialist economy and an important hallmark of socialism's superiority over capitalism. Our national economy must be developed

in a planned way, while our system of administration through planning must be adapted to the actual situation, that is, to the existence of diverse economic forms in our country and to the real level of our economic development. While specifying that "the state practices economic planning on the basis of the socialist public ownership," the draft stipulates that the state "ensures the proportionate and co-ordinated growth of the national economy through overall balancing by economic planning and the supplementary role of regulation by the market." That is to say, the state should put the production and circulation of essential goods under unified planning, consisting of mandatory and guidance planning. As for the enterprises producing goods which fall outside the unified plans, the state allows them the freedom to adjust production according to variations in market demand and supply. To ensure the proper functioning of the social economy and the authority of the state plan, the draft stipulates, "Disturbance of the orderly functioning of the social economy or disruption of the state economic plan by any organization or individual is prohibited."

The state in the past tended to exercise excessive and rigid control in planning. In view of this drawback, apart from the adoption of diverse forms of planning to suit different conditions, enterprises should be given varying degrees of decision-making power so as to combine unified leadership through state planning with initiative by the production units. The draft stipulates that "state enterprises have decision-making power in operation and management within the limits prescribed by law, on condition that they submit to unified leadership by the state and fulfill all their obligations under the state plan" and that "collective economic organizations have decision-making power in conducting independent economic activities, on condition that they accept the guidance of the state plan and abide by the relevant laws." Furthermore, the draft stipulates that the state must institute "the socialist system of responsibility in various forms." All this will be of great importance in enhancing the enthusiasm and initiative of production units and workers, invigorating the economy and pooling the knowledge and efforts of the people for socialist modernization.

With the establishment of socialist public ownership, the system of exploitation of man by man was abolished, and "from each according to his ability, to each according to his work" became a basic principle in our socialist economy. This is reaffirmed in the draft. The principle of "to each according to his work" is linked to that of "from each according to his ability." In applying the principle "to each according to his work," we must do ideological work among the workers while providing material benefits so that they will work for society to the best of their ability. Though conditions are still lacking to enable everyone to develop his talent in an all-round way, the nature of work in our socialist society has fundamentally changed compared with that in a society under an exploitative system. The draft stipulates, "All working people in state enterprises and in urban and rural economic collectives should perform their tasks with an attitude consonant with their status as masters of the country." On its part, society, in which work is planned and organized, should see to it that the workers are paid according to the quantity and quality of their work and that all possible conditions are created for them to develop their talent.

Our economy is rather backward. To change this situation and build China into a modern socialist country as quickly as possible, it is imperative to give full play to the superiority of the socialist system, fully mobilize the broad masses of the people, rely on our own efforts and work hard. Furthermore, as China has a vast territory, its economic, technological and cultural development is very uneven between different regions, departments and enterprises. Our socialist economy must be guided by principles and have flexibility, must be both unified and diversified. This will help bring into full play the enthusiasm of the localities, departments, enterprises and workers under the centralized and unified leadership of the central authorities and suit our measures to differing conditions in terms of locality, time, issue and persons involved, so that both human and material resources, including land, are turned to best account and a free flow of goods is achieved. It is in this spirit that the articles on the economy are formulated. The present restructuring of our economic systems has already brought significant results, and it will be continued in a comprehensive and deep-going way. The relevant provisions of the draft lay down the principles for this work. Proceeding along these lines, we can assuredly build and develop a socialist economy with distinctive Chinese features so as to turn China into a rich and powerful country step by step.

3. SOCIALIST SPIRITUAL CIVILIZATION

The Chinese people have the fundamental task of striving to build a high level of socialist spiritual civilization while working for a high level of material civilization in building socialism. The addition of articles on socialist spiritual civilization marks an important step forward in the revision of the Constitution.

With regard to the cultural aspect of building a socialist spiritual civilization, the chapter on General Principles in the draft, in accordance with opinions expressed in the nationwide discussion, devotes an article each to education, to science, to public health and physical culture and to culture. This carries more weight than the composite article contained in the original draft and also enriches the content.

The expansion of education includes both making it universal and improving its standards so as to raise the educational level of the workers, peasants and cadres, to increase the number of intellectuals and to train specialized personnel in all fields. This is the foundation for the growth of science and culture as a whole and a condition for raising the people's political consciousness; it is also an indispensable prerequisite for developing material civilization. Citizens have the duty as well as the right to receive education, which includes compulsory primary education for school-age children, proper types of political, cultural, scientific, technical and professional education for working adults and pre-employment vocational training. The general cultural level in China is rather low. A more rapid growth of education calls for both regular schooling and spare-time education in various forms. The state will allocate adequate resources for educational purposes and at the same time encourage all social forces, including economic collectives, state enterprises and undertakings, public organizations and individuals who have the approval of the state to run educational facilities in various forms and with mass support. Modernization of science and technology is a key link in our four modernizations. The development of the natural and social sciences, research in basic and applied sciences, and the dissemination of scientific and technological knowledge are of paramount importance for socialist construction. Obviously public health and physical culture undertakings are important in protecting the people's health, building up their physique and raising their efficiency in work and study. Literature and art, the press, publishing and other cultural undertakings are also essential for enriching and improving the people's cultural life. The development of all these undertakings, however, cannot rely solely on the resources of the state; efforts by all social forces and wide-ranging activities of a mass character will be needed. These principles and requirements are incorporated in the relevant articles of the draft.

The policy of "letting a hundred flowers blossom and a hundred schools of thought contend" is not included in the articles on cultural work. This was based on the following considerations: First, the draft already includes among the fundamental rights of citizens freedom of speech and of the press, and freedom to engage in scientific research, literary and artistic creation and other cultural pursuits, that is, the substance of the policy is embodied in legal terms and, moreover, is given a broader interpretation. Second, apart from this policy, there are other basic policies governing work in science and culture, and it is unnecessary and impossible to write them all into the Constitution. Of course, there is no doubt that "letting a hundred flowers blossom and a hundred schools of thought contend" remains one of the basic principles guiding our scientific and cultural work and that it must be firmly implemented to make socialist science and culture flourish.

With regard to the ideological aspect of building socialist spiritual civilization, it must be noted, first of all, that Marxism-Leninism and Mao Zedong Thought is our fundamental guiding ideology. This is expressed in the Preamble as one of the Four Cardinal Principles.

Article 24 of the draft stipulates, "The state strengthens the building of socialist spiritual civilization through spreading education in high ideals and morality, general education and education in discipline and the legal system, and through promoting the formulation and observance of rules of conduct and common pledges by different sections of the people in urban and rural areas." This means that efforts must be made to imbue more and more citizens with high ideals, moral integrity, general education, and a sense of discipline so that a new standard of social morality is fostered and our nation acquires a revolutionary and vigorous mental outlook.

The same article also stipulates, "The state advocates the civic virtues of love for the motherland, for the people, for labour, for science and for socialism." This has been developed on the basis of the five requirements (love of the motherland, the people, labour and science, and care of public property) defining civic virtues in the Common Programme adopted in the early years of the People's Republic. These five requirements were explicit and plain. They proved to be useful in educating the masses of people and left a deep impression on them. In the conditions prevailing then, it was not yet opportune to put forward "love for socialism" as a requirement in the Common Programme. Today, it has become a matter of course to include it, and so it replaces "care of public property" in the original five requirements. Love for socialism is not an abstract idea. The care of public property is an important part of it.

Article 24 also calls for ideological education in communism among the people. Communist ideology is the heart of socialist spiritual civilization. In the period of the new-democratic revolution, Comrade Mao Zedong already pointed out clearly: "So far as the orientation of our national culture is concerned, communist ideology plays the guiding role." Now that we have established the socialist system, we should and can strengthen nationwide education in communism among cadres and the people, with everyone taking part. Only in this way will it be possible to keep the socialist orientation in our modernization drive and to ensure that our social development keeps heading for the correct goal and retains its ethical motivation. Education in communist ideology should take the form of helping a growing number of citizens acquire a dialectical and historical materialist world outlook and the work ethic of serving the people wholeheartedly, and integrate personal with collective and national interests, integrate immediate with long-term interests, and subordinate immediate personal interests to long-term common interests. Such education, of course, does not mean skipping a stage of historical development and pushing an economic and social system that can be realized only at a higher stage, the stage of communism with its highly developed productive forces. On the contrary, it must be in line with socialist principles such as "to each according to his work" and clear-cut economic responsibility to which we firmly adhere in our economic and social life at the present stage. Only under the guidance of such ideological education can socialist principles and policies be implemented fully and correctly.

Another provision in the same article is that the state "combats capitalist, feudalist and other decadent ideas," which sets the fighting task on the ideological front. Historical and practical reasons as well as domestic factors and the international environment make this fighting task protracted, and we should in no way relax our efforts.

Here I would like to make one further point: the requirements for building socialist spiritual civilization are in fact implied in many of the articles in the draft on the fundamental rights and duties of citizens. In our socialist country, ideological education, public opinion, standards of social conduct and the law are interrelated. Our Constitution provides for the rights of citizens and at the same time requires that they raise their consciousness as masters of the country and society and safeguard and exercise their rights in a correct manner. Safeguarding one's own rights and respecting those of others are inseparable. This requires that every citizen should safeguard the interests of the state, society and the collective and respect the freedoms and rights of others while safeguarding his own rights. The duties of citizens stipulated in the Constitution are legally obligatory. But it is more important that, as the country's masters, citizens should enhance their sense of responsibility to the state, to society and to other citizens and conscientiously perform their duties including those of safeguarding the socialist system and the unity of the country and of all our nationalities, safeguarding the security, honour and interests of the motherland, observing the Constitution, the law, discipline and public order, and taking care of public property. In order to build socialist spiritual civilization in the whole society, it is important that all citizens raise such consciousness and sense of responsibility, handle their relations with the state and society and with other citizens on the principles of socialism and collectivism, cultivate a recognition of their rights and duties and a sense of organization and discipline consonant with the socialist political system, and acquire awareness as socialist citizens.

4. THE STRUCTURE OF THE STATE

The draft of the revised Constitution stipulates that "the state organs of the People's Republic of China apply the principle of democratic centralism." In the light of this principle and the experience we have gained over the last thirty and more years in the building of state power, a number of new and important provisions about the state structure have been incorporated into the draft. They mainly deal with the following aspects:

(1) Strengthening the system of people's congresses. Some of the functions and powers which originally belonged to the National People's Congress are now delegated to its Standing Committee. The functions and powers of the Standing Committee have been expanded, and the Committee has been strengthened organizationally. Both the National People's Congress and its Standing Committee exercise the legislative power of the state; while the basic statutes are enacted by the former, other statutes are enacted by the latter. Members of the NPC Standing Committee may not hold posts in any of the administrative, judicial and procuratorial organs of the state, which means that a considerable number of them devote their full time to this work. The work of the National People's Congress is strengthened by the establishment of special committees to examine, discuss and draw up relevant bills or draft resolutions under the direction of the National People's Congress and its Standing Committee.

*(2) Restoring the posts of president and vice-president of the People's Republic.** Practice since the founding of the People's Republic proves that these posts are necessary for a sound state system and are better suited to the custom and desire of our people of all nationalities.

(3) Establishing the state Central Military Commission to direct the armed forces of the country. The Chairman of the Central Military Commission exercises overall responsibility for the Commission. He is elected by the National People's Congress and is responsible to it and its Standing Committee. The People's Liberation Army, created and led by the Chinese Communist Party, has been the national army since the founding of the People's Republic. On the basis of summing up the historical experience since the founding of the People's Republic and in accordance with the actual conditions and needs of our country, the draft properly defines the position of the armed forces in the state system. The leadership by the Chinese Communist Party over the armed forces will not change with the establishment of the state Central Military Commission. The Party's leading role in the life of the state, which is explicitly affirmed in the Preamble, naturally includes its leadership over the armed forces.

---

*Previously translated as chairman and vice-chairman of the People's Republic—*translator's note.*

(4) The Premier exercises overall responsibility for the State Council. Executive meetings by the State Council are composed of the Premier, Vice-Premiers, State Councillors and Secretary-General of the State Council; the Premier convenes and presides over executive and plenary meetings of the State Council. The ministers exercise overall responsibility for the respective ministries or commissions under their charge; the ministers convene and preside over executive meetings or commission meetings of the ministries or commissions under their charge.

In order to strengthen supervision over finances and financial and accounting activities, the State Council newly establishes an auditing body which will independently exercise its power to supervise through auditing in accordance with the law. Local governments at different levels also establish auditing bodies correspondingly.

(5) Strengthening the building of the local organs of state power under the unified leadership of the central authorities. The local people's congresses at and above the county level establish their standing committees. The people's congresses of the provinces and municipalities directly under the Central Government and their standing committees have the power to adopt and issue local regulations. Local people's governments at different levels practice the system of overall responsibility by governors, mayors, county heads, district heads, township heads and town heads. These provisions apply to the organs of self-government of national autonomous areas as well.

(6) Changing the system of the rural people's commune which combines government administration and economic management and establishing organs of state power at the township level. The people's commune will be solely an organizational form of the rural collective economy. This change will serve to strengthen the organs of state power at the grass-roots level in the rural areas and also to expand the collective economy. As for the concrete step to separate government administration from economic management, this calls for meticulous efforts, and the authorities in different localities should, in the light of the actual local conditions, conduct the work under leadership, step by step and in a planned way, refraining from rashness.

The status and role of self-governing mass organizations such as residents' committees and villagers' committees, which have long proved to be effective, are written into the Constitution.

(7) It is stipulated that state leaders, including the president and vice-president of the People's Republic, the chairman and vice-chairmen of the Standing Committee of the National People's Congress and the premier and vice-premiers of the State Council, shall serve no more than two consecutive terms. Thus, the *de facto* system of life-long tenure of leading posts is abolished.

Now, I would like to explain in particular the intentions of the above provisions and the requirements embodied in them.

First, To Enable the Whole People To Exercise State Power Better

Any reform of our political institutions and establishment of state organs should be aimed at ensuring politically and organizationally that the whole people wield state power and are real masters of the country. According to this principle, the main thing to do at the level of the central authorities is to strengthen the National People's Congress. As China is a big and populous country, the number of deputies to the National People's Congress should not be too small; but too large a number will make its regular work cumbersome. The Standing Committee is the permanent body of the National People's Congress, and all those on the committee can be described as executive deputies to the congress. Being few in number, they can meet frequently and carry a heavy load of legislation and day-to-day work. Therefore, appropriate extension of the functions and powers of the Standing Committee is an effective way to strengthen the system of the people's congress. At the local levels, the main thing to do is to broaden the democratic basis of organs of state power at different levels (including those at the grass-roots level) and, at the same time, extend their functions and powers appropriately so that, under unified central leadership, the localities may carry out their own development plans in the light of their own conditions. The mass organizations of self-management in grass-roots community life ought to be strengthened so that the people are mobilized to manage their own public affairs and social services. Putting these provisions into practice will develop socialist democracy in China more fully.

During the nationwide discussion, it was suggested that, while extending the functions and powers of the Standing Committee of the National People's Congress, we should fully ensure the status of the National People's Congress as the highest organ of state power. This opinion is correct. Therefore, the qualifying clause "provided that they do not contravene the basic principles of these statutes" is added to the third item of the functions and powers of the Standing Committee contained in Article 67 of the draft, which originally says that it may introduce, when the National People's Congress is not in session, partial supplements and amendments to the statutes enacted by the National People's Congress. Besides, an item—the 11th—which reads, "to alter or annual inappropriate decisions of the Standing Committee of the National People's Congress," is added to Article 62 which stipulates the functions and powers of the National People's Congress.

Second, To Enable the State Organs To Guide and Organize the Work of Socialist Construction More Effectively

State organs should be established and their functions and powers defined in the following spirit: Organs of state power, namely, the National People's Congress and the local people's congresses, should fully discuss the formulation of laws and policies on major issues and decide on them through democratic procedures so that they truly concentrate the will and represent the interests of the people; and there must be a strict system of responsibility in implementing laws and major policy decisions so as to raise efficiency. The system of responsibility is indispensable in developing socialist democracy and ensuring that the people exercise state power. The will of the people can be carried out only when the decisions they have made through the organs of state power are implemented promptly and effectively by the administrative organs.

Third, To Enable the Different State Organs To Co-operate With One Another Better on the Basis of a Proper Division of Labour

Under the socialist system, there is a community of fundamental interests of the whole people. Therefore, the people's congresses can and must exercise state power in a unified way. Given this premise, there should at the same time be a clear division of power among the administrative, judicial and procuratorial authorities and leadership over the armed forces so that the organs of state power and the other state organs, administrative, judicial and procuratorial, may work in concert and harmony. The President of the People's Republic, the State Council, the Central Military Commission, the Supreme People's Court and the Supreme People's Procuratorate are all elected or created by the National People's Congress, and they are all responsible to it and subject to its supervision. The National People's Congress, the President of the People's Republic and other state organs all work within the scope of their respective functions and powers. The rational division of labour among state organs can avoid over-concentration of power and at the same time serve to enhance the efficiency of work by the state in all fields.

At present, the work of restructuring the state organs is going on in our country. The provisions of the draft on the state structure give expression to the principles and results in this respect and will serve to push the work further ahead.

5. *UNITY OF THE COUNTRY AND UNITY OF ALL THE NATIONALITIES*

The history of the thirty and more years since the founding of the People's Republic shows that the unity of the country and the unity of all our nationalities achieved so far are of tremendous importance for the advance of our socialist cause and the well-being of the whole Chinese nation. Just as Comrade Mao Zedong put it: "The unification of our country, the unity of our people and the unity of our various nationalities—these are the basic guarantees of the sure triumph of our cause."

At present, reunification of our great motherland is not yet complete, and we must strive to accomplish it. The Preamble of the draft states: "Taiwan is part of the sacred territory of the People's Republic of China. It is the lofty duty of the entire Chinese people, including our compatriots in Taiwan, to accomplish the great task of reunifying the motherland." The separation of Taiwan from the motherland in the last three decades and more is absolutely contrary to the interests of our nation and the wishes of our people. An early end to this separation will be highly conducive to the prosperity of the Taiwan region and our motherland as a whole, and to the maintenance of peace in the Far East and in the whold world. It is an inevitable trend in accord with the desires of the people, a trend which no party, political force or individual can resist. It is an internal affair of China, which brooks no interference by any foreign country. On the eve of our National Day last year, Comrade Ye Jianying, Chairman of the Standing Committee of the National People's Congress, pointed out in a statement that, after peaceful reunification, Taiwan can enjoy a high degree of autonomy as a special administrative region. This autonomy means, among other things, that the current social and economic systems in Taiwan, its way of life and its economic and cultural relations with foreign countries will remain unchanged. Considering the needs of this particular situation, Article 31 of the draft stipulates: "The state may establish special administrative regions when necessary. The systems to be instituted in special administrative regions shall be prescribed by law enacted by the National People's Congress in the light of the specific conditions." We are absolutely unequivocal on the principle of safeguarding China's sovereignty, unity and territorial integrity. At the same time, we are highly flexible as regards specific policies and measures and will give full consideration to the concrete situation in the Taiwan region and the wishes of the people in Taiwan and those of all personages concerned. This is our basic position in handling problems of a similar kind.

It is a basic principle followed by the Communist Party of China and the state to work for the equality, unity and common prosperity of all our nationalities. We have scored tremendous success in this respect in the thirty and more years since the founding of the People's Republic. But we also committed "Left" mistakes during this period, especially during the "cultural revolution," when the policies of the Party and the state on nationality affairs were distorted and undermined, and many cadres and ordinary folk of minority nationalities were made to suffer. This is a serious lesson. In revising the Constitution this time, we have paid full attention to summing up the historical experience in this respect and drawn on the important results of setting things to rights in our work among the minority nationalities in recent years.

The Preamble of the draft points out, "In the struggle to safeguard the unity of the nationalities, it is necessary to combat big-nation chauvinism, mainly Han chauvinism, and also necessary to combat local-national chauvinism." This is because both are harmful to the unity of our nationalities. Combating big-nation chauvinism chiefly means combating it among the people of Han nationality. This is determined by the fact that the Han nationality makes up for the overwhelming majority of China's population and exerts the greatest influence on the political, economic and cultural life of the country. Comrades of Han nationality should be highly conscientious and mindful in guarding against and overcoming big-Han chauvinism. Like combating big-nation chauvinism, combating local-national chauvinism is also necessary to guarantee unity among all our nationalities. However, the mistake of grievously broadening the scope of struggle in this regard was committed in the past: First, many comrades not guilty of local-national chauvinism were wrongly accused; secondly, ideological mistakes were wrongly dealt with as contradictions between ourselves and the enemy. Like big-nation chauvinism, local-national chauvinism is a matter of wrong thinking and understanding which belongs to the category of contradictions among the people, except in cases of those who engage in rebellious and secessionist activities in collaboration with foreign quarters. Big-nation chauvinism and local-national chauvinism should be combated in a correct way, mainly through ideological education and adoption of necessary political, economic and cultural measures.

The system of autonomy in regions inhabited by minority nationalities is a correct system which proves suited to our country's conditions through the test of practice. China is a unitary multi-national country jointly created by all our nationalities. Suffering in common from imperialist aggression before liberation, the Han people and the people of minority nationalities forged close ties of mutual help in times of dire need. After the founding of the People's Republic, all our nationalities established a close political, economic and cultural relationship of interdependence and mutual assistance while advancing along the common road of socialism. Regional national autonomy within a unified country not only can ensure the lawful rights and interests of the minority nationalities and speed up the economic and cultural development of the areas they inhabit, but also serve to resist aggression and subversion from outside and guarantee the independence and prosperity of the country as a whole. That is why the draft stipulates that "all the national autonomous areas are inalienable parts of the People's Republic of China," and that "it is the duty of citizens of the People's Republic of China to safeguard the unity of the country and the unity of all its nationalities." This fully accords with the fundamental interests and common will of all our nationalities.

The provisions on regional national autonomy have restored some important principles contained in the 1954 Constitution and, moreover, acquired new content in keeping with the changes which have taken place in our country. It is stipulated in Section VI, "The Organs of Self-Government of National Autonomous Areas," in the chapter on the structure of the state that the chairmanship and vice-chairmanships of the standing committee of the people's congress of any national autonomous area shall include a citizen or citizens of the nationality or nationalities exercising regional autonomy in the area concerned; that the administrative head of an autonomous region, prefecture or county shall be a citizen of the nationality, or of one of the nationalities, exercising regional autonomy in the area concerned; and that organs of self-government independently arrange for and administer local economic development under the guidance of state plans and independently administer educational, scientific, cultural, public health and physical culture affairs in their areas. It is also stipulated that, in exploiting natural resources and building enterprises in the national autonomous areas, the state shall give due consideration to the interests of those areas; that the state shall give financial, material and technical assistance to the minority nationalities to accelerate their economic and cultural development and help the national autonomous areas train large numbers of cadres at different levels and specialized personnel and skilled workers of different professions and trades from among the nationality or nationalities in those areas. The provisions in the draft on the right of autonomy of the national autonomous areas show that the state fully respects and ensures the democratic right of the minority nationalities to manage their internal affairs.

6. INDEPENDENT FOREIGN POLICY

The Preamble of the draft lays down the basic principles of China's foreign policy. They are: independence; development of diplomatic relations and economic and cultural exchanges with other countries on the basis of the five principles of mutual respect for sovereignty and territorial integrity, mutual nonaggression, non-interference in each other's internal affairs, equality and mutual benefit and peaceful coexistence; opposing imperialism, hegemonism and colonialism, strengthening unity with the people of other countries, supporting the oppressed nations and developing countries in their just struggle to win and preserve national independence and develop their national economies, and striving to safeguard world peace and promote the cause of human progress.

Our adherence to these principles of foreign policy is dictated by the nature of our state and our social system. Having suffered for a century before the founding of the People's Republic, the Chinese people know full well that without national independence, the people of a country have no possibility to enjoy democratic rights and build a prosperous and powerful country. From their experience in the long years of revolution and construction, the Chinese people are deeply aware that their own future is closely bound up with that of the people of the world. The establishment of the socialist system has rooted out the social causes both of China's submission to any foreign oppression and of any possibility of China committing aggression abroad in any form. The world today is in the throes of intense turbulence, and this turbulent situation will not end so long as imperialism and hegemonism exist in the world. No matter what happens outside China, we will adhere to the policy of independence. As Comrade Deng Xiaoping said at the 12th National Congress of the Chinese Communist Party: "No foreign country can expect China to be its vassal, nor can it expect China to swallow any bitter fruit harmful to China's interests." We will also persist in treating all countries, big or small, as equals and consistently stand on the side of all oppressed nations and developing countries as well as all other countries and people working for world peace. China will never seek hegemony and will never allow any hegemonists to ride on its back.

Our country follows the policy of opening to the outside world on the premise of independence and will continue to do so in the days to come. China will continue to expand its economic, technical and cultural exchanges with other countries on the principle of equality and mutual benefit. The draft stipulates that foreign economic organizations and individual foreigners may invest in China and enter into economic co-operation with Chinese economic organizations. Of course, all foreign economic organizations in China must abide by the law of the People's Republic of China, and their lawful rights and interests will be protected by the law of the People's Republic of China.

In accordance with international practice, China protects the legitimate rights and interests of Chinese nationals residing abroad, and at the same time, calls on them to abide by the law of the country in which they reside and to live in harmony with the people of that country. China protects the lawful rights and interests of foreigners residing in China and, at the same time, requires that they abide by the law of the People's Republic of China. These are all set forth in the draft.

The Chinese people have waged protracted and arduous struggles to win and safeguard their national independence. Our foreign policy represents the fundamental interests of the Chinese people and accords with those of the people of the world. The draft stipulates that the state shall educate the people both in patriotism and in internationalism. The Chinese people's tradition of patriotism and internationalism must be handed down from generation to generation. This is the basic guarantee for adhering to our independent foreign policy.

Fellow deputies, after its discussion and formal adoption by the current session of the National People's Congress, the draft revised Constitution will go into operation as the fundamental law of the state with supreme authority and legal force. It will be the general statute for China's good administration and stability in the new historical period. We are convinced that the new Constitution will be strictly observed and implemented. Summing up both the positive and negative historical experience in formulating and implementing the constitutions since the founding of the People's Republic, the Preamble of the draft clearly states that, "The people of all nationalities, all state organs, the armed forces, all political parties and public organizations and all enterprises and undertakings in the country must take the Constitution as the basic norm of conduct, and they have the duty to uphold the dignity of the Constitution and ensure its implementation." Both the National People's Congress and its Standing Committee have the function and power of supervising the enforcement of the Constitution; the local people's congresses at different levels should ensure the observance and implementation of the Constitution in their respective administrative areas. In his report to the 12th National Congress of the Communist Party of China, Comrade Hu Yaobang solemnly declared: "In particular, Party members should be educated and urged to take the lead in observing the Constitution and laws. The stipulation in the new Party Constitution that 'the Party must conduct its activities with the limits permitted by the Constitution and laws of the state' embodies a most important principle. It is impermissible for any Party organization or member, from the Central Committee down to the grass roots, to act in contravention of the Constitution and laws." The Chinese people and the Communist Party of China fully recognize that the authority of the Constitution concerns the political stability and the future of our country, and that it is absolutely impermissible to undermine the Constitution in any way. All power in our country belongs to the people. The destiny of our country is in the hands of the awakened people. The Communist Party of China is the political party of the working class that represents the interests of the Chinese people and acts on their will. It has no interests of its own apart from the interests of the people. The Chinese Communist Party has attached great importance to the revision of the Constitution, on which the Political Bureau and the Secretariat of its Central Committee conducted special discussions. Most of the members of the Political Bureau and the Secretariat are concurrently members of the Committee for Revision of the Constitution, and the opinions of the Party Central Committee have found full expression in the draft. Having led the people in formulating the new Constitution, the Chinese Communist Party will uphold the dignity of the Constitution and ensure its implementation together with the people of all our nationalities and the democratic parties and people's organizations. After the Constitution is adopted, it is necessary to give the Constitution wide publicity by various means so that it will be made known to every household. When our one billion people all cultivate the consciousness and habit of observing and upholding the Constitution and fight against all acts violating and undermining the Constitution, this will become a mighty force. With efforts by all the people and the Chinese Communist Party to ensure its implementation, the new Constitution that embodies the will of the people and the correct propositions of the Chinese Communist Party is bound to play a great role in promoting the success of China's socialist modernization.

The version of the new state constitution adopted by the Fifth National People's Congress differs only slightly from the draft, which is not printed in this volume. The differences are mainly editorial and essentially affect the level of emphasis given to certain matters. In the final version, for example, less emphasis is given to the inheritability of private property and to the right of foreign firms to invest and carry on joint enterprises in China, and the retirement of overage officials is stressed more heavily. It should be noted that the chief of state, designated by the Chinese term zhu xi [chairman], is now officially rendered president. Thus there is no more chairman in the Party— only a secretary general—and there is a president rather than a chairman (in English, although not in Chinese) in the state, an indication perhaps of the gradual fading of the era of Mao Zedong. In the draft constitution, the number of vice-premiers was specified as two to four, but there is no such limitation in the final version.

PREAMBLE

China is one of the countries with the longest histories in the world. The people of all nationalities in China have jointly created a splendid culture and have a glorious revolutionary tradition.

Feudal China was gradually reduced after 1840 to a semi-colonial and semi-feudal country. The Chinese people waged wave upon wave of heroic struggles for national independence and liberation and for democracy and freedom.

Great and earth-shaking historical changes have taken place in China in the 20th century.

The Revolution of 1911, led by Dr. Sun Yat-sen, abolished the feudal monarchy and gave birth to the Republic of China. But the Chinese people had yet to fulfill their historical task of overthrowing imperialism and feudalism.

After waging hard, protracted and tortuous struggles, armed and otherwise, the Chinese people of all nationalities led by the Communist Party of China with Chairman Mao Zedong as its leader ultimately, in 1949, overthrew the rule of imperialism, feudalism and bureaucrat-capitalism, won the great victory of the new-democratic revolution and founded the People's Republic of China. Thereupon the Chinese people took state power into their own hands and became masters of the country.

After the founding of the People's Republic, the transition of Chinese society from a new-democratic to a socialist society was effected step by step. The socialist transformation of the private ownership of the means of production was completed, the system of exploitation of

man by man eliminated and the socialist system established. The people's democratic dictatorship led by the working class and based on the alliance of workers and peasants, which is in essence the dictatorship of the proletariat, has been consolidated and developed. The Chinese people and the Chinese People's Liberation Army have thwarted aggression, sabotage and armed provocations by imperialists and hegemonists, safeguarded China's national independence and security and strengthened its national defense. Major successes have been achieved in economic development. An independent and fairly comprehensive socialist system of industry has in the main been established. There has been a marked increase in agricultural production. Significant progress has been made in educational, scientific, cultural and other undertakings, and socialist ideological education has yielded noteworthy results. The living standards of the people have improved considerably.

Both the victory of China's new-democratic revolution and the successes of its socialist cause have been achieved by the Chinese people of all nationalities under the leadership of the Communist Party of China and the guidance of Marxism-Leninism and Mao Zedong Thought, and by upholding truth, correcting errors and overcoming numerous difficulties and hardships. The basic task of the nation in the years to come is to concentrate its effort on socialist modernization. Under the leadership of the Communist Party of China and the guidance of Marxism-Leninism and Mao Zedong Thought, the Chinese people of all nationalities will continue to adhere to the people's democratic dictatorship and follow the socialist road, steadily improve socialist institutions, develop socialist democracy, improve the socialist legal system and work

[New China News Agency, 4 December 1982.]

hard and self-reliantly to modernize industry, agriculture, national defense and science and technology step by step to turn China into a socialist country with a high level of culture and democracy.

The exploiting classes as such have been eliminated in our country. However, class struggle will continue to exist within certain limits for a long time to come. The Chinese people must fight against those forces ane elements, both at home and abroad, that are hostile to China's socialist system and try to undermine it.

Taiwan is part of the sacred territory of the People's Republic of China. It is the lofty duty of the entire Chinese people, including our compatriots in Taiwan, to accomplish the great task of reunifying the motherland.

In building socialism it is imperative to rely on the workers, peasants and intellectuals and unite with all the forces that can be united. In the long years of revolution and construction, there has been formed under the leadership of the Communist Party of China a broad patriotic united front that is composed of democratic parties and people's organizations and embraces all socialist working people, all patriots who support socialism and all patriots who stand for reunification of the motherland. This united front will continue to be consolidated and developed. The Chinese People's Political Consultative Conference is a broadly representative organization of the united front, which has played a significant historical role and will continue to do so in the struggle for socialist modernization and for the reunification and unity of the country.

The People's Republic of China is a unitary multinational state built up jointly by the people of all its nationalities. Socialist relations of equality, unity and mutual assistance have been established among them and will continue to be strengthened. In the struggle to safeguard the unity of the nationalities, it is necessary to combat big-nation chauvinism, mainly Han chauvinism, and also necessary to combat local-national chauvinism. The state does its utmost to promote the common prosperity of all nationalities in the country.

China's achievements in revolution and construction are inseparable from support by the people of the world. The future of China is closely linked with that of the whole world. China adheres to an independent foreign policy as well as to the five principles of mutual respect for sovereignty and territorial integrity, mutual non-aggression, non-interference in each other's internal affairs, equality and mutual benefit, and peaceful coexistence in developing diplomatic relations and economic and cultural exchanges with other countries, China consistently opposes imperialism, hegemonism and colonialism, works to strengthen unity with the people of other countries, supports the oppressed nations and the developing countries in their just struggle to win and preserve national independence and develop their national economies, and strives to safeguard world peace and promote the cause of human progress.

This constitution affirms the achievements of the struggles of the Chinese people of all nationalities and defines the basic system and basic tasks of the state in legal form; it is the fundamental law of the state and has supreme legal authority. The people of all nationalities, all state organs, the armed forces, all political parties and public organizations and all enterprises and undertakings in the country must take the constitution as the basic norm of conduct, and they have the duty to uphold the dignity of the constitution and ensure its implementation.

CHAPTER ONE: GENERAL PRINCIPLES

Article 1. The People's Republic of China is a socialist state under the people's democratic dictatorship led by the working class and based on the alliance of workers and peasants.

The socialist system is the basic system of the People's Republic of China. Sabotage of the socialist system by any organization or individual is prohibited.

Article 2. All power in the People's Republic of China belongs to the people.

The organs through which the people exercise state power are the National People's Congress and the local people's congresses at different levels.

The people administer state affairs and manage economic, cultural and social affairs through various channels and in various ways in accordance with the law.

Article 3. The state organs of the People's Republic of China apply the principle of democratic centralism.

The National People's Congress and the local people's congresses at different levels are instituted through democratic election. They are responsible to the people and subject to their supervision.

All administrative, judicial and procuratorial organs of the state are created by the people's congresses to which they are responsible and under whose supervision they operate.

The division of functions and powers between the central and local state organs is guided by the principle of giving full play to the initiative and enthusiasm of the local authorities under the unified leadership of the central authorities.

Article 4. All nationalities in the People's Republic of China are equal. The state protects the lawful rights and interests of the minority nationalities and upholds and develops the relationship of equality, unity and mutual assistance among all of China's nationalities. Discrimination against and oppression of any nationality are prohibited; any acts that undermine the unity of the nationalities or instigate their secession are prohibited.

The state helps the areas inhabited by minority nationalities speed up their economic and cultural development in accordance with the peculiarities and needs of the different minority nationalities.

Regional autonomy is practiced in areas where people of minority nationalities live in compact communities; in these areas organs of self-government are established for the exercise of the right of autonomy. All the national autonomous areas are inalienable parts of the People's Republic of China.

The people of all nationalities have the freedom to use and develop their own spoken and written languages, and to preserve or reform their own ways and customs.

Article 5. The state upholds the uniformity and dignity of the socialist legal system.

No law or administrative or local rules and regulations shall contravene the constitution.

All state organs, the armed forces, all political parties

and public organizations and all enterprises and undertakings must abide by the constitution and the law. All acts in violation of the constitution and the law must be looked into.

No organization or individual may enjoy the privilege of being above the constitution and the law.

Article 6. The basis of the socialist economic system of the People's Republic of China is socialist public ownership of the means of production, namely, ownership by the whole people and collective ownership by the working people.

The system of socialist public ownership supersedes the system of exploitation of man by man; it applies the principle of "from each according to his ability, to each according to his work."

Article 7. The state economy is the sector of socialist economy under ownership by the whole people; it is the leading force in the national economy. The state ensures the consolidation and growth of the state economy.

Article 8. Rural people's communes, agricultural producers' co-operatives, and other forms of co-operative economy, such as producers, supply and marketing, credit and consumers' co-operatives, belong to the sector of socialist economy under collective ownership by the working people. Working people who are members of rural economic collectives have the right, within the limits prescribed by law, to farm private plots of cropland and hilly land, engage in household sideline production and raise privately owned livestock.

The various forms of co-operative economy in the cities and towns, such as those in the handicraft, industrial, building, transport, commercial and service trades, all belong to the sector of socialist economy under collective ownership by the working people.

The state protects the lawful rights and interests of the urban and rural economic collectives and encourages, guides and helps the growth of the collective economy.

Article 9. Mineral resources, waters, forests, mountains, grassland, unreclaimed land, beaches and other natural resources are owned by the state, that is, by the whole people, with the exception of the forests, mountains, grasslands, unreclaimed land and reaches that are owned by collectives in accordance with the law.

The state ensures the rational use of natural resources and protects rare animals and plants. The appropriation or damage of natural resources by any organization or individual by whatever means is prohibited.

Article 10. Land in the cities is owned by the state.

Land in the rural and suburban areas is owned by collectives except for those portions which belong to the state in accordance with the law; house sites and private plots of cropland and hilly land are also owned by collectives.

The state may in the public interest take over land for its use in accordance with the law.

No organization or individual may appropriate, buy, sell or lease land, or unlawfully transfer land in other ways.

All organizations and individuals who use land must make rational use of the land.

Article 11. The individual economy of urban and rural working people, operated within the limits prescribed by law, is a complement to the socialist public economy. The state protects the lawful rights and interests of the individual economy.

The state guides, helps and supervises the individual economy by exercising administrative control.

Article 12. Socialist public property is sacred and inviolable.

The state protects socialist public property. Appropriation or damage of state or collective property by any organization or individual by whatever means is prohibited.

Article 13. The state protects the right of citizens to own lawfully earned income, savings, houses and other lawful property.

The state protects by law the right of citizens to inherit private property.

Article 14. The state continuously raises labour productivity, improves economic results and develops the productive forces by enhancing the enthusiasm of the working people, raising the level of their technical skill, disseminating advanced science and technology, improving the systems of economic administration and enterprise operation and management, instituting the socialist system of responsibility in various forms and improving organization of work.

The state practices strict economy and combats waste.

The state properly apportions accumulation and consumption, pays attention to the interests of the collective and the individual as well as of the state and, on the basis of expanded production, gradually improves the material and cultural life of the people.

Article 15. The state practices economic planning on the basis of socialist public ownership. It ensures the proportionate and co-ordinated growth of the national economy through overall balancing by economic planning and the supplementary role of regulation by the market.

Disturbance of the orderly functioning of the social economy or disruption of the state economic plan by any organization or individual is prohibited.

Article 16. State enterprises have decision-making power in operation and management within the limits prescribed by law, on condition that they submit to unified leadership by the state and fulfill all their obligations under the state law.

Article 17. Collective economic organizations have decision-making power in conducting independent economic activities, on condition that they accept the guidance of the state plan and abide by the relevant laws.

Collective economic organizations practice democratic management in accordance with the law, with the entire body of their workers electing or removing their managerial personnel and deciding on major issues concerning operation and management.

Article 18. The People's Republic of China permits foreign enterprises, other foreign economic organizations and individual foreigners to invest in China and to enter into various forms of economic co-operation with Chinese enterprises and other economic organizations in accordance with the law of the People's Republic of China.

All foreign enterprises and other foreign economic organizations in China, as well as joint ventures with Chinese and foreign investment located in China, shall abide by the law of the People's Republic of China. Their lawful rights and interests are protected by the law of the People's Republic of China.

Article 19. The state develops socialist educational undertakings and works to raise the scientific and cultural level of the whole nation.

The state runs schools of various types, makes primary education compulsory and universal, develops secondary, vocational and higher education and promotes pre-school education.

The state develops educational facilities of various types in order to wipe out illiteracy and provide political, cultural, scientific, technical and professional education for workers, peasants, state functionaries and other working people. It encourages people to become educated through self-study.

The state encourages the collective economic organizations, state enterprises and undertakings and other social forces to set up educational institutions of various types in accordance with the law.

The state promotes the nationwide use of putonghua (common speech based on Beijing pronunciation.)

Article 20. The state promotes the development of the natural and social sciences, disseminates scientific and technical knowledge, and commends and rewards achievements in scientific research as well as technological discoveries and inventions.

Article 21. The state develops medical and health services, promotes modern medicine and traditional Chinese medicine, encourages and supports the setting up of various medical and health facilities by the rural economic collectives, state enterprises and undertakings and neighbourhood organizations, and promotes sanitation activities of a mass character, all to protect the people's health.

The state develops physical culture and promotes mass sports activities to build up the people's physique.

Article 22. The state promotes the development of literature and art, the press, broadcasting and television undertakings, publishing and distribution services, libraries, museums, cultural centres and other cultural undertakings, that serve the people and socialism, and sponsors mass cultural activities.

The state protects places of scenic and historical interest, valuable cultural monuments and relics and other important items of China's historical and cultural heritage.

Article 23. The state trains specialized personnel in all fields who serve socialism, increases the number of intellectuals and creates conditions to give full scope to their role in socialist modernization.

Article 24. The state strengthens the building of socialist spiritual civilization through spreading education in high ideals and morality, general education and education in discipline and the legal system, and through promoting the formulation and observance of rules of conduct and common pledges by different sections of the people in urban and rural areas.

The state advocates the civic virtues of love for the motherland, for the people, for labour, for science and for socialism, it educates the people in patriotism, collectivism, internationalism and communism and in dialectical and historical materialism; it combats capitalist, feudalist and other decadent ideas.

Article 25. The state promotes family planning so that population growth may fit the plans for economic and social development.

Article 26. The state protects and improves the living environment and the ecological environment, and prevents and remedies pollution and other public hazards.

The state organizes and encourages afforestation and the protection of forests.

Article 27. All state organs carry out the principle of simple and efficient administration, the system of responsibility for work and the system of training functionaries and appraising their work in order constantly to improve quality of work and efficiency and combat bureaucratism.

All state organs and functionaries must rely on the support of the people, keep in close touch with them, heed their opinions and suggestions, accept their supervision and work hard to serve them.

Article 28. The state maintains public order and suppresses treasonable and other counter-revolutionary activities; it penalizes actions that endanger public security and disrupt the socialist economy and other criminal activities, and punishes and reforms criminals.

Article 29. The armed forces of the People's Republic of China belong to the people. Their tasks are to strengthen national defence, resist aggression, defend the motherland, safeguard the people's peaceful labour, participate in national reconstruction, and work hard to serve the people.

The state strengthens the revolutionization, modernization and regularization of the armed forces in order to increase the national defence capability.

Article 30. The administrative division of the People's Republic of China is as follows:

(1) The country is divided into provinces, autonomous regions and municipalities directly under the central government;

(2) Provinces and autonomous regions are divided into autonomous prefectures, counties, autonomous counties and cities;

(3) Counties and autonomous counties are divided into townships, nationality townships and towns.

Municipalities directly under the central government and other large cities are divided into districts and counties. Autonomous prefectures are divided into counties, autonomous counties, and cities.

All autonomous regions, autonomous prefectures and autonomous counties are national autonomous areas.

Article 31. The state may establish special administrative regions when necessary. The systems to be instituted in special administrative regions shall be prescribed by law enacted by the National People's Congress in the light of the specific conditions.

Article 32. The People's Republic of China protects the lawful rights and interests of foreigners within Chinese territory, and while on Chinese territory foreigners must abide by the law of the People's Republic of China.

The People's Republic of China may grant asylum to foreigners who request it for political reasons.

CHAPTER TWO: THE FUNDAMENTAL RIGHTS AND DUTIES OF CITIZENS

Article 33. All persons holding the nationality of the People's Republic of China are citizens of the People's Republic of China.

All citizens of the People's Republic of China are equal before the law.

Every citizen enjoys the rights and at the same time must perform the duties prescribed by the constitution and the law.

Article 34. All citizens of the People's Republic of China who have reached the age of 18 have the right to vote and stand for election, regardless of nationality, race, sex, occupation, family background, religious belief, education, property status, or length of residence, except persons deprived of political rights according to law.

Article 35. Citizens of the People's Republic of China enjoy freedom of speech, of the press, of assembly, of association, of procession and of demonstration.

Article 36. Citizens of the People's Republic of China enjoy freedom of religious belief.

No state organ, public organization or individual may compel citizens to believe in, or not to believe in, any religion; nor may they discriminate against citizens who believe in, or do not believe in, any religion.

The state protects normal religious activities. No one may make use of religion to engage in activities that disrupt public order, impair the health of citizens or interfere with the educational system of the state.

Religious bodies and religious affairs are not subject to any foreign domination.

Article 37. The freedom of person of citizens of the People's Republic of China is inviolable.

No citizen may be arrested except with the approval or by decision of a people's procuratorate or by decision of a people's court, and arrests must be made by a public security organ.

Unlawful deprivation or restriction of citizens' freedom of person by detention or other means is prohibited; and unlawful search of the person of citizens is prohibited.

Article 38. The personal dignity of citizens of the People's Republic of China is inviolable. Insult, libel, false charge or frame-up directed against citizens by any means is prohibited.

Article 39. The home of citizens of the People's Republic of China is inviolable. Unlawful search of, or intrusion into, a citizen's home is prohibited.

Article 40. The freedom and privacy of correspondence of citizens of the People's Republic of China are protected by law. No organization or individual may, on any ground, infringe upon the freedom and privacy of citizens' correspondence except in cases where, to meet the needs of state security or of investigation into criminal offenses, public security or procuratorial organs are permitted to censor correspondence in accordance with procedures prescribed by law.

Article 41. Citizens of the People's Republic of China have the right to criticize and make suggestions to any state organ or functionary. Citizens have the right to make to relevant state organs complaints and charges against, or exposures of, violation of the law or dereliction of duty by any state organ or functionary; but fabrication or distortion of facts with the intention of libel or frame-up is prohibited.

In case of complaints, charges or exposures made by citizens, the state organ concerned must deal with them in a responsible manner after ascertaining the facts. No one may suppress such complaints, charges and exposures, or retaliate against the citizens making them.

Citizens who have suffered losses through infringement of their civic rights by any state organ or functionary have the right to compensation in accordance with the law.

Article 42. Citizens of the People's Republic of China have the right as well as the duty to work.

Using various channels, the state creates conditions for employment, strengthens labour protection, improves working conditions and, on the basis of expanded production, increases remuneration for work and social benefits.

Work is the glorious duty of every able-bodied citizen. All working people in state enterprises and in urban and rural economic collectives should perform their tasks with an attitude consonant with their status as masters of the country. The state promotes socialist labour emulation, and commends and rewards model and advanced workers. The state encourages citizens to take part in voluntary labour.

The state provides necessary vocational training to citizens before they are employed.

Article 43. Working people in the People's Republic of China have the right to rest.

The state expands facilities for rest and recuperation of working people, and prescribes working hours and vacations for workers and staff.

Article 44. The state prescribes by law the system of retirement for workers and staff in enterprises and undertakings and for functionaries of organs of state. The livelihood of retired personnel is ensured by the state and society.

Article 45. Citizens of the People's Republic of China have the right to material assistance from the state and society when they are old, ill or disabled. The state develops the social insurance, social relief and medical and health services that are required to enable citizens to enjoy this right.

The state and society ensure the livelihood of disabled members of the armed forces, provide pensions to the families of martyrs and give preferential treatment to the families of military personnel.

The state and society help make arrangements for the work, livelihood and education of the blind, deaf-mute and other handicapped citizens.

Article 46. Citizens of the People's Republic of China have the duty as well as the right to receive education.

The state promotes the all-round moral, intellectual and physical development of children and young people.

Article 47. Citizens of the People's Republic of China have the freedom to engage in scientific research, literary and artistic creation and other cultural pursuits. The state encourages and assists creative endeavours conducive to the interests of the people that are made by citizens engaged in education, science, technology, literature, art and other cultural work.

Article 48. Women in the People's Republic of China enjoy equal rights with men in all spheres of life, political, economic, cultural and social, including family life.

The state protects the rights and interests of women, applies the principle of equal pay for equal work for men and women alike and trains and selects cadres from among women.

Article 49. Marriage, the family and mother and child are protected by the state.

Both husband and wife have the duty to practice family planning.

Parents have the duty to rear and educate their minor children, and children who have come of age have the duty to support and assist their parents.

Violation of the freedom of marriage is prohibited. Maltreatment of old people, women and children is prohibited.

Article 50. The People's Republic of China protects the legitimate rights and interests of Chinese nationals residing abroad and protects the lawful rights and interests of returned overseas Chinese and of the family members of Chinese nationals residing abroad.

Article 51. The exercise by citizens of the People's Republic of China of their freedom and rights may not infringe upon the interests of the state, of society and of the collective, or upon the lawful freedoms and rights of other citizens.

Article 52. It is the duty of citizens of the People's Republic of China to safeguard the unity of the country and the unity of all its nationalities.

Article 53. Citizens of the People's Republic of China must abide by the constitution and the law, keep state secrets, protect public property and observe labour discipline and public order and respect social ethics.

Article 54. It is the duty of citizens of the People's Republic of China to safeguard the security, honour and interests of the motherland, they must not commit acts detrimental to the security, honour and interests of the motherland.

Article 55. It is the sacred obligation of every citizen of the People's Republic of China to defend the motherland and resist aggression.

It is the honourable duty of citizens of the People's Republic of China to perform military service and join the militia in accordance with the law.

Article 56. It is the duty of citizens of the People's Republic of China to pay taxes in accordance with the law.

CHAPTER THREE: THE STRUCTURE OF THE STATE

Section I: The National People's Congress

Article 57. The National People's Congress of the People's Republic of China is the highest organ of state power. Its permanent body is the Standing Committee of the National People's Congress.

Article 58. The National People's Congress and its Standing Committee exercise the legislative power of the state.

Article 59. The National People's Congress is composed of deputies elected by the provinces, autonomous regions and municipalities directly under the central government, and by the armed forces. All the minority nationalities are entitled to appropriate representation.

Election of deputies to the National People's Congress is conducted by the Standing Committee of the National People's Congress.

The number of deputies to the National People's Congress and the manner of their election are prescribed by law.

Article 60. The National People's Congress is elected for a term of five years.

Two months before the expiration of the term of office of a National People's Congress, its Standing Committee must ensure that the election of deputies to the succeeding National People's Congress is completed. Should exceptional circumstances prevent such an election, it may be postponed by decision of a majority vote of more than two-thirds of all those on the Standing Committee of the incumbent National People's Congress, and the term of office of the incumbent National People's Congress may be extended. The election of deputies to the succeeding National People's Congress must be completed within one year after the termination of such exceptional circumstances.

Article 61. The National People's Congress meets in session once a year and is convened by its Standing Committee. A session of the National People's Congress may be convened at any time the Standing Committee deems this necessary, or when more than one-fifth of the deputies to the National People's Congress so propose.

Article 62. The National People's Congress exercises the following functions and powers:

(1) to amend the constitution;

(2) to supervise the enforcement of the constitution;

(3) to enact and amend basic statutes concerning criminal offenses, civil affairs, the state organs and other matters;

(4) to elect the president and the vice-president of the People's Republic of China; (previously translated as chairman and vice-chairman of the People's Republic of China—translator's note)

(5) to decide on the choice of the premier of the State Council upon nomination by the president of the People's Republic of China, and to decide on the choice of the vice-premiers, state councillors, ministers in charge of ministries or commissions and the auditor-general and the secretary-general of the State Council upon nomination by the premier;

(6) to elect the chairman of the Central Military Commission and, upon his nomination, to decide on the choice of all the others on the Central Military Commission;

(7) to elect the president of the Supreme People's Court;

(8) to elect the procurator-general of the Supreme People's Procuratorate;

(9) to examine and approve the plan for national economic and social development and the reports on its implementation;

(10) to examine and approve the state budget and the report on its implementation;

(11) to alter or annul inappropriate decisions of the Standing Committee of the National People's Congress;

(12) to approve the establishment of provinces, autonomous regions, and municipalities directly under the central government;

(13) to decide on the establishment of special administrative regions and the systems to be instituted there;

(14) to decide on questions of war and peace; and

(15) to exercise such other functions and powers as the highest organ of state power should exercise.

Article 63. The National People's Congress has the power to recall or remove from office the following persons:

(1) the president and the vice-president of the People's Republic of China;

(2) the premier, vice-premiers, state councillors, ministers in charge of ministries or commissions and the auditor-general and the secretary-general of the State Council;

(3) the chairman of the Central Military Commission and others on the commission;

(4) the president of the Supreme People's Court; and

(5) the procurator-general of the Supreme People's Procuratorate.

Article 64. Amendments to the constitution are to be proposed by the Standing Committee of the National People's Congress or by more than one-fifth of the deputies to the National People's Congress and adopted by a majority vote of more than two-thirds of all the deputies to the congress.

Statutes and resolutions are adopted by a majority vote of more than one half of all the deputies to the National People's Congress.

Article 65. The Standing Committee of the National People's Congress is composed of the following: the chairman, the vice-chairmen; the secretary-general; and members.

Minority nationalities are entitled to appropriate representation on the Standing Committee of the National People's Congress.

The National People's Congress elects, and has the power to recall, all those on its Standing Committee.

No one on the Standing Committee of the National People's Congress shall hold any post in any of the administrative, judicial or procuratorial organs of the state.

Article 66. The Standing Committee of the National People's Congress is elected for the same term as the National People's Congress; it exercises its functions and powers until a new Standing Committee is elected by the succeeding National People's Congress.

The chairman and vice-chairmen of the Standing Committee shall serve no more than two consecutive terms.

Article 67. The Standing Committee of the National People's Congress exercises the following functions and powers;

(1) to interpret the constitution and supervise its enforcement;

(2) to enact and amend statutes with the exception of those which should be enacted by the National People's Congress;

(3) to enact, when the National People's Congress is not in session, partial supplements and amendments to statutes enacted by the National People's Congress provided that they do not contravene the basic principles of these statutes;

(4) to interpret statutes;

(5) to examine and approve, when the National People's Congress is not in session, partial adjustments to the plan for national economic and social development and to the state budget that prove necessary in the course of their implementation;

(6) to supervise the work of the State Council, the Central Military Commission, the Supreme People's Court and the Supreme People's Procuratorate;

(7) to annul those administrative rules and regulations, decisions or orders of the State Council that contravene the constitution or the statutes;

(8) to annul those local regulations or decisions of the organs of state power of provinces, autonomous regions and municipalities directly under the central government that contravene the constitution, the statutes or the administrative rules and regulations;

(9) to decide, when the National People's Congress is not in session, on the choice of ministers in charge of ministries or commissions or the auditor-general and the secretary-general of the State Council upon nomination by the premier of the State Council;

(10) to decide, upon nomination by the chairman of the Central Military Commission, on the choice of others on the commission, when the National People's Congress is not in session;

(11) to appoint and remove the vice-presidents and judges of the Supreme People's Court, members of its Judicial Committee and the president of the Military Court at the suggestion of the president of the Supreme People's Court;

(12) to appoint and remove the deputy procurators-general and procurators of the Supreme People's Procuratorate, members of its Procuratorial Committee and the chief procurator of the Military Procuratorate at the request of the procurator-general of the Supreme People's Procuratorate, and to approve the appointment and removal of the chief procurators of the people's procuratorates of provinces, autonomous regions and municipalities directly under the central government;

(13) to decide on the appointment and recall of plenipotentiary representatives abroad;

(14) to decide on the ratification and abrogation of treaties and important agreements concluded with foreign states;

(15) to institute systems of titles and ranks for military and diplomatic personnel and of other specific titles and ranks;

(16) to institute state medals and titles of honour and decide on their conferment;

(17) to decide on the granting of special pardons;

(18) to decide, when the National People's Congress is not in session, on the proclamation of a state of war in the event of an armed attack on the country or in fulfillment of international treaty obligations concerning common defense against aggression;

(19) to decide on general mobilization or partial mobilization;

(20) to decide on the enforcement of martial law throughout the country or in particular provinces, autonomous regions or municipalities directly under the central government; and

(21) to exercise such other functions and powers as the National People's Congress may assign to it.

Article 68. The chairman of the Standing Committee of the National People's Congress presides over the work of the Standing Committee and convenes its meetings. The vice-chairmen and the secretary-general assist the chairman in his work.

Chairmanship meetings with the participation of the chairman, vice-chairmen and secretary-general handle the important day-to-day work of the Standing Committee of the National People's Congress.

Article 69. The Standing Committee of the National People's Congress is responsible to the National People's Congress and reports on its work to the congress.

Article 70. The National People's Congress establishes a nationalities committee, a law committee, a finance and economic committee, an education, science, culture and public health committee, a foreign affairs committee, an overseas Chinese committee and such other special committees as are necessary. These special committees work under the direction of the Standing Committee of the National People's Congress when the congress is not in session.

The special committees examine, discuss and draw up relevant bills and draft resolutions under the direction of the National People's Congress and its Standing Committee.

Article 71. The National People's Congress and its Standing Committee may, when they deem it necessary, appoint committees of inquiry into specific questions and adopt relevant resolutions in the light of their reports.

All organs of state, public organizations and citizens concerned are obliged to supply the necessary information to those committees of inquiry when they conduct investigations.

Article 72. Deputies to the National People's Congress and all those on its Standing Committee have the right, in accordance with procedures prescribed by law, to submit bills and proposals within the scope of the respective functions and powers of the National People's Congress and its Standing Committee.

Article 73. Deputies to the National People's Congress during its sessions, and all those on its Standing Committee during its meetings, have the right to address questions, in accordance with procedures prescribed by law, to the State Council or the ministries and commissions under the State Council, which must answer the questions in a responsible manner.

Article 74. No deputy to the National People's Congress may be arrested or placed on criminal trial without the consent of the presidium of the current session of the National People's Congress or, when the National People's Congress is not in session, without the consent of its Standing Committee.

Article 75. Deputies to the National People's Congress may not be called to legal account for their speeches or votes at its meetings.

Article 76. Deputies to the National People's Congress must play an exemplary role in abiding by the constitution and the law and keeping state secrets and, in production and other work and their public activities, assist in the enforcement of the constitution and the law.

Deputies to the National People's Congress should maintain close contact with the units which elected them and with the people, listen to and convey the opinions and demands of the people and work hard to serve them.

Article 77. Deputies to the National People's Congress are subject to the supervision of the units which elected them. The electoral units have the power, through procedures prescribed by law, to recall the deputies whom they elected.

Article 78. The organization and working procedures of the National People's Congress and its Standing Committee are prescribed by law.

Section II: The President of the People's Republic of China

Article 79. The president and vice-president of the People's Republic of China are elected by the National People's Congress.

Citizens of the People's Republic of China who have the right to vote and to stand for election and who have reached the age of 45 are eligible for election as president or vice-president of the People's Republic of China.

The term of office of the president and vice-president of the People's Republic of China is the same as that of the National People's Congress, and they shall serve no more than two consecutive terms.

Article 80. The president of the People's Republic of China, in pursuance of decisions of the National People's Congress and its Standing Committee, promulgates statutes, appoints and removes the premier, vice-premiers, state councillors, ministers in charge of ministries or commissions, and the auditor-general and the secretary-general of the State Council; confers state medals and titles of honour; issues orders of special pardons; proclaims martial law; proclaims a state of war; and issues mobilization orders.

Article 81. The president of the People's Republic of China receives foreign diplomatic representatives on behalf of the People's Republic of China and, in pursuance of decisions of the Standing Committee of the National People's Congress, appoints and recalls plenipotentiary representatives abroad, and ratifies and abrogates treaties and important agreements concluded with foreign states.

Article 82. The vice-president of the People's Republic of China assists the president in his work.

The vice-president of the People's Republic of China may exercise such parts of the functions and powers of the president as the president may entrust to him.

Article 83. The president and vice-president of the People's Republic of China exercise their functions and powers until the new president and vice-president elected by the succeeding National People's Congress assume office.

Article 84. In case the office of the president of the People's Republic of China falls vacant, the vice-president succeeds to the office of president.

In case the office of the vice-president of the People's Republic of China falls vacant, the National People's Congress shall elect a new vice-president to fill the vacancy.

In the event that the offices of both the president and the vice-president of the People's Republic of China fall vacant, the National People's Congress shall elect a new president and a new vice-president. Prior to such election, the chairman of the Standing Committee of the National People's Congress shall temporarily act as the president of the People's Republic of China.

Section III: The State Council

Article 85. The State Council, that is, the central people's government, of the People's Republic of China is the executive body of the highest organ of state power; it is the highest organ of state administration.

Article 86. The State Council is composed of the following:

The premier; the vice-premiers; the state councillors; the ministers in charge of ministries; the ministers in charge of commissions; the auditor-general; and the secretary-general.

The premier has overall responsibility for the State Council. The ministers have overall responsibility for the respective ministries or commissions under their charge.

The organization of the State Council is prescribed by law.

Article 87. The term of office of the State Council is the same as that of the National People's Congress.

The premier, vice-premiers and state councillors shall serve no more than two consecutive terms.

Article 88. The premier directs the work of the State Council. The vice-premiers and state councillors assist the premier in his work.

Executive meetings of the State Council are composed of the premier, the vice-premiers, the state councillors and the secretary-general of the State Council.

The premier convenes and presides over the executive meetings and plenary meetings of the State Council.

Article 89. The State Council exercises the following functions and powers:

(1) to adopt administrative measures, enact administrative rules and regulations and issue decisions and orders in accordance with the constitution and the statutes;

(2) to submit proposals to the National People's Congress or its Standing Committee;

(3) to lay down the tasks and responsibilities of the ministries and commissions of the State Council, to exercise unified leadership over the work of the ministries and commissions and to direct all other administrative work of a national character that does not fall within the jurisdiction of the ministries and commissions;

(4) to exercise unified leadership over the work of local organs of state administration at different levels throughout the country, and to lay down the detailed division of functions and powers between the central government and the organs of state administration of provinces, autonomous regions and municipalities directly under the central government;

(5) to draw up and implement the plan for national economic and social development and the state budget;

(6) to direct and administer economic work and urban and rural development;

(7) to direct and administer the work concerning education, science, culture, public health, physical culture and family planning;

(8) to direct and administer the work concerning civil affairs, public security, judicial administration, supervision and other related matters;

(9) to conduct foreign affairs and conclude treaties and agreements with foreign states;

(10) to direct and administer the building of national defense;

(11) to direct and administer affairs concerning the nationalities, and to safeguard the equal rights of minority nationalities and the right of autonomy of the national autonomous areas;

(12) to protect the legitimate rights and interests of Chinese nationals residing abroad and protect the lawful rights and interests of returned overseas Chinese and of the family members of Chinese nationals residing abroad;

(13) to alter or annul inappropriate orders, directives and regulations issued by the ministries or commissions;

(14) to alter or annul inappropriate decisions and orders issued by local organs of state administration at different levels;

(15) to approve the geographic division of provinces, autonomous regions and municipalities directly under the central government, and to approve the establishment and geographic division of autonomous prefectures, counties, autonomous counties and cities;

(16) to decide on the enforcement of martial law in parts of provinces, autonomous regions and municipalities directly under the central government;

(17) to examine and decide on the size of administrative organs and, in accordance with the law, to appoint, remove and train administrative officers, appraise their work and reward or punish them; and

(18) to exercise such other functions and powers as the National People's Congress or its Standing Committee may assign it.

Article 90. The ministers in charge of ministries or commissions of the State Council are responsible for the work of their respective departments and convene and preside over their ministerial meetings or commission meetings that discuss and decide on major issues in the work of their respective departments.

The ministries and commissions issue orders, directives and regulations within the jurisdiction of their respective departments and in accordance with the statutes and the administrative rules and regulations, decisions and orders issued by the State Council.

Article 91. The State Council establishes an auditing body to supervise through auditing the revenue and expenditure of all departments under the state council and of the local governments at different levels, and those of the state financial and monetary organizations and of enterprises and undertakings.

Under the direction of the premier of the State Council, the auditing body independently exercises its power to supervise through auditing in accordance with the law, subject to no interference by any other administrative organ or any public organization or individual.

Article 92. The State Council is responsible, and reports on its work, to the National People's Congress or when the National People's Congress is not in session, to its Standing Committee.

Section IV: The Central Military Commission

Article 93. The Central Military Commission of the People's Republic of China directs the armed forces of the country.

The Central Military Commission is composed of the following:

The chairman; the vice-chairmen; and members.

The chairman of the Central Military Commission has overall responsibility for the commission.

The term of office of the Central Military Commission is the same as that of the National People's Congress.

Article 94. The chairman of the Central Military Commission is responsible to the National People's Congress and its Standing Committee.

Section V: The Local People's Congresses and the Local People's Governments at Different Levels

Article 95. People's congresses and people's governments are established in provinces, municipalities directly under the central government, counties, cities, municipal districts, townships, nationality townships and towns.

The organization of local people's congresses and local people's governments at different levels is prescribed by law.

Organs of self-government are established in autonomous regions, autonomous prefectures and autonomous counties. The organization and working procedures of organs of self-government are prescribed by law in accordance with the basic principles laid down in sections V and VI of Chapter Three of the constitution.

Article 96. Local people's congresses at different levels are local organs of state power.

Local people's congresses at and above the county level establish standing committees.

Article 97. Deputies to the people's congresses of provinces, municipalities directly under the central government, and cities divided into districts are elected by the people's congresses at the next lower level; deputies to the people's congresses of counties, cities not divided into districts, municipal districts, townships, nationality townships and towns are elected directly by their constituencies.

The number of deputies to local people's congresses at different levels and the manner of their election are prescribed by law.

Article 98. The term of office of the people's congresses of provinces, municipalities directly under the central government and cities divided into districts is five years. The term of office of the people's congresses of counties, cities not divided into districts, municipal districts, townships, nationality townships and towns is three years.

Article 99. Local people's congresses at different levels ensure the observance and implementation of the constitution, the statutes and the administrative rules and regulations in their respective administrative areas. Within the limits of their authority as prescribed by law, they adopt and issue resolutions and examine and decide on plans for local economic and cultural development and for the development of public services.

Local people's congresses at and above the county level examine and approve the plans for economic and social development and the budgets of their respective administrative areas and examine and approve reports on their implementation. They have the power to alter or annul inappropriate decisions of their own standing committees.

The people's congresses of nationality townships may, within the limits of their authority as prescribed by law, take specific measures suited to the peculiarities of the nationalities concerned.

Article 100. The people's congresses of provinces and municipalities directly under the central government, and their standing committees, may adopt local regulations, which must not contravene the constitution, the statutes and the administrative rules and regulations, and they shall report such local regulations to the Standing Committee of the National People's Congress for the record.

Article 101. At their respective levels, local people's congresses elect, and have the power to recall, governors and deputy governors, or mayors and deputy mayors, or heads and deputy heads of counties, districts, townships and towns.

Local people's congresses at and above the county level elect, and have the power to recall, presidents of people's courts and chief procurators of people's procuratorates at the corresponding level. The election or recall of chief procurators of people's procuratorates shall be reported to the chief procurators of the people's procuratorates at the next higher level for submission to the standing committees of the people's congresses at the corresponding level for approval.

Article 102. Deputies to the people's congresses of provinces, municipalities directly under the central government and cities divided into districts are subject to supervision by the units which elected them, deputies to the people's congresses of counties, cities not divided into districts, municipal districts, townships, nationality townships and towns are subject to supervision by their constituencies.

The electoral units and constituencies which elect deputies to local people's congresses at different levels have the power, according to procedures prescribed by law, to recall deputies whom they elected.

Article 103. The standing committee of a local people's congress at and above the county level is composed of a chairman, vice-chairmen and members, and is responsible, and reports on its work, to the people's congress at the corresponding level.

The local people's congress at and above the county level elects, and has the power to recall, anyone on the standing committee of the people's congress at the corresponding level.

No one on the standing committee of a local people's congress at and above the county level shall hold any post in state administrative, judicial and procuratorial organs.

Article 104. The standing committee of a local people's congress at and above the county level discusses and decides on major issues in all fields of work in its administrative area; supervises the work of the people's government, people's court and people's procuratorate at the corresponding level; annuls inappropriate decisions and orders of the people's government at the corresponding level, annuls inappropriate resolutions of the people's congress at the next lower level, decides on the appointment and removal of functionaries of state organs within its jurisdiction as prescribed by law; and, when the people's congress at the corresponding level is not in session, recalls individual deputies to the people's congress at the next higher level and elects individual deputies to fill vacancies in that people's congress.

Article 105. Local people's governments at different levels are the executive bodies of local organs of state power as well as the local organs of state administration at the corresponding level.

Local people's governments at different levels practice the system of overall responsibility by governors, mayors, county heads, district heads, township heads and town heads.

Article 106. The term of office of local people's governments at different levels is the same as that of the people's congresses at the corresponding level.

Article 107. Local people's governments at and above the county level, within the limits of their authority as prescribed by law, conduct the administrative work concerning the economy, education, science, culture, public health, physical culture, urban and rural development, finance, civil affairs, public security, nationalities affairs, judicial administration, supervision and family planning in their respective administrative areas; issue decisions and orders; appoint, remove and train administrative functionaries, appraise their work and reward or punish them.

People's governments of townships, nationality townships and towns carry out the resolutions of the people's congress at the corresponding level as well as the decisions and orders of the state administrative organs at the next higher level and conduct administrative work in their respective administrative areas.

Article 108. Local people's governments at and above the county level direct the work of their subordinate departments and of people's governments at lower levels, and have the power to alter or annul inappropriate decisions of their subordinate departments and people's governments at lower levels.

Article 109. Auditing bodies are established by local people's governments at and above the county level. Local auditing bodies at different levels independently exercise their power to supervise through auditing in accordance with the law and are responsible to the people's government at the corresponding level and to the auditing body at the next higher level.

Article 110. Local people's governments at different levels are responsible, and report on their work, to people's congresses at the corresponding level. Local people's governments at and above the county level are responsible, and report on their work, to the standing committee of the people's congress at the corresponding level when the congress is not in session.

Local people's governments at different levels are responsible, and report on their work, to the state administrative organs at the next higher level. Local people's governments at different levels throughout the country are state administrative organs under the unified leadership of the state council and are subordinate to it.

Article 111. The residents' committees and villagers' committees established among urban and rural residents on the basis of their place of residence are mass organizations of self-management at the grass-roots level. The chairman, vice-chairmen and members of each residents' or villagers' committee are elected by the residents. The relationship between the residents' and villagers' committees and the grass-roots organs of state power is prescribed by law.

The residents' and villagers' committees establish committees for people's mediation, public security, public health and other matters in order to manage public affairs and social services in their areas, mediate civil disputes, help maintain public order and convey residents' opinions and demands and make suggestions to the people's government.

Section VI: The Organs of Self-Government of National Autonomous Areas

Article 112. The organs of self-government of national autonomous areas are the people's congresses and people's governments of autonomous regions, autonomous prefectures and autonomous counties.

Article 113. In the people's congress of an autonomous region, prefecture or county, in addition to the deputies of the nationality or nationalities exercising regional autonomy in the administrative area, the other nationalities inhabiting the area are also entitled to appropriate representation.

The chairmanship and vice-chairmenships of the standing committee of the people's congress of an autonomous region, prefecture or county shall include a citizen or citizens of the nationality or nationalities exercising regional autonomy in the area concerned.

Article 114. The administrative head of an autonomous region, prefecture or county shall be a citizen of the nationality, or of one of the nationalities, exercising regional autonomy in the area concerned.

Article 115. The organs of self-government of autonomous regions, prefectures and counties exercise the functions and powers of local organs of state as specified in Section V of Chapter Three of the constitution. At the same time, they exercise the right of autonomy within the limits of their authority as prescribed by the constitution, the law of regional national autonomy and other laws, and implement the laws and policies of the state in the light of the existing local situation.

Article 116. People's congresses of national autonomous areas have the power to enact autonomy regulations and specific regulations in the light of the political, economic and cultural characteristics of the nationality or nationalities in the areas concerned. The autonomy regulations and specific regulations of autonomous regions shall be submitted to the Standing Committee of the National People's Congress for approval before they go into effect. Those of autonomous prefectures and counties shall be submitted to the standing committees of the people's congresses of provinces or autonomous regions for approval before they go into effect, and they shall be reported to the Standing Committee of the National People's Congress for the record.

Article 117. The organs of self-government of the national autonomous areas have the power of autonomy in administering the finances of their areas. All revenues accruing to the national autonomous areas under the financial system of the state shall be managed and used by the organs of self-government of those areas on their own.

Article 118. The organs of self-government of the national autonomous areas independently arrange for and administer local economic development under the guidance of state plans.

In exploiting natural resources and building enterprises in the national autonomous areas, the state shall give due consideration to the interests of those areas.

Article 119. The organs of self-government of the national autonomous areas independently administer educational, scientific, cultural, public health and physical culture affairs in their respective areas, protect and cull through the cultural heritage of the nationalities and work for the development and prosperity of their cultures.

Article 120. The organs of self-government of the national autonomous areas may, in accordance with the military system of the state and concrete local needs and with the approval of the State Council, organize local public security forces for the maintenance of public order.

Article 121. In performing their functions, the organs of self-government of the national autonomous areas, in accordance with the autonomy regulations of the respective areas, employ the spoken and written language or languages in common use in the locality.

Article 122. The state gives financial, material and technical assistance to the minority nationalities to accelerate their economic and cultural development.

The state helps the national autonomous areas train large numbers of cadres at different levels and specialized personnel and skilled workers of different professions and trades from among the nationality or nationalities in those areas.

Section VII: The People's Courts and the People's Procuratorates

Article 123. The people's courts in the People's Republic of China are the judicial organs of the state.

Article 124. The People's Republic of China established the Supreme People's Court and the local people's courts at different levels, military courts and other special people's courts.

The term of office of the president of the Supreme People's Court is the same as that of the National People's Congress; he shall serve no more than two consecutive terms.

The organization of people's courts is prescribed by law.

Article 125. All cases handled by the people's courts, except for those involving special circumstances as specified by law, shall be heard in public. The accused has the right of defense.

Article 126. The people's courts shall, in accordance with the law, exercise judicial power independently and are not subject to interference by administrative organs, public organizations or individuals.

Article 127. The Supreme People's Court is the highest judicial organ.

The Supreme People's Court supervises the administration of justice by the local people's courts at different levels and by the special people's courts; people's courts at higher levels supervise the administration of justice by those at lower levels.

Article 128. The Supreme People's Court is responsible to the National People's Congress and its Standing Committee. Local people's courts at different levels are responsible to the organs of state power which created them.

Article 129. The people's procuratorates of the People's Republic of China are state organs for legal supervision.

Article 130. The People's Republic of China establishes the Supreme People's Procuratorate and the local people's procuratorates at different levels, military procuratorates and other special people's procuratorates.

The term of office of the procurator-general of the Supreme People's Procuratorate is the same as that of the National People's Congress; he shall serve no more than two consecutive terms.

The organization of people's procuratorates is prescribed by law.

Article 131. People's procuratorates shall, in accordance with the law, exercise procuratorial power independently and are not subject to interference by administrative organs, public organizations or individuals.

Article 132. The Supreme People's Procuratorate is the highest procuratorial organ.

The Supreme People's Procuratorate directs the work of the local people's procuratorates at different levels and of the special people's procuratorates; people's procuratorates at higher levels direct the work of those at lower levels.

Article 133. The Supreme People's Procuratorate is responsible to the National People's Congress and its Standing Committee. Local people's procuratorates at different levels are responsible to the organs of state power at the corresponding levels which created them and to the people's procuratorates at the higher level.

Article 134. Citizens of all nationalities have the right to use the spoken and written languages of their own nationalities in court proceedings. The people's courts and people's procuratorates should provide translation for any party to the court proceedings who is not familiar with the spoken or written languages in common use in the locality.

In an area where people of a minority nationality live in a compact community or where a number of nationalities live together, hearings should be conducted in the language or languages in common use in the locality; indictments, judgments, notices and other documents should be written, according to actual needs, in the language or languages in common use in the locality.

Article 135. The people's courts, people's procuratorates and public security organs shall, in handling criminal cases, divide their functions, each taking responsibility for its own work, and they shall co-ordinate their efforts and check

each other to ensure correct and effective enforcement of law.

CHAPTER FOUR: THE NATIONAL FLAG, THE NATIONAL EMBLEM AND THE CAPITAL

Article 136. The national flag of the People's Republic of China is a red flag with five stars.

Article 137. The national emblem of the People's Republic of China is Tiananmen in the centre illuminated by five stars and encircled by ears of grain and a cogwheel.

Article 138. The capital of the People's Republic of China is Beijing.

Organic Law of the State Council, 10 December 1982

48

This law, adopted by the Fifth National People's Congress, spells out the revelant provisions (Articles 85–92) of the constitution. The emphasis here is on the operation, not the power or functions, of the State Council.

Article 1. This organic law is formulated in accordance with the stipulations concerning the State Council provided by the PRC Constitution.

Article 2. The State Council is composed of a premier, vice premiers, state councillors, ministers in charge of ministries, ministers in charge of commissions, an auditor-general and a secretary-general.

The State Council applies the system of decision by the premier. The premier directs the work of the State Council. The vice premiers and state councillors assist the premier in his work.

Article 4. The State Council holds the plenary meetings of the State Council and the executive meetings of the State Council. The plenary meetings of the State Council are composed of all members of the State Council. The executive meetings of the State Council are composed of the premier, the vice premiers, the state councillors and the secretary general. The premier convenes and presides over the plenary meetings and executive meetings of the State Council. The important issues in the work of the State Council must be discussed and decided by the executive meetings of the State Council or the plenary meetings of the State Council.

Article 5. The decisions, orders, administrative rules and regulations issued by the State Council, the bills submitted by the State Council to the NPC or the Standing Committee of the NPC, and the appointment and removal of personnel of the State Council are signed by the premier.

Article 6. The state councillors are entrusted by the premier with taking charge of the work in certain fields or certain special tasks. They may handle foreign affairs on behalf of the State Council.

Article 7. The secretary general of the State Council, working under the direction of the premier, is responsible for handling the day-to-day work of the State Council.

The State Council has a certain number of deputy secretaries-general who assist the secretary-general in his work.

The State Council establishes a general office which is led by the secretary-general.

Article 8. The establishment, dissolution or merger of ministries and commissions of the State Council is recommended by the premier and decided by the NPC, or by the Standing Committee of the NPC when the NPC is not in session.

Article 9. Each ministry has a minister and two to four vice ministers. Each commission has a minister, 2 to 4 vice ministers and 5 to 10 commission members.

The ministries and commissions apply the system of decision by the ministers in charge of ministries or commissions. The ministers in charge of ministries or commissions direct the work of their respective departments, convene and preside over their ministerial meetings of commission meetings and commission work meetings, and sign important requests or reports submitted to the State Council and the orders and instructions issued to lower level units. The vice ministers or commissions assist the ministers in charge of ministries or commissions in the latter's work.

[New China News Agency, 14 December 1982.]

Article 10. The principles, policies, plans and important administrative measures concerning the work of the ministries and commissions should be reported to, and decided by the State Council. The ministries and commissions may issue orders, directives and rules and regulations within the limit of their powers in accordance with laws and the decisions of the State Council.

Article 11. According to work requirements and the principle of simplified organization, the State Council may set up a certain number of directly-subordinate organizations in charge of various specialized businesses and a certain number of working bodies that assist the premier in handling specialized businesses, with each organization or working body having two to five responsible persons.

Constitution of the Chinese People's Political Consultative Conference, 11 December 1982

49

The CPPCC is a large body national in scope, with local branches supposedly representing the broad "united front" on which Communist rule in China theoretically rests. It has even less power than the National People's Congress and serves mainly as a propaganda sounding board for the programs of the Communist Party, which is not only represented in the CPPCC, as are other public bodies, but which also controls the CPPCC.

GENERAL PROGRAM

During the protracted course of revolution and construction, the Chinese people have developed the broadest patriotic united front, which is led by the CPC and participated in by various democratic parties, nonparty democratics, mass organizations, personages of minority nationalities and patriotic personages of all circles, and which embraces all socialist workers and patriots who support socialism, or who support the reunification of the motherland, including our compatriots in Taiwan, Hong Kong and Macao, and Chinese nationals residing abroad.

The CPPCC is a patriotic united front organization of the Chinese people. In September 1949, the first plenary session of the CPPCC, exercising the functions of the NPC in an acting capacity and representing the will of the whole nation, declared the founding of the PRC, thus giving play to its important historical role. Following the First NPC in 1954, the CPPCC made important contributions by continuing to do a great deal of work in the state's political life and in social life as well as in promoting friendship with foreign countries. In the future, the CPPCC will continue to play its important part in intensifying socialist modernization, in achieving the reunification of the motherland, including Taiwan, and in struggling against hegemonism and safeguarding world peace.

Under the leadership of the CPC, Chinese people of all nationalities have eradicated the exploitative system and established the socialist system. Fundamental changes have taken place with regard to the classes in Chinese

society. The worker-peasant alliance has been more consolidated. The intellectuals, like the workers and peasants, have become a force upon which socialist undertakings rely. Most of those who used to belong to the exploitative classes have become laborers who earn their own living. All democratic parties, which have advanced, gone through tests and made important contributions together with the CPC in the course of people's revolution and construction, have become political alliances of those parts of the socialist workers and the patriots supporting socialism they keep in touch with, and they are playing an increasingly important part. People of all nationalities in the countries have developed a national relationship marked by unity, fraternity and mutual assistance. Patriots with religious beliefs have taken an active part in the motherland's socialist construction. Our compatriots in Taiwan, Hong Kong and Macao and our overseas Chinese ardently love their motherland, support the reunification of the motherland and support the country's modernization. Under the new historical period, our country's patriotic united front has an even stronger vitality. It is still an important magic weapon to unite the Chinese people to struggle, and to construct and reunify our motherland, and it will be further consolidated and developed.

Now that the exploitative classes have been eliminated as such, class struggle no longer constitutes a principal contradiction in our society. But owing to domestic factors and international influence, the Chinese people's struggle against the hostile forces at home and abroad will still be protracted, and class struggle will continue to exist within certain limits for a long time.

[New China News Agency, 11 December 1982.]

The principal contradictions our country faces are the contradictions between the people's increasing material and cultural needs and backward social production. The general task of the Chinese people of all nationalities in the new historical period is to rely on our own efforts and work hard to achieve, step by step, the modernization of our industry, agriculture, national defense and science and technology and to make China a culturally advanced and highly democratic socialist country. The CPPCC must, on the political basis of ardently loving the PRC and supporting the leadership of the CPC and the socialist cause, do its utmost to further consolidate and develop the patriotic united front, bring all positive factors into play, unite with all the forces that can be united, and work with one mind and with concerted efforts to maintain and develop the political situation of stability and unity, enhance the building of a socialist democracy and legal system and strive to create a new situation of socialist modernization and realize the general task of the Chinese people of all nationalities.

The CPPCC is an important form of fostering socialist democracy in our country's political life. In accordance with the CPC's policy of "long-term coexistence and mutual supervision" and the principle of "treating each other with all sincerity and sharing weal and woe" with all democratic parties and nonparty persons, the CPPCC will carry out political consultations on the state's cardinal policies and the important issues of the people's livelihood, and will, through making proposals and criticisms, bring its democratic supervisory role into play.

The PRC Constitution is the fundamental guiding principle for all the activities of the CPPCC.

CHAPTER ONE: GENERAL PRINCIPLES OF WORK

Article 1. The National Committee and local committees of the CPPCC operate according to the CPPCC constitution.

Article 2. The National Committee and local committees of the CPPCC participate in the discussion of important issues of the state and local affairs by various means.

The National Committee and local committees of the CPPCC, in accordance with the proposals of the CPC, or democratic parties and people's organizations, hold consultative meetings attended by leading members of various parties and organizations and representatives of patriotic personages of all circles.

Article 3. The National Committee and local committees of the CPPCC propagate and implement the state's constitution, laws and various principles and policies, give impetus to social forces to actively take part in building a highly material civilization and a civilization with a high socialist spirit, and assist state organs in striking at criminal activities undermining socialism in the economic and other spheres.

Article 4. The National Committee and local committees of the CPPCC maintain close ties with the personages of all quarters, reflect their opinions and demands and those of the people they keep in touch with, give suggestions and make criticisms of the work of the state organs and state functionaries, assist the state organs in carrying out organizational and administrative reforms, improve operation, increase efficiency and combat bureaucracy.

Article 5. The National Committee and local committees of the CPPCC readjust and handle the relationship among all spheres of the united front and the important matters concerning cooperation within the CPPCC.

Article 6. The National Committee and local committees of the CPPCC, through various means, actively propagate advanced thought, launch propaganda and education on the social ethics of loving the motherland, the people, labor, science and socialism as well as on revolutionary ideals, morality and discipline.

Article 7. The National Committee and local committees of the CPPCC adhere to the principle of "letting a hundred flowers blossom and a hundred schools of thought contend"—a principle of developing science and flourishing culture—maintain close ties with the state organs and other organs concerned, carry out investigation and study in the political, legal, education, scientific and technological, cultural, and art, medical and health, sports and other fields, encourage the free airing of views, open all avenues for people of talent and bring their members' specializations and roles into full play.

The National Committee and local committees of the CPPCC give impetus and render assistance to social forces to start all types of undertakings conducive to socialist construction.

Article 8. The National Committee and local committees of the CPPCC organize their members to inspect, visit and investigate so that they can understand the various situations, study the various undertakings and the important issues regarding the people's livelihood, and submit proposals and criticisms to the state organs and other organs concerned.

Article 9. The National Committee and local committees of the CPPCC organize and promote the study of Marxism-Leninism and Mao Zedong Thought, the study of current events and political matters and the study and exchange of professional, scientific and technological knowledge on the basis of voluntary participation so as to improve the ability of each to serve the motherland.

Article 10. The National Committee and local committees of the CPPCC popularize and participate in implementing the state policy with regard to the reunification of the motherland, actively develop ties with the compatriots and the people of all walks of life in Taiwan and promote the realization of the great cause of the reunification of the motherland.

Efforts must be made to strengthen ties and unity with the compatriots in Hong Kong and Macao, and encourage them to make contributions to building and reunifying the motherland.

Article 11. The National Committee and local committees of the CPPCC propagate and help implement the state's policy on intellectuals, so as to create favorable conditions for bringing the role of intellectuals into full play in socialist modernization.

Article 12. The National Committee and local committees of the CPPCC propagate and help implement the state's nationalities policy, reflect the opinions and demands of the national minorities, and make contributions to developing the economies and cultures of districts inhabited by people of national minorities, to safeguard their lawful rights and interests, to improving and developing socialist relations among all nationalities, to strengthening the great unity among the people of all nationalities and to defending the reunification of the motherland.

Article 13. The National Committee and local committees of the CPPCC propagate and help implement the state's policy on religion, and unify the patriots in the field of religion and religious believers in offering their share to building and reunifying the motherland.

Article 14. The National Committee and local committees of the CPPCC propagate and help implement the state policy on overseas Chinese affairs, strengthen ties and unity with Chinese residents abroad and encourage them to make contributions to building the motherland and to the great cause of reunifying the motherland.

Article 15. The National Committee and local committees of the CPPCC propagate and help implement the state's foreign policy, actively and on their own initiative develop people's diplomatic activities according to specific conditions, and strengthen the exchange of friendly visits and cooperation with the peoples of various countries.

Article 16. The National Committee and local committees of the CPPCC engage in compiling, studying and publishing reference materials on modern and contemporary Chinese history on the basis of their special feature as an united front organization.

Article 17. The National Committee of the CPPCC strengthens its ties with its local committees, facilitates the flow of information on the current situation, exchanges experiences and joins the local committees in studying problems of a common nature.

CHAPTER TWO: GENERAL ORGANIZATIONAL PRINCIPLES

Article 18. The CPPCC sets up a National Committee and local committees.

Article 19. The National Committee of the CPPCC is composed of representatives of the CPC, the various democratic parties, nonparty democratic personnel, various people's organizations, representatives of the national minorities, compatriots from Taiwan, Hong Kong and Macao, returned overseas Chinese and specially invited persons. The local committees of the CPPCC are formed according to local conditions and with reference to the formation of the National Committee.

Article 20. With the consultation and concurrence of the Standing Committee of the National Committee of the CPPCC, those parties and organizations that agree with this current constitution may participate in the National Committee of the CPPCC. Individuals may participate in the National Committee of the CPPCC after consultation and upon invitation by the Standing Committee of the National Committee of the CPPCC. Those that participate in the local committees are handled by the local committees at various levels according to the above-mentioned provision of this article.

Article 21. The units and individuals participating in the

National Committee or local committees of the CPPCC have the obligation to abide by and implement this constitution.

Article 22. The local committees of the CPPCC have the obligation to abide by and implement nationwide resolutions adopted by the National Committee, and a local committee at a lower level has the obligation to abide by and implement region-wide resolutions adopted by the local committee at a higher level.

Article 23. The relations between the National Committee of the CPPCC and its local committees and the relation between a local committee at a high level and local committees at a lower level are one of guidance.

Article 24. A motion at the plenary session of the National Committee of the CPPCC should be adopted only after the motion has won the support of more than half of the members of the plenary session. A motion put forward to the Standing Committee of the National Committee should be adopted only after it has won the support of more than half of the Standing Committee members. All the units and individuals participating in the CPPCC have the obligation to abide by and implement its resolutions. If they have different opinions, they may announce that they have reservations while resolutely implementing the resolutions. The local committees may do the same.

Article 25. Members of the National Committee and the local committees of the CPPCC have the right to vote, elect and stand for election in the CPPCC meeting at the corresponding level and to offer criticisms and proposals on the work of the meeting.

Article 26. The units and individuals participating in the National Committee and the local committees of the CPPCC have the right to participate in discussing the major policies of the state and the major events in their own localities and in offering proposals and criticisms on the work of state organs and state functionaries through the CPPCC meeting and organization of the corresponding level.

Article 27. The units and individuals participating in the National Committee and local committees of the CPPCC have the freedom to announce the withdrawal of their participation.

Article 28. If the units and individuals participating in the National Committee and the local committees of the CPPCC have seriously violated the CPPCC constitution or the resolution adopted by the CPPCC plenary session and Standing Committee, the Standing Committee of the National Committee or that of a local committee can separately issue a warning to the offender on the basis of the seriousness of the case, or cancel its qualifications to participate in the National Committee or local committees of the CPPCC.

If the unit or individual disagrees with the judgment, he or it may request to have the case reviewed.

CHAPTER THREE: THE NATIONAL COMMITTEE

Article 29. The participating units, the number and the choice of members of each National Committee of the CPPCC are decided on by the Standing Committee of the previous National Committee through consultation.

When the National Committee deems it necessary to increase or change the participating units or the number and the choice of members during its term of office, its Standing Committee should make decisions through consultation.

Article 30. The National Committee of the CPPCC is elected for a term of 5 years. In exceptional circumstances, its term of office may be extended; such an extension must be approved by a majority vote of more than ⅔ of all the members of its Standing Committee.

Article 31. The National Committee of the CPPCC has a chairman, a number of vice chairmen and a secretary general.

Article 32. The National Committee of the CPPCC holds a plenary session once every year. When the Standing Committee deems it necessary, extraordinary sessions may be convened.

Article 33. The following functions and powers of the National Committee of the CPPCC are exercised by the plenary session:

1. revising the CPPCC constitution;

2. electing the chairman, a number of vice chairmen and the secretary general of the National Committee and members of its Standing Committee;

3. hearing and examining the report on the work of the Standing Committee;

4. discussing and deciding the CPPCC's major working principles and tasks; and

5. Participating in discussions on the general orientation and major policy decisions of the country and offering suggestions and criticisms.

Article 34. The National Committee of the CPPCC sets up a Standing Committee to handle its affairs.

The Standing Committee is composed of the chairman of the National Committee, the vice chairmen, the secretary general and a number of members. Candidates for the Standing Committee are nominated through consultation by the participating parties, organizations, nationalities and personages from various circles of the National Committee, and elected by a plenary session of the National Committee.

Article 35. The Standing Committee of the National Committee of the CPPCC exercises the following functions and powers:

1. convening and conducting plenary sessions of the National Committee of the CPPCC; the first plenary session of each National Committee elects a presidium to conduct the session;

2. organizing efforts to fulfill the tasks as provided by the CPPCC constitution;

3. implementing the decisions of plenary sessions of the National Committee;

4. examining and approving, when the plenary session of the National Committee is not in session, important proposals to be sent to the NPC and its Standing Committee or the State Council;

5. appointing and removing deputy secretaries-general of the National Committee upon the recommendation of the secretary general; and

6. deciding on the setting up and changing of working organizations or the National Committee of the CPPCC and appointing and removing their leading members.

Article 36. The chairman of the National Committee of the CPPCC presides over the work of the Standing Committee. The vice chairmen and the secretary general assist the chairman in his work.

The chairman, vice chairmen and the secretary general are the participants in the chairmanship conference to attend to the important routine work of the Standing Committee.

Article 37. The National Committee of the CPPCC has a number of deputy secretaries-general to assist the secretary general in his work. It sets up a general office to work under the leadership of the secretary general.

Article 38. The National Committee of the CPPCC may set up a number of working organizations when necessary; this should be decided by the Standing Committee.

CHAPTER FOUR: THE LOCAL COMMITTEES

Article 39. Provincial committees, autonomous regional committees and municipal committees of the CPPCC are established in the provinces, autonomous regions and municipalities directly under the central government; autonomous prefectures, cities divided into districts, counties, autonomous counties, cities not divided into districts, and municipal districts, where conditions are available, may establish their own local committees.

Article 40. The participating units, the number and the choice of members of each local committee of the CPPCC are decided on through consultation by the standing committee of the previous local committee.

When a local committee deems it necessary to increase or change the participating units or the number and the choice of members during its term of office, its standing committee should make the decisions through consultation.

Article 41. The local CPPCC committees of provinces, autonomous regions, municipalities directly under the central government, autonomous prefectures and cities divided into districts are elected for a term of 5 years. The local committees of counties, autonomous counties, cities not divided into districts and municipal districts are elected for a term of 3 years.

Article 42. A local CPPCC committee at any level has a chairman, a number of vice chairmen and a secretary general. Local committees of counties, autonomous counties, cities not divided into districts and municipal districts may decide not to have a secretary general based on actual conditions.

Article 43. The plenary session of a local CPPCC committee is to be convened at least once a year.

Article 44. The following functions and powers of a local CPPCC committee are exercised by its plenary session:

1. electing the local committee chairman, vice chairmen, secretary general and members of the standing committee;

2. hearing and examining the report on the work of the standing committee;

3. discussing and approving relevant resolutions; and

4. participating in discussions on important national and local affairs and to offer suggestions and criticisms.

Article 45. A local CPPCC committee at any level sets up a standing committee to handle its affairs.

The standing committee is composed of the chairman of the local committees, the vice chairmen, the secretary general and a number of members. Candidates for the standing committee are nominated through consultation by the participating parties, organizations, nationalities and personages from various circles in the local committee, and elected by a plenary session of the local committee.

Article 46. The standing committee of a local CPPCC committee exercises the following functions and powers:

1. convening and conducting plenary sessions of the local committee; the first plenary session of each local committee elects a presidium to conduct the session;

2. organizing efforts to fulfill the tasks as provided by the CPPCC constitution and implementing the decisions of a country-wide nature made by the National Committee and those concerning an entire area made by a higher local committee;

3. implementing resolutions of the plenary session of the local committee;

4. examining and approving, when the plenary session of the local committee is not in session, important proposals to be sent to the local people's congress at the corresponding level and its standing committee or the people's government;

5. appointing and removing deputy secretaries general of the local committee upon the recommendation of the secretary general; and

6. deciding on setting up and changing work organizations of the local committee and appointing and removing their leading members.

Article 47. The chairman of a local CPPCC committee at any level presides over the work of its standing committee. The vice chairmen and the secretary general assist the chairman in his work.

The chairman, vice chairmen and the secretary general are the participants in the chairmanship conference to attend to the important routine work of the standing committee.

Article 48. A local CPPCC committee at any level may have one or more deputy secretaries general when necessary to assist the secretary general in his work.

Article 49. The local committees of provinces, autonomous regions and municipalities directly under the central government have a general office. The establishment of other work organizations should be decided by their standing committees according to actual local conditions and work requirements.

The establishment of work organizations for the local committees of autonomous prefectures, cities divided into districts, counties, autonomous counties, cities not divided into districts and municipal districts should be decided by their standing committees according to actual local conditions and work requirements.

CHAPTER FIVE: SUPPLEMENTARY ARTICLES

Article 50. This constitution will be implemented following its adoption by the plenary session of the National Committee of the CPPCC.

JIANG HUA   50
On the Work of the Supreme People's Court, 7 June 1983

As president of the Supreme People's Court, Jiang Hua's report reaffirms that in China, as in other Communist countries, the law and the courts are highly politicized.

Fellow deputies: I fully agree with the opening speech made by Peng Zhen, vice chairman of the NPC Standing Committee, and the government work report made by Premier Zhao Ziyang.

[New China News Agency, 25 June 1983.]

Since the First Session of the Fifth NPC in February 1978, tremendous changes have taken place in our country's political and economic situation. Guided by the line of the 3d Plenary Session of the 11th CPC Central Committee, the party and the state have accomplished the arduous task of eliminating chaos and restoring order in our guiding thought, switched the emphasis of work to modern socialist economic construction, and brought about a great historical change. The national economy has been set on a course of steady and sound development. The country's political stability and unity have been more consolidated. Socialist democracy has been restored and developed. The socialist legal system is being gradually perfected. All this has contributed to an excellent political and economic situation in China rarely seen since the founding of the PRC. In the past 5 years the people's court has given substance to and strengthened, perfected, and developed its organization and work and has taken the correct path of seeking truth from facts and doing things according to the law. Marked achievements have been made in all fields of work. I will now briefly report on the major work the people's courts at all levels have done in the past 5 years:

1. Holding the eighth national people's judicial work conference to thoroughly expose and criticize the crimes of the Lin Biao-Jiang Qing counterrevolutionary cliques in "smashing public security and procuratorial organs and people's courts" and disrupting people's judicial work. During the 10 years of internal disorder the Lin Biao-Jiang Qing counterrevolutionary cliques frantically committed crimes of "smashing public security and procuratorial organs and people's courts," tore down the organization and structure of the people's court, persecuted judicial cadres and disrupted the socialist legal system. From April to May 1978 the Supreme People's Court held the eighth national people's judicial work conference which exposed and criticized the crimes of the Lin Biao-Jiang Qing counterrevolutionary cliques, began to sum up the good experience gained in the effective people's court work done since the founding of the PRC, and called for restoring the fine tradition in people's judicial work as soon as possible. After the meeting the people's courts at all levels throughout China conscientiously relayed and implemented the meeting's guidelines, basing themselves on actual conditions, thoroughly exposing and criticizing the Lin Biao-Jiang Qing counterrevolutionary cliques and eliminating their pernicious influence. This facilitated the efforts to bring order out of chaos in people's judicial work.

2. Emancipating minds, overcoming obstructions, and firmly reviewing and redressing unjust, false, and wrong cases tried during the "Great Cultural Revolution." The eighth national people's judicial work conference laid down the principle of "completely redressing cases that are completely wrong, partially redressing cases that are partially wrong and not redressing cases that are not wrong" in reviewing and reversing unjust, false, and wrong cases. Since the latter half of 1978 the Supreme People's Court has vigorously reviewed cases by holding meetings, issuing documents, making investigations, and selecting and compiling typical cases.

Following the guidelines of the 3d Plenary Session of the 11th CPC Central Committee, people's courts at all levels throughout China have upheld the principle of seeking truth from facts and making corrections whenever mistakes are found, and have step by step made an extensive and profound review. By the end of 1981, 1.2 million criminal cases tried during the "Great Cultural Revolution" had been reviewed. More than 301,000 unjust, false, and wrong cases, involving more than 326,000 people, had been retried and redressed in accordance with the related policies of

the CPC Central Committee. The injustice done to large numbers of people persecuted by the Lin Biao-Jiang Qing counterrevolutionary cliques were thus remedied. Numerous convincing facts show that the review and redress of unjust, false, and wrong cases served as an effective way to expose and denounce the excruciating crimes of the Lin Biao-Jiang Qing counterrevolutionary cliques; that it was an important step in bringing order out of chaos; and that it greatly helped to heal the gaping wound inflicted on the people by the 10 years of internal disorder, to promote stability and unity and to mobilize all positive factors for achieving the four modernizations with one heart and one mind.

Although the work of reviewing and redressing unjust, false and wrong cases from the "Great Cultural Revolution" has now basically been completed, some problems remain to be solved in various localities. Some major, important, difficult, and complicated cases still have to be reviewed. Among the cases that have been reviewed, some should be redressed but have not been redressed; some have not thoroughly been redressed, resulting in unnecessary complications; and some require efforts to bring the case to completion. In some aspects, unjust, false, and wrong verdicts were also passed on criminal cases tried before the "Great Cultural Revolution" because of limited understanding or because of mistakes in the work at that time. In recent years the people's courts at all levels have retried and redressed some of these unjust, false, and wrong cases left over from history by handling petitions. Other cases are being reviewed and redressed. We are urging the people's courts at all levels to take effective measures to keep up their efforts and do this work well. All unjust, false, and wrong cases tried by people's courts that have not been redressed should be resolutely redressed.

3. Trying the chief culprits of the case of the Lin Biao-Jiang Qing counterrevolutionary cliques according to law. In accordance with the decision of the 16th Session of the 5th NPC Standing Committee, a special court under the Supreme People's Court tried the 10 chief culprits of the case of the Lin Biao-Jiang Qing counterrevolutionary cliques according to law from 20 November 1980 to 25 January 1981. During that trial a great amount of conclusive evidence was presented fully exposing the serious crimes of the Lin Biao-Jiang Qing counterrevolutionary cliques. The chief culprits, Jiang Qing and Zhang Chunqiao, were sentenced to death with a 2-year reprieve and with permanent deprivation of their political rights. The eight other chief culprits were also given appropriate penalties. This stern judgment upheld justice, educated the people, aroused the masses' socialist enthusiasm, and further promoted political stability and unity. The trial was based on facts and used the law as a yardstick. It strictly distinguished between criminal offense and political mistake. It was a typical example of handling a case according to law. More than 60,000 people from all parts of the country attended the hearings and press agencies, newspapers, and radio and television stations gave full coverage to the trial. This provided hundreds of millions of people with a universal and lively education on the legal system.

The period of serving their terms of death sentence with a 2-year reprieve for the criminals Jiang Qing and Zhang Chunqiao expired on 25 January this year.

The Supreme People's Court formed a collegiate bench according to the law to examine the performance of Jiang Qing and Zhang Chunqiao while serving their terms of death sentence with reprieve. It was found that during the period Jiang Qing and Zhang Chunqiao did not in any flagrant way resist reform. Based on a decision of the judicial committee and based on law, it was ruled that the original verdict of death sentence with a 2-year reprieve for the criminals Jiang Qing and Zhang Chunqiao be reduced to life imprisonment, and that the original verdict of permanent deprivation of political rights remain unchanged.

Since 1982 the Higher and Intermediate People's Courts in Shanghai, Beijing, Sichuan, Hubei, Jiangxi, Yunnan, Zhejiang, and Liaoning have separately conducted open trials, according to law, of backbone elements of the Jiang Qing counterrevolutionary clique in their respective localities and meted out appropriate penalties. The Chinese PLA Military Court has also conducted open trials, according to law, of backbone elements of the Lin Biao counterrevolutionary clique in the Army and meted out appropriate penalties. The historical task of trying the case of the Lin Biao-Jiang Qing counterrevolutionary cliques has now been fulfilled.

4. Punishing, according to law, counterrevolutionary criminals and criminal offenders who have seriously disrupted social order, safeguarding public security, and protecting the interests of the state and the people. Statistics show that from January 1978 to December 1982 local people's courts at all levels tried and completed a total of more than 939,000 criminal cases of the first instance, and more than 157,000 criminal cases of the second instance, and more than 1,289,000 petitions concerning criminal cases. The Supreme People's Court handled and completed 2,944 cases of appeals, retrials, and reviews of death sentences concerning criminal offenses. It handled more than 638,600 letters of petition concerning criminal cases and received petitioners concerning criminal cases on more than 155,100 occasions.

Presently the domestic political situation has undergone a fundamental change. With above 99 percent of the population belonging to the category of the people, class struggle is no longer the major contradiction of society in our country. Of course, class struggle will continue to exist to a certain extent for a long time to come and will even intensify under certain conditions. The change in the political situation is reflected markedly by the criminal cases handled by the people's courts. The number of counterrevolutionaries cases dropped markedly in 1982 and represented only 0.5 percent of the total number of criminal cases. Among criminal cases in general, common criminal cases make up the majority. Although serious criminal cases seriously disrupting the social order constitute a minority, the damages they cause are great. The composition of criminals has also changed. Immediately after the founding of the People's Republic, the majority of criminals were elements of the antagonistic classes and dregs of the old society. But now the overwhelming majority of criminals are working people and their sons and daughters. In many places, some 80 percent of the number of major cases like murders and explosions were committed because contradictions among the people had not been timely resolved. This shows that crimes committed among the people have become the major issue jeopardizing public security.

In view of the above, it is necessary to firmly implement, in the work of criminal trials, the principle of hitting at the minority while winning over and educating the majority, and to carry out the policy of combining punishment with leniency as stipulated by the party and the state. In accordance with the guidelines of the urban public security conference, a handful of criminals who have seriously disrupted social order by committing murders, robberies, rapes, explosions, and arsons, particularly the chief recidivists, abettors and accomplices among the criminals, were severely and promptly punished according to law. A few found guilty of most heinous crimes were given death penalties according to law. As a result, heavy blows were dealt to rampant criminal activities and the people's interests were protected.

The majority of other criminals have been appropriately punished by law according to the seriousness of their crimes and the circumstances of their cases. In some borderline cases, the criminals were not given sentences but were accepted by the public security departments for reeducation through labor, or were assigned to the care and education of factories, neighborhoods, schools or guardians to assist them in turning over a new leaf. Youths and teenagers who have erred and committed crimes were handled, according to law, with leniency by redeeming them through education and persuasion. Through judicial activities, the people's courts in various localities have actively participated in comprehensive work for improving public security, mainly by publicizing the legal system, educating the masses to self-consciously abide by the law, and boldly waging struggle against law offenders. By making judicial suggestions, the concerned units were assisted in perfecting their rules and regulations, sealing loopholes, and preventing crimes. All these efforts have produced fine results.

Through criminal trials the people's courts have effectively brought into play their function of exercising dictatorship over the enemy and protecting the people, as well as the significance of efforts to achieve a fundamental turn for the better in public security.

5. Severely punishing criminals who have seriously disrupted the economy in order to ensure the smooth progress of socialist economic construction. Over the past few years China has scored marked results in carrying out the policy of externally opening up to the outside world and domestically enlivening the economy. However, there are still problems in economic and political life. The incidence of crime seriously disrupting the economy such as embezzlement, bribery, smuggling, speculation, swindling, and theft of public property has markedly increased. In some areas and among some people these criminal activities have become rather rampant. Since 1982 the people's courts at various levels have seriously implemented the CPC Central Committee's and State Council's "Decision on Hitting at Serious Criminal Activities in the Economic Field" and the Fifth NPC Standing Committee's "Decision on Severely Punishing Criminals Who Cause Great Damage to the Economy." The people's courts have regarded the trial of economic criminal cases as an important task and have particularly concentrated forces on handling major and serious cases.

According to statistics, in 1982 the local people's courts at various levels and the railway transportation courts handled a total of 33,265 economic criminal cases of various types and meted out punishment to 37,123 culprits. Among the culprits, 6,115 were former government personnel (including 53 cadres at the county level and 2 cadres at the prefectural level); 1,862 culprits each illegally appropriated more than 10,000 yuan. The people's courts in various localities have meted out severe punishment to criminals who illegally appropriated huge sums or were involved in serious cases. In a few particular serious cases, the criminals have been given death penalties according to law. For instance, Wang Zhong, deputy director of the political and legal affairs committee under the Shantou Prefectural CPC Committee in Guangdong Province, misusing his authority in leading and commanding anti-smuggling work during his tenure as secretary of the Haifeng County party committee from the second half of 1979 to May 1981, embezzled large quantities of contraband goods and asked for and accepted bribes amounting to over 69,700 yuan. Because of the huge illegally appropriated sum, the circumstances under which the crimes were committed, and the particularly serious damages caused, he was sentenced to death according to law. When he was given the death sentence, the broad masses of cadres and the people applauded and pledged firm support for the solemn verdict of the people's court.

Since 1982 the Supreme People's Court has strengthened its supervision over the work of people's courts in various localities in handling economic criminal cases. It has also selectively edited and published some data on typical cases of economic crime in which relevant policies and laws have been carried out in a relatively satisfactory manner. At the beginning of this year it held a discussion meeting on the work of handling economic criminal cases by higher people's courts and special people's courts. Those attending the meeting learned about each other's situation, exchanged experiences, and discussed issues on how to better crack priority cases and draw a clear-cut line between the guilty and the innocent. To strike at serious economic crimes is a long-range major task. It constitutes an important guarantee for upholding the socialist road and developing the modernization program. We must continue to implement the two "resolutions" and do a still better job in handling economic criminal cases.

6. Handling a large number of civil cases and protecting the rights and interests of the state, the collective and the individual. According to statistics, over 2,648,000 civil cases of the first instance and over 165,000 civil cases of the second instance were brought to a conclusion, and more than 31,700 cases of civil appeal were handled by local people's courts at all levels from January 1978 to December 1982. At the same time a large number of simple disputes were solved. The Supreme People's Court brought 87 cases of civil appeal and retrial to a conclusion, handled more than 39,800 people's letters of civil appeal, and received people who had lodged civil appeals on more than 43,900 occasions.

During the past 5 years the number of civil cases accepted by people's courts greatly increased with each passing year. In 1982 more than 770,000 civil cases were brought to a conclusion after the first trial, marking an increase of 17 percent over 1981 and of 170 percent over 1978. Among those civil cases brought to a conclusion, not only cases concerning marriage, family, inheritance, housing, and residential land, and claims for compensation of damage markedly increased, but also many new disputes concerning land, forests, water conservancy facilities, farm tools, draft animals, fertilizer, and others emerged. Civil cases involving foreigners have also cropped up, and the number of such cases is on the increase. Generally speaking, the increase and changes among civil cases are a normal sign. On the one hand, this is because of the strengthening of socialist democracy and the socialist legal system; the people now have the courage to file lawsuits to solve civil disputes, and the people's courts actively accept civil cases to safeguard the lawful rights and interests of citizens. On the other hand, a number of new problems have cropped up due to the implementation of the policy of externally opening up the country to the outside world and domestically invigorating the economy. Reflected in civil relations, these new problems have resulted in new disputes.

In light of the above–mentioned situation, we have strengthened our work of handling civil cases. In December 1978 and July 1982 we separately convened two national conferences on the trial of civil cases. At these two conferences we further gained a better understanding of the importance of handling civil cases, studied the new situation and new problems which cropped up in the course of handling civil cases, and discussed problems in implementing the Law of Civil Procedure (for trial implementation). Mainly using mediation, the people's courts in various localities promptly handled millions of civil cases of all types on the spot while implementing the guidelines laid down by the two conferences, acting upon the relevant policies of the party, the Marriage Law and other laws, and relying on the masses, the basic-level organizations and the units concerned. Many people's courts also paid attention to preventing contradictions from sharpening, and took the initiative to carry out mediation and enlighten the litigants in solving their civil disputes. This effectively prevented the occurrence of many major crimes.

In implementing the Law of Civil Procedure (for trial implementation), the people's courts in various localities toured places to handle cases on the spot, carry out mediation well in the course of handling lawsuits, and scored initial successes in strengthening their basic work and their work at grassroots units. The basic-level people's courts in many localities stepped up the building of people's tribunals and their professional guidance to people's mediation committees, provided conveniences for the masses, improved their efficiency in handling cases, and timely settled many civil disputes at the grassroots level. This won wide acclaim from the masses.

7. Making vigorous efforts to try economic disputes in order to readjust economic relations and maintain economic order. In accordance with the Organic Law of the People's Courts, the Supreme People's Court and the higher people's courts at all levels established their respective economic divisions between the second half of 1979 and the end of 1982. The intermediate people's courts, except those in some individual localities, also set up their economic divisions. In accordance with the guidelines laid down by the Third Session of the Fifth NPC on strengthening judicial work in the economic field, people's courts at all levels vigorously tried economic disputes and handled a total of more than 49,000 such cases by the end of 1982. As the Economic Contract Law came into force and the Law of Civil Procedure was implemented on a trial basis, the people's courts in various parts of the country immediately began to enforce the provisions of the two laws; they tried economic contract disputes between per-

sons, economic disputes involving foreigners, economic disputes between foreign enterprises or organizations that should be handled by a law court of our country according to agreement, as well as administrative cases which should be tried by people's courts according to law. In trying economic disputes, many people's courts stressed the principle of mediation in accordance with the provisions of the Law of Civil Procedure (for trial implementation). Ascertaining the facts, distinguishing right from wrong and making sure who should be held responsible, the people's courts did everything possible to mediate the economic disputes that could be mediated. When such mediation failed, then such economic disputes were tried. While trying cases, many people's courts also paid attention to publicizing the legal system and making judicial suggestions in order to make relevant units understand and observe the law and to prevent or limit economic disputes.

8. Making efforts to restructure the people's courts and to strengthen the building of the judges' corps. In the past 5 years a large number of cadres were transferred to people's courts at various levels, thus initially strengthening the judges' corps and judicial organs. With the gradual improvement of the country's legal system, various trial systems have been instituted. In line with the unified plan for organizational reform at the central and local levels and in accordance with the legal procedure, the Supreme People's Court and the higher people's courts in various provinces, municipalities and autonomous regions have since last year initially carried out organizational reform and readjusted and consolidated their leading bodies. The intermediate and basic-level people's courts are now also carrying out organizational reform. In carrying out organizational reform, the people's courts at various levels have paid attention to selecting and promoting to leading positions outstanding young and middle-aged cadres who have both ability and political integrity and have better professional knowledge of law and practical judicial experience, especially intellectual cadres with professional knowledge of law. Members of the readjusted leading bodies are more revolutionary, younger in age, professionally more competent, and better educated to a certain extent.

To meet the needs in their work, the people's courts in various localities have in the past few years strengthened the building of the judges' corps ideologically and professionally. A number of cadres have been trained in various ways at their respective posts. Practice proves that it is essential for judges to have good political quality.

But this alone is not enough; judges must also have professional knowledge of law as well as knowledge of science and culture. Otherwise it will be difficult for them to do increasingly arduous trial work. The Supreme People's Court convened a national conference on judicial work of people's courts in March this year, which worked out a preliminary plan for cadre training. This plan calls for making every effort to enable the overwhelming majority of judges to greatly increase their professional knowledge of law and to greatly raise their scientific and cultural level in not too long a period of time.

Deputies: generally speaking, the achievements made by the people's courts in the past 5 years are a result of their upholding the four fundamental principles, implementing the party's line, principles and policies laid down since the 3d Plenary Session of the 11th CPC Central Committee and their making continuous efforts to straighten

out things and eliminate the influence of "leftist" mistakes. By trying current cases and reinvestigating unjust, frameup and wrong cases, the people's courts at various levels have since 1978 accumulated a wealth of practical trial experience, both positive and negative. Their main experiences are:

First, it is imperative to uphold the principle of seeking truth from facts and to faithfully adhere to the truth. Judges must follow the dialectic-materialist ideological line and base themselves on facts in trying a case. This is a prerequisite for handling cases correctly. Only by faithfully adhering to the truth can a judge be faithful to the law and the system and to the interests of the people. Many unjust, frameup and wrong cases tried during the "Great Cultural Revolution" resulted from judges readily believing in fabricated or distorted evidence. Both positive and negative experience shows us that in trying a case, it is imperative to correctly ascertain the facts and that it is not allowed to exaggerate or play down facts, much less to distort facts or change the nature of a crime. To ascertain the facts in a case, it is necessary to have ample evidence; no conclusion can be reached on a case only on the strength of a statement made by evidence, whether it proves the accused to be guilty or not to be guilty, or to have committed a serious or minor crime, must be conscientiously investigated and verified in order to base judgment on verified facts. In handling a civil case or an economic dispute, the facts must also be investigated and the evidence must also be verified. Only in this way can a case we try or handle stand the test of history.

Second, it is imperative to correctly enforce the law of the state and to act in strict accordance with it. In trying a criminal case, it is necessary to convict and mete out the penalty to the accused according to the Criminal Law. Criminal cases should be tried in public, and the procedure and system prescribed in the Criminal Law must be implemented in earnest in trying such cases. In handling civil cases and economic disputes, it is necessary to distinguish right from wrong and to be clear about who should be held responsible in accordance with relevant laws and policies. Moreover, such cases should be handled according to the procedure and system prescribed in the Law of Civil Procedure (for trial implementation). Experience over many years proves that only by acting in strict accordance with the law will it be possible to ensure quality in handling cases, to accurately punish criminals, and to effectively protect the legitimate interests of the people. If a judge deviates from the law, he will have no criterion for handling a case. If that happens, the quality of handling the case cannot be ensured, and unjust, frameup, and wrong cases may even occur. The socialist legal system was completely disrupted during the "Great Cultural Revolution." During that period criminal cases, especially counterrevolutionary cases, were not at all tried according to law; enemies were taken for comrades, and vice versa, and the distinction between crime and innocence was blurred.

As a result, many good, innocent people were mistakenly convicted. Since the implementation of the Criminal Law and the Law of Criminal Procedure, the people's courts at various levels have persistently acted according to law, thus basically ensuring the quality of handling a case. Now even if a case were mistakenly handled, it could in time be remedied according to law. Practice over the past 5 years shows that acting according to law is not smooth sailing; there are interferences and obstructions in this regard. Therefore, judges must enforce the provision of the Constitution that the people's courts, in accordance with the law, exercise judicial power independently, they must have a firm faith, uphold principle, and dare to struggle against unconstitutional acts of illegally interfering with judicial work.

Third, it is necessary to implement the mass line and to combine special organs with the masses. In trying a criminal case, it is essential to collect information from among members of the masses who know the facts concerning the case, to put stress on the weight of evidence and not to readily believe any statement made by the accused under examination. Both the statement made by the accused under examination and the evidence presented must be checked and verified. In handling a civil case, it is necessary to go among the masses to investigate the details behind the case in order to understand the crux of the dispute among the parties concerned. Moreover, the masses and basic-level organizations should be relied on to help the parties in the dispute to see what is right or reasonable and to do a good job in mediating their dispute. Trying civil cases is a kind of mass work as well as political and ideological work. If the mass work and the political and ideological work are done thoroughly, the dispute is handled properly; then the parties in the dispute are sincerely convinced, the masses are educated, and a good social effect is produced. In a word, the people's courts should be good at following the mass line; they should listen attentively to the views of the various quarters through investigation and study, and at the same time, be good at thinking things out for themselves and handling cases independently and responsibly.

Deputies: Although the people's courts have made the above achievements in their work, they still have some shortcomings and problems. The main shortcomings and problems are: Some cadres have not yet emancipated their minds sufficiently. As a result, they are slow in understanding the importance of reinvestigating and remedying unjust, frameup, and wrong cases and act slow in handling them. In handling some criminal cases, they are not daring enough to act according to law. Responsible cadres of some people's courts fail to pay sufficient attention to trying civil cases. The courts are still short of cadres, and their cadres whose level of knowledge of law, science, and culture is generally rather low cannot meet the needs of their work. There are also many difficulties in equipment and funds.

Effective measures must be taken to correct such shortcomings and solve such problems.

Fellow deputies, the 12th CPC National Congress indicates that our party and state have entered a historical stage for bringing about a new situation in all fields of socialist construction. Meanwhile, the promulgation of the new Constitution and its enforcement have ushered in a new stage of development of socialist democracy and legality in China. In this new situation, the party and the people expect that new and higher demands should be met by the people's courts. Necessary reforms must be carried out to improve the work of the people's courts. Only thus can they meet the needs of the new situation and successfully fulfill the glorious tasks of protecting the people, dealing blows at the enemy, and safeguarding the socialist legal system and socialist modernization.

The people's courts at all levels must further improve their criminal judicial work and use the weapon of the law to accurately and timely punish counterrevolutionary criminals and other criminals who endanger social order and undermine the socialist economy; they must also improve their work of trying civil cases and economic disputes, correctly readjust the relationship between individual and property, and effectively protect the lawful rights of the state, the collective, and the individual. In conducting trials, the people's courts must uphold the principles of seeking truth from facts, of handling matters in strict adherence to law, of relying on the masses, and of accommodating them. In addition, the people's courts must actively participate in the comprehensive program to improve social order by coordinating with other departments concerned, extensively publicizing the legal system, launching activities to improve judicial work, educating and saving juvenile delinquents in order to achieve the aim of reducing disputes and preventing crime. To realize all this, we must fulfill one important condition, that is, we must discover, select, and bring up talented people and build a contingent of judges who are revolutionized, young in age, better educated, and professionally competent. Following the guidelines of the 12th CPC National Congress and the First Session of the Sixth NPC, the people's courts at all levels must conscientiously abide by the new Constitution, strive to improve their work by reforming it, create a new situation in court work, and make due contributions to the socialist modernization drive.

Fellow deputies, please consider the report I have just presented.

YANG SHANGKUN

On the Work of the Standing Committee of the National People's Congress, 7 June 1983

Yang, an important veteran Party official, reports on the work of the Standing Committee. Like other state bodies, it is dominated by the Communist Party, operating essentially through the Party members belonging to it. For the functions of the Standing Committee, see Articles 64–69 of the 1982 state constitution (Doc. 47).

Fellow deputies: The work of the NPC Standing Committee before the Fifth Session of the Fifth NPC was reported to and approved by the past NPC sessions. Entrusted by the Fifth NPC Standing Committee, I will now make a report on the work of the NPC Standing Committee since the Fifth Session of the Fifth NPC to the First Session of the Sixth NPC.

In the past 6 months, the Standing Committee has performed its work under the guidance of the principle of creating a new situation in socialist modernization across the country, in line with its tasks as prescribed in the new Constitution, and in accordance with a resolution adopted by the Fifth Session of the Fifth NPC on the functions and powers of the present NPC Standing Committee, with its work centering on presiding over the election of deputies to the Sixth NPC and the preparations made for convening the First Session of the Sixth NPC.

I

The new Constitution adopted and promulgated by the Fifth Session of the Fifth NPC for implementation has received warm support from the people of all nationalities throughout the country. What the broad masses of people are now most concerned about is how to effectively ensure its implementation. This is a matter of great importance that has a bearing on the political stability and prosperity of our country. The new Constitution must be the basic norm of conduct for all state organs, the Armed Forces, all political parties and public organizations, all enterprises and undertakings, as well as each and every citizen. It is the sacred duty of the people of all nationalities throughout the country to abide by the Constitution and uphold its sanctity.

To this end, it is first necessary to further publicize the new Constitution and further conduct education on it throughout the country. Since its promulgation, the study of the new Constitution, the publicity given to it, and the education conducted on it have played a very important role in enabling the cadres and masses to enhance their understanding of the new Constitution and raise their consciousness in observing it. However, it should be noted that arduous work has to be done for a long time in order to translate abiding by the Constitution and upholding its sanctity into conscientious action of the cadres and masses. The Constitution should be regularly, persistently, and thoroughly studied and publicized in connection with problems in practical work and questions of ideology and understanding. Particularly, cadres at all levels should conscientiously study and publicize the new Constitution and observe and implement it strictly. It is necessary to prevent and correct any violations of the Constitution and laws and enable the 1 billion people to grasp the new Constitution. This is the basic guarantee for the implementation of the Constitution.

Since its promulgation, some past rules and practices may not conform to the new Constitution or may have contravened it. Such problems must be solved in good time. For this reason, Vice Chairman Peng Zhen of the NPC Standing Committee proposed at a meeting last February that all public security, procuratorial, and judicial departments take the initiative in systematically checking on whether or not there are any instances of failing to conform to the new Constitution in their work, and that vigorous efforts be made to conscientiously rectify them, if any. The NPC Standing Committee holds that all state organs, the Armed Forces, all political parties, and public organizations as well as all basic units, without exception, must act in strict accordance with the Constitution. Local people's congresses and their standing committees at various levels must ensure the observance and implementation of the Constitution in their respective administrative areas, and deputies to people's congresses at all levels must be models in observing and implementing the Constitution. Any acts in violation of the Constitution should be investigated. This is an important aspect in effectively ensuring the implementation of the Constitution.

In legislative work, the Standing Committee has considered and approved the "Regulations on the Direct Election of People's Congresses at or Below the County Level," the "Decision on the Ministry of Foreign Economic Relations and Trade Exercising the Examining and Approving Authority of the Former Foreign Investment Administration

[New China News Agency, 25 June 1983.]

Committee" and "Decision on the Early Election of City People's Congresses After the Merger of Prefectures and Cities." The Legislative Affairs Commission of the Standing Committee, in coordination with departments concerned, has also studied and revised some laws, such as the "Military Service Law (draft)," the "Law on Safety of Maritime Transport (draft)," and the "Law on Statistics (draft)" which, after further revision, will be submitted one by one to the NPC Standing Committee for examination and approval.

On the one hand, vigorous efforts should be made to continue enacting necessary laws according to the needs and possibilities from now on. On the other hand, there should not be too many laws loaded with trivial details. Moreover, our laws must be carefully worked out, and they must be feasible and capable of solving practical problems. To prevent haste, lack of careful consideration, inconsistencies, and mutual contradictions in law enactment and avoid problems in law enforcement so as to maintain the stability and solemnity of the law, the chairmanship meeting of the Standing Committee has decided: Before a draft law is submitted to the Standing Committee for examination and approval, explanations on it must first be made to a meeting of the Standing Committee. Then, the draft law may be submitted to the NPC Standing Committee or its special committees concerned for examination and revision.

At the same time, members of the Standing Committee should also study the draft law. After all this, the draft law may be submitted to the Standing Committee for approval. This is an important measure to improve the lawmaking procedure.

II

In this period, the Standing Committee devoted its attention mainly to presiding over the election of deputies to the Sixth NPC and preparing for the convocation of the First Session of the Sixth NPC.

The election of deputies to the Sixth NPC and the convocation of its first session are a major task in strengthening and improving state organs and the leadership system and creating a new situation in all fields of socialist modernization. The Standing Committee examined and approved the "Plan for the Number of Deputies to be Elected From Minority Nationalities to the Sixth NPC" and the "Plan for the Election Through Consultation of Taiwan Province's Deputies to the Sixth NPC." In early March of this year, the NPC Standing Committee held a forum of responsible persons of the standing committees of the people's congresses of various provinces, autonomous regions, and municipalities directly under the central government. At the forum, Vice Chairmen Yang Shangkun and Xi Zhongxun made important speeches on questions raised by various localities on the election of new people's congresses and the electoral work, and Deputy Secretary General Wang Hanbin gave a briefing on several legal questions on the election of new people's congresses and the electoral work. This forum solved, from the legal point of view, some questions regarding the election of new people's congresses and the electoral work in various localities and ensured the smooth progress of the electoral work. All provinces, autonomous regions, and municipalities directly under the central government convened their new people's congresses which

elected deputies to the Sixth NPC according to law before the end of April. The Chinese PLA also elected its deputies to the Sixth NPC according to law.

In mid-April, the Standing Committee sponsored a meeting in Beijing to elect Taiwan Province's deputies through consultation to the Sixth NPC. Through deliberations and consultations, 13 deputies to the Sixth NPC were elected from among 110 candidates nominated by compatriots of Taiwan origin in various provinces, autonomous regions, and municipalities directly under the central government, as well as in the PLA. The balance of the quota to be elected in proportion to the province's population is reserved. This shows the concern and expectations of the people throughout the country that the Taiwan compatriots will administer state affairs along with the people of all nationalities in the unified family of the motherland.

In accordance with the "Electoral Law," all constituencies nominated more candidates than the number of deputies to be elected. The nomination was made through consultations and discussions among the CPC, the various democratic parties, and people's organizations. Candidates participating in the election also jointly nominated their own candidates according to law. Because too many candidates were nominated in some localities, preliminary elections were held there. Then, the official lists of candidates were determined according to the opinions of the majority. In the course of the election, stress was put on giving consideration to various aspects. While giving consideration to the proportion of women and people who are not members of the Communist Party, the number of deputies to be elected from various minority nationalities was ensured. The results in this respect are good. In the course of the election, some problems of failing to comply with the provisions of the law or failing to complete the legal formalities occurred in some localities.

In coordination with the localities concerned, the Standing Committee made vigorous efforts to study and solve such problems and to sum up experiences and lessons in this regard. The Standing Committee also stressed that it is imperative to hold elections in accordance with the Constitution and the "Electoral Law," uphold the sanctity of the law, and to strengthen the concept of the legal system. Therefore, generally speaking, this election proceeded well and the masses of people were rather satisfied.

The 27th Standing Committee meeting held in early May this year discussed the examining report submitted by the deputies' Credentials Committee, affirmed that qualifications of the 2,978 deputies elected by all constituencies were valid, and issued a public notice on 9 May making public the namelist of all deputies elected.

The deputies elected show the following characteristics:

1. They are representatives from various quarters. Among them are all democratic party and nonparty personages and representative figures from all mass bodies and from the circles of science, technology, literature and art, education, sports, public health, press, publication, religion, and returned Overseas Chinese. They also include noted personages from the industrial, business, financial, and cultural circles in Hong Kong and Macao. In addition, workers and peasants still constitute 26.6 percent and women, 21.2 percent of the deputies. This shows the Chinese people have further strengthened their unity and that the patriotic united front has been increasingly consolidated.

2. They include a number of advanced personages who have made contributions to the four modernizations and reform. Of all deputies, the advanced figures emerging on all fronts since the 3d Plenary Session of the 11th CPC Central Committee account for 23 percent. Most of them are in their 30's and not older than 40 years of age. Among them are model workers and peasants, the Jiang Zhuying and Luo Jianfu type scientific and technical workers, leading cadres who are good at enterprise administration and management, and heroic personages who defend our motherland and safeguard public order. These advanced deputies' participation in the management of state affairs embodies the wishes of the broad masses and shows the superiority of the socialist system under which the people are masters.

3. The numbers of intellectuals among the deputies has markedly increased in proportion. There are 1,324 college-educated deputies, constituting 44.5 percent of the total. This shows the policy on intellectuals has been further implemented and that the state and the people have faith in knowledge and intellectuals. This will help bring the important role of intellectuals in socialist modernization into full play.

4. The minority nationalities are represented by their own deputies. Each of China's 55 minority nationalities has at least one deputy representing it. In all, 403 deputies have been elected from among minority nationalities, constituting 13.5 percent of the total. This percentage is double the percentage of the population of minority nationalities in the entire population of China, which is 6.7 percent. This will help develop the socialist relationships among all nationalities in terms of equality, unity, and mutual assistance.

We believe that the new National People's Congress will certainly further strengthen the unity of people of all nationalities in China, adhere to the tasks set by the new Constitution, and strive to build China in a still better way into a culturally advanced and highly democratic modern socialist state.

III

The Standing Committee listened to Premier Zhao Ziyang's "Report on Visiting 11 African Countries" and fully approved it. The committee considers Premier Zhao's visit very successful and regarded it as a great event in the history of Sino-African relations since Premier Zhou Enlai's visit to Africa in the 1960's. In addition, the Standing Committee members suggested that we should strengthen education in patriotism and internationalism among the broad masses in accordance with the stipulations of the Constitution, extensively unite with the people of all countries in the world, particularly with those in the Third World and regard this as an ideological education to promote socialist spiritual civilization, and strive to develop the diplomatic relations and economic and cultural cooperation between our country and the Third World countries. These suggestions are good and should be taken into consideration in our practical work.

Exchange of friendly visits with parliaments of all countries is one of the important tasks of the NPC. Last March, the NPC delegation led by Vice Chairman Ngapoi Ngawang Jigme visited two friendly countries: Sri Lanka and Nepal. The Standing Committee also separately received parliamentary delegations from Yugoslavia, France, the United States, Western Samoa, and Tanzania. In exchanging visits with the parliaments of these countries, we introduced to them China's NPC system, the development of China's socialist democracy, and the improvement of its socialist legal system. We also introduced to them China's achievements in socialist construction and reform in the new historical period of socialism and China's foreign policy based on maintaining independence and keeping the initiative in our own hands and the five principles of peaceful coexistence. We have made great efforts to develop the relations of friendly cooperation with parliaments and peoples of all countries. In addition, with regard to major issues concerning China's sovereignty and national interests, we elucidated our country's solemn and just stand, stressing that no foreign country can expect China to swallow any bitter fruit that damages our country's interests. As a result, we have strengthened mutual understanding and friendly relations with parliaments of all countries.

Our practical experience proves that it is of important significance to carry out friendly activities between the NPC and parliaments of all countries. We did not make enough efforts in this regard in the past. Though we have caught up in the last few years, we should still further expand and develop these activities.

The Standing Committee also discussed and approved the "Convention on Banning and Punishing Crime of Apartheid" and the "Convention of Preventing and Punishing Genocidal Crimes," and joined the "Treaty on the Antarctic."

Deputies: The First Session of the Sixth NPC has been held, and the Fifth NPC Standing Committee has successfully fulfilled its historical task. In the past 5 years, the Fifth NPC and its Standing Committee, under the direction of Chairman Ye Jianying, have resolutely eliminated chaos and restored order and formulated the new Constitution and a number of important basic laws which can run the country well and give the people peace and security. They have done much work in improving the people's congress system, developing socialist democracy, and strengthening the socialist legal system. Last March, Chairman Ye Jianying asked the Standing Committee members not to nominate and elect him deputy to the Sixth NPC. He also asked them not to nominate him as a candidate for the chairmanship of the NPC Standing Committee. Cherishing a feeling of great reverence for him, the Standing Committee agreed to his request. Now on behalf of the Fifth NPC Standing Committee, I avail myself of this opportunity to renew to Chairman Ye Jianying the assurances of my highest consideration and extend him my heartfelt thanks for his outstanding contributions during his tenure of office as chairman of the Fifth NPC Standing Committee.

Above is the major work the Standing Committee has done in the past 6 months. All proposals, appointments, and removals approved at two meetings held by the Standing Committee during this period have been put into print and distributed to all deputies. Your examination of them is requested.

Report on the Work of the Government, 6 June 1983

A long report by the premier on the work of the government, essentially the State Council, is a regular feature of the sessions of the National People's Congress. Zhao places emphasis on the economy, which, like any socialist one in a Communist country, is the main business of the government. The most interesting part of this report, however, lies in the establishment of a Ministry of State Security, whose primary responsibility is to protect the state against espionage.

Fellow Deputies, on behalf of the State Council, I now submit a report on the work of the government for examination and approval by the present congress.

REVIEW OF THE GOVERNMENT'S WORK IN THE PAST FIVE YEARS

Under the leadership of the Chinese Communist Party, our country has won big successes bringing about great changes in all fields of work during the period of the Fifth National People's Congress, thanks to concerted efforts by governments at all levels and the people of all our nationalities.

We have achieved and enhanced political stability and unity throughout the country and made more efforts to improve socialist democracy and legality. During the past five years, our political life has steadily returned to normal; the relations among all our nationalities, based on equality, solidarity, mutual assistance and fraternity, have been reinforced; the patriotic united front has been broadened; and society as a whole has enjoyed increasing stability with each passing year. The National People's Congress and its Standing Committee adopted a number of laws, and the State Council promulgated a series of statutes, and all this has helped strengthen democratic management in economic, political and other activities of the country and ensure public order and order in production and other work across the land. In particular, the promulgation of China's new Constitution marked a new stage in our effort to build up socialist democracy and legality. The organizational reforms made in the State Council and in the provincial, municipal and autonomous region governments have met with initial success, as illustrated by the closer contact between government and people and greater efficiency in administrative work. Because they have ease of mind, the people of all our nationalities show a growing enthusiasm in socialist construction. To win honour for the socialist motherland and contribute one's share to its

socialist modernization has become the watchword of our time. We have in recent years properly solved a series of problems left over from the past. We re-examined large numbers of cases involving unjust, false and wrong charges and reversed the verdicts that had been passed on them. People who had been wrongly labelled bourgeois rightists received redress, as did small tradespeople, peddlers and handicraftsmen who were wrongly classified as capitalists. Landlords, rich peasants, counter-revolutionaries and bad elements who have become law–abiding working people through remoulding have had their designations removed, and large numbers of former Kuomintang Party, government and Army personnel and special agents were released from prison in conformity with our policy of leniency.

Our struggle against serious crimes in the economic and other fields has helped ensure the socialist character and orientation of our efforts in various spheres of national construction. Although some destabilizing factors still exist in our society which we must make continued efforts to eliminate, people have every reason to believe that the present situation of stability and unity is irreversible and that our great motherland will enjoy a long period of order and stability. No force on earth can hold back or undermine this historical trend.

China's economy has freed itself from the instability caused by serious imbalance among its major branches and has gradually moved on to a path of sound growth. The implementation of the principle of readjusting, restructuring, consolidating and improving the national economy over the past few years has led to a radical change in the long-standing high rate of accumulation and serious backwardness of agriculture and light industry. As a result of readjustment, by 1982, the accumulation rate had fallen to 29 percent, as against 36.5 percent in 1978, while funds for consumption showed a fairly big increase. The proportion that agriculture accounted for in the total value of industrial and agricultural production rose from 27.8 percent in 1978 to 33.6 percent in 1982 and light industry from 31.1 percent to 33.4 percent. In conjunction with readjustment of the ratios between accumulation and con-

[New China News Agency, 23 June 1983.]

sumption and between agriculture and light industry on the one hand and heavy industry on the other, the State Council took firm steps to eliminate the rather serious financial deficit and strike a basic balance between state revenue and expenditure and between credit receipts and payments. We have maintained both an overall stability and a fairly high rate of economic growth during this period of readjustment. The total output value of industry and agriculture shot up to 829.1 billion yuan in 1982, 32.6 percent over 1978, averaging an annual increase of 7.3 percent. This confirms the correctness of the principle of economic readjustment, which has produced significant results.

China's agriculture has extricated itself from protracted stagnation and achieved a sustained overall upsurge. The State Council has implemented a series of rural policies in the past few years to stimulate labour enthusiasm of the peasants. We have raised the purchase prices of farm and sideline products by a wide margin, increased the import of grain and reduced the quotas of grain purchase by the state in some areas. All this has helped revitalize the countryside. Compared with 1978, the peasants' income rose by as much as 26 billion yuan in 1982 from the increased purchase prices of farm and sideline products alone. Meanwhile, we have readjusted crop patterns and the agricultural structure and promoted diversification of the rural economy without allowing grain production to fall off. Of particular importance is the fact that the peasants, under the leadership of the party, have created varied forms of contracted responsibility system based on the household, with remuneration linked to output. This has enabled us to change the long-term practice of issuing arbitrary orders about production and of distributing the product in an equalitarian way. It combines small-scale management on the household basis with specialized and socialized production, preserving the advantages of the agricultural cooperative movement, and thus integrates the superiority of collective ownership with peasant initiative in household management of production, allowing both to develop fully. As a solution to a fundamental problem that has long plagued China's socialist agriculture, it represents a step forward which is of profound and far-reaching historic significance. Although much remains to be improved in our rural work, in the past few years we have, on the whole, reinforced the worker-peasant alliance under new historical conditions, fired the enthusiasm of the hundreds of millions of Chinese peasants and provided a powerful stimulus to production.

Compared with 1978, China's output of grain went up by 16 percent in 1982; cotton, by 66 percent; oil-bearing crops, by 126 percent; sugar crops, by 83 percent; and cured tobacco, mulberry silkworn cocoons, pork, beef, mutton, etc. by more than 50 percent each. Everybody knows that there was no lack of natural calamities in the past few years. Nevertheless, the total value of agricultural output rose by an annual average of 7.5 percent, which is 2.3 times the average annual increase during the 26 years preceding 1978. By and large, the overwhelming majority of the population in the more than 240 poor counties with low farm yields now have adequate food and clothing. Certain counties, notorious for their poverty, have improved by leaps and bounds and become new centres of commodity production. The steadily growing prosperity of the rural areas has opened the way for the improved economic and political situation.

China's consumer goods industry has ended its long-term backwardness, heavy industry has gradually corrected its service orientation and industry as a whole has been expanding steadily in the course of readjustment. We have attached importance in recent years to the production of consumer goods so that light industry has been able to expand more quickly than heavy industry. From 1979 through 1982, the average annual increase in the output value of light industry has been 11.8 percent, as against 3.4 percent for heavy industry. There has been considerable growth in the production of many commodities in short supply. As compared with 1978, the output of bicycles was up by 180 percent in 1982; of sewing machines, by 160 percent; of wristwatches, by 140 percent; of TV sets, 11.4 times; and of chemical fibres, cotton cloth, woollen fabrics, sugar, leather shoes, etc., all by wide margins. The metallurgical, chemical, building material, machine-making and other heavy industries have readjusted their product mix and worked to broaden their range of services. They have supplied an increasing quantity and growing variety of products of better quality for agriculture, the textile and other light industries, the market, enterprises undergoing technical transformation and the export trade. The downward trend of heavy industrial production has been reversed in the course of readjustment. As we have readjusted the ratio between light and heavy industries, tightened energy control and carried out technical transformation for saving energy, 40 million tons of standard coal were saved in 1981 and 1982 alone. As the industrial structure has become sounder following readjustment and consolidation, industrial production as a whole has averaged an annual increase of 7.2 percent in the last four years, despite an average annual increase of only 1.9 percent in energy consumption for the same period. This is a signal victory for our economic readjustment.

Urban and rural markets are thriving as seldom seen before in the history of our People's Republic, and foreign economic and technical exchange has expanded greatly. Total volume of retail sales was 257 billion yuan in 1982 as against 155.9 billion yuan in 1978, an increase of 64.8 percent. This means the increase averaged 25.3 billion yuan annually, which is over five times the corresponding figure of 4.9 billion yuan for the 26 years prior to 1978. The chronic shortage in the supply of nonstaple foodstuffs has been eased considerably, as volume of retail sales of meat, poultry and eggs in 1982 was 110 percent more than in 1978 and the supply of edible oils has improved significantly. Nearly all manufactured goods for daily use are now in ample supply.

Most commodities that used to be rationed are now available without restriction. Customers today have a wider choice of consumer goods. The total volume of China's import and export trade reached 77.2 billion yuan in 1982, as against 35.5 billion yuan in 1978, a 120 percent increase in four years. There has been a welcome change in the export mix, with the proportion of manufactured goods going up from 46.5 percent to 55 percent of total export value. We have imported 440 items of technology and equipment since 1979 under unified state plans, and this has helped stimulate production. We decided to import 22 sets of equipment in 1978, and by the end of 1982 we basically repaid the high-interest foreign loans to cover the portion delivered. Good preliminary results have been obtained in the trial running of the four special economic zones of Zhenzhen, Zhuhai and Shantou in Guangdong Province and Xiamen in Fujian Province. We have also promoted tourism in recent years, which serves to expand our friendly contacts with the rest of the world. The continuous growth of our economy and the rapid expansion of our foreign trade and other foreign economic relations have all been achieved in the context of a current worldwide economic depression and shrinking international markets, thus demonstrating the superiority of the socialist economic system and the correctness of our policy of opening to the outside world, which has been carried out on an ever wider scale.

Initial restructuring of our economy has brought significant results and fruitful experience. While introducing a major reform in the agricultural system in the past few years, we initiated reforms to diversify the economy of towns and cities, expand the decision-making power of industrial and commercial enterprises, improve circulation of goods between town and country and extend the role of key cities. With the predominance of the state economy ensured, the number of workers and staff employed in collective units in towns and cities rose by 6,030,000 in the past four years, their industrial output value increased by 49 percent and the number of self-employed workers in towns and cities jumped from 150,000 to 1,470,000. Various forms of responsibility system for operation have been adopted by most state industrial and commercial enterprises. A number of small state-owned shops, restaurants and other catering businesses and small enterprises have begun to introduce the system of collective operation or contractual operation by workers and staff as a collective or as individuals, all under state ownership. Flexible and varied forms of supply for the convenience of customers have been adopted for many industrial means of production that used to be under unified state distribution. Such forms as planned state purchase, purchase by order, selective purchasing and sales by enterprises on their own are beginning to be adopted for manufactured consumer goods that used to be under unified state purchase and marketing. Moreover, we have changed the system of circulating manufactured goods in the urban and rural areas through separate channels and this has improved the interflow of commodities between town and country. We are working to extend the role of key cities, break down the barriers between localities and departments and establish various forms of economic association and economic zones. We have also instituted necessary reforms in the control of capital construction and in the foreign trade system. These measures have been effective in arousing the initiative of localities, departments, enterprises and workers and staff, invigorating the urban and rural economy, bringing more convenience to the people in their daily life and improving economic results, and have furnished experience for further reform.

The persistent, erroneous tendency to belittle knowledge and discriminate against intellectuals has gradually been corrected, and education, science and culture have improved. The number of institutions of higher education in China increased from 598 in 1978 to 715 in 1982, with the number of students rising from 856,000 to 1,154,000. More than 43,000 graduate students have been admitted in the past five years, 83 percent more than the total number enrolled in the 17 years before the "Cultural Revolution." A total of 18 doctor's, nearly 15,000 master's, and over

300,000 bachelor's degrees have been conferred by graduate schools and colleges through strict examinations. The conferring of doctorates is a big event in the history of modern Chinese education. In 1982, more than 640,000 students enrolled in various courses of adult higher education, including TV and correspondence university classes and evening colleges. The unitary system of secondary education has begun to be changed and total enrollment in secondary vocational schools has tripled in the past three years. There were 207 million people in schools of all types and levels by the end of 1982. People are becoming more and more convinced that the guiding principle for science and technology is that they must be related to economic development. Large numbers of scientific and technological personnel are tackling major projects in their own fields. In the five years under review they achieved important results in over 13,000 scientific and technological items in agriculture, industry, national defense, new and sophisticated technologies and basic research, of which 418 inventions won state awards and some were up to advanced world levels. Growing numbers of people recognize and stress the importance of science and technology for our modernization. Research in social sciences has also made headway. Art and culture show liveliness of thought and rich creativity and the quality of works has gradually improved. More than 2,400 works of literature and art won prizes in national award programmes or at national festivals in recent years. One hundred and ten thousand books and other publications were published in a total of over 23.9 billion copies in the five years under review. Medical and public health work have made progress. Between 1978 and 1982, the number of hospital beds rose from 1,856,000 to 2,054,000 and that of professional medical workers from 2,464,000 to 3,143,000. The deepening of the nationwide patriotic public health campaign has brought varying degrees of improvement in sanitary conditions in town and country. The promotion of mass sports activities has helped build up the people's physique. Chinese athletes have broken many world records and won a fair number of championship titles in international competitions. The Chinese people in their hundreds of millions have been fired with patriotism and dedication to national rejuvenation by these outstanding achievements.

The living standards of the people in town and country have improved significantly on the basis of expanded production. Net income of Chinese peasants averaged 270 yuan in 1982, double that in 1978. In the past five years, tens of millions of peasant households have moved into the 2.2 billion square metres of new housing built in the rural areas. More than 38 million people in towns and cities were given jobs. This, plus wage increases and bonuses, has markedly improved the living standards of workers and staff members. The annual per capita income of urban workers and staff that can be used as living expenses averaged 500 yuan in 1982, 38.3 percent over 1978, after allowing for price rises. State investment in this period in housing for urban workers and staff members totalled 48 billion yuan and 350 million square metres of new housing were completed, equivalent to all housing built in the 19 years before 1977.

Considerable advances have also been made in social security and welfare services. Bank savings in town and country amounted to 67.5 billion yuan at the end of 1982, 3.2 times the 1978 figure. Our personal experience shows us the notable improvement in the living standards of the urban and rural population in recent years.

Our national defence and defence forces have been strengthened and the independence and security of our motherland safeguarded. With all-round implementation of the policy of modernizing and regularizing our revolutionary Army, the military capability and political consciousness of the People's Liberation Army have risen appreciably. Initial structural reform and administrative streamlining and reorganization in the organization and command of troops has meant a step forward towards combined arms units. Military training and ideological and political work in the Armed Forces, the work of military academies and schools, logistics and research in military sciences have all been strengthened, and the professional level of the officer corps and their competence to command have been raised. The Army's fine traditions have been carried forward and the relations between Army and government and between Army and people have become ever closer. Owing to repeated wild armed provocations by the Vietnamese authorities along the borders of China's Guangxi Zhuang Autonomous Region and Yunnan Province, our Army was compelled in the spring of 1979 to carry out limited counter-attack in self-defence, which was successful. The militia are now fewer in number and better in quality, thanks to reform and readjustment. Scientific research and production related to national defence have forged ahead. Fresh progress has been made in the development of new tactical and strategic weapons. The steady enhancement of our defence capability is an important guarantee that the people of all our nationalities will be able to dedicate themselves wholeheartedly to the modernization programme.

We have adhered to an independent foreign policy and achieved new successes in foreign affairs. We have continued to expand relations with other countries on the basis of the five principles of mutual respect for sovereignty and territorial integrity, mutual non-aggression, non-interference in each other's internal affairs, equality and mutual benefit and peaceful coexistence. In the past five years, we have established diplomatic relations with 15 more countries, bringing the total to 129. During this period, Chinese leaders paid visits to 90 countries and leaders from 81 countries came to visit China. Our unity and friendship with Third World and non-aligned countries have grown and become stronger. We have made unceasing efforts to combat hegemonism and safeguard world peace. We have upheld principle and justice and are playing an ever bigger role on major international issues in a complex international situation.

Fellow deputies, during the past five years our country followed the path of sound growth after surmounting various political and economic difficulties, and these are years in which the people enjoyed ease of mind and the state grew more prosperous.

Our successes in this period were not easily won. They were achieved as a result of the fundamental changes in our guidelines and principles. When the current government took office in early 1978, "left" errors in our guidelines and practical work had not yet, for the most part, been straightened out and corrected.

In addition to politically reaffirming the erroneous theory of the "Cultual Revolution" the report on government work, submitted by the State Council to the First Session of the Fifth National People's Congress in February 1978, set unrealistically high targets for economic development so that the scale of construction far exceeded our national capabilities and aggravated the imbalance between the major branches of our economy and other economic difficulties created by the decade of domestic turmoil. If this state of affairs had not been corrected promptly, the consequences would have been disastrous. The Third Plenary Session of the Eleventh Central Committee of the Chinese Communist Party held at the end of 1978 formulated a correct political, ideological and organizational line, decided to shift the focus of our work to socialist modernizations and began to set things to rights in all spheres, thus bringing about a historic change. In keeping with the line of the third plenary session and the decisions adopted by the Fifth National People's Congress and its Standing Committee, politically, we have made determined efforts in recent years to eliminate various persistent pernicious effects arising from the so-called theory of continuing the revolution under the dictatorship of the proletariat, while at the same time upholding the four cardinal principles by eliminating interference of all sorts from the right. Economically, we have overcome with firmness the persistent error of construction, and adhered to the principle of proceeding from China's actual conditions and capability, working hard and advancing step by step. The policy of readjustment, restructuring, consolidation and improvement put forward in 1979 and, in particular, the decision made at the end of 1980 to further readjust the national economy were of decisive significance in setting to rights the guideline for economic work and constituted a fundamental turning point in the growth of China's economy along sound lines.

Past experience, if not forgotten, is a guide for the future. China is a developing socialist country with a huge population, and her material and technical foundation remains rather weak. This determines the protracted, arduous and complicated nature of our modernization programme. The basic points of departure for a correct economic development policy are the integration of the basic tenets of Marxism with the concrete realities of China and adherence to the principle of seeking truth from facts and doing things in accordance with China's concrete conditions. We can reach our goal of modernization only step by step and in stages. We should not overstep objective conditions and attempt the impossible, but, where objective conditions permit, we should strive for what can be achieved through efforts. The major setbacks we suffered in the past in economic development were all due to, among other things, a divorce from China's realities as manifested in the excessively high demands and impetuosity for quick results in our guideline. The primary condition for ensuring continued development of the current favourable situation and avoidance of repeating our past mistakes is to bear firmly in mind the historical lessons, remain clear-headed at all times and unswervingly adhere to the principles of seeking truth from facts and of steady advance in national construction.

Because things have been set to rights, the confidence of the whole nation in the socialist system has been reinforced and the people are once again showing great enthusiasm in building the socialist motherland. This is the source of strength on which we can draw in striving for victory.

Large numbers of model and advanced workers have come to the fore in the past five years, and over 38,500 were cited as labour heroes at the national and the provincial, municipal, and autonomous region levels, over 42,900 as pace-setters in the new "Long March" and more than 71,800 as "March 8 red flag bearers". The soul-stirring exploits and fine spirit of Comrades Zhao Chune, Luan Fu, Zhang Hua, Jiang Zhuying, Luo Jianfu, Lei Yushun, An Ke, Zhu Boru, Li Junjia and Zhang Haidi have been an inspiration to hundreds of millions of people, old and young, throughout the country. On behalf of the State Council, I would like to extend a high salute to the workers, peasants, People's Liberation Army men, intellectuals and public figures of various circles who are working hard everywhere and to express sincere thanks to the people of all our nationalities for their support for the work of the government. Our government work still leaves much to be desired and we face many difficulties on the road ahead. As regards production, capital construction and circulation, economic results are still unsatisfactory and the waste of manpower and material and financial resources is appalling. Owing to inadequate control over the market and prices, open or disguised increases in the prices of certain commodities, particularly non-staple foodstuffs, have occurred in quite a few places. The building of a socialist spiritual civilization has not yet received adequate attention in some localities, departments and units. There are certain unwholesome things in the spheres of ideology, culture and art. The unhealthy tendencies and practices in society have not been forcefully and completely checked, and there is no lack of economic crimes and some other serious crimes. Some government functionaries have not yet effectively corrected the reprehensible habit of bureaucratism and the unhealthy practice of seeking personal gain through abuse of government power. We must be soberly aware of these problems and solve them conscientiously in order to consolidate and expand the present favourable situation.

THE MAIN TASKS FOR THE NEXT FIVE YEARS

Based on our analysis of the work done in the past five years as well as on the current situation and problems, this State Council deems it necessary to make the following suggestions in regard to the work of the incoming administration for the congress to examine.

The main tasks of the government for the coming five years should be to mobilize the people of all our nationalities to fulfill or overfulfill the Sixth Five-Year Plan, draw up and carry out the Seventh Five-Year Plan, continue to push ahead with work in various fields centering on economic developing, bring about a fundamental turn for the better in the financial and economic situation and in standards of social conduct as put forward by the Twelfth National Congress of the Chinese Communist Party, and thus win a signal victory in the struggle to create a new situation in all fields of socialist modernization.

I. On Economic Development

The party's twelfth national congress decided that the strategic goal of quadrupling the gross annual output value of industry and agriculture by the end of the century should be realized in two steps. In the decade 1981–90, our main objective is to lay a solid foundation for the following decade, 1991–2000, when we shall strive for new vigorous economic growth. This is a correct decision based on objective reality.

The next five years are of key importance in laying the foundation. During this period, we must do a good job of readjusting the national economy, speed up reforms, concentrate on key construction projects and technical transformation, ensure the stable growth of the economy, accumulate strength and create conditions for subsequent advance.

In the next five years, we must first of all ensure that agriculture and light and heavy industries grow in a balanced way. Taking as our premise constant improvement of economic results, we must strive for a realistic rate of growth in production, which can be achieved through exertion. As things stand now, the growth rate set in the Sixth Five-Year Plan period can be surpassed, and we can set a somewhat higher rate for the Seventh Five-Year Plan period. The rate of growth must of course be predicated on steady improvement of economic results, and under no circumstances should we stress quantity and output value one-sidedly. We must ensure constant improvement in quality and increased variety of all products that have a ready market so as to expand real social wealth. The objective of quadrupling gross annual industrial and agricultural output value in 20 years was set for the country as a whole. When it comes to specific localities, departments or enterprises, some will have to increase their output value more than four times and some less. All must proceed from their own concrete conditions, stress better economic results and make their plans subject to nationwide balance. We must not change but must firmly implement the basic rural policies adopted sinced the third plenary session of the eleventh Central Committee of the party and must continue to stabilize and improve the various forms of the system of contracted household responsibility related to output and implement the principle of "sparing no effort in promoting grain production and actively developing diversified undertakings" so as to ensure development in agriculture, forestry, animal husbandry, sideline occupations and fishery in the coming five years. At the same time, investment in agriculture should be gradually increased and the production and technological conditions of agriculture vigorously improved. Water conservancy works should be better built, with stress on improving drainage and irrigation facilities in areas producing commodity grain and cotton. The chemical fertilizer industry should be expanded rapidly and the proportion of compound and phosphate and potash fertilizers gradually increased. We should energetically expand the fodder industry, substantially increase the output of mixed feed and step up the improvement of grasslands so as to promote the growth of animal husbandry. We should strengthen research in agricultural science and technology and apply them more widely, stress breeding improved seed strains and popularize them and adopt comprehensive technical measures suited to local conditions for improving soils, reforming cultivation methods, and preventing and wiping out plant diseases and insect pests so as to raise per-unit yield. We should step up afforestation, rationally use forest reserves and continue to curb indiscriminate felling of trees through resolute measures. While promoting the steady growth of agricultural production, we should get heavy industry to better serve agriculture, light industry and technical transformation and should continue to apply the principle of giving light industry priority in the supply of energy and raw and semi-finished materials, access to transport facilities, allocation of investment and loans and use of foreign exchange.

As for light industry, we should constantly improve the quality of its products, increase designs and varieties, develop new lines of products and ensure a fairly high rate of growth in the production of consumer goods so as to maintain and expand the present fairly ample market supply.

In the next five years, we must work harder to build key energy and transport projects and promote the technical transformation of existing enterprises. The success or failure of the key construction projects has a vital bearing on the future of China's modernization and on the fundamental interests of our people. The whole nation should support these projects and the entire working class and the people of all our nationalities should contribute to their construction. There are 890 large and medium-sized projects to be continued or started during the Sixth Five-Year Plan period. Of these, 93 major ones, each calling for investment of 500 million yuan or more, are already under way. More major projects will be undertaken in the Seventh Five-Year Plan period. We should step up expansion of the power industry by building hydro-electric, thermal and nuclear power stations. A number of large hydro-electric stations should be gradually constructed along the upper reaches of the Huanghe River and the upper and middle reaches of the Changjiang River and its tributaries, and in the Hongshui River Basin. A number of electric power stations should be built one after another near the coal mines in Shanxi Province, Nei Monggol, Huainan and Huaibei regions in Anhui Province and the Liupanshui region in Guizhou Province. On the one hand, we should concentrate on exploiting the big opencut mines in Shanxi Province and Nei Monggol to increase the small and medium-sized mines in a planned way. In the petroleum industry, we should stress general surveying and prospecting both inland and offshore and strive to verify as soon as possible the reserves of a number of new oil and gas fields. In tackling the energy problem, it is essential to continue to apply the policy of laying equal stress on development and conservation. In every new project we should make rational use of energy by adopting new energy-saving techniques and technologies. With regard to railways, we should focus on augmenting their capacity to carry coal while actively transforming old lines and building new ones where necessary. To meet the needs of domestic economic development and foreign trade, we should increse the capacity of harbours, inland waterways, roads and air transport, and further improve post and telecommunications facilities. While concentrating on the energy and transport industries, we should ensure a corresponding expansion of the metallurgical, chemical, building materials, electronics and machine-making industries and strengthen geological prospecting. Like construction of the key projects, energetic promotion of technical transformation of enterprises is an important condition for all-round fulfillment of the Sixth Five-Year Plan and for ushering in a new period of vigorous economic growth. Under unified planning, in the next five years we will step up technical transformation of existing enterprises, especially of major enterprises in key industries and important cities, so as to raise the tech-

nological level of production in a significant way. The focus of such technical transformation will be the improvement of the properties and quality of products and the lowering of consumption of energy and raw and semi-finished materials.

We must continue to improve the people's living standards in both town and country and strictly control population growth in the next five years. Both income and consumption levels in town and country will go up with expanded production and higher productivity.

The supply of non-staple foodstuffs will steadily improve, as will the quality of people's clothing. General durable goods such as bicycles and wrist watches will by and large meet market demand and more and more home electrical appliances such as TV sets and washing machines will be available to both urban and rural families. We must vigorously tighten market and price control and continue to keep commodity prices basically stable. A large amount of housing will continue to be built in urban and rural areas. The growth of urban infrastructure should match expanded production and construction of residential areas. Special effort should be made to increase the supply of water and gas to big cities and to improve public transportation services. We will strive to expand medical, public health and social welfare services in both town and country and ensure environmental protection. Stimulating production and improving the people's living standards both require that we continue to lay special stress on population control. This is our national policy, a policy of fundamental, strategic importance. We must persistently advocate late marriage and one child per couple, strictly control second births, prevent additional births by all means, earnestly carry out effective birth control measures and firmly protect infant girls and their mothers. In order to promote family planning, we must use all available means to provide diverse forms of old-age care.

In performing our tasks in the coming five years, we must pay special attention to helping the areas inhabited by minority nationalities develop their economy and culture and enhance their prosperity.

While working to accomplish these tasks, particularly of giving priority to key construction projects, we face the most urgent problem of inadequate financial resources with serious decentralized use of funds. In the four years from 1979 through 1982, the total output value increased by 33.6 percent, which is not a small figure, but our state revenue in the same period dropped by 3.3 percent. We must carefully analyse the reasons for this state of affairs, arrive at a common understanding and take resolute and effective measures to bring about a speedy change. Otherwise, there will be no adequate financial and material guarantees for our key construction projects and our plan for laying a solid foundation in the 1980s and entering a new period of vigorous economic growth in the 1990s will fail. The State Council holds that the problem should be solved earnestly through the following three channels:

First, strive for better economic results and open up new sources of revenue. A major reason for the decline in state revenues over the past few years was poor economic results as manifested in the continuing high cost of industrial production and transport and the large amount of funds being tied up in commodity circulation. The costs of comparable products of industrial enterprises rose by 0.9

percent in 1980 and 1 percent in 1981, and failed to drop in 1982. This alone meant a decrease of 4–5 billion yuan in state revenue. In 1982, the combined deficit of industrial enterprises that ran at a loss came to 4.2 billion yuan. Add to this the operating losses in grain and commercial enterprises, and the total loss rises to over 10 billion yuan. Unless this situation is changed soon, it is bound to seriously affect our construction and production. All departments, localities, and enterprises must bear firmly in mind the need for improving economic results and must never stress input to the neglect of output, stress state investment to the neglect of making contributions to the state in return.

Shifting the focus of our economic work to improvement of economic results must not remain a general call, but must be turned into effective action. Be it economic readjustment or consolidation, technical transformation or structural reform, the objective must always be improvement of economic results and an increase in state revenues. Consolidation of enterprises is essential for obtaining better economic results and should be speeded up and improved so that this task is done earnestly in all existing enterprises before 1985. All departments, localities, enterprises and institutions should unfailingly cut down production costs and other expenses specified in the state plan. Any enterprise that fails to do so will incur a proportional deduction in the portion of profit retained for its own use. All units must turn over all the funds assigned them by the state in the form of taxes and profits quotas. Any unit that fails to do so because of poor management is, in principle, not entitled to give wage increases to its workers and staff members. Appropriate quotas must be set according to the merits of each case for the amount of circulating funds used by enterprises, and any unauthorized increase is forbidden. All enterprises that run at a loss due to poor operation must reverse this trend within a given time limit. Otherwise, they must be ordered to shut down, suspend operations, amalgamate with others or switch to the manufacture of other products. All units and workers and staff members should immediately swing into action and increase production and practice economy, restore or strengthen labour discipline, raise work efficiency and firmly struggle against any extravagance and waste, in discipline and irresponsibility. All localities, departments, enterprises and institutions must set specific goals for improving economic results and adopt and carry out concrete measures to achieve them.

Second, properly distribute national income and increase the proportion in it of financial revenue. Another important reason for the state's inadequate financial resources in recent years is excessive decentralization of funds, which means that too little is concentrated in the hands of the state. The proportion of financial revenue in the national income dropped from 37.2 percent in 1978 to 25.5 percent in 1982. The numerous problems accumulated over the years demand that we spend more money on improving the people's standard of living and on increasing the funds at the disposal of enterprises, and it is also reasonable to reduce the proportion of financial revenue in the national income to some extent. But some of our measures are a bit too drastic and this, coupled with the fact that financial control is not strict enough, leaving many loopholes, has caused the proportion of financial revenue to drop too much. This is in sharp contrast to extra-budgetary funds

which have increased considerably, rising from 37.1 billion yuan in 1978 to 65 billion yuan in 1982, a 75.2 percent growth within just four years. Because of the serious over-decentralization of funds, it has been impossible to control the overall scale of capital construction, resulting in overlapping or blind construction, and it has also been difficult to check the growth of funds for consumption and, in particular, the rapid growth in the indiscriminate handing out of bonuses and subsidies in cash or in kind. Under no circumstances should this state of affairs be allowed to continue. Otherwise, the country's key construction projects cannot be carried out, normal economic order and the appropriate ratios restored through painstaking efforts may be upset again, the major policy decisions and measures of the central authorities may not be implemented, and the progress of China's socialist modernization may be impeded.

Both the Twelfth National Congress of the Chinese Communist Party and the Fifth Session of the Fifth National People's Congress clearly enunciated the policy of concentrating funds for key construction projects and of strictly controlling the scale of capital construction. But this problem has not yet been solved in a satisfactory way due to a generally deficient recognition of its importance and urgency, the failure of the government to take sufficiently forceful measures, and the lack of strict check-up and supervision. The State Council holds that, in future, rational distribution of national income, prevention of excessive decentralization of funds, and appropriate increases in the proportion of financial revenue in the national income must be placed on the agenda as an extremely important task of our government work. In distributing the national income, we must give consideration to both the overall interests of the people and those of the individual and to both long-term and immediate interests. We should gradually enable the people to become well-off and enterprises to increase their earnings on the basis of growing production and national income; at the same time, we should see that state revenue rises steadily and the state as a whole prospers step by step. The rate of increase for wages, bonuses and welfare funds for workers and staff members must be less than that for profits and taxes turned over to the state by the enterprises, and the practice of indiscriminately issuing bonuses must be stopped. The increase in peasant income must come mainly from expanded production and lower costs. The state provides 32 billion yuan in price subsidies for farm produce and other kinds of subsidies at present. If measures are not taken, this figure may continue to rise sharply in the future. This is beyond the state's financial capability and must be checked. In regard to enterprises, we must not return to the former practice of "unified receipts and allocations by the state." Nevertheless, the state must be assured of the largest share of the increased profits of the enterprises, mainly through taxation and the fixing of a rational ratio between the after-tax profits to be kept by the enterprises and the amount to be turned over to the state. The centrally controlled proportion of state revenue must be raised appropriately so as to meet the needs of key construction projects and other state expenditures. China is still rather poor and we must strongly advocate hard work and thrift in building the country and the viewpoints of taking overall interests into account and of subordinating the part to the whole. There is now violation of the law and discipline in some establishments, including misuse of and underjustified additions to production costs, tax evasion, withholding of revenue that ought to be turned over to the state, appropriation of state property for use by individual units, and appropriation of public property for private use. These practices must be investigated and rectified. Leading cadres at all levels should act courageously in safeguarding the state interests, strictly enforce financial and economic discipline and unflinchingly struggle against such bad practices.

Third, correctly determine the overall scale of capital construction and strive to ensure funds to key construction projects and to increase returns on investment. Capital construction must be done on an appropriate scale in order to lay a solid foundation for vigorous economic growth. But the scale must match our national strength and must not exceed our financial and material capabilities. If we fail to observe this objective economic law, we shall be punished by reality. Our present capital construction is already on a fairly large scale.

The problem is that state budgetary investment in key construction projects in the fields of energy and transport has failed to reach the amount planned, while capital construction by localities, departments, and enterprises using their own funds or different kinds of loans is out of control and construction of ordinary processing industries and nonproductive enterprises far exceeds the plan. We must change this situation in good time and exercise strict control over the overall scale of capital construction so as to muster the resources of the whole country for building a group of modern backbone projects and transforming a number of present key enterprises and thereby lay a solid foundation and prepare adequate reserve forces for China's economic growth.

The large, backbone projects undertaken as key items call for enormous investment, entail a long construction cycle and require a series of auxiliary projects. Therefore, we must not undertake too many such projects at the same time. We must act according to our capabilities, make comprehensive plans and take all factors into consideration. Otherwise, there will be no funds to build construction projects that bring quick economic returns, or to expand agricultural production, the market for manufactured goods turned out by light industry and our intellectual resources. This will seriously pull down our economic growth rate in the near future and may even once again cause an imbalance in national economic growth. There must be a high degree of centralized and unified management of capital construction as a whole, with the State Planning Commission responsible for ensuring an overall balance. With regard to the key construction projects, the State Planning Commission, the economic departments in charge and relevant local governments should make adequate preparations, act strictly in accordance with capital construction procedures and plan, design and build meticulously, as they did for construction of the 156 major projects during the period of the First Five-Year Plan (1953–57). At present, waste in capital construction is appalling, and investment in many key projects is above budgetary estimates. According to a survey of 176 large and medium-sized projects now being put up, investment to date already exceeds the original budgetary estimates by 18.5 billion yuan. For some items, this is admittedly due to the original estimates having been set too low, but in most cases it is due to a variety of

irrational factors. In future, a strict economic responsibility system must be practiced in capital construction and waste of all kinds eliminated. No locality, department, unit, or individual is allowed to collect fees arbitrarily or extort anything from the organizations charged with building the key construction projects. The State Council has decided to organize, after this session, necessary forces to conduct investigations at the key projects. Units which have done their work well will be commended and those whose work is poor exposed and criticized. Those who have caused serious losses and waste by neglect of duty must be punished according to administrative discipline and the law. We must live up to the expectations of the people by displaying a high sense of responsibility to the state and the people and making good use of the funds they have accumulated through diligent labour.

II. Restructuring the Economy

It is imperative to speed up structural reform of the economy so as to meet the requirements of economic development. At its Fifth Session, the Fifth National People's Congress approved the measures submitted by the State Council to be taken in the last three years of the Sixth Five-Year Plan period to restructure the economy.

They are being implemented as follows: After six months of preparatory work, the first step in instituting a system of taxation instead of delivery of profits to the state has been taken in all state-owned industrial and commercial enterprises as of June 1. In conjunction with the restructuring of government administration, we are expanding experiments in encouraging key cities to organize production and circulation better as a way to handle properly the contradictions between higher and lower levels and between departments and regions. The plan for reform of the system of rural commodity circulation has been put into effect on a trial basis throughout the country. These three reforms, being a breakthrough in the present organization of the economy, have already started, but much remains to be done and we should continue to push the work ahead.

We have stepped up study and overall planning for restructuring the economy as a whole and will try to work out as soon as possible a programme for trial application at selected points and in a few given regions so that it can be extended step by step throughout the country during the Seventh Five-Year Plan period. Comprehensive restructuring of the economy requires special efforts to solve the following problems:

First, to reform the planning system and strengthen the state's effective control over the national economy and guidance to it. The reform of the planning system is an important link in restructuring the economy as a whole. Under the principle of ensuring the leading role of the planned economy supplemented by market regulation, we should adopt such methods of management as mandatory planning, guidance planning or market regulation with regard to different enterprises, products and tasks. We should do a better job of economic forecasting and step by step devise scientific regulations for planning as regards decision-making, programming, overall balancing, appraising and job responsibility so as to improve and refine the entire planning system. While making proper use of administrative and legislative means, the state should use more effectively such economic levers as pricing, taxation and credits, strengthen statistical work and supervision by statistical means and guide the economic activities of localities, departments and enterprises in the right direction, so as to ensure fulfillment of the state plan.

Second, to organize production and circulation according to the requirements of large-scale socialized production and develop a single socialist market. The main points are as follows: Take cities as centres and organize economic activities according to the inherent laws of economic growth, breaking down the barriers between regions, departments, and town and county. We must continue to reorganize or merge enterprises on the principle of achieving coordination among specialized departments and improving economic results, and gradually rationalize the organization of enterprises and their system of management. We must earnestly remove barriers and blockades, open up diverse channels of circulation and reduce intermediate links in circulation to ensure the free flow of commodities and gradually form inter-trade and trans-regional economic zones and networks. Work in this respect should be started in the large and medium-sized coastal cities, selected cities in the hinterland and some new major economic bases. Such work can be undertaken later in economically underdeveloped regions where conditions are not yet ripe.

Third, to reform the financial system and the wage and labour systems. The system of taxation instead of the delivery of profits to the state should be improved, some new taxes introduced where necessary, tax rates properly readjusted and revenue going to the central and local authorities and that shared by both according to different categories of taxes be clearly defined, with a view to improving and stabilizing the relations between the state and enterprises and between the central and local authorities in distribution of revenue. Reform the wage system step by step, carry out the principle of "to each according to his work" and overcome equalitarianism so as to link the income of the workers and staff members closely with economic results, the success or failure of enterprise operation and their own contributions in work. Reform the personnel system step by step so that people can be transferred to other jobs or go to a higher or a lower post as required, departments or enterprises can employ or appoint people according to their merits and the labour force can be handled flexibly under the guidance of the state plan so that trained personnel can be used rationally and can make professional progress.

The reforms we are carrying out or are about to carry out are aimed at overcoming the shortcomings and defects in the present organization of the economy which hamstring the growth of the productive forces, gradually creating a new economic structure suited to China's conditions and building socialism with distinct Chinese characteristics. Though being a revolution in themselves, such reforms are of course not designed to bring about a fundamental change in the social system. They are not meant to shake or go against the socialist system; on the contrary, they constitute a process of its self-improvement and self-perfection. They are conducted consciously on the strength of the socialist system itself and through the practice of hundreds of millions of people under the leadership of the party and the state and the guidance of Marxism-Leninism and Mao Zedong Thought. Through these reforms, the basic system of socialism will be consolidated and developed and its specific systems improved and refined so as to promote the smooth growth of the productive forces. Of course, after the newly restructured economy is established for a time following our concentrated efforts for comprehensive reform, it will still be necessary, as production and technology grow and other conditions change, to continue reforming one link or another in the economy.

In recent years, we have made significant successes in reforms in the rural areas. There are both similarities and dissimilarities between the reforms in agriculture and those in urban industrial and commercial enterprises. The similarities are evident in that in both cases the reforms have made it possible for the production and commercial units and the working people to link their material interests closely with the fruits of their labour and with the expansion of the material production of all society and hence unleash their initiative. However, as there are different types of ownership, levels of the productive forces and extent of socialization, reforms in the cities are more complex than in the countryside. Therefore, we should draw from the experience in rural reforms only what is common to both and must not mechanically apply the specific forms of operation and management suited only to agriculture to urban industrial and commercial enterprises and other undertakings. Since more than 80 percent of the state revenue comes from urban industrial and commercial enterprises, the outcome of reforms in the cities has a vital bearing on the national economy as a whole. We must pay special attention to the fact that while we are restructuring our economy, we are continuing economic readjustment and striving to bring about a fundamental change for the better in the financial and economic situation.

This means that in making reforms we must pay full attention to our economic capability and that while we must be firm, we should also guard against impetuosity. Wherever necessary and feasible, experiments should be conducted in order to gain experience and then it should be spread step by step.

The State Council holds that, while minor defects are unavoidable and not difficult to remedy in the course of reform, we must see to it that major defects are avoided. Each step or measure taken in reform must help fulfill the tasks set in the state plan and lead to the harmonious growth of the national economy, to the achievement of better economic results from various economic activities and to the interests of the state, the collective and the individual and to the guarantee of a steady and rational growth of state revenues. All localities, departments and enterprises must give first priority to safeguarding the overall interests of the state and those of the consumers in carrying out reforms. This is the only way to ensure a successful restructuring of the economy.

Some comrades now hold that reform simply means decentralization of power and interests. This view is both incorrect and harmful. It is wrong to exercise excessive and rigid control over specific economic activities of enterprises which hamstrings their initiative. A proper measure of flexibility is entirely necessary. But major economic activities that concern overall interests should nevertheless be centralized. Any attempt to weaken such centralization means retrogression rather than progress and cannot ensure the growth of our economy along socialist lines. Powers and interests appropriate to enterprises must be respected. But it must first of all be made clear that as the reform gradually spreads, much higher demands and ever heavier responsibility will be placed on the enterprises. For the various forms of responsibility system characterized by the combination of responsibility, power and interests, responsibility is of primary importance. A determined reformer should not fight for partial interests and power, but should be fully aware of his or her responsibility and fulfill it, strive to improve operation and management, promote technical progress, strengthen labour discipline, do such work as bookkeeping well and achieve better economic results. All enterprises and all workers and staff members should focus their attention on these points. Leading economic bodies at different levels and all enterprises should exert themselves to raise the quality of their work to meet the standards required by the reform.

The restructuring of our economy is a big event in our economic life and in society at large. Leaders at all levels must have a clear idea of the fundamental objective of the reform and adhere to its correct orientation and principles. In instituting any reform, we should take into account not only its own merits but also its relationship and co-ordination with other reforms, and not only the immediate effect but the long-term impact. We should closely combine the reform with the readjustment of the economic structure and the consolidation and technical transformation of the enterprises so that they help and promote each other. In the course of reform, we must strengthen and persevere in ideological and political work, bring about a common understanding through intensive, meticulous and convincing publicity and education and overcome erroneous ideas that hinder the successful institution of the reform. Governments at all levels, including the State Council, must exercise better leadership, support and set value on any innovation by the masses that is in keeping with the orientation of the reform, promptly study and solve any new problems that crop up in the process and systematically guide and push the restructuring of the economy forward.

III. On the Development of Education, Science and Technology, and Culture

From now on we should stress the development of intellectual resources, giving priority to the development of culture which focuses on the promotion of education and science and technology. This is a prerequisite for invigorating China's national economy. By greatly enhancing the people's scientific and educational level as well as their political awareness and moral standards, we will be able to provide a tremendous dynamic force for economic and social development and for advancing socialist material and spiritual civilization. This is a question of great concern to the whole nation, and many comrades have made a good number of useful suggestions. Governments at all levels must firmly overcome the erroneous tendency of belittling cultural work and make the development of intellectual resources an important item on their agenda.

We must now give prominence to developing higher education and quickly training personnel for all trades and professions. The State Council recently approved the report submitted by the Ministry of Education and the State Planning Commission on speeding up the expansion of higher education in different forms. Enrollment in regular colleges and universities is to rise from 315,000 in 1982 to 550,000 in 1987, a 75 percent jump in those five years. We will also try to provide higher education through such forms as radio, TV and correspondence university classes and evening colleges, and college for training managerial personnel and for advanced training of teachers so that their enrollment can grow from 290,000 in 1982 to 1,100,000 in 1987, a 280 percent rise. To carry out this plan, the state will ensure the investment and materials for major construction projects. We will also adopt necessary policies and organizational measures to encourage people to become educated through independent study and to train young and middle-aged cadres in rotation and in a planned way, so that there will be more specialists in all trades and professions.

China's specialized secondary school education has been slow in growing over the years, with the result that the ratio of intermediate and high-level specialists is seriously out of balance. This holds back expansion of the technical force at the frontline of production, resulting in an enormous waste of investment in education. We must lose no time in restructuring secondary education and setting up vocational and technical schools in a planned way. Senior middle vocational school students should account for over 40 percent of the total senior middle school enrollment in the next five years. This requires training more teachers for vocational and technical schools, encouraging qualified scientific and technical personnel and master craftsmen to join the staff of vocational schools or give courses in them, and urging factories and mines to run classes jointly with regular schools.

More and more workers, peasants and young people have now come to realize from their own experience the importance of learning scientific and general knowledge and political theory. There is a rising enthusiasm for studying. Governments at all levels, enterprises, communes and production brigades must do their best to develop education to satisfy the demand of workers and peasants. Primary and secondary education constitutes the foundation. We must make great efforts to train primary and secondary school teachers, help them improve the teaching standard, and create a fine atmosphere of respect for teachers in society at large. We must strive to make primary education universal and wipe out illiteracy, first and foremost, among adults. Pre-school education is highly important and must be developed in a planned way. We must train more and better teachers for such education and improve it gradually. We must do a good job of compiling teaching materials, improve teaching methods, and steadily raise the quality of education of all kinds and at all levels.

Economic growth is dependent on scientific and technological advances. Last February we brought together several hundred scientists, technical experts and leading members of the departments concerned to work out a 15-year scientific and technical development programme (1986–2000) that would coordinate scientific and technological advance with economic and social development. Policies concerning technology and equipment will likewise be worked out for agriculture, energy, communications and transport, computers, the machine-building industry, raw and semi-finished materials and consumer goods. These should provide a sound scientific and technological basis for drawing up a long-term programme for overall economic and social development. Efforts should be continued during the Sixth Five-Year Plan period to build the 38 key research projects and to disseminate and apply 40 major scientific and technological research achievements. Apart from key research projects designated by the state, various departments, localities and enterprises should undertake research according to their own needs and possibilities. In addition, the government is organizing the scientific and technical personnel concerned to make first-phase preparations and begin research on important construction subjects for the 279 major projects now planned. We should also strive to digest, assimilate and spread advanced technology introduced from other countries so as to raise China's level of production and technology more quickly through imported technology and joint production.

The most pressing problem confronting us is the unified arrangement and proper use of scientific and technical personnel. In order to do this, we will take the following measures: 1) Break down the barriers between departments and between regions and work out unified placement and appropriate use of scientific and technical personnel on a nationwide scale through the drawing up of the development programme, the joint tackling of key scientific and technical projects and establishment of technological development centres. 2) Transfer in a planned way a number of scientific and technical personnel from heavy and defense industries to energy, transport, light industry and agriculture where such personnel are few; transfer a number of personnel from institutions of higher education and scientific research that are well staffed to secondary schools or vocational schools to augment their teaching staff. 3) Set up a system of rational interflow of scientific and technical personnel so that they can move from overstaffed to understaffed departments and to encourage them to go to small and medium-sized cities, the rural areas, national minority areas and remote border regions. 4) Create a system of dual control over the country's scientific and technical personnel, grading them according to whether they come under the management of the central or local authorities and according to their trades or professions and specialities. 5) Improve the systems of appraisal, promotion and awards and the conferring of academic titles on scientific and technical personnel so as to raise the professional competence of those who are young and middle-aged.

Under the guidance of Marxism-Leninism and Mao Zedong Thought and the principles of integrating theory with practice and of "letting a hundred flowers blossom and a hundred schools of thought contend," people specialized in philosophy and other social sciences should conduct creative research into the major ideological, theoretical and practical problems arising from our socialist modernization, summarize from a historical perspective the achievements and lessons gained in all fields since the founding of the People's Republic and analytically study and criticize different trends of thought in the world so as to assimilate what is useful and produce research results of high quality.

After some years of effort, we will establish a modern, nationwide research network step by step in philosophy and other social sciences that embraces a complete range of disciplines and subjects, each with distinctive characteristics but coordinated in their development, and is rational in geographical distribution.

The departments of culture, the arts, the press, publishing, broadcasting and television should constantly educate the people in patriotism and collectivism and in socialist and communist ideology so as to promote socialist spiritual civilization. Focusing on raising the quality of their works or products, these departments should adjust and restructure their administrative systems, consolidate their ranks, update their basic facilities and enrich the people's cultural life by meeting the diverse needs of the people who differ in age, occupation, educational level and interests, creating and providing more and better works that are to the people's liking and organizing all kinds of cultural, recreational and sports activities for every section of the people. We must improve our radio and TV programmes, the movie industry and the work of publishing, printing and distribution and build more and better libraries, scientific and technological centres, museums, archives, cultural centres, youth and children's palaces and sports facilities so as to meet the needs of our people, especially the young, for study and recreation. We must continue to protect historical relics well. We must do our best to spread scientific knowledge among the people and familiarize them with the fine ideological and cultural heritage of mankind in different ways through modern techniques of reproduction and transmission. Our works should reflect the activities of the people in the great modernization drive in a profound and graphic way so as to arouse boundless enthusiasm for progress. Our objective in providing nourishment for the mind should be not only to meet the people's requirements for proper entertainment and aesthetic enjoyment but, above all, to satisfy their thirst for knowledge in all fields. We should not only help them enrich their mental world and live by higher moral standards, but also significantly raise their ability to know and change the objective world.

The leading bodies in charge of ideological and cultural work at all levels must ensure the quality of our intellectual and artistic products by respecting artistic principles and the creative work of writers and artists. Our literary and artistic systems should be reformed step by step and under guidance. Our aim is to ensure the flourishing of socialist literature and art and enhance the ideological and artistic quality of writers and artists and of their works. While continuing to overcome "left" errors, we must constantly watch out for the tendency of some works towards crass commercialism regardless of social consequences; this has already appeared and had a pernicious influence. We should adopt effective measures to rectify this tendency. For a considerably long time to come, we will strive to expand socialist production and commodity exchange, which nevertheless are essentially different from the profit-grabbing and anarchic commodity production characteristic of the capitalist system of private ownership. Most intellectual and artistic products circulate in the form of commodities, but in no case must we allow the decadent ideology of "putting money above everything else" to spread unchecked in our society. All honest, patriotic and revolutionary writers and artists must not treat their works and performances as a means of grabbing fame and fortune. The tendency towards bourgeois liberalism in ideological and cultural work and disregard for social consequences are incompatible with the policy of serving the people and socialism, and we must continue to criticize such trends. All ideological, cultural and art workers must cultivate a deep sense of responsibility to the people and live up to their expectations.

We must run our medical and health services better. Attention should be paid to the promotion of traditional Chinese medicine while developing modern medicine. The tendency of ignoring the treasure-house of medicine of our motherland must be overcome. We must continue to uphold the principles of putting prevention first, of giving consideration to both town and country and of combining Chinese and Western medicine. We must gradually reform the present medical systems, strengthen the building and management of medical and public health facilities at all levels, and raise the quality of medical service and treatment. We must continue the mass patriotic public health campaign and prevent and cure infectious and endemic diseases of all kinds. We should encourage mass sports activities in urban and rural areas with the focus on improving physical culture in schools and strive to raise our athletic standards.

The key to strengthening cultural work lies in implementing more fully our policies on intellectuals so as to bring their enthusiasm into full play. All departments and localities should, in the light of their own conditions, adopt measures to improve their work towards intellectuals in real earnest. Intellectuals should receive gradual and appropriate increases in remuneration for their work. Since the salaries of those middle-aged intellectuals who play the backbone role are far too low, the state will, despite financial difficulties, do its best to raise their salaries gradually to a level corresponding to their posts and titles.

In order to tap our intellectual resources and promote the advance of education, science, literature, and art, physical culture and public health, thus ensuring a balanced and proportionate economic and social development in our country, the State Council has decided to increase investment in these areas year by year. However, apart from financial allocations by the state, it is necessary to arouse the enthusiasm of localities, departments, mines, factories, enterprises, rural people's communes and production brigades and the people at large for investment in the development of intellectual resources. The state, the collective and the individual should make joint efforts to promote cultural advance.

IV. On State Power and Law Enforcement

The success of China's modernization requires us to redouble our efforts to build socialist democracy and the legal system, improve the work of public security, the procuratorate and the judiciary, curb violations of the law and social discipline, make a fundamental turn for the better in the standards of social conduct and continue to strengthen political stability and unity.

The new Constitution is the basic statute for the Chinese people in running the affairs of the state. The people must be educated and organized to enforce it conscientiously. Governments at all levels and their functionaries should set an example by resolutely upholding the inviolability of the Constitution and become models in abiding by it. We hope that deputies to the people's congresses at all levels and the people at large will strictly supervise government functionaries in this respect. We shall continue to reform and improve government institutions and the system of leadership in accordance with the provisions of the Constitution. Provincial, municipal and autonomous regional governments should carry forward their organizational reform and do it well. Government institutions at the county and grass-roots levels will be gradually reformed in the coming winter and the following spring.

Governments at all levels should aim for better systems and style of leadership and better responsibility systems, closer ties with the masses and effective forms of supervision both from above and below, so as to overcome manifestations of bureaucratism and increase work efficiency. All government functionaries should strictly abide by the law and discipline, work selflessly in the public interest and serve the people wholeheartedly. Disciplinary measures, including demotion and dismissal, must be firmly adopted against bureaucrats responsible for big financial and material losses to the state. Those who commit criminal offenses must be called to account to criminal law. Whoever defies the law and discipline and willfully encroaches upon the democratic rights of the people, seeks personal gain by abusing his position and power, or participates in economic and other criminal activity must be dealt with according to law. There must be no connivance with wrongdoing.

We shall continue to speed up economic and administrative legislation. The State Council will have a number of economic statutes enacted so as to serve the requirements of China's modernization. Leading members of government economic departments and other economic organizations should learn how to use legal means to supervise economic activities so as to plug the loopholes and overcome weak points that criminals of different stripes may exploit and to safeguard socialist economic order.

Reform and strengthening of public security, procuratorial and judicial work and coordinated efforts by all quarters concerned constitute the key to making a fundamental turn for the better in public order and social conduct. There has been improvement in recent years thanks to the efforts made by various quarters, but public order is still not as good as in the best years after the founding of the People's Republic. Such criminal offenses as murder, robbery, rape and larceny pose quite a problem in some places. The recent plane hijacking indicates that there are serious loopholes and defects in our system of management, that public security, procuratorial and judicial departments have failed to perform some of their functions effectively as organs of dictatorship, and that some departments are intolerably apathetic both politically and ideologically, maintaining not the slightest vigilance against enemies. We must draw lessons from this incident. We assuredly can fight more effectively to prevent and eliminate such cases if governments at all levels, the public security, procuratorial and judicial departments and the entire people cooperate closely. The handful of hostile elements and incorrigible, inveterate criminals, regardless of what they do through covert sabotage or reckless moves, shall not be able to escape due punishment. We must suppress counterrevolutionary activities and deal powerful blows at criminal offenses in the economic and other spheres, and we must not relax our efforts under any circumstances. The public security, procuratorial and judicial organs at all levels, for their part, should maintain close ties with the masses, rely on them, organize all social forces and coordinate all efforts to prevent the commission of crimes and educate and redeem those who have gone astray. It is imperative to build up urban residents' committees, villagers' committees and public security and people's mediation organizations under them and to encourage the urban residents and peasants to draw up common pledges and work regulations, so as to foster the initiative of the masses in maintaining public order and observing social morality as masters of the country. We must help the people to solve ideological problems and to mediate disputes among themselves so that these can be resolved before they get out of control. Centres for reforming criminals or educating offenders through labour should be consolidated and the various forms of work-study schools for juvenile delinquents should be run well. We should inspire self-respect among young offenders and provide those who have mended their ways with the opportunity to turn over a new leaf.

We should make great efforts to strengthen the ranks of the public security, procuratorial and judicial personnel to meet the needs of their work, enhance their political quality and professional competence, raise their social status, improve their skills and facilities and increase their ability to combat crime. All those working in this field, leading cadres at different levels in particular, must acquire the political quality of utter devotion to the state and the people as well as the revolutionary spirit of "fearing neither hardship nor death," and they must constantly improve their attitude towards the masses, democracy and legality and heighten their sense of organization and strict conformity with the Constitution and law. They should see that the laws are strictly observed and enforced and that law-breakers are punished. More secondary schools and institutes of political science and law should be established to provide regular training for in-service personnel so that the public security, procuratorial and judicial contingents become a well-trained force cherished by the people as the pillar of public order.

Fellow deputies, China's socialist modernization is being carried out in a complex and turbulent international situation. To protect the security of the state and strengthen our struggle against espionage, the State Council is submitting to the present congress for its approval the request to establish a Ministry of State Security which will provide more effective leadership over such work.

We must continue to modernize our national defence and raise our national defence capabilities to keep pace with current international developments. The Chinese People's Liberation Army must step up its military and political training, strive to revolutionize, modernize and regularize itself, and increase its capability for operations by combined Army units and for quick response under conditions of modern war. We should speed up research, testing and manufacturing of weapons and update their technological level. We should improve the system of military service and build a strong militia. We should continue to carry forward the fine traditions of supporting the government and cherishing the people, supporting the Army and giving preferential treatment to families of servicemen and martyrs and to strengthen the unity between Army and government and between Army and people. We should never forget our sacred duty to strengthen our national

defence so as to ensure the success of China's socialist modernization.

V. On Foreign Affairs

Our socialist modernization requires a peaceful international environment. The preservation of peace is the common desire of the people of China and the rest of the world. The superpower contention for world hegemony is the main source of turmoil in the world today. It is imperative to oppose hegemonism in order to safeguard world peace. The Chinese Government takes opposing hegemonism and safeguarding world peace as the basic point of departure for its foreign policy and seeks to develop relations with other countries on the basis of the five principles of peaceful coexistence and to promote the progress of mankind.

The Third World constitutes a powerful force against imperialism, colonialism and hegemonism. China is part of the Third World. Our basic stand in foreign affairs is to strengthen solidarity and cooperation with other Third World countries. It is our sacred duty to support other Third World countries and people in their struggles to win and uphold their national rights. We firmly support the people of Kampuchea and Afghanistan in their struggle against aggression.

Vietnam and the Soviet Union must withdraw their troops immediately, unconditionally and totally from Kampuchea and Afghanistan respectively, leaving the people of these countries to settle their own affairs. We firmly support the Arab people, and particularly the Palestinian people, in their struggle against Israeli aggression and expansion. Israel must withdraw from the Arab territories it has occupied. The national rights of the Palestinian people must be restored to them. We resolutely support the Namibian people in their struggle for national independence and the people of South Africa in their struggle against racial discrimination and apartheid and for national liberation. We resolutely support the peoples of Central America, and particularly of the Caribbean region, in their struggle to uphold independence and sovereignty and to oppose foreign intervention.

Many Third World countries in Asia, Africa and Latin America have entered the new historical stage of consolidating their political independence through expanding their national economy and have done very well in developing their economy. However, they are still faced with grave economic difficulties due to prolonged rule and plunder by foreign powers in the past and to the shackles of present unfair and unequal international economic relationships. The Third World countries strongly demand that this irrational state of affairs be changed and that a new international economic order be established. The Chinese Government firmly support this just stand. We believe that cooperation among the Third World countries, known as South-South cooperation, is most important for propelling North-South negotiations and changing the old international economic order. Having always supported each other and helped supply each other's needs, we and other Third World countries have moved further ahead in economic and technical cooperation in recent years. And we shall make still greater efforts to promote such cooperation, keeping to the principle of "equality and mutual benefit, stress on practical results, diversity in form and common progress".

Ever since its emergence, the Non-Aligned Movement has played an increasingly important role in safeguarding world peace. The seventh conference of heads of state and government of the non-aligned countries recently held in New Delhi put forward many constructive proposals for solving the major problems of the world today. We sincerely wish the Non-Aligned Movement new successes in pursuing its aim and principles of independence and non-participation in any blocs and in combating imperialism, colonialism and power politics of all descriptions.

China always attaches importance to maintaining and expanding friendly relations with its neighbouring countries.

The Democratic People's Republic of Korea, our fraternal neighbour whose relations with us are as close as lips and teeth, is marching forward unswervingly along the socialist road. We, the Chinese people, will always treasure our friendship with the Korean people, which has been cemented with blood. We wish to extend them our warm congratulations on their achievements on all fronts, and we resolutely support them in their struggle for independent and peaceful reunification of their fatherland.

Since the signing of the Sino-Japanese treaty of peace and friendship in 1977, much progress has been made in the relations between our two countries. For the further development of Sino-Japanese relations we put forward in 1982 the three principles of "Peace and friendship, equality and mutual benefit, and prolonged stability," which have won the support of all sections of Japanese society. The Chinese and Japanese people alike share the desire to perpetuate such friendly relations from generation to generation. We are convinced that, provided the governments and people of both countries join their efforts to overcome interference, friendship and cooperation between the two countries are bound to grow steadily.

We are distressed by the fact that the once friendly Sino-Vietnamese relations have deteriorated to the point of serious confrontation in recent years as a result of the invasion and occupation of Kampuchea by the Vietnamese authorities who have pursued regional hegemony in Indochina and Southeast Asia, discriminated against Chinese residents and opposed China. Nevertheless, we are ready to continue our efforts to improve Sino-Vietnamese relations. The Chinese Foreign Ministry issued a statement last March expounding China's position and proposals for settling the Kampuchean question and improving Sino-Vietnamese relations, and this has won international public support. We hope that the Vietnamese Government will set store by the fundamental interests of the Vietnamese and Chinese people and give our proposals serious consideration.

We are happy to see that our relations with the ASEAN countries have developed in the struggle to safeguard peace and security in Southeast Asia. We also note with satisfaction that our traditional friendship and cooperation with Bangladesh, Burma, Nepal, Pakistan and Sri Lanka are being constantly strengthened. There has also been some improvement in the relations between China and India in recent years. With two thousand years of peaceful relations behind them, China and India ought to be able to get along with each other well. The Sino-Indian boundary question left over from the past can without doubt be settled through consultations in the spirit of mutual understanding and mutual accommodation. Even if it cannot be settled for the time being, it should not stand in the way of improving our relations. We are ready to strive for better Sino-Indian relations.

There has been steady growth in the close solidarity and friendly cooperation between China and the Socialist Republic of Romania and the Socialist Federal Republic of Yugoslavia. The Chinese people are gratified to see the remarkable achievements made by the people of Romania and Yugoslavia in socialist construction. We can learn much from their valuable experience. The friendship between us can stand all tests.

The Chinese people also cherish friendly feelings towards the people of the other East European countries. We are interested in their accomplishments and experience in socialist construction. In recent years, our economic, cultural and sports exchanges with these countries have been increasing. We believe that, through joint efforts, the relations between China and these countries will continue to improve.

China appreciates and supports the efforts made by West European countries to strengthen their unity and the positive role they have played in international affairs. It maintains good relations with many developed countries in Western Europe, North America and Oceania. Facts have shown that countries with different social systems can coexist in peace and cooperate on an equal footing. We shall, as always, continue our efforts to expand and deepen our cooperation and exchanges with these countries in the political, economic, cultural, scientific, and technological and other fields.

Since the establishment of diplomatic relations between China and the United States in 1979, there has been some development in the relations between the two countries, but it falls far short of what could have been achieved. The United States has formulated the so-called Taiwan Relations Act and continues to sell arms to Taiwan in serious violation of the public commitments it undertook in all the Sino-U.S. communiques and the principles governing the establishment of Sino-U.S. diplomatic relations that both parties agreed to.

The Chinese Government and people set store by Sino-U.S. relations, but they will never tolerate any infringement on China's sovereignty or any interference in its internal affairs. The U.S. Government should strictly observe the Sino-U.S. communiques and stop doing anything that harms Sino-U.S. relations and hurts the Chinese people's feelings. This is the only way to ensure sound development of Sino-U.S. relations.

The relations between China and the Soviet Union have been strained over a long period of time, and this is not to the advantage of either party. The people of China and the Soviet Union are all interested in the normalization of relations between the two countries. The Chinese side put forward positive proposals for normalization during the Sino-Soviet consultations which started last October. We hold that to improve Sino-Soviet relations, the first step to be taken is for the Soviet side to remove the real threat to China's security. This is a major issue that cannot be evaded. We are waiting for the Soviet side to prove its good faith by deeds.

The fundamental principles governing China's foreign policy have been written into our new Constitution. These principles are entirely correct and the Chinese Government will unswervingly carry them out. As always, we shall join all countries and people that love peace and uphold justice in firmly opposing hegemonism and striving for the progress of mankind and world peace.

Fellow deputies, the reunification of the country and the unity of the people of all our nationalities provide the fundamental guarantee for the growing strength and prosperity of our motherland. The people of all our nationalities, including our compatriots in Taiwan, Xianggang (Hong Kong) and Aomen (Macao) and Chinese nationals residing abroad, eagerly look forward to the reunification of the motherland at an early date and this is our most sacred task. All Chinese at home and abroad who wish to see their motherland reunified, strong and prosperous have been working in various ways to promote the peaceful reunification of the motherland. Let us express our appreciation to all those who have contributed to this goal. We must continue our efforts to remove as soon as possible this artificial barrier that separates the people on both sides of the Taiwan Strait. We shall, at an opportune moment, recover Chinese sovereignty over Xianggang and take appropriate measures to maintain its prosperity. We will continue to exert ourselves in all fields, further broaden the patriotic united front and strengthen the great unity of all our nationalities, people of various strata and from all walks of life, and all patriotic elements, in order to make common efforts to build a socialist system with distinctive Chinese characteristics and to create a unified, flourishing and prosperous motherland.

The next five years are years of vital importance to our socialist economic growth and other work. The tasks facing us are at once glorious and arduous. Many difficulties still lie ahead. We must foster the pioneering spirit of hard struggle, seek truth from facts and work assiduously. Provided we keep this up, we will be able to surmount all obstacles on our way forward, tide over this relatively difficult period and put our socialist modernization onto a broader road.

The Party and the Military

Provisional Regulations on Military Offenses, 10 June 1981

53

These provisional regulations were adopted by the Standing Committee of the National People's Congress. They appear rather severe and suggest that there may be considerable disciplinary problems in the armed forces.

On the basis of the guiding ideology and fundamental principles of the "Criminal Law of the People's Republic of China," these regulations are formulated with a view to punishing servicemen for offenses they commit against their duties, educating them to conscientiously carry out their duties and strengthening the combat capability of army units.

Article 2. Any act of an active duty PLA serviceman that infringes on his duties and endangers that state's military interests and is punishable by law is considered a serviceman's offense against his duties. However, in cases of markedly mild offenses and when not too much harm has been caused, the act is not considered an offense and will be dealt with in accordance with military discipline.

Article 3. Any person who violates the regulations on using firearms and equipment and causes serious accidents arising from his negligence and resulting in severe injury or death of others may in serious cases be sentenced to fixed-term imprisonment of not more than 3 years or detention at hard labor, and in cases with particularly serious consequences to fixed-term imprisonment of not less than 3 years and not more than 7 years.

Article 4. Any person who violates the law and regulations on guarding the state's military secrets by betraying or losing important state military secrets may in serious cases be sentenced to fixed-term imprisonment of not more than 7 years or detention at hard labor.

Any person who commits the above offense during wartime may be sentenced to fixed-term imprisonment of not less than 3 years and not more than 10 years, and in particularly serious cases to fixed-term imprisonment of not less than 10 years or life imprisonment.

Any person who steals, collects or furnishes military secrets for enemies or foreigners may be sentenced to fixed-term imprisonment of not less than 10 years, life imprisonment or death.

Article 5. Any personnel in command or on duty who causes serious consequences by leaving his post or neglecting his duties may be sentenced to fixed-term imprisonment of not more than 7 years or detention at hard labor.

Any person who commits the above offense during wartime may be sentenced to fixed-term imprisonment of not less than 5 years.

Article 6. Any person who deserts the army in violation of the military service law may in serious cases be sentenced

[New China News Agency, 10 June 1981.]

by fixed-term imprisonment of not more than 3 years or detention at hard labor.

Any person who commits the above offense during wartime may be sentenced to fixed-term imprisonment of not less than 3 years and not more than 7 years.

Article 7. Any person who crosses the boundary (border) illegally to flee the country may be sentenced to fixed-term imprisonment of not more than 3 years or detention at hard labor, and in serious cases to fixed-term imprisonment of not less than 3 years and not more than 10 years.

During wartime, offenders may be subject to heavier punishment.

Article 8. Any serviceman on active duty at the border or coastal defense line who practices favoritism or commits other irregularities or allows another person to cross the boundary (border) without authorization may be sentenced to fixed-term imprisonment of not more than 5 years or detention at hard labor, and in serious cases to imprisonment of not less than 5 years. During wartime, the punishment may be more severe.

Article 9. Any serviceman who abuses his power of office to maltreat or persecute a subordinate and whose offenses are so vile as to have caused serious injuries or other serious consequences may be sentenced to fixed-term imprisonment of not more than 5 years or detention at hard labor. For offenses that result in the death of a person, offenders may be sentenced to fixed-term imprisonment of not less than 5 years.

Article 10. Any person who resorts to violence or threat to obstruct command personnel or personnel on shift or station duty from performing their duties may be sentenced to fixed-term imprisonment of not more than 5 years or detention at hard labor, and in serious cases to fixed-term imprisonment of not less than 5 years. In especially serious cases or in cases of serious injuries or deaths resulting from such offenses, offenders may be sentenced to life imprisonment or death. During wartime, the punishment may be more severe.

Article 11. In cases of theft of weapons, equipment or military supplies, offenders may be sentenced to fixed-term imprisonment of not more than 5 years or detention at hard labor, and in serious cases, to fixed-term imprisonment of not less than 5 years and not more than 10 years. In especially serious cases, offenders may be sentenced to fixed-term imprisonment of not less than 10 years or life imprisonment. During wartime, the punishment may be more severe, and offenders may be given the death sentence if the offenses are especially serious.

Article 12. Any person who commits the crime of sabotaging weapons, equipment or military installations may be sentenced to fixed-term imprisonment of not more than 3 years or detention at hard labor. In cases of sabotage of major weapons, equipment or military installations, offenders may be sentenced to fixed-term imprisonment of not less than 3 years and not more than 10 years. In especially serious cases, offenders may be sentenced to fixed-term imprisonment of not less than 10 years, life imprisonment or death. During wartime the punishment may be more severe.

Article 13. Any serviceman who deliberately inflicts injuries to himself in order to evade his military obligations during wartime may be sentenced to fixed-term imprisonment of not more than 3 years, and in serious cases to fixed-term imprisonment of not less than 3 years and not more than 7 years.

Article 14. Any person who fabricates rumors to mislead others and undermine army morale during wartime may be sentenced to fixed-term imprisonment of not more than 3 years, and in serious cases to fixed-term imprisonment of not less than 3 years but not more than 10 years.

Any person who colludes with the enemy to spread rumors so as to mislead others and undermine army morale may be sentenced to fixed-term imprisonment of not less than 10 years or life imprisonment. In especially serious cases, offenders may be given the death sentence.

Article 15. Any person who is directly responsible for deliberate abandonment of wounded on the battlefield, particularly in those cases that are considered abominable, may be sentenced to fixed-term imprisonment of not more than 3 years.

Article 16. All servicemen who are afraid of fighting and desert from battlefield will be sentenced to 3 years' imprisonment or less; in serious cases, they will be sentenced to 3 to 10 years' imprisonment; and in cases which caused major losses in battle or war, they will be sentenced to 10 years to life imprisonment or death.

Article 17. All servicemen who disobey orders during a battle, thus jeopardizing the outcome of a war, will be sentenced to 3 to 10 years' imprisonment, and in cases of serious harm to the battle or war effort they will be sentenced to 10 years to life imprisonment or death.

Article 18. All servicemen who intentionally make a false report about the military situation and fake military orders, thus jeopardizing military operations, will be sentenced to 3 to 10 years' imprisonment, and in cases of serious harm to the battle and war effort they will be sentenced to 10 years to life imprisonment or death.

Article 19. All servicemen who are afraid of death in battle and voluntarily lay down weapons and surrender to the enemy will be sentenced to 3 to 10 years' imprisonment, and in cases of a serious nature they will be sentenced to 10 years to life imprisonment.

All servicemen who, after surrendering to the enemy, help the enemy will be sentenced to 10 years to life imprisonment or death.

Article 20. All servicemen who plunder and harm innocent residents in military operational areas will be sentenced to 7 years or less; in serious cases, they will be sentenced to more than 7 years' imprisonment; and in cases of a particularly serious nature, they will be sentenced to life imprisonment or death.

Article 21. All servicemen who seriously maltreat captives will be sentenced to 3 years imprisonment or less.

Article 22. In times of war, servicemen who are sentenced to 3 years' imprisonment or less with a reprieve because there is no actual danger may be allowed to atone for their crimes by performing good services. When they have performed really good services, the original sentence may be rescinded, and they will no longer be considered criminals.

Article 23. All servicemen on active duty who commit crimes not listed in these regulations will be handled in accordance with the related articles of "The Criminal Law of the People's Republic of China."

Article 24. As to servicemen who commit serious crimes, their decorations, medals and titles of honor may be recalled, in addition to their being punished.

Article 25. All staff members and workers of the military establishment who commit crimes listed in these regulations will be punished in accordance with these regulations.

Article 26. These regulations will become effective as of 1 January 1982.

The Party and the Armed Forces in Historical Perspective, 1 July 1981

54

The chief of staff of the People's Liberation Army (PLA) restates the important principle, sacred in the Chinese Communist movement since the rise of Mao Zedong in the late 1920s, that the Party must always control the armed forces, never the other way around. Although Yang Dezhi does not say so, senior generals have been among Deng Xiaoping's main opponents, essentially because they believe he is sacrificing too much of the pre-1949 Maoist tradition. Deng accordingly has retained the chairmanship of the Party's powerful Military Affairs Committee rather than passing it to General Secretary Hu Yaobang, who would normally hold it ex officio. Many senior officers are being retired.

As we solemnly commemorate its 60th founding anniversary, our party has successfully held the 6th Plenary Session of the 11th CCP Central Committee. The session adopted the "Resolution on Certain Questions in the History of Our Party Since the Founding of the People's Republic of China," reelected principal leading members of the Central Committee and elected new ones. This is an event of great, immediate and far-reaching historical significance. It shows that our party, which dares to uphold the truth, is good at correcting its mistakes and, through the tests of twists and turns as well as victories, has further united and become stronger and greater and is worthy to be called a proletarian revolutionary party guided by Marxism-Leninism-Mao Zedong Thought. Under the great banner of Marxism-Leninism-Mao Zedong Thought, the whole party, the entire army and people of all the nationalities in the country are closely rallying around the party Central Committee and building a modern and powerful socialist country with one heart and one mind. Our cause will certainly surge forward with great vitality.

The CCP is the force at the core leading the people throughout China. During the new historical period, the nucleus of the four basic principles we uphold is firm perseverance in the leadership of the CCP. When this is related to the people's army, it means upholding the principle of "the party commands the gun" or adhering to the party's absolute leadership over the army. An army of the proletariat is the prime requirement for a proletarian party to seize political power and consolidate it. It is an armed group implementing revolutionary political tasks. The purpose of our army, since the date of its birth, has been one of serving the Chinese people heart and soul. It has taken on its shoulders the mission of fulfilling the historic tasks of the proletarian party in this country. Its nature and missions dictate that only under the CCP's absolute leadership can it fulfill its great historic tasks. Without party leadership, our army cannot accomplish its revolutionary political missions, nor can it serve its purpose nor retain its proletarian nature.

The Chinese PLA was founded by Comrade Mao Zedong and the other proletarian revolutionaries of the older generation and, under the CCP's absolute leadership, has grown in strength through the tests of protracted periods of war. One of the special characteristics of the democratic revolution in China is resorting to armed revolution to oppose armed counterrevolution. In this country, without the leadership of the CCP and without armed struggle, the people's army cannot exist or grow and the cause of revolution cannot be victorious.

Since its defeat in the first great revolution, our party has understood the truth that "political power grows out the barrel of a gun." It led armed uprisings in many parts of the country and began to establish the people's army. On 1 August of 1927, Comrades Zhou Enlai, Zhu De, He Long, Ye Ting and Liu Bocheng, acting in accordance with the instructions given them by the party, led more than 30,000 troops of the northern expedition army to stage the Nanchang uprising, firing the first shots against the Kuomintang reactionaries. In pursuance of the decision of the party's "7 August" conference, Comrade Mao Zedong led the autumn harvest uprising in the Hunan-Jiangxi border area on 9 September that same year and directed the uprising troops to the Jianggangshan Mountains to establish an armed independent regime of workers and peasants. In April 1928, the troops led by Comrades Zhu De and Chen Yi that were left behind after taking part in the Nanchang uprising and the units participating in the insurrection in southern Hunan arrived at the Jinggangshan Mountains after repeated fighting and joined the force led by Comrade Mao Zedong. These forces merged into the 4th Army of the Chinese workers and peasants' Red Army.

During this period, our party led more than 100 armed uprisings in Guangzhou, Pingjiang and in the areas of Hubei-Henan-Anhui, western Hunan-Hubei, Fujian-Zhejiang-Jiangxi, Hunan-Hubei-Jiangxi, Haifeng-Lufeng and in the

[Yang Dezhi, "Unswervingly Uphold Our Party's Absolute Leadership Over the Army," *Red Flag*, no. 13, 1 July 1981.]

regions on the left and right sides of Xijiang River and Hainan Island. With the founding of a number of Red armies of workers and peasants, the flames of the Chinese revolution were kindled.

By 1930 the Red Army units had grown to nearly 100,000 men. Several armies and corps were formed. These later developed into the First, Second and Fourth Front Armies. The party not only launched but also carefully cultivated the people's army. From the very beginning of our army's founding, the party attached great significance to building party organizations and to political and ideological work in the army. At that time the Red Army was mainly composed of peasants and those who had crossed over from the old armies. Consequently there was a rather serious problem of unhealthy trends prevailing in the Red Army such as slackness in discipline, ultrademocracy, anarchism and warlord style. In view of this problem, Comrade Mao Zedong himself called the ninth party congress of the Fourth Red Army in December 1929 at Gutian Village in Shanghang County, Fujian Province, and delivered the report "On Correcting Mistaken Ideas in the Party." With the dissemination of the guidelines of the resolution adopted at the Gutian Congress, a wide-scale ideological education to eliminate nonproletarian ideas was carried out in all army units.

In the course of the long revolutionary war in the ensuing years, the party launched several new-type ideological education movements in the army, thereby gradually putting our army on the basis of Marxism-Leninism-Mao Zedong Thought and making it an entirely new people's army different from any army in the old days. At the same time the principle that party branches should be organized on a company basis was formulated and party organizations and political departments at various levels along with a system of political work were established in our army. Our army's purpose was defined as that of serving the people wholeheartedly. The army was required to display the three major styles of work—integrating theory with practice, making criticism and self-criticism and forging close ties with the masses—to carry out the tasks as a fighting force, a working force and a productive force, to adhere to the three basic principles of unity between the army and the people, between officers and men, and of disintegrating the enemy troops, to put into practice the three major democracies—political democracy, economic democracy and military democracy—and to abide by the three main rules of discipline and the eight points for attention. This ensured the party's absolute leadership over the army and enabled the army to preserve its proletarian nature.

It was for this reason that during the 22 years of unprecedentedly arduous revolutionary war, our army was able to grow from small to large, to become stronger and stronger in the course of fighting and to fight valiantly together with the people. It was because of this that our army was able to smash the enemy's encirclement and the suppression, interceptions and attacks in the agrarian revolutionary war, to defeat the Japanese imperialist aggressors in the war of resistance against Japan and to put the Kuomintang reactionaries to rout in the war of liberation. It was also because of this that our army was able to overthrow the reactionary rule by imperialism, feudalism and bureaucrat-capitalism. Following the nationwide liberation, our army maintained its fine traditions, continued to advance and successfully safeguarded the socialist revolution and construction of the motherland. Today it has developed into a relatively sizable people's army composed of numerous services and branches, a mighty force against aggression and expansion by imperialism and hegemonism and for the defense of peace in the Far East and in the world.

It was for this reason that during the past decades our army was able to forge close flesh-and-blood ties and maintain fish-and-water relations with the people. Either on heavy-combat battlefields or in rescue efforts, our army's commanders and fighters were willing to sacrifice themselves in order to protect the interests of the masses. For this purpose thousands upon thousands of our fine comrades gave their lives. On the other hand the people have always regarded our army men as their own soldiers. The people have lived frugally in order to support army units: They have shielded wounded soldiers from enemy search even at the cost of their own lives. They warmly love and trust the people's army.

It was for this reason that our army was able to repeatedly smash the criminal acts of careerists and conspirators in splitting the party and the armed forces, to rally closely and consistently around the party Central Committee, to unite on the basis of Marxism-Leninism-Mao Zedong Thought and to stand as a mainstay loyal to the party and the people's revolutionary cause. During the Long March Zhang Guotao plotted to set up another Central Committee and to split the party and the Red Army, but in the end he met with the ignominious fate of having to flee alone without even his bodyguards. After liberation Gao Gang dished up the "army party theory" in a futile attempt to use the gun to command the party, but finally this scheme failed and was exposed, and he had to reap the bitter fruit of his own sowing. Lin Biao plotted to usurp the party and state leadership, wildly clamoring that he wanted to "command everything" and "arrange everything." In the end, however, he was unable to win over to his side even a squad or a platoon. All he could do was to hurriedly escape with his wife, his son and a few sworn followers, and in the end he died in the wilderness. With a dream of becoming "empress of the Red capital," Jiang Qing tried sometimes to attack and sometimes to win over our army, but she could never succeed. Finally she was arrested and was brought to the judgment of history by the party and the people. These ironclad facts eloquently prove that the party's absolute leadership played a decisive role in the growth and development of our army.

Historical experience, positive and negative, tell us that without the CCP's absolute leadership, our people's army cannot exist even for a single day. To resolutely uphold the party's absolute leadership or to oppose it amounts to a question which is not only crucial to the growth and development of our army but which also concerns the success or failure of our revolutionary cause. We must bear in mind this incontestable truth, which has been verified through decades of practice. Any idea or action attempting to weaken or do away with the party's absolute leadership in the army is extremely detrimental and must be resolutely opposed.

We are now at a new historic juncture. The army not only shoulders the task of building and defending the four modernizations, but also has to do well in consolidating, improving and building itself. This is a matter of importance that the people of all nationalities in the country have entrusted to the people's soldiers and a great historical task that the party has assigned to our army. To accomplish this hard yet glorious task, it is imperative to resolutely uphold the party's absolute leadership of the army.

The most fundamental thing about resolutely upholding the party's absolute leadership is to firmly keep to the leadership of the party's Marxism revolutionary line and its principles and policies. As proved by our army's experience over the decades, by firmly supporting the strategic changes made by the party and by resolutely carrying out its correct line, principles and policies at major historical junctures, we have been able to overcome the twists and turns and the difficulties encountered on the road and to advance from victory to victory.

At the beginning of the war of resistance against Japan, our party decided to carry out a second Kuomintang-CCP cooperation effort in the interest of the whole nation and reorganized the Red Army, our main armed forces, as the 8th Route Army, while the guerrillas remaining in the southern provinces after the Long March were reorganized to form the New 4th Army. Our party then ordered the various army units to penetrate deeply into the enemy's rear areas to engage in guerrilla warfare and build anti-Japanese bases in order to contribute, through our concrete action, to the formation of a national united front against Japanese aggression.

This marked a major strategic change in our party's history. Resolutely supporting the party's strategic change and implementing its strategic policy decision, the broad masses of commanders and fighters of our army set out to various battlefields in high morale to fight bloody battles with the Japanese aggressors. Vigorous flames of anti-Japanese battles were kindled here and there, from the area of the Changbai Mountains to the foot of the Wuzhi Mountains and from the banks of the Huanghe to the Chang Jiang valley. Comrades Zhu De, Peng Dehuai, Liu Bocheng, Deng Xiaoping, He Long, Luo Ronghuan, Xu Xiangqian and Nie Rongzhen separately led the main force of the 8th Route Army, namely the 115th, 120th and 129th Divisions, to northern China. After that the New 4th Army led by Comrades Ye Ting, Xiang Ying and Chen Yi marched to southern and northern Jiangsu to carry out anti-Japanese guerrilla operations. Taking advantage of the topography of the Luliang, Wutai, Taihang and Yimeng Mountains and relying on the broad masses, our 8th Route Army carried out guerrilla operations, appearing and disappearing mysteriously and fighting flexibly and skillfully to strike at the Japanese aggressors. It always won the battle and performed many superb feats. It fought at Pingxingguan, carried out a night raid on Yangmingbao, defeated the "encircling attacks from nine directions," smashed the "Iron-wall encirclement," and shattered the "containment policy." It smashed the numerous "village mopping-up," "nibbling" and "sweeping" campaigns, wiped out large numbers of enemy and puppet troops, frustrated the three anticommunist high tides launched by the Kuomintang reactionaries, recovered the vast expanse of lost land and built the Shanxi-Qahar-Hebei, Shanxi-Hebei-Shandong-Henan, Shanxi-Suiyuan and Shandong anti-Japanese bases. It used its concrete actions to tell the people of all nationalities and of all strata in the country the fact that the people's army led by the CCP stood at the forefront of the war of resistance against Japan, was a main force to save the nation from peril and represented the genuine hope of the people to be extricated from the abyss of misery. At the same time, it made the enemy aware that the Chinese people, now armed, could in no way be defeated. This encouraged and spurred on the anti-Japanese war on a nationwide scale.

The period from 1941 to 1943 was the hardest time in the war of resistance against Japan. At that time the Hebei-Shandong-Henan border region, where I worked, was hit by drought 3 years in a row, and there were also epidemic diseases. The stubborn forces made up of the Japanese and puppet troops continued their ceaseless wild mopping-up operations, implementing the cruel "triple atrocity" policy of burning all, killing all and looting all. In the face of the precedented difficulties, our Hebei-Shandong-Henan army units resolutely carried out the party's policy of "consolidating the basic areas, developing the guerrilla areas, persisting in the struggle in border areas and preserving and saving our forces."

On the one hand, they went all out to deal blows at the invading enemy troops. During those 3 years, they fought some 2,300 battles, killing more than 19,000 enemy and puppet troops and capturing some 9,000. On the other hand, they mobilized the soldiers and people to provide for and help themselves by engaging in production. A call was issued to bear all hardships and to surmount every difficulty. Finally, the difficult period was over. Historical experience shows that at the crucial moment the army must support the party's strategic changes and resolutely implement its correct line, principles and policies. This is a vital guarantee for the victory of the revolution.

Since the 3d Plenary Session of the 11th CCP Central Committee held in 1978, our party has, systematically and thoroughly, set to rights things that had been thrown into disorder, eliminated the old, erected the new and established the path to carry out modernization according to China's actual situation. The central work conference held in 1980 again made a major policy decision, working hard to carry out further economic readjustments and to achieve greater political stability.

Now the 6th Plenary Session of the 11th CCP Central Committee once again calls on the whole party, the entire army and the people of all nationalities throughout the country to continue carrying forward the spirit of the foolish old man who removed the mountain, to work with one heart and one mind, and to turn China into a modern and powerful socialist country with a high degree of democracy and civilization. At this crucial moment when this major change is taking place, we should all the more carry forward our glorious traditions, resolutely implement the line, guidelines and policies laid down since the 3d Plenary Session of the 11th CCP Central Committee; continue to emancipate our thinking; firmly uphold the four basic principles; eliminate interferences from left and right erroneous thinking; further straighten out the ideological line; closely keep pace with the party's strategic changes both in one's own thinking and one's own actions; and make fresh contributions to developing and safeguarding the four modernizations program.

To follow the party's absolute leadership means to obey the party's command in everything. In fulfilling the task assigned by the party, we must be all the more set on driving forward when there is danger ahead. We should fight wherever the party directs us. By no means shall we fear difficulties and retreat. This is our army's fine work style that has been handed down from one generation to another.

During the difficult years of war, Comrade Mao Zedong and the proletarian revolutionaries of the older generation as well as the broad masses of commanders and fighters of our army had already set examples. In the second year of the war of liberation when our army had just entered the stage of launching a strategic counterattack against the Kuomintang reactionaries, all the conditions our army met were very difficult. To draw the war to the Kuomintang controlled area, wipe out the enemy on exterior lines and thoroughly smash to pieces Chiang Kaishek's counterrevolutionary plan to shift the war to the liberated areas, Chairman Mao resolutely decided to send a part of our army to penetrate the Kuomintang-controlled area in order to attract the enemy's main force and relieve the enemy's threat against the liberated area in Shandong. Our main forces led by Liu Bocheng and Deng Xiaoping resolutely implemented the orders issued by the party Central Committee, courageously shouldered this arduous but glorious task, valiantly marched south and broke through many enemy defense lines. They made a leap forward of a thousand li, fought the enemy for state power and boldly drove into the Tabieshan area. Like a sharp knife thrust into the enemy's heart, they directly threatened Kuomintang lairs in Wuhan and Nanjing and drew up the great curtain of our army's strategic counterattack. At that time, on the question of whether or not the Tabieshan revolutionary base area could be consolidated, the party Central Committee and Chairman Mao envisaged three possibilities: 1) Our army would be unable to hold its ground and would have to turn back after paying a price. 2) It would be unable to hold its ground and would have to fight guerilla warfare in the vicinity after paying a price. 3) It would be able to hold its ground after paying a price. Senior officers Liu and Deng as well as the broad masses of army commanders and fighters remarkably accomplished their task with actual deeds, firmly held their ground in the Tabieshan area and realized the best possibility. It was in that same year that under the leadership of Comrade Nie Rongzhen, our Shanxi-Qahar-Hebei troops triumphantly fought the Qingfengdian campaign. First of all, they drew out of their lairs the enemy troops guarding Shijiazhuang. Then, they made a forced march like a strong wind, wiped out the whole enemy division in the movement and captured over 10,000 enemy soldiers, including the commander of the enemy's 3d Army, Luo Lirong. After that, they once again brought into full play the work style of continuous fighting and fearing no fatigue, and concentrated the main force of the Shanxi-Qahar-Hebei field army and some local troops in central Hebei to liberate Shijiazhuang, which was heavily guarded by the enemy.

In the Shijiazhuang campaign, over 20,000 enemy soldiers guarding the city were totally wiped out. This joined the Shanxi-Qahar-Hebei liberated area with the Shanxi-Hebei-Shandong-Henan liberated area and played an important role in further developing a large-scale counterattack on the north China battlefield.

Commander in Chief Zhu De praised this campaign highly as a "new example of seizing a big city," and jubilantly wrote a poem: "Heroes in our party have emerged one after another. From now on, we do not have to worry about our hair graying at the temples." This kind of revolutionary spirit in our army of resolutely implementing orders issued by the party, of advancing wave upon wave and of pressing forward with an indomitable will is not only a priceless treasure for defeating the enemy and winning victories in war years, but also a gigantic force for developing and safeguarding the four modernizations program today. To safeguard the security of the motherland's territorial land, air space and waters, and to oppose aggression and threats to China by imperialism and hegemonism, our army must display the heroic spirit of pressing forward with indomitable will and of vowing not to coexist with our enemy, and must resolutely carry out the orders issued by our party. Following certain changes in the state system, the system of the army will also undergo certain changes. Under the new historical conditions, all cadres and fighters of our army must bring into full play the fine traditions and work style of the members of the old Red Army and the old 8th Route Army; resolutely accept the party's assignments; learn from Comrade Lei Feng, who cherished whatever assignment he was given, did his best, devoted himself to his duties and remarkably fulfilled missions assigned by the party; and support and strengthen the party's absolute leadership over the army. They must do so whether they are stationed in the cities, guard the border regions, remain PLA troops, or have been transferred to work in local areas or engage in any revolutionary tasks.

To uphold the party's absolute leadership, we must persistently regard political work as the lifeline of our army and incessantly use Marxism-Leninism-Mao Zedong Thought to educate the army. This is a solid foundation in ensuring the party's absolute leadership over the army. The fundamental distinction between a proletarian army and a bourgeois army is that the proletarian army has a set of revolutionary political functions and that the ideological and theoretical foundation in guiding this army is Marxism-Leninism-Mao Zedong Thought. Our army is a revolutionary armed force composed mainly of peasants, coming from the many different parts of the country, diverse in origin, experience and disposition. What kind of strength has made this army united as one under the banner of the party for scores of years? What kind of strength has made this army courageous, fearless and invincible? One important factor is the education the PLA troops receive in Marxism-Leninism-Mao Zedong Thought. This education helps all the commanders and fighters understand why they join the army and what they are fighting for, acquire a highly developed political consciousness and common revolutionary ideals and attain a common goal of struggle. Therefore, the broad masses of commanders and fighters of our army are able to consciously place themselves under the absolute leadership of the party and unremittingly fight for the noble interests of the party and the people at all times. In the 22-year long democratic revolution in which armed struggle was regarded as the main form of struggle and in 32 years of socialist revolution and socialist construction, many heroes and models have emerged from our army. They are brilliant representatives in this regard. Our experience in the past tells us that to persistently educate the PLA troops with Marxism-Leninism-Mao Zedong Thought will create vitality in political work and militancy in PLA troops. After the decade of disorder in the country, some comrades have a misunderstanding that since Comrade Mao Zedong made mistakes in his late years, it looks like we do not have to uphold Mao Zedong Thought any more. This view is erroneous. We must deal with Mao Zedong and Mao Zedong Thought with a scientific approach. Comrade Mao Zedong made mistakes in the 10-year "Great Cultural Revolution." However, if we judge his activities as a whole, he made indelible contributions to founding and developing the party and the people's liberation and to the birth of the People's Republic of China and the advance of socialism in our country.

He has been publicly recognized as a great Marxist, a great proletarian revolutionary and strategist and the great leader of the whole party, the entire army and the people of all nationalities throughout the country. Our party and the people of all nationalities in the country would have had to grope in the dark much longer had it not been for Comrade Mao Zedong and the party Central Committee he led more than once to rescue the Chinese revolution from grave danger and chart the firm, correct political course for the party and the army. As a product that integrates the universal truth of Marxism-Leninism with the concrete practice of the Chinese revolution, Mao Zedong Thought is recognized as the guiding ideology of the party. So far as our army is concerned, Comrade Mao Zedong's theories on the building of the people's army, his theses on political work in the army and his series on strategy and tactics in a people's war are even more powerful ideological weapons, which have always been used to overcome difficulties and obstacles and defeat the enemy.

For decades, Mao Zedong Thought has nurtured the cadres and the fighters of our armed forces. Those who were admitted during the era of the Red Army, during the war of resistance against Japanese aggression, during the war of liberation or after the founding of the PRC have all been highly educated by Mao Zedong Thought. The growth and development of our armed forces have never strayed from the path of Marxism-Leninism-Mao Zedong Thought. Of course, our advocacy of upholding Mao Zedong Thought is by no means an attempt to restore the erroneous leftist ideology which prevailed prior to the third plenary session. It is necessary to sum up the experiences and lessons learned from the mistakes committed by Comrade Mao Zedong in his later years. Without doing so, more and more serious mistakes might possibly be made. However, in summing up such experiences and lessons of history, certain historical conditions must be taken into consideration. We not only oppose adopting a dogmatic attitude toward Mao Zedong Thought, mechanically memorizing certain existing ways of handling things or engaging in the so-called "two whatevers," but also oppose adopting an attitude of completely negating Mao Zedong Thought, thinking that it has lost is practical significance of guidance or refusing to study and apply it. We should uphold the correct principle put forth at the third plenary session, understand completely and correctly the scientific nature of Mao Zedong Thought, adopt a dialectical and historical materialistic viewpoint toward Comrade Mao Zedong and his theses, and use the Marxism doctrine that everything has two different aspects to replace the subjective idealism and the metaphysical method that adopt either an absolutely affirmative or absolutely negative attitude toward everything. The cadres and fighters of our armed forces, in particular those ranking cadres, should take the lead in studying Comrade Mao Zedong's works, in particular his philosophical and military writings, study his stand, viewpoint and method of analyzing and handling problems, and study his high skill in building the armed forces, directing warfare

and defeating a strong enemy. This is particularly significant for ensuring the ceaseless advancement of our armed forces under the party's absolute leadership and for winning victory in any future war against aggression.

In upholding the party's absolute leadership, it is essential to have firm confidence in the party and to establish the faith that the cause of revolution will surely be victorious. History has undisputedly attested that the CCP is the motive force leading our cause forward and that only the party can guide the Chinese people in extricating themselves from the predicament of being exploited and enslaved and marching onto the brilliant road to socialism; that only the party can make the Chinese nation stand erect in the East and become an important force in supporting the just struggle of the peoples of various countries in the world, in opposing imperialism and hegemonism, in defeating all anti-China activities and in defending peace in the East and the world. Without the CCP's leadership, there are neither the brilliant victories already won by the Chinese people nor the bright future of socialist modernization. It is the resolute confidence of the whole party, the whole armed forces and the people of various nationalities throughout the country to uphold the strengthening and improvement of the party's leadership.

It cannot be denied that our party committed mistakes in the past decade and more and is still facing many difficulties. However, our party has had the fine work style of conducting criticism and self-criticism and the ability to correct its mistakes and surmount the obstacles along the path toward advancement.

After the failure of the 1927 revolution, Chiang Kai-shek slaughtered tens of thousands of our party members and hundreds of thousands of workers and peasants. The blood we shed could fill a stream. Nevertheless, the CCP members were not intimidated. They wiped away their blood stains, buried the dead bodies of their companions, held high the revolutionary banner and continued to advance forward. Because of Wang Ming's mistaken "left" adventurist leadership during the land reform revolutionary period, the Red Army lost all the White areas and 95 percent of the Soviet areas. The Red Army was forced to withdraw from the Soviet areas and almost landed itself in an impasse. But after the Zunyi conference, our party gained a new life and the Red Army was able to continue to develop. Although there are still many problems at present and the tasks are arduous, our party has since the third plenary session formulated the correct line, principles and polities for solving these problems and the situation has greatly changed. The party's sixth plenary session further summed up the experience and lessons learned since the founding of the PRC and adjusted and strengthened the leadership of the party Central Committee. This fully shows that our party is good at maintaining and strengthening party unity and raising the party's fighting capability by adhering to Marxism. This is our reliable guarantee for accomplishing the great tasks of the new era. We must be firm and optimistic about the future and possess the confidence for winning victory. Any doubts and waverings about the future are unfounded.

Recalling the past and looking toward the future, we feel an upsurge of emotion and are filled with confidence. So long as we bear in mind that we are the great Chinese PLA led by the CCP and that we always should follow the instructions of the party Central Committee, this people's army will forever be invincible. This has been borne out by our army's history of hard struggle over the past decades and will be borne out by the sacred struggle of defending the security and independence of the great motherland.

On the Continuing Validity of Mao Zedong's Military Thought, 1 August 1981

55

It is a sacred principle in Chinese Communist military affairs that Mao's military science, including its emphasis on the people's war, remains valid and that it must be reconciled with the PRC's drive for military modernization.

It has been 60 years since the birth of the most loyal and farsighted and the bravest vanguard of the working class—the Chinese Communist Party! One of the immortal contributions made by the Chinese communists to our motherland and the people over the past 60 years was to found and nurture a completely new type of people's army—the Chinese People's Liberation Army. We all know that 1 August 1981 makes the 54th year since this people's army embarked on the brilliant and militant course of struggle.

Under the leadership of the party, the Chinese People's Liberation Army entered the agrarian revolutionary war, the war of resistance against Japan and the war of liberation. It fought successively for more than 20 years and wiped out a total of 11 million domestic and foreign enemies. A new China grew out of the barrel of the people's gun. The disaster-ridden Chinese nation eventually was able to stand on its own feet in the family of nations! Now this army has developed from a ground force into a combined arms unit which includes various armed services armed with self-defensive missiles and nuclear weapons. Just like a great wall of steel, it is defending the independence and security of the motherland as well as the socialist modernization of our country.

Comrade Mao Zedong was a great Marxist and proletarian revolutionary. He was also a world famous great strategist and outstanding military expert. Proceeding from the basic principle of Marxism and our country's national condition, Comrade Mao Zedong and his comrades-in-arms created and accumulated abundant and unique experiences which guided the Chinese revolutionary war. After a theoretical distillation, it became a science—Mao Zedong military science. Under its guidance, the Chinese people used armed revolution to defeat the armed counterrevolution and win the final victory.

Mao Zedong military science has played a very important part in the whole scientific system of Mao Zedong Thought. It was a product of combining Marxism-Leninism with the specific practice of the Chinese revolutionary war. It is an invincible and correct proletarian military theory and principle which have been repeatedly proven by war practice over scores of years. It is a comprehensive and complete scientific system. Therefore, it is completely worthy of the name Mao Zedong military science. Mao Zedong military science was named after Mao Zedong. Just like Mao Zedong Thought, it was a crystallization of the collective wisdom of the entire party and army. Many outstanding leaders of our party and army have made important contributions to the growth and development of Mao Zedong military science. Mao Zedong military science was a brilliant achievement of Marxism-Leninism in the military field. Furthermore, it enriched and developed theory of knowledge of Marxism and dialectics. Mao Zedong military science is our powerful ideological weapon for building and defending our socialist motherland and striving for world peace and progress of mankind.

The "Resolution on Certain Questions in the History of Our Party Since the Founding of the People's Republic of China" adopted by the 6th plenary session of the 11th party Central Committee highly evaluates Comrade Mao Zedong's theories on the building of a revolutionary army and his military strategy. It points out that Mao Zedong's military thought was his most outstanding contribution to the military theories of Marxism-Leninism. This is a matter of vital importance for us to learn, study, carry out and maintain Mao Zedong military science as well as apply and develop it under the new historical conditions.

WITHOUT THE PEOPLE'S ARMY, THERE WOULD BE NO LIBERATION OF THE PEOPLE OR INDEPENDENCE OF THE NATION

In the mid-19th century, Marx and Engels earnestly hoped that workers would arm themselves to organize an "independent proletarian guard." ("Selected Works of Marx and Engels," vol. 1, p. 112) After the failure of Paris Commune, Marx explicitly pointed out: "A proletarian army is the first condition for the proletarian dictatorship." ("Selected Works

[Fu Zhong, "Mao Zedong Military Science is Forever the Chinese People's Treasure," *Red Flag*, no. 15, 1 August 1981.]

of Marx and Engels," vol. 2, p. 443) In order to defend the newborn Soviet power, Lenin and Stalin organized the Workers and Peasants Red Army and gained the experiences of revolutionary war. However, just as Comrade Mao Zedong pointed out, although the experience of civil war in the Soviet Union led by Lenin and Stalin was of world significance, we should not copy it mechanically. The building of the Chinese revolutionary army and the guidance of Chinese revolutionary war bore their own characteristics which were different from those of the Soviet civil war. In accordance with the real condition in China and the reality of the Chinese revolutionary war, Comrade Mao Zedong founded the army and guided the war.

When our party was in its infancy, it did not realize the importance of organizing an army. During the period of the northern expedition, it had some idea of it, but it was still insufficient. It was only after the failure of the great revolution and learning a bitter lesson that the party truly realized the paramount importance of the revolutionary army. It was Comrade Mao Zedong who profoundly grasped and had a most farsighted view on this subject. When he was investigating the peasant movement in Hunan, he stressed the importance of organizing the armed forces of peasants. When he was in charge of the institutes of peasants' movement in Guangzhou and Wuhan, he paid close attention to military training. After the failure of the great revolution in 1927, the Kuomintang launched a surprise attack and ruthlessly slaughtered the Chinese communists. However, the Chinese communists held high the banner of revolution and carried out armed resistance. Since the Nanchang uprising which fired the first shot against the Kuomintang reactionaries, the party successively organized more than a hundred uprisings in various places. At the "7 August meeting," Comrade Mao Zedong maintained that the central authorities should attach importance to military affairs, pointing out: "We should know that political power grows out of the barrel of a gun." After that, he led the autumn harvest uprising in the Hunan-Jiangxi border region and succeeded in leading the army which took part in the uprising to the Jianggang Mountains and establishing the first revolutionary base. In the meantime, he expanded the revolutionary forces in the rural area and pioneered the method of using the countryside to encircle the cities and seizing power by armed force.

In the practice of revolutionary war, Comrade Mao Zedong systematically solved the problem of turning the revolutionary army mostly composed of peasants into a new-type people's army which was of a proletarian nature, and observed strict discipline and maintained close ties with the masses of people. He maintained that to serve the people wholeheartedly was the sole purpose of the army and that our principle was that the party commands the gun, and the gun must never be allowed to command the party. He formulated the three main rules of discipline and the eight points for attention and stressed the implementation of democracy in the three main fields of politics, economics and military affairs and the principles of unity between commanders and soldiers on the one hand and between the army and the people on the other, as well as other methods of disintegrating the enemy forces. In addition, he put forward and summed up a whole set of guiding principles and methods for political work in the army.

The key to building a people's army lies in maintaining the party's absolute leadership over the army. This is the fundamental method for retaining the proletarian nature of the army. Practice has proved that it is always a matter of great importance, whether in peacetime or war, to implement the responsibility system on the part of senior officers under the collective leadership of the party committee and give full play to the leading role of the unified leadership of the party committee, to the role of the party branch as a fighting bastion and to the vanguard and exemplary role of communists. This is a matter which we should never neglect. We should promote and consolidate the work of our army in various fields through strengthening the leadership and building of our party.

The party's leadership over the army is realized and ensured by political work, which includes the party's organizational and ideological work. History has proved that to turn an army mainly composed of peasants into an armed group which truly shoulders a revolutionary political task, it is necessary to conduct a Marxist and Leninist education so that it will constantly raise its proletarian class consciousness, establish a lofty ideal of communism and raise its awareness of resolutely implementing the programs, guiding principles and policies of the party, willingly abide by the strict discipline and unceasingly overcome the ideological influence of petty producers, the bourgeoisie and feudalism. Political work should ensure that the fighting power of the army be constantly consolidated and enhanced so that the broad masses of commanders and soldiers possess the heroic spirit of "fearing neither hardship nor death," devoting oneself to revolution and crushing all enemies.

Comrade Mao Zedong always maintained that "revolutionary political work led by the Communist Party is the lifeblood of the revolutionary army." After nationwide liberation, Comrade Mao Zedong personally instructed that the principle "political work is the lifeblood of our army" should be included in the "rules and regulations of the political work of the Chinese People's Liberation Army." History has proved that political work and the people's army are as indispensable as air and water to life. We should neither abandon nor weaken it. We should follow the correct thesis "political work is the lifeblood of economic work and all other work" stated in the "Resolution on Certain Questions in the History of Our Party Since the Founding of the People's Republic of China." Only by vigorously strengthening political work, upholding the four basic principles, building both the high degree of socialist material civilization and spiritual civilization and carrying forward all patriotic spirit and the spirit of making contributions to modernization and hard struggle, can we work with one heart and one mind, surmount every difficulty and strive for the realization of the party's objectives in the new historical period.

After the founding of the People's Republic of China, Comrade Mao Zedong called for strengthening our national defense and building modernized army forces and acquiring modern defense technology which included self-defensive nuclear weapons. We are now following the teachings of the party and Comrade Mao Zedong to strengthen our military training, political work, logistic work and the study of military science. In so doing, we will further enhance our fighting power and gradually turn our army into a powerful and modernized revolutionary army which masters advanced technology and advanced military science. Historical practice has proved: "Without the people's army there would be no people's liberation and national independence." This was the case in the past and it has and will remain so at present and in the future. This is a basic experience paid for with blood, which we must never forget. During the socialist period, the People's Liberation Army is a mighty pillar of the people's democratic dictatorship, that is, the proletarian dictatorship. Without such a complete new-type people's army which has close ties with the people, it is impossible to effectively defend our national independence and socialist modernization.

PEOPLE'S WAR AND ITS STRATEGY AND TACTICS CAN CERTAINLY DEFEAT ALL POWERFUL ENEMIES

"The army and the people are the foundation of victory." "The richest source of power to wage war lies in the masses of people."

Comrade Mao Zedong applied the basic principle of historical materialism—"history is created by people"—to the revolutionary war and formed a guiding line for the people's war, which regarded the people's army as the mainstay and relied on the masses of people.

The people's revolutionary war in our country was actually a peasants' war led by the proletariat. The party and Comrade Mao Zedong closely linked armed struggle with peasants' agrarian problems.

Due to the fact that millions upon millions of peasants owned the land and their rent for land and interest on loans were reduced, they realized, through their own immediate and vital interests, that the revolutionary war led by the Communist Party was truly for their own liberation. Therefore, they wholeheartedly supported and assisted and took part in the revolutionary war. This was the inexhaustible source of power for the people's war. Extensive and profound political mobilization was the basic condition for carrying out the people's war. Once the masses of people were mobilized, they could engulf the enemy in the boundless ocean. During the years of the war of resistance against Japan, mine warfare, tunnel warfare, sabotage operations and sparrow warfare were the great creation of the masses of people. During the decisive battles in the later stage of the war of liberation, millions upon millions of people delivered grain and ammunition and supported the front. They organized stretcher teams and transport corps, using their shoulders and caravans to carry goods and wounded soldiers. The wheels rolled on and mountains stretched over a thousand li. What a magnificent sight it was! Without the irresistible force of the masses, it was impossible to win the nationwide victory.

Comrade Mao Zedong formulated the system of armed force which combined field army, local armed forces and people's militia. Under the unified leadership of the party, main formations and regional troops were combined. Regular forces and guerrillas as well as people's militia were combined. The armed masses and unarmed masses were also combined. The main forces were ready at all times to shoulder the fighting tasks over the local level and dealt with and wiped out the enemy's regular forces. Working in coordination with people's militias, local armed forces defended the bases and supported the main forces to attack and eliminate local enemies. A dragnet of fighting against the enemy was thus spread.

To develop the people's war and defeat our powerful enemies, we should unite with forces that can be united, form the most extensive revolutionary united front and organize thousands upon thousands into an enormous and powerful revolutionary army. Comrade Mao Zedong pointed out that the united front and armed struggle were the two basic weapons for defeating the enemy.

War should not be separated from politics even for a single moment. The purely military viewpoint which paid no attention to politics was wrong. The peaceful settlement of the Xian incident and the anti-Japanese national united front jointly formed by the Kuomintang and the Communist Party were a turning point of the situation at that time. After the formation of the united front, the people's armed forces were greatly expanded. During the liberation war, the democratic and revolutionary united front formed by our party and various democratic parties and patriotic personages of various circles was the second battle front in the Kuomintang-controlled area. Chiang Kai-shek was thus surrounded by the whole people. The revolts of the Kuomintang troops and "Beiping-type" as well as "Suiyuan-type" peaceful liberation accelerated the victorious process of the liberation war.

The victory of the people's war in China declared the bankruptcy of the bourgeois theory that weapons alone decided the outcome of war. Comrade Mao Zedong said: Weapons are an important factor in war, but not the decisive factor; it is people, not things, that are decisive. Have historical facts not proved this? The weapons of the Chinese troops were not as sophisticated as those of the Japanese troops, but it was the Chinese people who won the victory. Chiang Kai-shek's troops armed with modern U.S. weapons were wiped out one division after another by the People's Liberation Army whose weapons were inadequate. Chiang Kai-shek became our "chief of supply corps." In the Korean battlefield, the U.S. ground forces had more tanks and artillery than we did. Besides, the U.S. Air Force and Navy held the upper hand. However, they were defeated by the Chinese and Korean peoples. In the past, when our weapons and equipment were inferior, the people's war was our magic weapon for defeating the enemy; now our weapons and equipment have been further improved and the forms of war have also changed, but we still rely on the people's war to wipe out the aggressors. We should never misunderstand or doubt this.

Of course, new situations and new problems are bound to occur in the people's war under the present conditions, which we should consciously study and explore. They are different from the people's war in the past. For instance, with regard to guerrilla warfare, due to the fact that the enemy employs grand tactics and that it is armed with advanced technology and equipment and possesses stronger surveillance and mobilization capabilities, new conditions will occur when the people's guerrilla warfare is carried out. Although the enemy is powerful, it has its own difficulties. Although it is strong, it still has its weak points. The possibility of exploiting its weakness always exists. We can still actively carry out various kinds of guerrilla warfare, attack the enemy's rear bases, undermine its communications apparatus and communications and transportation, cut off its supply lines, tire out, wear down and pin down the enemy. In so doing, we will be able to fight in coordination with the main force.

During the long period of revolutionary war in our

country, our enemy was strong and we were weak. During the period of agrarian revolutionary war, Comrade Mao Zedong pointed out: "The enemy is strong and the Red Army is weak." When the war of resistance against Japan had just started, we had only 30,000 troops, but we had to face the Japanese aggressor troops armed with sophisticated weapons. When the liberation war had just started, we had only about 1 million troops scattered in a dozen bases, but we had to face 4.3 million Kuomintang troops armed and supported by the U.S. imperialists. When the war to resist U.S. aggression and aid Korea had just begun, our enemy was the U.S. aggressors who dominated the world and possessed atom bombs. However, Comrade Mao Zedong deserved to be called a contemporary giant of the proletariat and the greatest national hero of the Chinese nation. He showed great foresight and dared to struggle and win victory. With brilliant and scientific foresight, he delineated that the enemy was a paper tiger which was outwardly strong, but inwardly weak. He repeatedly told our cadres and soldiers that the small stone of revolution could smash the big water vat of the imperialists and the Kuomintang. He armed the minds of our people and our army with the principle "strategically we should despise all our enemies, but tactically we should take them all seriously," so that we were confident of our victory. In the meantime, Comrade Mao Zedong creatively applied Marxist dialectics to the military field and laid down a whole series of the strategies and tactics of the people's war for the weak to defeat the strong. Their characteristics which we usually call the "three general rules" were: quick decisions within a protracted war, offense within strategic defense and exterior lines within strategic interior lines. This was the basic strategic experience of giving play to the strong points and avoiding the weaknesses as well as making use of advantages and avoiding disadvantages. Concentrating an absolutely superior force to thoroughly wipe out the enemies was the basic method taken by the weak army to defeat its strong enemies. By adopting such a method, our troops succeeded in turning their strategic inferiority into superiority in the battles. During the "second counter-campaigns against encirclement" in the agrarian revolutionary war, we had only 30,000 troops, but we had to cope with 200,000 enemy troops who were 7 times our strength. However, under the guidance of Comrade Mao Zedong, we concentrated our absolutely superior force to attack one of the enemy's routes. As a result, we wiped out the greater part of an enemy division and part of another division. After that, we pushed on in the flush of victory and successively won 5 battles and eliminated more than 30,000 enemy troops. In his poem "To the Tune of Yu Chia Ao—Against the Second 'Encirclement' Campaign," Chairman Mao wrote: "In 15 days we have marched 700 li crossing misty kan waters and green Fukien hills, rolling back the enemy as we would a mat." This was a vivid description of the battle. This was also a successful combination of offense within defense, quick decisions within a protracted war and exterior lines within interior lines. By adopting such a strategy, our troops completely smashed the "encirclement" by a large number of the enemy troops.

Another example was a battle in the liberation war, Chiang Kai-shek concentrated his superior force to attack our bases in Shandong and Shaanxi. Comrade Mao Zedong instructed the south China field army to pretend to fight the enemy for the eastern part of Shandong Province so that the enemy's "right fist" was stretched to the coast of Bohai. In the meantime, he personally directed the northwest field army to hit out in Yulin so that the enemy's "left fist" was stretched to the verge of the desert. In so doing, Chiang Kai-shek's two fists were set far apart and "his chest was exposed." Just at that time, Comrade Mao Zedong ordered the main forces of Liu and Deng to cross the Huanghe River and march toward the Dabie Mountain, just like a dagger thrust at the enemy's chest. The war situation of the whole country was thus changed, reducing the enemy's strategic offense to strategic defense. Thus we turned our strategic defense into strategic offense.

Comrade Mao Zedong was good at correctly changing military strategy as the war developed. He adopted different kinds of warfare—guerrilla warfare, mobile warfare and positional warfare—in light of the changes in the balance of forces between the enemy and ourselves. At the beginning of the war of resistance against Japan, Comrade Mao Zedong regarded independent warfare guerrilla as a strategy. It was entirely new in the history of war to regard tactical guerrilla warfare as a strategy. During the liberation war, under the guidance of Comrade Mao Zedong, we adopted the strategy of mobile warfare. In other words, we advanced or retreated in big strides and wiped out the enemy's effective strength. During the later stage of the war to resist the U.S. aggressors and aid Korea, we adopted the strategy of active defense to carry out positional warfare mainly by making use of tunnels. Working in cooperation with the Korean people and army, we battered the enemy, forcing the United States to agree to a truce. During the war, Comrade Mao Zedong appropriately adopted different kinds of strategy in light of local conditions so that we could give full play to our advantages and exploit the enemy's weakness.

While commanding our troops in a war, Comrade Mao Zedong always adopted a flexible strategy and avoided sticking to one pattern. His basic principle was to tie down the enemy but never let the enemy hinder us from attacking. He directed military operations with miraculous skill and devised strategies from a command tent. He not only directed our powerful troops with high proficiency, but also subdued our enemy. During the Long March, Comrade Mao Zedong personally directed the battle of "crossing the Cheshui River on four occasions" and our troops penetrated and cut up the enemy forces. When the enemy thought that we were marching toward the east, we outflanked it from the west. When the enemy thought that we were crossing the river, we gave it a back thrust from the east. In so doing, we puzzled the enemy and kept it constantly on the run. When the enemy was building blockhouses to check us crossing the Changjiang River from the north, our troops suddenly turned back to Guizhou from the south, crossing the Wujiang River and pressing up to Guiyang. Chiang Kai-shek who was "supervising operations" in Guiyang was compelled to move troops from Yunnan to protect him. Therefore, the main forces of the Red Army directed by Comrade Mao Zedong headed directly for Yunnan and passed the province to march northward. The superb art of military command in making a feint to the east and attacking in the west and defeating the opponent by a surprise move was extolled as a great success of Comrade Mao Zedong. During the war of liberation, Comrade Mao Zedong commanded our army to take the initiative and withdraw from Yanan, while he himself persisted in staying in northern Shaanxi and contended with the enemy using his "mushroom" tactic. Comrade Mao Zedong once remarked humorously: I am a piece of meat and I can attract Hu Zongnan and his swarm of flies. Under the wise command of Comrade Mao Zedong, our army finally annihilated, with only inferior forces the crack troops of the Chiang army under Hu Zongnan's command, thus laying a solid foundation for liberating the northwest region.

Comrade Mao Zedong theorized the successful military strategies of our army in the protracted fighting against the enemies at home and abroad and summed them up into 10 major military principles. These principles played a very significant guiding role in the rapid ultimate victory in the war of liberation.

As was pointed out by Comrade Ye Jianying: "The idea of fighting strategically decisive battles is a significant integral part of Comrade Mao Zedong's complete military science." When the war of liberation entered its third year, and without missing the opportunity, Comrade Mao Zedong organized the three major campaigns of Liaoxi-Shenyang, Huai-Hai and Beiping-Tianjin and commanded the PLA in waging strategically decisive battles against the KMT army. Our army followed the instructions of Comrade Mao Zedong and achieved great success. In the Laioxi-Shenyang campaign, it adopted the combat principle of bolting the door behind and beating the dog, "ignoring the enemy troops in Changchun and Shenyang and concentrating its forces against the enemy troops in Jinzhou, Yulin and Tangshan." In the Huai-Hai campaign, it adopted the principle of annihilating the enemy's main force north of the Changjiang River. In the Beiping-Tianjin campaign, in order to attract the enemy forces in Beiping and Tianjin so that they would not make the decision to flee by sea, it adopted the principle of "encircling without attacking" or "blocking without encircling." The great victories in the three major campaigns were victories of Comrade Mao Zedong's idea of fighting strategically decisive battles.

When we make a comprehensive observation of Comrade Mao Zedong's systematic theory on the building of the people's army, carrying out the people's war and employing strategy and tactics in a flexible way, and when we make a comprehensive observation of Comrade Mao Zedong's great practice in leading the revolutionary war for several decades and the birth and course of development of Mao Zedong military science, we can clearly see that seeking truth from facts is the most important axis running through his military science. Seeking truth from facts is his concentrated and conspicuous demonstration of employing and developing the theory of knowledge and dialectics of Marxism-Leninism in the military field and is the quintessence and living spirit of Mao Zedong military science.

As the objective situation changes in the future, we have to revise or use new conclusions to replace certain military principles and methods of fighting formulated by Comrade Mao Zedong under particular conditions in the past. However, the stand, viewpoint, methods and the ideological line of seeking truth from facts based on dialectical materialism and historical materialism have the greatest vitality running through Mao Zedong military science. They are like the sun and moon in the sky and will remain fresh forever. We have mentioned that Mao Zedong military science is forever the Chinese people's treasure and they are the most valuable parts of the treasure.

What is seeking truth from facts? Comrade Mao Zedong gave an incisive explanation during the Yanan rectification campaign. He said: "Facts" exist objectively, "truth" means their internal relations and "to seek" means to study. We should derive from them, as our guide to action, laws that are inherent in them and not imaginary.

The "Resolution on Certain Questions in the History of Our Party Since the Founding of the People's Republic of China" adopted by the 6th Plenary Session of the 11th CCP Central Committee also points out: "Seek truth from facts. This means proceed from reality and combine theory with practice, that is, integrate the universal principles of Marxism-Leninism with the concrete practice of the Chinese revolution."

The formation and the course of development of Mao Zedong military science itself is a course of strictly proceeding from reality, closely combining theory with practice and closely integrating the universal principles of Marxism-Leninism with the concrete practice of the Chinese revolutionary war.

Comrade Mao Zedong employed the stand, viewpoint and methods of Marxism-Leninism, followed the line of dynamic theory of knowledge as a reflection of reality in accordance with dialectical materialism, carried out meticulous and systematic investigations and study, and painstakingly and carefully pondered over the abundant direct experiences of the Chinese revolutionary war (including both successful and unsuccessful experiences), namely the perceptual materials.

He eliminated the dross and selected the essential, discarded the false and retained the true, proceeded from one point to another and from outward appearance to inner essence, and modified them. In this way, the perceptual knowledge leaped into rational knowledge and was subsequently raised to the level of theory. He used the theory in the practice of guiding the war and tested it through practice. He then continued to sum up the new practical experiences from war and further enriched and raised the level of his military theory.

Through this recurring process, the theory became more and more correct and profound and could more comprehensively reflect the objective law of war.

Comrade Mao Zedong's military theory which was based on his scientific summation of the practice of the protracted war and was tested in the practice of war, is in complete accord with the "scientific abstraction abstraction" noted by Lenin. Therefore, it can objectively instead of subjectively, comprehensively instead of one-sidedly and essentially instead of superficially reflect the law of Chinese revolutionary war.

The scientific approach of seeking truth from facts was followed and manifested in the course of the shaping and development of Mao Zedong military science. To study, uphold, inherit and develop Mao Zedong military science, we, too, have to keep to this scientific approach. If we only learn the superficial meaning of the words of each principle or concept, we will never learn the essence and truth, or, the living soul, conveyed between principles and concepts. Some comrades are worried about their lack of combat experience. This, indeed, is not necessary. Comrade Mao Zedong himself went through the process from understanding nothing to understanding something and then from understanding something to understanding quite a lot in military affairs. If we follow Comrade Mao Zedong's example of sticking to the principle of seeking truth from facts, in constantly practicing and making investigation and study and in assiduously studying and digging into what we study, we will certainly be able to learn warfare from peacetime training and other military work and, once war breaks out, we will learn warfare from warfare.

Comrade Mao Zedong's concept of seeking truth from facts in directing military affairs has profound significance in many aspects.

First of all, he strictly proceeded from the practical condition of our country while formulating military strategy.

Comrade Mao Zedong pointed out: "Fully understanding the condition of China is the fundamental basis for understanding all problems of the revolution." Of course, this is also the fundamental basis for studying the laws of the revolutionary war in China and for formulating military strategy and tactics for our army.

According to Comrade Mao Zedong's teachings, to persist in seeking truth from facts, we have to study not only the universality of contradictions in objective things, but, more importantly, their particularity. We have to study not only the particularity of the contradiction in the movement of an objective thing as such but, in in-depth study, the particularity of the contradictions in given stages of the development of things. At all times, we have to concretely analyze the specific conditions and study and direct warfare in view of the specific time and place.

Comrade Mao Zedong repeatedly stressed that we have to study not only the laws of war of a general nature but, in particular, revolutionary war and the still more particular Chinese revolutionary war. We must study the summed-up experience in warfare by ancient and contemporary people. However, we must verify these conclusions through our own experience, absorbing what is useful, rejecting what is not useful and adding in what is special of our own.

Comrade Mao Zedong waged a persistent and resolute struggle against the erroneous tendency of making Marxism a dogma and deifying foreign experience in military affairs just as he did in political affairs. He opposed both foreign and local dogmas. He opposed both the mechanical copying of the laws of the civil war in the Soviet Union and the application of the military regulations of Chinese reactionary governments in a procrustean manner. Even our own very successful experience should be altered as the objective conditions and our missions change. Comrade Mao Zedong said in 1958: The 10 cardinal principles of military operation can be applied at present and in many instances in the future. However, Marxism is not stationary but developing as time goes by. So the 10 cardinal principles of military operation will have to be supplemented and developed and some of them revised in the light of the practical condition of war in future. In short, Comrade Mao Zedong's famous, concise, yet comprehensive saying "have the particularity and its development in mind" contains very profound Marxist philosophy. It is the fundamental principle for seeking truth from facts and directing war. We should make it a maxim in doing military work, thoroughly understand it and determinedly apply it.

In order to seek truth from facts in directing a war, it is necessary to follow Comrade Mao Zedong's Marxist theory on knowledge which he elucidated in his article, "On Practice." It is essential to try our best to ensure that the subjective direction of a war corresponds to the constantly changing objective realities of both the enemy and ourselves. There is absolutely no consideration for personal feelings in a war. Whoever acts in defiance of the principle of "making the subjective correspond to the objective" will be punished by blood immediately.

To know the enemy and yourself is the fundamental way to solve contradictions between the subjective and the objective in a war. In conducting a war, we must firmly regard investigations and studies as the first step in directing battles. We must neither exaggerate the enemy's strengths and superiority nor belittle its shortcomings and inferiority. We must oppose the tendency to ignore the enemy's superiority in certain areas and, at the same time oppose any tendency to be overawed by the ferocious enemy. We must also adopt a clear-cut stand among ourselves. We must realize our own shortcomings as well as our strengths. When the situation or the balance of strength between the enemy and ourselves changes and when a war or campaign enters a new stage of development, we should make timely changes in our strategy and tactics. Because both sides in a war or a battle are composed of living human beings bearing arms, keeping their secrets from each other and making false moves to confuse each other, the phenomenon of war is more elusive and is characterized by greater uncertainty than any other social phenomenon. It is extremely difficult to make subjective direction correspond entirely to the objective situation in a war. However, we must strive to achieve a basic conformity between the two. This means that those elements which play a decisive role in a campaign or battle should conform to each other. Only in this way will we lay the foundation for victories.

In order to solve the contradiction between the subjective and the objective in fighting a war, a campaign must be carried out in the war from beginning to end. Continuous efforts must be made to examine and revise the original military plans throughout the course of the ever-changing military operation. Whenever it is discovered that the subjective direction does not correspond, or corresponds only in part, to the objective situation, we must demonstrate the courage to resolutely make timely changes. Anyone who does not understand the need for such changes or is unwilling to make them, and who acts blindly, is bound to fail.

Utilizing the dialectical-materialist theory of knowledge, Comrade Mao Zedong systematically described the source of a commander's correct thinking in directing war and what form it takes. In his article, "Strategy in China's Revolutionary War," he wrote: "A commander's correct disposition stems from his correct decisions, his correct decisions stem from his correct judgments, and his correct judgments stem from a thorough and necessary reconnaissance and from analyzing and piecing together various kinds of data gathered from reconnaissance."

The commander employs all possible and necessary methods of reconnaissance, analyzes the information gathered about the enemy's situation, takes his own conditions into account and then makes a study of both sides and their interrelations. Through this process, he forms his judgments, makes up his mind and works out his plans. This is the sequence and the complete process of assessing a situation which a military commander goes through before he formulates a strategic plan, a campaign plan or a battle plan. Under no circumstances should we reverse such an order, particularly since a modern war is highly mobile and the military situation may undergo myriad changes in the twinkling of an eye. It is extremely difficult to know the enemy and to know yourself. This calls for even greater efforts on our part to achieve this. In ordinary times, we should also make full preparations for this and we should make strenuous efforts to conduct systematic and careful investigations and studies of the military, political, economic, cultural and other situations of the enemy and fraternal units as well as our own situation.

Comrade Mao Zedong applied the dialectical-materialist theory of knowledge to war and completely placed our army's art in directing war on a scientific basis.

There is an erroneous saying among some comrades—which we have already refuted—that holds that the serious accidents in economic construction in the past, which were caused by the arbitrary issuance of subjective orders, resulted from the adoption of the same methods used for giving battle commands when giving directions for construction. Those comrades who support such sayings apparently fail to understand that our army is most scientific and realistic in directing war and in opposing rashness and foolhardiness.

To direct a war by persistently seeking truth from facts according to Comrade Mao Zedong's teaching, we fully respect the objective conditions and refrain from becoming "armchair strategists." Nor should we depend on wishful thinking. We should fight no battle unprepared, fight no battle we are not sure of winning; make every effort to ensure victory in the given set of conditions as between the army and ourselves, and oppose impetuousness and military adventurism. However, we must not regard our efforts to respect objective conditions as an excuse not to bring into full play our subjective dynamic role. Comrade Mao Zedong emphatically pointed out more than once: "In their endeavor to win a war, those who direct war cannot overstep the limitations imposed by the objective conditions; within those limitations, however, they can and must play a dynamic role in striving for victory." He also pointed out: "It is a human characteristic in war." It was also on the stage built upon objective conditions that, in war, Comrade Mao Zedong himself directed the performance of one live drama after another, full of sound and color. Going into battle with a relatively weak force against the stronger enemy, he directed our army to strategically "pit one against ten" and tactically "pit ten against one." He turned strategic inferiority into a superiority in a campaign or battle. This is an important point in the dynamic role in war.

In explaining Comrade Mao Zedong's art in directing military affairs, Comrade Ye Jianying often cited the story about Sun Bin's advice to Tian Ji, a general of the state of Qin on chariot races to show the dynamic role in war.

Tian Ji bet heavily on races between his chariots and those of the young lords of Qi. Sun Bin saw that the three sets of teams were well matched. Seeing this, Sun Bin said to Tian Ji: "Bet heavily. I shall see that you win." Taking him at his word, Tian Ji bet a thousand gold pieces with the king and lords. Just before the race started, Sun Bin said: "Now, run your worst team against their best, your best against their second-best and your second-best against their worst." After three races, Tian Ji lost one race but won

the two others, getting a thousand gold pieces from the king. After this, he recommended Sun Bin to King Wei, who consulted him on military theory and then made him his chief of staff. (Sun Zi: Biography of Wu Qi)

This story on the "records of the historian" vividly and metaphorically explains that to defeat a superior force with an inferior force, we cannot rely on foolhardiness, we must depend on planning with a scientific approach. Despite the fact that the practice of bringing the subjective dynamic role into full play is inevitably limited by objective conditions, we will open up vast vistas in giving full play to our subjective dynamic role—just as the ancient saying goes: "Ingenuity in varying tactics depends on mother wit"—as long as we comprehensively and fully understand the objective situation and pay attention to objective laws. On the other hand, we will never be able to make a good move in a chess game if we fail to take the entire situation into account. Mao Zedong's military science has properly and highly appraised the subjective dynamic role, and dialectically elucidated the relations between objective conditions and the subjective dynamic role. Not only does it not run counter to materialism, it has also avoided the practice of mechanical materialism and upheld dialectical materialism.

As far as giving guidance in a war is concerned, to persist in seeking truth from facts and proceeding from reality in doing everything is the only correct way to have a good grasp of the law of the unity of opposites, which is the very core of Marxist dialectics. In a war, the strong and the weak, the big and the small, the attacker and the defender, the winning side and the losing side, the side with the initiative and the side thrown into a passive position as well as the concentration or the dispersion of the forces used, and so on, all represent a unity of the opposites that tend to transfer themselves and reverse with each other. To guard against adventurism when on the offensive, against conservatism when on the defensive and against flightism when on the move are the basic strategic and tactical principles worked out by Comrade Mao Zedong by applying the law of the unity of opposites. When there are more than two different contradictions, the way to handle them as stressed by Comrade Mao Zedong is to be good at grasping the main contradiction. Specifically, this means to pay attention to the use of the forces. In other words, it is necessary to concentrate the forces and guard against egalitarianism. He said that concentration of the forces appears to be easy, but it is not when it comes to actually doing it. Everyone knows that the best way to win victory is to use more forces than the other side. But many people cannot achieve this. The reason is that they do not have a strategic mind and adopt a perfunctory attitude as one who allows himself to be dominated by the circumstances. This makes it clear that when we are not good at analyzing the contradictions and fail to have a good grasp of the main one, or the key, we will be confused and at a loss for what to do and it would be impossible for us to guide the war to victory in the manner of seeking truth from facts.

To seek truth from facts is also of utmost importance to building the people's army, just as it is to providing guidance in a war. When offering his incisive exposition of Comrade Mao Zedong's concept of seeking truth from facts in the all-army political work conference held in June, 1978,

Comrade Deng Xiaoping pointed out emphatically that it is necessary to proceed from reality both in doing the army's political work and in army-building as a whole. We said that it is necessary to pay attention to analyzing the new situation and solving the new problems emerging under the new historical conditions, to decide on the principles for our work in accordance with the actual conditions instead of acting in the manner of "an office handling incoming and outgoing documents" to simply copy and convey the messages transmitted from above, and to carry out work in a creative way by combining the instructions of the central authorities or instructions from other superior authorities with the actual conditions in our own units.

The major military works written by Comrade Mao Zedong contain a wealth of penetrating philosophical concepts of Marxism. As has been noted in the "Resolution on Certain Questions in the History of Our Party Since the Founding of the PRC," Comrade Mao Zedong's important works on the question of the Chinese revolutionary war represent the most brilliant examples of applying and developing the Marxist theory of knowledge in the course of practice. In concept, we must more clearly understand that Comrade Mao Zedong's philosophical works are not limited only to such articles as "On Practice" and "On Contradiction." "On Correcting Mistaken Ideas in the Party," "Problems of Strategy in China's Revolutionary War," "Problems of Strategy in Guerrilla War Against Japan," "On Protracted War" and "Problems of War and Strategy" and other military works are also important philosophic works of Marxism written by Comrade Mao Zedong.

In 1935, after the Red Army reached northern Shaanxi in its Long March, Comrade Mao Zedong delved into the study of philosophy, despite his busy schedule, in an effort to find theoretical answers to the extremely complex problems facing China's revolution at the time. He told us on many occasions that one important condition for winning victory is to study theory. He also said: My advice to you, comrades, is to study philosophy. Marxism encompasses several schools of knowledge, but what is fundamental in it is Marxist philosophy. We should regard the study philosophy as a matter of importance not to be neglected if we are to push revolution and construction forward.

Mao Zedong Thought, which is the outgrowth of the collective struggle of the party and the people, has educated one after another generation of us. It will remain the guiding thought of our party in the future. By the same token, Mao Zedong military science, which likewise is an outgrowth of the collective struggle, is a valuable spiritual wealth of the people of our country. It will continue to guide our actions for a long time in the future. Furthermore, its significance and role will far exceed the military field.

Mao Zedong military science has displayed its tremendous might in China's revolution. This historical fact fully demonstrates that our party has the ability to solve the most complex and difficult problem in the revolutionary war and the superb art of military command with which we can change from an inferior to a superior position. Comrade Mao Zedong has left this world forever. Now the glorious duty to inherit and develop Mao Zedong military science has been passed onto our shoulders. In the new historical period in which we will carry on our cause and forge ahead, as long as we assiduously study Comrade Mao

Zedong's military theory of materialism and military dialectics and see that Mao Zedong military science is passed on from generation to generation, we surely will be able to use our relatively inferior equipment to prevail over a relatively superiorly equipped enemy in any future war against aggression.

The basic principles and scientific methods of Mao Zedong military science will never become outdated. We must unswervingly affirm its scientific value, seriously study it, inherit it and apply it at all times. Of course, we must study Mao Zedong military science in such a way that it is accurately and comprehensively understood. We must adopt the scientific attitude of seeking truth from facts and persist in the method of combining theory with practice, instead of mechanically copying isolated phrases or words or ready-made formulas. The important thing is to use "the arrow" of Mao Zedong military science to shoot at "the target" in the war against aggression in the future, strive to use its stand, viewpoints and methods to study the new situation and solve the new problems emerging in the course of national defense modernization—the many new problems emerging from a future war against aggression in particular—and strive to sum up the new experience expected in the course of new practice, so as to enrich and develop Mao Zedong military science with new principles and new conclusions that conform with the reality.

We should not neglect the need to study Mao Zedong Thought and Mao Zedong military science simply on the grounds that Comrade Mao Zedong made mistakes in his later years. Nor should we doubt or play down the role of Mao Zedong military science just because the development of modern military technology has brought about such new conditions as the emergence of guided missiles and nuclear weapons. However, the types of weapons may change, however, the forms of war operations may change, we must always uphold the basic principles of Mao Zedong military science, particularly the dialectical materialistic and historical materialistic concepts and the principle of seeking truth from facts contained in it.

Modern military science and military technology is changing and developing with each passing day. If we are blind to this new situation, we would be practicing conservatism militarily. This would only bring about backwardness in our military science and technology and such backwardness would mean nothing else but taking a beating. Therefore, we must keep our eyes wide open, strive to learn and study the achievements made in modern military science, attach importance to the accomplishments made in new military technologies and practically enhance our efforts in investigating and studying the military situations of foreign countries. We must understand and learn from both positive and negative experiences gained by foreign countries in the military field. In short, we should "make foreign things serve China" and be good at absorbing the good things of foreign countries and at developing and creating the new things of our own.

At present, the world has become even more turbulent and uneasy. The factors of war are continuously increasing and the danger of war remains. The whole party, the whole army and the people of all nationalities of the whole country must maintain a high degree of vigilance and pay attention to military matters. For this reason, we must particularly cherish Mao Zedong military science and make efforts to study and understand it. It is the powerful ideological and theoretical weapon with which to strengthen the national defense, build a modernized revolutionary army and win victory in a future war against aggression. It will forever remain the treasure of the people of our country in defeating and prevailing over the enemy.

Deng Xiaoping Cultivates His Image as a Military Leader, 19 September 1981

56

In 1981 and 1982, Deng, wearing a military uniform, was prominently publicized as having taken part in summer maneuvers. This speech is one of the footprints left by this effort to demonstrate his ultimate authority over the armed forces, as well as to associate himself conspicuously with the goal and process of strengthening China's defense capabilities.

Fellow commanders, fighters and comrades: You have triumphantly accomplished your military exercise tasks. On behalf of the CPC Central Committee, the State Council, and the Military Commission of the CPC Central Committee, I wish to convey my warm congratulations and cordial regards to you.

The present exercise has tested the achievements of modernization and regularization building of our troops and has quite successfully embodied the characteristics of modern warfare. You have gained experience in various armed services fighting in coordination under modern conditions and have enhanced military and political quality, and the level of actual combat of the troops. This will be a vigorous impetus for the building, war preparedness, and training of the whole Army. You have attained the anticipated results in the military exercise and have been successful. This fully shows that the People's Army created by our party and armed with Mao Zedong Thought has good military and political quality, fine fighting style and strict organizational discipline, and combat effectiveness. We fully believe that with such a fine Army and the support of the broad masses, we will certainly be able to defeat any aggressor.

Our country is now at an important period in history when we are carrying forward the revolutionary cause and forging ahead into the future. Due to the effective implementation of the party's correct line, principles, and policies, there is further political stability and unity in the whole party, army, and nation, and the situation at all fronts is getting more and more favorable. Anti-hegemonism struggles are forging ahead in the international arena and the hegemonists are being further isolated. However, we must be aware that under the sharp contention between the superpowers and the acceleration of the Soviet hege-

monist in its global strategic plan, world peace and China's security will be seriously menaced. Therefore, we must be highly vigilant.

Our Army is the firm pillar of the people's democratic dictatorship and it shoulders the glorious mission of defending the socialist motherland and the modernization program. Therefore, it is imperative to build our Army into a powerful, modern, and regular revolutionary Army.

We must adhere to the four cardinal principles, strengthen political and ideological building, and strive to enable our troops to become a fine example in carrying out the party's line, principles, and policies.

We must, on the basis of constantly developing the national economy, improve our weaponry, and speed up the modernization of our national defense.

We must establish close ties between the Army and the government and the Army and people, strengthen unity within the Army, step up militia building, and inherit and carry forward the glorious tradition of the People's Army.

We must enhance military and political training, further improve the military and political quality of our troops, and strive to raise the ability of various armed services in fighting in coordination under modern conditions.

We must be modest and prudent, guard ourselves against arrogance and rashness, carry out the activities of "four haves, three stresses, and two fearlessnesses," and enhance the fostering of our style, so that our troops will have strict oganizationsl discipline. (In February 1981, according to a call by the CPC Central Committee on building socialist spiritual civilization and the characteristics of the Army, the PLA General Political Department put forward the slogan of "four haves, three stresses and two fearlessnesses" in the "Directives for Strengthening Youth Work in the Army." The slogan is: "Have ideals, morality, knowledge, and physical health; stress a soldier's appearance and bearing, courtesy, and discipline; and fear neither hardship nor sacrifice." In January 1983, in light of the relative wording in the documents of the 12th CPC Con-

---

[Deng Xiaoping, "Build a Powerful, Modern, and Regular Revolutionary Army," 19 September 1981 (in *Selected Works of Deng Xiaoping*, pp. 349–50).]

gress on building socialist spiritual civilization, the slogan was changed into "have ideals, morality, better education, and discipline; stress a soldier's appearance and bearing, courtesy, and hygiene; and fear neither hardship nor sacrifice.")

We must, in a down-to-earth manner, be prepared for anti-aggressive wars and make new contributions to the defending of world peace and the security of our territory, to the early return of Taiwan to the motherland, and to realizing the sacred great cause of reunification.

The Military Service Law, 31 May 1984

57

In 1955 the PRC had acquired a reasonably modern, as well as Communist, military system, including conscription, but it had been disrupted by the radical Defense Minister Lin Biao in 1965. Almost two decades later the gradual re-regularization of the PLA has received a boost from the adoption of this military service law, more comprehensive than anything of the kind that the PRC has had before.

CHAPTER ONE: GENERAL PRINCIPLES

Article 1. This law is formulated in accordance with Article 55 of the Constitution of the People's Republic of China: "it is the sacred obligation of every citizen of the People's Republic of China to defend the motherland and resist aggression. It is the honorable duty of citizens of the People's Republic of China to perform military service and join the militia in accordance with the law," and other related provisions.

Article 2. The military service system of the People's Republic of China utilizes compulsory military service for its main body while combining compulsory servicemen with volunteers, and militia with reserves.

Article 3. All citizens of the People's Republic of China, regardless of their nationality, race, profession, family background, religious belief and level of education, have the obligation to perform military service in accordance with this law. Those who are unsuitable for military service because of serious physiological defects or disability are exempted from military service.

Article 4. The armed forces of the People's Republic of China are composed of the Chinese People's Liberation Army, the Chinese People's Armed Police and the militia.

Article 5. Military service falls into active duty and reserve duty categories. Those who serve on active duty in the Chinese People's Liberation Army are called active military servicemen while those who are organized into militia units or have registered for reserve service are called reserve military servicemen.

Article 6. All active military servicemen and reserve military servicemen must observe the Constitution and the law and perform citizen's duties prescribed by the Constitution and the law and at the same time enjoy citizen's rights. The rights and obligations as a result of performing military service will be governed by this law and other military regulations.

Article 7. Active military servicemen must obey military rules and regulations, be faithful to their duties, and be ready to fight and defend the motherland at all times. Reserve military servicemen must take part in military training according to regulations and be ready at all times to join the Army and fight for the defense of the motherland.

Article 8. Those active or reserve military servicemen who have performed meritorious service may be conferred with medals, decorations or honorary titles.

Article 9. The system of military ranks is to be implemented in the Chinese People's Liberation Army.

Article 10. The Ministry of National Defense is responsible for military service work in the whole country under the leadership of the State Council and the Central Military Commission.

Various military regions are responsible for military service work within the jurisdiction of the respective regions in accordance with the tasks entrusted to them by the Ministry of National Defense.

Provincial military districts (garrison commands, garrison districts), military subdistricts (garrison districts), people's armed forces departments of various counties, autonomous counties, cities and districts under the jurisdiction of cities are responsible for military service work within their own jurisdiction under the leadership of higher military organizations and the people's governments at the same level.

Various organs, organizations, enterprises and people's governments of various townships, nationality

[New China News Agency, 4 June 1984.]

townships and towns are to implement military service work in accordance with the stipulations of this law. In units with people's armed forces departments, military service work is to be handled by people's armed forces departments. In units without people's armed forces departments, military service work is to be handled by designated departments.

CHAPTER TWO: PEACETIME CALL-UP

Article 11. The number, requirements and times of requirements and times of recruitment for active service in the whole country each year are to be decided by the orders of the State Council and the Central Military Commission.

Article 12. Male citizens reaching 18 years of age before 31 December each year should be drafted for active service. Those who are not drafted during that year may be drafted for active military service before they reach 22 years of age.

According to the need of military units, female citizens may be drafted in accordance with the above stipulation.

According to the needs of military units and on a voluntary basis, male and female citizens who do not reach the age of 18 before 31 December of that year may be drafted for active service.

Article 13. All male citizens who reach the age of 18 before 31 December of the year should register for military service no later than 30 September of the year according to the arrangements made by the military service organs of counties, autonomous counties, cities or districts under the jurisdiction of cities. Those who have registered for military service and been qualified in preliminary screening shall be called conscript citizens.

Article 14. During the conscription period, the conscript citizens should report to designated physical examination stations at prescribed times for physical examination in accordance with the notifications issued by the military service organs of counties, autonomous counties, cities or districts under the jurisdiction of cities.

The conscript citizens who meet active service requirements and whose conscription has been approved by the military service organs of counties, autonomous counties, cities or districts under the jurisdiction of cities shall be conscripted into active service.

Article 15. The military service of a conscript citizen may be deferred if he is the only person working to support his family or if he is a student attending a full-time school.

Article 16. A conscript citizen who is detained pending investigation, prosecution or trial; or who has been sentenced to imprisonment or forced labor; or is under surveillance or serving a sentence shall not be conscripted.

CHAPTER THREE: ACTIVE SERVICE AND RESERVE SERVICE OF ENLISTED MEN

Article 17. Enlisted men include compulsory servicemen and volunteers.

Article 18. The term of active service for compulsory servicemen is 3 years in the Army or 4 years in the Navy or Air Force.

After completion of the term of active service, the compulsory servicemen may serve an extra term of active service according to the needs of the armed forces and the servicemen's own free will. The extra term of active service shall be 1 to 2 years in the Army, or 1 year in the Navy or in the Air Force.

Article 19. Compulsory servicemen who have become specialized technical personnel after 5 years of active service, including the extra term of active service, may change their service status into one of volunteer if they apply for such a status change and if their applications are approved by organs at or above division level.

The term of voluntary active service shall be at least 8 years and no more than 12 years counting from the day of the status change. Volunteers shall not be older than 35 years of age. Voluntary service may be appropriately extended if the armed forces have special needs, the volunteers are willing to serve the extended service and the extension is approved by organs at or above the corps level.

Article 20. Enlisted men should be discharged from active service after they complete their terms of active service. They may be discharged from active service sooner if earlier discharge is justified by the need for strength reduction in the armed forces, by the enlisted men's physical unfitness certified by a military hospital, or by other special reasons, and is approved by organs at or above the division level.

Article 21. After enlisted men are discharged from active service, the armed forces shall place them in enlisted reserve service if they meet the reserve requirements, or place them in officer reserve service if they are evaluated as suitable for officer duties.

Enlisted men who have been discharged from active service and placed in reserve service by the armed forces should register for reserve service with the military service organs of counties, autonomous counties, cities or districts under the jurisdiction of cities within 30 days after they return to their places of residence.

Article 22. The conscript citizens who have registered for military service in accordance with the stipulations of Article 13 of this law, but who have not been conscripted, should serve enlisted reserve service.

Article 23. The ages for enlisted reserve service are from 18 to 35 years.

Article 24. Enlisted reserve service is classified into first category and second category.

First category enlisted reserve service includes the following personnel: 1) persons organized into the primary militia organizations in accordance with the stipulations of Article 38 of this law; 2) enlisted men under the age of 28 who have been discharged from active service and registered for reserve service and are working in units where there are no militia organizations; and 3) specialized technical personnel under the age of 28 who have registered for reserve service.

Second category enlisted reserve service includes the following personnel: 1) persons organized into ordinary militia organizations in accordance with the stipulations of Article 38 of this law; 2) enlisted men between 29 and 35 years of age who have been discharged from active service, registered for reserve service, working in units where there are no militia organizations, and other male citizens who meet enlisted reserve service requirements.

Persons serving in first category enlisted reserve service shall shift to second category reserve service after they reach the age of 29. Persons serving in second category enlisted reserve service shall be discharged from reserve service after they reach the age of 35.

CHAPTER FOUR: ACTIVE AND RESERVE DUTIES OF OFFICERS

Article 25. Active-duty officers are replenished by the following personnel:

1. Graduates from military institutions and academies;

2. Enlisted men who have received officer training in an organization that operates with the approval of the Central Military Commission and who have passed the fitness tests for officers;

3. Graduates from institutions of higher learning and special and technical secondary schools, who are suited to serve as officers;

4. Non-military cadres and individual vocational and technical personnel recruited by non-military departments in the Army.

In time of war, active-duty officers are also replenished by the following personnel:

1. Enlisted men who can be directly appointed as officers;

2. Officers on reserve duty who have been called up, and cadres in non-military departments who are suited to serving in the Army on active duty.

Article 26. Officers on reserve duty include the following personnel:

1. Officers who withdraw from active duty to become reserves;

2. Enlisted men who are discharged from active military service and are made to serve as reserve officers;

3. Graduates from institutions of higher learning who are made to serve as reserve officers;

4. Professional People's Armed Forces cadres and military cadres who are made to serve as reserve officers;

5. Cadres and professional and technical personnel in non-military departments who are made to serve as reserve officers.

Article 27. The top age limit for active and reserve duty officers is specified by the officers' service regulations of the Chinese PLA.

Article 28. Active-duty officers who have reached the specified upper age limit should withdraw from active duty. Those who have not reached the upper age limit may also withdraw from active duty if they need to do so because of exceptional circumstances. This withdrawal is subject to approval.

When an officer withdraws from active duty, he should serve as a reserve officer if he meets the requirements.

Article 29. An active-duty officer who withdraws from active duty and serves as a reserve officer, a soldier who withdraws from active duty and is made to serve as a reserve officer or a graduate from an institute of higher learning who is made to serve as a reserve officer should report to the local military service organ in the county, autonomous county, city or municipal district to register himself as an Army reserve officer within a period of 30 days after he arrives in the work unit or in the locality where he resides.

The military service organs of the county, autonomous county, city or municipal district should accept registration from professional People's Armed Forces cadres, militia cadres and those cadres and professional and technical personnel in non-military departments who are suited to serve as officers and report them to the military organ at the higher level for approval so that they may serve as reserve officers.

Reserve officers who have reached the upper age limit, set for reserves should withdraw from reserve duty.

CHAPTER FIVE: CADETS RECRUITED FROM AMONG YOUNG STUDENTS BY MILITARY INSTITUTIONS AND ACADEMIES

Article 30. In accordance with the needs of army building, military institutions and academies may recruit cadets from among young students. The age of cadets is not restricted by the age limit for those recruits who serve active duty.

Article 31. After passing the examinations for their studies, the cadets will be issued graduation diplomas by the military institutions and academies appointed as active-duty officers or non-military cadres according to the regulations.

Article 32. Cadres who have failed to pass the examinations after completing their studies in specified courses will be issued certificates by the military institutions and academies for the completion of the courses. They should return to the place of their household registration before they attended the military institution or academy, and arrangements will be made by the people's government of the county, autonomous county, city or municipal district to help them settle down according to the measures specified by the state in dealing with those who have completed the courses in similar institutions and academies.

Article 33. Cadets who are unsuited to continue their studies in military institutions and academies due to chronic diseases or other reasons and whose requests for withdrawal have been approved will be issued certificates of attendance by institutions and academies. Arrangements will be made by the people's government in the county, autonomous county, city or municipal district where their household registration was before they attended the military institution or academy to meet them and help them settle down.

Article 34. Cadets who are expelled from the institutions and academies should be taken care of by the people's government in the county, autonomous county, city or municipal district where their household registrations were before they attended the military institution or academy, and handled according to the measures specified by the state in dealing with those who have been expelled by similar institutions and academies.

Article 35. The stipulations in Article 31, Article 32, Article

33 and Article 34 of this law are also applicable to cadets recruited from among active-duty enlisted men.

CHAPTER SIX: THE MILITIA

Article 36. The militia is an armed mass organization which is not divorced from production and is the Chinese People's Liberation Army's assistant and reserve force.

The tasks of the militia are as follows:

1. The militia actively takes part in building socialist modernization and takes the lead in accomplishing production and other tasks.

2. The militia undertakes tasks in preparation against war, defends the frontiers and maintains social security.

3. The militia is ready at all times to join the Army and take part in military operations to resist aggression and defend the motherland.

Article 37. Various townships, nationality townships, towns and enterprises are to set up militia organizations. Male citizens from age 18 to 35 who meet the requirements for performing military service, with the exception of those who are drafted for active military service, are to be organized into militia organizations as reserves. The age for militia cadres may be extended in an appropriate manner.

In units which do not set up militia organizations, male citizens who meet the conditions for performing military service are to register for reserve service.

Article 38. Militiamen are divided into primary militiamen and general militiamen. Soldiers retired from active service and those who have received military training or those who have been selected to receive military training under age 28 are organized into primary militia units, while other male citizens from 18 to 35 who meet the conditions for performing military service are organized into general militia units.

According to need, female citizens may be absorbed into primary militia units.

The age for primary militiamen in frontier and coastal areas, minority nationality regions and units in cities with special situations may be extended in an appropriate manner.

CHAPTER SEVEN: MILITARY TRAINING FOR RESERVE PERSONNEL

Article 39. Military training for soldiers in reserve service is to be conducted by militia organizations or conducted independently.

Primary militiamen from 18 to 20 who have not served active military duty are to receive 30 to 40 days' military training. The training period for specialized and technical militiamen may be extended appropriately according to the actual need.

The retraining of militiamen who have served active military duty and received military training and the training of general militiamen and reserve soldiers who have not been organized into militia units are to be conducted

in accordance with the regulations of the Central Military Commission.

Article 40. Reserve officers should receive 3 to 6 months' military training during their service period.

Article 41. In times of necessity, the State Council and the Central Military Commission may order reserve personnel to take part in crash training programs.

Article 42. The original work units of the reserves in various organs, organizations, enterprises and establishments are to pay wages and bonuses and provide other welfare treatment as usual to personnel in reserve service when they take part in military training.

The people's governments of various townships, nationality townships and towns are to pay subsidies to reserve servicemen in rural areas when they take part in military training to make up for their loss of working time based on the method of sharing the burden and the income of similar labor.

CHAPTER EIGHT: MILITARY TRAINING FOR STUDENTS OF SCHOOLS OF HIGHER LEARNING AND SENIOR MIDDLE SCHOOLS

Article 43. Students of schools of higher learning must receive basic military training during their period of schooling.

According to the needs of national defense building, students who are suitable for assuming officer's duties are to receive additional short-term concentrated training. Those who pass examination and evaluation will serve as reserve officers with the approval of military organizations.

Article 44. Schools of higher learning should set up military training organizations, assign military instructors and organize students to undergo military training.

The short-term concentrated training for reserve officers stipulated in the second paragraph of Article 43 shall be jointly organized and conducted by officers on active service dispatched by military departments and the military training organizations of schools of higher learning.

Article 45. Senior middle schools and schools equivalent to senior middle schools should assign military instructors to conduct military training among students.

Article 46. The Ministry of Education and the Ministry of National Defense shall be responsible for the military training at schools of higher learning and senior middle schools. Education and military departments should set up working organizations in charge of students' military training or assign special personnel to take charge of the work.

CHAPTER NINE: MOBILIZATION OF MILITARY PERSONNEL IN WARTIME

Article 47. In order to deal with the enemy's surprise attack and resist aggression, people's governments and military organizations at all levels should make sufficient preparations in peacetime for the mobilization of military personnel in wartime.

Article 48. After the state issues a mobilization order, people's governments and military organizations at all levels should take the following mobilization actions immediately:

1. The discharge of armymen from active service should be stopped and armymen on leave or visiting relatives should immediately return to their own units;

2. Reserve personnel should be prepared to respond to the call to active service at any time and must report to the designated place on time upon receiving the notice;

3. Responsible persons of offices, organizations, enterprises and institutions, as well as people's governments of townships and nationality townships and towns, must organize the reserve personnel of each unit, who have been called up, to report to the designated place on time; and

4. Transportation departments must give priority to transporting reserve personnel who have been called up and armymen on active service who are returning to their own units.

Article 49. In the event of an extraordinary situation in wartime, the State Council and the Central Military Commission can make the decision to conscript male citizens between the ages of 36 to 45 to serve active duty.

Article 50. Armymen on active service who need to be demobilized at the end of a war should be discharged in groups and by stages in accordance with the demobilization order of the State Council and the Central Military Commission and should be given proper arrangements by people's governments at various levels.

CHAPTER TEN: PREFERENTIAL TREATMENT TO ARMYMEN ON ACTIVE SERVICE AND ARRANGEMENTS FOR DISCHARGED ARMYMEN

Article 51. Armymen on active service, disabled revolutionary armymen, armymen discharged from active service, and families of revolutionary martyrs, armymen who sacrificed their life or died of ailments, and armymen on active service should be respected by the community and given preferential treatment by the state and the masses of people.

Article 52. Disabled revolutionary armymen have priority in purchasing tickets for trains, steamboats, airplanes and long-distance buses and shall be given a discount in accordance with regulations.

Surface mail sent by compulsory servicemen from their units shall be delivered without postage.

Article 53. Armymen on active service who become disabled because of an injury during a war or performing an official duty shall be issued a disabled revolutionary armyman's compensation certificate by the PLA units according to the degree of the disability. Discharged special-and-first-class disabled revolutionary armymen shall be given a lifetime pension by the state. Second- and third-class disabled revolutionary armymen living in cities or towns shall be given whatever job they can do by the people's government of the county, autonomous county, city or district directly under the city where they take up residence, and those living in rural areas shall be given suitable jobs in local

enterprises and institutions whenever available, otherwise they shall be given disability pension according to regulations to ensure their livelihood.

Article 54. Families of compulsory servicemen living in the countryside shall be given preferential treatment in balancing the burden by the people's government of township, nationality township or town.

The specific methods and standards for the preferential treatment shall be decided upon by provincial, autonomous regional and municipal people's governments.

Families of compulsory servicemen living in urban areas who have difficulty in their daily life shall be given proper subsidy by the people's government of the county, autonomous county, city or district directly under the city.

Article 55. Families of armymen on active service who sacrifice their life or die of ailments shall be given pension by the state in a lump sum. Those who are incapable of working or do not have a fixed income to maintain their daily life shall be given an additional pension by the state on a regular basis.

Article 56. After being discharged from active service, compulsory servicemen shall, in accordance with the principle of returning to where they came from, be taken care of by the people's government of the county, autonomous county, city or district directly under the city that has drafted them:

1. The township, nationality township and town people's governments shall arrange for the production and livelihood of compulsory servicemen residing in rural areas after they are discharged from active service. Offices, organizations, enterprises, and institutions should give them appropriate preferential treatment when recruiting staff members and workers from rural areas.

2. After being discharged from active service, compulsory servicemen residing in urban areas shall be assigned jobs by the people's government of the county, autonomous county, city or district directly under the city. Those who were regular staff members and workers in offices, organizations, enterprises and institutions before the draft are allowed to be reinstated to their former posts.

3. After being discharged from active service, compulsory servicemen shall be given priority in entrance examinations for institutes of higher learning and secondary specialized schools, provided they make the same score as other applicants.

Article 57. Compulsory servicemen who contract mental disease during service shall be sent to local hospitals for treatment or home for convalescence, depending on the degree of the seriousness of the disease, after being discharged from active service. All the necessary medical and living expenses shall be taken care of by the people's government of the county, autonomous county, city or district directly under the city.

Compulsory servicemen who contract chronic disease while in the service and who have a relapse after being discharged and need to receive medical treatment shall be taken care of by local health institutions. The people's government of the county, autonomous county, city or district directly under the city shall subsidize all necessary medical and living expenses if the patient cannot afford to pay them.

Article 58. After being discharged from active service, volunteers shall be assigned jobs by the people's government of the county, autonomous county, city or district directly under the city that has recruited them. Under special circumstances, their jobs can be arranged in an overall manner by the people's government at the next higher level, or by provincial, autonomous regional, or municipal people's governments. Those who volunteer to return to the countryside to take part in agricultural production should be encouraged and given additional allowances for setting up a home in a new place.

Volunteers who become disabled while taking part in war or performing official duty or who have basically lost the capability to work because of breakdown from constant overwork during active service shall, upon completing discharge procedures, be taken care of by the people's government of the county, autonomous county, city or district directly under the city that recruited them or where their parents, spouse or children reside.

Article 59. Proper arrangements shall be made by the state for officers after being discharged.

Article 60. Militiamen who sacrifice their life or become disabled while participating in war or performing official duty and reserve personnel and students who sacrifice their lives or become disabled while taking part in military training, shall be given compensation and preferential treatment by local people's governments according to the regulations concerning compensation and preferential treatment to militiamen.

CHAPTER ELEVEN: PENALTIES

Article 61. According to the regulations of this law, citizens who have the obligation but refuse and evade registration for military service, citizens who have been enlisted but refuse and evade enlistment, and reserve personnel who refuse and evade military training after repeated admonition shall be forced by grassroot people's governments to fulfill the obligation to perform military service.

In wartime, reserve personnel who refuse and evade enlistment or military training to a serious degree shall be punished in accordance with the first section of Article 6 of the "Provisional Regulations of the People's Republic of China on Punishing Dereliction of Duty by Armymen."

Article 62. State functionaries who accept bribes, engage in malpractice to seek private gains, or commit dereliction of duty while handling conscription work and thus inflict serious losses to the work shall be respectively punished according to Article 185 and Article 187 of the "Criminal Law of the People's Republic of China." Those with mild offenses can be given administrative discipline.

CHAPTER TWELVE: APPENDIX

Article 63. This law applies to the Chinese People's Armed Police Force.

Article 64. Regulations shall be formulated separately for the posts of civilian cadres which the Chinese People's Liberation Army sets up in accordance with the needs.

Article 65. This law comes into force on 1 October 1984.

Intellectuals, Dissent, and Human Rights

The Trial of Wei Jingsheng, 16 October 1979

This article endorses, in almost savage language, the fifteen-year sentence passed on Wei, a dissenting intellectual who was found guilty of giving military secrets (actually, seemingly harmless information relating to the Sino-Vietnamese War of 1979) to foreign journalists. This case was intended to make an example of Wei and to signal an abrupt end of the so-called Beijing Spring of 1978–79, during which it appears that, for the purpose of undermining Hua Guofeng, somewhat greater freedom of speech, as well as the putting up of posters critical of the regime, had been permitted. For excerpts of the prosecution's statement and Wei's defense at the trial, see the New York Times, *15 November 1979 and the* Asian Wall Street Journal, *24 November 1979. These excerpts are based on the posters put up at Democracy Wall and circulated by dissident sources.*

In accordance with the provisions of our laws, the Beijing Municipal Intermediate People's Court openly tried Wei Jingsheng on 16 October for his counterrevolutionary crimes, sentenced him to 15 years' imprisonment and deprived him of his political rights for 3 years after he serves his term. This judgment has upheld the sanctity of our country's legal system and is in the basic interest of the Chinese people, and it is bound to be supported by the broad masses of people.

Ours is a socialist state of the dictatorship of the proletariat led by the working class and based on the alliance of workers and peasants. This state was finally founded through a protracted heroic struggle by the Chinese people who, under the leadership of the CCP, had shed their blood and made sacrifices to overcome all difficulties. Our country has won tremendous victories in the socialist revolution and construction over the past 30 years. Earth-shaking revolutionary changes have taken place in our motherland, which has been built into a socialist country with the beginnings of prosperity. The great future of the Chinese people is linked closely with the great prospects of the socialist system.

Only socialism can save China. The CCP is the core of leadership of the whole Chinese people. The guiding ideology of the PRC is Marxism-Leninism-Mao Zedong Thought. All this is explicitly stipulated in the Constitution of our country. Every citizen must support the leadership of the CCP and the socialist system, uphold the unification of the motherland and the unity of all nationalities and abide by the Constitution and laws. This is also explicitly stipulated in the Constitution. If anyone carries out criminal activities with a view to rejecting Marxism-Leninism-

Mao Zedong Thought and CCP leadership and subverting the socialist system of the dictatorship of the proletariat, he violates the Constitution and harms the basic interests of the state and the people and should be punished according to the law.

The Constitution of our country guarantees the democratic rights of the broad masses of the people. The people have the right to criticize the work of the government, and the people's government welcomes criticisms from the broad masses of people and has the courage to make self-criticism.

However, it is absolutely impermissible for anyone in our socialist country to plot and engage in sabotage to subvert the dictatorship of the proletariat and the socialist system in the name of socialist democracy. To overthrow the dictatorship of the proletariat and the socialist system, Wei Jingsheng viciously slandered Marxism-Leninism-Mao Zedong Thought and the CCP in his "articles" and journal. He cursed the socialist system as an "evil system" and agitated the masses to "engage in a reform of the socialist system" and "seize power." These are out-and-out counterrevolutionary crimes. The criminal Wei Jingsheng was so frenzied that he provided a foreigner with military intelligence concerning our country's self-defensive counterattacks against Vietnam. He thus committed the crime of betraying his motherland. The Constitution of our country stipulates: "The state safeguards the socialist system, suppresses all treasonable and counterrevolutionary activities and punishes all traitors and counterrevolutionaries." It is completely correct and much to the satisfaction of the people for the people's court to convict the criminal Wei Jingsheng in accordance with the related stipulations of the "PRC Regulations Concerning Punishment for Counterrevolution," so that the socialist system can be safeguarded, the dictatorship of the proletariat can be consolidated and socialist modernization can be smoothly

---

["Resolutely Punish Counterrevolutionary Criminals," *People's Daily*, 17 October 1979.]

carried forward. As to the criminal Wei Jingsheng, he simply deserves the punishment.

For a time there were even people who tried to defend such a counterrevolutionary criminal as Wei Jingsheng, even praising him as a "pioneer for human rights" and as a "democratic fighter." Some of these people might have been ignorant of the truth and the inside details about Wei Jingsheng, and they were thus deceived. There was also a very small number of people whose aims were similar to Wei Jingsheng's and who tried to take advantage of his criminal activities to undermine our country's stability and unity, sabotage our socialist modernization and subvert our dictatorship of the proletariat and socialist system. We want to advise these people: Your calculations are wrong. You had better stop daydreaming!

Although there are still counterrevolutionaries like Wei Jingsheng in our country at this time, they are just a handful. The masses of people in our country support the Chinese Communist Party and ardently love the socialist motherland. Our socialist system under the dictatorship of the proletariat is now more consolidated than ever before. Our country's sovereignty and the dignity of its laws brook

no violation. Regardless of the banners of so-called "human rights," "democracy" and what-not flaunted by Wei Jingsheng and regardless of who openly tried to defend him, because of the irrefutable evidence of his counterrevolutionary crimes he must be punished according to the law.

Here we also want to advise those people who were fooled and deceived to fully understand: Socialist democracy must be developed and the socialist legal system must be strengthened. But anyone who actually engages in counterrevolutionary activities in the name of "democracy" must know that the people throughout the country will not let him.

At present, under the leadership of the party Central Committee, the people throughout our country are dedicated heart and soul to realizing the four modernizations, and the situation is becoming better and better. Of course, we also know that in our country there still exist a very small number of counterrevolutionaries and criminals who are hostile to and are sabotaging the socialist modernization of our country. We should never slacken our efforts for class struggle with them. Our dictatorship of the proletariat must never be weakened to any extent.

Human Rights as a Bourgeois Invention, 26 October 1979

The slogan and concept of human rights have had considerable appeal in China, especially among intellectuals. Here the human rights issue is semiofficially dismissed as a bourgeois notion having no real relevance to a socialist society.

The human rights question is an important topic in modern international political activities. In China, in the process of promoting socialist democracy, people have been discussing this question for some time now. How, after all, should we understand and deal with the human rights question? Only by making a historical and concrete analysis from a Marxist standpoint can we arrive at a more appropriate conclusion.

HUMAN RIGHTS ARE A PRODUCT OF HISTORY

The bourgeoisie raised the slogan of human rights in the past. Its theoretical basis was the theory of "the natural rights of man."

As early as the Renaissance in Europe, the antecedents of emerging bourgeois thinkers conceived the early ideas on human rights. Enlightened thinkers of 17th and 18th century Europe, inspired by bourgeois philosophers

of the time, systematically expounded the theory of the natural rights of man in their writings to attack the privileges and divine right of feudal aristocrats and of priests. The Englishman Locke (1632–1704) said: "Man is born free, equal and independent" and "nobody should infringe upon others' lives, health, freedom or property" ("On Government," Part II, published by the Commercial Press in 1964, pp. 59, 6). He added: "The people have a natural right, which does not change nor can it be denied" (quoted from "Major Viewpoints of Bourgeois Jurists Concerning Questions of the State and Legal Rights," pp. 15–16). Rousseau (1712–1778), a prominent exponent of enlightened thought in France, asserted: "Everyone is born free and equal. To renounce one's freedom is to renounce one's moral stature and to cede one's rights to a general will of which one is part" ("The Social Contract," published in 1963 by the Commercial Press, pp. 7, 13). According to enlightened thinkers, all men are born free and equal and they have the right to live and acquire property. "The people have the right to decide for themselves." If the rulers became despotic tyrants and infringed upon people's rights, the latter had the right to topple the despotic rule and restore their natural rights.

["A Brief Discussion of Human Rights," Beijing *Guangming Daily*, 26 October 1979.]

The theory of the natural rights of man embodied the interests and aspirations of the emerging bourgeoisie. What the enlightened thinkers aspired to was nothing but the utopian kingdom of the bourgeoisie where freedom and equality would be theirs for the asking. However, this theory basically negated the autocratic rule of feudal monarchs and basically negated the religious doctrine that all things were for God and that man should dedicate all he had to God. This theory was considered revolutionary at that time.

The theory of "the natural rights of man" was a powerful ideological weapon of the emerging bourgeoisie in their revolution against the feudal system. Human rights were their major slogan, and the basic content of the bourgeois political program.

The war of independence in the American colonies broke out in 1775. This was "a great and truly emancipating and revolutionary war in American history" ("Selected Works of Lenin," Vol. 3, p. 586). On 4 July 1776, a continental conference composed of the representatives of 13 colonies adopted the "Declaration of Independence," which proclaimed the separation of 13 North American colonies from British rule and the inauguration of the United States of America. The declaration was drafted by Jefferson, an exponent of the natural rights of man. According to the declaration, "All men are created equal, and they are endowed by their creator with certain unalienable rights, such as life, liberty and the pursuit of happiness." The declaration pointed out that to safeguard these rights people set up a government and if any government infringes upon these rights, people have the right to change it, replace it and set up a new government. For the first time this declaration used a political program to define the principle of human rights. This was of progressive significance at a time when the European continent was dominated by feudal autocracy. Marx called it "the first declaration of human rights" (Collected Works of Marx and Engels, Vol. 16, p. 20).

The French Revolution broke out in 1789. A constituent assembly was formed in August to adopt "The Declaration of Human and Civic Rights." This was called "A Declaration of Human Rights," which for the first time raised the slogan of "human rights." It upheld that "all men are born free and enjoy equal rights." "Any political alliance aims to protect people's inalienable and natural rights, which consist of freedom, property, security and the right to resist oppression." The French Constituent Assembly enacted the Constitution in 1791 and inserted this declaration as a preface to the Constitution. Thus, "The Declaration of Human Rights" for the first time legally affirmed the principles of human rights including freedom and equality put forward by bourgeois enlightened thinkers. This contributed significantly to inspiring people's struggle and promoting the bourgeois revolution.

Marx pointed out that human rights represented "the most general form of rights" (Collected Works of Marx and Engels, Vol. 3, p. 228). In form, human rights recognize no differences between people in nationality, sex, religion and creed and especially in class, cover all men and are of a universal nature. The bourgeoisie regard such rights as inborn and natural. But demands and concepts of human rights were born historically. Before the bourgeoisie, various classes waged struggles to win or maintain their own political, economic and even survival rights and put forward various slogans. But they never put forward such a universal slogan as human rights. The slave-owning classes

and feudal and landlord classes openly asserted their traditional privileges. Not being representative of new forms of production, the slave class and the peasant class also did not raise a universal human rights slogan. As far as the economic foundation is concerned, the human rights slogan in universal form can only be a product of capitalist commodity and money relations. Capital represents inborn "equals." Whether they are capitalists owning money or proletarians who have only their own labor to sell as a commodity, possessors of commodities are equal before the law. The relations between them as possessors of commodities are equal, operating on the principle of exchange of equal values. Capitalist owners of commodities must also be free men unrestricted in action. This applies to the capitalists and is also true of hired workers. The latter must get rid of feudal shackles to become free men who can freely sell their labor. When the development of capitalism had reached a certain stage, it sharply clashed with the feudal system. Feudal guilds and various feudal privileges became serious obstacles standing in the way of further capitalist progress. Such demands as getting rid of feudal shackles, removing feudal inequality and establishing equal rights and freedom of action were put on the agenda and quickly spread to become universal demands that went beyond the limits of individual countries. Thus, freedom and equality were naturally declared as human rights. The idea of human rights was born on such a social foundation. Just as Engels pointed out, "Only on this foundation can we discuss man's equality and the problem of human rights" (Anti-Duhring, p. 101).

The human rights put forward by the bourgeoisie, although universal and including all people in form, absolutely cannot include all people in reality. They can only be bourgeois rights. In capitalist society, the bourgeoisie possess the means of production and have the right to exploit and enslave the proletariat. Yet the proletariat have nothing, and their most fundamental right is actually nothing but freedom or equality in selling their own labor. Marx and Engels pointed out: "One of the human rights declared as most important is bourgeois ownership" (Anti-Duhring, p. 15). "Equality in exploiting labor is a primary human right of capital" (Capital, Vol. 1, p. 324). Though the bourgeoisie treat the contents of human rights as civil rights and clearly set them in the constitution, yet in real life in capitalist society only the bourgeoisie fully enjoy human rights. Marx said, "Human rights themselves are privileges" (Collected Works of Marx and Engels, Vol. 3, p. 229). The bourgeoisie merely substituted the privileges of money for the feudalistic class privileges and hereditary privileges. In relation to the feudalistic privileges, the human rights proclaimed by the bourgeoisie were a historical progress. However, this kind of human rights was narrow and extremely hypocritical for the proletariat and the masses of working people.

In the past 200 to 300 years, the slogan of human rights put forward by the bourgeoisie has had a widespread influence in the capitalistic countries. However, human rights have remained a principle of internal political life and of legislation in the capitalist countries. It was during World War II that human rights really became an instrument of international political struggle and a guiding principle of international law.

In 1942, the 26 nations (including the United States, China and the Soviet Union) fighting against the German, Italian and Japanese fascists signed the "Charter of the

United Nations" and pointed out: "We deeply believe that total victory over the enemy is extremely necessary for safeguarding life, liberty, independence and religious freedom and also protecting human rights and justice within our own and other countries." In 1945, the United Nations was formally set up. The "Charter of the United Nations" declared: "We are determined to preserve the future generations from the indescribable tragedy of war twice visited on mankind within our generation, and we reiterate our belief in basic human rights, the respect and value of human character and equality between men and women and between all nations big and small." The promotion of human rights is one of the guiding principles of the United Nations.

In World War II the atrocities committed by the German, Italian and Japanese fascists resulted in great sufferings for mankind. They evoked strong indignation on the part of people of all countries throughout the world, who universally called for upholding human rights. The articles of the "Charter of the United Nations" on human rights reflect the demands and aspirations of people throughout the world and are of progressive significance in opposing fascism.

On 10 December 1948, the United Nations passed the "Declaration of Human Rights." This declaration defined the specific contents of individual freedom and the political rights as well as social, economic and cultural rights of the individual. The "Declaration of Human Rights" holds: "All men are born free and are equal in dignity and rights." Its basic idea is still the "theory of natural rights" of the bourgeoisie. However, because the contents of this declaration have to a certain extent reflected the anti-war feeling of the people of various countries after the war and their desire for democracy, peace and the protection of their social and economic rights, it is still of progressive significance and has a very great impact internationally.

In recent years, many Third World countries have made new demands on the human rights question. They question interpretations of the human rights concept, and they oppose the fact that UN activities relating to human rights are dominated solely by European standards. They point out that human rights are not only the rights and basic freedom of the individual, but should also include the rights of the nation. They are not only political rights, but should also include social, economic and cultural rights. They advocate that the human rights activities of the United Nations should give priority to solving problems of serious large-scale international violations of human rights, solving racial segregation, all forms of racial discrimination, colonialism, foreign domination, occupation and aggression and threats to national sovereignty, unity and territorial integrity and also serious large-scale violations of the human rights of various nations and individuals caused by the refusal to acknowledge the full rights of various countries to have their own say regarding their own wealth and natural resources. In short, they stress that it is necessary to insure the collective rights of all nations and peoples in international relations and to link the struggle to safeguard human rights with the struggle against aggression, for national independence, against international exploitation and to develop the national economy. Obviously, such demands for human rights are anti-imperialist, anticolonialist and antihegemonist in nature and have a positive significance.

Any country which practices hegemony and oppresses the people of other countries, either on a world scale or in a region, will inevitably at the same time oppress the people of its own country. Where the rights of the people are violated on a large scale, it often creates or leads to the creation of large numbers of refugees. The current Indochinese refugee problem is a large-scale violation of human rights. It is causing tens of thousands of people to drown in the ocean. It is only natural that this is strongly condemned by international opinion.

"Human rights" is also a slogan used by the imperialists and the bourgeoisie to attack our dictatorship of the proletariat and our socialist system. Seeing things through the eyes of bourgeois individualist freedom, they regard our socialist order, which combines centralism with democracy and discipline with freedom, as the absence of human rights in a socialist country. They viciously attack measures taken by our dictatorship of the proletariat(such as suppression of counterrevolutionaries) as a violation of human rights. These attacks and vilifications must be resolutely refuted. We have realized the public ownership of the means of production and abolished the system of exploitation of man by man. In our Constitution it is provided that all citizens enjoy broad democratic rights. Although our system must be constantly perfected and there are still some problems in our work, our socialist system guarantees the masses of laboring people all kinds of basic rights from the very foundation. This is a fact for all to see. We have not forgotten that in old China a sign at the gate of a park read "No Admittance for Dogs and Chinese." In this barbarous and shameless way, the foreign aggressors humiliated the Chinese people and denied outright that the Chinese people had any human rights at all. It was only after the Chinese people strongly resisted and, especially under the leadership of the Chinese Communist Party, overthrew the three big mountains of imperialism, feudalism and bureaucrat capitalism, that such ugly things were eliminated forever, that the Chinese people straightened up, raised their heads and gained their basic rights as human beings. What right do the imperialists have to discuss so-called human rights in China?

It should be pointed out that because the concept of human rights itself is abstract and indefinite, it can be interpreted in different ways and given different content from different angles. Now internationally human rights have almost become an all-embracing concept of rights, and everyone has his own interpretation. At the same time, because political systems and concrete conditions differ from country to country, the rights of citizens provided by law are also different. This is an internal affair of each country. We should analyze on the basis of concrete conditions and adopt a proper attitude and flexible tactics in dealing with the human rights question. We must not deal with it in a simplistic manner.

THE BASIC SLOGAN OF THE PROLETARIAT IS TO ELIMINATE CLASSES

How should the proletariat approach the slogan of human rights? In the "Introduction of 'Criticism of the Hegelian Philosophy'" he wrote between the end of 1843 and January 1844, Marx pointed out that the proletariat "can no longer seek help from its historical rights, but only from human rights" ("Selected Works of Marx and Engels," Vol. 1, p. 14). But the same article also pointed out that the proletariat "cannot liberate itself unless, in liberating itself from all other social spheres, it liberates all these social spheres at the same time." Obviously, the human rights mentioned by Marx in the article referred to the elimination of private ownership and of classes, liberation of all mankind and realization of communism. At that time, Marx had already turned from idealism to materialism and from revolutionary democracy to communism, but in his expounding of theoretical viewpoints and in his choice of words the influence and traces of the former were still visible. Later on, Marx and Engels definitely expressed their principled attitude toward human rights: "When mentioning rights, we and many other people have emphatically pointed out the communist stand against political rights, personal rights and the most ordinary form of rights, that is, human rights" ("Collected Works of Marx and Engels," Vol. 3, pp. 228–229). Any rights take inequality as the premise and are applied to different persons with the same yardstick. Therefore, they actually mean inequality. The goal of the communists is to liberate all mankind and realize actual equality among all members of society. For this reason, communists absolutely should not take the slogan of human rights as their basic slogan. In "the earliest mature Marxist works, the 'Impoverishment of Philosophy' and the 'Communist Manifesto,'" (quoting Lenin), the slogan of human rights was not mentioned. Not mentioning the slogan of human rights in such programmatic communist documents as the "Communist Manifesto" naturally should be regarded as an oversight or omission. Later on, in leading the international workers' movement, Marx again did not advocate the use of the slogan of human rights. There was only one exception, which appeared in 1864 when Marx drafted the provisional regulations of the International Workers' Association (the First International). A sentence in the preface to these regulations read: "One has the duty to demand human rights and citizen rights not only for oneself but also for anyone who fulfills his obligations" ("Collected Works of Marx and Engels," Vol. 16, p. 16). However, this sentence was added because other members of the drafting committee (this committee comprised representatives of different "socialist" sects) insisted on it. Marx explained this in his letter of 4 November of the same year to Engels. He said: "I had to adopt the two words 'obligations' and 'rights' and such other terms as 'truth, morals and justice.' However, they have been properly arranged so that they can cause no harm" ("Collected Works of Marx and Engels," Vol. 31, p. 17). Marx suggested deleting the sentence on human rights when he prepared the 1871 edition of these regulations (see "Collected Works of Marx and Engels," Vol. 17, p. 476).

The historical mission of the proletariat is to abolish the system of exploitation of one man by another and to completely liberate all mankind. Marx and Engels gave a profound explanation of this idea in the "Communist Manifesto." They pointed out: "Communist theory may be summed up in the single sentence: Abolition of private property" ("Selected Works of Marx and Engels," Vol. 1, p. 265). They also refuted the slander that the elimination of private property meant the elimination of individuality, independence and freedom and exposed the class nature of individuality, freedom and so forth. The basic slogan of the proletariat is to eliminate classes. Lenin pointed out clearly: "It took a whole era in world history to eliminate feudalism and its vestiges and to implement the principles of the bourgeois system (which can be entirely called a bourgeois democratic system). The slogan of this era of world history invariably was: Liberty, equality, ownership and Bentham. The elimination of capitalism and its vestiges and the implementation of the principles of the communist system constitute the content of the new era that has already begun in the history of the whole world. The slogan of this era inevitably will and should be: Eliminate classes, enforce the dictatorship of the proletariat in order to fulfill this goal, mercilessly expose the prejudices of the petty-bourgeois democrats on freedom and equality and wage a relentless struggle against these prejudices" ("Collected Works of Lenin," Vol. 31, p. 354).

Then isn't it true that the proletariat must not mention the slogan of human rights at all? That isn't true. Although as far as the proletariat is concerned the principle of human rights (such as liberty and equality) put forth by the bourgeoisie is essentially hypocritical, the proletariat should make use of it to demand that the bourgeoisie themselves put the principle into practice. In this way the proletariat can use the slogan as a weapon in its struggle against the bourgeoisie. Therefore, it does not negate it in general. However, it must be made clear that such rights as liberty, equality and so forth are after all "PURELY DEMOCRATIC DEMANDS" (quoting Engels). The proletariat cannot restrict itself to this kind of slogan and these kinds of demands. It should put forth its own higher demand and goal, that is, the realization of socialism and communism. It follows that for this, proletarian democratic dictatorship must be realized, otherwise, any so-called human rights, liberty and equality can only be something to fool the people. Engels once pointed out while criticizing the Gotha program: "The idea of socialist society as the realm of equality is a one-sided French idea resting upon the old 'liberty, equality, fraternity, an idea which was justified as a stage of development in its own time and place but which, like all the one-sided ideas of earlier socialist schools, should now be overcome. Such ideas only produce confusion in people's heads, and more precise methods of presenting the matter have been found" ("Selected Works of Marx and Engels," Vol. 3, p. 31). Putting the democratic dictatorship of the proletariat into practice, abolishing private ownership, eliminating classes, emancipating all of humanity and realizing communism—this is the explicit Marxist elaboration of this question. Real equality among all members of society can be guaranteed and ample material wealth enjoyed by everyone only after communism is realized. Only then can man's strength and intellect be fully and freely developed and applied. Only under such conditions can man truly become master of nature and society. Putting forth the slogan of human rights devoid of the proletariat's fundamental aim, especially under the current situation in which the slogan of human rights has become extremely complicated, only dims our objective and causes confused thinking.

The slogan of human rights was once raised by our party in leading the struggle of democratic revolution. The slogan of "fighting for freedom and human rights" was raised in the "7 Febuary" general strike in 1923 (Secretariat of the China Labor Association: "The '7 February' Massacre," 27 February 1923, see *Xiang Dao [Guide]*, 20th Issue). The slogan of "fighting for human rights and freedom" was put forward in the "Letter to All Compatriots on the Fight Against Japan and for National Salvation" (that is, the "'1 August' Declaration") jointly issued by the Chinese Central Soviet Government and the CCP Central Committee in Memory of the 4th Anniversary of the Outbreak of the War of Resistance Against Japanese Aggression"). The human rights put forward by us represented a slogan of mobilization against imperialism and feudalism. It was a concrete policy for democracy (chiefly for safeguarding personal freedom). Under such conditions that the existence of the whole Chinese nation was threatened by the invasion of imperialism and that the broad masses of people were brutally oppressed by the feudal warlords, such slogans and policies doubtless played a positive role in exposing the brutality of imperialism and feudals and mobilizing people of all walks of life to form an extensive united front against imperialism and feudalism.

However, human rights was not our party's major slogan, even in the democratic revolutionary period. It is not too difficult to understand that since the beginning of the socialist period in our country, the slogan of human rights has seldom been used in the documents of our party, in the laws of our country and in our political life. This is because our revolution has entered a new historical stage of struggle which directly aims at abolishing private ownership and eliminating classes. In formulating our guiding principles and slogans and conducting ideological and theoretical propaganda, it is more important to adopt the precise Marxist formulation; it is no longer necessary to emphasize such slogans as human rights.

THE SOCIALIST SYSTEM IS CAPABLE OF GUARANTEEING THE COMPLETE REALIZATION OF PEOPLE'S RIGHTS

Rights are invariably bound by some kind of norms. In fact, the capitalist countries have long included the contents of human rights as acknowledged by the bourgeoisie in their constitutions and laws and stipulated that these would be their citizen rights. In this way, human rights are expressed in the form of citizen rights.

After seizing political power and establishing a state under its dictatorship, the proletariat also stipulated its own laws (primarily the Constitution) and laid down in legal form all rights won by the people. Our country's Constitution stipulates the fundamental rights of all citizens of the People's Republic of China in the political, economic and cultural spheres. All these citizen rights as stipulated in our Constitution refer, in a special way, to "human rights." But compared with the different socialist systems of the capitalist countries, the citizen rights of a socialist country have at least two fundamental characteristics: Firstly, regarding private property as sacred and inviolable, the capitalist countries stipulate that property is the most fundamental right of a citizen. Our Constitution, however, emphasizes that "socialist public property shall be inviolable" and that "citizens must take care of and protect public property." Secondly, speaking of every citizen in our country, particularly the working class and all other laboring masses who account for the overwhelming majority of our population, our citizen rights are real and not pretentious or hypocritical. This is because we have abolished private ownership of the means of production. All members of our society equally share the fruit of production, and the broad masses of people have become masters of the country. Only a tiny handful of hostile elements, counterrevolutionaries

and other criminals among our population, who are regarded as the objective of the dictatorship, shall be deprived of their political rights of citizenship for a certain period of time in accordance with law. In the capitalist countries, although the bourgeoisie has included human rights in the Constitution and legally recognized such rights of all citizens, only a tiny handful of bourgeois elements among the population actually enjoy such rights. As for the proletariat and laboring masses who represent the overwhelming majority of the population, the rights they enjoy are incomplete, restricted and very pitiful. Furthermore, even though certain changes have taken place in the capitalist countries, the essentials of this question remain unchanged today. It is very difficult for the proletariat and the bourgeoisie to speak the same language on the issue of human rights.

We say that the socialist system safeguards, in the main, each and every right that should actually be enjoyed by every citizen according to law. But this does not necessarily mean that under socialist conditions people should automatically and uninterruptedly enjoy all citizen rights. Due to the imperfect sectors of the superstructure in our socialist society, the existence of bureaucratism, the shortcomings in certain links of our government system and the incomplete legal system, it is difficult to provide reliable protection from time to time to the people's democratic rights, personal freedom and legal economic rights and benefits. What we should never overlook is the fact that the reactionary force left behind by the old society may again bring about great disasters to the broad masses of the people at a certain time or under certain special conditions. For instance, in order to usurp party and state power, Lin Biao and the "gang of four" wantonly trampled on the legal system and seriously violated the citizen rights of our people. However, it is very clear that the dictatorship of the proletariat and the socialist system have nothing to do with this situation. On the contrary, what we see in this situation is precisely the result of distorting and undermining the dictatorship of the proletariat and the socialist system. Therefore, in order to avoid a recurrence of this situation, we should never change our fundamental system. What we should do is to revive, uphold and unceasingly perfect our socialist system, give full play to democracy, strengthen the legal system and consolidate and enhance the dictatorship of the proletariat.

We must clearly analyze the issue of "human rights" which was discussed in our society some time ago. The enticing slogans put forward by a tiny handful of individuals are actually aimed at uglifying the socialist system, beautifying capital-imperialism and using the "human rights" issue to oppose the four fundamental principles with ulterior motives. We must resolutely expose and criticize any individual with such motives. Keeping in mind the bitter past lesson of how the legal system was trampled on and citizen rights seriously violated when Lin Biao and the "gang of four" were on a rampage and keeping in mind the fact that suppression of democracy, violation of law and intrusion of citizen rights still exist in actual life in certain localities, some other people have urgently demanded that the people's fundamental rights be protected and socialist democracy perfected and put into full practice. Even though the language and methods of presentation used to put forward these demands may not be adequate, we must understand that many of the actual demands are reasonable and proper. In dealing with them, we should provide guidance, eliminate some misunderstandings and help draw a clear distinction between bourgeois democracy and proletarian democracy. On the one hand, we must now conscientiously solve the question of how to institutionalize our democracy and guarantee it by law, effectively do a good job in promoting socialist democracy and adopt effective measures to protect the people's fundamental rights. We must solemnly criticize and educate those who do not respect people's rights and who willfully restrict and interfere with the exercise of legitimate citizen rights and resolutely correct their mistakes so that they will understand the solemnness of citizen rights. We must conscientiously find out and seriously handle those people who violate the law and discipline and infringe on citizen rights no matter how high their position may be. It is wrong to defend or cover up for these people, no matter what reason we give ourselves.

On the other hand, any right is invariably restricted by certain material conditions and cultural levels. Without a relatively developed economy, it will be difficult to enable every citizen to enjoy fully the right to work and rest and other economic rights; without certain necessary cultural achievements, it will be impossible for a citizen to fully enjoy each and every cultural right and benefit. Thus only by raising economic and cultural levels can citizen rights of democracy and freedom be fully realized. This is the Marxist viewpoint of historical materialism in dealing with the question of rights. Therefore, in order to protect each and every right of the citizens as stipulated by the Constitution, it is most important to concentrate all our efforts and do an even better job in the four modernizations and rapidly raise our country's productive forces—which are still very backward—to modern levels and at the same time to raise the scientific and cultural levels of the entire nation to a much higher level.

DENG XIAOPING   **60**
Address to a Writers and Artists Congress, 30 October 1979

Deng insists on the necessary compatability between intellectual freedom and creativity on the one hand and Party control on the other.

Fellow deputies and comrades:

It is an event of historic importance that the representatives of our writers, dramatists, artists, musicians, art performers, film workers and other literary and art workers of various nationalities are gathering in this hall to sum up together their basic experience of literary and art work in the past 30 years in order to enhance achievements, overcome shortcomings and discuss how to promote literature and art in the new historical period. On behalf of the CCP Central Committee and the State Council, I would like to extend my warm greetings to the congress.

Present at this meeting are writers and artists of the older generation who have joined the new cultural movement since the "May 4th movement" period; writers and artists who have contributed to the cause of the people's liberation in various stages of our revolution after the "May 4th movement;" writers and artists who grew up after the founding of the PRC; writers and artists who emerged during the struggle against Lin Biao and the "gang of four"; and also writers and artists from among our compatriots in Taiwan, Hong Kong and Macao. This meeting marks an unprecedented unity of the literary and art workers throughout our country.

Our line of literature and art was correct and our

achievements in literature and art were remarkable during the 17 years prior to the Great Cultural Revolution. The so-called "dictatorship of a sinister line in literature and art" was a complete slander fabricated by Lin Biao and the "gang of four." During the 10 years that Lin Biao and the "gang of four" ran rampant, a host of good literary and art works were banned and the broad masses of literary and art workers were framed and persecuted. During that period, many of our comrades and friends in the literary and art circle uprightly resisted and struggled against Lin Biao and the gang. During the struggle in which our party and people defeated Lin Biao and the gang, the literary and art workers made admirable and indelible contributions. I would like to express my cordial regards to you.

Since the overthrow of the "gang of four," the literary and art circle, under the leadership of the party Central Committee, has been implementing the party's policy concerning intellectuals. A number of literary and art works welcomed by the people have reappeared. With ease of mind, the literary and art workers have displayed increasing enthusiasm for creative work. In a short period of only several years, many good novels, poems, songs, dramas, films, quyi (ballads and cross talk), reportages, musical works, dances and photographic and art works have appeared in the course of settling accounts with the ultra-leftist line of Lin Biao and the "gang of four." These works

[New China News Agency, 30 October 1979.]

play an active role in smashing the mental shackles imposed on people by Lin Biao and the "gang of four," eliminating their pernicious influence, liberating the mind, heightening our fighting spirit and inspiring the people to dedicate themselves heart and soul to the four modernizations. In the last 3 years, the literary and art circle, I think, is one of the fields in which very good achievements have been made. The literary and art workers deserve the trust, love and respect of the party and the people. Rigorous testing by the storm of struggle has shown that our contingent of literary and art workers in general is good. The party and the people are very pleased to have such a contingent of literary and art workers.

Fellow deputies and comrades: Our country has entered a new period of socialist modernization. While striving to enhance the productive forces by a big margin, we should improve and perfect the socialist economic and political systems, practice ample socialist democracy and develop an adequate socialist legal system. While striving to build a high material civilization, we should also raise the scientific and cultural levels of the whole nation, develop a noble, rich and colorful cultural life and create a highly socialist spiritual civilization.

The dedication of heart and soul to the accomplishment of the four modernizations is the overriding central task of people throughout China for a considerably long time to come. It is a great and long term undertaking which decides the destiny of our motherland.

The masses and the cadres on all fronts should be activists in emancipating the mind, promoting stability and unity, defending the motherland's unification and accomplishing the four modernizations. Whether a thing is advantageous or detrimental to the accomplishment of the four modernizations should be the most fundamental criterion for determining the right or wrong of all work. The literary and art workers should cooperate with educational workers, theoretical workers, journalist workers, political workers and other related comrades in waging a protracted and effective ideological struggle against ideas and habits that impede the four modernizations. It is imperative to criticize the ideas of the exploiting classes, the influences of the conservative and narrow-minded small producer mentality and anarchism and extreme individualism and to overcome bureaucracy. It is necessary to restore and carry forward the revolutionary traditions of our party and the people, to foster fine morality and social practices and make positive contributions to a highly developed socialist spiritual civilization.

In beginning this undertaking, there is plenty of room for us to develop literature and art. The literary and art department has an important responsibility, which cannot be shifted to other departments, to satisfy the people's varying demands in spiritual life, foster new socialist people and raise the ideological, cultural and moral levels of the whole society.

Our literature and art belong to the people. Our people are industrious, brave, firm and indomitable. They have wisdom and ideals, love the motherland and socialism, consider the interests of the whole and observe discipline. In the past several thousand years, particularly in the half century and more after the May 4th movement, they have had full confidence, worked hard, overcome all resistance and written one brilliant chapter after another of Chinese history. No powerful enemies have ever been able to overpower them. No difficulties, no matter how serious, have been able to block their advance. Literary and artistic creation must fully show the fine quality of our people and praise the great victories they have won in revolution and construction as well as in their struggles against various enemies and various difficulties.

Our writers and artists should exert still greater efforts and make still more achievements in depicting and fostering new socialist people. They should portray the pioneers in the four modernizations and depict the pioneers' brand new feature in having revolutionary ideals, noble sentiments, creative ability and a wide field of vision and in assuming a scientific attitude and realistic approach. They should use the image of the new people to fire the enthusiasm for socialism among the broad masses and give impetus to the masses' historic creative activities in the course of undertaking the four modernizations.

Our socialist literature and art should use vivid and touching artistic images to portray people's innate character in various social relations, express the demand of the times for progress and show the trend of historical development. It should strive to educate the people in socialist ideology and imbue them with a spirit of struggle for a better future.

China has a long history, vast land and a large population. People of different nationalities, professions, ages, experience and educational levels have different habits, customs, cultural traditions and artistic inclinations. Any artistic creation that provides education, enlightenment, entertainment and aesthetic enjoyment on a grand scale or small, written in a serious or humorous vein, lyrical or philosophical, all should be given a place in our literary and art field. Feats of heroism or daily labor, the struggle of ordinary people, their joys and sorrows, the life of today's people as well as that of the ancients should all be portrayed by literature and art. We should learn from all progressive and fine pieces of literary and art works and performing arts of China's ancient times and foreign countries and use them for reference.

We should continue to stick to the orientation set by Comrade Mao Zedong for literary and art creation of serving the people, the worker-peasant-soldier masses in the first place, and to keep to his principle of letting a hundred flowers bloom and a hundred schools of thought contend. Things foreign and ancient should be used to serve modern China, and we must weed through the old to bring forth the new. In artistic creation, we should advocate free style. In artistic theory, we should advocate free discussion among those with different viewpoints and among different schools of thought. Lenin said: "In literature, it is absolutely necessary to have plenty of room for individual creation and inclination and plenty of room for different ideas, imaginations, forms and contents." In order to attain our common objective of accomplishing the four modernizations, we should open up a broader avenue for our literature and art and have daily increasing varieties of ideas guiding our literary and art creation, themes and techniques. We should dare to create new things. We should prevent and overcome the tendency of monotonous, mechanical formulation and generalization.

Any art workers who recognize their responsibility to the people should consistently gear their work to the needs of the broad masses, endeavor to improve their work constantly and guard against rough and slipshod work. They should seriously weigh the social effect of their work and strive to provide the people with the best food for thought. In the past, Lin Biao and the "gang of four" corrupted people's souls with the reactionary and decadent ideology of the exploiting class and poisoned the social atmosphere, thus seriously undermining our revolutionary tradition and fine habits. Our writers and artists should provide the people with a broader mental outlook through their creative work and continue to wage a resolute struggle against the pernicious influence of Lin Biao and the "gang of four." They should be sober-minded toward the pressure from the "left" and from the right to stir up social disorder and disrupt political stability and unity through all forms of activities. These were erroneous tendencies that went contrary to the interests and wishes of the majority of the people. They should join other forces in society and, through their literary and art creation and by closely coordinating with other work in the ideological sphere, alert the people to these dangers and condemn and oppose them.

Writers and artists should exert themselves in the study of Marxism-Leninism-Mao Zedong Thought and enhance their ability to comprehend and analyze life as well as the ability to grasp the essence of things through reality. It is our hope that more and more comrades among the writers and artists will become engineers in fact as well as in name to shape the soul of mankind.

Those who educate others must themselves be educated. Those who give the people nourishment must first absorb nourishment themselves. Who, then, should be the ones to give the writers and artists an education and provide them nourishment? The answer provided by Marxism is: the people. The people are the mothers of writers and artists. All progressive writers and artists owe their artistic lives to their flesh-and-blood relations with the people. Artistic life would wither for those who neglected or severed such a relationship. The people need art, and art needs the people even more. The basic way to make our socialist literature and art flourish is for the writers and artists to conscientiously draw raw material, themes, plots, words, poetic sentiment and picturesque meaning from the people's lives and to nurture themselves in the hardworking spirit of making history. We are convinced that our writers and artists will continue to advance unswervingly along this road.

Writers and artists should continue to improve and enhance their ability to express themselves artistically. All writers and artists should study painstakingly and absorb, apply and develop all fine artistic skills, domestic and foreign, and create perfect artistic forms with the national character and the spirit of the times. Only by defying difficulties, studying and practicing diligently and exploring dauntlessly will the writers and artists be able to scale the heights in art. We sincerely hope that the literary and art contingent will unite even closer and grow. All writers and artists, professional or amateur, socialist and patriotic writers and artists and all those who hope for the reunification of the motherland should help one another and learn from each other and devote all their energy to literary and art creation, research and criticism. The people should be the

ones to appraise the literary and art creations in the light of ideological and artistic achievements. Writers and artists should heed criticism and accept constructive opinion from all circles that are the impetus to their progress and improvement in their work.

Within the literary and art contingents, there should be comradely and friendly discussion among writers and artists of different categories and schools, between comrades engaging in literary and art creation and criticism and between writers and arists and their readers. They should present facts and reason things out. They should tolerate criticism and countercriticism, uphold truth and correct mistakes as necessary.

Writers and artists are burdened with the heavy responsibility of discovering and training young writers and artists. Young writers and artists in their prime of life have sharp minds. They represent the future of our literary and art undertakings. We should give them enthusiastic help and at the same time set strict demands on them, so that they will not deviate from real life and will make continuous ideological progress in the pursuit of art. Middle-aged writers and artists who form the backbone of our literary and art contingents should be fully utilized.

Great importance should be attached to the training of literary and artistic talents. They are indeed too few outstanding writers and artists in a big country such as ours with a population of over 900 million. This situation is very incompatible with our time. We have to create the essential conditions ideologically and on the strength of our work system to cultivate and bring up outstanding talents.

The party committees at all levels should exercise effective leadership over literary and art work. In leading literary and art work, the party committees should, based on the characteristics of literature and art and the law of development, help writers and artists acquire the conditions for making literary and art undertakings flourish, raise the literary and art level and create fine literary and art creations as well as develop performing skills worthy of our great people and great era. The party committees should not indulge in issuing orders or insist that literature and art be subordinate to a temporary, specific and direct political task.

At present, sustained efforts should be made to help writers and artists continue to emancipate their minds, break loose from the mental shackles imposed by Lin Biao and the "gang of four" and uphold the correct political orientation and to give them support from every field, including material support, to insure that the writers and artists can fully utilize their wisdom and talents. We recommend that leading members exchange views with writers and artists as equals; on the other hand, writers who are party members should play an exemplary role with their own achievements in uniting and drawing the broad masses of writers and artists together to move forward. The bureaucratic way of doing things must be discarded. Administrative orders in the sphere of literary and art creation and criticism must be abolished. Such things will have a counterproductive effect if they are looked upon as upholding party leadership. We should uphold the ideological line of dialectical materialism, analyze both positive and negative experience in the history of literary and art development over the past 30 years, free ourselves from the trammels of all sorts of outmoded ideas, study new situations and solve new problems based on the characteristics of the new period. The absurd way pursued by Lin Biao and the "gang of four" undermined the party leadership over literary and art work and stifled literary and art life. It is very essential for writers and artists to fully utilize the individual creative spirit, since literary and art undertakings involve complicated mental labor. The subject matter and the method of presentation can only be explored and decided step by step by the writers and artists themselves in their artistic work. No outside interference should be permitted.

Fellow delegates and comrades: Comrade Mao Zedong pointed out at the founding of new China: "An upsurge of cultural construction will naturally appear with the approach of the upsurge in economic construction."

Through arduous struggle and by surmounting increasing difficulties, we have smashed the "gang of four" and swept away the big stumbling block that stood on our road to progress. We can now say with full confidence that this situation will soon emerge; conditions for putting into practice the Marxist principle of "letting a hundred flowers bloom and a hundred schools of thought contend" are daily ripening. Only by working hard will the broad masses of writers and artists unfold a new prospect of making our literature and art flourish and bloom.

This congress is the first grand gathering of writers and artists from all parts of the country who are on the new Long March. The comrades attending this congress are those who have made fruitful achievements. It is our conviction that following the closing of this congress, comrades will produce more and better artistic work for the motherland and the people. I wish this congress full success.

ZHOU YANG
On Cultural Creativity Under Socialism, 1 November 1979

For many years Zhou Yang has been one of the Party's principal hatchetmen in dealing with the intellectual community. In his speech to the Fourth National Congress of Writers and Artists, Zhou Yang had the almost hopeless task of convincing his constituency that freedom to express cultural creativity exists when it fact it does not.

While joyously celebrating the 30th anniversary of the founding of the PRC, we are gathered here today for the Fourth National Congress of Writers and Artists. Nineteen years have elapsed since the convocation of the third congress and three decades have passed since the first. During this period which is nearly one-third of a century, our country has undergone great changes and severe tests and the people have weathered numerous violent and frightening storms in their march to victory. History is made up of changes. There are bound to be twists and turns, and at times things will take a turn for the worse. However, nothing can stop the rolling wheels of time. After all, the strength of the people is invincible.

The 10 years of turmoil wrought by Lin Biao and the "gang of four" spelled calamity for our people. Representing the aspirations of the people, the party Central Committee headed by Comrade Hua Guofeng set things right, brought the country out of danger and initially achieved stability and unity. At present, all our undertakings are once again

victoriously forging ahead along the correct course. At the end of last year, the party convened the 3d plenary session of its 11th Central Committee. Upholding the dialectical materialist ideological line, the plenary session clearly affirmed the principle of practice being the sole criterion for testing truth and urged the whole party and people throughout the country to shift their work focus to socialist modernization and to rapidly build China into a powerful socialist country. This was an important strategic decision, a historic turning point and a grant objective which set the hearts of millions of people aflame. As the continuations and developments of the guidelines of the party's plenary session the 2d session of the 5th NPC that was convened not long ago, the recent 4th plenary session of the 11th CCP Central Committee and Comrade Ye Jianying's speech at the meeting in celebration of the 30th anniversary of the founding of the PRC have further heightened people's confidence in surmounting every difficulty to win new victories.

The present national Congress of Writers and Artists is convened under these circumstances. At this congress, we will earnestly discuss how our literature and art should shoulder the glorious mission entrusted by the times, strive for greater prosperity and improvement, and play its proper

[Zhou Yang, "Inherit from the Past and Go Forward, Make Literature and Art Flourish in the New Period of Socialism," New China News Agency, 20 November 1979.]

role in serving the four modernizations by training new socialist people, raising the people's cultural level, promoting social progress and development and constantly satisfying the growing cultural needs of the masses. The people expect us to provide them with correct and practical answers to these questions. We cannot let them down.

The present congress will be of particularly great significance in the history of the development of socialist literature and art in our country. It marks the end of the dark era in which Lin Biao and the "gang of four" practiced feudal fascist dictatorship and destroyed literature and art and the beginning of a new era of prosperity for socialist literature and art. The historical task of carrying forward our heritage and forging ahead into the future falls on our shoulders. We should turn our present congress into one for seeking truth from facts, sum up our work and exchange experiences, during the course of which both criticism and self-criticism will be made. It will be a democratic and lively congress in which everyone will work together with one heart in the march toward socialist modernization.

Literature and art are a very important and complicated part of ideology. It is not easy to sum up experiences over the past 30 years. My report here will only offer a few commonplace remarks by way of introduction so that others may discuss it and draw correct conclusions.

AN ARDUOUS FIGHTING COURSE

Like all other causes, our socialist literature and art have gone through a great and arduous course in the three decades since the founding of our People's Republic. We have achieved great successes and accumulated rich experiences, both positive and negative. We must sum up those experiences, draw lessons and wisdom from them, explore their governing laws and steadily forge ahead. Ours is a socialist society, and our literature and art are socialist literature and art which bear our national characteristics. The socialist society is a historical process. It will steadily develop from a not quite perfect society to a fairly perfect one. However, it cannot ultimately make the transition to communism unless it has created the necessary material and spiritual conditions. This process will mainly be brought about by consciously and steadily making improvements and readjustments over a long period of time. Literature and art, as a part of the ideology of a socialist society, also go through steady reform and development. We must pay attention to practice, heed the opinions of the masses, use history as a mirror and make a continuous effort to study and explore the laws governing the development of our socialist literature and art.

Socialist literature and art were born more than a century ago during the time of Marx and Engels. They were not born peacefully, and it was only after arduous struggles that they finally won the right to exist. Because of the Great October Revolution, Russian literature became the advance guard of socialist literature and art in the world. China's new literature and art benefited from the literature and art of Russia, northern Europe, southeastern Europe and the Soviet Union. Written during the "May 4th" new culture movement, Lu Xun's "Call to Arms" and Guo Moruo's "The Goddesses" laid a solid foundation for our modern literature and art in both prose writing and poetry. The "literary revolution" during the "May 4th" period and subsequently the "revolutionary literature" during the period of the great revolution represented a great leap in the history of Chinese literature and art. Under the leadership of the party and with the great Lu Xun acting as the standard bearer, the leftwing literary and art movement of the 1930's held high the banner of proletarian literature, boldly foiled the counterrevolutionary cultural "encirclement and suppression" put up by the Kuomintang reactionaries and wrote a new page in Chinese proletarian literature and art with the blood of revolutionary writers and artists. The history of modern Chinese literature was replete with brilliant deeds of how writers gave their lives for truth. For example, there were the execution of Ruo Shi, Hu Yepin and three other martyrs in the 1930's and the assassination of Wen Yiduo in the 1940s. With their strong militant spirit, the revolutionary literature and art of the 1930's enhanced the morale of the masses of people who were under national and class oppression and performed indelible meritorious services toward bringing about the victory of the anti-imperialist and anti-feudal new deomcratic revolution and the war of national literation. Lu Xun's militant essays, prose and other works, Mao Dun's "Midnight" and other novels, Ye Shaojun's "Ni Huanzhi," Ba Jin's "Family," Cao Yu's "Storm," Lao She's "Camel Xiangzi," Li Jieren's "Small Billows in a Pool of Stagnant Water" and so on all won universal praise. The literary and theatrical works produced by Tian Han, Xia Yan, Jiang Guangci, Zhang Tianyi and many other revolutionary writers sowed the seeds of revolution among the broad masses and educated young people. "Identured Laborers," the first book to portray the miserable life of the industrial workers in our country, gave new life to our efforts. The newly emerging wood carving movement championed and fostered by Lu Xun became an important front army of the leftwing literary and art movement. The mass movement or singing national salvation songs such as "March of the Volunteers" and the drama groups which played an active part on the anti-Japanese front performing plays like "Put Down Your Whip" aroused and inspired the masses to enthusiastically plunge into the struggle to resist Japanese aggression for national salvation. In novels like "Village in August" and "Life and Death Struggle," which were true records of the struggle at that time, the bourgeoning young writers of the northern provinces told of the suffering of and resistance put up by the 30 million fellow countrymen in the enemy-occupied areas. All these were the splendid achievements of revolutionary literature and art in this period. Meanwhile, old revolutionary base areas like Jiangxi and northern Shaanxi had also accumulated valuable experiences in literary and art creation and mass literary and art activities. Of course, our proletarian literature and art were still in their infancy at that time because these were unprecedented in Chinese history. Most of the works were immature in thinking and in art. Many of the writers had not yet freed themselves from the influence of petty bourgeois ideas. The activists of the leftwing literary and art movement at that time, such as Qu Qiubai, Yang Hansheng, Feng Xuefeng and A Ying, had done a tremendous amount of work in disseminating the Marxist theory of literature and art and building up the ranks of leftwing writers and artists. However, because we had not fully prepared ourselves with Marxist theory and kept abreast of the actual conditions of the Chinese revolution, we lacked knowledge of history and social experiences we engendered dogmatic and sectarian tendencies of varying degrees while disseminating Marxist ideas of literature and art and assimilating the experiences of the revolutionary literary and art movement launched by the international proletariat. Lu Xun, with his profound ideas, broad erudition and rich experience in struggle, had made enormous contributions toward the development of the revolutionary literary movement and left us with the most valuable heritage.

Comrade Mao Zedong's "Talks at the Yanan Forum on Literature and Art," published in 1942, was a document of epoch-making significance in the history of literature and art. The "Talks" clearly advanced the brilliant concept that literature and art should serve the workers, peasants and armymen and the people at large and that writers and artists should become one with the people living in a new era. The biggest merit of the "Talks" was that they correctly solved the fundamental theoretical question of literature and art—whom to serve and how to serve. This resulted in tremendous changes in the content and form of our revolutionary literature and art. Around the time of the publication of the "Talks," the writers and artists of the revolutionary base areas all went into the midst of the worker-peasant-armymen masses and integrated themselves with the masses. They set great store by folk art and people's new creative writings and were greatly influenced by the thoughts, feelings and aesthetic standards of the people. Our literature and art assumed a new aspect at that time. The new rural folk dance movement represented by the dance "Brother and Sister Reclaiming Wasteland" sprang up. The new opera "The White-Haired Girl," the new Beijing Opera "Driven to Join the Liangshan Mountain Rebels" and the new Shaanxi Opera "Debts of Blood and Tears" all turned out to be great successes. The new folk song "The East Is Red" and revolutionary songs like "The Huanghe Cantata," "The 38th Route Army's March" and "The Song of Guerrillas" were written and performed. Modern wood carvings and new year pictures were in vogue. The long poems "Self-Defense Corps in the Border Areas" and "Wang Gui and Lu Xiangxiang," the unique medium-length novel "Stories Told by Li Youcai" and novels like "The Sun Shines on the Sanggan River," "The Hurricane," "Gao Ganda" and "Flowers That Will Never Wither" were published. All these featured the revolutionary changes of the new era. Disregarding personal safety, large numbers of cultural troupes plunged into the flames of revolutionary wars. They actively took part in democratic national construction in the base areas and made important contributions toward the revolutionary cause. These were our initial achievements in consciously applying Mao Zedong's concepts on literature and art. The valuable experiences provided by them helped open up vast vistas for the development of socialist literature and art.

In the Kuomintang-ruled areas, many revolutionary and progressive writers and artists also produced outstanding works. Among the important works of this period were the poems "Torch" and "To the Fighters," the novel "Gold Rush" and modern dramas such as "Before and After the Qingming Festival," "The Germs of Fascism" and "Foggy Chongqing." Guo Moruo's modern drama "Qu Yuan," which boldly challenged the Kuomintang reactionaries by drawing historical parables, created a furor. Under the leadership of the party, progressive literary and art activities exerted widespread and profound influence among the masses of students and intellectuals. "Unity Means Strength" and other revolutionary songs heightened the morale of the people.

The First National Congress of Writers and Artists held in Beijing in 1949 represented the joining of two revolutionary literary and art forces—one coming from the liberated areas and the other from the Kuomintang-controlled areas. At that time, our party had just won political power in the whole country and moved from wartime circumstances to peaceful construction and from the countryside to the cities. The first congress was convened under these new historical conditions. In response to Comrade Mao Zedong's call, the writers and artists who attended the congress unanimously said they would strive to keep to the new orientation of literature and art. The establishment of the PRC marked the basic termination of the period of the new democratic revolution and the beginning of the socialist revolution. It also marked the establishment of the people's democratic dictatorship, or the dictatorship of the proletariat, in the whole country. This meant new tasks for our literary and art workers. First, our literature and art should now serve socialist revolution and socialist construction instead of serving the new democratic revolution as they did in the past. Literature and art should render service on a larger scale, in a wider scope and in many more fields. This gave rise to the question of how literature and art should become one with the people living in a new era. In the past, writers and artists had traveled a tortuous and uneven road, made numerous explorations, steeled themselves and stood up to rigorous tests in trying to integrate themselves with the masses. Now they were confronted with new ordeals. How should literature and art as an ideology better conform to the socialist economic base, reflect the new life and the struggle, thoughts and feelings of the people living in this historical period in a rich and varied way and satisfy the daily growing cultural needs of the masses is a problem which must be correctly solved. After liberating the whole country and becoming the ruling party, our party was confronted with the new task of guiding literature and art to develop along the socialist path and in a direction favorable to the people. We had gained rich experiences, both positive and negative, on these questions.

Under the leadership of the party Central Committee and Comrade Mao Zedong, the literary and art circles began to wage struggles against bourgeois and feudal ideologies. These included the criticism of the film "The Life of Wu Xun," the idealist approach of the Hu Shi school or study on the classical novel "The Dream of the Red Chamber" and Hu Feng's political and literary views. These struggles were essential and significant as ideological and literary criticism. However, when they were launched with great fanfare throughout the country as political movements, they produced serious negative results. At that time, China had already entered the socialist period. The socialist transformation was a profound change aimed at eliminating the private ownership of the means of production. Socialist economy and politics both required a corresponding ideology. Since bourgeois and feudal ideas were deep-rooted in the sphere of ideology, ideological struggles inevitably took place in various parts of this sphere. This made it necessary for us to use Marxism to vanquish all brands of exploiting class ideologies and strive to make proletarian ideologies dominate this sphere. After waging these struggles, the party Central Committee and Comrade

Mao Zedong promptly advanced the policy of "letting a hundred flowers blossom and a hundred schools of thought contend" in 1956, when the socialist transformation was basically completed. This policy had tremendous significance in developing and promoting the prosperity of socialist culture and art.

Right after the founding of the PRC, we were confronted with the question of how to deal with traditional operas, including Beijing Operas and other local operas. This not only involved the cultural needs of the people but was a socialist problem which would affect the jobs of tens of thousands of artists. Operas formed an extremely rich part of the valuable heritage created by the Chinese people over a long period. However, they had to be reformed because, as products of old times, they carried with them not only the quintessence of democracy but also the dregs of feudalism. Together with the opera singers, we sorted out and reformed many traditional theatrical pieces and performing arts in accordance with the criteria laid down by Comrade Mao Zedong for useful, harmless and harmful categories. As a result, many types of dramas which were on the verge of extinction before liberation gained a new lease on life and large numbers of traditional theatrical pieces again shone with dazzling splendor in terms of script, music and performance after discarding the dross and retaining the essential. We had achieved substantial successes and accumulated considerable experiences in almost every field, from the creation and adaption of theatrical pieces and the reform of performing skills and stage art to the training of young performers. Good operas dominated the stage during the first 17 years after the country's liberation, although bad pieces did appear from time to time. Many outstanding Beijing Operas and other local operas were produced. For example, "Generals and Ministers in Harmony," "Liang Shanbo and Zhu Yingtai," "The Story of the White Snake," "The Story of Funu," "Fifteen Strings of Coins," "Lady Generals of the Yang Family," "Capital Punishment," "Sparks Amid the Reeds," "The Red Lantern," "Jie Zhenguo," "The Young Son-in-Law," "Liu Qiader," "Union With a Fairy," "Searching the College," "The Monkey Subdues the Demon" and "The Chaoyang Canal" were all rich in the spirit of reform and strong in artistic appeal. Most important of all, we succeeded in our attempts to adapt traditional operas to contemporary life. The 1964 festival of revolutionary Beijing operas on contemporary themes was a review of successes made in this field. We had also achieved positive results and experiences in systematizing and reforming our traditional painting, music, dance, ballad singing, puppet shows, shadow shows and acrobatics and in collecting and collating the folk literature of various nationalities.

New China devoted major efforts to developing its own film-making industry. Back in the 1930s, our leftwing film workers started the work of pioneering China's film-making industry under the leadership of the party despite the pressure exerted by the Kuomintang reactionaries. Outstanding films made since the 1930s, such as "The Fisherman's Song," "The School Tragedy," "A Myriad of Twinkling Lights," "The Crow and the Sparrow" and "The River Flows East and Never Returns" still live in people's memories. With the unprecedented development of the film-making industry after the country's liberation, the new world and the new people living in it were unfolded before the audience. During this time, our film artists produced a great number of good and popular films. These included "Sons and Daughters of the Chinese Nation," "The Steel Fighters," "The White-Haired Girl," "Red Flags on the Green Mound," "Dong Cunrui," "The Red Detachment of Women," "Acacia Village," "Li Shuangshuang," "Radio Wages That Never Die Away," "Sangkunryung," "The Storm," "New Anecdotes of a Veteran," "Lin Zexu," "1894 Storm," "The New Year's Sacrifice," "Big Waves Washing Away the Sand," "Serfs," "The Siege," "Sisters on Stage," "Early Spring" and "Heroic Sons and Daughters." Newsreels, as the testimony of the times, recorded valuable information about what had happened in our party and country. The newsreel "The Powerful Army Marches Down to the Lower Reaches of the Yangzijiang" once broke the box office record. We also have some excellent and unique popular science films and art films.

During the first 17 years after liberation, literary creations, including novels, dramas, poems and prose, flourished and well-received outstanding works emerged in large numbers. Comrade Guo Moruo assiduously wrote a number of outstanding literary and academic works despite his heavy leadership duties in the fields of science and culture. Lao She also plunged into writing with immense zeal shortly after returning to China. In his works "The Longxu Canal," "The Teahouse" and a few others, he portrayed the life of the people in Beijing which he was well acquainted with, exposed the darkness of old China with a heavy heart and warmly praised the new people's regime. Guo Moruo's "Cai Weniu" and Tian Han's "Guan Hanqing" and "Princess Wencheng," which gave historical personages new appraisals and depicted the fraternal relations between the Han and other minority nationalities from a new standpoint, demonstrated the artistic courage and explorative spirit of these two old writers. Modern dramas like "Growing Up in Battles," "Ten Thousand Crags and Torrents" and "Never Forget" and operas like "Red Guards of Lake Honghu," "Little Erhei Is Getting Married," "Liu Hulan," "Red Coral," "Sister Jiang" and "Third Sister Liu" all reflected contemporary and past struggles from different angles. We have read many novels which described the heroic scenes of the revolutionary struggles waged by the Chinese people over the past half a century and novels about historical personages. For long novels, we have "The History of Pioneers," "Red Flag Manua," "Red Crag," "The Song of Youth," "First Records of the Storm," "Tracks in the Snowy Forest," "Annals of a Small Town," "Three-Family Alley," "Sanliwan," "Great Changes in a Mountain Village," "The Red Sun," "Railroad Guerrillas," "Bitter Cauliflower," "Defending Yanan," "Bastion of Iron," "Motive Force," "Tempered in Struggle," "Militant Youth," "Morning in Shanghai," "Jinshazhou," "The Aroma That Lingers Throughout the Four Seasons," "Storm and Thunder," "The Song of Quyang Hai" and "Li Zicheng." For medium-length novels and collections of short stories, we have "Political Commissar," "This Land of 3,000 Li," "The Snowy Night," "Dawn by the Riverside," "Party Fee," "Lily," "Story of Li Shuangshuang," "My First Boss" and "Spring Sowing and Autumn Harvesting." These were all well-known to and praised by the reading public. The report "Who Is the Most Lovely Person" became a popular seller noted for its strong international sentiments and warm praises for the People's Army. "The Story of Luo Wenying" was well-received by young readers and played an important part in guiding and educating youngsters. The short story "The Young Man Who Has Just Joined the Organizational Department," the report "On the Bridge-Construction

Worksite" and other works caught the attention of the reading public for having boldly and keenly reflected the contradictions among the people during the socialist period and are to play the role of literature as a weapon of criticism. With respect to poetry, we have Comrade Mao Zedong's world-renowned poems, the modern and old-styled poems written by Comrade Chen Yi and other proletarian revolutionaries of the older generation, new folk songs written by the worker-peasant-soldier masses as well as outstanding poems such as "The Sugarcane Forest—To the Tune of Qing Sha Zhang," "Hearty Singing" and "Petroleum" written by popular poets. These poems have warmly eulogized the new socialist life.

Major developments and new creations were also made in painting, sculpture, music, dance, ballad singing, puppet shows, shadow shows, acrobatics, photography and other art forms. With their paint brushes, our traditional Chinese artists painted the magnificent landscape of our motherland and sang praises of the people's new life. Paintings such as "The Founding Ceremony," "How Wonderful Is our Land" and "The Bloodstained Coat," the relief sculptures which are monuments depicting the people's heroes, the giant sculpture "The Revenue Office," the full-length song-and-dance epic "The East Is Red," cantatas such as "The Long March Suite" and "Gada Meilin Symphonic Poem" and the ballets "Small Dagger Society" and "The Red Detachment of Women" were all new creations depicting the people's revolutionary struggle. They were invaluable attempts which contributed to giving socialist literature and art a national and mass character. Ballad singing and the double talk between comedians played the part of light cavalry in the new period and new stories became a new form of storytelling. Outstanding achievements were also made in the production of picture books and children's plays.

During this period, tremendous headway was made in literary and art education, and large numbers of talented people were trained for the state. Those comrades who devoted themselves to the cause of literary and art education deserve our respect.

The fruits of our literary and art creation during the first 17 years after the country's liberation were rather impressive. They played an important part in inspiring the masses to carry out socialist revolution and construction, fostering socialist ethics and values among people of the younger generation, satisfying the aesthetic needs of the people and enriching their spiritual life. Our literature and art are worthy of the title of mirror of the great era. At the same time, they are also textbooks in life from which we draw wisdom and strength. These brilliant achievements on the literary and art front can never be erased by Lin Biao and the "gang of four." History is impartial as are the people. If we take a look at how the reading public and audience warmly welcomed the long-banned films and literary and art works of those 17 years after the downfall of the "gang of four" we can see the will of the people and the masses' fair judgment.

Since the founding of the People's Republic, we have built a contingent of professional and amateur writers and artists under the leadership of the party Central Committee, the fosterage of Mao Zedong Thought and the kind attention of Comrade Zhou Enlai. Many writers and artists have grown up among the workers, peasants and army-

men. They are the new blood of socialist literature and art. This honored contingent is loyal to the party, the people and the socialist cause.

The first move of Lin Biao and the "gang of four" in their conspiracy to usurp supreme party and state power was to control the cultural field. They started by bringing false charges against "The Dismissal of Hai Rui." The so-called "Summary of the Forum on the Work in Literature and Art in the Armed Forces" signaled their all-round seizure of power and was their program for exercising "all-round dictatorship" over literary and art circles. Taking advantage of their usurped political power, they pushed the most reactionary cultural policy, vigorously practiced feudal fascist cultural autocracy and cultural nihilism and brought about the darkest days into the history of modern culture. They not only totally negated our achievements in literature and art during those 17 years but also negated the magnificent fruits and glorious traditions of our revolutionary literature and art since the 1930s, or in worse cases, since the "May 4th" movement. They slanderously described the socialist literature and art of our country as "an antiparty and antisocialist black line of literature and art," slandered the revolutionary writers and artists as "people who represented the black line" and denigrated the party's leadership over literary and art work as "the dictatorship of the black line." They banned all outstanding literary and art works, modern or ancient, Chinese or foreign, in a vain attempt to wipe out all the progressive culture of mankind. The China Federation of Literary and Art Circles and other associations were branded as "Petoefi Clubs" and arbitrarily disbanded. Large numbers of writers and artists were persecuted or humiliated. China's socialist literature and art experienced an unprecedented disaster. Just now, the congress has already expressed our profound mourning and deep feelings for the great numbers of deceased writers, artists and literary and art workers who were persecuted and falsely charged by Lin Biao and the "gang of four."

The "gang of four" pushed an ultraleftist line which served their conspiracy to usurp party and state power. They tampered with and distorted Comrade Mao Zedong's concepts on literature and art, cut off the flesh-and-blood ties between literature and art on the one hand and the people on the other, denied that social life is the only source of literary and art creation, replaced true life and art with lies and fabrications and gravely defamed revolutionary literature and art. They distorted the proper relationship between literature and art on the one hand and politics on the other, subjected art to the enslavement of counterrevolutionary politics and turned our literature and art into "conspiratorial literature and art" and the slave of reactionary politics. By spreading fallacies like "giving prominence to three things" and "letting the main theme take precedence," promoting the disgusting style of their stereotyped gang writing and pushing all kinds of preposterous measures in literature and art, they led our party's literary and art cause into a serious disaster. Their pernicious influence is so widespread that it has not yet been completely eliminated.

However, the interference and sabotage of Lin Biao and the "gang of four" were rather transient when viewed from the angle of historical development. They did not completely disrupt the process of the development of socialist literature and art and could not have done so even if they had wanted to. The overwhelming majority of literary and art workers did not submit to the despotic power of the "gang of four." Instead, they persisted in waging struggles either openly or by covert and indirect means. Those fighters in the literary and art circles who feared no sacrifice and risked their lives to wage struggle against Lin Biao and the "gang of four" deserve to be admired and learned from. The struggle between the revolutionary literary and art workers and Lin Biao and the "gang of four" was a struggle between revolutionary people and counterrevolutionary careerists and conspirators and between the party's policy of "letting a hundred flowers blossom and a hundred schools of thought contend" on the one hand and feudal fascist cultural autocracy and cultural nihilism on the other. It was also a struggle between dialectical materialism and subjective idealism and between revolutionary realism on the one hand and formulaism and stereotyped gang writing on the other in literary and art concepts. This was an acute struggle. Instead of growing passive, many writers and artists who lived under these adverse circumstances applied themselves to their works and quietly proceeded with their writing, or made preparations for writing. The party's good daughter Zhang Zhixin boldly upheld truth and broke down modern superstitions. With the prison as her platform and poems and songs as weapons, she resisted brutality and did not yield unto death. Her moving deeds will live forever in our hearts. It has been proven through rigorous tests that with the exception of a few scum and opportunists, our literary and art contingent is a revolutionary contingent which cannot be subdued or destroyed.

Although Comrade Zhou Enlai was seriously ill and had problems with his work, he still showed concern for the party's literary and art cause and the destiny of the writers and artists. He saved many writers and artists and literary and art works from ill fate where his power permitted. He was always of the same heart with the masses of literary and art workers. When the "gang of four" criticized the so-called "sinister pictures" and "absolute music," the films "Pioneers" and "Morning Glow Over the Sea," the novel "Water Margin" and other literary and art works, they always pointed their sinister spearhead at proletarian revolutionaries of the older generation represented by Comrade Zhou Enlai.

The great "April 5th" movement which used poems as the fighting weapon was a heroic and mighty struggle waged by the Chinese people against the "gang of four." It also wrote a unique and immortal page in the history of proletarian literature and art in our country. The photographers defied difficulties and dangers to shoot the majestic scenes of this struggle. This mass mourning of Premier Zhou and angry denunciation of the "gang of four" mobilized the nation ideologically and prepared public opinion for our subsequent victory in smashing the gang. History is ruthless and highly dramatic. The "gang of four" made the literary and art front the first target of attack in their conspiracy to usurp party and state power; the people used the great hammer of literature and art to sound their death knell.

In the 3 years following the smashing of the "gang of four," the past 2 years in particular, literary and art circles have brought order out of chaos and criticized the theory of the "dictatorship of the sinister line" advocated by Lin Biao and the "gang of four" along with other fallacies. The literary and art principles worked out by the party Central Committee and Comrade Mao Zedong have once again been correctly explained and conscientiously implemented. Our socialist literature and art have begun to recover and develop. The spirit of the 3d plenary session of the 11th party Central Committee and the discussions concerning the truth criterion have greatly promoted the emancipation of thinking in literary and art circles. Once the "gang of four" fell, cartoons and comic dialogs came to the fore and became daggers stabbing at the enemies. Revolutionary poems and poetry recitals dispelled the long silence and expressed the militant fervor of the masses. It is particularly worth mentioning here the "Poems of Tiananmen" which were once popular among the masses and poems written by new and veteran poets which sang the praises of the people's heroes and criticized the "gang of four," such as "Autumn in Tuanpowa," "October in China," "The Jubilant Festivals of the Revolutionary People," "On the Wave Peak," "Premier Zhou, Where Are You?" "Sad Memories in January" and so forth. They evoked a strong reaction among the masses. The newsreel "Eternal Glory to Our Esteemed and Beloved Premier Zhou" expressed the grief and memories of millions upon millions of people. People in the literary and art circles have now dared to break through, discuss and explore problems which they did not dare to touch for a long time. Literary and art workers have not only smashed the shackles imposed on them by the "gang of four" and broken through many forbidden areas, but also abolished many restrictions and taboos imposed during the 17 years after the founding of new China. Various literary and art works have constantly emerged in large number like asparagus after spring rain. Medium-length novels and short stories such as "Teacher in Charge of Class," "A Sacred Mission," "Window," "Our Army Commander," "Scars," "Director Qiao Assumes Office," "Red Magnolia Under a Big Wall" and "Little 8th Route Army on the Grasslands," the feature story "Between Man and Monster," plays such as "The Score of Loyalty," "Where Silence Is," "Make Youth More Beautiful," "The Future Is Calling" and "Flowers That Usher in Spring," and the opera "Star Light, Oh, Star Light" have been welcomed by the people because of their inspiring themes, militant style and creative artistry. The dance drama "The Silk Road and Flower Rain" praises, with its completely new, beautiful artistic style and distinctive national features, the friendship between the Chinese and foreign peoples in ancient times and the undaunted fighting spirit of the people's artists in their creative works. It has won the praise of the audiences. In addition, plays which portray proletarian revolutionaries of the older generation have also appeared, such as "Newspaper Boy," "First Light of Morning," "Chen Yi Leaves the Mountain" and so forth. Some veteran writers have summoned up their vigor and continued to write. "The East," a long novel which describes the struggle to resist U.S. aggression and aid Korea and protect homes and the motherland; "Wang Zhaojun" and "The Song of Gale," plays which describes historical figures in ancient times; and "Goldback's Conjecture," a story which describes contemporary scientists, were examples of their achievements. New progress has been made in the themes and artistic style of movies. Movies such as "From a Slave to General," "Ji

Honghchang," "Little Flowers," and so forth were produced. In the self-defensive counterattack against Vietnamese aggressors, many literary and art workers, especially those in the army, rushed to the front and wrote works reflecting the great patriotic and revolutionary heroic spirit of our people and army.

The full emancipation of artistic creative power has led to admirable results in mural paintings. A newly completed grand mural painting erected in Beijing International Airport and other relevant artistic works have been highly praised by Chinese and foreign writers and artists. They have initiated a new path for our country's mural paintings. The painters of these murals are mostly talented young people who have emancipated their minds and dared to think new ideas about combining our traditional national characteristics of mural paintings with modern techniques to express the spirit of the new epoch. All these mural paintings are the products of their coordinated efforts with ceramic handicraft artists and architects. Their artistic achievements with distinctive styles and characteristics and creative experiences are worth summing up and popularizing.

Many works in this period, short novels and plays in particular, promoted the realistic traditions of socialist literature and art in portraying the acute struggle of the masses against the "gang of four" and various complicated social contradictions arising in those difficult years. They also depicted proletarian revolutionaries of the older generation and advanced figures coming to the fore in the new Long March and exposed various stumbling blocks and malpractices hampering the realization of socialist modernization. In timely and incisive ways, using various themes, they brought forth problems in practical life awaiting urgent solution. They strongly reflected the desire, ideal, feelings and demands of the masses. These works are the products of the great trend in the movement of the emancipation of the mind in our country and in return affect and promote the development of the trend. These works were created by comparatively young writers. They truly expressed their personal experience and understanding with a keen eye and the courage to explore. They wanted to denounce, protest and shout loudly because their experiences were imbued with bitterness, blood, tears, resentment and grief. Their awakening and struggle after being hoodwinked could also be found in their works. With pungent style, they shattered restrictions and fetters to express their profound experiences and described what they had seen and heard. This has shocked readers. These works reflected the deep scars inflicted by Lin Biao and the "gang of four" on the people's life and minds and exposed their towering crimes. On no account must we randomly accuse them of being "literature of scars" or "literature of exposure." The scars of the people and scars inflicted by the counterrevolutionary factional setup objectively do exist. How could our writers cover them up or whitewash them? How could our writers turn a blind eye to various contradictions arising in practical life. Of course, we never agreed to the naturalist approach of reflecting these scars and spreading passive, listless and nihilist ideas and feelings. The people need healthy literature and art. We need the strength of literature and art to help the people deepen their understanding of their past miserable sufferings, heal their scars, draw experiences and avoid the recurrence of these tragedies.

These works came from the vast sea of the people. They were imbued with a rich flavor of life and strong spirit of the times. Most of their writers were new. Sometimes they were not mature enough. Shortcomings of various kinds were hard to avoid. It is natural that people hold different views on them. Free discussion and debate should be allowed. These writers should also humbly listen to opinions from different quarters. In a word, these new writers are now deeply thinking, fighting and advancing. They represent the young generation of our country's literary circles. They are in the process of growing up and maturing. They have brilliant prospects. We must enthusiastically welcome them, encourage them and correctly guide them. Our literature and art should unite people, not demoralize them; they should encourage people to go all out and make progress, not lose heart and they should make people become broadminded, not shortsighted. Any work which corrodes the people's soul and corrupts the general mood of society should be resisted and criticized.

Reviewing the course of the 30-year development of our literature and art, for most of the time, with the exception of 10-year catastrophic period when Lin Biao and the "gang of four" ran amuck, we have basically implemented in our literature and art work, the literature and art line advocated by the party and Comrade Mao Zedong. We have, as a whole, taken Marxism-Leninism-Mao Zedong Thought as our guiding principle. Mao Zedong Thought on literature and art is an important component part of Mao Zedong Thought. It has taught our literary and art workers from generation to generation. Comrade Zhou Enlai was our model in practicing Mao Zedong Thought on literature and art. He always specified and further developed literary and art principles put forward by Comrade Mao Zedong by integrating them with practice. Several important speeches delivered by him and Comrade Chen Yi on literary and art problems fully stressed the utmost importance of promoting democracy in socialist literature and art. They had an immense guiding significance for our literature and art. It was under the guidance of Comrades Zhou Enlai and Chen Yi that we succeeded in holding the Xinqiao meeting and Guangzhou meeting in 1961 and 1962 respectively, which discussed the problems of films and drama. To deal with shortcomings and mistakes arising in our literature and art work at a certain period, the Ministry of Culture and the party group of the federation of literature and art circles put forward in 1962 certain suggestions for improving literature and art work—the "eight-point decision on literature and art."

These suggestions were basically correct. Undoubtedly, we have scored essential and immense success in our literature and art work. Our main current is correct and healthy. However, it is equally undeniable that we have many shortcomings and made mistakes in our work. It should be particularly stressed that the "leftist" guiding ideology has caused severe damage to the party's cause of literature and art. While slandering the correct line we pursued as a counterrevolutionary revisionist line, Lin Biao and the "gang of four" utilized and malignantly developed some shortcomings and mistakes in our work from the ultraleftist angle. Of course, certain "leftist" mistakes we committed in our work were entirely different in nature from the ultraleftist line pursued by Lin Biao and the "gang of four" in a bid to usurp party and state power. However, we must not excuse our faults by citing the interference and sabotage of Lin Biao and the "gang of four." While fully affirming our achievements, we must acknowledge the shortcomings and mistakes in our work. We must be good at learning something from the past bitter experiences, drawing a lesson and avoiding future mistakes.

Under certain historical conditions and backgrounds, some of our leaders who were in charge of literature and art work failed to overcome the "leftist" ideology in their minds. As a result, they sometimes could not correctly and practically assess the situation of class struggle in literature and art circles. They could not correctly handle the relations between literature and art and politics. They enlarged class struggle, and confused contradictions among the people with contradictions between ourselves and the enemy. While criticizing ideology, art and literature, they improperly used the methods for political movements and mass struggle to deal with the problems of the spiritual world. Some comrades were injured. Practice has proven that it was harmful to adopt administrative means and methods for mass struggle to deal with problems arising in ideological spheres. It should be particularly pointed out that the anti-rightist struggle launched in 1957 in literature and art circles severely confused the two different kinds of contradictions. Many comrades were improperly attacked. Some correct or basically correct literature and art viewpoints and works were wrongly criticized. A large number of literature and art workers were injured, including those who were talented, promising and bold in exploring. The flourishing situation in the literature and art circles brought about as a result of implementing the policy of "letting a hundred flowers blossom and a hundred schools of thought contend" was sabotaged. The proneness to boasting and exaggeration and tendencies to effect the transition to communism prematurely which prevailed throughout the country in 1958 and the movement of "pulling up white flags" launched in intellectual circles also affected literature and art circles, thereby again encouraging "leftist" tendencies. While staging ideological struggles and explaining and handling some literature and art problems, we committed mistakes by oversimplifying and vulgarizing things, thereby encouraging the evil tendencies of formalism and generalization in literature and art theories and creativity. We criticized in a crude way and injured artistic democracy. This lesson was a profound one, and we should take warning from it.

What lessons should we learn from our previous errors after all? In the final analysis, we should mainly exert efforts to correctly handle the following three relationships: The relationship between literature and art and politics, including the problem of how the party should lead literature and art work; the relationship between literature and art and the people's life with emphasis on artistic practice, that is, the problem of realism in literary and art creation; and the relationship between the inherited traditions and reform in literature and art, that is, the problems concerning implementation of the policies of weeding out the old to let the new grow, making the past serve the present and making foreign things serve China. Whether or not we can correctly handle the three relationships is closely bound up with success and failure of our socialist literature and art.

Among the three relationships, the relationship between art and literature and the people's life is the most basic and decisive one. Art and literature are the reflection of social life. Literature and art take life, as a whole, as their subject of description. They proceed from life, grow roots in life and greatly influence life. Writers should, at all times, go deep into life and be faithful to life. They should write about things which they are familiar with, things they are interested in and things which impress them deeply. They should write only after careful consideration. Instead of proceeding from a "temporary" policy, writers should observe, describe and assess life in accordance with a broader historical background. In this sense, the truthfulness of literature and art is identical with politics. We advocate revolutionary realism and revolutionary romanticism. We also advocate that we should portray the heroic figures of our era in our socialist literature and art. We admit that a correct world outlook will play a leading role in our literary and art creation. All these are correct. The problems such as "truthful writing," the road of realism, portraying heroic characters and "portraying middle characters" and so forth are all academic problems. They can be solved through free discussion. It is wrong to oppose and regard in simple and general terms "truthful writing," "portraying middle characters" and so forth as bourgeois or revisionist literary and art ideology. The Dalian meeting held in 1962 and the criticism of the theory of "portraying middle characters" did not tally with reality. Truthfulness is the heart of art. It is impossible for us to talk about the ideological and artistic contents of works if we depart from truthfulness. As for writers and artists, life is their primary importance. The practice of life, including the practice in creative activities, affects not only the writers and artists themselves, but also their world outlook. This will lead to a change and a leap in their world outlook. The idea of combining revolutionary realism with revolutionary romanticism advocated by Comrade Mao Zedong has helped writers observe and portray life with a correct vision. This idea is a guiding principle. However, revolutionary realism and revolutionary romanticism should both take root in the soil of realistic life. Revolutionary realism always includes the factors of revolutionary romanticism because it must reflect the prospects of reality as its base. Even fiction must not lack reality. Of course, no slogan for creative writings should on any account become a formula and dogma which stifles the vitality of creative writing. Under the prerequisite that literature and art should observe the objective laws of reflecting real life, every writer and artist must enjoy the freedom of adopting any method in their creative works. We should advocate the creative methods which we consider the best. In the meantime, we should encourage diversified creative methods and style. Uniformity should not be imposed. It is not advisable to unify the whole of literature and art creation under a certain fixed creative method. It is impossible to do so and it would not be beneficial in giving full scope to the creative talent of writers and artists who possess individual characteristics. Such a practice will not be beneficial to the flourishing and development of literature and art creations.

Writers and artists must conscientiously seek guidance from the scientific Marxist world outlook in their efforts to understand and reflect life. This world outlook acknowledges that society is full of contradictions and that the world cannot exist without contradictions. Socialist literature and art must be daring in exposing and reflecting contradictions and struggles in life. Whether to squarely face and expose contradictions or to dodge and cover them up is what marks the distinction between the two different world outlooks and the two different outlooks on art. The two functions of literature and art, the so-called exposure or praise are not opposed to or irreconcilable with each other, but are only two sides to the question. The crux of the matter lies in what stand to take, what to praise and what to expose. Literary and artistic creations must give expression both to the bright side of the people's life and to the seamy side of society. If there is a bright side, there will be a seamy side; if there is praise, there can also be criticism. Socialist literature and art are entrusted with the task of criticism and self-criticism. "Dialectics does not treat anything as an object of worship for it is critical and revolutionary by nature." (Marx) Once Marxism is deprived of its critical spirit, it loses its revolutionary nature. We must not only criticize our enemy, but also adopt a critical attitude toward ourselves and our practice; otherwise, we can no longer make progress. Socialist writers and artists must be vigilant. They must remain sober-minded and be attentive to all sorts of contradictions in life and their development. They must use their keen insight to reflect the new conditions and questions. They must be good at discovering all the newborn things and progressive forces and also be courageous in exposing everything standing in the way of our advance.

The relationship between politics and literature and art is, in essence, that between the people and literature and art. Our literature and art must reflect the people's life and their needs and interests in various revolutionary periods. The kind of politics we are referring to here is the politics of the proletarian class and of the masses, not any politics in which a few statesmen immerse themselves, still less is it the kind of politics into which a handful of careerists and conspirators plunge themselves. The political line and policies formulated by our party are, in the final analysis, aimed at serving the present and long-term interests of the people. Therefore, in trying to reflect life, literature and art cannot keep themselves aloof from politics, in fact, they are closely related to politics. So long as literature and art give true expression to the needs and interests of the people, it is inevitable that they will exert a great influence on politics. Advocating the divorce of literature and art from politics will only lead literature and art astray. Among the various forms of class struggle such as in the political, economic and theoretical arenas, politics always remains in the center of the picture. However, no statesman, no matter whether he is a proletarian statesman or otherwise, can guarantee that he is always correct. Mistakes are unavoidable for anyone. The political line and concrete policies always have to be adapted to changes in the foreign and domestic situations. They must be complemented and revised in accordance with the result of the test by practice and altered in light of changes in the local situation at the given time. What was considered to be correct in a place at a time in the past may become incorrect in another place at another time. Hence, to faithfully reflect life, literature and art must meet the requirements of the politics of a given political period. In today's context, they must suit the requirements of socialist modernization. Everything that is conducive to socialist modernization and that can directly or indirectly inspire people to dedicate themselves to the construction of our socialist motherland is desirable to the proletariat and is in the interests of the proletariat and the broad masses of the people. We must

not entertain the narrow view that the relationship between politics and literature and art is only a one way street with literature and art playing a supporting role in the implementation of a certain concrete policy or political task for a certain locality at a certain time. In no way can politics take the place of art, nor is politics equal to art. Literary or artistic works that are in the forms of illustrative diagrams of policies, sermons or slogans or posters, or that are turned into formulas or generalities have no hope of being welcomed by the people due to the lack of truthfulness in their way of reflecting life and the absence of artistic appeal. It follows that such works cannot do a good job in playing the political role expected of literature and art.

Our literature and art is aimed at bringing up a new generation of socialist-minded people, improving the people's spiritual complexion, promoting the development and further perfection of socialist society and satisfying the ever growing needs of the people's cultural life. Such is the objective of socialist literature and art and such is the political task they are facing. It is wrong to say that literature and art are merely implements of class struggle; it is also wrong to oversimplify the relationship between politics and literature and art. Literature and art influence politics through the typified artistic images they create and the varied artistic means they employ. The artistic appeal of literary and artistic works and the influence on politics they can exercise are in proportion to the diversity of the artistic means used and the degree to which characters in such works are typified. The kind of mentality that "I am not after fame in art but only want to be exempted from punishment by looking out against political mistakes" is detrimental to the people's cause no matter whether it is some leading cadres or the writers or artists themselves who are actually suffering from this mentality.

How should the party exercise its leadership in literature and art? This most important question is central to the question of the relationship between politics and literature and art. The correct way for the party to exercise leadership is to do so by relying on the masses, including the specialists, and by implementing the mass line. In this respect, we must try our best to turn those among us who are nonprofessionals into connoisseurs. We must base our leadership on the principle of seeking truth from facts and act according to the laws governing art. We must never try to provide guidance in a peremptory patriarchal manner or by indulging in personal whims. Writers and artists must enjoy the freedom to decide what or how to write. Instead of flagrantly interfering in their creative activities, our leading comrades must be good at giving systematic guidance on the correct course of action, encourage discussions and debates among people holding divergent views, allow those who have made mistakes to correct them and allow criticisms and countercriticisms.

Today's literature and art originated from the literature and art of the past. There is historical continuity in this respect with national characteristics in literature and art. However, socialist literature and art are a brand new kind of literature and art different from any of their counterparts in bygone eras. We now come face to face with the question of the relationship between continuing the tradition and carrying out reforms. Not long ago we publicized Comrade Mao Zedong's talk with some musicians back in 1956. In it Comrade Mao Zedong gave brilliant expositions on how to preserve the national characteristics of our art and how to create what is new in the sense that it is socialist and what is original in the sense that it is proletarian. We must appropriately handle the relationship between the continuation of tradition and the institution of reforms. After conservative tendencies are criticized, we must guard against the tendency of national nihilism; after the tendency of recklessness is criticized, we must be on our guard lest conservative tendencies again rear their heads. Many traditional plays have now reappeared on our stage and been welcomed by the masses. Nevertheless, there are people who worry about the return of "emperors, kings, generals and ministers as well as scholars and beauties." Such a situation demands our concrete analysis. Some of the emperors, kings, generals and ministers of the past have been outstanding personages who once rendered meritorious service to the people, or personages who performed meritorious deeds in the defense of or unification of the motherland. Some of the scholars or beauties were rebels against feudal rites and laws in search of personal liberty and happiness. Although we need positive characters on our stage, there should also be negative ones as objects of condemnation and castigation; we must not ban them from the stage in an indiscriminate manner. Instead, we should reappraise them in the light of historical materialism and restore them to whatever positions they should occupy in traditional operas. Stagnation or ossification will render them lifeless. Traditional operas have their time-honored repertoires, mature, artistic, stylized ways and consummate stagecraft. They imbue the people with historical knowledge and help them develop the ability to distinguish between what is just and unjust, right and wrong, as well as beautiful and ugly. People often feel overwhelmed with admiration for the national style and aesthetic power in traditional operas. However, under the agelong influence of feudal ideology, many traditional operatic plays contain oversimplified or distorted descriptions of historical facts, impart incorrect ideas about what is right and what is wrong and introduce incorrect ethical standards. At the same time, traditional operatic plays often lead to fixed habits of appreciation. Therefore, the reform of traditional operas is a very arduous task. Such reform must be active and prudent, daring but not rash. We are opposed both to sticking to conventions and to rudeness and impetuosity in this respect. In any reform, attention must be paid to preserving the national styles and the cream of their artistry and to enriching their technique of expression and improving and perfecting their overall achievements. We must not only reform traditional operas, but also create new plays on historical themes based on historical materialist principles. Using traditional operas to reflect the people and their life today is a requirement of the times and the people as well as the development of art itself. We must not be content with our old national styles but must exert ourselves to develop and create new national styles. On the one hand, we must weed out the old to create the new and make the past serve the present; on the other hand, we must make foreign things serve China by reforming and utilizing whatever is good in foreign countries. We must set great store by the achievements gained in the field of revolutionary modern drama. We must not adopt the attitude toward these plays of "excluding and rejecting all" just because they were once tampered with by the "gang of four," who credited the achievements

in this respect to themselves, abused them and preposterously called them "model plays." We must thoroughly clean up the mire left by the "gang of four" with regard to these revolutionary modern plays and correctly summarize experiences gained in this respect so that they can give off their fresh glow.

THE GLORIOUS TASK OF THE NEW ERA

Our country has entered a new stage in history. Our historical task is to stimulate the flourishing of socialist culture and art while promoting socialist economic development. Our literature and art should reflect the great struggle of the people in marching toward socialist modernization, help the people understand and overcome the difficulties and obstacles standing in the way of progress, arouse their fighting spirit and inspire them with confidence. Our literature and art are of great significance in training new socialist persons and educating the younger generation.

In the past 3 years, the literary and art front has overcome various obstacles. It has taken a courageous step forward on the new Long March. However, it should be admitted that current literature and art still fall far short of the needs of the four modernizations and fail to meet the needs of the masses. The kind of life reflected by our literary and art works is not in line with the spectacular or lively struggle being waged by the masses in actual life. Literary and art works are not wide-ranging enough in subject matter, nor are they varied enough in artistic style. They reflect a lack of depth in thinking. Artistic skills also call for further improvement. The masses of people fare rather badly in their cultural and artistic life. Their call for changing this situation is a strident one. Every literary and art worker deeply feels the urgency and importance of his own job. We should strive to further develop and enliven various kinds of literature and art so they can play a still greater role in inspiring and educating the masses of people, especially the youths.

Achieving the four socialist modernizations is a great reform in productivity and also a profound reform from the economic foundation to ideology. This requires people to emancipate their minds in a big way. From "4 May" to "5 April," revolutionary literature and art have traditionally been an important part of the Chinese people's movement to emancipate the mind. Lu Xun, founder of our revolutionary literature and art, was a great pioneer and pacesetter in the movement to emancipate the mind. Our revolutionary writers and artists have played their part in various movements to emancipate the mind. The 1942 literary and art rectification campaign in Yanan was coordinated with the great rectification movement launched by the whole party. The revolutionary poems and songs of Tiananmen in 1976 sounded the bugle call for the attack on the "gang of four" and threw wide open the gates for the emancipation of the people's minds. Our literature and art should penetratingly reflect the great course of our Chinese people's movement to emancipate the mind and promote and stimulate the sustained and penetrating development of this movement.

For the very reason that our literature and art are charged with such a historical task, literary and art work itself calls for a great emancipation. Literature and art are highly creative mental work. Creating new socialist literature and art that serve the four modernizations is a grand

and very arduous task. In doing such work can we get into a rut? Can we become set in our ways? Can we mechanically start to borrow things in their entirety? Can we stop moving ahead? Can we be without great ambitions? We must be emancipated from the mental shackles of the ultraleftist line of Lin Biao and the "gang of four." We must be emancipated from the bonds of modern superstitions created by them. We must be emancipated from the influence and habits of feudalist and capitalist thinking and from the narrow views of small producers that exist to a serious extent. We must be emancipated from the influence of literary and artistic dogmatism and various idealist and metaphysical concepts. Our literature and art must really advance in a direction guided by the law of development of socialist literature and art. Our literature and art must be really rooted in the people's life. They must really reflect objective realities, faithfully give expression to the thoughts and wishes of the people and wholeheartedly serve the people. They must really be literature and art freed from the ideological shackles of exploiting classes and freed from everything that caters to low tastes—to be literature and art predicated by Lenin.

At present, there are still hindrances to the emancipation of the mind on the literature and art front. Certain comrades charge that the emancipation of the mind in literature and art circles has been "carried too far" with the masses left ideologically "confused." They attribute to literature and art certain mistakes that have appeared in society. This does not agree with facts. Of course, we must criticize various erroneous ideas and oppose anarchism, extreme individualism and the tendency toward capitalist "liberalization." However, as things now stand, it is not a case of the emancipation of the mind having been carried too far. Instead, it is a matter of not enough having been done in emancipating the mind. There are still great hindrances to the emancipation of the mind. There is still no lack of people with ossified or semiossified thinking. We can only encourage and not discourage, correctly guide and not suppress the emancipation of people's minds. To require literary and art workers to emancipate their minds, those in charge of literature and art work must first take the lead in emancipating their own minds.

At present, those in literature and art circles are continuously discussing the criterion of truth and have further criticized the "notes on literary and art work forum of PLA units." The aim is to thoroughly eliminate the remnant poison of the ultraleftist line. This is of extremely great significance in turning chaos into order on the literature and art front and in carrying out the party's general lines and specific policies for literature and art. Without eliminating the remnant poison of the ultraleftist line and without following a correct ideological line, our literature and art cannot steadily advance.

To emancipate the mind, those in literature and art circles must firmly and unswervingly carry out the guideline "let a hundred flowers bloom and a hundred schools of thought contend." This guideline is a new experiment in socialist cultural policy. Both our positive and negative experiences show that carrying out this guideline makes for relatively active and lively literature and art and that running counter to it leads to sluggishness and regression in literature and art.

For many years, frequent and enlarged ideological and political struggles have made it impossible on many occasions to carry out this guideline well. For example, Lin Biao and the "gang of four" thoroughly ruined this guideline. Due to their rebelling against and damaging this guideline, the development of literature and art has suffered immensely. This is a very profound lesson.

The "blooming and contending" guideline has now been incorporated in our Constitution which guarantees the right of the people to carry out scientific research and create literature and art and insures mutual competition and debate in creating literature and art and commenting on them. This is to say that we use the mass line and free competition and free debate as a means to develop socialist literature and art and all literature and art that benefit the people. We must have faith in the ideological power of Marxism and in the creativity and judgment of the masses. We must create an atmosphere most congenial for the free development of science and art. We must encourage freedom in literary creation and the free airing of views and open all avenues for people of talent. We must give the fullest play to the enthusiasm and creativity of literature and art workers and wage a joint struggle to bring about a new period of flourishing socialist literature and art.

To achieve this aim, what are the primary tasks confronting our literary and art workers?

First, we must energetically develop various kinds of literature and art and raise the ideological and artistic levels. From various angles, our literature and art should reflect the life and struggle of the people amid the great historical changes of our era. The struggle being waged by our people to achieve modernization bears on the destiny of the whole country and the people and on the fate and struggle of everyone and every family. We must encourage writers and artists to plunge into life and draw on these richest sources of material for art. Writers and artists must reflect in their works the progress of the arduous struggle to achieve socialist modernization. They must put forward and answer the problems of the new era which are of great concern to the people. They must create artistic images of contemporary figures who have come to the fore. They must paint a rosy picture of the new Long March. Writers must chiefly describe the life and fate of various kinds of people and their complexities, and tap the recesses of people's minds as a rich source of material in depicting the profound changes in their spiritual outlook in the struggle for modernization. Our literature and art must not only depict heroic figures but also people of all kinds including middle-of-the-road characters, backward characters and negative characters. Our literature and art must more energetically and penetratingly expose conspirators and careerists like Lin Biao and the "gang of four" and their factional networks and their social roots. In the spirit of criticism and self-criticism, our literature and art must also expose and criticize the bureaucratic style or practice, the feudalist concept of privileged treatment, the narrow views of small producers, conservative ideas and all hackneyed ideas and ingrained habits of olden times. Our literature and art must criticize bourgeois, petty-bourgeois and anarchist thinking that hampers social progress. Our literature and art should fully reflect the complicated and arduous nature of this struggle to help the masses of people understand and reform life.

Our literature and art works should also reflect the heroic exploits of proletarian revolutionaries of the older generation and numerous revolutionary martyrs, set straight the revolutionary history distorted and altered by Lin Biao and the "gang of four" and restore history to what it should be; help the people, especially the younger generation, correctly understand history and know the price paid for the victory of our revolution; use revolutionary traditions to educate the people and encourage people to embark on the new Long March. This is not only of great immediate significance but will be an example for the generations to come.

In portraying revolutionary history, we must uphold the use of historical materialism to create typical images of proletarian revolutionaries. With proletarian fervor, our writers and artists should describe the deeds that our revolutionary leaders and many proletarian revolutionaries of the older generation have accomplished in the Chinese revolution. They should do so only after obtaining all the relevant historical data. It is not easy to portray revolutionary leaders but we must remain true to historical facts and their personalities. This requires careful attention and must not be neglected.

It is gratifying to note that after many years of unjustified prohibition, the novel "Liu Zhidan" has reappeared. Many writers have made commendable efforts in portraying revolutionaries of the older generation. Theatrical works depicting Chairman Mao, Premier Zhou, NPC Standing Committee Chairman Zhu, Chen Yi, Ho Long and others from various angles have appeared: Revolutionary memoirs have also come out in large numbers. Apart from their historical value, these memoirs have laid the foundation for writing biographies of proletarian revolutionaries. While describing revolutionary leaders and revolutionaries with their lofty qualities and their noble spirit, literary and art works must correctly give expression to the relationship between leaders and the masses of people. While depicting leaders in their important capacities, they must give expression to the masses being the driving force behind history. Leaders are the people's guides and are public servants wholeheartedly devoted to serving the people. They are by no means "omniscient and omnipotent" saviours staying high above the masses. Any concepts of deifying leading figures or bestowing favors upon the people run counter to the objective realities of life and historical materialism and are distortions of leading figures and sneers at the people.

Second, we must encourage literature and art to reflect the current great struggle for socialist modernization and the glorious history of our proletarian revolutionary struggle. We must also encourage writers and artists to take up various other themes on history and real life in different styles, forms and manner and portray persons of all types and kinds so that people can understand all patterns of life and struggles of past and present eras, broaden their horizon, strengthen their fighting spirit and enhance their knowledge. Things past and present, at home and abroad, up in the sky and down on earth—things spanning a period of several thousand years and covering a distance of several tens of thousands of li—should receive the attention of writers and artists and be their sources of material.

Of various artistic forms, films are the most popular while simultaneously being the most modern means of presentation. People hope that the subject matter of films, their categories, their patterns and their styles can show greater diversity and variety. Our films must not only satisfy the needs of domestic audiences but also win praise abroad. Traditional plays, songs and folk art forms must be further restructured and developed to create more and better programs on history and the contemporary era. For local plays,

modern operas, dance dramas, juvenile plays, radio plays, television plays, ballads and symphonies, the art of presentation of singing should be further improved. We must train a large number of artists capable of performing well. Cinema houses and opera troupes must be reorganized to improve their management to further pave the way for developing and raising the standards of films and operas. Scientific and educational films should be better geared to the needs of the four modernizations so they can contribute something new. People feel that the present singing activity is not lively enough and often recall the moving scenes in the years on the way to liberation. Not only do we now need marching songs to arouse people's fighting spirit but also entertaining lyrics and light music. It is hoped that our musicians and broadcasting stations can satisfy the people's fervent wishes. Works of sculpture, frescoes, traditional Chinese paintings, oils, wood engravings, cartoons and new year pictures must be energetically developed and their standards raised. Industrial art which is closely related to the people's daily life should be further streamlined and improved on the basis of retaining traditional features. Organs specializing in sculpture and frescoes should be established. Traditional Chinese paintings and oils should be duplicated and circulated so they can reach the general public. For all kinds of literature and art, we must continuously strive to raise the ideological level and craftsmanship. All media and means of spreading literature and art, including the quality of printing and the format of publications, technical facilities, stage acoustics and cinematic techniques, equipment and facilities must be modernized to achieve increasing perfection.

Juvenile literature and art, such as reading matter, plays and cartoons, are of especially great significance in educating the younger generation, satisfying their cultural needs, cultivating their socialist moral outlook and helping their healthy growth. This is a major problem bearing on the training of successors to the communist cause. Such literature and art should be given serious attention and energetically promoted. It rests with our writers and artists to make their own contributions.

Third, we must energetically carry out mass cultural activities so that socialist literature and art can be further popularized. Our country has 900 million people, 800 million of whom are peasants. Thus, mass culture chiefly means socialist rural culture. If we do not use new socialist culture to educate the masses of peasants and raise their standards, then we are leaving hundreds of millions of our fraternal peasants to the fate of being continuously bound by the shackles of feudal superstitions, ignorance and the various backward habits of small producers. If they can not be mentally emancipated, then all talk about raising the scientific and cultural levels of the whole Chinese people will be nonsense. On the one hand, the presentation of cultural and art programs by professionals, the showing of films, the publication and distribution of books and magazines—all such activities—should be taken to the countryside, industrial and mining enterprises and PLA companies by all possible means and made available to the general public. The broadcasting facilities in the countryside should be further expanded, their film-projecting networks further developed and their projecting equipment and stage costumes and properties made as simple and easy to handle as possible to facilitate crossing mountains and forging streams and developing a mobile cultural setup of the Ulan Muchi type in a planned manner. On the other hand, we must energetically develop spare-time cultural and artistic activities among the people in industrial and mining enterprises, the countryside, army units and cities and hunt for talent from among them so we can have cultural and art reserve forces constantly on tap. We must pay attention to and energetically promote the development of a healthy cultural life for urban residents. To develop socialist culture and art, we cannot just rely on professional cultural and art groups. We must also rely on the cultural and art devotees and active spare-time cultural and art enthusiasts so we can unite in advancing together. Mass spare-time cultural activities must be promoted based on the needs of the masses and according to the principle of voluntariness and cannot be allowed to interfere with production and add to the masses' burden.

Fourth, the areas inhabited by people of minority nationalities in our country account for around 60 percent of its whole area. They have lived where they are for generations and have their own time-honored cultures and traditions. They have made their respective tremendous contributions toward the development of our culture. In the future, we must further energetically develop the culture and art of various fraternal nationalities in order to strengthen the cultural exchange between them.

Since the founding of the state, various fraternal nationalities have scored tremendous achievements in cultural and artistic work. The resources of the treasurehouse of traditional art have been tapped and sorted out. New creations are continuously being turned out. The lengthy poem "The Dress for 100 Birds," the novels "Flowers on the Grassland" and "The Smiling Jinshan River," the film "Qin Liangmei," and the dance drama "Shaoshu Village and Nanmu Ruona" have added luster to our multinational literature and art. Culture prepresented by these works received a heavy mauling and an almost fatal blow at the hands of Lin Biao and the "gang of four." Rooted in the life of people of various nationalities for centuries, it has survived like an ever-flowing river incapable of being exhausted. "A Shima" has lasted all this time as a work recited by people. The manuscript of the well-known and longest epic in the world "Gerusalemme" was saved from destruction by singers at the risk of their own lives. "Shirmu Kamu," a great treasure in the history of oriental music in circulation for over a thousand years is being continuously collated. Epics "Jiang Geer" and "Manasi" are also being collated.

The task now confronting us is to collect and sort out a number of valuable works of art from various fraternal nationalities. We must use scientific means to record and collate various fine verbal literary works so they can be preserved and carried forward. Many folk cultural and artistic activities consigned to oblivion should be resumed and improved upon, so long as they are beneficial to the cultural and artistic life of fraternal nationalities. We must restore and develop troupes and research organs handling literature and art of various minority nationalities. We must attach importance to and train writers and artists among fraternal nationalities. We must pay particular attention to developing the features peculiar to literature and art of various fraternal nationalities. In no way can we downplay such features. Cultural exchanges between various fraternal nationalities should result in their respective literature and art being more enriched and more independent. In no way should we simply let the culture and art of one nationality supplant that of another. Such an approach alienates us from the masses and is not in line with the interests of the nationality concerned. It also does not help the development of a rich and colorful multinational culture.

Fifth, strengthening the Marxist criticism of literature and art and its theory is of vital significance in developing our socialist literature and art. Our efforts in literary and artistic theoretical criticism played a positive and militant role in the struggle to expose and criticize the "gang of four" and eliminate the remnant poison of the ultraleftist line, and have stimulated the emancipation of the mind and the creation of literature and art. But generally speaking, we have not done enough research in literature and art theory. Our literature and art criticism is still not forceful enough. The forces devoted to criticizing theory are not powerful enough. The needs of the developing situation cannot be fully met.

Mao Zedong Thought, including his thinking on literature and art, has always been and is still our guide to progress in literature and art work. Out of the need to usurp party and state power, Lin Biao and the "gang of four" freely emasculated, altered and trampled upon Comrade Mao Zedong's thinking on literature and art, casted away its dream or the universal truth and fundamental principles expounded by it, seized on sentences taken out of context and individual viewpoints suited for certain conditions and scopes, and turned them into absolutes as a charm to practice deception and a stick brought to bear. Such an extremely bad state of things can never be allowed to happen again. The remnants of factions and their remaining pernicious influence have not been thoroughly eliminated. To completely solve this problem still calls for tremendous efforts on our part. How to correctly treat Mao Zedong Thought is a major problem of principle in the ideological line. We should not regard Marxism-Leninism-Mao Zedong Thought as dogma not to be changed for the generations to come. Instead we should use it as a guide in our actions. With many new situations and new problems unknown to writers of Marxist classics, including Comrade Mao Zedong, we cannot demand readymade answers from the works of revolutionary teachers to all problems now existing in literature and art. Based on our personal experiences and guided by current realities, we must again study and examine Comrade Mao Zedong's writings, his observations and his studies on literature and art matters and try to cope with the new situations and new problems now appearing in the realm of literature and art. We should not only uphold the fundamental principles expounded by Comrade Mao Zedong on literature and art but simultaneously apply and develop them concretely, showing the courage to properly revise and supplement them where all his criticisms and writings on certain individual problems are not suited or appropriate to actual conditions. We should make our own contributions toward enriching and developing the Marxist theory on literature and art and Mao Zedong's thinking on literature and art.

The Marxist theory on literature and art was introduced from abroad but must be developed on the basis of our own national foundation. We must integrate it with the practice of the literature and art movement of China and with our country's time-honored cultural traditions. Our country has a 2,000-year history of literary and artistic theoretical criticism. There have been many well-known works commenting on essays, plays, music, paintings, poems of all kinds and novels, sagas and so forth. Great writers, poets, painters, thinkers and commentators through the ages have given many valuable opinions on literature and art. This is a treasurehouse of national thinking on aesthetics. We must uphold Marxist viewpoints in sorting out, studying and critically carrying on this valuable heritage in order to facilitate the development of the Marxist literature and art theory marked with our own national features.

Workers devoted to the literary and artistic theoretical criticism must pay attention to studying and finding out about life and getting acquainted with writers and readers. Professional theory commentators must mix well with mass commentators and admit that the masses of people are the most authoritative commentators on literary and artistic creations.

Sixth, the fine cultural heritages of various nations in the world and contemporary advanced literature and art are the common spiritual wealth of mankind. To meet the needs of socialist modernization and the development of literature and art, we must strengthen and expand international cultural exchange activities and develop and establish friendly relations with writers and artists of various countries in the world. We must broaden our horizon and let all the splendid fruits of culture enrich our people's cultural life and serve the building of a socialist culture. Meanwhile, we must energetically introduce our socialist new culture and fine traditional arts to the people of the world. Such cultural exchanges are of great significance in not only enriching our socialist literature and art but also developing friendship between peoples and uniting the peoples of various countries in the struggle to oppose imperialism and hegemonism and safeguard whole peace.

While taking the initiative to develop international cultural and artistic exchanges, we must implement what Comrade Mao Zedong taught us and acquire the strong points of all nations or countries and learn what is really good. But we must "learn things in an analytical and critical manner and not do so blindly, copying everything in its entirety mechanically." We "must not copy their weaknesses or shortcomings." It is very clear that in our cultural exchanges with foreign countries, if we neglect the danger of capitalist cultural thinking and capitalist living patterns corrupting our people and youths, and if we fail to strengthen the ideological arming of the people and to raise their ability to recognize and resist such corruptive forces, and instead accept Western cultural thinking with such devotion as to forfeit our own national self-confidence and self-respect, we will be in danger and we must guard against this. We must oppose both overestimating and underestimating ourselves.

THE DUTIES OF THE CHINA FEDERATION OF LITERARY AND ART CIRCLES AND VARIOUS LITERARY AND ART ASSOCIATIONS

To fulfill the glorious duties mentioned above, the China Federation of Literary and Art Circles and the various literary and art associations in all parts of the country must energetically resume and realistically improve and strengthen their own work to meet the needs of the new situation. Certain areas and units have still not really carried out the relevant policies. Certain frameups and wrong verdicts have still not been completely straightened out. This does not help the unity in literature and art circles

or the development of literature and art. The primary task now is to do all we can to unite all literary and art workers that can be united (including those patriotic literature and art workers in Taiwan, Hong Kong and Macao) and develop their talents and their knowledge to stimulate the development and flourishing of various literary and artistic creations and the business theoretical criticism in a joint effort to achieve the main goal of the four modernizations.

The China Federation of Literary and Art Circles is a union of various literature and art associations. Various literature and art associations are professional groups of literary and art workers in various fields (including those engaged in creating, performing, writing commentaries, research, translating and editing, art teachers, workers, and organization workers of literature and art units) who have voluntarily come together to study and practice art on their own initiative to stimulate artistic creation, the criticism of theory and international cultural exchanges.

The federation and the various literature and art associations must pay particular attention to recruiting young and middle-aged literature and art workers to participate in the leadership work of the various associations. Regarding work methods, we must widely adopt social ways of doing things, uphold democratic principles, really give expression to the nature of a group representing the people, and strictly guard against simple and rigid administrative ways of doing things. We must keep in close touch with the masses of literature and art workers, so that the federation and the various literature and art associations can become organizations for the creation and criticism of various kinds of literature and art—organizations which are full of life and vigor and rich in originality and not lifeless managerial organs entangled in red tape. The federation and the various associations must make improvements and achieve new features in their structure, in their style and in various fields. Those organs in charge of relevant organizational work must strive to achieve perfection and do their work with flying colors.

Literature and art are a kind of creative mental work, a product of individual and also collective efforts. In all their activities and their work, the leading groups of the federation and the various associations should pay adequate attention to the features of literary and artistic creations. They should fully respect the laws peculiar to the creation of literature and art and respect the different individual creations of every writer and artist and their individual style. Diversity in subject matter, form and style should be encouraged. Free competition among different schools of art should also be encouraged. People representing different views on literature and art should be allowed to contend.

Through various channels, the federation and the various associations in all parts of the country contact and unite all those groups or individuals in literature and art circles who are willing to serve the motherland and the people. All those persons who are specialized in a certain field and have contributed something should be encouraged to become their member by various relevant literature and art associations. Members should be made to take collective interests and the whole situation into consideration, seek unity, help each other and oppose sectarianism, individualism and anarchism. Communists among the members of various associations should play an exemplary role in uniting others.

Under the leadership of the party, the federation and the various associations should do their work in close cooperation with the administrative leadership departments in charge of culture and with workers, youths, women and other public bodies, and get our work done in a positive and vigorous manner.

First, the federation and the various associations must make proper arrangements for full-time and spare-time literary and art workers and adopt various proper measures to provide the necessary conditions for writing, research, study, and deep involvement in life on the part of old, middle-aged and young forces in literature and art circles. A favorable atmosphere and the necessary sites for creation must also be created for their benefit. In light of the concrete conditions of writers and artists, we must adopt effective flexible means to organize them to live deep amid industrial and mining enterprises, rural areas and army units and various lines and businesses. They are to stay at fixed points or make rounds to make inspections. Thus artistic exchanges and mutual discussions can be conducted, so that they can broaden their horizon, enhance their knowledge and accumulate a store of material for creation.

Second, we must energetically help association members and the masses of literature and art workers link reality with the study and examination of Marxism-Leninism-Mao Zedong Thought and the study and examination of the history and current conditions of literature and art in our country and in the world, study and sum up the experiences of revolutionary literary and art movements, and continuously raise their own ideological and theoretical levels and energetically carry out various activities in criticizing literature and art. The various associations should establish appropriate theory research organs, train theory workers well and publish various literature and art magazines in a proper way.

Third, the federation and the various associations should do everything they can to help the administrative leadership departments in charge of culture in training various kinds of literature and art workers in order to gradually change and overcome the serious situation marked by a current shortage of workers in literature and art circles, the lack of successors or the failure to make full use of talent. The various associations may launch various study institutions or forums to strengthen basic training for literature and art workers and raise their artistic standards. They must strive to run literary and art periodicals and serials well and publish literary and art magazines for the benefit of young readers in literature and art. Practice shows that the proper handling of magazines is a good way to guide and enliven creation and discover and train talent. We must encourage older writers, artists and commentators to help their assistants, their apprentices and their students and teach the latter what they know so proper successors can be trained. They must create more conditions for the artistic practice of young literature and art workers. Concerning literature and art criticism, they should pay particular attention to training young talent and resolutely oppose suppressing new forces. Editors of literature and art magazines shoulder great responsibilities in this respect. It is hoped that they will become hardworking gardeners and discerning Bo Le's. Their job is a glorious one.

Fourth, the federation and the associations should assist the Ministry of Education, the Ministry of Culture and the Central Committee of the CYL in strengthening art education over primary and middle school students, raising the young people's standard of art appreciation and artistic accomplishments, molding their temperament and enriching their spiritual life. Under the socialist system, art education is a powerful means of cultivating communist ethics and values. A good job of conducting art education not only can help us train a big reserve army of writers and artists but is of extremely far reaching significance in remolding the spiritual outlook of the Chinese nation and raising the scientific and cultural levels and artistic accomplishments of the whole nation.

Fifth, it is necessary to protect the creative work of writers and artists, secure their legitimate rights and safeguard their freedom to create, perform and do academic research. Toward writers and artists who suffered because of unlawful practices—for example, when their fruits of labor were attacked or suppressed or when their right to work was willfully infringed upon or deprived—the federation and the associations have the duty and right to speak in their defense and appeal to the procuratorial and judicial departments for public prosecution according to law.

It is also necessary to pay attention to the welfare of the writers and artists and cooperate with cultural publication departments to revise or work out reasonable regulations regarding fees, royalties and performance in keeping with the principle of "from each according to his ability, to each according to his work" and the present economic conditions in our country. In cooperation with cultural administration departments, the federation and associations must set up a system of awards, decide on awards through discussion and pay particular attention to awarding young people and amateur writers. They must show concern for the well-being of writers and artists and give subsidies and preferential treatment to those who have lost their ability to work and have livelihood problems due to old age, poor health or other factors beyond human control.

Sixth, it is necessary to develop international cultural exchanges more systematically, energetically and actively, along with the development of our modernization program and the launching of diplomatic activities, such cultural exchanges will become increasingly more frequent and important. We must try our best to do this work well. Not only must we make more friends and learn from progressive literature and art and the literature and art workers of other countries through these activities, but we must try to acquaint ourselves better with the struggle and life of the people of other lands to promote our creation on international themes, give the people a better education in internationalism and support the world people's struggle for freedom and liberation.

Comrades, after going through a difficult and tortuous course over the past three decades and with the people of the whole country uniting in struggle, China will stand as a brand new, powerful and modern socialist country in the East in the not too distant future. This powerful country will create a brand new culture and art which the Chinese people and their ancestors will be proud of and will enrich the spiritual life of the masses and add new wealth to the world's treasure house of literature and art.

We are full of confidence before this glorious but heavy task. We have the glorious traditions of revolutionary literature and art since the "May 4th" movement and the guidance of Marxism-Leninism-Mao Zedong Thought. In particular, we have the precious experiences and lessons of the past three decades for which we have paid a tremendous price. At present, the 900 million Chinese people are engaged in the great but arduous struggle to build China into a powerful and modern socialist country under the leadership of the party Central Committee. The exciting life stirred up by this struggle and the subsequent changes in people's thoughts, feelings and mental outlook are the richest, deepest and broadest source of literary and art creation and the most powerful motive force for our writers and artists. The great changes in the motherland have created the most favorable time factor for the new prosperity of our literature and art. We will still encounter numerous difficulties, obstacles and setbacks on our road of advance. However, as long as we dare to struggle and blaze new trails, no hardships and dangers can subdue us.

To create a great culture and usher in a new period of flourishing literature and art, we cannot do without "pathbreakers." In a big country like ours, the literature and art cause does not need just a few or several dozen pathbreakers but thousands and thousands of them. In the days of old China, Lu Xun deeply regretted the "silent China" and prayed for a "valorous pathbreaker" who would dare to "break away from traditional ideas and methods" and break the silence that reigned in the cultural arena. During the 1950's, Comrade Mao Zedong fervently hoped to see "several dozen or hundred columns of proletarian literary and art fighters" moving about freely and quickly on the road of advance in literature and art. Although Lin Biao and the "gang of four" nearly succeeded in turning new China into the old "silent China," they were unable to subdue the voice of the liberated and highly conscious people.

We firmly believe that there will be several tens and several hundred route armies and millions and millions of "pathbreakers" on our literary and art front. Together, they will sing the battle song of our era and produce the strongest repercussion and response among the people of our country and the whole world. They will break the present horizon of Chinese literature and art and become honored vanguards in ushering in a new period of flourishing socialist literature and art.

Reviewing the past and looking into the future, we are full of confidence. There had been one peak after another in the history of ancient literature and art. For example, there were the book of songs, poems of the State of Chu, folk songs and ballads in the Han and Wei style, poetry of the Tang and Song dynasties, verse of the Yuan Dynasty and novels of the Ming and Qing dynasties. In the history of contemporary literature and art, we have great men of letters like Guo Moruo, Mao Dun and Ba Jin, who are headed by Lu Xun. We also have outstanding artists like Nie Er, Xian Xinghai, Mei Lanfang, Ouyang Yuqian, Cheng Yanqiu, Zhou Xinfang, Qi Baishi and Xu Beihong. Today, we are living in a socialist era. After going through the most torrential and complicated struggle, the people of our country are now taking part in a new and greater struggle. Under these new historical conditions, as long as we unite in struggle, we can definitely reach a state never before reached by our predecessors and scale heights that are more imposing than those scaled at any time in the past.

Let us forge ahead courageously and create tirelessly. A renaissance of new China's socialist literature and art is bound to arrive, with brilliant and talented people coming forth in large numbers.

The End of Democracy Wall, 30 November 1979

62

The decision by the Beijing municipal authorities to do away with Democracy Wall was obviously taken under pressure by the Party center and was clearly a controversial move.

At the fifth (enlarged) meeting of the Beijing Municipal Revolutionary Committee on 30 November, the participants heatedly discussed the issue of the "Xidan Wall" put forward by the 12th meeting of the 5th NPC Standing Committee. They reviewed the situation in the past year since the "Xidan Wall" appeared, and cited numerous facts on how a small number of people with ulterior motives have used the "Xidan Wall" to cause trouble and to sabotage stability and unity and the building of the four modernizations. They held that practice has now proven that the

[Hong Kong *Wen Wei Po*, 2 December 1979.]

"Xidan Wall" has only disadvantages and no advantages, and should be disposed of as rapidly as possible.

Han Zuoli, a member of the municipal revolutionary committee and a responsible person of the municipal education bureau, said: Since the "gang of four" were smashed, our country has greatly needed a political environment of stability and unity to insure the smooth progress of building the four modernizations. This is the desire of the people of the whole country, and also of the people of the capital. However, Wei Jingsheng and his ilk want to cause chaos everywhere. They made use of the "Xidan Wall" to vigorously create counterrevolutionary public opinion, attack the leadership of the party, attack the socialist system, and sabotage stability and unity, in a vain attempt to overthrow the leadership of the party and the socialist system. In view of this situation, the "Xidan Wall" cannot be allowed to continue.

Zhang Binggui, a member of the municipal revolutionary committee and a national labor model, said: Practice has proven that the "Xidan Wall" has not played any good role. The people causing trouble there are all loafers who refuse to go to work or attend school. What person genuinely content with getting on with production and wholeheartedly pursuing the four modernizations has gone to that place? After they saw the news in the 28 November press about the demand to dispose of the "Xidan Wall," many workers in our unit joyfully declared: "A very good thing, too! The 'Xidan Wall' can now be abandoned."

Chen Fuhan, a member of the municipal revolutionary committee and vice chairman of the trade union of the Beijing railways, said: The people of the whole country are going all out to promote the four modernizations, while a small number of people with ulterior motives have made use of the "Xidan Wall" to stir up trouble and chaos everywhere so that people know no peace. How can the focus of work be shifted if things go on like this? How can the four modernizations be accomplished? As I see it, the people making trouble there are the very ones who do not promote the four modernizations, and who want to destroy socialism.

Li Qiaoyun, vice chairman of the municipal revolutionary committee, said: A small number of people with ulterior motives have stirred up trouble by rumormongering at the "Xidan Wall," causing a storm throughout the city, sapping the morale of the masses, spoiling the appearance of the city and blocking traffic. There are 100 bad things and not 1 good thing about the existence of the "Xidan Wall." If things go on like this, how can order in society, work and production in the capital be guaranteed?

Lu Zijing, member of the municipal revolutionary committee and secretary of the Shijingshan District CCP Committee, said: There are not many people involved in making trouble at the "Xidan Wall," but their influence is extremely bad. They make use of the "Xidan Wall" to level false charges against and attack the leaders of the party and state, leak party and state secrets and offer intelligence for sale. This place has already become an important center for a number of foreigners with ulterior motives to fish for intelligence, endangering the fundamental interests of the people of the whole country. The cadres and masses in Shijingshan District have demanded many times that the departments concerned take suitable action to solve the problem.

Wang Xueli, a member of the municipal revolutionary committee and a national labor model, said: Those people making trouble at the "Xidan Wall" are always shouting about "democracy," but what do they mean by that? If the masses fail to agree with the viewpoints they disseminate at the "Xidan Wall," those people surround, attack and abuse them. Some of them have even openly proposed the establishment of brothels in China. Is this also democracy?

Guan Shixiong, a member of the municipal revolutionary committee and director of the municipal industry and agriculture education office, said: As some people see it, "Xidan Wall" is the only place in the whole country where there is "democracy;" does that mean that there is no democracy anywhere else? Actually these people are opposing socialism under the pretext of democracy.

Now there are very many channels for bringing democracy into play; if you have views on something they can be reported according to your organization and system and you can also bypass the immediate leadership and go to higher levels. So long as the problems you report are correct, they can be rationally solved. To insure democracy for the great majority of the people, the public security organs, procuratorates and courts must resolutely uphold the socialist legal system and seriously implement the municipal revolutionary committee's notice of last March. They must severely and mercilessly punish a handful of black sheep who collect crowds for troublemaking and to sabotage law and order in society. If we allow these people to go on making trouble, we will endanger the democracy of the masses and harm their fundamental interests.

A Controlled Substitute for Democracy Wall, 6 December 1979

63

A new provisional stipulation calls for posters to be moved to a much less conspicuous location, and, contrary to what is mentioned here, their content is to be officially vetted.

To protect the people's democratic rights, safeguard social order, facilitate the handling of proposals and reasonable demands set forth in some big-character posters and prevent the use of such posters anonymously or under pseudonyms for conducting law-breaking activities, the following provisional stipulations are hereby promulgated:

1. In the future, all big-character posters, as well as small-character posters, to be posted in places other than one's own unit shall be put up only at the designated posting site in Yetan Park. Posting of big-character posters at Xidan Wall and other places is prohibited.

[Beijing Municipal Revolutionary Committee notice, 6 December 1979. Text broadcast by Beijing Domestic Service, 6 December 1979.]

2. A big-character poster registration center shall be set up near the site where the big-character posters are to be put up. Those who put up the big-character posters are required, before posting, to register their real names, addresses and units to which they belong. The contents of the big-character posters shall not be examined by the registration center.

3. Those who put up the big-character posters shall be held responsible for the political and legal implications of the content. It is forbidden to reveal state secrets, to fabricate information and make false charges, to libel and conduct other activities that violate the law.

4. Creating disturbances or riots at the site where posters are put up is prohibited. Violators shall be only duly punished according to the law.

5. The above stipulations shall go into effect 8 December 1979.

The National People's Congress Limits Freedom of Speech, 10 September 1980

This resolution amends Article 45 of the state constitution of 1978, thereby limiting freedom of speech and the putting up of posters.

The Third Session of the Fifth NPC approves the motion of revising Article 45 of the PRC Constitution put forward by the Standing Committee of the Fifth NPC and, in order to give full scope to socialist democracy, improve the socialist legal system, maintain the political situation of stability and unity and ensure the smooth progress of the socialist modernization program, decides that Article 45 of

[Resolution of the Third Session of the Fifth National People's Congress, 10 September 1980, New China News Agency, 10 September 1980.]

the PRC Constitution—"Citizens enjoy freedom of speech, correspondence, the press, assembly, association, procession, demonstration and the freedom to strike and have the right to 'speak out freely, air their views fully, hold great debates and write big-character posters'"—will be revised to read "Citizens enjoy freedom of speech, correspondence, the press, assembly, association, procession, demonstration and the freedom to strike," deleting "have the right to 'speak out freely, air their views fully, hold great debates and write big-character posters'" which is stipulated in the original Article 45.

For One Hundred Homogeneous Flowers, 24 October 1980

65

The terminology used in this article is intended to recall Mao Zedong's famous but shortlived, liberal initiative of 1956—the Hundred Flowers Campaign. However, the message is repressively different: in a socialist society, such as the PRC, not only bourgeois (modern Western) but also feudal (traditional Chinese) values and ideas have no legitimate place.

A particular line of reasoning has been in vogue in academic discussions and literary and artistic criticism for a long time: Contending among a hundred schools of thought

[Lei Shenghong, "Does Contending Among a Hundred Schools of Thought Actually Amount to 'Contending Between Two Schools of Thought'?" *People's Daily*, 24 October 1980.]

actually amounts to contending between two schools of thought, meaning between the proletarian and the bourgeois schools of thought. This oversimplified method of understanding and propagandizing the principle of letting a hundred schools of thought contend does not conform to the actual conditions in the academic and literary and art fronts. It has already brought harmful results to our scientific and cultural undertakings. Without clarifying this concept, it would be difficult to correctly implement the principle of letting a hundred schools of thought contend.

I

Viewed from the actual conditions in our country at this time, aside from the proletarian and the bourgeois schools of thought, the petit bourgeois and the feudal schools of thought also exist in the realm of consciousness. The proposition that "only two schools of thought are contending" does away with the serious task of eliminating the influence of feudal thought confronting us and overlooks the existence of petty bourgeois thinking.

We have been inadequate in understanding and guarding against the feudal school of thought for a very long period of time, particularly in the 30 years after the founding of the People's Republic. Thus, we have neglected criticism against this school of thought.

China was an ancient feudal empire and feudal society lasted for more than 2,000 years. The feudal system comprised a complete set of political, economic, ideological and theoretical systems and moral and legal concepts. The dominance of feudal thought was deeprooted. After the liberation of our country, the anti-imperialist and anti-feudal democratic revolution developed into the socialist revolution. Generally speaking, it is correct to say that the main target of the socialist revolution is the bourgeoisie. However, the Chinese revolution was staged under semi-feudal and semicolonial historical conditions. Capitalism had never been well developed in China. From the economic base to the superstructure, the Chinese bourgeoisie had never occupied a dominant position like the feudal landlord class. Its influence in the realm of consciousness was very far behind that of the federal landlord class. The great victory of the anti-imperialist and antifeudal democratic revolution eliminated feudal production relationships and the political system, but feudal ideology did not pass away with the passing away of the economic base because it was relatively autonomous and tenacious. In terms of guiding thought, after the founding of the People's Republic, we have always propagandized that the basic contradiction in socialist society is the contradiction between the socialist and the capitalist road and between the proletariat and the bourgeoisie. In ideology, we have been stressing criticism against bourgeois and revisionist thinking. Thus, we overlooked criticism against feudal thinking. In the new situation, feudal thinking had changed its appearance, even putting on the mantle of "socialism" and passing itself off as socialism to wreak havoc. Its apparition not only wanders in society but is also reflected in the ruling party and manifested in some leaders.

It often forms an abnormal union with other ideologies of the exploiting class in exerting harmful influence on the revolutionary cause. The thinking of antiparty conspirators and careerists like Lin Biao, Kang Sheng and the "gang of four" was a bizarre offspring of such a union. During the 10 years of turmoil, they vigorously engaged in the cult of personality, waged a mass deification movement, enforced barbarism, implemented obscurantist policies and formed gangs and factions in their attempt to usurp party and state power. All this resulted in the rampant spread of the pernicious influence of feudalism. Facts have shown that: Whether or not we want to admit it, the feudal school of thought has long been "contending" with the other schools and it is still "contending." Moreover, it is a very vigorous school of thought. This has become very clear. Under such circumstances, if we sum up contending among a hundred schools of thought as merely the "contending between two schools of thought," that is, between the proletarian and the bourgeois schools, we are bound to overlook the existence of feudal thinking, lower the people's vigilance against the danger of feudal thinking and, in effect, serve the purpose of protecting feudal thinking. This will be harmful to our efforts at eliminating remnant feudal ideas, expanding the position of Marxist thought and developing science and art through struggle in the realm of consciousness.

Furthermore, the view on "contending between two schools of thought" rejects the petit bourgeois school of thought and this results in overlooking the existence and influence of petit bourgeois thinking and sometimes, oversimplifying and classifying petit bourgeois thinking as the same as bourgeois thinking.

In old China, due to various social and historical reasons, there was a large number of small producers both in the cities and in the countryside. In terms of social status, they belonged to the middle class. The social position of the petit bourgeoisie determined that they had a revolutionary side and also a weak and vacillating side. It was different from the proletariat but could not also be simply classified as bourgeoisie. We cannot equate the two and cannot raise petit bourgeois thinking to the higher plane of principle and criticize it as bourgeois thinking. Unfortunately, under the slogan that a hundred schools of thought contending is actually "two schools of thought contending," and in various campaigns of ideological criticism and criticism in literature and art in the past, petit bourgeois thinking was often criticized and struggled against as bourgeois thinking. This was even more outstanding and obvious in literary and artistic creation. When some writers betrayed some petit bourgeois temperament or tendency, some people would make a great fuss and conduct criticism and struggle against them. Once their questions were raised to the level of bourgeois thinking, the targets of criticism not only did not have the right to defend themselves but were actually deprived of their right to continue writing. These methods have brought great harm to our literary and artistic undertaking. Today, in implementing the principle of letting a hundred schools of thought contend, we must correctly handle petit bourgeois thinking and must not push it to the side of bourgeois thinking.

II

When Comrade Mao Zedong put forth the "double hundred" principle, he correctly pointed out: "Questions of right and wrong in the arts and sciences should be settled through free discussion in artistic and scientific circles and through practical work in these fields. They should not be settled in an overly simple manner." ("On the Correct Handling of Contradictions Among the People") The view that "there are only two schools contending" often leads to using administrative means and political struggles to resolve questions in the realm of consciousness and using oversimplified methods to resolve very complex problems in literature and art and academic questions.

For many years, under the influence of ultraleftist thinking, the principle of letting a hundred schools of thought contend was summed up as "letting two schools of thought contend". Therefore, differences in opinion in the course of academic study and literary and art criticism were viewed as the direct manifestation of the struggle between "two classes, two roads, two lines and two world outlooks." Particularly after the antirightist struggle of 1957, all academic contention in science and art was considered to be class struggle. Even today, there are people who hold on to this view and method and who seek to flagrantly interfere in questions of literature and art and academic questions. Problems in the realm of consciousness are very complex. Only thoroughgoing and meticulous work can be effective in solving these problems. Employing a simple method would often lead to the opposite of what one wishes to accomplish. According to the stipulation of the "double hundred" principle, we must never adopt the simple method of political struggle to destroy bourgeois writers and works and bourgeois ideas and works in the academic fields. Even bourgeois literature and art has its period of rise and decline. We must fully acknowledge the historical role of bourgeois writers, artists and works during the period of the rise of the bourgeoisie and recognize their historical significance, while pointing out their class and historical limitation. Moreover, we must selectively inherit their progressive ideological content and sophisticated artistic techniques. They constitute a very precious cultural inheritance. We must not allow and should not attempt its destruction. Even in dealing with bourgeois literature and art during its period of decline, we must conduct concrete analysis of individual writers and works. It is certainly not a question of indiscriminate destruction. During the 19th century, criticism against realism emerged in bourgeois literature and art. Balzac and Tolstoy were great masters of art who criticized realism. However, Marx, Engels and Lenin did not adopt a destructive attitude toward them just because they were bourgeois writers who criticized realism. We only know that the revolution mentors called for unity of the proletariat to destroy the capitalist system and all exploitative systems, but they never taught us to destroy bourgeois writers and works. Engels clearly saw that "politically, Balzac belonged to the orthodox school." "He was all sympathetic for the doomed class." However, Engels also said: "I think Balzac is a greater realist master than all Zolas in the past, present and future." His works contain penetrating cognitive values. "In his poetic judgment, there is splendid revolutionary dialectics!" In the same manner, Tolstoy, who came from a noble class, "was a landlord who fanatically believed in the Christian religion." He was a Tolstoyist [as published] who fervently advocated "nonviolence in resisting evil." However, Lenin said: Tolstoy was "a talented artist. He not only created an incomparable picture of Russian life but also produced first class works in world literature." "In his literary inheritance, one could not find anything that only belonged to the past, but things that belong to the future. The Russian proletariat must accept and study this inheritance." The same attitude must be adopted toward academic works of the bourgeois class. Everyone knows that Marxism came from three sources: classical German philosophy, classical English political economy and French utopian socialism. The representative personalities of these three schools of thought all belonged to the bourgeois or petit bourgeois class. If Marx and Engels did not selectively inherit their thought but simply destroyed them, we would not have Marxism!

III

The view which claims that "there are only two schools contending" takes the proletarian class as constituting only one school of thought. It denies the existence of differences in consciousness within the proletariat itself and the movement of contradictions and the dialectical law involved in the process of human cognition. Thus, it violates the Marxist line on cognition.

For many years, under the influence of ultraleftist thinking, people have been afraid to express their views, not only on political questions, but also on academic questions. The highhanded method of political struggle was used to maintain superficial unanimity, as if the proletariat has been really "united" as one school, and condemn all dissenting views as belonging to the "bourgeois class." This phenomenon is very abnormal.

The Marxist theory of cognition holds that human cognition of objective things is not absolute and is not achieved in one attempt. Even under the guidance of the correct world outlook and methodology, people's knowledge about unknown realms and new things differ in thousands of ways. This is true in art and in science as well. Therefore, even within the ranks of the proletariat, we must not and it is impossible to demand that understanding of some concrete questions be completely identical and without any difference. This kind of demand is unrealistic. Of course, in terms of ideological system, that is, world outlook, there is only one school of thought for the proletariat which is the scientific framework of Marxism with dialectical materialism and historical materialism as its theoretical basis. However, within the ranks of the proletariat, the understanding of many academic questions, questions of literature and art and other questions is often varied or even opposed to each other. This is because human cognition is always limited by the objective conditions and subjective cognitive ability. People usually perceive one aspect of the matter first and go from the particular to the general. People's cognition of a particular aspect of a matter is fragmentary and usually one-sided. Therefore, differences are common. According to the dialectical materialist understanding of the world, the objective world which is independent of human will is an ever changing and rejuvenating movement process. New things continuously come forth while old ones continuously die out. People's knowledge about new things and unknown realms deepens only by the repeated process of practice-cognition, until they grasp the essence, that is, the internal law of movement of matter. Before the law of a matter is known to people, we must advocate the spirit of courageous search for truth, engage in different types of practice and conduct bold experiments and explorations from different angles. Here, we indeed need the courage of an adventurer. In this process, errors, difficulties, failures and setbacks are almost inevitable. We must not put political name tags on a person, "dismiss" him from the family of the proletariat and drive him to the ranks of the bourgeoisie just because he made this or that mistake and met this or that failure in the process of his search for truth. Literary and artistic creation and scientific research are complex spiritual labor. It is simply impossible to demand that all writers and scientists not commit errors and complete their cognition of objective things on one try. Such does not conform with the Marxist line on cognition.

To facilitate the discussion and cognition of objective truth, we must also advocate free contention among various schools of thought within the ranks of the proletariat. Regarding the various objectively existing schools of thought which have differences among them or are opposed to each other, we must not be impatient in forcing an artificial "unity" on them and in arriving at a conclusion. Conclusions to many questions have to be tested by time and practice. Even after the test of time and practice has proved that a certain school of thought is indeed wrong, we still must not apply the simple rule of "only two schools contending" and plainly put the name tag of "bourgeois thinking" on that school. This is because in the realm of literature, art and social science, differences and opposition of views on many problems are not a result of opposing class standpoints. It is usual for several different views to be held on a particular question, each one having its own basis and contending equally. Even if one of the schools made a mistake, we must not use this as a basis to brand it as "bourgeois." In the past, we were used to using the "rule"

of the struggle between two classes, two roads, and two lines to judge all questions. We have instinctively acquired the following habit: Whenever there are differences in opinion, there is struggle between two classes, two roads and two lines; once we see contention of any kind, we must find out which school is bourgeois and which is proletarian. This metaphysical way of thinking and working method has indeed brought us great damage and profound lessons.

In short, the principle of letting a hundred schools of thought contend encourages people to be bold in practicing, diligent in thinking about problems and courageous in exploring. It points out to people the correct principle in understanding the world and actively changing the world. On the other hand, the view that "only two schools of thought must contend" restricts people's thinking and action and results in hesitation, leading to the atmosphere where "ten thousand horses were all muted and a hundred flowers were all withered, fallen and scattered about." To make the socialist literary and artistic undertaking flourish and develop academic research, we must firmly implement the principle of "letting a hundred flowers blossom and a hundred schools of thought contend" to enable literary and artistic work and academic research to serve socialism and the people better.

A Condemnation of the Film Script, "Bitter Love," 20 April 1981

66

From this description of what is essentially an essay in individualistic artistic self-expression, it can be seen why the film script was anathema to the authorities. It is interesting and also significant that the propaganda charge against "Bitter Love" was led by the PLA. The older generals, and probably the younger ones as well, want a disciplined society and do not like the effusions of undisciplined intellectuals.

Since the downfall of the "gang of four", particularly since the 3d Plenary Session of the 11th CCP Central Committee, the broad masses of literary and art workers have emancipated their thinking and acquired ease of mind under the guidance of Marixism-Leninism-Mao Zedong Thought.

Their enthusiasm for creativity has been running high. As a result, a prosperous scene has appeared in the field of socialist literature and art in our country and a large number of outstanding works have come to the fore in our army. Alongside the great achievements, shortcomings and

problems have also found their way into literary and art creations by army writers. On the one hand, there is the influence of erroneous "leftist" ideology which must be further eliminated. On the other hand, there is a tendency toward bourgeois liberalization which must be rectified. Both of these tendencies run counter to the four basic principles. The film script "Bitter Love" by Comrade Bai Hua, an army writer, not only runs counter to the four basic principles but also practically reaches the point of negating patriotism. We hold that it is necessary to criticize this work according to the principle of seeking truth from facts. Such criticism will help deepen our understanding of the four basic principles, raise our consciousness of adhering to and safeguarding the four basic principles, carry forward the spirit of patriotism and make the creation of literary and art works prosper.

["The Four Basic Principles Brook No Violation—A Comment on the Film Script, 'Bitter Love,'" *Liberation Army Daily*, 20 April 1981, reprinted in *Sichuan Daily*, 21 April 1981.]

I

"Bitter Love" describes the tragedy of a painter who fervently loved the motherland all his life but was "trampled upon" by the motherland. The story begins with the pursuit of painter Ling Chenguang and his flight to Weidang in the summer of 1976, recalls his experiences during his youth and goes on to describe his tragic end, freezing and starving to death in a snow-covered field. In old China, the young Ling Chenguang was poor, but he was well looked after by charitable persons and held in high regard by those who appreciated his talents wherever he went. For example, an artist who specialized in colored drawings taught him the techniques of coloring; Mr. Chen, a scientist, called him a friend; Juanjuan, Mr. Chen's daughter, gave him a carving knife with a lover's knot tied to it and sang him the song "We Love Under the Light of the Stars;" an elder of a Buddhist monastery had Ling Chenguang's painting of orchids mounted and presented to him in return for a scroll dedicated to "the esteemed secular Buddhist Ling Chenguang," on which was written these lines taken from Qu Yuan's poem "Li Sao" [falling into trouble]: "If deep down I consider it a worthy cause, I would pursue it even at the cost of my life." When the Kuomintang press-ganged able-bodied men, the young Ling Chenguang was rescued by a boatgirl named Lu Niang. The two fell deeply in love. He later took part in the movement against hunger, against civil war and against persecution. When he was pursued by secret agents, he hid himself in an oceanliner and fled abroad. In a country in the Americas, he became famous and enjoyed the luxuries of "a villa with a garden," "a black sedan," "black maids," "a studio with lighting fixtures." He held exhibitions and won the applause and esteem of foreigners. In his own gallery, he ran into Lu Niang by chance and the two eventually got married. After liberation, the couple gave up everything they had abroad and returned to the motherland. When the oceanliner entered the territorial waters of the motherland and the five-starred red flag was in sight, Lu Niang gave birth to their daughter, whom they named "Xingxing," meaning star. However, the painter only enjoyed a brief span of happiness in their socialist motherland before the disastrous "Great Cultural Revolution" set in. In contrast to the eagerness of this family to show their love for their motherland, the story goes into great lengths to play up how the motherland did not show any love for them. It tells of how their family was forced to move to a dusky small room "without windows, without sunlight and without air;" how the painter was flogged on his birthday. Feeling that there was no place for her "in this country," his daughter Xingxing decided to take refuge elsewhere, but Ling Chenguang disapproved of her plan. The daughter then asked: "You love our country and have suffered for your bitter love. . . . But does this country love you as you love it?" Ling Chenguang "could not find the words to answer this question." As he was being pursued, he kept asking himself "why a man living in the socialist motherland still has to flee his home" and remained perplexed despite much thought.

During his exile in Ludang, he swallowed raw fish and ate the pickings of rats just like a barbarian. Toward the end of the film, the snow stopped and the sun came out again. Everyone ran out in search of the missing Ling Chenguang. However, the flame of life inside the body of the painter had already burned out. With his last ounce of energy, he drew "a huge question mark" by crawling on the snowy soil, and the dot of the question mark was "his frozen body." His life had come to an end, but "his eyes remained open" and his hands were stretched toward the sky. This was the so-called "glorious and arduous course" traversed by the painter Ling Chenguang as described in the film script "Bitter Love."

II

The author of "Bitter Love" declares to the people that the theme of this work is love—the love of the protagonist for the motherland and also the love of the author for the motherland. However, after reading this work, we cannot help but say that the sentiments he describes and expresses are not exactly "love" for the motherland, but a resentment against our party and socialist motherland under the guise of "love."

Loving one's country and the spirit of patriotism have never been abstract things. They have different contents under different historical conditions and in different classes and societies. Today, when we talk about loving our country, we do not just mean cherishing the vast territory, abundant resources, beautiful mountains and rivers and age-old and splendid culture and traditions of the motherland. We also mean cherishing the 1 billion industrious and heroic people led by the Chinese Communist Party, cherishing the socialist country under the people's democratic dictatorship (that is, the dictatorship of the proletariat), and cherishing the great cause of socialist modernization led by the party. This kind of patriotism has the broadest and most profound social base. It has brand-new social, economic, political and ideological contents and is beyond any kind of patriotism in history. It reflects the new relationship between the people and their country, which is being shaped and developed in the course of socialist construction. Today, how can we think of love for the motherland and love for the party and for socialism as conflicting? However, what "Bitter Love" reflects is just that. According to its description, there remained some friendly feelings and warmth in the old society; but in the new, socialist China, there is bitterness and tragedy everywhere. In the old society, there were people who would come to the rescue of the persecuted patriots; but in new China, patriots not only continue to be persecuted but are driven to the wall. In that country in the Americas, there was "radiant sunshine" throughout the land; but in the socialist motherland, there is nothing but darkness. "Bitter Love" describes how Ling Chenguang loved his country as a way to show how the motherland did not love him. In this work, even the five-starred red flag was faded. The painter's daughter was born under the five-starred red flag but could not find a place for herself under this flag. Xingxing's flight is portrayed by alternating shots of the "fluttering" five-starred red flag and a "tearful" Xingxing, accompanied by the dialogue of her parents at the time of her birth: "What shall we call her?" "Let's call her Xingxing." The five-starred red flag is the solemn symbol of the socialist motherland. Every patriotic person is bound to feel humiliated beyond tolerance to see this symbol thus mocked. In contravention to the truth of history and life, "Bitter Love" uses sharp contrasts to clearly express this theme: New China is inferior to old China; the Communist Party is inferior to the Kuomintang; socialism is inferior to capitalism; and the socialist motherland not only has nothing lovable but is abominable and horrible.

It is precisely under the leadership of the Chinese Communist Party that the Chinese nation has been able to fundamentally change its destiny and stand up in the world in the past 60 years. The great cause of people's liberation led by our party has entered a most brilliant and shining page in the chronicles of patriotism of the Chinese nation.

Today, our party is again leading the people of various nationalities throughout the country to embark on the great cause of socialist modernization. This is a concentrated expression of the spirit of patriotism of the Chinese nation. "Without the Communist Party, there is no new China;" "Only socialism can save China." This is the truth of history and the aspiration of the people. Despite the fact that our party had made mistakes in its work and suffered setbacks, particularly the fact that we have not been able to fully bring into play the superiority of the socialist system due to the sabotage of the Lin Biao and Jiang Qing counterrevolutionary cliques, we still have made tremendous achievements in the 30 years since the founding of the People's Republic. A person who seizes on the mistakes made by the party to negate our socialist country under the leadership of our party and negate the four basic principles is definitely not singing the praise of patriotism but is slinging mud on it.

Through artistic images, "Bitter Love" spreads the sentiment of fleeing from the socialist motherland. Although the writer noted that the film script intends to "show the congealment and centripetal force of the Chinese nation," yet what people see in this work is just how this sort of "congealment and centripetal force" is ruined. Through the mouth of the painter's daughter, the film script put forth the acute question "You love our country. . . . But does this country love you as you love it?" This is indeed the real theme of this work. The whole story actually elucidates this theme. The painter Ling Chenguang "obsessively loves the motherland," but in the end his family was broken up, some fled, some dead. The historian Feng Hansheng, who met the painter in a reed marsh, gave up his "high standard of living" overseas, but the result was that he fell into a sort of "unrequited love" toward the motherland for the rest of his life. The poet Xie Qiushan and his wife, who returned to the motherland aboard the same ship with the painter, were forced to separate, with "the husband living in the south and the wife living in the north." When the poet received the "notification of the death" of his wife Yunying, and looked at her picture, there was the echo of his wife's coughing and her words on board the ship returning to the motherland: "I'll be all right. I'll be all right since we are returning to the motherland. Everything will be fine." All these have practically constituted an accusation and curse of the motherland, spreading the sentiment of suspicion and resentment toward the motherland. As a matter of fact, what does this sort of sentiment have in common with the innocent hearts of China's broad masses of the working people and intellectuals in ardently loving the motherland and the party? Recently, there have been extensive reports in the newspapers and magazines about Luan Fu, a former assistant professor at Taiyuan Industrial College. He returned from the University of Taiwan to the mainland in 1949. Despite the fact that he suffered persecution during the 10 years of great turmoil, he always

had full confidence in the party, the socialist cause and the bright future of the motherland. Undaunted by repeated setbacks, he contributed all his painstaking efforts to the socialist motherland, and the people of the motherland will remember him for ever. Over the years, many Chinese scientists and technicians living overseas have returned to the motherland one after another to participate in the four modernizations. "No matter how poor and backward my motherland is, she is still my motherland. Just like my mother, no matter how poor she is, she is still my mother." This is indeed a common statement from the depths of their hearts. The patriotic spirit of the Chinese people, being the congealment and centripetal force, is a significant ideological foundation for the great unity of the people of all nationalities throughout the country today, including the Taiwan compatriots and all Overseas Chinese. It is a great spiritual force for building a modern socialist motherland. However, the centrifugal sentiment which permeates the film script "Bitter Love" undermines the patriotic spirit and national self-confidence of we the Chinese people. It is detrimental to stability and unity and the four modernizations we are now embarking on.

III

The author noted that this work is meant to expose and try the "gang of four." However, people are not able to see from it which were the counterrevolutionary crimes of the "gang of four," nor could they see the struggles of the party and the people against the "gang of four." The writer made use of a large number of images, metaphors, symbols and words to repeatedly show the spiritual enslavement of the people by the "deity," the miserable fate of the people under the "sun" as well as the tragedies which occurred on the land over which the five-starred red flag flutters. Quite obviously, what the deity and the sun in the film script mean to insinuate is by no means the "gang of four"; and the deliberate arrangement for the tragedies to occur under the five-starred red flag was never intended for the trial of the "gang of four." Besides, there is indeed no reason we say that "this country" as mentioned by Xingxing referred to the "gang of four." The motherland and the "gang of four" are two entirely different concepts; and by the same token, the party and the "gang of four" are also two entirely different concepts. How could a writer who is responsible to the people distort history in such a way and take the perverse acts of the "gang of four" as the grim ruthlessness of the motherland toward its own children? How could he put all the blame of the sufferings of the 10 years of great turmoil on the socialist system and even equate the party with the "gang of four" and castigate it all the same? None of us can ever forget the sufferings endured during the time when the "gang of four" ran amok. It was the "gang of four" who trampled upon the motherland and its children. The country and the people suffered together, and our party, army and state also suffered serious damage. However, despite the fact that Lin Biao and the "gang of four" usurped part of the party and state powers, the broad masses of our party members, cadres and people never stopped resisting and struggling against them. Finally, it was precisely the people under the leadership of the party who rose up against and smashed Lin Biao and the "gang of four." All these have demonstrated that our party and state share the same fate as the broad masses of the people and that our party and socialist motherland belong to the people. Since the smashing of the "gang of four," many literary and artistic works have correctly reflected this historical event. With clear love and hatred, they have given people inspiration, confidence and strength. For example, the film "Night Rain in Bashan" has demonstrated that the broad masses of the people were basically antagonistic to Lin Biao and the "gang of four." Nevertheless, "Bitter Love" is different. It separates the party from the people (including the intellectuals) and confuses the party and the motherland with Lin Biao and the "gang of four." In the film script, the poet Xie Qiushan recited a poem: "Since we are comrades, comrades in arms and compatriots, why should you set up a trap for me? Since you have decided to put me in chains, why should you wear smiles on your faces? Since you have prepared to stab me in the back, why should you embrace me in your arms? You have sealed our mouths with tape, but the questions rebound inside our heads!..." This clearly demonstrates that what the film script wants to expose and try is not Lin Biao and the "gang of four," but our party, the leader of our party and our socialist state power under the people's democratic dictatorship.

The other theme of the film script is vilifying the leadership of the party and the state power under the people's democratic dictatorship. The writer noted: "China's modern feudalism is even more formidable than feudalism before the 1911 revolution." The artistic images pieced together in "Bitter Love" are in fact illustrations of this concept. The writer also gave the following explanation about his intentions in the creation of "Bitter Love": "Emperors of the past dynasties and those people in power could never be the symbols of the motherland. Never! On the contrary, they were the people who trampled upon the motherland." Here although the term "those people in power" through the ages is obscure, yet the meaning is not difficult to understand.

It covers the ruling party of our country under the people's democratic dictatorship—including the Chinese Communist Party and its leader. In the film script "Bitter Love," there are scenes about deification, God worshipping and how the masses were fooled by the deity all through the work. There are repeated dialogues such as: "Why is this deity so very dark?" "He has been blackened by the smoke of burning joss sticks and candles of faithful believers...." These are echoed with scenes of the Beijing streets "filled with people waving the little books of quotations, and of numerous devout, innocent but fanatic faces." The central meaning of the dialogue between the elder of the Buddhist monastery and young Ling Chenguang on deities, joss sticks and candles and temples is: The temples create the deities, fool the faithful believers and cheat them for their donations for joss sticks and candles. The only possible social effects of this sort of metaphors and suggestions could only guide the people's hatred of the "gang of four" toward the party, the leader of the party, the people's democratic dictatorship and the socialist system.

We oppose both feudal superstition and modern superstition. Nevertheless, we cannot negate basic Marxist principles concerning the relationship between the masses, the classes, the ruling party and the leaders because we oppose modern superstition. The proletarian ruling party and its leaders have come forward after undergoing long-term tests in the course of the people's revolutionary struggles. They are not idols carved in wood or molded in clay, nor illusions created through superstition. They gain the support of the masses simply because they represented the interests of the masses. But leaders are not gods after all. Comrade Mao Zedong was a great Marxist. He performed immortal feats for our party, our army and the people of all nationalities in our country. Although in his later years he committed mistakes, which were disastrous to the party and the country, we must primarily affirm his immortal feats and admit that his mistakes were secondary. Mao Zedong Thought is a coproduct of basic Marxist principles and the concrete practice of the Chinese revolution, and is simultaneously the treasure, cemented with sweat and toil, of the tens of millions of our party members and hundreds of millions of our people. The basic principles of Mao Zedong Thought will forever be the spiritual weapon of party members, the PLA commanders and fighters and the Chinese people, and will guide us to incessantly push forward the revolution. In holding discussions on the criterion of truth and doing away with modern superstition, the party demands that the people emancipate their minds, use their brains, seek truth from facts, be united as one to look forward, proceed from reality in observing and dealing with problems, and smash the shackles of "bookism" and the two "whatevers." All this is not meant to negate Comrade Mao Zedong and his thought. On the contrary, it is to evaluate Comrade Mao Zedong in a truthseeking way, restore the true features of Mao Zedong Thought and uphold and develop Mao Zedong Thought. This is in fact the fundamental interest of the whole party, entire army and all the people. Yet, the writer of "Bitter Love" mentions our party and its leaders in the same breath with "past emperors," portrays them as "those who trample upon the motherland," and defiles the broad masses and cadres as "innocent and superstitious people." The writer is in fact antagonistic to the party and the people when he says such things and gives such descriptions.

IV

Wild geese in the formation of a chevron flying freely in the sky repeatedly appear in "Bitter Love" and the theme song "While We Fly, We Write the Character Man in the Sky," and man as "the noblest image both in heaven and on earth" is repeatedly mentioned. These are used to contrast with the miserable experiences of the people all over our motherland. It is said that this way of working out the plot "will urge the people to think: 'What is man's dignity? What is man's value?'"

Comrade Mao Zedong once said: "Of all things in the world, man is the most valuable." Many fine sons and daughters of our nation and our party, for the interests of the people, stepped into the breach as another fell and, for the people's dignity, would rather die than submit. In the struggle for social progress and for the cause of the people's liberation, they realized the value of man. We respect man's dignity and man's value, but we do not put aside historical, realistic and concrete man to talk about abstract "love of mankind." In the old society, the Chinese people were not entitled to any rights. Of course, they were without dignity or value. Only in the socialist new China and under the leadership of the party were the people able to become masters of the country, were the intellectuals able to do worthwhile things and were the Overseas Chinese able to end the discrimination against them abroad. The Chinese Communists are armed with Marxism-Leninism-Mao Zedong Thought. Their aim is to serve the people wholeheartedly and their ultimate goal is the liberation of all mankind. In this sense, the communists are explorers and promoters of the most glorious cause of mankind and they are truly revolutionary humanitarians. But how is this written in the work "Bitter Love"? It misrepresents our party's aim of struggling for the people's interests as protection and blessings of a god which are only written in a prayer book or hanging high up in the sky, visible but not available. The film script repeatedly uses flocks of wild geese in chevron formation in the sky and the theme song of "The Noblest Image Both in Heaven and On Earth" to set off by contrast the miserable destiny of man on earth and accuses our party of trampling upon man's dignity, ignoring man's value and causing tragedy to the people all over our motherland. The odes to man in the film script are not only similar to those views of striving for the so-called "human rights" which appeared on the walls of Xi Dan 2 years ago but are also similar to the meaningless deliberations on realizing man's nature put forth over 100 years ago by the so-called "true" socialists who represented the interests of the urban petit bourgeois in Germany and who opposed the communist revolution. Marx and Engels made a thorough analysis of these kinds of viewpoints: They "do not represent the interests of the proletariat but represent the interests of man's nature, that is, the interests of ordinary men. These kinds of men do not belong to any class and do not exist in reality at all. They only exist in the cloudy and foggy figment of philosophical imagination." ("The Communist Manifesto") The "man" eulogized by "Bitter Love" is exactly one of these kinds of men. The film script does not represent the fundamental interests and needs of the broad masses of people living in socialist China. It is fabricated by the writer from the concepts of bourgeois humanism. It is detached from the reality of Chinese society and is only a tool for accusing the party and socialism.

"Bitter Love" quotes verses from Qu Yuan's "Li Sao": "It is a long and tortuous road leading to a lofty realm of thought, yet I will persist in taking it despite any difficulty" and uses them repeatedly throughout the film script. It also uses other verses from "Li Sao": "If deep down I consider it a worthy cause, I would pursue it without regret even at the cost of my life" to express the indomitable spirit of "persistence" of the painter Ling Chenguang. In reality, Qu Yuan's love for his motherland was manifested in his loyalty to the kingdom of Chu and in his sympathy for the people. What Qu Yuan persisted in was mainly shown in his determination to carry out reforms and in his progressive idea of advocating "making laws to promote the country's prosperity." But the kind of "persistence" preached in "Bitter Love" is to "persist" in doubting the party and socialism, to "persist" in departing from the four basic principles and to "persist" in urging the people to turn away from our motherland. This was not carrying forth Qu Yuan's spirit but is going against it. The film script distorts Qu Yuan's spirit but copies Qu Yuan's story to create the tragic image of the painter Ling Chenguang. The work also uses as its ending a climax similar to the ancient tragedy of Qu Yuan who drowned himself in the Milo River more than 2,000 years ago. On a boundless snowy field, as a flock of wild geese disappear over the horizon, the painter uses his body to crawl out a question mark on the breast of the motherland and ends his "persistence" as the dot of the question mark. Although Ling Chenguang is dead, a "growing" question mark is laid before the people's eyes.

The writer provides the answer in his own words: In developing a plot like this, it is "hoped that people can draw a grievous lesson from the lives of the brokenhearted, cast aside their illusions of those who styled themselves as symbols of the motherland and carry out indomitable struggle!" Then, who are those people who style themselves as symbols of the motherland? And against whom should we carry out indomitable struggle? The questions raised by this film script can only lead to this conclusion: Its spearhead is directed at the party and at the four basic principles.

V

The four basic principles are the foundation of our great socialist motherland and their contents have been written in our constitution. The whole party, the entire army and all people of all nationalities of the country should abide by them and the work on all fronts should follow them. Literary and artistic work is not exempted from this. The appearance of the film script "Bitter Love" in *Dianying Wenxue [Cinema Literature]* is not an isolated phenomenon. It reflects the erroneous trend of thought of anarchism, ultraindividualism and the bourgeois liberalism to the extent of negating the four basic principles. This trend exists among a very small number of people. If this kind of erroneous trend of thought is allowed to run rampant, it will certainly endanger the political situation of stability and unity and we shall not be able to smoothly carry out economic readjustment and the four modernizations. This goes against the fundamental interests of the people of the whole country. The purpose of our criticism of the erroneous tendency of "Bitter Love" is to uphold and safeguard the four basic principles, consolidate and develop stability and unity and defend the socialist four modernizations.

The policy of letting a hundred flowers bloom and a hundred schools of thought contend is a policy to bring about the prosperity of socialist literature and art. This means free competition between various forms and styles in literature and art, free academic discussions and opposition to pursuing only one style and one school by means of administrative measures. If we think that it means unlimited and absolute freedom which may even violate the four basic principles, then we shall embark on the evil road of bourgeois liberalism going against the interests of the broad masses of people. Therefore, criticizing erroneous tendencies by argument and reasoning and waging necessary ideological struggle will not affect the implementation of the policy of letting a hundred flowers bloom and a hundred schools of thought contend but is conducive to its correct implementation. If we conceal mistakes, stop criticism and avoid struggle, this will not be conducive to upholding the four basic principles, to developing socialist literature and art and to helping those comrades who have committed mistakes. We hope to raise the consciousness of our army's literary and artistic workers in upholding the four basic principles by criticizing this work "Bitter Love." We also hope that the writer of "Bitter Love" can draw a lesson from this mistake, correct his creative ideas and write works beneficial to our socialist motherland and the people.

In order to uphold and safeguard the four basic principles, we must carry out with perfect assurance and persistently struggle against erroneous tendencies which violate the four basic principles. The four basic principles are the fundamental prerequisites for our army's implementation of the line, principles and policies formulated since the party's third plenary session and the means to build itself into a modern revolutionary army. They are also the firm and correct political orientation for all the work of our army including literary and artistic work. Each of our army's cadres and fighters, especially party members, should look upon upholding and safeguarding the four basic principles as his sacred duty. The core to upholding the four basic principles is upholding the party's leadership.

Every literary and artistic worker who loves his country, serves the people and serves socialism should unite closely around the party and should on the basis of upholding the four basic principles, continue to emancipate his mind, correctly implement the policy of letting a hundred flowers bloom and a hundred schools contend and promote the prosperity and development of socialist literature and art. He should strive to make his work reflect correctly the new era we are in and to spur on the whole party, the whole army and the whole people of all nationalities of the country to make new contributions to the great cause of the four modernizations with concerted efforts and with one mind. Only in this way can we do credit to the party and the people who have nurtured us and to our dear socialist motherland.

On Regional Autonomy and the National Minorities, 14 July 1981

67

Ulanhu is a sinicized Mongol who, for many years, has been the Party's chief spokesman on the concerns of the 6 percent of the total population who are not Han (ethnic Chinese). Although Communist Party rule since 1949 has brought the minorities some of the benefits of modernization, it has trampled on their traditions and deprived them of freedom behind a facade of autonomy.

The past 60 years were years in which all nationalities of the Chinese nation pursued common liberation and happiness under the leadership of the CCP.

The founding of the PRC in 1949 marked the end of the oppression of the Chinese nation by imperialists and the oppression of minority nationalities in China by the KMT reactionaries. It also opened an epoch of complete equality of all nationalities in China. The elimination of the exploiting system and the establishment of the socialist system has eradicated the social roots of struggles among different nationalities and opened a new historical chapter on national unity. At present, we are marching on the road of socialism and are struggling for the common development and prosperity of all nationalities.

Over the past 60 years, the Chinese communists with Comrade Mao Zedong as the principal representative have integrated the basic principles of Marxism-Leninism with the practical situation of China's nationalities and formulated, implemented and developed a policy on regional autonomy of minority nationalities. The essence of our policy on regional autonomy of minority nationalities is the establishment of autonomous areas of minority nationalities on the basis of regions where minority nationalities live in compact communities within the country's integral and inseparable territories and under the unified leadership of the supreme state organs. Autonomous organs are formed consisting mainly of personnel of the minority nationalities which practice autonomy. They can fully exercise their autonomous rights on the basis of the principle of democratic centralism. In accordance with the state's general principles and policies and with reference to the practical situations of their own nationalities and areas, they can decide for themselves their specific principles and policies and act on their own in managing the affairs of their own nationalities and areas. This policy can both uphold the common rights and interests of all nationalities throughout the country and at the same time uphold the special rights and interests of all minority nationalities which live in compact communities in different regions throughout the country.

In reviewing the glorious journey undertaken by China's nationalities struggling in unity and standing together through thick and thin in winning the victories of the new democratic revolution and the socialist revolution and construction, we have clearly understood that the party's policy on regional autonomy of minority nationalities is a significant integral part of Mao Zedong Thought

[Ulanhu, "The Glorious Course of Regional Autonomy of National Minorities," *People's Daily*, 14 July 1981.]

and is the sole correct basic policy for solving China's nationalities problem.

I. THE PARTY'S POLICY ON REGIONAL AUTONOMY FOR MINORITY NATIONALITIES IS A BASIC POLICY FOR CORRECTLY SOLVING CHINA'S NATIONALITIES PROBLEM

Since it was first founded, our party has wholeheartedly struggled for the liberation and happiness of all nationalities in China during the period of the democratic revolution. In opposing the oppression of minority nationalities by imperialists, the feudal warlords and the KMT reactionaries, our party put forth different tentative plans and proposals to realize a complete liberation of the Chinese nation and equality and unity among all nationalities in China. Under the guidance of Marxism-Leninism-Mao Zedong Thought, and through long-term investigations and practice, our party finally decided upon taking the policy on regional autonomy of minority nationalities as the basic policy for solving China's nationalities problem, thus winning the wholehearted support of the people and leaders of all nationalities.

Through their own personal experience, they have clearly understood that practicing regional autonomy for minority nationalities, strengthening unity among different nationalities, upholding the unification of the motherland and developing socialism constitute a promising road for common development and prosperity for all nationalities. All courses of action which deviate from this road violate the common desire and fundamental interests of the people of all nationalities and will simply get us nowhere.

At the CPPCC in 1949, representatives of different nationalities decided together on the establishment of a unified PRC. At the same time, it also determined as a national policy the practice of regional autonomy for minority nationalities in regions where minority nationalities live in compact communities. This choice of great historical significance was in fact determined by the following characteristics of the relations among different nationalities in China:

1. A longstanding unified country with centralized state power constitutes a historical basis for practicing regional autonomy for minority nationalities. China is made up of different nationalities, and it has been a unified country with centralized state power ever since the Qin Dynasty. Despite the fact that the situation of a feudal separatist country could not be completely eliminated, and that there had been several changes of separation and reunification over the more than 2,000 years from the Qin Dynasty to the Qing Dynasty, a unified country has somehow been the main trend. Since China is a country founded by all nationalities of the Chinese nation, China's minority nationalities are therefore generally inward-looking when they are not subject to outside intervention. Even when the ruling classes of minority nationalities in the border regions actually "became the masters of the central plains," they inevitably considered themselves as the orthodox rulers of China, this country of great fame and cultural heritage. During the last several centuries, a unified country has really become something irreversible.

2. The situation of different nationalities living together and depending upon one another is a favorable condition for practicing regional autonomy of minority nationalities. In their prolonged history, China's nationalities have migrated frequently, penetrating into one another's areas. They have gradually formed a situation in which different nationalities live together but in their respective large or small compact communities, live mingled with one another or live in scattered areas. In addition, they have also formed a relationship in which they depend on one another economically. In these circumstances, it is obviously inappropriate to establish separate states for different nationalities. Regional autonomy for minority nationalities, on the other hand, is a practice based on regions where minority nationalities live together in compact communities. On the basis of the relations among different nationalities and the conditions of economic development and with reference to the historical conditions, we may establish different types of autonomous areas for minority nationalities so as to make it easier for the different minority nationalities to exercise their rights as masters of their own affairs in matters concerning their own nationalities and localities.

3. The nature of Chinese society and the international situation since the opium wars determined that national alliance is a prerequisite for national liberation, and upholding the unification of the country is a prerequisite for ensuring national freedom. Modern China was a semifeudal and semicolonial country subject to the aggression of several imperialist countries. The contradiction between the imperialists and the Chinese nation was one that played a principal role in modern Chinese society. If China's nationalities had each gone its own way and given no thought to the others, they would have been partitioned and even annexed by the imperialist countries. Only by uniting together was it possible to join forces to triumph over the enemy and win victory in the struggle for national liberation. After the victory of the struggle for national liberation against the imperialists, and especially after the overthrow of the reactionary rule of the KMT and the establishment of the PRC, when the people of different nationalities really became the masters of the state, it was even more necessary for China's nationalities to uphold the unification of the country in order to tackle the disintegration, infiltration, subversion and aggression by the imperialists and hegemonists and to ensure national freedom.

In short, the country will survive when united, and perish when split up. It is either one or the other. In order to save the country from subjugation and ensure its survival, to promote the prosperity of all nationalities and to build a powerful modern socialist country, the people of all nationalities in China have upheld unification and opposed splitting up.

4. The correct leadership of a unified proletarian political party has formed the core force for practicing regional autonomy for minority nationalities in a unified country. In the history of modern China, many nationality movements with different political tendencies emerged in regions inhabited by minority nationalities. However, they all ended in failure. All possible ways were explored and all possible methods were tried. Facts have demonstrated that only a proletarian political party could shoulder the heavy responsibility of leading China's nationalities in seeking liberation, assisting the minority nationalities in gaining the rights of managing their own affairs on an equal basis and guiding them onto the socialist road of happiness. In the history of China's movement for national liberation, it was not the political parties of any other class, but the CCP, a proletarian political party, which first put

forth and which has persistently upheld a program for complete national liberation which included the policy of regional autonomy for minority nationalities and has thereby won the wholehearted trust, and love and esteem of the people of different nationalities. The revolutionary people of all nationalities with lofty ideals have converged under the banner of the CCP just like all rivers flowing to the sea. The correct program, strong organization and great prestige of the party and the party's many cadres of different nationalities have formed the core force in practicing regional autonomy for minority nationalities in a unified country.

5. The protracted common revolutionary struggles of the people of all nationalities has created a political basis for carrying out nationality regional autonomy. The revolution led by our party has always been the common cause of all nationalities in our country. Under the leadership of the party, the national democratic united front was formed. During protracted revolutionary struggles, the party has sown the seed of revolution in many areas inhabited by minority peoples, trained minority nationality cadres, waged armed struggles and even set up Red political power. Up to the liberation war period, almost all nationalities in our country had converged into a revolutionary torrent, and formed an entity dedicated heart and soul to the same cause, thus creating a solid basis for carrying out nationality regional autonomy.

6. The imbalance in the distribution of natural resources and in economic development determines that carrying out nationality regional autonomy in a unified country is an important guarantee of realizing common national prosperity. There are 55 confirmed different minority nationalities in our country. Compared with the Han nationality, our minority nationalities are small in population, accounting for barely 6 percent of the total population of the whole country, but they live in widely scattered areas, accounting for about 50 to 60 percent of the total area of our country. In areas inhabited by minority nationalities, there are dense forests and luxurious grasslands and rich mineral resources underground. It is obvious that in the areas inhabited by minority nationalities the level of economic development is generally lower than that in the areas inhabited by the Han nationality. The modernization of the areas inhabited by minority nationalities is a component part of the modernization of the whole country. The modernization of the areas inhabited by the Han nationality cannot be carried out without the help of rich resources in the areas inhabited by minority nationalities. The modernization of the areas inhabited by minority nationalities cannot be carried out without the financial support of the state and the technical help from the areas inhabited by the Han nationality. Therefore, judging from the prospects for the socialist cause, both the Han nationality and the minority nationalities will benefit if they are united and will suffer if they are divided.

To sum up, we have both the historical and realistic basis, both the internal and external reasons for and both the political and economic conditions to carry out nationality regional autonomy, which are the needs of both revolution and construction. In a word, it suits the conditions of our country, conforms to the will of the people and is the choice of history.

The policy of nationality regional autonomy of the party has gradually matured following the development of the situation and the accumulation of experience.

Starting from the second national party congress, the party has, in each stage of the development of the revolution, stated its stand on regional autonomy. In 1929, it was proposed in the "Proclamations by Headquarters of the 4th Army of the Red Army" signed by Comrades Mao Zedong and Zhu De: "the Han, Monggol, Hui and Zang nationalities can draw up the rules by themselves." In 1938, at the sixth plenary session of the sixth party committee, Comrade Mao Zedong explicitly expounded the party policy on nationality regional autonomy. Comrade Mao Zedong pointed out: All minority nationalities "have the same rights as the Han nationality and, on the principle of joining forces to oppose Japan, have the right to manage their own affairs and at the same time unite with the Han nationality in founding a unified country." Prior to the victory of the anti-Japanese war, the party had helped the minority nationalities to found a few nationality autonomous areas. Owing to the limitations of the objective conditions at that time, these nationality autonomous areas were not large in scope and did not exist for a long time. After the victory of the anti-Japanese war, Comrade Zhou Enlai and others put forth on behalf of the parrty Central Committee the "draft program for building up our country in peace," in which it was pointed out explicitly that "within the areas inhabited by minority nationalities, the equal status of all nationalities and their right to autonomy should be accepted." During the liberation war period, our party explicitly declared we "accept that all minority nationalities within the Chinese boundaries have equal rights with regard to autonomy." The party led the autonomous movement in Nei Monggol and formed the autonomous government of Nei Monggol in 1947, thus setting up in China the first autonomous region on a fairly large scale.

I personally participated in the birth of the Nei Monggol Autonomous Region. I realize deeply that the policy of nationality regional autonomy of the party alone is the basic policy in solving correctly the national problems of our country.

In striving for national liberation, the Monggol nationality groped in the dark for a long time. Enemies of every Hui, Monggol and non-Monggol, at home and abroad, made use of such pleasant words as "independence" and "autonomy" to inveigle the Monggol nationality into their traps. After the revolution of 1911 broke out, at the instigation of czarist Russia, a few princes and dukes of the Nei Monggol nationality who were hostile to revolution asserted their "independence" and, opposed by the broad masses and patriotic upper circles of the Nei Monggol nationality, soon ceased all activities. Later, under the pressure of events, the Kuomintang headed by Chiang Kai-shek promised "autonomy" to Nei Monggol, but facts proved that this promise was a mere scrap of paper. Under the aegis of Japanese imperialism, Mongolian traitor Demchukdondub and his ilk carried out sham "autonomy." They carried out traitorous activities under the guise of "autonomy," working in the service of the Japanese imperialists which practiced the "policy of Manchuria and Mongolia," enslaved and ruled the Monggol nationality. In order to oppose national and class oppression, the broad masses of the people of the disaster-ridden Monggol nationality waged spontaneous struggles, one stepping into the breach as another fell. These spontaneous struggles, including the Gadameilin uprisings, unfortunately failed.

Only the Communist Party of China pointed out for the Monggol nationality the road to liberation, so that the

Monggol nationality living in the dark saw the light. As early as in the first revolutionary civil war period, the party set up party organizations in Nei Monggol, unfolded the work of the party and trained the first generation of communist fighters of the Monggol nationality. During the second revolutionary civil war period, the party persisted in the revolutionary struggles in the Nei Monggol region. During the anti-Japanese war period, the party trained large numbers of cadres of the Monggol nationality and set up the Daqingshan revolutionary base area.

As soon as the anti-Japanese war ended, the so-called provisional government of the republic of Nei Monggol appeared in Sonid Youqi. Through the propaganda and education of the party, the broad masses of the Monggol nationality in the region unanimously agreed to follow the path laid out by the party of carrying out nationality regional autonomy on the basis of national equality, thus isolating and defeating the one or two splittists in this government. In November 1945, the federation of autonomous movements of Nei Monggol led by the party was set up in Zhangjiakou to replace the "provisional government of the republic of Nei Monggol." In January 1946, the "autonomous government of the people of East Monggol" appeared again in Gegenmia. Through the federation of autonomous movements of Nei Monggol, the party did arduous and meticulous work with the regime, so that the party's policy of nationality regional autonomy struck chords in the hearts of the people and the splittist views of one or two members in the government were boycotted and opposed. In April that year, through consultations at the "3 April" conference, it was decided to dismiss the government and set up the east Monggol general branch of the federation of autonomous movements of Nei Monggol. Henceforth, led by the party, the autonomous movements of Nei Monggol were united and marched along the path of healthy growth. Following the victorious development of the people's democratic revolution throughout the country, the autonomous government of Nei Monggol was officially set up on 1 May 1947 for which Chairman Mao Zedong and Commander in Chief Zhu De jointly sent a cordial cable of congratulations to the autonomous government. The founding of the autonomous government of Nei Monggol enabled the masses of the people of the Monggol nationality to obtain the right of being the masters of their own affairs, which they had never been able to be throughout history, to strengthen national unity and to uphold the unification of the motherland. The cavalry units of the Nei Monggol people wiped out the remnant Kuomintang forces and robbers in the Nei Monggol region and supported the liberation war in other places, making a due contribution to the liberation of Nei Monggol and the whole of China.

The successful founding of the Nei Monggol Autonomous Region signified that the party's policy on nationality regional autonomy had successfully stood up to the tests of practice and entered the stage of maturity.

II. ACHIEVEMENTS AND LESSONS IN THE IMPLEMENTATION OF REGIONAL AUTONOMY FOR MINORITY NATIONALITIES

The victory of the people's revolutionary war brought in a spring of unity and equality among nationalities. Since then, regional autonomy for minority nationalities has blossomed and reaped rich fruits in the vast territory of the motherland.

As of June 1981, 5 autonomous regions, 29 autonomous prefectures and 75 autonomous counties had been established in China.

Practice over the past 30-odd years has verified that regional autonomy for minority nationalities as initiated by our party has at least the following four overwhelmingly superior features:

1. The implementation of regional autonomy for minority nationalities is conducive to the integration of the country's centralization and unity with the self-determination by and equality among the nationalities.

The founding of the PRC marked a fundamental change in the relations between the nationalities in China. Since then, the people of minority nationalities have begun to take part in the administration of state affairs on an equal footing with other people. Since then, they have established a socialist national relationship characterized by equality and mutual help with the Han nationality.

Our country is one in which the nationalities are united and cooperative. With regard to state affairs, both the Han nationality and the minority nationalities send representatives to the NPC, the organ of the state's highest authority, to discuss the major issues. This is an unprecedented undertaking.

With regard to local affairs, the minority nationalities enjoy the right to be masters of their own affairs because the state implements regional autonomy. This is a great undertaking and achievement after hundreds and thousands of years. The main purpose of regional autonomy for minority nationalities is to allow minority nationality cadres, who are able to faithfully implement the principles and policies of the party and the state, [to] maintain close ties with the local people, fully grasp the characteristics of various nationalities and deeply understand the mentality of various nationalities, to take charge of their own affairs. Facts have proven that as long as we conscientiously exercise regional autonomy for minority nationalities, energetically train and boldly use minority nationality cadres, we will be able to change distrust between different nationalities into mutual trust and change misunderstanding between different nationalities into mutual understanding. Organs of self-government in autonomous regions will serve as important ties between the state and the people of minority nationalities, and the state will be able to maintain flesh-and-blood ties with the people of minority nationalities and achieve genuine centralization and unity on the basis of safeguarding the right of self-determination of and equality among the nationalities.

2. Regional autonomy for minority nationalities is conducive to the integration of the general principles and policies of the party and the state with the specific conditions of various minority nationality regions. The various nationalities in China have many different specific conditions. Let us take a look at the forms of society before the democratic reform. Some minority nationalities and the Han nationality were largely identical with only slight differences. Serfdom existed in some nationality areas, slavery existed in others and primitive communes existed in still others. Together, they practically constitute a living history of social development. We should by no means mechanically apply the successful experiences of the Han nationality and other minority nationality regions as a formula so that all nationalities in different stages of social

development will move onto the socialist road, nor should we ask them to "progress at the same pace" and "do things rigidly regardless of specific conditions." Much less should we do what Lenin spoke against, "drive people up to the clouds with a stick." We should allow them to adopt their own methods and steps which suit their specific conditions so that they can reach the same goal by different routes. Stalin once said: "It is possible that a specific solution of the question will be required for each nation. If the dialectical approach to a question is required anywhere it is required here, in the national question." ("Collected Works of Stalin," vol. 2, p. 309)

When exercising regional autonomy for the minority nationalities, we should adhere to dialectics and allow the minority nationalities to make steady progress under the guidance of the general principles and policies of the party and the state, to adopt their own methods and steps in accordance with their specific conditions and to move onto the socialist road. For example, we carried out land reforms through peaceful consultations and abolished the feudal lords system in the Dehong and Xishuangbanna Autonomous Prefectures of Tai nationality. We adopted the policy of redeeming serfs from their owners, thereby emancipating the serfs in some Zang regions. We did not carry out the democratic reform as a movement in minority nationality regions which, in varying degrees, still maintained primitive communes, and where class polarization was not clear and not serious. Instead, we gradually accomplished the tasks of democratic reform through developing the economy and culture and through socialist transformation. These principles and policies have proved successful. The Nei Monggol Autonomous Region has had similar experiences. In the winter of 1947, some comrades of the Ju Ud League carried out democratic reforms in the pastoral area of the Monggol nationality by mechanically applying the methods adopted by the Han nationality to carry out the land reform in its pastoral area. As a result, a large quantity of livestock died. The Nei Monggol party and government leading organs corrected this mistake.

In accordance with the specific conditions of the pastoral areas inhabited by the Monggols, they thoroughly abolished the nobility's privileges and implemented the "three don'ts and two benefits" policy—don't struggle, don't discriminate and don't determine class status (don't determine class status in public, but handle it as an internal matter); benefit both the herd owners and herdsmen and aid the poor herdsmen. They eliminated the feudal exploitation system and promoted the rapid development of animal husbandry. Later, in the process of socialist transformation, the Nei Monggol party and government leading organs also paid attention to proceeding from the specific conditions of the local nationality. For example, they adopted the principle of "stable policies, flexible methods and adequate time" toward the collectivization of animal husbandry. When carrying out socialist transformation of the herd owners' economy, they primarily adopted the policy of redemption, which was used in running joint state-private pastures. All these correct principles and policies were unique achievements made in the implementation of the party's policy of regional autonomy for minority nationalities.

3. The implementation of regional autonomy for minority nationalities is conducive to the integration of the prosperity of the state with the prosperity of the nationalities.

While carrying out construction work, we should not follow the old capitalist road, maintain or expand the differences in the degrees of prosperity among different nationalities. We should take the socialist road, gradually reduce or eliminate such differences. Otherwise, we will no longer be communists who firmly uphold equality among nationalities. Regional autonomy for the minority nationalities is a good system for establishing political, economic and cultural cooperation among nationalities. When a country is unified, it can vigorously help minority nationalities develop the economy and culture and organize them to help each other. By conscientiously implementing regional autonomy for minority nationalities, we will be able to mobilize the positive material factors in nationality autonomous regions through mobilizing the positive role played by the people in these regions. This will play an enormous role in the socialist construction of our country. The road of regional autonomy of minority nationalities leads to prosperity of the country as well as of various nationalities.

Since the founding of the PRC, the socialist construction in the nationality autonomous regions has developed by a big margin. The total output value of industry, agriculture and animal husbandry of various nationality autonomous regions in 1979 registered an increase of 926 percent over 1949. The number of university students of minority nationalities in 1979 was 1,290 percent that of 1952, the number of secondary students was 2,316 percent that of 1952, while the number of primary students was 500 percent that of 1952. Without exercising the regional autonomy of minority nationalities, it would be impossible to imagine such achievements.

4. Carrying out regional autonomy for minority nationalities helps to link the love of the people of the various nationalities for national unity with their love for their own nationalities.

Good relations among the various nationalities have always been an important factor for the stability of the political situation in our country, tranquillity on our borders and the strengthening of our national defenses. Eighty to 90 percent of our vast borderlands are inhabited by minority nationalities. So long as the regional autonomy for minority nationalities is carried out well, the people of the minority nationalities will have confidence that they are the masters of both their homeland and their country, and their enthusiasm in loving their country and their nationalities will be brought to full play. At present the people of the Monggol and other nationalities in Nei Monggol are guarding the north gate of our country, the people of the Uygur and other nationalities in Xinjiang are guarding our west gate, the people of the Tibetan and other nationalities on the roof of the world in Xizang are making their valuable contributions to the cause of guarding the southwest border of our motherland, while the people of the Zhuang and other nationalities in the south have performed heroic deeds in the struggle against Vietnamese aggressors.

In short, many fraternal nationalities together with the PLA shoulder the sacred responsibilities of guarding our motherland, and together they have formed a bastion of iron on our border. Before the liberation, some of the minority nationalities were driven by the reactionary ruling classes to remote, thickly forested mountains and were on the verge of extinction. Since the liberation, they have revived, and rebuilt their homelands. Regional national autonomy was even given to the Oroqen nationality, which had a population of only about 2,000, in the early post-liberation period. The pride of the people of all the minority nationalities in being the masters of their motherland and in being a part of the nation with a long history and magnificent future has been unprecedentedly enhanced.

The tremendous superiority of our system of regional autonomy of minority nationalities is, in a word, that each nationality has its proper place and plays its proper role in harmony, and helps the other. For more than 30 years, we have achieved great success in carrying out regional autonomy for minority nationalities. We can foretell that on our common road toward socialism, the regional autonomy of minority nationalities will certainly bring about a variety of blooms in both the material and the spiritual civilization of our motherland.

We must point out here that in the course of carrying out regional autonomy for minority nationalities there have also been great twists and turns which caused losses and left us lessons from bitter experience.

Problems occurred after the accomplishment in the main of socialist transformation. Owing to our lack of experience in carrying out regional autonomy for minority nationalities and especially owing to the influence of erroneous leftist guiding thought, we made a wrong appreciation of the national relations at home and began to be impatient to eliminate the differences between nationalities. As a result we made mistakes and errors in our work. After the accomplishment in the main of socialist transformation, the relations among nationalities were basically relations between the laboring people of various nationalities. However, for a long time we still wrongly stressed that "the nationality problem is in essence a problem of classes," confused the nationality problem with that of class and mixed up contradictions among the people with those between the enemy and ourselves. Therefore, not only were the same mistakes of unduly broadening the scope of the struggle against the rightists made in the areas of minority nationalities as in the areas of Han nationality, but a movement against local nationalism was wrongly launched. The ideology of local nationalism, like that of the Han chauvinism, is a kind of contradiction among the people to be overcome in our ranks. However, in the movement against local nationalism it was taken as a contradiction between the enemy and ourselves. Moreover, some justifiable national feeling and normal opinions on work were taken as manifestations of local nationalism and wrongly criticized, and harm was done to many cadres of minority nationalities, intellectuals and people of the upper strata. During the "Cultural Revolution" the mistakes in broadening the scope of class struggle on the nationality problem grew especially severe, and harm was done to still more nationality cadres and masses. Another particular expression of mistakes in our work on nationalities was that we paid inadequate respect to the power of autonomy of minority nationalities. During a certain period the nationalization of the cadres of autonomous organs was taken as conflicting with their communization. The power of autonomous organs was put on the same footing as that of ordinary local state organs. The result was that the policy of regional autonomy for minority nationalities could not be really implemented, and even some of the autonomous powers provided in our constitution became empty words. The above lessons must be kept firmly in our minds.

During the "Cultural Revolution", the Lin Biao-Jiang Qing cliques sowed prejudice among nationalities and created troubles among them. They slandered our party's policy of regional autonomy of minority nationalities and described it as "sowing discord." We were distressed to see that through the 10 years of chaos, the relations among nationalities took a turn for the worse and the regional autonomy of minority nationalities existed in name only. A calamity was suffered by the people of both the minority nationalities and the Han nationality.

Our party, representing the will of the people of all nationalities, smashed first the Lin Biao then the Jiang Qing counterrevolutionary cliques and frankly exposed and resolutely overcame the obstructions of the leftist mistakes in our work on minority nationalities. In particular, since the 3d plenary session of the 11th Central Committee of our party in December 1978, the party and government have reaffirmed the policy of regional autonomy of minority nationalities and the other policies on minority nationalities and has time and again checked on their implementation. The state grants large financial subsidies to nationality autonomous areas every year to help them to develop their economy and culture. In 1979 our party convened a special conference to emphatically study and forcefully promote the work on minority nationalities. Since its establishment in 1980 the Secretariat of the Central Committee of the party has attached great importance to work on minority nationalities, especially the work on regional autonomy for minority nationalities. The Central Committee made an important decision on policies for work in Xizang, and its basic spirit suits other nationality autonomous areas. This important decision embodies the correct line of the party since the 3d plenary session of its 11th Central Committee, and developed the party's policy of regional autonomy of minority nationalities. It has drawn enthusiastic responses from and won the sincere support of the people of the various nationalities all over the country. In less than 1 year, the situation in Xizang took a turn for the better faster than expected. In all the other nationality autonomous areas, new measures were studied and formulated in accordance with the basic spirit of this important decision and in line with the specific national characteristics of the nationalities and the actual conditions, to strengthen the work on minority nationalities and to implement national policies. Marked success has been achieved. The people of all our nationalities enthusiastically rejoice that after a period of standstill and retrogression the work of regional autonomy for minority nationalities is making rapid progress again.

III. PERSIST IN CARRYING OUT REGIONAL AUTONOMY OF MINORITY NATIONALITIES AND FIGHT FOR FULFILLING THE NEW TASKS IN THE NEW PERIOD

At present, our country is entering a new period of waging a struggle for building a powerful modern socialist state. Accordingly, minority nationality work with respect to regional autonomy for minority nationalities and in other respects is entering a new stage too.

The nationality relations at present are mainly good. But in some areas and in some respects there are still quite a few urgent problems in these relations that we cannot neglect. During the past few years the party and the government have always listened to the voice of the minority nationalities and looked into their desires. What the cadres and masses of the minority nationalities want at present are mainly listed in the following five points:

1. They want to enjoy the autonomy rights in accordance with the regulations in the constitution and the relevant laws of our country, so that they may independently manage the affairs of their own nationalities and in their own areas, and all their work can proceed from the actual conditions of their nationalities and areas. They do not agree to making no distinction between autonomous and nonautonomous areas or to treat the work in their areas on the same footing as in other areas.

2. They want to properly protect and rationally exploit the natural resources in their areas and safeguard the economic rights and interests of their nationalities and areas, under the unified economic and financial systems of the country. They want to rationally solve the contradictions between agriculture and animal husbandry, between farms and communes and between the enterprises on higher levels and the nationality autonomous areas themselves. The key to their wishes is that, under the general policies and unified planning of the state, a proper distinction be made between the power and right to manage and exploit the natural resources under the jurisdiction of the central or higher-level state organs on the one hand and those under the jurisdiction of nationality autonomous areas on the other, and that concrete systems and methods of management be clearly formulated. They also want a prompt check on the blind movement of people into their areas and an appropriate solution to this problem.

3. They call for thoroughly overcoming poverty and backwardness and for coming up to prosperous and civilized standards as quickly as possible. They hope that on the basis of self-reliance, they can obtain energetic assistance from the state and regions of the Han nationality. They also hope that higher authorities will relax restrictions on the financial and economic policies for the autonomous areas of minority nationalities.

4. They call for strengthening education on nationality policies for cadres, especially leading cadres and training of cadres of minority nationalities. They also call for improving the quality of and expanding the minority cadre ranks and for further promoting socialist relations among our various nationalities on the basis of equality and mutual aid. They hope that socialist democracy will be continuously promoted, that our socialist legal system will be perfected, that the political situation, of stability, unity and liveliness, will be consolidated and developed, and that firm blows will be dealt at internal and external enemies' counterrevolutionary activities, such as inciting national secession and attempting to disrupt China's unification.

5. They demand that the cultural heritages of minority nationalities be rescued and sorted out, that the spoken and written languages of minority nationalities be used and developed, that efforts be made to enable the cultures of minority nationalities to flourish, and that minority nationalities' customs and religious beliefs be respected.

The above-mentioned demands are undoubtedly reasonable ones and we should conscientiously handle them. We must try to solve in a timely manner those problems which can be solved rather quickly; we must actively try to solve step-by-step those problems which cannot be solved within a short period of time. We should believe that the broad masses of the people of minority nationalities are reasonable.

To improve and promote socialist relations among our various nationalities and to strengthen the ties of unity among people of all nationalities in China for fulfilling new tasks for the new period, we must persist in the practice of regional autonomy for minority nationalities and conscientiously guarantee our minority nationalities' right to autonomy. The "Resolution on Certain Questions in the History of Our Party Since the Founding of the People's Republic of China," adopted by the 6th Plenary Session of the 11th CCP Central Committee, contains special provisions for improving and promoting socialist relations among our various nationalities and for strengthening national unity. The resolution correctly sums up our country's experiences in carrying out nationalities work and indicates the way to advance in this work. We should regard these provisions as the basis for seeking unity in ideology, thinking and action. All cadres and people in areas of minority nationalities must resolutely implement these provisions. In the days to come, in accordance with the resolution's provisions concerning nationalities issues, we must stress the following three aspects of our nationalities work:

1. We Should Have a Correct Understanding of Regional Autonomy of Minority Nationalities

Prior to the "Great Cultural Revolution," leftist mistakes had already created ideological confusion on issues concerning regional autonomy for minority nationalities. The "Great Cultural Revolution" worsened this kind of ideological confusion. At present, not all of our comrades have a correct understanding of regional autonomy for minority nationalities.

With regard to the implementation of regional autonomy for minority nationalities, some comrades think that hanging up a signboard for this autonomy for show and recruiting a few cadres of minority nationalities to give us a hand will suffice. These comrades do not have a correct understanding of the party's policy on regional autonomy for minority nationalities and also lack a full understanding of the general principles of the Marxist-Leninist-Mao Zedong theory of nationalities. If we allow these comrades to carry out regional autonomy for minority nationalities, they certainly will turn this kind of autonomy into something more nominal than real or even into something only nominal.

Due to the influence of leftist mistakes, in their heart of hearts, these comrades think: Since we are now in the socialist period, there is no point in discussing minority nationalities and promoting autonomy! They do not understand that although the merging of nationalities is a splendid ideal indeed, such a merging can only be realized in a communist society. As for the socialist period, although the generalities among nationalities will be increased gradually, generally speaking, this is a flourishing period for various nationalities. If we attempted to bring about the merging of nationalities in the socialist period, things would go contrary to our wishes. A policy on bringing about the merging of nationalities by coercion and commandism would be "tantamount to a policy of assimilation." Of course, "the policy of assimilation is absolutely excluded from the arsenal of Marxism-Leninism." ("Collected Works of Stalin," vol. 2, pp. 298–299) Now these comrades should understand this point: Nationalities will exist for a long time to come and so will nationalities problems. Therefore, regional autonomy for minority nationalities will also exist for a long time to come.

Some comrades unavoidably have ideas characteristic of Han chauvinism which is primarily a legacy of feudal despotism. In their heart of hearts, some of our comrades still have not completely eliminated the traditional concept which holds Huaxia [an ancient name for China] in honor and despises barbarous tribes to the east and the north. This concept prevailed in feudal times. The intriguing thing is that this outworn concept has actually fitted in easily with the wrong leftist thinking. Some comrades have always distrusted cadres and people of minority nationalities and do not show due respect for our minority nationalities' right to autonomy. Therefore, although they also pay lip service to promoting regional autonomy for minority nationalities, they, in fact, are prone to carry out this autonomy perfunctorily as a routine practice or to run things all by themselves without consulting others. Isn't it true that due to the practice of running things all by oneself without consulting others there have been many cases of failure to improve relations among various nationalities over a long period of time? We should conscientiously draw lessons from these cases. Through education we must conscientiously overcome the ideas characteristic of Han chauvinism.

At the same time, we must also pay attention to guarding against local nationalism. In particular, we must oppose splittism. In the view of some people, a federal republic necessarily means a greater amount of freedom than a centralized republic. Such a view is a muddled one, to say the least. Lenin pointedly noted: "The really democratic centralized republic gave more freedom than the federal republic." ("Collected Works of Lenin," vol. 25, p. 435) As stated above, it goes without saying that our various nationalities have united and lived together in China over a long period of time. Through the revolution, we have strengthened this unity and achieved an unprecedentedly great solidarity. To attempt to turn this unity into disunity would be going against the historical trend.

We must do well in propagating the Marxist-Leninist-Mao Zedong theory of nationalities and the party's policy on regional autonomy of minority nationalities. We must always propagate them, carry out this propaganda work in close connection with real problems and carry out this propaganda work in all party, government, military and mass organizations. We must use this theory and this policy to educate the masses, especially the cadres, and use them to educate cadres of minority nationalities, especially cadres of the Han nationality. In addition to using them to educate ordinary cadres, we must attach major importance to using them to educate leading cadres. After successfully carrying out this propaganda work, we can correct the wrong ideological trend and do a still better job of implementing the party's policy on regional autonomy for minority nationalities.

2. The Party's Policy on Regional Autonomy for Minority Nationalities Should Be Carried Out in an All-Round Way and in a Timely Manner

The implementation of the party's policy on regional autonomy for minority nationalities involves two basic issues, namely nationalization and the right to autonomy.

Nationalization is a prerequisite to exercising the right to autonomy. There are several aspects of nationalization. The key link is the nationalization of cadres in autonomous offices. The organization and work of autonomous offices should be primarily handled by personnel of local minority nationalities. This means: Principal leading posts in autonomous offices must be held by people of local minority nationalities, and the number of cadres of minority nationalities should be proportionate to the size of their population. It is imperative to guarantee that every cadre of a minority nationality be truly entrusted with the responsibility and authority that should go with his post. At the same time, in accordance with the composition of local nationalities, it is imperative to put representative figures of other nationalities in suitable positions. All leading cadres of various nationalities in autonomous offices must conform to the standards for selecting cadres as set by the party and the state and have both ability and political integrity. It is imperative to rationally put people in leading positions in autonomous offices after full deliberations and consultations among the parties concerned. Have all autonomous offices in our autonomous regions realized the nationalization of their cadres? Most of them are approaching this target. There are quite a few problems in allocating cadres within some other departments in autonomous areas of minority nationalities. In some autonomous areas of minority nationalities, very few cadres of minority nationalities are unit chiefs, very few are leading cadres, very few work for important departments, very few are staff of party organizations, and very few leading cadres of minority nationalities can really exercise the functions and powers that go with their posts. We must make great efforts to train and promote cadres of minority nationalities and resolutely change the above-mentioned conditions as quickly as possible.

Because in many autonomous areas of minority nationalities, there are more Han people than minority nationality people, some comrades do not agree to the predominance in the autonomy organs of personnel of the nationalities exercising autonomy and even think that this is unfair to the Han people. This is obviously wrong. Here, two points need explaining: First, citizens of all nationalities in autonomous areas of minority nationalities are masters of the country and they all enjoy equal rights and have to perform equal duties. This is a different question from having the predominance in the autonomy organs of the nationalities exercising autonomy. Second, when we say regional autonomy of nationalities, the word "nationalities" means minority nationalities making up the main body of the population there. The word "regional" means places where minority nationalities making up the main body of the population live in compact communities, and the word "autonomy" means autonomy of minority nationalities making up the main body of the population there. The Han nationality makes up the great majority of the population of the country and there is no need for them to practice autonomy in the autonomous areas of minority nationalities, nor is it necessary to have Hans predominate in the autonomy organs. If personnel of the nationalities exercising autonomy do not predominate in the autonomy organs, then we are no longer practicing regional autonomy for minority nationalities. Comrade Mao Zedong pointed out that regional autonomy for minority nationalities means taking in earnest the predominance of minority nationalities and the supplementary role of the Han nationality in minority nationality regions. We must adhere to this correct principle. Of course, all autonomy organs of autonomous regions of minority nationalities should definitely ensure equal rights among different nationalities, encourage different nationalities to respect one another, to learn from one another and to help one another, continuously strengthen solidarity among nationalities, make the relationships among nationalities closer and eliminate prejudice and estrangement among nationalities. Failing to make efforts to this end is also wrong. In the past decades, a great number of Han cadres working in autonomous regions of minority nationalities have made indelible contributions to the revolution and construction of autonomous regions of minority nationalities, and they will continue to make important contributions. It is also a glorious task for Han cadres working in autonomous regions of minority nationalities to increase the number of minority nationality cadres in autonomy organs. The broad masses of minority nationality people will never forget the important meritorious deeds of Han cadres who have worked arduously for a long time in autonomous regions of minority nationalities and have earnestly and sincerely served the minority nationalities.

Evidently, the autonomy of existing autonomous regions of minority nationalities is imperfect.

Affairs concerning the whole country should of course be handled in a unified way only by the state. As to affairs concerning localities, they can and must be handled independently by autonomy organs in accordance with legal stipulations. Compared with ordinary local state organs with similar administrative status, the functions and powers of autonomy organs are undoubtedly more and greater.

With the development of socialist construction, autonomy in economic management and financial administration in autonomous regions of minority nationalities has become a conspicuous problem demanding great attention and a prompt solution. As early as 25 years ago, Comrade Mao Zedong said, "In regions of the minority nationalities, it is necessary to study carefully to find out what kind of economic management system and financial system are really suitable." ("Selected Works of Mao Zedong," vol. 5, p. 278) At present, there has been some improvement in the financial system and the economic management system of some sectors. More improvement should be made from now on.

The economic management system and financial system must fully respect the rights and interests of autonomous regions of minority nationalities and in particular the rights and interests of managing independently resources and enterprises in accordance with the state's laws. In exploiting and utilizing resources in autonomous regions of minority nationalities, state organs at a higher level should hold thorough consultations with autonomy organs and make proper arrangements so that the project will be conducive to both the development of the whole national economy and the development of the economy of the autonomous regions. It must be beneficial to the local people. In order to promote the development and prosperity of the economy and culture of autonomous regions of minority nationalities and to eliminate actual inequality among different nationalities, the state should do its best to give financial and technological assistance to autonomous regions in addition to promoting the self-reliance of autonomous regions of minority nationalities.

Comrade Zhou Enlai pointed out: ". . . because in the past, reactionary rulers of the Han nationality oppressed and exploited the minority nationalities, it is natural and unavoidable that the minority nationalities take a skeptical attitude toward the Han nationality." ("On Several Problems of Our Country's Policies for Minority Nationalities" by Zhou Enlai) Therefore, in treating problems such as increasing the number of minority-nationality cadres in autonomy organs, autonomy and other problems concerning relationships among nationalities, the Han nationality should follow Lenin's teaching: "If we really want to handle problems with a true proletarian attitude, we must be very careful and must adopt an attitude of showing concern and making concessions. . . . It is better to make more concessions and be more moderate toward minority nationalities than to make insufficient concessions and not be moderate enough." ("Collected Works of Lenin," vol. 36, p. 632)

3. Strengthen the Legal System of Regional Autonomy for Minority Nationalities

"The Resolution on Certain Questions in the History of Our Party Since the Founding of the People's Republic of China" adopted at the 6th Plenary Session of the 11th CCP Central Committee pointed out: "It is necessary to persist in regional autonomy and enact laws and regulations to ensure this autonomy and the decisionmaking power in applying party and government policies according to the actual conditions in the regions." Stipulations on autonomy in our existing constitution are far from being sound. In his speech made on 15 September 1980 at the first meeting of the committee for revising the constitution, Vice-Chairman Ye Jianying pointed out that autonomy should be explicitly stipulated in the constitution. At present, the work of revising the constitution is under way. We believe that through revising the constitution, important legal guarantees for regional autonomy for minority nationalities will surely be provided.

Twenty-nine years ago, we formulated the "outline for enforcing regional autonomy for minority nationalities of the People's Republic of China" which played an important role in practicing regional autonomy for minority nationalities. However, some contents of this law no longer meet the present needs. Therefore, it is our country's urgent need to formulate a law for regional autonomy for minority nationalities on the basis of 30 years' experience in practicing regional autonomy for minority nationalities and in accordance with the present new situation. At present, serious study on formulating this new law is being carried out by the departments concerned.

Rules and specific regulations on autonomy formulated by autonomy organs in autonomous areas of minority nationalities are important measures to strengthen the legal system of regional autonomy of minority nationalities. In May 1980, while in the Xizang Autonomous Region Comrade Hu Yaobang stated, "Laws and regulations in accordance with respective characteristics should be formulated to protect the autonomy of minority nationalities and the special interests of the minority nationalities." At present, some autonomous areas of minority nationalities have started to formulate rules and specific regulations on autonomy. This is gratifying progress.

Lessons of the past years have taught us that without the guarantee of a sound socialist legal system, it is difficult to implement policies for regional autonomy for minority nationalities. At present, in strengthening the legal system of regional autonomy for minority nationalities, we are confirming through laws the requirements of the policies for regional autonomy for minority nationalities and ensuring through compulsory means the implementation of policies for regional autonomy for minority nationalities. Only by strengthening the legal system of regional autonomy for minority nationalities, improving propaganda on the legal system of minority nationalities and resolutely acting according to legal stipulations can we truly implement policies for regional autonomy for minority nationalities. Therefore, this is a pressing matter of the moment and also a measure for a long time to come.

The experience of the past 60 years has amply proved that the CCP is the faithful representative of the interests of all the people of the Chinese nationalities and is the leading core of all the people of the Chinese nationalities. The party's policies for regional autonomy for minority nationalities have guided the minority nationalities to traverse a tortuous yet glorious course. Having survived the obstructions and sabotage of internal and external enemies and interferences of erroneous inner-party trends, the party has shown even more clearly its tremendous superiority and vigorous vitality. Without the party's leadership and without the policies for regional autonomy for minority nationalities, there is no thorough liberation, free development or happy life for the minority nationalities.

The 3d Plenary Session of the 11th CCP Central Committee, which was of great historical significance, and the 4th and 5th plenary sessions that followed put forth and implemented step-by-step a series of important decisions on ideology, politics, organization and all fields of the socialist construction, totally reversed the erroneous leftist orientation and, in accordance with new historical conditions, progressively opened up a correct road for socialist modernization suitable for China's conditions. The 6th Plenary Session of the 11th CCP Central Committee, which ended victoriously not long ago, unanimously adopted "The Resolution on Certain Questions in the History of Our Party Since the Founding of the People's Republic of China," reelected principal leading members of the Central Committee and elected new ones. This session was another important meeting of our party and was a new milestone of our party and country in bringing order out of chaos and carrying forward the revolutionary cause and forging ahead into the future. In our work for minority nationalities we are now facing a very favorable situation which we have not seen for years.

As long as we adhere to the four basic principles, resolutely implement the Marxist line, principles and policies, seriously study and implement the spirit of the sixth plenary session of the CCP Central Committee, seriously study "The Resolution on Certain Questions in the History of Our Party Since the Founding of the People's Republic of China" and resolutely work hard along the direction indicated by the "resolution," the Party's policies on regional autonomy for minority nationalities can be comprehensively implemented and pushed forward in good time. In addition, regional autonomy for minority nationalities will be strengthened and become better with each passing day, the unity of the country will surely be unprecedentedly consolidated, and the minority nationalities and the Han nationality will certainly realize common prosperity on the socialist road. Under the guidance of the party's policies on regional autonomy for minority nationalities, the minority nationalities are forging ahead with full confidence toward a bright future.

HU YAOBANG

68

On Literature and Art, 27 December 1981

In this speech to a conference on filmmaking, the rather unconventional and outspoken general secretary attempts to cheer up his audience and urges everyone to remain apolitical while somehow serving the Party's political goals.

I am a rooter for ball games, a rooter for radio and television broadcasts, a rooter for the movie industry. In short, I am your avid supporter. Our comrades of all party committees and propaganda departments must assign such a task for themselves: to be rooters, to cheer everybody up.

Literature and art, like sports, have a broad mass character. We must organize and lead the people to use all means possible to boost anything which has a broad mass character, which is beneficial to the people, which can inspire and educate people to aim high and which is

[Hu Yaobang, "Uphold the Concept of One Dividing Into Two; Attain a Still Higher Goal," *Red Flag*, no. 21, 1 November 1982.]

popular among the people. Because only by doing this can we prove ourselves to have what our party constantly claims as a mass viewpoint.

The year 1981 will pass and a new year will come in only 4 more days. How should we view our work this year and greet the new year? Let me present these remarks to you comrades: Uphold the concept of one divides into two; attain a still higher goal. If there should be a "dui lian" [a Chinese couplet often written and mounted on scrolls to be hung on the wall] for the new year, can these remarks be considered as fit for this purpose?

All our comrades must uphold the concept of one divides into two at all times. This is a conclusion reached at the meeting sponsored by the party Central Committee for the first secretaries of various provinces, municipalities and autonomous regions to review the work of this year. To view things with the concept of one divides into two, we can see, on the one hand, our party has achieved great progress in its work and the result has generally been good, but, on the other, we can also see that we have not been performing very well in other work, including that in which we ought to have done better, such as political and ideological work, [stabilizing the] commodity prices and so forth. How does literary and art work fare? I hope you comrades will have this issue analyzed with the scientific attitude of one divides into two so that the work next year will be done better.

As far as the movie industry is concerned, we must fully affirm that much progress was made during the past several years, and that new progress has been made this year. Therefore, good and generally acceptable movies have been the mainstream. This also tells us that the majority of our comrades have been working very hard. Some middle-aged and young directors and playwrights have been maturing very quickly. Our workers, peasants, soldiers and intellectuals, our Communist Party members, CYL members and Young Pioneers, in short people of all nationalities throughout the country, male and female, young and old, people residing in cities and rural areas, are pleased with and welcome the accomplishments and progress achieved by the people of the movie industry and their hard work and contributions. They can see these accomplishments with their own eyes, and they will remember them and are thankful for them. This is what we usually mean as the rights and wrongs of a case will be judged by the public. This is a fact, and this is the kind of confidence we should have.

Of course, there is another side of the coin. This is to say that certain movies are really not good enough, that certain comrades have not worked hard enough, and that relatively serious shortcomings and errors still can be found in certain works and among certain individual comrades. The two main problems are simply thus:

First, the political sentiments of certain works and certain comrades are not healthy. Where are these unhealthy political sentiments reflected? They are reflected mainly in their attitude of ignoring, and even writing off, the great accomplishments achieved by the Chinese people in pursuing their socialist cause, and in their attitude of blaming the entire state, the entire revolutionary rank and file and the entire socialist system for the mistakes in our revolutionary process and for the destructions done by the Lin Biao and Jiang Qing counterrevolutionary cliques. Because of such attitudes, they conclude that communism has no future, and that communism is but a dim illusion. That is what I mean by unhealthy political thinking or political sentiments.

Why do we have to criticize Comrade Bai Hua? It is because his work "Unrequited Love" is unhealthy in political thinking and harmful to the people's minds. Things have now turned out very well since he has been criticized and since he has realized his mistakes and made a self-criticism. Comrade Bai Hua is still a party member and a writer, and he will continue to write. Comrade Bai Hua produced some good works in the past. We hope he will produce more good works. People can see from this case that the party Central Committee's policies and ways of doing things are vastly different from those in the past, and these differences have demonstrated that our party has indeed learned a beneficial lesson from its mistakes and setbacks and has become more mature.

There is no doubt that we must convincingly and seriously criticize erroneous things. Here, we must adhere to truths and never try to save face. It is best that one conducts self-criticism earnestly instead of shielding a shortcoming or fault. The comrades, readers and audience must help him. This is not only true for writers, but also true for the responsible comrades of our party committees at all levels. Can we criticize the Standing Committee members of the party Central Committee's Political Bureau and the comrades of the Secretariat if they have committed mistakes? Naturally we can criticize them. We can even criticize Comrade Mao Zedong's errors. Why can't we criticize ourselves, if we commit mistakes? For our great cause, whoever makes mistakes in our revolutionary ranks should be criticized or told to conduct self-criticism. However, we must face facts, be good to others and pay attention to science and policy. We must not wantonly criticize people. Perhaps some comrades would say that one's enthusiasm will be affected once criticism has started. We say: It all depends on what kind of enthusiasm you have. If it is the kind of enthusiasm detrimental to the socialist cause, should we not dampen this kind of enthusiasm? This kind of dampening would help the healthy enthusiasm to further develop at the same time.

Second, some comrades have failed to attain a lofty realm of thought in some of their works. Their realm of thought is even very low. Where does this phenomenon manifest itself? Mainly it shows up when they are unable to correctly handle the relations between love affairs and the revolution and between love affairs and the socialist cause, while inappropriately overemphasizing the love affairs.

Naturally, love affairs constitute an important theme in literature and art. We not only may write on this theme, but should write on this theme. I had mentioned this at the symposium on script writing held last year. Who says that we cannot write about love affairs? They represent an integral part of human life and an important phenomenon in social life. The question is what role we let love affairs play. All communists, revolutionaries and patriots should be even more broadminded and farsighted. Ardently loving only our great motherland, our great people and our socialist cause is most valuable. If we can classify our sentiments of ardent love into number one, number two and number three, the number one should be this type of ardent love. Literature and art in the socialist period should be much more progressive than that in the new democratic revolution period. First of all, our literary and art works should educate the people, particularly the young people, to love the socialist cause of the motherland and our people. Fundamentally, love affairs should be identical with the revolutionary cause. For the people's interests and for the socialist cause, a revolutionary should be able to completely sacrifice one's own love affairs and even life, if it is necessary to do so.

People still remember the Hungarian poet Petofi's famous poem: "Life is indeed valuable, but the price of love is even more valuable. However, for the sake of freedom, I can give up both." For the nation's independence and the people's freedom in the motherland, this democratic revolutionary in the mid-19th century was able to attain this kind of lofty realm of thought. How can our socialist literature and art today retreat to the realm of thought where love is considered as something supreme? We should not let love between the sexes overtake the revolution and prevail over the revolution. Nor should we give publicity to love being the noblest and doing everything for the sake of love. Our literary and art works should always be aimed at broadening the people's spiritual realm and at encouraging and inspiring the people to dedicate themselves to the socialist modernization of the motherland.

Only by upholding the concept of "one divides into two," will it be possible for us to attain a still higher goal. In the next year, not only must you attain a higher goal, you must also work hard to attain a higher goal in doing the work of our party and the work of all trades and professions. You said that in the next year, you would produce 100 feature films. This is fine. However, the question is what kind of feature films. Everyone believes the quantity of 100 feature films should be ensured. The quality of these films should also be better than those produced in 1981. It is, therefore, necessary for you comrades to work harder than ever to conscientiously solve the series of questions in the realms of ideology and art and in all fields of your work.

As for economic development, there must be a practical and "unexaggerated" growth rate next year. This means a certain quantitative as well as a strict qualitative requirement or combining of quantity with quality in this regard. I think this requirement is also completely applicable to film production.

If we make no big mistakes, adopt a scientific approach and go all out to push the national economy forward, it will be possible gradually to accelerate the improvement of the people's living standards a little bit. However, generally speaking, it will not be quite possible for our living standards to catch up with those in the most economically developed countries in the next 50 years or until the 2020's or 2030's. Let us review some history. China was gradually reduced to a semicolonial and semifeudal society since the middle of the 19th century. After more than a century, a tremendous social change took place in China in the middle of the 20th century—China entered the period of socialism. It might take another century or so for the fundamental and tremendous socioeconomic change to occur in our country so that China will be among the advanced of the world—or such a change might not take place until the middle of the 21st century. Therefore, the course of social history has determined that we Chinese have to bear more hardships in this century and the next. What is so serious about bearing some hardships? Difficulties and hardships will help you succeed in your undertakings. This century and the next will be the two centuries in which the Chinese nation will bring about tremendous changes and make tremendous progress.

Such historical development and changes require our comrades to conscientiously experience all kinds of hardships and tempering. After this difficult historical stage, our nation will have a bright future. This is the realm of thought in which our minds are emancipated. Such a realm of thought is one of revolutionary romanticism and revolutionary realism. Is this not realistic? We must be determined to work hard in the next 5 decades to make China a modern, powerful socialist country with political stability, economic prosperity, developed education and high ethical standards and to make our country really stand up. This will be a close integration of revolutionary realism with revolutionary romanticism. Could one be called a revolutionary realist if one disregards the nature of historical development and regards the people's cause and ideals as worthless or devoid of any merit? That is shortsighted, naturalistic and indicative of a declining mentality.

Comrades, this question concerning the realm of thought is one of a fundamental character and characteristic of the times. Among our people, party members and cadres, there will definitely be more and more people who firmly believe that our country will effect a tremendous change or progress from disorder to order and from poverty to prosperity and who conscientiously work hard for this purpose. Now some people eagerly look forward to this, others are half believing and half doubting and still a very small number of people determinedly oppose such a tremendous change and progress and want to go backward. This requires us to turn our party's correct lines and objectives, through our ideological, political, theoretical, propaganda, literary and art, journalistic and educational work, into the firm will and conviction of large numbers of party members, cadres and people, into the ideas, consciousness and public opinion of hundreds of millions of people of various nationalities and into their actions. There will be no future for our literature and art if they do not serve this purpose. If our writers and artists fail to stand ahead of the times but stand aside and only write, perform or sing something about the "wind, flowers, snow and moon" and "love," or if they stand behind the times and only write, perform or sing something "miserable" or which is "unbearable to recall," then, what future will they have? There will be no future at all for those who stand opposed to use and distort and curse the revolution with a mentality marked by antipathy and gloom and with the language of hatred, and they are bound to be cast aside by the people. Of course, this does not in the slightest degree mean that ugly phenomena in our social life cannot be criticized. We have said on several occasions that they can and should be criticized. The question here is what stand you take and your frame of thought.

Comrade Xia Yan has just asked me to say more about the question of study. I think this is an extremely important question. The question of restudy faces not only you in your profession but also the whole party and people of all nationalities throughout the country, including us. Of course, the division of work in society varies from people to people. However, there are common yet different requirements for people in study. As far as writers and artists are concerned, I think that they must step up their study of Marxism, social life, culture, science and history.

Marxism, which came into being more than 100 years ago, has its rich theory of literature and art. But this does not mean that authors of classical works of Marxism have provided readymade answers to all questions about literary and art work. Our study of Marxism today is for no other purpose than guiding our artistic practice with the Marxist stand, viewpoint and method. We should strive to attain a higher ideological and a higher artistic level and to integrate the one with the other or to merge them into a single whole. Only in this way will we be able to greatly raise our realm of thought and to promote social progress in a particular way.

I do not know if you have read Comrade Wang Chaowen's "The Concept of Aesthetics" and some other comrades' aesthetical works. I have read some of the book but have not yet finished it. I feel that there may be some shortcomings in all books on aesthetics, but they still can help us understand some concepts or common sense of aesthetics so that we can avoid detours in this regard. Now some of our comrades do not pay sufficient attention to theoretical questions, and our achievements in the theory of literature and art are very few indeed.

Writers and artists should go deep into the realities of life in order to observe, experience and analyze persons and social phenomena of various kinds—this is a prerequisite for our literary and art creation. If a writer does not do so, he can only fabricate stories according to his subjective needs. Take the plot of having a love affair in a tank for example. People only have to ask this: Since the number of personnel assigned to a tank is limited, how can another person be added to it so casually? Gorki once sincerely advised a young writer: Do not write anything in a hurry but study it first. He also said: One must pay attention to reality in order to portray new life vividly and effectively. There are three kinds of realities—the past reality, the present reality and the sketchy reality of the future.

In studying science, culture and history, one must pay particular attention to language. I think it necessary to remind comrades, especially young comrades, to pay close attention to this matter.

"A writing that is devoid of literary grace will not last long." This is quite right. It shows that a writing devoid of literary grace and refined language cannot touch people to the heart. This is an extremely important experience. Literary language is an art. A work without literary grace definitely has little vitality. Please take a look at Lu Xun, Guo Moruo, Mao Dun, Ba Jin, Gao Yu, Lao She, Zhao Zhuli and other literary giants of modern times. Is any of them not a great master of the art of language? However, it appears that some young comrades have not paid close attention to this matter. If one does not have sufficient literary accomplishment and is unwilling to study some classical Chinese poems and prose, his writing will be insipid and devoid of the effect of touching people to the heart. If one goes on like this, how can one do one's job?

Certain comrades mentioned the movie "Bosom Friend." I think a movie like this can be produced. Cai E indeed rendered outstanding service in the struggle of overthrowing Yuan Shikai during the old democratic revolutionary period, and Xiao Fengxian can be regarded as a woman with foresight and courage. However, I do not know whether the movie's playwright and director read Xiao Fengxian's elegiac couplet for Cai E. The first part of the couplet reads: "Over the boundless horizon in the south, you ascended like a roc that wings skyward, lifted by the cyclone. How can I, a survivor of a chaotic world, bear the fact that our union has become a mere dream?" The second half reads: "During your several years of stay in the north, I pitied myself for having led an aimless life. But after having

you, a hero, as my bosom friend, what is fleeting will be remembered forever." You can see that this couplet, which mentions Cai's lofty ambition and Xiao Fengxian herself, as well as her relationship with Cai, has a fairly deep perception and literary grace. I hear that it was written by a literati in Xiao Fengxian's name. Nevertheless, it has a certain literary value. I think it would be nice if the movie "Bosom Friend" used this couplet as its theme and even used its words for the lyrics of a theme song. From this we can see that we must continue to brush up on history and culture. If our works have a correct theme and tell a touching story with a rich, graceful language, they certainly can powerfully educate and inspire our people.

Some comrades maintain that our movies, like ball games, should be up to the standard that they can compete with other countries on the international movie scene. I think this issue must be analyzed because we will lose our bearings if it is not clearly analyzed. Nowadays, the international sports tournaments are matches of athletic skills conducted under unified competition regulations and judging standards that are internationally acknowledged. In light of these regulations and standards, who wins and who loses can be clearly distinguished, and the results, which do not have a class character, are spontaneously recognized by the whole world. However, literature and art, including motion pictures, are different. It is one of the ideological departments that has a strong class and social character. The same literary and art work may be judged differently, or even diametrically, by different people because of differences in their social status and world outlook. Of course, different peoples and different countries can and should learn from each other in the field of artistic forms and skills of their literature and art. All the positive results from the literature and art of all nations will contribute to mankind's cultural development. In the final analysis, however, whether our literature and art has a great vitality depends only on whether it meets the needs for the progress of people of all nationalities. Therefore, the goal of struggle of our literature and art is not what it can accomplish internationally, but how it can penetrate the hearts of the broad masses of Chinese people and become a powerful spiritual weapon that can arouse hundreds of millions of Chinese people to struggle for socialist modernization. If our literature and art really attains this goal, it has expressed its major international significance. If our own culture can be developed and thrive healthily in a great country like China, which has ¼ of the world's population, and if our people will emerge in the world as a highly civilized nation, it will be an inestimable contribution to and a tremendous motivating force in the world's cultural development. Is it possible then that this will not be recorded in full detail in the cultural history of the world?

In short, in the interest of our country and people, we must heighten our spirits, rise up and be ready to exert sustained and strenuous efforts to build a stronger and more prosperous country. We must also emulate the Chinese women's volleyball team's spirit of winning glory for the motherland and the people. Some comrades say that their burden is heavy and they already feel the "pressure." I think this is good. When tap water cannot reach the upper floors of tall buildings, it is because there is not enough pressure. There must be some pressure, but, of course, it should not be too large. In the final analysis, we rely on our legs in order to attain a still higher goal. Whether our legs can make large steps depends on how loyal we are to our motherland, the people, the party and the socialist cause.

This meeting is being held quite successfully. I propose that a meeting like this be held every December. The meeting should be larger so it will be attended by directors, playwrights and some performers and singers. The purpose for settling the general account at the end of the year is to be prepared for the fighting during the new year. Let me repeat what I said: We must wage a hard struggle in order to attain a still higher goal!